Film Study

Film Study

An Analytical Bibliography

VOLUME 4

Frank Manchel

Rutherford ● Madison ● Teaneck
Fairleigh Dickinson University Press
London and Toronto: Associated University Presses

Associated University Presses
440 Forsgate Drive
Cranbury, NJ 08512

Associated University Presses
25 Sicilian Avenue
London WC1A 2QH, England

Associated University Presses
P.O. Box 488, Port Credit
Mississauga, Ontario
Canada L5G 4M2

The paper used in this publication meets the requirements
of the American National Standard for Permanence of Paper
for Printed Library Materials Z39.48-1984.

Library of Congress Cataloging-in-Publication Data

Manchel, Frank.
    Film study: an analytical bibliography / Frank Manchel.
        p.   cm.
    ISBN 0-8386-3414-1 (v. 4: alk. paper)
    1. Motion pictures—Bibliography.   2. Motion pictures—Study and teaching.   I. Title.
    Z5784.M9M34   1990
    [PN1994]
    016.79143—dc20   84-45026
                                                                   CIP

Contents of Volume 4

GLOSSARY   2211

APPENDIX I   2240
A SELECTED LIST OF FILM CRITICS AND
  PERIODICALS   2240

APPENDIX II   2249
SELECTED LIST OF 16MM FILM DISTRIBUTORS   2249
SELECTED LIST OF 8MM FILM DISTRIBUTORS   2254
SELECTED LIST OF VIDEO DISTRIBUTORS   2254

APPENDIX III   2257
"THE DON'TS AND BE CAREFULS"—1927–1930   2257

APPENDIX IV   2260
THE PRODUCTION CODE OF THE MOTION
  PICTURES PRODUCERS AND DIRECTORS OF
  AMERICA, INC.—1930–1934   2260
  PREAMBLE   2260
  GENERAL PRINCIPLES   2260
  REASONS SUPPORTING PREAMBLE OF CODE   2263

APPENDIX V   2266
SELECTED LIST OF SOURCES OF FURTHER FILM
  STUDY   2266
  ARCHIVES   2266
  LIBRARY RESOURCES   2272
  BIOGRAPHICAL AND REFERENCE TOOLS   2272
  BOOKSTORES   2273
  STILLS   2274

APPENDIX VI   2277
UNITED STATES ECONOMIC REVIEW OF 1984   2277

APPENDIX VII   2286
WALDORF CONFERENCE STATEMENT (1947)   2286

APPENDIX VIII   2287
A SELECTED LIST OF PUBLISHERS   2287

APPENDIX IX   2302
U.S. MOTION PICTURE THEATRES' BOX OFFICE   2302

ARTICLE TITLES INDEX   2303

AUTHORS-ARTICLES INDEX   2396

AUTHORS-BOOKS INDEX   2453

BOOK TITLES INDEX   2514

FILM PERSONALITIES INDEX   2601

SUBJECT INDEX   2700

FILM TITLES INDEX   2757

Film Study

Glossary

This Glossary includes many of the most commonly held terms cited in books about the art of the film. The purpose is to offer a beginning student a basic descriptive vocabulary in film study. The assumption is that a familarity with the language that critics, educators, and filmmakers use in discussing film facilitates learning. No attempt is made to be either comprehensive or definitive.[1]

A and B CUTTING/ROLLS/PRINTING: Two matching rolls of film are used by a filmmaker to mask splices and to provide special effects. An alternating process allows the appropriate shots to be printed on a third roll that eliminates any signs of editing.

ABC: (1) American Broadcasting Company. (2) A British distributing Company.

ABERRATION: distortion of the image by optical elements, e.g., lens, prism, and mirror.

ABOVE THE LINE: The costs associated with the creative talent of a film: e.g., performers, screenwriters, directors, and producers.

ABRASIONS: The unwanted mark or scratch on the surface of films caused by improper threading, projection, or handling.

ABSTRACT FILM: A non-representational film in which the separate shots create formal relationships, but ignore traditional patterns and content.

ACADEMY LEADER: The black film at the beginning of each reel containing numbers in descending order to indicate the starting point for projection of the film, and near the end to indicate when to switch over to next reel.

ACADEMY MASK: A camera mask used to fix the rectangularity of the camera

---

[1]   For more extensive information, see *Harry M. Geduld and Ronald Gottesman, AN ILLUSTRATED GLOSSARY OF FILM TERMS (New York: Holt, Rinehart and Winston, 1973); *Thurston C. Jordan, Jr., GLOSSARY OF MOTION PICTURE TERMINOLOGY (Menlo Park: Pacific Coast Publishers, 1968); *John Mercer, THE UNIVERSITY FILM ASSOCIATION MONOGRAPH 2: GLOSSARY OF FILM TERMS, rev. ed. (Houston: University of Houston, 1979); *James Monaco, HOW TO READ A FILM: THE ART, TECHNOLOGY, LANGUAGE, HISTORY, AND THEORY OF FILM AND MEDIA, rev. ed. (New York: Oxford University Press, 1981); and *Ralph S. Singleton, FILM MAKER'S DICTIONARY (Beverly Hills: Lone Eagle Publishing Company, 1986).

image on the screen to approximately a 3:4 ratio. Since the Academy of Motion Picture Arts and Sciences set the standards, the enclosed area is known as an Academy aperture. During the heyday of the Hollywood studio years, the ratio was 1: 1.3.

ACADEMY RATIO: The regulated shape of film frames in theatrical films, as determined by the Academy of Motion Picture Arts and Sciences. The most current standard is 1.85 (width) to 1:1.85 (height).

ACETATE: A slow-burning base for movie film composed mainly of cellulose triacetate, often referred to as a safety base.

ACHROMATIC: A lens designed for handling chromatic aberrations and for achieving a common focus.

ACTION: The movement that takes place in front of the lens.

ACTION!: The director's signal to begin filming.

ACTION CUTTING: Editing shots to give the impression that the action is continuous and uninterrupted.

ACTUAL TIME: The amount of time that it takes to see the film. It also refers to "real" time in lifelike situations.

ADAPTATION: The screen transformation of a work from another medium to the film.

ADDITIVE PROCESS: The system used in color reproduction that reconstitutes the images of a scene into their primary colors.

AD LIB: Improvised dialogue not found in the script or rehearsed before filming.

ADVERTISING: The means of promotion that inform the public about the film. In modern filmmaking, it often become more costly than the production of the film itself.

AFFECTIVE THEORY: The concept that emphasizes how a film's meaning is determined by filmmakers AND spectators.

AFTER-IMAGE: An impression of a shot that remains in the spectator's memory when the next shot appears.

AGENT: The individual(s) responsible not only for handling the contracts of people working in the film industry, but also for arranging "package deals" for a complete film.

AGITKI: A short Soviet propaganda film used during World War I that was put on agit-trains and exhibited around the Soviet Union.

AJYM: A film production company run by Claude Chabrol and instrumental in launching LA NOUVELLE VAGUE.

AMBIENT NOISE: The sounds occurring during production that are stored for possible use on the sound track.

AFI: The American Film Institute, which was established in 1967.

ANALYSIS: The detailed examination of a film rather than a review of its basic plot, cast, and credits.

ANAMORPHIC LENS: A lens that allows the width of the film image to be narrowed during recording and then "normalized" during projection. It produces the "letter envelope" effect in CinemaScope.

ANGLE: The point of view from which the action in front of the lens is filmed.

ANIMATED FILM: The shots of inanimate objects (or drawings) recorded frame by frame.

ANIMATION: The ability to make static objects appear to move.

ANIMATION STAND: A piece of equipment that holds the camera and allows the filmmaker to shoot one frame at a time and to create the illusion of motion.

ANSWER PRINT: The first of the "final" prints of the film combining sight and sound, used for measuring the time of each shot and the quality of the photography.

APERTURE: An optical device in the camera that determines how each frame is exposed. The lens aperture controls the amount of entering light, the printer aperture regulates the light needed to expose film being reproduced, and the projector aperture limits the section of each projected frame.

ART DEPARTMENT: The department responsible for staging and maintaining

the sets on a film production.

ART DIRECTOR: The individual responsible for designing and supervising
the sets for a film production.

ART HOUSE: A movie theater that caters to specialty audiences who prefer
intellectual experiences, rather than escapist entertainment. The
emphasis is on AUTEUR productions, rather than on popular movies.

ASA: The lens settings determined by the American Standards Association
that indicate the "film speed" required for recording light on
film.

ASPECT RATIO: The ratio, by height and width, of a single movie frame. It
also refers to the appropriate projection of a film on screen. The
standardization process is controlled by the Academy of Motion
Picture Arts and Sciences.

ASSOCIATIONAL EDITING: Matching several shots to create a specific and
immediate interpretation of a person's behavior or the meaning of an
event.

ASYNCHRONOUS SOUND: The source of the sound is not seen on screen, but
often indicates the antithesis of what is being shown.

ATMOSPHERE: The mood, setting, or background effect of a shot, what the
French call, MISE EN SCENE. It also refers to the staging of crowd
scenes.

AUDIENCE: An anonymous group of people who watch a film. It suggests that
the viewers are indiscriminate and manipulated unconsciously by the
filmmaker.

AUTEUR: The individual often considered responsible for the total film.

AUTEUR THEORY: The concept that one person determines the "look" and
"quality" of film, oOriginated in France by Francois Truffaut and
popularized in America by Andrew Sarris.

AVANT-GARDE: A non-traditional approach to filmmaking that either
introduces a new perspective, or functions outside the mainstream
of the film industry.

B-PICTURE: A low-budget movie run as a second feature or on Saturday

morning television shows.

BACKER: The individual who puts up the money for the film.

BACKGROUND MUSIC: The music in narrative films that underscores a
character's personality or the mood of a scene.

BACK-LIGHTING: In order to contrast lighting effects, lights are set
up behind or facing the lens (without distorting the len's control of
light). Generally used to glamorize a star's appearance.

BACKLOT: A storage area for old sets and stage properties.

BACK PROJECTION: The use of images projected on a transparent screen
to serve as the setting of the action.

BARN DOORS: The black metal flaps put on lights to shape the effect of
the lights.

BASE (film): The transparent, flexible material mixed with chemicals to
create film. Initially base was nitrate
now it is acetate.

BELOW-THE-LINE COSTS: Expenses accumulated during shooting and during the
postproduction process.

BENSHI: Japanese performers who narrated silent films. Also known as
"Katsuben."

BEST BOY: The chief assistant to the head electrician (gaffer).

BIT PART: A minor role.

BLACK COMEDY: An unfortunate term that connotes absurd humor.

BLACKLIST: An unofficial list used mainly during the late 1940s and 1950s
to prevent suspected Communists and sympathizers from working in the
film industry.

BLAXPLOITATION: Hollywood's exploitation of African-Americans in
mainstream filmmaking during the late 1960s and early 1970s.

BLIMP: The part of a camera that muffles the sound of the camera

operating.

BLIND BIDDING: A system in which exhibitors are forced to select a film, sight unseen.

BLOCK BOOKING: A system in which exhibitors are forced to buy a number of films in order to get a preferred film.

BLOCKBUSTER: An extremely popular film that often justifies formula filmmaking.

BLOW-UP: An enlargement of a screen image by means of an optical printer.

BLUE SCREEN: A process that allows additional material to be added to a scene. Used primarily for special effects.

BOMB: Something you never want. A box-office disaster!

BOOKING: Renting a film.

BOOM: A device that carries mobile cameras to allow shots to be taken from almost any angle. Microphone booms provide the same flexibility.

BOX OFFICE: The place where tickets are sold. More often, it refers to a film's appeal to mass audiences.

BREAKAWAY: The fragile, specially constructed props designed for action sequences.

BREAKDOWN: The shot-by-shot planning of a scene or a film.

BRIDGING SHOT: An inserted shot that condenses time or shortens distances--e.g., a moving clock hand, or pages falling off a calender.

BUDGET: The total itemized expenses associated with film.

BUFF: A person who loves films but demonstrates little interest in intellectual analysis or criticism.

BUSHIDO: The code of the Samurai used in Japanese historical dramas.

BUSINESS: Gestures or behavior that texture a character's image or a scene's "look."

CABLE TELEVISION: A service that provides alternatives to network television programming. Unlike network broadcasting, Cable TV is a service for a monthly fee.

CALL: The schedule sheet that tells everyone connected with the production when to report.

CAMEO ROLE: A bit part played by a celebrity.

CAMERA STYLO: A term coined by Alexandre Astruc for creating, with a camera, the way a writer works with a pen.

CAN: The container for a reel of film. Also an idiom for announcing that the film is ready for release: e.g., "It's in the can!"

CANON: A group of films selected by people in authority to represent the best examples of formula filmmaking, noted directors, and/or the cinema.

CANNED MUSIC: Prerecorded music not produced for a specific film.

CHAIN-DRAMA: See RENJA-GEKI.

CINEASTE: People who love to watch and/or make films.

CINEMA: A high-brow definition of film as an art form. It is an attempt to convince the elite that film is the equal of the traditional arts.

CINEMA VERITE: The on-the-scene, "natural" documentary effect that suggests that reality is being recorded just as it happened.

CINEMATOGRAPHER: The individual in charge of photography and lighting.

CIRCUIT: A chain of theaters operated by one organization booking films for several locations.

CLAP BOARD: The wooden chalkboard used to signal the start of a take and to provide visual and oral cues to the editor.

CLOSE-UP: A tight shot of a person's face or an object.

CODE: A linguistic concept asserting that there is a scientific system
    for analyzing film's meaning. It is also used to refer to the
    Motion Picture Production Code: See Appendix IV.

COIC: COMITE D'ORGANIZATION DE L'INDUSTRIE CINEMATOGRAPHIQUE, a French
    committee set up by the Nazi occupation forces to handle film
    resources during World War II in France.

COMPILATION FILM: A film anthology using footage from other films.

COMPOSITION: The artistic arrangement of the visual aspects in a frame
    before shooting.

CONTEXTUAL CRITICISM: Anchoring analysis in the time in which the film
    was made and/or in the framework of a filmmaker's total output.

CONTINUITY: Invisible, easy-flowing transitions that move the plot,
    dialogue, and characters from start to finish.

CONTRAST: The manipulation of light and shadows within a shot.

CONVENTIONS: A stock character, setting, theme, dialogue, situation, or
    cinematic technique used repeatedly in a film formula to reassure
    audiences that the movie will meet their preconceived expectations.

CRANE SHOT: A camera shooting from a boom.

CRAWL: The titles or words that begin at the top of the screen and roll
    down.

CREDITS: The technical people who worked in and on the film.

CRITICS: Serious film students who take time to analyze a film and to
    direct their insights to informed audiences.

CROSSCUT: Frequent, rapid switching from one shot to another for purposes
    of showing simultaneous action.

CUE: An action, sound, or gesture that indicates the start of something
    new.

CUE SHEET: A silent film technique indicating where a musician should play certain types of music for mood or effect.

CULT MOVIE: A film that appeals almost exclusively to a hardy group of individuals who find it contains characters, incidents, and themes unfathomable or unappealing to mass audiences.

CULTURAL HEGEMONY: A complex process involving a series of relationships that collectively reflect a nation's values.

CULTURAL RADIFICATION MODEL: A method for testing how media function as agencies of political control in society.

CUT: A visual transition from one shot to another.

CUT!: The director's signal to call a halt to the shooting.

CUT AWAY: A fast shift away from the main action. A cut back returns you quickly to the main action.

CUTTER: A synonym for editor.

DAILIES: The work print of the sight and sound image shot the previous day and used for evaluating the progress of the filming. Also called "Rushes."

DAY-FOR-NIGHT: Shooting a film during the day but using blue filters to create the illusion of night.

DECONSTRUCTIONISM: Theoretically reducing the structure of a film to its individual parts.

DECOUPAGE: A French term that describes the characteristics of the classic Hollywood film. The emphasis is on separating the plot into separate shots before shooting begins in order to create the illusion of "invisible" or "seamless" editing.

DEFINITION: The sharpness of the visual image.

DEEP-FOCUS CINEMATOGRAPHY: The ability to keep the foreground and the background in balanced focus.

DEPTH OF FIELD: The visual range between the foreground and the

background.

DETAIL SHOT: More extreme than a close-up.

DIACHRONIC: A linguistic concept that accounts for the change in
something because of a time factor.

DIALECTIC: A Marxist concept contrasting opposing elements in a system
to expose important differences.

DIAPHRAGM: The instrument that monitors the light going through the lens.

DIFFUSION: Softening the light effect on an individual.

DIRECT CINEMA: A variation of CINEMA VERITE, stressing non-fiction
films made with light and portable equipment and giving the illusion
of objectivity. It is the American version of the French approach.

DISSOLVE: A visual effect that causes a transition between one shot and
another by first dimming and then brightening.

DISTRIBUTION: Booking and selling films.

DOCU-DRAMAS: Highly controversial TV re-creations of historical events
in quasi-factual narratives.

DOCUMENTARY: Non-fiction filmmaking that purports to record actual places
and events as they appear, rather than as they are created. Also
known as "factual Films" or "realistic Films."

DOLBY SYSTEM: A name for a noise-reduction system for optical and/or
tape-recording and high-fidelity amplification.

DOLLY: A wheeled platform used for moving the camera and camera crew to
make the action flow smoothly.

DOUBLE EXPOSURE: Recording two or more images on one piece of film.

DOUBLE FEATURE: Showing two films on the same program.

DOWSER: An electric device for masking changes from one reel to another.

DUBBING: The substitution of a sound track in the national language for the foreign speech.

DUPE: A duplicate film.

EDGE NUMBERING: A technique employing numbers on a work print and a final print that coordinates the editing of images and sounds during the last stages of editing. Also known as "Key Numbers" or "Rubber Numbering."

EDITING: The process of putting together the shots, scenes, sequences, and sounds in a film. A frequent issue is who--e.g., the director or the producer--does the cutting along with the editor.

EMULSION: The dull side of film stock containing light-sensitive chemicals (gelatin and silver halide) used for recording screen images.

ESTABLISHING SHOT: The placement of the scene in a specific context: time, place, mood, and setting. Also known as a "Cover Shot."

EXECUTIVE PRODUCER: The person credited with obtaining or giving the money to make the film.

EXHIBITION: A film that is shown in a movie theater, on television, or during a special screening.

EXPERIMENTAL FILM: A film that is concerned with images and/or sounds for the sake of innovation, rather than for profit and mass consumption.

EXPLOITATION FILM: A schlock film that is produced and marketed to capitalize on the lowest common denominator--e.g. gratuitous sex and violence--in the minds of the audience.

EXPOSURE: Allowing too much (overexposed) or too little (underexposed) light to strike the film stock. The former is used for dreamlike effects, the latter for terrifying effects.

EXPRESSIONISM: A film style that emphasizes visual distortions as objective representations of a character's psychological state.

EXTRA: A bit player who has no dialogue and who is used in crowd scenes for the sake of atmosphere.

EXTREME CLOSE-UP: A camera shot that allows a person or object to dominate the entire frame.

EXTREME LONG SHOT: A camera shot that makes the subject appear far away.

FADE IN/OUT: Motion from darkness to light or from light to darkness in visual terms.

FAST MOTION: Slowing the camera's recording speed so that the projected action on the screen moves unnaturally fast. Also known as "Accelerated Motion."

FEATURE FILM: A narrative film, running at least eighty-five minutes, that appears in movie theaters.

FEATURE PLAYER: An individual who plays a key role in the film, but who is not the star.

FIAF: Federation of International Film Archives.

FEERIE: A nineteenth-century melodrama that specialized in mime, acrobatics, and music for special effects.

FEMINIST FILM CRITICISM: A specific political and analytical perspective in which methodologies from sociology, psychology, film studies, semiotics, and related areas are used to analyze films in which the relationship between women on the screen and women in society is depicted.

FESTIVALS: A planned event for the exclusive screening of films that are to be honored, merchandized, and remembered.

FILM: (1) Movies, motion pictures, and the cinema. (2) A strip of celluloid that can record and/or project fixed images and/or sounds to create the illusion of motion.

FBO: Film Booking Office, a silent film company run by Joseph P. Kennedy.

FILM CONTINUUM: The complete process of filmmaking from the origin of an idea for a film, to the released film's reception.

FILM D'ART: A movement in silent French films that used stage plays and

performers so as to make movies respectable.

FILM ICONOGRAPHY: The ways in which filmmakers, through the language of
    film--e.g., editing, camera angles, lighting, composition, acting,
    music, dialogue, and sound effects--construct a film's meaning and
    ideology.

FILM LEADER: A short piece of film at the beginning and end of each reel
    of film, mainly used for protecting the film being edited or
    projected.

FILM SPACE: The space determined by the filmmaker for viewing, as opposed
    to actual space.

FILM THEORY: An attempt to analyze film principles.

FILM TIME: The emotional time of the action, as compared to its actual
    time.

FILM NOIR: A film formula that deals with greed, lust, and murder, set
    in urban settings noted for dark streets, long shadows, and
    uncontrollable passions.

FILTER: A device for screening out unwanted sounds, images, and colors.

FINAL CUT: The print used to mix the images with sound.

FIRST RUN: The initial release of the movie.

FLASHBACK: A shot, scene, or sequence that jumps back in time.

FLASH FORWARD: A shot, scene, or sequence that jumps forward in time.

FLOODLIGHTS: A light that distributes rays broadly, rather than focusing
    them on a specific area.

FOOTAGE: The amount of celluloid shot for a scene, sequence, or film.

FORMAT: A film's size--e.g., 8mm, 16mm, 35mm, 70 mm--or image--e.g.
    1:1.85--in width and height.

FORMULA FILMS: A narrative film with fixed conventions routinely made

and designed to satisfy audience expectations. The best ones often use innovative techniques to upgrade the conventions for modern tastes.

FORMALISM: A film theory that emphasizes the importance of form over content in creating a film's preferred meaning.

FOUR-WALL: Renting a theater for a fixed sum to show a film and to take all the box office risks.

FRAME: The individual picture on a strip of celluloid, or the actual composition of the shot. The traditional projection method used for silent films was sixteen frames per second; sound has twenty-four frames per second.

FRAMING: That section of reality shown to the audience. Three major types of framing are (1) dramatic--used to heighten suspense and to accent differences; (2) oblique--used for psychological effects and to indicate abnormal behavior; and (3) split--to show two or more different characters or actions.

FREE CINEMA: A British semi-documentary movement in the fifties dealing with the difficulties in everyday life.

FREEZE FRAME: The use of a single picture printed and projected repeatedly to convey the impression of a photographic still.

FRONT PROJECTION: The type of screen projection used in movie theaters.

F-STOP: A numerical calculation for lens apertures that indicates the amount of light transmitted to the lens.

FUNCTIONALISM: A theory for evaluating the mass media as social and economic systems that interconnect with each other.

FX: An abbreviation for effects.

GAFFER: The head electrician on a film production.

GATE: The camera or projector aperture that exposes the film moving through the camera or projector. Also known as "Picture Gate" or "Film Gate."

GAUGE: A film width measured in millimeters. The higher the gauge number, the sharper the image.

GEL: A flexible sheet of transparent colored plastic used for affecting color recording.

GENDAI-GEKI: Japanese historical films.

GENERAL RELEASE: The standard practice in distributing and exhibiting a film.

GENRE: A literary term applied to movie types with consistent patterns that go beyond individual films and respond to well-known audience expectations. See also FORMULA FILMS.

GERMAN EXPRESSIONIST MOVEMENT: A famous era in silent German films that began in 1919 and ended in the mid-twenties when Hollywood raided the famous German studios and brought the best talent to America. The movement reflected the cinema's debt to expressionist experiments in the AVANT-GARDE literary and art world of the period.

GLASS SHOT: A technique in which paintings or titles are placed on a section of a glass plate
live action is then shot through the
glass to create the illusion that the action is occurring in a specific setting.

GRAIN: A silver particle in the emulsion of a film, sometimes grouped together to create special effects.

GRIP: An individual who does general handy work on a film set.

GUARANTEE: A contractual arrangement for special arrangements in directing or acting in a film. Also used between distributors and exhibitors to determine the conditions of a film booking.

GROSS: The total amount of money a film earns from exhibition.

HAND-CRANKED: The standard practice in silent films, whereby the cinematographer operated the camera during shooting to control film speed. Sometimes used in the early days of projection.

HAND-HELD: a shot made by a cinematographer using a light, portable

camera.

HAYS OFFICE: An abbreviation for the period between 1922 and 1945, when
William Harrison Hays was head of the Motion Picture Producers and
Distributors Association. Also known as "The Breen Office," after
Joseph I. Breen, who regulated the Movie Code from 1934 to the 1950s.

HEAVY: The villain in a movie.

HIGH-KEY LIGHTING: A bright image typical of light-hearted
films, especially musicals and screwball comedies.

HOLLYWOOD TEN: A group of individual filmmakers convicted of contempt
of Congress because they refused to knuckle under to the Fascist
behavior of the 1947 House Un-American Activities Committee.

HOLOGRAM: A 3-D image produced by laser photography.

HOOK: An attention-grabbing device to get the audience involved at the
start of a film.

HORSE OPERA: A B-Western.

HYPE: Excessive advertising.

IDEOLOGY: The images and symbols used by a specific society to define its
view of the "real world," and to perpetuate itself.

IMP: The Independent Motion Picture Company, a silent film distribution
company run by Carl Laemmle.

INCIDENTAL MUSIC: Mood music that helps create the screen emotion
in the scene being projected.

INDEPENDENTS: The name originally associated with individuals opposed to
the members of the Motion Picture Trust. Later associated with
individuals working outside mainstream film production, distribution,
and exhibition.

INFORMATION THEORY: The concept dealing with how messages are transmitted
and received.

INTELLECTUAL MONTAGE: Editing a series of shots to create an abstract concept.

INTENTIONAL FALLACY: The mistake of judging a film's meaning by the presumed intentions of the filmmaker(s).

INTERMITTENT MOVEMENT: The process of moving the film through the camera and the projector in a stop-go fashion, thus making it possible for individual frames to be exposed, projected, and then replaced by the following frame.

I.A.T.S.E: The International Alliance of Theatrical Stage Employees and Moving Picture Machine Operators of the United States and Canada, the central organization of craft employees and film projectionists.

IRIS: The gradual opening or closing of the lens, designed for dramatic effect.

JIDAI-GEKI: A Japanese period-drama.

JOHNSTON OFFICE: Named after Eric A. Johnston, who took over Hays's job in 1945 and changed the name of the MPPDA to the Motion Picture Association of America. Johnston died in 1963.

JUMP CUT: Abrupt cutting from shot to shot, and from scene to scene.

KAMMERSPIEL: A German Expressionist formula film that specialized in psychological characterizations of ordinary people in trouble.

KATSUBEN: See Benshi.

KEY LIGHT: The major source of light on a subject, used for creating the primary mood.

KEY NUMBERS: See EDGE NUMBERING.

KEYSTONE KOPS: The zany police force that starred in Mack Sennett's Keystone Comedies.

KILL: Turning off the lights.

KINETOSCOPE: The peephole viewer invented by William Kennedy Laurie Dickson and marketed by the Edison Manufacturing Company.

KINO-EYE: Soviet AVANT-GARDE documentaries in the silent era.

KLIEG LIGHT: Very powerful spotlights, often used at premieres.

LEGION OF DECENCY: A censorship body created by the Catholic church in the United States in 1933. It was the guiding force behind the creation of the Motion Picture Production Code. Many other religious groups in America also supported the legion's activities.

LEGS: A business term that means that a film will have an extended run.

LENS: An optical system that organizes light rays in order to create an image.

LIGHTING: Illuminating a scene or a shot to create a specific mood or effect.

LIMITED RELEASE: A marketing strategy to test the box office success of a new film.

LINKAGE: A Soviet editing concept emphasizing a psychological connection between shots that emerges "naturally," rather than "dramatically." Often used to contrast the methods of V. I. Pudovkin (who invented "linkage" editing) with those of Sergei M. Eisenstein (who stressed the "collision" of shots to produce a psychological meaning).

LIVE ACTION: Ordinary action as compared to the illusion created by animation or special effects.

LOCATION SHOOTING: Filming scenes outside the studio.

LONG SHOT: A complete shot of a subject or action.

LONG TAKE: Shooting for an extended period of time without the use of edited shots.

LOT: A piece of studio property used for building a set.

LOW-ANGLE SHOT: Shooting up at a subject.

LOW-KEY LIGHTING: An emphasis on dark, dramatic lighting, especially in thrillers and melodramas.

MAINSTREAM FILMMAKING: (1) From the teens to the late fifties, it referred to the Hollywood theatrical film during the heyday of the studio system. (2) Currently, it refers to patterns determined by the major American film distributors who control the film market.

MALE GAZE: A feminist term referring to the way in which Hollywood filmmakers use viewing as a means of providing sexual pleasure and of reinforcing a patriarchal point of view.

MASK: A device designed to control light transmission.

MASTER SHOT: A long take of a scene that editors use in determining how the scene will be cut. Also known as a "Cover Shot."

MATCH CUT: Editing that stresses metaphorical relationships, rather than continuous action.

MATTE: A masking technique used to block out a particular part of the frame.

MATTE SHOT: Mixing actual shots with artificial scenes to create a new setting.

McGUFFIN: The gimmick created by Alfred Hitchcock for keeping audiences in suspense.

MELODRAMA: The action that centers on exaggerated conflicts between heroes and villains.

METTEUR EN SCENE: The French term for director.

MIRROR SHOT: A special effects shot using a mirror to record an image.

MISE EN SCENE: A French term translated as "putting into the scene" and

used for describing how a shot or scene is directed. The "look" of a set and the placement of the performers as compared to the editing of a scene.

MIXER: An individual who combines various sound tracks.

MIXES: A form of superimposition in visuals. In sound, a blend of sound tracks.

MONTAGE: The French term for editing. Also, a collection of shots rapidly projected to create the illusion of time passing or of a collection of memories.

MONTAGE OF ATTRACTIONS: An editing concept developed by Sergei M. Eisenstein to show specific relationships among disparate shots.

MOTIF: A significant stylistic device that occurs repeatedly in the film.

MOTION PICTURE PATENTS COMPANY: An organization of ten silent film companies that banded together on January 1, 1909, for the purpose of monopolizing the film industry. It went out of existence in 1915. See also TRUST.

MOTION PICTURE PRODUCTION CODE: A collection of principles for regulating the content of American films from 1930 until the mid-1960s. It became effective only after the Legion of Decency forced the MPPDA to let Joseph I. Breen oversee the implementation of the principles beginning in June 1934.

MOVIOLA: A machine used to examine film foot by foot and to coordinate the visual and the audio.

MPPA: The Motion Picture Production Agency set up to enforce the Motion Picture production Code.

MPPC: See MOTION PICTURE PRODUCTION CODE.

MPPDA: The Motion Picture Producers and Distributors of America, created in 1921, to regulate the film industry and to ward off external censorship. The name was changed in 1945 to the Motion Picture Association of America.
MUTOSCOPE: A flip-card peepshow that was put out by Thomas Edison's rivals, The American Mutoscope Company (later known as Biograph). One of the major partners was William Kennedy Laurie Dickson, the man who invented the Kinetoscope, the Edison peepshow machine.

NARRATION: Offscreen commentary.

NARRATIVE: The story. A "film narrative" refers to the causal relationships that constitute the actions and the messages contained in a specific film text.

NATURALISM: A concept that assumes that we are at the mercy of social forces. The slice-of-life action presumes a scientific and objective interpretation of life.

NEGATIVE IMAGE: A photographic image devoid of color and that reverses the standard use of light and shadows.

NEOREALISM: A cinematic style that emerged during the final days of World War II in Italy. Characterized by non-professional actors portraying the hardships of daily life and shot with light, portable cameras in semi-documentary fashion.

NEP: New Economic Policy, a plan used by the Soviet government in the late twenties that failed and that was instrumental in ushering in socialist realism.

NEW AMERICAN CINEMA: The American AVANT-GARDE movement in the 1960s, primarily reacting against Hollywood production techniques and conventions.

NOUVELLE VAGUE: A form of filmmaking developed by young French film critics during the mid- to late 1950s. In part a homage to Hollywood formula films and AUTEUR directors, the low-budget films relied on light camera equipment and location shooting to tell pyschological stories. More a name for a group of exciting film talents, than a coherent theory.

ONE-REELER: A film running less than twelve minutes.

ONNAGATA: Japanese female impersonators in silent films. See also OXAMA.

OPTICALS: Special effects made either on a special printer or in the camera.

OUTLINE: The initial step in the screenwriting process.

OUT-TAKES: Shots and scenes that have been deleted from the final print of the film.

OXAMA: See ONNAGATA.

PACKAGE: A deal in which a screenplay, performers, a director, and a producer are contracted for a specific film project.

PAN: A horizontal camera movement.

PARADIGM: A semiotic term denoting a potential, rather than an actual relationship.

PARALLEL EDITING: Alternating shots between simultaneous actions to create the impression that the spectator is watching both events at the same time. See also CROSS-CUTTING.

PERSISTENCE OF VISION: The brief retention of an image by the retina of the eye after that image has been replaced by another. At one time, the phenomenon was thought to explain the illusion of motion in films.

PHI PHENOMENON: A psychological effect that gives the illusion of motion when one image is quickly replaced by another. It differs from the "peristence of vision" effect, which is physiological.

PLOT: The structuring of events in a narrative film.

POINT OF VIEW: (1) The distance between the camera and the subject. (2) The camera angle used in recording a shot. (3) The perspective of the filmmaker toward the subject.

POINT OF VIEW SHOT: A camera shot taken from the presumed position of a character. See also SUBJECTIVE SHOT.

PORNOGRAPHY: A work with no redeeming social values, presumably, works that concentrate on gratuitous sex.

POSTPRODUCTION: The work done on a new film after it is "in the can." The process involves editing the recorded images and sounds.

PREMIERE: The first public exhibition of a new film.

PRE-PRODUCTION: The work done before shooting begins. The process

involves determining the locations, scheduling the cast and crew, creating a shooting script, constructing the sets, and designing the costumes.

PREVIEW: (1) A pre-release screening of a new film. (2) Publicity clips from a new film shown before a feature film. See also TRAILERS.

PRINT: A positive copy made from a negative film (one that has its primary tone inverted).

PROCESS SHOT: A process in which background footage is projected through a transparent screen while live action takes place in front of the screen.

PRODUCER: The person in charge of managing and financing a production.

PRODUCTION CODE OFFICE: The MPPA agency in charge of implementing the Production Code. Originally known as the Breen Office.

PROPAGANDA: A means to subordinate the intellect to the emotions. Its purpose is to discourage debate, to create widespread acceptance of a particular point of view, and to rationalize where necessary the doubts audiences may have concerning a controversial policy.

PULLING FOCUS: See RACK FOCUS.

QUICK CUT: See JUMP CUT

RACK FOCUS: A system whereby the focus is changed within a shot. The purpose is to direct the viewer's attention to a particular object or person. Also known as "Pulling Focus."

RATINGS: (1) Classifications determined by a film board to indicate appropriate audiences. (2) A means of measuring the size of a TV audience.

RAW STOCK: Unprocessed or unused film.

REACTION SHOT: A shot of an individual reacting to an event or to another individual.

READING A FILM: Paying close attention to the way in which the

various elements--e.g., lighting, dialogue, performers, editing, and sound effects, etc.--communicate ideas that contribute to the reception of the film.

REALISM: A presumed objective treatment of an event and/or a relationship.

REAR PROJECTION: See BACK PROJECTION.

REFLECTOR: A piece of equipment that directs light to a desired spot.

REFLEXIVE FILMS: Works that call attention to the fact that they are movies and not reality. Generally, this is accomplished by one of the characters looking at the audience or commenting on what's happening on screen.

RELEASE PRINT: The print used by distributors to rent, lease, or sell to exhibitors.

RENJA-GEKI: A Japanese drama using film footage of outdoor locations. See CHAIN-DRAMA.

REPRESENTATIONS: The illusion created by filmmakers to approximate reality.

RETAKE: New shots of bad rushes.

REVIEW: A short commentary dwelling on cast, credits, plot summary, and personal reaction to a work. Generally for purposes of advising the reader on what's in the film, rather than critically analyzing it.

ROUGH CUT: A crudely put together silent version of an evolving film. It is not in sequence.

RUBBER NUMBERING: See EDGE NUMBERING.

RUNAWAY PRODUCTION: An American movie made in a foreign country in order to minimize costs.

RUNNING TIME: The time that the actual picture takes when projected from start to finish.

RUSHES: The immediate screening of recently developed shots as yet

unedited. See DAILIES.

SCENE: A specific section of the film shot in one set-up.

SCENARIO: A general idea of a proposed film. See TREATMENT.

SCORE: Music composed for a film.

SCREENPLAY: The basis of the narrative film. Always written, it goes
    through various stages: e.g., outline, treatment, shooting script,
    and continuity script,

SCRIPT: An extensive description of the action, plot, characters,
    dialogue, and theme in a proposed film.

SECOND UNIT: A special team assigned to shoot specific scenes.

SEMIOTICS: In film, a theory for analyzing how messages are
    produced and received (signification) through a set of codes and
    signs.

SEQUENCE: A scene(s) in a film.

SET-UP: The fixing of equipment and blocking of performers prior to
    shooting.

SFX: An abbreviation for "special effects."

SHOOT: The filming of a shot, scene, or sequence.

SHOOTING SCHEDULE: A breakdown of the shots to be taken, the performers
    used, and the camera shots needed.

SHOOTING SCRIPT: A shot-by-shot breakdown of the script for purposes of
    actual production. Also known as "continuity script."

SHOT: A single piece of film imagery without interruptions or editing.

SHOWCASE: Special release pattern for bringing attention to a new film.

SHUTTER: A device in the camera and projector that protects the film

from light.

SIGN: A semilogical term describing the two basic elements of
signification: the "signifier" (the meaning) and the "signified"
(the object being communicated). In oversimplified terms, a police
car is the signifier; the notion of a police car is the signified.
Together, they compromise the sign.

SLEEPER: A surprise hit. BAGHDAD CAFE (1988) rather than INDIANA
JONES AND THE LAST CRUSADE (1989).

SLON: SOCIETE POUR LE LANCEMENT DES OUVRES NOUVELLES, a film co-operative
started by Chris Marker in 1967.

SLOW MOTION: The technique by which the camera is run quicker than
usual so that the projected film moves slower than normal.

SOCIALIST REALISM: A style of Soviet filmmaking that emphasized everyday
life and proper conduct for Soviet citizens, but avoided the more
detached qualities of the early Soviet films.

SOFT FOCUS: The hazy photographic effect that glamorizes fading stars.

SOAP OPERA: An endless serialized drama once considered low-brow, but now
considered a rich source of information about contemporary drama and
society.

SOUND TRACK: A place along the side of film prints where sound is
recorded. The sound can either be recorded optically or magnetically.

SPLICE: Joining two pieces of film together.

SPLIT SCREEN: A separate image juxtaposed but not overlapping on the
screen at the same time.

SPOTLIGHTS: Light used for special effects.

SPROCKETS: The small "teeth" that grab holes on the edge of film strips
to move film through camera and projectors.

STAR SYSTEM: A public relations ploy for focusing the audience's
attention on a performer's personality rather than on his or her
acting ability.

STEADICAM: A device developed by the cinematographer Garrett Brown that allows an individual to strap on a camera and move easily during hand-held shooting. It creates the same effect as a "tracking shot," but is less expensive to shoot.

STEREOTYPES: A controversial means of organizing information.

STOCK SHOTS: Film footage of events, locations, and personalities that are housed in film libraries for later use.

STORYBOARD: A visual breakdown of the material to be filmed. Done in the form of sketches sequentially presented.

STRUCTURALISM: A theoretical concept that emphasizes conflicting relationships ("binary opposition") between groups and individuals.

SUBJECTIVE CAMERA: See POINT OF VIEW.

TAKE: The total scene shot, numbered, and ready for processing. Also, a means for calculating the number of times a shot took to complete.

TEAR-JERKER: A highly sentimental film.

TEXT: The organic unity of the film and the manner in which its various elements contribute to the communication of ideas about the characters, setting, theme, etc. Also, the narrative in a book.

THEATRICAL FILM: A film whose major objective is exhibition in a movie theater.

THEME: The purpose of the story.

THREE-D: A screen process using two projected images that creates the illusion of three-dimensional imagery. In order for this process to be effective, the viewer must wear special glasses.

TIE-IN: The sale of products associated with a particular film.

TIE-UP: Efforts by the film industry to relate a particular film to a particular activity.

TILTING: Moving the camera vertically.

2238   GLOSSARY

TINTING: Coloring a film during processing rather than in the shooting. The major form of color films in the silent era, the major source of professional shame in the modern era.

TONE: The manipulation of cinematic elements to create a specific feeling and/or mood. Also used to indicate color contrasts.

TRACKING: The parallel movement of the camera with the subject being shot. It can also be used to photograph a continuous, but motionless, scene. The best examples are found in the films of LA NOUVELLE VAGUE.

TRAILER: Shots from a film used in advertising to announce the film will soon be shown in your neighborhood theater.

TRAVELING SHOT: Moving the camera sideways or in and out. Also known as a "Tracking Shot."

TREATMENT: An outline of a proposed film, used for getting people interested in the project.

TRUST: See MOTION PICTURE PATENTS COMPANY.

TURN-OVER: The technique of having the entire screen image flip flop in the frame.

TYPECASTING: The selection of the cast by use of stereotypes.

UFA: University Film Association. Later changed to UFVA.

UFVA: University Film and Video Association.

UNDERGROUND CINEMA: Term for experimental and AVANT-GARDE films.

UNIT: A group assembled to make a film.

USCC: U. S. Catholic Conference, an organization providing media reviews and educational services.

USES AND GRATIFICATION MODEL: A strategy for evaluating how people

are educated and satisfied by the mass media.

VGIK: VSESOYUZN GOSUDARSTVENYI INSTITUT KINEMATOGRAFIA, a Soviet film
school where theories about montage were developed.

VOICE OVER: An off-screen voice to explain the action on screen.

WALK-ON: A bit player.

WIDE ANGLE: A lens with limited focal length but with the ability to
record a vast area of action.

WIPE: The technique in which one image pushes another image off the
screen.

WOMEN'S FILM: A formula film featuring narrative patterns, stereotypes,
themes, and production qualities appealing primarily to female
audiences.

WORK PRINT: A duplicate of the principal film that is used in
postproduction editing.

WPA: Works Project Administration, the organization responsible for the
Federal Writers' Project.

ZOOM: The quick movement by the camera toward or away from the center of
attention.

Appendix I

A SELECTED LIST OF FILM CRITICS AND PERIODICALS

Films are regularly reviewed in the following publications: THE BLACK AMERICAN, Dwight Brown; CHICAGO SUN TIME, Roger Ebert; CHICAGO TRIBUNE, Gene Siskel; THE CHRISTIAN SCIENCE MONITOR, David Sterritt; THE CITY SUN, Armond White; COMING ATTRACTIONS, Judith Crist; COMMONWEAL, Tom O'Brien; ESQUIRE, Toby Thompson; Gannett Newspapers, William Wolf; GLAMOUR, Jay Gould Boyum; HOLLYWOOD REPORTER, Robert Osborne; LOS ANGELES TIMES, Charles Champlin and Sheila Benson; LOS ANGELES WEEKLY, Michael Wilmington; THE NATIONAL REVIEW, John Simon; THE NEW REPUBLIC, Stanley Kauffmann; NEW YORK DAILY NEWS, Kathleen Carroll; NEW YORK MAGAZINE, David Denby; NEW YORK OBSERVER, Rex Reed; NEW YORK POST, David Edelstein; NEW YORK TIMES, Vincent Canby and Janet Maslin; THE NEW YORKER, Terrence Rafferty and Pauline Kael; NEWHOUSE NEWSPAPERS, Richard Freedman; NEWSDAY, Joseph Gelmis and Lynn Darling; NEWSWEEK, David Ansen and Jack Kroll; PENTHOUSE, Roger Greenspun; PEOPLE, Peter Travers; PLAYBOY, Bruce Williamson; THE PROGRESSIVE MAGAZINE, Michael H. Seitz; SEVEN DAYS, Georgia Brown; TIME, Richard Corliss and Richard Schickel; THE TORONTO GLOBE AND MAIL, Jay Scott; THE VILLAGE VOICE, Andrew Sarris and J. Hoberman; VOGUE, Molly Haskel; THE WALL STREET JOURNAL, Julie Salamon; and WOMEN'S WEAR DAILY, Howard Kissel. In addition, there are TV film reviewers like Gene Siskel, Rogert Ebert, Rex Reed, and Jeffrey Lyons.

Films are also reviewed and discussed regularly in the following periodicals:

ACTION. 7950 Sunset Boulevard, Hollywood, California 90046. $4 per year.

AFTERIMAGE. Visual Studies Workshop, 31 Prince Street, Rochester, New York 14607. $2.75 per copy, $28 per year for individuals; $32 for institutions; overseas: individuals, $32; $36, institutions.

AFI EDUCATION NEWSLETTER. American Film Institute, Department PD, P. O. Box 27999, 2021 North Western Avenue, Los Angeles, California 90027. $5 per year.

AMAZING CINEMA. 12 Moray Court, Baltimore, Maryland 21236. $18.50 per year.

AMERICA. American Press, 106 W. 56th Street, New York, New York 10019. $28 per year.

AMERICAN CINEMATOGRAPHER. ASC Holding Corporation, 1782 N. Orange Dr., Hollywood, California 90028. $2.95 per copy, $22 per year.

AMERICAN CINEMEDITOR. P. O. Box 16490, Encino, California 91416. $15 per year for individuals; $12 for students; and $23 for overseas subscriptions.

AMERICAN CLASSIC SCREEN. 7800 Conser, Shawnee Mission, Kansas 66204.

AMERICAN FILM. 1515 Broadway, New York, New York 10036. $2.50 per copy, $25 per year (outside U. S., add $7).

AMERICAN IMAGO, Wayne State University Press, Leonard N. Simons Bldg., 5959 Woodward Avenue, Detroit, Michigan 48202. $41 per year Institutions and Libraries; $29, individuals.

AMERICAN QUARTERLY, Smithsonian Institution, NAMH-4601, Washington, D. C. 20560. Subscriptions according to Income (i.e., Income under $12,000 is $15 per year).

AMERICAN SCHOLAR. United Chapters of Phi Beta Kappa, 1811 Q Street, N. W., Washington, D. C. 20009. $18 per year.

ANIMANIA. 3112 Holmes Avenue South, Minneapolis, Minnesota 55408. $2 per copy, $46 per year.

A-V COMMUNICATION REVIEW. Department of Audio-Visual Instruction, NEA, 1201 16th Street, N. W., Washington, D. C. 20036. $8 per year.

BACK STAGE. 330 West 42nd Street, New York, New York 10036. $50 per year.

THE BIG REEL. Route #3, Box 83, Madison, North Carolina 27025. $3 per copy, $20.00 per year.

BOXOFFICE. 1800 North Highland Avenue, Suite 710, P. O. Box 226, Hollywood, California 90028. $3.95 per copy, $35 per year.

BROADCASTING. Broadcasting Publications Inc., 1735 De Sales Street, NW Washington D. C. 20036.

BRIGHT LIGHTS. P. O. Box 26081, Los Angeles, California 90026. $2 per copy, $8 for 4 issues.

BRITISH JOURNAL OF AESTHETICS, Oxford University Press, Press Rd., Nearsdon, London NW 10 ODD England (Quarterly)

CAHIERS DU CINEMA. 9 Passage de la Boule-Blanche, 50 Rue du Faubourg-Saint Antoine, 7501 2, Paris, France.

CAMERA OBSCURA. The John Hopkins University Press, 701 West 40th Street, Suite 275, Baltimore, Maryland 21211. $28 institution price, single issue $8.

CANTRILL'S FILMNOTES. Box 12951, CPO Melbourne, Victoria, Australia.

CENEFAN. 3378 Valley Forge Way, San Jose, California 95117. $2.50 per issue.

CHANNELS. 19 West 44th Street, New York, New York 10036. $65.00 per year.

CINEASTE. 200 Park Avenue S, Suite 1320, New York, New York 10003. $13 per year (individuals), $19 foreign; $21 for libraries, $25 foreign.

CINEFANTASTIQUE. P. O. Box 270, Oak Park, Illinois 60303. $4.95 per copy, $18 for 4 issues.

CINEFEX. P. O. Box 20027, Riverside, California 92516. $5.25 per copy, $17 for 4 issues.

CINEMA CANADA. Box 398, Station Outremont, Montreal, Quebec, H2V 4NG, Canada. $26 per year for individuals; $30 for institution (plus $15 for overseas postage).

CINEMA JOURNAL. 217 Flint Hall, University of Kansas, Lawrence, Kansas 66044. $3.50 per copy, $7 per year.

CINEMA PAPERS. 644 Victoria Street, North Melbourne, Victoria, 3051 Australia. $7 per year.

CINEMATOGRAPH. 480 Potrero Ave, San Francisco, California 94110. $7.50 per year (individuals), $13 (institutions).

CINEMASCORE. P. O. Box 70868, Sunnyvale, California 94086. $8 per year, $4.00 each.

CINE-TRACTS. 4111 Esplanade Avenue, Montreal, Quebec, H3W 1S9, Canada. $60 per year.

CLASSIC IMAGES. 301 E. 3rd Street, Muscatine, Iowa 52761. $25 for 12 issues.

CONTACT STRATEGIES. 4289 Bunche Hall, University of California, Los Angeles, California 90024.

CONTINUUM. Western Australian College of Advanced Education, Box 66, Mount Lawley, WA 6050, Australia.

COPIE ZERO 360 Rue McGill, Montreal, Quebec H2Y 2E9, Canada (Quarterly)

CRITICAL INQUIRY. University of Chicago Press, 5720 S. Woodlawn Ave., Chicago, Illinois 60637. $29 per year (individuals), $58 (institutions), $20 (students).

CRITICAL STUDIES IN MASS COMMUNICATION. Department of Communication, University of Utah, Salt Lake City, Utah, 84112. $12 per copy, $40 per year (members), $45 (institutions).

CTVD: CINEMA-TV-DIGEST. Hampton Books, Route 1, Box 202, Newberry, South Carolina 29108. $.85 per copy, $3 for 4 issues.

DAILY VARIETY. 1400 North Cahuenga Boulevard, Hollywood, California 90028. $70 for six months, $85 per year.

DEEP FOCUS. 94 Charles Campbell Road, Cox Town, Bangalore, 560 005, India.

DIGEST OF THE UNIVERSITY FILM AND VIDEO ASSOCIATION. Department of Cinema and Photography, Southern Illinois University, Carbondale, Illinois 62901. Inquire for rates.

EAST-WEST FILM JOURNAL. Institute of Culture and Communication, East-West Center, 1777 East-West Road, Honolulu, Hawaii 96848, USA. Subscription Address: Journals Department, University of Hawaii Press, 2840 Kolowalu Street, Honolulu, Hawaii 96822. $15 per year for individuals; $25 per institution. Outside the United States: $17 per year for individuals; $30 per year for institutions.

FILAMENT. Department of Theatre Arts, Wright State University, Dayton, Ohio 45435. free.

FILM. British Federation of Film Societies Unit, BFI, 21 Stephen Street, London W1P 1PL, England.

FILM AND HISTORY. Historians Film Committee, New Jersey Institute of Technology, Newark, New Jersey 07102. $14 per year for individuals, $20 per year institutions.

FILM BULLETIN. 1239 Vine Street, Philadelphia, Pennsylvania 19107.

FILM COMMENT. 140 West 65th Street, New York, New York 10023. $14.95 for 6 issues.

FILM CRITICISM. Box D. Allegheny College, Meadville, Pennsylvania 16335. $9 a year for individuals; $10, institutions/library; $12, foreign (air mail, $15).

FILM CULTURE. GPO Box 1499, New York, New York 10001. $12 for 4 issues.

FILM DOPE. 40 Willifield Way, London, NW11 7XT England.   (Irregularly)

FILM JOURNAL. Ed. Thomas R. Atkins, P. O. Box 9602, Hollins College, Virginia 24020.

FILM LIBRARY QUARTERLY. P. O. Box 348, Radio City Station, New York, New York 10019.

FILMMAKERS MONTHLY. P. O. Box 115, Ward Hill, Massachusetts 01830.

FILMMAKERS' NEWSLETTER. 80 Wooster Street, New York, New York 10012. $40 per year.

FILM QUARTERLY. University of California Press, 2120 Berkeley Way, Berkeley, California 94720. $3.50 per copy, $14 per year.

FILM READER. Film Division, Northwestern University, 1905 Sheridan Road, Evanston, Illinois 60201. $10 per issue.

FILM REVIEW. Old Court House, Old Court Place, London W8 4PD, England.

FILMS. 34 Buckingham Palace Road, London SW1 WORE, England. $3.25 per issue.

FILMS AND FILMING. 248 High Street, Croydon, Surrey CRO 1NF, England.

FILMS ILLUSTRATED. 13-35 Bridge Street, Hemel Hempstead, Hertfordshire, England. $2.95 per copy, $26 per year.

FILMS IN REVIEW. P. O. Box 589, New York, New York 10021. $18 per year.

FILMS ON SCREEN AND VIDEO. 22-24 Buckingham Palace Road, London SW1, England.

FILMVIEWS. P. O. Box 204, Albert Park, Victoria 3206, Australia. $4 for four issues/ overseas, $24 for four issues.

FILMTEXAS. Texas Film Commission, P. O. Box 12428, Austin, Texas 78711. Subscriptions free.

FOCUS! Doc Films, 5811 South Ellis Avenue, Chicago, Illinois 60637. $1 per issue.

FOCUS MAGAZINE. Film Studies Program, University of California, Santa Barbara, California 93106. Free upon request.

FOCUS ON FILM. The Tantivy Press, Magdalen House, 136 Tooley Street, London SE1 2TT, England.

FRAMEWORK. Comedia, 9 Poland Street, London W1V 3DG, England.

HISTORICAL JOURNAL OF FILM, RADIO AND TELEVISION. School of Communication, 636AH, University of Houston, 4800 Calhoun Avenue, Houston, Texas 77004. Personal Member $28, Institutional Members $84.

THE HOLLYWOOD IMAGE. 336 North Foothill Road, Beverly Hills, California 90210. $2 per copy, $24 per year.

THE HOLLYWOOD REPORTER. P.O. Box 1431, Hollywood, California 90018. $0.75 per copy, $63 per year.

IRIS. Institute for Cinema and Culture, University of Iowa, 162 Communications Studies Building, Iowa City, Iowa 52242. $14.00 a year. $8.00 single issue.

JOURNAL OF FILM AND VIDEO. Division of Mass Communication, Emerson College, 100 Beacon Street, Boston, Massachusetts 02116. $4 per copy domestic ($5 foreign); $12.00 per year ($20 foreign).

JOURNAL OF FILM AND VIDEO. Division of Communication, Emerson College,   100 Beacon Street, Boston, Massachusetts 02116. For Institutional non-members, $12 per year; $20 foreign.

JOURNAL OF POPULAR FILM AND TELEVISION. Popular Culture Center, Bowling Green State University, Bowling Green, Ohio 43403. $10.75 per copy, $21.95 per year for individuals, $42.50 for institutions.

JUMP CUT. P. O. 2620 N. Richmond, Chicago, Illinois 60647. $4 per copy, $14 for 4 issues for individuals; $20 for for issues for institutions. Foreign subscriptions: $16 for 4 copies for individuals; $22 for 4 copies for institutions.

LITERATURE/FILM QUARTERLY. Salisbury State College, Salisbury, MD, 21801. $6 per copy, $12 per year (individuals), $24 (institutions)

MEDIA INFORMATION AUSTRALIA. Australian Film, TV and Radio School.   P. O. Box 126, North Ryde, NSW 2113, Australia. $32 per year for Individuals; $40 for organizations. Overseas: $55 for individuals, $65 for organizations.

MEMORIES. P. O. Box 50071, Boulder, Colorado 80321-0071. $9.97 per year.

MILLENNIUM: FILM JOURNAL. 66 East 46th Street, New York, New York 10017. $12.00 per year.

MISE-EN-SCENE. 10950 Euclid Avenue, Cleveland, Ohio 44106. $1 per copy.

MONTHLY FILM BULLETIN. The British Film Institute, 21 Stephen Street, London, WIP IPL, England. $28 per year.

MOTION PICTURE: A TRI-QUARTERLY FILM JOURNAL. Collective for Living Cinema, 41 White Street, New York, New York 10013. $11 per year.

MOTION PICTURE DAILY. 1270 Sixth Avenue, New York, New York 10020. $15 per year.

MOTION PICTURE HERALD. 1270 Sixth Avenue, New York, New York 10020. $5 per year.

MOVIE. 25 Lloyd Baker Street, London WC1X 9AT, England. $5 per copy ($6.50 per double issue).

MOVIEGOER. 545 Market Street, Knoxville, Tennessee 37902. Free.

MOVING IMAGE. 1 Videofilm Plaza, Marion, Ohio 43305. $1.95 per copy, $18 per year.

MOVING IMAGE REVIEW. Northeast Historic Film, Blue Hill Falls, Maine 04615. Student, $15.00 a year; Regular member, $25.00.

OCTOBER. MIT Press Journals, 28 Carleton Street, Cambridge, Massachusetts 02142.

ON FILM. College of Fine Arts, UCLA, 405 Hilgard Avenue, Los Angeles, California 90024. $2.50 per copy, $7.50 for subscription of three copies.

PERSISTENCE OF VISION. 53-24 63rd Street, Maspeth, New York 11378. $13.50 for subscription of three copies for individuals; $15, for institutions; $20 for foreign subscriptions. Published irregularly.

POST SCRIPT. Jacksonville University, 2800 University Boulevard N, Jacksonville, Florida 32211. $12 per year for individuals, $20 for institutions. Overseas, $17 a year for individuals; $25 for institutions.

PREMIERE: THE MOVIE MAGAZINE, 2 Park Avenue, New York, New York 10016. $18 per year.

PROGRESSIVE MAGAZINE. 409 East Main Street, Madison, Wisconsin 53703. $2.50 per copy, $23.50 per year.

QUARTERLY REVIEW OF FILM AND VIDEO. S. T. B. S. Marketing Department, P. O. Box 786, Cooper Station, New York, New York 10276. $40 individual, $106 academic library, $130 corporate.

SCREEN ACTOR MAGAZINE. 7065 Hollywood Boulevard, Hollywood, California 90028. $1.00 per copy, $7 per year.

SCREEN. 29 Old Compton Street, London, W1V 5P, England.   Individual, $38 per year; Institution, $58 per year.

SCREEN DIGEST. 37 Gower Street, London, WC1E 6HH, England.

SCREEN FACTS. P. O. Box 154, Kew Gardens, New York 11415. $7 per year.

SEMIOTICA. Mouton de Gruyter, Walter de Gruyter, Inc., 200 Saw Mill River Road, Hawthorne, NY 10532.

SEQUENCES. 4005 Rue de Bellechasse, Montreal, Quebec H1X 1J6, Canada (Quarterly).

SHAKESPEARE ON FILM NEWSLETTER. 70 Glen Cove Drive, Glen Head, New York 11545. $4 a year; $7 for two years.

SIGHT AND SOUND. The British Film Institute, 21 Stephen Street, London, W1P 1PL, England. $16 per year.

SILENT PICTURE, THE. 613 Harrow Road, London, W20, England. $3 per year.

STARLOG. 475 Park Avenue South, New York, New York 10016. $3.50 per copy, $29.97 per year.

STILLS. 10 Museum Street, London WC1A 1LE, England. $70.00 per year.

TECHTRENDS. 1126 16th Street, N. W., #700, Washington, D. C.   20036. $24 for 6 issues.

VARIETY. 475 Park Ave. S., New York, New York 10016. $1.25 per copy, $50 per year.

THE VELVET LIGHT TRAP, THE. University of Texas Press, Journal Department, P. O. Box 7819, Austin Texas 78713. $15.00 per copy for individuals ($17.50 Outside U. S. A.), $28 for institutions ($30.50 Outside U. S. A.).

VISIONS. Boston Film/Video Foundation, 1126 Boylston Street, Boston, Massachusetts 02215. $25 per year.

WIDE ANGLE. Johns Hopkins University Press, Baltimore, Maryland 21211. $3 per copy, $18 per year for individuals; $37 for institutions.

WOMEN AND FILM. 2802 Arizona Avenue, Santa Monica, California 90404. $2 per year.

Appendix II

SELECTED LIST OF 16MM FILM DISTRIBUTORS

Almi Cinema 5 (CIV), 1585 Broadway, New York, New York 10036.

Arthur Cantor, Inc. (ACI), 2112 Broadway, Suite 400, New York, New York 10023. (212) 496-5710

Audio Brandon (AUD/BRA) see MAC (Macmillan Films)

Aument Film Library (AUM), 1047 Orchard Avenue, S. E., Grand Rapids, Michigan 49506-3544. (616) 454-8157, (313) 961-5982

Benchmark Films, Inc. (BEN), 145 Scarborough Road, Briarcliff Manor, New York 10510. (914) 762-3838

Blackhawk Films (BLA), 1 Old Eagle Brewery, P. O. 3990, Davenport, Iowa 52808. (319) 323-9736, (800) 553-1163

Budget Films (BUD), 4590 Santa Monica Boulevard, Los Angeles, California 90029. (213) 660-0187

CAL (See University of California)

Carousel Films (CAR), 241 E. 49th St., New York, New York 10036. (212) 683-1660

Charard Motion Pictures (CHA), 2110 E. 24th Street, Brooklyn, New York 11229. (718) 891-4339

Churchill Films (CHU), 662 N. Robertson, Los Angeles, California 90069. (213) 657-5110

CIN (See Hurlock)

Cinema 5 (CIV), 1588 Broadway, New York, New York 10036. (212) 975-0550

CIV ((See Almi)

Clem Williams Films (CWF), 2240 Noblestown Road, Pittsburgh, Pennsylvania 15205. (412) 921-5810, (800) 245-1146

CRM/McGraw-Hill Films (CRM), P. O. Box 641, Del Mar, California 92014. (619) 453-5000

Creative Film Society (CFS), 8435 Geyser Ave., Northridge, California 91324. (818) 885-7288

Direct Cinema Ltd. (DCL), Box 69589, Los Angeles, California 90069. (213) 656-4700

Don Bosco Multimedia (DBM), 475 North Avenue, New Rochelle, New York 10802. (914) 632-6562

Em Gee Film Library (EMG), 6924 Canby Avenue, Suite 103, Reseda, California 91335. (818) 981-5506

EMC (See CAL)

Festival Films (FES), 2841 Irving Avenue South, Minneapolis, Minnesota 55408. (612) 870-4744

Film and Video Library (FVL), University of Michigan , 400 Street, Ann Arbor, Michigan 48103. (313) 764-5360

Films for the Humanities, Inc. (FFH), Box 2053, Princeton, New Jersey 08540. (201) 329-6912

Films Incorporated (FNC), 1144 Wilmette Ave., Wilmette, Illinois, 60091. (312) 256-3200, (800) 323-4222

Filmmakers Cooperative (FMC), 175 Lexington Avenue, New York, New York 10016. (212) 889-3820

Grove Press Film Division (GRO), 196 West Houston Street, New York, New York 10014. (212) 242-4900

Historical Films (HIF), P. O. Box 46505, Los Angeles, California 90046.

Hurlock-Cine World (CIN), 2858 Mendenhall Loop Road, P. O. Box 34619 Juneau, Alaska 99803-4619.

Icarus Films/Cinema Perspectives (ICP), 200 Park Avenue South, Suite 1319, New York, New York 10003. (212) 674-3375

Images Film Archive (IMA), 300 Phillips Park Road, Mamaroneck, New York 10543.
(914) 381-2993

Indiana University (IND), Audio-Visual Center, Bloomington, Indiana 47405. (812)
332-0211

International Film Bureau (IFB), 332 South Michigan Avenue, Chicago, Illinois 60604.
(312) 427-4545

International Film Exchange (IFE), 201 West 52nd Street, New York, New York 10019.
(212) 582-4318

Iowa Film (IOW), University of Iowa, C-5 Seashore Hall, Iowa City, Iowa 52242. (319)
353-5885

Ivy Film/16 (IVY), 165 West 46th Street, New York, New York 10036. (212) 382-0111

JAN (See FNC)

Jason Films (JAS), 2621 Palisades Avenue, Riverdale, New York 10463.   (914)
884-7648

Kino International Corporation (KNO), 250 W. 57th Street, New York, New York
10019. (212) 586-8720

Kit Parker Films (KIT), 1245 Tenth Street, Monterey, California 93940-3692. (408)
649-5573, (800) 538-5838

Learning Corporation of America (LCA), Coronet/MTI Film and Video, 108 Wilmot
Road, Deerfield, Illinois 60015. (800) 323-6301

The Liberty Company (LCF), 695 West 7th Street, Plainfield, New Jersey 07060. (201)
757-1450

Louisiana State University Instructional Resource Center (LSU), Himes Hall, Room 118,
Baton Rouge, Louisiana 70803. (504) 388-1135

Lucerne Films (LUC), 37 Ground Pine Road, Morris Plains, New Jersey 07950. (201)
538-1401

Macmillan Films/Audio Brandon (MAC), 34 MacQuestern Parkway S., Mount Vernon,
New York 10550. (914) 664-5051

Mass Media Ministries (MMM), 2116 N. Charles Street, Baltimore, Maryland 21218. (301) 727-3270

McGraw-Hill Films (MCG), see CRM (CRM/McGraw-Hill)

The Media Guild (MEG), 11526 Sorrento Valley Road, San Diego, California 92121. (619) 755-9191

MGM/United Artists Entertainment Company (MGM), 1350 Avenue of the Americas, New York, New York 10019. (800) 223-0933

Modern Sound Pictures (MOD), 1402 Howard St., Omaha, Nebraska 68102. (800) 228-9584

Mogull's (MOG), 1280 North Ave., Plainfield, New Jersey 07062. (201) 753-6004

Museum of Modern Art (MMA), Department of Film, 11 West 53rd St., New York, New York 10019. (212) 956-4204

National Audio-Visual Ctr. (NAC), General Services Administration, Washington, D. C. 20409. (310) 763-1896.

National Film Board of Canada (NFB), 1251 Avenue of the Americas, New York, New York 10020. (212) 586-5131

National Gallery of Art Extension Services (NGA), Washington, D. C. 20565. (202) 737-4215

National Geographic Society, Educational Services (NGE), 17th and M Streets, Washington, D. C. 20036 (202) 857-7000

National Telefilm Associates (NTA), 12636 Beatrice Street, Los Angeles, California 90066. (213) 306-4040

New Line Cinema (NLC), 575 Eighth Avenue, New York, New York 10018. (212) 674-7460

New Yorker Films (NYF), 16 W. 61st Street, New York, New York 10023. (212) 247-6110

New York University Film Library (NYU), 26 Washington Place, New York, New York 10003. (212) 777-2000

Productions Unlimited (PRU), 1301 Avenue of the Americas, New York, New York 10021. (212) 541-6770

Pyramid Films and Video (PYR), Box 1048, Santa Monica, California 90406. (213) 828-7577

Reel Images (REE), P. O. Box C, Sandy Hook, Connecticut 06482. (203) 426-2574

RKO General Pics (RKO), 1440 Broadway, New York, New York 10018. (212) 764-7108.

Roa's Films (ROA), 914 North 4th Street, P. O. Box 661, Milwaukee, Wisconsin 53201. (414) 271-0861, (800) 558-9015

Sterling Educational Films (STE), 241 E. 34th Street, New York, New York 10016. (212) 683-6300

SIN (See Hurlock)

Swank Motion Pictures (SWA), 201 So. Jefferson Avenue, St. Louis, Missouri 63166. (314) 534-6300, (800) 325-3344

Syracuse University Film Center (SUF), 1455 East Colvin Street, Syracuse, New York 13210. (315) 423-2452

Tamarelle's International Films (TIF), 110 Cohasset Stage Road, Chico, California 95926. (916) 895-3429

Texture Films Inc. (TEX), 5547 N. Ravenwood Avenue, Chicago, Illinois 60076.

Time-Life Films (TIM), 100 Eisenhower Drive, Paramus, New Jersey 07653. (201) 843-4545

Trans-World Films (TWF), 332 So. Michigan Avenue, Chicago, Illinois 60604. (312) 922-1530

Twyman Films (TWY), 4700 Wadsworth Road, Box 605, Dayton, Ohio 45401. (513) 276-5941, (800) 543-9594

University of California (CAL), Extension Media Center, 2716 Shattuck Avenue, Berkeley, California 94704. (415) 642-0460

University of Iowa (IOW), C-5 Seashore Hall, Iowa City, Iowa 52242. (319) 353-5885

Vidamerica (VAF), 235 East 55th Street, New York, New York 10022. (212) 355-1600

Video Communications Inc. (VCI), 6555 E. Skelly Drive, Tulsa, Oklahoma 74145. (918) 662-6460

Warner Brothers (WSA), see Swank Motion Pictures, Inc.

Welling Motion Pictures (WMP), 454 Meacham Ave., Elmont, New York 11003. (516) 354-1066

Westcoast Films (WCF), 25 Lusk Street, San Francisco, California 94107. (415) 362-4700, (800) 227-3058

Williams Films (WFM), 2240 Noblestown Road, Pittsburgh, Pennsylvania 15205. (412) 921-5810

Willoughby-Peerless (WIL), 115 W. 31st Street, New York, New York 10001. (212) 929-6477

World Northal (WOR), 1 Dag Hammarskjold Plaza, New York, New York 10017. (212) 223-8169

Zipporah Films Inc. (ZPH), 1 Richdale Avenue, Unit #4, Cambridge, Massachusetts 02140 (617) 576-3603

For a more extensive list consult FEATURE FILMS: A DIRECTORY OF FEATURE FILMS ON 16MM AND VIDEOTAPE, 8th edition. Compiled and ed. James L. Limbacher (New York: R. R. Bowker Co., 1985)

SELECTED LIST OF 8MM FILM DISTRIBUTORS

Blackhawk Films (BLA), 1 Old Eagle Brewery, P. O. 3390, Davenport, Iowa, 52808. (319) 323-9736, (800) 553-1163

Film Classic Exchange (FCE), 1914 So. Vermont Avenue, P. O. Box 77568, Los Angeles, California 90007. (213) 731-3854

For a more complete list, see 8MM FILM DIRECTORY: A COMPREHENSIVE AND DESCRIPTIVE INDEX. Compiled and Edited by Grace Ann Kone (New York: Comprehensive Service Corporation, 1969-70).

SELECTED LIST OF VIDEO DISTRIBUTORS

Blackhawk Films (BLA), 1 Old Eagle Brewery, P. O. 3990, Davenport, Iowa 52808. (319) 323-9736, (800) 533-1163

Clem Williams Films (CWF), 2240 Noblestown Road, Pittsburgh, Pennsylvania 15205.
(412) 9021-5810, (800) 245-1146

CRM/McGraw-Hill Films (CRM), P. O. Box 641, Del Mar, California 92014.   (619)
463-5000

Direct Cinema Ltd., (DCL), Box 69589, Los Angeles, California 90069.   (213)
656-4700.

Festival Films (FES), 2841 Irving Avenue South, Minneapolis, Minnesota 55408. (671)
870-4744

Films Incorporated (FNC), 1213 Wilmette Ave., Wilmette, Illinois 60091. (312)
256-3200, (800) 323-4222

Golden Tapes Video Library (GTV), 336 Foothill Road, Beverly Hills, California 90213.
(213) 550-8156

Images Film Archive (IMA), 300 Phillips Park Road, Mamaroneck, New York 10543.
(914) 381-2993

Ivy Film/16 (IVY), 165 West 46th Street, New York, New York 10036. (212) 382 -0111

Kit Parker Films (KPF), 1245 Tenth Street, Monterey, California 93940. (408)
649-5573, (800) 538-5838

Magnetic Video (MVC), 23705 Industrial Park Drive, Farmington Hills, Michigan 48018.
(313) 477-6066

MGM/United Artists Entertainment Company (MGM), 1350 Avenue of the Americas,
New York, New York 10019. (800) 223-0933

National Audio-Visual Center (NAC), General Services Administration, Washington,
D. C. 20409. (310) 763-1896

Pyramid Films and Video (PYR), Box 1048, Santa Monica, California 90406. (213)
818-7577

Swank Motion Pictures (SWA), 201 So. Jefferson Avenue, St. Louis, Missouri 63166.
(314) 534-6300, (800) 325-3344

Tamarelle's French Film House (TFF), 110 Cohasset Stage Road, Chico, California
95925. ((916) 895-3429

Appendix II

Time-Life Video (TIM), 100 Eisenhower Drive, Paramus, New Jersey 07653.   (201) 843-4545

Trans-World Films (TWF), 332 So. Michigan Avenue, Chicago, Illinois 60604. (312) 922-1530

Twyman Films (TWY), 4700 Wadsworth Road, Box 605, Dayton, Ohio   45401.   (513) 276-5941, (800) 543-9594

United Training Media (UTM), 6633 W. Howard Street, Niles, Illinois 60648. (800) 558-9015. Illinois residents call collect (312) 647-0600.

University of California (CAL), Extension Media Center, 2223 Fulton Street, Berkeley, California 94720. (415) 642-0460

The Voyager Company (VOY), 2139 Manning Avenue, Los Angeles, California 90025. (213) 474-0032

Zipporah Films (ZIP), 1 Richdale Avenue, Cambridge, Massachusetts 02140.   (617) 576-3603

Appendix III

I. CRIMES AGAINST THE LAW: These shall never be presented in such a way as to throw sympathy with the crime against the law and justice or to inspire others with a desire for imitating.

A. MURDER

1. The technique of murder must be presented in such a way that will not inspire imitation.

2. Brutal killings are not to be presented in detail.

3. Revenge in modern times shall not be justified.

B. METHODS OF CRIME should not be explicitly presented.

1. Theft, robbery, safe-cracking and dynamiting of trains, mines, buildings, etc., should not be detailed in methods.

2. Arson must be subject to the same safeguards.

3. The use of firearms should be restricted to essentials.

4. Methods of smuggling should not be presented.

C. THE ILLEGAL DRUG TRAFFIC must not be portrayed in such a way as to stimulate curiosity concerning the use of, or traffic in, such drugs; nor shall scenes be approved which show the use of illegal drugs or their effects in detail (as amended Sept. 22, 1946.)

D. THE USE OF LIQUOR in American life, when not required by the plot or for characterizations, will not be shown.

II. SEX
The sanctity of the institution of marriage and the home shall be upheld. Pictures shall not imply that low forms of sex relationships are the accepted or common thing.

A. ADULTERY AND ILLICIT SEX, sometimes necessary plot material, must not be explicitly treated or justified or presented attractively.

B. SCENES OF PASSION

1. These should not be introduced except where they are definitely essential to the plot.

2. Excessive and lustful kissing, lustful embraces, suggestive postures and gestures are not to be shown.

2257

Appendix III

3. In general, passion should be treated in such a manner as not to stimulate the lower or baser emotions.

C. SEDUCTION OR RAPE

1. These should never be more than suggested, and then only when essential to the plot. They must never be shown by explicit method.

2. They are never the proper subject for comedy.

D. SEX PERVERSION or any inference to it is forbidden.

E. WHITE SLAVERY shall not be treated.

F. Miscegenation (sex relationship between black and white races) is forbidden.

G. SEX HYGIENE and venereal diseases are not proper subjects for theatrical motion pictures.

H. Scenes of ACTUAL CHILDBIRTH, in fact or silhouette, are never to be presented.

I. Children's sex organs are never to be exposed.

III. VULGARITY
The treatment of low, disgusting, unpleasant, though not necessarily evil subjects should be guided always by the dictates of good taste and a proper regard for the sensibilities of the audience.

IV. OBSCENITY in word, gesture, reference, song, joke, or by suggestion (even when likely to be understood only by part of the audience) is forbidden.

V. PROFANITY
Pointed profanity and every other profane or vulgar expression, however used, is forbidden. No approval by the Production Code Administration shall be given to the use of words and phrases in motion pictures including, but not limited to, the following:
Alley cat (applied to a woman); bat (applied to a woman); broad (applied to a woman); Bronx cheer (the sound); chippie, cocotte; God; Lord, Jesus, Christ (unless used reverently); cripes; fanny; fairy (in a vulgar sense); finger (the); fire, cries of; Gawd; goose (in a vulgar sense); "hold your hat"; louse; lousy; hot (applied to a woman); "in your hat," nance; nerts; nuts (except when meaning crazy); pansy; razzberry (the sound); slut (applied to a woman); S.O.B., son-of-a-tart; toilet gags; tom cat (applied to a man); traveling salesman and farmer's daughter jokes; whore; damn; hell; (excepting when the use of said last two words shall be essential and required for portrayal, in historical fact or folklore, or for the presentation in proper literary context of a Biblical, or other religious quotation, or a quotation from a literary work provided that no such use shall be permitted which is intrinsically objectionable or offends good taste.)
In the administration of Section V of the Production Code, the Production Code Administration may take cognizance of the fact that the following words are offensive to the patrons of motion pictures in the United States and more particularly to the patrons of motion pictures in foreign countries: Chink, Dago, Frog, Greaser, Hunkie, Kike, Nigger, Spic, Wop, Yid.

VI. COSTUME

A. COMPLETE NUDITY is never permitted. This includes nudity to the fact
or in silhouette, or any licentious notice thereof by other characters
in the pictures.

B. UNDRESSING SCENES should be avoided, and never used save where
essential to the plot.

C. INDECENT OR UNDUE EXPOSURE is forbidden.

D. DANCING COSTUMES intended to permit undue exposure or indecent
movements in the dance are forbidden.

VII. DANCES

A. Dances suggesting or representing sexual actions or indecent passion
are forbidden.

B. Dances which emphasize indecent movements are to be regarded as
obscene.

VIII. RELIGION

A. No film or episode may throw ridicule on any religious faith.

B. MINISTERS OF RELIGION in their characters as ministers of religion
should not be used as comic characters or villains.

C. Ceremonies of any definite religion should be carefully avoided and
respectfully handled.

IX. LOCATIONS

The treatment of bedrooms must be governed by good taste and delicacy.

X. NATIONAL FEELINGS

A. The use of the flag shall be consistently respectful.

B. The history, institutions, prominent people and citizenry of all
nations shall be represented fairly.

XI. TITLES

Salacious, indecent or obscene titles shall not be used.

XII. REPELLENT SUBJECTS

The following subjects must be treated within careful limits of good
taste:

Appendix IV

THE PRODUCTION CODE OF THE MOTION PICTURES PRODUCERS AND DIRECTORS OF AMERICA, INC.---1930-1934

PREAMBLE

Motion picture producers recognize the high trust and confidence which have been placed in them by the people of the world and which have made motion pictures a universal form of entertainment.

They recognize their responsibility to the public because of this trust and because entertainment and art are important influences in the life of a nation.

Hence, though regarding motion pictures primarily as entertainment without any explicit purpose of teaching or propaganda, they know that the motion picture within its own field of entertainment may be directly responsible for spiritual or moral progress, for higher types of social life, and for much correct thinking.

During the rapid transition from silent to talking pictures they realized the necessity and the opportunity of subscribing to a Code to govern the production of talking pictures and of reacknowledging this responsibility.

On their part, they ask from the public and from public leaders a sympathetic understanding of their purposes and problems and a spirit of cooperation that will allow them the freedom and opportunity necessary to bring the motion picture to a still higher level of wholesome entertainment for all the people.

GENERAL PRINCIPLES

1. No picture shall be produced which will lower the moral standards of those who see it. Hence the sympathy of the audience shall never be thrown to the side of crime, wrong-doing, evil or sin.

2. Correct standards of life, subject only to the requirements of drama and entertainment, shall be presented.

3. Law, natural or human, shall not be ridiculed, nor shall sympathy be created for its violation.

I. Crimes Against the Law

These shall never be presented in such a way as to throw sympathy with the crime as against law and justice or to inspire others with a desire for imitation.

1. Murder
    a) The technique of murder must be presented in a way that will not inspire imitation.
    b) Brutal killings are not to be presented in detail.
    c) Revenge in modern times shall not be justified.

2. Methods of crime should not be explicitly presented.
    a) Theft, robbery, safe-cracking, and dynamiting of trains, mines, buildings, etc., should not be detailed in method.
    b) Arson must be subject to the same safeguards.
    c) The use of firearms should be restricted to essentials.
    d) Methods of smuggling should not be presented.

3. The illegal drug traffic must not be portrayed in such a way as to stimulate curiosity concerning the use of, or traffic in, such drugs; nor shall scenes be approved which show the use of illegal drugs, or their effects, in detail (as amended

September 11, 1946).

4. The use of liquor in American life, when not required by the plot or for proper characterization, will not be shown.

II. Sex
The sanctity of the institution of marriage and the home shall be upheld. Pictures shall not infer [sic] that low forms of sex relationship are the accepted or common thing.

1. Adultery and illicit sex, sometimes necessary plot material, must not be explicitly treated or justified, or presented attractively.

2. Scenes of passion
   a) These should not be introduced except where they are definitely essential to the plot.
   b) Excessive and lustful kissing, lustful embraces, suggestive postures and gestures are not to be shown.
   c) In general, passion should be treated in such manner as not to stimulate the lower and baser emotions.

3. Seduction or rape
   a) These should never be more than suggested, and then only when essential for the plot. They must never be shown by explicit method.
   b) They are never the proper subject for comedy.

4. Sex perversion or any inference [sic] to it is forbidden.

5. White slavery shall not be treated.

6. Miscegenation (sex relationship between the white and black races) is forbidden.

7. Sex hygiene and venereal diseases are not proper subjects for theatrical motion pictures.

8. Scenes of actual childbirth, in fact or in silhouette, are never to be presented.

9. Children's sex organs are never to be exposed.

III. Vulgarity
The treatment of low, disgusting, unpleasant, though not necessarily evil, subjects should be guided always by the dictates of good taste and a proper regard for the sensibilities of the audience.

IV. Obscenity
Obscenity in word, gesture, reference, song, joke, or by suggestion (even when likely to be understood only by part of the audience) is forbidden.

V. Profanity
Pointed profanity and every other profane or vulgar expression, however used, is forbidden.

No approval by the Production Code Administration shall be given to the use of words and phrases in motion pictures including, but not limited to, the following:

Alley cat (applied to a woman); bat (applied to a woman); broad (applied to a woman); Bronx cheer (the sound); chippie; cocotte; God, Lord, Jesus, Christ (unless used reverently); cripes; fanny; fairy (in a vulgar sense); finger (the); fire, cries of; Gawd; goose (in a vulgar sense); "hold your hat" or "hats"; hot (applied to a woman); "in your hat"; louse; lousy; Madam (relating to prostitution); nance; nerts; nuts (except when meaning crazy); pansy; razzberry (the sound); slut (applied to a woman); S.O.B.; son-of-a; tart; toilet gags; tom cat (applied to a man); traveling salesman and farmer's daughter jokes; whore; damn, hell (excepting when the use of said last two words shall be essential and required for portrayal, in proper historical context, of any scene or dialogue based upon historical fact or folklore, or for the presentation in proper literary context of a Biblical, or other religious quotation, or a quotation from a literary work provided that no such use shall be permitted which is intrinsically objectionable or offends good taste).

In the administration of Section V of the Production Code, the Production Code Administration may take cognizance of the fact that the following words and phrases are obviously offensive to the patrons of motion pictures in the United States and more particularly to the patrons of motion pictures in foreign countries: Chink, Dago, Frog, Greaser, Hunkie, Kike, Nigger, Spig, Wop, Yid.

VI. Costume
  1. Complete nudity is never permitted. This includes nudity in fact or in silhouette, or any licentious notice thereof by other characters in the pictures.

  2. Undressing scenes should be avoided, and never used save where essential to the plot.

  3. Indecent or undue exposure is forbidden.

  4. Dancing costumes intended to permit undue exposure or indecent movements in the dance are forbidden.

VII. Dances
  1. Dances suggesting or representing sexual actions or indecent passion are forbidden.

  2. Dances which emphasize indecent movements are regarded as obscene.

VIII. Religion
  1. No film or episode may throw ridicule on any religious faith.

  2. Ministers of religion in their character as ministers of religion should not be used as comic characters or as villains.

  3. Ceremonies of any definite religion should be carefully and respectfully handled.

IX. Locations
   The treatment of bedrooms must be governed by good taste and
   delicacy.

X. National Feelings
   1. The use of the flag shall be consistently respectful.

   2. The history, institutions, prominent people and citizenry of all
      nations shall be represented fairly.

XI. Titles
   Salacious, indecent, or obscene titles shall not be used.

XII. Repellent Subjects
   The following subjects must be treated within the careful limits of
   good taste:
   1) Actual hangings or electrocutions as legal punishments for crime.
   2) Third-degree methods.
   3) Brutality and possible gruesomeness.
   4) Branding of people or animals.
   5) Apparent cruelty to children or animals.
   6) The sale of women, or a woman selling her virtue.
   7) Surgical operations.

REASONS SUPPORTING PREAMBLE OF CODE

1. Theatrical motion pictures, that is, pictures intended for the
theatre as distinct from pictures intended for churches, schools,
lecture halls, educational movements, social reform movements, etc., are
primarily to be regarded as ENTERTAINMENT.
   Mankind has always recognized the importance of entertainment and
   its value in rebuilding the bodies and souls of human beings.
   But it has always recognized that entertainment can be of a
   character either HELPFUL or HARMFUL to the human race, and in
   consequence has clearly distinguished between:
   a) Entertainment which tends to improve the race, or at least to
      recreate and rebuild human beings exhausted with the realities
      of life; and
   b) Entertainment which tends to degrade human beings, or to lower
      their standards of life and living.
   Hence the MORAL IMPORTANCE of entertainment is something which has
   been universally recognized. It enters intimately into the lives
   of men and women and affects them closely; it occupies their minds
   and affections during leisure hours; and ultimately touches the
   whole of their lives. A man may be judged by his standard of
   entertainment as easily as by the standard of his work.
   So correct entertainment raises the whole standard of a nation.
   Wrong entertainment lowers the whole living conditions and moral
   ideals of a race.
      Note, for example, the healthy reactions to healthful sports,
      like baseball, golf; the unhealthy reactions to sports like
      cockfighting, bullfighting, bear baiting, etc.
   Note, too, the effect on ancient nations of gladiatorial combats,
   the obscene plays of Roman times, etc.

2. Motion pictures are very important as ART.
Though a new art, possibly a combination art, it has the same
objects as the other arts, the presentation of human thought, emotion,
and experience, in terms of an appeal to the soul through the senses.

Here, as in entertainment,
Art enters intimately into the lives of human beings.

Art can be morally good, lifting men to higher levels. This has
been done through good music, great painting, authentic fiction,
poetry, drama.

Art can be morally evil in its effects. This is the case clearly
enough with unclean art, indecent books, suggestive drama. The
effect on the lives of men and women is obvious.

Note: It has often been argued that art in itself is unmoral,
neither good nor bad. This is perhaps true of the THING PRODUCT
of some person's mind, and the intention of that mind was either
good or bad morally when it produced the thing. Besides, the thing
has its EFFECT upon those who come into contact with it. In both
these ways, that is, as a product of a mind and as the cause of
definite effects, it has a deep moral significance and
unmistakable moral quality.

Hence: The motion pictures, which are the most popular of modern
arts for the masses, have their moral quality from the intention
of the minds which produce them and from their effects on the
moral lives and reactions of their audiences. This gives them a
most important morality.

1. They reproduce the morality of the men who use the pictures as
   a medium for the expression of their ideas and ideals.

2. They affect the moral standards of those who, through the
   screen, take in these ideas and ideals.
   In the case of the motion pictures, this effect may be
   particularly emphasized because no art has so quick and so
   widespread an appeal to the masses. It has become in an
   incredibly short period the art of the multitudes.

3. The motion picture, because of its importance as entertainment
   and because of the trust placed in it by the peoples of the
   world, has special MORAL OBLIGATIONS:
   A. Most arts appeal to the mature. This art appeals at once to
      every class, mature, immature, developed, undeveloped,
      law-abiding, criminal. Music has its grades for different
      classes; so has literature and drama. This art of the motion
      picture, combining as it does the two fundamental appeals of
      looking at a picture and listening to a story, at once
      reaches every class of society.

   B. By reason of the mobility of a film and the ease of picture
      distribution, and because of the possibility of duplicating
      positives in large quantities, this art reaches places
      unpenetrated by other forms of art.

   C. Because of these two facts, it is difficult to produce films

intended for only certain classes of people. The exhibitor's
theatres are built for the masses, for the cultivated and
the rude, the mature and the immature, the self-respecting
and the criminal. Films, unlike books and music, can
with difficulty be confined to certain selected groups.

D. The latitude given to film material cannot, in consequence,
   be as wide as the latitude given to book material. In
   addition:
   a) A book describes; a film vividly presents. One presents
      on a cold page; the other by apparently living people.
   b) A book reaches the mind through words merely; a film
      reaches the eyes and ears through the reproduction of
      actual events.
   c) The reaction of a reader to a book depends largely on the
      keenness of the reader's imagination; the reaction to a
      film depends on the vividness of presentation.
      Hence many things which might be described or presented
      in a book could not possibly be presented in a film.

E. This is also true when comparing the film with the
   newspaper.
   a) Newspapers present by description, films by actual
      presentation.
   b) Newspapers are after the fact and present things as
      having taken place; the film gives the events in the
      process of enactment and with apparent reality of life.

F. Everything possible in a play is not possible in a film:
   a) Because of the larger audience of the film, and its
      consequential mixed character. Psychologically, the
      larger the audience, the lower the moral mass resistance
      to suggestion.
   b) Because through light, enlargement of character,
      presentation, scenic emphasis, etc., the screen story is
      brought closer to the audience than the play.
   c) The enthusiasm for and interest in the film actors and
      actresses, developed beyond anything of the sort in
      history, makes the audience largely sympathetic toward
      the characters they portray and the stories in which they
      figure. Hence the audience is more ready to confuse actor
      and actress and the characters they portray, and it is
      most receptive of the emotions and ideals presented by
      their favorite stars.

G. Small communities, remote from sophistication and from the
   hardening process which often takes place in the ethical and
   moral standards of groups in larger cities, are easily and
   and readily reached by any sort of film.

H. The grandeur of mass settings, large action, spectacular
   features, etc., affects and arouses more intensely the
   emotional side of the audience.

In general, the mobility, popularity, accessibility, emotional appeal, vividness,
straight-forward presentation of fact in the film make for more intimate contact with
a larger audience and for greater emotional appeal.

Hence the larger moral responsibilities of the motion pictures.

Appendix V

SELECTED LIST OF SOURCES FOR FURTHER FILM STUDY

ARCHIVES

A word of caution in using the following resources. Some of them are private foundations that restrict access to their material. Problems exist as well in arranging convenient times or in getting permission to cite the material in the collection. It is absolutely necessary to call or to write these archives and museums to get information on which is the best way to proceed.[1]

AUSTRALIA

Australian Film Institute, 47 Little La Trobe Street, Melbourne VIC 3000, Australia

National Film and Sound Archive, McCoy Circuit, Acton, Canberra, A.C.T. 2601, Australia.

BRAZIL

Museu de Arte Moderna do Rio de Janerio, Cinemateca, Avenida Beira-Mar Caixa Postal 44, 20000, Rio De Janeiro, Brazil, 231 18 71.

BRITAIN

British Film Institute, Information & Documentation, 127 Charing Cross Road, London, WCH 2; and 81 Dean Street, London, WIV 6AA England.

Imperial War Museum, Lambeth Road, London SE1 6HZ, England.

National Film Archive, 21 Stephen Street, London WIP 1PL, England.

Scottish Film Archive, Scottish Film Council, 74 Victoria Crescent Road, Dowanhill, Glasgow G12 9JN, Scotland.

CANADA

---

[1] This appendix is indebted to Jay Leyda et al., "Special Features on Film Scholarship," FILM QUARTERLY 16:2 (Winter 1962-63): 29-50; William Siska, "Directory of Useful Addresses," CINEMA JOURNAL 27:2 (Winter 1988):76-80; and ___, "Directory of Useful Addresses," ibid., 28:2 (Winter 1989):82-5. For a good description of what the archives include, see Frances Thorpe, ed. INTERNATIONAL DIRECTORY OF FILM AND TV DOCUMENTATION CENTRES (Chicago: St. James Press, 1988).

Cinematheque Quebecoise/Musee du Cinema, 335 est de Maisonneuve, Montreal, Quebec, H2X 1K1, Canada. (514) 842-9673.

Moving Image and Sound Archives, 395 Wellington St., Ottawa, Ontario, K1A 0N3 Canada. (613) 995-1311.

National Film Board of Canada, 3155 Cote de Liesse Road, Ville St. Laurent, Quebec, H3C 3H5, Canada. (514) 283-9045.

CZECHOSLOVAKIA

Czechoslovakia Film Archives, Czechoslovak Film Institute, Narodni 40, 110 00 Praha 1, Czechoslovakia, 2600 87.

DENMARK

Det Danske Filmmuseum, St. Sondervoldstraede, 1419 Copenhagen K, Denmark, Asta 6500.

FRANCE

La Cinematheque Francaise, 82 Rue de Courcelles, Paris 8e France.

Institut des Hautes Etudes Cinematographiques, 92 Champs Elyssees, 75008, Paris, France, 539-22-86.

Service des Archives du Film C. N. C., 78390-Bois D'Arcy, Paris, France 3460 20 50

HUNGRY

Hungarian Cinematheque and Film Research Institute, Nepstadion ut 97, Budapest XIV Hungary.

INDIA

National Film Archives of India, Law College Road, Poona 441004, India, 58516.

ISRAEL

Israel Film Archine/Cinematheque, 43 Jabotinsky Street, Jerusalem, Israel, 67121.

Appendix V

ITALY

Cineteca Nazionale, Centro Sperimentale di Sperimentale di Cinematografia, Via Ruscolana 1524, 00173 Rome, Italy, 740-046.

Museo Nazionale del Cinema, 10122 Turin, Palazzo Chiablese, Plaza San Giovanni 2, 10122 Italy 510-370.

JAPAN

Japan Film Library/Council, Ginza-Hata Building, 4-5, 4-chome, Ginza, Chuo-Ku, Tokyo, Japan, (03) 561-6719.

Matsuda Eigasha, 3-18-8 Towa, Adachi-Ku, Tokyo, Japan 120

Tokyo National Museum of Modern Art Film Center, 3-7-6, Kyobashi, Chio-Ku, Tokyo 104 Japan.

NORWAY

Norsk Filminstitut, Aslaksveien, 14 B, Postboks 5 Roa, Oslo 7, Norway, (12) 24 29 94.

POLAND

Filmoteka Polska, Ul Pulawaka Nr 61, 00-975 Warsaw 12, Poland 45-50-74.

SOVIET UNION

Gosfilmfond, Stancia Bielye Stolby, Moskovskaia Oblast, USSR, 136-10-18.

SPAIN

Filmteca Nacional de Espana, Carratera de la Dalesa de la Villa s/n, Madrid 35, Spain, 243 47 95.

SWEDEN

Svenska Filminstitutet Filmhuset Box 271 26, S 102 52, Stockholm, Sweden, 63 05 10.

UNITED STATES

Ackerman Imagi-Movie Archives, 2495 Glendower Avenue, Hollywood, California 90027. (213) 666 6326.

The American Archives of the Factual Film, Iowa State University Library, Ames, Iowa 50011.

American Film Institute, Kennedy center for the Performing Arts, Washington, D. C. 20566. (202) 833-9800.

American Museum of the Moving Image, 35th Avenue at 36th Street, Astoria, Queens (718) 784-0077.

Anthology Film Archives, 32-34 Second Avenue, New York, New York 10003. (212-477-2714).

Black Film Center/Archive, Memorial Hall East, Indiana University, Bloomington, Indiana 47405.

CBS News Archives, 524 West 57th Street, New York, New York 10019.   (212) 975-2834.

Charles K. Feldman Library, American Film Institute of Advanced Film Studies, 2021 Northwestern Avenue, Los Angeles, California 90027.   (213) 856-7600.

Cinema-Television Library and Archives of the Performing Arts, University Library, University of Southern California, Los Angeles, California 90089-0812. (213) 743-6058. Warner Bros. Archives: (213) 748-7747.

Edison National Historic Site, Main Street and Lakeside Avenue, West Orange, New Jersey 07052.

The Robert and Frances Flaherty Study Center, School of Technology, Claremont, California 91711. (714) 626-3521.

Folger Library Shakespeare Film Study Collection, Folger Shakespeare Library, 201 East Capitol Street, Washington, D. C. 20003.

Free Library of Philadelphia, Theater Collection, Logan Circle, Philadelphia, Pennsylvania 19103.

Hollywood Film Archive, 8344 Melrose Avenue, Hollywood, California 90069. (213) 933-3345.

Hollywood Museum, 852 Melrose Avenue, Los Angeles, California 90028.

Louis B. Mayer Library, The American Film Institute, 2021 Northwestern Avenue, Los Angeles, California 90027. Reference phone 1:00 to 3:00 p.m. only: (213) 856-7655.

Indiana University, Lily Library, Bloomington, Indiana 47401. (812) 337-2452.

International Museum of Photography, George Eastman House, 900 East Avenue, Rochester, New York 14607. (716) 271-3361.

Keith/Albee Collection, University of Iowa Library, University of Iowa, Iowa City, Iowa 52242. (319) 335-5291.

Los Angeles County Museum of Natural History, History Division, 900 Exposition Park B1., Los Angeles, California 90007.

Motion Picture, Broadcasting and Recorded Sound Division, Library of Congress, Washington, D.C. 20540. (202) 287-5840

Museum of Broadcasting, 1 East 53rd Street, New York, New York, 10022. (212) 752-4690.

Museum of Modern Art, Film Study Center, 11 West 53rd Street, New York, New York 10019. (212) 708-9631.

National Archives and Records Service, Audio Visual Archives Division, Pennsylvania Avenue between 7th and 9th Streets NW, Washington, D. C. 20408. (202) 523-3063.

National Center for Film and Video Preservation, The American Film Institute, The John F. Kennedy Center for the Performing Arts, Washington, D. C. 20566. (202) 828-4070; and National Center for Film and Video Preservation, The American Film Institute, P. O. Box 27999, 2021 North Western Avenue, Los Angeles, California 90027.   (213) 856-7637.

The National Center for Jewish Film Library, Brandeis University/Lown 102, Waltham, Massachusetts 02154.

NBC, Inc., 30 Rockefeller Plaza, New York, New York 10112.

Oregon Historical Society, 1230 Southwest Park Avenue, Portland, Oregon 97205. For rental films contact: Education Department; for for purchase of films or archival footage contact: Film Archives.

Pacific Film Archive, University Art Museum, 2625 Durant Avenue, Berkeley, California 94720. (415) 642-1412/1437.

Raff and Gammon Collection, Manuscripts and Archives Department, Baker Library, Harvard Business School, Cambridge, Massachusetts 02163.

RKO Pictures, Corporate Archives and Records Center, 129 N. Vermont Avenue, Los Angeles, California 90004. (213) 383-5525.

UCLA Film Archives, Department of Theater Arts, University of California, Los Angeles, California 90024. (213) 825-7253.

UCLA Special Collections Library, A1713 URL, 405 Hilgard Ave., Los Angeles, California 90024-1575. (213) 825-4988.

Universal City Studios, Research department, 100 Universal City Plaza, Universal City, California 91608. (818) 777-2493.

Uiversity of Illinois, Communications Library, 122 Gregory Hall, 810 S. Wright Street, Urbana, IL 61801.

Walt Disney Archives, 500 South Buena Vista Street, Burbank, California 91521. (818) 840-5424.

Wesleyan University Cinema Archives, Middletown, Connecticut 06457.

Wisconsin Center for Film & Theater Research, 816 State Street (Photo Archives), Madison, Wisconsin 53706. (608) 262-0585; 6040 Vilas Hall (Administrative Offices), University of Wisconsin-Madison, Madison, Wisconsin 53706.

WEST GERMANY

Deutschen Film und Fernseha Kademie, Pommernalle 1, 1000 Berlin 19, West Germany, 3036-212 and 234.

Deutsches Institut fur Filmkunde, Schloss, 6202 Wiesbaden, Biebrich, West Germany, 69074-75.

Deutsche Kinemathek Siftung, 1000 Berlin 19, Pommernalle 1, West Germany, 3036-233 and 234.

Photo-Und Filmmuseum, Munchner Stadmuseum, St. Jakobs-Paltz 1, D8 Munich 2 West Germany.

Appendix V

LIBRARY RESOURCES

Columbia University Libraries, 535 West 114th Street, New York, New York 10027.

Dartmouth College, Baker Library, Hanover, New Hampshire 03755.

De Forest Research Service, 780 North Gower Street, Los Angeles, California 90038.

The Free Library of Philadelphia, Logan Square, Philadelphia, Pennsylvania 19144.

The Library of Congress, Motion Picture, Broadcasting and Recorded Sound Division, Washington, D. C. 20540. (202) 287-5840.

Margaret Herrick library, Academy of Motion Picture Arts & Sciences & Academy Foundation, 8949 Wilshire Boulevard, Beverly Hills, California 90211. (213) 278-4313

New York Museum of the Performing Arts, Lincoln Center at 111 Amsterdam Avenue, New York, New York 10023.

New York Public Library, Fifth Avenue and 42nd Street, New York, New York 10023.

New York Public Library at Lincoln Center, Library and Museum of the Performing Arts, 111 Amsterdam Avenue, New York, New York 10023. (212) 870-1639.

Sterling Memorial Library, Yale University, New Haven, Connecticut 06520.

Twentieth Century Fox Film Corporation Research Library, 10201 W. Pico Boulevard, Los Angeles, California 90064.

UCLA Library, Department of Special Collection, Powell Library, UCLA, Los Angeles, California 90024.

University of Southern California, Cinema Library, Department of Special Collections, Room 206, Doheny Library, USC, Los Angeles, California 90007. (213) 746-6058.

BIOGRAPHICAL AND REFERENCE TOOLS

Library of Congress Catalogue Books National Union Catalogue
Union List of Serials
Readers' Guide to Periodicals
Subject Index to Periodicals
Film as Art
New York Times Index
How and Where to Look It Up
American Library Resources: a bibliographical guide, Supplement

BOOKSTORES

Birns and Sawyer, 1026 North Highland Avenue, Hollywood, California 90038.

Book City Collectibles, 6631 Hollywoood Boulevard, Hollywood, California 90028.

Book City of Burbank, 308 North Golden Mall, Burbank, California 91502.

Booklord's, P. O. Box 177, Peter Stuyvesant Station, New York, New York 10009.

Books, Books, Books, 301 East 3rd Street, Muscatine, Iowa 52761.

Cinema Specialties, Inc., 217 East 86th Street, Suite 282, New York, New York 10028.

David Henry, 36 Meon Road, London w3 8An, London, England.

Drama Book Shop, 723 Seventh Avenue, New York, New York 10019.

Drama Books, 134 Ninth Street, San Francisco, California 94103.   (415) 255-0604.

Gotham Book Mart, 41 West 47th Street, New York, New York 10036.

Hampton Books, Route 1, Box 202, Newberry, South Carolina 29108.

Hollywood Book City, 6625-6627 Hollywood Boulevard, Hollywood, California 90028.

Hunt's Bookshop, 1063 North Spaulding Avenue, West Hollywood, California 90046.

Jean Noel Herlin, 40 Harrison Street, New York, New York 10013.

Larry Edmunds Bookshop, 6658 Hollywood Boulevard, Hollywood, California 90028;
  and 11969 Ventura Boulevard, Studio City, California 90028.

Limelight Film and Theatre Bookstore, 1803 Market Street, San Francisco, California
  94103.

Movie Madness, 1642 Massachusetts Avenue, Cambridge, Massachusetts 02138.

Richard Stoddard-Performing Arts Books, 18 East 16th Street, Room 202, New York, New York 10003. (212) 645-9576.

STILLS

The Bettmann Archive, Inc., 136 East 57th Street, New York, New York 10022. (212) 758-0362.

BFI Stills, Poster and Designs, 21 Stephen Street, London W1P 1PL, England.

Billy Rose Theater Collection, The New York Public Library at Lincoln Center, 111 Amsterdam Avenue, New York, New York 10023. (212) 870-1639.

Bison Archive, 650 N. Bronson Avenue, Hollywood, California 90210. (213) 276-9491.

British Film Institute, 21 Stephen Street, London W1P 1PL, England.

The Cinema Shop, 604 Geary Street, San Francisco, California 94102. (415) 885-6785.

Chapman's Picture Palace, 1757 North Las Palmas, Hollywood, California 90028. (213) 467-1739.

Collectors Book Store, 6763 Hollywood Boulevard, Hollywood, California 90028. (213) 467-3298.

Douglas J. Hart, 7278-A Sunset Boulevard, Hollywood, California 90046. (213) 876-6070.

Eddie Brandt's Saturday Matinee, 6310 Colfax Avenue, North Hollywood, California 91609. (213) 856-7600.

Film Favorites, P.O. Box 133, Canton, Oklahoma 73724. (405) 886-3358.

Hollywood Book and Poster Company, 1706 North Las Palmas Street, Hollywood, California 90028. (213) 465-8764.

Hollywood Poster Exchange, 965 North LaCienega Boulevard, Los Angeles, California 90069. (213) 657-2461.

International Museum of Photography, Film Department, George Eastman House, 900 East Avenue, Rochester, New York 14607. (716) 271-3361.

Larry Edmunds Bookshop, Inc., 6658 Hollywood Boulevard, Hollywood, California 90028. (213) 463-3273.

Los Angeles Public Library, 630 West Fifth Street, Los Angeles, California 90071. (213) 612-3200.

Margaret Herrick Library, Academy of Motion Picture Arts and Sciences, and Academy Foundation, 8949 Wilshire Boulevard, Beverly Hills, California 90211. (213) 278-8900

Memory Shop, 109 East 12th Street, New York, New York 10003. (212) 473-2404.

Memory Shop West, 3450 16th Street, San Francisco, California 94114. (415) 626-4873.

Movie Star News, 212 East 14th Street, New York, New York 10003. (212) 777-5564.

Museum of Modern Art, Department of Film, Film Stills Archive, 11 West 53rd Street, New York, New York 10019. (212) 708-9830/9831.

New York Public Library at Lincoln Center, Billy Rose Theatre Collection, 111 Amsterdam Avenue, New York, New York 10023. (212) 870-1639.

Jerry Ohlinger's Movie Materials Store, 242 West 14th Street, New York, New York 10011. (212) 989-0869.

Pacific Federal Savings and Loan Association, 6801 Hollywood Boulevard, Hollywood, California 90028. (213) 463-4141.

Quality First, 6546 Hollywood Boulevard, Suite 201, Hollywood, California 90028.

Quigley Photographic Archive, Georgetown University Library, Special Collections Division, 37th and O Street, N W, Washington, D. C. 20057. (202) 687-7444.

Stephen Sally, 339 West 44th Street, New York, New York 10036. (212) 246-4972.

Texas Movie Emporium, 501 W. Powell Ln #213, Austin, Texas 78753. (512) 836-9075.

University of California at Los Angeles (UCLA), University Research Library, Room 22478, Theater Arts Library, 405 Hilgard Avenue, Los Angeles, California 90024. (213) 825-4880.

Theatre Arts Collection, Harry Ransom Humanities Research Center, The University of Texas at Austin, P. O. Drawer 7219, Austin, Texas 78713-7219. (512) 471-9122.

Wisconsin Center for Film and Theater Research, Film Archive, 816 State Street, Madison, Wisconsin 53706. (608) 262-0585.

Appendix VI

(THEATRICAL, TELEVISION, HOME VIDEO, PAY-TV)

1. GENERAL THEATRICAL DATA: UNITED STATES

BOX OFFICE GROSS

1984 was the fourth consecutive year of record breaking box office revenues, and a milestone in the history of the industry - the first year that the $4 billion level has ever been attained.

1984's total box office gross of $4,030.6 million was $264.6 million higher than last year, a +7.0% increase.

YEAR	BOX OFFICE GROSS (MILLION)	YEARLY PERCENT CHANGE	1984 VERSUS
1984	$4,030.6	+7.0%	-
1983	$3,766.0	+9.1%	+7.0%
1982	$3,452.7	+16.4%	+16.7%
1981	$2,965.6	+7.9%	+35.9%
1980	$2,748.5	-2.6%	+46.6%

The growth pattern, at the box office, was sporadic, with a fairly poor first quarter, followed by an excellent second quarter, then a dip in the third quarter, and finally a quite strong last quarter of the year.

QUARTERLY COMPARISON OF BOX OFFICE GROSS
1984 vs. 1983
(MILLIONS)

	1984	1983	Per Cent Change
First	$815.0	$816.5	-0.18%
Second	$1,144.5	$1,039.7	+10.08%
Third	$1,135.5	$1,081.1	+5.03%
Fourth	$935.6	$828.7	+12.90%
Year	$4,030.6	$3,766.0	+7.03%

ADMISSIONS

While the admissions advance, for 1984, was small--only 2.2 million--we finished the year with 1.199 billion admissions, the highest level reached since 1961. U.S. theatre admissions for the past five years were:

Year	Admissions	Yearly Percent Change	1984 Versus
	(millions)		
1984	1,199.1	+0.18%	-
1983	1,196.9	+1.8%	+0.18%
1982	1,175.4	+10.2%	+2.02%
1981	1,060.0	+4.5%	+13.12%
1980	1,021.5	-8.9%	+17.39%

ADMISSION PRICES

Admission prices closed out 1984 at $3.45, compared to a December, 1983, $3.22 ticket price, an increase of +7.1%.

The 1984 full-year average price was $3.361, an increase of +6.8% when compared to 1983's $3.146.

The Consumer Price Index (All Items) increase for 1984 was +4.0%.

HIGH GROSSING FEATURES

In 1984, there were 33 feature films that achieved U.S. film rentals of $10 million or more.

Of these, 13 films reached the $20+ million level in film rentals, down from 18 a year ago, and slightly below the average of the previous four years.

Year	$10 Million Or More	$20 Million Or More
1984	33	13
1983	34	18
1982	36	14
1981	30	10
1980	36	17

THEATRES

1984 was a record year for theatre screens in the United States, with 20,200 reported at the latest count--up from 18,884 in 1983, an increase of +6.9%.

There are now 17,368 hardtop/conventional theatre screens, up 1,336 (+8.3%) over last year.

There are also 2,832 drive-in screens, down but 20 (-0.01%) from a year ago.

CARA RATINGS (Classification and Ratings Administration)

In 1984, CARA rated 323 feature films, down -4.4% from 1983's 338 level.
A distribution of how many films were rated G, PG, PG-13, R, and X, is shown
below, for 1984 and 1983.

Rating	1984 #	1984 %	1983 #	1983 %
G	7	2.2%	11	3.3%
PG	98	30.3%	117	34.6%
PG-13	18	5.6%	-	-
R	196	60.7%	208	61.5%
X	4	1.2%	2	0.6%

Since 1968, the Classification and Rating Administration (CARA) has rated
6,795 feature films, whose ratings were distributed as follows:

Rating	1968- 1984	1968- 1984
G	891	13.1%
PG	2,469	36.3%
PG-13	18	0.3%
R	3,053	44.9%
X	364	5.4%
	6,795	100.0%

EMPLOYMENT

During the first eight months of 1984, the motion picture industry employed
an average of 216,050 people, compared to 210,088 during the like period a year
ago. This was a substantial increase of 5,962 people, +2.8%.
Production and Services personnel increased to 96,275, up from 83,400,
+15.4%, while the count of Distribution employees slumped somewhat, from 10,375
to 10,288, a decline of 0.8%.
Theatre employment dropped significantly, for the second straight year, from
116,313 to 109,488 currently, a fall of -5.9%.

ADVERTISING

In 1983, the latest year for which figures are available, a total of $828.8 million was spent to advertise motion pictures in newspapers, on television, on radio, and in magazines. This was an increase of $60.0 million (+7.8%) compared to 1982.

Advertising expenditures for Network television expanded by +20.4%, $130.0 million vs. $109.6 million, while Local television spending fell by -13.7%.

Newspaper advertising advanced by +8.9%, from $543.7 million to $592.0 million.

The following table illustrates the share of the 1983 advertising dollar captured by each of the media:

Media	Per Cent Share	$ Millions
Newspapers	71.4%	$592.0
Network TV	15.9%	132.0
Local TV	9.4%	78.0
(All TV)	(25.3%)	(210.0)
Radio	2.7%	22.0
Magazines	0.6%	4.8
Total	100.0%	$828.8

RELEASES

In 1984, our [CARA] computerized tracking system identified 87 distributors, including MPAA member companies, who released a total of 398 new features and 122 reissues, for a grand total of 520 films.

Year	New	Reissues	Total
1984	398	122	520
1983	395	106	501
1982	365	68	433

The number of films released yearly by our member companies, from 1980 through 1984, is shown below:

Year	New	Reissues	Total
1984	151(25)	15(1)	166(26)
1983	165(33)	25(5)	190(38)
1982	149(14)	26(7)	175(21)
1981	145(8)	28(1)	173(9)
1980	136(-)	30(-)	166(-)

NEGATIVE COSTS

The average negative cost of new features financed in whole or in part by MPAA companies and released in 1984 jumped by +21.3%, from $11.9 million to $14.4 million. This was the first truly significant advance in this area since 1981, when a +20.8% increase was recorded.

The median cost of these films rose from $10.8 million a year ago to $11.5 million in 1984, an increase of +6.0%.

Year	Average Production Cost Per Feature (000)	Increase Over Prior Year	%Increase 1984 Compared To
1984	$14,412.6	+21.27%	–
1983	$11,884.8	+0.30%	+21.27%
1982	$11,849.5	+4.53%	+21.63%
1981	$11,335.6	+20.82%	+27.14%
1980	9,382.5	+5.26%	+53.61%

II: GENERAL VCR AND CABLE (BASIC, ADDRESSABLE, PAY) DATA: U.S. ONLY

A. VCR HOUSEHOLDS

Since 1980, the VCR Household count has increased seven fold, with 1984's increase +80%.

Year	VCR Households	% Increase Over Prior Year	% Increase 1984 Compared To
1984	15,000,000	+80.0%	-
1983	8,300,000	+72.9%	+80.0%
1982	4,800,000	+92.0%	+212.5%
1981	2,500,000	+35.1%	+500.0%
1980	1,850,000	-	+710.8%

B. VCR PENETRATION RATES IN U.S. TV HOUSEHOLDS

Year	VCR Households	TV Households	Percent
1984	15,000,000	85,300,000	17.6%
1983	8,300,000	84,200,000	9.9%
1982	4,800,000	83,700,000	5.7%
1981	2,500,000	81,900,000	3.1%
1980	1,850,000	78,000,000	2.4%

C. SALES OF PRE-RECORDED VIDEOCASSETTES TO U.S. DEALERS
(Excludes "Adult" Material)

Year	Pre-Recorded Cassettes	% Incease Over Prior Year	% Increase 1984 Compared To
1984	22,000,000	+131.6%	-
1983	9,500,000	+58.3%	+131.6%
1982	6,000,000	+9.1%	+266.6%
1981	5,500,000	+83.3%	+300.0%
1980	3,000,000	-	+633.3%

D. SALES OF BLANK VIDEOCASSETTES TO U.S. CONSUMER MARKET

Year	% Increase Blank Cassettes	% Increase Over Prior Year	1984 Compared To
1984	109,000,000	+91.2%	-
1983	57,000,000	+130.8%	+91.2%
1982	24,700,000	+9.8%	+341.3%
1981	22,500,000	+50.0%	+384.4%
1980	15,000,000	-	+626.7%

E. BASIC CABLE HOUSEHOLDS

The growth in the number of basic cable households has been fairly constant at between 15% and 19% per year, and +88% over the past five years.

Year	Basic Cable Households	% Increase Over Prior Year	% Increase 1984 Compared To
1984	36,900,000	+14.9%	-
1983	32,100,000	+18.0%	+14.9%
1982	27,200,000	+16.7%	+35.6%
1981	23,300,000	+18.8%	+58.3%
1980	19,600,000	-	+88.2%

F. ADDRESSABLE CABLE HOUSEHOLDS

The number of addressable cable households almost doubled in 1984, and have more than tripled since 1982.

Year	Addressable Cable Households	% Increase Over Prior Year	% Increase 1984 Compared To
1984	6,600,000	+83.3%	-
1983	3,600,000	+140.0%	+83.3%
1982	1,500,000	-	+340.0%
1981	N/A	-	-
1980	N/A	-	-

G. PAY CABLE SUBSCRIPTIONS AND SUBSCRIBERS

Pay cable subscriptions (which include multi-pay homes) increased +7.5% in 1984, while the number of subscribers increased by +12.2%.

Year	Pay Cable Subscriptions	% Increase Over Prior Year	% Increase 1984 Compared To
1984	30,100,000	+7.5%	-
1983	28,000,000	+35.9%	+7.5%
1982	20,600,000	+36.4%	+46.1%
1981	15,100,000	+69.6%	+99.3%
1980	8,900,000	-	+238.2%

Year	Pay Cable Subscribers	% Increase Over Prior Year	% Increase 1984 Compared To
1984	20,200,000	+12.2%	-
1983	18,000,000	+34.3%	+12.2%
1982	13,400,000	-	+50.5%
1981	N/A	N/A	-
1980	N/A	N/A	-

Appendix VII

Members of the Association of Motion Picture Producers deplore the action of the ten Hollywood men who have been cited for contempt of the House of Representatives. We do not desire to pre-judge their legal rights, but their actions have been a disservice to their employers and have impaired their usefulness to the industry.

We will forthwith discharge or suspend without compensation those in our employ and we will not re-employ any of the ten until such time as he is acquitted or has purged himself of contempt and declares under oath that he is not a Communist.

On the broader issue of alleged subversive and disloyal elements in Hollywood, our members are likewise prepared to take positive action.

We will not knowingly employ a Communist or a member of any party or group which advocates the overthrow of the Government of the United States by force or by any illegal or unconstitutional methods.

In pursuing this policy, we are not going to be swayed by hysteria or intimidation from any source. We are frank to recognize that such a policy involves dangers and risks. There is the danger of hurting innocent people. There is the risk of creating an atmosphere of fear. Creative work at its best cannot be carried on in an atmosphere of fear. We will guard against this danger, this risk, this fear.

To this end we will invite the Hollywood talent guilds to work with us to eliminate any subversives; to protect the innocent; and to safeguard free speech and a free screen wherever threatened.

The absence of a national policy, established by Congress with respect to the employment of Communists in private industry, makes our task difficult. Ours is a nation of laws. We request Congress to enact legislation to assist American industry to rid itself of subversive, disloyal elements.

Nothing subversive or un-American has appeared on the screen. Nor can any number of Hollywood investigations obscure the patriotic services of the 30,000 Americans employed in Hollywood who have given our Government invaluable aid in war and peace.

Appendix VIII

A SELECTED LIST OF PUBLISHERS

Abbeville Press, Inc., 488 Madison Avenue, New York, New York 10022[1]

Ablex Publishing Corporation, 355 Chestnut Street, Norwood, New Jersey 07648

Ace Books, 200 Madison Avenue, New York, New York 10016

Aero Associates, Incorporated, 8033 Emerson Avenue, Los Angles, California 90045

Alfred Knopf, 201 East 50th Street, New York, New York 10022

Allen and Unwin (See Unwin Hyman)

Allison & Busby Ltd., 44 Hill Street, London W1X 8CB, England

ALPHA EDITIONS (See Burgess Publishing Company)

American Heritage Press (McGraw-Hill Book Co.), 605 Avenue of the Americas, New York, New York 10011

American Library Association, 50 E. Huron Street, Chicago, Illinois, 60611

Andrews and McMell, 4900 Main Street, Kansas City, Missouri 64112

Arbor House Publishers (See William Morrow and Company).

Arden Press, Inc., P. O. Box 418, Denver, Colorado 80201

---

[1] At the time this appendix was being completed, a massive amalgamation of publishing houses was underway. Typical of the problem it creates for teachers is an experience I had on April 3, 1989. After identifying the texts for my classes in the fall, I took in the book order form to the University Bookstore. Book 1, published from Little, Brown and Company, was now ordered from Scott-Foresman. Book 2, published by Alfred Knopf, was now ordered from McGraw-Hill. And book 3, published by Prentice-Hall, was now ordered from Simon and Schuster. The following list of publishers, therefore, may be outdated at the very moment I am writing this footnote. It is offered as a reminder of what was and is no more. My advice is to use it as an illustration of how the publishing world is changing.

Ardis Publications, 2901 Heatherway, Ann Arbor, Michigan 48104

Arlington House Publishers (See Crown)

Arno Press, Inc. (See Ayer Company Publishers) New York 10017

A. S. Barnes & Company, Inc., Box 421, Cranbury, New Jersey 08512

Ash & Grant, 9 Henrietta Street, Covent Garden, London, England WC2E 8PS

Associated University Presses, 440 Forsgate Drive, Cranbury, New Jersey, 08512.

Atheneum Publishers, 866 Third Avenue, New York, New York 10022

Augsburg Publishing House, 426 South Fifth Street, Minneapolis, Minnesota 55415

Avon Book Division (The Hearst Corporation), 105 Madison Avenue, New York, New York 10016

Ayer Company Publishers, Inc., 302 Main Street, P. O. Box 958, Salem, New Hampshire 03079

Ballantine Books (Div. of Random House), 201 East 50th Street, New York, New York 10022

Balch Institute For Ethnic Studies (See Assocaited University Presses)

Bantam Books, Inc., 666 Fifth Avenue, New York, New York 10019

Bartholomew House, Ltd. (Bartell Media Corp.), 205 East 42nd Street, New York, New York 10022

Basic Books, Inc., 10 East 53rd Street, New York, New York 10022

Basil Blackwell, Inc., 432 Park Avenue S., Suite 1503, New York, New York 10016

Beacon Press, 25 Beacon Street, Boston, Massachusetts 02108

Beaufort Books, 9 East 40th Street, New York, New York 10016

Berkley Publishing Corporation, 200 Madison Avenue, New York, New York 10016

Between the Lines, 394 Euclid Avenue Surle 203, Toronto, Ontario, M6G 259

B. Klein Publishers, Inc., P. O. Box 8503, Coral Springs, Florida 33065

Black Sparrow Press, 24 Tenth Street, Santa Rosa, California 95401

Bobbs-Merrill Company, 866 Third Avenue, New York, New York 10022

Bodley-Head, Ltd., 32 Bedford Square, London, England WC1B 3EL

Booklegger Press, 555 29th Street, San Francisco, California 94131

Books for Libraries Comm., Inc., 50 Liberty Avenue, Freeport, New York 11520

R. R. Bowker Company, 245 W. 17th Street, New York, New York 10011

The Boxwood Press, 183 Ocean View Boulevard, Pacific Grove, California 93950

British Film Institute (National Film Theatre Bookshop), South Bank, Waterloo, London SE1 8XT, England

British Film Institute publications (See University of Illinois Press)

Bucknell University Press (See Associated University Presses)

Burgess Publishing Company/ALPHA EDITIONS, 7108 Ohmns Lane, Minneapolis, Minnesota 55435

Burt Franklin Company, P. O. Box 856, New York, New York 10014

Cambridge University Press, 32 East 57th Street, New York, New York 10022

Canadian Film Institute, 150 Rideau Street, Ottawa, Ontario KIN 5X6

Castle Books, P. O. Box 17262, Memphis, Tennessee 38187

Chandler Publishing Company, (Intext Educational Publishers), 257 Park Avenue South, New York, New York 10010

Chronicle Books, 275 Fifth Street, San Francisco, California 94103

Cinefax, Box 151, Kew Gardens, New York 11415

Citadel Press, Inc., 120 Enterprise Avenue, Secaucus, New Jersey 07094

Clarkson N. Potter/Crown Publishers, 225 Park Avenue South, New York, New York 10003

Co-Libri (Marketing & Sales Co. for Mouton), P. O. Box 482, NL-2501 CL, Gravehage, Netherlands

Cornell University Press (also address for University of Illinois Press), P. O. Box 250, Ithaca, New York 14851

Coward-McCann Publishers (Geoghegan, Inc.), 200 Madison Avenue, New York, New York 10016

Croom Helm, 51 Washington Street, Dover, New Hampshire 03820

Criterion Books, Inc., 257 Park Avenue South, New York, New York 10010

The Crossing Press, 22D Roache Road, P. O. Box 1048, Freedom, California 95019

Crown Publishers (See Clarkson N. Potter)

David McKay, Inc., 201 East 5oth Street, New York, New York 10022

Delacorte Press (Dell Publishing Co., Inc.) 1 Dag Hammarskjold Plaza, New York, New York 10017

Delilah Communications, Ltd., 118 East 25th Street, New York, New York 10010

Derbibooks, Inc., Secaucus, New Jersey 07094

Dial Press (Dell Publishing Co., Inc.), 1 Dag Hammarskjold Plaza, New York, 10017

Dodd, Mead & Company, 71 Fifth Avenue, New York, New York 10003-3004

Dorrance & Company, 828 Lancaster Avenue, Bryn Mawr, Pennsylvania 19010

Doubleday & Company, Inc., 501 Franklin Avenue, Garden City, New York 11530

Dover Publications, Inc., 180 Varick Street, New York, New York 10013

Drake Publishers, Inc., 381 Park Avenue South, New York, New York 10016

Duke University Press, Box 6697 College Station, Durham, North Carolina 27708

E. P. Dutton & Company, Inc., 2 Park Avenue, New York, New York 10016

Educational Film Library Association, 17 West 60th Street, New York, New York 10023

Elsevier Scientific Publishing Company, 52 Vanderbilt Avenue, New York, New York 10017

Evergreen Press, Box 306, Avalon, California 90704

Exposition Press, Inc., Box 33, Norris, Tennessee 37828

Facts on File, 460 Park Avenue South, New York, New York 10016

Faber and Faber, Inc., 50 Cross Street, Winchester, Massachussetts 01890

Fairleigh Dickinson University Press (See Associated University Presses)

Farrar, Straus & Giroux, 19 Union Square West, New York, New York 10003

Federal Legal Publications, Inc., 157 Chambers Street, New York, New York 10007

Film/Video Arts, Inc. (formerly Young Filmakers Foundation), 817 Broadway, New York, New York 10003-4797.

Florida State University Press, Institute for Social Research, Tallahasse, Florida 32306

Frederick Fell, Inc., 2131 Hollywood Boulevard, Suite 204, Hollywood, Florida 33020

Films, Inc., 5447 N. Ravenwood Avenue, Chicago, Illinois 60640

Folger Books, 440 Forsgate Drive, Cranbury, New Jersey 08512

Fortress Press, 2900 Queen Lane, Philadelphia, Pennsylvania 19129

Funk & Wagnalls, 10 East 53rd Street, New York, New York 10022

Gale Research Co., Book Tower, Detroit, Michigan 48226

Garland Publishing, Inc., 136 Madison Avenue, New York, New York 10016

Geoghegan, Inc. (See Coward-McCann Publishers)

G. K. Hall & Company, 70 Lincoln Street, Boston, Massachusetts 02111

Globe Book Co., Inc., 190 Sylvan Avenue, Englewood Cliffs, New Jersey 07632

Greenhouse Publications Pty Ltd., 385 Bridge Road, Richmond Victoria 3121, Australia

Greenwood Press Inc., 88 Post Road West, Box 5007, Westport, Connecticut 06881

Grossman Publishers, 625 Madison Avenue, New York, New York 10022

Grove Press, Inc., 920 Broadway, New York, New York 10010

Hallmark Cards, Inc., 25th & McGee Streets, Kansas City, Missouri 64141

Harcourt Brace Jovanovich, Inc., 1250 Sixth Avenue, San Diego, California 92101

Harper & Row Publishers, 10 East 53rd Street, New York, New York 10022

Harry N. Abrams, Inc., 100 Fifth Avenue, New York, New York 10011

Hartmore House, 1363 Fairfield Avenue, Bridgeport, Connecticut 06605

Hart Publishing Company, Inc., 15 West Fourth Street, New York, New York 10012

Hastings House Publishers, Inc., 9 East 40th Street, New York, New York 10016

Hawthorne Books, Inc., 260 Madison Avenue, New York, New York 10016

Heineman Educational Books, Ltd., 70 Court Street, Portsmouth, New Hampshire 03801

Heinmann-William, Ltd., Michelin House, 81 Fulham Road, London 5W3 GRB England

Hemingway Western Studies Series, Boise State University, Boise, Idaho 83725

Hewitt House, Old Tappan, New Jersey 07675

Hippocrene Books, Inc., 171 Madison Avenue, New York, New York 10016

Hill & Wang Publishers (Farrar, Straus & Giroux), 19 Union Square West, New York, New York 10003

Historical Films, Box 46505, Los Angeles, California 90046

Holloway House Publishing Company, 8060 Melrose Avenue, Los Angeles, California 90069

Hollywood Film Archive, 8344 Melrose Avenue, Hollywood, California 90069

Holt, Rinehart & Winston, Inc., 111 Fifth Avenue, New York, New York 10003

Houghton Mifflin Company, 1 Beacon Street, Boston, Massachusetts 02107

Hudson Hills Press, Suite 1308, 230 Fifth Avenue, New York, New York 10001-7704

Humanities Press, Inc., 171 1st Avenue, Atlantic Highland, New Jersey 07716-1289

H. W. Allen & Co., Ltd., 43 Essex Street, London, England

H. W. Wilson Company, 950 University Avenue, Bronx, New York 10452

Imported Publications, Inc., 320 West Ohio Street, Chicago, Illinois 60610

Indiana University Press, 10th & Morton Streets, Bloomington, Indiana 47401

International Arts & Sciences Press, 901 North Broadway, White Plains, New York 10603

Intext Educational Publishers (See Chandler Publishing Company)

Iowa State University Press, 2121 South State Avenue, Ames, Iowa 50010

J. B. Lippincott Company, East Washington Square, Philadelphia, Pennsylvania 19105

Jewish Film Festival, 2600 Tenth Street #102, Berkeley, California 94710

Jonathan David Publishers, Inc., 68 Elliott Avenue, Middle Village, New York 11379

Johns Hopkins University Press, 701 West 40th Street, Suite 275, Baltimore, Maryland 21211

Kodansha International/USA, Ltd., Harper Row, 10 East 53rd Street, New York, New York 10022

Kraus-Thomson Organization, Ltd., Route 100, Millwood, New York 10546

KTO Microform, Route 100, Millwood, New York 10546

Lake View Press, P.O. Box 578279, Chicago, Illinois 60657

Lancer Books, Inc., 1560 Broadway, New York, New York 10036

Lawrence and Wisehart, 39 Museum Street, London WC1A 1LQ

League of Women Voters of the U.S., 1730 M. Street, N. W., Washington, D. C. 20036

Lester & Orpen Dennys Ltd., 78 Sullivan Street, Toronto, Ontario MST 1C1, Canada

Limelight Editions, 118 East 30th Street, New York, New York 10016

Little, Brown & Company, Inc., 34 Beacon Street, Boston, Massachusetts 02106

Locare Research Group, 910 North Fairfax Avenue, Los Angeles, California 90046

Locust Hill Press, P. O. Box 260, West Cornwall, Connecticut 06796

Longman, 95 Church Street, White Plains, New York 10601

Lorrimer Publishers, Ltd., 16 Tite Street, London, SW3 4HZ, England

Louisiana State University Press, Hill Memorial Building, Highland Road, Louisiana State University, Baton Rouge, Louisiana 70803

Loyola University Press, 3441 North Ashland Avenue, Chicago, Illinois 60657

Lutterworth Press, P. O. Box 60, Cambridge CBI 2NT, England

Macmillan Company, 866 Third Avenue, New York, New York 10022

Manor Books, 329 Fifth Avenue, New York, New York 10016

Mayfield Publishing Company, 1240 Villa Street, Mountain View, California 94301

McFadden-Bartell Corporation, 205 East 42nd Street, New York, New York 10017

McFarland and Company, Inc., Box 611 N, Jefferson, North Carolina 28640

McGraw-Hill Book Company, 1221 Avenue of the Americas, New York, New York 10020

Mercury House, 300 Montgomery Street, Suite 700, San Francisco, California 94109

Michael Joseph, Ltd., 27 Wright's Lane, London, W8 5TZ, England; Microsoft Press, 16011 N. E. 36th, Box 97017, Redmond, Washington 98073-9717

M. I. T. Press, 55 Hayward Street, Cambridge, Massachusetts 02142

Moonstone Press, P.O. Box 142, Beverly Hills, California 90213

Museum of Modern Art, 11 West 53rd Street, New York, New York 10019

Naiburg Publishing Corporation, 27 West 44th Street, Box 19, New York, New York 10036

Thomas Nelson, Inc., P. O. Box 141000, Nashville, Tennessee 37214

Netherlands Government Information Service, The Hague, 43, Noordeinde, Netherlands

New American Library, 1633 Broadway, New York, New York, 10019

The Newark Museum, 49 Washington Street, P. O. Box 540, Newark, New Jersey, 07101

Newmarket Press, 3 East 48 Street, New York, New York 10017

New York Graphic Society Publishers, Ltd., 39 Beacon Street, Boston, Massachusetts 02108

W. W. Norton & Company, Inc., 500 Fifth Avenue, New York, New York 10001

O'Hara Publications, Inc., 1813 Victory Place, Burbank California 91504

Overlook Press, RR1 Box 496, Woodstock, New York 12498

Oxford University Press, 200 Madison Avenue, New York, New York 10017

Jerome S. Ozer Publishers, 340 Tenatly Place, Englewood Cliffs, New Jersey 07631

Pantheon Books, Inc., (Random House, Inc.), 201 East 50th Street, New York, New York 10022

Paragon House Publishers, 90 Fifth Avenue, New York, New York 10011

Paul Hamlyn, Inc., 205 East 42nd Street, New York, New York 10036

Penguin Books, Inc., 40 W. 23rd Street, New York, New York 10010

Pergamon Press, Maxwell House-Fairview Park, Elmsford, New York 10523

Peter H. Wyden Company, 201 E. 50th Street, New York, New York 10022

Peter Martin Associates, Ltd., 35 Britain Street, Toronto, Ontario, M5A 1R7, Canada

Pflaum Publishing, 3024 Springboro West, Dayton, Ohio 45439

Pitman Publishing Corporation, 6 East 43rd Street, New York, New York 10017

Playboy Press, 919 North Michigan Avenue, Chicago, Illinois 60611

Plexus Publishers, Ltd., 30 Craven Street, London, WC2N SNT England

Pocket Books (Ace Distribution Corp.), 1230 Avenue of the Americas, New York, New York 10020

Pomegranate Arts Books, Incorporated, P. O. Box 980, Corte Maders, California 94925

Popular Library, 600 Third Avenue, New York, New York 10016

Praeger Publishers, One Madison Avenue, New York, New York 10010

Prentice-Hall, Inc., Rte 9W. Englewood Cliffs, New Jersey 07632

The Preservation Press, National Trust for Historic Preservation, 1785 Massachusetts Avenue, N. W., Washington, D. C. 20036

Primestyle Publishers, Ltd., 21 Highfield Avenue, St. Austell, Cornwall, England

Primus: Donald I. Fine, Inc., 128 East 36th Street, New York, New York 10016

Princeton University Press, 41 Williams Street, Princeton, New Jersey 08540

G. P. Putnam's Sons, 200 Madison Avenue, New York, New York 10016

Quadrangle Books, (A N.Y. Times Book Co.), 10 East 53rd Street, New York, New York 10022

Quick Fox, 33 West 60th Street, New York, New York, 10023

Rampart Press, P. O. Box 50128, Palo Alto, California 94303

Random House, Inc., 201 East 50th Street, New York, New York 10022

Red Dembner Enterprises Corp., 80 Eighth Avenue, New York, New York 10011

Redgrave Publishing Company, 380 Adams Street, Bedford Hills, New York 10507

Regency Press, Ltd., 125 High Holborn, London, WC1V 6QA England

Henry Regnery Company, Contemporary Books, Inc., 180 North Michigan Avenue, Chicago, Illinois 60601

Max Reinhardt Archive, State University of New York at Binghamton, Binghamton, New York 13901

Re/Search Publications, 20 Romolo #B, San Francisco, California 94133

Routledge, Chapman and Hall, 29 West 35th Street, New York, New York 10001

R. R. Bowker Company, 1180 Avenue of the Americas, New York, New York 10036

Rutgers University Press, 109 Church Street, New Brunswick, New Jersey 08903

St. James Press, 425 N. Michigan Avenue, Suite 600, Chicago, Illinois 60611

St. Martin's Press, Inc., 175 Fifth Avenue, New York, New York 10010

Salem House, Merrimac Publishers Circle, 462 Bolton Street, Topsfield, Massachusetts 01983

W. B. Saunders Company, Curtis Center, Independence Square W, Philadelphia, Pennsylvania 19106

Scarecrow Press, Inc., P. O. Box 656, 52 Liberty Street, Metuchen, New Jersey 08840

Scott-Foresman & Company, 1900 East Lake Avenue, Glenview, Illinois 60025

Charles Scribner's Sons, 866 Third Avenue, New York, New York 10022

Seaview Press, 861 Sea View Drive, El Cerrito, California 94530

Secker & Warburg, Ltd., Michelin House, 81 Fulham Road, London SW3 6RB, England

Serina Press, 70 Kennedy Street, Alexandria, Virginia 22305

Signet Books (New American Library), 1633 Broadway, New York, New York 10019

Simon & Schuster, Inc., Simon and Schuster Building, 1230 Avenue of the Americas, York, New York 10020

Smyrna Press, Box 1803-GPO, Brooklyn, New York 11202

Southern Methodist University Press, P. O. Box 415, Dallas, Texas 75275

Southern Illinois University Press, P. O. Box 3697, Carbondale, Illinois 62901

Stein and Day Publishers, 7 East 48th Street, New York, New York 10017

Stewart, Tabori, and Chang. (See Workman Publishing)

Stipes Publishing Company, 10-12 Chester Street, Champaign, Illinois 61820

Lyle Stuart, Inc., 120 Enterprise Avenue, Secaucus, New Jersey 07094

Swallow Press Books, Scott Quadrangle Room 144, The Ohio University Press, Athens, Ohio 45701

Tab Books, P. O. Box 40, Blue Ridge Summit, Pennsylvania 17214

The Tantivy Press, 2 Bedford Gardens, London, W8 7EH, England

Thames and Hudson, 30-34 Bloomsbury Street, London, WC1, England

Thessaly Press, P. O. Box 130, London E11 1BP, England

Thomas Y. Crowell Company, 10 East 53rd Street, New York, New York 10022

Trident Press (Simon & Schuster, Inc.), 630 Fifth Avenue, New York, New York 10020

Frederick Ungar Publishing Co., Inc., 370 Lexington Avenue, New York, New York 10017

Universe Books, 381 Park Avenue South, New York, New York 10016

University of California Press, 2120 Berkeley Way, Berkeley, California 94720

University of Chicago Press, 5801 South Ellis Avenue, Chicago, Illinois 60637

University of Delaware Press (See Associated University Presses)

University of Georgia Press, Terrell Hall, Athens, Georgia 30602

University of Illinois Press (See Cornell University Press)

University of Massachusetts Press, P. O. Box 429, Amherst, Massachusetts 01002

University of Michigan Press, P. O. Box 1104, Ann Arbor, Michigan 48106

University of Minnesota Press, 2037 University Avenue S. E., Minneapolis, Minnesota 55414

University of Missouri Press, 200 Lewis Hall, Columbia, Missouri 65201

University of New Mexico Press, Journalism Building Room 220, Albuquerque, New Mexico 87131

University of Oklahoma Press, 1005 Asp Avenue, Norman, Oklahoma 73069

University of South Dakota, Vermillion, South Dakota 57069

University of Tennessee Press, 293 Communications Building, Knoxville, Tennessee 37916

University of Texas Press, Post Office Box 7819, Austin, Texas 78713

University of Toronto Press, Front Campus, Toronto, Ontario M5S 1 A6

University Press of America, 4720 Boston Way, Lanham, Maryland 20706

University Press of Mississippi, 3825 Ridgewood Road, Jackson, Mississippi 39211

University Press of New England, 17 1/2 Lebanon Street, Hanover, New Hampshire 03755

University Publications of America, 44 North Market Street, Frederick, Maryland 21701

Unwin Hyman (formerly George Allen & Unwin), 8 Winchester Place, Winchester, Massachussetts 01890.

Van Nostrand Reinhold Company, 115 Fifth Avenue, New York, New York 10003

Vantage Press, Inc., 516 West 34th Street, New York, New York 10001

The Vestal Press, P. O. Box 97, 320 North Jensen Road, Vestal, New York 13850

Viking Press, Inc., 40 West 23rd Street, New York, New York 10010

Walt Lee Company, P. O. Box 27800, Van Arsdale Road, Potter Valley, California 95469

Warner Brothers Publishers, Inc., 666 Fifth Avenue, New York, New York 10013

Warner Paperback Library, 75 Rockefeller Plaza, New York, New York 10019

Wayne State University Press, Leonard N. Simons Building, 5959 Woodward Avenue, Detroit, Michigan 48202

Weidenfeld and Nicolson, 841 Broadway, New York, New York 10003-4793

William Collins & World Publishing Company, Inc., 2080 West 117th Street, Cleveland, Ohio 44111

William Morrow Company, Inc., 105 Madison Avenue, New York, New York 10016

Windmill Press, 2005 W. Balboa Boulevard, No.262, Newport Beach, California 92663

Women's History Research Center, Inc., 2325 Oak Street, Berkeley, California 94708

Workman Publishing, 708 Broadway, New York, New York 10013

Wyden Books, P.O. Box 151, Ridgefield, Connecticut 06877

Young Filmakers Foundation (See Film/Video Arts, Inc.)

Appendix IX

U.S. MOTION PICTURE THEATRES' BOX OFFICE

U.S. MOTION PICTURE THEATRES' BOX OFFICE
AVERAGE PRICE PER ADMISSION AND NUMBER OF ADMISSIONS

| Year | U.S. BOX OFFICE GROSS ($MILLIONS) | | | | Average Price per Admission (Including Admission Taxes) | Number of Admissions (Millions) |
	Excluding Admission Taxes	Federal Admission Tax	State & Local Admission Taxes	Including Admission Taxes		
1946	$1,398.3	$ 279.7	$ 14.0	$1,692.0	$ 0.416	4,067.3
1947	1,317.8	263.5	13.2	1,594.0	0.435	3,664.4
1948*	1,244.6	248.9	12.5	1,506.0	0.440	3,422.7
1949	1,196.7	239.3	12.0	1,448.0	0.457	3,168.5
1950	1,138.7	227.8	12.5	1,379.0	0.457	3,017.5
1951	1,099.0	219.8	13.2	1,332.0	0.469	2,840.1
1952	1,092.3	218.5	14.2	1,325.0	0.477	2,777.7
1953	1,103.0	220.6	15.4	1,339.0	0.509	2,630.6
1954*	1,117.8	116.7	16.5	1,251.0	0.551	2,270.4
1955	2,224.3	74.7	15.0	1,204.0	0.581	2,072.3
1956	1,042.6	69.9	12.5	1,125.0	0.594	1,893.9
1957	1,016.5	50.8	10.7	1,078.0	0.624	1,727.6
1958*	984.4	16.8	8.8	1,010.0	0.650	1,553.8
1959	981.1	16.7	8.2	1,006.0	0.676	1,488.2
1960	925.5	15.7	7.2	984.4	0.727	1,304.5
1961	923.3	15.7	6.5	945.5	0.772	1,224.7
1962	855.2	14.5	5.2	874.9	0.810	1,080.1
1963*	904.3	15.3	5.4	925.0	0.846	1,093.4
1964	926.1	15.7	5.8	947.6	0.925	1,024.4
1965	1,018.0	17.2	6.6	1,041.8	1,010	1,031.5
1966	1,059.7	None	7.4	1,067.1	1,094	975.4
1967*	1,101.7	None	8.3	1,110.0	1,198	926.5
1968	1,272.5	None	9.5	1,282.0	1,310	978.6
1969	1,284.4	None	9.6	1,294.0	1,419	911.9
1970	1,418.6	None	10.6	1,429.2	1,552	920.6
1971	1,338.8	None	10.7	1,349.5	1,645	820.3
1972*	1,570.5	None	12.6	1,583.1	1,695	934.1
1973	1,511.4	None	12.1	1,523.5	1,762	864.6
1974	1,891.4	None	16.1	1,908.5	1,888	1,010.7
1975	2,093.9	None	20.9	2,114.8	2,048	1,032.8
1976	2,016.2	None	20.2	2,036.4	2,128	957.1
1977	2,348.8	None	23.5	2,372.3	2,231	1,063.2
1978	2,617.1	None	26.3	2,643.4	2,343	1,128.2
1979	2,793.4	None	27.9	2,821.3	2,517	1,120.9
1980	2,721.3	None	27.2	2,748.5	2,691	1,021.5
1981	2,936.2	None	29.4	2,965.6	2,779	1,067.0
1982	3,418.5	None	34.2	3,452.7	2,937	1,175.4
1983	3,728.7	None	37.3	3,766.0	3,246	1,196.9
1984	3,990.7	None	39.9	4,030.6	3,361	1,199.1

*Estimates based on Census of Business

SOURCE: Motion Picture Association of America, Inc. (M.P.A.A.),
Information Services, Research Department.

2302

Article Titles Index

A

A Bas--Everything! 474
ABC Admits an Error in Airing Russian's Views 489
ABC Criticized for Move After Soviet Threat 489
ABC Delays AMERIKA, Discloses Soviet Warning 489
ABC Discontinues Movie Operations 678
ABC Will Proceed with AMERIKA 549
Abel Gance's Accusation Against War 1712
Abel Gance: Prometheus Bound 1712
Abolish Term "Black Films" 904, 905
Abraham Polonsky 1094
Absence of Malice 1017
Absence Which Becomes a Legendary Presence: John Ford's Use of Off-Screen
  Space, An 1674
Absences of Sandra, The 1874
ACCIDENT 2161
Accounting Rule Masking Future Profits 743
Accusations Against Charles Chaplin for Political and Moral Offenses 1433
Achieving the Fantastic in the Animated Film 416
Across the Awareness Divide: Reviving THE EMPEROR JONES (2) 876
Across the Board 2084
Acting Art, The 1434
Action All the Way 1672
Action But No Consensus on Film Coloring 656
Actor and His Mask, The 1022
Actor, Director Cassavetes Dies from Cirrhosis of Liver 2048
Adaptation of Cinematic Dreams, The 578, 593
Adaptations in Evelyn Waugh's Fiction 1294
Add Film to Rhetoric 39
Adirondack Film Maker Seeks Big-City Success 671
Adult-Appeal Releases On Rise During Summer B. O. Season 764
Aesthetic and Feminist Theory: Rethinking Women's Cinema 471
Aesthetic Becomes Political: A History of Film Criticism in CAHIERS DU CINEMA,
  The 1997, 2103
Aesthetic Defense of the Star System in Films, An 1437
Aesthetic of Reality: Cinematic Realism and the Italian School of Liberation,
  An 1922
Aesthetic Relevance of the Organization of Film Production, The 1512
Aesthetics of the Zoom Lens, The 79
Aesthetics, Social Commentary and Analysis 144
AFI Celebrates Directing Workshop 681
Afro-American Literature as a Cultural Resource for a Black Cinema
  Aesthetic 949
After a Decade, Poitier Returns as an Actor to a Changing Hollywood 890
After Bergman 2182
After the Ball 400
After the Fall: Post-Cimino Hollywood 2201
After the Film Generation 34
After the Nouvelle Vague 2093
After The Revolution 2181
After The Strike 2034
After 70 Pictures 1680
Afterthoughts on "Visual Pleasure and Narrative Cinema" Inspired by DUEL IN
  THE SUN (King Vidor, 1946) 531, 532
Afterword 1462

Afterword to THE ROAD TO GLORY: A SCREENPLAY 1103
Against the System of Suture 591
Age of the Replicant, The 409
Agent Power Now Rules Hollywood: No Film Czars to Snub Them 2197
Agnes Varda Sings: An Interview 2114
Alain Resnais: The War Is Over 2116
Alain Resnais: Toward the Certainty of Doubt 2116
Alain Resnais: "Memory Is Kept Alive with Dreams" 2116
Alain Robbe-Grillet: The Novelist as Director 1301
Alan Schneider, 66, Director of Beckett Dies 2067
Aldrich Interview 2071
Alex Jacobs: The Best (and Least) Known Screenwriter In Hollywood 2073
Alexander Black's Picture Plays: 1893-1894 1601
ALFIE 2161
Alfred Adler, Individual Psychology, and Marilyn Monroe 586
Alfred Guzzetti's Family Portrait Sittings 982
Alfred Hitchcock 1835
Alfred Hitchcock and the Ghost of Thomas Hobbes 1835
Alfred Hitchcock Dies; A Master of Suspense 1854
Alfred Hitchcock Index, An 1835
Alfred Hitchcock Talking . . . 1835
Alfred Hitchcock Was the Poet of Civilized Suspense 1854
Alfred Hitchcock's Working Credo 1835
Alfred Hitchcock, Prankster of Paradox 1837
Alfred Hitchcock, 80, Dies in Hollywood 1854
Alfred Hitchcock: Allegory of Ambiguous Sexuality 1838
Alfred Hitchcock: Lost in the Wood 1837
Alfred Hitchcock: Master of Morality 1836
Alfred Hitchcock: The Film-maker as Englishman and Exile 1839
Alfred Joseph Hitchcock 1834
Alfred Newman 83
Ali McGraw: A Return to Basics 2191
Alice Doesn't Live Here Anymore 1011
ALICE'S RESTAURANT and the Tradition of the Plotless Film 163
All About Bette 1981
All About Eve 1981
All Guns and Gangsters: A Report on the Present Situation of the French
  Cinema 1999, 2093
All In the Family: Alfred Hitchcock's SHADOW OF A DOUBT 1835
All is not Welles 1023
All Talking! All Singing! All Lubitsch: Ernst Lubitsch in the Thirties--Part
  Two 1694
All the Better Books 1297, 1301
All the King's Men 1012
All the Right Moves 670
Allen, Woody 2072
Ally Sheedy's Film Career Tracks the Image of Youth in the 1980's 972
Alternation, Segmentation, Hypnosis: Interview with Raymond Bellour 471
Alvah Bessie 1178
Alvah Bessie, 81, Of Hollywood 10, Dies In California 1178
Amadeus, Shamadeus 1330
AMAZING STORIES Tries New Tactics 760
America Rediscovers Its Black Actors 901
American B Film: A Fond Appreciation, The 651
American Cinema of the Sixties 2041, 2088
American Dream on Film, The 39, 52
American Family, An 982
American Film and Television Schools and the Search for Cultural Identity 42

American Film Industry of the 1970's: Stasis in the "New Hollywood," The 660
American Films and Foreign Audiences 748
American Graffiti 993
American Intellectual History: A Critical Appraisal 258
American Jews and the Holocaust 291
American Melies, The 1604
American Star of the Hindi Screen, An 2168
American Tendencies 1749
AMERICAN TRAGEDY, AN 1866
American Vitagraph: 1897-1901 615, 618, 1462, 1590, 1601
American Way West, The 424
American Western and American Society, The 559
American Western: Myth and Anti-Myth, The 424
American Young in Uproar 817
Americanization of the Holocaust on Stage and Screen, The 291, 837
America, "Mass Society" and Mass Media 459
America: The Celluloid Myth 815
AMERIKA--an Irresponsible TV Series 489
AMERIKA--Slogging Through a Muddle 489
Amerikan Broadcasting 549
Amerikan Way on TV, The 489
An Unlikely Movie Mecca 658
Analysis of Motion Picture Financing, An 608
And Justice for Some 1292
AND NOW MY LOVE 2119
And Reflects on Life and Art 2168
And The Pursuit of Happiness 2074
And Then There Was Nunn 903
And Time Marched On: The Creation of the MARCH OF TIME 227
Anderson Shooting IF . . . 1001
Androgynous Scribes, Duplicitous Inscriptions: Isaac Bashevis Singer's
  Cinematic Dreamscapes 598
Andrzej Wajda 2180
Andrzej Wajda, Director With Double Vision 2180
Andy 2039
Andy Warhol, Pop Artist, Dies 2040
Andy Warhol: Iconographer 2039
Angels on the Screen 815
Angle and Reality: Godard and Gorin in America 2111
Anguish: Alphaville 2151
Animated Cinema: The Way Forward 76
Animation in Zagreb 77
Anne of the Thousand Days 1347
ANNEE DERNIERE A MARIENBAD, L' 2153
Another Dreamer Who Wants To Stop All War 1376
Another Trip to the Pawnshop 2084
Answering Film With Film: The Hampton Epilogue, A Positive Alternative to the
  Negative Black Stereotypes 1367
Anthony Quinn 1015
Anthropology and Film: The Social Science Implications of Regarding Film As
  Communication 52
Anti-Militarism of Stanley Kubrick, The 2083
Antiblind-Bidding Contributed to Downbeat B. O.: Mancuso 676
Antitrust Policies and the Motion Picture Industry 697
Antonioni In Transit 1874
Antonioni Men 1874
Antonioni, Michelangelo 1874
Any Which Way He Could 1257, 1258, 1261
Aparajito 1004

Apocalypse Then: Hollywood Looks Back at Vietnam   335
Appalachia on Film: The Making of SERGEANT YORK   913
Apparatus: An Introduction, The   584
Appeal of the Moving Picture, The   455, 744
Appeal to Lillian Hellman and Mary McCarthy, An   1322
Applications of Communication Theory: IV, Immediate Experience of Movies   463
Apprenticeship of John Ford, The   1674
Approaches to Film Teaching: A Seminar Discussion   40
Approaching the Work of Dorothy Arzner   471, 475
Arab Image in American Film and Television, The   826
Archeology of Cinema Architecture: The Origins of the Movie Theater, The   617,
  1600
Archetypal American, The   40, 424
Archetypal Reading of JULIET OF THE SPIRITS, An   593
Archie Bunker's Bigotry: A Study in Selective Perception and Exposure   835
Architecture of Reception, The   252, 485, 486, 714
Are Feminist Heroines An Endangered Species?   2207
Are Movies Ready for Real Orientals?   826
Are the Ratings Just Alphabet Soup?   959
Are YOU Waving THE Flag at Me?; Samuel Fuller and Politics   1976
Are "New" Women's Films Guilty of Sexism in Reverse?   793
Argentina Way   2157
Argentina Way--Part One   2157
Argentina Way--Part Two   2157
Argument in Film: Applying Rhetorical Theory to Film Criticism, The   41
Armat-Jenkins Dispute and the Museums, The   1586
Arrival and Departure   2160
Ars Longa, Vita Brevis   610
Art and Artlessness: Peter Ustinov   2010
Art and Death of D. W. Griffith   1368
Art and Film in Francois Truffaut's JULES AND JIM and TWO ENGLISH
  GIRLS   2155
Art and the Holocaust: Trivializing Memory   290
Art Carney: I Brought the Pouch to the Part   1006
Art Direction   79
Art of Cineplastics, The   1710
Art of Dreaming in THREE WOMEN and PROVIDENCE: Structures of the Self,
  The   593
Art of Jacques Tati, The   2001
Art of Noncompromise: You've Got to Love Something Enough to Kill It,
  The   2197
Art of the Actor   1434
Art of Vision, The   1974
Art of Yasujiro Ozu, The   1742
Arthur Freed   83
Arthur Penn In Canada   2088
Arthur Penn: Directing Films and Plays   2088
Arthur Penn: The Flight from Identity   2088
Articulation of Color in a Filmic System: Two or Three Things I Know About
  Her, The   80, 654
Artist as Pornographer: Borowczyk Interviewed, The   2192
Artist Warhol, 58, Dies of Heart Attack   2040
Artistic Recipe for MY DINNER WITH ANDRE, The   2119
Artistic Vision of Sam Peckinpah, The   2087
Artistry of Psychotics, The   580
As Many Notes As Required   1330
ASC, The   79
Ashby, Hal   2195

Asides on Godard 2108
Aspects of British Feminist Film Theory 471
Aspects of the Familiar: A Defense of Minority Group Stereotyping in the Popular
 Film 1367
Assessing Time Warner Data Offer a Glimpse 2205
At CBS-TV, They're Testing 1, 2, 3 . . . 726
At Independent Film Festival, Hail and Farewell 671
At Last I Can Tell It to Someone! Feminine Point of View and Subjectivity in the
 Gothic Romance Films of the 1940s 792
At Last--Brother Caring for Brother 898
At The Boundary of Film and Theatre 1062
At the Movies 1292
At War With Ourselves 368
ATALANTE, L' 1828
ATALANTE: A Review, L' 1828
Atlanta Child Murders, The 548
Audience as Protagonist in Three Hitchcock Films 2079
Audience Research in the Movie Field 707, 728, 736, 738
Audio-Visualism versus Education 39
Audit of Marquee Values: April 1940 735
Audrey Hepburn 1988
Audrey Rose: In Search of a Soul 1987
Australia Stands In as a Television Hollywood 672
Australian Silent Films, 1904-1907: The Features Begin 1590
Authorial and Systemic Self-Consciousness in Literature and Film 1297
Authors, Auteurs, and Adaptations: Literature as Film/Film as Literature 1025
AUTOBIOGRAPHY OF JANE PITMAN: How to Make a White Film from a Black
 Novel 1300
Autobiography of Peter Pan, The 2196
Autobiography of Woody Allen, The 2072
Autumn of Jean Renoir, The 1813
Autumnal Ozu: THE END OF SUMMER 2024
Aux Armes!: The Rise of the Hollywood War Film, 1916-1930 223
Avant-Garde and Its Imaginary, The 471, 476, 480, 481, 527, 531, 585, 590
Avant-Garde Films in Struggle to Stay Alive 2205
Average High-Priced Movie: Where All the Money Goes, An 670
AVVENTURA, L' 2172
Ayn Rand in the Stockyard of the Spirit 1315

B

B . . . for Black: No Business Like Micheaux Business 860, 867, 868, 869,
 882
Back to the Future 2197
Backing Britain 2159
Bad and the Beautiful, The 1290
Bad Guys Wear Pin Stripes 486
Bakshi, Ralph 2195
Ban on Vadim 2119
Bank Shots: Interviews with Two Film Financiers 645
Banker Looks at the Picture Business--1971, A 659
Banker Looks at the Picture Business, A 659
Bankers Star Behind the Scenes 743
Banned in Britain 1024
Barbara Stanwyck 799
Barefoot Contessa, The 1290
Baron, The Count and Their Ghoul Friends 388
Baryshnikov Takes On Another Role--Movie Star 1016

Baseball on the Screen 815
Bashful Hero in American Film of the Nineteen Forties, The 803, 804
Basic Demand of Life for Love, The 2189
BATMAN Sets Sales Record: 4100 Million in 10 Days 2206
Battle for Time Inc.: Bottom Line Is Cash 2204
BATTLE OF ALGIERS, THE 2176
Battle Over Video Cassettes: Millions in Tape Rentals at Stake, A 762
Bazin & Renoir: An Uncanny Rapport 1819
Beautiful Music from a Twisted Time 1896
Bebe Daniels 1703
Because They're Young--Part One 816, 998
Because They're Young--Part Two 816, 998
Becker 1994
Beethoven, Chopin and Tammy Wynette: Heroine and Archetypes in FIVE EASY
  PIECES 789
Before and After Television: The South African Cinema Audience 771
Before Laurel: Oliver Hardy and the Vim Comedy Company, a Studio
  Biography 621, 627
Behind a Corporate Courtship 2205
Behind the Strike at NBC 672
Behind TV's Angelgate Mess: How Dirty Deals Work and Why Hollywood Loves
  Them 610
Beige, Brown or Black 884, 941
BELLE ET LA BETE, LA 2009
Belmondo 2151
Ben Hecht 1224
Ben Hecht: A Sampler 85, 1064, 1224
BEN HUR Journal, The 1748
Bending of a Mind 1292
Benjamin Will Survive: Interview With Charles Webb 2086
Bergman and Anderson for Sophomores 1141
Bergman and Dream 593
Bergman's Portrait of Women: Sexism or Suggestive Metaphor? 497
Bergmanorama 2183
Berlin II. The Retrospective 203
Berlin on $50,000 a Year 1322
Bernard Herrmann 83
Bernardo Bertolucci: An Interview 2174
Bertolucci On THE CONFORMIST 2174
Bessie Love 1367
Best and Worst of It, The 2090
Best of All Possible Worlds, The 410
Best Second Fiddle, The 384
BEST YEARS OF OUR LIVES: A Review, THE 375
Bette Davis 1981
Bette Davis: Part One 1981
Bette Davis: Part Two 1981
Better Late Than Never 2012
Better Than Metro Isn't Good Enough!: Hecht and MacArthur's Own Movies 1224
Between Art and Life 2109
Between Explosions 1651
Between Heaven and Hell: Interview With Carl Dreyer 2190
Between The Acts 1648, 2182
Between Theater and Life: Jean Renoir and RULES OF THE GAME 1827
Between Two Worlds: Jewish Images in American Films 827
Between 2001 and STAR WARS 410
Beyond Cinema: Notes on Some Films by Andy Warhol 2039

Beyond East and West: The American Western and Rise of the Chinese Swordplay Movie 424
Beyond The Frame 656
BEYOND THE LIMIT: Familiar Shadows From the World of Graham Greene 1301
Beyond The Powers That Be 1137
Bibliography of Latin American Cinema, A 2178
Bibliography on Sound in Film 632
BICYCLE THIEF 1933
BICYCLE THIEF, THE 1004
Bidding Adieu to the Feminine Mystique 789
Big Boom in Outdoor Movies 649
Big Boy Tells His Story, The 1453
Big Brawl: Hollywood vs. Television--Part III, The 648
Big Brawl: Hollywood vs. Television--Part II, The 648
Big Brawl: Hollywood vs. Television--Part I, The 648
Big Film Trend Stories of '73 2194
Big Gains for Video Cassettes: Revenues Nearing Box Office Income 672
Big Hitch: Is the Director a Prisoner of his Own Virtuosity?, The 2080
Big Knife, The 1290
Big Movie Houses Going Way of Dinosaurs; Minis Reign 752
Big One Gets Away 472
Big Screen Takes on New Meaning 674
Big Screens, The 656
Big Sleep, The 798
Big Video Picture From Japan, The 675
Bigger Than Life 673
Billy Budd 1018
BILLY BUDD Script Extract 1018
BILLY JACK Phenomenon, The 666
Billy Liar 994
Billy Wilder 1987
Billy Wilder: Closet Romanticist 1987
Biofilmography 1014
Biofilmography of Anthony Mann 1982
Biofilmography of Robert Rossen 1985
Biographical Hogwash 1374
Biograph, Griffith and Fate 1362
Birth and Rebirth in Current Fantasy Films 410
Birth of a Film Poet, The 1362
Birth of a New Avant-Garde: LA CAMERA-STYLO, The 1996, 2123
Birth of a Notion, The 874
Birth of a Style, The 1674, 1704
Birth of BIRTH OF A NATION, The 941
Birth of CHILDREN OF PARADISE, The 1910
Birth of Hollywood, The 1595
Birth of RULES OF THE GAME, The 1822
Birth of WAY DOWN EAST, The 1391
Biting the Hand of Hollywood 1295
Bitter Harvest: AIDS and the Arts 2204
Bitter Life of Money, The 1022
Black Action Film: The End of the Patiently Enduring Black Hero, The 898
Black and White Buddies: How Sincere Is the Harmony? 904
Black Cinema: Supernigger Strikes 896
Black Dramatists Offer New Visions of Old Icons 906
Black Film Experience, The 860, 861, 1577
Black Films 898
Black Films and Film Makers; Movies in the Ghetto, B. P. (Before Poitier) 860
Black Films of Old 852
BLACK GOD AND WHITE DEVIL 2158

Black Images in American TV: The First Two Decades 854
Black Man as Movie Hero, The 900
Black Men or Good Niggers? 942
Black Motion Pictures: The Past 871
Black Movies 898, 899, 916, 942
Black Odyssey: Sweet Sweetback's Baadasssss Song 942
Black Reaction to GONE WITH THE WIND, The 812
Black Woman's Outlook in Whitney Film Series 902
Black Women in Films: A Mixed Bag of Tricks 942
Black Women's Responses to THE COLOR PURPLE 905
Black Years of Dalton Trumbo, The 1084
Blackboard Jungle, The 1000
Blackface, Hollywood Style 880
Blacklisted 1084
Blacklisting 1084
Blacklist=Black Market 1084, 1097
BLACKMAIL: The Opening of Hitchcock's Surrealistic Eye 1864
Blacks and the Academy Awards; Can We Get Them? 877
Blacks Flex Muscles in Film and TV 905
Blacks in American Films 559
Blacks in Television: A Selective, Annotated Bibliography 855
Blacks in the Arts: Evaluating Recent Success 903
Blacks, Loyalty, and Motion Picture Propaganda in World War II 856
Blake Edwards in Tiff Over "S. O. B." 1295
Blake Edwards' Revenge 1295
Blanche Sweet 1365
Blanche Sweet, Actress; An Early Star of Silent Films 1365
BLAUE ENGEL, DER 1831
Blaxploitation Films and High School Youth: SWAT SUPER FLY 978
Blazing the Trail: Harry Saltzman 1319
Blessed Isle or Fool's Paradise 994
Blind-Bidding Factions Nearing Deal; Blocks Still Remain 676
Blood on the Nash Ambassador: Cars in American Films, The 559
Blow-Up 2173
Blow-Up, The 2173
BLUE ANGEL, THE 1831
Blue Denim 1001
Blue Notes 2037
Blueprints for Feature Films: Hollywood's Continuity Scripts 637
BLUME and HEARTBREAK KID--What Kind of Jews Are They? 834
Bobby Harron 1365
Bogart, Hawks, and THE BIG SLEEP Revisited--Frequently 798, 1978
Bogdanovich--Will NICKELODEON Be His Last Picture Show? 1294
Bogdanovich, Peter 2195
Bonanza at the Top of Disney 681
Bonaparte et la Revolution 1712
BONNIE AND CLYDE Revisited: Part One 2088
BONNIE AND CLYDE Revisited: Part Two 2088
Book of Numbers 941
Book Reviews 560
Book Reviews of WOMEN'S PICTURES and WOMEN IN FILM 586
Book Review: AMERICA IN THE MOVIES 576
Book Review: AN ALBUM OF GREAT SCIENCE FICTION FILMS, Rev. ed. 413
Book Review: AN ALBUM OF MODERN HORROR FILMS 393
Book Review: CAMERAS WEST 430
Book Review: FILM AND THE DREAM SCREEN: A SLEEP AND A
  FORGETTING 584, 596
Book Review: GANGSTERS ON THE SCREEN 386

Book Review: HITCHCOCK'S BRITISH FILMS 1857
Book Review: HOLLYWOOD FROM VIETNAM TO REAGAN 604
Book Review: HOLLYWOOD'S IMAGE OF THE JEW 839
Book Review: JEAN RENOIR: THE FRENCH FILMS, 1924-1935 1823
Book Review: JOHN FORD 1685
Book Review: LOVING WITH A VENGEANCE: MASS-PRODUCED FANTASIES FOR
WOMEN 517
Book Review: PUBLIC OPINION 546
Book Review: RUNNING AWAY FROM MYSELF 495
Book Review: SCREENING OUT THE PAST: THE BIRTH OF MASS CULTURE AND
THE MOTION PICTURE INDUSTRY 784
Book Review: SEXUAL STRATAGEMS: THE WORLD OF WOMEN IN FILM 497
Book Review: THE AMERICAN MOVIE INDUSTRY 697
Book Review: THE BOX-OFFICE CLOWNS 1954
Book Review: THE CITIZEN KANE BOOK 1793
Book Review: THE DARK SIDE OF GENIUS 1855
Book Review: THE IMAGE, OR, WHAT HAPPENED TO THE AMERICAN
DREAM? 547
Book Review: THE JEW IN AMERICAN CINEMA 839
Book Review: THE JOHN FORD MOVIE MYSTERY 1685
Book Review: THE OXFORD COMPANION TO FILM 1522
Book Review: THE SAMURAI FILM 1744
Book Review: THE SOCIAL BASIS OF AMERICAN COMMUNISM and WRITERS ON
THE LEFT 830
Book Review: THE STRANGE CASE OF ALFRED HITCHCOCK and THE ART OF
ALFRED HITCHCOCK 1844
Book Review: THE WAVES AT GENJI'S GATE 2026
Book Review: WHEN MOVIES BEGAN TO SPEAK 1755
Book Review: WHEN PICTURES BEGAN TO MOVE 1614
Book Review: WHEN THE MOVIES WERE YOUNG 1377
Book Review: WOMEN AND FILM: BOTH SIDES OF THE CAMERA 506
Book Review: WOMEN ON FILM: THE CRITICAL EYE 513, 515, 531
Book Review: WOMEN'S PICTURES and WOMEN IN FILM 506
Book Review: YESTERDAY'S CLOWNS: THE RISE OF FILM COMEDY 1678
Bookkeeping on an Analyst's Coach: A French Critic's Approach to
Hitchcock 1836
Books 576, 1185, 1419
Books as Films 1028
Books of the Times 571
Books of the Times: CINEMA OF PARADOX 1905
Books: BIG BAD WOLVES: MASCULINITY IN THE AMERICAN FILM 809
Books: Faulkner Scripts for Film on De Gaulle 260
Books: Hitchcock's Dark Side 1853
Books: HOLLYWOOD DIRECTORS, 1914-1940 1551
Books: HOLLYWOOD IN THE THIRTIES 1752
Books: LUIS BUNUEL 1721
Books: PARE LORENTZ AND THE DOCUMENTARY FILM 1872
Books: THE CUBIST CINEMA 1711, 1717
Books: THE DISNEY VERSION 1769
Books: THE DREAM THAT KICKS and HISTORY MUST ANSWER TO MAN 1510
Books: THE MOTION PICTURE GUIDE 1755
Boom Is Really an Echo, The 863
Boom Summer for Sequels 2200
Borden Chase: An Interview 1982
Boris Karloff 388
Boris Karloff: The Man Behind The Myth 1808
Born in Fire: The Ontology of the Monster 416
Bostonians: Visually Stunning Feature About Emotional Conflicts 1324
Both Sides of the Camera 1984

BOULEVARD NIGHTS S. F. Run Ends at Mayor's Request 974
Box Office Abroad Now More Valuable 672
Box Office Drawl: An Analysis of the Films of James Stewart 1982
Boy Meets Boy--Or Where the Girls Aren't 2193
Boy Meets Facts 710, 735
Boys in the Back Room, The 1028
Brakhage Lectures, The 1974
Brakhage's Eyes 1974
Brave New Worlds of Production Design, The 410
Break with the Past: Part One 1889
Break with The Past: Part Two 2018
BREAKER MORANT: Quibbling Over Imperialism 448
Breaking Away 1004
Breaking Down the Conventional Barriers 1301
Breathless 2151
Brecht and the Cinema 1335
Bresson on Location 2008
Bresson's Stylistics Revisited 1994
Brief, Tragical History of the Science-Fiction Film, A 409
Bringing in the Sheaves 1674
Bringing the Movies to Life 674
Bringing The War Home 365
Britain in America 2159
British and American Motion Picture Wage Rates Compared 607, 647
British Board of Film Censors and Content Control in the 1930s, II: Foreign
  Affairs 225
British Board of Film Censors and Content Control in the 1930s, I: Images of
  Britain 225
British Documentaries in the War 217
British Feature Directors: An Index to Their Work 2159
British Film Censorship and Propaganda Policy During the Second World
  War 202
British Official Attitudes Towards Propaganda Abroad, 1918-39 217, 242
Broadway's Grand Cinemas Are Fading Away 629
Brooks, Mel 2073
Bruce Connor 2039
Budd Schulberg 1155
Budd Schulberg--On Hollywood, On the Waterfront, and On the Spot 1277
Budd Schulberg: The Screen Playwright as Author 1277
Buffoons and Brave Hearts: Hollywood Portrays the Russians 259
Bull In the China Shop: Godard's LA CHINOISE 2109
Burning Memories, Mississippi 1964 255
Business for Art's Sake 2203
Buster Keaton on Gags 1672
Buster Keaton: An Interview 1672
But Can Hollywood Live Without George Lucas? 2196
But Compared to the Original 1301
Buts & Rebuts--Hitchcock: A Defense and Update 1835
Buttonpusher or Partner? 71
Bye Bye Musicals 400

C

CA Interview With Waldo Salt 1090
Cabinet of Dr. Caligari, The 1309
Cactus Rosebud, or THE MAN WHO SHOT LIBERTY VALANCE 2075
Cahiers du Cinema's Rereading of Hollywood Cinema: An Analysis of
 Method 477
CAHIERS DU Peckinpah 2087
Calamity, With Sound Effects 634
California Leads States in Money From Filming 658
California's Literary Regionalism 1028, 1042, 1044, 1108
Call for a New Generation of Film Makers, A 2039
Camera as a God, The 489
Camera as Snowball: France 1918-1927, The 1711
Camera Movement and Cinematic Space 79
Camera Movement in Edison and Biograph Films, 1900-1906 1608
Cameraman: Part II, The 79
Cameraman: Part I, The 79
Camille 1012
Campaign Propels LA BAMBA 611
Campus Denizens Go-For-Pix, Disks, Radio, But Not TV 754
Can Great Books Make Good Movies? 7 Writers Just Say No! 1029
Can TV Save the Films? 664
Can We Now Forget the Evil She Did? 321
Can't Stop the Musicals 2199
Canada Celebrates a Mission In Film 2162
Canadian Dilemma: A Problem of Identity, The 2162
Canadian Feature Films in the Chicago Theatrical Market, 1978-1981: Economic
 Relations 681
Cannon Faces New Copyright Charges 535
Cannon Group Loses $9.9 Million in Quarter 535
Cannon Loses Some Luster 535
Cannon Seeks Respectability: Grudge Seen in Hollywood 535
Cannon to Buy Chain of Theaters 682
Cannon's Box-Office Respect 535
Capital at Play: Form in Popular Film 485, 533, 552, 590
Capra and Langdon 1672
Capsule of John Sturges 1987
Captive Audience: The Troubled Odyssey of Cinema Advertising, The 771
Career of Dudley Nichols, The 85, 1064
Career of Erich Von Stroheim, The 1674
Career of Rudolph Valentino, The 1674
Career that Spans Half a Century, A 1671
Carl Dreyer's Shorts 2190
Carl Foreman 1093
CARMEN JONES: The Dark Is Light Enough 941
Carol Reed in the Context of His Time: Part One 1021
Carol Reed in the Context of His Time: Part Two 1021
Carole Lombard in Macy's Window, The 488
Cartridges Are Coming, The 672
CASABLANCA: It Lingers Deliciously in Memory "As Time Goes By" 372
Case Against Film Censorship, The 966
Case of Artistic Inflation, A 2169
Case of the Missing Mother: Maternal Images in Vidor's STELLA DALLAS,
 The 794, 796
Case Study of Film Antitrust Legislation: R. D. Goldberg v. Tri-State Theatre
 Corporation, A 639
Casino as a Movie Setting and Metaphor, The 527
Cassavetes on Cassevetes 2074

Cassettes 672
Cassettes Imperil Post-Oscar Profits 545
Cast a Cold Eye: The Films of Billy Wilder 799, 1987
Casting 1666
Castration or Decapitation 471
Cat On a Hot Tin Roof 1352
CAT PEOPLE: Paul Schrader Changes Spots 2195
Caught 2010
CAUGHT and REBECCA: The Inscription of Femininity as Absence 615, 714, 1835
Cecil B. DeMille's Virtues 1680
Cecil B. DeMille: August 12, 1881-January 21, 1959 1680
Celebrating France's Directors Who Rode the New Wave 2095
Celluloid Assimilation: Jews in American Silent Films 820, 823
Celluloid Noose, The 832
Celluloid Sedition?: The Strange Case of the Hollywood Ten 1084
Cellulose Nitrate Roots: Popular Entertainments and the Birth of Film Narrative 1583, 1587
Censorship of BLONDE VENUS: Textual Analysis and Historical Methods, The 529
Central Tendency of the French Cinema, A 129
Ceremonies of Innocence: Two Films by John Ford 1673
Certain Tendency of The French Cinema, A 1998, 2145
Chabrol 2098
Chabrol and Truffaut 2098
Chabrol Films a Henry Miller Tale 2098
Chabrol Puts de Beauvoir on Film 2098, 2101
Chabrol's Schizophrenic Spider 2098, 2101
Chabrol, Claude 2099
Chabrol: The Lyrical Mystery Master 2098, 2099
Chains Seek Film House Domination 682
Chandler and Marlowe are the Toast of a Party 1197
Changes in Black Films 904
Changing Cognitive Structure as a Basis for the Sleeper Effect 745
Changing of the Guard, The 665, 2034
Changing Status of the Actor, The 1587
Chaplin and Chaplinism 1414
Chaplin and Sound 1417
Chaplin and the Progressive Era: The Neglected Politics of a Clown 1414
Chaplin as Composer 1414
Chaplin Files: Can It Happen Again?, The 1418
Chaplin Redux 1414
Chaplin World-View, The 1419
Chaplin's Collaborators 1419
Chaplin: Of Crime and Genius 1414
Characteristics of Propaganda 204
Chariots of Fire 1013
CHARIOTS OF FIRE: Traditional Values/False History 1013
Chariots of Mixed Feelings 1013
Charles Brackett 84
Charles Chaplin's Tryst with Spain 1417
Charles Chaplin: A Study in Contradictions 1414
Charles Chaplin: Chaplin Directs Brando and Loren 1418
Charlie Chaplin 1414
Charlie Chaplin's Films and American Cultural Patterns 1414
Charlie Chaplin's MONSIEUR VERDOUX Press Conference 1433
Charlie Chaplin: An Authorized Interview 1420
Charlie Dearest 1433

Charlie's Chaplin   1419
Cheap Thrills That Degrade Blacks   897, 898
Checklist of Materials about Science Fiction, A   410
Child Custody: Jurists Weigh Film Vs. Life   1007
Children and Film   978
Children and Youth in America   972
Children Not Nearly as Afraid of "The Bomb" as Popularly Believed, Psychiatrist
  Concludes   1024
Children of the Light   416
Children's Innocence Getting Lost?   981
Children's Shelf: When Movies Were Young   1755
China   2163
CHINA IS NEAR   2173
China: The Red Sons   2163
CHINOISE: Child's Play?, LA   2130
Chris Marker and the Mutants   2115
Chris Marker: The SLON Films   2115, 2116
Christmas Film Sales Set Record   756
CHRONICLE OF A SUMMER   2154
Chronicler of Power: Interview With Franklin Schaffner   2090
CHRONIQUE D'UN ETE   2154
CINE-TRANSE: The Vision of Jean Rouch   2094, 2120
Cinefeminism and Its Discontents   506, 511
Cinema and Its Double: Alfred Hitchcock, The   1836
Cinema and Suture   82, 591
Cinema and Television: Jean Renoir and Roberto Rossellini   648
Cinema as a Gun: An Interview With Fernando Solanas   2110
Cinema Dilemma: Films from The Underground   2039
Cinema for the Millions: Soviet Socialist Realism and the Problem of Film Comedy,
  A   261
Cinema in Cuba, The   2163
Cinema Italiano 1962   2169
Cinema Novo vs. Cultural Colonialism: An Interview With Glauber Rocha   2158
Cinema Novo: Pitfalls of Cultural Nationalism   2158
Cinema of Adolescence, The   974, 975
Cinema of Appearance   2093
Cinema of Attraction: Early Film, Its Spectator and the Avant-Garde, The   1602
Cinema of Common Sense   2040
Cinema of Illusion   409
Cinema of Marguerite Duras: Sound and Voice in a Closed Room, The   2152
Cinema of Nicholas Ray, The   1984, 1985
Cinema of Poetry, The   2176
Cinema Sex: From THE KISS to DEEP THROAT   2037
Cinema Sings the Blues   400
CINEMA VERITE, or Fantastic Realism   2120
Cinema Weekly and Cinema Truth: Dziga Vertov and the Leninist
  Proportion   1645
CINEMA-VERITE in France   2040
Cinemascope   656
Cinemascope: Before and After   655
Cinematic Ambiguity: James' THE TURN OF THE SCREW and Clayton's THE
  INNOCENTS   1324
Cinematic Essence, The   142
Cinematic Model for Film Studies in Higher Education: Center for Media
  Study/SUNY at Buffalo   38
Cinematic Reflections on Jewish Life in 15-Work Festival at 92d Street Y   836
Cinematography With Tears!   1866
Cinema/Ideology/Criticism   470, 474, 475, 479
Cinema: Langue ou Langage?, Le   134

Cinema: The New Pictures 952
Cinerama 656
Cinevideo and Psychology 1583
Circle of Pain: The Cinema of Nicholas Ray 1985
Circles and Squares 1509
Circles of Desire: Narration and Representation in LA RONDE, The 2010
CITIZEN KANE 1750, 1807
Citizen Kane Book, The 1101, 1793
CITIZEN KANE: The American Baroque 1807
City Lights 1430
City Lights: Immigrant Women and the Movies 719
Civil Rights Burned 255
Civil War, The 1673
Classics Fans Oppose Colorizing 656
Classics Revisited: LA GRANDE ILLUSION 1827
Claude Chabrol 2151
Claude Chabrol Interviewed 2098
Claude Chabrol into the 'Seventies 2098, 2101
Claude Lelouch Discusses his Work, Francis Lai, Film Distribution, American
  History and Justice 2119
CLAUDINE: A Movie That Blacks Can Relate To 1005
Clean Germans and Dirty Politics 264
CLEO DE 5 a 7: Script Excerpt 2157
Cleo's Joe: Part I--The Typewriter Years 1981
Cleo's Joe: Part II--All About Eve and Others 1981
Cliff-Hanger at M. G. M., The 630
Clockwork Violence 2083
Close Encounters of the Authoritarian Kind 410
Close Encounters of the Fourth Kind 409
Close Encounters With Steven Spielberg 2196
Closely Watched Trains 994
Coca Cola and the Golden Pavilion 1740
Cocking A Snook 1981
Cocteau and Orpheus 2009
Cocteau's ORPHEUS Analyzed 2009
Coffee, Brandy and Cigars 30 1018
Coke Unit, Tri-Star to Join Operations 678
Cold War Against David Wark Griffith, The 1363
Cold War Cinema I 1098
Cold War Cinema II 1098
Coleco to Add RAMBO Line 437
Colette--and A Modern Devil: Second Part of Autant-Lara's Work for the
  Cinema 1993
Collapse of the Federated Motion Picture Crafts: A Case Study of Class
  Collaboration in the Motion Picture Industry, The 1750
Collapse of Watkins' Nuclear War Film, The 1024
Colleen Moore 1695
Colleen Moore, Ultimate Flapper of the Silent Screen, Is Dead at 87 1695
College Course File: Film as History 252
College Students' Attitudes Toward Movies 462
Collision with the Party Line 1091, 1092
Colonialism, Racism and Representation: An Introduction 858
Color and Cinema: Problems in the Writing of History 654, 1509
Color Film Crisis, The 1514
Color's An Old Device 79
Colored Paper Pans Connelly's "Pastures" Cast 874
Colorizing Film Classics: A Boon or Bane? 656
Colour and Concepts 2084

Colour Problem 1514
Columbia Studio Chief Faces Industry Doubts 667
Columbia Working to Manage Word of Mouth on Pictures 670
Combination and Litigation: Structures of U. S. Film Distribution,
   1896-1917 607, 616, 1462
Comeback of the Movies, The 651
Comedy In Which Class Tells, A 1005
Comedy of Ozu and Chaplin: A Study in Contrast, The 1414
Comedy That Smirks at Itself 2194
Comedy's Greatest Era 144, 306
Comic Art of Jacques Tati, The 2001
Comic Strip and Film Language, The 1584
Coming Home a Hero: The Changing Image of the Vietnam Vet on Prime Time
   Television 259
Coming of Sound: Technological Change in the American Film Industry,
   The 632
Coming of Television and the "Lost Motion Picture Audience," The 678
Coming of the Camera and the Projection, The 615
Coming to Terms with Color 79
Comment on the Hawksian Woman, A 1747
Comments on Blacklisting and BLOCKADE 376
Comment: The Family Connection 982
Commercials at Movies: The Filmgoers' Burden 487
Commitment and the Strait-Jacket 1010, 1016
Commodity Fetishism: Women in GOLD DIGGERS OF 1933 461
Communication and the Arts 135
Communication Research and the Concept of Mass 705
Communication Research and the Image of Society: Convergence of Two
   Traditions 745
Communism and the Movies: A Study in Film Content 1098
Companion to Violence and Sadism in the Cinema 750
Company Town Pastoral: The Role of Big Business in EXECUTIVE SUITE 814
Comparative Approach to the Form and Function of Novel and Film: Dorothy
   Richardson's Theory of Art, A 1297
Competition Among Mass Media and the Public Interest 648
Complacency, Competition and Cooperation: The Film Industry Responds to the
   Challenge of Television 648, 656
Composing for the Screen 83
Concept of History in American Produced Films: An Analysis of the Films Made
   in the Period 1950-1961, The 256
Conceptualizing the Use of Film Study to Study History: A
   Bibliofilmography 39
Conceptualizing the Use of Film to Study History 252
Conference Report: Conference on Feminist Film Criticism 467, 475, 476, 530
Confessions of a Frustrated Screenwriter 85, 1035, 1094
Confessions of a Nazi Spy 203
Confessions of a Number One Son 826
Conflict of Conscience, A 1988
CONFORMISTA, IL (THE CONFORMIST) 2174
Confrontations: Norman Jewison Interviewed 2082
Conglomerates and Content: Remakes, Sequels, and Series in the New
   Hollywood 673, 772
CONNECTION--Con, THE 1348
CONNECTION--Pro, THE 1348
Connection, The 1348
Conrad and Hitchcock: THE SECRET AGENT Inspires SABOTAGE 1838
Conrad Hall: An Interview 2079
Conrad on the Screen 1301
Conscience of a Director, The 2084

Considering De Palma 2196
Constance Talmadge 1366
Construction of the Castrated Woman in Psychoanalysis and Cinema, The 470
Content Analysis of the Treatment of Black Americans on Television, A 854
Contentious but Catalytic 1849
Continental Westerns 424
Contradicting the Hollywood Image 2083
Contribution of the French Literary Avant-Garde to Film Theory and Criticism
  (1907-1924), The 1709, 1710
Convenient Villain: The Early Cinema Views the Mexican-American, The 826
Conventional-Unconventional 1994
Conversation With Francois Truffaut 2107
Conversation With George Cukor 1012
Conversation with Hitchcock 1835
Conversation With Jean Renoir 1813
Conversation With Marguerite Duras 2152
Conversation With Nicholas Ray and Joseph Losey 2161
Conversation With Preston Sturges 1014
Conversation With Resnais, A 2116
Conversation With Roger Edens 1464
Conversation With Sam Peckinpah, A 2087
Conversation With Satyajit Ray 2168
Conversation With Truffaut 1006
Conversations With Bunuel 1002
Conversations With Lillian Gish 1365
Conversion of the Jews, The 820, 822
Convoluted Memoir of the '30s, A 1322
Cool Head, Hot Images 2196
Coppola Films Conrad in Vietnam 367
Coppola's Vietnam Movie is a Battle Royal 367
Coppola, Francis Ford 2196
Coppola, Heavily in Debt, Decides to Sell Studio 536
Coppola, Inc. 2196
Copyright and Early Theater, Vaudeville and Film Competition 1599
Cornel Wilde: Producer/Director 2092
Corporate Ownership and Control of the US Film Industry 660
Corrections: LETTER FROM AN UNKNOWN WOMAN 1984
Correction: Motion Picture Attendance and Social Isolation 745
Correspondence: Sternberg and Stroheim 1674
Costa-Gavras' MISSING: A Legal and Political Battlefield 772
Country Boys: An Aspect of Rural America in the Age of Innocence, The 1363
Country Girl, The 1350
Country of the Past Revisited: Losey, Galileo, and the Romantic Englishwoman,
  The 1981
Court Declines to Block Time Inc. Meeting 2204
Covered Wagon, The 1702
Cowardly Cuban Film Critics? 2163
Cowboy Hero and the American West . . . as Directed by John Ford,
  The 1673
Cowboy, Pioneer and American Soldier 232
Cranes are Flying, The 1001
Creating a Reality that Doesn't Exist: An Interview With Louis Malle 2119
Creative Remembering and Other Perils of Film Study 593
Creator-Audience Relationship in the Mass Media: An Analysis of Movie Making,
  The 553
Crime 384
Crisis of Naming in Feminist Film Criticism, The 465
Crisis that Led to Better Things: Final Part of a History of Italian Cinema 1607

Critic as Consumer: Film Study In the University, VERTIGO, and the Film
  Canon, The   2081
Critic Keeps Her Cool on UP TIGHT   916
Critic's Notebook: 4 Films at Once on Holocaust Offer a Dialogue   291
Critical Camera of Joseph Losey, The   1981
Critical Evaluation of the Controversies Engendered by D. W. Griffith's BIRTH
  OF A NATION, A   864
Critical Question, The   131
Critical Question: Another View, The   132
Criticism and/as History: Rereading BLACKMAIL   1864
Critique of Cine-Structuralism (Part II)   477, 478
Crossing the Line to Stardom   1437
Crowd, The   1707
Crown Film Unit, 1940-43, The   216
Cuba   2163
Cult Movies: NORTH BY NORTHWEST, The   2079
Cultivated Folks and the Better Classes: Class Conflict and Representation in
  Early American Film   1603
Cultural Barometer   219
Cultural History Written With Lightning: The Significance of THE BIRTH OF A
  NATION   1366
Cultural Identity and the European Economic Community   664
Cultural Influences on Film Interpretation Among Chinese and American
  Students   749, 770
Cultural Restitution and Independent Black Cinema   950
Cultural Revolution, Collectivization, and Soviet Cinema: Eisenstein's EARTH and
  Dovzhenko's EARTH   1645
Current 'Teen Movies: Good News and Bad   971
Current Cinema: Langdon, The   1672
Cuts in Film LOST HORIZON Restored   1799
Cycles and Genres   176
Cycles and Gyres of Hollywood History, The   2190
Czech In New York: An Interview With Milos Forman, A   2164
Czechoslovakia   2165
C. B. DeMille's Human Side   1680

D

Dalton Trumbo   1282
Dalton Trumbo: An Interview   1084
Damn Your A Priori Principles--Look!: W. R. Robinson Discusses the Movies as
  Narrative Art   1026
Dancing Images: Busby Berkeley's Kaleidescope   1797
Danger is Seduction: An Interview With Haskell Wexler, The   1350
Dangerous Recuperations: Red Dawn, Rambo, and the New Decaturism   335, 336
Dark Aspects of John Ford Go Unlighted In Sinclair's Biog   1685
Dark at the Top of the Stairs, The   1349
Dark Passages: A Feminist Analysis of PSYCHO   2080
Dark Struggle, The   1641
Darkness and Light: Carl Dreyer   1729, 2190
Darwinian World of Claude Chabrol, The   2098, 2099
David and Lisa   995
David Wark Griffith   1360, 1363, 1368
David Wark Griffith: Creator of Film Form   1363
David Wark Griffith: In Retrospect, 1965   1363
Day Black Movie Stars Got Militant, The   942
Day of the Butterfly, The   1434

DAY OF THE LOCUST--Comparing John Schlesinger's Film and Nathanael West's
  Novel, THE   1291
DAY OF THE LOCUST, A Night at the Movies, THE   1291
DAY OF THE LOCUST: John Schlesinger Interviewed, THE   1291
Daydreams and Nightmares: Reflections on the Criticism of Mass Culture   534
Days in the Gardens of Hollywood   1031
De Palma, Brian   2196
Deal for MGM/UA Assets   2205
Deal Is Expected For Sony to Buy Columbia Pictures   2205
Dean--Ten Years After   1005
Dear Dean Korzybski   132
Death of Marilyn Monroe, The   1290
Death of Mickey Mouse, The   77
Death of Rastus: Negroes in American Films Since 1945, The   883, 888, 915, 941
Debate Over Shylock Simmers Once Again   822
Decade: Britain--We're All Right Jack, The   2159
Decade: France--A Mirror for Marianne, The   2093
Decade: Spain, The   2182
Decay of the Motion Picture Patents Company, The   607, 1359, 1461
Decision on Time by Friday Seen   2205
Decision-Making in the Film Industry: The Influence of the TV Market   648
Declaration of Independence   671
Declarations of Independence: A History of Cagney Productions   643
Decline of a Mandarin, The   1368
DEER HUNTER and the Demythification of the American Hero, THE   801
Defeat   1389
Defeated by Pornography   960
Delaware Court Refuses to Block Time-Warner Link, A   2205
DELIVERANCE From Novel to Film: Where is Our Hero?   1301
DELIVERANCE: Four Variations of the American Adam   801, 1300
Demise of the Cult of True Womanhood in Early American Film, 1900-1930: Two
  Modes of Subversion, The   621
Demons on the Screen   815
Demy Calls the Tune   2119
Demy, Jacques   2119
Descriptive Phenomenology and Film: An Introduction   132
Design and Teaching of Dramatic Films: An Approach to Values Education,
  The   39
Designed for Film   79
Desire in SUNRISE   1706
Desperately Seeking Hollywood   681
Despite Defeat, Paramount Is Expected to Persevere   2205
Destruction of Neo-Realism, The   1922, 1923, 1924
Detective in Hitchcock's FRENZY: His Ancestors and Significance, The   1836
Detective Work at GIK   1866
Detours in Film Narrative: The Development of Cross-cutting   1361, 1605
Development and Decline of the Drive-In Movie Theater, The   649
Development of Realism with a Sense of Humour: Fifth Part of a History of Italian
  Cinema, The   1607
Development of the Contemporary Black Film Movement, The   949
Developments in Feminist Film Criticism   495
Dexterity in a Void: The Formal Aesthetics of Alfred Hitchcock   1835
Dialogue of Film: Joan Tewkesbury   2195
Dialogue of the Deaf   2109
Dialogue on Film   1037
Dialogue on Film: Alan J. Pakula,   2195
Dialogue on Film: An Interview With Jeanne Moreau   2155
Dialogue on Film: Billy Wilder and I. A. L. Diamond   1987

Dialogue on Film: Gore Vidal 2089
Dialogue on Film: Hal Ashby 2195
Dialogue on Film: Horton Foote 1210
Dialogue on Film: Images of Adolescence 973
Dialogue on Film: Interview With Francois Truffaut 2106
Dialogue on Film: John Frankenheimer 2077
Dialogue on Film: Joseph Losey 1981
Dialogue on Film: Paul Schrader 2195
Dialogue on Film: Peter Bogdanovich 2195
Dialogue on Film: Robert Towne 2195
Dialogue on Film: Robert Wise 1987
Dialogue on Film: Sidney Poitier 887
Dialogue on Film: Steven Spielberg 2196
Dialogue on Film: Sydney Pollack 2089
Dialogue on Film: William Friedkin 2195
Dialogue on Film: William Wyler 1748
Dialogue: Ann Kaplan Replies to Linda Williams's "Something Else Besides a Mother" 795
Dialogue: Patrice Petro and Carol Flinn on Feminist Film Theory 795
Diane Keaton Grapples With Sex and Maternity 1003
DIARY OF A COUNTRY PRIEST 2008
Diary of Anne Frank, The 849
Dick Diver and Constance Talmadge 1115
Dick Tracy Meets MURIEL 2116
Dickens and Hitchcock 1837
Dickens Garland, A 1301
Dickens on the Screen 1300
Dickens, Griffith, and the Film Today 1301, 1657
Did Cooper and Stewart Have To Be So Stupid? 789
Didion & Dunne: The Rewards of a Literary Marriage 530
Diener Builds Ties to Movies 678
Difference of George Axelrod, The 84
Differential Movie Appeals as Correlates of Attendance 533, 745
Differential Movie-Viewing Behavior of Male and Female 745
Difficulties of LITTLE BIG MAN, The 1320
Difficulty of Being Jean-Luc Godard, The 2109
Difficulty of Difference, The 471
Dimension Pictures: Portrait of a 70's Independent 643
Diner 995
Dinesen a Big Seller Again With Film Tie-In 488
Director as Superstar, The 2175
Director Dared Use Race Humor; "Soul" as Lure For "Cotton's" B. O. Bale 896
Director In Aspic 1985
Director Raoul Walsh to Be Buried in Simi Valley 1672
Director's Progress: John Huston in Perspective, A 1321
Directorate, The 1547
Directory of Useful Addresses 2266
Dirk Bogarde 2161
Dirty Books, Dirty Films, and Dirty Data 565
Dis-Embodying the Female Voice 495
Disabled Vietnam Vet in Hollywood Films, The 259
Disaster Strikes Disaster Films 753
Discontented Bourgeois: Bourgeois Morality and the Interplay of Light and Dark Strains in Hitchcock's Films, The 1834
Discontinuity and Film History: The Case of Heidegger and Benjamin 252
Discussion: Personal Creation In Hollywood--Is it Possible? 1988, 2034
Disenchantment of Scott Fitzgerald, The 1133
Disney Banking on TEX To Rewin Teen-Agers 998
Disney Expansion Set 672

Dissolves by Gaslight: Antecedents to the Motion Picture in Nineteenth-Century Melodrama 711, 1584
Distance and Style: The Visual Rhetoric of Max Ophuls--LETTER FROM AN UNKNOWN WOMAN, 1984
Distantiation and Douglas Sirk 794
DIStory: Cinema and Historical Discourse 256
Distributors Challenge Indies Exhibitors to Improve Service 763
Divided Woman: Bree Daniels in KLUTE, The 799
Dividing Labor for Production Control: Thomas Ince and the Rise of the Studio System 697, 1463, 1622
Dixon, Griffith, and the Southern Legend 1366, 1385
Do I Get to Play the Drunk This Time: An Encounter With Howard Hawks 1747
Do Movies Predict the Public Mood? 454
Do Movies' Titles Affect Box Offices? 738
Do the Race Thing: Spike Lee's Afro-Fascist Chic 903
DO THE RIGHT THING: Issues and Images 903
Do the Sty Thing 903
Doctor on the Screen, The 815
Docudrama Strikes Again 549
Documentary and Hollywood, The 230, 255, 295
Documentary Films and the Problem of "Truth," The 280
Documentary Film, The 295
Documentary Idea: A Frame of Reference, The 295
Does Rudy Speak from the Beyond? 1453
Does the Holocaust Defy Dramatization? 291
Dog Days in the Movie 1749
Doing It All At Once 1018
Doing What Comes Naturally 1749, 1795
Dolce Vita, La 1023
Doll, a Truck, a Loving Adult Going Beyond Critical Viewing, A 978
Dolores de Rio 1709
Don't Blame the Screenwriter When the Glue Is Missing 1030
Don't Look Where We're Going: Visions of the Future in Science Fiction Films, 1970-1982 416
Donahue: Spectator Positioning in the Talk Show Genre 544
Donald Crisp's Memory 1365
Donald Ogden Stewart 1104
Dorothy Arzner: Critical Strategies 1798
Dorothy Gish 1365
Dossier on Melodrama 792
Dostoyevsky to Disney, The Dickensian Legacy 1301
DOUBLE INDEMNITY 799
Doubles of Fantasy and the Space of Desire, The 410
Douglas Sirk: Melo Maestro 1986
Dovzhenko Papers, The 1665
Dovzhenko: Notes on the Director's Work Before ZVENIGORA 1645
Dovzhenko: Poet of Life Eternal 1645
Drama Inches Up on Comedy at the Movies 762, 764
Drama of Non-Existence 1874
Drama's Melos: Max Steiner and MILDRED PIERCE, The 800
Drawings that Are Alive: The Story of the Animated Film Cartoon 76
Dream and Photography in a Psychoanalytic Film: SECRETS OF A SOUL 579, 593
Dream and Reality 142
Dream as Reality: Bunuel/Dali's UN CHIEN ANDALOU 598, 1728
Dream Visions in Pre-Hollywood Film 1587
Dreaming and Thinking: S. O. B. and Its relationship to Blake Edwards' Genre Films 598

Dreams and Visions in Fellini's CITY OF WOMEN 593
Dreams in the Dream Factory 816
Dreamscapes 410
Dreyer at 65 1729
Drive Reducing Function of Fantasy Behavior, The 749
Drive-In at Twilight, The 649
Drive-In Movies: An Innovation Hits 50 and Passes Its Prime 649
Drive-In Time 649
Drive-Ins 649
Drums Along the Mekong: I Love America, I am Apolitical 1673
Dr. Jackson: Ratings Services Show Minority Discrimination 855
DR. STRANGELOVE 40, 2083
Duck Soup For The Rest Of Your Life 1749
Duplicity in MILDRED PIERCE 471, 800
Durgnat vs. Paul: Last Round in the Great Hawks Debate 1747
Dutch Films 2179
Dutchman 1349
DWG: A Bibliographic Update 1368
Dynamic Frame 656
Dynamic Gesture: New American Independents, The 2039
Dynamics of Cultural Resistance, The 462, 543, 545, 715
Dziga Vertov as Theorist 1645, 1668
Dziga Vertov Film Group In America: An Interview With Jean-Luc Godard and
  Jean-Pierre Gorin, The 2111
Dziga Vertov: An Introduction 1645
D. W. Griffith and Anarchy in American Films 1363
D. W. Griffith and the Banks: A Case Study in Film Financing 1367
D. W. Griffith and the Possibilities of ENOCH ARDEN 1363
D. W. Griffith and the Use of Off-Screen Space 1362, 1364
D. W. Griffith at Biograph From June-December 1908: The Pragmatic Artist 1362
D. W. Griffith Influence, The 1363
D. W. Griffith's Film Version of Browning's PIPPA PASSES: Some Problems in
  the Early Literature to Film Adaptation 1363
D. W. Griffith: Kentucky to Hollywood 1360
D. W. Griffith: THE BIRTH OF A NATION 1383

E

Eagle-Lion: The Violent Years 1935
Earliest Images: The Lumiere Brothers' Films, The 1599
Early Cinema of Edwin Porter, The 618, 1361, 1605
Early Days of William Wyler, The 1748
Early Film Production in England: The Origin of Montage, Close-ups, and Chase
  Sequence 1606
Early Franklin J. Schaffner, The 2090
Early Griffith: A Wider View 1361
Early History of Animation: Saturday Morning TV Discovers 1915, The 1583
Early Sound Comedy 1745
Early Works of Robert Bresson, The 2008
East of Eden 1005, 1325
Eastern Western 367
Eastern Writer in Hollywood, The 1037, 1062, 1065, 1101, 1103
Eastwood Top Event at Cannes 437
EASY RIDER 2081
EASY RIDER Revisited 2081
EASY RIDER: Comic Epic Poem in FILM 2081
EASY RIDER: Critique of the New Hedonism? 2081
EASY RIDER: The Initiation of Dennis Hopper 2081

Eavesdropping on Female Voices: A Who's Who of Contemporary Women
  Filmmakers 2207
Economic Imperative: Why Was the B-Movie Necessary?, The 651, 652
Economic Perspective on Formula in Popular Culture, An 173
Economic Struggle and Hollywood Imperialism: Europe Converts to Sound 632
Economics of Film: What Is the Method?, The 608, 675, 676
Economics of the Motion Picture Industry: A Survey, The 608, 639
Economics of the Television Market for Theatrical Movies, The 656
Eddie Constantine 2151
Edison's Dream: A Brief History of the Kinetophone 1585
Editing and Other Foibles of Movies on Cassettes 762
Editing HIROSHIMA MON AMOUR 2152
Editor Fights Violence in Movies 960
Editor's Comment 108
Education Comes First 40
Educational Film Propaganda and the Nazi Youth 251
Educational Programs for the Improvement of Race Relations: Motion Pictures,
  Radio, the Press, and Libraries 880
Edward Dmytryk 368
Edward G. Robinson 1804
Edwin J. Hadley: Travelling Film Exhibitor 615, 1599
Edwin S. Porter 1361, 1605
Effect of Criticism on Urban Film Tastes 745
Effect of Film Violence on Inhibition Against Subsequent Aggression 745
Effect of the Motion Picture GENTLEMEN'S AGREEMENT on Attitudes Towards
  Jews, The 832
Effects of Film Material Upon Children's Behavior 754
Effects of Films on the Importance of Behavioral Freedom, The 546
Effects of Mass Media on the Sexual Behavior of Adolescent Females 546
Effects of Observing Violence, The 745
Effects of Pentagon Influence on War Movies, 1948-70 230
Effects of Television on Film in Argentina, Brazil, and Mexico 771
Effects of Television on the Motion Picture Industry: 1948-1960, The 648, 649,
  650, 697
Effects of Vicariously Experiencing Supernatural-Violent Events: A Case Study
  of THE EXORCIST's Impact, The 546
Eighties Hollywood: Dominant Tendencies 484
Eisenstein as Theorist 1646
Eisenstein in Hollywood 1865
Eisenstein-Prokofiev Correspondence, The 1645
Eisenstein's Aesthetics: A Dissenting View 1645
Eisenstein's BEZHIN MEADOW 1645
Eisenstein's Epistemological Shift 1645
Eisenstein's Images and Mexican Art 1867
Eisenstein's Mexican Tragedy 1867
Eisenstein, Kracauer and Marx: Socio-political Influence in Film Theory 41
Eisenstein: Ideology and Intellectual Cinema 1645
Eleanor Perry Dies; Wrote Screenplays 995
Elective Affinities: Aspects of JULES AND JIM 2155
Elegy for Wonderland 1122
Eleven East 14th Street 1361
Elia Kazan and the House Un-American Activities Committee 1084, 1089
Elia Kazan on "The Young Agony" 1018
Elia Kazan--The Genius of a Style 1018
Ellipsis on Dread and the Specular Seduction 471
Emancipation Orgasm: Sweetback in Wonderland, The 894
Emotion-Eliciting Qualities in the Motion Picture Viewing Situation and Audience
  Evaluations 771

Emotionally Speaking, It's Still the Same Old Story 761
EMPEROR JONES, THE 876
Empty Streets, The 997, 1335
Encore! From Stage to Screen 666
Encounter with John Huston, An 1321
Encounters With Josef Von Sternberg 1674
End of the Road 2034, 2041, 2081
Enfants Terribles, Les 2093
English Influences on the Work of Edwin S. Porter 1361
English Professor Who Created Rambo Says Colleagues Don't Scoff at His
  Work 437
Entertainer, The 1013, 2079
Entertainment and Utopia 460, 461
Entertainment, Politics, and the Movie Business 888, 906
ENTHUSIASM: From Kino-Eye to Radio-Ear 1645
Entreprenuers, Engineers, and Hobbyists: The Formation of a Definition of
  Amateur Film, 1897-1923 772
Enunciation and Sexual Difference 471
Epic 656
Epic Film for Kurosawa, The 2019
Epic! Heroic! American! 843
Era of the Auteur: An Interview With Jean Renoir 1822
Eric Rohmer 2102, 2105
Eric Rohmer: An Interview 2094, 2102, 2104
Eric Rohmer: Bibliography 2102
Eric Rohmer: L'Amour Sage 2101, 2102, 2104
Erich Pommer, Part I 1632
Erich Pommer, Part II 1632
Erich Von Stroheim 1019
Erich Von Stroheim: The Legend and the Fact 1018
Erich Wolfgang Korngold 83
Eroticism and the Good Italian Earth: Fourth Part of a History of Italian
  Cinema 1607
Eroticism in Cinema: Definitions and Points of Departure--The Dark Gods 999
Eroticism in Cinema: Midnight Sun 1000
Eroticism in Cinema: Mind and Matter, An Analysis of French and Italian
  Styles--Some Mad Love and the Sweet Life 1000
Eroticism in Cinema: Symbolism--Another Word For It 1000
Eroticism in Cinema: The Deviationists--Saturnalia in Cans 999
Eroticism in Cinema: The Mass Media and Their Public--Cupid Versus the
  Legions 999
Eroticism in Cinema: The Sacred and the Profane--Flames of Passion, All Next
  Week 999
Eroticism in Cinema: The Subconscious--From Pleasure Castle to Libido
  Motel 999
Escapist Realism, An 2093
Essay Towards MAN WITH A MOVIE CAMERA, An 1669
Esther Shub's Unrealized Project 213
Esther Shub: Cinema is My Life 213
Esthetics of Courage, The 2179
Eternal Rebellion of Luis Bunuel, The 1002
Ethical Issues in the Film Industry 537
Ethnic Humor Bubbles to the Surface of the Melting Pot 859
Ethnic Images: What We See Isn't Always What We Are 440
Ethnic Prejudice and Susceptibility to Persuasion 546
Eugene Pallette 1366
Euro-English Movies: More British Than Not 2206
Europe Produces Westerns Too 424
European Western: A Chapter from the History of the Western Film, The 424

Evasion of Propaganda: How Prejudiced People Respond to Anti-Prejudice
  Propaganda 209
Even Misfits Can Live Happily Ever After 816
Even Wands Can't Create Magic at the Box Office 756
Evening With Meyer and Masoch: Aspects of VIXENS and VENUS IN FURS,
  An 2037
Event and the Image: Michelangelo Antonioni, The 1012, 1874
Every Year in Marienbad or The Discipline of Uncertainty 2153
Evolution and Shape of the American Western 2035
Evolution of Film Language, The 2123
Evolution of the Language of Cinema, The 129, 167, 1807
Evolution of the Western, The 1802
Evolutionary Image of the Jew in American Films, The 822, 824, 828, 831, 833
Evolving Art, An 142
Excerpts From Final Report of Attorney General's Panel on Pornography 961,
  962
Exhibition Contract--A Scrap of Paper, The 676, 677
Exhibition License--Part II, The 676
Exhibitors, The 2034
Exhibs As Pards in Pic Sale Plan 677
Exile in Hollywood: John Schlesinger 1291
Exorcising the Past: Jewish Figures in Contemporary Films 834
Expanding World of Sidney Poitier: Superstar, Director, Producer Eyes the
  Future, The 889
Expensive Manipulations Behind the Oscar Nominations, The 545
Experimental Cinema in America 1921-1947 262, 710, 864, 1359, 1576
Exploitation Films and Feminism 789
Export or Die 2182
Extended Family, American Style, The 1006
Extent and Diversity of Degree Programs in Film and Video 34, 35
Eye of a Cynic: A Monograph on Billy Wilder, The 799, 1987
Eye of Knowledge: Voyeuristic Games in Film and Literature, The 1838
E. Ann Kaplan Replies 794, 796

F

Fabulous Decade Ending in Risky Multi-Million-$ Films; Diller on 'Cycles' 611
Fabulous Saints and Sinners: Second Part of an Analysis of Preminger's Work
  for the Cinema 1984
Face of '63: Britain, The 1016
Face of '63: France, The 2093
Face of '63: Germany, The 2165
Face of '63: Italy, The 1012, 2169
Face of '63: Japan, The 2176
Face of '63: The Spanish Influence, The 2182
Face of '63: United States, The 2034
Face of Horror, The 388
Face of Independence, The 1014, 1090, 1985
Face the Music 83, 400
Face Was Familiar, The 1666
FACES 2074
Fact and Affirmation: Thoughts on the Methodology of Film History and the
  Relation of Theory to Historiography 1509, 1623
Fact of Mortality, The 2030
Fact Vs. Fiction in Mississippi 255
Facts About Films and Facts of Films 252, 1509, 1512
Facts into Fiction: An Interview With Alain Resnais 2116

Fact, Fiction and History Were In The Beginning: History of Italian Cinema 1607
Faded Out 654
Fadeout for Movie Palace in Brooklyn 629
Fading, Fading, Faded: The Color Film Crisis 654
Failed Opportunities: The Integration of the Motion Picture and Television
 Industries 678
Fair Enough 1105
Faith and Idolatry in the Horror Film 185, 2080
Fallen Idols 1674
Fallen Woman and the Virtuous Wife: Musical Stereotypes in THE INFORMER,
 GONE WITH THE WIND, and LAURA, The 400, 461
False Art of the Propaganda Film, The 444
Falstaff 1353
Family in a Ford, A 982
Family Movies--Catch Them While You Can 978
Family Spree of FILM NOIR, The 1003
Family Tree of Monsters, A 388
Fanning the Flames: Anti-American Reaction to OPERATION BURMA (1945) 349
Fantasms of Andrew Oehler, The 1602
Fantasy, Science Fiction, Mystery, Horror 416
Fascinating Fascism 321
Fascism in the Contemporary Cinema 577, 1985
Fascist Guns in the West, The 446, 2198
Fashioning and Re-fashioning: Framing Narratives in the Novel and Film 1297
Fassbinder on Sirk 1986
Fathers and Sons 2174
Fathers, Feminism and Domination: Marxist Theory on Ideology in Popular
 Film 484, 976
Father, the Son, and the Holy Revolution (I), The 1021
Faulkner and Film: Two Versions of SANCTUARY 1300
Faulkner Filmography, A 1214
Faulkner Trove of Never-Produced Hollywood Scripts, A 1214
Fay Wray Writes the Story of Her Life 1800
Fear of Spying 1836
Federico Fellini 1927
FEDORA 1291
Fellini Builds Reggiolo, The Town of His Dreams 1927
Fellini on Men, Women, Love, Life, Art and His New Movie 1927
Fellini Satyricon: A Structural Analysis 2175
Fellini's Voices 1927
FELLINI-SATYRICON 2175
Fellini: An Interview 1927
Fellini: Master of Ageless Comedy 1927
Feminism and Film: Critical Approaches 483
Feminist Critical Practice: Female Discourse in MILDRED PIERCE 800
Feminist Film Criticism 471
Feminist Film Criticism: An Introduction 465
Feminist Film Criticism: Theory and Practice 57, 444, 497
Feminist Politics and Film History 471
Feminist Readership, Violence, and MARNIE 793
FEMME DU BOULANGER, LA 1826
Fernando Solanas: An Interview 2157
Festivals 2178
Fever Yields Merchandising Gold; Promoter Gives Input 488
Few Offers Accrue to Actors in ROOTS 855
Few Reminiscences, A 1018, 1671
Fiction and Film: A Study for New Sources 1025
Fiction and Film: An Interview With George Garrett 1026
Fiction Film and Historical Analysis, The 261

Fiction of Fact--and the Fact of Fiction, The   254
Fiction of the Managerial Class   1132, 1133
Fictional Realism: Watt and Bazin on the Pleasures of Novels and Films   1297
Fictious Justice   255
FIDDLER ON THE ROOF   850
Fifteen Cents Before 6:00 P.M.: The Wonderful Movies of the 'Thirties   221, 454
Fifteen Years After: Notes from West Germany   2165
Fifteenth State Outlaws Blind Bidding on Films   676
Fifth Columnists, The   1002
Fifty Years of Italian Cinema   1607
Figure in the Red Carpet, The   1835
Figures in a Landscape: Narrative Strategies in MAJOR DUNDEE   2087
Files of F.B.I. Tell of Contacts Between Hoover and Disney   488
Film Adaptation of Waugh Tests the Limits of Moving Books to the Screen,
   A   1028
Film Adaptations Drawing Criticism   1032
Film Advertising, the Film Industry, and the Pin-up: The Industry's
   Accommodations to Social Forces   1437
Film Analysis: The Structural Approach   252
Film and American Studies: Questions, Activities, Guides   39
Film and Cultural Pluralism   661
Film and Dream   593
Film and Esthetics   53
Film and European Competition Law   664
Film and Fiction   1298
Film and Foreign Policy: The USIA, 1962-1967   230, 231, 295, 2034
Film and Labor: What the Credits Mean   609
Film and Literature; The Case of DEATH IN VENICE: Luchino Visconti and
   Thomas Mann   1308
Film and Revolution in Nicaragua: An Interview With Incine Filmmakers   2178
Film and Revolution: An Interview With Jean-Luc Godard   2109
Film and System: Terms of Analysis, Part I   585
Film and System: Terms of Analysis, Part II   585
Film and the Masquerade: Theorizing the Female Spectator   589, 590
Film and the Other Arts   142
Film and the Photo League: Radical Cinema in the 1930s   225
Film and the Physiology of Dreaming Sleep: The Brain As a
   Camera-Projector   579, 593
Film and the Radical Aspiration   2109
Film and the Visual Arts   53
Film and Theatre   1332
Film as an Agent, Product and Source of History   253
Film as Educator   37, 40, 51
Film as Experience: Nicholas Ray--The Director Turns Teacher   1985
Film as International Business: The Role of American Multinationals   647
Film as Social and Intellectual History at the University of Pennsylvania   39
Film as Source Material for History, The   252
Film at Expo '74   674
Film Attendance: Why College Students Chose to See Their Most Recent
   Film   751
Film Audience Research, 1960-1980: An Annotated Bibliography   705
Film Audience Research, 1960-1980: An Update   705
Film Books: SCREENING OUT THE PAST   783
Film Bureau Phenomenon in America: State and Municipal Advocacy   658
Film Career of John Barrymore, The   1798
Film Conglomerate "Blockbusters"   748
Film Critique No. 3: CITIZEN KANE   1807
Film Critique No. 4: LORD OF THE FLIES   1001

Film Critique No. 5: BATTLESHIP POTEMKIN 1666
Film Critique No. 6: BICYCLE THIEF 1932
Film Culture: The State of the Art 1523
Film Directors Who Have Lost Focus in the Theater 1334
Film Economics and Film Content: 1946-1983 608, 671, 673, 771
Film Editing: I 82
Film Editing: II 82
Film Education and Film Culture 40
Film Education in Our Time 40
Film Education Research: An Overview 34, 41
Film Favorites: BIGGER THAN LIFE 1985
Film Favorites: William Pechter on THE WILD BUNCH 2087
Film Financing and Banking 631, 672
Film Form, 1900-1906 1604
Film Genre to Film Experience 410
Film Giant With No Studio, The 662
Film Has Nothing to Do with Literature 1298
Film History and Film Histories 252, 1509, 1513, 1514, 1515
Film History for Exhibitors 1670
Film History: A Revisionist Perspective 1510, 1513, 1516
Film History: The Narrow Discourse 1509, 1514
Film In China 2163
Film Industry Studies: The Search for a Theory 612
Film Industry Today, The 661
Film Industry, Its Audience, and New Communications Technologies, The 756, 762, 770
Film Is a Film: Some Notes on Jean-Luc Godard, A 2109
Film is Modern Theatre 1105
Film Library and How It Grew, The 1522
Film Literacy 979
Film Mailbag: Debating the Role of Psychiatrists in Life and on Film 816
Film Mailbag: On THE DEER HUNTER 367
Film Maker Reflects on a 12-Year Project, A 903
Film Music: A Survey 400
FILM NOIR and the Genre Continuum 1947
FILM NOIR: A Modest Proposal 1947
FILM NOIR: Style and Content 1947
FILM NOIR: The Director--Fritz Lang's American Nightmare 1637
FILM NOIR: The Politics of the Maladjusted Text 1947
FILM NOIR: the Writer: Raymond Chandler and the World You Live In 1301
Film Notes: Hollywood Focuses on Hollywood 1143
Film Propaganda and Its Audience: The Example of Britain's Official Films During the First World War 212
Film Propaganda in the Soviet Union, 1941-1945: Two Views 208, 213, 281, 282
Film Reality: The Cinema and the Theater 144
Film Review: LUCAS 997
Film Review: NIGHT OF THE SHOOTING STARS 377
Film Review: NO WAY OUT 890
Film Scholarship: Dead or Alive? 1523
Film Scholarship: Past and Prospective 1522
Film SEXUAL PERVERSITY Is Getting a New Name 738
Film Society Pays Tribute to "Il Maestro" 1927
Film Spectacles 656
Film Student's Guide to the Reference Shelf, A 1520
Film Studio's Chief Fails to Establish Brave New World 670
Film Studios Buying Up Theaters in Major Cities 681
Film Study and the History Classroom 51
Film Study and the University of Chicago 38

Film Study, Literary Criticism, and Science: A Polemical Response to Richard Dyer MacCann   1523
Film Study: NOTHING BUT A MAN   40, 952
Film Style   2190
Film Style and Technology In the Forties   1944
Film Style and Technology in the Thirties   1745
Film Version of Everyman Wins Mexico   454
Film Viewer as Consumer, The   621
Film View: For Today's Screenwriter, What's in a Name?   1037
Film-Maker as Romantic Poet: Brakhage and Olson, The   1974
Filmgoing and Bertram Lewin's Three Worlds of Experience   593
Filmic Art and Training   1332
Filmic Dream and Point of View, The   593
Filming Henry James--Britain vs. America   1324
Filming JULIUS CAESAR   1354
Filming of Updike Book Divides a Seaside Town   1316
Filming THE ICEMAN COMETH   1351
Filmmaking: Special Effects in STAR WARS   812
Filmography of Betty Comden and Adolph Green   83
Filmography of Elia Kazan   1005
Filmography of FILM NOIR, A   1947
Filmography of Preston Sturges   1912
Filmography: Busby Berkeley   1797
Films   1027
Films and Dreams   593
Films and Edith Wharton   1300
Films and Rhetoric   53
Films Are Contemporary: Notes on Film Education   40
Films by Jean Rouch   2120
Films for the Classroom: Pedagogical Luxury or Rental Rip-Off?   132
Films in Focus   1292
Films of Billy Wilder, The   799, 1987
Films of Chabrol--A Priest Among Clowns, The   2098, 2100, 2101
Films of Claude Chabrol, The   2098
Films of D. W. Griffith: A Style for the Times, The   1367
Films of D. W. Griffith: The Development of Themes and Techniques in 42 of His Films, The   1362
Films of Fred Zinnemann, The   1989
Films of George Cukor   1012
Films of Heinosuke Gosho, The   1740
Films of Joseph L. Mankiewicz, The   1981
Films of Kurosawa, The   2019, 2029
Films of Luis Bunuel, The   1002, 1714
Films of Mary Pickford, The   1391
Films of Oscar Micheaux: America's First Fabulous Black Filmmaker, The   866
Films of Ring Lardner, Jr., The   379
Films of Robert Rossen, The   1090, 1985
Films of Sidney Lumet: Adaptation as Art, The   2084
Films of Stan Brakhage, The   1974
Films of Thomas H. Ince, The   1350
Films Out of Books: Bergman, Visconti, and Mann   1297
Films Reflect a Brash New Spain   2182
Films: S. O. B.   1295
Filmusicals   400
Film, Politics and the Press: The Influence of ALL THE PRESIDENT'S MEN   438
Film: Blake Edwards' "S. O. B.," a Farce   1295
Film: Documentary on Views About the Atom Bomb   324
Film: Godard In His Mafia KING LEAR   2112

Film: Hearst Newsreels in a 100-Minute Feature 300
Film: HOLLYWOOD SHUFFLE, Satire by Robert Townsend 903
Film: The "Literary Approach" 1297
Film: Welles in "Filming OTHELLO" 1353
Filth V. Lucre: The Black Community's Tough Choice 897
Financial Battle to Make TV Series, A 678
Financing of Film Production in Europe 664
Financing on Independent Feature Films, The 645
Financing the Production and Distribution of Motion Pictures 618
Fire This Time 255
First Eight Serials of Republic, The 1455
First Golden Age, The 1745
First Movie Audiences, The 710
First Picture Shows: Austin, Texas (1894-1913), The 719, 1599
First Reality: Film Censorship in Liberal England, The 211
First-Time Directors: A New Breed 2197
Fitzgerald Filmography 1110
Fitzgerald In Hollywood 1121, 1126
Fitzgerald's "Crazy Sundays": Cinderella in Hollywood 1119
Fitzgerald, Hollywood, and THE LAST TYCOON 1293
Five Films 1012, 1874
Five Worlds of John Ford, The 1007, 1674
Five-Year Struggle to make COMING HOME, The 376
Flaherty's Quest for Life 1671
FLASHDANCE: Eroticism and the American Dream 598
Flawed Genius: The Works of Robert Mulligan 1325
Florence Lawrence 1365
Florida: The Forgotten Film Capital 719, 1599
Flying High: An Interview With George Roy Hill 2079
Focus on a Peregrinating Poitier 890
Focusing on Youth: A New Breed of Movie Attracts the Young, Shakes Up
  Hollywood 748
Folk Values in a New Medium 941
Following My Actor's Instinct 1016
Fond Salutes and Naked Hate: Mel Brooks Interviewed 2073
Fond Son Is Reviving Preston Sturges's Fame, A 1912
Fonda 2081
Fonda is Rebuffed by V.F.W. 552
Footage Fetish: Recovering LOST HORIZON 1799
Footnote to the History of Riefenstahl's OLYMPIA 321
For a Close Cinematic Analysis 1143
For Film Director, 78, a Second Wind of Success 1942
For Film Moguls, Salaries in Megabucks 536
For Polish Film, A Mood of Cautious Optimism 2179
For the Movies 1034
For the Theatre 1034
For Us and By Us 40
For 25 Cents, Every Moviegoer was Royalty 486
Forbidden Fruit: The Nazi Feature Film, 1933-1945 322
Ford and Kennedy on the Western 424
Ford in Person 1673
Ford in Print 1673
Ford on Ford 1674
Ford's Lost World 1673
Foreign 'Piracy' of TV Signals Stirs Concern 226
Foreign Distribution of American Foreign Motion Pictures 625
Foreign Films on Soviet Screens, 1921-1931 1646
Foreword to HOLLYWOOD ON HOLLYWOOD 1042

Forgotten First: The Armat-Jenkins Partnership and the Atlanta Projection, The 1586
Forgotten Ford 1673
Formal Strategies as an Index to the Evolution of Film History 1583, 1584
Forms of Coherence In Woody Allen Comedies 2072
FORT APACHE 1673
Forty Point Two Million Dollars to Disney Chief 537
Forty Years a Queen: The Joan Crawford Story 1803
Forty Years After, Artists Still Struggle with the Holocaust 291
Forty Years of Cliffhanging 1455
FOUR HORSEMAN OF THE APOCALYPSE, THE 1707
Four Hundred Blows of Francois Truffaut, The 2155
FOUR HUNDRED BLOWS, THE 1005
Four Recent French Documentaries 2117
Four Years in a Bottle: A Critical Study of French Film Production Under the Occupation 1903
Fourth Commitment: Interview With John Frankenheimer, Part II, The 2077
Fox Plans a TV Program Service 678
Fox's Barry Diller Gambles on a Fourth TV Network 678
Fragments of a Fashionable Discourse 470
Fragments of a Mirror: Uses of Landscape in Hitchcock 1835
Frames: The Quality of Preminger 1984
FRANCES 1292
Frances Marion: Part I 84
Frances Marion: Part II 84
Francis Ford Coppola Interviewed 1322, 2196
Franco in Hollywood 1322
Francois Truffaut 2106
Francois Truffaut Dies at 52; Key New Wave Director 2108
Francois Truffaut on the New Wave: Truffaut Looks Back 2094
Francois Truffaut, 1932-1984 2108, 2156
Francois Truffaut: A Man Can Serve Two Masters 2106
Francois Truffaut: An Interview 2106
Francois Truffaut: Anarchist Imagination 1005, 2106
Francois Truffaut: Feminist Filmmaker? 2106
Franju 2119
Franju, Georges 2119
Frank and Eleanor Perry 995
Frank Capra and the Popular Front 1075
Frank Capra: NAME ABOVE THE TITLE One of the Best Books on H'wood That Was 1763
Frankenheimer 2077
Franklin Schaffner 2090
Franklin Schaffner, 69, Oscar-Winning Director 2067
Franklin Schaffner: From PLANET OF THE APES to PATTON 2090
Franz Waxman 83
Fred Wiseman: TITICUT Revisted 2092
Fred Zinnemann Filmography 1989
Fred Zinnemann Has Succeeded with New Actors in Real Settings 1988
Fred Zinnemann: An Interview 1989
Fred Zinnemann: Quiet Man on the Set 1988
Frederick Wiseman 2092
Free Cinema 295
French Cinema .   .   . The Old and the New 1711
French Cinema During the Occupation, The 1903
French Cinema Under the German Occupation, The 1903
French Cinema, 1940-1944, and Its Socio-Psychological Significance: A Preliminary Probe 247, 1903

French Culture and Critical Theory: CINETHIQUE 479
French Film Culture and Critical Theory: CINETHIQUE 2103
French Films During the Occupation 1903
French Gave Me My Freedom, The 1002
French Line, The 131, 1998
French Outsider With the Inside Look: A Monograph of Robert Bresson's Early
  Work 1994
French Social Cinema and the Popular Front 225
French Writers Turned Filmmakers 2112, 2113
Frenchman in Hollywood 2119
Fresh Assay of the Comic Gold of Preston Sturges, A 1912
Fresh Light on Racial Themes: On Blacks in American Films 933
FRESHMAN, THE 1672
Freud at the Movies 816
Freud: Effets Speciaux; Mise En Scene: U.S.A. 531
Freundschaft 1276
Friendly Citizens: Images of Women and the Feminization of the Audience in
  Vietnam Films 442
Friese-Greene Is a Legend 1585
Fritz Lang on Godard and CONTEMPT 2110
Fritz Lang Remembered 1637
Fritz Lang Talks About the Problems of Life Today 1637
Fritz Lang's America: Part One 1018, 1637
Fritz Lang's America: Part Two 1018, 1637
Fritz Lang, Incorporated 643
Fritz Lang: Only Melodrama 1642
From a Written Film History to a Visual Film History 1511
From AIDA to ZAUBERFLOTE: The Opera Film 400
From AMERICAN GRAFFITI to Outer Space 2196
From Berlin to Neubabelsberg: Nazi Film Propaganda and Hitler Youth
  Quex 206
From Book to Film--Via John Huston 1319
From Book to Film: Simplification 1300
From Comic Strips to Animation: Some Perspective on Winsor McCay 1584
From Depths to Heights 667
From Dictatorship to Democracy: Carlos Saura's CARMEN 598
From Entertainment to Social Force: The Discovery of the Motion Picture
  1918-1945 725, 770
From Fetish to Subject: The Containment of Sexual Difference in Hollywood's
  Wartime Cinema 789
From Film to Film 1004, 2168
From Generation to Generation 2181
From Here to Eternity 1988
From Identification to Ideology: The Male System of Hitchcock's
  NOTORIOUS 1835
From Jews to JAWS 820
From Olive Oyl to Sweet Polly Purebread: Sex Roles, Stereotypes and Televised
  Cartoons 789
From Page to Screen in Smalltown America: Early Motion Picture Exhibition in
  Winona, Minnesota 719
From PSYCHO to DRESSED TO KILL: The Decline and Fall of the Psychiatrist
  in Movies 816
From Repressive Tolerance to Erotic Liberation: MAEDCHEN IN UNIFORM 495
From Rock Around the Clock to The Trip: The Truth About Teen Movies 743
From Screen To Screen: Cinema Films on Television 648
From Stage to Screen 1464
From Technology to Adultery 2034
From the AMERICAN SHADCHAN to ANNIE HALL: The Life and Legacy of Yiddish
  Film In America 829

From the Editor 1142
From the Outdoors to Outer Space: The Motion Picture Industry in the
  1970s 753
From THE 400 BLOWS to SMALL CHANGE 2106
Front Office, Box Office, and Artistic Freedom: An Aspect of the Film Industry
  1945-1969 736
Frustrated Warner Head Sees His Dream Threatened, A 2204
Fuller Up 1977
Function of the Narrative in Literature and Film: Some Issues, The 1297
Funny Is Money 2073
Funny Money 1137
Funny Side of Life, The 1672
Future . . . A Slight Return, The 1987
Future Film Historian: Less Art and More Craft, The 1511
Future Imperfect 410
Future Isn't What It Used to Be, The 410
F.B.I. is a Strange Hero for MISSISSIPPI BURNING 255

          G

Gahan Wilson Horror Movie Pocket Computer, The 1234
Gallery of Great Artists: Alec Guinness 1942
Gallery of Great Artists: Anna Magnani 1933
Gallery of Great Artists: Anthony Quinn 1022
Gallery of Great Artists: Orson Welles 1023
Gallery of Great Artists: Spencer Tracy 994
Gallery of Great Artists: Trevor Howard 1010, 1943
Game Theory and THE RULES OF THE GAME 1827
Gangster as A Tragic Hero, The 384
Gangsters, Vampires, and J. A. P.'s: The Jew Surfaces in American
  Movies 819, 834, 835
Garbo 1012
Garbo--How Good Was She? 1012
Gas 1837
Gathered Light: History, Criticism and THE RISE OF THE AMERICAN FILM,
  The 1509, 1512
Gatsby 1321
Gatsby Flap, The 1322
Gays, Gals, Goys, and All Those Other Minorities on Media 831
Gencorp to Sell RKO Pictures 663
Gender and Genre 621
Gene Kelly 1980
General, The 1704
Generation Without a Cause 1003
Genetic Structuralism and the Cinema: A Look at Fritz Lang's METROPOLIS 1642
Genre and the Resurrection of the Past 416
Genre Criticism 176
Genre Films and the Status Quo 463
Genre Film: Myth, Ritual, and Sociodrama 452
Genre, Director and Stars in John Ford's Westerns 1674
Genre: Theory and Malpractice 174
GENTLEMEN PREFER BLONDES 471, 487
George Axelrod and THE MANCHURIAN CANDIDATE 2078
George Coulouris, 85 is Dead; Actor Relished Villainous Roles 1807
George Cukor 1012
George Cukor: An Interview 1012
George Jean Nathan and the Dramatist in Hollywood 1104, 1106

George Lucas Goes Far Out 2196
George Lucas--Burden of Dreams 2196
George Lucas: The Stinky Kid Hits the Big Time 2196
George O'Brien 1706
George Seaton 1805
George Stevens 849, 1009
George Stevens and the American Dream 1009
George Stevens: His Work, Part One 1009
George Stevens: His Work, Part Two 1009
Georges Franju: The Haunted Void 2119
Georges Melies and the FEERIE 1590, 1604
Georgy Girl 1006
Gerald Mast Replies to Janet Staiger's "The Politics of Film Canons" 447
German Film In 1964: Stuck at Zero, The 2165
German Film Industry and the New Order, The 227
German Wasteland, The 2165
Germany A Lost Decade 207
Germany: The Past that Will Not Go Away 2165
GERTRUD 2189
Getting Better 1005
Getting Even 1295
Getting His Break in BREAKING AWAY 1005
Getting Things Right 1007
Gig Finally Made It, Didn't He? 2089
Gig Young 2089
Gilded Age 1049
Girls on Film: Fantasy, Desire and Desperation 469, 706
Gish and Garbo: The Executive War on Stars 1012
Giving Them What They Want: Movie Audience Research Before 1950 710, 733
Glasnost In the Soviet Union 2182
Glasnost in Wide Screen: Hush, Hush, Old Stalinist 2182
Glimpses of Hitch 1856
Glimpses of the Moon: Science Fiction 409
Glimpses of the Nazi Cinema (1933-1945) 2165
Gloria Swanson 1454
Gloria Swanson Dies; 20's Film Idol 1454
Glory That Was Hollywood, The 1044
Glory That Was Hollywood: The Babylon of the West Is Being Revisited by Every
  Filmmaker In Town. Why? 2195
Goal-Oriented Individual Psychology--Alfred Adler's Theory 586, 587
Godard and Me: Jean-Pierre Gorin Talks 2111
Godard and Revolution 2109
Godard and the Dziga Vertov Group: Film and Dialect 2111
Godard and the US 2109
GODARD ON GODARD: Notes for a Reading 2110
Godard--Cult or Culture? 2109
Godard's MASCULINE-FEMININE: The Cinematic Essay 163
Godard's Truths 2110
Godard's WEEKEND: Totem, Taboo and the Fifth Republic 2109
Godard, Jean-Luc 2108
Goddesses, The 1434
Goddess, The 1292
Godzilla and the Japanese Nightmare: When Them! is U.S. 390
Goebbels and the Function of Propaganda 251
Goebbels' Work 282
Going for Extra Innings: Billy Wilder Interviewed 1987
Going Hollywood 1672
Golden Age of Republic Serials, The 1455
GONE WITH THE WIND 812

Good at Games 590
Good Guys and Bad Guys 801
Good-Bad Girl, The 602
Gook-Hunter, The 367
Gordon Parks: Beyond Black Film 900
Gosho, Heinosuke 1888
Government Financial Support to the Film Industry in the United States 771
Grading Hollywood's Ratings System 960
Graduate Flunks Out, The 2085
GRADUATE'S Photography, THE 2086
GRADUATE, THE 2085, 2086
GRAFFITI Is the Story of His Life 993
Graham Greene as Film Critic 1329
Graham Greene's Movies 1300
Graham Greene, How Do You Do It? 1329
Grand Illusions 1827
Grand Illusion: Hollywood and World War II, The 258
GRANDE ILLUSION, LA 1827
GRAPES OF WRATH, THE 1326, 1673
GRAPES OF WRATH: A Visual Analysis, THE 1326
Graphic In Filmic Writing: A BOUT DE SOUFFLE or the Erratic Alphabet,
 The 2151
Gravity of SUNRISE, The 1706
Gray Thoughts on RED SHOES 1943
Great Blank Page, The 1672
Great Books Are Not the Stuff of Great Movies 1029
Great Britain 1934, 1936
Great D. W., The 1368
Great Films of the Century: CITIZEN KANE 1807
Great Films of the Century: LE REGLE DU JEU 1827
Great Films of the Century: THE COVERED WAGON 1702
Great Films of the Century: THE GENERAL 1704
Great Films of the Century: THE INFORMER 1019
Great Films of the Century: THE MALTESE FALCON 373
Great Films of the Century: THE MAN WITH THE MOVIE CAMERA 1669
Great Films of the Century: THE PASSION OF JOAN OF ARC 1729
Great Films of the Century: THE SEVENTH SEAL 2189
GREAT GATSBY, THE 1322
Great Locomotive Chase, The 1672
Great Northern Film Company: Nordisk Film in the American Motion Picture
 Market, The 1626
Great Rewrite, The 1297
Great Stone Face, The 1672
Great Three-In-One 1004
Great War Viewed From the Twenties: THE BIG PARADE, The 221
Greatest Gangster Movie Ever Filmed: PRELUDE TO WAR, The 232
Green Thoughts in a Technicolor Shade: A Reevaluation of THE GREAT
 GATSBY 1322
Greene Criticizes Film Adaptations of His Books 1033
Greta Garbo's Secret 1012
Grierson Movement, The 215
Griffith and Poe 1363
Griffith and the Development of the Silent Film 1362
Griffith and the Technical Innovations 1363
Griffith in Hollywood 1368
Griffith Tradition, The 1362
Griffith's BROKEN BLOSSOMS and the Problem of Historical Specificity 1509
Griffith's Family Discourse: Griffith and Freud 1364

Griffith's Film Career before THE ADVENTURES OF DOLLIE 1361
Griffith's Talkies 1368
Griffith, a Big Step Forward and Judith 1365
Griffith, Maker of Battle Scenes, Sees Real War 1376
Griffith: The Triangle Productions 1368
Group Celebrates a Decade of Distributing Black Films 907
Groups Protest Toys With War Theme 437
Growing Independence, A 559
Growing Up Among the Stars 410
Growing Up Is Hard to Put in Focus: Recent Films Illustrate the Difficulty of
  Capturing Adolescence 972
Growth of Movie Monopolies: The Case of Balaban & Katz, The 622
Growth of the Feature Film 1627
Guide to Video Systems: Disk and Cassette 762
Guiletta and Federico: Visits With Fellini 1927
Gunplay and Horses: Howard Hawks Talks About His Way With Westerns 424
G. B. S. on the Screen 1300
G. M. "Bronco Billy" Anderson: The Screen Cowboy Hero Who Meant
  Business 429
G. W. Pabst 1643

H

HAIL THE CONQUERING HERO 1014, 1912
Hal Ashby, 59, an Oscar Winner Whose Films Included SHAMPOO 2082
Hal B. Wallis Dies at 88; Produced Classic Films 1289
Hal B. Wallis Dies at 88; Veteran Film Producer 1289
Hal Roach on Film Comedy 1695
Hale's Tours: Ultrarealism in the Pre-1910 Motion Picture 1605
HAMLET 1353
Hamlet to Clown 1013, 1354
Handle with Care 1031
Handmaiden of Villainy: Methods and Problems in Studying the Historical
  Reception of a Film, The 485
Hands Up, Hans! 2165
Hanging Out Movie--DINER, The 995
Happily Ever After 2203
Happy Birthday, Blanche Sweet 1365
Hard Part, III: Getting it Right--The Aesthetics of Failure, The 669
Hard Part, II: Getting it Shown--Shelf Life, The 669
Hard Part, I: Getting it Made--Breathless Diary, The 669
Harlequin's Stick, Charlie's Cane 1419
Harold Arlen 83
Harold Lloyd 1672
Harold Lloyd Made a Fortune by Combining Comedy and Thrills 1672
Harold Lloyd: A Reassessment of His Comedy 1672
Harry Brown, 69, a Screenwriter 1147
Harry Langdon 1410, 1672
Hats Off to ABC For Not Applying Rambo Mentality 549
HAUNTING, THE 1323
Have Horror Films Gone Too Far? 387
Hawkeye in Hollywood 1300
Hawks Isn't Good Enough 1747
Hawks vs. Durgnat 1747
Haywire in Hollywood: Girlhood Memories By Movieland Daughters 970
HBO Nears Fox, Paramount Accord 678
HBO Versus the Studios 653
He Drew From His Boyhood to Make DINER 995

He Who Gets Hitched   1836
He Who Treads the Tiger's Tale   2195
Heart Attack Fells Producer/Director Peckinpah at 59   2062
HEART IS A LONELY HUNTER, THE   996
HEART Survives Crisis: Zoetrope Delivers Paychecks   536
Heart Transplant   367
HEARTS IN DIXIE (The First Real Talking Film)   941
HEAVY TRAFFIC and AMERICAN GRAFFITI   993
Hegemonic Female: Fantasy in AN UNMARRIED WOMAN and CRAIG'S WIFE, The   472
Heiress, The   1007
Hellman and the Communists   1096
Hellman Word Assailed Again   1322
Help! They're Back   765
Hemingway into Film   1301
Hemingway on the Screen   1300
Hemingway Tradition in American Film, The   373
Hemingway, Hollywood and Female Representation: THE MACOMBER AFFAIR   1231
Henry B. Walthall   1365
Henry James, James Ivory, and That Nice Mr. Emerson   1324
Here Come the Czechs: Grass Roots   2164
Here was an Actor: Henry B. Walthall's Magic Has Had a Long Effect   1365
Here's Looking at You, Kid: How I Learned to Stop Worrying and Love the Baby   1003
Heretic's Look at Musicals, A   400
Heretic's View of Westerns, A   424
Herman Mankiewicz   1266, 1269
Hero in Black Film: An Analysis of the Film Industry and Problems in Black Cinema, The   860, 876, 899, 900
Heroes are Tired, The   424
Heroine, The   789
Hero, The   806
Hero, the Harlot, and the Glorified Horse as Mythic Americans, The   789
Herrmann, Hitchcock, and the Music of the Irrational   1835
High Court Refines Standard on Obscenity Cases   962
HIGH NOON   1019
High Price of Nostalgia for Things Cinematic, The   2193
High Price of Screen Love-Making, The   1453
High 40's, The   1944
Highest Honor to Pickford   1391
Hill, George Roy   2079
His Crowning Achievement   1432
HIS GIRL FRIDAY: Production for Use   1747
Historian and Film, The   275
Historians and Movies: The State of the Art   252
Historical Inception of Stage and Film, The   1340
Historical Notes on Dr. Frankenstein and His Monster   1808
Historical Reception of Hitchcock's MARNIE, The   1835
Historical Trends in the Criticism of the Newsreel & Television News 1930-1945   208
Historicism and Historism in Recent Film Historiography   252
Historiography as Cinematography: A Prolegomenon to Film Work for Historians   257
History of Film Teaching in the American School System, The   39, 40
History of Hollywood's Jews, A   820
History of Mentalities: The New Map of Cultural History, The   261
History of Negro Motion Pictures   942

History of World Cinema: Models for Economic Analysis, The 618
History with Lightning: The Forgotten Film WILSON 366
History--Before and After Mussolini: Second Part of a History of Italian
  Cinema 1607
Hitch 1836
Hitch Your Genre to a Star 1671
Hitchcock 1835, 1978
Hitchcock and Bunuel: Desire and the Law 1838
Hitchcock and the Art of Suspense: Part II 1836
Hitchcock and the Art of Suspense: The Paranoia of Fear 1836
Hitchcock and the Ethics of Vision 1836
Hitchcock and the Mechanisms of Suspense 1836
Hitchcock Confronts Evil 1836
Hitchcock Versus Hitchcock 1836
Hitchcock Versus Truffaut: If I Lose My Leg I Lose Rosie 1857
Hitchcock's REAR WINDOW: Reflexivity and the Critique of Voyeurism 1978
Hitchcock's Wasteland Vision: An Examination of FRENZY 1836
Hitchcock's Women 1838
Hitchcock's World 1835
Hitchcock, The Enunciator 1835
Hitchcock, Truffaut, and the Irresponsible Audience 1857
Hitchcock: Auteur or Hack--How the Filmmaker Reshaped His Reputation Among
  Critics 1835
Hitchcock: Suspense and Meaning 1836
Hitler's Favorite Filmmaker Honored at Colorado Festival 321
Hitler's Impact on the Lower Middle Class 251
Hollow Victories 1672
Hollywood and Broadway Share a Wealth of Talent 1331
Hollywood and Pedagogy 39
Hollywood and the Collective Myth 576
Hollywood and the Indian 454
Hollywood and the Novelist--A Fickle Romance at Best 1028
Hollywood and the Pentagon: When the Military Assists a Production 232
Hollywood and the South, 1930-1960 860
Hollywood and the Vietnam War 335
Hollywood and the "Art Cinema" as a Bipolar Modeling System: A BOUT DE
  SOUFFLE and BREATHLESS 2152
Hollywood and World War I, 1914-1918 223
Hollywood Arab: 1984-1986, The 826
Hollywood at the Crossroads 659
Hollywood at War: The American Motion Picture and World War II 262
Hollywood Battles Killer Budgets 670, 671, 676
Hollywood Before the Blacklist: Radical Impact Re-Examined 1099
Hollywood Cluster Syndrome, The 463
Hollywood Debates HBO Role in Film Financing 653
Hollywood Does Broadway 2204
Hollywood Dream: 1983, The 1535
Hollywood Entices Japanese 2206
Hollywood Fights Anti-Semitism 1431
Hollywood Filmmaking and Reputation Building : Hitchcock's THE BIRDS 1835
Hollywood Films on the British Screens: An Analysis of the Functions of American
  Popular Culture Abroad 722
Hollywood Focuses on Vietnam at Last 335
Hollywood G-Man, 1934-1945, The 384
Hollywood Game Grows Rich--and Desperate, The 536, 611
Hollywood Harakiri: On the Decline of an Industry and an Art 653, 665, 2191
Hollywood Highrollers 1137
Hollywood History Lesson 1321

Hollywood in Britain: The Postwar Embargo on Exporting Feature Films to
  Britain 771
Hollywood in Fiction 1028
Hollywood In the Age of Television 1944
Hollywood is Sick 640
Hollywood Is Taking Aim at the Funny Bone 2201
Hollywood Lays an Egg 669
Hollywood Lullaby 1295
Hollywood Market Research 739
Hollywood Moves to Tap Video Market 762
Hollywood Musical: An Annotated Bibliography, The 83
Hollywood Novel, The 1297
Hollywood on Hollywood 1028, 1044, 1944
Hollywood on the Mekong 337
Hollywood Report 942
Hollywood Revisited 656
Hollywood Revisited: A Sad Homecoming 1294
Hollywood Romantic: A Monograph on George Stevens 1009
Hollywood Scene: The American Minority Problem, The 832
Hollywood Screenwriter, The 85, 1036, 1066
Hollywood Sells Off The Splendor 1464
HOLLYWOOD SHUFFLE 903
Hollywood Spent More for TV Ads Last Year 2205
Hollywood Stardom 1377
Hollywood Survival: 50 Years of Success and Oblivion 1037
Hollywood Thinks Small in a Big Way 647
Hollywood Travels: Sturges and Sullivan 1921
Hollywood Under Water--Elia Kazan on THE LAST TYCOON 1293
Hollywood War Films: 1942-1944 200, 281
Hollywood War of Independence, The 1944, 2034
Hollywood Worried by Growing Cassette Rentals 672
Hollywood 1965 2034
Hollywood 1985 669
Hollywood (Hot Dog) Days 2192
Hollywood--It Wasn't All That Bad 1130
Hollywood's Anti-Red Boomerang 1084
Hollywood's Color Problem 902
Hollywood's Conversion to Color: The Technological, Economic, and Aesthetic
  Factors 654, 748, 1670
Hollywood's Crashing Epics 669
Hollywood's Dirty Little Secret 902, 903, 904, 905
Hollywood's Favorite Fable 2034
Hollywood's Gamble on Big Hits--Fewer Movies and Emptier Theaters 752, 755
Hollywood's Handsomest Director 1707
Hollywood's International Market 625, 1993
Hollywood's Mean Season Ends 756
Hollywood's Most Secret Agent 2197
Hollywood's Movie Star System: A Historical Overview 735
Hollywood's New Heroines 1322, 2199
Hollywood's New "Feminist" Heroines 680
Hollywood's Newest Heavyweight: Victor A. Kaufman--Taking Tri-Star Into the
  Big Time 678
Hollywood's Search For Stars 651
Hollywood's Spotty Record on Foreign Affairs 454
Hollywood's Summer Sweepstakes 762
Hollywood's Unmarried Husbands and Wives 1453
Hollywood's Youth Cult Films 2207
Hollywood's "Political" Cinema 439

Hollywood, New Technology and International Banking: A Formula for
  Success 681
Hollywood, The Jewish Experience, and Popular Culture 820, 821
Hollywood, the National Recovery Administration, and the Question of Monopoly
  Power 640, 1068
Hollywood, The National Recovery Administration, and the Question of
  Sound 697
Hollywood: Broke--And Getting Rich 960
Hollywood: The Blessed and the Cursed 1105
Hollywood: The Shock of Freedom in Films 2038
Hollywood: The Toll of the Frenzied Forties 646
Holocaust: Of Plays and Playwrights, The 290
Holographic Motion Pictures for Theater and Television 655
Homage to an Artist 1018
Home Box Office Moves in on Hollywood 653
Home in the Wilderness: Visual Imagery in John Ford's Westerns, A 1673
Home Video Recorders: A Useful Survey 756
Home Video Recorders: Rights and Ratings 760
Hoodlums: The Myth 384
Hooray for Providence, Wilkes-Barre, Saranac Lake--and Hollywood 1621
HORA DE LOS HORNOS, LA 2157
Horror Films 388
Hot Guns and Cold Women 424
Hot Tickets May Burn Up Record Books 764
How a Classic Clown Keeps Inspiring Comedy 1414
How AMADEUS was Translated from Play to Film 1330
How Dare They 678
How Do We Teach It? A Primer for the Basic Film/Literature Course 39, 52
How Do We Teach It? A Primer for the Basic Literature/Film Course 1026
How Effective was Nazi Propaganda? 251
How Endings Have Affected Two Recent Movies 1308
How Griffith Picks His Leading Women 1366
How Hollywood Fixed an Election 1069
How Hollywood is Smashing the Colour Bar 885
How I Make Films: An Interview With John Huston 1321
How I Stopped Worrying and Love the Cinema 2083
How Much Did Hitchcock Know? 1857
How Old Movie Serials Inspired Lucas and Spielberg 2196
How Reagan Always Gets the Best Lines 437
How Rock is Changing Hollywood's Tune 2203
How School Achievement Relates to Mass Media Use 754
How the Blacklist Worked in Hollywood 1084
How the Graphic Arts Feats in ZELIG Were Done 786
How the West Was Lost 1987
How to Distribute a Film 676
How to Take It All Seriously (From Antonioni to Andy) 56
How TV and Film Portrayals Affect Sexual Satisfaction in College Students 546
How Warner Got Back Its Glitter 663
How (And Where) the Powerful, the Rich & the Sexy Spend Their Money 1137
Howard Hawks 1747
Howard Hawks--Masculine Feminine 798
Howard Hawks, 81, Story Teller Who Became a Pantheon Figure 798
Howard Hawks: A Private Interview 1747
Howard Hawks: An Interview 1747
Howard Hawks: Hawks Thief--Patterns of Continuity in RIO BRAVO, EL
  DORADO, and RIO LOBO 1747
Howard Hawks: Masculine Feminine 1747
Hugo Friedhofer 83
Hulot: Or the Common Man as Observer and Critic 2001

Human Artifice and the Science Fiction Film   409
Human Landscape of John Ford's South   912
Human Need in THE DAY OF THE LOCUST: Problems of Adaption   1291
Human Side of D. W. Griffith, The   1361
Humphrey Bogart's SAHARA: Propaganda, Cinema and the American Character
   in World War II   375
Humphrey Jennings: Surrealist Observer   316
Hungarian Cinema: The Fight for Freedom   2167
Hungary   2167
HUSTLER, THE   1014
Hybrid Plots in PSYCHO   2080
Hyperion to a Satyr   1233
Hysteria and Authoritarianism in the Films of Robert Aldrich   2071
H. G. Wells on the Screen   1301

I

I Can't Get Jimmy Carter to See My Movie   2071
I Can't Get That Monster Out of My Mind   530
I Dream for a Living: Steven Spielberg, the Prince of Hollywood, Is Still a Little
   Boy at Heart   2196
I Have Nothing Against Sally Field, but. . . .   1017
I Know Where I'm Going   1813
I Prefer the Sun to the Rain   2119
I See Dassin Make the Law   1975
I Surrender, Mama   997
I Think I Liked the Book Better: Nineteen Novelists Look at the Film Version
   of Their Work   1039, 1040
I Want to Treat SHOOT THE PIANO PLAYER Like a Tale by Perrault: An
   Interview With Francois Truffaut   2156
I Was a Young Woman of Parts: An Interview With Angela Lansbury   2078
I Was Born for The Cinema   1927
I Wasn't Always a Filmmaker   2163
I Wish: An Interview With Francois Truffaut   2106
I'd Rather Be Like I Am: Some Comments on THE LONELINESS OF THE LONG
   DISTANCE RUNNER   997
Iceman Cometh Too Close, The   1351
ICEMAN COMETH, THE   1351
Ichikawa and the Wanderers   2177
Ichikawa, Kon   2022
Ici Se Habla Euro-English   2206
Idea of Genre in the American Cinema, The   176
Idea of Montage in Soviet Art and Cinema, The   1646
Ideas on Authorship   1999
Identity: An Interview With Nicholas Roeg   2160
Ideological and Technological Determinism in Deep-Space Cinema Images   1814
Ideological Effects of the Basic Cinematographic Apparatus   470, 479, 480
Ideological Foundations of the Czech New Wave, The   2165
Ideological Gunfight at the RKO Corral: Notes on Howard Hughes' I MARRIED
   A COMMUNIST   1949
Ideology and Hypotheses In the Criticism of Neo-Realism   1921
Ideology of the Social Consciousness Movie: Three Films of Darryl F.
   Zanuck   1204
Ideology, Genre, Auteur   1046
IF . . .   1001
If Hollywood is Dead or Dying, Perhaps The Following Are Some of The
   Reasons   1105

If Willis Gets $5 Million, How Much for Redford? 1437
IKIRU 2030
Illicit Pleasures: Feminist Spectators and PERSONAL BEST 590
Illustrious Career of Jean Renoir, The 1813
Image in Film Worries Mississippians 255
Image Mirrored: Reflexivity and the Documentary Film, The 280
Image of New Orleans on Film, The 913
Image of Patriarchal Power in YOUNG MR. LINCOLN (1939) and IVAN THE
 TERRIBLE, PART I (1944), The 477
Image of the Jew in Recent European Pics, The 834
Image of Woman as Image: The Optical Politics of DAMES, The 497
Image Revisionism: Unlikely Hero, Guaranteed Villain 802
Images and Words In Ingmar Bergman's Films 2183
Images of Canada 1590
Images of the Mind: Psychiatry in the Commercial Field 816
Image, or, What Happened to the American Dream?, The 547
Imaginary Signifier, The 528
Imitation of Film-Mediated Aggressive Models 745
Immigrants and Spectators 718, 765
Impact of Griffith's BIRTH OF A NATION on the Modern Ku Klux Klan,
 The 1367
Impact of THE JAZZ SINGER on the Conversion to Sound, The 1746
Impact of the Paramount Decision on Motion Picture Production and
 Distribution:1908-1915 607
Importance of the Entertainment Film, The 455
Improbable Ethnic Hero: William Powell and the Transformation of Ethnic
 Hollywood 454
In a Lonely Place 1985
In a New Film, Spike Lee Tries to Do the Right Thing 903
In Appreciation: Lucy's Enduring Comedy Captured Our Hearts 1757
IN COLD BLOOD: The Filmic Novel and the Problem of Adaptation 1300
In Defense of Myself 1420
In Defense of Popular Taste: Film Ratings Among Professionals and Lay
 Audiences 462
In Defense of Sam Peckinpah 2087
In Defense of the KKK 1367
In Defense of Violence 2124
In Dispute on Bias, Stanford Is Likely to Alter Western Culture Program 446
In Harlem, a James Bond With a Soul? 941
In Movies Whitey Is Still King 942
In Re: Columbia Pictures and Puttnam's Orphans 671
In Search of a Revolution: Peter Hall 1355
In Search of Stanley Kubrick 2083
In Search of the Greatest Gatsby 1322
In Search of the MISSING 1021
In Search of the Real South 914
In the Name of Feminist Film Criticism 465
In the Picture: A Matter of Conviction 2077
In the Picture: Cassevetes in London 2074
In the Picture: 99 and 44/100% Dead 2077
In The RED DESERT 2173
In the Service of Ideology: How Betty Grable's Legs Won the War 769
In The Time Inc. Game, Warner Head Has Aces 2204
In the Wake of THE GREAT GATSBY 1322
In Time Inc. Battle, All Eyes On the Courts 2204
In Very Early Days 1585
Independence With a Vengeance 645
Independent Producer, The 643
Independent's Day 671

India Is on Our Minds, But Whose India?   548
Indian Cinema Today   2168
Indian Family   1004
Indian on the Screen, The   454
Indiana's Little 500 Speeds Into the Big Time   1005
Indie Boom Turns Bust   2203
Individual Differences in Affective, Evaluative, and Behavorial Responses to an
    Erotic Film   546
Individualism Against Machinery: An Interview With Fred Zinnemann   1989
Individualism Versus Collectivism: The Shift to Independent Production in the
    US Film Industry   658, 661
Indpendents   666
Industrialization of Entertainment in the United States   711
Industry   666, 754
Industry Economic Review and Audience Profile   754
Industry Highlights   1670
Industry--Grosses Gloss: Breaking Away at the Box-Office   668
Industry, The   665, 666
Industry: Campaigns and Caveat   670
Industry: Four-Walling, The   666
Industry: Seventh Annual Grosses Gloss   669
Industry: Tenth Annual Grosses Gloss   761, 2194
Influence of Personal Values on Movie Preferences, The   535
Influence of the MPAA's Film-Rating System on Motion Picture Attendance: A
    Pilot Study, The   959
Influence of the Paramount Decision on Network Television in America, The   646
Ingmar Bergman and the Devil   2183
Ingmar Bergman Film Index, An   2183
Innis Points a Finger at the Media   855
Innocence, An Originality, A Clear Eye: A Retrospective Look at the Films of
    D. W. Griffith and Andy Warhol, An   2040
INNOCENTS and What Passes for Experience, THE   1014, 1324
INNOCENTS, THE   1324
Insects in a Glass Case: Random Thoughts on the Films of Claude Chabrol   2098,
    2099
Inside Hollywood   1139
Inside Story of WATERFRONT, The   1277
Insistence of the Letter in the Unconscious, The   480
Integrated Approach to Teaching of Film and Literature, An   1025
Integrating Marxist and Psychoanalytical Approaches in Feminist Film
    Criticism   471, 587, 588, 593
Intertitles   1748
Interview and Filmography of Robert Aldrich   2071
Interview With Andy Warhol, An   2039
Interview With Anthony Mann   1982
Interview With Antonioni, An   1012, 1874
Interview With British Cine-feminists   471
Interview With Buster Keaton, An   1672
Interview With Carl Foreman   1019
Interview With Chabrol   2098
Interview with Dreyer, An   1729
Interview With Federico Fellini, An   1023, 1927
Interview With Frank Perry, An   995
Interview With Franklin Schaffner, An   2090
Interview With Frederick Wiseman, An   2092
Interview With George Roy Hill   2078
Interview With Georges de Beauregard   2110
Interview With Godard   2110

Interview With Harold Lloyd 1672
Interview With Horton Foote, An 1325
Interview With Jacques Demy 2119
Interview With Jacques Rivette, An 2098
Interview With Jean Renoir 1813
Interview With Jean-Pierre Melville, An 2000, 2093
Interview With John Ford 1351
Interview With Josef Von Sternberg 1674
Interview With Kihachi Okamoto, An 1894
Interview with Marilyn Monroe 586
Interview With Mel Brooks 2073
Interview With Mike Nichols 2085
Interview With Otto Preminger 1984
Interview With Otto Preminger, An 1984
Interview With Peter Brook 1002
Interview With Roberto Rossellini, February 22-25, 1971, In Houston,
  Texas 1933
Interview With Roger Corman 2075
Interview With Roger Leenhardt and Jacques Rivette 2098
Interview With Sidney Lumet, An 2084
Interview With Truffaut 2106
Interviewing Bunuel 1002, 1714
Interview: Albert and David Maysles, An 2085
Into Another World 368
Into the '90s: The Future of Talking Pictures 2204
Into the Sixties 2159
INTOLERANCE and the Soviets: An Historical Investigation 1367, 1646
Introducing Film Study in an Undergraduate Context: Queens University 38
Introduction to ANGER AND BEYOND 540
Introduction to Film Bibliographies, An 1520
Introduction to RAGGED DICK And MARK, THE MATCH BOY 1052
Introduction to THE PAT HOBBY STORIES BY F. SCOTT FITZGERALD 1128
Introduction to THE RISE OF SILAS LAPHAM 1051
Introduction: Metahistory of Films 252, 1509, 1511
Introduction: Recent Ideas of Narrative Order 1297
Introduction: Symposium on the Methodology of Film History 1510
Introduction: The Symbolic Annihilation of Women by the Mass Media 459, 460
Investigating Africa's Past 918
Irish on the Screen, The 454
Irving Thalberg 1492
Is Action or Politics the Real Attraction? 483
Is Hollywood Really "S. O. B." Decadent? 1295
Is it Better to be Shaft than Uncle Tom? 862
Is It Worth Making Blockbuster Films? 611
Is That Old Hollywood Tradition--the Sneak Preview--Fading Out? 574
Is There a Cure for Film Criticism 1027
Is Truffaut the Happiest Man on Earth? Yes 2106
ISHTAR: A $51 Million Film Project in Trouble 535
ISLAND OF THE BLUE DOLPHINS, THE 996
Islands of the Mind 2073
Isolated Hero of Ingmar Bergman, The 2183
Israel 2169
Israeli Cinema 2169
It Depends How You Look At It 2086
It Wasn't Like That in the Book 1301
It Wasn't Like That in the Play 1335
It's a Family Affair 998
It's a New Age for Father-Son Relationships 971
It's Gonna Blow Whitey's Mind 916, 941

It's Here! Hollywood's Ninth Era!   2196
It's How You Play the Game   2177
It's My Fault--I Never Followed the Rules   2154
It's Not Quite All True   1792
It's Only a Movie   40
It's Technology to the Rescue of the Drive-In Movie Theaters   649
It's the Fans Who Make the Films   710, 738
It's the Manner of Telling: Interview With Alfred Hitchcock   1836
It's the Truth Even If It Didn't Happen That Way: Ken Kesey's ONE FLEW OVER
   THE CUCKOO'S NEST   1324
Italian Film Renaissance, The   1607
Italian Neorealism: A Mirror Construction of Reality   1922
Italian-American Demur Gangster Image in Film   826
Italy   2169, 2173
Italy Sotto Voce   2169
Italy's Angry Young Directors   2169
Italy: The Moral Cinema   1922
Itinerant Movie Show and the Development of the Film Industry, The   615, 710,
   1599
Ivan the Magnificent   1001, 2181
IVAN THE TERRIBLE: A Peak In Darien   1645
I. A. L. Diamond is Dead at 67; Won Oscar for THE APARTMENT   1291
I. B. Singer Talks to I. B. Singer About the Movie YENTL   1033
I, Governor of California, and How I Ended Poverty   1233

J

Jack Clayton Interviewed: "I'm Proud of That Film"   1322
Jack Pickford   1392
Jack Valenti's State Department   647
Jackboot Cinema: The Political Propaganda Film in the Third Reich   322
Jacques Becker   1994
Jacques Demy and His Other World   2119
Jacques Demy: Interview   2119
Jacques Rivette   2098
Jail, Freedom and the Screenwriting Profession   1084
James Baldwin: Writing and Talking   540
James Bond and America in the Sixties: An Investigation of the Formula Film in
   Popular Culture   422
James Coburn: His Life and HARD TIMES   2087
James Cruze   1702
James Murray   1707
James M. Cain and the Movies of the Thirties and Forties   1039
James Stewart   1982
James Whale   1808
James Wong Howe   79
Jane Fonda Finds Peace in Her Time   552
Jane Wyatt   1328
Janet Staiger Replies to Dudley Andrew and Gerald Mast   446
Japan   2015, 2016, 2017, 2024, 2177
Japan's Best Movies Don't Travel Well   2177
Japanese Film-Making Today   2024
Japanese Put Up $100 Million to Back Films in Hollywood   2206
Japanese Swordfighters and American Gunfighters   1733, 1737, 1739
Japan: Bullish on Pandas and Pets   2177
Japan: The Younger Talents   2024
Jay Leyda, Film Historian, Writer and a Student of Sergei Eisenstein   1651

Jazzing Up the Old Movie House   752
Jean Cocteau   1995
Jean Renoir and the Popular Front   1813
Jean Renoir's Death Breaks the Line of French Masters   1814
Jean Renoir: A Colossus Among Cinema Directors, Dies at 84   1814
Jean Rouch In Conversation   2120
Jean Rouch: A Pastoral Perspective   2120
Jean Rouch: A Personal Perspective   2120
Jean Vigo   1811, 1828
Jean-Luc Godard   2109
Jean-Luc Godard and Americanism   2109
Jean-Luc Godard and the Childhood of Art   2109
Jean-Luc Godard: Nihilism Versus Aesthetic Direction   2130
Jean-Luc Godard: 2 into 3   2109
Jean-Pierre Leaud: Coming of Age   2155
Jerry Wald and SONS AND LOVERS   1010
Jerzy Skolimowski: Portrait of a Debutant Director   2180
Jessica Lange, Film Star Whose Future is Here   1292
JEUX INTERDITS, LES   2008
Jew on the Screen, The   820
Jewish Gangster: Crime as "Unzer Shtik," The   833
Jewish Images in the French Cinema of the 1930s   227
Jewish Theme in Contemporary Cinema, The   820
Jewison, Norman   2082
JEZEBEL and the Emergence of the Hollywood Tradition of a Decadent
  South   857
JIGOKUMON   2029
Joan Crawford   1803
Joan Crawford's Latest Decade   1803
John Bright, 81, a Screen Writer   1070
John Cassavetes, Major Director in U. S. Cinema Verite, Dies at 59   2048
John Cassavetes, Peter Falk   2074
John Cassavetes: Film's Bad Boy   2074
John Ford   1674, 1802
John Ford and Monument Valley   1674
John Ford 1895-1973   1673
John Ford's Literary Sources: From Realism to Romance   1674
John Ford's THE SEARCHERS: Capitalist Claptrap   2076
John Ford's THE SEARCHERS: Heroic Romance   2076
John Ford's Wilderness--THE MAN WHO SHOT LIBERTY VALANCE   2076
John Ford's YOUNG MR. LINCOLN   477
John Ford: A Reassessment   1673
John Ford: An Epic Half-Century of American Filmmaking   1673
John Ford: Assessing the Reassessment   1673
John Ford: Midway--The War Documentaries   1673
John Frankenheimer   2077
John Frankenheimer: His Rise and Fall   2077
John Frankenheimer: The Smile on the Face of the Tiger   2078
John Grierson and the Documentary Film Movement   215
John Grierson's First Years at the National Film Board   215
John Henry and Mr. Goldberg: The Relationship Between Blacks and Jews   859
John Huston and the Figure in the Carpet   373
John Huston and THE MALTESE FALCON   373
John Huston 1906-1987   1915
John Huston--The Hemingway Tradition in American Film   1321
John Huston, Film Director, Writer, and Actor, Dies at 81   1087, 1915
John Milius   2197
John Mills   1301
John Schlesinger and THE DAY OF THE LOCUST   1291

John Schlesinger: Social Realist 994
JOLI MAI, LE 2152
Joris Ivens Interviewed by Gordon Hitchens, November 20, 1968, American
  Documentaries 217
Joris Ivens, 90, Dutch Documentary Film Maker 314
Joris Ivens: Artist in Documentary 319
Josef Von Sternberg 1674
Joseph Losey, or the Camera Calls 372, 1981
Joseph Rauh: 50 Years, and Counting, of Doing Good 1096
Joshua Logan, Stage and Screen Director, Dies at 79 1264
JOUR DE FETE 2001, 2010
JOUR SE LEVE, LE 1825
JOURNAL D'UN CURE DE CAMPAGNE 2008
Journey Into Fear 903
Journey into the Night 1711
Journey Through India 1004, 2168
Jules Dassin: An Interview 1975
JULIA 1322
JULIUS CAESAR [1953] 1354
Jung/Sign/Symbol/Film, Part One 594
Jung/Sign/Symbol/Film, Part Two 594
Jupiter Revisited--the Odyssey of "2010" 2083
Just How Brechtian is Rossellini? 1922
Justices, in 6-3 Ruling, Ease Curb on Seizure of X-Rated Materials 960
J. Edgar Hoover and the Detective Hero 384

K

KABUKI 1734
Kaddish for the Fading Image of Jews in Film 820, 834
Kanchenjunga: Satyajit Ray at Work on His Film 2168
Kane Mutiny, The 1263
Karl Freund 1640
Katharine Hepburn 1352
Kazan in the Fifties 1980
Keaton at Venice 1672
Keep Them on the Hook 2084
Keeping Up With The Antonionis 1874
Keeping Up With The Beatles 2161
Kelly: Part One . . . Dancer, . . . Director 1980
Kelly: Part Two 1980
Ken Darby 83
Kenji Mizoguchi 1739
Kenneth MacGowan 1577
Keystone to Kojack: The Hollywood Cop 559
Killers, Kisses . . . LOLITA: An Analysis of Stanley Kubrick's Work for
  the Cinema 2083
Kim Hunter 1346
KING KONG 1800
King Vidor 367, 1671
King Vidor at NYU 1671
King Vidor's Play Fails to Go Over 873
King Vidor: A Career That Spans Half A Century 1806
King Vidor: Part 1 1671, 1713
King Vidor: Part 2 1671
KISS ME DEADLY: Evidence of a Style 2072
Kiss Tomorrow Goodbye 2199

KLUTE 1: A Contemporary Film Noir and Feminist Criticism 469, 799
KLUTE 2: Feminism and Klute 799
Knight Without Meaning? Marlowe on the Screen 798
Knocking on Hollywood's Door: Black Filmmakers Like Spike Lee's Struggle to
   See and Be Seen 903
Kon Ichikawa 2023
KOYAANISQATSI: Godfrey Reggio's Filmic definition of the Hopi Concept of "Life
   out of Balance" 598
KRAMER VS. KRAMER 1007
KRAMER VS. KRAMER: A Symposium 1007
KRAMER: When Smaller is Better 1007
Kubrick and His Discontents 2083
Kubrick and the Structures of Popular Culture 2083
Kubrick Goes Gothic 2083
Kubrick's Brilliant Vision 2083
Kuleshov 1645, 1646
Kuleshov: Prophet Without Honor? 1645
Kuntzel's Law and UNCOMMON VALOR, Or, Reshaping the National
   Consciousness in Six Minutes Flat 442
Kurosawa in Winter 2020
Kurosawa on Kurosawa 2019
Kurosawa's Humanism 2019
Kurosawa, Akira 2021

L

L'Avventura 1012
LA DOLCE VITA 1023
LA STRADA 1022
LA STRADA--A Poem on Saintly Folly 1022
LA (The) DOLCE (Sweet) VITA (Life) 1023
Label on 3 Films Backed by Court 962
Labor Relations in Hollywood 1069
LACOMBE LUCIEN 2119
Laddies' Fox Exit Won't Be Prolonged 536
LADRI DI BICICLETTE 1926
Lady and the Director: Bette Davis and William Wyler, The 1348, 1748, 1981
LADY EVE, THE 1921
Lady Vanishes: Women, Magic, and the Movies, The 1590
Land of Promise: The Projection of Peace Aims in Britain, The 216
Landscape of a Mind: Interview With Roman Polanski 2180
Landscape of the Desert, The 1874
Language of Hollywood, The 1310
Laocoon for the Movies, A 1030
Large-Screen Film: A Viable Entertainment Alternative to High Definition
   Television, The 674
LAST ANGRY MAN, THE 1020
Last Days of Alfred Hitchcock, The 1844
LAST PICTURE SHOW, THE 996
Last Sequence of ON THE WATERFRONT, The 1980
LAST TYCOON, THE 1134, 1293
Last Words on Last Year: A Discussion with Alain Resnais and Alain
   Robbe-Grillet 2153
Last Years of Von Stroheim, The 1018
Lately, Seeing Isn't Believing 490
Later Films of William Wyler, The 1748
Later Films of Yasujiro Ozu, The 2024, 2032
Later Years: King Vidor's Hollywood Progress, The 1806

Latest Films Show "Blaxploitation" 906
Latin America: On the Periphery of the Periphery 2178
Latin in Hollywood Films Often Caricature to Latin 826
Laurence Harvey 1016
Laurence Olivier, 82, Classical Actor Is Dead 1862
Lean--Lover of Life 1943
Lear Back in TV Production in a Venture with Columbia 672
Lee Harvey Oswald: An Adlerian Interpretation 586
Lee Rich's Stubborn Optimism 662
Left Bank: Marker, Varda, Resnais, The 2116
Legendary John Ford, 78, Dies; Personally Honored by U. S. 1673
Legion of Lost Films: Part I, The 1674
Leisure and Monopoly Capital: Concentration and Standardization in Franco-U.
  S. Trade in Film 771
Lelouch, Claude 2119
Lena 942
Lena Horne 879
Leni and the Wolf: Interview With Leni Riefenstahl 321
Leni Riefenstahl 321
Leni Riefenstahl: Artifice and Truth in a World Apart 321
Leni Riefenstahl: The Deceptive Myth 539
LES ALLURES DU CHEVAL, Eadweard James Muybridge's Contribution to the
  Motion Picture 1585
LES QUATRE CENT COUPS (THE 400 BLOWS) 1005
Leslie Fiedler and the School of Ekstatics 1028
Lesson in Cinema: Interview With Anthony Mann, An 1982
Lessons Learned in Combat: Interview With Robert Rossen 1014, 1985
Lester Cole, a Screenwriter In "Hollywood 10," Dies at 81 1201
Let's Uproot TV's Image of Blacks 855
Letter from An Unknown Woman 1984
Letter From MANHATTAN 530
Letter from Roger Corman, A 2075
Letters: Harry Langdon 1672
Letters: Hitchcock 1855
Letters: SCHOOL DAZE Days 903
Letters: Spike Lee 903
Libel Suit Is Filed Against MISSING 1021
Liberation in Chains: "The Woman Question" In Hollywood 2207
Library of Congress, The 1522
Life on the Black List 1084
Life Style of Homo Cinematicus 2106
Light of Day 2109
Like Acid: Interview With Louis Malle 2119
Lilith and I 1985
Lillian Gish 1365
Lillian Gish . . . Director 1365
Lillian Gish: Life and Living 1365
Lillian Hellman's Gift to a Young Playwright 1095
Lillian Hellman, Playwright, Author and Rebel, Dies at 77 1095
Limitations of Kracauer, The 100
Limits of Silent Comedy, The 1672
Limits of Spectacle, The 471
Linguistic Models in Early Soviet Cinema 1648
Linkage: Pudovkin's Classics Revisited 1645, 1667, 1668
Linking of Legends: THE GREAT GATSBY and CITIZEN KANE, A 1322
Links in a Chain: PSYCHO and Film Classicism 1843, 2080
Lion Rampant: The Record of M-G-M 1464
Lionel Barrymore 1365

Lionel Barrymore Index, A 1365, 1803
Literary and Film Genres: Toward a Taxonomy of Film 176
Literary Approach, The 39
Literary Origins: Sternberg's THE BLUE ANGEL 1831
Literary Sophistication of Francois Truffaut 2106
Literati Gripe About Crassness But Can't Resist the Rewards, The 1030, 1066
Literature and Film: A Review of Criticism 1163
Literature and Film: Marking Out Some Boundaries 1026
Literature and Philosophy as Narrative Writing 1297
Literature of the Archeology of Cinema, The 1580, 1581, 1615
Literature/Film: A Bibliography 1162, 1163
LITTLE BIG MAN 1320
LITTLE BIG MAN. The Novel and the Film: A Study of Narrative Structure 1320
LITTLE CAESAR and its Role in the Gangster Film Genre 384
Little Fellow's Self Portrait, The 1419
Little Larger than Life: First Part of an Analysis of Wyler's Work for the Cinema,
  A 1006, 1748
Little Larger Than Life: Second Part--A Comparison of Size, A 1006, 1748
LITTLE THIEF: Scenes from the Last Truffaut, The 2106
Little World and the Big: Concerning Ingmar Bergman's FANNY AND
  ALEXANDER 2183
Living on with Lenin 1648, 2181
Living with Laughter 1410
Living-Room War: VCR-Day--World War II Combat Films on Tape 365
Local Hero: Workin' 40 Acres and a Mule in Brooklyn 903
Loew's Inc. 630
Loews Theatres Sold in $160 Million Deal 678
Lola in Los Angeles 2119
London Festival 1000
LONELINESS OF THE LONG DISTANCE RUNNER, THE 997
LONELY VILLA and Griffith's Paradigmatic Style, THE 1390
Lonelyhearts 1301
LONG DAY'S JOURNEY INTO NIGHT 1350
LONG DAY'S JOURNEY INTO NIGHT: An Interview with Sidney Lumet 1350
LONG GOODBYE and CHINATOWN: Debunking the Private Eye Tradition,
  THE 1300
Long Goodbye, The 1301
Long Take, The 100
Long Time on the Little Road, A 1004
Long, Long Road to Brenda Patimkin, The 916
Look at Britain 2159
Looking for Documentary 1869
Looking for the "Great Whatzit": KISS ME DEADLY and FILM NOIR 2072
Looking Homeward--In Vain: The Family in American Film 980
LORD OF THE FLIES 1001, 1002
Lorimar and Warner Case 663
Lorimar's Retreat From Films 536
Losey: Modesty and Eve 1981, 2161
Losey: Puritan Maids 1981
Losses Lead RCA to Cancel Videodisk Player Production 764
Lost Films of Orson Welles, The 1751
Lost Objects and Mistaken Subjects: Film Theory's Structuring Lack 471
Lou Gossett Jr. Battles the Hollywood Stereotype 905
Louis Delluc, Film Theorist, Critic, and Prophet 1711, 1712
Louis Malle 2119
Louis Malle Diagnoses His MURMUR OF THE HEART 2119
Louis Malle on LACOMBE LUCIEN 2119
Louis Malle's Fascination With Life's Turning Points 2119
Louis Malle's France 2119

Louis Malle: An Outsider's Odyssey 2119
Louis Malle: From THE LOVERS to PRETTY BABY 2119
Louis Wolheim 371
LOVED ONE, THE 1294
LOVED ONE: An Irreverent, Invective, Dark Film Comedy, THE 1294
LOVES OF A BLONDE 2164
Lubitsch in the Thirties: Part One 1694
Lucas, George 2197
LUCAS: Teen-Age Romance 997
Luchino Visconti 1874
Luchino Visconti and the Italian Cinema 1874
LUCIA 497
Lucille Ball Dies; Leaves Legacy of Laughter 1757
Lucille Ball, Spirited Doyenne of TV Comedies, Dies at 77 1757
Luigi Pirandello and the Cinema 1335
Luis Alcoriza and the Films of Luis Bunuel 1714
Luis Bunuel: Spanish and Surrealist 1714
Lumet In '69 2084
LUST FOR LIFE 1015

M

M 1831
M-G-M's Backlot 1464
M-G-M's First 30 Years 1464
M-G-M: War Among the Lion Tamers 630
Ma Barker to Von Richthofen: An Interview With Roger Corman 2075
MACBETH 1355
MACBETH into THRONE OF BLOOD 1356
Mack Sennett 1411
MACK & MABEL and Silent Film Era 1410
MADAME DE 2010
MADAME DE: a Musical Passage 497
Madcap Mabel Normand: The True Story of a Great Comedienne 1412
Made for Each Other: The Melodrama of Hollywood and the House Committee on
  Un-American Activities, 1947 559
Madness, Authority, and Ideology in the Domestic Melodramas of the 1950's 792
Mad, Mad World of Mel Brooks, The 2073
Mae Marsh 1365
Mae Marsh Since '32 1365
Mae Marsh, Robert Harron, and D. W. Griffith 1365
Maesto on Fantasy, Finance and the Art of Film, The 1927
Mafia on Film, The 384
MAGNIFICENT AMBERSONS, THE 1327
MAGNIFICENT SEVEN, THE 2031
Major Directions of German Feminist Cinema, The 2165
Make Money, Not War 2200
Making an Old Thing New: Kurosawa's Film Adaptation of Shakespeare's
  MACBETH 1356
Making of Denmark Vesey's Rebellion, The 252
Making of Mervyn LeRoy, The 1804
Making of ONE FLEW OVER THE CUCKOO'S NEST, The 1324
Making Peace with the 60s 2088
Making the Devil Useful 39
Making the Past Live: Inaccuracy in Historical Films 254
Making the Screen Speak 1330
Malle: PRETTY BABY Could Be Called "The Apprenticeship of Corruption" 2119

Malling of the Movies, The   670, 2203
MALTESE FALCON, THE   373
Mamet's Dark View of Hollywood As a Heaven for the Virtueless   1136
Mamet, Foote and Words on Film   1039
Man for All Movies: The Films of Fred Zinnemann, A   1989
MAN FOR ALL SEASONS, A   1020
Man From Casablanca (Julius J. Epstein), The   1083
MAN IN THE WHITE SUIT, THE   1942
Man Ray as Film Maker: Part I   1713
Man Ray as Film Maker: Part II   1713
Man Who Made GONE WITH THE WIND, The   812
Man Who Made Serials, The   1455
MAN WHO SHOT LIBERTY VALANCE, THE   2076
MAN WHO SHOT LIBERTY VALANCE: A Study of John Ford's Film, THE   2076
Man Who Turned Art Upside Down, Inside Out, The   2040
Man With the Movie Camera, The   1669
Man's Right to Know Before He Dies: A Powerful New Anti-War Film From Britain,
   THE WAR GAME   1024
Man's World, A   424
Man's World: An Analysis of the Films of William Wellman, A   1674
Man's World: Concluding An Analysis of the Films of William Wellman, A   1674
Manchild In the Promised Land   2196
Mandates of Good Taste: The Self-Regulation of Film Advertising in the
   Thirties   1438
Manhandling the Movies   1316
Mankiewicz: The Thinking Man's Director, The   1981
Mann and His Environment: First Part of an Analysis of Anthony Mann's Work
   for the Cinema   1982
Mann In the Dark   1982
Mannerisms--in the Grand Manner   1981
Many Voices of Donald Ogden Stewart, The   1104
Marcel Carne and the Nazis   1910
MARIENBAD Revisited   2153
Mario Bellocchio: An Interview   2173
Marion Mack Is Dead; Silent-Film Actress, 87   1687
Mark Robson   375
Mark Twain on the Screen   1300
Marker and Resnais: Myth and Reality   2115, 2117
Market Place: Dramatic Rise of Vistar Films   535
Market Research: Beyond the Fanny of Cohn   754
Marketing a Movie is More Than Selling Jell-o   611
Marketing Magic, With Rabbit, for Disney Films   668
Marketing Movies for Children   610
Marshall Neilan   1393
Martin Scorsese Fights Back   2197
MARTY   1008, 2197
Martyr Complexes   1324
Marxism and Formalism in the Films of Luchino Visconti   1884
Mary   1391
Mary Astor, 81, Is Dead; Star of MALTESE FALCON   373
Mary Beth Hughes   1021
Mary Miles Minter   966
Mary Pickford   1391, 1392
Mary Pickford (1893-1979): The Star the Working Class Found   1391
Mary Pickford's Directors   1391, 1392
Mary Pickford: Herself and Her Career   1391
Masculinity in the Movies: TO LIVE AND DIE IN L. A.   806
Masks and Faces: An Interview With John Cassavetes   2074
Masochism and Subjectivity   470

Masochism and the Perverse Pleasure of the Cinema   470
Masquage: The Multi-Image Film   2039
Masque: An Extrapolation of Eisenstein's Theory of Montage-as-Conflict to the
    Multi-Image Film   1645
Mass Communication and Para-Social Interaction: Observations on Intimacy at a
    Distance   544, 545
Mass Communication and the Social Sciences: Some Neglected Areas   745
Mass Communications   749
Mass Communications Research: An Old Road Resurveyed   745
Mass Culture and the Creative Artist: Some Personal Notes   220
Mass Culture Revisited   548, 552
Mass Entertainment in Perspective: The Need for a Theory of the Middle
    Range   855
Mass Media and Children: A Study of Exposure Habits and Cognitive
    Effects   745
Mass Produced Photoplays: Economic and Signifying Practices in the First Years
    of Hollywood   1463
Mass Society and Mass Culture   459, 461
Master of Poetic Confusion: John Cassavetes   2048
Master of Suspense: An Analysis of Hitchcock's Work for the Cinema, Part 1,
    A   1836
Master of Suspense: An Analysis of Hitchcock's Work for the Cinema, Part 2,
    A   1836
Master of the Movies   2108
Mastery of Movement: An Appreciation of Max Ophuls   2010
Max Linder   1419
Max Ophuls   2010
Max Ophuls: An Introduction   2010
Max Steiner   83
Maysles Brothers and "Direct Cinema," The   2041
Maysles: Filming the Impossible   2085
MCA Turns Hand to Acquisitions   662
Meadow, The   1234
Mean, Moody and Magnificent   388
Measure for Measure: Interview With Joseph L. Mankiewicz   1039, 1981
Mechanized Muse, The   1105
Media and Manners: Film and Society In Some Current British Films   2159
Media as Business: A Brief History   613
Meditation, the Novelistic, and Film Narrative   1297
Meet Me In Las Vegas   2196
Meet the New Director: Robert Redford of ORDINARY PEOPLE   1009
Meet Whiplash Wilder   1987
Mel Brooks and the Cinema of Exhaustion   837
Mel Gussow's Biog of Zanuck Cues an Untold Story Yet to Be Written   1501
Melodrama   712
Melodrama and the American Cinema   713, 716
Melodrama: Postmortem for a Phantom Genre   712, 715
Melting Pot and the Humoring of America: Hollywood and the Jew, The   820,
    824
Melville on the Screen   1300
Melville, Jean-Pierre   2000
Melvin Van Peebles   879
MEMBER OF THE WEDDING, THE   997
Memories of a Past Master   1814
MEMORIES OF PRISON   2158
Memories of Prison: An Interview With Nelson Pereira Dos Santos   2158
Memories of Resnais   2116
Men Who Made "GREY GARDENS": What Makes the Maysles Run?, The   2085

Mentshlekhkayt Conquers All: The Yiddish Cinema in America 829, 830
Merely Players: The Impact of Shakespeare on International Cinema 1009, 1342
Merely Stupendous 1745
Merit of Flying Lead, The 1987
Mervyn LeRoy, 86, Dies; Director and 1748
Metafictional Hitchcock: The Experience of Viewing and the Viewing of
 Experience in REAR WINDOW and PSYCHO 1978
Metaphor: An Interview With Arthur Penn 1320
Method and Why: An Account of the Actor's Studio, The 1434
Method Master: Rod Steiger's Career 1980
Method of Constructing Lost Films, A 1524
Method of John Ford, The 1351
Method of THE SEARCHERS, The 980, 2076
Method of WHY WE FIGHT, The 281
Methodological Evaluation of Thurstone's Movie Attitude Scale 462
Metro-Goldwyn-Mayer 630
METROPOLIS 1642
METROPOLIS: The Lights Fantastic--Semiotic Analysis of Lighting Codes in
 Relation to Character and Theme 1642
Mexican Bunuel, The 1002
Mexican Cinema: A Panoramic View 2167, 2178
Mexico: From the Golden Age to the Present 2178
MGM/UA Accepts New Quintex Bid 2205
MGM/UA May Sell Unit Assets 663
MGM/UA's Plan to Spin Off a Studio Collapses 662
MGM/UA, HBO in Film Deal 678
MGM, Its Image Bruised, Is Straining to Find Hits 663
Mice in the Milk 1981
Michael Curtiz 372, 800
Michael Powell: Myths and Supermen 801
Michael Roemer and Robert Young: Film Makers of NOTHING BUT A MAN 952
Michelangelo Antonioni and the Imagery of Disintegration 1874
Michelangelo in Disneyland: ZABRISKIE POINT 1874
Middle Chabrol 2098, 2099, 2105
MIDSUMMER NIGHT'S DREAM, A 1355
Mighty Money Machine, The 622
Mike Nichols: The Special Risks and Rewards of the Director's Art 2085
Miklos Rozsa 83
Mildred Pierce Meets the Bad Seed 1003
MILDRED PIERCE Reconsidered 800
Milestones Can be Millstones 889
Milius the Barbarian 2197
Milos Forman's America Is Like Kafka's--Basically Comic 2164
Mind of the Mob: Hollywood and Popular Culture in the 1930s, The 559
Mind's Eye 2083
Mini-Series Mogul Dips Into History Again, A 549
Mini-Series Teaches ABC Hard Lessons, A 2205
Minnelli and Melodrama 714
Minnelli's Magic 1983
Minor Disappointments 1985
MIRACLE OF MORGAN'S CREEK, THE 1921
Miracle of the Movie, The 723
Mirror of Discontent: THE MARCH OF TIME and Its Politically Controversial Film
 Issues 281
Mirror Phase as Formative of the Function of the "I," The 480
Mirth, Sexuality, and Suspense: Alfred Hitchcock's Adaptation of THE
 THIRTY-NINE STEPS 1864
Mise-En-Scene in John Ford's MY DARLING CLEMENTINE 1976
MISSING 1021

MISSING By Costa-Gavras 1021
Missing Idol, The 1234
MISSING in Action: Costa-Gavras Interviewed 1021
Mississippi Theater Bans Film on Death of Rights Workers 255
Mixed Reviews for Wyman 678
Mizoguchi and Modernism: Structure, Culture, Point of View 1739
Mizoguchi and Ozu--Two Masters from Japan 2018
Mizoguchi Spectrum 1739, 1890
Mizoguchi's Oppressed Women 497
Mizoguchi: The Ghost Princess and the Seaweed Gatherer 1739
Modern Apocalypse: THE WAR GAME, The 1024
Modern Hero: The Nongenue, A 789
Modern Times 1432
Modes of Definition: Running Order Through Chaos 1297
Modesty and Pretension in Two New Films 2015, 2031
Mogul--That's a Jewish Word 819, 820
Monogram: Its Rise and Fall in the 1940s 640
Monopoly in Motion Picture Production and Distribution: 1908-1915 607, 697,
  1459, 1462
Monsieur Verdoux 1433
Monster and Victim: Women in the Horror Film 529
Monster Marathon, The 2089
Monster Movies: A Sexual Theory 388, 975
Monster Movies: They Came from Beneath the Fifties 388
Monsters from the Id--an Examination of the Science Fiction Film Genre 409
Montage of Attractions 1646
Montana Becomes 21st State to Outlaw Blind-Bid Practice 676
Mood Music: An Inquiry into Narrative Film Music 400
Moral Dimension in Documentary, The 214
Morality of PLATOON, The 368
More British Sounds 2159
Mormons as Silent Cinema Villains: Propaganda and Entertainment 826
Morning Comes for Frances 1292
Mort Sahl Called Me a 1939 American 2087
Mosaic of Moviegoing, The 2106
Moscow K.O.'s ABC in the First Round 549
Mother of the New Wave: An Interview With Agnes Varda 2114, 2115
Motion Picture and the Novel, The 1298
Motion Picture as Metaphor in the Works of F. Scott Fitzgerald, The 1108, 1110,
  1115
Motion Picture Attendance and Social Isolation 744
Motion Picture Attendance: A Market Segmentation Approach 748, 770
Motion Picture Audience: A Neglected Aspect of Film Research, The 768
Motion Picture Economics 607, 635, 641, 736
Motion Picture Exhibition in Manhattan, 1906-1912: Beyond the Nickelodeon 719
Motion Picture Experience as Modified by Social Background and Personality,
  The 749
Motion Picture Film Widths 655
Motion Picture Patents Company: A Reevaluation, The 607, 619, 1460, 1461
Motion Picture Technique: A Basic Library 71
Motion Pictures and Crime 724
Motion to Reinstate Ban on Splits Denied Distrib'rs by Calif. Court 677
Motive, Mischief and Melodrama: The State of Film Narrative in 1907 1361
Movement, Color and Sound in a "Darke Roome" 1580
Movie and Myth 814
Movie Audiences, Urban Geography, and the History of the American Film 623,
  705
Movie Chronicle: The Westerner 424

Movie Code: A View from Parents and Teenagers 959
Movie Genres: Toward a Conceptualized Model and Standardized Definitions 771
Movie House, The 1234
Movie Investments, Not Always Stars 743
Movie Jew as an Image of Assimilation, 1903-1927, The 819, 824, 825
Movie Magic Returns 1013
Movie Mailbag: And Now--The War of the Welles 1792
Movie Majors, The 667
Movie Merchandise: The Rush Is On 488
Movie Palaces and Exhibition 622
Movie Pre-History 1582
Movie Ratings System, The 960
Movie Review: KAGEMUSHA (SHADOW WARRIOR) 2019
Movie Review: THE WARRIORS 973
Movie Studios Prepare for a Record Summer 2206
Movie Theater of the Future: The Home? 2202
Movie Theater Owners are Bullish on Future 755
MOVIE vs. Kael 2096
Movie's and Man's Humanity 40
Movie-Themed Films Aimed at Large Record-Buying Audience 488, 611
Moviegoing and American Culture 553
Moviemakers Come to Main Street 658
Movies and Audiences: A Reasonable Approach to American Film Criticism 581
Movies and Man's Humanity 952
Movies and Poetry, The 1025
Movies and Propaganda 218
Movies and Reality, The 1309
Movies and the Teenager 748
Movies Are Better than Ever--On Television 653, 2202
Movies Become Big Business: Public Theatres and the Chain-Store Strategy,
  The 697
Movies by Metronome 2156
Movies in Vaudeville: Historical Context of the Movies as Popular Entertainment,
  The 621, 718
Movies Look Abroad for Profit 488
Movies on Television 753, 779
Movies Swing an Election, The 226
Movies that Play for Keeps 2081
Movies to Sell the Reich 227
Movies, Mommies, and the American Dream 982
Movies, Mr. Griffith, and Us, The 1382
Movies, Race, and World War II: TENNESSEE JOHNSON as an Anticipation of the
  Strategies of the Civil Rights Movement 856
Movies: Stereotypes or Realities?, The 546
Movies: The Celluloid President 1088
Moving Picture and Historical Research, The 265
MPAA Figures For 1976, Contrasts VARIETY Index 752
Mr. Film Noir Stays at the Table: An Interview With Robert Aldrich 2071
Mr. Ford and Mr. Rogers: The Will Rogers Trilogy 1673
Mr. Hulot and Time 2007
Multiplexes Add 2,300 Movie Screens in 5 Years 752
Murder: A Big Problem 220
Murdoch Officially Closes Fox Deal to be Sole Studio Owner 663
Murdoch to Unite Fox 678
Murnau's Midnight and Sunrise 1706
Museum Cancels China Film 489
Music Makers: Elmer Bernstein and Jerry Goldsmith, The 83
Music of the Fears 83
Music Video and the Spectator: Television, Ideology and Dream 584

Musical Fantasy: THE LITTLE PRINCE   416
Musketeers of Pig Alley and the Well-made Sausage   1363
Mutual Approval of Keaton and Lloyd, The   1672
My Experience   2010
My Life on the Blacklist   1084
My Name is Joseph H. Lewis   743
My Name Isn't Costello   1076
My Three Powerfully Effective Commandments   2183
My Way of Working Is In Relation to the Future: A Conversation With Carl
  Dreyer   2189
Mysteries of Cassette Love   2202
Mysteries of Cocteau's ORPHEUS, The   2009
Myth and Reality   177
Myth Maker: The Creative Mind of Novelist E. L. Doctorow, The   1032
Myth of Old Movies: An Interpretation of Dreams, The   547
Myth of Persistence of Vision, The   1583
Myth of the Southern Box Office: A Factor in Racial Stereotyping in American
  Movies, 1920-1940, The   854
Myth of Total Cinema, The   129, 167
Myth That Won't Go Away: Selling Out in Hollywood, The   1028, 1031, 1038
Mythical Method: Fictionalizing the Vietnam War, The   442
Mythos of Stardom: Judy Garland and Liza Minnelli, The   1138
Mythos of "The Sickness Unto Death": Kurosawa's IKIRU and Tolstoy's THE
  DEATH OF IVAN ILLYCH, The   2030
M. P. A. A. Ratings and the Box Office: Some Tantalizing Statistics   753, 2202
M*A*S*H, McCloud and McCabe: An Interview With Robert Altman   379
M: A Reconsideration   1641, 1831

N

N Word, The   2206
NAKED CITY, THE   1975
Naming Names: Sam Ornitz, James Cagney, the Hollywood Reds, and Me   1084,
  1085
NANOOK OF THE NORTH   1703
NAPOLEON Campaigns in the Battle for Preservation   1726
Napoleon of the Cinema   1605
Narrated Cinema: The Pioneer Story Films of James A. Williamson, A   1606
Narrative and Infra-Narrative in Film   1297
Narrative Discourse in Film and Fiction: The Question of the Present Tense,
  The   1297
Nathanael West's Dream Dump   1162
Nation in Crisis: Hollywood's Response to the 1940s, The   559
National Conference on the Teaching of Film, The   39
National Types as Hollywood Presents Them   857
Native American Women in Westerns: Reality and Myth   454
Nativism and Assimilation: the Hollywood Aspect   823
Natural Phenomenon: Interview With Elia Kazan, A   1005
Nature of Evidence   282
Nature of Propaganda, The   206
Nature of the Viewing Experience: The Missing Variable in the Effects Equation,
  The   490
Nazi Architecture--A Blueprint for World Domination   251
Nazi Control of the German Film Industry, The   227
Nazi Film Propaganda In Occupied France   1903
Nazi Musicologist as Myth Maker in the Third Reich, The   209
Nazi Party Election Films, 1927-1938   321

Nazi Propaganda in Occupied Western Europe: The Case of the Netherlands   251
Nazi Reframes: Negative Stereotyping In American Reviews of New German
  Films   2165
Nazi Retro Films: Experiencing the Mistakes of the Ordinary Citizen   358
Nazi Wartime Newsreel Propaganda   202, 255
Nazis and Japs   374
Nazis Return, The   322
Necessity of Confrontation Cinema: Peter Watkins Interviewed, The   1024
Need for Statistical Research   738
Needs of Film/TV Education, 1977, The   42
Needs of Motion Picture Audiences, The   706, 734, 736, 742, 752
Neglected Pioneer, A   1586
Negro Actor and the American Movies, The   873, 942
Negro and the Cinema, The   942
Negro in American Films, The   860, 871
Negro in American Films: Some Recent Works, The   893, 894, 942
Negro in Hollywood: A Critical Study of Entertainment Films Containing Negro
  Themes, A   860
Negro in THE BIRTH OF A NATION, The   1383
Negro Invades Hollywood, The   881, 942
NEGRO SOLDIER (1944): Propaganda in Black and White, THE   303
Negroes Ask for Better Shade in Pictures   879
Negroes in Films   890
Netherlands, The   2179
Networks Raise Ratings By Showing More Films   678
Never to Be Thirty-Six Years Old: REBECCA as Female Oedipal Drama   1835
Never-Ending Western Movie, The   1234
New Allies for Studios In Challenge of Networks   2205
New American Gothic   1985
New Approach to Film History, A   252, 1509, 1515, 1516
New Ballgame: The Cartridge Revolution, The   672
New Black Cinema and Uses of the Past   949
New Czech Film, The   2164
New Departures for Two Major Directors   2196
New Documentaries of Frederick Wiseman, The   2092
New Egyptian Cinema: Adapting Genre Conventions to a Changing Society,
  The   2178
New Electronic Media: An Overview, The   764
New Films From Poland   2179
New Hollywood Cinema   471
New Hollywood: De Laurentiis's Moves Point Up the Changes in Economics of
  Films   658
New Hollywood: Mel Brooks Interviewed   2073
New Hollywood: Myth and Anti-Myth, The   815, 2034
New Issue as VCR's Expand: Violent Films and the Young   961
New Kid on Bloc   2167
New Laocoon: Artistic Composites and the Talking Film, A   1030
New Lease on Life for New World   673
New Lon Chaney Index, A   1702
New Mexican Cinema, The   2178
New Money in Movies, The   488
New Negro on the Screen, The   893
New Road to Progress: The Use and Production of Films by the Labour
  Movement, 1929-39, The   214
New Serbo-Creationism, The   2014
New Sex Symbols, The   1137
New Studies Examine Sexual Guilt   1000
New Technology Moving into Films   675
New Trends in Exhibition   676

New Trends in Exhibition Deals 676
New TV Technologies Alter Viewing Habits 545
New Tycoons of Hollywood, The 2197
New Video Technologies: System Will Permit Shopping at Home, The 762
New Vietnam Films: Is the Movie Over?, The 442
New Wave and French Cinema 2093
New Wave or Gestures 2093
New World Accepts Offer by Pathe 673
New World of Roger Corman, The 2075
New World's New Order 673
New York as Film Setting and as Star 658
New York Film Festival 580
New York Letter: Towards a Spontaneous Cinema 2039
New "Great Era" For Movies: What's Behind the Comeback 751, 2195
News Media at War, The 255
Next Steps in Film History Research 1513
Next Stop, Tinseltown 2206
Nicholas Ray on the Years at RKO 1984
Nicholas Ray, Without a Cause 1985
Nicholas Ray, 67; Director of Films 1985
Nicholas Ray: Rebel! 1984
Nicholas Ray: The Last Movies 1985
Nicholas Ray: The Years at RKO--Part One 1984
Nicholas Ray: The Years at RKO--Part Two 1984
Nichols, Mike 2085
Nickelodeon Theaters, 1905-1914: Building an Audience for the Movies 710, 719,
   722
Nickelodeons and Common Shows Over the Hill 1310
Night and Day, Truffaut Is the One 2154
NIGHT OF THE HUNTER 1315
NIGHT OF THE SHOOTING STARS from Italy 377
NIGHT OF THE SHOOTING STARS, THE 377
Night or Day, Truffaut's the One 2154
Nightmare and Nostalgia: The Cinema of Sam Peckinpah 2087
Nightmare and the Horror Film: The Symbolic Biology of Fantastic Beings 593
Nightmare World of Hitchcock's Women, The 598
Night, Eclipse, Dawn: An Interview With Michelangelo Antonioni 1874
Nina Mae McKinney Is Big Hit At Lafayette 873
Nineteen Fifties' Production 740
Nineteen Fifties: The Case of Elia Kazan and ON THE WATERFRONT, The 559
Nineteen Seventy-Five Film Biz: At 12-Year High; Some Big Buts 2198
Nineteen Seventy-Five to Nineteen-Eighty Five: Ten Years that Shoot the
   World 2190
Nineteen-Fifty-Four in Japan 2024
Nineteen-Twenty-Four Olympics Recreated in English Work 1013
Ninteen Seventy-Five Film Biz: At 12-Year High 2198
No Attempt at Artiness, Profundity, or Significance: FIRESIDE THEATER and
   the Rise of Filmed Television Programming 653
No Depth on WUTHERING HEIGHTS 1327
NO LIES: Direct Cinema as Rape 295
No More Suzie Wongs: Chinese Women in the Movies 789
No Villains, No Heroes--Part One: A Curious Madness 1082, 1084
No Villains, No Heroes--Part Two: A Time of Evil 1084
No Way Out: Existential Motifs in the FILM NOIR 1947
Nobody Has Any Fun in Bergman's Movies 2183
Nobody Waved Goodbye 1008
Non Humans, The 409
NORTH BY NORTHWEST 2079

North Lights and Cigarette Bulb: Conversations with Cameramen   79
Nostalgia Isn't What It Used To Be: The Middle Ages in Literature and
  Film   416
Not a Garbo or a Gilbert in the Bunch: Alan Pakula Talks With Tom Milne   800,
  2195
Not Developing An Indigenous Film Industry: The Case of the New German
  Cinema   618
Not Just Another Charlie Bluhdorn   2205
Not Just Child's Play   970
Not What They Seem   576
Note From the Editors . . . , A   482
Note on Eisenstein's Shot Montage of a Monologue from Pushkin's Drama BORIS
  GODUNOV, A   1645
Note on Novels and Films, A   1298
Note on Progress, A   1522
Note on the Film, A   144
Notes on a New Generation   2093
Notes on an Early Losey   1981
Notes on Black Movies   896, 897, 942
Notes on Columbia Pictures Corp., 1926-41   252, 1509, 1515
Notes on Current Griffith Research   1360
Notes on Evolving Heroes, Morals, Audiences   801
Notes on Experience and the Teaching of Film: Brock University   38
Notes on Film Acting   1327, 1434
Notes on FILM NOIR   1947
Notes on Film Scholarship, Criticism, Methodology, and What Are We Doing Here
  Anyway?   1523
Notes on LES ENFANTS DU PARADIS   1910
Notes on Preston Sturges and America   1912
Notes on Propaganda   201
Notes on Robert Bresson   1023, 1994
Notes on Robert Rossen   1014, 1985
Notes on Rossen Films   1014, 1985
Notes on Sirk & Melodrama   794, 1986
Notes on Suture   591
Notes on the Art of John Ford   1019, 1673
Notes on the Auteur Theory in 1962   2097
Notes on THE BIG SLEEP--Thirty Years After   798
Notes on the Melodrama and the Family under Capitalism   792
Notes on the New American Cinema   2074, 2075
Notes on the New Stylization   2034
Notes on the Spatial System of Ozu's Early Films   1742
Notes on the Style of Von Stroheim   1018
Notes on the Text, "John Ford's YOUNG MR. LINCOLN"   477
Notes on Theater-and-Film   1105
Notes on Warner Brothers Foreign Policy, 1918-1948   227
Notes on "Camp"   144
Notes Towards a Structural Analysis of the Films of Samuel Fuller   1977
Nothing to Lose: Interview With Andy Warhol   2039
Notion of Genre, The   176
Nouvelle Vague or Jeune Cinema   2093
Novel into Film   1297
Novel Into Film: An Experimental Course   1297
Novel Novel: Fable Fable?   1301
Novelist Looks At Hollywood, A   1105, 1297
Novelists in the Dream Factory   1043
Novels and Films: A Limited Inquiry   1297
Now and Nowhere: Roeg's BAD TIMING   495
Now You See It: Landscape and Anthony Mann   1982

NOW, VOYAGER: Some Problems of Enunciation and Sexual Difference   801
NR=MC2: Rossellini, "Neo-Realism," and Croce   1922
Nuclear Family War   605
Nurturance and Rejection in Woody Allen's INTERIORS and Ingmar Bergman's
  Melodramas   2072

O

O Young Men of the New Age   1013
O'Neill on the Screen   1335
Obits: Sam Peckinpah--No Bleeding Heart   2062
Obituary on Dorothy Gish   1365
Obituary on Eugene Pallette   1366
Obituary on Florence Lawrence   1365
Obituary on Harry Carey   1366
Obituary on Lionel Barrymore   1365
Obituary on Mae Marsh   1365
Obituary on Marshall Neilan   1393
Obscene Undertaking, An   1301
Observations on Keaton's STEAMBOAT BILL   1672
Obsession   2196
Obsession in the Melodrama: Amy Jones' LOVE LETTERS   792
Obstinate Audience, The   745
Obvious and the Code, The   82
Odd Couple, The   1352
Odd Jobs and Subsidies: Nathanael West in Hollywood   1291
Oddities and One-Shots   2074
Ode to the Old Left   379
Of Canons and Quietism: Dudley Andrew Responds to Janet Staiger's "The
  Politics of Film Canons"   447
Of Motion Pictures   880
Of Movies and Men   809
Of the Movies   941
Off-Screen: Konography   2022, 2023
Offscreen Space: Images of Early Cinema Production and Exhibition   1587
Oh! Oh! Antonioni   1012, 2172
Oh, You Sundance Kid!   2079
Oklahoma Kid   998
Old Age of Alfred Hitchcock, The   1835
Old Dependables, The   1944, 1988
Old Lie, The   265
Old Master Re-Visited   1674
Old Movies Come Alive   2193
Old Pix Don't Die, They Just Fade Away   1514
Oliver Stone   368
Olivier's RICHARD III: A Reevaluation   1354
Olivier, Hamlet, and Freud   1353
Olivier: Exit the Emperor   1862
Olvidados, Los   1002
Omegaville   2109
On Akira Kurosawa   2019
On Andy Warhol   2039
On Being Under a Director's Spell   1016
On Cinematography   79
On Cocteau   2009
On Film   1309
On Film Editing   82

On Film Music 83
On Hollywood--and Valentino 1674
On Independent Black Cinema 853, 950
On Jewish Hollywood 845
On Kenji Mizoguchi 1739
On Location With Billy Wellman 1674
On Mae Marsh 1365
On Playing Wilson 366
On Style 978
On Suspense and Other Film Matters: An Interview With Alfred Hitchcock 1836
On the Future of the Movies 753
On the History and Ideology of Film Lighting 79, 719
On the Naked Thighs of Miss Dietrich 1831
On the Road to MGM: A History of Metro Pictures Corporation 1465
On the Search for the Real Nitty-Gritty: Problems and Possibilities in CINEMA
  VERITE 2040
On the Track of Hiroshi Shimizu 1891, 1892
On the Trail of the Unknown Chaplin 1414
On The Use of the Mass Media as Escape: Clarification of a Concept 745
On the Warpath: John Ford and the Indians 1673
On Turning Books into Movies 1032, 1037
On Violence . . . 750
On War and the Movies: A Reappraisal 257
On Writing for the Films 1309
Once Again, the White Liberal to the Rescue 900
ONE FLEW OVER THE CUCKOO'S NEST 1324
ONE FLEW OVER THE CUCKOO'S NEST: Some Reasons for One Happy
  Adaptation 1324
One Man's China: An Interview With Felix Greene 2163
One of the Hollywood 10 Revisits Moscow 1180
One or Two Things 2109
One Path to Colour: An Autobiographical Fragment 1645
One Psychological Moment, Please 816
One. . . Two. . . Three. . .: A Study of the War Film 280
Only Connect: Some Aspects of the Work of Humphrey Jennings 317
Only in Hollywood 536
Open Approach to Film Study and the Situation at Iowa, An 37, 38
Open City 1933
Operating on Metaphor: Using Film/Activities to Explore Feelings 978
Ophuls and the Romantic Tradition 2010
Oppositional Exhibition: Notes and Problems 471
Optical Effects 79
Oral Tradition, the Written Word and the Screen Image, The 1299
Ordeal by Disney: Little Bit Goes a Long Way 1084, 1085
ORDINARY PEOPLE 1009
Organic Unity and Pathos in the Composition of POTEMKIN 1666
Oriental Bad Boys 1000
Origin of the Star System 1434
Origins of United Artists, The 1464
ORPHEE 2009
Orson Welles 1022
Orson Welles and John Ford: History and Myth in Film 175
Orson Welles and the Big Experimental Film Cult 1022
Orson Welles and the Great American Dummy 1327
Orson Welles Began An Ongoing Revolution 1751
Orson Welles is Dead at 70; Innovator of Film and Stage 1751
Orson Welles: An Introduction 1750
Oscar Micheaux: Pioneer Filmmaker 866
Oscar Syndrome, The 1099

Oscar-Winning DEER HUNTER is Under Attack as "Racist" Film   367
Other Brando: The Surprising World of Paul Newman, The   1014
Other Hitchcock, The   1836
Other Side of the Curtain, The   2181
Our Awkward Ally   259
Our Crowd   836
Our Dream Cinema: Western Historiography and the Japanese Cinema   2018
Our Foreign Trade in Motion Pictures   226, 625
Our Own Past, Lost and Gone, is in GRAFFITI   993
Our Resources for Film Scholarship   1522
Out of Affluence   761
Out of This World   409
Out Of What Past? Notes on the "B" Film Noir   1947
Outrage: A Print Documentary on Westerns   424
Over the Brink   264
Overview   481, 482
Overview of Cinema on the Fairgrounds, The   1599
OWI Goes to the Movies: The Bureau of Intelligence's Criticism of Hollywood, 1942-1943   229
Ozu   1742
Ozu Spectrum   1742, 1892, 1902

P

Packaging Pop Mythology   180
Pageantry Colors a Historical Portrait   548
Pagnol, From the Source   1809
Pained Lucas Ponders Attack on WILLOW, A   673
Paint It Black: The Family Tree of FILM NOIR   1947
Painting the Leaves Black: Rouben Mamoulian Interviewed   1803
PAISA   1925
Pakula's Approach   799
Pakula, Alan J.   2195
Pale Black Imitation: All-Colored Films, 1930-60, A   860, 882
Pam Grier: Coming into Focus   897
Panel Calls on Citizens to Wage National Assault on Pornography   961
Pantheon Directors   1674
Paradigmatic Structures in YOUNG MR. LINCOLN   477
Parameters of the Open Film: LES VACANCES DE MONSIEUR HULOT   2011
Paramount   635
Paramount Adds to Bid for Time   2205
Paramount Bid Lifts Time by $44   2204
Paramount Bids for Time Inc.; Battle With Warner Is Likely   2204
Paramount Deal With Showtime Shakes Pay-TV   653
Paramount Decrees Reconsidered, The   663
Paramount Delay Cited by Citibank   2205
Paramount Faults Time Over Stockholder Data   2205
Paramount Pictures   621
Paramount Pictures' Success Key to Revamping at G&W   2205
Paramount Raises Bid For Time   2205
Paramount to Acquire Right to 5 TV Stations   672
Paramount, Part II   635
Paramount: Oscar for Profits   621
Paranoia and the Film System   471
PARIS NOUS APPARTIENT   2098
Part Four: The Russian Cinema   1648

Participation of Our Schools in the Defense and Diffusion of Our National
  Culture, The 42
Parting of the Ways: A Cuban-American View 2163
Parting of the Ways: An Interview With Jesus Diaz 2163
Pascal's Wagner and the Feminist Dilemma in Eric Rohmer's MY NIGHT AT
  MAUD'S 598
Pasolini 2171
Passing of a Master, The 1854
Passion of Henri Langlois, The 2006
Passion of Joan of Arc, The 1729
Pat Hobby: Anti-Hero 1128, 1129, 1133
Pather Panchali and Aparajito 1004
Patterns in Wartime Documentaries 284
Patterns of Cinema: American Youth in Uproar 982
Patterns of Power 1939
Patterns of Power and Potency, Repression and Violence: Sirk's Films of the
  1950s 1986
Patterns of Production and Employment in Hollywood 607, 610
Paul Robeson and Black Identity in American Movies 875
Paul Robeson: His Career in the Theatre, in Motion Pictures, and on the Concert
  Stage 875
Paul Robeson: The Black Man as Film Hero 875
Paying Homage to Mozart 1330
Payment Anticipated 1234
Peace With Honor: Cowboys and Viet Cong 367
Peckinpah In from the Cold Mexico 2087
Peckinpah In Mexico 2087
Peckinpah's Return 2087
Penn, Arthur 2088
People and the Pictures. The British Working Class and Film in the 1930's,
  The 214, 242
People Who Need People 1323
People's Attitudes Toward Motion Pictures 751
PERFORMANCE 2160
Perils of Pauline, The 151
PERSONAL BEST: Women in Love 590
Personal Record, A 2176
Personality Correlates of Physiological Responses to Motion Pictures 754
Personality Determinants of Mass Media Preferences 533
Perspectives on War: A Teaching Unit of Films 200
Persuasion At The Pictures 243
Peter Pan Generation Makes Room for Small Fry, The 971
Peter Watkins Discusses His Suppressed Nuclear Film THE WAR GAME 1024
Phantom India 2119
Phantom of Personality, The 2183
Phases of Cinema Unity: II 1033
Philip Marlows: Which Is Chandler's Ideal Detective? The Case of Raymond
  Chandler 1947
Philosophy and Film 52
Photography/Cinematography 1587
Pickford Story 1391
PICKUP ON SOUTH STREET and the Metamorphosis of the Thriller 1977
PICNIC 1002
Pictorial Imagery in Kozintsev's KING LEAR 1355
Picture Palace: Economic Sense or Hollywood Nonsense, The 636
Pier Paolo Pasolini: An Epical-Religious View of the World 2176
Pier Paolo Pasolini: An Interview 2176
Pinning Down the Quicksilver: Interview With Anthony Perkins 1023, 2080
Pioneering the Talkies 1746

Pistols and Cherry Pies: LOLITA From Page to Screen   1272, 1273
PLACE IN THE SUN, A   1015, 1039
Plague of Locusts, A   1291
Plain Words on Underground Film Programs   2039
Plan to Split MGM/UA Is Reported   662
Plastic Material, The   142
Playboy in a Monastery: An Interview With John Bormann   2073
PLAYBOY Interview: John Cassavetes   2074
PLAYBOY Interview: Sam Peckinpah   2087
PLAYBOY Interview: Stanley Kubrick   2054, 2083
Playground of Jean Vigo, The   1828
Playing Dirty: Michael Caine   2161
Playing The Game: Stanley Baker   2161
Plea From Los Angeles: Big Films, Come Home   658
Pleasure, Ambivalence, Identification: Valentino and Female Spectatorship   471
Plight of Indies Emerges as Major Issue at Show West   763
Pod Society Versus the Rugged Individualists, The   384
Pods, Blobs, and Ideology in American Films of the Fifties   416
Poe on the Screen   1300
Poet of Poverty: Part One--The Great Years   1004, 1933
Poet of Poverty: Part Two--Umberto-And After   1004, 1933
Poetic of Horror: More than Meets the Eye, The   388
Poe, Hitchcock, and the Well-Wrought Effect   1837
Point Man: Oliver Stone Interviewed   368
Point of View and Narrative Voice in THE GRAPES OF WRATH: Steinbeck and
    Ford   1326
Point of View and "Intrarealism" in Hitchcock   1835
Point-of-View Shot, The   79
Pointed Horror: The Films of Luis Bunuel and Georges Franju   1714
Poitier Represents Millions of Negroes   889
Pola Negri, "Vamp" of Silent Films, Dies   1632
Poland   2179
Poland's Banned Films   2179
Polish Drama, The   2012
Polishing the Teen-age Image   972
Political Censorship of Films In Britain Between the Wars, The   210, 216
Political Economy of Hollywood: The Studio System, The   559, 630
Political Polarization and the French Cinema   225
Political Program of CAHIERS DU CINEMA, 1969-1977, The   2103
Politics and Film: Strange Bedfellows?   443
Politics and Pontecorvo   2176
Politics and Popular Culture: Hollywood at Bay, 1933-1953   820
Politics Catches Up to THE CANDIDATE   455
Politics in Film: How Moviemakers Handle Hot Issues   444
Politics of African Cinema, The   949
Politics of Compromise in Hollywood: A Case Study, The   219
Politics of Cultural Anthropolgy: An Interview With Jean Rouch, The   2120,
    2121, 2154
Politics of Film Canons, The   445, 446, 473, 474, 1514
Politics of Narration: Capra's MR. SMITH GOES TO WASHINGTON   1799
Politics of Nostalgia, The   995
Politics on Celluloid   1021
Politics, Painting and the Language of Signs in Godard's MADE IN USA   2110
POLITIQUE DES AUTEURS, LA   1102, 2096, 2097
POLITIQUE DES AUTEURS, THE   2123
POLITIQUE DES AUTEURS: Part One--World View as Aesthetic, LA   1999, 2106
POLITIQUE DES AUTEURS: Part Two--Truffaut's Manifesto, LA   2106
Pollack's Hollywood History   2089

Pop Art Pitfalls: Interview With John Frankenheimer, Part I   2077
Popular Asian Film: A Checklist of Sources, Part I   2018
Popular Asian Film: A Checklist of Sources, Part II   2018
Popular Culture in America: Social Problem in a Mass Society or Social Asset in
  a Pluralist Society?   459, 461
Popular Film as a Progressive Text--A Discussion of COMA, Part 1, The   787
Popular Film as a Progressive Text--A Discussion of COMA, Part 2, The   787
Popular Hero Symbols and Audience Gratifications   745, 801
Popularity of Filmgoing in the US, 1930-1950, The   634, 667
Porter and Griffith   1361
Porter or Ambivalence   1605
Portrait in Human Frailty: Concluding an Analysis of the Films of James
  Stewart   1982
Portrait of a First-Run Audience   745
Portrait of a Young Actor on His Way Up to the Top: Keir Dullea   995
Portrait of the Artist as an Old Man: Groucho Marx   1749
Portraying Life with Dignity: An Analysis of Daniel Mann's Work for the
  Cinema   1020
Position of Women in Hollywood Melodramas, The   792, 793
Positive Thinking: Hal Ashby   2195
Possibly the Greatest: MY LIFE AND MY FILMS   1823
Postmodernism, or the Cultural Logic of Late Capitalism   417
Postwar French Cinema: Of Waves in the Sea   1992, 1993
Postwar Performance of the Motion Picture Industry, The   661
Postwar Struggle for Color, The   654, 655
Potential: The Mirisch Brothers   374
Powell Retrospective Reflects a Happy Life in Film   1833
Power of Adaptation in APOCALYPSE NOW, The   367
Power of the Gun, The   1987
Power of the Screen; The Influence of Edith Head's Film Designs on the Retail
  Fashion Market, The   610
Power Today: Majors' Majors   1137
Power Yesterday and Today: A Conversation With Greg Bautzer   1136
Power Yesterday: A Conversation With Henry Hathaway   366
Practice of Film Teaching: Vanier College, The   38
PRAXIS as a Cinematic Principle in Films by Robert Bresson   1994
Prayer of Thanks, Dreams of Vengeance   437
Pre-History and Early Years of the Cinema, The   1583
Pre-Text and Text in GENTLEMEN PREFER BLONDES   533
Preface to an Interview   1005
Preminger's 2 Periods--Studio and Solo   1984
Preminger, 80, Dead of Cancer in New York   1984
Preminger: Two Cheers for the Film-Flam Man   1984
Preparation of Teachers of Media, The   40
Presence of Discourse/Discourse of Presence: Representing Vietnam   442
Preston Sturges   1014, 1912, 1921
Preston Sturges and the Theory of Decline   1014, 1912
Preston Sturges in the Thirties   1912
Preston Sturges or Laughter Betrayed   1014, 1912
Preston Sturges: Success in the Movies   1014, 1912
PRETTY BABY: Love in Storyville   2119
Prevert, Jacques   1813
Prey to Catastrophe, A   1637
Pride Without Prejudice: Sidney Poitier's Career   887
Primal Conditions and Conventions: The Genres of Comedy and Science
  Fiction   410
Primal Scream: An Interview With Steven Spielberg   2196
PRIME OF MISS JEAN BRODIE, THE   1003
Prime Time Soap Opera   982

Primitive Cinema--A Frame-up? or The Trick's on Us 1602
Print the Fact: For and Against the Films of John Ford 1673
Prisoner of the Desert 1802
Private Eye, The 373
Private Films of Billy Wilder, The 1987
Private Life of Billy Wilder, The 1987
PRIVATE LIFE OF HENRY VIII, THE 1865
Private Madness and Public Lunacy 1985, 2080
Private War of Robert Aldrich, The 2071
Private World of William Inge, The 1349
Pro-Negro Films in Atlanta 884, 941
Problem of Film Genre: A Mentalistic Approach 176
Problem of High Culture and Mass Culture, The 455, 548
Problem of Monopoly, The 607, 635, 636, 644
Problem of Realizing Medieval Romance in Film: John Boorman's EXCALIBUR,
  The 416
Problem With G, The 982
Problems in Film History: How Fox Innovated Sound 633
Problems of Filming NATIVE SON 903
PROCES DE JEANNE D'ARC, LE 1023
Producer Likely to Head Sony-Owned Columbia 2205
Producer Will Head Fox Studio 663
Profiles: How About a Little Game? 2083
Program Notes: A STAR IS BORN (1937) 1675
Program Notes: ALICE'S RESTAURANT 2088
Program Notes: AN AMERICAN IN PARIS 1983
Program Notes: BATTLEGROUND 1675
Program Notes: BODU SAVED FROM DROWNING 1814
Program Notes: BREATHLESS 2152
Program Notes: BRINGING UP BABY 1803
Program Notes: DIRECTED BY JOHN FORD 1674
Program Notes: DR. STRANGELOVE, OR: HOW I LEARNED TO STOP WORRYING
  AND LOVE THE BOMB 2083
Program Notes: FELLINI SATYRICON 1927
Program Notes: FRENCH CAN CAN 1814
Program Notes: HALLELUJAH! 1806
Program Notes: HIROSHIMA MON AMOUR 2152
Program Notes: HIS GIRL FRIDAY 1747
Program Notes: I VITELLONI 1927
Program Notes: JULES AND JIM 2155
Program Notes: KISS ME DEADLY 2072
Program Notes: KLUTE 800
Program Notes: KRAMER VS. KRAMER 1007
Program Notes: L'ANNEE DERNIERE A MARIENBAD 2153
Program Notes: L'ASCENSEUR POUR L'ECHAFAUD 2119
Program Notes: L'ATALANTE 1828
Program Notes: LA GRANDE ILLUSION 1827
Program Notes: LA REGLE DU JEU 1827
Program Notes: LE CRIME DE MONSIEUR LANGE 1814
Program Notes: LES BONNES FEMMES 2098
Program Notes: LES COUSINS 2098
Program Notes: LES QUATRE CENT COUPS 2155
Program Notes: MARTY 1983
Program Notes: MILDRED PIERCE 800
Program Notes: MR. SMITH GOES TO WASHINGTON 1799
Program Notes: MURMUR OF THE HEART 2119
Program Notes: MY DARLING CLEMENTINE 1976
Program Notes: NORTH BY NORTHWEST 2079

Program Notes: PSYCHO 2080
Program Notes: REBEL WITHOUT A CAUSE 998
Program Notes: RED RIVER 1747
Program Notes: SCARFACE: THE SHAME OF A NATION 1747
Program Notes: SERGEANT YORK 365
Program Notes: SHADOWS 2074
Program Notes: SHOOT THE PIANO PLAYER 2156
Program Notes: STAGECOACH (1939) 1802
Program Notes: THE BICYCLE THIEF 1933
Program Notes: THE BIG SLEEP 798, 1747
Program Notes: THE DIRTY DOZEN 2071
Program Notes: THE GRADUATE 2085
Program Notes: THE LINE OF DEMARCATION 2098
Program Notes: THE LOWER DEPTHS 1814
Program Notes: THE MAN WHO SHOT LIBERTY VALANCE 2075
Program Notes: THE SEARCHERS 2076
Program Notes: THE SEVENTH SEAL 2189
Program Notes: THE SOUTHERNER 1814
Program Notes: THE STORY OF G. I. JOE 1675
Program Notes: THE WILD BUNCH 2087
Program Notes: Three Films by Brakhage 1974
Program Notes: THX 1138 2196
Program Notes: TO HAVE AND HAVE NOT 1747
Program Notes: TONI 1814
Program Notes: TOUCH OF EVIL 2091
Program Notes: TWENTIETH CENTURY 1747
Program Notes: UMBERTO D 1933
Program Notes: WHO'S AFRAID OF VIRGINIA WOOLF? 2086
Program Notes: WILD BOYS OF THE ROAD 1675
Program Notes: YOUNG MR. LINCOLN 477
Program Notes: ZAZIE DANS LE METRO 2119
Program Notes: 8 1/2 1927
Program Playback Preferences in VCR Households 760
Projector and the Camera: Intergrating Courses in Cinema Studies and
  Filmmaking, The 39
Prolegomena to a Contextualist Genre Criticism 38
Proletarian Cinema and the Weimar Republic, The 212
Propaganda as Vision--TRIUMPH OF THE WILL 321
Propaganda Films About the War in Vietnam 325
Propaganda in International Politics, 1919-1939 211, 212
Propaganda, Autarky and the German Housewife 251
Prophet Louis Ducos Du Hauron, The 1585
Proposal for a Course on Films and History 39
Proposed Production of War Pictures 1376
Prospects of the Ethnographic Film 2039, 2120
Protecting the Children: HUCKLEBERRY FINN, E.T., and the Politics of
  Censorship 979
Protolite Screen: Drive-In Breakthrough 649
Psychiatrist in Today's Movies: He's Everywhere and in Deep Trouble, The 816
Psychiatry Looks at the Appeal of RAIN MAN 815
PSYCHO and the Rollercoaster 2080
PSYCHO Therapy 2080
Psychoanalysis and Cinema: The Imaginary Discourse 593
Psychoanalysis, Film, and Television 579
Psychological Appeal of the Hollywood Western, The 534
Psychological Effects of the Western Film 745
Psychopathic Characters on Stage 453
Psychosis, Neurosis, Perversion 585, 1843, 2080
PSYCHO, Rosie and a Touch of Orson: Janet Leigh Talks 2080

PSYCHO: The Institutionalization of Female Sexuality 1843, 2080
Public Appraises Movies, The 742
Public Image and the Private Eye of Richard Attenborough, The 374
Public Opinion and CROSSFIRE 832
Publishing: CLOCKWORK ORANGE Regains Chapter 21 1317
Puritanism of Joseph Losey, The Cubist 1981
Puritans Anonymous 751
Pursuing the Dream: Sexy, Straight-on and Ambitious, Kevin Costner is a
  Grownup Hero With Brains 801
Pursuit of the Falcon 373, 1301
Pursuits of Happiness; A Reading of THE LADY EVE 1921
Putting Music in Its Place 83
Puttnam's New Mission 537

Q

Qu'est-ce que la Nouvelle Vague 2093, 2094, 2096, 2112
Quantitative Analysis of Motion Picture Content 742
Quantitative View of Soviet Cinema, A 1648
QUATRE CENT COUPS, LES 2155
Que Viva Prohibition? 1315
Question Marks on the New Czechoslovak Cinema 2164
Question of Class and Color: Spike Lee Takes a Hard Look at Black College Life,
  A 903
Question of Standard, A 1019
Questions and Answers With Jean Renoir 1814
Questions No One Asks about Willy, The 1748
Question: Interview With Robert Bresson, The 1994
Quiet Man, The 1674
Quiet, Influential Investor: Laurence A. Tisch, A 678
Quite Apart from Miklos Jansso . . . Some Notes on the New Hungarian
  Cinema 2167

R

R-H Factor and the New Cinema, The 1012
Radley Metzger: Aristocrat of the Erotic 2037
RAIDERS OF THE LOST ARK and How it Was Filmed 2196
RAISIN IN THE SUN, A 1009, 1348
RAISIN IN THE SUN: Expect Movie Version to Rival Stage Play's Huge Success,
  A 1009
Ralph Ellison and the Uses of the Imagination 452
Ralph Richardson 1943
Rambo Doctrine, The 472
Rank's Attempt at the American Market 1935
Raoul Walsh on D. W. Griffith 1366
Raoul Walsh Talks About D. W. Griffith 1366
Raoul Walsh--His Silent Films 1671
Raoul Walsh: He Used to be a Big Shot 1672
Raoul Walsh: 1887-1981 1672
Rating Game, The 960
Raw Reactions to a Film on Racial Tensions 903
Raymond Chandler and Hollywood 1301
Raymond Chandler on Screen 1198
Re-Thinking U. S. Film History: The Depression Decade and Monopoly
  Control 632

Reaction of the Negro to the Motion Picture THE BIRTH OF A NATION 865, 1383
Reading Hitchcock 1835
Reading Intertitles 1388
Reading Process: A Phenomenological Approach, The 485
Ready for Vietnam? A Talk with Michael Cimino 367
Real Crisis In American Films, The 2201
Real Estate: A Movie House Boom In Manhattan 682
Real Sins of Hollywood, The 1310
Real "Eve" Sues to Film the Rest of Her Story, The 791
Realism and Beyond: The Films of John Frankenheimer 2077
Realism and Film Historical Practice 252
Realism and Romance In the Films of John Ford 1674
Realism and the Cinema 1333
Realists--A Return to Life, The 1922
REAR WINDOW: A Construction Story 1978
Reason and Unreason In Federico Fellini's I VITELLONI 1927
Rebel In Kimono: First Part Of An Analysis Of Kurosawa's Work for The Cinema, The 2019
Rebel With a Camera 2152
Rebel With Kid Gloves: First Part of an Analysis of Autant-Lara's Work for the Cinema, The 1993
Rebel Without a Cause: Nicholas Ray in the Fifties 1985
Rebels in Jackboots, The 322
Rebels With a Cause 2108
Rebels Without Causes 816, 1003
Recent Books on Chinese Films 2163
Recent Developments in Feminist Criticism 466, 467, 471
Recent Rivette: An Inter-Re-View 2098
Recent Work in Genre 173
Reception Theory and the Avant-Garde 485
Reckless Moment, The 2010
Reckoning of the Miracle: An Analysis of Czechoslovak Cinematography, A 2164
Reconciling Entertainment and Thought: An Interview With Julio Garcia Espinosa 2163
Reconstitution of A CORNER IN WHEAT, A 1366
Red Badge of Courage, The 1321
Red China 2163
RED DESERT 2173
RED DESERT, The 2173
Red Harvest 2163
Red Recollections 1184
RED SHOES, THE 1016
Redford Broadens Pet Project 671
Redford's Second Debut 1009
Rediscovery of Oscar Micheaux, Black Film Pioneer, The 866
Rediscovery: Buster 1672
Rediscovery: STRIKE 1667
Rediscovery: TOO HOT TO HANDLE 1672
Red, Blue Godard 2109
Reedification and Utopia in Mass Culture 537
Reference Works for Film Study 1520
References, Please: On Film Encyclopedias 1522
Refighting the War: Why the Movies are in Vietnam 337
Reflections in a Golden Lens 1233
Reflections on the Breast 593
Reflections: An Interview With Alan Bates 2077
REGLE DU JEU 1827
Regrets for the Road Not Taken 1016

Rehearsing the Middle Ages   2102
Rejoinder   2151
Relation of the Poet to Daydreaming, The   452
Relationship Between Religious Beliefs and Attending the Fear-Provoking
  Religiously Oriented Movie--THE EXORCIST, The   546
Relationship of Constrained Anxiety: Historians and Film, A   39
Relationship of Ingmar Bergman to E. T. A. Hoffmann, The   2183
Reluctant Exile: Joseph Losey, The   1981
Remembered Vitality of King Vidor, The   1671
Remembering Adolph Zukor   1505
Remembering D. W. Griffith   1368
Remembering D. W. Griffith: A Filmography   1368
Reminder From Script   1142
Reminiscenes   1985
Rene Clair in Hollywood   1724
Rene Clair, LE MILLION, and The Coming of Sound   1810, 1825
Renee Adoree   367
Renoir and Realism   1813
Renoir in America   1813
Repeat Audience for Movies on TV, The   545
Reply to Samuels' Article on Hitchcock   1835
Reply, A   375
Report Cites Unequal Pay for Female Writers   2207
Report Draws Strong Praise and Criticism   961
Report From China   2163
Report From Cuba   2163
Report From Poland   2179
Report on New Dimensions   656
Report on Reagan--F.B.I. Ties   1088
Report on the Weekend School   792
Report to the Board of Directors, University Film and Video Association   35
Report Warns School Reforms May Fall Short   439
Reports: The Symposium on Movie Business and Finance   659
Representation of Violence to Women: Hitchcock's FRENZY, The   1838
Rereading Femininity   532
Research on the Film Audience: An Annotated Bibliography, 1982-1985   705
Resnais and Reality   2116
Resnais, Alain   2116, 2117
Resnais: L'ANNEE DERNIERE A MARIENBAD   2153
Responses of Blacks and Other Minorities to Television Shows of the 1970s About
  Their Groups   855
Resurgence of Von Stroheim, The   1019
Rethinking American Film History: The Depression Decade and Monopoly
  Power   640
Retractions and Reiterations on Films and Dreams   593
Retrospective Look at the Films of D. W. Griffith and Andy Warhol, A   1368
Retrospective: THE MANCHURIAN CANDIDATE   2078
Return of Busby Berkeley, The   1797
Return of SHANE, The   1009
Return of the Dean, The   388
Return of the Grown-up Movie, The   2202
Return of the Repressed, The   409
Return of the Repressed: The Jew on Film, The   837
Return of the Repressed: The Palestinian Wave in Recent Israeli Cinema,
  The   2169
Return of the Return of the Summer Sequel   2200
Return to Melies: Reflections on the Science Fiction Film   410
Returning Soldier: A Dissent, The   375

Revamping of Fox Film Puts Emphasis on Movies, A   2205, 2206
Revelations   1989
Reveling in Unembarrassed Trash   537
Revenge Fuels the Cold War Movies of the 80's   334
Reversing the Process   40
Review of CLOSELY WATCHED TRAINS   994
Review of DELIVERANCE and Filmography of John Boorman   2073
Review of LES BICHES   2151
Review of MOVIES AND MONEY: FINANCING THE AMERICAN FILM
  INDUSTRY   634
Revolution in China   2163
Rewards of Quality, The   1711
Rex Ingram and Alice Terry: Part One   1707
Rex Ingram and Alice Terry: Part Two--The Studio at Nice and the End of a
  Career   1707
RHAPSODY IN BLUE   1007
Rhetoric of Hitchcock Thrillers, The   1836
Rhetoric of WILD STRAWBERRIES, The   2189
Ricardou and LAST YEAR AT MARIENBAD   2153
Richard Barthelmess   1705
Richard Conte Getting Offers He Can't Refuse as Ideal Mafia Type   826
Riches of Jean Renoir, The   1814
Riddled With Errors   1502
RIDE THE HIGH COUNTRY   2087
Right of Re-Vision: Michelle Citron's DAUGHTER RITE, The   794
Right-Hemisphere Processing in Dreams and Films   593
RIO LOBO By Howard Hawks   1747
Rise and Fall of the American West: Borden Chase Interviewed, The   424
Rise and Fall of the Rock Film: Part II--From WOODSTOCK to STARDUST, The
  Parade's Gone By, The   2199
Rise and Fall of the Rock Film: Part I, The   2199
Rise of Anti-Americanism in France: French Intellectuals and the American Film
  Industry, 1927-1932, The   626
Rise of The Telefilm and the Networks' Hegemony Over the Motion Picture
  Industry, The   678
Ritual and Heroism in the Fantasy Film   801
RKO Radio: An Overview   622
RKO Years, Part II   622
RKO: It's Only Money   622
Road Back, The   1037
Road to Neorealism, The   1874, 1877
Road to THE VICTORS, The   368
Robbe-Grillet on Novels and Films   2113
Robert Aldrich   2071
Robert Aldrich: The Director as Phoenix   1136, 2071
Robert Bresson   1023, 1994
Robert Flaherty and the Naturalist Documentary   1671
Robert Flaherty (Barnouw's File)   1671
Robert Flaherty, 1884-1851   1671
Robert Flaherty: The Man In the Iron Myth   1671
Robert Harron   1365
Robert Redford Goes Behind the Camera for a New Image   1009
Robert Rossen   1985
Robert Rossen and the Filming of LILITH   1985
Robert Rossen: A Retrospective   1090
Robert Wise   1987
Robert Wise at Fox   1988
Robert Wise at RKO   1988
Robert Wise Continued   1988

Robert Wise Filmography (1) 1988
Robert Wise Filmography (2) 1988
Robert Wise Filmography (3) 1988
Robert Wise Filmography (4) 1988
Robert Wise Talks about the New Hollywood 1988
Robert Wise To Date 1988
Robin Hood on the Screen 1301
Rock of Life, The 2183
Roger Corman Interview 2075
Roger Corman: A Double Life 2075
Rohmer at Work: Tea for Two 2105
Rohmer Interviewed 2101, 2104
Rohmer's Perceval 2101, 2103
Roland H. Totheroh Interviewed: Chaplin Films 1416
Role of Movies in Morale, The 233
Role of the Mass Media and the Effect of Aggressive Film Content Upon Children's
  Aggressive Responses, The 455
Role of the Western Film Genre in Industry Competition, 1907-1911, The 619,
  1517
Role of Women In SEVEN WOMEN, The 1673
Role of 3-D in Motion Pictures, The 655
Roman Polanski In New York 2180
Romance of Money, The 1115
ROMEO AND JULIET (1954) 1009
ROMEO AND JULIET (1968) 1356
Ronald Colman 1305
Ronald Colman's Career: Part One 1305
Ronald Colman's Career: Part Two 1305
Rondo Gallant 2119
ROOM AT THE TOP 1016
Room at the Top? 1016
Room Where Scott Died, The 1109
Roots of Neorealism 1921
ROOTS: Eight Points of View 780
Rosalind Russell 1002
ROSEBUD and the Illusions of Childhood Innocence in CITIZEN KANE 598
Ross and Dross 1016
Rossen Index, A 1014, 1985
Rouben Mamoulian, Stage and Film Director, Dies 1748
Round About Moscow 2182
Rowland V. Lee 1204
Rule of Nobody: Myth and Reality In Swedish Cinema, The 2183
Rumpled Anarchy of Bill Murray, The 2202
Running, Jumping and Standing Still 1672
Rural Preferences in Motion Pictures 710, 726
Russ Meyer: King of the Nudies 2037
Russia Revisited 2182
Russian Youth in an Uproar 2181
Ruth Roland 1455

S

Sadoul and Film Research 1361
SAG Vows Redoubled Effort to End Inequitable Minority Hiring 895
Sale to Sony Approved by Columbia Pictures   .artauth
 Sanger, David E. 2205
SALESMAN 2085
Sam Fuller Lands with THE BIG RED ONE 1977
Sam Fuller's War 1977
Sam Fuller: The Gold Beneath the Brass 1977
Sam Peckinpah and THE WILD BUNCH 2087
Sam Peckinpah Lets It All Hang Out 2087
Sam Peckinpah's Television Work 2087
Sam Peckinpah's West 2087
Sam Peckinpah, Robert Ardrey and the Notion of Ideology 2087
Sam Peckinpah: The Survivor and the Individual 2087
Same Old Story: Stereotypes and Difference, The 550
Samuel Fuller 1960, 1977
Samuel Fuller's Action Films 1977
Samuel Fuller's Gangster Films 1977
Samuel Fuller: Two Interviews 1977, 2078
Samuel Goldwyn 1464
Samurai and Small Beer: Part Two 2019
Samurai Film and the Western, The 2019
Samurai to Shomin-geki 2176
Sand Castles: Steven Spielberg Interviewed 2196
SANG D'UN POETE, LE 1826
Sanitizing a Novel for the Screen 1029
SANSHO DAYU 2031
Sarah Bernhardt 1463
Satire and Sympathy: A New Wave of Yugoslavian Filmmakers 2014
Satisfaction--A Most Unpopular Feeling 2180
Satisfying Soap 1016
Satyajit Ray Gives Ibsen A Bengali Spin   .   .   . 2168
Satyajit Ray: A Study 1004, 2168
Satyajit Ray: An Interview 2168
SATYRICON 2175
Say the Right Thing 903
Scar of Shame: Skin Color and Caste in Black Silent Melodrama, The 868
Scarlet Women: The Depiction of Female Communists In Hollywood Film 1945
Scene Design and Early Film 1587
Scenes from a Mind 2072
Schrader, Paul 2195
Science Fiction Film Criticism in the Seventies: A Selected Bibliography 410
SciFi Hits the Big Time 409
Scott Fitzgerald in Hollywood 1118
Scoundrel Tome 1257, 1261
Screen Adaptation 1301
Screen and the Book: A Solution for Slow Learners, The 35
Screen Answers Back 1984
Screen at the End of the Tunnel, The 337
Screen Education in American High Schools 40
Screen Extract from THE LONELINESS OF THE LONG DISTANCE RUNNER 997
Screen Fans Organize to Bite Hand that Feeds Double Features 640
Screen in Hitchcock's BLACKMAIL, The 1835
Screen's New Look--Wider and Deeper, The 655
Screenwriters 666
Screenwriters Symposium 85
Screen: KAGEMUSHA, Kurosawa's 27TH Film 2019

Screen: NATIVE SON, Based on Wright's Novel   903
Screen: Redford's ORDINARY PEOPLE   1009
Screen: Redgrave in James' BOSTONIANS, The   1324
Script Extract from THE INNOCENTS   1324
Script Extract of LA DOLCE VITA   1023
Script to Screen with Max Ophuls   2010
Scrooge's Permutations are Part of Popular Lore   1301
Search for a New Style in Musicals: Sixth Part of a History of Italian Cinema,
  The   1607
SEARCHERS and the Pleasure Principle, THE   449, 478, 529
SEARCHERS, THE   2076
SEARCHERS: Cult Movie of the New Hollywood, THE   2076
Searching for a Scapegoat: The Portrait of Rotwang as a "Jewish Scientist" in
  Fritz Lang's METROPOLIS   1642
SEARCH, THE   1988
Second Thoughts on Stroheim   1674
Secret Lair of the Jedi, the Grail and the Green Slimers   2196
Secret Life of Federico Fellini, The   1022, 1927
See No Evil   2181
See You at Mao   2110
Seeing and Perceiving   40
Seeing Through Movies   252
Seeking Out Legendary Hollywood   1042
Seeking Planets That Do Not Exist   2165
Seeking to Take the Longest Journey: A Conversation With Albert Maysles   2085
Selected and Annotated Bibliography of Books and Articles on Music in the
  Cinema, A   400
Selected Characteristics of the X-Rated Movie Audience: Toward a National
  Profile of the Recidivist   754
Selected Films for Young Adults 1978   978
Selected Films for Young Adults 1979   978
Selective Exposure: The Potential Boomerang Effect   543
Self-Censorship in the Movie Industry: A Historical Perspective on Law and
  Social Change   697
Self-Criticism   2124
Self-Reflective Musical and the Myth of Entertainment, The   400
Sell It Again, Sam!   761
Selling Power of Stars, The   1137
Semi-Precious Age of TV, The   653
Senate Isolationists Run Afoul of Wilkie in "Warmonger" Hearings   203
Senjamyson: An Interview With Jay Sayer on the Making of THE VIKING WOMEN
  AND THE SEA SERPENT   2075
Sensuality in the Cinema   999
SEPARATE PEACE: Filming the War Within, A   1300
Sequel Becomes the New Bankable Film Star, The   761
Sergeant Rutledge   1673
Sergei Eisenstein   1645
Sergio Leone, 67, Italian Director Who Revitalized Westerns   2171
Serial Lovers, The   1455
Serials of Republic, The   1455
Serials with Sound   1455
Series Stars Moonlight in TV Films   678
Serpent's Skin, The   2183
Services on Friday for Sir Alfred, Master of Suspense   1854
Seven from the Past: Aspects of the Pre-War Japanese Cinema   1740, 1894
Seven Revelations about Mel Brooks   2073
Seven Ways with SEVEN DAYS IN MAY   2077
Seven Years Without Directing, and Billy Wilder is Feeling Itchy   1987

SEVENTH SEAL, THE 2189
Seventy 2159
Seventy-Six--And Still Diamond Lil 1749, 1795
Several Sides of Kon Ichikawa, The 2022, 2024
Sex and DR. STRANGELOVE 2083
Sex and Sexism in the Eroduction 2037
Sex and the Single Family 1003
Sex in America: Conservative Attitudes Prevail 977
Sex Symbol: Marilyn, Prime Time, and the Nielsens, The 789, 1138, 1178
Sexual Imagery and the Black Woman in American Cinema 872, 949
Sexuality at a Loss: The Films of F. W. Murnau 471
Sex, Violence and Drugs: All In Good Fun! Russ Meyer Interviewed 2037
Shadow and Act 865, 883
Shadow of the Swastika 322
Shakespeare and Hollywood: Two Film Cliches 1354
Shakespeare on Film in the Classroom 39
Shakespeare on the Screen 1342
Shakespeare on Three Screens: Peter Brook Interviewed 1342
Shall We Gather at the River: The Late Films of John Ford 2076
SHANE 1009
SHANE and George Stevens 1009
Shape of Theaters to Come, The 674, 2202
Shaping the Film Business in Postwar Germany 647
She Wants to Change TV's Image of Blacks 855
SHERIFF: Alexandre Astruc Does Justice to Howard Hawks 1747
Sherlock Holmes on the Screen 1300
Sherlock Holmes: Genre and Industrial Practice 608, 640
Shift at Columbia Pictures, A 670
Shochiku and Violence Too 1737
Shoot!--Sam Peckinpah 2087
Short History of Latin American Film Histories, A 252
Short History of the Soviet Cinema, A 1648
Short Take 703
Should Films Be Politically Committed? 2156
Should Shylock Be Suppressed? 822
Showing the World What It Owed to Britain: Foreign Policy and "Cultural
  Propaganda," 1935-45 242
Showscan Moving With Theatres, Films 674
Showscan: A New Type of Exhibition for a Revolutionary Film Process 674
Showscan: Coming Soon to a Theatre Near You 674
Showscan: Doug Trumbull's New 70mm Format 674
Side Glance at Medusa: Hollywood, the Literature Boys, and Nathanael West,
  A 1028
Sideshows: Hollywood in Vietnam 367
Sidney Buchman 1093
Sidney Lumet 2084
Sidney Lumet: An Interview 1350
Sidney Poitier 892
Sidney Poitier as Black Militant 889
Sidney Poitier on 40 Years of Change 892
Sign of the Times: The Computer as Character in TRON, WAR GAMES, and
  SUPERMAN III 409
Significance of Sidney, The 892
Signification, Representation, Ideology: Althusser and the Post-Structualist
  debates 587
Signs of the Predicament: Italian Notes, The 1922
Silence is Golden 1106
Silence Was Our Virtue 1365
Silent Serial, The 1455

Silents Weren't Just Voiceless Talkies, The 1514, 1578
Silliest Film: Will Machinery Make Robots of Men? 1309
Silver Screen Under Glass, The 760
Sinclair Lewis and the Movies 1300
SINGIN' IN THE RAIN 1295
Sir Alexander Korda 1865
Sir Richard Attenborough 548
Sirk's THE TARNISHED ANGELS: PYLON Recreated 1039
Sirkumstantial Evidence 1986
Sisyphus in Hollywood: Refocusing F. Scott Fitzgerald 1109, 1126, 1130
Sitting, Eating Popcorn as Alienation Grows 900
Six Authors In Pursuit of THE SEARCHERS 2076
Six Films of Josef Von Sternberg 1674
Six-Gun Galahad, The 424
SJUNDE INSEGLET, DET 2189
Skeleton Key to 2001, A 2055
Skeleton Keys 1920
Skin Games 2116
Skirting a Time Inc. Barrier, Paramount Lines Up 7 Banks 2205
Skull Beneath the Skin, The 2021, 2024
SLAUGHTERHOUSE-FIVE: Novel and Film 1300
Slavery Motif in Recent Popular Cinema: THE COLOR PURPLE and THE BROTHER
  FROM ANOTHER PLANET, The 905
Sling the Lamps Low 1747
SLON 2115, 2116
Slow Fade to Afro: The Black Presence In Brazilian Cinema 2158
Slut, Bitch, Virgin, Mother: The Role of Women in Some Recent Films 789
Small Change 998
Small People in a Big World: A Monograph on John Huston, Part 2--A Touch of
  Melville 373, 1321
Small Rise in TV Viewing Reported 545
Small Screens Breed Small Movies 678
Small Studios' Tough Season 670, 672
Smiley the Redeemer 881
SMULTRONSTALLET 2189
So He Became a Lady's Man: First Part of Cukor's Work for the Cinema 1012
So Much and Yet So Little: A Survey of Books on Chaplin 1419
Social Context and Mass Media Reception 745
Social Documentary in Yugoslavia 2014
Social Engineering for a Democratic Society at War 320
Social History of Film: Heterogeneity and Mediation, The 449, 450, 1509, 1516,
  1556
Social History of Movies, The 783
Social History of the Motion Picture, A 710
Social-Science Fiction 410
Socialist Realism and the Soviet Cinema 2181
Socially Acceptable Immigrant Minority Group: The Image of the Jew in American
  Popular Films, The 818, 827, 828, 831, 832
Society: Violence and the Bitch Goddess, The 800
Sociology of Parent-Youth Conflict, The 1003
Soft Edges: The Art of Literature, The Medium of Film 1297
Solidarity and Violence 2163
Some Aspects of the Interaction of the British Entertainment Media with
  Contemporary Race Relations 854
Some Aspects of the Work of Humphrey Jennings 216
Some Comments on the Design of Large-Screen Motion-Picture Theaters 655
Some Desirable Goals For Motion Pictures 622
Some Economic Aspects of Motion Picture Production and Marketing 607, 638

Some Effects of Films of Successful Blacks on Racial Self-Concept 546
Some Ideas on the Cinema   1922, 1924
Some Like It Chilled   388
Some Notes on the Source of LA REGLE DU JEU   1827
Some Observations on Sternberg and Dietrich   1674
Some Patterns of Mass Media Use in Santiago de Chile   748
Some Personal Visions   1711
Some Questions About The Depiction of Jews in New Films   820, 835
Some Questions Answered   1988
Some Remarks   1974
Some Sociological Notes on the Boom in Film Interest   534
Some Visual Motifs of FILM NOIR   1948
Somebody Must Put a Lid on Budgets   2200
Somerset Maugham and the Cinema   1329, 1330
Something Else Besides a Mother: STELLA DALLAS and the Maternal
  Melodrama   795
Sometimes "Small" Movies Can Be Very Big   2201
Son of Uncle Sam   1019
Song of Innocence: THE CREATURE FROM THE BLACK LAGOON   410
Songs of Innocence and Experience: The Blakean Vision of George Lucas   2196
Songs of Innocence: Chabrol and Franju   2098
SONS AND LOVERS   1010
Sony Has High Hopes for Columbia Pictures   2205
Sophomoric Scholarship   1753
Sorcerer's Apprentice: Bazin and Truffaut on Renoir, The   1819
Sorcerers or Apprentices: Some Aspects of Propaganda Films   215, 241, 282
Sound and Color   632
Sound and the Fuhrer, The   203
Sound of One Wing Flapping, The   1835
Sound Track: RULES OF THE GAME   1827
SOUNDER--A Hollywood Fantasy?   941
Sources of FILM NOIR, The   1947
Southern Exposure: KUDZU and IT'S GRITS   913
Southern Heroine in the Films of the 1930's, The   857
Soviet Actress Talks About Sex and Symbolism   2182
Soviet Cinema: The New Way   1648, 2182
Soviet Director's Debt to Griffith, The   1363
Soviet Directors Mix Illusion and Reality   2182
Soviet Documentaries that Face Up to Reality   2182
Soviet Film Criticism   2182
Soviet Film Today, The   2182
Soviet Films Since 1945--Part One   2182
Soviet Films Since 1945--Part Two   2182
Soviets Assail RAMBO Film Cult   437
Space ILIAD: THE "STAR WARS" War: I, A   812
Spaces Between: American Criticism of Japanese Film, The   1738
Spain and THE SPANISH EARTH   319
Spain: Spanish Film Under Franco--Do Not Disturb   2182
Special Features on Film Scholarship   2266
Special FILM CULTURE Issue on Erich Von Stroheim   1674
Special Issue on Orson Welles   1751
Special Issue: Graham Greene   1329
Special Truffaut Issue   1005, 2106
Spectacle   656
Spectacle Film: 1967, The   656
Spectacle of Theory: An Historical Speculation, The   485
Spectator of American Symbolic Forms: Re-Reading John Ford's YOUNG MR.
  LINCOLN, The   477
Spectator-in-the-Text: The Rhetoric in STAGECOACH, The   79, 1802

Spectator's Comments   123
Spielberg at 40: The Man and The Child   2196
Spielberg's Elixir Shows Signs of Mature Magic   2196
Spielberg, Steven   2196
Spike Lee Raises the Movies' Black Voice   903
Spike Lee's Blacks: Are They Real People?   903
Spike Lee's Gotta Have It   903
Spinning Reels of Memory on a Master's Centenary   1414
SPLENDOR IN THE GRASS   1010
Splitting Jaws with the Happy Booker: A Talk with a Circuit Buyer   676
Spoken Silents in the Japanese Cinema, Essay on the Necessity of
  Katsuben   1736
Squeezing the Wide into a Narrow Temple   2004
Stage and Screen Go Their Separate Ways   1035
STAGE FRIGHT and Hitchcock   1920
Stahl into Sirk   1986
Stalinist Ideology Seen Through CHAPAYEV   261
Standards for Film Education   35
Standing Still   903
Stanley Kubrick   2083
Star as Market Strategy: Bette Davis in Another Light, The   637
Star Drek: The "STAR WARS" War: Part II   812
STAR IS BORN, A (1954)   1296
Star Library Attraction: Loaning Video Cassettes   760
Star Role for Hollywood Offices   537
STAR WARS Trilogy   812
Star-Crossed In Prague   2164
Starmaker Whose Dreams Turned to Dust   1368
Stars   1434
Stars in Our Hearts--A Critical Commentary on George Lucas' STAR WARS,
  The   812
Stars They Couldn't Photograph, The   2155
State of the Studios   2159
Statistical Style Analysis of Motion Pictures   79, 2198
Steinbeck's "String of Pictures" in THE GRAPES OF WRATH   1326
STELLA DALLAS and Feminist Film Theory   794
Stella, Reborn as an Unmarried Mother   794
Stepin Fetchit Talks Back   877
Stereotypes   543, 865
Stereotypes and the Media: A Re-evaluation   436
Stereotyping as a Method of Exploitation   851
Sterling Hayden   1092
Sternberg: The Context of Passion   1674
Steve Ross's Days of Deal-Making   2205
Steve's Summer Magic: E. T. And POLTERGEIST--Two From The Heart   2196
Steven Spielberg In His Adventures on Earth   2196
Stilled Life   1006
STILTE ROND CHRISTINE M (A QUESTION OF SILENCE), DE   526
Store Promotions Are Trivializing E. T., The   488
Story Into Script   1985
Story of Asdiwal, The   175
Story of Gosta Berling, The   1630
Strange Case of Alfred Hitchcock--Part 10, The   1835
Strange Case of Alfred Hitchcock--Part 1, The   1835
Strange Case of Alfred Hitchcock--Part 2, The   1835
Strange Case of Alfred Hitchcock--Part 3, The   1835
Strange Case of Alfred Hitchcock--Part 4, The   1835
Strange Case of Alfred Hitchcock--Part 5, The   1835

Strange Case of Alfred Hitchcock--Part 6, The 1835
Strange Case of Alfred Hitchcock--Part 7, The 1835
Strange Case of Alfred Hitchcock--Part 8, The 1835
Strange Case of Alfred Hitchcock--Part 9, The 1835
Stranger in a Strange Land 534
Stranger in a Strange Land: A Moviegoer at the Theater 1033
Stranger in Paradise 1032
Strategy of Soviet Propaganda, The 201
STREETCAR NAMED DESIRE, A 1352
Stroheim Revisted: The Missing Third in the American Cinema 1018
Stroheim: The Legend and the Fact 1674
Structural Patterning in the Lumiere Films 1590
Structurally Equivalent Stories in Movie and Text and the Effect of the Medium
  on Recall 533
Structure of Film Music, The 83
Structures of Consensus and Coercion: Workers' Morale and the Maintenance of
  Work Discipline, 1939-1945 251
Structures of Narrativity in Fritz Lang's METROPOLIS 1642
Student Attitudes Toward the Foreign Film 748
Students and the Occupational World 1011
Studios Move into Prime Time: Hollywood and the Television Industry in the
  1950s, The 653, 656, 678
Studios Woo Cassette Mass Market 672
STUDS LONIGAN 1301
Study Conducted for the Motion Picture Association of America, Inc. by Opinion
  Research Corporation 756
Study Guide to BILLY BUDD 1018
Study Guide to BILLY LIAR 994
Study Guide to LORD OF THE FLIES 1001
Study Guide: THE HUSTLER 40, 1014
Study in Practical Philosophy, A 732
Study of Carol Reed, A 1021
Study of Children's Attitudes and the Influence of a Commercial Motion
  Picture 737
Study of Racial Images: A Structural Approach, The 856
Study of The Effects In-Home Entertainment Alternatives Have on Film
  Attendance, A 755
Study of the Negro Problem in Motion Pictures, A 859
Study of the Professional Color Motion Picture Antitrust Decrees and Their
  Effects, A 654
Study Through Stills of MY DARLING CLEMENTINE, A 1976
Study to Determine the Drawing Power of Male and Female Stars Upon
  Movie-Goers of Their Own Sex, A 738
Stunt Men: They Should Be As Well Known As The Stars For Whom They Often
  Double 424, 1405
Style and Instinct: Part 1 1975
Style and Instinct: Part 2 1975
Style and Medium in the Moving Pictures 136, 144, 1332
Style in Film-Making: I--This Damned Eternal Triangle 978
Style in Film-Making: II--Truth is Stranger Than Fiction 978
Style in Film-Making: III--Getting Cinema on the Right Wave Length 978
Style in Film-Making: IV--Alexander and the Greats 978
Style in Film-Making: V--Who Really Makes the Movies? 978
Style in Film-Making: VI--Expressing Life in Celluloid 978
Style Is Born, A 1922, 2169
Style of Rene Clement: Part I 1995
Style of Rene Clement: Part II 1995
Style of Spectacle: Interview With Busby Berkeley, A 1797
Style, Function, and Ideology: A Problem in Film History 479

Style, Grammar, and the Movies 476, 477
Sub-New York Sensibility, The 2039
Subcultural Studies and the Film Audience: Rethinking the Film Viewing
  Context 458, 770
Subject is Money, The 897, 942
Suburbs and Proverbs 2106
Subversive Form, A 1587, 1604
Subversive Play: Fantasy in Robbe-Grillet's Films 416
Success Begins at Forty 1014
Successful Failure of Therapy in NOW, VOYAGER: The Women's Picture as
  Unresponsive Symptom, The 801
SUDDENLY LAST SUMMER 1353
Suicide of Robert Bresson, The 1994
SULLIVAN'S TRAVELS 1921
Summer of Fox's Discontent, The 536
Summing Up the Seventies 2201
SUN ALSO RISES, THE 1323
Sunflowers and Commissars 1648, 2182
SUNRISE 1706
SUNRISE: A Film Meets Its Public 1706
SUNRISE: A Murnau Masterpiece 1706
Superstar Returns to the Screen: Sidney Poitier at 60, A 906
Superstar=Superset 2039
Supplying the Props for War Films 232
Suppressing Controversial Films: From OBJECTIVE BURMA to MONTY PYTHON'S
  LIFE OF BRIAN 705
Surrealist and Spanish Giant: An Analysis of Bunuel's Work for the
  Cinema 1002, 1714
Survival! 2092
Survivors, The 1944
Suspense Master Alfred Hitchcock Dead at 80 1854
Susumu Hani 2176
Susumu Hani: An Interview 1000
Suzanne Simonin, Diderot's Nun 2098
Sweden: Paradise or Paradox 2182
Sweden: Past and Present 2183
Swedish Films at Sorrento 2182
Swedish Paradox, The 2182
Sweetening of America: The Image of the Jew in Film, The 835
SWEET, SWEETBACK'S BAADASSSSS SONG and the Development of the
  Contemporary Black Film Movement 949, 953
Swiss Film Bares Another Chapter of the Holocaust, A 377
Syberberg's Germany 362
Sydney Didn't Want to Shoot "Horses" 2089
Sydney Pollack: The Way We Are 2089
Symposium on Arbitration in the Motion Picture Industry 641
Symposium on Published Film Scripts: The Value of Close Analysis 1141
Symposium on Soviet Documentary 255
Symposium on the Methodology of Film History 252
S. O. B. 1295
S/Z and RULES OF THE GAME 472, 1827

T

TABU (TABOO), A Story of the South Seas   1671
Take Two: ROMAN HOLIDAY   1748
Take Woody Allen--Please!   2072
Takeover!   763
Taking Chances, Interview With Leo McCarey   1805
Taking Life Seriously: A Monograph on John Huston, Part I--A Touch of
  Hemingway   373, 1321
Taking Some Liberties With THE SUN ALSO RISES   1323
Tale of Two Movies: Charlie Chaplin, United Artists, and the Red Scare,
  A   1418
Tales of Sound and Fury: Observations on the Family Melodrama   712, 977
Talk With Mary   1391
Talk with Mr. Schulberg   1039
Talking About Sex: Notes on First Coitus and the Double Sexual Standard   977
Talking with Peckinpah   2087
Tame Authors and the Corporate Laboratory: Stories, Writers, and Scenarios in
  Hollywood   1035, 1455
Tame Wolves and Phony Claims: Paranoia and FILM NOIR   1947
TAMING OF THE SHREW, THE (1966)   1356
Tape Changes the Home Movie Picture   31
Tartikoff Escorts NBC Into the Movie Business   678
Tati Speaks   2001
Teaching History to the Disadvantaged College Student: A History Through Film
  Approach   39
Teaching the Screen Language: A Basic Method   95
Teaching the Sound Track   83
Teaching Through Genre   173
Technicolor   79
Technique and Ideology: Camera Perspective, Depth of Field   479
Technological and Aesthetic Influences Upon the Development of Deep Focus
  Cinematography in the United States   79, 1807
Technology and Ideology in the Cinema   479
Technology in the Void: Politics and Science in Four Contemporary Space
  Movies   410
Technology of Narrative: Notes on the Esthetics of Nonexistent Fictions,
  The   1297
Ted Turner in the Lion's Den   663
Ted Turner's Screen Test   663
Teenagers and Teenpics, 1955-1957: A Study of Exploitation Filmmaking   739,
  743, 770
Television and Film Ignored Vietnam Until the Late 1960's, Scholars Argue   443
Television and Hollywood: Economic Relations in the 1970s   653
Television and the Future of Motion Picture Exhibition   648
Television Apposite Reactions   653
Television as a Dream   180
Television Melodrama   180
Television/Film Attitudes of Upper-Middle Class Professionals   754
Television, Hollywood, and the Development of Movies Made-for-Television   678
Telling It on the Mountain: Black Filmmakers Are Outside . . .   860, 901, 902
Temples of the Seventh Art   1507
Temporality and Narrativity in Early Cinema   1590
Ten Points About the Crisis in the British Film Industry   607, 751
Ten Seconds to Eternity   1013
Ten Years After Marienbad   2153
Ten Years of Truffaut   2106
Ten-Speed Rite of Passage, A   1004
Tender Comrades   1084, 1085

Tense Situation: Interview With William Friedkin   2195
Tension at Twilight: Second Part of an Analysis of Anthony Mann's Work for the Cinema   1982
Tenth Annual Grosses Gloss   670
Tenth Muse Climbs Parnassus, The   1632
Terrible Buildings: The World of Georges Franju   2119
Terror of Pleasure: The Contemporary Horror Film and Postmodern Theory, The   388
Test of Time: William Wyler, The   1748
Test Screenings of New Movies Put Demographics Over Creativity   738
Testament   2009
Testament of Jean Cocteau, The   2009
TEX   998
Text and Social Process: The Case of James Bond   486
TEX, Parentless Boys in Oklahoma   998
Thank God--I Am Still an Atheist: Luis Bunuel and VIRIDIANA   1992
Thank Heaven for Little Girls   789
That Great Blank Page, The Screen   1029
That Stockholm Venus   1453
That's Hollywood: The Strike That Never Was   1083
That's Wormwood: THE DAY OF THE LOCUST   1291
The Goldbergs--Stereotypes Loved by Americans   833
Theater and Cinema: Part One   1334
Theater and Cinema: Part Two   1334
Theatre Supplies the Funny Men: Third Part of a History of Italian Cinema, The   1607
Theatricality, Narrativity, and Trickality: Reevaluating the Cinema of Georges Melies   1604
Theatricals in Jean Renoir's THE RULES OF THE GAME and GRAND ILLUSION   1827
Theda Bara   1434
Their Holocaust, Upon Watching Ours: THE DR. JOHN HANEY SESSIONS and OPEN SECRETS   291
Theme, Felt Life, and the Last-Minute Rescue in Griffith After INTOLERANCE   1363
Theodore Dreiser and the Film   1300
Theoretical-Historical Survey: Films and Dreams, A   582, 583
Theories of Film Music   83, 400
Theory and Film: Principles of Realism and Pleasure   588, 605
Theory and Practice of Blockbusters, The   656
Theory and Practice: The Criticism of Jean-Luc Godard   2109
Theory of Mass Culture, A   455
Theory: LOVING WITH A VENGEANCE: MASS-PRODUCED FANTASIES FOR WOMEN   517
There Are No Simple Solutions--Frederick Wiseman on Viewing Film   2092
There Isn't Enough Time: An Interview With Alain Resnais   2116
There's More to Malle Than Sex, Sex, Sex   2119
They Call Me a Do-It-Yourself Man   888
They Liked to Break the Rules   1410
They Shaft Writers Don't They?: Interview With James Poe   85, 1037
They Tell It Like It wasn't   1013
They Turned Old Movies Into a Timely Film About Nuclear War   324
They've Turned Gatsby to Goo   1322
Thin Slice of Americana, A   1002
Thinking it Differently: Television and the Film Industry   678
Thinking of Corruption   1009
Third Audience, The   1022
This Damned Eternal Triangle   1297

THIS IS AMERICA: Documentaries for Theaters, 1942-1951 280
THIS MAN MUST DIE: Chabrol's ILIAD 2098
THIS SPORTING LIFE 2160
Thomas H. Ince 1350
Thomas Ince 1577
Thorny Issues from the Seeds of Controversy 2098
Thought in Film: The Case of Kozintsev's HAMLET 1353
Thoughts About the Fear of Kids in Current American Movies 974
Thoughts on CINEMA VERITE and a Discussion with the Maysles Brothers 2041
Thoughts on My Craft 1729, 2190
THOUSAND CLOWNS, A 1022
Thousands of E. T.'s Are Heading for Stores 488
Three Ages of the Musical, The 400
Three by Aldrich 2071
Three Comedians of the Horse Opera 1447
Three Designers: Ken Adams, Edward Marshall, Richard MacDonald 79
Three Faces of Evil 834
Three Faces of FILM NOIR 1947
Three Frankenheimer Films: A Sociological Approach 2077
Three Novelists Criticize Hollywood 1032
Three Thousand Hours of Cinema 2109
Three Women's Films 526
Three X Sam: The Flavor of Ketchup--Sam Fuller Interviewed 1977
Three-D on the Screen 656
Three-D or Not Three-D 655
Three-D: Cinema's Slowest Revolution 655
Threepenny Lawsuit, The 2124
Thrill a Minute: Adventure Movies of the 60's 372
THRONE OF BLOOD 1356
Through the Devil's Door: The Early Westerns of Anthony Mann 1982
Through the Looking Glass: Frank Pierson 85
Thunder & Lightning 409
Tight Close-Up, The 2084
Tim McCoy 424
Time and Space of Alain Resnais, The 2116
Time and Warner Look to Europe and Pacific 2204
Time Case Is Dividing Wall Street 2205
Time Flickers Out: Notes on the Passing of THE MARCH OF TIME 281
Time Inc. and Warner Prepare a Counterattack 2205
Time Inc. and Warner to Merge, Creating Largest Media Company 2204
TIME Inc. Is Everything 653
Time Inc.'s Board Plots A Defense 2205
Time Inc., Rejecting Bid by Paramount, Will Pursue Warner 2205
Time of Crisis 2159
Time Overflowing: Rivette In Interview With Jacques Aumont, Jean-Louis Comolli,
  Jean Narboni 2121
Time Turns Paramount Bid Down 2205
Times Change, The 379
TIREZ SUR LE PIANISTE 2156
TITICUT FOLLIES Audience and the Double Bind of Court-Restricted Exhibition,
  The 772
To Catch a Hitch 1835
To Have (Written) and Have Not (Directed): Reflections on Authorship 1323,
  1747
TO KILL A MOCKINGBIRD 1325
To Rescue GERTRUD 2189
To Sci-Fi Writers Hollywood Is Mostly Alien 410
To See or Not to See: The Case Against Censorship 966
To What Extent Does One Have to Learn to Interpret Movies 538

Tom H. Ince   1463
TOM JONES   1328
Tom Mix   424
Tom Mix was a Softie   810
Tomorrow and Tomorrow and TOMORROW   913
Tomorrow the Movies: Is Hollywood Growing Up?   646
Tomorrow's Animation   77
Toning Down Ad Campaign   973
Tony Richardson: An Interview in Los Angeles   1013
Top Stars, Top Dollars   1137
Tough Guy: James M. Cain Interviewed   1039
Tough Race, The   1705
Toward a Cinema of Cruelty   2087
Toward a Harmony of Interests? Rockefeller, the YMCA and the Company Movie
  Theater in Colorado   630
Toward a Historical Methodology for Film Scholarship   1509
Toward a History of Film Exhibition: The Case of the Picture Palace   1670
Toward a Non-Bourgeois Camera Style   2110
Toward a Theory of Film Suspense   1836
Toward a Theory of the Engaging Narrator: Earnest Interventions in Gaskell,
  Stowe, and Eliot   116
Toward a "Politique des Adaptations"   1297
Toward an Historical Methodology for Film Scholarship   252
Toward Film Study   39
Toward Filmic literacy: The Role of the American Film Institute   40
Towards a Brechtian Criticism of Cinema   2124
Towards a Feminist Aesthetic: Reflection-Revolution-Ritual   497
Towards a Historiography of American Film   252, 874, 1509, 1516
Towards a History of Screen Practice   1580, 1582, 1601, 1603
Towards a Theory of a Black Cinema Aesthetic   869, 949, 953
Trade Winds   1130
Traditional Theater and Film in Japan   1335
Traditions of Trickery: The Role of Special Effects in the Science Fiction
  Film   416
Trailblazer and Rebel   1671
Transformation of THE STERILE CUCKOO, The   1039
Transient Olympian: The Psychology of the Male Movie Star, The   801
Translations of Passages from the Two Editions of Athanasius Kircher's ARS
  MAGNA LUCIS ET UMBRAE   1580
Treatment of Social Problems   817
Tri-Ergon, Tobias-Klangfilm, and the Coming of Sound   632
Tri-Star Ok'd to Play Loews, Though Indie Plight Recognized   763
Tri-Star Planning Loews Expansion   682
Tri-Star Sets Exhib Example   682
Tri-Star to Become Part of Columbia Pictures   678
Tri-Star's Bid for Movie Stardom   678
Tri-Star's Screen Buy Moves Studio to Industry Forefront   682
Trial of Joan of Arc, The   1023
Trial of Orson Welles, The   1023
Trials   1022
Trial, The   1022, 1023
Trib-Star Checks Out Film Fans, And Where They Get Info (Not TV)   753
Tribute to Raoul Walsh, A   1672
TRIUMPH OF THE WILL: Document or Artifice?   321
Trouble in Paradise   646
Troubles on the Home Front   972
TRUE HEART SUSIE and the Art of Lillian Gish   1391
Truffaut Re Renoir, Hitchcock, "Man" Vs "Situation" Interest   2107

Truffaut's Gorgeous Killers 2106
Truffaut's LA CHAMBRE VERT: Homage to Henry James 2106
Truffaut's Manifesto: Part Two 1999
Truffaut: Heir to Apollinaire 2106
Truffaut: The Man Was Revealed Through His Art 2108
Truffaut: Twenty Years After 2106
Trumbull's Progress 674
Truth About Leni, The 321
Truth About Pearl White 1455, 1457
Trying To Understand My Own Film 2153
Turia, An Original Story 1671
Turner Wants His MGM TV 678
Tutor-Code of Classical Cinema, The 82, 591
TV Docudrama: Question of Ethics 549
TV Families: Clinging to the Tried and Untrue 972, 973
TV Mailbag: Leni Could Have Said No 321
TV Movies--Better Than the Real Thing (Are You Kidding?) 2202
TV Recycles THE ENTERTAINER As Entertainment 1014
TV Subjects Share Lives With Mixed Feelings 549
TV's Effect on Film Esthetics 648
TV's Historical Dramas: Fact or Fiction? 222
TV's Portrayal of Children Criticized 972
TV's Young Turks: Part One 1939
TV's Young Turks: Part Two 1939
TV: Eva Peron's Argentina and Shylock's Venice 822
TV: The End of the Beginning 653
Twelve Tarzans, The 1455
Twentieth Century-Fox 635
Twentieth Century-Fox Presents a Cinemascope Picture 655
Twentieth-Century's Backlot 1464
Twenty-First Century Nervous Breakdown 409
Twenty-Five Films to Become US Treasures 1514
Twilight of the Drive-In, The 649
Two . . . But Not of a Kind: A Comparison of Two Controversial
  Documentaries 816
Two Arts in One 2109
Two Aspects of Jungian Perspective Upon Film: Jung and Freud 594
Two Cents on the Ruble 1301
Two Chambermaids, The 1994
Two Decades in Another Country: Hollywood and the Cinephiles 1997
Two Faces of Drama, The 1334
Two Faces of FACES 2125
Two Inches off the Ground 2024
Two on U. S. Commission Dissent on Pornography 961
TWO OR THREE THINGS I KNOW ABOUT HER: Godard's Analysis of Women in
  Capitalist Society 497
Two Rode Together 1673
Two Sides of the Civil Rights Coin: A Discussion of TROUBLEMAKERS and A
  TIME FOR BURNING 813
Two Studies in Space-Time 409
Two Studies Link Teen-Age Suicides to TV Programs 745
Two Types of Film Theory 100, 1645
Two Views of THE ICEMAN COMETH 1351
Two Ways Art Gives Shape to Political Horrors 1977
Two Who Were There View PLATOON: The Correspondent 368
Two Who Were There View PLATOON: The Marine Officer 368
Two Women Succeeded as Producers, But Easy Street Is Down the Road 2207
Two-Faced Woman: The "Double" in Women's Melodrama of the 1940's 792
Two-Reel Comedy--Its Rise and Fall, The 1410

Type and Stereotype: Chicano Images in Film 826
Typically Swedish In Ingmar Bergman, The 2183
T. E. B. Clarke, Writer, Dies at 81 1937

U

UA Communications Sold to TCI; Tri-Star Buying Screens 682
UA Unveils Future Film Plans 663
UA's 35th Birthday 1464
Ultimately We Are All Outsiders: The Ethics of Documentary Filming 537
Uncle Tom Will Never Die! 941
UNCLE TOM'S CABIN in American Film History 718
Uncovering the Female Body 1587
Under the Shadow of Hollywood 1935, 1936
Underground Chic: Performance 2160
Underground River, The 2114, 2157
Underground River: Agnes Varda, The 2039
Underground U. S. A. and the Sexploitation Market 2039
Undiscovered Country, The 2159
Uneasy East: Aleksander Ford and the Polish Cinema, The 2012
Unfinished Business of THE LAST TYCOON, The 1109, 1294
Unheroic Age? It is a Screaming Theme 807
Union of Soviet Socialist Republics 2182
Unique Film, The 1985
Uniqueness of Kon Ichikawa: A Translated Symposium, The 2022
United Artists Executive Ousted After HEAVEN'S GATE Fiasco 535
United Artists Sale Backed 2204
United Artists' Script Calls for Divorce 662
United Artists: Final Shooting Script 635
United States Versus the Princes of Porn 2192
United States v. Charlie Chaplin, The 1418
United States v. Motion Picture Film THE SPIRIT OF '76: The Espionage Case
  of Producer Robert Goldstein (1917) 223
Universal Classroom, The 40
Universal Hitchcock, The 1835
Universal Pictures Aide Resigns Under Pressure 535
Universe of Robert Bresson, The 2003
Unknown Cinema of Britain, The 1937
Unlikely Elements: Alan J. Pakula Interviewed 2195
Unmasking of a Political Film, The 1315
Unseen Energy Swallows Space: The Space in Early Films and Its Relation to
  American Avant-Garde, An 1590, 1600
Unwanted PLATOON Finds Success as U. S. Examines the Vietnam War 368
Up from the Underground, Part 1: Curtis Harrington 2039
Up from The Underground, Part 2: Conrad Rooks 2039
Up to Date with Robert Aldrich 2071
Upset by SADAT, Egypt Bars Columbia Films 488
USA: Confidential 816, 998
Use and Abuses of the Zoom Lens, The 79
Useful Modes of Thinking Contribute to the Power of Prejudice 904
Uses and Gratifications Approach in the Study of "Entertainment" and Leisure
  Use, The 855
Using the Partnership Model 71
Utopia 'Tis of Thee 547
U. A. Theatre and Cable Deal 662
U. S. and Soviet Film Makers Debate Stereotypes 440
U. S. Black Films Failing in Europe 898

U. S. Film Exhibition: The Formation of Big Business   621, 636, 639
U. S. Literature: Canon Under Siege   445
U. S. Market Needs Specialty Pix   671
U. S. Motion Picture Theatres' Box Office Average Price Per Admission and Number of Admissions   751
U. S. Takes Issue With Costa-Gavras Film on Chile   1021
U. S. Ticket Sales $1,750,000,000   753
U. S. & Canada Theater Circuits Ranked By Size   682

V

VACANCES DE MONSIEUR HULOT, LES   2011
Vadim and Zola   2119
Vadim, Roger   2120
Valenti Justifies Prediction of Doom from Home VCRs   760
VALLEY GIRL   999
Value Implications of Popular Films, The   453, 455
Vamp and the Machine: Technology and Sexuality in Fritz Lang's METROPOLIS, The   1642
Vanishing Jew of Our Popular Culture: The Little Man Who Is No Longer There   830
Varda, Agnes   2114
VCR's and Disks Now Star at Show   31
VCR's Bring Big Changes in the Use of Leisure   31, 545
Verbal Taboo in SHAMPOO   438
Vertical Integration, Horizontal Regulation: The Growth of Rupert Murdoch's US Media Empire   663
VERTIGO Re-Visited   2081
Vertov Papers, The   1645
Very Narrow Path: The Politics of Edward Dmytryk, A   1092
Veteran's View of Hollywood Authenticity, A   254
Viacom Most Likely Turner Partner for MGM/UA Buy   662
Vibrations: An Interview With John Phillip Law   2082
Victory of Vittorio De Sica, The   1877, 1925
Video Cassettes Get a Big Play: Videodisk Sales Face Problems   764
Video Disc: Shining a New Light, The   760
Video Recorders Change Daily Habits   762
Video Reshaping Film Industry: TV Technology Erodes Control of Distribution   762
Video Sales Expected to Set Records: Industry Offers Its Latest Wares in Chicago Show   762
Videodisc Revolution, The   760
Videodisks Battle for Consumer Favor   764
Videology of Science Fiction, The   416
Vietnam and the Hollywood Genre Film: Inversions of American Mythology in THE DEER HUNTER and APOCALYPSE NOW   178
Vietnam Filmography, A   335
Vietnam Hero Worship   376
Vietnam! Vietnam!--An Exclusive Report on John Ford's Propaganda Documentary for the USIA   1674
Vietnam: Representations of the Self and War   442
VIEW FROM THE BRIDGE, A   1349
Viewing Japanese Film: Some Considerations   1738
Viewing Report of SHANE   1009
Viewing Report: TREASURE OF THE SIERRA MADRE   1022
Viewing, Viewed: A Critique of Subject-Generated Documentary   280
Vincente Minnelli Dies; Movie Director was 76   1983
Vincente Minnelli: The Decorative Auteur   1983

Violence in Television Drama: Trends and Symbolic Functions   459
Violence in the Cinema   71
Violence Leads to Modified Ads for Par's WARRIORS   974
VIRGIN SPRING: Anatomy of a Mythic Image, THE   2183
Virginity of Astronauts: Sex and the Science   416
VIRIDIANA   1991
Virtues and Limitations of Montage, The   129
Visibility and Feminist Film Criticism   476
Vision and Dream in the Cinema   593
Visit to the Trenches   1376
Visual Distancing in Godard   2110
Visual History: The Craft of the Historian Filmmaker   252
Visual Pleasure and Narrative Cinema   471, 473, 527, 529, 531, 532
Visualizing the Warsaw Ghetto: Nazi Images of the Jews Refiltered by the
  BBC   222
Vitaphone--Pro and Con, The   633
Vitascope/Cinematographe: Initial Patterns of American Film Industrial
  Practice   615, 1602
Voices of the Documentarist, The   280
Vote for Britain: A Cinemagoer's Guide to the General Election   817
Vsevolod Pudovkin   1645, 1668
Vt. Theaters Struggle for Films, Survival   764

W

Wait and See: Chabrol's Films Not Yet Shown in Britain   2098, 2099
Waking From a New "Nightmare" to New Profits   2206
Waldo Salt   1090
Waldo Salt, 72, Dies; Oscar-Winning Writer   1090
Walking the Hollywood Color Line   851
Wall Street Awaits Video Wunderkind   31
Wallace Reid   966
Walt Disney Innovates the Television Showcase   653
Walt Disney's Private Snafu: The Use of Humor in World War II Army Film   320
Wanted, An Ethics of Employment for Our Time   1186
Wanted: More Events, More Heroes   547
War Against War Movies, The   258
War and the Arts, The   335
War as a Spiritual Exercise: Japan's "National Policy Films"   1894, 1895, 1896,
  1898
War Between the Writers and the Directors: Part II--The Directors   2077
War Cinema of Imperial Japan, The   1894, 1895
War Films, The   232
War Game, The   1024
War Is, Was, and Always Will Be, Hell   282
War Makers, The   325
War of the Wizards   2199
War Over Justice: An Interview With Marcel Ophuls, A   324
War That's Fit to Shoot   1977
War Within: The making of KNOW YOUR ENEMY--JAPAN, A   281
Warhol's Underground   2039
Warhol, Andy (with Paul Morrissey)   2040
Warner Brothers   622
Warner in a Deal to Acquire Lorimar   663
Warner Is Acquired by Time Inc. Within Hours of Court Approval   2205
Warner's Financial Aid Helps Rescue Cannon   535
Warner's Scenario for Hits   663

Warner-Vitaphone Peril: The American Film Industry Reacts to the Innovation of Sound, The 633, 697
Warner, HBO Deal Reported: Rights to Films Set to be Sold 653
WARRIORS Off to Good Start in N.Y. 973
Warriors Return: Normal or Neurotic? 375
War, Wheat and Steel: King Vidor Interviewed 367, 1671
Was Welles a Wizard or a Whirling Dervish? 1751
Way Out West: Nathanael West in Lotus Land 1291
Way They Were, The 1084
Way We weren't, The 981
WBBM in Live-Lens Survey; 75% of Kids Testing Chicago Theatres Admitted to 'R' Pics 753
We Aren't Family: Movies for Non-Nuclear People 1003
We Lost it at the Movies: The Generation that Grew Up on THE GRADUATE Took Over Hollywood--and Went into Plastics 666, 667, 2191
We Lost So Much Dignity as We Came of Age 1007, 1365
We're Living In a Hitchcock World, All Right 1836
We've Gotta Have It: Spike Lee and a New Black Cinema 903
Weapons: An Interview with Joseph Losey 1981
Weaving a Narrative: Style and Economic Background in Griffith's   Biograph Films 1362
Weinberg Touch: Harry Langdon, The 1672
Well-Worn Muse: Adaptation in Film History and Theory 1297
Welles Before Kane 1807
Welles' CHIMES AT MIDNIGHT 1353
Wellman's WILD BOYS OF THE ROAD: The Rhetoric of a Depression Movie 1675
Western Landscape of Raoul Walsh, The 1672
Western--Old and New, The 424
Westerner, The 144
What Do Those Birds in Hollywood Have that I Don't?: Early Filmmaking in Colorado 626
What Do We Know About Audiences? 745
What Ever Happened to American Movies? 2071
What Every Girl Wants to Know 1453
What Has Stephane Audran Got? Glamour 2098
What Is A Star 1981
What Is Hollywood Trying To Tell Us? 971
What Is Transamerica? 662
What Isn't Cinema? 1509
What Lies Between the Objects 2134
What makes a Star?--Howard Hawks Knew Best of All 1747
What Makes Hollywood Bid Big for a Hot Novel 1028
What Makes Hollywood Run Now? 1046
What Makes Mel Brooks Run? 2073
What Makes Two Olympic Heroes Run in the British CHARIOTS OF FIRE 1013
What Shining Phantom: Writers and the Movies 1028, 1106
What to Show the World: The Office of War Information and Hollywood, 1942-1945 229
What TV Drama Is Teaching Our Children 440
What's Hollywood Saying to You, Or Why Nostalgia 973
What's Love Got to Do with It?: A Kiss Is Still a Kiss, But the Rules Have Changed 2204
What's New at the Movies 2207
What's Real? What's True? 2084
What's So Funny About Japan? 2177
What's Wrong With Today's Films? 2202
Whatever Happened to Bette Davis? 1981
Whatever Happened to Film Noir?: THE POSTMAN ALWAYS RINGS TWICE (1946-1981) 505

When a Tame Film Inspires Violence 974
When Disney Buys a TV Station 672
When Hollywood Asks the Pentagon For Help 231
When I do It, It's Not Gore, Says Writer Paul Schrader 2195
When Is an Independent Producer Independent?: The Case of United Artists after
  1948 643
When Kids Get Mad 722
When Movies Are Political Harbingers 444
When Movies Were Very Young 1362
When the Lights Went Out--Hollywood, the Depression and the Thirties 733,
  736
When The Movies Go Abroad 213
When the New Wave Became Old Hat: The Films of Claude Chabrol--Part 1 2098
When the New Wave Became Old Hat: The Films of Claude Chabrol--Part 2 2098,
  2101
When the Soundtrack Makes the Film 611
When the Woman Looks 495
When We Dead Awaken: Writing as Re-Vision 468
When Women Wept 793
When Writers Turn the Tables Rather than the Other Cheek 143
Where America Feels at Home: The Sitcom Living Room 544
Where Are All the Women Who Fell for 007? 680
Where Are the Films About Real Black Men and Women? 897, 1005
Where Are the Women? 790
Where Have All the Heroes Gone? 437, 803
Where Have All the Stylists Gone? 1434
Where Love Has Gone 982
Where the Action Was 2040
Which Way the Black Film 941
White Light, White Heat 324
Whitehall With Warhol 2040
Who are Those Guys? The Movie Western During the TV Era 2035
Who Goes to the Cinema? 755
Who Is Without Sin? The Maternal Melodrama in American Film, 1930-1939 794
Who Owns the Media: The Conglomerates Have a Stranglehold on Mass
  Entertainment 671, 675
Who Really Wrote CITIZEN KANE? 1263
Who's Afraid of Alfred Hitchcock 1835
WHO'S AFRAID OF VIRGINIA WOOLF? 2086
Whose Crisis 2159
Why 'Faithful' Adaptations Fail 1291
Why Are They Being So Mean to THE GREAT GATSBY? 1322
Why Can't the Movies Play Ball? 816
Why Do We Cheer Vigilante Cops? 801
Why Does White America Love Sidney Poitier So? 890, 891
Why E. T. Must Go Home: The New Family in American Cinema 410
Why Hollywood Never Asks the God Question 1139
Why Indians Can't Be Villains Any More 826
Why Is Sidney Poitier the Only One? 890
Why Jewish Movie Moguls: An Exploration in American Culture 820, 821
Why More Top Novelists Don't Go Hollywood 1028
Why Neo-Realism Failed 1004, 1922
Why Some Novelists Cast Hollywood as the Heavy 1136
Why the Movie Majors Are Major 607, 614, 659, 660
Why THE SILENT CLOWNS Isn't All That Original 1677
Why Today's Films Turn to History 256
Why TV Is Buying From Hollywood 1005
Why Women Go to the Movies 528, 585, 588

Why Women Wept 615
Why Write If You Can't Sell It? 1028
Why You Go to the Pictures Or Stay Away: The BBC Gives the Industry the
  Facts . . . 744
Why "S. O. B." Deserves to Be S. R. O. 1295
Why, Even You and I Can Be Stars 2085
Wider Scope: Hollywood Is Expanding Its Business Horizons 653
Widescreen 655
Wild Bill William A. Wellman 1674
Wild Bill's Wild Boys 1675
WILD BUNCH and the Problem of Idealist Aesthetics, or How Long Would Sam
  Peckinpah Last In Plato's Republic?, The 2087
WILD BUNCH Versus STRAW DOGS 2087
Wild Ones, The 2207
Wilder Life, A 1973
Wilder Times 799
Will Movie Theaters Survive Video? 760
Will Success Spoil Brazilian Cinema? 2158
Will These 'New Era' Movies Bring Out the Snob in You? 1034
William Faulkner: Novel Into Film 1321
William Fox Presents SUNRISE 1706
William Wyler: A Great Director Exploits His Virtuosity 1007
William Wyler: A Great Director Has Been Reduced to Exploiting His
  Virtuosity 1748
William Wyler: A Life in Film 1748
William Wyler: An Interview 1748
WILSON 366
WILSON: Hollywood Propaganda for World Peace 366
Wings of Eagles, The 1673
With Malice Toward Some 1017
Without a Dinosaur: Peter Bogdanovich Interviewed 2195
Wiz Kid 2084
Wizardry of Fellini, The 1927
Wodehouse World of Hollywood, The 1058
Woman at the Keyhole: Women's Cinema and Feminist Criticism, The 495, 528,
  614
WOMAN IN THE DUNES 2177
Woman Is a Woman, A 2109
Woman's Film: Possession and Address, The 495
Woman's Nightmare: Masculinity in DAY OF THE DEAD 806
Women and Film: A Discussion of Feminine Aesthetics 470
Women and Still More Women: Part II 1012
Women as Caricature in Films 789
Women at Work: Warners in the Thirties 471
Women Growing 2156
Women in Film 789
Women in Film . . . Just Barely 789
Women in Western Films: The Civilizer, the Saloon Singer, and Their Modern
  Sister 431
Women's Cinema and Feminist Film Criticism 471
Women's Cinema as Counter-Cinema 451, 497
Women's Film, The 792
Women's Place: The Absent Family 642
Women, Representation and the Image 789
Wooden Acting of Woody Allen, The 2072
Woody Allen at the Peak of Parody 786
Woody Allen Continues to Refine His Art 786
Woody Allen Is Feeling Better 2072
Woody Allen: Stumbling through the Looking Glass 2072

Woody Allen: The Failure of the Therapeutic 837
Words and Movies 2083
Workers' Film Movement in Britain, 1929-39, The 214
Working Class Goes to War, The 559
WORKING GIRL in Reagan Country 470
Working with Bresson 1994
Working with Hitch 1838
Working with Hitchcock 1844
World of Carl Dreyer, The 1729
World of Comedy 1410
World of Howard Hawks, The 1747
World of Samuel Fuller, The 1977
World War I Aviation Film 371
World War I on the Screen: Part I 262
World War I on the Screen: Part II 262
World War II in the Movies: A Selected Bibliography of Sources 262
World War II on Japanese Screens 282
World War II: Armed Forces Documentary 230, 295
Worlds Apart: Aldrich Since THE DIRTY DOZEN 2071
Worldwide Merchandising Yields Heavily For Factors 488, 611
Wounded Vet in Postwar Film, The 259
Writer and Motion Pictures, The 84
Writer II: An Interview With Alexander Jacobs, The 85
Writer in American Films, The 85
Writer's Wave, A 2159
Writer: Raymond Chandler and the World You Live In, The 798
Writing Film History: The Struggle for Synthesis 613
Writing for Musicals: Interview With Betty Comden and Adolph Green 83
Writing For the Movies is Harder Than It Looks 1028
Writing History with Film: Two Views of the 1937 Strike Against General Motors
  by the UAW 252
Writings of Dziga Vertov, The 1645
Written on the Screen: Anita Loos 85, 1035
WUTHERING HEIGHTS: He Hated the Star, . . . Story, . . . Ending,
  But . . . 1474
Wyler Is Dead at 79; Director Had Won 3 Academy Awards 1796
Wyler on Wyler 1748
Wyler, Wellman, and Huston: Three Directors With a Past and a Future 1748
Wyler, William 1748

X

X-Rated Industry in a Slump 960

Y

Yasujiro Ozu 1742
Yasujiro Ozu: The Syntax of His Films 1893, 1894
Year of LA DOLCE VITA, The 1023, 2169
Yesterday and Tomorrow: New Hungarian Films 2167
Yesterday's Hollywood: Gangster Heroes 384
Yesterday's Hollywood: Musicals and Comedies 401
Yesterday's Hollywood: Western Heroes 424
Yiddish Origins and Jewish-American Transformations 836
Yiddish Transit 820

You Name It, I'll Eat It: A Monologue Discussion of Morrissey's FLESH, TRASH,
  HEAT 2040
Young and Innocent 1835
Young German Film 2165
YOUNG MR. LINCOLN, 1939 477
Young Swedish Cinema: In Relation to Swedish Film Tradition 2182
Your Taste, My Taste . . . and the Censor's 1984
Youth and the Cinema: Part I--The Teenage Rave 970, 982
Youth and the Cinema: Part II--Candid Camera 970, 982
Youth of Francis Ford Coppola, The 2196
Yugoslavia: Multi-Faceted Cinema 2014

Z

Z Films 2049
ZERO DE CONDUITE 1828
Zinnemann on the Verge 1988
Zoetrope and APOCALYPSE NOW 2196
Zoetrope Saga, The 2196
Zoetrope Up For Sale 536

Authors-Articles Index

A

Abel, Richard 477, 1709, 1710, 1843
Aberbach, David 1414
Abramson, Dan 879
Ackerman, Dan 1675
Ackerman, Forrest J. 412
Acker, Robert 2165
Adair, Gilbert 2101, 2103
Adamson, Joe 1749
Adamson, Judith 1329
Adams, Michael 913, 1110, 1115
Adams, Robert L., Jr. 1362, 1364
Adelson, Andrea 672
Adler, Renata 151, 514, 916
Admussen, Richard L. 1297
Afron, Charles 1748
Agee, James 53, 137, 140, 144, 145, 306, 366, 915, 1368, 1383, 1548, 1677, 1693, 1845
Agostino, Donald E. 760
Agress, Lynne 789
Ajame, Pierre 2147
Albarino, R. 1351
Albert, Robert 455
Aldrich, Robert 2071
Aldridge, Kay 498
Alea, Thomas Guitierrez 2163
Alexander, A. J. 789
Alexander, Francis W. 851
Alexander, Max 1726
Alexander, S. G. P. 2031
Allegro, Anthony T. 2195
Allen, Don 2106, 2151
Allen, Eric 656
Allen, Jeanne Thomas 607, 621, 1359, 1461, 1462, 1510, 1513, 1516, 1590, 1599, 1838
Allen, Robert C. 252, 615, 617, 621, 685, 697, 718, 719, 1509, 1514, 1590, 1602, 1706
Allen, Steve 1692
Allen, Tom 653
Almendarez, Valentin 1814, 2156
Almendros, Nestor 2163
Alpert, Hollis 53, 142, 1000, 1105, 1293, 2085, 2156
Altman, Charles F. 252, 593, 874, 1509, 1516
Altman, Rick 1390
Altman, Robert 1749
Alvey, Mark 1007, 1921
Alwyn, William 83
Amberg, George 139, 1525, 2005, 2009
Ames, Aydelott 966
Ames, Roy 2000
Anast, Philip 533, 745
Anderegg, Jeanne 604
Anderegg, Michael A. 39, 1838
Anderson, Carolyn 772

Anderson, Earl 141, 1753
Anderson, Joseph L.   1335, 1583, 1733, 1736, 1737, 1738, 1739, 1740, 1894, 2182
Anderson, Lindsay 216, 295, 317, 1012, 1351, 1548, 1674, 1802, 1845, 1980, 2024, 2076
Anderson, Robert 607, 619, 685, 1460, 1461, 1517
Andrews, Nigel 2087
Andrews, Rena 321
Andrew, James Dudley 446, 447, 654, 655, 1141, 1297, 1706, 1914, 1992, 1993, 1994, 2008, 2156
Andrew, J. Dudley 37, 38
Andrew, Paul 1739
Angell, Roger 1007
Ansbacher, Heinz L. 586, 587
Ansen, David 906, 995, 998, 1016, 1295
Ansinall, Sue 1569
Antonioni, Michelangelo 53, 141
Appelbaum, Ralph 1987, 2077, 2079
Appel, Alfred, Jr. 1637, 1838
Applebaum, Ralph 2195
Appleman, Daniel 2178
Aranda, J. Francisco 1002, 1714, 1721, 1723
Arbasino, Alberto 1878
Arbit, Roberta L. 386
Arbuthnot, Lucie 533
Archer, Eugene 53, 373, 1003, 1009, 1018, 1321, 2010, 2183
Ardsley, Robert 646
Aristarco, Guido 1012
Armes, Roy 1548, 1711, 1826, 1995, 2009, 2116, 2151, 2153, 2171
Armour, Robert A. 801, 912, 1300, 1312
Armstrong, Michael 388, 750, 1355, 1356, 1856
Arms, George 1051
Arnheim, Rudolf 53, 54, 142, 144, 580, 1030, 1754, 1955
Arnold, Edwin T. 1108, 1110, 1115
Arnold, Francis 409
Arnold, Gary 1392
Arnold, James W. 416
Arnold, Robert 252, 485, 486, 714
Arrowsmith, William 37, 40, 51
Arthur, Art 1680
Arthur, Paul 1974
Asendio, James 942
Asheim, Lester Eugene 1300
Ash, Rene L. 1536
Asimov, Isaac 415
Asquith, Anthony 1632
Astaire, Fred 1962
Astruc, Alexandre 1747, 1996, 2123
Atkinson, Brooks 1351
Atkins, Irene Kahn 1294, 1322
Atlas, Jacoba 2073
Atlas, James 2119
Attenborough, Richard 1571
Atwell, Lee 409
Au Werter, Russell 2077
Aufderheide, Patricia 2158, 2163
Austen, David 424, 816, 998, 1082, 1084, 1999, 2074, 2086, 2093, 2161
Auster, Albert 259, 559, 1391, 2041, 2088
Austin, Bruce A. 573, 649, 705, 751, 753, 756, 762, 768, 769, 770, 771, 959, 2202

Austin, Wade 912
Avakian, Aram 2042
Axeen, David 367
Ayer, Douglas 697
Ayfre, Amedee 2003

B

Babener, Liahna 970
Baby, Yvonne 2130, 2135, 2156
Bachmann, Gideon 1023, 1321, 1927, 2093
Baez, Joan 62
Baggett, Patricia 533
Bailin, Rebecca 793
Bailyn, Lotte 745
Baird, Jay W. 206
Baker, Peter G. 997, 1000, 1001, 1014, 1020, 1323, 1324, 1328, 1349, 1352,
    1353, 1981, 2157, 2181
Baker, Ross K. 549
Baker, Russell 472
Bakshy, Alexander 1339
Balazs, Bela 65, 144, 1312
Balcon, Michael 81
Baldwin, James 220, 892, 941, 1309
Balio, Tino 643, 685, 686
Bandura, Albert 745
Banks, Cherry A. McGee 854
Bannerman, Julia 462
Baran, Stanley J. 546
Barbaro, Nick 1828, 1933, 1976, 2098
Barbera, Jack 913
Barbour, Alan 1447
Barker, W. W. 1084
Barkhausen, Hans 321
Barkin, Michael 1019, 1673
Barna, Yon 1513
Barnes, Clive 1410
Barnes, Peter 1350
Barnouw, Erik 85, 247, 1593, 1602, 1671
Barringer, Felicity 2182
Barron, Frank 488, 611, 752
Barron, Fred 2102
Barry, Bridget 855
Barry, Iris 1522
Barr, Charles 655, 2003, 2130
Barsam, Richard Meran 280, 295, 296, 321, 1312
Barsness, John A. 1019
Barthes, Roland 118, 566
Barth, Jack 2081
Bartlett, Nicholas 1641
Bart, Pauline B. 565
Basinger, Jeanine 365, 508, 615, 793, 801, 1921
Baskakov, Vladimir 2181
Basler, Barbara 486
Bass, Warren 573
Batchelor, Jennifer 400
Bates, Robin 2165

Bates, Roy E. 697
Battcock, Gregory 2039
Battestin, Martin C. 1316
Baudry, Jean-Louis 118, 470, 479, 480, 584
Bauer, Alice H. 459
Bauer, Ralph A. 564, 733
Bauer, Raymond A. 459, 745
Baumgarten, Marjorie 1814, 2119
Baxter, John 1548, 1561, 1831, 2082, 2120, 2154, 2195
Baxter, Peter 79, 719, 1831
Bayer, William 995
Bazin, Andre 53, 129, 167, 350, 648, 1002, 1102, 1334, 1414, 1548, 1723, 1802, 1807, 1816, 1836, 1845, 1922, 1933, 2007, 2096, 2097, 2123
Beale, Lewis 424
Beal, Greg 1675
Bean, Robin 85, 325, 816, 994, 995, 998, 1005, 1010, 1014, 1018, 1023, 1319, 2010, 2080, 2161, 2165
Beardslee, David C. 1011
Beaton, James 1315
Beaupre, Lee 666, 668, 676
Beauregard, Georges de 2131
Beauvoir, Simone de 508
Beckerman, Jim 1312
Becker, Boris W. 535, 769
Beck, Philip 175, 252
Bedell, Sally 973
Behlmer, Rudy 79, 83, 371, 1301, 1980
Behrens, Laurence 41
Beinhorn, Courtenay 1976
Belkin, Lisa 972
Bellah, James Warner 2075
Beller, Miles 1005
Bellour, Raymond 82, 118, 585, 1835, 1843, 2080
Bellush, Bernard 1074, 1076, 1080
Bell, Wendy 2088
Belton, Ellen R. 1673
Belton, John 1835, 1976
Benayoun, Robert 2131
Benchley, Robert 916, 941
Benderson, Albert 593
Bender, Eillen T. 598
Benet, Stephen Vincent 1134
Bennetts, Leslie 328, 656, 681, 1003, 1291, 1912, 1927
Bennett, Lerone, Jr. 894
Bennett, Tony 486
Benoit-Levy, Jean 50
Benson, Edward 771
Benson, Harold 141
Bentley, Eric 712, 1333, 1336
Beranger, Jean 1813
Bercovici, Konrad 1420
Berger, John 2159
Berger, Joseph 445
Berger, Spencer M. 1798
Bergman, Ingmar 141, 1298, 2183
Bergstrom, Janet 471
Berg, A. Scott 1474
Berg, Charles 400, 1933, 2098
Berg, Gretchen 2039, 2110

Berkowitz, Leonard 745
Berkowitz, Stan 2037
Berlowitz, Marvin J. 978
Bernhardt, William 2030
Bernstein, Barbara 508
Bernstein, Elmer 83
Bernstein, Jeremy 2083
Bernstein, Matthew 643
Bernstein, Richard 446
Berson, Arnold 321
Bessie, Alvah 1084, 1089
Bevins, Winfred 2087
Biggers, Thompson 771
Billard, Ginette 2110, 2119
Billings, Pat 1989
Bishop, Christopher 1672
Biskind, Peter 303, 416, 1084, 1985
Bjorkman, Stig 1977, 2078
Blache, Alice Guy 508
Blackburn, Steve 1747, 2083
Black, Gregory D. 229, 856
Black, Louis 1535, 1747, 1806, 2088
Blades, John 798
Blakefield, William J. 281
Blanchard, Simon 1569
Blangsted, Folmer 82
Blobner, Helmut 322
Bloch, Robert 415
Blotner, Joseph 1316
Blowen, Michael 904, 905
Bluem, A. William 73, 295
Bluestone, George 53, 142
Blue, James 1000, 1024, 1672, 2041, 2120, 2168, 2176
Blumberg, James F. 1142
Blumenberg, Richard M. 280, 2035, 2153
Blumenthal, J. 1356
Blumer, Ronald H. 1711
Blum, William 2087
Bobo, Jacqueline 905
Bobrow, Andrew 1291
Bock, Audie E. 2021, 2196
Boddy, William 653, 656, 678
Bodeen, DeWitt 84, 966, 1042, 1248, 1300, 1365, 1366, 1434, 1680, 1703, 1707, 1709
Bogan, Louise 514
Bogdanovich, Peter 1263, 1673, 1674, 1776, 2084
Bogle, Donald 860, 867, 868, 869, 882
Bombyk, David 1836
Bondanella, Peter 1914, 2169, 2173
Bond, Kirk 1729, 1836, 2164, 2189
Bonelli, Eugene 2186
Bone, Robert 452
Bonitzer, Pascal 118
Bontemps, Jacques 1039, 1961, 1981, 1985
Boorman, John 1032
Borders, William 548
Borde, Raymonde 1947
Bordwell, David 39, 79, 118, 1644, 1645, 1646, 1750, 2018, 2076, 2106

Bordzuk, Gary 1536
Borges, Jorge Luis 1792
Bork, Eric 2072
Borneman, Ernest 686, 1022
Boultenhouse, Charles 489
Bourdain, G. S. 2095, 2113
Bourget, Jean Loup 190
Bourne, St. Clair 949
Bowers, Ronald L. 1803, 2009, 2160
Bowles, Stephen E. 227
Bowser, Eileen 252, 1361, 1366, 1510, 1694
Bowser, Pearl 863, 866, 872, 949
Boyer, Jay 1093
Boyer, Peter J. 489, 549, 678
Boyle, James F. 1142
Bracher, Frederick 1028, 1042, 1044, 1108
Brackett, Leigh 508, 1747
Brackman, Jacob 53, 2086
Bradbury, Ray 1234
Bradlow, Paul 816
Brady, Frank 1751
Brady, Robert A. 607, 635, 636, 644
Braff, Richard E. 1365, 1702
Brakhage, Stanley 1955, 1974
Brandon, James R. 1734
Branigan, Edward 79, 80, 654, 1509
Brantley, Robin 1747
Braudy, Leo 416, 1320, 1846, 1857, 2093
Brauer, Ralph 736, 2035
Braun, Eric 1434, 1749, 1795, 1803
Braverman, Barret 1363
Brecht, Bertolt 1309, 2124
Brehm, Randi 994, 1018
Breitbart, Eric 2000, 2093
Breitrose, Henry 2040
Breit, Harvey 1039
Breton, Andre 1720
Brewster, Ben 477
Bridges, James 700
Bright, John 1084, 1085
Brill, Leslie W. 1843
Brion, Patrick 83, 1005, 1014, 1797, 1982, 1985
Britton, Andrew 367
Britt, Donna 905
Britt, Gwenneth 996
Brody, S. 1645
Broeck, John 83
Brogan, D. W. 455, 547, 548
Bromwich, David 576
Brooks, John 1132, 1133
Brooks, Louise 508, 1012, 1674
Brooks, Mel 700
Brook, Peter 1002, 1342
Broughton, Garry 2098, 2099
Broun, Heywood Hale 862
Brouse, Ann G. 393
Brouwer, Martin 745
Browne, Nick 79, 118, 477, 579, 593, 1364, 1799, 1802
Brownlow, Kevin 1236, 1414, 1577, 1609, 1712, 1748

Brown, Anne 1463, 1747, 1994
Brown, Constance A. 1354
Brown, Geoff 1224, 1842
Brown, Georgia A. 2177, 2196
Brown, John Lindsay 2073
Brown, Karl 1368
Brown, Patricia Leigh 544
Brown, Roscoe C. 855
Brown, Royal S. 1835, 2130, 2196
Brown, Sterling A. 941
Brown, Thornton K. 1463, 1747, 1994
Brozan, Nadine 791
Broz, Jaroslav 2164
Brunas, John 1446
Bruner, Jerome 177
Brunetta, Gian Piero 1876
Brunette, Peter 1039, 1314, 1922
Brunius, Jacques B. 1718, 2153
Brustein, Robert 53, 137, 815, 2034
Bryan, James H. 754
Bryan, Julien 282
Buchanan, Angus 1328
Buckley, Michael 993, 1017, 1346, 2089
Buckner, Garth 1321
Buck, Pearl S. 54
Budd, Michael 1673, 1674, 1912
Budgen, Suzanne 1827
Bukalski, Peter J. 35
Bukowiecki, Leon 2009
Bunuel, Juan 1723
Bunuel, Luis 53, 1548, 1722, 1723
Burch, Noel 118, 1542, 1605, 2093, 2094, 2096, 2112, 2116, 2117
Burgess, Jackson 995, 1001, 2083
Burgess, John 1012, 1320
Burke, Franke M. 1927
Burke, Kenneth 1752
Burke, P. E. 2183
Burk, Debbie 2155
Burnett, Ron 38
Burns, Bradford E. 252
Burns, Dan E. 1272, 1273
Burns, E. Bradford 39, 2178
Burns, E. Jane 416
Burns, Fred 416
Burns, Paul E. 1645, 1667, 1668
Burstyn, Varda 603
Burton, Henry 1014, 1985
Burton, Julianne 471, 2178
Buscombe, Edward 176, 190, 252, 632, 678, 1509, 1511, 1515, 1516, 1837, 1999
Butler, Terence 2088
Buxton, Rod 1814
Byers, Jackie 1983
Bygrave, Mike 669, 2196, 2197
Byrge, Duane 903, 997, 1104
Byrne, Donn 546
Byron, Stuart 665, 666, 1324, 2071, 2076

C

Cadbury, William 1363
Caen, Michael 379
Cagle, Anthony 1827
Cain, James M. 1039
Calder, Robert L. 1329, 1330
Callahan, John F. 1109, 1294
Callenbach, Ernest 132, 139, 513, 1022, 1349, 1350, 1507, 1512, 1523, 1974,
2086, 2087
Calverton, V. F. 219
Cameron, Elisabeth 2098
Cameron, Ian 1752, 1835, 1836, 1843, 1978, 1984, 2003, 2071, 2096, 2098, 2099,
2123, 2130
Cameron, Julia 2204
Campbell, Edward D. C., Jr. 912
Campbell, Gregg M. 789
Campbell, Marilyn 1674
Campbell, Peter 1315
Campbell, Russell 225, 1204, 1673, 1675
Camper, Fred 1984
Canby and Akira Kurosawa 2019
Canby and Cold War films 334
Canby and documentaries 324
Canby and Federico Fellini 1927
Canby and film budgets 2200
Canby and film buffs 56
Canby and film criticism 430
Canby and Japanese movies 2177
Canby and national film characteristics 2206
Canby and self-reflexive comedies 2194
Canby and Spike Lee 903
Canby and Steven Spielberg 2196
Canby and THE NIGHT OF THE SHOOTING STARS 377
Canby and the star system 2085
Canby and Vietnam War films 335
Canby and "small" films 2201
Canby, Vincent 444, 483, 537, 590, 674, 678, 756, 761, 786, 889, 901, 903,
959, 974, 993, 1005, 1007, 1009, 1021, 1029, 1035, 1037, 1292, 1295, 1322, 1351,
1353, 1751, 1814, 1854, 1912, 2098, 2108, 2112, 2154
Canel, Fausto 2163
Canham, Kingsley 1674, 1961, 1977, 1981
Cannella, Mario 1921
Cantwell, Mary 1927
Capote, Truman 1309
Capra, Frank 609, 1160, 1377
Carducci, Mark 2083
Carduner, Art 2183
Card, James 1391, 1772
Carey, Gary 85, 916, 1035, 1104, 1348, 1542, 1748, 1793, 1981, 2010
Carey, John 573
Carlson, Harry C. 748
Carns, Donald 977
Carringer, Robert 1263, 1327
Carroll, Kent E. 2109, 2130
Carroll, Noel 593, 1312, 1836
Carroll, Raymond L. 270
Carr, H. C. 1366, 1376
Carr, Jay 971

Carson, Diane 598
Carson, L. M. Kit 2196
Carter, Bill 2205
Carter, Ed 1013
Carter, Everett 1366
Carter, Roy E. 749
Cartnal, Alan 1748
Carynnyk, Marco 1645, 1665
Cashill, John R. 180
Cashman, Jerome 1755
Casper, Kent 2165
Cassady, Ralph, Jr. 607, 638, 697, 1459, 1462
Cassanova, Manuel Gonzales 42
Cassavetes, John 566, 2074
Castello, Giulio Cesare 1874, 2169
Casty, Alan 1090, 1367, 1985, 2077
Cast, David 2110
Casus, Victor 1723
Catton, W. R. 745
Cavalcanti, Alberto 64, 141, 1754
Cavander, Kenneth 1010, 1019, 1356, 2159
Cavell, Stanley 1843, 1921
Cawelti, John G. 189, 2088
Cawley, Leo 337
Cecil, Norman 1001, 1002
Cels, Roger 676
Ceplair, Larry S. 219
Cerf, Bennett 1130
Chabot, Jean 2123
Chabrol, Claude 1836, 2123
Chalfen, Richard 573
Chamberlin, Phillip 994
Chambers, Robert W. 738
Champlin, Charles 566, 653, 664, 1757, 2186
Chanan, Michael 1569
Chandler, Raymond 1846
Changas, Estelle 53, 789
Chang, Joseph S. M. J. 1641, 1831
Chanko, Kenneth M. 995, 1350
Chaplin, Charles Spencer 157, 1420, 1757
Chase, Chris 1292, 1295
Chase, Donald 2199
Chaudhuri, Arun Kumar 859
Chaumeton, Etienne 1947
Chavance, Louis 1697
Chemasi, Antonio 982, 2119
Cherkasov, Nikolai 1866
Cherry, Richard 1987
Chierichetti, David 1446
Chin, Frank 826
Chisholm, Brad 1388
Chloe, Aaron 672
Christians, Clifford G. 537, 771
Christy, George 1137
Chrystal, William G. 321
Chunovic, Louis 678
Chute, David 2075
Chutkow, Paul 2105, 2119

Ciment, Michel 2098, 2123
CineAction! Collective, The 483
Cipnic, Dennis J. 2039
Citron, Michelle 470
Cixous, Helene 471
Clair, Rene 142, 144
Clarens, Carlos 384, 409, 590, 819, 820, 1356, 1542, 2098, 2101, 2102, 2104, 2192
Clarke, Gerald 2165
Clark, Alfred E. 1985
Clark, Arthur B. 1010
Clark, Michael 442
Clark, Randall 1224
Clegg, Cyndia 416
Clermont-Tonnerre, Antoine De 2206
Clifton, Charles H. 1356
Clines, Francis X. 437, 1329
Clouzot, Claire 1024, 2074, 2109, 2164, 2173
Cobos, Juan 1792, 2182
Cochran, Thomas C. 613
Cocks, Jay 1985
Cocteau, Jean 144, 1789
Coen, John 2092
Coffey, Barbara 2155
Cogley, John 686
Cohen, Joe 1773
Cohen, Mitchell S. 1291
Cohen, Robert 1739
Cohen, Sarah Blacher 836
Cohen, Saul B. 952, 1985
Coleman, Horace W. 879
Coles, Robert 1024
Cole, Clayton 1325
Cole, Robert J. 2204, 2205
Cole, Stewart G. 737
Collet, Jean 1874, 2069, 2130, 2133
Collier, Eugenia 900
Collins, Alan 2075
Collins, Forrest 754
Collins, Gary 1980
Collins, Glenn 905, 1807, 2040, 2082, 2182, 2196
Colpi, Henri 2152
Columbus, Chris 799
Combs, Richard 1007, 1008, 1291, 1293, 1295, 1981, 2077, 2078
Comedy's Greatest Era 145
Comerford, Adelaide 1294, 1356, 2086
Comolli, Jean-Louis 118, 470, 474, 475, 479, 1797, 2124, 2125, 2126, 2183
Conant, Jennet 903
Conant, Michael 663, 686
Conaway, James 2164
Concon, Helen W. 40
Conley, Walter 1671
Conniff, Kathleen R. 2182
Connolly, Cyril 1722
Connor, Edward 388, 656, 815, 1300, 1455
Conrad, Herbert S. 710, 726
Conrad, Randall 1827
Conroy, William T., Jr. 1674
Considine, David M. 974, 975

Constable, Rita 1312
Cook, Bruce 1084, 1977, 2077, 2162, 2196
Cook, Page 83, 1356
Cook, Pam 466, 471, 475, 507, 587, 789, 798, 800
Coombs, Richard 2071, 2196
Cooper, Eunice 209
Coopman, Mira 2179
Coppola, Francis Ford 2041
Corbin, Louise 1005, 1015
Cordero, Frank J. 1502
Corliss, Mary 1293
Corliss, Richard 85, 100, 255, 295, 666, 667, 761, 801, 1036, 1066, 1184, 1292,
  1542, 1671, 1912, 1921, 2037, 2080, 2191, 2196
Corman, Avery 995
Corrigan, Philip 1568
Corry, John 291, 548
Cortez, Stanley 2042
Costello, Marjorie 675
Cotes, Peter 1419
Cott, Jeremy 1672
Cott, Jonathan 2110
Coulouris, George 1793
Coulson, Alan A. 1943
Cournot, Michel 2130, 2131
Coursen, David F. 1673, 2076
Coursodon, Jean-Pierre 1548
Courtenay, Tom 997
Coutard, Raoul 2109, 2131
Covington, Floyd C. 881, 915, 942
Cowie, Elizabeth 787, 789
Cowie, Peter 994, 1002, 1016, 1023, 1352, 1354, 1729, 2179, 2182, 2189
Cowley, Malcolm 1115
Cozarinsky, Edgardo 2098
Craddock, John 1001
Crandall, Ralph 1797
Crandall, Robert W. 661
Crane, Jeffrey L. 754
Crane, Stephen 53
Crawley, Budge 1835
Creed, Barbara 792, 793
Cressy, Paul 732, 749
Cripps, Thomas R. 247, 248, 303, 566, 783, 819, 824, 825, 854, 856, 860, 865,
  875, 883, 888, 915, 919, 933, 941, 949, 1382, 1383, 1511
Crispin Miller, Mark 2087
Crisp, Donald 1007, 1365
Crisp, Quentin 1442
Crist, Judith 514, 1215, 1295, 1770
Croce, Arlene 1004, 1005, 1013, 1348, 1542, 2151
Crofts, Stephen 448, 1669
Croft, Jeremy 202, 1569
Croizier, Ralph 424
Cronyn, Hume 1855
Crossette, Barbara 2168
Crouch, Stanley 903
Crowdus, Gary 996, 2158, 2163
Crowther, Bosley 50, 70, 710, 738, 790, 890, 892, 916, 941, 1362, 1630, 1672,
  1702, 1703, 1704, 1707, 1800, 1933, 1966, 1988, 2071, 2173
Crow, Duncan 648, 1745, 2159

Croyden, Margaret 1927
Crutchfield, Will 1896
Cruze, Harold 919
Culbert, David 259, 303, 320
Culhane, John 799, 2119
Culkin, John 71
Cummings, Judith 658
Cunningham, Frank R. 598
Curran, Trisha 912, 1009, 1312
Curry, Jack 764
Curry, Robert 593
Curtin, John 2162
Curtin, Philip D. 918
Curtiss, Thomas Quinn 1018
Curtis, James C. 39, 51
Cushman, R. B. 1365
Custen, George F. 573
Cutts, John 379, 400, 1009, 1018, 1023, 1084, 1348, 1349, 1807, 1980, 2087

D

Dagle, Joan 1297
Dale, R. C. 1724
Dallard, Muriel 889
Dalrymple, Ian 216, 242
Dalton, (Susan) Elizabeth 471, 508
Daly, David A. 132
Damico, James 564, 1542, 1947
Daniels, Don 2055
Daniels, Edgar F. 2039
Daniels, Gordon 247
Daniels, Thomas E. 1128, 1129, 1133
Daniels, William 2042
Dardis, Tom 1028, 1031, 1038
Darrach, Brad 2073
Das Gupta, Chidananda 2168
Dasco, Dan 812
Dassin, Jules 1975
Daudelin, Robert 2123
Davalle, Peter 1356
Davey, Serge 1805
Davidson, Bill 222, 2079
Davidson, James F. 2028
Davies, Brenda 1020
Davies, Philip 559
Davies, Wallace E. 1455, 1457
Davis, Bette 1170, 1756, 1777, 1981
Davis, D. William 1418
Davis, George 871
Davis, Howard 1853
Davis, John 227, 345, 1314
Davis, Kingsley 1003
Davis, L. J. 2197
Davis, Peter 1006
Davis, Praxton 798, 1978
Davis, Richard 996
Davis, Thulani 903
Dawidowicz, Lucy S. 222, 291, 830

Dawson, Anthony H.   607, 610, 635, 641, 647, 736
Dawson, Jan   993, 2159, 2160, 2174
Dawson, Jim   2086
Dayan, Daniel   82, 591
Day, Barry   656, 2086
de Gramont, Sanche   474
De La Roche, Catherine   1008, 1434, 1835
De Lauretis, Teresa   118, 471, 495, 496
De Laurot, Edouard L.   39, 1022
De Leon, Eddie   1927
Dean, Joan F.   410
Debrix, Jean R.   82, 648, 1025, 2009
Decker, Thomas   227
Deer, Harriet   2083
Deer, Irving   2083
Degenfelder, E. Pauline   1039, 1315
Deinum, Andries   1185
Delahaye, Michel   321, 1005, 1994, 2109, 2180, 2190
DeMille, Cecil B.   1680
Deming, Caren J.   789
Dempsey, Michael   85, 902, 993, 1037, 1673, 2072, 2201
Demy, Jacques   2119
Denby, David   295, 1033, 1294
Denig, L.   1376
Denkin, Harvey   1648
Deren, Maya   53, 140, 514, 1955
Derry, Charles   2099, 2196
Dervin, Daniel   410, 593
Desilets, Michael   2092
Desnos, Robert   582
Desowitz, Bill   663, 674, 1137, 2062
Desser, David   837
Deutelbaum, Marshall   598, 1363, 1590, 1843
DeVita, Guido   2155
Dewey, John   546
Di Nubila, Domingo   2157
Dickens, Milton   749
Dickinson, Margaret   1569
Dickson, Robert C.   1577
Dickson, Thorold   1362
Dick, Bernard F.   1025, 1297
Didion, Joan   514, 530, 566
Dieckmann, Katherine   981
Diehl, Digby   2075
Dienstfrey, Harris   1671
Dismond, Geraldyn   873, 942
Disney, Walt   1756
Dittmar, Linda   1297
Doane, Mary Ann   118, 465, 495, 496, 589, 590, 615, 714, 1706, 1835
Docherty, David   755
Doctorow, E. L.   62
Doeckel, Ken   83, 1006, 1748
Doherty, Thomas   739, 743, 770
Dombkowski, Dennis J.   653
Dominick, Joseph R.   608, 671, 673, 771
Donaldson, Peter   1353
Dongen, Helen Van   1671
Doniol-Valcroze, Jacques   1002, 1012

Donner, Clive 1336
Dooley, Roger B. 454, 1328
Dorner, Jorn 2183
Dorr, John H. 1362, 1368
Dort, Bernard 2124
Dos Passos, John 1309
Douchet, Jean 1843, 2008
Dougherty, Phil 678
Douglas, Mark 1414
Douglas, William O. 1764
Dowell, Pat 673
Downer, Alan S. 1316
Downing, Francis 1133
Downing, Robert 1352, 1365
Dowson, Jan 2149
Draper, Arthur 941
Dratch, Howard 2178
Dreiser, Theodore 1309, 1310
Drew, Bernard 2072, 2077
Drew, William M. 1712
Dreyer, Carl Theodor 65, 1729, 1955, 2190
Drobashenko, Sergei 208, 213, 243, 247, 281
Dronberger, Ilse 748
Drowne, Tatiana Balkoff 1001
Drum, Dale S. 1361, 2190
Du Pasquier, Sylvain 1672
Ducibella, Joseph 1506
Dudar, Helen 670
Dudinsky, Donna 2106
Dukes, Ashley 1339
Dullea, Georgia 1007
Dunagan, Clyde Kelly 812
Dunham, Harold 1365, 1367
Dunlap, David W. 629
Dunne, Philip 230, 255, 295, 1159
Dupis, Diane L. 1090
Dupre, John 2087
Durgnat, Raymond 656, 750, 751, 817, 978, 999, 1008, 1023, 1294, 1297, 1312, 1323, 1348, 1349, 1410, 1548, 1671, 1713, 1723, 1747, 1752, 1835, 1845, 1939, 1947, 1961, 1981, 1993, 2003, 2008, 2009, 2037, 2093, 2108, 2116, 2130, 2157, 2161
Dworkin, Martin 264, 893
Dyer, Peter John 322, 424, 817, 849, 970, 982, 1000, 1001, 1004, 1016, 1018, 1356, 1368, 1410, 1711, 1747, 1813, 1835, 1922, 1994, 2030, 2049, 2164, 2181
Dyer, Richard 460, 461, 507
Dynia, Philip 1835

E

Eames, Marian 1943
Earnest, Olen J. 768
Easley, Greg 252
Eastin, Kent D. 1359
Eaton, Mike 2133
Ebert, Alan 897
Ebert, Roger 609, 900, 2037
Eberwein, Robert T. 593
Eckert, Charles 488

Eckholm, Erik   745
Edelman, Rob   1536, 1668, 1975, 2119, 2196
Edelstein, David   997, 1324
Edgerton, Gary   646, 658, 771
Editors of CAHIERS DU CINEMA   477
Editors of CAMERA OBSCURA   483
Edward, Roy   1002
Ehrenstein, David   669, 2039
Ehrlich, Evelyn   912
Eidsvik, Charles   1297, 1353
Eisenberg, Adam   2083
Eisenstein, Sergei M.   65, 141, 144, 1301, 1332, 1336, 1645, 1646, 1655, 1657,
  1666, 1866, 1939
Eisner, Lotte H.   1018, 1995
Elber, Lynn   756
Eliot, T. S.   1309
Elkin, Frederick   453, 455, 533, 745, 801
Eller, Claudia   681
Elliott, William R.   439
Ellison, Harlan   415
Ellison, Mary   559
Ellison, Ralph   865, 883
Ellis, Jack   54
Ellis, Jack C.   215
Ellis, Kirk   1673
Ellis, Terry   2081
Ellsworth, Elizabeth   590
Ellul, Jacques   204
Ellwood, David W.   242, 247
Elsaesser, Thomas   118, 189, 479, 712, 977, 1961, 1986, 1997, 2103
Elson, Robert T.   296, 303
Elton, Arthur   252
Embler, Jeffrey   83
Emery, F. E.   745
Emory, Doug   1326
Endore, Guy   1084
Engel, Andi   2123, 2163
Englebach, David   2073
Engle, Harrison   295, 2180
Ephron, Delia   972, 973
Ephron, Nora   566
Epstein, Carol   1536
Erengis, George P.   1464
Erens, Patricia   497, 819, 827, 829, 830, 834, 835, 839, 1142, 2022, 2089, 2169
Esrock, Ellen   1297
Estrin, Mark W.   2085
Eswara, H. S.   754
Evans, Robert   700
Evans, Walter   388, 564, 975
Everett, E. K.   1361
Everson, William K.   303, 388, 424, 656, 807, 1019, 1315, 1350, 1360, 1363, 1405,
  1455, 1577, 1672, 1673, 1674
Ewen, Elizabeth   719
Ewig, Iain   2081
Ewing, Dale E., Jr.   1947
Eyles, Allen   373, 415, 1006, 1014, 1352, 1673, 1674, 1804, 1988, 1989, 2071,
  2119
Eyman, Scott   1637, 1674

Eynon, Christine 262
Eyquem, Olivier 1982

F

Fabrikant, Geraldine 31, 535, 610, 611, 653, 662, 663, 667, 670, 672, 673, 678, 681, 682, 755, 974, 2205
Fadiman, William 1301
Fairbanks, Douglas, Jr. 1695
Fairchild, B. H. 2196
Falewicz, Jan 745
Falkenberg, Pamela 2152
Fantel, Hans 31, 675, 762, 764
Farber, Jim 998
Farber, Manny 1014, 1548, 1912, 1972
Farber, Raoul 1672
Farber, Stephen 53, 85, 549, 566, 656, 669, 672, 678, 799, 800, 995, 998, 1003, 1143, 1327, 1352, 1356, 1799, 1985, 1987, 2034, 2041, 2081, 2084, 2086, 2087, 2089, 2161, 2196, 2202
Faris, Gerald 1632
Farnsworth, Clyde H. 647
Farrell, James T. 1309, 1310
Farrell, Tom 1985
Fassbinder, Rainer Werner 2098, 2099
Fast, Howard 1234
Faulkner, William 1309
Faure, Elie 1710
Fearing, Frank 375
Featherstone, Joseph 972
Federman, Raymond 2109
Feiffer, Jules 62
Feingold, Stanley 1910
Fein, Esther B. 972
Feldmann, Hans 2083
Feldman, Harry 1363, 1680
Feldman, Joseph 1363
Feldman, Seth 280, 1645
Feld, Fritz 1451
Fellini, Federico 63, 140, 1022
Fell, John L. 132, 711, 783, 1361, 1520, 1583, 1584, 1587
Felman, Shoshana 532
Fenin, George N. 424, 1019, 2034
Fenwick, J. H. 1982
Fergusson, Francis 1752
Fergusson, Otis 1548
Fernandez, Enrique 1003, 2163
Fernow, Donald Lloyd 817
Ferrara, Patricia 1834
Ferro, Marc 253, 261, 276
Feshback, Seymour 749
Feuer, Jane 83, 400
Fiedler, Leslie 1028, 1106, 1316
Fielding, Raymond 71, 281, 1590, 1605
Field, Mary 254
Field, Sidney 424
Fieschi, Jean-Andre 1985, 2098, 2099, 2109, 2180
Fife, Marilyn Diane 854
Filmer, Paul 2077

Finehout, Robert   1746
Fink, Rychard   1052
Finler, Joel W.   1699, 1822
Firda, Richard Arthur   1831
Fischer, Lucy   497, 792, 1590, 1645, 1810, 1825
Fishbein, Leslie   621
Fisher, Barbara   1583
Fisher, William A.   546
Fiske, Edward B.   439
Fitzgerald, F. Scott   1309
Fitzpatrick, Ellen   1001, 1012
Flaherty, David   1671
Flaherty, Frances   140, 1671, 1681, 1703
Flaherty, Robert J.   141, 1671, 1939
Flake, Carol   534
Flatley, Guy   889, 1877, 1925
Flaus, John   1023
Fledelius, Karsten   252
Fleener, Nickie   1367
Fleischer, Frederic   2182
Fleischer, Richard   1023
Fleischer, Stefan   1976
Fletcher, John   816
Flinn, Carol   795
Flinn, Tom   1314, 1947
Flint, Peter B.   314, 373, 1087, 1454, 1671, 1748, 1757, 1854, 1915, 2171
Flitterman-Lewis, Sandy   579
Flynn, Charles   651, 652, 2078
Foister, Tony   978
Folks, Jeffrey J.   913
Follain, Jean   712
Folsberg, Myra   2196
Forbes, Jill   850, 2109
Forbes, Ryan   2083
Ford, Charles   1463, 1994
Ford, Greg   2040
Ford, John   424, 1772
Foreman, Carl   85, 368, 1034, 1035, 1094
Forester, C. S.   1234
Fore, Steve   442, 2072
Forman, Betty Yetta   829
Forman, Lady Helen   242
Forsdale, Joan Rosengren   979
Forsdale, Louis   979
Forsyth, Scott   484, 485, 533, 552, 590, 976
Fosburgh, Lacey   1028
Fothergill, Richard   83
Foulkes, D.   745
Fowler, Glenn   1695
Fowler, Roy A.   1792
Fox, Julian   1305, 1363, 1671, 1674
Fox, Terry Curtis   812, 1983, 1985
Franchi, R. M.   1006, 2107
Francovich, Alan   2158
Frankenheimer, John   1351, 2077
Franklin, H. Bruce   410, 416
Fraser, C. Gerald   760, 855, 902, 903, 907, 1070
Frayling, Christopher   559

Frazer, John   1583
Fredrickson, Don   594, 1523
Freedman, Samuel G.   335
Freeman, David   1844
Freeman, Lincoln   651
Freidson, Eliot   705
French, Philip   71, 1297, 1301, 1320, 1685, 1839, 2130, 2160
French, Warren   1725, 1726, 1963, 2053, 2066
Freud, Sigmund   452, 453
Friedenberg, Edgar Z.   53, 2086
Friedmann, Thomas   291
Friedman, Arthur B.   1672
Friedman, Lester D.   820, 822, 823, 1092, 1312
Friedman, M. R.   834
Friedman, Norman L.   534, 820, 821, 855
Frith, Simon   400
Frost, George E.   654
Fruchter, Norman   1349, 1666
Fuchs, Daniel   1031
Fuentes, Carlos   1548, 1723
Fullertin, John   769
Fuller, Sam   85
Fuller, Samuel   1977
Fuller, Stanley   1300
Fuller, Stephen   1064, 1224
Fulton, A. R.   685
Furstenberg, Jean   443

G

Gabbard, Glen O.   816
Gabbard, Krin   816
Gabler, Neal   486
Gaggi, Silvio   2115, 2117
Gaines, Jane   769, 868
Gallagher, John   2197
Gallagher, Tag   980, 1673, 1922, 2134
Gallez, Douglas W.   83, 284, 400
Galling, Dennis Lee   83
Galloway, David   1162
Gamarekian, Barbara   961
Gans, Herbert J.   459, 461, 521, 553, 722, 776
Garbo, Greta   508
Garcon, Francois   1903
Garis, Leslie   530
Garmes, Lee   79, 2042
Garnham, Nicholas   2135
Garrett, George   1103
Garringer, Newson E.   1672
Garrison, Lee C.   706, 734, 736, 742, 752
Gartenberg, Jon   1608
Gassner, John   366
Gaudreault, Andre   1361, 1590, 1604, 1605
Gavronsky, Serge   2039
Geduld, Carolyn   1314
Geduld, Harry M.   400, 410
Gehring, Wes D.   1414
Geist, Kenneth   379, 1981, 2090

Geist, William   649
Gelb, Barbara   2085
Gelb, Leslie   454
Gelder, Lawrence Van   2085
Geller, Robert   40
Gelmis, Joseph   850
Geltzer, George   1455, 1672, 1702, 1707
Geng, Veronica   590
Georgakas, Dan   1277, 2120, 2121, 2154, 2163
Geraghty, Christine   526
Gerard, David   2154
Gerard, Jeremy   1039
Gerard, Lillian   1808
Gerasimov, Sergei   1023, 2181
Gerbner, George   459, 462, 543, 545, 715
Gerima, Haile   853, 950
Gerstein, Evelyn   303, 1645
Gerstle, Ralph   79, 1325
Gerstle, Robert   1005
Gessner, Robert   65
Giacci, Vittorio   1838
Giannetti, Louis   1322
Giannini, Attilio H.   618
Giard, Robert   2098
Gibbs, Harriet   1352
Gibney, Alex   2200
Gibson, Helen   1585
Gibson, John   1827, 2083
Giddis, Diane   508, 799
Gide, Andre   1309
Gielgud, John   1463, 1676
Gifford, Dennis   1672
Gilbert, Billy   1754
Gilcrease, Virginia   596
Gilles, Jacob   2115, 2155
Gillett, John   207, 656, 1010, 1012, 1648, 1672, 1740, 1939, 1944, 2015, 2023,
   2159, 2161, 2182
Gilliatt, Penelope   1348, 1418, 1672
Gilliat, Sidney   1865
Gilling, Ted   1793
Gill, Brendan   1291, 1419, 2037
Gill, Jerry H.   52
Gill, Michael   1024
Gilman, Richard   1336
Gilson, Rene   1797
Ginensky, Richard   1000
Gingrich, Arnold   1128, 1129
Ginibre, Jean-Louis   366
Giroux, Robert   1411
Gish, Lillian   1365
Gittens, Tony   950
Glassco, David   1297
Glassman, Marc   1084
Glass, Fred   409
Gledhill, Christine   466, 467, 469, 471, 495, 496, 507, 794, 799
Glicksman, Marlaine   789
Godard, Jean-Luc   53, 1874, 1961, 1994, 2109, 2123, 2124, 2183
Goddard, Donald   2196

Godfrey, Lionel 83, 400, 424, 816, 998, 1301, 1325, 1335, 1349
Goldbeck, Willis 2075
Goldberger, Paul 658
Goldberg, Robert 2098, 2101, 2197
Goldin, Marilyn 2174
Goldman, Debra 2203
Goldman, John 1682
Goldman, Judith 2109
Goldman, William 62, 700
Goldwyn, Samuel 640
Gold, Herbert 2073
Gold, Richard 671
Gold, Ronald 896
Goleman, Daniel 904, 1000
Gollub, Judith 2112, 2113
Gomery, J. Douglas 573, 608, 612, 617, 618, 621, 622, 623, 632, 633, 634, 636, 639, 640, 660, 661, 663, 667, 675, 676, 678, 685, 697, 703, 705, 1068, 1315, 1510, 1551, 1670, 1976
Goodlad, Sinclair 855
Goodman, Ezra 65
Goodman, Joan 2196, 2197
Goodman, Paul 140, 1363
Goodman, Walter 300, 443, 454, 527, 859, 960, 997, 1032, 1136, 1291
Goodwin, James 1163, 1312, 1645
Goodwin, Michael 415, 1747, 1984, 2111
Gorbman, Claudia 83, 632, 800
Gordon, David 607, 614, 659, 667, 751
Gordon, Thomas F. 771
Gorky, Maxim 1309
Gosser, H. Mark 1580, 1581, 1586, 1615
Gottesman, Ronald 1523, 1792
Gottlieb, Sidney 1315
Gough-Yates, Kevin 789, 806, 1922, 1923, 1924, 2080, 2161
Gouveia, Georgette 960
Gow and Alan Bates 2077
Gow and Alan J. Pakula 2195
Gow and HAIL THE CONQUERING HERO 1014
Gow and IF . . . 1001
Gow and L'AVVENTURA 1012
Gow and LA STRADA 1022
Gow and LITTLE BIG MAN 1320
Gow and LONG DAY'S JOURNEY INTO NIGHT 1350
Gow and Peter Bogdanovich 2195
Gow and SONS AND LOVERS 1010
Gow and THE PRIME OF MISS JEAN BRODIE 1003
Gow and TO KILL A MOCKINGBIRD 1325
Gow and WHO'S AFRAID OF VIRGINIA WOOLF? 2086
Gow, Gordon 372, 373, 374, 409, 995, 1023, 1301, 1347, 1353, 1355, 1391, 1561, 1874, 1981, 1989, 2039, 2073, 2078, 2079, 2082, 2084, 2092, 2098, 2101, 2114, 2119, 2157, 2160, 2164, 2180
Gozlan, Gerard 2123
Grace, Harry A. 1414
Graham, John 1026, 2092
Graham, Olive 1747, 2085
Graham, Peter 2040, 2093
Graham, Ron 794
Graham, Sheila 1109
Gramont, Sanche de 2106
Granger, Rod 1324

Grant, Barry Keith   38, 410
Graubard, Allen   839
Grauman, Lawrence   1301
Gray, Bert   1365, 1803
Gray, Hugh   54, 85, 128, 1671
Greeley, Andrew   1139
Green-Armytage, Jonathan   1982
Greenberg, Dan   697, 1755
Greenberg, Harvey R.   335, 336
Greenberg, James   836
Greenberg, Joel   79, 367, 1012, 1561, 1671
Greene, Graham   1309, 1432, 1548
Greene, Marjorie   1023, 1994
Greenfield, Pierre   1673
Greenspun, Roger   1673, 1684, 1823, 1973, 1984, 2018, 2155
Green, Ian   1569
Green, J. Ronald   573
Green, Theophilus   900
Green, Tom   764
Gree, O. O.   1674
Gregory, Charles T.   384, 798, 801, 1301
Gregor, Ulrich   2165
Grenier, Cynthia   1648, 1975, 2119, 2182
Grenier, Richard   1855
Grey, Lennox   135
Gribbel, Jack   1393
Grierson and screen education   50
Grierson, John   206, 303, 1548, 1754, 1828
Griffin, George   77
Griffin, Nancy   2196
Griffith, Ann   1981
Griffith, Richard   50, 124, 176, 1574, 1628, 1693, 1748, 1754
Griggs, John   1365
Grinker, Roy E.   375
Grogg, Sam L., Jr.   35, 581
Grossberg, Mike   2196
Gross, John   1028, 1905
Gross, Joseph   2163
Grove, Martin   682, 764
Gruber, Frank   85
Gruen, John   1016
Grundberg, Andy   1599
Grupenhoff, Richard   866
Guarner, Jose Luis   2130
Guback, Thomas H.   625, 647, 653, 661, 664, 686, 769, 771, 1993
Guber, Peter   672
Guerin, Ann   1981
Guerrero, Ed   905
Guillemot, Agnes   2131
Gundlach, Ralph   546
Gunning, Tom   1362, 1382, 1383, 1590, 1600, 1602
Gunston, David   321
Gupta, Udayan   902
Gussow, Mel   143, 666, 1862, 2067
Gustafson, Robert   573, 609, 610
Guthrie, Tyrone   1034
Guynn, William   2103
Guy, Rory   1323

H

Haberman, Clyde 1927, 2098
Hachem, Samir 903
Hackett, Hazel 1903
Haggard, Mark 1673
Hagopian, Kevin 643
Haislip, William 789
Halas, John 77
Halberstadt, Ira 295, 2072
Halberstam, David 368
Haleff, Maxine 2041
Haley, Jay 455, 744
Halliwell, Leslie 264, 388, 815, 1745
Hall, Dennis John 887, 1980, 1982
Hall, Peter 1862
Hall, Stuart 587
Halpern, Ben 858
Halpern, Sue 671
Hamden S. 1360
Hames, Peter 2164
Hamilton, Harlan 1586
Hamilton, Marie L. 740
Hammer, Joshua 2206
Hammond, John H. 1580
Hammond, Robert M. 1714
Hampton, Charles 2081
Hampton, Wilborn 658
Handelman, Janet 303, 2092
Handel, Leo A. 738, 739
Handzo, Stephen 1874, 1982
Hanhardt, John 2078
Hansard, David 2152
Hansen, Miriam 471
Hanson, Gayle 764
Haponek, Jean 2024
Haralovich, Mary Beth 449, 450, 511, 608, 640, 769, 1437, 1438, 1509, 1516, 1556
Harcourt-Smith, Simon 1920
Harcourt, Peter 994, 997, 1022, 1714, 1927, 1930, 1932, 2098, 2099, 2105, 2116
Hardison, O. B. 1316, 1836
Hardy, Forsyth 217, 1871
Hardy, James Earl 903
Hardy, Phil 1961, 2003
Harmetz and Alan Ladd, Jr. 536
Harmetz and AMERICAN GRAFFITI 993
Harmetz and box-office receipts 762, 764
Harmetz and Charles Crichton 1942
Harmetz and comedy films in the 1980s 2201
Harmetz and David Puttnam 671
Harmetz and disaster films 753
Harmetz and Fay Wray 1800
Harmetz and film classics 1514
Harmetz and film nostalgia 2193
Harmetz and film sequels 2200
Harmetz and film tie-ins 488
Harmetz and Francis Ford Coppola 536
Harmetz and George Lucas 2196
Harmetz and Hollywood in the 1950s 647

Harmetz and Independent film festivals   671
Harmetz and male bonding   2193
Harmetz and marketing   668
Harmetz and MGM   662
Harmetz and NATIVE SON (1986)   903
Harmetz and Robert Redford   671
Harmetz and Rupert Murdoch   663
Harmetz and sequels   761, 2206
Harmetz and sneak previews   574
Harmetz and studio executives   536, 537
Harmetz and studios in the 1980s   671
Harmetz and television ratings   760
Harmetz and TEX   998
Harmetz and the Walt Disney Company   672
Harmetz and theater boom   681
Harmetz and tie-ins   488
Harmetz and Tri-Star Pictures   678
Harmetz and Universal Pictures   535
Harmetz and videocassette rentals   762
Harmetz and Warner Bros.   1083
Harmetz and women in film   2207
Harmetz and 20th Century-Fox   2205
Harmetz, Aljean   367, 368, 437, 440, 463, 535, 545, 670, 672, 673, 676, 678,
   738, 756, 890, 1028, 1029, 1037, 1197, 1292, 1295, 1308, 1437, 1987, 2089
Harmon, Sidney   885
Harpole, Charles H.   674, 1814
Harrington, Clifford V.   2024
Harrington, Curtis   1806
Harrington, Mona   470
Harrison, Carey   1356, 2173
Harrison, Harry   415
Harrison, William   942
Harrisson, Tom   242
Harris, Adrienne   506, 586
Harris, Mark   1965
Harris, Neil   1587, 1604
Harris, Warren G.   1446
Hartack, Don   2075
Harte, Judith   1775
Hartley, Dean Wilson   39, 52, 1026
Hartog, Simon   1569
Hart, Henry   656, 672, 1003, 1004, 1008, 1010, 1014, 1022, 1023, 1290, 1296,
   1323, 1325, 1347, 1349, 1350, 1353, 1354, 1355, 1985, 1988, 2086
Harvey, James   1986
Harvey, Laurence   1016
Harvey, Stephen   256, 1809, 1849
Harvey, Sylvia   507, 642, 1569
Haskell, Molly   497, 508, 792, 798, 843, 971, 1006, 1315, 1322, 1542, 1706, 1747,
   1984, 2098, 2100, 2101, 2102, 2105, 2109
Hatch, Robert   1295
Hauduroy, Jean-Francois   83
Haun, Harry   83, 1083
Hauser, Arnold   53
Haverhill, Lawrence   1536
Haver, Ron   622
Hayakawa, Sessue   70, 374
Haycox, Ernest   1772
Hayes, Helen   1782

Hayes, Thomas C. 663, 743
Hazarika, Sanjoy 2168
Heard, Colin 2039
Heath, Stephen 118, 585, 591, 1966, 2069
Hecht, Ben 566, 1105, 1122, 1234
Hecht, Leo 2182
Heck-Rabi, Louise 2114
Hedges, H. M. 1030
Heilbronn, Lisa M. 259
Heinrich, Ray 673
Heinz, Linda 1300
Heisler, Gerald H. 546
Heller, Joseph 1037
Heller, Scott 437
Hellmann, John 178, 367
Henderson, Brian 100, 477, 478, 1645, 2110
Hendriks, Gordon 685
Henley, John 365, 1927, 2091
Henry, Catherine 1831
Hepburn, Katharine 1288
Hepworth, Cecil M. 1757
Herman, Peter J. 697
Herman, Robin 324
Hernacki, Thomas 1874
Herrmann, Bernard 1793, 2081
Herron, William 996
Hershman, Arlene 488
Hersholt, Jean 1699
Herzog, Charlotte 617, 622, 1600
Hess, John 1999, 2106
Hess, Judith W. 190, 463
Heston, Charlton 1748
Heung, Marina 410
Hibbin, Nina 1001, 1648, 2181
Hickey, Terry 1433
Higginbotham, Virginia 2182
Higham, Charles 79, 367, 799, 1561, 1671, 1792, 1835, 1987, 2019, 2077, 2195
Higham, John 258
Highsmith, Patricia 1197
High, Peter B. 1894, 1895
Hilenski, Ferdinand Alexi 1363
Hillier, Bevis 1841
Hill, Deborah J. 598
Hill, Derek 388, 2159
Hill, Herbert 540
Hill, Jerome 1974
Hill, John 1569
Hill, Stephen P. 1645, 1648, 2182
Hine, Al 890
Hinson, Hal 410
Hinton, David B. 321
Hirano, Kyoko 1888, 2016, 2017, 2024, 2177
Hirschfeld, Gerhard 251
Hirsch, Foster 1322, 2010, 2160
Hirshfield, Claire 39
Hirsh, Allan 1324
Hirt-Manheimer, Aron 820
Hitchcock, Alfred 1835, 1837, 1913
Hitchcock, Peggy 1012

Hitchens, Gordon 217, 1808
Hoare, J. B. 1942
Hoberman, J. B. 324, 337, 368, 446, 666, 820, 1003, 2020, 2106, 2108, 2156, 2167, 2190, 2198
Hobson, J. Allan 579, 593
Hobson, Sheila Smith 852
Hochman, Charles N. 93
Hochman, Stanley 1830
Hodgens, R. M. 409, 1009, 1010, 1014, 1324, 1325, 1348
Hodgkinson, Anthony W. 40, 95
Hodgkinson, A. W. 1019
Hoekzema, Dorothea 1747
Hoekzem, Loren 1738
Hoffer, Tom W. 1584
Hoffman, Alice 649
Hoffman, Stanley 317
Hoffner, Tom W. 429
Hofsess, Jack 2083
Hogenkamp, Bert 214, 242
Holben, Herbert 322
Holdenfield, Chris 2197
Holden, Stephen 906, 2203
Holdstein, Deborah H. 995, 2081, 2195
Holland, Larry Lee 1365, 1392
Holland, Norman H. 137
Holloway, Ronald 2014
Hollyman, Burnes St. Patrick 719, 1599, 1601
Holly, Ellen 897, 1005
Holmes, John Clellon 221, 454
Holm, Wilton R. 655
Honeycutt, Kirk 376, 2197
Honore, Hal 86
Hood, Stuart 215, 1569
Hook, Sidney 1186
Hoover, Marjorie L. 1414
Hope-Wallace, Philip 1355
Hope, Bob 1165, 1449
Horak, Jan-Christopher 1314
Horne, Lena 942
Horowitz, Irving Louis 1723
Horowitz, Joy 902, 903, 904, 905
Horowitz, Margaret M. 1843
Horton, Andrew 1914, 2014, 2119
Horton, Donald 544, 545
Houseman, John 1354, 1419, 1966, 2034
Houston, Beverle 1981, 2106, 2175, 2176
Houston, Penelope 131, 282, 373, 409, 656, 816, 1000, 1002, 1003, 1007, 1008, 1009, 1012, 1013, 1015, 1016, 1019, 1024, 1084, 1198, 1290, 1296, 1321, 1324, 1542, 1548, 1672, 1711, 1835, 1874, 1912, 1944, 2034, 2153, 2159, 2161, 2173
Hoveyda, Fereydoun 2120, 2124, 2126
Howard Reid, John 1984
Howard, Clifford 1749, 1865
Howard, Juanita R. 900
Howe, A. H. 659
Howe, James Wong 2042
Howe, Joyce 789
Ho, Sam 2087
Hrusa, Bernard 1022, 1939

Hudson, Roger 79
Huettig, Mae D. 686
Huffman, John L. 769
Huff, Theodore 1028, 1044, 1361, 1414, 1674, 1944
Hughes, John Emmett 630
Hughes, Pennethorne 1340
Hughes, Robert 220
Hughes, Rupert 634
Hughes, William 39
Hull, David Stewart 322, 2179
Hulseberg, Richard 1297
Hunnings, Neville 664
Hunt, Albert 47
Hunt, Barbara 1297
Hunwitz, Barbara 1580
Hurlbut, Marilyn 438
Husband, Charles 854
Huss, Roy 1300
Huston, John 140, 145
Huston, Nancy 2080
Hutchins, Charles L. 864
Hutchmaker, J. Joseph 51
Huthmacher, J. Joseph 39
Hutton, Patrick H. 261
Huxley, Aldous 201, 1106, 1233, 1309
Huyssen, Andreas 1642
Hwang, David 826
Hyde, Thomas 1843

I

Iiri, Goro 1742
Imeson, Jo 1295
Ingels, Marty 1137
Inglis, Ruth 686
Insdorf, Annette 377, 1312, 2094, 2106, 2143, 2179, 2180
Irwin, Bill 1414
Isaac, Dan 820, 835
Isaksson, Folke 2168
Isenberg, Michael T. 39, 221, 252, 1509
Iser, Wolfgang 485
Ivens, Joris 319
Ivory, James 2167
Iwabutchi, Masayoshi 2024
Izod, John 653

J

Jablonski, Edward 83, 400, 1295
Jack Kerouac 53
Jackson, Lynne 2207
Jacobowitz, Florence 792, 806
Jacobson, Harlan 669, 1330, 1514
Jacobson, Herbert L. 232
Jacobs, Diane 367, 982, 1312
Jacobs, Jack 79, 83, 1305, 1705
Jacobs, Lea 529, 801

Jacobs, Lewis   141, 144, 262, 566, 710, 864, 1359, 1383, 1576, 1718
Jacoby, Lois   85
Jacob, Gilles   372, 1981, 2093, 2130
Jaehne, Karen   674, 2207
Jahoda, Maria   209
Jameson, Fredric   417, 537, 1835
Jameson, Richard T.   1316, 1323
James, Caryn   291, 490, 738, 971, 972, 1301, 1327, 1977, 2098, 2205, 2207
James, David   442, 1974
James, George   1365
James, Watson S. "Jay"   764
Janos, Leo   536, 611
Jarvie, Ian C.   252, 349, 573, 705, 769, 1324, 2071, 2163
Jarvik, Laurence   2202
Jeffords, Susan   442
Jeffrey, Richard   1835, 1843
Jeffries, Georgia   982
Jensen, Paul   85, 798, 1064, 1301, 1642, 1808
Jerome, V. J.   911
Jester, Ralph   39
Jeter, Ida   857, 912, 1750
Jhiard, Susan   1838
Joannides, Paul   79
Johnson, Albert   849, 884, 893, 894, 941, 942, 1004, 1350, 1352, 1353, 1464,
   2039, 2074
Johnson, Dale   1912
Johnson, Diane   1028
Johnson, Ian   750, 751, 1009, 1022, 1342, 1925
Johnson, Julian   1391
Johnson, Nora   1043
Johnson, Timothy   2029
Johnson, William   79, 83, 400, 994, 1011, 1361, 1792, 2034, 2069, 2098, 2163,
   2177
Johnstone, J. W. C.   745
Johnston, Claire   451, 466, 471, 473, 497, 507, 508, 587, 799, 1798, 2159
Johnston, Kenneth G.   1119
Johnston, Sheila   526
Joly, Jacques   1827
Jones, Dorothy B.   140, 200, 281, 524, 646, 742, 1098, 1321, 1706
Jones, DuPre   1987
Jones, Edward T.   1291, 1322
Jones, Harold Ellis   710, 726
Jones, Ken   1366
Jones, Quincy   2042
Jonsson, Eric (see Andrew Sarris)   1014, 1912
Jordon, Marion   1569
Josslin, Daniel   1954
Jouffroy, Alain   2131
Jowett, Garth S.   256, 564, 573, 617, 710, 725, 733, 769, 770, 1590
Jozsa, Margaret   565
Jurkiewicz, Kenneth   410

K

Kabak, Wayne 666
Kael and film criticism 137, 142
Kael, Pauline 40, 53, 54, 62, 63, 141, 430, 779, 801, 896, 897, 942, 979, 1010, 1014, 1016, 1018, 1027, 1324, 1509, 1548, 2034, 2096, 2133
Kagan, Norman 876
Kahlenberg, Richard 672
Kahn, Gordon 816
Kakutani, Michiko 291, 822, 1030, 1066, 1301, 1330, 2119
Kalinak, Kathryn 400, 461, 506
Kaminsky, Stuart M. 79, 183, 373, 384, 410, 565, 1315, 1672, 2019, 2073
Kanin, Garson 1291, 1440, 1686
Kanin, Michael 2028
Kaplan, David A. 2196
Kaplan, Deborah 972
Kaplan, E. Ann 471, 507, 508, 587, 588, 593, 794, 795, 796, 1231
Kaplan, Fred 1674
Kaplan, George (Robin Wood) 1837
Kapsis, Robert E. 1835
Karnoff, Joel E. 1926
Karp, Alan 674
Karr, Kathleen 1621
Kasindorf, Martin 2193
Kass, Judith M. 1536
Kass, Robert 1354, 1607
Kast, Pierre 1927
Katz, E. 745
Katz, John 1025
Kauffmann, Stanley 34, 53, 124, 137, 141, 1013, 1016, 1033, 1105, 1312, 1322, 1336, 1548, 1748, 2030, 2156
Kauffman, Stanley 124
Kaufman, Michael T. 903
Kaufman, Stanley Lloyd, Jr. 2090
Kawin, Bruce 1914
Kawin, Bruce F. 416, 593, 1214, 1297
Kay, Karyn 508
Kazan, Elia 84
Keane, Marian E. 1843
Kearney, Jill 2202
Kearns, James 374
Kehl, D. G. 1326
Kehr, Dave 2011, 2199
Kelkres, Gene G. 1586
Kelly, Gene 1506
Kelly, Keith 1094, 1099
Kelman, Ken 318, 321
Kemp, Philip 1813, 1825, 2088
Kenez, Peter 208, 213, 248, 281, 282
Kennedy, Burt 424
Kennedy, Harlan 409, 2083
Kennedy, Lisa 903
Kennedy, Margaret 1105
Kennedy, Shawn G. 682
Kent, Leticia 367, 2119
Kenyon, Judy 744
Kepley, Betty 1646
Kepley, Vance, Jr. 1363, 1367, 1509, 1646
Kerbel, Michael 655, 1984

Kerouac, Jack 1309
Kerr, Deborah 1940
Kerr, Paul 743, 1947
Kerr, Peter 226
Kerr, Walter 1030, 1331, 1334, 1414
Kershaw, Ian 251
Kershner, Irvin 2034
Kettenacher, Lothar 251
Keyan G. 771
Keyser, Lester J. 834
Kilbourne, Don 1266, 1269
Kilday, Gregg 670, 678
Kimmelman, Michael 2204
Kimmel, Daniel M. 282
Kindem, Gorham 573, 654, 697, 735, 748, 913, 1670
Kinder, Marsha 367, 477, 578, 584, 593, 1874, 1981, 2106, 2119, 2175, 2176
Kingston, Jeremy 1637
King, Andrea 2206
King, Edith Morgan 2009
King, Gayle 771
King, Nel 1912
King, Wayne 255
Kinney, Judy Lee 442
Kinskey, Leonid 372
Kinzle, David 1584
Kirk, Tom 2066
Kitses, Jim 424, 1982
Klagsburn, Francine 833
Klapper, Joseph T. 745
Klaprat, Cathy 637, 686
Kleinfield, N. R. 662, 764, 2205
Kleinfield, Sonny 653
Kleinhans, Chuck 497, 792
Klein, Gillian 1675
Klein, Martin J. 815
Klein, Michael 2106
Klemesrud, Judy 680, 993, 2154
Klenow, Daniel J. 754
Klinger, Barbara 467, 475, 476, 530, 1843, 2080
Knapp, Steven 748, 770
Knebel, Fletcher 960
Kneeland, Douglas 649
Knight, Arthur 54, 140, 166, 303, 377, 565, 566, 1000, 1004, 1017, 1301, 1410,
    1770, 1792, 1814, 1854, 1977, 1988, 2071
Knight, Roy 47
Knoedelseder, William K. 535
Knox, Alexander 366
Koch, Gertrud 528, 585, 587, 588
Koch, Howard W. 1173, 1966, 2010
Koch, Stephen 1025
Kohler, Richard 656
Kolkein, R. P. 2111
Koningsberger, Hans 1319
Kopper, Philip 2202
Koppes, Clayton R. 229, 856
Kornick, Mike 1585
Kornweibel, Theodore, Jr. 375
Korte, Jr., Walter F. 1884

Koskinen, Maaret 2183
Koszarski, Richard 508, 1587, 2196
Kotlarz, Irene 874
Kottack, Conrad 410
Kovacks, Steven 1713
Kovacs, Katherine Singer 1590, 1604
Kowinski, William Severini 670, 2203
Kozintsev, Grigori 1656
Kozloff, Max 2173
Kracauer, Siegfried 140, 144, 566, 857, 1014, 1548, 1697, 1811, 1912
Kramer, Stanley 140
Kramer, Steven Philip 1712
Krebs, Albin 2048
Krishnamurthy, Nadig 754
Kristein, Lincoln 1903
Kristeva, Julia 118, 471
Kristof, Nicholas D. 535, 960
Krohn, Bill 674
Kroll, Jack 376, 1009, 1013, 1322, 2199
Krueger, Eric 982
Kubrick, Stanley 2083
Kuehl, Jerry 275
Kuhn, Annette 471
Kuhn, Helen Weldon 849
Kula, Sam 40, 1577
Kupferberg, Audrey E. 1536
Kurosawa, Akira 1574
Kustow, Michael 1349, 1354
Kuter, Leo K. 79
Kyrou, Ado 1723

L

Labarthe, Andre S. 2131
Labaton, Stephen 2204
LaBlanc, Michael L. 1092
Lacan, Jacques 480
Lacassin, Francis 1584, 2116
Lackner, Helen 477
Laemmle, Ann 998, 1921
Lafferty, William 653
Lalich, Glenn 2076
Lambert, Gavin 656, 1007, 1018, 1023, 1301, 1321, 1354, 1637, 1836, 1922, 1994, 2009
Lamb, Blaine P. 826
Lamb, Derek 77
Lamont, Austin 671
Lam, R. Errol 855
Landro, Laura 658
Landrum, Larry N. 173, 262, 410, 565, 2018
Landsbergis, A. 1009
Lane, John Francis 1012, 1023, 1356, 1922, 1975, 2169, 2172
Langer, Lawrence L. 291, 837
Langer, Susanne 144
Langlois, Henri 1776
Lang, Fritz 1637
Lang, Robert 2072
Lardner, Ring, Jr. 845, 1084, 1096

Lareau, Normand 1323
Larkin, Robert 454
Larner, Jeremy 455
Larrabee, Eric 814
Larson, Rodger 2040
Laskas, Kristin 1814
Lasky, Jesse L., Jr. 85
Lasky, Jesse L., Sr. 1756
Lassally, Walter 656
Lasswell, Harold D. 201
Lauder, Frank 1939
Laurot, Edouard 1321
LaValley, Albert J. 416, 605, 1314, 1846
Lawson, Carol 995
Lawson, John Howard 45, 141, 376, 566, 1321
Lawson, R. 1368
Lawson, W. P. 723
Lawton, Ben 1922
Lazarsfeld, Paul F. 521, 707, 728, 736, 738
Leab, Daniel J. 252, 882
Lean, David 1939
Leary, Richard 1672
Lebovici, Serge 582
Lebow, Jeanne 598
Lederer, Joseph 1985
Lederman, Marie Jean 593
Lee, David D. 913
Lee, Sharon 2152
Lee, Spike 903
Leff, Leonard J. 366, 1142, 1843
Lehmann-Haupt, Christopher 571
Lehman, Ernest 1836, 1844
Lehman, Peter 479, 812, 1674, 1747
Leiber, Nicholas 2088
Leites, Nathan 602
Lejune, C. A. (Caroline) 514
Lenne, Gerard 497, 529
Lennig, Arthur 1391
Lenning, Arthur 65
Leonard, Dean 1138
Leonard, Neil 1300
Lerner, Carl 2189
Lerner, Irving 1301
LeRoy, Mervyn 50, 1804
Lesage, Julia 57, 444, 445, 448, 466, 472, 497, 587, 1827, 2110
Lesser, Stephen O. 1155
Levaco, Ronald 1645, 1646
Levi-Strauss, Claude 175, 714
Levine, Irving R. 1927
Levine, Joseph E. 610
Levinson, Richard M. 789
Levin, Harvey J. 648
Levitin, Jacqueline 2114, 2115
Levy, Herbert M. 966
Levy, Mark R. 756, 760
Lev, Michael 2205
Lev, Peter 2119
Lewis, Anthony 472

Lewis, Herschell Gordon 393
Lewis, Jerry M. 462
Lewis, Kevin 1365
Lewis, Marshall 1006, 2107
Lewis, Roger 2041
Lewis, Stephen 1015
Leyda, Jay 140, 164, 319, 1368, 1522, 1587, 1644, 1645, 1651, 1655, 1658, 1663, 1867, 2015, 2019, 2029, 2031, 2266
Leydon, Joseph 2087
Lichty, Lawrence W. 270
Liebman, Stuart 1711, 1717
Liehm, Antonin J. 2164
Lifton, Mitchell 1001
Lightman, Herb A. 674
Lillich, Richard B. 1300
Limbacher, James, L. 79
Lindell, Richard L. 1162, 1163
Linderman, Deborah 118, 1835
Linder, Carl 1955
Lindsay, Robert 2197
Lindsay, Vachel 1336
Lindsey, Robert 31, 545, 549, 653, 662, 752, 755, 762, 1042
Linton, James M. 214, 490, 573
Linville, Susan 2165
Lipkin, Steve 771, 1706
Lippe, Richard 603, 792, 806
Lippmann, Walter 543, 865
Lithgow, James 2039
Litle, Michael 1827
Litman, Barry R. 648, 656
Littich, Meredith 1342
Lloyd, Harold 1672, 1693
Locke, Alain 941
Lockhart, Kimball 1874
Lokke, Virgil L. 1028
Londoner, David J. 686
London, Herbert 440
London, Jack 1309
Lond, Harley 674
Long, Littleton 1084, 1354
Lopez, Ana 252
Lorentz, Pare 303
Lounsbury, Myron O. 1509, 1512
Lourie, Eugene 1827
Lovell, Alan 449, 478, 529, 1937, 1961
Lowell, Constance 1006
Lowry, Edward 615, 643, 1599, 1802, 1974, 2040, 2071, 2075, 2076, 2079, 2119
Low, Rachel 1842
Loynd, Ray 536, 663
Lubin, David 1835
Lubow, Arthur 812
Lucas, George 81
Luciano, Dale 1350
Luft, Herbert G. 322, 375, 849, 1009, 1464, 1505, 1632, 1640, 1643, 1671, 1674, 1729, 1806
Lugg, Andrew M. 2039
Luhr, William 1297, 1312, 1747
Lukinbill, Laurence 2079
Lumet, Sidney 2041, 2084

Lund, Daniel Manny 573, 613
Lurie, Rod 232
Lurie, Susan 470
Luther, Rodney 648
Lynch, Joan D. 34, 41
Lyons, Richard D. 977
Lyons, Timothy J. 34, 35, 223, 1416, 1418

M

Maben, Adrian 2116, 2119
MacBean, James Roy 2110, 2111, 2157
MacCabe, Colin 118, 537
MacCann, Richard Dyer 139, 230, 231, 295, 645, 1512, 1520, 1523, 2034
Maccoby, Eleanor 745
Macdonald, Dwight 63, 140, 158, 455, 1548, 1648, 1955, 2170
MacDougall, David 2039, 2120
MacFadden, Patrick 1024, 2085
MacGowan, Kenneth 615, 655
MacKaye, Milton 648
MacKenzie, Kent 2034
Macklin, F. Anthony 1674, 2081, 2083, 2086, 2087
Mack, John E. 489
Macliammoir, Michael 1022
Maclochlainn, Alf 1714
Macorelles, Louis 2124
MacShane, Frank 1301
Madden, David 1039, 1419, 2183
Maddison, John 1002
Madge, Charles 317
Madsen, Axel 665, 1835, 2034, 2077, 2087, 2089
Mage, David A. 648, 1813
Magistrale, Anthony 979
Magliozzi, Ron 1536
Mahoney, Dennis F. 1642
Mahoney, Marie 800, 1799
Mailer, Norman 566, 1315, 1322
Majdalany, Fred 1022
Malkmus, Lizabeth 2178
Maloney, Russell 1834
Malraux, Andre 53, 582
Maltby, Ralph 559
Maltby, Richard 630, 1947
Maltin, Leonard 1536, 1577, 2072
Maltz, Albert 1975
Mamber, Stephen 2092
Mamis, Joshua 763
Manceaux, Michele 1012, 1874, 2130, 2173
Manchel, Frank 35, 40, 324, 424, 560, 952, 1014, 1721, 1752, 1769, 1872
Mancini, Elaine 1360, 1914, 2179
Mancini, Marc 409
Maneaty, Leah 497
Mannock, P. L. 1002, 1022
Mann, Delbert 84
Mann, Heinrich 1309
Mann, Thomas 1309
Mansfield, Joseph 1315

Manvell, Roger 315, 1001, 1013, 1624, 1635, 1729, 2015, 2189
Mapp, Edward 942
Marchetti, Gina 458, 770
Marcorelles, Louis 1711, 1813, 2098, 2106, 2126, 2152, 2165, 2167
Marcus, Robert D. 553
Mardone, Michel 2126
Mareth, Paul 760
Margolis, Barbara 2178
Margolis, Herbert F. 832
Margulies, Lee 760
Mariani, John 804
Marill, Alvin H. 1015, 1301
Marinucci, Vinicio 1607
Marion, Dennis 1018, 1674
Marker, Frederick J. 2183
Marker, Lise-Lone Marker 2183
Markey, Constance 410
Markopoulous, Gregory 1955
Marks, Louis 1290
Marple, B. G. 1321
Marriott, Michel 903
Marsden, Michael T. 564
Marshall, Herbert 125, 1645
Martineau, Barbara Halpern 508
Martinez, Enrique 1023
Martin, Andre 76
Martin, David 1706
Martin, Douglas 752
Martin, James M. 410
Martin, Linda 816
Marx, Groucho 1783
Maslin, Janet 488, 508, 514, 676, 762, 786, 903, 998, 1007, 1009, 1017, 1324, 1796, 2196, 2202
Mason, Clifford 890, 891, 916, 937
Mass, Roslyn 1322
Mastin, M. 1368
Mast, Gerald 252, 446, 447, 1509, 1513, 1514, 1515, 1548, 2072, 2106, 2190
Mast,Gerald 38
Matias, Diana 477, 479
Mattox, Michael 942
Maugham, W. Somerset 1309
Mayersberg, Paul 1000, 1297, 1752, 2071, 2077
Mayer, Andrew C. 2001
Mayer, Arthur 50, 54, 1464, 2034
Mayer, Martin 547
Mayer, Michael F. 676, 677, 700
Mayne, Judith 471, 476, 495, 496, 528, 614, 718, 765, 1297, 1587
May, Elaine Tyler 820, 821
May, Lary L. 820, 821
McArthur, Colin 1961, 1977, 2087
McBride, Joseph 877, 981, 1044, 1353, 1672, 1673, 1747, 1802, 1807, 1987, 2175, 2195, 2196
McCabe, Colin 588, 605
McCabe, John 1691
McCaffrey, Donald W. 1294, 1672
McCall, Mary 1076
McCann, Eleanor 2189
McCarthy, Todd 651, 652, 1535, 1674, 1685, 1814, 1854, 1987, 2196
McCarty, John 2087

McClelland, Douglas 1446
McClure, Arthur F. 262
McConnell, Frank D. 190, 410, 416, 565, 1977
McCormick, Ruth 508, 1324
McCourt, James 1986
McCreadie, Marsha 1324
McCreary, Eugene C. 1711, 1712
McDonald, Gerald D. 1434, 1464
McDonnell, Anna 2203
McDonough, Tom 1029
McDougal, Stuart Y. 1864
McDowell, Edwin 260, 488, 1028, 1032, 1317, 1322
McGann, Kevin 1315
McGilligan, Patrick 368, 508, 645, 653, 1084, 1085, 1257, 1261, 2202
McGillivray, David 2073
McGill, Douglas C. 2040
McGrory, Mary 549
McGuigan, Cathleen 970
McInerney, Peter 335
McInroy, Patrick 1604
McKee, Allen 1034
McLaughlin, James B. 1835, 1843
McLuhan, Marshall 63
McMahon, Ed. 1770
McManigal, Rod 1352
McNamara, Brooks 1587
McNamara, Susan 722
McNiven, Roger 1672
McPherson, Bruce 579, 593
McPherson, James Alan 255
McQueen, Butterfly 1318
McVay, Douglas 799, 1004, 1007, 1009, 1013, 1354, 1434, 1674, 1933, 1942,
  1943, 1987, 2019, 2119
McWilliams, Donald E. 2092
Mebane, Mary E. ("Liza") 898
Medjuck, Joe 1348, 2075
Meeker, Hubert 2173
Meisel, Myron 669, 2048
Mekas, Jonas 65, 137, 140, 141, 1955, 2039, 2074, 2075
Mellen, Joan 415, 439, 577, 1985, 2019
Melling, P. H. 559
Mellor, David 317
Melnik, Stefan 855
Menaker, Daniel 653
Menashe, Louis 2182
Mencken, H. L. 1309, 1674
Merralls, James 1013
Merritt, Russell 617, 685, 710, 712, 715, 718, 719, 722, 803, 804, 1366, 1385,
  1587
Meryman, Richard 586
Merz, Charles 213
Messaris, Paul 538, 573
Messinger, James R. 1039, 1040
Metz, Christian 118, 134, 528
Metz, Robert 662
Meyerhold, Vsevolod 1414
Meyersohn, Rolf B. 745
Meyers, Sidney 319

Meyer, Michael 209
Meyer, Richard J. 1362
Meyer, Russ 700
Meyer, William R. 800
Michaelson, Annette 2109
Michael, Earl 1455
Michalczyk, John J. 772
Michalek, Boleslaw 2012
Michals, John 593
Michelson, Annette 167, 514
Michels, Robert G. 809
Michel, Manuel 2167, 2178
Michener, Charles 898, 899, 916, 942, 1004, 1362, 2193
Middleton, Russell 546
Mieher, Stuart 903
Miles, Bernard 1434
Miles, Lynda 2196
Milicia, Joseph 2153
Millar, Daniel 1813, 2003
Millar, Gavin 1857, 1960, 1977
Miller, Arthur 2042
Miller, Don 651, 1935
Miller, Gabriel 789, 1138, 1178, 1836
Miller, Henry 1723
Miller, Judith 488
Miller, Mark Crispin 810
Miller, Randall M. 813, 814
Miller, William 1142
Mills, Bart 410
Milne, Tom 84, 800, 996, 1001, 1002, 1011, 1320, 1542, 1729, 1977, 1994, 2021, 2024, 2083, 2098, 2101, 2119, 2130, 2133, 2154, 2160, 2161, 2190
Minnelli, Vincente 1959
Minor, Bill 255
Minot, Drew 422
Missiaen, Jean-Claude 1982
Mitchell, Donald 1365
Mitchell, George 79
Mitchell, George J. 424, 1350, 1463, 1522, 1671, 1673, 1674
Mitchell, Greg 1069, 2020
Mitgang, Herbert 489, 1214
Mitry, Jean 1351, 1674, 1704
Modleski, Tania 388, 1835, 1966
Mohoney, Marie 2155
Molotsky, Irvin 1418
Monaco, Eitel 664
Monaco, James 671, 675, 760, 798, 1542, 1836, 2116, 2155
Monegal, Emir Rodriguez 295
Moneysmith, Marie 1137
Monod, Roland 1994
Monroe, Dale 2090
Montagu, Ivor 65, 1645, 1667, 1838
Montgomery, Patrick 1366
Moore, James 1155, 1282
Moore, Marcia 1414
Morandini, Merando 1023, 2169
Moran, Malcolm 1005, 1013
Morgan, James 1290, 1295
Morgan, Ted 2192
Morgan, Thomas 678, 2067

Morgenstern, Joseph 994, 1006, 2106
Morley, Alison 1084
Morley, Sheridan 1020, 1365, 1377
Morrison, Susan 469, 706
Morrissett, Ann 2182
Morris, C. Brian 1417
Morris, George 1987
Morris, Peter 1590
Mosier, John 2167, 2179
Moskowitz, Gene 2012, 2084
Moskowitz, Ken 2083
Moss, Carlton 860, 871
Moss, Geoffrey 1389
Moss, Robert F. 410, 834
Mottram, Eric 559
Mottram, Ron 1509, 1623, 1626
Mould, David H. 208
Moullet, Luc 2109
Mourlet, Michel 2124
Moynihan, Julian 1312
Mulholland, Robert E. 672
Mullen, Pat 1681
Mulvey, Laura 118, 466, 471, 473, 508, 527, 529, 531, 532, 587, 712, 715, 794, 1986, 2133
Munden, Kenneth 1300
Muni, Paul 1756
Murnau, F. W. 1671
Murphy, A. 1675
Murphy, A. D. 700, 753, 756, 1322, 2194
Murphy, Brian 388, 565
Murphy, Kathleen 2062
Murphy, Robert 1569, 1935, 1936
Murphy, William Thomas 281
Murray, Edward 1300
Murray, James P. 897, 942
Murray, Lawrence L. 648, 656
Murray, Leo 1023, 2003
Murray, William 1797, 2087
Musser, Charles 615, 618, 1361, 1462, 1580, 1582, 1587, 1590, 1601, 1603, 1605

N

Nachbar, John C. 581
Naficy, Hamid 2120
Nakamura, Haruji 1739, 1742, 1890, 1892, 1902, 2022
Narboni, Jean 2124
Narboni, Paul 470, 474, 475, 479
Narducy, Ray 2079, 2195
Naremore, James 373, 1391
Nash, Alanna 1366, 1368
Nash, Eleanor H. 1352
Nathan, Robert 1105, 1297
Neale, Steve 471, 550, 792, 2087
Neal, Robert W. 39
Neff, Andrew 536
Nelson, Donald 643
Nelson, Joyce 800, 1300

Nelson, Richard Alan 621, 627, 719, 771, 826, 1599
Neve, Brian 559
Nevins, Francis M., Jr. 2081
Ney, Joanna 2154
Nicholls, David 2109
Nicholson, Tom 653
Nichols, Bill 38, 176, 476, 477
Nichols, Dudley 140, 142, 366, 1351
Nichols, L. 1391
Nichols, Nina 1747, 1814, 1921, 2156
Nicoll, Allardyce 50, 144, 1336
Niemeyer, G. Charles 1363
Niven, David, Jr. 1057
Niver, Kemp 655
Nix, Crystal 904
Noames, Jean-Louis 1014, 1805, 1961, 1985
Noble, Gill 888, 906
Noble, Peter 1383
Noble, Robin 2083
Nock, Thomas J. 366
Nogueira, Rui 1813, 1988, 2080, 2098, 2101, 2104
Nolan, Jack Edmund 372, 800, 1300, 1846, 2151
Nolan, Lloyd 1771
Noorau, Michael 2034
Nordbert, Carl Eric 1012
Norden, Martin F. 259, 749, 770, 912
Nordheimer, Jon 961
Nord, David 173
Noriega, Chon 390
Norman, Marsha 1095
Norris, Floyd 2204
Norris, Frank 1309
North, Christopher J. 226, 625, 1670
Novik, William 1903
Nowell-Smith, Geoffrey 252, 316, 714, 814, 1012, 1509, 1512, 1874, 2076, 2106, 2169
Nulf, Frank 1335

O

O'Brien, Kenneth 857
O'Connell, Bill 654
O'Connor, John E. 51
O'Connor, John J. 489, 822
O'Dell, Paul 1362
O'Donnell, Victoria 913
O'Dowd, Donald D. 1011
O'Grady, Gerald 40
O'Hara, John 1792
O'Leary, Liam 1707
O'Malley, Tim 2119
O'Mealy, Joseph 2175
O'Neal, Frederick 886, 951
Oakes, Philip 1014
Obalil, Linda J. 2083, 2195
Oberbeck, S. K. 2176
Oberholtzer, Ellis 778
Oderman, Stuart 1454

Odets, Clifford 801
Oes, Ingvald C. 1627
Ogilvy, David 735
Ogle, Patrick 79, 1807
Oliver, William 1300
Olsen, Marvin E. 744, 745
Olsen, Ray 978
Oms, Marcel 1697
Ong, Walter J. 71
Onipege, Oladipo 919
Onosko, Tom 640, 1987
Ophuls, Marcel 2006
Ophuls, Max 1966, 2010
Opinion Research Corporation 742
Oppenheim, S. Chesterfield 654
Ort, Dan 40, 1014
Osborne, Robert 998, 1021, 1164, 1292, 2019
Osborn, Elodie 77
Oshana, Maryann 454
Oshatz, Lorrie 2153
Oudart, Jean-Pierre 82, 477
Overstreet, Richard 1039, 1981
Oxenhandler, Neal 2009, 2106, 2153, 2167
Ozu, Yasujiro 1902

P

Pace, Eric 762, 903, 1983, 2108
Page, Tim 1289
Paletz, David L. 543, 1294, 2034
Pally, Marcia 820, 834
Palmer, James W. 1324
Palmer, R. Barton 108, 801, 1947, 1978
Panofsky, Erwin 53, 136, 144, 1332
Parker, Gillian 1312
Pasetta, Marty 1164
Pasolini, Pier Paolo 2176
Patalas, Enno 2165
Patrick, Robert 789
Patterson, Frances Taylor 1020, 1352
Patterson, Lindsay 853, 916, 919, 941, 942
Pattison, Barrie 1982
Pauley, Thomas H. 565
Paul, David 2179
Paul, William 653, 665, 1747, 2010, 2191
Pearson, Gabriel 2093
Pearson, Roberta 1603, 1843, 1978
Peary, Dennis 508
Peary, Gerald 415, 508, 1039, 1314
Pear, Robert 961
Pease, Nick 801
Peat, Hal W. 1301
Peavy, Charles D. 924
Pechter, William S. 1022, 2087
Peckham, Morse 547
Pegler, Westbrook 1105
Pellow, C. Kenneth 1039

Pena, Richard 252
Pendakur, Manjunath 681, 771
Penley, Constance 471, 476, 480, 481, 483, 527, 531, 585, 590
Penna, Anthony 39
Pennington, Ron 973
Penn, Stanley 748
Perebinossoff, Philippe R. 1827
Pereboom, Pieter 252
Perier, Martin 1006
Peritore, N. Patrick 132
Peri, Enzo 1927
Perkins, Carolyn 1983, 2098
Perkins, Victor F. 1752, 1835, 1961, 1978, 1984, 1985, 2130
Perlmutter, Ruth 39, 820, 824, 835, 1978
Perry, Edward 1542, 1548, 1583, 1584, 1874, 1877, 1921
Peterson, Bernard L. Jr. 866
Peterson, Iver 290
Peterson, Jane A. 1948
Peterson, Maurice 1005
Petric, Vlada 39, 213, 582, 583, 593, 1143, 1511, 1542, 1645, 1668
Petrie, Graham 1419, 2084, 2094, 2104, 2119
Petro, Patrice 252, 485, 795, 1843
Petterson, Maurice 941
Pettit, Arthur G. 2087
Pett, John 1836
Peyser, Tony 366
Pfaff, Gunter 71
Phillips, Gene D., S. J. 564, 994, 1012, 1291, 1294, 1300, 1329, 1748, 1981, 1989
Phillips, Joseph D. 748
Phillips, Michael S. 227, 1001
Pickard, Roy 1705, 1987
Picker, David V. 700, 2041
Pickford, Mary 1374
Pierre, Sylvie 2125
Pilger, John 367
Pinchel, Irving 1999
Pines, Jim 856
Pinsker, Mark 837
Pinter, Harold 1336
Pipolo, Tony 2004
Pirie, David 1961
Piso, Michelle 1843
Pit 1013
Pithon, Remy 247
Pitt, David E. 2182
Place, Janey A. 471, 477, 507, 982, 1326, 1948
Plaza, Alex 2086
Plecki, Gerald 912
Pletnyov, Valeri 1658
Plotkin, Harris M. 649
Poague, Leland A. 176, 1836, 1843, 1864, 2080, 2155
Podany, Edward C. 546
Poffenberger, A. T. 724, 778
Poggi, Gianfranco 1874
Pohl, Constance 1315
Pohl, Frederick 415
Pointer, Michael 1301
Poitier, Sidney 1009

Polan, Dana B. 1646
Polito, Ronald 39, 40
Pollack, Andrew 762, 764
Pollack, Sydney 76, 700
Pollock, Dale 667, 677, 2107
Pollock, Griselda 792
Polonsky, Abraham 375, 1084
Polskin, Howard 653
Polt, Harriet R. 77, 2034, 2081
Pom 322
Pommer, Erich 1635
Popkin, Harry 830
Porfiro, Robert G. 505, 1947
Porter, Jack Nusan 859
Porter, Vincent 1569
Poster, W. S. 1014, 1912
Potamkin, Harry Alan 303, 1033, 1749
Potter, Vilma Raskin 1300
Pound, Ezra 1752
Poussaint, Alvin 897, 898
Powell, Dilys 514, 1441
Powers, James 887
Powers, John 365
Powers, R. G. 384
Pratley, Gerald 1835, 2090
Pratt, Cathy 646
Preminger, Otto 1984
Price, James 1353, 2086, 2109
Price, Vincent 388
Priestley, J.B. 53
Prima, Jesse 1001
Pringle, Harry 226
Prokosch, Mike 1750, 1994
Pronay, Nicholas 202, 210, 211, 216, 242, 247, 248, 255, 265, 1569
Proppe, Hans 2158
Prouse, Derek 656, 1002, 1005, 1012, 1292, 1325, 1327, 1434, 1714
Pryluck, Calvin 537, 564, 615, 710, 711, 736, 771, 1512, 1599, 2085
Pryor, Thomas M. 611, 651, 1501, 1763, 2197
Pudovkin, V. I. 53, 142, 144, 1312
Pulleine, Tim 1986
Pulliam, Rebecca 1326, 1673
Purdum, Todd S. 437
Pusch, Henry F. 200
Putnam, Harold 258
Puttnam, David 1842

Q

Quart, Barbara 1293
Quart, Leonard 259, 559, 1075, 1293, 2041, 2088
Quigley, Isabel 1547, 2169
Quigley, Martin 455
Quinn, Anthony 1022
Quirk, Lawrence J. 1803, 1981

R

Raack, R. C. 257
Rabinowitz, Lauren 515, 531, 1747
Rabinowitz, Paula 461
Raborn, George 83
Raeburn, Anna 1766
Raimirez-Berg, Charles 1827, 1828
Raine, Kathleen 317
Ramsaye, Terry 50, 566, 1585
Ramsey, Cynthia 598
Ramsey, Hartley 1290
Randall, Richard S. 686
Ranvaud, Don 1922
Raper, Michell 1981
Rape, Joe 2155
Rapf, Joanna E. 1291
Raphaelson, Samson 1276
Rappaport, Mark 1020
Rapper, Irving 1495
Rapping, Elayne 680, 2207
Raths, Louis 832
Ravage, Maria-Teresa 384
Ravo, Nick 552
Rawlings, E. 745
Rayns, Tony 2084
Ray, Nicholas 1985
Ray, Satyajit 1004, 1548, 2168
Ray, W. 1866
Reade, Eric 1590
Reade, Walter, Jr. 2042
Read, Herbert 1752, 1939
Rebello, Stephen 2195
Reddick, Lawrence D. 880, 915, 920, 924, 937, 939, 941
Reed, Carol 1939
Reeves, Geoffrey 1342
Reeves, Jimmie L. 798, 1675, 1747
Reeves, Nicholas 212
Reid, John Howard 384, 812, 1006, 1012, 1020, 1748, 1981, 1982, 1989
Reid, Mark A. 898
Reif, Tony 2081
Reilly, Adam 1536
Reimer, Robert C. 358
Reiner, Robert 559
Reisz, Karel 997, 1015, 1084, 1352, 1748, 1939
Renoir, Jean 140, 167, 1813
Renov, Michael 789, 1835
Rentschler, Eric 2165
Resnais, Alain 2153
Rhode, Eric 137, 999, 1004, 1005, 1023, 1434, 1828, 1922, 1927, 2010, 2093, 2168, 2180
Richardson, A. W. 1002, 1005, 2079
Richardson, Tony 1434, 1548, 1714
Richards, Jeffrey 225, 875, 1569, 1673
Richie, Donald 141, 1000, 1335, 1542, 1548, 1723, 1738, 1739, 1740, 1886, 1893, 1894, 1898, 2019, 2022, 2024, 2028, 2032, 2037
Richler, Mordecai 1032, 1037, 1101, 1793
Richter, Hans 140, 1718, 1955
Rich, Adrienne 468, 495

Rich, B. Ruby 465, 466, 495, 506, 511, 533, 539, 794
Rich, Frank 816, 1136, 1322
Rich, Hermione 1007, 1352
Rickey, Carrie 515, 998, 1017, 1292, 2197
Rider, David 996
Rierra, Emilio G. 1002, 1723, 1991
Riesman, David 814, 1299
Riesman, Evelyn 1298
Riley, Brooks 367
Riley, Clayton 938
Riley, Dan 1137
Ringel, Harry 1136, 1864, 2071
Ringgold, Gene 799, 1002, 1988
Ring, Frances 1109, 1126, 1130
Ritter, Walter E. 255
Ritzer, Teri 677, 763
Rivette, Jacques 1747, 1813, 1999, 2121
Roach, Hal 1410
Roaman, Chet 74
Robbe-Grillet, Alain 2153
Robbins, Fred 2073
Robbins, Jim 682
Robb, David 895
Robertson, Nan 752
Roberts, Steven V. 1749, 1795
Robertus, Patricia 959
Robinson, David 265, 656, 1001, 1012, 1096, 1377, 1441, 1542, 1561, 1645, 1672,
     1803, 1869, 1965, 1992, 2012, 2167, 2182
Robinson, Deanna Campbell 754
Robinson, George 2071
Robinson, Louie 889
Rockwell, John 611
Rodowick, David N. 471, 792
Rodrigues, Eusebio 2119
Roemer, Michael 1548
Roessler, Robert 754
Rogers, Ginger 1759
Rogoff, Rosalind 1585
Rohauer, Raymond 1687, 1770
Rokeach, Milton 835
Rolling, Gwen 1803
Rollins, Peter C. 39
Roman, Robert C. 388, 1300, 1335, 1804, 2030
Romm, Mikhail 1866
Ronder, Paul 2106
Rondolino, Gianni 247
Ropars, Marie-Claire 2151
Rosefelt, Reid 1084
Rosenbaum, Jonathan 1674, 1742, 1985, 2098, 2109
Rosenberg, Bernard 548, 552
Rosenberg, James L. 712
Rosenblatt, Daniel 816
Rosen, Irwin C. 832
Rosen, Marjorie 982, 1322, 2196
Rosen, Miriam 2178
Rose, Brian 564, 753
Rose, Chuck 1137
Rose, Cynthia 999

Rose, Ernest D. 42
Rose, Jacqueline 471
Rose, Olivia 1669
Rose, Philip G. 1419
Rose, Vattel T. 949
Rossen, Robert 1014, 1090, 1985, 2183
Ross, Chuck 678
Ross, Jean W. 1090
Ross, Lillian 1321
Ross, Michael E. 892, 904
Ross, Murray 1069
Ross, Steven J. 659
Ross, T. J. 1028, 1981
Rosten, Leo C. 218, 656
Rotha, Paul 144, 1005, 1015, 1292, 1636
Rother, Larry 454
Rothman, Cliff 663, 678, 682, 1137
Rothman, N. L. 820
Rothman, William 591, 982, 1315, 1843, 1857
Roth, Lane 429, 1642
Rotzoll, Kim B. 537, 771
Roud, Richard 131, 997, 1012, 1301, 1335, 1874, 1960, 1981, 1994, 1998, 2008,
   2115, 2116, 2119, 2133, 2151, 2152, 2159, 2173, 2174
Rowling, Gwen 798, 1747
Royal, Susan 2196
Rubenstein, Elliott 1672, 1921
Rubenstein, Leonard 2163
Rubin, Martin 1673
Ruby, Jay 52, 280
Ruby, Michael 1139
Ruhe, Edward 1297
Ruhe, E. L. 39
Ruppert, Peter 1297
Russell, John 2040, 2074
Russell, Lee (Peter Wollen) 1835, 1977, 2083, 2119
Rutherford, Charles S. 565
Ryall, Tom 173, 176
Ryan, Trevor 214, 1569
Ryo, Namikawa 247
Ryu, Chishu 1742

S

Sadoul, Georges 144, 1361, 1605, 1606, 1992, 2093, 2130
Safer, Elaine B. 1324
Safer, Morley 566
Safran, Don 488, 974, 1814
Sallitt, David 1835
Salmans, Sandra 535, 536, 678, 726, 743
Salter, James 2042
Salter, Stephen 251
Salt, Barry 79, 1604, 1697, 1745, 1944, 2198
Salvato, Larry 2075
Samsell, R. L. 1109, 1126, 1130
Samuels, Charles Thomas 1723, 1835
Samuels, Stuart 39, 822, 824, 828, 831, 833
Sandall, Roger 1012, 2120
Sandburg, Carl 1309

Sandeen, Eric J.   203
Sanders, Gregory   2152
Sanders, Terry B.   645
Sanger, David A.   31
Sarka, Kobita   1004
Sarris and ABSENCE OF MALICE   1017
Sarris and Andre Bazin   1819
Sarris and CITIZEN KANE   1807
Sarris and DOCTOR ZHIVAGO   1027
Sarris and EAST OF EDEN   1325
Sarris and feminist film theories   508
Sarris and film criticism   137, 141
Sarris and Francois Truffaut   2108
Sarris and HAIL THE CONQUERING HERO   1014
Sarris and Jean-Luc Godard   2109, 2133
Sarris and John Huston   1915
Sarris and King Vidor   1671
Sarris and LETTER TO AN UNKNOWN WOMAN   1966
Sarris and LOST HORIZON   1799
Sarris and MISSING   1021
Sarris and movie myths   547
Sarris and ODD MAN OUT   1021
Sarris and Otis Ferguson   148
Sarris and screenwriters   1145
Sarris and screenwriting   1029
Sarris and Sidney Poitier   887
Sarris and the AUTEUR theory   2097
Sarris and THE TURNING POINT   1016
Sarris and Woody Allen   786
Sarris, Andrew   53, 337, 377, 379, 1002, 1005, 1013, 1292, 1432, 1542, 1548,
   1674, 1677, 1694, 1747, 1751, 1776, 1788, 1837, 1845, 1912, 1955, 1972, 1977,
   1983, 1984, 1985, 1987, 2010, 2039, 2042, 2074, 2075, 2076, 2106
Sartre, Jean-Paul   1309
Sato, Tadao   1414, 1739, 1742, 1894, 1895, 1896, 1898
Sauvage, Pierre   2071
Sawyer, Paul   1005
Sayre, Nora   514, 789, 1098
Schackel, Sandra Kay   431
Schaffner, Franklin   2090
Schary, Dore   140
Schatz, Thomas   189
Schechner, Mark   837
Scheckley, Robert   415
Schecter, Leona Protas   282
Schenck-Hamlin, William J.   438
Scher, Mark J.   2163
Scheuer, Philip K.   2119
Scheurer, Timothy E.   564
Schickel, Richard   62, 170, 415, 495, 566, 765, 826, 994, 1295, 1514, 1578, 1701,
   1836, 1988
Schillaci, O. P., Rev. A.   200
Schillaci, Peter   803
Schiller, Patricia   546
Schlesinger, Arthur M., Jr.   254, 270, 576
Schlesinger, John   994
Schlesinger, Mark   1536
Schlosser, Arnold   875
Schmalz, Wayne   1355

Schmidt, Jackson 1465
Schneider, Alan 2067
Schneider, Harold W. 1026
Schneider, Irving 816
Schneider, Wolf 662
Schonert, Vernon L. 1410, 1672, 1707
Schrader, Leonard 1739, 1742, 1890, 1892, 1902, 2022
Schrader, Paul 189, 1001, 1947
Schramm, Wilbur 70
Schulberg, Budd 832, 1028, 1046, 1091, 1092, 1121, 1126, 1257, 1258, 1261, 1277, 1297
Schultheiss, John 1037, 1062, 1065, 1101, 1103, 1104, 1106
Schultz, Victoria 1933
Schuster, Mel 1446
Schuth, H. Wayne 913
Schuyten, Peter 662
Schwartz, Nancy 1314, 1673
Schwartz, Tanis 754
Schwartz, Tony 653
Schwerin, Jules V. 76, 1019
Schwichtenberg, Cathy 639, 771
Scobie, W. I. 896
Sconce, Jeff 477
Scott, Jay 2195, 2207
Scott, Joan 1084, 1085
Scott, Kenneth W. 1300
Seaman, Ann Rowe 800, 1814, 2074
Seaver, Richard 2116
Seberg, Jean 1985
Sebestyn, Istvan 760
Secrest, Chris 2080, 2152
Segal, Mark 1332
Segers, Frank 752
Seguin, Louis 1723
Seidman, Robert 2088
Seiter, Ellen 436, 517
Seldes, Gilbert 70, 1358
Selig, Michael A. 223, 262, 462, 489, 618, 800, 1014, 1035, 1747, 2076
Seneca, Gail 533
Sennett, Mack 142
Sepulveda, Orlando 748
Serceau, Daniel 497
Sesonske, Alexander 1356
Seton, Marie 303, 1004, 1867, 2168
Settle, Mary Lee 789
Seydor, Paul 1645, 2085, 2086
Shaffer, Lawrence 2087
Shaffer, Peter 1330
Shaheen, Jack 826
Shain, Russell 230
Shales, Tom 876, 1577
Shalit, Gene 960
Shamroy, Leon 2042
Shannon, Jeff 2076
Shapiro, Mitchell E. 755, 769, 771
Shapiro, Owen 291
Sharits, Paul J. 38, 2109
Sharkey, Betsy 903, 2200
Sharples, Win, Jr. 400

Shatnoff, Judith 1005, 2106, 2177
Shatzkin, Roger 1315
Shaw, George Bernard 1309, 1336
Shay, Don 2083
Sheckley, Robert 1234
Shedlin, Michael 2079
Sheed, Wilfrid 816
Sheehan, Robert 630
Shenon, Philip 961
Shepard, David 1577
Shepard, Richard F. 836, 1783
Shepard, Thomas 900
Sherman, Barry L. 748, 770
Sherman, Eric 166
Sherwood, Robert E. 1105
Shewey, Don 2204
Shils, Edward 534
Shipman, David 1981, 2151
Shivas, Mark 1977, 2071, 2098, 2099
Shohat, Ella 2169
Short, Kenneth R. M. 247, 1431
Short, Ray Leroy 710
Showalter, Dennis E. 826
Siciliano, Enzo 2171
Siclier, Jacques 2093
Sidney, George 400
Siegel, Gary 1315
Siegel, Joel E. 590, 2109
Siegler, Robert 1645, 2039
Signoret, Simone 1016
Silberman, Marc 528, 585
Silet, Charles L. P. 1843
Silke, James 2071
Silverberg, Robert 415
Silverman, Joan L. 912
Silverman, Kaja 118, 470, 471, 495, 496
Silverstein, Norman 1363, 1672, 2109
Silver, Alain J. 1835, 2071, 2072
Silver, Charles 1293, 1414, 1674
Silver, Joan Micklin 700
Silvey, Robert J. 70, 744
Simcovitch, Maxim 1367
Siminoski, Ted 666
Simmons, Garner 2087
Simmons, Jerold 366
Simonet, Thomas 673, 754, 772
Simone, R. Thomas 2030
Simon, Jerome S. 1805
Simon, John 53, 994, 1322, 1723, 2001, 2109, 2131, 2172
Simon, Michel 2093
Simon, Rita James 959
Simper, Deloy 1837
Sinatra, Frank 1962
Sinclair, Andrew 1655, 1914, 1934, 1936
Sinclair, Upton 1233, 1309
Singer, David 833
Singer, Isaac Bashevis 1033
Siodmak, Robert 384

Sirkin, Elliott 1003
Siska, William C. 1674, 1685, 2266
Siskel, Gene 437, 753
Sitton, Bob 2085
Skinner, Richard Dana 1430
Skivington, Andrea M. 430
Sklar, Robert 444, 784
Skoller, Donald S. 1994, 2189
Skvorecky, Josef 2165
Slade, Joseph W. 565
Slavin, Barbara 649
Slavitt, David 166
Slide, Anthony 1440, 1446, 1536, 1672, 1695, 1865
Sloan, William 813
Slout, William L. 718
Slusser, George 416
Small, Edward S. 176
Small, Melvin 259
Smith, Conrad 1583
Smith, Frank Leon 1455
Smith, Frederick 1113
Smith, Julian 564, 1327
Smith, Liz 1914
Smith, Paul 243
Smith, Robert 1982
Smith, Sally Bedell 545, 549
Smith, Sarah W. R. 1297, 1312
Smith, William Thomas 942
Smythe, Dallas W. 745
Smyth, Rosaleen 1569
Snieder, S. 653
Snyder, Thomas 812, 2197
Snyder, Tom 2196
Sobchack, Thomas 190
Sobchack, Vivian C. 295, 410, 416, 452, 565, 573
Sobol, Joshua 290
Soderbergh, Peter A. 223, 232, 257, 258, 860
Sodowsky, Alice 565
Sohn, David 200
Solin, Pierre 247
Solomon, Stanley J. 65
Sonbert, Warren 1836
Sontag, Susan 63, 144, 321, 362, 508, 514, 978, 1298, 1332, 1548, 1955, 2133
Sopocy, Martin 1606
Sorgen, Richard A. 368
Sorlin, Pierre 227
Southall, Derek J. 655
Southern, Terry 2042
Sparshott, F. E. 582, 593
Spears, Jack 262, 371, 454, 815, 1361, 1391, 1392, 1419, 1605, 1695
Spector, Warren 1535
Spehr, Paul C. 654, 1514, 1577
Spellerberg, James 479
Spence, Louise 858
Spiegel, Alan 2142
Spiegel, John P. 375
Spielberg, Steven 2196
Spottiswoode, Raymond 54
Springer, Alicia 761

Springer, John 84, 1014, 1981, 1985
Springer, Karen 903
Spring, D. W. 243
Squire, Jason E. 754
Sragrow, Michael 1020, 1347
Staayer, Chris 506
Stabiner, Karen 674, 2202
Stadler, Harald 485
Staehling, Richard 743
Staiger, Janet Kay 445, 446, 473, 474, 485, 607, 616, 618, 637, 658, 661, 685,
  697, 861, 1035, 1062, 1455, 1462, 1463, 1514, 1622
Stainton, Walter H. 1582, 1585, 1586
Stam, Robert 858, 1838, 1843, 1978, 2158
Stanbrook, Alan 669, 1009, 1016, 1019, 1702, 1729, 1889, 1891, 1892, 1989,
  2018, 2116, 2155
Stang, Joanne 1009
Staples, Brent 903
Stark, Samuel 1987
Starman, Ray 1492
Starr, William 1084, 2158, 2173
Stead, Peter 214, 242
Stecker, Dora H. 622
Steele, Richard W. 232
Steele, Robert 71, 139, 1334, 2084
Steene, Birgitta 497, 2183
Stegman, Allan 674
Steiger, Rod 2042
Steinman, Clay 980, 2076
Stein, Elliot 387, 2022, 2023, 2098
Stephanick, Michael 1792
Stephenson, William 463, 1058
Stephens, Lenora Clodfelter 913
Stern, Michael 655, 1986
Stern, Nina Weiss 1009
Stern, Seymour 140, 141, 1361, 1363, 1367, 1368, 1374
Sterritt, David 1673
Stevenson, James 2074
Stevenson, Richard W. 662, 672, 673, 674, 678, 2205, 2206
Stevens, George, Jr. 1748
Stevens, John D. 812
Stewart, David C. 39
Stewart, Garrett 409, 416
Stewart, Glen 608
Still, William Grant 916
Stoller, James 2039
Stolzfus, Ben 416
Stoney, George C. 54, 140
Stone, Herbert 1365
Stonier, G. W. 1014, 1912
Storm, Ole 1726
Stowell, H. Peter 1674
Strasberg, Lee 1965
Straubher, Joseph Dean 771
Strauss, William V. 625
Straus, David 626
Strebel, Elizabeth Grottle 225, 242, 247, 1813, 1903
Strickland, Nancy 2202
Strick, John C. 608, 639, 781

Strick, Philip   409, 415, 1704, 1981, 2001, 2010, 2075, 2119
Strug, Cordell   2087
Struss, Karl   2042
Stuart, Frederic   648, 649, 650, 697
Studlar, Gaylyn   470, 584, 596
Sturges, John   1987
Sturhahn, Larry   1324
Suber, Howard   820, 831, 1019, 2085
Suggs, Donald   903
Sugy, Catherine   942
Suid, Larry   335
Sulik, Boleslaw   1807, 2180
Sullivan, Mary Rose   2081
Sullivan, Mike   1802, 2075
Sullivan, Thomas R.   2081
Sullivan, William   914
Summers, Murray   1447
Surowiec, Catherine A.   1842
Surtees, Robert L.   2086
Sussex, Elizabeth   995
Sutherland, Sidney   1412
Sutherland, Zena   1614, 1755
Svatel, Peter   1814
Svehla, Gary   801
Swahn, Lennart   2183
Swann, Paul   771
Swartz, Mark E.   1599
Sweet, Blanche   1365
Sweigart, William R.   83, 1982
Swindell, Larry   1522, 1748
Symmes, Daniel L.   655
Symons, Julian   1947
Szabo, Will   655
Szekely, Kalman S.   855

T

Taaffe, William   1013
Tailleur, Roger   1084, 1089
Tajima, Renee   903, 1737
Tankel, Johnathan D.   1746
Tanner, Louise   368, 548, 1325
Tarratt, Margaret   409, 1233, 1301, 2161
Tarr, Susan   2158
Tart, Charles   582
Tate, Allen   1752
Tate, Greg   881
Taubman, Philip   1180
Taves, Brian   1433
Taylor, Anna Marie   497
Taylor, Dwight   1118
Taylor, Elizabeth   1971
Taylor, Frank   649
Taylor, Howard   855
Taylor, John Russell   373, 635, 801, 1022, 1294, 1325, 1450, 1542, 1930, 1944,
   2159, 2161
Taylor, Paul   1292
Taylor, Philip M.   211, 212, 217, 242, 247

Taylor, Richard 251, 261
Taylor, Ryland A. 545
Taylor, Stephen 2083, 2093
Taylor, Stuart, Jr. 960, 962, 1021
Teahan, John E. 546
Teddlie, Charles 573
Telberg, Val 1645
Telotte, J. P. 185, 409, 410, 912, 2080
Templin, Yvonne 1606
Terry, Clifford 1009
Tesich-Savage, Nadja 2102
Teush, Bart 1828
Thackery, Ted, Jr. 1632
Thalberg, I. and screen education 50
TheBerge, Rita 1674, 1827, 1927
Theodore, Terry 860
Thies, Jochen 251
Thomaier, William 1301, 1745, 1808
Thomason, David 415
Thomas, Anthony 83, 424
Thomas, Bob 1854
Thomas, David O. 617, 719, 1142
Thomas, John 1022, 2078
Thomas, Lowell 298
Thomas, Paul 998, 1819, 1823, 1844, 1855
Thompson, Anne 761, 2194, 2200
Thompson, Howard 890
Thompson, Kristin 118, 1742, 2011
Thompson, Lawrence D. 335
Thompson, Richard 1673, 1977
Thompson, Toby 649
Thomson, David 1548, 1985, 2080, 2201
Thom, Robert 166
Thornburn, David 180
Thornton, Sybil 1744, 2026
Thorp, Margaret 1298
Tiessen, Paul 1297
Tinsley, Elisa 437
Tinter, Adeline R. 2106
Tired Critics, The 40
Toeplitz, Jerzy 1522
Toeplitz, Krzysztof-Teodor 2180
Toffler, Alvin 62
Tolchin, Martin 437
Tolkin, Michael 2085
Tolstoy, Leo 1309
Tomaselli, Ruth 771
Tomasulo, Frank P. 544
Tonecki, Zygmunt 1062
Toplin, Robert Brent 252
Tornabene, Lyn 2083
Tornqvist, Egil 2183
Tors, Ivan 85
Towne, Robert 1037
Tozzi, Romano 368, 1012, 1365
Trachtenberg, Alan 1587
Trager, Frank 832
Trainor, Bernard E. 368

Traubner, Richard 203
Trauth, Denise M. 769
Tremblay, Anne 1323
Tretyakov, S. 255
Trevino, Jesus Salvador 2178
Trilling, Diana 514, 1290
Trilling, Lionel 1076
Trimmer, Joseph F. 1314
Trolle, Boerge 1729
Truchaud, Francois 1813
Trudeau, Garry 62
Truffaut and Andre Bazin 167
Truffaut and film criticism 142
Truffaut, Francois 129, 140, 1419, 1548, 1747, 1789, 1792, 1813, 1905, 1909, 1920, 1996, 1998, 2006, 2106, 2131, 2145, 2156
Trumbo, Dalton 880, 1084, 1097, 1099
Truscott, Harold 1672
Tuchman, Gaye 459, 460
Tuchman, Mitch 671
Tucker, N. 1321
Tudor, Andrew 174, 190, 2087, 2172
Tugent, Tom 820
Tuller, David 658
Tulloch, John 1642
Tumlin, John S. 2079
Tupper, Lucy 1300
Turim, Maureen 471, 487, 511, 1997, 2103
Turk, Edward Baron 1910
Turner, George E. 674
Turner, John B. 1836
Turner, John W. 1320
Turner, Ronald 1104
Turton, H. 1018
Tuten, Frederick 2081
Tyler, Parker 53, 142, 303, 1022, 1955, 2028
Tyler, Ralph 1014
Tyler, Susan 769
Tynan, Kenneth 1012, 2037

U

Uhry, Joanna 978
Ullmann, Liv 1941
Ulrichsen, Erik 2183
Ursini, James 1744
Uselton, Roi A. 367
Ustinov, Peter 1018, 1057, 1841
Utterback, Ann S. 280

V

Vager, Hans Rudolf 1308
Valenti, Jack 700, 960, 2198
Van Den Ecker, Louis 254
Van Dongen, Helen 295
Van Dyke, Dick 1691
Van Dyke, Willard 54, 139

Van Gelder, Lawrence 972, 1004, 1013
Van Peebles, Melvin 942
Van Wert, William F. 1748, 2115, 2116, 2152
Vanderbeek, Stan 1955, 2039
Vanderwood, Paul J. 576
Varshavsky, Y. 2181
Vas, Robert 215, 241, 282, 1023, 1648, 2160, 2165, 2167, 2182
Vaughan, Dai 317, 1669
Vaughan, David 400
Vaughn, Olwen 1903
Venturi, Lauro 1009
Vermilye, Jerry 1835, 2183
Vernet, Marc 531
Verret, Catherine 2155
Vesselo, Arthur 1016, 1353
Vianello, Robert 678
Vidmar, Neil 835
Vigo, Jean 1722
Vincent, Richard C. 1520
Vincenzo, Joseph 546
Visconti, Luchino 1874
Viviani, Christian 794
Vlahos, Petro 655
Vogel, Amos 321, 1955, 2174
Volpi, Gianni 2110
Volunteers for La Mancha 40
Von Brauchitsch, Mathias 39
Von Sternberg, Josef 53, 1336, 1697
Von Stroheim, Erich 1699, 1955
Vorkapich, Slavko 140

W

Wagner, Robert W. 42
Wahlstrom, Billie J. 789
Waldekranz, Rune 2182
Waldman, Diane 626, 630, 792
Wald, Jerry 1301
Wald, Malvin 1093, 1975
Walker, Alexander 508
Walker, Franklin 1028
Walker, Janet 800
Walker, Mary Jo 413
Walker, Michael 713, 716, 1835, 2098, 2101, 2123
Walkowitz, Daniel 252
Wallace, Irving 642, 690
Walling, William 1315
Walsh, Martin 2111
Walsh, Michael 1330
Walsh, Peter 1323
Walters, Barry 1003
Walter, Eugene 1927
Wanderer, Jules J. 462
Wanger, Walter 233
Ward, Brendan 1013
Ward, Frank 1729
Ward, John 1301

Warfield, Nancy 1910, 2076
Warhol, Robyn R. 116
Warner, Alan 384, 401, 424
Warner, Virginia 303
Warshow, Paul 1315
Warshow, Robert 53, 62, 144, 160, 350, 384, 424, 430, 1433, 1548
Washington, Michael 978
Wasko, Janet 573, 631, 672, 681, 769, 1367
Wasserman, Harry 1949, 2072
Wasson, Richard 1312
Watkins, Mel 540
Watts, Richard 1018
Wead, George 1595, 1672
Weales, Gerald 576, 884, 941
Weaver, Harold 949
Weaver, William 1885
Webb, Charles 2085
Weber, Barbara 978
Weber, Bruce 1032, 2196
Weber, Eugen 2093
Wegner, Hart 912
Weill, Kurt 65
Weinberg, David 818, 826, 828, 831, 832
Weinberg, Herman G. 140, 1018, 1297, 1645, 1669, 1672, 1674, 1699, 1754, 1955
Weiner, Bernard 2072
Weiner, Debra 508
Weinraub, Bernard 489
Weis, Elisabeth 1835, 1843
Weitz, Paul 580
Welch, David 202, 212, 247, 251, 255
Wellesley, Arthur 610
Welles, Orson 1022
Wellington, Mike 2175
Wells, H. G. 1309
Wells, Jeffrey 1007
Wells, Therese L. 535, 763
Wells, Walter 1161
Welsch, Janice 508, 1312
Welsh, James Michael 1024, 1141, 1277, 1712
Wenden, D. J. 274
Werner, Gosta 1524
Weschler, Lawrence 2179
Wesley, Richard 941
Westerbeck, Colin 367
West, Dennis 2163, 2178
Wexman, Virginia Wright 2081
Whannel, Paddy 40
Wharton, Flavia 995, 1324
Whitehall, Richard 280, 384, 424, 1010, 1012, 1827, 1831, 1933, 1943, 2040, 2087, 2161
Whitehead, O. Z. 1441
White, Armond 860, 901, 902
White, Dennis L. 388
White, Erdmute Wenzel 598, 1728
White, M. B. 1828, 2116, 2117
White, Timothy 2202
Whiting, J. H. 1362
Whitney, John S. 1947
Whitney, Simon N. 697

Whyte, Alistair 2131
Wickham, DeWayne 906
Wicking, Christopher 1982
Wicks, Ulrich 1162, 1163
Wiener, Thomas 2197, 2199
Wiesel, Elie 290
Wiese, Mildred J. 737
Wilbur, Richard 1316
Wilensky, Harold 459, 461
Wilks, Bob 71
Willemen, Paul 118, 794, 1966
Willett, Ralph 424, 559, 823
Williams, Alan 470, 1642, 2010
Williams, Barbara Morrow 897
Williams, Forrest 1927, 2010
Williams, Frederick 749
Williams, Linda 118, 495, 496, 590, 795, 826
Williams, Raymond 1568
Williams, Tony 410
Williams, Wenmouth, Jr. 755, 769
Williford, Stanley O. 877
williman, Joseph 166
Willing, Diana 1008, 1022
Willis, Don 1642, 1674
Willis, Ellen 508
Wilmington, Michael 1673, 1747, 1802, 1984, 1987
Wilson, David 2090, 2176
Wilson, Edmund 1028
Wilson, Gahan 1234
Wilson, Richard 1792
Wilson, Robert F., Jr. 1301, 1354
Wimberly, Darryl 2189
Winge, John Hans 1335
Winick, Charles 1666
Winkler, Karen J. 443
Winnington, Richard 1004, 1012, 1981
Winokur, Mark 454
Wirt, Frederick M. 966
Wise, Naomi 1747, 1984
Wohl, R. Richard 544, 545
Wolfenstein, Martha 602
Wolfe, Charles 1297, 2098, 2099
Wolfe, Tom 62
Wolff, Jurgen M. 1142
Wolfgang, Ernst 256
Wolfson, Kim 749, 770
Wolf, Barbara 2019
Wollenberg, H. H. 820
Wollen, Peter 118, 477, 478, 1835, 1961, 1977, 2080
Woll, A. 826
Woodside, Harold 2001
Woods, Frederick 424
Wood, Denis 410, 812
Wood, George, Jr. 1827
Wood, Michael 1021, 2199
Wood, Peter H. 180

Wood, Robin 189, 409, 484, 806, 1046, 1315, 1323, 1522, 1542, 1548, 1706, 1739, 1747, 1827, 1828, 1836, 1843, 1845, 1857, 1966, 1985, 2031, 2076, 2088, 2098, 2108, 2119, 2123, 2130, 2133
Woolf, Virginia 1309
Woollacott, Janet 1569
Worchel, Stephen 546
Worth, Sol 573
Wray, Karl 1204
Wright, Basil 303, 1021, 1348, 1939
Wright, Damon 2207
Wright, Elsa Gress 2189
Wuilleumier, Marie-Claire 2131
Wu, Ying Ying 2114
Wycliff, Don 437
Wylie, Thomas F. 41
Wyndham, Francis 1350

X

Xavier, Ismail 2158

Y

Yacowar, Maurice 183, 565, 1367, 1437, 1843, 2072
Yakir, Dan 611, 670, 1021, 2084, 2094, 2119, 2120
Yarrow, Andrew L. 656, 682, 1651
Yates, John 565
Yates, Kevin-Gough Yates 1985
Yates, Peter 1004
Yau, Esther 2163
Yearwood, Gladstone L. 860, 869, 876, 899, 900, 949, 953
Yoaken, Lola G. 1666
Yost, Kim 1945
Youngson, Robert 1290
Young, Charles M. 2073
Young, Colin 40, 139, 1013, 1944, 1988, 1994, 2034, 2040, 2093, 2173
Young, George M., Jr. 802
Young, Kristin 1024
Young, Vernon 137, 141, 1922, 2182
Yourenev, R. 1648

Z

Zack, A. J. 1136
Zakia, Richard D. 2037
Zalaffi, Nicoletta 2098
Zalman, Jan 2164
Zavattini, Cesare 140, 1922, 1924
Zeavin, Lynne 506, 586
Zeller, Dorothy M. 255
Zemon, Marvin 1994   .
Zimmermann, Patricia R. 772
Zimmerman, Paul D. 2073, 2083
Zinnemann, Fred 1988, 2034
Zita, Jacquelyn N. 2080
Zito, Stephen F. 860, 861, 982, 1577, 2196

Authors-Books Index

A

Aaron, Daniel 830
Abadie, Ann J. 1209
Abbott, L. B. 79
Abe, Kobo 2177
Abolin, R. W. 72
Abrams, M. H. 445, 448
Academy of Motion Pictures Arts and Sciences, the 1144
Ackerman, Forrest J. 417
Adair, Gilbert 218, 341, 2055
Adamson, Joe 1780, 1783
Adamson, Judith 1218
Adams, Brian 2158
Adams, Les 424
Adams, Samuel Hopkins 1311
Adkinson, R. V. 1635
Adler, Bill 1294, 2044, 2047
Adler, Mortimer J. 732, 955
Adler, Renata 145, 2085
Adler, Richard P. 180, 835
Adorno, T. W. 774, 778
Affron, Charles 1388, 1438, 1751, 2170
Afron, Mirella Jona 2143
Agan, Patrick 1439
Agate, James Evershed 1320, 1327, 1329, 1330, 1357
Agee, James 145, 531, 1014, 1021, 1022, 1296, 1298, 1322, 1353, 1354, 1357, 1433, 1688
Agel, Jerome 553, 2054
Ahlers, Arvel W. 71
Aitken, Gillon R. 1319, 1655, 1663
Aitken, Roy E. 1369
Akutagawa, Ryunosuke 2028
Albee, Edward 2086
Aldgate, Anthony 253, 265, 298, 540, 1938
Aldrich, Thomas Bailey 1389
Aleichem, Sholom 828, 847, 850
Alexandre, Marianne 1722, 1822
Alger, Horatio, Jr. 1052, 1139
Allain, Marcel 1617
Allan, Blaine 1968
Allan, Elkan 1521
Alleman, Richard 1232
Allen, Beverly 2171
Allen, Charlotte Vale 1041
Allen, Don 62, 2143, 2144
Allen, Jane 1104
Allen, Jeanne Thomas 797, 800
Allen, J. C. 1640
Allen, Nancy 1521
Allen, Richard 1238
Allen, Robert C. 440, 579, 612, 613, 618, 632, 707, 709, 710, 719, 721, 722, 766, 767, 1068, 1437, 1509, 1511, 1513, 1514, 1518, 1520, 1554, 1706
Allen, Woody 2045, 2208
Allep, Alfred, Jr. 1272
Allister, Ray 1610

Alloway, Lawrence   383, 452
Allvine, Grendon   1470
Allyson, June   1759
Alpert, Hollis   146, 565, 849, 1023, 1290, 1349, 1352, 1354, 1760, 1929, 1940, 2052
Althshuer, Thelma   1335
Althusser, Louis   479
Altman, Charles F.   1520
Altman, Richard   400, 460, 1163
Altomara, Rita Ecke   621
Alton, John   79
Alton, Stanley R.   86
Ambler, Nancy Morrison   1507
Amelio, Ralph J.   43
Anbinder, Paul   1583, 1587
Anderegg, Michael A.   322, 1086, 1988
Andersen, Yvonne   87
Anderson, Alexandra   1816
Anderson, Carolyn   2070
Anderson, Joseph L.   1574, 1731, 1734, 1735, 1736, 1737, 1739, 1740, 1741, 1742, 1885, 1889, 1892, 1894, 1895, 2015, 2016
Anderson, Lindsay   1682
Anderson, Michael   1795
Anderson, Patrick Donald   1044, 1060, 1136, 1137, 1144, 1244, 1290, 1292, 1295, 1296
Anderson, Robert   619, 1679
Anderson, Sherwood   1316
Andrade-Watkins, Claire   901
Andrew, James Dudley   119, 124, 125, 132, 133, 134, 135, 161, 162, 167, 169, 442, 1105, 1706, 1900, 1996, 1997, 2129
Andrew, Paul   1900
Andrzejewski, Jerzy   2180
Anger, Kenneth   1057, 1241, 1242
Annan, David   387, 409
Anobile, Richard J.   388, 1687, 1690, 1770, 1772, 1781, 1783, 1784, 1914, 2053, 2208
Anski, Solomon Z.   828
Antell, Gerson   612
Antonioni, Michelangelo   1012, 1881, 2169
Applebaum, Stanley   401, 1724
Apra, Adriano   1875, 1878
Aranda, J. Francisco   1719, 1990
Arce, Hector   1138, 1765, 1783, 1784, 1785
Archer, Leonard Courtney   879
Arijon, Daniel   71
Arliss, George   1759
Armer, Alan A.   71
Armes, Roy   113, 162, 324, 1565, 1571, 1606, 1618, 1715, 1910, 1928, 1992, 2000, 2001, 2112, 2115, 2122, 2135, 2189
Armour, Robert A.   1521, 1636
Armstrong, William H.   565
Arnheim, Rudolf   127, 166
Arnold, Alan   1060, 1463, 1695
Arnold, Edwin T.   2043, 2072
Arnold, James W.   42
Arnold, William   1292
Aros, Andrew A.   2033
Arrowsmith, William   1881

Artel, Linda   490
Arthur, Tom   1769
Arvidson, Linda   1376
Arzooni, O. G. J.   2168
Asheim, Lester Eugene   1305, 1306
Asplund, Uno   1419
Astaire, Fred   1759
Astor, Mary   1679
Atkins, Irene Kahn   401, 1636
Atkins, Thomas R.   410, 2070
Attansio, Salvator   1767
Atwan, Robert   747
Auden, W. H.   1871
Aumont, Jacques   1655
Aumont, Jean-Pierre   1909
Austen, Jane   1312, 1327
Austin, Bruce A.   458, 534, 537, 649, 681, 705, 711, 719, 720, 739, 748, 756, 767, 768, 770, 771, 772
Auty, Martyn   2159
Averson, Richard   70
Avisar, Ilan   310

B

Babich, Lawrence J.   422
Babington, Bruce   401
Babitsky, Paul   1648
Bacall, Lauren   798, 832, 1078
Bacher, Lutz   112, 113, 1632
Bach, Steven   535, 553
Bacon, James   1057, 1241
Baddeley, W. Hugh   82
Baechlin, Peter   1870
Bahrenburg, Bruce   553, 1322
Bailey, Adrian   1767
Bainbridge, John   1686
Baird, Jay W.   206, 208, 228
Baker, Carroll   1957
Baker, Fred   2041
Baker, M. Joyce   341, 789
Baker, W. W.   560
Balazs, Bela   125, 166
Balcon, Michael   216, 1841, 1871
Balderston, John L.   1798
Baldwin, James   860, 895
Baldwin, Neil   1727
Balio, Tino   607, 621, 625, 630, 632, 635, 639, 642, 653, 664, 676, 684, 686, 710, 736, 797, 930, 1369, 1370, 1460, 1465, 1466
Ball-Rokeach, Sandra   747
Ballantyne, James   310
Ball, John Dudley   2082
Ball, Robert Hamilton   1342
Balshofer, Fred J.   1587
Balsley, Daisey F.   860
Baltake, Joe   2058
Balzac, Honore de   1317, 2099
Banaszkiewicz, Wladyslaw   2013
Bandler, Bernard, II   1752

Bankhead, Tallulah 1760
Bann, Richard W. 1691
Banta, Martha 1047
Baran, Paul 765
Barber, Rowland 1064, 1784
Barbour, Alan G. 1078, 1081, 1456, 1761, 1778, 1788
Bardeche, Maurice 627, 1519, 1558, 1625
Bare, Richard 71
Barker, Felix 1861
Barker, Martin 962
Barnard, Tim 2157
Barna, Yon 1644, 1655
Barnes, John 1610
Barnett, Louise K. 2171
Barnouw, Erik 246, 292, 1588, 2167
Barrault, Jean-Louis 1909
Barrett, Edward L., Jr. 1079
Barrett, Gerald R. 1957
Barrett, Gregory 787, 788, 801, 802, 1575, 1733, 1734, 1735, 1736, 1737, 1740, 1742, 1743, 1888, 1891, 1895, 1898, 2016, 2020
Barrett, William E. 952
Barrie, James 1703
Barris, Alex 408, 1246
Barrymore, John 1760
Barrymore, Lionel 1760
Barry, Iris 514, 1370, 1519, 1558, 1625, 1675
Barr, Charles 1566, 1567, 1690, 1839, 1935
Barsam, Richard Meran 101, 215, 217, 230, 246, 255, 280, 284, 294, 295, 317, 319, 320, 1681
Barson, Alfred T. 145
Barson, Michael 1783
Barthes, Roland 177, 482, 487, 495
Bartolini, Luigi 1004
Basinger, Jeanine 341, 1787, 1964
Bassani, Giorgio 2174
Bassinger, Jeanine 280
Basten, Fred E. 654
Bast, William 1959
Bataille, Gretchen M. 425
Batchelor, John Calvin 428
Bathrick, Serafina Kent 794
Batschelet, Ralph J. 609
Battcock, Gregory 489, 1955
Batty, Linda 1522
Baudelaire, Charles-Pierre 2129
Bauer, Barbara 1350
Bauer, Raymond 778
Baum, L. Frank 1801
Baum, Vicki 1802
Bavar, Michael 1795
Bawden, Liz-Anne 1522
Baxter, Anne 1957
Baxter, John 384, 410, 661, 1067, 1081, 1675, 1683, 1696, 1752, 2157
Baxter, Peter 1697
Bayer, William 71
Bazelon, Irwin 402
Bazin, Andre 128, 167, 1297, 1334, 1337, 1419, 1432, 1509, 1789, 1814, 1819, 1905, 1922, 1924

Beadle, Erastus 175
Beal, J. David 71
Bean, Robin 1344, 1354
Beards, P. H. 93
Beath, Warren Newton 1959
Beaton, Cecil 1760
Beattie, Eleanor 2162
Beaumont, LePrince De 2008
Beauvoir, Simone de 514
Beaver, Frank E. 147, 1519, 1558, 1584, 1625
Beaver, James N., Jr. 1093
Becker, Howard 459, 461
Beckett, Samuel 2067
Beckman, Henry 71
Beckoff, Samuel 43
Beck, Calvin 388
Beck, Carl 1077
Bego, Mark. 1962
Behlmer, Rudy 1032, 1044, 1124, 1246, 1249, 1290, 1296, 1486, 1493, 1945
Behrman, Samuel Nathaniel 1176
Beja, Morris 1308
Belafonte, Dennis 1785
Bell-Metereau, Rebecca 487, 491, 553, 589
Bellamy, Ralph 1761
Belling, Curt 227
Bellone, Julius 137
Bellour, Raymond 511
Bell, Clive 457
Bell, Mary Hayley 1941
Belton, John 1702, 1774, 1964
Beman, Lamar Taney 963
Benchley, Nathaniel 1078, 1761
Benderson, Albert Edward 2170
Benderson, Bruce 1909
Benedict, Ruth 1894, 1898
Benet, James 462
Benjamin, Walter 550
Bennett, Charles 1864
Bennett, Tony 422
Benoit-Levy, Jean 101
Benson, Kathleen 885
Benson, Thomas W. 2070
Bentley, Eric 712, 1067, 1075, 1080, 1091, 1178, 1179, 1333
Beograd Film Institute 185, 186
Berelson, Bernard 708, 778
Bergan, Ronald 421, 1371, 1547
Berger, John 531, 538, 637
Berger, Thomas 1320
Bergman, Andrew 441, 554, 555, 556, 559, 1078, 1762
Bergman, Ingmar 2182, 2184
Bergman, Ingrid 1761
Bergom-Larsson, Maria 2184
Bergson, Henri 1425
Bergsten, Bebe 1593, 1626', 1627
Berg, A. Scott 1471
Berg, Charles Merrell 402
Berkowitz, Leonard 749
Berkowitz, Stan 698
Berk, Lynn M. 180

Berman, Connie 951
Berman, Marshall 550
Bernanos, Georges 2008
Bernstein, Irving 658
Berrigan, Daniel, S. J. 553
Bertrand, Daniel 607, 619, 625, 687
Besas, Peter 235
Bessie, Alvah 832, 1177
Bessie, John 1067
Bessy, Maurice 1790
Best, Marc 990, 991
Betancourt, Jeanne 491
Betrock, Alan 982
Betts, Ernest 540, 1567, 1568, 1936
Beveridge, James 215
Biberman, Herbert 1089
Bierce, Ambrose 1316
Billard, Pierre 2129
Billings, Pat 660, 2042
Birkos, Alexander S. 1649
Biro, Yvette 162
Bishop, George 1081, 1788
Biskind, Peter 1952
Bittner, John R. 747
Bitzer, G. W. 1362, 1371
Bjorkman, Stig 2185
Black, Gregory D. 229, 351
Black, Lendley C. 1648
Black, Shirley Temple 1787
Blades, Joseph Dalton, Jr. 119, 137
Blair, Alan 2184, 2188
Blake, Edith 553
Blake, Richard Aloysius 2185
Blake, William 1013
Blanchard, E. L. 687
Blanchard, Nina 72, 1232
Blanchard, Phyllis 726, 778
Bland, Alexander 1296
Blatty, William 554, 1317
Bleicher, Norman L. 72
Blesh, Rudi 1677, 1687, 1705
Bliss, Michael 2209
Blonski, Annette 491
Bloom, Samuel W. 882
Bluem, A. William 607, 676, 687
Bluestone, George 1019, 1021, 1309, 1311, 1314, 1327
Blumenberg, Richard M. 43
Blumer, Herbert 729, 730, 775, 776
Blum, Daniel 1523, 1613, 1752
Blum, Eleanor 1523
Bobker, Lee R. 72, 101, 110
Bocek, Jaroslav 2013
Bock, Audie E. 1735, 1738, 1739, 1886, 1887, 1890, 1891, 1893, 1894, 1895,
   1898, 1899, 2016, 2021, 2022
Bodeen, DeWitt 1681, 1765
Bodon, Jean 1419
Bogdanovich, Peter 146, 876, 1401, 1636, 1683, 1775, 1843, 2076
Boggs, Joseph M. 62, 102

Bogle, Donald 277, 852, 860, 885, 920, 921, 922, 923, 924
Bohannan, Paul 918
Bohnenkamp, Dennis R. 33, 43
Bohn, Thomas W. 281, 1519, 1559, 1586, 1671, 1749
Boileau, Pierre 2080
Bojarski, Richard 1778, 1782
Boker, Carlos 177, 312, 319
Boller, Paul F., Jr. 1233
Bolt, Robert 970, 1020
Bonanno, Margaret Wander 1917
Bonazza, Blaze O 109
Bona, Damien 1174, 1175
Bondanella, Peter 1885, 1928, 1929
Bone, Edith 125
Bone, Jan 105
Bonn, Thomas W. 1714
Bookbinder, Robert 1350
Boorstin, Daniel J. 255, 457, 546, 547, 549, 556, 1027, 1139, 1434
Booth, Michael 712
Booton, Hendon 1398
Bordwell, David 57, 59, 60, 61, 63, 94, 95, 102, 112, 113, 616, 1062, 1519, 1628, 1725, 1729
Boskin, Joseph 861, 907
Boswell, John 1081, 1788
Bosworth, Patricia 1958
Botham, Noel 1060
Boucicault, Dion 862
Boulding, Kenneth E. 258
Boulle, Pierre 2090
Bourgeois, Jacques 87
Bouzereau, Laurent 2208
Bowers, Q. David 1440, 1588, 1600
Bowers, Ronald L. 1484, 1487
Bower, Dallas 1339
Bowles, Jerry 1767
Bowles, Stephen E. 1523, 2058
Bowser, Eileen 1370
Bowser, Pearl 901
Bowskill, Derek 87
Boyarsky, Bill 1088
Boyer, Deena 2170
Boyum, Joy Gould 137, 1309
Bozzetti, Piergiuseppe 2005
Brabner, Wendy 1957
Bradford, Roark 930
Bradford, Sarah 1350, 1962
Brady, Anna 1523
Brady, Frank 1790
Brady, John 84
Bragg, Melvyn 1940
Braine, John 1016
Brando, Anna Kashfi 1957
Brand, Max 425
Branson, Clark 1775
Brasch, Walter M. 76
Brasillach, Robert 627, 1519, 1558, 1625
Braudy, Leo 179, 180, 186, 1547, 1819, 2144
Brauer, Donna 425
Brauer, Ralph 425

Braum, Myron 1786
Brehm, Jack W. 543
Brenner, Debbie 1524
Brenner, Marie 1233
Breton, Andre 1713
Brewer, Terry 1359, 1412
Brewster, Ben 479
Brian, Denis 1760
Bridges, Herb 1318
Brill, A. A. 531
Brill, Lesley 1843
Brinnin, John Malcolm 1196
British Board of Film Censors (BBFC) 225
British National Film Archive 1611
Britton, Andrew 603
Britton, Celia 169
Brodbeck, Emil E. 72
Brode, Douglas 1953, 2045, 2054, 2061
Brodsky, Louis Daniel 260, 1206
Brogan, D. W. 778
Broman, Sven 1686
Bronfeld, Stewart 84
Bronte, Charlotte 1312
Bronte, Emily 1312, 1327
Bron, Elizabeth Lee 1767
Brooker-Bowers, Nancy 1145
Brooke, Dinah 1816, 1909
Brooke, Peter 712, 714, 716
Brooks, Alfred G. 1635
Brooks, Mel 2047
Brooks, Richard 375, 849
Brooks, Van Wyck 1053
Brosnan, John 388, 411, 417, 422
Broughton, James 80
Brough, James 799, 1057, 1243, 2050
Browne, Nick 114
Brownlow, Kevin 204, 205, 209, 210, 212, 213, 223, 259, 262, 263, 296, 617,
  1392, 1519, 1609, 1675, 1677, 1726
Brown, Alec 1817
Brown, Curtis F. 1761, 1774
Brown, Harry 354
Brown, Jared 1179, 1782
Brown, Karl 1372
Brown, Les 650
Brown, Lewis S. 1581, 1597
Brown, Roland G. 44
Brown, Royal S. 2130
Brown, Wesley 906
Brown, William 1860
Broz, Jaroslav 2013
Bruccoli, Matthew J. 1110, 1111, 1114, 1116, 1118, 1119, 1121, 1122, 1125,
  1127, 1129, 1130, 1132, 1133, 1207, 1215, 1273, 1280, 1975
Bruce, Graham 402
Brunette, Peter 1882
Brunsdon, Charlotte 491
Bryer, Jackson R. 1227
Bryher, Winifred 1062, 1340, 1754, 2176
Buache, Freddy 1720, 1989

Buchanan, Singer Alfred 860
Buchan, Jack 212
Buchan, John 1838, 1864
Bucher, Felix 1572
Buchman, Herman 84
Buck, Pearl 1320
Budgen, Suzanne 1930
Bukalski, Peter 1524
Bukowski, Charles 1042
Bull, Clarence Sinclair 1440
Bulman, J. C. 1342
Bunuel, Luis 1720, 1990
Burch, Noel 112, 167, 733, 1601, 1731, 1732, 1733, 1734, 1735, 1738, 1739,
   1740, 1741, 1742, 1743, 1744, 1745, 1887, 1889, 1890, 1892, 1896, 1897, 1901,
   1902, 2018
Burder, John 82
Burfield, Diana 70
Burgess, Alan 1761
Burgess, Anthony 2055
Burgess, Muriel 1862
Burke, Jim 2046
Burke, Thomas 1388
Burke, William Lee 860
Burns, E. Bradford 2177
Burns, Rex 1046, 1049, 1051
Burns, Robert Elliot 1804
Burroughs, Edgar Rice 919
Burrows, Michael 2059
Burton, Arthur 586
Burton, Dwight L. 980
Burton, Julianne 2177
Buscombe, Edward 1520
Bussing, Sabine 389
Buss, Robin 1572
Butler, Ivan 44, 63, 342, 389, 1568, 1609, 2179, 2180
Byrge, Duane 1752
Bywater, Tim 37, 119, 120, 121, 125, 138

C

Cable, Frances 1446
Cadbury, William 138
Cagin, Seth 558, 576, 684
Cagney, James 1078, 1762
Cahan, Abraham 1313, 1314
Cahn, William 1692
Cain, James M. 797, 798, 800, 1037, 1042, 1161, 1314, 1924
Calder-Marshall, Arthur 1681
Calder, Jenni 425
Caldwell, Erskine 858, 914, 1924
Calistro, Paddy 1777
Callaghan, Barry 87
Callahan, John F. 1048, 1052, 1120
Callenbach, Ernest 44, 1012, 1019, 1021
Callow, Simon 1860
Cameron, Evan W. 632
Cameron, Ian 1881, 2003, 2094, 2123, 2130
Cameron, Ken 86

Cameron, Shipp 1760
Campaine, Benjamin M.   607, 613, 626, 647, 660, 678, 748
Campbell, Edward D. C., Jr.   440, 857, 871, 895, 907, 912
Campbell, Joanna 2059
Campbell, Russell 87
Canadian Film Archives   1522
Canemaker, John 76
Canfield, Alyce 1780
Canham, Kingsley 800, 1766, 1779
Cannom, Robert 1788
Cannon, Doran William 554
Capote, Truman 605, 1318
Capra, Frank 281, 1762
Cardullo, Bert 138
Carey, Gary 226, 1272, 1400, 1402, 1407, 1479, 1524, 1777, 1958
Carmen, Ira H.   225, 963, 2038
Carnegie, Andrew 555
Carney, Raymond 1763, 2047
Carne, Marcel 1909
Carpozi, George, Jr.   365, 1081, 1138, 1765, 1772, 1964
Carrick, Edward 79
Carrier, Rick 87
Carringer, Robert L.   44, 1639, 1790
Carroll, David 87, 1440
Carroll, John M.   893
Carroll, Lewis 1031
Carroll, Noel 162
Carroll, Peter N.   2050
Carr, Gary 1264
Carr, Larry 1440
Carr, Robert K.   1077
Carson, Robert 1158
Carter, Huntley 1649
Carter, Tasile 1068
Carvainis, Maria 1768
Carynnyk, Marco 1645, 1654, 1665
Cary, Diana Sierra (Baby Peggy) 426, 991
Casebier, Allan 102
Cashin, Fergus 1356, 1940
Casper, Joseph Andrew 1784
Cassavetes, John 2048
Castell, David 1862, 2066
Castle, Charles 1676, 1765
Casty, Alan 63, 103, 1012, 1519, 1559, 1969
Cater, Douglass 180
Catling, Gordon 87
Caughey, John 1057, 1233
Caughey, LaRee 1057, 1233
Caughie, John 162, 1999
Caunter, Julien 87
Caute, David 1077
Cavell, Stanley 64, 528, 531, 576
Cawelti, John G.   182, 185, 188, 350, 430, 564, 712, 716, 1047, 1049, 1051, 2064
Cawkwell, Tim 1543
Cayen, Ron 1325
Ceplair, Larry 203, 219, 226, 1063, 1065, 1075, 1099, 1181
Ceram, C. W. (Kurt W. Marek) 1581, 1589
Chabrol, Claude 1850

Chaillet, Jean-Paul 2208
Chambers, Whittaker 1190
Champlin, Charles 661, 1519, 1913, 1944, 1951, 2038
Cham, Mybe B. 901
Chanan, Michael 1510, 1583, 1611, 1938, 2163
Chandler, Raymond 738, 1037, 1042, 1161, 1162, 1197, 1199, 1977
Chaneles, Sol 1524
Chanslor, Ray 1984
Chaplin, Charles Spencer 1414, 1419, 1420, 1427
Chaplin, Charles, Jr. 1420, 1421
Chaplin, Lita Grey 1431
Charney, Maurice 594
Charters, W. W. 729, 773
Chase, David 609
Chase, Richard 178
Chatman, Seymour 114, 1881
Chell, David 1548
Chenoweth, Lawrence 1047
Chevalier, Maurice 1764, 1765
Choate, Julian Ernest, Jr. 427
Choukas, Michael 213
Chowan, Jeffrey 2208
Christensen, Terry 558
Christie, Agatha 1197
Christie, Ian 1653
Christopher Fryer 2061
Churchill, Hugh B. 82
Ciment, Michel 1093, 1257, 1962, 2055, 2161
Cini, Zelda 1058, 1233
Clair, Rene 1724, 2005
Clarens, Carlos 384, 389
Clarke, Arthur C. 1311, 2054, 2083
Clarke, Charles G. 80
Clarke, Gerald 1196
Clarke, Simon 479
Clark, Al 1196
Clark, M. J. 252
Clark, Paul 2163
Clark, Randall 1145, 1154
Clark, Walter Van Tilburg 1021
Cleaue, Alan 88
Clerk, Caroline 1765
Clifton, N. Roy 114
Clinch, Minty 1078
Coates, Paul 2013
Cobb, Humphrey 1314
Cocchi, John 426
Cocteau, Jean 1816, 1817, 2005, 2009
Coe, Brian 1589
Cogley, John 1067, 1074, 1087, 1096, 1185
Cohen-Seat, Gilbert 2002
Cohen, Arthur 543
Cohen, Hennig 258
Cohen, John 2171
Cohen, Keith 115
Cohen, Louis Harris 1649
Cohen, Marshall 164, 1332
Cohen, Sarah Blacher 819, 836
Cohn, Art 1971

Cohn, Lawrence 298
Colette (See Sidonie Gabrielle) 147
Cole, Lester 1067, 1075, 1083, 1098
Collet, Jean 2130
Colle, Royal D. 860
Collier, Jo Leslie 1633
Collins, W. H. 86
Colman, Hila 88
Colman, Juliet Benita 1679
Columbia, David Patrick 1969
Comito, Terry 2069
Comstock, G. A. 459
Conant, Michael 607, 623, 630, 634, 641, 675, 687, 742
Condon, Richard 2077
Conger, Syndy M. 1297
Connelly, Marc 930, 931
Connell, Brian 1401, 1402
Connors, Marie 1215
Conot, Robert 1586, 1615
Conover, David 1138
Conrad, Earl 886, 950, 1771
Conrad, Joseph 1114, 1312, 1316, 1838
Considine, David M. 983
Constantine, Mildred 1650
Conver, David 1965
Conway, Michael 1138, 1686, 1774, 1965
Cooke, Alistair 138, 1398, 1399, 1403, 1406, 1432
Cook, Bruce 1067, 1282
Cook, David A. 655, 1519, 1560, 1583, 1605, 1607, 1624, 1631, 1633, 1644, 1646,
    1714, 1747, 1812, 1814, 1876, 1950, 2016, 2021
Cook, Michael 72
Cook, Olive 1584, 1589, 1590
Cooper, Jackie 1679
Cooper, James Fenimore 175
Cooper, John C. 45
Cooper, Martin M. 1164
Cooper, Miriam 1366, 1373
Cooper, Ross 2157
Coppedge, Walter 1779
Coppola, Eleanor 367
Corey, David 1836
Corliss, Richard 1029, 1093, 1101, 1140, 1145, 1147, 1266, 1285, 1802, 1912
Corman, Avery 110, 1007
Corneau, Ernest N. 426
Corrigan, R. W. 712
Corrigan, Timothy 2165, 2166
Cortazar, Julio 1311, 2173
Costanzo, William V. 45
Costa, Sylvia Allen 72
Costello, Donald P. 1023, 1344, 1930
Coster, Patience 1525
Cotes, Peter 1420
Cotton, Joseph 1765
Cottrell, John 1356, 1862, 1940
Coursen, H. R. 1342
Coursodon, Jean-Pierre 1548
Cowie, Peter 1525, 1560, 1561, 1624, 1627, 1628, 1629, 1791, 1882, 2178, 2185
Cowley, Malcolm 765, 1113, 1116, 1119

Coyle, Wallace 2056
Coynik, David 45, 88
Crafton, Donald 1623
Crane, Cheryl 1971
Crane, Robert David, 2061
Crane, Stephen 1316, 1321
Crawford, Christina 1765
Creel, George 223
Cremer, Robert 1782
Cressey, Paul G. 729
Crichton, Kyle 1783
Cripps, Thomas R. 277, 709, 859, 860, 861, 863, 867, 868, 876, 878, 923, 924, 926, 927, 929, 930, 931, 943, 952, 953, 1341, 1382
Crisp, C. G. 2102, 2103, 2141, 2144
Cristall, Ferne 492
Crist, Judith 147, 609, 1008, 1020
Croce, Arlene 1759
Cross, Brenda 1353
Crowson, Lydia Lallas 1818
Crowther, Bosley 226, 963, 1019, 1408, 1480, 1482, 1576, 1672, 1702, 1703, 1704, 1707, 1800, 1825, 1933, 2173
Crowther, Bruce 1947, 1956
Croy, Homer 1374
Cruze, Harold 916
Culbert, David 343, 569, 1542
Culkin, John M. 53, 200, 1354
Cumbo, Robert C. 2171
Cunningham, John W. 1019
Curran, James 1568, 1935
Currie, Hector 45, 1335
Curry, George 1318
Curtin, Philip D. 919
Curtiss, Thomas Quinn 1698
Curtis, Anthony 1440
Curtis, David 582, 1715
Curtis, James 1918
Curti, Carlo 1492
Cvetic, Matthew 1190
Cyr, Helen W. 916, 917
Cywinski, Ray 1918
Czitrom, Daniel J. 458, 723, 772

D

Dahl, David 1773
Dale, Edgar 729, 730
Dale, R. C. 1724, 1826
Dalton, David 1325, 1959
Daly, David A. 488, 753
Dandridge, Dorothy 886, 950
Daniels, Arlene Kaplan 462
Danischewsky, M. 1842
Danko, X. 1658
Danziger, Marlies K. 109
Dardis, Tom 1063, 1066, 1125, 1129, 1134, 1147, 1216, 1687, 1693, 1705
Dart, Peter 1662
Darvi, Andrea 991
Das Gupta, Chidananda 2167

Davidson, Bill 1057, 1242, 1788
David, Jay 1081, 1788
David, Saul 690
Davies, Philip 559
Davis, Bette 1766
Davis, Brian 384
Davis, Robert Edward 456, 725
Davis, Ronald L. 1233
Davis, Sammy, Jr. 950
Davy, Charles 1753
Dawidowicz, Lucy 311
Dawson, Bonnie 492
Dawson, Jan 514, 2131
Day, Beth 1057, 1233
Day, Douglas 1265
De Beauvoir, Simone 2098
De Fleur, Melvin L. 721, 747
De Grazia, Edward 963
De Grazia, Sebastian 457
De La Roche, Catherine 1650
De Lauretis, Teresa 168, 467, 481, 492, 493, 494, 496, 532
De Maurier, George 1798
De Saussure, Ferdinand 482
De Sica, Vittorio 1928, 1929
Deals, Kenneth 1778
Deane, Hamilton 1798
Deans, Mickey 1138, 1773
Dean, Basil 1842
Debes, John 55
Debrix, J.R. 97, 98, 100, 106
DeFelice, James 1939
Defoe, Daniel 557, 1311
Delamater, Jerome 402
Deleuze, Gilles 162
DeLiso, Oscar 2170
Deloria, Vine Jr. 916
DeMille, Cecil B. 1680
DeMille, William C. 32, 1680
Deming, Barbara 494, 576
Denby, David 139
DeNeut, Richard 2059
DeNitto, Dennis 103, 110, 119, 120, 125
Denton, Clive 1696, 1779
Deren, Maya 1955
Derks, Mik 72
Derry, Charles 389, 1526
Des Pres, Terrence 222, 311
Deschner, Donald 1770, 1774, 1788
DeSourdis, Ron 1917
Desser, David 205, 807, 1731, 1732, 1734, 1735, 1888, 2019, 2023, 2024, 2026, 2027, 2030, 2176, 2177
Deutelbaum, Marshall 1836, 1843
Devries, Daniel 2056
Dewey, Langdon 2013
Di Franco, J. Philip 2049
Di Lauro, Al 2037
Diakite, Madubuko 867, 869, 909, 911, 953
Dickens, Charles 822, 1301, 1304, 1305, 1306, 1307, 1308, 1312, 1316

Dickens, Homer 365, 1078, 1081, 1762, 1765, 1767, 1777, 1786
Dickens, Norman 2061
Dickinson, Leo 72
Dickinson, Thorold 64, 1650
Dickos, Andrew 1918, 1920
Dickstein, Morris 1547
Dick, Bernard F. 104, 203, 329, 345, 799, 1029, 1225, 1291, 1341, 1971
Diderot, Denis 2098
Didion, Joan 1041, 1042
Diehl, Digby 609
Dies, Martin 832, 1077
Dietrich, Marlene 1767
Dillard, R. H. W. 389
Dimmitt, Richard B. 1752, 2033
DiMona, Joseph 1244
Dineen, Joseph F. 2078
DiOrio, Al 799, 1138, 1773
Dixon, Thomas 700, 940, 1366, 1387
Dixon, Wheeler Winston 1216, 1548
Dmytryk, Edward 72, 1029, 1092, 1201
Doane, Mary Ann 465, 466, 495
Doctorow, E. L. 1032, 1037
Doherty, Thomas 983
Dolan, Jill 496
Doll, Susan 1534, 1535
Dolmatovskaya, Galina 2181
Dombkowski, Dennis J. 678
Donahue, Suzanne Mary 608, 622, 623, 640, 644, 649, 658, 663, 665, 667, 690, 954, 959, 960, 1463
Donaldson, Maureen 1774
Donddis, Donis A. 45
Donnelly, Dorothy 1390
Donnelly, Peter 1060
Donner, Jorn 2185
Doolittle, Hilda (H. D.) 514
Dos Passos, John 1037, 1042, 1316
Douglas, Kirk 1959
Douglas, Lloyd C. 1986
Douglas, Melvyn 1769
Dowdy, Andrew 647, 658, 1951, 1953
Dower, John W. 236, 1897
Downing, David 799, 1958, 2050, 2061
Downing, John D. H. 559
Doyle, Arthur Conan 381
Drabinsky, Garth H. 781
Drake, Douglas 390
Dray, Philip 558, 576, 684
Dreiser, Theodore 1015
Drinkwater, John 1475
Driscoll, John P. 45
Druxman, Michael B. 403, 1328, 1330, 1785, 1863, 2052
Du Maurier, Daphne 469, 1029
Duberman, Martin Bauml 951
Dufty, William 1091
Duggan, Margaret M. 1108
Dukore, Bernard F. 1344
Dumas, Alexander 1012, 1802
Duncan, Ronald 2005, 2009
Dunne, Philip 272, 1059, 1067, 1087, 1203, 1204

Dunn, Linwood, G.   80
Durgnat, Raymond   64, 535, 580, 1004, 1012, 1022, 1327, 1676, 1696, 1721, 1728, 1729, 1820, 1843, 1939, 2128
Durham, Philip   893
Dworkin, Susan   554, 2208
Dyer, Richard   487, 511, 875, 999, 1293, 1436, 1437, 1441, 1556
Dye, David   983
Dyment, Alan .R.   1525
Dysinger, W. S.   729

E

Eames, John Douglas   1482, 1503
Earley, Steven C.   188
Easton, Carol   1129, 1471
Eaton, Mike   2143
Ebert, Alan   609
Ebert, Roger   437, 1526, 1548
Eberwein, Robert T.   584, 594, 596, 606
Eckert, Charles W.   1342
Edelson, Edward   385, 991
Edera, Bruno   77
Edgerton, Gary R.   621, 690
Editors of Eastman Kodak   80, 86, 88
Editors of FILMS IN REVIEW   1526
Editors of SUPER 8 FILMMAKER   80
Editors of the Associated Press   1174
Edmonds, I. G.   1164, 1475, 1503
Edmonds, Robert   64, 84
Edmunds, Hugh H.   781
Edwards, Anne .1138, 1773, 1787, 1861
Edwards, Lee   1088, 1113
Eels, George   1786
Ehrenpreis, Ivin   181
Ehrlich, Evelyn   247, 1903, 1905
Eidsvik, Charles   46
Eisenstein, Elizabeth   782
Eisenstein, Sergei M.   208, 582, 583, 1301, 1509, 1647, 1656, 1657, 1658
Eisler, Hans   83
Eisner, Lotte   514, 582, 1573, 1633, 1637, 1638, 1640, 1641, 1642
Eliot, George   116
Elisofon, Eliot   1057, 1236
Elley, Derek   382
Elliot, Godfrey M.   46
Ellis, A. E.   1866
Ellis, Jack C.   653, 655, 740, 1519, 1526, 1561, 1584, 1626, 1630, 1632, 1644, 1714, 1733, 1738, 1911, 1913, 1949
Ellis, John   549, 559
Ellrod, J. G.   1442
Ellsworth, Liz   2070
Ellul, Jacques   204, 205, 241, 550
Elson, Brigid   1821
Elton, G. R.   288
Emanuel, Barbara   492
Emboden, William   1463
Emerson, Mark   2209
Emmens, Carol A.   1526

Encyclopaedia Britannica Films 1000
Englander, A. Arthur 91
Englander, David A. 88
English, John W. 139
Englund, Steven 203, 219, 226, 1063, 1065, 1075, 1181
Enser, A. G. S. 1150
Ephron, Amy 1041
Ephron, Henry 1206
Epstein, Edward Z. 1060, 1679, 1772, 1773, 1797, 1914, 1971
Erens, Patricia 444, 451, 465, 471, 496, 498, 709, 819, 823, 825, 838, 839, 850, 851, 2019, 2027
Erhmann, J. 480
Ernst, Morris 964
Essoe, Gabe 1527, 1680, 1703, 1772
Estrin, Allen 1764
Etzkowitz, Janice 2136
Evanchuck, P. M. 2058, 2162
Evans, Arthur B. 1818
Evans, Bertrand 36
Evans, Gary 215, 236
Evans, Mark 403
Evans, Max 2061
Evans, Patrick 2147
Evans, Peter 1941
Evans, Peter Williams 401
Evans, W. Duane 687
Everest, F. Alton 86
Everson, William K. 263, 380, 385, 426, 427, 498, 1409, 1512, 1519, 1576, 1613, 1677, 1690, 1695, 1765, 1770
Ewen, Stuart 1051
Ewers, Carolyn H. 886, 888, 951
Ewing, Sam 72
Eyesenck H. J. 2037
Eyles, Allen 381, 390, 426, 660, 1078, 1081, 1761, 1783, 1788, 1951, 2042
Eyman, Scott 1519, 1669

F

Facey, Paul W. 219, 964
Fadiman, Regina K. 1037, 1049, 1208, 1321
Fadiman, William 642, 661, 690, 691, 1028
Fahey, David 1576
Fairbanks, Douglas, Jr. 1404
Fairbanks, Douglas, Sr. 1400
Fairbanks, Letitia 1403, 1409
Fajans, Milt 49
Falk, Irving A. 89
Falk, Quentin 1219
Faller, Greg S. 1545, 1546
Fanon, Franz 917
Fanshel, Susan 299
Farber, Manny 148, 1013, 1015, 1296, 1325, 1352, 1912, 1981, 2085, 2086
Farber, Stephen 691, 964,' 1234
Farmer, Frances 1292
Farrell, Barry 2059
Farrell, Edmund J. 46
Farrell, James T. 1037
Faulkner, Christopher 1820

Faulkner, Trader 1941
Faulkner, William 557, 858, 914, 1037, 1103, 1206, 1207, 1209, 1215, 1316, 1924, 2114
Faulk, John Henry 1100
Fawcett, Marion 1527
Fayen, Sharon 980
Feibleman, Peter 1227
Feiffer, Jules 2209
Feild, Robert D. 1768
Feineman, Neil 785, 2209
Feingold, Henry L. 831
Feinman, Jeffrey 1057, 1242, 1294, 2044, 2047
Feldman, Charles Matthew 964
Feldman, Harry 64, 101, 1300
Feldman, Joseph 64, 101, 1300
Feldman, Seth R. 1663, 1664
Fellini, Federico 2170, 2171
Fell, John L. 104, 115, 1519, 1561, 1590
Fenin, George N. 427
Fensch, Thomas 46
Feret, Bill 498
Ferguson, Otis 994, 1012, 1018, 1320, 1326, 1327, 1328, 1330, 1348, 1351, 1357, 1431
Ferguson, Robert 88
Fernett, Gene 1456, 1466
Fern, Alan 1650
Ferro, Marc 258, 261, 269
Festinger, Leon 543
Fetherling, Doug 1224
Feuer, Jane 403
Feyen, Sharon 46
Fielding, Henry 1029, 1312
Fielding, Raymond 80, 98, 208, 217, 224, 227, 254, 280, 281, 283, 284, 296, 298, 299, 301, 303, 319, 654, 842, 1590
Fielding, Tom 1328
Fields, Ronald J. 1770
Fields, W. C. 1770
Field, Stanley 82
Field, Sy 84
Finch, Christopher 80, 411, 1059, 1138, 1234, 1768, 1773
Fine, Richard A. 1150
Finler, Joel W. 1018, 1242, 1549, 1698, 1699
Fiore, Carlo 1958
Firestone, Ross 609, 2041
Fischer, Edward 46
Fischer, Heinz-Dietrich 459, 853
Fischer, Lucy 2007
Fish, Stanley 485
Fite, Gilbert C. 211
Fitzgerald, F. Scott 820, 1037, 1041, 1042, 1104, 1109, 1110, 1111, 1113, 1114, 1115, 1116, 1117, 1119, 1120, 1122, 1125, 1129, 1131, 1132, 1133, 1134, 1135, 1142, 1145, 1158, 1161, 1216, 1247, 1316, 1321
Fitzgerald, Michael G. 1476
Fitzgerald, Zelda 1110, 1119
Flaherty, Frances 1681, 1704
Flamini, Roland 1125, 1318
Flanagan, Hallie 1077
Flaubert, Gustave 1316, 1317

Fleming, Alice 1549
Fleming, Ian 422
Fleming, Michael 580, 597, 598, 605, 801
Florescu, Radu 395
Flores, Sam 2148
Flynn, Charles 651
Flynn, Errol 989, 1771
Focillon, Henri 194
Fontaine, Joan 1914
Foort, Reginald 83
Foote, Horton 1325
Fordin, Hugh 403, 404
Ford, Dan 1683
Ford, John 1772
Forester, C. S. 1979
Forman, Henry James 732, 778
Forsdale, Louis 65
Forslund, Bengt 1629
Forster, E. M. 548
Fountain, Leatrice Gilbert 1440, 1686
Fowler, Douglas 598
Fowler, Gene 1411, 1760, 1770
Fowler, Roy 1903, 1909
Fowles, John 1293
Fox, Stuart 825, 839
Fraenkel, Heinrich 1573
Fraigneau, Andre 1817
Francis, David 1409, 1414, 1415, 1427
Francovich, Allan 1823
Frankau, Gilbert 1797
Franklin, Joe 1609
Frank, Gerald 1109, 1138
Frantz, Joe B. 427
Fraser, George MacDonald 254, 269
Frater, Charles B. 86
Frayling, Christopher 427
Frayne, John G. 86
Frazer, John 1604, 1616
Fredrik, Nathalie 1165
Freedland, Michael 643, 827, 1078, 1493, 1759, 1762, 1771, 1778, 1917, 2050, 2058
Freeman, David 1042, 1844
French, Brandon 368, 375, 498, 657, 791
French, Philip 1466
French, T. L. 1997
French, Warren 912, 1326, 1684
Freud, Sigmund 531
Frewin, Leslie 1767
Friar, Natasha 427, 434
Friar, Ralph 427, 434
Frick, John W. 1600
Friedman, Daniel 1507
Friedman, Lester D. 667, 819, 822, 825, 839, 840, 841, 842, 850
Friedrich, Otto 1234
Frischauer, Willi 643, 1966
Fromm, Eric 430
Froug, William 1104, 1150
Frye, Northrop 177, 178, 540, 1017, 1153
Fry, Nicholas 1990, 2070, 2092, 2135, 2146

Fuchs, Daniel 1041, 1314
Fuksiewicz, Jacek 2013
Fulton, Albert 46
Fulton, A. R. 1303, 1306, 1307, 1333, 1613, 1943
Fundlater, Richard 1863
Furhammar, Leif 204, 208, 209, 236
Fussell, Betty Harper 1411

G

Gabler, Neal 819, 825, 832, 833, 843, 853
Gable, Kathleen 1772
Gabree, John 385
Gabrielle, Sidonie 147, 508
Gabriel, Teshome H. 917, 918
Gado, Frank 2185
Gaffney, Maureen 983
Gagne, Paul R. 390
Gale, Stephen H. 1275
Gallagher, J. P. 1415
Gans, Herbert J. 706
Garbicz, Adam 1527
Garcia Marquez, Gabriel 2163
Gardiner, Dorothy 1197
Gardner, Gerald 964
Gard, Elizabeth 2178
Garfield, Brian 428
Garnham, Nicholas 1639, 1830, 1960, 1961, 1977, 2134
Garrett, George P. 798, 1210
Garry, Stephen 165, 208
Gartley, Lynn 1080, 1767
Gaskell, Elizabeth 116
Gaskill, Arthur L. 88
Gassner, John 370, 378, 799, 1007, 1014, 1015, 1018, 1021, 1210, 1326, 1327
Gates, Phyllis 1962
Gaupp, Charles John, Jr. 1336
Geduld, Carolyn 2057
Geduld, Harry M. 609, 1309, 1374, 1420, 1528, 1549, 1656, 1661, 1689, 1753, 1866, 2211
Gehman, Richard 1078, 1081, 1761
Gehring, Wes D. 1420, 1426, 1770
Geist, Kenneth L. 363, 1123, 1269, 1354
Gelb, Alan 1958
Gelfman, Jane R. 798
Gellermann, William 832, 1077
Gelman, Barbara 1453
Gelman, Howard 1093
Gelmis, Joseph 609, 1549
Gelsey, Erwin 1798
Gentile, Mary C. 440, 470, 499, 529, 530, 533, 534, 587, 590
Georgakas, Dan 609, 900
Gerlach, John C. 1528
Gerlach, Lana 1528
Gernsheim, Alison 1591
Gernsheim, Helmut 1591
Gershuny, Theodore 554, 643
Gertner, Richard 1756

Gessner, Robert 88, 94
Giannetti, Louis D. 104, 119, 122, 128, 131, 163, 1519, 1549, 1669
Giardino, Thomas F. 89
Gibson, Arthur 2186
Gidley, M. .bookauth Wicks, Stephen 47
Gielgud, John 1842
Gifford, David 1611
Gifford, Denis 390, 1421, 1570, 1778
Gilliatt, Penelope 148, 149, 514, 1821
Gill, Brendan 1760
Gill, Jerry H. 2186
Gill, Sam 1677
Gilman, John 1529
Gilson, Rene 1818, 1995
Gingrich, Arnold 1127, 1129
Giono, Jean 1826
Gish, Lillian 1369, 1375
Giustini, Rolando 84
Glasgow, Ellen 914
Glassman, Marc 560
Glassner, Lester 940
Glatzer, Richard 1763
Glazier, Nathan 830
Gledhill, Christine 466, 587
Glimcher, Sumner 72
Glut, Donald F. 390, 391
Gmur, Leonhard H. 1572
Godfrey, Lionel 1774, 2060
Goldberg, Judith N. 845
Goldblatt, Burt 417, 1759, 1784
Golding, William 1001
Goldman, Eric A. 825, 828, 847, 848
Goldman, Herbert G. 827, 1778
Goldman, William 554, 1150, 1318
Goldstein, Laurence 88
Goldstein, Ruth M. 978, 983, 984
Goldwyn, Samuel 1472
Golovskoy, Val S. 2181
Golson, G. Barry 609
Gombrich, E. H. 493, 540, 603
Gomery, J. Douglas 607, 612, 613, 617, 618, 621, 622, 623, 625, 630, 632, 634, 635, 643, 662, 663, 691, 693, 707, 709, 719, 1068, 1437, 1509, 1511, 1513, 1514, 1518, 1520, 1554, 1706
Gomes, P. E. Salles 1823
Goodell, Gregory 72
Goode, James 554
Goodgold, Ed 1457
Goodis, David 2155
Goodman, Ezra 739, 1234, 1242, 1382, 1761
Goodman, Walter 1077, 1078
Goodrich, Frances 837
Gorbman, Claudia 404
Gordon, George N. 89
Gordon, Malcolm 47
Gorky, Maksim (Aleksey Maksimovich Peshkov) 1667
Gosser, H. Mark 655, 1585, 1591
Gottesman, Ronald 1528, 1656, 1661, 1689, 1690, 1792, 1866, 2211
Gottlieb, Carl 554
Goulart, Elwood 111

Goulding, Daniel J.   2014
Gould, Michael   1716
Gourlay, Logan   1862
Gow, Gordon   220, 391, 662, 1953
Graham, Carroll   1031, 1041, 1104, 1135
Graham, Cooper C.   318, 1376
Graham, Don   428, 433
Graham, Garrett   1031, 1041, 1104, 1135
Graham, Peter   1102, 1529, 1720, 2123
Graham, Sheila   1057, 1109, 1114, 1120, 1121, 1123, 1127, 1129, 1131, 1132, 1148, 1216, 1247
Gramsci, Antonio   442, 443, 521
Granger, Stewart   1941
Grant, Barry Keith   47, 189
Grau, Robert   1519, 1555, 1614
Grayson, David   1081
Gray, Hugh   1334, 1414, 1509, 1814
Gray, Simon   990
Grazia, Edward D.   2037
Grazzini, Giovanni   1930, 2170
Greaves, Roger   1574
Greenberger, Howard   798
Greenberg, Alan   2166
Greenberg, Harvey R.   582, 598
Greenberg, Joel   609, 1550, 1753, 1913
Greenberg, Martin Harry   1234
Greenberg, Stanley   2142
Greene, Graham   1037, 1218, 1219, 1320, 1327, 1328, 1329
Greene, Naomi   258, 261, 269, 1725
Greene, Ward   859
Greenfield, Howard   2171
Greenwood, Elizabeth   1932
Green, Gerald   1020
Green, Judith   1932, 2171, 2172
Green, Marc   691, 1234
Green, Martin   1427
Green, Stanley   404, 1759
Gregg, Eugene S.   1753
Gregory, Mollie   73
Grey, Lita   1421
Grey, Zane   425
Griffin, Jonathan   1909
Griffith, David Wark   1367, 1376
Griffith, Mrs. D. W. (Linda Arvidson)   1376
Griffith, Richard   245, 280, 872, 1057, 1442, 1473, 1519, 1520, 1564, 1571, 1576, 1681, 1764
Grimm, Jacob and Ludwig   601
Grimstead, David   712
Grisham, William Franklin   621
Grogg, Sam L., Jr.   564
Groom, Winston   363
Gross, Miriam   1197
Grualt, Jean   2150
Grupenhoff, Richard   931
Guarner, Jose Luis   1883
Guback, Thomas H.   607, 647, 656, 661, 676, 693, 694
Guber, Peter   554
Guerra, Tonino   2169

Guest, Judith 1008
Guild, Leo 1499
Guiles, Fred Lawrence 1065, 1138, 1151, 1690, 1965
Gunning, Thomas Robert 1362
Gunter, Jonathan F. 73
Gurko, Leo 1045
Gussow, Mel 1499
Guthrie, Lee 2045
Gutman, Stanley T. 1044, 1135
Guzzetti, Alfred 2110, 2111, 2131

H

Haas, Robert Bartlett 1596
Habberjam, Barbara 162
Hackett, Albert 837
Hackett, Pat 2068
Haddad-Garcia, George 799, 2050
Hadleigh, Boze 1442
Hagen, John Milton 1242
Haggard, H. Rider 919
Haining, Peter 1421
Halas, John 77, 84
Haldeman, Joe W. 363
Haley, Michael 1845
Hale, Bryant 1564
Hale, William Storm 66
Hallgren, Mauritz 954
Halliday, Jon 1970, 1986
Hallin, Daniel C. 347
Halliwell, Leslie 391, 1529, 1677
Hallmundsson, Hallberg 1965
Hall, Ben M. 1506
Hall, James Norman 1330
Hall, Katy 81
Hall, Stuart 47, 521
Halsey II, W. W. 1819
Hamblett, Charles 1234, 2060
Hamblin, Robert W. 260, 1206
Hames, Peter 2164
Hamilton, John R. 428
Hammett, Dashiell 1037, 1222, 1806, 1915
Hammond, John H. 1614
Hammond, Paul 1604, 1616
Hammond, Robert M. 2005
Hample, Stuart 2045
Hampton, Benjamin B. 607, 622, 628, 710, 1056, 1393, 1467, 1519
Hancock, Ralph 1403, 1409
Handel, Leo A. 660, 706, 734, 739, 740, 774
Handlin, Oscar 457
Hanke, Ken 381
Hanlon, Lindley 2003
Hanna, David 1761, 2066 '
Hannigan, Jane Anne 41
Happe, L. Bernard 73
Haralovich, Mary Beth 792, 1520
Harbinson, Allen 2067
Harcourt, Amanda 73

Harcourt, Peter 2162
Hardin, Nancy 2051
Hardwood, Ronald 1842
Hardy, Forsyth 202, 207, 215, 237, 248, 1624, 1628
Hardy, Phil 411, 1961
Hardy, Thomas 1312
Harmetz, Aljean 554, 643, 1235
Harpole, Charles Henry 115, 1814
Harrington, Evans 1209
Harrison, Helen P. 73
Harrison, O. B., Jr. 798
Harrison, Rex 1842
Harris, George 1138
Harris, Morgan 73
Harris, Radie 1057, 1243
Harris, Robert A. 1845
Harris, Thomas J. 404, 560
Harris, Valarie 901
Harris, Warren G. 1772, 1774, 1973
Harryhausen, Ray 411
Hartog, Simon 1004, 1928
Hart, Douglas C. 381
Hart, Harold H. 964
Hart, James 1377
Harvey, Stephen 800, 1759, 1765
Harvey, Sylvia 474
Harwell, Richard 1125, 1310
Harwood, Ronald 554, 1319
Haskell, Molly 465, 471, 501, 502, 503, 505, 512, 514, 591, 592, 709, 791, 1056
Haskins, James 885
Hassell, R. Chris, Jr. 1342
Haun, Harry 1529
Hauser, Arnold 778
Hauser, Philip M. 729
Hauser, Thomas 1020
Havelock, Eric 782
Haver, Ronald 1248, 1487
Hawthorne, Nathaniel 1298, 1312
Haycox, Ernest 1311, 1802
Hayden, Nicola 1724, 1728, 1816, 2064
Hayden, Sterling 1092, 1097
Hayes, Roberta 609
Hayes, R. M. 694
Haymes, Nora Eddington Flynn 1771
Hayne, Donald 1680
Hayward, Stan 84
Hay, James 464, 1873, 1874, 1877
Head, Edith 1777
Heath, Stephen 167, 168, 475, 592
Hecht, Ben 1038, 1042, 1057, 1224, 1265
Hedges, Inez 1716
Heide, Robert 1529
Heilbroner, Richard L. 1047, 1050
Heilbut, Anthony 1067
Heilman, Robert 712
Heimann, Jim 1442
Helfman, Harry 89
Heller, Joseph 1037

Hellman, Lillian 858, 1037, 1096, 1148, 1225, 1227, 1228, 1229
Hellman, Sam 1976
Hemingway, Ernest 1037, 1211, 1231, 1274, 1316, 1322, 1323, 1924
Hemingway, Paul T. M. 34
Hemming, Roy 404
Henderson, Brian 119, 120, 163, 444, 1919
Henderson, Kathy 1530
Henderson, Robert M. 1360, 1378, 1389
Hendricks, Gordon 860, 1592, 1596, 1615
Henry, Joseph 1930, 2170
Henstell, Bruce 141, 1608
Hepburn, Katharine 554, 1915, 1979
Hepworth, Cecil 1611
Heraldson, Donald 1623
Herman, Gary 799, 2050
Herman, Lewis 84, 85
Herman, William 103
Herndon, Bonnie 1366
Herndon, Booton 1403, 1406
Herndon, Venable 1325, 1959
Herrick, Margaret 1542
Herrmann, Dorothy 609, 1275
Herskowitz, Michael 1766
Herx, Henry 1530
Herzog, Herta 778
Herzog, Martje 2166
Herzog, Werner 2166
Hess, Thomas B. 977
Heston, Charlton 2052
Hetherington, John 1658, 1666
Heyer, Robert 47
Hibbin, Nina 2012
Hibbin, Sally 423
Hickman, Gail Morgan 411
Higashi, Sumiko 466, 503, 631, 632, 791, 1365, 1374, 1391
Higginbotham, Virginia 1721, 1729
Higham, Charles 609, 801, 1235, 1288, 1494, 1519, 1550, 1680, 1753, 1766, 1767, 1771, 1774, 1777, 1792, 1860, 1913, 2042
Hilberg, Raul 311
Hildreth, Lee 1655
Hillier, Jim 474, 1996, 1997, 1998, 1999, 2002, 2035, 2096, 2103, 2123
Hill, Gary 1524
Hill, Herbert 452, 540
Hill, Joseph F. 2187
Hill, Stephen P. 2181
Hilton, James 1328, 1799
Himes, Chester 896
Himmelstein, Hal 179, 180
Hinton, David B. 318
Hinton, S. E. 998
Hirschhorn, Clive 405, 1476, 1962
Hirschhorn, Joel 1443
Hirsch, Foster 799, 1091, 1785, 1947, 1956, 1962, 1980, 2161, 2162
Hirshbein, Peretz 828
Hitchens, Neal 1965
Hitt, Jim 428
Hoban, Charles 746
Hoberman, J. B. 392
Hobson, Andrew 89

Hobson, Laura Z.   1018, 1029
Hobson, Mark   89
Hochman, Stanley   139, 1550, 1850, 1905, 2142
Hodgdon, Dana H.   73
Hodgkinson, Anthony W.   47, 244, 315, 323
Hoffer, Thomas W.   77
Hoffman, William   886, 888, 951
Hofmann, Charles   405
Hogan, David J.   392
Hogben, Lancelot   1592
Hogenkamp, Bert   1832, 1840
Hoggart, Richard   778
Holaday, P. W.   729
Holden, Anthony   1862
Holland, Norman   485
Holland, Ted   429
Hollinger, Karen   1966, 1983, 2007
Holloway, Ronald   2013, 2014
Hollo, Anselm   2149
Hollyman, Burnes Saint Patrick   2158
Holman, L. Bruce   77
Holtzman, William   1350, 1778, 2047, 2058
Holt, Robert T.   201
Holzer, Hans   1235
Honore, Paul M.   86
Hoos, Gunther   90
Hopkinson, Peter   1870
Hopper, Hedda   1057, 1243
Hopwood, Henry V.   1592
Horkheimer, Max   774
Horner, William R.   429
Horne, Lena   879, 880, 950
Horn, Maurice   77
Horn, Zsuzsanna   2012, 2013
Horowitz, Gad   604
Horowitz, James   429
Horst   1452
Horton, Andrew S.   1139, 1310, 2052
Horvath, Joan   89
Hotchner, A. E.   643, 1958
Houseman, John   1340
Houston, Beverle   141, 163, 1641
Houston, Penelope   514, 1925
Howard, Leslie Ruth   1778, 1858
Howard, Richard   1435, 1448, 1818
Howells, William Dean   1051
Howitt, Dennis   438, 439, 445, 746
Howlett, James   1325
Howlett, John   1917, 1959
Hoyt, Edwin P.   1138, 1965
Hrabal, Bohumil   994, 2164
Hrabal, Bohumil   2165
Huaco, George A.   1633, 1719, 1923, 1924, 1925
Huber, Richard M.   1047, 1053
Hubler, Richard G.   1088, 1785
Hudson, Richard   1454
Huettig, Mae D.   607, 624, 630, 634, 636, 639, 694, 769, 1103
Huff, Theodore   1367, 1421, 1422, 1426

Hughes, Eileen Lanouette 2170
Hughes, Langston 860
Hughes, Robert 140, 220
Hughes, Rupert 1104
Hugo, Victor 1702
Hull, David Stewart 219, 238, 321
Hunnings, Neville March 225, 965
Hunter-Blair, Kitty 2181
Hunter, Evan 1000
Hunter, Linda 1237
Hunter, Lise 1644, 1655
Huntley, John 84
Hurley, Neil P. 47
Hurt, James 1105, 1333, 1336
Huss, Roy 140, 392, 448, 453, 578, 586, 600, 601, 602, 2170
Huston, John 1087, 1915
Hutchinson, Tom 392, 1057
Hutchins, Charles L. 1367
Huxley, Aldous 751, 1037, 1158
Hyams, Joe 1057, 1078, 1243, 1761, 1762, 2043
Hyatt, Marshall 931
Hyland, Wende 609
Hyman, Barbara Davis 1766
Hyman, Jeremy A. 1766
H. D. (Hilda Doolittle) 514

I

Ibanez, Vincent Blasco 1707
Iden, Peter 2166
Infield, Glenn B. 318
Ingals, Thomas 1487
Inglis, Ruth A. 233, 965
Innis, Harold 774
Insdorf, Annette 222, 310, 311, 2093, 2095, 2096, 2107, 2145, 2155
Irwin, Will 1504
Isaksson, Folke 204, 208, 209, 236
Isaksson, Ulla 2186
Isenberg, Michael T. 203, 223, 267
Iser, Wolfgang 447, 485
Isherwood, Christopher 1031, 1042, 1102
Ishihara, Shintaro 2023
Israel, Abigail 1720, 1990
Israel, Lee 1760
Ivens, Joris 314, 319
Ivory, James 2167
Izod, John 608, 616, 642, 643, 647, 655, 658, 663, 664, 668, 677, 696, 706, 720, 743, 744, 747, 752, 1982, 2107

J

Jackson, Arthur 408
Jackson, Charles 1029, 1987
Jackson, Kathy Merlock 970, 971, 972, 985
Jackson, Martin A. 221, 259, 270
Jackson, Shirley 1312, 1323
Jacobs, David 1422

Jacobs, Denis Raab 2208
Jacobs, Jack 1786
Jacobs, Lewis 65, 140, 141, 155, 207, 216, 248, 254, 255, 262, 282, 303, 319, 556, 633, 710, 864, 872, 915, 1033, 1340, 1351, 1359, 1467, 1519, 1555, 1560, 1576, 1739, 1758
Jacques, Richard 1724, 1728
Jahr, Cliff 1971
Jameson, Fredric 417
James, David E. 2033
James, Henry 601, 1006, 1316, 1323, 1324
Janaro, Richard Paul 1335
Jarratt, Vernon 1573
Jarrell, Randall 457
Jarvie, Ian C. 163, 450, 471, 540, 550, 552, 679, 705, 728, 775, 777, 854, 978, 1556
Jay, Michael 808
Jeeves, Mahatma Kane (W. C. Fields). 1770
Jenkinson, Philip 405
Jenkins, Bruce 1754
Jenkins, Reese V. 1614
Jennings, Dean 1498
Jennings, Gary 1235
Jennings, Mary-Lou 316
Jensen, Paul M. 1638, 1639, 1779
Jerome, Stuart 1495
Jerome, V. J. 924, 931
Jewell, Derek 1918
Jewell, Richard B. 1546
Jhabvala, Ruth Prawer 548
Jobes, Gertrude 607, 1075, 1467
Johnes, Carl 1765
Johnson, Albert' 73
Johnson, Bertha 73
Johnson, Diane 1221
Johnson, Dorothy M. 1311, 2075
Johnson, Dorris 1036, 1130, 1249
Johnson, Lincoln F. 105
Johnson, Nora 1065, 1114, 1252
Johnson, Randal 2158, 2159
Johnson, Robert K. 2208
Johnson, Ron 105
Johnson, Timothy Wayne 1045
Johnson, Warren 72
Johnson, William 412
Johnson, W. Stacy 109
Johnston, Alva 1473
Johnston, Claire 471, 475
Johnston, Mireille 317
Johnston, Ollie 1769
Jones, Dorothy B. 1706
Jones, Emily S. 48
Jones, Everett L. 893
Jones, G. William 48, 2186
Jones, James 368, 1029, 1037
Jones, Ken D. 347, 430, 1443, 1544, 1787
Jones, R. E. 583
Jones, Stephen G. 239
Jong, Erica 1041

Jordan, Rene 1081, 1765, 1772, 1958
Jordan, Thurston C., Jr. 1530, 2211
Jordon, Winthrop 918
Jorgens, Jack J. 1343
Jowett, Garth S. 227, 239, 329, 439, 463, 488, 560, 577, 607, 611, 613, 625, 639, 640, 646, 648, 649, 650, 674, 676, 677, 710, 711, 718, 721, 728, 732, 733, 736, 743, 752, 780, 782, 1057
Joyce, James 101, 557, 1311
Juneau, James 1138, 1773
Juno, Andrea 418

K

Kael and A MAN FOR ALL SEASONS 1020
Kael and A PLACE IN THE SUN 1015
Kael and A STREETCAR NAMED DESIRE 1352
Kael and A VIEW FROM THE BRIDGE 1349
Kael and ALICE DOESN'T LIVE HERE ANYMORE 1011
Kael and AMERICAN GRAFITTI 993
Kael and ANNE OF THE THOUSAND DAYS 1347
Kael and BILLY BUDD 1018
Kael and CAMILLE 1012
Kael and CITIZEN KANE 1807
Kael and EAST OF EDEN 1005, 1325
Kael and film criticism 149, 150, 151
Kael and GEORGY GIRL 1006
Kael and GOODBYE, MR. CHIPS 1328
Kael and HIGH NOON 1019
Kael and IF . . . 1001
Kael and JULIUS CASEAR 1354
Kael and LITTLE BIG MAN 1320
Kael and LONELINESS OF THE LONG DISTANCE RUNNER 997
Kael and LONG DAY'S JOURNEY INTO NIGHT 1350
Kael and LOS OLVIDADOS 1002
Kael and MACBETH 1355
Kael and ROMEO AND JULIET 1356
Kael and screenwriters 1101, 1142
Kael and SMALL CHANGE 998
Kael and SPLENDOR IN THE GRASS 1010
Kael and THE BLACKBOARD JUNGLE 1000
Kael and THE CRANES ARE FLYING 1001
Kael and THE ENTERTAINER 1013
Kael and THE GRADUATE 2085
Kael and THE GRAPES OF WRATH 1326
Kael and THE HAUNTING 1323
Kael and THE LAST PICTURE SHOW 996
Kael and THE MAGNIFICENT AMBERSONS 1327
Kael and THE MEMBER OF THE WEDDING 997
Kael and THE PRIME OF MISS JEAN BRODIE 1003
Kael and THE TREASURE OF THE SIERRA MADRE 1022
Kael and THE TURNING POINT 1016
Kael, Pauline 151, 514, 896, 1290, 1292, 1294, 1296, 1509, 1793, 1868
Kael, P. and screenwriters 1063
Kafka, Franz 1022, 2091
Kagan, Norman 348, 561, 785, 1175, 2056
Kahle, Roger 48
Kahn, Gordon 1067, 1186
Kaminsky, Stuart M. 73, 178, 179, 190, 191, 322, 1081, 1087, 1765, 1916, 2187

Kando, Thomas 457, 458, 733
Kane, Kathryn 174, 175, 178, 233, 328, 341, 349, 350
Kanfer, Stefan 229, 1045, 1067, 1074, 1076, 1080, 1096, 1100, 1187
Kanin, Garson 832, 1041, 1057, 1236, 1777
Kantor, Bernard R. 609, 1550
Kaplan, Alice Yaeger 1558
Kaplan, Allen 1025
Kaplan, E. Ann 466, 469, 471, 504, 507, 532, 533, 585, 587, 591, 792, 794, 798, 1637, 1638, 1947
Kaplan, Mike 1530, 1531
Kardish, Lawrence 1562
Karen, Robert 82
Karimi, Amir Massoud 1947, 1956
Karl, Frederick R. 1211
Karney, Robyn 1531
Karpf, Stephen Louis 385
Karp, Alan 785
Karp, Patti 73
Karr, Kathleen 1576, 1577
Karyn, Kay 1781
Kass, Judith 1762, 1767
Katz, Ephraim 1531
Katz, John Stuart 48
Katz, William Loren 893
Kauffmann, Stanley 33, 141, 151, 152, 153, 221, 994, 995, 997, 1001, 1003, 1004, 1005, 1009, 1010, 1013, 1014, 1016, 1018, 1022, 1023, 1295, 1323, 1324, 1325, 1328, 1348, 1349, 1350, 1352, 1353, 1356, 1608, 2086
Kaufman, Deborah 848
Kaufman, Jay 88
Kawin, Bruce F. 105, 111, 116, 1103, 1207, 1211, 1214, 1310
Kaye, M. M. 548
Kay, Karyn 465, 471, 507
Kazan, Elia 1257, 1261, 1979
Keaton, Buster 1688
Keats, John 1274
Kehoe, Barry 1773
Kehoe, Vincent J. R. 84
Keirstead, Phillip O. 91
Kelleher, Brian 1849
Kellen, Konrad 204, 205
Keller, Gary D. 826
Keller, Marjorie 1818
Kelley, Kitty 1918
Kelley, Samuel Lawrence 886, 887, 888, 890, 951
Kellner, Douglas 569
Kellogg, Robert 175
Kelly, Mary Pat 2209
Kelly, Terence 1939
Kempton, Murray 550
Kemp, Jerrold E. 89
Kendricks, Gordon 1610
Kennedy, Joseph P. 619
Kennedy, Keith 89
Kepley, Vance, Jr. 1655
Kerbel, Michael 1771, 2060
Kern, Sharon 1526
Kerr, Laura 1057, 1238
Kerr, Paul 696

Kerr, Walter 1677
Ketchum, Charles B. 1930
Keyser, Barbara 1754
Keyser, Les 660, 1754
Key, Wilson Bryan 2037
Kezich, Tullio 2171
Khatchadourian, Haig 141
Kiernan, Thomas 799, 1355, 2050, 2179
Kiesling, Barrett C. 1754
Kilgore, Al 1691
Kilpatrick, James Jackson 955
Kim, Erwin 2066, 2089
Kindem, Gorham 73, 607, 615, 676, 696, 748, 1459, 1462
Kinder, Marsha 141, 163, 1641
King, Barry 1441
King, Stephen 393
Kinsey, Anthony 77
Kipling, Rudyard 994, 1312, 1806
Kirby, Jack Temple 864, 913
Kirkpatrick, Sidney D. 1412
Kirschner, Allen 65
Kirschner, Linda 65
Kirsten, Lincoln 1754
Kitses, Jim 48, 174, 192, 350, 429, 1982
Kittredge, William 1311
Kitt, Eartha 885, 950
Klapper, Joseph T. 747, 773
Klapp, Orrin E. 437, 551, 552, 562, 791, 807, 817
Kleiner, Dick 1679, 1780, 1804
Klein, Michael 367, 1311
Klein, Walter J. 73
Kleist, Heinrich von 2142
Kline, T. Jefferson 2170
Klingender, Francis D. 630, 1103
Klinge, Peter 164
Klinge, Sandra 164
Klinowski, Jacek 1527
Klotman, Phyllis Rauch 931
Knapton, James 36
Knecht, Kenneth 92
Knight, Arthur 233, 263, 556, 1057, 1236, 1359, 1438, 1519, 1555, 1560, 1562
Knight, Vivienne 1941
Knowles, Dorothy 225
Kobal, John 617, 1138, 1236, 1443, 1444, 1634, 1675, 1752, 1753, 1766, 1767, 1772, 1914, 1965
Kobler, John 1760
Koch, Howard W. 1067, 1262
Koch, Stephen 2068, 2091
Kolyer, Diane 1786
Kone, Grace Ann 1532
Konopelski, Leonard 80
Koppes, Clayton R. 229, 351
Korda, Michael 1859
Korte, Walter, Jr. 1874
Kostin, Vladislav 2181
Koszarski, Richard 1550, 1551, 1699, 1708
Kotsilibas-Davis, James 1760, 1781
Kotz, David 634
Kovacks, Steven 1716, 1729

Kowalski, Rosemary Ribich   509
Kozintsev, Grigori   1342, 1343
Kozloff, Sarah   113, 116
Kracauer, Siegfried   130, 168, 206, 318, 321, 441, 474, 555, 576, 776, 778, 1027,
   1304, 1339, 1573, 1635, 1639, 1719, 1829
Kramer, Dale   1505
Kramer, Steven Philip   1712, 1713, 1726, 1730
Krane, Susan   1754
Krauzer, Steven M.   1311
Kreidl, John Francis   1968, 2112, 2117, 2132, 2137, 2151
Kreuger, Miles   405
Krishnaswamy, Subrahmanyam   2167
Krogh, Daniel   392
Kuhns, William   43, 48, 49, 65, 89
Kuhn, Annette   466, 471, 475, 509, 521, 587, 588
Kuhn, Thomas   1571
Kulik, Karol   1858
Kurosawa, Akira   1735, 1738, 1739, 1886, 1891, 1895, 1899, 2016, 2028
Kushner, David   2184
Kwiatkowski, Aleksander   1625, 1628
Kybett, Harry   92
Kyrou, Ado   582, 1722

L

LaBrecque, Ron   698
Lacan, Jacques   480, 596
Lacey, Richard A.   49
LaGuardia, Robert   1958
Lahue, Kalton C.   429, 1359, 1412, 1444, 1456, 1457, 1458, 1532, 1677
Lake, Stuart N.   1982
Lamarr, Hedy   1780
Lambert, Gavin   1041, 1042, 1125, 1318
Lambray, Maureen   1551
Lamparski, Richard   1444, 1445, 1446
Lampell, Millard   837
Lanchester, Elsa   1860
Landau, Jacob M.   2178
Landay, Eileen   932
Landon, John W.   406
Lane, Helen R.   167
Lane, Jeffrey   1786
Lane, Tamar   725, 778
Langerlof, Selma   1624
Langer, Susanne K.   450, 582, 583, 955
Langman, Larry   49, 1152, 1532
Lang, Fritz   1639
Lardner, James   672
Lardner, Ring, Jr.   1074
Larkin, Rochelle   1469
Larmett, John   610
Larsen, Otto N.   749
Larson, Cedric   223
Larson, David Alan   678
Larson, Randall D.   412
Larson, Rodger   89
Larson, Rodger, Jr.   49

Lary, N. M. 1650
Lasky, Betty 1477
Lasky, Jesse L., Jr. 1478, 1861
Lasky, Jesse L., Sr. 1477, 1479
Lasky, Michael S. 1845
Lasky, William R. 1479
Lassally, Walter 80
Lasswell, Harold 773
Latham, Aaron 1113, 1118, 1124, 1216, 1217
Laurence, Frank M. 1231
Laurents, Arthur 375, 859, 952
Lauritzen, Einar 1628, 1630
LaValley, Albert J. 797, 800, 1845
Lavers, Annette 177
Lawder, Standish D. 1717, 1730
Lawford, Patricia Seaton 1780
Lawrence, D. H. 751, 1010, 1312
Lawrence, Fred 1785
Lawrence, Jerome 1785
Lawson, John Howard 85, 164, 232, 790, 1070, 1298, 1299, 1363
Lawton, Ben 2171
Lawton, Richard 1451
Lax, Eric 2046
Laybourne, Kit 77
Layman, Richard 1223
Lazarou, George A. 1495
Lazarus, Paul N., III 73
Leab, Daniel J. 277, 860, 862, 865, 880, 888, 924, 927, 932, 933, 934, 935, 943, 1005, 1341
Leach, Edmund 175, 177
Leach, Jim 2189
Leahy, James 371, 1963
Leaming, Barbara 1355, 1793, 2179
Lebel, Jean-Patrick 1688
Leckie, William H. 893
Lederer, Laura 565
Leebron, Elizabeth 1080
Lees, David 698
Lee, Harper 858, 1325
Lee, Raymond 385, 1394, 1446, 1454, 1457, 1680, 1703
Lee, Robert E. A. 48
Lee, Walter 412
Leff, Leonard J. 1846, 1852, 1951
Legg, Stuart 630, 1103
LeGrice, Malcolm 1717
Lehman, Ernest 2053, 2086
Lehman, Peter 117
Leighton, Frances Spatz 1759
Leigh, Janet 1962
Leiser, Erwin 207, 240
Leites, Nathan 576, 581, 602, 732, 734, 740, 798
Lejeune, Caroline Alice 1322, 1327
Lellis, George 70, 474, 477, 1689, 1997, 1998, 2102, 2103, 2111, 2125
LeMay, Alan 2076
Lembourn, Hans Jorgen 1138, 1965
Lemery, Christine 2150
Lenglet, Philippe 2167
Lenihan, John H. 429
Lenne, Gerard 529

Lennig, Arthur 1592, 1610, 1782
Lentz, Harris M., III. 412
Leonard, Harold 1526, 1532, 1533
Leprohon, Pierre 1574, 1608, 1821, 1873, 1882, 1933
Lerner, Jean 204
Lerner, Max 1045
Leroux, Gaston 396
LeRoy, Mervyn 1780, 1804
Lesage, Julia 2110, 2132
Lesser, Stephen O. 1154
Lester, Sandra 1527
Levaco, Ronald 1662
Leventhal, Ellen 1036, 1130, 1249
Levine, Michael 1533
Levin, G. Roy 1870
Levitan, Eli L. 77
Levy, Emanuel 680, 791, 969, 1165, 1788
Levy, William Turner 1764
Lev, Peter 2135
Lewin, Linda 2150
Lewis, Arthur H. 1236
Lewis, Brian 132, 133, 169
Lewis, George H. 457
Lewis, Howard Thompson 607, 617, 626, 733
Lewis, Jerry 90
Lewis, M. K. 76
Lewis, Rosemary 76
Leyda, Jay 208, 209, 213, 304, 583, 1650, 1656, 1657, 1658, 1659, 1660, 2163
Libby, Bill 1169
Library of Congress 1533
Library Staff of Women's History Research Center 512
Lidstone, John ' 90
Lieberman, Susan 1446
Liehm, Antonin J. 2011, 2013, 2164
Liehm, Mira 1876, 1926, 1928, 2011, 2013
Limbacher, James L. 30, 406, 420, 654, 655, 1533, 1534, 1546, 2033
Lincoln, Jairus 91
Linden, George 582
Linden, George W. 142
Linder, Carl 73
Lindgren, Ernest 66, 583, 1562
Lindsay, Cynthia 1779
Lindsay, Vachel 123, 124, 168, 1033, 1389
Linet, Beverly 1081, 1777, 1917
Linton, James M. 439, 463, 488, 577, 611, 613, 650, 674, 676, 677, 711, 752, 780
Lippe, Richard 399
Lippmann, Walter 541, 542, 546, 773
Lipton, Lenny 73, 74
Litwak, Mark 698
Livingston, Don 90
Livingston, Paisley 2187
Llewellyn, Richard 1007, 1029
Lloyd, Harold 1693
Lloyd, Ronald 1551
Loader, Jayne 1041
Lockwood, Charles 1236
Logan, Joshua L. 1264

Lokke, Virgil L. 1028, 1134
London, Mel 74
London, Rose 393
Longwell, Dennis 76
LOOK Editors 263, 283, 346
Lookstein, Haskel 291
Loos, Anita 1060, 1061, 1148, 1379, 1380, 1399
Loos, Mary 1041
Lorentz, Pare 153, 964
Lotman, Jurij 164
Lounsbury, Myron Osborn 120, 123, 124, 126, 142
Lovell, Hugh G. 1068
Lowenthal, Leo 457, 774
Lowery, Sandra 747
Lowe, Corinne 1473
Lowndes, Douglas 90
Lowry, Edward 2002
Low, Rachel 315, 1607, 1612, 1745, 1831, 1832, 1840
Loy, Myrna 1781
Lucanio, Patrick 412
Luhr, William 117, 798, 1198, 1519, 1914
Lukas, Christopher 74
Lundbergh, Holger 2185
Lyman, Richard 1108
Lynch, F. Dennis 164
Lynch, Joan Driscoll 33, 34, 49
Lynch, William 50
Lynn, Kenneth S. 1047, 1052
Lyons, Robert Joseph 1928, 1960
Lyons, Timothy J. 1421, 1422, 1622
Lyon, Christopher 1534, 1535, 1545
Lyon, James K. 1196

M

MacAfee, Norman 2171
MacCabe, Colin 2110, 2111, 2112, 2133
MacCann, Richard Dyer 50, 142, 203, 224, 230, 305, 1105, 1236, 1298, 1331, 1467, 1526, 1535, 1951, 1998
MacColl, Gail 1174, 1175
Macdonald, Dwight 153, 154, 778, 997, 1001, 1005, 1010, 1022, 1023, 1328, 1348, 1349, 1350, 1353, 1354, 1356, 1648
Macdonald, Ross (Kenneth Millar) 1041, 1042
MacDonnell, Kevin 1596, 1597
MacDougall, Roger 1942
MacGowan, Kenneth 1359, 1577
Mackinnon, Kenneth 1336
Mackintosh, Mary 1342
MacLeod, Celeste 1047, 1050
Macnicol, Fred 2012, 2013
MacPherson, Kenneth 924, 1062, 1340, 1754, 2176
MacShane, Frank 1274
Madden, David 146, 1041.
Maddock, Brent 2001, 2007
Madsen, Axel 322, 662, 675, 799, 1086, 1087, 1454, 1796, 1916, 1972
Madsen, Roy 78
Madsen, Roy Paul 66
Maeder, Edward 269

Magny, Claude-Edmonde 514, 1104, 1152
Magretta, Joan 1139, 1310
Mailer, Norman 550, 820, 1041, 1042, 1135, 1138, 1158, 1965
Maisel, David 1904
Malamud, Bernard 2076, 2077
Maland, Charles J. 1423, 1764
Malerba, Luigi 1574
Malkiewicz, J. Kris 80
Mallery, David 50, 191
Malle, Louis 377
Malstrom, Lars 2184
Maltby, Richard 563
Maltin, Leonard 66, 80, 992, 1236, 1446, 1529, 1535, 1623, 1691, 1754, 1768,
  1781
Manchel, Frank 66, 386, 393, 413, 421, 430, 471, 513, 791, 833, 976, 1294,
  1614, 1678, 1755, 1946, 1947, 1954, 2035
Mancini, Elaine 1872, 1875, 1878
Mandelbaum, Howard 1754
Mander, Gertrud 240, 1637, 1638, 1642
Manfull, Helen 1039, 1063, 1067, 1083, 1084, 1100, 1282, 1285
Mankiewicz, Joseph L. 1272
Mank, Chaw 1060
Mank, Gregory William 394, 1248, 1484
Manning, David 70
Manning, Robert N. 74
Mann, Heinrich 1830, 1831
Mann, Thomas 1042, 1308
Manoogian, Haig P. 90
Manvell, Roger 50, 77, 78, 84, 106, 142, 216, 244, 351, 580, 597, 598, 605,
  801, 1021, 1337, 1343, 1408, 1423, 1447, 1536, 1572, 1573, 1607, 1612, 1718,
  1739, 1832, 1939, 1954, 2187, 2189
Maple, Jessie 81
Mapp, Edward 936, 1341
Marchak, Alice 1237
Marcorelles, Louis 51
Marcuse, Herbert 430, 604
Marcus, Fred H. 1312
Marek, Kurt W. (C. W. Ceram) 1581, 1589
Marill, Alvin H. 799, 886, 887, 888, 951, 1091, 1473, 1536, 1778, 1785, 1964,
  1968
Marily, Henry 1917
Marinis, Louise 72
Marino, T. J. 90
Marion, Frances 1394
Marker, Frederick J. 2187
Marker, Lise-Lone 2187
Markmann, Charles Lam 2170
Marlowe, Don 1237
Marner, Terence St. John 74, 79
Marquand, J. P. 1042
Marquis, Dorothy 729
Marrus, Michael R. 1903
Marsden, Michael T. 564, 581, 733, 736, 753
Marshall Cavendish Learning System, the 1562
Marshall, Herbert 1651, 1656, 1659, 1661, 1866
Marsh, Ken 92
Martin-Sperry, Carol 1817, 2005
Martinengo, Luciano 2171

Martinetti, Ronald   1959
Martin, Linda   513
Martin, Marcel   1572, 1652
Martin, Olga J.   965
Martin, Pete   1768
Marx, Arthur   1474, 1783
Marx, Groucho   1783, 1784
Marx, Harpo   1064, 1784
Marx, Maxine   1784
Marx, Samuel   226, 1117, 1118, 1153, 1483
Mascelli, Joseph V.   81
Masoch, Sacher   2037
Mason, Jeffrey D.   1064
Massey, Raymond   1325, 1861
Masterson, Whit   2069
Mast, Gerald   164, 798, 1332, 1407, 1519, 1520, 1536, 1562, 1600, 1678, 1775, 1821
Mathias, Harry   81
Matias, Diana   1658, 1663
Matthews, Jane DeHart   1077
Matthews, Jessie   1718, 1862
Maugham, W. Somerset   1037, 1312
Maupassant, Henri-Rene-Albert-Guy de   2129
Maxim, John R.   1440, 1686
Mayersberg, Paul   1041, 1056, 1058, 1237
Mayer, Arthur   1571, 1576, 1676
Mayer, David   1659, 1666
Mayer, J. P.   580
Mayer, Michael F.   607, 675, 676, 698, 1954
Mayhew, Leonard   2094, 2148
Maynard, Richard A.   51, 241, 430, 892, 915, 916, 918, 919, 985, 986
May, Lary   711, 717, 718, 719, 720, 782, 784
May, Mark A.   51, 729, 732
McArthur, Colin   174, 192, 350, 386
McBride, Joseph   371, 609, 798, 1552, 1592, 1684, 1776, 1793, 1794, 1959
McCabe, John   1415, 1421, 1423, 1691
McCaffrey, Donald W.   1421, 1424, 1672, 1678, 1693
McCambridge, Mercedes   1964
McCartey, John   1849
McCarthy, Todd   651
McCarty, Clifford   1078, 1153, 1762, 1918
McCarty, John   392, 394, 1916
McClain, Bebe Ferrell   74
McClelland, Doug   965, 1088, 1189, 1244, 1447, 1777
McClellan, C. Kirk   554
McClintick, David   537
McClintock, Marsha Hamilton   2178
McClure, Arthur F.   347, 430, 565, 1451, 1544
McConnell, Frank   798, 1153
McCormick, Ruth   2166
McCoy, Horace   1037, 1042, 1161, 1314, 2088
McCoy, Malachy   2059
McCreadie, Marsha   513, 514, 515, 531
McCrindle, Joseph F.   1552
McCullers, Carson   858, 995, 997
McDonald, Archie P.   430
McDonald, Bruce   51
McDonald, Gerald D.   1424
McDonald, Keiko I.   1900, 2025

McDonnell, Gordon   1920
McDonough, Tom   81
McFarlane, Brian   2157
McGee, Mark   2050
McGee, Mark Thomas   973, 986
McGerr, Cecilia   1725
McGilligan, Patrick   1078, 1154, 1762, 1786
McGrath, John   1822
McGuinnis, Joe   550
McIntosh, Don   90
McKinney, Doug   2062
McKowen, Clark   51
McLaughlin, Robert   656, 1335, 1336, 1951
McLean, Albert F., Jr.   564, 718
McLuhan, Marshall   782
McMurtry, Larry   996, 1237
McNally, Raymond T.   395
McQuail, Denis   438, 578, 721, 746
McVay, Douglas   406
Meade, Ellen   89
Mead, Shepherd   1345, 1346
Mehr, Linda Harris   1537
Meisner, Sanford   76
Mekas, Jonas   531, 1955
Mellencamp, Patricia   168, 495
Mellen, Joan   465, 471, 514, 515, 527, 669, 791, 805, 808, 1138, 1722, 1731,
   1732, 1733, 1738, 1888, 1965, 2015, 2021, 2023, 2024, 2025, 2026, 2029, 2031,
   2172, 2176
Melnik, Stefan Reinhard   459, 853
Melton, David   1773
Meltzer, Milton   860
Melville, Herman   156, 1018, 1312
Mencken, H. L.   29
Mendelsohn, Harold   455, 456, 461
Mendelson, Lois   165
Menjou, Adolphe Jean   1081
Menville, Douglas   413, 414
Menville, R. Reginald   414
Menzel, Jiri   2164
Mercer, Ann   48
Mercer, John   81, 1528, 1530, 1537, 2211
Meredith, Scott   1064
Merleau-Ponty, Maurice   183, 185
Meryman, Richard   1266, 1271
Metz, Christian   133, 168, 169, 480, 584, 596
Meyers, Richard   414
Meyers, Warren   1447
Meyer, Anthony   47
Meyer, William R.   431, 800, 1495
Michael, David   554
Michael, Paul   1169, 1753, 1762
Michalczyk, John J.   566, 577, 1313, 2169
Michatek, Bolestaw   2014, 2179
Michelson, Annette   733, 1601, 1743
Miklos, Mark   90
Milford, Nancy   1110, 1114, 1115, 1116, 1118
Milland, Ray   1964
Millar, Kenneth (Ross Macdonald)   1041, 1042

Millerson, Gerald 92
Miller, Arthur 1265
Miller, Arthur C. 837, 1587
Miller, Diane Disney 1768
Miller, Don 431
Miller, Edwin 609
Miller, Eugene L., Jr. 2043, 2072
Miller, Gabriel 1313
Miller, Gavin 82
Miller, Henry 557, 1042
Miller, Lynn Fieldman 517
Miller, Pat P. 85
Miller, Patricia George 74
Miller, Patsy Ruth 1695
Miller, Randall M. 813, 820, 826
Miller, Richard 482
Miller, Robert Milton 1752
Miller, Tony 74
Miller, Vernon L. 729
Millichap, Joseph R. 1281, 1326
Mills, C. Wright 457, 462, 550
Mills, Earl 886, 950
Mills, John 1941
Milner, Michael 999, 2037
Milne, Tom 371, 1629, 1782, 1963, 2133
Mimura, Reiko 1164, 1503
Minnelli, Vincente 1138, 1784
Minney, R. J. 1357, 1841
Minus, Johnny 66
Mitchatek, Bolestaw 2181
Mitchell, Alice Miller 710, 727
Mitchell, Margaret 121, 812, 929, 944, 1029, 1435, 1436, 1801
Mitry, Jean 132, 169
Mizener, Arthur 1110, 1113, 1148
Mizruchi, Ephraim 1047
Mock, James R. 210, 223
Modiano, Patrick 377
Modleski, Tania 463, 468, 469, 517, 521, 528, 537, 538, 592, 718, 1849
Moews, Daniel 1677, 1688
Moley, Raymond 629, 728, 732, 778, 966, 1055
Molt, Cynthia Marylee 1318
Molyneaux, Gerard, F. S. C. 1424, 1430
Monaco, James 67, 96, 324, 566, 662, 667, 1519, 1538, 2094, 2095, 2097, 2114,
  2117, 2126, 2138, 2211
Monaco, Paul 441, 1631, 1718, 1923, 1924, 2122
Monier, Pierre 90
Monroe, Marilyn 1138, 1965
Montagu, Ivor 101, 142, 208, 1660, 1661, 1662, 1866, 1867
Monti, Carlotta 1770
Moore, Barbara Ann 678
Moore, Colleen 1695
Moore, Dickie 992
Moore, Marianne 514
Moore, Robin 363
Moravia, Alberto 2174
Mora, Carl J. 2178
Mordden, Ethan 406, 1467
Morella, Joe 1060, 1447, 1679, 1772, 1773, 1797, 1914, 1971
Moreno, Eduardo 1777

Morgan, Hal 655, 699
Morgenstern, Joseph 994
Morin, Edgar 1435, 1448
Morley, Christopher 1282
Morley, Margaret 1862
Morley, Raymond 641
Morrell, David 437
Morris, C. B. 1723
Morris, George 643, 1771, 1958
Morris, Peter 1343, 1543, 1553, 2162
Morris, Wright 1042
Morrow, James 74
Morsberger, Robert E. 1064, 1067, 1093, 1104, 1154, 1282, 1326
Moseley, Roy 1774
Mosley, Leonard 1319, 1501, 1768
Mosley, Nicholas 2161
Mosley, Philip 2187
Moss, Robert F. 395, 1425, 1941
Mott, Donald R. 2209
Mould, David H. 269
Moussinac, Leon 1660, 1666
MOVEMENTS IN ANIMATION 78
Muller-Strauss, Maurice 1870
Muller, Don 651
Mulvey, Laura 514, 1986
Munden, Kenneth W. 1538
Munshower, Suzanne 2047
Munsterberg, Hugo 124, 169, 582, 778
Murphy, Michael J. 395
Murphy, Robert 1841
Murphy, William T. 1681, 1682
Murray, Edward 143, 1108, 1113, 1114, 1155, 1930
Murray, Eunice 1138, 1965
Murray, Feg 1242
Murray, James P. 852, 895, 902, 936, 937, 938, 953, 2092
Musser, Charles 1586, 1600, 1615
Mussman, Tony 2133
Muybridge, Eadweard 1581, 1597, 1598
Myerson, Michael 2164
Myers, Eric 1754
Myles, Linda 661

N

Nabokov, Vladimir 1273
Nachbar, John G. 431, 564
Naha, Ed 395, 2050, 2075
Narboni, Jean 2133
Narcejac, Thomas 2080
Naremore, James 1022, 1448, 1794, 2054
Nash, Jay Robert 1755
Nathanson, E. M. 2071
Nathan, George Jean 1034
Naumberg, Nancy 1756
Navasky, Victor S. 1067, 1075, 1085, 1086, 1092, 1093, 1096, 1097, 1098, 1099,
  1100, 1155, 1178, 1189, 1205, 1282, 1284
Naylor, David 1506

Neagle, Anna 1862
Neale, Stephen 174, 192, 1563
Neal, Patricia 2059
Negri, Pola 1695
Neibaur, James L. 812
Nelson, Al P. 1369
Nelson, Richard Alan 621
Nelson, Thomas Allen 2057
Nemeskurty, Istvan 2012, 2013
Nestyev, Israel 1868
Neugroschel, Joachim 362
Nevares, Beatriz Reyes 2178
Neve, Brian 559
New York Library Association 987
Newcomb, Horace 780
Newman, Kim 396
Newman, Roger K. 963, 2037
Newquist, Roy 1766, 1778
Nias, D. K. B. 2037
Nicholls, Peter 414
Nichols, Bill 170, 176, 182, 184, 464, 712, 715, 799
Nichols, Dudley 370, 378, 799, 1007, 1014, 1015, 1018, 1021, 1210, 1326, 1327, 1772
Nicoll, Allardyce 557, 711, 1331, 1332, 1337
Niklaus, Thelma 1420
Nilsen, Vladimir 165
Nin, Anais 514
Nisbett, Alec 86
Nisbet, Robert 1050
Niver, Kemp R. 1380, 1395, 1593
Niville, John T. 1770
Nizer, Louis 966
Nizhny, Vladimir 208, 1660
Noble, Peter 277, 866, 877, 920, 938, 939, 1341, 1700, 1766, 1794
Nochlin, Linda 977
Noguchi, Thomas T. 1244
Nogueira, Rui 2006
Nolan, William F. 1087, 1223, 1916, 2059
Nollen, Scott Allen 1692
Norden, Martin F. 69, 1298
Nordoff, Charles 1330
Norris, Frank 1018, 1299
North, Joseph H. 1593, 1601
Norton, Graham 1939
Nowell-Smith, Geoffrey 1884
Nowlan, Gwendolyn Wright 420
Nowlan, Robert A. 420
Nowotny, Robert Allen 654
Null, Gary 872, 882, 940

O

O'Brien, Mary Ellen 76
O'Connor, Flannery 1316
O'Connor, Garry 1863
O'Connor, Jane 81
O'Connor, John E. 51, 221, 259, 270
O'Dell, Paul 1381, 1595

O'Dell, Scott 996
O'Donnell, Victoria 239
O'Flaherty, Liam 1019
O'Hara, John 1037, 1042, 1162, 1274
O'Higgins, Paul 225
O'Leary, Liam 1610, 1687
O'Neill, Eugene 875, 944
Oaka, Shohei 2029
Oakley, Charles 1613
Oates, Stephen B. 1215
Oberfirst, Robert 827, 1778
Oboler, Eli M. 966
Offen, Ron 1078, 1762, 1958
Ogden, Raymond August 1077
Ohlgre, Thomas H. 180
Oringel, Robert S. 92
Orlandello, John 1038, 1340, 1351
Orlik, Peter B. 74
Ornitz, Samuel 1071
Orriss, Bruce W. 380
Orr, Mary 1981
Orton, Barry 747
Orwell, George 78, 1076
Osborne, John 601, 1328
Osborne, Robert 1170
Oshana, Maryann 940
Oshman, Robert L. 1448
Ottoson, Robert 699, 1947, 1956
Ott, Frederick W. 1639
Oumano, Ellen 1539, 1552
Overbey, David 1928
Overstreet, Harry 1054
Owen, Anita 43

P

Paine, Albert Bigelow 1365
Palmer, Myles 2046
Parish, James Robert 386, 415, 420, 423, 432, 799, 993, 1042, 1057, 1091, 1248,
  1448, 1470, 1484, 1539, 1540, 1756, 1771, 1785, 2073
Parker, Barry M. 1344
Parker, David L. 107
Parker, Dorothy 1037, 1111
Parker, Gillian 367, 1311
Parker, Lottie Blair 1391
Parks, Rita 432
Park, James 540, 1539
Parlato, Salvatore, Jr. 1539
Parrill, William 2063, 2087
Parrish, Robert 1275
Pashdag, John 1237
Pasolini, Pier Paolo 2171
Pate, Michael 1539 ·
Patterson, Lindsay 896, 898, 924, 940
Patterson, Richard 81
Pauly, Thomas H. 1095, 1262, 1293
Paul, David W. 2013

Paul, William 1781
Paxton, Robert O. 1903
Payne, Robert 1425
Peary, Danny 415
Peary, Gerald 471, 507, 1314, 1315, 1914
Pechter, William S. 154, 1327
Peck, William A. 92
Pellegrino, Ronald 86
Pendo, Stephen 380, 798, 1198
Penley, Constance 518
Pepitone, Lena 1138, 1965
Pepper, Stephen C. 38
Perelman, S. J. 1037
Perisic, Zoran 78
Perkins, V. F. 106
Perosa, Sergio 1115, 1128
Perry, Donald LeRoy 607, 628, 630, 634, 646, 648
Perry, Edward S. 1526, 1535, 1998
Perry, Eleanor 1041
Perry, George 396, 1570, 1841, 1850, 1918, 1936, 1937, 1939, 1940, 2159
Perry, Jeb H. 1540
Perry, Louis B. 1068
Perry, Richard S. 1068
Perry, Ted 2170, 2175
Peshkov, Aleksey Maksimovich (See Gorky, Makism) 1667
Petaja, Emil 1453
Petersen, Carl 1211
Peterson, Horace C. 211
Peterson, Marcelene 1564
Peterson, Ruth C. 729, 730, 732, 865
Peters, Arthur King 1818
Peters, Charles C. 729
Peters, J. M. 67
Peters, J. M. L. 52, 1329
Petit, Arthur G. 826
Petley, Julian 241
Petrey, D. Sandy 1660, 1666
Petric, Vlada 582, 583, 1520, 1664, 1669, 2187
Petrie, Graham 1510, 1676, 2146, 2167
Petri, Bruce 1787
Pettigrew, Terence 812
Petzold, Paul 74, 75, 81, 91
Peyton, Patricia 52
Pfaff, Eugene E., Jr. 2209
Pfaff, Francoise 919
Pflaum, Hans Gunther 2165
Phelan, John M. 52
Phelan, J. J. 626, 710, 724, 727, 778
Phelps, Guy 225
Phelps, Robert 1818
Philbrick, Herb 1190
Phillips, Baxter 966
Phillips, David Graham 1313, 1314
Phillips, Gene D., S. J. 1039, 1215, 1218, 1219, 1296, 1552, 2057
Phillips, Klaus 2166
Phillips, William H. 67
Pickard, Roy 192, 415, 1171, 1467
Pickard, R. A. E. 1540
Pickford, Mary 1395

Pike, Andrew 2157
Pildas, Ave 1506
Pilkington, William T. 433
Pinchot, Ann 1138, 1375, 1773
Pincus, Edward 91
Pines, Jim 277, 859, 860, 861, 878, 895, 927, 943, 944, 945, 946
Pinter, Harold 1293
Piper, Henry Dan 1111, 1114, 1123, 1126, 1148
Piper, James 75
Pirie, David 396, 1940
Pistagnesi, Patrizia 1875, 1878
Pitts, Michael R. 386, 396, 415, 423, 432, 433, 1248, 1539, 2073
Place, Janey A. 1684, 1685, 2076
Plotkin, Janis 848
Poague, Leland 138
Poague, Leland A. 1694, 1706, 1836, 1843
Poe, Edgar Allan 1730, 1837, 2129
Pohle, Robert W. 381
Poitier, Sidney 886, 951
Polanski, Roman 1355, 2179
Polan, Dana B. 1651, 2078
Pollack, Dale 2209
Porter, Katherine Anne 2062
Porter, Melinda Camber 2050, 2127
Porter, Vincent 1568, 1935
Poster, Steve 72
Postman, Neil 135
Poteet, G. Howard 52
Powdermaker, Hortense 514, 536, 550, 609, 614, 734, 742, 1046, 1057, 1238
Powell, Anthony 1148
Powell, David J. 41
Powers, Anne 946
Pratley, Gerald 322, 643, 1087, 1860, 1917, 1967, 2051, 2052, 2077, 2162
Prats, A. J. 117
Pratt, Douglas 1540
Pratt, George C. 1594
Prawer, S. S. 397
Preminger, Otto 643, 1967
Prendergast, Roy M. 407
Prevots, Naima 1676
Price, Barbara Anne 1931, 1932
Price, Michael H. 399
Price, Theodore 1931, 1932
Prindle, David F. 1156
Probst, Leonard 609
Pronay, Nicholas 210, 211, 212, 213, 214, 216, 217, 225, 242, 255
Prosonby, Arthur 211
Proust, Marcel 2137
Prouty, Olive Higgins 797, 800
Proviser, Henry 91
Pryluck, Calvin 34, 1520
Pudovkin, V. I. 208, 1662
Purdy, Jim 448, 449, 567, 568, 569, 716
Pushkin, Aleksandr Sergeyevich 1645
Puzo, Mario 1029
Pye, Michael 662, 1951
Pym, John 2167

Q

Quigley, Isabel 51, 1426
Quigley, Martin, Jr. 1580, 1581, 1594, 1599, 1756
Quinlan, David 1540, 1552
Quinn, Anthony 1968
Quirk, Lawrence J. 800, 1679, 1761, 1766, 1778, 1781, 1782, 1786, 1920, 1973, 2047, 2060

R

Rabiger, Michael 82
Rabkin, Eric S. 416
Rabkin, Gerald 2037
Rabourdin, Dominique 2147, 2155
Rachuk, Igor 1653
Rader, Dotson 1345
Radway, Janice A. 469
Raeburn, John 1763
Ragan, David 1541
Ragaway, Martin 691
Rahill, Frank 712
Rainey, Buck 424
Ramsaye, Terry 1382, 1467, 1519, 1555, 1615
Randall, Richard S. 225, 967
Rand, Ayn 229, 1037
Rapee, Erno 407
Rau, M. 1420
Rau, N. 1420
Rawlings, Majorie Kinnan 1010
Rayns, Tony 2166
Ray, Man 1727
Ray, Robert B. 165, 2194
Ray, Satyajit 1566
Ray, Sidney F. 81
Reader, Keith 444, 474, 489, 566, 1563
Reade, Eric 1594, 2157
Read, Herbert 457, 1025
Read, James Morgan 211
Reagan, Ronald 1088, 1785
Rebello, Stephen, 1238
Redding, Robert 1177
Redgrave, Michael 1863
Reed, Carol 1219, 1329
Reed, Donald A. 2066
Reed, John 1667
Reed, Rex 155
Reeves, Richard 1144
Rehrauer, George 66, 394, 422, 513, 1526, 1541
Reid, Alison 2058, 2162
Reiff, Stephanie 554, 1319
Reisz, Karel 82
Remarque, Erich Maria 371, 1805
Renan, Sheldon 1955
Renoir, Jean 1822
Renov, Michael 353
Renshaw, Samuel 729
Rentschler, Eric 2166

Reppen, Joseph 594
Reynerston, A. J. 75
Reynolds, Debbie 1969
Rheuban, Joyce 1692, 2166
Rhode, Eric 1519, 1553, 1563, 1624, 1645, 1703, 1712, 1715, 1829, 1869, 1923, 1924, 1927, 1935, 1946, 1997, 2093, 2095
Ricci, Mark 1138, 1774, 1789, 1965
Rice, Cy 1770
Richardson, Dorothy 514, 1297
Richardson, Robert 1026, 1298, 1315
Richards, David 1970
Richards, Dick 1786
Richards, Jeffrey 423, 540, 1833, 1839, 1938
Richie, Donald 1574, 1575, 1731, 1734, 1735, 1736, 1737, 1739, 1740, 1741, 1742, 1885, 1887, 1889, 1892, 1893, 1894, 1897, 1900, 2015, 2016, 2021, 2028
Richin, Moses 1047, 1055
Richler, Mordecai 1032, 1037
Rich, Linda 1576
Rich, Adrienne 468
Ridgeway, Julie 1767
Ridgeway, Steve 1767
Rieff, Philip 452
Riese, Randall 1965
Riesman, David 430, 774
Rifkin, Ned 1882
Riley, Philip J. 1679
Rilla, Wolf 91
Rimbaud, Jean-Nicholas-Arthur 2129
Rimberg, John David 1648, 1652, 2181
Rinehart, Stanley Ray 648
Ringel, Fred J. 1105
Ringgold, Gene 801, 1681, 1765, 1914, 1918
Rivkin, Allen 1057, 1238
Road, Sinclair 245
Robbe-Grillet, Alain 2139, 2140
Robbins, Tod 1311
Robertson, James C. 967
Robertson, Joseph F. 75, 82
Robertson, Patrick 1542
Robertson, R. J. 973, 986
Roberts, Kenneth H. 91
Robinson, David 1410, 1414, 1415, 1416, 1418, 1419, 1423, 1425, 1426, 1519, 1563, 1606, 1626, 1631, 1637, 1638, 1642, 1644, 1652, 1670, 1676, 1678, 1689, 1714, 1719, 1869, 1876, 1990
Robinson, Edward G. 799, 1091, 1786
Robinson, Jeffrey 801
Robinson, Jill 1041
Robinson, J. F. 93
Robinson, Patrick 1950
Robinson, W. R. 1028, 1316
Robyns, Gwen 1861
Roche, Henri-Pierre 2147, 2155
Rockwell, John 1918
Rockwood, Louis 91
Roddenberry, Gene 554
Roddick, Nick 1496, 2159
Rodriguez, Elena 2054
Roffman, Peter 448, 449, 567, 568, 569, 716

Rogers, Robert E. 80
Rogin, Michael Paul 1785, 2077
Rohmer, Eric 1850
Rollins, Peter C. 271
Rollyson, Carl E., Jr. 1138, 1230, 1965
Rondi, Gian Luigi 1876
Rooney, Frank 1311
Rooney, Mickey 1786
Rosenbaum, Jonathan 392, 1789
Rosenberg, Bernard 67, 455, 457, 547, 548, 552, 609, 814, 1468
Rosenberg, James L. 712
Rosenberg, Jan 451, 519
Rosenblum, Ralph 82
Rosenkrantz, Linda 1059, 1234
Rosenthal, Alan 2042
Rosenthal, Stuart 1762, 1931
Rosen, Marjorie 465, 471, 497, 512, 514, 518, 576, 791
Rosen, Philip 117
Rose, Ernest D. 52
Rose, Jacqueline 519
Rosow, Eugene 386
Rossen, Robert 1090
Rossen, Steven 1090
Rossi, Patrizio 1883
Rossner, Judith 1032, 1037
Ross, Helen 1448
Ross, Leonard Q. (Leo C. Rosten) 1238
Ross, Lillian 554, 1319, 1321, 1426, 1448
Ross, Murray 1068, 1069, 1156, 1173
Ross, T. J. 53, 392
Rosten, Leo C. 226, 457, 736, 1041, 1049, 1057, 1121, 1238, 1435, 1437
Rotha, Paul 216, 243, 245, 246, 294, 302, 872, 1520, 1564, 1625, 1681, 1682
Rothel, David 433
Rothert, Edward 2014, 2181
Rothman, William 1851
Rotsler, William 2037
Roud, Richard 1542, 2006, 2134
Rousseau, Jean Jacque 1257
Rouzet-Albagli, Nicole 51
Rovin, Jeff 415, 416, 2052
Rowan, Bonnie G. 1542
Rowlands, Avril 85
Roy, Emil 109
Ruban, Al 2048
Rubenstein, Elliot 1689, 2143
Rubenstein, Lenny 609, 900
Rubinstein, E. A. 459
Rubin, Martin 609, 2042
Rubin, Steven Jay 220, 231, 341, 350, 354, 423
Rubin, Theodore Isaac 995
Ruby, Jay 1682
Ruckmick, Christian A. 729
Rudisill, Richard 1594
Ruppert, Peter 1297
Russell, Jane 1917
Russell, Sharon A. 165
Russett, Robert 78
Russo, John 397
Russ, Joanna 519

Ryall, Tom 1851
Ryan, Michael 569
Ryan, Roderick T. 654
Rynew, Arden 91

S

Sabath, Barry 1639
Sackett, Susan 554
Sadoul, Georges 1543, 1553, 1572, 1618, 1665, 1910, 2178
Salachas, Gilbert 1931
Saleman, Barrie 2184
Salem, James M. 1010, 1756
Saltus, Carol 1816
Salt, Brian G. D. 78
Samples, Gordon 1157
Sampson, Henry T. 860, 868, 870, 943, 946, 947, 948
Samuelson, David W. 81
Samuels, Charles 879, 951
Samuels, Charles Thomas 53, 165, 1688, 1773, 2034
Sanderson, Richard Arlo 615, 1600
Sanders, George 1969
Sanders, M. L. 212
Sandro, Paul 579, 1723
Sands, Frederick 1686
Sands, Pierre Norman 1069, 1171
Sanford, Charles 1326
Sanford, Nevitt 1011
Sarf, Wayne Michael 433
Sarris, Andrew 53, 132, 155, 156, 531, 609, 980, 994, 1002, 1006, 1015, 1023,
  1321, 1327, 1328, 1349, 1351, 1553, 1685, 1697, 1756, 1788, 1926, 2086
Sartre, Jean-Paul 2129, 2147
Sato, Tadao 787, 788, 801, 802, 1575, 1731, 1733, 1734, 1735, 1736, 1737, 1740,
  1742, 1888, 1891, 1892, 1895, 2016, 2020
Saunders, Cheryl McAllister 2209
Sauvage, Pierre 1548
Sayles, John 554
Sayre, Joel 1103, 1207
Schaefer, Jack 1009
Schaefer, Susan 43
Schary, Dore 1071, 1485
Schatz, Thomas 173, 176, 179, 193, 194, 699, 1464, 1466
Schechter, Harold 987
Scheer, James F. 1479
Scherle, Victor 1764
Scherman, David E. 1757
Scheuer, Steven H. 68, 1529
Schewel, Amy 1544
Schickel, Richard 143, 156, 234, 307, 549, 569, 879, 880, 942, 950, 994, 995,
  1001, 1024, 1080, 1206, 1359, 1360, 1361, 1362, 1363, 1364, 1366, 1367, 1372,
  1381, 1388, 1390, 1398, 1399, 1404, 1406, 1407, 1435, 1436, 1449, 1553, 1564,
  1693, 1769
Schiff, Lillian 91
Schillaci, Anthony 53, 200
Schlesinger, Arthur 457, 736
Schlesinger, Arthur, Jr. 733
Schlossberg, Marilyn 2051

Schlozman, Kay Lehman 1046, 1051
Schnapper, Amy 656, 678
Schnitman, Jorge A. 699
Schnitzer, Jean 1652
Schnitzer, Luda 1652
Schoell, William 397
Scholes, Robert 175
Schrader, Paul 1893, 2004
Schramm, Wilbur 201
Schreivogel, Paul A. 324, 379
Schulberg, Budd 820, 1029, 1037, 1041, 1042, 1058, 1091, 1104, 1106, 1109, 1116, 1117, 1118, 1121, 1126, 1127, 1135, 1148, 1158, 1161, 1162, 1193, 1233, 1277, 1278
Schulman, Gary 543
Schumach, Murray 967
Schuster, Mel 1543, 1554, 2166
Schuth, H. Wayne 2060
Schwartz, Nancy Lynn 1065, 1069, 1185, 1191
Schwartz, Ronald 2182
Schwartz, Sheila 1065, 1069, 1191
Schwarz, Arturo 1727, 1731
Schwarz, Ted 1780
Sciacca, Tony 1918
Scotland, John 1757
Scott, Adrienne 137
Scott, Evelyn F. 1239
Scott, Helen G. 1566, 1856, 1864, 2148, 2149
Scott, James F. 68
Scott, Jay 157
Scott, Kathryn Leigh 1449
Scott, Paul 548
Seabury, William Marston 627, 781
Sealy, Shirley 609
Seaver, Richard 2136, 2137, 2152
Seelye, John 1363
See, Carolyn 1028, 1042, 2037
Segrave, Kerry 513
Seidman, Steve 799, 1972
Seiter, Ellen 792
Selby, Stuart 39
Selby, Stuart Alan 54
Selden, Raman 120
Seldes, Gilbert 157, 158, 173, 306, 1055, 1056, 1358, 1676, 1757
Sellers, Michael 1941
Selznick, Irene Mayer 1488
Semprun, Jorge 379
Semsel, George Stephen 2163
Sennett, Mack 1413
Sennett, Richard 550
Sennett, Ted 397, 407, 1497
Serjeant, Richard 87
Servadio, Gaia 1884, 1922
Sesonske, Alexander 1823
Seton, Marie 830, 951, 1646, 1647, 1656, 1660, 1661, 1667, 1865, 2167
Seydor, Paul 2063
Shade, Rose 1138, 1965
Shadoian, Jack 387
Shaheen, Jack G. 355, 454
Shain, Russell Earl 200, 231, 328, 350

Shakanov, L. 2181
Shakespeare, William 438, 822, 862, 2078
Shale, Richard 283, 306, 321, 1080, 1173
Sharff, Stefan 68
Sharples, Win, Jr. 91
Sharp, Dennis 1507
Shatzkin, Roger 1314, 1315
Shavelson, Melville 848
Shaw, Arnold 885, 950, 1918
Shaw, George Bernard 1344, 2058
Shaw, Irwin 1041
Sheed, Wilfrid 158
Sheldon, Edward 862
Shelley, Mary 394, 1312, 1808
Shepherd, David 1081
Shepley, John 2171
Sheratsky, Rodney E. 54, 315, 323
Sheridan, Alan 480
Sheridan, Marion 54, 1021, 1807
Sherman, Barry L. 75
Sherman, Eric 609, 2042
Sherwood, Robert 1060
Shewey, Don 1278
Shihara, Shintaro 2023
Shilova, Irina 2181
Shils, Edward 457, 778
Shindler, Colin 218, 272
Shipley, Lee 1104
Shipman, David 1391, 1449, 1450, 1958
Shipman, Nell 1450
Shirley, Graham 2158
Shi, Cameron 1413
Shores, Edward 2053
Short, Kenneth R. M. 201, 208, 211, 213, 216, 223, 246, 253, 255, 265, 273,
  281
Short, Luke 425
Shulman, Irving 986, 1060, 1695, 1774
Shuttleworth, Frank K. 729, 732
Siciliano, Enzo 2171
Sidney, George 1106
Sieben, Pearl 827, 1778
Signoret, Simone 1910
Silet, Charles L. P. 425
Silke, James R. 1498, 1764, 1782, 1927
Silva, Fred 865, 1383
Silverman, Kaja 165, 519
Silverstein, Harry 609, 1468
Silverstein, Norman 140
Silver, Alain 398, 1732, 1743, 1861, 1947, 1956, 2044
Silver, Charles 434, 1767
Silver, Pat 1861
Simmons, Garner 2063
Simmon, Scott 1696
Simonet, Thomas S. 735, 1174
Simone, Sam P. 1851
Simon, John 143, 158, 159, 160, 993, 994, 995, 996, 1001, 1003, 1006, 1007,
  1008, 1011, 1016, 1020, 1022, 1023, 1024, 1296, 1328, 1347, 1349, 1350, 1356,
  2086, 2187

Simon, Neil 2060
Simon, William G. 1824, 1828
Simon, William H. 1819
Sinatra, Nancy 1918
Sinclair, Andrew 1490, 1685, 1822
Sinclair, Upton 624, 1471
Singer, Isaac Bashevis 1032, 1037
Singer, Kurt 1860
Singer, Michael 1554
Singleton, Ralph S. 75, 2211
Siniscalo, Carmine 1574
Sinyard, Neil 2209
Sir-Cliff, Bernard 2170
Siska, William Charles 118
Sitney, P. Adams 582, 1757, 1955, 2039
Sjoman, Vilgot 2188
Skaggs, Calvin 1316
Skenazy, Paul 1196
Skiles, Marlin 75
Sklar, Robert 228, 560, 572, 576, 607, 640, 728, 729, 957, 1057, 1129, 1133
Skoller, Donald 1629
Skolsky, Sidney 1057, 1244
Skorman, Richard 1543
Skrade, Carl 45
Skretvedt, Randy 1692
Skvorecky, Josef 2164
Slade, Mark 68
Slatzer, Robert F. 1081, 1138, 1966
Slide, Anthony 143, 519, 620, 654, 655, 699, 881, 1365, 1381, 1383, 1384, 1385,
   1390, 1391, 1412, 1450, 1557, 1572, 1595, 1757, 1758, 2009
Sloan, James Park 363
Sloan, Joan 2005
Slotkin, Richard 175
Slusser, George E. 416
Smallman, Kirk 91
Smith, Ella 799, 1786
Smith, Henry Nash 175, 176, 1048
Smith, James L. 712
Smith, John M. 1543, 1824
Smith, Julian 199, 231, 283, 359
Smith, Lucinda 1506
Smith, Marsha 1544
Smith, Patrick S. 2069
Smith, Paul 259, 275
Smith, Robert 1986
Smith, Sarah W. R. 147
Smith, Sharon 520
Smith, Thomas G. 81
Snyder, John J. 146
Snyder, Robert L. 1871
Snyder, Stephen 2171, 2176
Sobanski, Oskar 2012, 2014
Sobchack, Thomas 37, 58, 59, 119, 120, 121, 125, 138, 1520
Sobchack, Tom 68
Sobchack, Vivian C. 58, 59, 68, 120, 121, 416, 417, 1520
Sobel, Raoul 1409, 1414, 1415, 1427
Sohn, David A. 69, 106
Solinas, PierNico 2172
Solmi, Angelo 1932

Solomon, Jon   383
Solomon, Stanley J.   69, 143, 197, 712, 715
Solzhenitsyn, Alexander   554, 1319
Sontag, Susan   144, 1298, 1356
Sophocles   601
Sorlin, Pierre   255, 276, 1387
Southern, Terry   1041
Souto, H. Mario Raimondo   81
Souvestre, Pierre   1617
Spada, James   1138, 1962, 2050, 2066
Spark, Muriel   30, 1003
Spatz, Jonas   1040, 1042, 1047, 1053, 1056, 1157
Spears, Jack   210, 1239
Spehr, Paul C.   1595
Spencer, Charles   1761
Spiegel, Alan   1316
Spiegel, Penina   2059
Spigelgass, Leonard   799, 1091, 1786
Spillane, Mickey   2071
Spoto, Donald   1607, 1848, 1852, 1853, 1856, 1978
Spottiswoode, Raymond   75, 98, 106
Spraos, John   608, 647, 699
Sprigge, Elizabeth   1817
Springer, John   407, 1758, 1771
Spring, D. W.   211, 212, 213, 214, 216, 217, 225, 242, 255
Squires, James Duane   211
Squire, Jason E.   607, 608, 676, 687, 699, 754
Stack, Oswald   2171
Stacy, Pat   1081
Stadiem, William   1138, 1965
Staiger, Janet Kay   60, 616, 1460, 1519
Stallings, Laurence   304
Stallybrass, Oliver   1574, 1726
Stampp, Kenneth M.   864
Stam, Robert   118, 2159
Stanke, Don E.   423
Stanley, John   398
Stanley, Robert   43, 49
Stanley, Robert H.   662, 700, 701
Stanton, Frank   457
Staples, Donald   45
Starks, Michael   988
Stark, Richard   2073
Starr, Cecile   54, 55, 78
Stauffacher, Frank   1955
Stecker, Elinor H.   75
Stedman, Raymond William   434, 1457
Steegmuller, Francis   1819
Steele, Joseph Henry   1761
Steele, Robert   1544
Steene, Birgitta   2188, 2189
Steen, Mike   1239
Stefan, Jerzy   2180
Steiger, Brad   1060, 1138, 1773
Steinbeck, John   135, 522, 1005, 1037, 1281, 1924
Steinberg, Try Corbett   608, 1544
Steinbrunner, Chris   417
Steinham, Gloria   1138

Stein, Ben 574
Stein, E. P. 1957
Stein, Joseph 850
Stempel, Tom 85, 1036, 1063, 1159, 1254
Stenn, David 1679
Stephen 168
Stephenson, Ralph 78, 97, 98, 100, 106
Stephenson, William 463, 778
Sternhill, Zeev 1904
Stern, Lee Edward 407
Stern, Michael 1970, 1971, 1986
Stern, Seymour 1367, 1382, 1758
Stevenson, Robert Louis 117, 1277, 1312
Steven, Peter 465, 573
Stewart, David C. 39, 54
Stewart, Donald Ogden 1124, 1278
Stewart, Jack 1771
Stewart, Lucy Ann Ligett 1782
Stewart, William T. 1544
Stine, Whitney 801, 1766
Stirling, Monica 1884
Stock, Dennis 1325, 1959
Stock, Stuart H. 418
Stoddard, George D. 729
Stoil, Michael Jon 1652, 2158
Stoker, Bram 398, 1312, 1642, 1798
Stoler, Mark A. 1509, 1510, 1518
Stoltzfus, Ben 2113, 2139
Stone, Alfred A. 1042
Stone, Gregory P. 457
Stone, Irving 1015
Stong, Phil 1104
Stott, William 1870
Stout, Wesley W. 1693
Stovin, P. D. 1688
Stowell, Peter 1685
Stowe, Harriet Beecher 116, 156, 718
Straczynski, J. Michael 85
Strasser, Alex 76
Stratemeyer Syndicate (Tom Swift) 1145
Stratton, David 2158
Strebel, Elizabeth Grottle 1811, 1812, 1813, 1814, 1815
Street, Douglas 989
Strickland, A. W. 417
Strick, Phillip 1450, 1882
Stromgren, Richard L. 69, 1298, 1519, 1559, 1586, 1671, 1714, 1749
Strong, Phillip Duffield 1041
Stuart, Campbell 212
Stuart, Frederic 648, 656
Stuart, Ray 1450
Stubbs, John C. 1932
Studlar, Gaylyn 1697
Styron, William 1032, 1037
St. John, Adela Rogers 1396
St. Laurent, Cecil 2009
Suber, Howard 1068, 1084
Suid, Lawrence Howard 231, 348, 350, 360
Suid, Murray 74
Suino, Mark E. 164

Sullivan, Ed 1423, 1428
Sullivan, Kaye 520
Sullivan, Sister Bede 55
Sultanik, Aaron 1564
Sussex, Elizabeth 215, 246, 248, 315, 316, 2159
Svensson, Arne 1575, 1627, 1888, 2018, 2029
Swallow, Norman 1661, 1667
Swanson, Gloria 1454
Swan, John 1427
Sweet, Freddy 2118, 2138
Sweezy, Paul M. 634, 765
Swenson, Karen 1138
Swift, Jonathan 2100
Swift, Tom (Stratemeyer Syndicate house pseudonym) 1145
Swindell, Larry 1093, 1781, 1788
Syberberg, Hans-Jurgen 362
Sylvester, Derek 1941, 2061
Symmes, Dan 655, 699
Symons, Julian 1224

T

Tabori, Paul 1859
Taft, Robert 1598
Tagore, Rabindranath 548
Tailleur, Roger 1089
Tajiri, Vincent 1060
Talbot, Daniel 136, 144, 1105, 1332, 1710
Tanitch, Robert 1862
Taraborrelli, J. Randy 951
Taranow, Gerda 1463
Tarbox, Charles H. 701, 1460, 1595, 1600
Tarkington, Booth 1327
Tarkovsky, Andrey 2181
Tauber, Irene B. 782
Taub, Eric 76
Taves, Brian 1771
Taylor, Deems 1564
Taylor, Derek 554
Taylor, Dwight 1977
Taylor, John Russell 408, 1220, 1320, 1795, 1848, 1853, 1855, 1857, 1940, 2170, 2208
Taylor, Philip M. 212
Taylor, Richard 1644, 1652, 1653, 1662
Taylor, Robert 1138
Taylor, Robert Lewis 1771
Taylor, Roger G. 1966
Taylor, Telford 1077
Taylor, Theodore 70
Taylor, William R. 2065
Tebbel, John 1047
Teichman, Howard 1064
Teitelbaum, Maureen 1822
Tenney, Jack B. 1079
Tevis, Walter 1014, 1311
Thackeray, William 1299, 1312
Thomas, Bob 78, 1958, 1962

Thomas, Dylan 101
Thomas, Frank 1769
Thomas, Robert 226, 368, 534, 609, 800, 1080, 1240, 1469, 1489, 1490, 1766, 1769
Thomas, Sam 1160
Thomas, Sari 452, 542, 573, 751
Thomas, Terry 1290, 1958, 1962
Thomas, Tony 408, 643, 1032, 1044, 1045, 1088, 1160, 1246, 1249, 1296, 1451, 1771, 1779, 1785, 1787, 1941, 1959
Thomey, Tedd 643, 1959
Thompson, Frank 1554
Thompson, Howard 70, 1760, 1787
Thompson, Kenneth 2060
Thompson, Kristin 60, 94, 95, 102, 108, 112, 616, 618, 701, 1519, 1867, 1868
Thomson, David 144, 1160, 1426, 2047
Thorpe, Edward 1057, 1198, 1240
Thorpe, Frances 1545
Thorp, Margaret Farrand 487, 488, 622, 732, 734, 784, 1057
Thrasher, Frederick M. 729, 1758
Thurstone, L. I. 462, 729, 730, 732
Tibbetts, John C. 1338, 1399, 1405, 1407
Todd, Ann 1863
Todd, Mike, Jr. 1971
Todd, Susan McCarthy 1971
Toffel, Neile McQueen 2059
Toffler, Arthur 457
Toll, Robert C. 862
Tolstoy, Count Lev Nikolayevich 557, 2030
Tomaselli, Keyan 2089
Tomkies, Mike 989, 1081, 1789, 1964
Tomlinson, Hugh 162
Tompkins, Jane P. 485
Torme, Mel 1138, 1774
Tornabene, Lyn 1773
Torrence, Bruce T. 1065
Tozzi, Romano 1788
Travaill, Vera 1817
Traven, B. 191, 1314, 1979
Travers, Peter 554, 1319
Trent, Paul 1451
Trewin, J. C. 1842
Trojanski, John 91
Trojan, Judith 987
Tromberg, Sheldon 76
Trow, W. S. 550
True, Marshall 1509, 1510, 1518
Truffaut, Francois 1566, 1819, 1843, 1856, 1864, 2094, 2148, 2149, 2150
Truitt, Evelyn Mack 1545
Trumbo, Dalton 1067, 1074, 1076, 1087, 1233, 1282, 1284, 1286
Truzzi, Marcello 457
Tuchman, Gaye 459, 462
Tucker, Richard N. 1575, 1731, 1735, 1736, 1740, 1887, 1890, 1902, 2016, 2018
Tudor, Andrew 165, 176, 780, 785
Tulloch, John 2158
Tunney, Kieran 1760
Tunstall, Jeremy 573
Tupino, Mario 1023
Turaj, Frank 2179
Turan, Kenneth 2037

Turconi, Davide 1412
Turim, Maureen Cheryn 1955
Turk, Edward Baron 1909
Turnbull, Andrew 1056, 1111, 1116, 1118, 1120, 1122, 1123, 1125, 1128, 1129,
  1148
Turner, George E. 80, 399
Turner, Graeme 55, 59
Turner, Lana 1971
Turner, Roland 1545
Turow, Joseph 812, 816
Turton, T. P. 1021
Tuska, Jon 381, 434, 1758, 1795, 1947, 1948, 1956
Twain, Mark 175, 1298
Twitchell, James B. 399
Twomey, Alfred E. 1451
Tyler, Parker 170, 171, 233, 576, 581, 1054, 1240, 1364, 1428, 1431, 1564, 1956
Tyler, Three W. 80
Tynan, Kenneth 1941

U

Ulanov, Barry 260
Umiker-Sebeok, Donna Jean 169
Umphlett, Wiley Lee 989, 1160
Underwood, Peter 1779
Upchurch, Alan Y. 1658
Updike, John 1316
Ursini, James 398, 1861, 1919
Usabel, Gaizka S. de 642, 701

V

Vadim, Roger 2050
Vahimagi, Tise 653
Valerio, Joseph M. 1507
Vale, Eugene 85
Vale, V. 418
Vallance, Tom 408
Valleau, Marjorie A. 219, 277
Van de Velde, Robert 201
Van den Haag, Ernest 457
Van Hecke, B. C. 385
Van Ormer, Edward 746
Van Peebles, Melvin 942, 953
Van Watson, William 2172
Van Wert, William F. 2112, 2113, 2114, 2127, 2140
Vardac, A. Nicholas 557, 711, 1331, 1338
Vassilokos, Vassili 577
Vasudev, Aruna 2167
Vaughan, Ciba 1790, 1818, 1995, 2130
Vaughan, Dai 249
Vaughn, Robert 1067, 1096, 1194
Vechten, Carl Van 1041
Veith, Richard 93
Verba, Sidney 1046, 1051
Vermilye, Jerry 643, 799, 801, 1766, 1774, 1782, 1786, 1940

Verne, Jules 1029, 1620
Vesterman, William 747
Viazzi, Glanco 1422
Vickers, Hugo 1761, 1861
Vidal, Gore 1041, 1042
Vidor, King 1081, 1696
Viertel, Salka 1914
Villon, Francois 2129
Vincent, Elizabeth 2208
Vincent, Richard C. 608, 651, 701, 702
Vinson, James 1541, 1545, 1546
Violet, Ultra 2069
Virmaux, Alain 147
Virmaux, Odette 147
Visconti, Luchino 1932, 2172
Vizzard, Jack 968
Von Gunden, Kenneth 418
Von Harbou, Thea 1639, 1830
Von Sternberg, Josef 1698, 1788, 1830
Voronstov, Yuri 1653

W

Wagenknecht, Edward 1290, 1385, 1410
Wagner, Geoffrey 1316
Wagner, Robert F. 76
Wagner, Robert W. 107
Wagner, Steven 2172
Wajda, Andrzej 2014
Wakeman, John 1554
Wake, Sandra 2064
Waldhorn, Arthur 1231
Waldman, Diane 794
Waldron, Gloria 55
Walker, Alexander 225, 1451, 1686, 1759, 1766, 1861, 1940, 2057
Walker, David 573
Walker, Franklin 1105
Walker, Joseph 1676
Walker, Juanita 1676
Walker, Katherine Sorley 1197
Walker, Michael 2128
Wallace, Lew 1029
Wallant, Edward Lewis 1314, 2084
Waller, Gregory Albert 1030, 1331, 1333, 1334, 1338
Waller, Gregory A. 399
Wallis, Hal 801, 1288
Wall, James M. 55
Walsh, Andrea S. 442, 443, 458, 461, 521, 522, 523, 543, 614, 638, 728, 791, 800, 801
Walsh, Raoul 1700
Walt Disney Productions 1769
Walter, Ernest 83
Walz, Eugene P. 2106, 2150
Wanger, Walter 2043
Wapshott, Nicholas 2160
Ward, Elizabeth 1947, 1956, 2044
Ward, John 324, 2139
Ward, Larry Wayne 308

Ware, Derek 76
Warham, John 76
Warhol, Andy 2069
Warner, Alan 405
Warner, Jack L. 226, 1498
Warren, Bill 418
Warren, Doug 1078
Warren, Patricia 1571
Warren, Robert Penn 884, 1012, 1029
Warshow, Robert 160, 464, 531, 1009, 1019, 1433
Wasko, Janet 608, 618, 627, 629, 630, 634, 637, 645, 662, 663, 702, 1367
Waters, Ethel 879, 951
Waters, John 2210
Watkins, Floyd 858
Watters, James 1452
Watt, Harry 308, 322
Watt, Ian 1297
Waugh, Charles 1234
Waugh, Evelyn 1028, 1041, 1042, 1158
Wayne, Jane Ellen 1773, 1920
Wead, George 70, 1689
Weales, Gerald 1095
Weatherby, W. J. 1138, 1966
Weaver, John T. 1546
Weaver, Kathleen 1546
Weaver, Richard 855
Weaver, William 1924
Webb, Charles 2085
Webb, Michael 1241
Weinberg, Herman G. 160, 1018, 1022, 1574, 1639, 1698, 1700, 1729
Weiner, Janet 55
Weintraub, Joseph 1795
Weiss, Ken 1457
Weiss, Marion 2209
Weiss, Paul 165, 201
Weiss, Richard 1047
Weis, Elisabeth 1392, 1418, 1452, 1857
Welch, David 202, 249, 251, 282
Welch, Jeffrey Egan 1163
Weldon, Don 1477
Weldon, Michael 419
Wellman, William A. 1701
Wells, H. G. 1037, 1312, 1620, 1789
Wells, John Warren 2037
Wells, Walter 1042, 1043, 1108
Wellwarth, George E. 1635
Welsch, Janice R. 466, 523, 524, 791, 1297
Welsh, James Michael 1399, 1405, 1407, 1712, 1713, 1726, 1730
Weltman, Manuel 1457
Wengraf, Susan 490
Wertmuller, Lina 2172
Westmoreland, Bob 93
West, Jessamyn 1319
West, Mae 1795
West, Nathanael 154, 820, 1037, 1041, 1042, 1058, 1103, 1104, 1135, 1145, 1158, 1161, 1162, 1226, 1291
Wexman, Virginia Wright 1966, 1983, 2007
Wheaton, Christopher D. 1068, 1546

Wheeler, Helen 525
Whitaker, Raymond W. 1813
Whitaker, Rod 70
Whitehead, Peter 1344, 1354
White, Alistair 2013
White, David 2158
White, David Manning 67, 455, 457, 547, 548, 552, 814
White, Pearl 1458
White, Tony 79
White, Walter 879
White, William 1289
Whitman, Walt 175
Whitney, Steven 1785
Whyte, Mal 398
Wicking, Christopher 653
Widener, Don 2058
Wiene, Robert 1635
Wilcock, John 2069
Wilcox, Herbert 1863
Wiley, Mason 1174, 1175
Wilk, Max 1241
Willener, Alfred 70
Williams, Alan Larson 2006
Williams, Bernard 968
Williams, Carol Traynor 525, 526
Williams, Chester 1773
Williams, Christopher 166
Williams, Clarence 55
Williams, Dakin 1345
Williams, Henry 648
Williams, John 2052
Williams, Linda 495
Williams, Mark 409
Williams, Martin 1386
Williams, Raymond 442, 521, 614, 778
Williams, Tennessee 858, 1345, 1346, 2052
Willis, Donald 419, 798, 1776
Willis, Donald C. 1764
Wills, Garry 550
Will, David 1961
Wilmington, Michael 1684
Wilner, Daniel M. 882
Wilson, Arthur 1499
Wilson, David 240, 1841
Wilson, Earl 1918
Wilson, Edmund 1028, 1031, 1104
Wilson, George M. 119
Wilson, Henry Leon 1041, 1059
Wilson, Ivy Crane 1914
Wilson, James C. 218, 363
Wilson, J. A. 473
Wilson, Robert 148
Windahl, Sven 438, 578, 746
Windler, Robert 643, 1396, 1787
Winkler, A. M. 229
Winquist, Sven G. 1627
Winston, Douglas Garrett 1163
Winters, Shelley 1973
Wiseman, Thomas 1565

Wise, Arthur   76
Wise, Jeffrey   1986
Witcombe, R. T.   2169
Withers, Robert S.   70, 96, 97
Witus, Barbara   554
Wlashchin, Ken   55
Wodehouse, P. G.   1037
Wolfenstein, Martha   576, 581, 602, 732, 734, 740, 798
Wolfe, Charles   1764
Wolfe, Halley   86
Wolfe, Tom   550
Wolf, Leonard   399
Wolf, Robert Erich   2147, 2155
Wolf, William   1784
Wollenberg, H. H.   1573
Wollen, Peter   133, 134, 171, 172, 1961
Wong, Eugene Franklin   453
Woodward, Ian   1961
Wood, Alan   1862
Wood, Leslie   1596
Wood, Michael   575, 580
Wood, Robin   365, 367, 399, 484, 603, 798, 1320, 1777, 1843, 1858, 1881, 2064,
  2128, 2168, 2188
Wood, Tom   799, 1972
Woolf, Virginia   514
Woollacott, Janet   422
Woolrich, Cornell   1311, 1978
Wordsworth, Christopher   76
Wray, Fay   1795
Wright, Basil   200, 216, 217, 1520, 1565, 1681, 1809, 1839, 1871, 1912, 1923,
  1924, 1926, 1934, 1936, 1937, 1938, 1946, 1949, 1993, 2012, 2018
Wright, Charles R.   543
Wright, Gene   400, 420
Wright, Richard   945, 1316
Wright, Will   175, 184, 197, 293
Wright, William   1096, 1230
Writers Guild of America, West, The   1144
Wurlitzer, Rudolph   1041
Wylie, Irwin   1047, 1049, 1054
Wyman, David S.   291
Wysotsky, Michael Z.   86

Y

Yablonsky, Lewis   1785
Yacowar, Maurice   1346, 1857, 2046, 2072
Yale French Studies   1815
Yanni, Nicholas   1771, 1800
Yearwood, Gladstone L.   949, 950
Yeats, William Butler   101
Yeck, Joanne   794
Yellin, David G.   1215
Yergin, Daniel   346
Yoakem, Lola Goelet   85
Youngblood, Denis J.   1653
Youngblood, Gene   144
Young, Christopher   1959

Young, Freddie 81
Young, Jordan R. 1451
Young, Philip 1231
Young, Vernon 161, 1326, 2188
Young, William C. 1547
Yule, Andrew 704
Yulsman, Jerry 91
Yurick, Sol 973

Z

Zanuck, Darryl F. 1500
Zavattini, Cesare 1884, 1885, 1924
Zaza, Tony 1530
Zeffirelli, Franco 2172
Zettl, Herbert 93, 107
Zierold, Norman 993, 1452, 1468, 1686
Zimmerman, Paul D. 1784
Zinman, David 421, 1328, 1577, 1954
Zito, Stephen F. 2037
Zola, Emile 1316, 2120
Zolotow, Maurice 799, 1081, 1973, 1987
Zornow, Edith 978, 983, 984
Zucker, Carole 1697
Zucker, Harvey Marc 422
Zucker, Joel Stewart 252, 2065
Zukor, Adolph 1505
Zweig, Stephen 1966, 1983

Book Titles Index

A

A NOUS LA LIBERTE/ENTR'ACTE: FILMS BY RENE CLAIR 1724, 1728
A-Z OF MOVIE DIRECTORS 1547
A-Z OF MOVIE-MAKING 91
ABANDONMENT OF THE JEWS: AMERICA AND THE HOLOCAUST, 1941-1945, THE 291
ABEL GANCE 1712, 1713, 1726, 1730
ABOUT JOHN FORD 1682
ABSTRACT FILM AND BEYOND 1717
ABSTRACTION IN AVANT-GARDE FILMS 1955
ACADEMIC AMERICAN ENCYCLOPEDIA 1049
ACADEMY AWARDS ILLUSTRATED: A COMPLETE HISTORY OF HOLLYWOOD'S ACADEMY AWARDS IN WORDS AND PICTURES 1170
ACADEMY AWARDS 1976: OSCAR ANNUAL 1170
ACADEMY AWARDS 1979: OSCAR ANNUAL 1164
ACADEMY AWARDS: A COMPLETE GUIDE FROM A TO Z, THE 1171
ACADEMY AWARDS: A PICTORIAL HISTORY, THE 1169
ACADEMY AWARDS: AN UNGAR REFERENCE INDEX 1173
ACADEMY LEADER 1174
ACADEMY PLAYERS DIRECTORY 1174, 1542
ACID TEST 158, 1023, 1296
ACOUSTIC MIRROR: THE FEMALE VOICE IN PSYCHOANALYSIS AND CINEMA, THE 519
ACROSS THE RIVER AND INTO THE TREES 1274
ACTING IN THE CINEMA 1448
ACTION! CAMERA! SUPER 8 CASSETTE FILM MAKING FOR BEGINNERS 87
ACTOR'S BOOK OF MOVIE MONOLOGUES, THE 1544
ACTOR'S LIFE: JOURNALS 1956-1976, THE 2052
ACTOR: THE LIFE AND TIMES OF PAUL MUNI 1785
ADDITIONAL DIALOGUE: LETTERS OF DALTON TRUMBO, 1942-1962 1039, 1063, 1067, 1083, 1084, 1100, 1282
ADMIRABLE CRICHTON, THE 1703
ADVENTURES IN THE SCREEN TRADE: A PERSONAL VIEW OF HOLLYWOOD AND SCREENWRITING 1150
ADVENTURES OF ANTOINE DOINEL: FOUR SCREENPLAYS, THE 2148
ADVENTURES WITH D. W. GRIFFITH 1372
ADVENTURE, MYSTERY, AND ROMANCE 182, 716
ADVENTUROUS FILM MAKING 71
ADVISE AND CONSENT 2067
AENEID, THE 1153
AESTHETIC OF JEAN COCTEAU, THE 1818
AFRICA AND AFRICANS 918
AFRICA ON FILM: MYTH AND REALITY 918, 919
AFRO-AMERICAN CINEMATIC EXPERIENCE: AN ANNOTATED BIBLIOGRAPHY & FILMOGRAPHY, THE 931
AFTER MANY A SUMMER DIES THE SWAN 1158
AFTER THE FALL 1261
AGAINST INTERPRETATION 1298
AGAINST INTERPRETATION AND OTHER ESSAYS 144
AGE D'OR, L'/UN CHIEN ANDALOU: FILMS BY LUIS BUNUEL 1722
AGE OF THE AMERICAN NOVEL: THE FILM AESTHETIC OF FICTION BETWEEN THE TWO WARS, THE 1104, 1152
AGE OF THE DREAM PALACE: CINEMA AND SOCIETY 1930-1939, THE 540

AGEE ON FILM, VOLUME ONE: REVIEWS AND COMMENTS 145, 1014, 1021,
  1022, 1296, 1322, 1353, 1354, 1357, 1433
AGEE ON FILM, VOLUME TWO 145
AGES OF GIELGUD: AN ACTOR AT EIGHTY, THE 1842
AGGRESSION: A SOCIAL PSYCHOLOGICAL ANALYSIS 749
AH, WILDERNESS 1341
AIR FORCE 360
AKIRA KUROSAWA: A GUIDE TO REFERENCES AND RESOURCES 2019, 2027
AL JOLSON: YOU AIN'T HEARD NOTHIN' YET 827, 1778
ALAIN RESNAIS 324, 2094, 2095, 2112, 2114, 2117, 2137, 2138
ALAIN RESNAIS, OR THE THEME OF TIME 324, 2139
ALAIN ROBBE-GRILLET: THE BODY OF THE TEXT 2113, 2139
ALBUM OF GREAT SCIENCE FICTION FILMS, AN 413
ALBUM OF GREAT SCIENCE FICTION FILMS, Rev. ed., AN 1946, 2035
ALBUM OF MODERN HORROR FILMS, AN 393, 791, 976, 2035
ALEC GUINNESS 1941
ALEXANDER DOVZHENKO: THE POET AS FILMMAKER--SELECTED
  WRITINGS 1654, 1665
ALEXANDER KORDA 1859
ALEXANDER KORDA: THE MAN WHO COULD WORK MIRACLES 1858
ALFRED HITCHCOCK ALBUM, THE 1845
ALFRED HITCHCOCK AND THE BRITISH CINEMA 1851
ALFRED HITCHCOCK PRESENTS: AN ILLUSTRATED GUIDE TO THE TEN-YEAR
  CAREER OF THE MASTER OF SUSPENSE 1849
ALFRED HITCHCOCK'S "PSYCHO" 2053
ALICE DOESN'T: FEMINISM, SEMIOTICS, CINEMA 467, 481, 492, 493, 494, 496,
  532
ALICE IN WONDERLAND 1031
ALIENS IN THE HOME: THE CHILD IN HORROR FICTION 389
ALL ABOUT CINEMA 87
ALL ABOUT EVE 1272
ALL GOD'S CHILLUN GOT WINGS 862
ALL IN THE FAMILY: A CRITICAL APPRAISAL 835
ALL MY SONS 1260
ALL MY YESTERDAYS: AN AUTOBIOGRAPHY 799, 1091, 1786
ALL OUR YESTERDAYS: 90 YEARS OF BRITISH CINEMA 1566, 1567, 1935
ALL QUIET ON THE WESTERN FRONT 1805
ALL TALKING! ALL SINGING! ALL DANCING! A PICTORIAL HISTORY OF THE
  MOVIE MUSICAL 407
ALL THE KING'S MEN 1012, 1029
ALL THE STARS IN HEAVEN: LOUIS B. MAYER'S M-G-M 226, 1479
ALL-IN-ONE MOVIE BOOK 74
ALLAN DWAN: THE LAST PIONEER 1401
ALLEGORIES OF CINEMA: AMERICAN FILM IN THE SIXTIES 2033
ALMOS' A MAN 1316
ALONE WITH ME: A NEW AUTOBIOGRAPHY 885, 950
AMATEUR FILMMAKER'S HANDBOOK OF SOUND SYNC & SCORING 86
AMAZING HERSCHELL GORDON LEWIS AND HIS WORLD OF EXPLOITATION
  FILMS, THE 392
AMAZING 3-D 655, 699
AMBIGUOUS IMAGE: NARRATIVE STYLE IN MODERN EUROPEAN CINEMA,
  THE 113
AMBOY DUKES, THE 986
AMERICA AS A CIVILIZATION 1045
AMERICA AS AMERICANS SEE IT 1105
AMERICA AT THE MOVIES 487, 488, 622, 732, 734, 784, 1057
AMERICA IN THE DARK: HOLLYWOOD AND THE GIFT OF UNREALITY 1160
AMERICA IN THE MOVIES: OR "SANTA MARIA, IT HAD SLIPPED MY
  MIND" 575, 580

AMERICA'S COMING OF AGE 1053
AMERICAN CINEMATOGRAPHER MANUAL. 5th ed. 80
AMERICAN CINEMA: DIRECTORS AND DIRECTIONS, 1929-1968, THE 132, 980,
1756
AMERICAN COLLEGE: A PSYCHOLOGICAL AND SOCIAL INTERPRETATION OF
THE HIGHER LEARNING, THE 1011
AMERICAN COMEDY, AN 1693
AMERICAN COWBOY: THE MYTH AND THE REALITY, THE 427
AMERICAN DIRECTORS 1548
AMERICAN DREAM OF SUCCESS: THE SEARCH FOR SELF IN THE TWENTIETH
CENTURY 1047
AMERICAN DREAMING: THE FILMS OF JOHN CASSAVETES AND THE AMERICAN
EXPERIENCE 2047
AMERICAN EXPERIENCE: APPROACHES TO THE STUDY OF THE UNITED
STATES 258
AMERICAN FAMILY LIFE FILMS 987
AMERICAN FILM CRITICISM: FROM THE BEGINNINGS TO "CITIZEN
KANE" 141, 1608
AMERICAN FILM DIRECTORS, THE 1551
AMERICAN FILM DIRECTORS: THE WORLD AS THEY SEE IT 1551
AMERICAN FILM DISTRIBUTION: THE CHANGING MARKETPLACE 608, 622,
623, 640, 644, 649, 658, 663, 665, 667, 690, 954, 959, 960, 1463
AMERICAN FILM EXHIBITION AND AN ANALYSIS OF THE MOTION PICTURE
INDUSTRY'S MARKET STRUCTURE, 1963-1980 621, 690
AMERICAN FILM GENRES, 2nd ed. 191
AMERICAN FILM GENRES: APPROACHES TO A CRITICAL THEORY OF POPULAR
FILM 178, 179, 190
AMERICAN FILM HERITAGE: IMPRESSIONS FROM THE AMERICAN FILM
INSTITUTE ARCHIVES, THE 1576, 1577
AMERICAN FILM INDUSTRY, Rev. ed., THE 607, 621, 625, 630, 632, 635, 639,
642, 653, 664, 676, 684, 710, 736, 1460
AMERICAN FILM INDUSTRY: A HISTORICAL DICTIONARY, THE 654, 655, 699,
881
AMERICAN FILM INSTITUTE CATALOG OF MOTION PICTURES PRODUCED IN
THE UNITED STATES: FEATURE FILMS 1921-30, THE 1538
AMERICAN FILM INSTITUTE GUIDE TO COLLEGE COURSES IN FILM AND
TELEVISION, THE 33, 43
AMERICAN FILM INSTITUTE SECOND SURVEY OF HIGHER EDUCATION,
THE 34
AMERICAN FILM MUSICAL, THE 400
AMERICAN FILM NOW: THE PEOPLE, THE POWER, THE MONEY, THE
MOVIES 662, 667, 1519
AMERICAN FILM STUDIOS: AN HISTORICAL ENCYCLOPEDIA 1466
AMERICAN GOSPEL OF SUCCESS: INDIVIDUALISM AND BEYOND, THE 1047,
1055
AMERICAN HISTORY/AMERICAN FILM: INTERPRETING THE HOLLYWOOD
IMAGE 221, 259, 270
AMERICAN HISTORY/AMERICAN FILM: INTERPRETING THE HOLLYWOOD
IMAGE, Expanded and Updated 270
AMERICAN HORRORS: ESSAYS ON THE MODERN HORROR FILM 399
AMERICAN IDEA OF SUCCESS, THE 1047, 1053
AMERICAN INTERNATIONAL PICTURES: A FILMOGRAPHY 699
AMERICAN JOURNEY WITH RICHARD REEVES 1144
AMERICAN MASS MEDIA: INDUSTRIES AND ISSUES 747
AMERICAN MOVIE GODDESS, THE 515
AMERICAN MOVIE INDUSTRY: THE BUSINESS OF MOTION PICTURES,
THE 607, 615, 647, 648, 656, 661, 676, 696, 735, 748, 1459, 1462
AMERICAN MOVIES REFERENCE BOOK: THE SOUND ERA, THE 1753

AMERICAN MOVIE, THE 1576
AMERICAN MUSICAL, THE 408
AMERICAN MYTH OF SUCCESS: FROM HORATIO ALGER TO NORMAN VINCENT PEALE, THE 1047
AMERICAN NEWSFILM 1914-1919: THE UNDEREXPOSED WAR 269
AMERICAN NEWSREEL, 1911-1967, THE 208, 217, 224, 254, 283, 284, 298, 299
AMERICAN NIGHTMARE: ESSAYS ON THE HORROR FILM 399
AMERICAN NOVEL AND ITS TRADITION, THE 178
AMERICAN ODYSSEY: ELIA KAZAN AND AMERICAN CULTURE, AN 1095, 1262, 1293
AMERICAN PICTURE PALACES: THE ARCHITECTURE OF FANTASY 1506
AMERICAN SHORT STORY, THE 1316
AMERICAN SILENT FILM 1409, 1519, 1613
AMERICAN SKEPTIC: ROBERT ALTMAN'S GENRE-COMMENTARY FILMS 785, 1175
AMERICAN THEATRICAL ARTS: GUIDE TO MANUSCRIPTS AND SPECIAL COLLECTIONS IN THE UNITED STATES AND CANADA 1547
AMERICAN THEATRICAL FILM, THE 1338
AMERICAN VAUDEVILLE AS RITUAL 718
AMERICAN VEIN: DIRECTORS AND DIRECTIONS IN TELEVISION, THE 653
AMERICAN VISION: THE FILMS OF FRANK CAPRA 1763
AMERICAN WEST FROM FICTION (1823-1976) INTO FILM (1909-1986), THE 428
AMERICAN WEST ON FILM: MYTH AND REALITY, THE 430
AN AFFAIR TO REMEMBER 1774
ANAGRAM OF IDEAS ON ART, FORM AND FILM, AN 1955
ANALYSIS AND CONCLUSIONS OF THE WASHINGTON TASK FORCE ON THE MOTION PICTURE INDUSTRY 610
ANALYSIS OF MOTION PICTURES ABOUT WAR RELEASED BY THE AMERICAN FILM INDUSTRY, 1939-1970, AN 200, 231, 328, 350
ANALYSIS OF THE FINANCIAL PLANS OF THE MOTION PICTURE INDUSTRY FOR THE PERIOD 1929 to 1962, AN 607, 628, 634, 646, 648
ANALYZING FILMS: A PRACTICAL GUIDE 67
ANATOMY OF CRITICISM: FOUR ESSAYS 177, 1153
ANATOMY OF FILM 104
ANATOMY OF LOCAL RADIO-TV COPY, 4th ed. 92
ANCIENT WORLD IN THE CINEMA, THE 383
AND THE ENVELOPE, PLEASE: A QUIZ BOOK ABOUT THE ACADEMY AWARDS 1163
AND THE WINNER IS . . . THE HISTORY AND POLITICS OF THE OSCAR AWARDS 1165
AND THE WINNER IS . . . THE HISTORY AND POLITICS OF THE OSCAR AWARDS 680, 791, 969
AND THEN THERE WERE NONE 1197
ANDRE BAZIN 167, 1996, 1997
ANDY WARHOL DIARIES, THE 2068
ANDY WARHOL'S ART AND FILMS 2069
ANGELA LANSBURY: A BIOGRAPHY 1917
ANGER AND BEYOND 452, 540
ANIMAL FARM 78
ANIMAL LOCOMOTION 1581, 1598
ANIMALS IN MOTION 1581, 1597
ANIMATED FILM, THE 78
ANIMATED FILM: CONCEPTS, METHODS, USES 78
ANIMATED RAGGEDY ANN & ANDY: AN INTIMATE LOOK AT THE ART OF ANIMATION--ITS HISTORY, TECHNIQUES 76
ANIMATING FILMS WITHOUT A CAMERA 87
ANIMATION BOOK: A COMPLETE GUIDE TO ANIMATED FILMMAKING--FROM FLIP-BOOKS TO SOUND CARTOONS 77
ANIMATION IN THE CINEMA 78

ANIMATION STAND, THE 78
ANIMATION: A REFERENCE GUIDE 77
ANIMATOR'S WORKBOOK, THE 79
ANNA NEAGLE SAYS "THERE'S ALWAYS A TOMORROW": AN
  AUTOBIOGRAPHY 1862
ANNE FRANK: THE DIARY OF A YOUNG GIRL 849
ANNIE 2060
ANNIE GET YOUR GUN 1264
ANNOTATED DRACULA, THE 398
ANNUAL OBITUARY 1980, THE 1545
ANSCO GUIDE TO PICTURE FUN MADE EASY, THE 71
ANTHONY MANN 1964
ANTHROPOLOGY-REALITY-CINEMA: THE FILMS OF JEAN ROUCH. 2143
ANTI-COMMUNIST BLACKLIST IN THE HOLLYWOOD MOTION PICTURE
  INDUSTRY, THE 1068, 1084
ANTITRUST IN THE MOTION PICTURE INDUSTRY: ECONOMIC AND LEGAL
  ANALYSIS 607, 623, 634, 641, 675, 687, 742
ANTONIONI 1881
ANTONIONI OR, THE SURFACE OF THE WORLD 1881
ANTONIONI'S VISUAL LANGUAGE 1882
ANTONIONI, BERGMAN, RESNAIS 1882
ANTONIONI: A MONOGRAPH 1882
APOSTLES OF THE SELF-MADE MAN 1047, 1049, 1051
APPOINTMENT IN SAMARRA 1274
APPRENTICESHIP OF DUDDY KRAVITZ 1032
APPROACHES TO FILM AS AN ART FORM: A HANDBOOK FOR COLLEGE
  TEACHERS 740
APU TRILOGY, THE 2168
ARCHAEOLOGY OF THE CINEMA 1581, 1589
ARCHETYPES IN JAPANESE FILMS: THE SOCIOPOLITICAL AND RELIGIOUS
  SIGNIFICANCE OF THE PRINCIPAL HEROES AND HEROINES 1743
ARE WE MOVIE MADE? 732, 778
ARE YOU NOW OR HAVE YOU EVER BEEN 1178
ARE YOU NOW OR HAVE YOU EVER BEEN, AND OTHER PLAYS 1067, 1075,
  1080, 1091, 1178
ARENA: THE HISTORY OF THE FEDERAL THEATRE 1077
ARGENTINE CINEMA 2157
AROUND CINEMAS 1320, 1327, 1329, 1330, 1357
AROUND THE WORLD IN EIGHTY DAYS 1029
ARRANGEMENT, THE 1261
ART AND ANIMATION: THE STORY OF HALAS & BATCHELOR ANIMATION
  STUDIO 1940/1980 78
ART AND ILLUSION 540, 603
ART AND PRUDENCE: A STUDY IN PRACTICAL PHILOSOPHY 732, 955
ART AND VISUAL PERCEPTION: A PSYCHOLOGY OF THE CREATIVE EYE 166
ART IN CINEMA: A SYMPOSIUM ON THE AVANT-GARDE FILM 1955
ART IN MOVEMENT: NEW DIRECTIONS IN ANIMATION 77
ART OF ALFRED HITCHCOCK: FIFTY YEARS OF HIS MOTION PICTURES,
  THE 1852, 1978
ART OF F. SCOTT FITZGERALD, THE 1115, 1128
ART OF READING, THE 447
ART OF THE AMERICAN FILM 1900-1971, THE 1519
ART OF THE CINEMA, THE 1815
ART OF THE FILM, THE 66, 583
ART OF THE MOTION PICTURE, THE 101
ART OF THE MOVING PICTURE, THE 123, 124, 168, 1033, 1389
ART OF WALT DISNEY, THE 1768

ART OF WALT DISNEY: FROM MICKEY MOUSE TO THE MAGIC KINGDOM, THE 1768
ART OF WATCHING FILMS, 2nd ed., THE 102
ART OF WATCHING MOVIES, 2nd ed. THE 62
ART OF W. C. FIELDS, THE 1770
ARTHUR PENN 1320, 2064
ARTHUR PENN: A GUIDE TO REFERENCES AND RESOURCES 2065
ARTIFICIALLY ARRANGED SCENES: THE FILMS OF GEORGES MELIES 1604, 1616
AS EVER, SCOTT FITZ--: LETTERS BETWEEN F. SCOTT FITZGERALD AND HIS LITERARY AGENT HAROLD OBER 1919-1940 1119
AS I AM: AN AUTOBIOGRAPHY 2059
AS TIME GOES BY: MEMOIRS OF A WRITER 1067, 1262
ASC TREASURY OF VISUAL EFFECTS, THE 80
ASPECTS OF AMERICAN FILM HISTORY PRIOR TO 1920 1383
AT THE TELEPHONE 1380
ATROCITY PROPAGANDA 211
ATTITUDE AS A DETERMINANT OF PERCEPTION IN THE MASS MEDIA OF COMMUNICATION: REACTIONS TO THE MOTION PICTURE "HOME" 882
AUDIO CONTROL HANDBOOK: FOR RADIO AND TELEVISION BROADCASTING 92
AUDIO IN MEDIA 86
AUDREY HEPBURN 1961
AUSTRALIAN CINEMA 2157
AUSTRALIAN CINEMA, THE 2157
AUSTRALIAN CINEMA: INDUSTRY, NARRATIVE AND MEANING 2158
AUSTRALIAN CINEMA: THE FIRST EIGHTY YEARS 2158
AUSTRALIAN FILM 1900-1977: A GUIDE TO FEATURE FILM PRODUCTION 2157
AUSTRALIAN MOVIES TO THE WORLD: THE INTERNATIONAL SUCCESS OF AUSTRALIAN FILMS SINCE 1970 2158
AUSTRALIAN SILENT FILMS: A PICTORIAL HISTORY, 1896-1929 1594
AUTHORS ON FILM 1309
AUTHORSHIP AND NARRATIVE IN THE CINEMA: ISSUES IN CONTEMPORARY AESTHETICS AND CRITICISM 117
AUTOBIOGRAPHY AND SEX LIFE OF ANDY WARHOL, THE 2069
AUTOBIOGRAPHY OF CECIL B. DEMILLE, THE 1680
AUTONOMOUS IMAGE: CINEMATIC NARRATION AND HUMANISM, THE 117
AVIATION IN THE CINEMA 380
AVVENTURA, L'(THE ADVENTURE) 2169
AWAKE IN THE DARK: AN ANTHOLOGY OF AMERICAN FILM CRITICISM, 1915 TO THE PRESENT 139

B

B DIRECTORS: A BIOGRAPHICAL DIRECTORY, THE 1548
B MOVIES 651
BABY DOLL: AN AUTOBIOGRAPHY. Rev. and updated edition 1957
BAD AT THE BIJOU 429
BAD GUYS: A PICTORIAL HISTORY OF THE MOVIE VILLAIN, THE 263, 385
BADGE OF EVIL 2069
BALKAN CINEMA: EVOLUTION AFTER THE REVOLUTION 2158
BAND OF ANGELS 884
BANK CONTROL OF LARGE CORPORATIONS IN THE UNITED STATES 634
BANNED FILMS: MOVIES, CENSORS, AND THE FIRST AMENDMENT 963, 2037
BANNED FILMS: MOVIES, CENSORS, AND THE FIRST AMMENDMENT 2037
BARBARA STANWYCK 799, 1786
BARBARA STANWYCK: A BIOGRAPHY 799
BARBAROUS COAST, THE 1041

BARDOT DENEUVE FONDA. 2050
BAREFOOT IN THE PARK 2060
BARREN GROUND 914
BARRY LYNDON 1312
BARRYMORES, THE 1760
BARRYMORES: THE ROYAL FAMILY IN HOLLYWOOD, THE 1760
BARTLEBY: A STORY OF WALL STREET 1312
BASIC ANIMATION STAND TECHNIQUES 78
BASIC BOOKS IN THE MASS MEDIA: AN ANNOTATED SELECT BOOKLIST 1523
BASIC FILM-MAKING 73
BASIC MOTION PICTURE TECHNOLOGY 73
BASIL RATHBONE: HIS LIFE AND HIS FILMS 1863
BASIS OF CRITICISM IN THE ARTS, THE 38
BATTLE OF ANGELS 1345
BATTLE OF BRITAIN: THE MAKING OF A FILM, THE 1319
BATTLESHIP POTEMKIN, THE 1659
BEAUTIFUL AND THE DAMNED, THE 1110, 1111, 1113, 1122
BEAUTY AND THE BEAST 2006
BEAUTY AND THE BEAST: DIARY OF A FILM 2005, 2009
BEAUTY AND THE BEAST: SCENARIO AND DIALOGS BY JEAN COCTEAU 2005
BEFORE HOLLYWOOD: TURN-OF-THE-CENTURY AMERICAN FILM 1583, 1587
BEFORE MICKEY: THE ANIMATED FILM 1898-1928 1623
BEFORE MY EYES: FILM CRITICISM AND COMMENT 152
BEGGARS ARE COMING, THE 1041
BEGINNINGS OF CINEMA IN ENGLAND, THE 1610
BEGINNINGS OF THE BIOGRAPH: THE STORY OF THE INVENTION OF THE
  MUTOSCOPE 1592
BEHIND THE CAMERA 89
BEHIND THE CAMERA: THE CINEMATOGRAPHER'S ART 80
BEHIND THE SCENES OF OTTO PREMINGER: AN UNAUTHORIZED
  BIOGRAPHY 643, 1966
BEHIND THE SCENES: THEATER AND FILM INTERVIEWS FROM "THE
  TRANSATLANTIC REVIEW" 1552
BEHIND THE SCREEN 1472
BEHIND THE SCREEN: THE HISTORY AND TECHNIQUES OF THE MOTION
  PICTURE 1577
BEHIND THE SPANISH LENS: SPANISH CINEMA UNDER FASCISM AND
  DEMOCRACY 235
BEHOLD THE MIGHTY WURLITZER: THE HISTORY OF THE THEATRE PIPE
  ORGAN 406
BELAFONTE: AN UNAUTHORIZED BIOGRAPHY 885, 950
BELOVED INFIDEL: THE EDUCATION OF A WOMAN 1032, 1109, 1120, 1121,
  1123, 1127, 1131, 1132, 1247
BEN HUR 1029
BEOWULF 1153
BERGMAN ON BERGMAN: INTERVIEWS WITH BERGMAN. 2185
BERNARD HERRMANN: FILM MUSIC AND NARRATIVE 402
BERNICE BOBS HER HAIR 1316
BERTOLT BRECHT IN AMERICA 1196
BERTOLT BRECHT: "CAHIERS DU CINEMA" AND CONTEMPORARY FILM
  THEORY 474, 477, 1997, 1998, 2102, 2103, 2111, 2125
BERTOLUCCI'S DREAM LOOM: A PSYCHOANALYTIC STUDY OF CINEMA 2170
BEST ACTOR: ACADEMY AWARDS 1170
BEST ACTRESS: ACADEMY AWARDS 1170
BEST AMERICAN SCREENPLAYS: FIRST SERIES--COMPLETE
  SCREENPLAYS 1160
BEST FILM PLAYS, 1943-1944 370, 1014, 1021
BEST FILM PLAYS, 1945 799, 1210

BEST MOVING PICTURES OF 1922-23, THE 1060
BEST OF M-G-M: THE GOLDEN YEARS (1928-59) 1484
BEST OF ROB WAGNER'S SCRIPT, THE 1758
BEST PICTURE: ACADEMY AWARDS 1170
BEST REMAINING SEATS; THE STORY OF THE GOLDEN AGE OF THE MOVIE,
  THE 1506
BEST SUPPORTING ACTOR, BEST SUPPORTING ACTRESS: ACADEMY
  AWARDS 1170
BETTE DAVIS 801, 1766
BETTE DAVIS: A BIOGRAPHY 1766
BETTE DAVIS: A CELEBRATION 1766
BETTE DAVIS: HER FILM TO STAGE CAREER 801
BETTER TIMES THAN THESE 363
BETTE: THE LIFE OF BETTE DAVIS 801, 1766
BETWEEN ACTION AND CUT: FIVE AMERICAN DIRECTORS 1554
BETWEEN FLOPS: A BIOGRAPHY OF PRESTON STURGES 1918
BETWEEN PICTURES 1041
BETWEEN THE SCREEN: THE HISTORY AND TECHNIQUES OF THE
  MOVIES 1359
BEYOND FORMULA: AMERICAN FILM GENRES 197
BIBLE, THE 382
BIBLIOGRAPHY: FIAF MEMBERS PUBLICATIONS 1522
BICYCLE THIEF: A FILM BY VITTORIO DE SICA, THE 1004, 1928
BIG BAD WOLVES: MASCULINITY IN THE AMERICAN FILM 805, 808
BIG SCREEN, LITTLE SCREEN 155
BIG SLEEP, THE 1978
BIG U: UNIVERSAL IN THE SILENT DAYS 1475
BIJOU 1041
BILLY BITZER: HIS STORY 1362, 1371
BILLY BUDD 1018
BILLY THE KID: A BIO-BIBLIOGRAPHY 434
BILLY WILDER 799, 1291, 1971, 1972
BILLY WILDER IN HOLLYWOOD 799, 1973, 1987
BING CROSBY 1350
BIOGRAPHY BULLETINS: 1896-1908 1593
BIOGRAPHY BULLETINS: 1908-1912 1370
BIRTH OF A NATION STORY, THE 1369
BIRTH OF A NATION, THE 1367
BIRTH OF THE TALKIES: FROM EDISON TO JOLSON, THE 1753
BITS OF PARADISE: 21 UNCOLLECTED STORIES BY F. SCOTT AND ZELDA
  FITZGERALD 1116, 1118
BLACK CINEMA AESTHETICS: ISSUES IN INDEPENDENT BLACK
  FILMMAKING 949, 950
BLACK FILM AS GENRE 860, 861, 923, 924, 952, 953
BLACK FILM STARS 932
BLACK FILMS AND FILM-MAKERS: A COMPREHENSIVE ANTHOLOGY FROM
  STEREOTYPE TO SUPERHERO 896, 898, 940
BLACK HOLLYWOOD: THE NEGRO IN MOTION PICTURES 872, 882, 940
BLACK MAGIC: A PICTORIAL HISTORY OF THE NEGRO IN AMERICAN
  ENTERTAINMENT 860
BLACK MAN ON FILM: RACIAL STEREOTYPING, THE 892, 915, 916
BLACK MILITARY EXPERIENCE IN THE AMERICAN WEST, THE 893
BLACK VALENTINO: THE STAGE AND SCREEN CAREER OF LORENZO TUCKER,
  THE 931
BLACK WEST, THE 893
BLACKFACE TO BLACKLIST: AL JOLSON, LARRY PARKS, AND "THE JOLSON
  STORY" 1189
BLACKFRAMES: CRITICAL PERSPECTIVES ON BLACK INDEPENDENT
  CINEMA 901

BLACKING UP: THE MINSTREL TRADITION IN NINETEENTH-CENTURY
  AMERICA 862
BLACKMAIL 1864
BLACKS IN AMERICAN FILMS: TODAY AND YESTERDAY 936, 1341
BLACKS IN AMERICAN MOVIES: A SELECTED BIBLIOGRAPHY 946
BLACKS IN BLACK AND WHITE: A SOURCE BOOK ON BLACK FILMS 860, 868,
  870, 946, 947, 948
BLACKS IN FILMS: A SURVEY OF RACIAL THEMES AND IMAGES IN THE
  AMERICAN FILM 859, 860, 861, 878, 895, 943, 944, 945, 946
BLEAK HOUSE 1153
BLOOD AND SAND 1707
BLOW-UP (1966) 1311, 2169
BLUE ANGEL: A FILM BY JOSEF VON STERNBERG, THE 1830
BLUE ANGEL: THE NOVEL AND THE FILM, THE 1830
BLUE HOTEL, THE 1316
BLUE MOVIE 1041
BLUE MOVIE: PORNOGRAPHY AND THE PORNOGRAPHERS--AN INTIMATE LOOK
  AT THE TWO-BILLION-DOLLAR FANTASY INDUSTRY 2037
BLUE PAGES 1041
BLUE SKIES AND SILVER LININGS: ASPECTS OF THE HOLLYWOOD
  MUSICAL 401
BLUFF YOUR WAY IN THE CINEMA 55
BODY AND SOUL: THE STORY OF JOHN GARFIELD 1093
BOGART 1078, 1761
BOGART AND BACALL: A LOVE STORY 1078, 1762
BOGEY'S BABY 798
BOGEY: THE FILMS OF HUMPHREY BOGART 1078, 1762
BOGEY: THE GOOD-BAD GUY 1078, 1761
BOGIE: THE BIOGRAPHY OF HUMPHREY BOGART 1078, 1761
BOND AND BEYOND: THE POLITICAL CAREER OF A POPULAR HERO 422
BONNIE AND CLYDE BOOK, THE 2064
BOOGIE WOOGIE AND BOOKER T. 906
BOOK OF DANIEL, THE 1032
BOOK OF MOVIE LISTS, THE 1527
BOOK OF TV LISTS, THE 1527
BOOKLESS CURRICULUM, A 44
BORIS KARLOFF AND HIS FILMS 1779
BORN TO LOSE: THE GANGSTER FILM IN AMERICA 386
BOSLEY CROWTHER: SOCIAL CRITIC OF FILM 1940-1967 147
BOUND AND GAGGED: THE STORY OF THE SILENT SERIALS 1456
BOUND FOR EAST CARDIFF 1350
BOX-OFFICE CLOWNS: BOB HOPE, JERRY LEWIS, MEL BROOKS, WOODY
  ALLEN, THE 833, 1294, 1954
BOYS, MOVIES AND CITY STREETS 729
BOYS: THE CINEMATIC WORLD OF LAUREL AND HARDY, THE 1692
BRANDO 1958
BRANDO FOR BREAKFAST 1957
BRAVO MAURICE! 1764
BRAZILIAN CINEMA 2159
BREAD AND A STONE 1177
BREAKING THROUGH, SELLING OUT, DROPPING DEAD, AND OTHER NOTES
  ON FILM MAKING 71
BREATHLESS: JEAN-LUC GODARD, DIRECTOR 2129
BRECHT BEFORE THE UN-AMERICAN ACTIVITIES COMMITTEE 1091
BRICK FOXHOLE, THE 375, 849
BRIEF EINER UNBEKANNTEN (LETTER FROM AN UNKNOWN WOMAN) 1983
BRIGHT SIDE OF BILLY WILDER, PRIMARILY, THE 799, 1972

BRITAIN CAN TAKE IT: THE BRITISH CINEMA IN THE SECOND WORLD
  WAR 1938
BRITISH BOARD OF CENSORS: FILM CENSORSHIP IN BRITAIN, 1896-1950,
  THE 967
BRITISH CINEMA AND SOCIETY, 1930-1970 540
BRITISH CINEMA HISTORY 1568, 1935
BRITISH CINEMA NOW 2159
BRITISH CINEMA: AN ILLUSTRATED GUIDE 1570
BRITISH FILM CATALOGUE 1895-1985: A REFERENCE GUIDE, THE 1611
BRITISH FILM COLLECTION 1896-1984: A HISTORY OF THE BRITISH CINEMA
  IN PICTURES, THE 1571
BRITISH LABOUR MOVEMENT AND FILM, 1918-1939, THE 239
BRITISH PROPAGANDA AT HOME AND IN THE UNITED STATES FROM 1914 to
  1917 211
BRITISH PROPAGANDA IN THE FIRST WORLD WAR 212
BROADCAST COPYWRITING, 3rd ed. 74
BROADWAY AND HOLLYWOOD: A HISTORY OF ECONOMIC INTERACTION 656,
  1335, 1336, 1951
BROWN SUGAR: EIGHTY YEARS OF AMERICA'S BLACK FEMALE
  SUPERSTARS 920
BRUISED FRUIT 1041
BUD: THE BRANDO I KNEW--THE UNTOLD STORY OF BRANDO'S PRIVATE
  LIFE 1958
BUFFALO SOLDIERS: A NARRATIVE OF THE NEGRO CAVALRY IN THE WEST,
  THE 893
BULGARIAN CINEMA, THE 2013
BURT LANCASTER 643
BURT LANCASTER: A PICTORIAL TREASURY OF HIS FILMS 643
BURTON 1940
BUSTER KEATON 1688, 1689
BUSTER KEATON AND THE DYNAMICS OF VISUAL WIT 1689
BUSTER KEATON'S "THE GENERAL" 1687
BUT FOR WHOM MR. CHARLIE 1261
BUTLEY 990
BUTTERFIELD 8 1274
BY A STROKE OF LUCK! AN AUTOBIOGRAPHY 1124, 1278
BY MYSELF 798, 832, 1078
BY THE EDITORS OF CONSUMER GUIDE: RATING THE MOVIE STARS FOR HOME
  VIDEO, TV, CABLE 1443

C

CABINET OF DR. CALIGARI, THE 1635
CADS AND CAVALIERS: THE GENTLEMEN ADVENTURERS OF THE
  SCREEN 1451
CAESAR'S THINGS 1110
CAGNEY 1078, 1762
CAGNEY BY CAGNEY 1078, 1762
CAGNEY: A BIOGRAPHY 1078
CAGNEY: THE ACTOR AS AUTEUR 1078, 1762
CAGNEY: THE AUTHORIZED BIOGRAPHY 1078
CAGNEY: THE STORY OF HIS FILM CAREER 1078
CAHIERS DU CINEMA 474, 1997
CAHIERS DU CINEMA: THE 1950s--NEO-REALISM, HOLLYWOOD, NEW
  WAVE 474, 1996, 1997, 1999, 2002
CAHIERS DU CINEMA: 1960-1968--NEW WAVE, NEW CINEMA, REEVALUATING
  HOLLYWOOD 474, 1998, 1999, 2035, 2096, 2103, 2123
CALIFORNIA LEGISLATOR 1079

CALIGARI'S CHILDREN: THE FILM AS TALE OF TERROR   397
CAME THE DAWN: MEMORIES OF A FILM PIONEER   1611
CAMERA AND I, THE   314, 319
CAMERA OBSCURA: A CHRONICLE, THE   1614
CAMERA POLITICA: THE POLITICS AND IDEOLOGY OF CONTEMPORARY
   HOLLYWOOD FILM   569
CAMERAS WEST   430, 1946
CAMILLE   1012
CANDIDE, AUNT POLLY'S STORY OF MANKIND   1278
CAPITAL AND CULTURE: GERMAN CINEMA 1933-45   241
CAPOTE: A BIOGRAPHY   1196
CAPTAINS COURAGEOUS   994
CAPTAINS OF CONSCIOUSNESS: ADVERTISING AND THE SOCIAL ROOTS OF
   THE CONSUMER CULTURE   1051
CARL THEODOR DREYER: FOUR SCREENPLAYS   1726
CARNAL KNOWLEDGE: A SCREENPLAY   2209
CAROLE LOMBARD   1781
CARTOON ANIMATION FOR EVERYONE   88
CARTOON MONICKERS: AN INSIGHT INTO THE ANIMATION INDUSTRY   76
CARY GRANT   1774
CARY GRANT: A CELEBRATION   569
CARY GRANT: A TOUCH OF ELEGANCE   1774
CARY GRANT: THE LIGHT TOUCH   1774
CARY GRANT: THE LONELY HEART   1774
CASEBOOK ON FILM, A   53
CAST OF KILLERS, A   1412
CAST OF THOUSANDS   1380
CAT ON A HOT TIN ROOF   1261, 1345
CATALOGING AND CLASSIFICATION OF CINEMA LITERATURE, THE   1544
CATALOGUE: SILENT FILMS   1611
CATCH-22   1312
CECIL BEATON: A BIOGRAPHY   1761
CECIL BEATON: MEMOIRS OF THE 40s   1760
CECIL BEATON: STAGE AND FILM DESIGNS   1761
CECIL B. DEMILLE   1680
CELEBRITY CIRCUS   609
CELEBRITY: THE MEDIA AS IMAGE MAKERS   566
CELLULOID AND SYMBOLS   45
CELLULOID CURRICULUM: HOW TO USE MOVIES IN THE CLASSROOM,
   THE   51
CELLULOID EGGHEAD: THE PORTRAYAL OF THE INTELLECTUAL IN THE
   AMERICAN FILM 1930-1976   1045
CELLULOID EGGHEAD: THE PORTRAYAL OF THE INTELLECTUAL IN THE
   AMERICAN FILM, 1930-1976   454
CELLULOID EMPIRE: A HISTORY OF THE AMERICAN MOVIE INDUSTRY,
   THE   662, 700, 701
CELLULOID MUSE: HOLLYWOOD DIRECTORS SPEAK, THE   609, 1550, 1753
CELLULOID ROCK: TWENTY YEARS OF MOVIE ROCK   405
CELLULOID SOUTH: HOLLYWOOD AND THE SOUTHERN MYTH, THE   440, 871,
   895, 907, 912
CELLULOID VAMPIRES: A HISTORY AND FILMOGRAPHY, 1897-1979   395
CENSORED: THE PRIVATE LIFE OF THE MOVIES   964
CENSORSHIP IN BRITAIN   225
CENSORSHIP OF THE MOVIES: THE SOCIAL AND POLITICAL CONTROL OF A
   MASS MEDIUM   225, 967
CENSORSHIP PAPERS: MOVIE CENSORSHIP LETTERS FROM THE HAYS OFFICE,
   1934-1948, THE   964
CENSORSHIP 1917   210

CENSORSHIP: FOR AND AGAINST 964
CENSOR, THE DRAMA AND THE FILM, THE 225
CERTAIN TENDENCY OF THE HOLLYWOOD CINEMA, 1930-1980, A 165, 2194
CHANDLERTOWN: THE LOS ANGELES OF PHILIP MARLOWE 1198
CHAPLIN 1421, 1423
CHAPLIN AND AMERICAN CULTURE: THE EVOLUTION OF A STAR
  IMAGE. 1423
CHAPLIN E LA CRITICIA 1422
CHAPLIN VS. CHAPLIN 1423, 1428
CHAPLIN'S FILMS 1419
CHAPLINANIA: A COMMENTARY ON CHARLIE CHAPLIN'S 81 MOVIES. VOLUME
  I--THE KEYSTONE FILMS 1420
CHAPLIN, THE MOVIES, & CHARLIE 1422
CHAPLIN: GENESIS OF A CLOWN 1409, 1414, 1415, 1427
CHAPLIN: HIS LIFE AND ART 1410, 1414, 1415, 1416, 1418, 1419, 1423, 1426
CHAPLIN: LAST OF THE CLOWNS 1428, 1431
CHAPLIN: THE MIRROR OF OPINION 1415, 1425
CHARACTER AND CULTURE 452
CHARACTER PEOPLE 1443
CHARLES CHAPLIN'S CITY LIGHTS: ITS PRODUCTION AND DIALECTICAL
  STRUCTURE 1424
CHARLES CHAPLIN: A GUIDE TO REFERENCES AND RESOURCES 1422
CHARLES LAUGHTON AND I 1860
CHARLES LAUGHTON: A DIFFICULT ACTOR 1860
CHARLES LAUGHTON: A PICTORIAL TREASURY OF HIS FILMS 1860
CHARLES LAUGHTON: AN INTIMATE BIOGRAPHY 1860
CHARLIE CHAN AT THE MOVIES: HISTORY, FILMOGRAPHY, AND
  CRITICISM 381
CHARLIE CHAPLIN 1415, 1423, 1425
CHARLIE CHAPLIN: A BIO-BIBLIOGRAPHY 1420
CHARLIE CHAPLIN: A BIOGRAPHY 1422
CHARLIE CHAPLIN: EARLY COMEDIES 1426
CHARLIE: THE IMPROBABLE LIFE AND TIMES OF CHARLES MACARTHUR 1265
CHARLTON HESTON 2052
CHARMED LIVES: A FAMILY ROMANCE 1859
CHESTNUTS IN HER LAP, 1936-46 1322, 1327
CHEVALIER: THE FILMS AND CAREER OF MAURICE CHEVALIER 1765
CHICANO CINEMA: RESEARCH, REVIEWS, AND RESOURCES 826
CHILD AND SOCIETY 726
CHILD AND YOUTH ACTORS: FILMOGRAPHIES OF THEIR ENTIRE CAREERS,
  1914-1985 983
CHILD OF PARADISE: MARCEL CARNE AND THE GOLDEN AGE OF FRENCH
  CINEMA 1909
CHILD OF THE CENTURY, A 1038, 1057, 1224
CHILD STARS, THE 993
CHILD STAR: AN AUTOBIOGRAPHY 1787
CHILDREN AND MOVIES 710, 727
CHILDREN AS FILM MAKERS 90
CHILDREN OF PARADISE: A FILM BY MARCEL CARNE 1909
CHILDREN OF STONE 1042
CHILDREN'S ATTENDANCE AT MOTION PICTURES 729
CHILDREN'S HOUR, THE 990
CHILDREN'S LIVE-ACTION MUSICAL FILMS: A CRITICAL SURVEY AND
  FILMOGRAPHY 404
CHILDREN'S NOVELS AND THE MOVIES 989
CHILDREN'S SLEEP 729
CHINESE CINEMA: CULTURE & POLITICS SINCE 1949 2163
CHINESE FILM: THE STATE OF THE ART IN THE PEOPLE'S REPUBLIC 2163
CHRISTMAS CAROL, A 1312

CHRYSANTHEMUM AND THE SWORD, PATTERNS IN JAPANESE CULTURE, THE 1894, 1898
CHURCH AND CINEMA: A WAY OF VIEWING FILM 55
CINEASTE INTERVIEWS ON THE ART AND POLITICS OF THE CINEMA, THE 609, 900
CINELITERACY 46
CINEMA 1565
CINEMA AND HISTORY 258, 261, 269
CINEMA AND HISTORY: BRITISH NEWSREELS AND THE SPANISH CIVIL WAR 253, 265, 298
CINEMA AND LANGUAGE 168
CINEMA AND SENTIMENT 1751
CINEMA AND SOCIETY: FRANCE AND GERMANY DURING THE TWENTIES 441
CINEMA AND TECHNOLOGY: IMAGE, SOUND, COLOUR 1563
CINEMA AND THE SCHOOL: A GUIDE TO 101 MAJOR AMERICAN FILMS 49
CINEMA AS ART, Rev. ed., THE 97, 98, 106
CINEMA AS ART, THE 100
CINEMA AS GRAPHIC ART (ON A THEORY OF REPRESENTATION IN THE CINEMA), THE 165, 208
CINEMA BEYOND THE DANUBE: THE CAMERA AND POLITICS 1652
CINEMA BOOKLIST 394, 1541
CINEMA BOREALIS: INGMAR BERGMAN AND THE SWEDISH ETHOS 2188
CINEMA DRAMA SCHEMA: EASTERN METAPHYSIC IN WESTERN ART 1335
CINEMA EAST: A CRITICAL STUDY OF MAJOR JAPANESE FILMS 2025
CINEMA ET HISTOIRE 269
CINEMA EYE CINEMA EAR: SOME KEY FILM-MAKERS OF THE SIXTIES 2170
CINEMA IN BRITAIN: AN ILLUSTRATED SURVEY 1568
CINEMA IN REVOLUTION: THE HEROIC ERA OF THE SOVIET FILM 1652
CINEMA IN THE ARAB COUNTRIES, THE 2178
CINEMA IN THE FEDERAL REPUBLIC OF GERMANY: THE NEW GERMAN FILM ORIGINS AND PRESENT SITUATION--A HANDBOOK 2165
CINEMA NOVO X 5: MASTERS OF CONTEMPORARY BRAZILIAN CINEMA 2158
CINEMA OF ADOLESCENE, THE 983
CINEMA OF ALAIN RESNAIS, THE 324, 2135
CINEMA OF ALFRED HITCHCOCK, THE 1843
CINEMA OF ANDRZEJ WAJDA, THE 2014, 2181
CINEMA OF APARTHEID: RACE AND CLASS IN SOUTH AFRICAN FILM, THE 2089
CINEMA OF CARL DREYER, THE 1629
CINEMA OF DAVID LEAN, THE 1860
CINEMA OF EDWARD G. ROBINSON, THE 799, 1091, 1785
CINEMA OF ERNST LUBITSCH, THE 1694, 1706
CINEMA OF FEDERICO FELLINI, THE 1931
CINEMA OF FRANCOIS TRUFFAUT, THE 2146
CINEMA OF FRITZ LANG, THE 1638, 1639
CINEMA OF HOWARD HAWKS, THE 1775
CINEMA OF JOHN FORD, THE 1683
CINEMA OF JOHN FRANKENHEIMER, THE 2051, 2052, 2077
CINEMA OF JOHN HUSTON, THE 322, 1087, 1917
CINEMA OF JOSEF VON STERNBERG, THE 1696
CINEMA OF JOSEPH LOSEY, THE 371, 1963
CINEMA OF LUIS BUNUEL, THE 1989
CINEMA OF MYSTERY 393
CINEMA OF MYSTERY AND FANTASY 387
CINEMA OF ORSON WELLES, THE 1791
CINEMA OF OTTO PREMINGER, THE 643, 1967
CINEMA OF OUSMANE SEMBENE: A PIONEER OF AFRICAN FILM, THE 919

CINEMA OF PARADOX: FRENCH FILMMAKING UNDER THE GERMAN OCCUPATION 247, 1903, 1905
CINEMA OF ROMAN POLANSKI, THE 2179, 2180
CINEMA OF SATYAJIT RAY, THE 2167
CINEMA OF STANLEY KUBRICK, THE 2056
CINEMA OF THE FANTASTIC 417
CINEMA ORGAN: A DESCRIPTION IN NON-TECHNICAL LANGUAGE OF A FASCINATATING INSTRUMENT AND HOW IT IS PLAYED, THE 83
CINEMA SEQUELS AND REMAKES, 1903-1987 420
CINEMA YESTERDAY AND TODAY 1724
CINEMA 1: THE MOVEMENT-IMAGE 162
CINEMA & SOCIETY: FRANCE AND GERMANY DURING THE TWENTIES 1631, 1718
CINEMATIC APPARATUS, THE 168
CINEMATIC IMAGINATION: WRITERS AND THE MOTION PICTURES, THE 1108, 1113, 1114, 1155
CINEMATIC VISION OF F. SCOTT FITZGERALD, THE 1216
CINEMATICS 165, 201
CINEMATOGRAPHY: A GUIDE FOR FILM MAKERS AND FILM TEACHERS 80
CINEMA, CENSORSHIP AND SEXUALITY, 1909-1925 509
CINEMA, POLITICS AND SOCIETY IN AMERICA 559
CINEMA, THE 473, 1563, 1939
CINEMA, THE MAGIC VEHICLE: A GUIDE TO ITS ACHIEVEMENTS 1527
CINEMA: A CRITICAL DICTIONARY--THE MAJOR FILM-MAKERS 1542
CIOCIARA, LA 2174
CITIZEN KANE BOOK: RAISING KANE, THE SHOOTING SCRIPT, BY HERMAN J. MANKIEWICZ AND ORSON WELLES, THE 149, 1063, 1101, 1142, 1793, 1807
CITIZEN WELLES: A BIOGRAPHY OF ORSON WELLES 1790
CITY OF ANGELS 1104
CITY OF GOD 1154
CITY OF NETS: A PORTRAIT OF HOLLYWOOD IN THE 1940'S 1234
CIVIL WAR ON THE SCREEN AND OTHER ESSAYS 210
CLAIR: FOUR SCREENPLAYS 2005
CLANDESTINE IN CHILE: THE ADVENTURES OF MIGUEL LITTIN. 2163
CLANSMAN, THE 700, 940, 1366, 1378, 1387
CLARA BOW: RUNNIN' WILD 1679
CLARK GABLE 1772
CLARK GABLE: A PERSONAL PORTRAIT 1772
CLASSIC AMERICAN NOVEL AND THE MOVIES, THE 1314, 1315
CLASSIC CINEMA: ESSAYS IN CRITICISM, THE 143
CLASSIC FILM SCRIPTS 1511
CLASSIC MOVIE MONSTERS 390
CLASSICAL HOLLYWOOD CINEMA: FILM STYLE & MODE OF PRODUCTION TO 1960, THE 57, 59, 60, 61, 63, 616, 1062, 1519
CLASSICS AND COMMERCIALS 1028, 1104
CLASSICS OF THE FILM 1592
CLASSICS OF THE FOREIGN FILM: A PICTORIAL TREASURY 1564
CLASSICS OF THE SILENT SCREEN: A PICTORIAL TREASURY 1609
CLAUDE CHABROL 2128
CLAUDE LELOUCH, FILM DIRECTOR 2135
CLAUDE LEVI-STRAUSS 177
CLAUDETTE COLBERT 1765
CLIFFORD ODETS: PLAYWRIGHT 1095
CLOCKWORK ORANGE, A 2055
CLOSE-UP: A CRITICAL PERSPECTIVE ON FILM 1641, 2176
CLOSE-UP: A CRITICAL PERSPECTIVE ON FILM. 141
CLOSE-UP: A MAGAZINE DEVOTED TO THE ART OF FILMS 1340
CLOSE-UP: THE CONTEMPORARY DIRECTOR 1758
CLOSE-UP: THE CONTRACT DIRECTOR 1758

CLOSE-UP: THE HOLLYWOOD DIRECTOR 1758
CLOSE-UP: 1927-1932 1062, 1754
CLOSELY WATCHED FILMS: THE CZECHOSLOVAK EXPERIENCE 2164
CLOSELY WATCHED TRAINS 994, 2164
CLOWN PRINCES AND COURT JESTERS: SOME GREAT COMICS OF THE SILENT
  SCREEN 1677
CLOZENTROPY: A TECHNIQUE FOR STUDYING AUDIENCE RESPONSE TO
  FILMS 164
COAT OF MANY COLOURS, A 1025
COCAINE FIENDS AND REEFER MADNESS: AN ILLUSTRATED HISTORY OF
  DRUGS IN THE MOVIES 988
COCTEAU ON THE FILM 1817
COCTEAU: A BIOGRAPHY 1819
COLETTE AT THE MOVIES: CRITICISM AND SCREENPLAYS 147
COLLECTED SCREENPLAYS OF BERNARD SHAW, THE 1344
COLLECTING FILM CLASSICS 1532
COLLECTING MOVIE MEMORABILIA 1524
COLLECTIVE BARGAINING IN THE MOTION PICTURE INDUSTRY 1068
COLLEGE OF ONE, A 1114, 1123, 1129
COMBAT FILMS 1945-1970 220, 231, 341, 350, 354
COMEDY WORLD OF STAN LAUREL, THE 1691
COMIC MIND: COMEDY AND THE MOVIES, THE 1678
COMING OF SOUND TO THE AMERICAN CINEMA: A HISTORY OF THE
  TRANSFORMATION OF AN INDUSTRY, THE 630, 632
COMMITTEE: THE EXTRAORDINARY CAREER OF THE HOUSE COMMITTEE ON
  UN-AMERICAN ACTIVITIES, THE 1077
COMMUNICATING ON FILM 45
COMMUNICATION MODELS FOR THE STUDY OF MASS COMMUNICATIONS 438,
  578, 746
COMMUNIST INFILTRATION IN THE UNITED STATES: ITS NATURE AND HOW
  TO COMBAT IT 1082
COMPANION TO THE MOVIES: FROM 1903 TO THE PRESENT DAY, A 192
COMPARATIVE STUDY OF SELECTED AMERICAN FILM CRITICS, 1958-1974,
  A 119, 137
COMPARATIVE STUDY OF THE CHANGES OF FIFTEEN FILM PLAYS ADAPTED
  FROM STAGE PLAYS, A 1336
COMPARISON OF EXHIBITION AND DISTRIBUTION PATTERNS IN THREE
  RECENT FEATURE MOTION PICTURES, A 488, 753
COMPETITIVE CINEMA, A 1939
COMPLEAT GUIDE TO FILM STUDY, THE 52
COMPLETE BOOK OF SCRIPTWRITING, THE 85
COMPLETE BOOK OF 8mm MOVIE MAKING, THE 91
COMPLETE FILMS OF EISENSTEIN: TOGETHER WITH AN UNPUBLISHED ESSAY
  BY EISENSTEIN, THE 1658, 1666
COMPLETE HANDBOOK OF VIDEOCASSETTE RECORDERS, THE 92
COMPLETE PHANTOM OF THE OPERA, THE 396
COMPLETE REFERENCE GUIDE TO WESTERNS OF THE SOUND ERA:
  SHOOT-EM-UPS, THE 424
COMPLETE TECHNIQUE OF MAKING FILMS, THE 90
COMPLETE "GREED" OF ERICH VON STROHEIM, THE 1018, 1700
COMPLETE "NIGHT OF THE LIVING DEAD" FILMBOOK, THE 397
COMPLETE "WEDDING MARCH" OF ERICH VON STROHEIM: A RECONSTRUCTION
  OF THE FILM, THE 1700
COMPOSING FOR THE FILMS 83
COMPOSITION OF TENDER IS THE NIGHT, THE 1119
COMPOUND CINEMA: THE FILM WRITINGS OF HARRY ALAN POTAMKIN,
  THE 155, 1033, 1340
COMPUTER ANIMATION 77

CONCEPTS IN FILM THEORY 119, 134, 135, 161, 442, 1105
CONCISE HISTORY OF THE CINEMA--VOLUME 1: BEFORE 1940, A 1560
CONCISE HISTORY OF THE CINEMA--VOLUME 2: SINCE 1940, A 1561
CONFESSIONS 1257
CONFESSIONS OF A CULTIST: ON THE CINEMA, 1955/1969 155, 994, 1023,
1321, 1327, 1328, 1349, 1926, 2086
CONFESSIONS OF A HOLLYWOOD COLUMNIST 1057
CONFESSIONS OF AN ACTOR 1760
CONRAD VEIDT: FROM "CALIGARI" TO "CASABLANCA" 1640
CONSTRUCTIVISM IN FILM: THE MAN WITH A MOVIE CAMERA--A CINEMATIC
ANALYSIS 1664, 1669
CONTEMPORARY CINEMA, THE 1925
CONTEMPORARY EROTIC CINEMA 2037
CONTEMPORARY GREEK CINEMA, THE 2166
CONTEMPORARY POLISH CINEMATOGRAPHY 2013
CONTEMPT OF CONGRESS: A STUDY OF THE PROSECUTIONS INITIATED BY
THE COMMITTEE ON UN-AMERICAN ACTIVITIES, 1945-1957 1077
CONTENT ANALYSIS IN COMMUNICATIONS RESEARCH 708
CONTENT ANALYSIS OF FILM: A SURVEY OF THE FIELD, AN EXHAUSTIVE
STUDY OF "QUAI DES BRUMES," AND A FUNCTIONAL DESCRIPTION 1813
CONTENT OF MOTION PICTURES, THE 729, 730
CONTEXT AND CRAFT OF DRAMA, THE 712
CONTINUED NEXT WEEK: A HISTORY OF THE MOVING PICTURE SERIAL 1457,
1458
CONVERSATIONS WITH JOAN CRAWFORD 1766
CONVERSATIONS WITH LILLIAN HELLMAN 1227
CONVERSATIONS WITH LOSEY 1962, 2161
CONVERSATIONS WITH MARILYN 1138, 1966
CONVERSATIONS WITH MY ELDERS 1442
COOP: THE LIFE AND LEGEND OF GARY COOPER 1081, 1765
COPPERFIELD '70: THE STORY OF THE MAKING OF THE OMNIBUS 20TH
CENTURY FILM DAVID COPPERFIELD 1318
COPYRIGHT ENTRIES (CUMULATIVE SERIES): MOTION PICTURES 1960-69 1525
CORONER 1244
COSTA-GAVRAS: THE POLITICAL FICTION FILM 566, 577
COTTON GOES TO HARLEM 896
COUNTRY GIRL: THE LIFE OF SISSY SPACEK 2209
COUNT: THE LIFE AND FILMS OF BELA "DRACULA" LUGOSI, THE 1782
COUPLE OF WRITERS, A 1197
COURSE IN GENERAL LINGUISTICS, A 482
COURTROOM'S FINEST HOUR IN AMERICAN CINEMA 560
COWBOYS AND CADILLACS: HOW HOLLYWOOD LOOKS AT TEXAS 428
CRACK-UP, THE 1031
CRACKPOT: THE OBSESSIONS OF JOHN WATERS 2210
CRAFT OF THE SCREENWRITER: INTERVIEWS WITH SIX CELEBRATED
WRITERS, THE 84
CRAWFORD: THE LAST YEARS 1765
Crawley, Tony 2209
CRAZY MIRROR: HOLLYWOOD COMEDY AND THE AMERICAN IMAGE, THE 1676
CRAZY SUNDAYS: F. SCOTT FITZGERALD IN HOLLYWOOD 1113, 1118, 1124,
1217
CREATIVE FILM-MAKING 91
CREATIVE WRITING THROUGH FILMS: AN INSTRUCTIONAL PROGRAM FOR
SECONDARY STUDENTS 51
CREATORS OF LIFE: A HISTORY OF ANIMATION 1623
CREATURE FEATURES MOVIE GUIDE: OR AN A TO Z ENCYCLOPEDIA TO THE
CINEMA OF THE FANTASTIC 398
CREDITS: VOLUME I--BY FILM TITLE, '85-'86 Edition 1524
CREDITS: VOLUME II--BY PRODUCTION CATEGORY, '85-'86 Edition 1524

CREDITS: VOLUME III--BY INDIVIDUAL, '85-'86 Edition 1524
CRIME MOVIES: FROM GRIFFITH TO "THE GODFATHER" AND BEYOND 384
CRISIS OF THE NEGRO INTELLECTUAL, THE 916
CRITICAL APPROACHES TO FEDERICO FELLINI'S 8 1/2 2170
CRITICAL EVALUATION OF THE CONTROVERSIES ENGENDERED BY D. W.
 GRIFFITH'S "BIRTH OF A NATION," A 1367
CRITICAL EXAMINATION OF RHETORICAL ARGUMENT IN NARRATIVE
 ENTERTAINMENT ON TELEVISION, A 111
CRITICAL FOCUS: AN INTRODUCTION TO FILM 43
CRITICAL HISTORY OF BRITISH CINEMA, A 1565
CRITICAL INDEX: A BIBLIOGRAPHY OF ARTICLES ON FILM IN ENGLISH,
 1946-1973, THE 1528
CRITICAL STUDY OF THE SCREWBALL COMEDY, A 1752
CRITICISM OF OTIS FERGUSON, THE 1018
CRITICIZING THE CRITICS 139
CRITIQUE OF FILM THEORY, A 119, 120, 163, 444
CUBAN IMAGE: CINEMA AND CULTURAL POLITICS IN CUBA, THE 2163
CUBIST CINEMA, THE 1717, 1730
CULTURAL-POLITICAL TRADITIONS AND DEVELOPMENTS OF THE SOVIET
 CINEMA 1917-1972, THE 1649
CULTURE AND SOCIETY, 1780-1950 614
CULTURES ON CELLULOID 444, 474, 489, 566
CUMULATED DRAMATIC INDEX 1909-19 1543
CURIOUS DEATH OF MARILYN MONROE, THE 1138, 1966
CURRENT RESEARCH IN FILM: AUDIENCES, ECONOMICS, AND LAW, Volume
 1 534, 649, 681, 711, 768
CURRENT RESEARCH IN FILM: AUDIENCES, ECONOMICS, AND LAW, Volume
 2 458, 537, 621, 739, 748, 756, 770, 771
CURRENT RESEARCH IN FILM: AUDIENCES, ECONOMICS, AND LAW, Volume
 3 771
CURRENT RESEARCH IN FILM: AUDIENCES, ECONOMICS, AND LAW, Volume
 4 772
CURRENTS IN JAPANESE CINEMA 787, 788, 801, 802, 1575, 1733, 1734, 1735,
 1736, 1737, 1740, 1742, 1888, 1891, 1892, 1895, 1898, 2016, 2020
CURSE OF CAPISTRANO, THE 1407
CUT! PRINT!: THE LANGUAGE AND STRUCTURE OF FILMMAKING 74
CUT: THE UNSEEN CINEMA 966
CYCLISTS' RAID 1311
CZECHOSLOVAK NEW WAVE, THE 2164

D

D'ENTRE LES MORTS 2080
DAIN CURSE, THE 1222
DALTON TRUMBO 1067, 1282
DAME AUX CAMELLIAS, LA 1802
DAMNED IN PARADISE: THE LIFE OF JOHN BARRYMORE 1760
DANCE IN THE HOLLYWOOD MUSICAL 402
DANCING IN THE SUN: HOLLYWOOD CHOREOGRAPHERS, 1915-1937 1676
DANS LE LABYRINTHE 2139
DANSE MACABRE 393
DARK AT THE TOP OF THE STAIRS, THE 1261
DARK CINEMA: AMERICAN FILM NOIR IN CULTURAL PERSPECTIVE 1947,
 1948, 1956
DARK DREAMS: A PSYCHOLOGICAL HISTORY OF THE HORROR FILM 389
DARK LADY OF THE SILENTS: MY LIFE IN EARLY HOLLYWOOD 1366, 1373

DARK SIDE OF GENIUS: THE LIFE OF ALFRED HITCHCOCK, THE   1607, 1853, 1856
DARK SIDE OF THE SCREEN: FILM NOIR, THE   1947, 1956
DARK STAR   1440, 1686
DASHIELL HAMMETT   1224
DASHIELL HAMMETT: A LIFE   1221
DAVID AND LISA   995
DAVID COPPERFIELD   1306, 1307, 1308, 1312
DAVID LEAN AND HIS FILMS   1861
DAVID O. SELZNICK'S HOLLYWOOD   1487
DAY FOR NIGHT: THE COMPLETE SCRIPT OF THE FILM   2148
DAY OF THE LOCUST, THE   1041, 1058, 1103, 1104, 1135, 1136, 1158, 1161, 1162, 1291
DAYS OF THRILLS AND ADVENTURE   1456
DE GAULLE STORY. VOLUME THREE OF FAULKNER: A COMPREHENSIVE GUIDE TO THE BRODSKY COLLECTION, THE   1206
DE GAULLE STORY, THE   260
DE PALMA CUT: THE FILMS OF AMERICA'S MOST CONTROVERSIAL DIRECTOR, THE   2208
DEAD END   2058
DEAD THAT WALK: DRACULA, FRANKENSTEIN, THE MUMMY, AND OTHER FAVORITE MOVIE MONSTERS, THE   391
DEADLY PARALLELS: FILM AND THE LEFT IN BRITAIN 1929-1939   1832, 1840
DEAR BORIS   1779
DEATH IN THE DEEP SOUTH   859
DEATH IN THE FAMILY, A   145
DEATH IN VENICE   1308
DEATH OF A SALESMAN   1260
DEATH OF ART, THE   858
DEATH OF IVAN ILLYCH, THE   2030
DEATH OF JAMES DEAN, THE   1959
DEBBIE: MY LIFE   1969
DECADE OF CUBAN DOCUMENTARY FILM: 1972-1982, A   299
DECLINE OF THE CINEMA: AN ECONOMIST'S REPORT, THE   608, 647, 699
DEEPER INTO MOVIES   149, 996, 1320, 1347, 1355
DEER PARK, THE   1041, 1135, 1136, 1158
DEMILLE: THE MAN AND HIS PICTURES   1680, 1703
DENNIS HOPPER: A MADNESS TO HIS METHOD   2054
DER BIKUK (THE DYBBUK)   828
DESCRIPTIVE STUDY OF REFERENCES MADE TO NEGROES AND OCCUPATIONAL ROLES REPRESENTED BY NEGROES IN SELECTED MASS MEDIA, A   860
DESIGNING FOR FILMS   79
DESIGNING & MAINTAINING THE CATV & THE SMALL TV STUDIO, 2nd ed.   92
DESIRE TO DESIRE: THE WOMAN'S FILM OF THE 1940s, THE   495
DESTRUCTION OF THE EUROPEAN JEWS, THE   311
DETECTIVE IN FICTION, THE   1956
DETECTIVE IN FILM, THE   380
DETECTIVE IN HOLLYWOOD, THE   381
DETOUR: A HOLLYWOOD STORY   1971
DEUX ANGLAIS ET LE CONTINENT   2147
DEVELOPMENT OF THE FILM: AN INTERPRETIVE HISTORY   1519, 1559
DEVIL FINDS WORK, THE   860, 895
DIALOGUE WITH THE WORLD   1000, 1001, 1018, 1021, 1022, 1807, 1981
DIANA   951
DIANA ROSS: SUPREME LADY   951
DIANYING: AN ACCOUNT OF FILMS AND THE FILM AUDIENCE IN CHINA   2163
DIARY OF A LOVER OF MARILYN MONROE   1138, 1965

DIARY OF ANNE FRANK, THE   837, 849
DICTIONARY OF FILMMAKERS   1553
DICTIONARY OF FILMS   1543, 1665
DICTIONARY OF LITERARY BIOGRAPHY, Volume 26: AMERICAN
  SCREENWRITERS   1064, 1067, 1093, 1104, 1154, 1282
DICTIONARY OF LITERARY BIOGRAPHY, VOLUME 44: AMERICAN
  SCREENWRITERS, SECOND SERIES   1145
DICTIONARY OF THE CINEMA, A   1529
DICTIONARY OF 1000 BEST FILMS   1540
DIES COMMITTEE, THE   1077
DIETRICH: THE STORY OF A STAR   1767
DIFFERENT STROKES: OR HOW I (GULP) WROTE, DIRECTED, AND STARRED
  IN AN X-RATED MOVIE   2037
DIFFICULTE D'ETRE, LA (THE DIFFICULTY OF BEING)   1817
DIFFICULTY OF BEING, THE (LA DIFFICULTE D'ETRE)   1817
DIRECTING FOR FILM AND TELEVISION   74
DIRECTING METHODS   73
DIRECTING MOTION PICTURES   74
DIRECTING TELEVISION AND FILM   71
DIRECTING THE DOCUMENTARY   82
DIRECTOR'S EVENT: INTERVIEWS WITH FIVE AMERICAN FILM-MAKERS,
  THE   609, 2042
DIRECTORS AND DIRECTIONS: CINEMA FOR THE SEVENTIES   2208
DIRECTORS AT WORK: INTERVIEWS WITH AMERICAN FILM-MAKERS   609, 1550
DIRECTORS IN ACTION: SELECTIONS FROM ACTION   609
DIRTY MOVIES: AN ILLUSTRATED HISTORY OF THE STAG FILM
  1915-1970   2037
DISCOVERY IN FILM   47
DISCOVERY IN FILM: BOOK TWO   47
DISCOVERY OF THE CINEMA, A   64
DISCRIMINATIONS: ESSAYS & AFTERTHOUGHTS 1938-1974   153
DISENCHANTED, THE   1041, 1058, 1106, 1109, 1116, 1121, 1126, 1127, 1135,
  1148, 1158
DISENCHANTMENT: MEANING AND MORALITY IN THE MEDIA   52
DISNEY ANIMATION: THE ILLUSION OF LIFE   1769
DISNEY FILMS, THE   1768
DISNEY POSTER BOOK, THE   1768
DISNEY VERSION: THE LIFE, TIMES, ART AND COMMERCE OF WALT DISNEY,
  THE   307, 569, 1080, 1206, 1769
DISNEY'S WORLD: A BIOGRAPHY   1768
DISNEY: A GUIDE TO REFERENCES AND RESOURCES   1080
DISPLACED PERSON, THE   1316
DISTRIBUTION OF THEATRICAL FEATURE FILMS TO TELEVISION, THE   656,
  678
DIVERSIONS OF PLEASURE: LUIS BUNUEL AND THE CRISES OF DESIRE   579,
  1723
DIVINE GARBO, THE   1686
DOCTOR's DILEMMA, THE   2058
DOCUMENTARY DIARY: AN INFORMAL HISTORY OF THE BRITISH
  DOCUMENTARY FILM, 1928-1939   216, 243, 246, 302
DOCUMENTARY EXPLORATIONS: 15 INTERVIEWS WITH FILMMAKERS   1870
DOCUMENTARY EXPRESSION AND THIRTIES AMERICA   1870
DOCUMENTARY FILM AND DEMOCRATIC GOVERNMENT: AN ADMINISTRATIVE
  HISTORY FROM PARE LORENTZ TO JOHN HUSTON   203
DOCUMENTARY FILM: THE USE OF THE FILM MEDIUM TO INTERPRET
  CREATIVELY AND IN SOCIAL TERMS THE LIFE OF THE PEOPLE   245, 280,
  294
DOCUMENTARY TRADITION, THE   207, 216, 222, 254, 255, 282, 303, 319

DOCUMENTARY: A HISTORY OF THE NON-FICTION FILM 292
DOG SOLDIERS 364
DOLCE VITA, LA 2170
DON QUIXOTE 1153
DON'T DRINK THE WATER 2044, 2046
DON'T GET ME WRONG--I LOVE HOLLYWOOD 1057, 1244
DON'T LOOK AT THE CAMERA 308, 322
DON'T SAY YES UNTIL I FINISH TALKING; A BIOGRAPHY OF DARRYL F.
  ZANUCK 1499
DON'T SHOOT, DARLING! WOMEN'S INDEPENDENT FILMMAKING IN
  AUSTRALIA 491
DONALD DUCK JOINS UP: THE WALT DISNEY STUDIO DURING WORLD WAR
  II 283, 306, 321, 1080
DORIS DAY 643, 1958, 1959
DORIS DAY SCRAPBOOK, THE 1958
DORIS DAY: HER OWN STORY 643, 1958
DOROTHY AND LILLIAN GISH 1375
DOROTHY DANDRIDGE: A PORTRAIT IN BLACK 886, 950
DOSTOEVSKY AND SOVIET FILM: VISIONS OF DEMONIC REALISM 1650
DOUBLE DE PALMA: A FILM STUDY WITH BRIAN DE PALMA 2208
DOUBLE EXPOSURE: COMPOSING THROUGH WRITING AND FILM 45
DOUBLE EXPOSURE: FICTION INTO FILM 1309
DOUBLE TAKE AND FADE AWAY: HALLIWELL ON COMEDIANS 1677
DOUBLE VISION: MY LIFE IN FILMS 2014
DOUG AND MARY: A BIOGRAPHY OF DOUGLAS FAIRBANKS AND MARY
  PICKFORD 1400, 1402, 1407
DOUGLAS FAIRBANKS: THE FIRST CELEBRITY 1404, 1407
DOUGLAS FAIRBANKS: THE FOURTH MUSKETEER 1403, 1409
DOUGLAS FAIRBANKS: THE MAKING OF A SCREEN CHARACTER 1403, 1406
DOUGLAS SIRK 1970, 1971, 1986
DOUGLAS SIRK: PROGRAM NOTES 1986
DOUGLAS SIRK: THE COMPLETE AMERICAN PERIOD 1986
DOVZHENKO BIBLIOGRAPHY, A 1645
DOWN THERE 2155
DRACULA 1312, 1642, 1798
DRACULA BOOK, THE 391
DRAMA SCHOLARS' INDEX TO PLAYS AND FILMSCRIPTS: A GUIDE TO PLAYS
  AND FILMSCRIPTS 1157
DRAMATIC ART OF THE FILM, THE 103
DRAMATIC IMAGINATION: REFLECTIONS AND SPECULATIONS ON THE ART
  OF THE THEATRE, THE 583
DRAT! BEING THE ENCAPSULATED VIEW OF LIFE OF W. C. FIELDS IN HIS
  OWN WORDS 1770
DREADFUL PLEASURES: AN ANATOMY OF MODERN HORROR 399
DREAM AND THE DREAMERS, THE 849, 1023, 1349, 1352, 1354
DREAM BESIDE ME: THE MOVIES AND THE CHILDREN OF THE FORTIES,
  THE 525, 526
DREAM OF DRACULA: IN SEARCH OF THE LIVING DEAD, A 399
DREAM OF SUCCESS: A STUDY OF THE MODERN AMERICAN IMAGINATION,
  THE 1047, 1052
DREAM PALACES: HOLLYWOOD AT HOME 1236
DREAM THAT KICKS: THE PREHISTORY AND EARLY YEARS OF CINEMA IN
  BRITAIN, THE 1510, 1583, 1611
DREAMS AND DEAD ENDS: THE AMERICAN GANGSTER/CRIME FILM 387
DREAMS AND THE DREAMERS, THE 1290
DREAMS AND THE DREAMERS: ADVENTURES OF A PROFESSIONAL MOVIE
  GOER, THE 146
DREAMS FOR SALE: THE RISE AND FALL OF THE TRIANGLE
  CORPORATION 1412

DREYER IN DOUBLE REFLECTION: TRANSLATION OF CARL TH. DREYER'S
  WRITINGS ABOUT THE FILM (OM FILMEN) 1629
DR. JEKYLL AND MR. HYDE 117, 1312
DUKE, A LOVE STORY, AN INTIMATE MEMOIR OF JOHN WAYNE'S YEARS 1081
DUKE: THE JOHN WAYNE ALBUM--THE LEGEND OF OUR TIME 1081, 1788
DUKE: THE LIFE AND TIMES OF JOHN WAYNE 1081
DUKE: THE STORY OF JOHN WAYNE 1081, 1789
DURGNAT ON FILM 535
DUTCH CINEMA: AN ILLUSTRATED HISTORY 2178
DWELL IN THE WILDERNESS 1177
DWIGHT MACDONALD ON MOVIES 997, 1001, 1005, 1010, 1022, 1023, 1328,
  1348, 1349, 1350, 1353, 1354, 1356, 1648
DYBBUK, THE (DER BIKUK) 828
DYNAMICS OF LITERARY RESPONSE, THE 485
DYNAMICS OF THE FILM 64, 101, 1300
DZIGA VERTOV: A GUIDE TO REFERENCES AND RESOURCES 1663
D. W. GRIFFITH AND THE BIOGRAPH COMPANY 1376
D. W. GRIFFITH AND THE NARRATOR-SYSTEM: NARRATIVE STRUCTURE AND
  INDUSTRY ORGANIZATION IN BIOGRAPH FILMS, 1908-1909 1362
D. W. GRIFFITH: AMERICAN FILMMAKER 1370
D. W. GRIFFITH: AN AMERICAN LIFE 569, 1360, 1361, 1362, 1363, 1364, 1366,
  1367, 1372, 1381, 1388, 1390
D. W. GRIFFITH: HIS BIOGRAPH FILMS IN PERSPECTIVE 1380
D. W. GRIFFITH: HIS LIFE AND HIS WORK 1360, 1378, 1389
D. W. GRIFFITH: THE YEARS AT BIOGRAPH 1378

E

EACH IN ITS ORDERED PLACE: A FAULKNER COLLECTOR'S NOTEBOOKS 1211
EACH MAN IN HIS TIME: THE STORY OF A DIRECTOR 1700
EADWEARD MUYBRIDGE: THE FATHER OF THE MOTION PICTURE 1596
EADWEARD MUYBRIDGE: THE MAN WHO INVENTED THE MOVING
  PICTURE 1596, 1597
EALING STUDIOS 1839
EARLY AMERICAN CINEMA 1595
EARLY DEVELOPMENT OF THE MOTION PICTURE 1887-1909, THE 1593, 1601
EARLY WOMEN DIRECTORS 519, 620
EAST OF EDEN 1005, 1281
EASTERN EUROPE: AN ILLUSTRATED GUIDE 2012
EASY RIDER: ORIGINAL SCREENPLAY 2051
ECLIPSE 1282
ECONOMIC CHANGES IN THE MOTION PICTURE INDUSTRY AS AFFECTED BY
  TELEVISION AND OTHER FACTORS 648
ECONOMIC CONTROL OF THE MOTION PICTURE INDUSTRY: A STUDY IN
  INDUSTRIAL ORGANIZATION 607, 624, 635, 636, 639, 694, 1103
ECONOMICS: INSTITUTIONS AND ANALYSIS 612
ECRITS: A SELECTION 480
ECSTASY AND ME: MY LIFE AS A WOMAN 1780
EDISON MOTION PICTURE MYTH, THE 1615
EDITH HEAD'S HOLLYWOOD 1777
EDUCATED IMAGINATION, THE 178, 540, 1017
EDUCATION OF H*Y*M*A*N K*A*P*L*A*N, THE 1238
EDUCATION OF THE FILM-MAKER: AN INTERNATIONAL VIEW, THE 76
EDUCATIONAL ACHIEVEMENTS: EXPLANATIONS AND IMPLICATIONS OF
  RECENT TRENDS 439
EDUCATIONAL FILMS: WRITING, DIRECTING AND PRODUCING FOR
  CLASSROOM TELEVISION AND INDUSTRY 84

EDWARD G. ROBINSON 799, 1091, 1785
EFFECTIVE TELEVISION PRODUCTION 92
EFFECTS OF MASS COMMUNICATION, THE 747
EFFECTS OF TELEVISION ON THE MOTION PICTURES AND RADIO INDUSTRIES,
  THE 648, 656
EIGHT MM SOUND FILM AND EDUCATION: PROCEEDINGS OF A CONFERENCE
  HELD AT TEACHERS COLLEGE 65
EIGHT MM/SIXTEEN MM MOVIE MAKING 91
EIGHT-AND-ONE/HALF: FEDERICO FELLINI, DIRECTOR 2170
EIGHT-MM FILM DIRECTORY: A COMPREHENSIVE DESCRIPTIVE INDEX 1532
EIGHTH VEIL--ANN TODD, THE 1863
EIGHTY YEARS OF CINEMA 1560
EISENSTEIN 1644, 1655
EISENSTEIN 2: A PREMATURE CELEBRATION OF EISENSTEIN'S
  CENTENARY 1658
EISENSTEIN'S "IVAN THE TERRIBLE": A NEOFORMALIST ANALYSIS 108, 1867,
  1868
EISENSTEIN: A BIOGRAPHY 1656
EISENSTEIN: A DOCUMENTARY PORTRAIT 1661, 1667
EISENSTEIN: THREE FILMS--BATTLESHIP POTEMKIN, OCTOBER, ALEXANDER
  NEVSKY 1658
ELECTRONIC ANTHOLOGY: PROBES INTO MASS MEDIA & POPULAR CULTURE,
  THE 62
ELECTRONIC ARTS OF SOUND AND LIGHT, THE 86
ELECTRONIC CINEMATOGRAPHY: ACHIEVING PHOTOGRAPHIC CONTROL OVER
  THE VIDEO IMAGE 81
ELECTRONIC IMAGING TECHNIQUES: A HANDBOOK OF CONVENTIONAL AND
  COMPUTER-CONTROLLED ANIMATION 77
ELEMENTS OF CINEMA: TOWARD A THEORY OF CINESTHETIC IMPACT,
  THE 68
ELEMENTS OF FILM 101
ELEMENTS OF FILM, 2nd ed. 110
ELEMENTS OF SEMIOLOGY 482
ELEMENTS OF SOUND RECORDING 86
ELIA KAZAN 1089
ELSA LANCHESTER HERSELF 1860
EMBATTLED SHADOWS: A HISTORY OF CANADIAN CINEMA 1895-1939 2162
EMERGENCE OF FILM ART: THE EVOLUTION AND DEVELOPMENT OF THE
  MOTION PICTURE AS AN ART, THE 140, 1351
EMERGENCE OF FILM ART: THE EVOLUTION AND DEVELOPMENT OF THE
  MOTION PICTURE AS AN ART, THE, 2nd ed. 141
EMOTIONAL RESPONSES OF CHILDREN TO THE MOTION PICTURE SITUATION,
  THE 729
EMPEROR JONES, THE 875, 944
EMPIRE OF THEIR OWN: HOW THE JEWS INVENTED HOLLYWOOD, AN 819, 832,
  833, 843, 853
ENCOUNTERING DIRECTORS 2034
ENCYCLOPEDIA OF AMERICAN FILM COMEDY 1532
ENCYCLOPEDIA OF THE MUSICAL FILM 404
ENGLISH MELODRAMA 712
ENGLISH NOVEL AND THE MOVIES, THE 367, 1311
ENGLISH, EDUCATION, AND THE ELECTRONIC REVOLUTION 46
ENTERTAINERS AND THE ENTERTAINED: ESSAYS ON THEATER, FILM AND
  TELEVISION 1340
ENTERTAINMENT: A CROSS-CULTURAL EXAMINATION 459, 853
EPIC FILM: MYTH AND HISTORY, THE 382
ERA OF RECONSTRUCTION 1865-1877, THE 864
ERIC ROHMER: REALIST AND MORALIST 2102, 2103, 2141
ERNST LUBITSCH'S AMERICAN COMEDY 1781

ERNST LUBITSCH'S "NINOTCHKA" STARRING GRETA GARBO AND MELVYN
 DOUGLAS 1781
ERNST LUBITSCH: A GUIDE TO REFERENCES AND RESOURCES 1639
EROS PLUS MASSACRE: AN INTRODUCTION TO THE JAPANESE NEW WAVE
 CINEMA 2023, 2176, 2177
ERROL AND ME 1771
ERROL FLYNN 1771
ERROL FLYNN: A MEMOIR 1771
ERROL FLYNN: THE UNTOLD STORY 1771
ESSAI SUR LES PRINCIPES D'UNE PHILOSOPHIE DU CINEMA. 2002
ESSAIS SUR LA SIGNIFICATION AU CINEMA 133
ESSAYS ON CHAPLIN 1419
ESTHETIQUE ET PSYCHOLOGIE DU CINEMA 132, 169
ETHNIC IMAGES IN AMERICAN FILM AND TELEVISION 813, 820, 826
EUROPEANS, THE 1323
EVENING WITH MIKE NICHOLS AND ELAINE MAY, AN 2060
EVERY DAY'S A MATINEE: MEMOIRS SCRIBBLED ON A DRESSING ROOM
 FLOOR 1241
EVERYTHING AND NOTHING: THE DOROTHY DANDRIDGE TRAGEDY 886, 950
EVOLUTION OF CHARACTER PORTRAYALS IN THE FILMS OF SIDNEY POITIER:
 1950-1978, THE 886, 887, 888, 890, 951
EVOLUTION OF FILM STYLES 164
EVOLUTION OF STYLE IN THE EARLY WORK OF DZIGA VERTOV 1664
EXECUTIVE HANDBOOK OF BUSINESS FILM AND VIDEOTAPE 72
EXILE'S RETURN, THE 765
EXILED IN PARADISE: GERMAN REFUGEE ARTISTS AND INTELLECTUALS IN
 AMERICA, FROM THE 1930s TO THE PRESENT 1067
EXPANDED CINEMA 144
EXPERIMENT IN THE FILM 1718
EXPERIMENTAL ANIMATION: AN ILLUSTRATED ANTHOLOGY 78
EXPERIMENTAL CINEMA 1715
EXPERIMENTAL CINEMA, 1930-1934 1758
EXPLORATIONS IN AMERICAN HISTORY: A SKILLS APPROACH 1509, 1510
EXPLORATIONS IN COGNITIVE DISSONANCE 543
EXPLORING CAREERS IN FILMMAKING 74
EXPLORING THE FILM 43, 49, 65
EXPORTING ENTERTAINMENT: AMERICA IN THE WORLD FILM MARKET
 1907-34 618, 701
EXTERMINATING ANGEL, NAZARI, AND LOS OLVIDADOS: THREE FILMS BY
 LUIS BUNUEL, THE 1990

F

FABULOUS FANTASY FILMS, THE 415
FABULOUS FONDAS, THE 799, 2050
FABULOUS LIFE AND TIMES OF PRESTON STURGES: AN AMERICAN DREAMER,
 THE 1919
FABULOUS LUNTS: A BIOGRAPHY OF ALFRED LUNT AND LYNN FONTANNE,
 THE 1782
FABULOUS ORSON WELLES, THE 1794
FABULOUS THIRTIES: ITALIAN CINEMA 1929-1944, THE 1875, 1878
FACE IN THE CROWD, A 1029
FACE ON THE CUTTING ROOM FLOOR: THE STORY OF MOVIE AND TELEVISION
 CENSORSHIP 967
FACE TO FACE 2184
FACES 2048
FACES OF HOLLYWOOD, THE 1440

FACES, FORMS, FILMS: THE ARTISTRY OF LON CHANEY 1679
FACTORS AFFECTING THE DECLINE OF THE MOTION PICTURE AUDIENCE IN
 THE UNITED STATES SINCE WORLD WAR II 648
FAILURE AND SUCCESS IN AMERICA: A LITERARY DEBATE 1047
FAIRBANKS ALBUM: DRAWN FROM THE FAMILY ARCHIVES BY DOUGLAS
 FAIRBANKS, JR., THE 1399, 1404, 1406
FALL OF THE HOUSE OF USHER, THE 1730
FALSEHOOD IN WARTIME 211
FAMILY GUIDE TO MOVIES ON VIDEO: THE MORAL AND ENTERTAINMENT
 VALUES OF 5,000 MOVIES ON TV AND VIDEOCASSETTE, THE 1530
FAMOUS FOR FIFTEEN MINUTES: MY YEARS WITH ANDY WARHOL 2069
FAMOUS IN AMERICA: THE PASSION TO SUCCEED--JANE FONDA, GEORGE
 WALLACE, PHYLLIS SCHLAFLY, JOHN GLENN 2050
FAMOUS PEOPLE ON FILM 1526
FANNY AND ALEXANDER 2184
FAR FROM THE MADDING CROWD 1312
FAR PAVILIONS, THE 548
FAR SIDE OF PARADISE: A BIOGRAPHY OF F. SCOTT FITZGERALD,
 THE 1110, 1113
FAREWELL TO ARMS, A 1231
FAREWELL, MY LOVELY 738, 1161, 1162
FARMER IN THE DELL, THE 1041, 1104
FASSBINDER 2166
FAST FADE: DAVID PUTTNAM, COLUMBIA PICTURES, AND THE BATTLE FOR
 HOLLYWOOD 704
FAST FORWARD: HOLLYWOOD, THE JAPANESE, AND THE ONSLAUGHT OF THE
 VCR 672
FATHER GOOSE: THE STORY OF MACK SENNETT 1411
FAULKNER AND FILM 1207, 1211
FAULKNER IN HOLLYWOOD: A STUDY OF HIS CAREER AS A SCENARIST 1106
FAULKNER'S INTRUDER IN THE DUST: NOVEL INTO FILM 1037, 1049, 1208,
 1321
FAULKNER'S MGM SCREENPLAYS 1103, 1207
FAULKNER, MODERNISM, AND FILM: FAULKNER AND YOKNAPATAWPHA,
 1978 1209
FEAR OF THE WORD: CENSORSHIP AND SEX 966
FEAR ON TRIAL 1100
FEARFUL SYMMETRIES: THE CONTEST OF AUTHORITY IN HITCHCOCK
 NARRATIVE 1836
FEATURE FILMS AS HISTORY 211, 253, 265, 273
FEATURE FILMS ON 8MM, 16MM, AND VIDEOTAPE. SIXTH EDITION. 30
FEATURE FILMS: A DIRECTORY OF FEATURE FILMS ON 16MM AND VIDEOTAPE
 AVAILABLE FOR RENTAL, SALE, AND LEASE 1534
FEDERAL THEATRE, 1935-1939: PLAYS, RELIEF, AND POLITICS, THE 1077
FEDERICO FELLINI 1927, 1931
FEDERICO FELLINI: A GUIDE TO REFERENCES AND RESOURCES 1932
FEDERICO FELLINI: AN ANNOTATED INTERNATIONAL BIBLIOGRAPHY 1931,
 1932
FEDERICO FELLINI: COMMENTS ON FILM 1930, 2170
FEDERICO FELLINI: ESSAYS IN CRITICISM 1929
FEDERICO FELLINI: THE SEARCH FOR A NEW MYTHOLOGY 1930
FEELING AND FORM: A THEORY OF ART DEVELOPED FROM "PHILOSOPHY IN
 A NEW KEY" 583, 955
FELLINI 1930, 1932
FELLINI THE ARTIST, Second, Enlarged edition 1930
FELLINI'S ROAD 1023, 1930
FELLINI: A LIFE 1929
FELLOW-TRAVELERS: A POSTSCRIPT TO THE ENLIGHTENMENT, THE 1077
FEMINISM AND FILM THEORY 518

FEMINIST SPECTATOR AS A CRITIC, THE   496
FIAF DIRECTORY AND TV DOCUMENTATION SOURCES   1545
FICTION AND THE CAMERA EYE: VISUAL CONSCIOUSNESS IN FILM AND THE
  MODERN NOVEL   1316
FICTION, FILM, AND FAULKNER: THE ART OF ADAPTATION   1215
FICTION, FILM, AND F. SCOTT FITZGERALD   1218
FIELD OF VIEW: FILM CRITICISM AND COMMENT   152
FIELDS FOR PRESIDENT   1770
FIFTY CLASSIC FRENCH FILMS, 1912-1982: A PICTORIAL RECORD   1572, 2009
FIFTY CLASSIC MOTION PICTURES: THE STUFF THAT DREAMS ARE MADE
  OF   1328, 1577
FIFTY FROM THE FIFTIES: VINTAGE FILMS FROM AMERICA'S
  MID-CENTURY   1954
FIFTY SUPER STARS   1443
FIFTY YEARS OF GERMAN FILM   1573
FIFTY YEARS OF ITALIAN CINEMA   1574
FIFTY YEARS OF MOVIE POSTERS   1444
FIFTY-YEAR DECLINE AND FALL OF HOLLYWOOD, THE   739, 1234
FIGURE IN FILM, THE   114
FIGURES OF LIGHT: FILM CRITICISM AND COMMENT   153, 995, 1001, 1003,
  1325, 1352, 2085
FILM   50, 2067
FILM ACTING: THE TECHNIQUES AND HISTORY OF ACTING FOR THE
  CAMERA   76
FILM ACTORS GUIDE: WESTERN EUROPE   1540
FILM ACTOR, THE   1539
FILM AND EDUCATION: A SYMPOSIUM ON THE ROLE OF FILM IN THE FIELD
  OF EDUCATION   46
FILM AND FICTION: THE DYNAMICS OF EXCHANGE   115
FILM AND ITS TECHNIQUES   75
FILM AND LITERATURE: AN INTRODUCTION   1308
FILM AND LITERATURE: CONTRAST IN MEDIA   1312
FILM AND POLITICS IN THE THIRD WORLD   559
FILM AND RADIO PROPAGANDA IN WORLD WAR II   201, 208, 211, 213, 216,
  223, 246, 255, 281
FILM AND REALITY: AN HISTORICAL SURVEY   162, 1715
FILM AND SOCIETY   50, 1331
FILM AND TELEVISION IN POLAND   2013
FILM AND TELEVISION MAKEUP   84
FILM AND TELEVISION YEARBOOK 1987   1525
FILM AND TELEVISION: AN ANALYTIC HISTORY OF ECONOMIC AND CREATIVE
  INTEGRATION   678
FILM AND THE CRITICAL EYE   103
FILM AND THE DREAM SCREEN: A SLEEP AND A FORGETTING   584, 594, 596,
  606
FILM AND THE HUMANITIES   51
FILM AND THE LIBERAL ARTS   53
FILM AND THE NARRATIVE TRADITION   115
FILM AND THEATRE   1331, 1332, 1337
FILM ANIMATION AS A HOBBY   89
FILM APPRECIATION   102
FILM ARCHETYPES: SISTERS, MISTRESSES, MOTHERS AND DAUGHTERS   523,
  524
FILM ART: AN INTRODUCTION   94, 95, 102, 112
FILM AS ART   127, 166
FILM AS FILM: CRITICAL RESPONSES TO FILM ART   137
FILM AS FILM: UNDERSTANDING AND JUDGING MOVIES   106
FILM AS SOCIAL CHANGE   59

FILM AS SOCIAL PRACTICE 55
FILM AUDIENCE: AN INTERNATIONAL BIBLIOGRAPHY OF RESEARCH, WITH
  ANNOTATIONS AND AN ESSAY, THE 705, 719, 720, 767, 768
FILM BEFORE GRIFFITH 1590
FILM BOOK BIBLIOGRAPHY, THE 1526
FILM BUSINESS: A HISTORY OF BRITISH CINEMA, 1896-1972, THE 540, 1567,
  1568, 1936
FILM CAREER OF ALAIN ROBBE-GRILLET, THE 2140
FILM CAREER OF BILLY WILDER, THE 799, 1972
FILM CAREER OF BUSTER KEATON, THE 1689
FILM CENSORS AND THE LAW 225, 965
FILM CENSORSHIP 225
FILM CRITICISM OF OTIS FERGUSON, THE 148, 994, 1012, 1320, 1326, 1327,
  1328, 1330, 1348, 1351, 1357, 1431
FILM CRITICISM: A COUNTER THEORY 138
FILM CULTURE READER 1955, 2039
FILM DAILY 1545
FILM DAILY YEAR BOOK OF MOTION PICTURES 1527
FILM DESIGN 79
FILM DIRECTOR AS SUPERSTAR, THE 609, 1549
FILM DIRECTORS GUIDE: WESTERN EUROPE 1540
FILM DIRECTORS: A COMPLETE GUIDE 1554
FILM DIRECTORS: A GUIDE TO THEIR AMERICAN FILMS 1539
FILM DIRECTOR: A PRACTICAL GUIDE TO MOTION PICTURE AND TELEVISION
  TECHNIQUES, THE 71
FILM EDITING HANDBOOK: TECHNIQUE OF 16MM FILM CUTTING 82
FILM EDUCATION IN SECONDARY SCHOOLS: A STUDY OF FILM USE IN
  SELECTED ENGLISH AND FILM COURSES 33, 34, 49
FILM EDUCATION: A COLLECTION OF EXPERIENCES AND IDEAS 47
FILM ENCYCLOPEDIA, THE 1531
FILM ESSAYS AND A LECTURE 1656
FILM EXPERIENCE: ELEMENTS OF MOTION PICTURE ART, THE 140
FILM FACTORY: RUSSIAN AND SOVIET CINEMA IN DOCUMENTS, THE 1653
FILM FANTASY SCRAPBOOK 411
FILM FEMINISMS: THEORY AND PRACTICE 440, 470, 499, 529, 530, 533, 534,
  590
FILM FLAM: ESSAYS ON HOLLYWOOD 1237
FILM FORM: ESSAYS IN FILM THEORY 208, 1301, 1509, 1647, 1657
FILM FORUM: THIRTY-FIVE TOP FILMMAKERS DISCUSS THEIR CRAFT 1552
FILM GENRE READER 189
FILM GENRES: AN ESSAY IN TERMINOLOGY AND DETERMINATION OF FILM
  GENRES 185, 186
FILM GENRE: THEORY AND CRITICISM 189
FILM GUIDE, 4th ed. 1529
FILM HAMLET: A RECORD OF ITS PRODUCTION, THE 1353
FILM HISTORY: THEORY AND PRACTICE 612, 613, 618, 632, 707, 709, 719,
  1068, 1437, 1509, 1511, 1513, 1514, 1518, 1554, 1706
FILM IDEA, THE 69
FILM IN FRANCE, THE 1903, 1909
FILM IN HISTORY: RESTAGING THE PAST, THE 255, 276, 1387
FILM IN STAAT UND PARTEI, DER 227
FILM IN THE AURA OF ART 162, 1706
FILM IN THE BATTLE OF IDEAS 232, 790, 1070, 1321
FILM IN THE CLASSROOM: WHY TO USE IT, HOW TO USE IT 43
FILM IN THE LIFE OF THE SCHOOL: PROGRAMS, PRACTICES AND NEW
  DIRECTIONS 50
FILM IN THE THIRD REICH: A STUDY OF THE GERMAN CINEMA 1933-1945 219,
  238, 321

FILM INDEX--A BIBLIOGRAPHY: THE FILM AS ART, VOLUME 1, THE   1526,
  1532
FILM INDEX--A BIBLIOGRAPHY: THE FILM AS INDUSTRY, VOLUME 2,
  THE   1533
FILM INDEX--A BIBLIOGRAPHY: THE FILM IN SOCIETY, VOLUME 3, THE   1533
FILM INDUSTRIES IN LATIN AMERICA: DEPENDENCY AND DEVELOPMENT   699
FILM INDUSTRIES: PRACTICAL BUSINESS/LEGAL PROBLEMS IN PRODUCTION,
  DISTRIBUTION AND EXHIBITION, THE, 2nd ed.   607, 675, 676, 698
FILM INDUSTRY IN BRAZIL: CULTURE AND THE STATE   2159
FILM LANGUAGE: A SEMIOTICS OF THE CINEMA   133, 168
FILM LIBRARY TECHNIQUES: PRINCIPLES OF ADMINISTRATION   73
FILM LIGHTING: TALKS WITH HOLLYWOOD'S CINEMATOGRAPHERS AND
  GAFFERS   80
FILM MAKER'S DICTIONARY   75, 2211
FILM MAKER'S GUIDE TO SUPER 8   80
FILM MAKERS ON FILM MAKING   609, 1549
FILM MAKING   72
FILM MAKING IN CREATIVE TEACHING   89
FILM MAKING IN SCHOOLS   90
FILM MUSIC AND KEEPING SCORE: FROM VIOLINS TO VIDEO   406
FILM NARRATIVES OF ALAIN RESNAIS, THE   2118, 2138
FILM NOIR: AN ENCYCLOPEDIC REFERENCE TO THE AMERICAN FILM
  STYLE   1947, 1956
FILM NOIR: REFLECTIONS IN A DARK MIRROR   1947, 1956
FILM NOTES   1592
FILM PROGRAMMER'S GUIDE TO 16MM RENTALS   1546
FILM READER 4   1632
FILM RESEARCH: A CRITICAL BIBLIOGRAPHY   1524
FILM SCHEDULING: OR, HOW LONG WILL IT TAKE TO SHOOT YOUR
  MOVIE?   75
FILM SCORE: THE VIEW FROM THE PODIUM   408
FILM SCRIPTS ONE   798, 1210
FILM SENSE, THE   208, 583, 1657
FILM SOCIETY PROGRAMMES: 1925-1939   1525
FILM STUDY AND THE ENGLISH TEACHER   69
FILM STUDY COLLECTIONS: A GUIDE TO THEIR DEVELOPMENT AND USE   1521
FILM STUDY GUIDES: NINE CLASSIC FILMS   44
FILM STUDY IN HIGHER EDUCATION   39, 41, 54
FILM STUDY IN THE UNDERGRADUATE CURRICULUM   47
FILM TEACHING: STUDIES IN THE TEACHING OF FILM WITHOUT FORMAL
  EDUCATION--FOUR COURSES DESCRIBED   47
FILM TECHNIQUE AND FILM ACTING   208, 1662
FILM THEORY AND CRITICISM: INTRODUCTORY READINGS   791, 1332
FILM THEORY AND CRITICISM: INTRODUCTORY READINGS. 3rd ed.   164
FILM TILL NOW: A SURVEY OF WORLD CINEMA, THE   245, 872, 1520, 1564,
  1625
FILM WORLD   101
FILM WORLD: A GUIDE TO CINEMA   142
FILM YEARBOOK, THE   1539
FILM 67/68   994
FILM 67/68: AN ANTHOLOGY OF THE NATIONAL SOCIETY OF FILM
  CRITICS   143
FILM-MAKER'S ART, THE   90
FILM-MAKER'S COOPERATIVE CATALOGUE   2090
FILMED BOOKS AND PLAYS: A LIST OF BOOKS AND PLAYS FROM WHICH FILMS
  HAVE BEEN MADE, 1928-1967   1150
FILMGOER'S COMPANION: AN INTERNATIONAL ENCYCLOPEDIA, THE   1529
FILMGUIDE TO TRIUMPH OF THE WILL   317

FILMGUIDE TO "LA PASSION DE JEANNE D'ARC" 1725, 1729
FILMGUIDE TO "ODD MAN OUT" 1939
FILMGUIDE TO "PSYCHO" 2054
FILMGUIDE TO "THE BATTLE OF ALGIERS" 2172
FILMGUIDE TO "THE GENERAL" 1689
FILMGUIDE TO "THE GRAPES OF WRATH" 1326, 1684
FILMGUIDE TO "THE RULES OF THE GAME" 1821
FILMGUIDE TO "2001: A SPACE ODYSSEY." 2057
FILMGUIDE TO "8 1/2" 2170, 2175
FILMING FOR TELEVISION 91
FILMING OF THE WEST, THE 434
FILMING OF "GONE WITH THE WIND," THE 1318
FILMING THE IMPOSSIBLE: TRAVELS IN SEARCH OF ADVENTURE 72
FILMING "THE GREAT GATSBY" 553, 1322
FILMMAKERS ON FILMMAKING: THE AMERICAN FILM INSTITUTE SEMINARS
  ON MOTION PICTURES AND TELEVISION 609, 1552
FILMMAKING FOR BEGINNERS 89
FILMMAKING FOR CHILDREN: INCLUDING MOTION PICTURE PRODUCTION
  HANDBOOK 91
FILMMAKING: A PRACTICAL GUIDE 73
FILMMAKING: THE COLLABORATIVE ART 609
FILMOGRAPHY OF FILMS ABOUT MOVIES AND MOVIE-MAKING, A 107
FILMOGRAPHY OF THE THIRD WORLD: AN ANNOTATED LIST OF 16mm Films,
  A 916, 917
FILMOLOGY MOVEMENT AND FILM STUDY IN FRANCE, THE 2002
FILMS AND CAREER OF ROBERT ALDRICH, THE 2043, 2072
FILMS AND DREAMS: AN APPROACH TO BERGMAN 582, 583, 2187
FILMS AND FEELINGS 64, 580, 1004, 1012, 1022, 1327, 1729
FILMS AND THE DIRECTOR: A HANDBOOK AND GUIDE TO FILM MAKING 90
FILMS AND THE SECOND WORLD WAR 216, 351
FILMS BEGET FILMS: COMPILATION FILMS FROM PROPAGANDA TO
  DRAMA 209, 304
FILMS BY AND/OR ABOUT WOMEN 512
FILMS DELIVER: TEACHING CREATIVELY WITH FILM 53, 200
FILMS FOR WOMEN 491
FILMS FOR YOUNG ADULTS: A SELECT LIST AND GUIDE TO PROGRAMMING,
  Revised edition 987
FILMS FOR, BY AND ABOUT WOMEN, Series II 520
FILMS IN AMERICA, 1929-1969: A PANORAMIC VIEW OF FOUR DECADES OF
  SOUND 1756
FILMS IN MY LIFE, THE 2094, 2148
FILMS IN REVIEW 1021
FILMS OF AKIRA KUROSAWA, THE 2021, 2028
FILMS OF ALAN LADD, THE 1917
FILMS OF ALFRED HITCHCOCK, THE 1845, 1850
FILMS OF ANTHONY ASQUITH, THE 1357, 1841
FILMS OF ANTHONY QUINN, THE 1968
FILMS OF BELA LUGOSI, THE 1782
FILMS OF BETTE DAVIS, THE 801
FILMS OF BING CROSBY, THE 1350
FILMS OF BORIS KARLOFF, THE 1778
FILMS OF CARL-THEODOR DREYER, THE 1628
FILMS OF CAROL REED, THE 1941
FILMS OF CARY GRANT, THE 1774
FILMS OF CECIL B. DEMILLE, THE 1681
FILMS OF CHARLIE CHAPLIN, THE 1424
FILMS OF CHARLTON HESTON, THE 2052
FILMS OF CLARK GABLE, THE 1772
FILMS OF DORIS DAY, THE 1959

FILMS OF DUSTIN HOFFMAN, THE 2054
FILMS OF D. W. GRIFFITH, THE 1385
FILMS OF ERROL FLYNN, THE 1771
FILMS OF FRANK CAPRA, THE 1764
FILMS OF FRANK SINATRA, THE 1918
FILMS OF FREDRIC MARCH, THE 1782
FILMS OF FRITZ LANG, THE 1639
FILMS OF GARY COOPER, THE 365, 1081, 1765
FILMS OF GENE KELLY: SON AND DANCE MAN, THE 1962
FILMS OF GEORGE PAL, THE 411
FILMS OF GEORGE ROY HILL, THE 2052
FILMS OF GINGER ROGERS, THE 1786
FILMS OF GRETA GARBO, THE 1686
FILMS OF HAL ROACH, THE 1695
FILMS OF HOWARD HAWKS, THE 798, 1776
FILMS OF INGMAR BERGMAN: FROM "TORMENT" TO "ALL THESE WOMEN,"
  THE 2185
FILMS OF INGRID BERGMAN, THE 1761
FILMS OF JACK LEMMON, THE 2058
FILMS OF JACK NICHOLSON, THE 2061
FILMS OF JACQUES TATI, THE 2001, 2007
FILMS OF JAMES CAGNEY, THE 1078, 1762
FILMS OF JAMES STEWART, THE 1787
FILMS OF JANE FONDA, THE 799, 2050
FILMS OF JEAN HARLOW, THE 1774
FILMS OF JEAN VIGO, THE 1824, 1828
FILMS OF JEAN-LUC GODARD, THE 2130
FILMS OF JOAN CRAWFORD, THE 800, 1766
FILMS OF JOHN GARFIELD, THE 1093
FILMS OF JOHN HUSTON, THE 1916
FILMS OF JOHN WAYNE, THE 1789
FILMS OF JOSEF VON STERNBERG, THE 1697, 1788
FILMS OF KATHARINE HEPBURN, THE 1777
FILMS OF KIRK DOUGLAS, THE 1959
FILMS OF LAUREL AND HARDY, THE 1690
FILMS OF LAURENCE OLIVIER, THE 1862
FILMS OF LENI RIEFENSTAHL, THE 318
FILMS OF MAE WEST, THE 1795
FILMS OF MARILYN MONROE, THE 1138, 1965
FILMS OF MARLENE DIETRICH, THE 1767
FILMS OF MARLON BRANDO, THE 1958
FILMS OF MARY PICKFORD, THE 1394
FILMS OF MYRNA LOY, THE 1781
FILMS OF NORMA SHEARER, THE 1786
FILMS OF ORSON WELLES, THE 1792
FILMS OF PAUL NEWMAN, THE 2060
FILMS OF RENE CLAIR, Vol. 1: EXPOSITION AND ANALYSIS, THE 1724, 1826
FILMS OF RENE CLAIR, Vol. 2: DOCUMENTATION, THE 1724
FILMS OF RITA HAYWORTH, THE 1914
FILMS OF ROBERT ALTMAN, THE 785
FILMS OF ROBERT BRESSON, THE 2003
FILMS OF ROBERT REDFORD, THE 2066
FILMS OF ROBERT ROSSEN, THE 1012, 1969
FILMS OF ROBERT TAYLOR, THE 1920
FILMS OF RODDY MCDOWALL, THE 1862
FILMS OF ROGER CORMAN: BRILLIANCE ON A BUDGET, THE 2050, 2075
FILMS OF RONALD COLMAN, THE 1679
FILMS OF RONALD REAGAN, THE 1088, 1785

FILMS OF SHIRLEY TEMPLE, THE 1787
FILMS OF SIDNEY POITIER, THE 886, 887, 888, 951
FILMS OF SPENCER TRACY, THE 1788
FILMS OF STANLEY KUBRICK, THE 2056
FILMS OF STEVE MCQUEEN, THE 2059
FILMS OF STEVEN SPIELBERG, THE 2209
FILMS OF SUSAN HAYWARD, THE 1777
FILMS OF THE FIFTIES: "SUNSET BOULEVARD" TO "ON THE BEACH,"
THE 1953
FILMS OF TYRONE POWER, THE 1785
FILMS OF WARREN BEATTY, THE 2047
FILMS OF WERNER HERZOG: BETWEEN MIRAGE AND HISTORY, THE 2166
FILMS OF WILLIAM HOLDEN, THE 1778
FILMS OF W. C. FIELDS, THE 1770
FILMS ON FILM HISTORY 1557
FILMS ON THE CAMPUS: CINEMA PRODUCTION IN COLLEGES AND
UNIVERSITIES 46
FILMSCRIPT: A WRITER'S GUIDE, THE 84
FILMS: A QUARTERLY OF DISCUSSION AND ANALYSIS 1754
FILM/CINEMA/MOVIE: A THEORY OF EXPERIENCE 164
FILM/CULTURE: EXPLORATIONS OF CINEMA IN ITS SOCIAL CONTEXT 452,
542, 573, 608, 751
FILM, CULTURE, AND THE BLACK FILMMAKER: A STUDY OF FUNCTIONAL
RELATIONSHIPS AND PARALLEL DEVELOPMENTS 867, 869, 909, 911, 953
FILM, THE 53
FILM: A MODERN ART 1564
FILM: A MONTAGE OF THEORIES 142, 1105, 1298
FILM: A PSYCHOLOGICAL STUDY, THE 169
FILM: A REFERENCE GUIDE 1521
FILM: AN ANTHOLOGY 136, 144, 1105, 1332
FILM: AN INTRODUCTION 104
FILM: BOOK 1--THE AUDIENCE AND THE FILMMAKER 140
FILM: BOOK 2--FILMS OF PEACE AND WAR 140, 220
FILM: ENCOUNTER 45
FILM: FORM AND FUNCTION 70
FILM: FORM & FEELING 103, 110, 119, 120, 125
FILM: READINGS IN THE MASS MEDIA 65
FILM: REAL TO REEL 45
FILM: SPACE, TIME, LIGHT, AND SOUND 105
FILM: THE CREATIVE EYE 106
FILM: THE CREATIVE PROCESS: THE SEARCH FOR AN AUDIO-VISUAL
LANGUAGE AND STRUCTURE 164, 1070, 1298, 1299, 1363
FILM: THE DEMOCRATIC ART 227, 329, 560, 607, 625, 639, 640, 646, 648, 649,
721, 732, 733, 736, 743, 1057
FILM: THE MEDIUM AND THE MAKER 68
FILM: THE REALITY OF BEING 54
FINAL CUT: DREAMS AND DISASTER IN THE MAKING OF "HEAVEN'S
GATE" 535, 553
FINAL DRESS 1340
FINALLY TRUFFAUT 2144
FINANCIAL CHARACTERISTICS OF SELECTED "B" FILM PRODUCTIONS OF
ALBERT J. COHEN, 1951-1957 608, 651, 701, 702
FINDING MARILYN: A ROMANCE 1138, 1965
FINE MESS: VERBAL AND VISUAL GEMS FROM THE CRAZY WORLD OF LAUREL
AND HARDY, THE 1690
FINNEGAN'S WAKE 1311
FINNISH CINEMA 1627
FIRST BLOOD 437
FIRST MEN ON THE MOON, THE 1620

FIRST STAGE: PROFILES OF NEW AMERICAN ACTORS 1530
FIRST TWENTY YEARS: A SEGMENT OF FILM HISTORY, THE 1593
FIRST TYCOONS, THE 1467
FIRST WORLD WAR, THE 304
FITZGERALD/HEMINGWAY ANNUAL 1969 1130
FITZGERALD/HEMINGWAY ANNUAL 1973 1109
FITZGERALD/HEMINGWAY ANNUAL 1977 1108, 1110, 1115
FIVE AGES OF THE CINEMA, THE 701, 1460
FIVE C'S OF CINEMATOGRAPHY, THE 81
FIVE HUNDRED BEST AMERICAN FILMS TO BUY, RENT OR VIDEOTAPE 1526
FIVE LIVES OF BEN HECHT, THE 1224
FIVE READERS READING 485
FIVE SCREENPLAYS BY PRESTON STURGES 1919
FIVE SCREENPLAYS: THE SERVANT/ THE PUMPKIN EATER/ THE QUILLER
  MEMORANDUM/ ACCIDENT/ THE GO-BETWEEN 1293
FIVE THOUSAND AND ONE NIGHTS AT THE MOVIES: A GUIDE FROM A TO
  Z 1868
FLASHBACK: A BRIEF HISTORY OF FILM 1519, 1669
FLASHBACK: NORA JOHNSON ON NUNNALLY JOHNSON 1065, 1114, 1252
FLASHMAN series 269
FLASK OF FIELDS: VERBAL AND VISUAL GEMS FROM THE FILMS OF W. C.
  FIELDS, A 1770
FLICK AND I, THE 609
FLORIDA AND THE AMERICAN MOTION PICTURE INDUSTRY, 1898-1980 621
FLYWHEEL, SHYSTER, AND FLYWHEEL: THE MARX BROTHERS' LOST RADIO
  SHOW 1783
FOCAL ENCYCLOPEDIA OF FILM AND TELEVISION TECHNIQUES, THE 75, 98
FOCUS ON CHAPLIN 1421, 1424
FOCUS ON D. W. GRIFFITH 1374
FOCUS ON FILM AND THEATRE 1333, 1336
FOCUS ON GODARD 2130
FOCUS ON HITCHCOCK 1845
FOCUS ON HOWARD HAWKS 1776
FOCUS ON ORSON WELLES 1792
FOCUS ON SCIENCE-FICTION FILM 412
FOCUS ON SHAKESPEARIAN FILMS 1342
FOCUS ON THE HORROR FILM 392
FOCUS ON THE WESTERN 431
FOCUS ON THEATRE AND FILM 1105
FOCUS ON "BLOW-UP" 2170
FOCUS ON "BONNIE AND CLYDE" 2064
FOCUS ON "CITIZEN KANE" 1792
FOCUS ON "RASHOMON" 2028
FOCUS ON "SHOOT THE PIANO PLAYER" 2144
FOCUS ON "THE BIRTH OF A NATION" 865, 1383
FOCUS ON "THE SEVENTH SEAL" 2188, 2189
FOLGER SHAKESPEARE FILMOGRAPHY, THE 1344
FONDA 1771
FONDAS: THE FILMS AND CAREERS OF HENRY, JANE, AND PETER FONDA,
  THE 1771
FONDA: HER LIFE IN PICTURES 2050
FOOTNOTES TO THE FILM 1753
FOR MARX 479
FOR WHOM THE BELL TOLLS 1217, 1231, 1322
FOREIGN FILMS ON AMERICAN SCREENS 1954
FOREVER EALING: A CELEBRATION OF THE GREAT BRITISH FILM
  STUDIO 1841, 1937

FOREVER HOLD YOUR BANNERS HIGH! THE STORY OF THE MICKEY MOUSE
  CLUB & WHAT HAPPENED TO THE MOUSEKETEERS 1767
FORGOTTEN FILMS TO REMEMBER: AND A BRIEF HISTORY OF FIFTY YEARS
  OF THE AMERICAN TALKING FILM 1758
FORGOTTEN HORRORS: EARLY TALKIES FROM POVERTY ROW 399
FORTY YEARS OF SCREEN CREDITS 1929-1969 1546
FOUNDATIONS OF STEREOSCOPIC CINEMA: A STUDY IN DEPTH 73
FOUR ASPECTS OF THE FILM 654, 655, 2033
FOUR FABULOUS FACES: GARBO, SWANSON, CRAWFORD, DIETRICH 1440
FOUR FILMS OF WOODY ALLEN: ANNIE HALL, INTERIORS, MANHATTAN,
  STARDUST MEMORIES 2208
FOUR GREAT COMEDIANS: CHAPLIN, LLOYD, KEATON, AND LANGDON 1421,
  1672, 1678
FOUR HORSEMEN OF THE APOCALYPSE, THE 1707
FOUR SCREENPLAYS OF INGMAR BERGMAN 2184
FOUR STORIES: "THE TOUCH," "CRIES AND WHISPERS," "THE HOUR OF THE
  WOLF," AND "THE PASSION OF ANNA" 2184
FOX GIRLS, THE 1470
FRAGMENTS: BRESSON'S FILM STYLE 2003
FRAME BY FRAME: A BLACK FILMOGRAPHY 931
FRAMEWORK: A HISTORY OF SCREENWRITING IN THE AMERICAN FILM 1159
FRANCE 1572
FRANCIS FORD COPPOLA 2208
FRANCOIS TRUFFAUT 2093, 2095, 2096, 2107, 2143, 2144, 2145, 2155
FRANCOIS TRUFFAUT: A GUIDE TO REFERENCES AND RESOURCES 2106, 2150
FRANJU 2128
FRANK CAPRA 1764
FRANK CAPRA: A GUIDE TO REFERENCES AND RESOURCES 1764
FRANK CAPRA: ONE MAN--ONE FILM 1764
FRANK CAPRA: THE MAN AND HIS FILMS 1763
FRANK CAPRA: THE NAME ABOVE THE TITLE 1762
FRANK SINATRA 1917
FRANK SINATRA, MY FATHER 1918
FRANK SINATRA: CELEBRATION 1918
FRANKENSTEIN 1312, 1808
FRANKENSTEIN CATALOG, THE 391
FRANKENSTEIN LEGEND: A TRIBUTE TO MARY SHELLEY AND BORIS
  KARLOFF, THE 391
FRANKLIN J. SCHAFFNER 2066, 2089
FRED ASTAIRE 1759
FRED ASTAIRE/GINGER ROGERS MOVIE BOOK, THE 1759
FRED ASTAIRE: A PICTORIAL TREASURY OF HIS FILMS 1760
FRED KARNO: MASTER OF MIRTH AND TEARS 1415
FREDERICK WISEMAN 2070
FREDERICK WISEMAN: A GUIDE TO REFERENCES AND RESOURCES 2070
FREE WOMEN OF MAGLIANO, THE 1023
FREEDOM OF THE MOVIES: A REPORT ON SELF-REGULATION FROM THE
  COMMISSION ON FREEDOM OF THE PRESS 233, 965
FRENCH CINEMA 1571, 1618, 1910, 1992
FRENCH CINEMA OF THE OCCUPATION AND THE RESISTANCE 1905
FRENCH CINEMA SINCE 1946: VOLUME ONE--THE GREAT TRADITION 2001
FRENCH CINEMA SINCE 1946: VOLUME TWO--THE PERSONAL STYLE 2000, 2122
FRENCH FILM 1571, 1572, 1606, 1618, 1910, 2112, 2115
FRENCH LIEUTENANT'S WOMAN: A SCREENPLAY, THE 1293
FRENCH LITERARY FILMMAKERS, THE 1313
FRENCH SOCIAL CINEMA OF THE NINETEEN THIRTIES: A CINEMATOGRAPHIC
  EXPRESSION OF POPULAR FRONT CONSCIOUSNESS 1811, 1812, 1813, 1814,
  1815
FRENCH THROUGH THEIR FILMS, THE 1572

FRIENDLY PERSUASION, THE 1319
FRIESE-GREENE: CLOSE-UP OF AN INVENTOR 1610
FRITZ LANG 1636, 1637, 1638, 1642
FRITZ LANG IN AMERICA 876, 1636
FRITZ LANG: A GUIDE TO REFERENCES AND RESOURCES 1637, 1638
FROM BOOK TO FILM: A COMPARATIVE ANALYSIS OF THE CONTENT OF
  SELECTED NOVELS AND THE MOTION PICTURES BASED UPON THEM 1305,
  1306
FROM CALIGARI TO HITLER: A PSYCHOLOGICAL HISTORY OF THE GERMAN
  FILM 206, 321, 441, 555, 776, 1573, 1635, 1639, 1829
FROM CAVE PAINTING TO COMIC STRIP 1592
FROM EARTH TO THE MOON 1620
FROM ENCHANTMENT TO RAGE: THE STORY OF SURREALIST CINEMA 1716,
  1729
FROM HERE TO ETERNITY 1029
FROM HESTER STREET TO HOLLYWOOD: THE JEWISH-AMERICAN STAGE AND
  SCREEN 819, 836
FROM QUASIMODO TO SCARLETT O'HARA: A NATIONAL BOARD OF REVIEW
  ANTHOLOGY 1920-1940 139
FROM RAGS TO RICHES: HORATIO ALGER, JR., AND THE AMERICAN
  DREAM 1047
FROM REVERENCE TO RAPE: THE TREATMENT OF WOMEN IN THE
  MOVIES 471, 501, 502, 503, 505, 591, 592, 1056
FROM SAMBO TO SUPERSPADE: THE BLACK EXPERIENCE IN MOTION
  PICTURES 860, 862, 865, 880, 888, 932, 933, 934, 935, 1005, 1341
FROM THE LIFE OF THE MARIONETTES 2184
FROM THE MEMOIRS OF PONTIUS PILATE 1178
FROM THE TERRACE 1274
FROM UNDER MY HAT 1057, 1243
FROM WAGNER TO MURNAU: THE TRANSPOSITION OF ROMANTICISM FROM
  STAGE TO SCREEN 1633
FRONT AND CENTER 1340
FULL LENGTH ANIMATED FEATURE FILMS 77
FUN IN A CHINESE LAUNDRY 1698
FUTURE TENSE: THE CINEMA OF SCIENCE FICTION 411, 417
F. SCOTT FITZGERALD AND THE LAST TYCOON 1111
F. SCOTT FITZGERALD's SCREENPLAY FOR ERICH MARIA REMARQUE'S
  "THREE COMRADES" 1114, 1215
F. SCOTT FITZGERALD: A CRITICAL PORTRAIT 1111, 1114, 1123, 1126
F. SCOTT FITZGERALD: THE LAST LAOCOON 1129

G

GABLE 1773
GABLE AND LOMBARD 1772
GABLE AND LOMBARD AND POWELL AND HARLOW 1772
GABLE'S WOMEN 1773
GAFFERS, GRIPS, AND BEST BOYS 76
GALLUP LOOKS AT THE MOVIES: AUDIENCE RESEARCH REPORTS
  1940-1950 735
GANGSTER FILM, THE 384
GANGSTER FILM: EMERGENCE, VARIATION AND DECAY 1930-1940, THE 385
GANGSTERS AND HOODLUMS: THE UNDERWORLD IN THE CINEMA 385
GANGSTERS ON THE SCREEN 386, 1947
GANGSTERS: FROM LITTLE CAESAR TO THE GODFATHER 385
GARBO 1686

GARBO AND THE NIGHT WATCHMAN: A SELECTION FROM THE WRITINGS OF BRITISH AND AMERICAN FILM CRITICS 138, 1432
GARBO: A PORTRAIT 1686
GARDEN OF THE FINZI-CONTINIS, THE (IL GIARDINO DEI FINZI-CONTINI) 2174
GARY COOPER 1081, 1765
GARY COOPER STORY, THE 365, 1081, 1765
GAUDY SPREE: THE LITERARY LIFE OF HOLLYWOOD WHEN THE WEST WAS FUN, A 1153
GENE KELLY: A BIOGRAPHY 1962
GENIUS OF THE SYSTEM: HOLLYWOOD FILMMAKING IN THE STUDIO ERA 699
GENRE 174, 192
GENRE: THE MUSICAL 400
GENTLEMAN'S AGREEMENT 1018, 1029
GENTLEMEN PREFER BLONDES 1379
GENTLEMEN TO THE RESCUE: THE HEROES OF THE SILENT SCREEN 1444
GEORGE C. SCOTT: THE MAN, THE ACTOR, AND THE LEGEND 2067
GEORGE RAFT 1785
GEORGE RAFT FILE: THE UNAUTHORIZED BIOGRAPHY, THE 1785
GEORGE ROY HILL 2053
GEORGE S. KAUFMAN AND HIS FRIENDS 1064
GEORGE S. KAUFMAN: AN INTIMATE PORTRAIT 1064
GERMAN CINEMA, THE 1573
GERMANY: AN ILLUSTRATED GUIDE 1572
GETTING EVEN 2045
GETTING IDEAS FROM THE MOVIES 729
GETTING INTO FILM 74
GETTING STARTED IN FILM-MAKING 91
GIELGUD: AN ACTOR AND HIS TIME 1842
GILLO PONTECORVO'S "THE BATTLE OF ALGIERS": A FILM WRITTEN BY FRANCO SOLINAS 2172
GINGER ROGERS 1786
GINGER, LORETTA, AND IRENE WHO? 1786
GINGER: TRIBUTE TO A STAR 1786
GIRL LIKE I, A 1061, 1379, 1399
GLASS KEY, THE 1222
GLASS MENAGERIE, THE 1345
GLAUBER ROCHA AND THE CINEMA NOVO: A STUDY OF HIS WRITINGS AND FILMS 2158
GLORIA AND JOE 1454
GLORIA SWANSON 1454
GLORIOUS TECHNICOLOR 654
GLOSSARY OF FILM TERMS, Rev. ed. 1530
GLOSSARY OF MOTION PICTURE TERMINOLOGY 1530, 2211
GOD BLESS YOU, BUFFALO BILL; A LAYMAN'S GUIDE TO HISTORY AND THE WESTERN FILM 433
GODARD AND OTHERS: ESSAYS ON FORM 163
GODARD ON GODARD: CRITICAL WRITINGS BY JEAN-LUC GODARD 2133
GODARD: IMAGES, SOUNDS, POLITICS 2110, 2111, 2112, 2133
GODARD: THREE FILMS--A WOMAN IS A WOMAN, A MARRIED WOMAN, TWO OR THREE THINGS I KNOW ABOUT HER 2131
GODFATHER, THE 1029
GODFREY DANIELS! VERBAL AND VISUAL GEMS FROM THE SHORT FILMS OF W. C. FIELD 1770
GOING HOLLYWOOD: AN INSIDER'S LOOK AT POWER AND PRETENSE IN THE MOVIE BUSINESS 1233
GOING STEADY 149, 1001, 1003, 1356, 2085
GOLDEN BOY 1259, 1292
GOLDWYN: A BIOGRAPHY 1471

GOLDWYN: A BIOGRAPHY OF THE MAN BEHIND THE MYTH 1474
GOMMES, LES 2139
GONE HOLLYWOOD 1059, 1234
GONE WITH THE WIND 929, 944, 1029, 1217, 1801
GONE WITH THE WIND AS BOOK AND FILM 1125
GONE WITH THE WIND ON FILM: A COMPLETE REFERENCE 1318
GONE WITH THE WIND: AS BOOK AND FILM 1310
GOOD EARTH, THE 1320
GOOD LITTLE DEVIL, A 1392
GOOD NIGHT SWEET PRINCE: THE LIFE AND TIMES OF JOHN
  BARRYMORE 1760
GOODBYE, MR. CHIPS 1328
GOODNESS HAD NOTHING TO DO WITH IT 1795
GRACE: THE SECRET LIVES OF A PRINCESS 1962
GRADIENTS OF DEPTH IN THE CINEMA IMAGE 115, 1814
GRAHAM GREENE AND THE CINEMA 1218
GRAHAM GREENE ON FILM 1327, 1328
GRAHAM GREENE: THE FILMS OF HIS FICTION 1219
GRAMMAR OF THE FILM LANGUAGE 71
GRAMMAR OF THE FILM: AN ANALYSIS OF FILM TECHNIQUE, A 106
GRAND ILLUSION: A FILM BY JEAN RENOIR 1822
GRAND INQUEST: THE STORY OF CONGRESSIONAL INVESTIGATIONS 1077
GRAPES OF WRATH, THE 1309, 1312
GREAT AMERICAN FILM DIRECTORS IN PHOTOGRAPHS 1550
GREAT AMERICAN MOVIE THEATERS 1506
GREAT AUDIENCE, THE 157, 306, 1056
GREAT BRITISH FILMS, THE 1940
GREAT BRITISH PICTURE SHOW, THE 1570, 1936
GREAT CHILD STARS 993
GREAT DANE AND THE GREAT NORTHERN FILM COMPANY, THE 1626, 1627
GREAT EXPECTATIONS 1301, 1304, 1305, 1307, 1308, 1312
GREAT FILM DIRECTORS 1547
GREAT FILM STILLS OF THE GERMAN SILENT ERA: 125 STILLS FROM THE
  STIFTUNG DEUTSCHE KINEMATHEK 1634
GREAT FILMS: FIFTY GOLDEN YEARS OF MOTION PICTURES, THE 1019, 1408,
  1576, 1672, 1702, 1703, 1704, 1707, 1800, 1825, 1933, 2173
GREAT FUNNIES: A HISTORY OF FILM COMEDY, THE 1678
GREAT GANGSTER FILMS, THE 2073
GREAT GANGSTER PICTURES, THE 386
GREAT GATSBY, THE 1110, 1114, 1273, 1321
GREAT GOD PAN: A BIOGRAPHY OF THE TRAMP PLAYED BY CHARLES
  CHAPLIN, THE 1425
GREAT GOLDWYN, THE 1473
GREAT KIDS OF THE MOVIES 991
GREAT MOVIE ACTRESSES 1450
GREAT MOVIE SERIES, THE 420
GREAT MOVIE SHORTS: THOSE WONDERFUL ONE- AND TWO-REELERS OF THE
  THIRTIES AND FORTIES, THE 1754
GREAT MOVIE STARS: THE GOLDEN YEARS, THE 1391, 1449
GREAT MOVIE STARS: THE INTERNATIONAL YEARS, THE 1450
GREAT RADIO PERSONALITIES IN HISTORIC PHOTOGRAPHS 1757
GREAT SCIENCE FICTION PICTURES, THE 415
GREAT SPORTS MOVIES 421, 791, 1946
GREAT SPY PICTURES, THE 423
GREAT WESTERN PICTURES II, THE 432
GREAT WESTERN PICTURES, THE 432
GREAT WESTERN STARS 432
GREATEST FOX OF THEM ALL, THE 1470

GREED 1018
GREED: A FILM BY ERICH VON STROHEIM 1699
GREEK TRAGEDY INTO FILM 1336
GREEN BERETS, THE 363, 364
GREEN FIELDS (GRINE FELDER) 828
GREEN PASTURES, THE 859, 876, 878, 930, 931
GREENHORNS: FOREIGN FILMMAKERS INTERPRET AMERICA 561
GREGORY PECK 643
GREGORY PECK: THE MAN BEHIND THE LEGEND 643, 1917
GRETA GARBO 1802
GRIERSON ON DOCUMENTARY 207, 237
GRIERSON ON DOCUMENTARY, Abridged edition 202
GRIFFITH ACTRESSES, THE 1365, 1384, 1390, 1391
GRIFFITH AND THE RISE OF HOLLYWOOD 1381
GRIFFITH: FIRST ARTIST OF THE MOVIES 1386
GRIFFITH: 1--"THE BIRTH OF A NATION" 1367
GRINE FELDER (GREEN FIELDS) 828
GROUCHO 1783
GROUCHO AND ME 1783
GROUCHO LETTERS: LETTERS FROM AND TO, THE 1784
GROUCHOPHILE, THE 1784
GROUCHO, CHICO, HARPO, AND SOMETIMES ZEPPO 1783
GROWING UP IN HOLLYWOOD 1057, 1275
GROWING UP WITH CHICO 1784
GUERRE EST FINIE: TEXT BY JORGE SEMPRUN FOR THE FILM BY ALAIN
  RESNAIS, LA 380, 2136
GUIDE FOR FILM TEACHERS TO FILMMAKING BY TEENAGERS, A 49
GUIDE TO AMERICAN SCREENWRITERS: THE SOUND ERA, 1929-1982. VOLUME
  II: FILMS, A 1152
GUIDE TO AMERICAN SCREENWRITERS: THE SOUND ERA, 1929-1982. VOLUME
  I: SCREENWRITERS, A 1152
GUIDE TO CRITICAL REVIEWS: PART II--THE MUSICAL, 1909-1974, 2nd ed.,
  A 1756
GUIDE TO CRITICAL REVIEWS: PART III--FOREIGN DRAMA, 1909-1977, 2nd
  ed., A 1756
GUIDE TO CRITICAL REVIEWS: PART IV--THE SCREENPLAY FROM "THE JAZZ
  SINGER" TO "DR. STRANGELOVE," A 1010, 1756
GUIDE TO FILMMAKING 91
GUIDE TO FILMS FEATURED IN THE JEWISH FILM FESTIVAL, A 848
GUIDE TO WORLD CINEMA, A 1521
GUIDEBOOK TO FILM: AN ELEVEN-IN-ONE REFERENCE 1528
GUNGA DIN 1806
GUTS AND GLORY: GREAT AMERICAN WAR MOVIES 231, 348, 350, 360
GWTW: THE MAKING OF "GONE WITH THE WIND" 1125, 1318

H

HABIT 1500
HAIL, COLUMBIA 1469
HALL OF FAME OF WESTERN FILM STARS, THE 426
HAMLET 1429
HAMMER: A CINEMA CASE STUDY 1940
HAMMETT: A LIFE AT THE EDGE 1223
HAND OF A STRANGER, THE (JOURNAL D'UN INCONNU) 1817
HAND THAT HOLDS THE CAMERA: INTERVIEWS WITH WOMEN FILM AND VIDEO
  DIRECTORS, THE 517
HANDBOOK OF ANIMATION TECHNIQUES 77
HANDBOOK OF BASIC MOTION PICTURE TECHNIQUES 72

HANDBOOK OF CANADIAN FILM, A 2162
HANDBOOK OF MULTICHANNEL RECORDING 86
HANDBOOK OF SOUND RECORDING: A TEXT FOR MOTION PICTURE AND
  GENERAL SOUND RECORDING, A 86
HANDBOOK OF SUPER 8 PRODUCTION 90
HANGING ON IN PARADISE 1065, 1151
HANNAH AND HER SISTERS 2208
HARLOW: AN INTIMATE BIOGRAPHY 1774
HARMLESS ENTERTAINMENT: HOLLYWOOD AND THE IDEOLOGY OF
  CONSENSUS 563
HAROLD LLOYD'S WORLD OF COMEDY 1692
HAROLD LLOYD: THE MAN ON THE CLOCK 1693
HAROLD LLOYD: THE SHAPE OF HIS LAUGHTER 569, 1693
HARPO SPEAKS! 1064, 1784
HARRIET 1259
HARRY LANGDON: THE COMEDIAN AS METTEUR-EN-SCENE 1692
HAUNCH, PAUNCH AND JOWL 1071
HAUNTED HOLLYWOOD 1235
HAUNTED SCREEN: EXPRESSIONISM IN THE GERMAN CINEMA AND THE
  INFLUENCE OF MAX REINHARDT, THE 1573, 1633, 1641
HAUNTING, THE 1323
HAVEN'T I SEEN YOU SOMEWHERE BEFORE?: REMAKES, SEQUELS, AND SERIES
  IN MOTION PICTURES AND TELEVISION 1896-1978 420
HAWKS ON HAWKS 798, 1776
HAYS OFFICE, THE 629, 641, 728, 966, 1055
HEART IS A LONELY HUNTER, THE 995
HEART OF DARKNESS 1312
HEARTH AND HOME: IMAGES OF WOMEN IN THE MASS MEDIA 459, 462
HEARTSONG 1489
HEAT AND DUST 548
HEAVENLY BODIES: FILM STARS AND SOCIETY 875, 1441
HELLMAN IN HOLLYWOOD 1029, 1225
HELLO, HOLLYWOOD: THE STORY OF THE MOVIES BY THE PEOPLE WHO MAKE
  THEM 1057, 1238
HEMINGWAY AND FILM 1039, 1231
HEMINGWAY AND THE MOVIES 1231
HENRY IV, PART I 1353
HENRY IV, PART II 1353
HENRY KING'S AMERICA 1779
HENRY KOSTER 1636
HENRY V 1353
HENRY, JANE AND PETER: THE FABULOUS FONDAS 1771
HERE'S LOOKING AT YOU, KID; 50 YEARS OF FIGHTING, WORKING, AND
  DREAMING AT WARNER BROS. 1498
HERETICAL EMPIRICISM 2171
HERITAGE OF HORROR: THE ENGLISH GOTHIC CINEMA 1946-1972 396
HEROES OF THE HORRORS 388
HEROES OF THE SILVER SCREEN 808
HEROES' TWILIGHT: THE FILMS OF SAM PECKINPAH 2063, 2087
HEROES, HEAVIES AND SAGEBRUSH: A PICTORIAL HISTORY OF THE "B"
  WESTERN PLAYERS 430
HEROES, HIGHBROWS AND THE POPULAR MIND 1045
HEROES, VILLAINS, AND FOOLS: REFLECTIONS ON THE AMERICAN
  CHARACTER 437, 551, 552, 562, 807, 817
HEYDAY: AN AUTOBIOGRAPHY 1071, 1485
HIGH NOON OF AMERICAN FILMS IN LATIN AMERICA, THE 642, 701
HIROSHIMA MON AMOUR: TEXT BY MARGUERITE DURAS FOR THE FILM BY
  ALAIN RESNAIS 2137, 2152

HIS EYE IS ON THE SPARROW: AN AUTOBIOGRAPHY 879, 951
HIS MAJESTY THE AMERICAN: THE FILMS OF DOUGLAS FAIRBANKS,
SR. 1399, 1405, 1407
HIS PICTURE IN THE PAPER: A SPECULATION ON CELEBRITY IN AMERICA
BASED ON THE LIFE OF DOUGLAS FAIRBANKS, SR. 569, 1398, 1404
HIS WAY: THE UNAUTHORIZED BIOGRAPHY OF FRANK SINATRA 1918
HISTORIAN AND FILM, THE 259, 275, 288
HISTORICAL AND CRITICAL SURVEY OF THE SCIENCE-FICTION FILM, A 413
HISTORICAL AND DESCRIPTIVE ANALYSIS OF THE WHY WE FIGHT SERIES,
AN 281
HISTORICAL STATISTICS OF THE U. S. COLONIAL TIMES TO 1970, Part
2 650, 736, 753
HISTORICAL STUDY OF THE ACADEMY OF MOTION PICTURE ARTS AND
SCIENCES (1927-1947), A 1069, 1171
HISTORICAL STUDY OF THE DEVELOPMENT OF AMERICAN MOTION PICTURE
CONTENT AND TECHNIQUE PRIOR TO 1904, A 615, 1600
HISTORY AND HEARTBURN: THE SAGA OF AUSTRALIAN FILM 1896-1978 2157
HISTORY MUST ANSWER TO MAN 1510
HISTORY OF AN ART AND AN INSTITUTION, THE 1359
HISTORY OF FILM, A 1519, 1561
HISTORY OF FILM, Second edition, A 1911, 1913, 1949
HISTORY OF FILM, 2nd ed., A 653, 655, 1561, 1584, 1626, 1630, 1632, 1644,
1714, 1733, 1738
HISTORY OF MOTION PICTURE COLOR TECHNOLOGY, A 654
HISTORY OF MOTION PICTURES, THE 627, 1519, 1558, 1625
HISTORY OF MOVIE PHOTOGRAPHY, THE 1589
HISTORY OF NARRATIVE FILM, A 655, 1519, 1560, 1583, 1605, 1607, 1624,
1631, 1633, 1644, 1646, 1747, 1812, 1814, 1876, 1950, 2016, 2021
HISTORY OF THE AMERICAN FILM INDUSTRY FROM ITS BEGINNINGS TO 1931,
A 607, 1519
HISTORY OF THE BRITISH FILM 1929-1939: FILM MAKING IN 1930s BRITAIN,
THE 1745, 1831, 1832, 1840
HISTORY OF THE BRITISH FILM: 1896-1906, THE 1607, 1612
HISTORY OF THE BRITISH FILM: 1906-1914, THE 1612
HISTORY OF THE BRITISH FILM: 1914-1918, THE 1612
HISTORY OF THE BRITISH FILM: 1918-1929, THE 1612
HISTORY OF THE CINEMA: FROM ITS ORIGINS TO 1970, A 1519, 1563, 1624,
1703, 1712, 1715, 1829, 1869, 1923, 1924, 1927, 1935, 1946, 1997, 2093, 2095
HISTORY OF THE IDEA OF PROGRESS 1050
HISTORY OF THE LOS ANGELES LABOR MOVEMENT, 1911-41, THE 1068
HISTORY OF THE MOVIES, A 607, 622, 628, 710, 1056, 1393, 1467
HISTORY OF THE SCREENWRITERS GUILD (1920-1924): THE WRITERS' QUEST
FOR A FREELY NEGOTIATED BASIC AGREEMENT 1068
HISTORY OF WORLD CINEMA, Revised and expanded edition, THE 1563, 1606,
1626, 1631, 1644, 1670, 1869, 1876
HISTORY OF WORLD CINEMA, rev. and expanded ed., THE 1519
HITCHCOCK 1566, 1850, 1856, 1864
HITCHCOCK AND SELZNICK: THE RICH AND STRANGE COLLABORATION OF
ALFRED HITCHCOCK AND DAVID O. SELZNICK IN HOLLYWOOD 1846, 1852,
1951
HITCHCOCK AS ACTIVIST: POLITICS AND THE WAR FILMS 1851
HITCHCOCK READER, A 1836, 1843
HITCHCOCK ROMANCE: LOVE AND IRONY IN HITCHCOCK'S FILMS, THE 1843
HITCHCOCK--THE MURDEROUS GAZE 1851
HITCHCOCK'S BRITISH FILMS 1857
HITCHCOCK'S FILMS 1858
HITCHCOCK: THE FIRST FORTY-FIVE FILMS 1850
HITCH: THE LIFE AND TIMES OF ALFRED HITCHCOCK 1853, 1855, 1857
HITLER: A FILM FROM GERMANY 362

HOLLIS FRAMPTON: RECOLLECTIONS, RECREATIONS 1754
HOLLY-WOULD! 1242
HOLLYWOOD 1042
HOLLYWOOD ACCORDING TO HOLLYWOOD 1246
HOLLYWOOD AND HISTORY: COSTUME DESIGN IN FILM 269
HOLLYWOOD AND THE ACADEMY AWARDS 1165
HOLLYWOOD AND THE AMERICAN IMAGE 1045, 1160
HOLLYWOOD AND THE BOX OFFICE, 1895-1986 608, 616, 642, 643, 647, 655,
  658, 663, 664, 668, 677, 696, 706, 720, 743, 744, 747, 752, 1982, 2107
HOLLYWOOD AND THE CATHOLIC CHURCH: THE IMAGE OF ROMAN
  CATHOLICISM IN AMERICAN MOVIES 1754
HOLLYWOOD AND THE PROFESSION OF AUTHORSHIP, 1928-1940 1150
HOLLYWOOD ANDROGYNY 487, 491, 553, 589
HOLLYWOOD ANECDOTES 1233
HOLLYWOOD AS HISTORIAN: AMERICAN FILM IN A CULTURAL CONTEXT 271
HOLLYWOOD AT SUNSET 1235
HOLLYWOOD AT THE CROSSROADS 658
HOLLYWOOD AT WAR: THE AMERICAN MOTION PICTURE AND WORLD WAR
  II 347
HOLLYWOOD AUTEUR: FRANCIS COPPOLA 2208
HOLLYWOOD BABYLON 1057, 1241
HOLLYWOOD BABYLON II 1057
HOLLYWOOD CAGE, THE 1234
HOLLYWOOD CAMERAMEN: SOURCES OF LIGHT 2042
HOLLYWOOD CONFIDENTIAL 1057, 1242
HOLLYWOOD CORRAL 431
HOLLYWOOD DESTINIES: EUROPEAN DIRECTORS IN AMERICA, 1922-1931 1676
HOLLYWOOD DIRECTORS 1914-1940 1550
HOLLYWOOD DIRECTORS 1941-1976 1551
HOLLYWOOD DOESN'T LIVE HERE ANYMORE 1275
HOLLYWOOD DYNASTIES 1234
HOLLYWOOD EDUCATION: TALES OF MOVIE DREAMS AND EASY MONEY 1042
HOLLYWOOD EXILES, THE 1675
HOLLYWOOD FILM INDUSTRY: A READER, THE 696
HOLLYWOOD FILMS OF THE SEVENTIES: SEX, DRUGS, VIOLENCE, ROCK 'N'
  ROLL & POLITICS 558, 576, 684
HOLLYWOOD FROM VIETNAM TO REAGAN 367, 484, 603, 604
HOLLYWOOD GENRES: FORMULAS, FILMMAKING, AND THE STUDIO
  SYSTEM 173, 193, 194
HOLLYWOOD GOES TO WAR: FILMS AND AMERICAN SOCIETY 1939-1952 218,
  272
HOLLYWOOD GOES TO WAR: HOW POLITICS, PROFITS, AND PROPAGANDA
  SHAPED WORLD WAR II MOVIES 229, 351
HOLLYWOOD GOLD: THE AWARD WINNING MOVIES 1171
HOLLYWOOD GREATS OF THE GOLDEN YEARS: THE LATE STARS OF THE 20s
  THROUGH THE 50s 1442
HOLLYWOOD HALLUCINATION, THE 170, 581, 1054, 1240, 1364
HOLLYWOOD HISTORY OF THE WORLD: FROM "ONE MILLION B. C." TO
  "APOCALYPSE NOW," THE 254, 269
HOLLYWOOD IN A SUITCASE 950
HOLLYWOOD IN FICTION: SOME VERSIONS OF THE AMERICAN MYTH 1040,
  1047, 1053, 1056, 1105, 1157
HOLLYWOOD IN THE FIFTIES 220, 662, 1953
HOLLYWOOD IN THE FORTIES 1913
HOLLYWOOD IN THE SEVENTIES 660
HOLLYWOOD IN THE SIXTIES 661
HOLLYWOOD IN THE THIRTIES 1067, 1752
HOLLYWOOD IN THE TWENTIES 1676

HOLLYWOOD IN THE 1940s: THE STARS' OWN STORIES 1914
HOLLYWOOD IN TRANSITION 1236, 1951
HOLLYWOOD IS A FOUR LETTER TOWN 1057, 1241
HOLLYWOOD KIDS 992
HOLLYWOOD LOOKS AT ITS AUDIENCE: A REPORT OF FILM AUDIENCE
  RESEARCH 660, 706, 739, 740, 774
HOLLYWOOD MODE OF PRODUCTION: THE CONSTRUCTION OF DIVIDED LABOR
  IN THE FILM INDUSTRY, THE 1460
HOLLYWOOD MUSICALS 407
HOLLYWOOD MUSICAL, THE 403, 405, 406, 408
HOLLYWOOD MUSICAL: A PICTURE QUIZ BOOK, THE 401
HOLLYWOOD NOVEL AND OTHER NOVELS ABOUT FILM, 1912-1982: AN
  ANNOTATED BIBLIOGRAPHY, THE 1145
HOLLYWOOD NOVEL: AN HISTORICAL AND CRITICAL STUDY, THE 1028, 1042
HOLLYWOOD NOW 642, 661, 690, 691, 1028
HOLLYWOOD OFF GUARD: A HIGH-SPIRITED, HUMOROUS, AND HILARIOUSLY
  ILLUSTRATED EXPOSE OF HOLLYWOOD STARS OFF GUARD 1448
HOLLYWOOD ON HOLLYWOOD 1042, 1248
HOLLYWOOD ON HOLLYWOOD: TINSEL TOWN TALKS 1244
HOLLYWOOD ON RONALD REAGAN: FRIENDS AND ENEMIES DISCUSS OUR
  PRESIDENT, THE ACTOR 1088
HOLLYWOOD ON THE PALISADES: A FILMOGRAPHY OF SILENT FILMS MADE
  IN FORT LEE, NEW JERSEY, 1903-1927 621
HOLLYWOOD ON TRIAL: THE STORY OF THE 10 WHO WERE INDICTED 1067,
  1074, 1186
HOLLYWOOD POSSE; THE STORY OF A GALLANT BAND OF HORSEMEN WHO
  MADE MOVIE HISTORY 426
HOLLYWOOD PROFESSIONALS (Volume 1), THE 800, 1766
HOLLYWOOD PROFESSIONALS (Volume 2): HENRY KING, LEWIS MILESTONE,
  SAM WOOD, THE 1779
HOLLYWOOD PROFESSIONALS (Volume 3): HOWARD HAWKS, FRANK BORZAGE,
  EDGAR G. ULMAR, THE 1702, 1774
HOLLYWOOD PROFESSIONALS (Volume 4): TOD BROWNING, DON SIEGEL,
  THE 1762
HOLLYWOOD PROFESSIONALS (Volume 5): KING VIDOR, JOHN CROMWELL,
  MERVYN LEROY, THE 1696
HOLLYWOOD PROFESSIONALS: FRANK CAPRA, GEORGE CUKOR, CLARENCE
  BROWN, THE 1764
HOLLYWOOD RAJAH: THE LIFE AND TIMES OF LOUIS B. MAYER 226, 1480
HOLLYWOOD RED: THE AUTOBIOGRAPHY OF LESTER COLE 1067, 1075, 1083,
  1098
HOLLYWOOD SAGA 32, 1680
HOLLYWOOD SCAPEGOAT: THE BIOGRAPHY OF ERICH VON STROHEIM 1700
HOLLYWOOD SCREENWRITERS, THE 1147
HOLLYWOOD SOCIAL PROBLEM FILM: MADNESS, DESPAIR, AND POLITICS
  FROM THE DEPRESSION TO THE FIFTIES, THE 448, 449, 567, 568, 569, 716
HOLLYWOOD SPEAKS! AN ORAL HISTORY 1239
HOLLYWOOD STORY, THE 1242
HOLLYWOOD STUDIO SYSTEM, THE 607, 612, 617, 621, 622, 623, 625, 634,
  635, 643, 662, 663, 691, 693
HOLLYWOOD STUDIOS, THE 1467
HOLLYWOOD STUDIOS: HOUSE STYLE IN THE GOLDEN AGE OF THE MOVIES,
  THE 1467
HOLLYWOOD STYLE, THE ·1057, 1236
HOLLYWOOD THAT WAS, THE 1237
HOLLYWOOD TODAY 660, 2042
HOLLYWOOD UNREEL: FANTASIES ABOUT HOLLYWOOD AND THE MOVIES 1234
HOLLYWOOD WRITERS' WARS, THE 1065, 1069, 1191, 1280
HOLLYWOOD 1920-1970 1561

HOLLYWOOD'S CHILDREN: AN INSIDE ACCOUNT OF THE CHILD STAR
  ERA 991
HOLLYWOOD'S GREAT LOVE TEAMS 1448
HOLLYWOOD'S HOLLYWOOD: THE MOVIES ABOUT THE MOVIES 1032, 1044,
  1246, 1249, 1290, 1296
HOLLYWOOD'S IMAGE OF THE JEW 667, 819, 839, 840, 841, 850
HOLLYWOOD'S MOVIE COMMANDMENTS: A HANDBOOK FOR MOTION PICTURE
  WRITERS AND REVIEWERS 965
HOLLYWOOD'S WARTIME WOMAN: REPRESENTATION AND IDEOLOGY 353
HOLLYWOODLAND U.S.A.: THE MOVIEGOER'S GUIDE TO SOUTHERN
  CALIFORNIA 1237
HOLLYWOOD; THE GOLDEN ERA 1239
HOLLYWOOD; WHEN SILENTS WERE GOLDEN 1239
HOLLYWOOD, UK: THE BRITISH FILM INDUSTRY IN THE SIXTIES 1940
HOLLYWOOD: LAND AND LEGEND 1058, 1233
HOLLYWOOD: LEGEND AND REALITY 1241
HOLLYWOOD: STARS AND STARLETS, TYCOONS AND FLESH-PEDDLERS,
  MOVIEMAKERS AND MONEYMAKERS 832, 1057, 1236
HOLLYWOOD: THE DREAM FACTORY 536, 550, 609, 614, 734, 742, 1046, 1057,
  1238
HOLLYWOOD: THE FIRST 100 YEARS 1065
HOLLYWOOD: THE HAUNTED HOUSE 1041, 1056, 1058, 1237
HOLLYWOOD: THE MOVIE COLONY, THE MOVIE MAKERS 226, 736, 1041, 1049,
  1057, 1121, 1238, 1435, 1437
HOLLYWOOD: THE MOVIE FACTORY 1236
HOLLYWOOD: THE PIONEERS 617, 1675
HOLLYWOOD: THE YEARS OF INNOCENCE 1236
HOMAGE TO CATALINA 1076
HOME AND THE WORLD, THE 548
HOME OF THE BRAVE 859, 952
HONORARY CONSUL, THE 1218
HOORAY FOR CAPTAIN SPAULDING! 1783
HOPE OF HEAVEN 1162, 1274
HORATIO ALGER, FAREWELL: THE END OF THE AMERICAN DREAM 1047, 1050
HORIZONS WEST: ANTHONY MANN, BUD BOETTICHER, SAM
  PECKINPAH--STUDIES OF AUTHORSHIP WITHIN THE WESTERN 174, 192, 350,
  429, 1982
HORROR 390
HORROR AND DOMESTICITY: THE MODERN GOTHIC ROMANCE FILM 794
HORROR AND FANTASY IN THE CINEMA 392
HORROR AND SCIENCE FICTION FILMS 419
HORROR FILM STARS 396
HORROR FILMS 389
HORROR FILM, THE 389
HORROR PEOPLE, THE 388
HORROR SHOWS: THE A-TO-Z OF HORROR IN FILM, TV, RADIO AND
  THEATER 400
HORRORS FROM SCREEN TO SCREAM: AN ENCYCLOPEDIC GUIDE TO THE
  GREATEST HORROR AND FANTASY FILMS OF ALL TIME 395
HORSE, THE GUN AND THE PIECE OF THE PROPERTY: CHANGING IMAGES
  OF THE TV WESTERN, THE 425
HOUND AND HORN: ESSAYS ON CINEMA 1752
HOUR WITH THE MOVIES AND THE TALKIES, AN 157, 1055, 1757
HOUSE COMMITTEE ON UN-AMERICAN ACTIVITIES, 1945-1950, THE 1077
HOUSE OF HORROR: THE COMPLETE STORY OF HAMMER FILMS, THE 387,
  390
HOUSE THAT SHADOWS BUILT, THE 1504
HOW GREEN WAS MY VALLEY 1007, 1029

HOW MOVIES WORK 105, 111
HOW TO APPRECIATE MOTION PICTURES 729
HOW TO BECOME A UNION CAMERAWOMAN FILM-VIDEOTAPE 81
HOW TO BREAK INTO MOTION PICTURES, TELEVISION, COMMERCIALS, AND
 MODELING 72, 1232
HOW TO DO SIMPLER TRICKS 87
HOW TO DO TRICKS 87
HOW TO MAKE A JEWISH MOVIE 848
HOW TO MAKE ANIMATED MOVIES: A STUDIO HANDBOOK 77
HOW TO MAKE GOOD SOUND MOVIES 86
HOW TO MAKE IT IN HOLLYWOOD 609
HOW TO MAKE MOVIE MAGIC IN AMATEUR FILMS 87
HOW TO MAKE MOVIES: A PRACTICAL GUIDE TO GROUP FILMMAKING 88
HOW TO MAKE NEWS & INFLUENCE PEOPLE 73
HOW TO ORGANIZE AND RUN A FILM SOCIETY 55
HOW TO PREPARE A PRODUCTION BUDGET FOR FILM & VIDEO TAPE. 2nd
 ed. 72
HOW TO REACH ANYONE WHO'S ANYONE 1533
HOW TO READ A FILM: THE ART, TECHNOLOGY, LANGUAGE, HISTORY, AND
 THEORY OF FILM AND MEDIA 67, 96
HOW TO READ A FILM: THE ART, TECHNOLOGY, LANGUAGE, HISTORY, AND
 THEORY OF FILM AND MEDIA, rev. ed. 2211
HOW TO SAVE YOUR OWN LIFE 1041
HOW TO SELL YOUR FILM PROJECT 71
HOW TO SHOOT A MOVIE STORY: THE TECHNIQUE OF PICTORIAL
 CONTINUITY 88
HOW TO SUCCEED IN BUSINESS WITHOUT REALLY TRYING 1346
HOW WE ADVERTISED AMERICA 223
HOWARD HAWKS 365, 798, 1777
HOWARD HAWKS STORYTELLER 798
HOWARD HAWKS: A JUNGIAN STUDY 1775
HOWARD HAWKS: STORYTELLER 1775
HUCKLEBERRY FINN 979
HUMAN FIGURE IN MOTION, THE 1598
HUMPHREY BOGART 1078, 1761, 1762
HUMPHREY JENNINGS: FILM-MAKER/PAINTER/POET 316
HUMPHREY JENNINGS: MORE THAN A MAKER OF FILMS 315, 323
HUNCHBACK OF NOTRE DAME, THE 1702
HUNDRED DIFFERENT LIVES: AN AUTOBIOGRAPHY, A 1325, 1861
HUNGARIAN CINEMA TODAY: HISTORY MUST ANSWER TO THE MAN 2167
HUSTLER, THE 1014, 1311

I

I AM A FOOL 1316
I AM A FUGITIVE FROM A CHAIN GANG 1804
I BLOW MY OWN HORN 1477, 1479
I LED THREE LIVES 1190
I LOST IT AT THE MOVIES 150, 997, 1000, 1001, 1005, 1010, 1013, 1018, 1323,
 1325, 1326, 1349, 1509
I LOST MY GIRLISH LAUGHTER 1104
I REMEMBER IT WELL 1138, 1784
I WAS A COMMUNIST FOR THE FBI 1190
I WAS A TEENAGE JUVENILE DELINQUENT ROCK'N'ROLL HORROR BEACH
 PARTY MOVIE BOOK, THE 982
ICEMAN COMETH, THE 1351
IDA LUPINO 1782
IDA LUPINO AS FILM DIRECTOR, 1949-1953: AN AUTEUR APPROACH 1782

IDEA OF THE IMAGE: JOSEF VON STERNBERG'S DIETRICH FILMS, THE   1697
IDEAS HAVE CONSEQUENCES   855
IDEAS OF ORDER IN LITERATURE AND FILM: SELECTED PAPERS   1297
IDEAS ON FILM: A HANDBOOK FOR THE 16mm. FILM USER   54
IDENTITY   985
IDEOLOGY AND IMAGERY   184
IDEOLOGY AND THE IMAGE: SOCIAL REPRESENTATION IN THE CINEMA AND
  OTHER MEDIA   170, 464
IDOLS OF SILENCE, THE   1450
IF WE ONLY HAD MONEY   1104
IKIRU: A FILM   2028
IL FE DELLE COMICHE   1412
ILIAD, THE   1153
ILLUSIONS OF A NATION: MYTH AND HISTORY IN THE NOVELS OF F. SCOTT
  FITZGERALD, THE   1048, 1052, 1120
ILLUSTRATED GLOSSARY OF FILM TERMS, AN   1528, 2211
ILLUSTRATED GUIDE TO FILM DIRECTORS, THE   1552
ILLUSTRATED HISTORY OF THE HORROR FILM, THE   389
ILLUSTRATED WHO'S WHO IN BRITISH FILMS, THE   1570
IMAGE AND INFLUENCE: STUDIES IN THE SOCIOLOGY OF FILM   785
IMAGE INDUSTRIES, THE   50
IMAGE MAKERS: SIXTY YEARS OF HOLLYWOOD GLAMOUR, THE   1451
IMAGES AND ENTERPRISE: TECHNOLOGY AND THE AMERICAN PHOTOGRAPHIC
  INDUSTRY 1839 TO 1925   1614
IMAGES IN ACTION: A GUIDE TO USING WOMEN'S FILM AND VIDEO   492
IMAGES IN LOW KEY: CINEMATOGRAPHER SOL POLITO, A. S. C. WITH A
  HISTORICAL SURVEY OF CINEMATOGRAPHY   1495
IMAGES OF AFRICA, THE   919
IMAGES OF CHILDREN IN AMERICAN FILM: A SOCIOCULTURAL
  ANALYSIS   970, 971, 972, 985
IMAGES OF MADNESS: THE PORTRAYAL OF INSANITY IN THE FEATURE
  FILM   580, 597, 598, 605, 801
IMAGES OF THE MEXICAN AMERICAN IN FICTION AND FILM   826
IMAGES OF WOMEN IN FILM: THE WAR YEARS, 1941-1945   341, 789
IMAGE, OR, WHAT HAPPENED TO THE AMERICAN DREAM?, THE   255, 546, 547,
  549, 556, 1027, 1434
IMAGE: A GUIDE TO PSEUDO-EVENTS IN AMERICA, THE   255, 547, 556, 1027,
  1139, 1434
IMAGE: KNOWLEDGE AND LIFE IN SOCIETY, THE   258
IMAGINARY SIGNIFIER: PSYCHOANALYSIS AND THE CINEMA, THE   169, 480,
  584
IMMEDIATE EXPERIENCE: MOVIES, COMICS, THEATRE, AND OTHER ASPECTS
  OF POPULAR CULTURE, THE   160, 464, 1009, 1019, 1433
IMMEDIATE SEATING: A LOOK AT MOVIE AUDIENCES   768
IMMORAL MEMORIES: AN AUTOBIOGRAPHY   1656
IMMORTAL JOLSON: HIS LIFE AND TIMES, THE   827, 1778
IMMORTALS OF THE SCREEN   1450
IMPACT OF FILM: HOW IDEAS ARE COMMUNICATED THROUGH CINEMA AND
  TELEVISION, THE   66
IMPLIED READER: PATTERNS IN COMMUNICATION IN PROSE FICTION FROM
  BUNYAN TO BECKETT, THE   485
IN A GROVE   2028
IN ABRAHAM'S BOSOM   862
IN COLD BLOOD   605
IN GENRE: THE MUSICAL: A READER   460
IN ITS OWN IMAGE: THE CINEMATIC VISION OF HOLLYWOOD   1044, 1060, 1136,
  1137, 1144, 1244, 1290, 1292, 1295, 1296
IN MY MIND'S I: AN ACTOR'S AUTOBIOGRAPHY   1863

IN SEARCH OF DRACULA: A TRUE HISTORY OF DRACULA AND OTHER
VAMPIRE LEGENDS   395
IN THE BEGINNING: PROGRAM NOTES TO ACCOMPANY ONE HUNDRED EARLY
MOTION PICTURES   1593
IN THE DARK: A PRIMER FOR THE MOVIES   101
IN THE SERVICE OF THE STATE: THE CINEMA OF ALEXANDER
DOVZHENKO   1655
IN THE ZONE   1350
INCIDENT AT VICHY   837
INCREDIBLE SARAH, THE   1463
INDECENT EXPOSURE: A TRUE STORY OF HOLLYWOOD AND WALL
STREET   537
INDELIBLE IMAGES: NEW PERSPECTIVES ON CLASSIC FILMS   138
INDELIBLE SHADOWS: FILM AND THE HOLOCAUST   222, 310, 311
INDEPENDENT BLACK AMERICAN CINEMA   901
INDEPENDENT FEATURE FILM PRODUCTION: A COMPLETE GUIDE FROM
CONCEPT THROUGH DISTRIBUTION   72
INDEPENDENT FILMMAKING   73
INDEPENDENT PRODUCER: FILM AND TELEVISION, THE   73
INDEPENDENT VIDEO: A COMPLETE GUIDE TO THE PHYSICS, OPERATION,
AND APPLICATION OF THE NEW TELEVISION   92
INDEX TO CRITICAL FILM REVIEWS IN BRITISH AND AMERICAN FILM
PERIODICALS TOGETHER WITH INDEX TO CRITICAL REVIEWS   1522, 1523
INDEX TO FILMS IN REVIEW 1950-1959, AN   1527
INDEX TO THE CREATIVE WORK OF DAVID WARK GRIFFITH   1367
INDIAN CINEMA SUPERBAZAAR   2167
INDIAN FILM   2167
INDUSTRIAL LIGHT AND MAGIC: THE ART OF SPECIAL EFFECTS   81
INDUSTRY: LIFE IN THE HOLLYWOOD FAST LANE, THE   690
INFORMATION FILM: A REPORT OF THE PUBLIC LIBRARY INQUIRY, THE   55
INFORMATIONAL FILM, THE   1537
INFORMER, THE   1309
INGMAR BERGMAN   2188
INGMAR BERGMAN AND SOCIETY   2184
INGMAR BERGMAN AND THE RITUALS OF ART   2187
INGMAR BERGMAN AND THE SEARCH FOR MEANING   2186
INGMAR BERGMAN DIRECTS   2187
INGMAR BERGMAN: A CRITICAL BIOGRAPHY   2185
INGMAR BERGMAN: A MONOGRAPH   2185
INGMAR BERGMAN: AN APPRECIATION   2187
INGMAR BERGMAN: ESSAYS IN CRITICISM   2187
INGMAR BERGMAN: FOUR DECADES IN THE THEATER   2187
INGMAR BERGMAN: THE CINEMA AS MISTRESS   2187
INGRID BERGMAN   1761
INGRID BERGMAN: AN INTIMATE PORTRAIT   1761
INGRID BERGMAN: MY STORY   1761
INJURY TO INSULT: UNEMPLOYMENT, CLASS, AND POLITICAL
RESPONSE   1046, 1051
INNOCENT EYE: THE LIFE OF ROBERT J. FLAHERTY, THE   1681
INQUISITION IN EDEN   1067, 1177
INQUISITION IN HOLLYWOOD: POLITICS IN THE FILM COMMUNITY 1930-1960,
THE   203, 219, 226, 1063, 1065, 1075, 1099, 1181, 1191, 1193
INSIDE DAISY CLOVER   1041
INSIDE OSCAR: THE UNOFFICIAL HISTORY OF THE ACADEMY AWARDS   1174,
1175
INSIDE WARNER BROS. (1935-1951)   1493, 1945
INSIDE "THE DEEP"   554
INSTRUCTIONAL FILM RESEARCH 1918-1950   746

INTEGRATION AND ATTEMPTED INTEGRATION BETWEEN THE MOTION
 PICTURE INDUSTRIES THROUGH 1956   678
INTERMISSION: A TRUE STORY   1957
INTERNATIONAL DICTIONARY OF FILMS AND FILMMAKERS: VOLUME I--FILMS,
 THE   1534
INTERNATIONAL DICTIONARY OF FILMS AND FILMMAKERS: VOLUME
 II--DIRECTORS/FILMMAKERS, THE   1535
INTERNATIONAL DICTIONARY OF FILMS AND FILMMAKERS: VOLUME
 III--ACTORS AND ACTRESSES, THE   1541, 1545
INTERNATIONAL DICTIONARY OF FILMS AND FILMMAKERS: VOLUME
 IV--WRITERS AND PRODUCTION ARTISTS, THE   1546
INTERNATIONAL DIRECTORY OF FILM AND TV DOCUMENTATION
 CENTRES   1545
INTERNATIONAL ENCYCLOPEDIA OF FILM, THE   1536, 1739, 1832
INTERNATIONAL FILM GUIDE   1525
INTERNATIONAL FILM INDUSTRY: WESTERN EUROPE AND AMERICA SINCE
 1945, THE   607, 676, 693, 694
INTERNATIONAL FILM NECROLOGY   1544
INTERNATIONAL PICTURE ALMANAC   1545
INTERPRETATION OF DREAMS, THE   531
INTERVIEWS WITH FILM DIRECTORS   609, 1002, 1351, 1553
INTERVIEWS WITH SCREENWRITERS OF HOLLYWOOD'S GOLDEN AGE   1154
INTIMACIES: STARS SHARE THEIR CONFIDENCES AND FEELINGS   609
INTIMATE STRANGERS: THE CULT OF CELEBRITY   549, 569, 1436
INTO FILM   88
INTOLERANCE: THE FILM BY DAVID WARK GRIFFITH, SHOT-BY-SHOT
 ANALYSIS   1367
INTREPID LAUGHTER: PRESTON STURGES AT THE MOVIES   1918, 1920
INTRODUCTION TO AMERICAN MOVIES, AN   188
INTRODUCTION TO CINEMATOGRAPHY, 3rd ed., AN   81
INTRODUCTION TO FILM   70
INTRODUCTION TO FILM CRITICISM: MAJOR CRITICAL APPROACHES TO
 NARRATIVE FILM   37, 120, 121, 125, 138
INTRODUCTION TO FILM, 2nd ed.   68
INTRODUCTION TO FILM, 2nd ed., AN   58, 59, 120, 121, 1520
INTRODUCTION TO FILM: A GUIDE TO THE ART, TECHNOLOGY, LANGUAGE,
 AND APPRECIATION OF FILM   96, 97
INTRODUCTION TO LITERARY CRITICISM   109
INTRODUCTION TO THE AMERICAN UNDERGROUND FILM, AN   1955
INTRODUCTION TO THE ART OF THE FILM   1706
INTRODUCTION TO THE ART OF THE MOVIES: AN ANTHOLOGY OF IDEAS ON
 THE NATURE OF MOVIE ART   140
INTRUDER IN THE DUST   1037
INVESTIGATION OF THE MOVIES FOR AND REALIZATION OF MUSIC TO
 ACCOMPANY THE AMERICAN SILENT FILM 1896-1927   402
INVISIBLE STORYTELLERS: VOICE-OVER NARRATION IN AMERICAN FICTION
 FILM   113, 116
IS THAT WHO I THINK IT IS? Volume 1   1439
IS THAT WHO I THINK IT IS? Volume 2   1439
IS THERE A TEXT IN THIS CLASS?: THE AUTHORITY OF INTERPRETIVE
 COMMUNITIES   485
ISLAND OF THE BLUE DOLPHINS   996
ISRAELI FILM: SOCIAL AND CULTURAL INFLUENCES 1912-1973, THE   2168
IT GIRL: THE INCREDIBLE STORY OF CLARA BOW, THE   1060, 1679
IT TAKES MORE THAN TALENT   1780
IT TOOK NINE TAILORS   1081
IT WAS FUN WHILE IT LASTED   1236

IT'S A HELL OF A LIFE BUT NOT A BAD LIVING: A HOLLYWOOD
  MEMOIR   1029, 1092, 1201
IT'S ALIVE! THE CLASSIC CINEMA SAGA OF FRANKENSTEIN 394
IT'S ONLY A MOVIE   51
ITALIAN CINEMA TODAY 1952-1965   1876
ITALIAN CINEMA, THE   1573, 1574, 1608, 1873, 1933
ITALIAN CINEMA: FROM NEOREALISM TO THE PRESENT 1885, 1928
ITALIAN POLITICAL FILMMAKERS, THE   2169
ITINERANT CAMERAMAN   80
IVAN THE TERRIBLE: A FILM BY SERGEI EISENSTEIN 1866
IVANHOE   822
I. E. AN AUTOBIOGRAPHY   1786

J

JACK LEMMON   2058
JACK NICHOLSON   2061
JACK NICHOLSON: A BIOGRAPHY   2061
JACK NICHOLSON: FACE TO FACE   2061
JACK NICHOLSON: THE SEARCH FOR A SUPERSTAR   2061
JACOBOWSKY AND THE COLONEL   1259
JACQUES TATI: A GUIDE TO REFERENCES AND RESOURCES   2007
JAMES AGEE: A STUDY OF HIS FILM CRITICISM   146
JAMES BOND FILMS: A BEHIND THE SCENES HISTORY, THE   423
JAMES BOND IN THE CINEMA   422
JAMES CAGNEY   1078, 1762
JAMES DEAN REVISITED   1325, 1959
JAMES DEAN STORY, THE   1959
JAMES DEAN, THE MUTANT KING: A BIOGRAPHY   1959
JAMES DEAN: A BIOGRAPHY   1325, 1959
JAMES DEAN: A SHORT LIFE   1325, 1959
JAMES DEAN: AMERICAN ICON   1325, 1959
JAMES DEAN: THE MUTANT KING   1325
JAMES M. CAIN   1196
JAMES STEWART   1787, 1951
JAMES WHALE'S FRANKENSTEIN   388
JANE EYRE   1312
JANE FONDA: A BIOGRAPHY   2050
JANE FONDA: ALL AMERICAN ANTI-HEROINE   799, 2050
JANE FONDA: HEROINE FOR OUR TIME   2050
JANE WYMAN, THE ACTRESS AND THE WOMAN: AN ILLUSTRATED
  BIOGRAPHY   1973
JANE: AN INTIMATE BIOGRAPHY OF JANE FONDA   799, 2050
JAPAN   1575, 1888, 2018, 2029
JAPANESE CINEMA: FILM STYLE   1575
JAPANESE FILM DIRECTORS   1887, 1890, 1891, 1893, 1894, 1898, 2021, 2022
JAPANESE FILM: ART AND INDUSTRY, THE   1574, 1734, 1735, 1736, 1737,
  1739, 1740, 1741, 1742, 1885, 1889, 1892, 1894, 2015, 2016
JAPANESE MOVIES   1574
JAPANESE MOVIE, Rev. ed., THE   1575, 1731, 1735, 1736, 1737, 1740, 1887,
  1897
JAPAN: FILM IMAGE   1575, 1731, 1735, 1736, 1740, 1887, 1890, 1902, 2016, 2018
JAWS LOG, THE   554
JEAN COCTEAU   1818, 1995
JEAN COCTEAU AND ANDRE GIDE: AN ABRASIVE FRIENDSHIP   1818
JEAN COCTEAU AND HIS FILMS OF ORPHIC IDENTITY   1818
JEAN COCTEAU AND THE FRENCH SCENE   1816, 1819
JEAN COCTEAU: AN INVESTIGATION INTO HIS FILMS AND PHILOSOPHY   1818

JEAN HARLOW 1774
JEAN LE BLUE 1826
JEAN MITRY AND THE AESTHETICS OF THE CINEMA 132, 133, 169
JEAN PIERRE LEFEBVRE 2162
JEAN RENOIR 1819, 1820, 1821
JEAN RENOIR: A GUIDE TO REFERENCES AND RESOURCES 1820
JEAN RENOIR: ESSAYS, CONVERSATIONS, REVIEWS 1821
JEAN RENOIR: THE FRENCH FILMS, 1924-1939 1823
JEAN RENOIR: THE WORLD OF HIS FILMS 1819
JEAN VIGO 1823, 1824
JEAN-LUC GODARD 2130, 2132, 2134, 2151
JEAN-LUC GODARD: A CRITICAL ANTHOLOGY 2133
JEAN-LUC GODARD: A GUIDE TO REFERENCES AND RESOURCES 2110, 2132
JEW IN AMERICAN CINEMA, THE 819, 823, 838, 839, 850, 851
JEWISH FILMS IN THE UNITED STATES: A COMPREHENSIVE SURVEY AND
  DESCRIPTIVE FILMOGRAPHY 839
JEWISH IMAGE IN AMERICAN FILM, THE 819, 822, 842
JIRI MENZEL AND THE HISTORY OF CLOSELY WATCHED TRAINS 2164
JOAN CRAWFORD 800, 1765, 1766
JOAN CRAWFORD: A BIOGRAPHY 800
JOAN CRAWFORD: THE RAGING STAR 1765
JOHN FORD 1683, 1684, 1685, 2076
JOHN FORD MOVIE MYSTERY, THE 1685
JOHN FORD'S "STAGECOACH" STARRING JOHN WAYNE 1772
JOHN FORD: A BIOGRAPHY 1685
JOHN GARFIELD; HIS LIFE AND FILMS 1093
JOHN GRIERSON AND THE NATIONAL FILM BOARD: THE POLITICS OF
  WARTIME PROPAGANDA 215, 236
JOHN GRIERSON FILM MASTER 215
JOHN GRIERSON: A DOCUMENTARY BIOGRAPHY 215
JOHN HUSTON 1087
JOHN HUSTON: A BIOGRAPHY 1087, 1916
JOHN HUSTON: KING REBEL 1087, 1916
JOHN HUSTON: MAKER OF MAGIC 322, 1087, 1916
JOHN WAYNE 1081, 1788
JOHN WAYNE AND THE MOVIES 1788
JOHN WAYNE STORY, THE 1081
JOHN WAYNE: PROPHET OF THE AMERICAN WAY OF LIFE 1788
JOHN WAYNE: THE ACTOR, THE MAN 1081, 1788
JOHNNY GOT HIS GUN 1233, 1282
JOLLY CORNER, THE 1316
JOLSON 827, 1778
JOLSON: THE LEGEND COMES TO LIFE 827, 1778
JORIS IVENS, FILM-MAKER: FACING REALITY 177, 312, 319
JOSEF VON STERNBERG: A CRITICAL STUDY OF THE GREAT DIRECTOR 1698
JOSEPH ANDREWS 1312
JOSEPH LOSEY 1962, 1980, 2161
JOSH: MY UP AND DOWN, IN AND OUT OF LIFE 1264
JOURNAL D'UN INCONNU (THE HAND OF A STRANGER) 1817
JOURNAL OF FORBIDDEN FILMS, THE 560
JOURNAL OF THE PLAGUE YEARS, A 229, 1045, 1067, 1074, 1076, 1080, 1096,
  1100, 1187
JOURNALIST'S NOTEBOOK OF LIVE RADIO-TV NEWS 91
JOURNALS OF JEAN COCTEAU, THE 1816
JUDY 1138
JUDY AND LIZA 1138
JUDY GARLAND 1138, 1773
JUDY GARLAND: A BIOGRAPHY 1138

JUDY: A REMEMBRANCE 1773
JUDY: THE FILMS AND CAREER OF JUDY GARLAND 1773
JULES AND JIM 2147
JULES AND JIM: A FILM BY FRANCOIS TRUFFAUT 2146
JULIET OF THE SPIRITS 2171
JULIUS CAESAR 438, 1789
JULIUS CAESAR: COMPLETE TEXT, WITH SCENES FROM THE
  SCREENPLAY 1354
JUMP CUT: HOLLYWOOD, POLITICS AND COUNTER-CINEMA 465, 573
JUNE ALLYSON 1759
JUST ME 1458
J. B. 1261
J. D. FILMS: JUVENILE DELINQUENCY IN THE MOVIES, THE 973, 986

K

KALEIDOSCOPIC LENS: HOW HOLLYWOOD VIEWS ETHNIC GROUPS, THE 826
KARL STRUSS: MAN WITH A CAMERA 1386
KARLOFF 1778, 1779
KARLOFF AND COMPANY: THE HORROR FILM 395
KARLOFF AND LUGOSI: THE STORY OF A HAUNTING COLLABORATION, WITH
  A COMPLETE FILMOGRAPHY OF THEIR FILMS TOGETHER 394
KARLOFF, THE MAN, THE MONSTER, THE MOVIES 1778
KATE: THE LIFE OF KATHARINE HEPBURN 1777
KATHARINE HEPBURN 1777, 1778
KAZAN ON KAZAN 1093, 1257
KEATON 1687, 1705
KEATON: THE MAN WHO WOULDN'T LIE DOWN 1687, 1705
KEATON: THE SILENT FILMS CLOSE UP 1677, 1688
KEEP WATCHING THE SKIES! AMERICAN SCIENCE FICTION MOVIES OF THE
  FIFTIES 418
KEN RUSSELL 1296
KENJI MIZOGUCHI: A GUIDE TO REFERENCES AND RESOURCES 1900
KIDVID: A PARENT'S GUIDE TO CHILDREN'S VIDEO 987
KINDERGARTEN OF THE MOVIES: A HISTORY OF THE FINE ARTS COMPANY,
  THE 1384, 1412
KINDNESS OF STRANGERS, THE 1914
KINETOSCOPE: AMERICA'S FIRST COMMERCIALLY SUCCESSFUL MOTION
  PICTURE EXHIBITOR, THE 860, 1615
KING COHN: THE LIFE AND TIMES OF HARRY COHN 368, 534, 1469
KING LEAR 2069, 2112
KING LEAR: THE SPACE OF TRAGEDY. THE DIARY OF A FILM
  DIRECTOR 1342
KING OF COMEDY 1413
KING OF THE Bs: WORKING WITHIN THE HOLLYWOOD SYSTEM 651
KING SOLOMON'S MINES 919
KING VIDOR 1081, 1696
KING VIDOR ON FILM MAKING 1696
KING VIDOR, AMERICAN 1696
KINGDOM OF DREAMS: SELECTED PAPERS FROM THE TENTH ANNUAL FLORIDA
  STATE UNIVERSITY CONFERENCE ON LITERATURE AND FILM 598
KING: A BIOGRAPHY OF CLARK GABLE, THE 1773
KINO: A HISTORY OF THE RUSSIAN AND SOVIET FILM 213, 1650
KIRK DOUGLAS 1959
KISS HOLLYWOOD GOODBYE 1380
KISS IS STILL A KISS: ROGER EBERT AT THE MOVIES, A 1548
KISS KISS BANG BANG 150, 997, 1002, 1006, 1012, 1015, 1019, 1020, 1022,
  1290, 1292, 1296, 1326, 1327, 1328, 1350, 1352, 1354

KITTY FOYLE 1282
KNIGHT ERRANT: A BIOGRAPHY OF DOUGLAS FAIRBANKS, JR. 1401, 1402
KNOWING THE MUSIC: NOTES ON FILM MUSIC 402
KODAK HOME MOVIE CAMERA GUIDE, THE 80
KOPS AND CUSTARDS: THE LEGEND OF KEYSTONE FILMS 1359, 1412
KORE DAKE YOMEBA WARE WA KATERU (READ THIS AND THE WAR IS
  WON) 1897
KRAMER VS. KRAMER 1007
KUBRICK 2055
KUBRICK: INSIDE A FILM ARTIST'S MAZE 2057
KULESHOV ON FILM: WRITINGS OF LEV KULESHOV 1662

L

LABOUR POWER IN THE BRITISH FILM INDUSTRY 1938
LACOMBE, LUCIEN 377
LADD: THE LIFE, THE LEGEND, THE LEGACY OF ALAN LADD 1917
LADIES IN DISTRESS 1444
LANA: THE LADY, THE LEGEND, AND THE TRUTH 1971
LANA: THE PUBLIC AND PRIVATE LIVES 1971
LANDSCAPE OF FREEDOM 954
LANGUAGE AND CINEMA 169
LANGUAGE OF CHANGE: MOVING IMAGES OF MAN 68
LANGUAGE OF FILM, THE 70
LANGUAGE OF THE SELF, THE 480
LANGUAGES OF REVOLT: DADA AND SURREALIST LITERATURE AND
  FILM 1716
LASER VIDEO DISC COMPANION: A GUIDE TO THE BEST (AND WORST) LASER
  VIDEO DISCS, THE 1540
LAST ANGRY MAN, THE 1020
LAST DAYS OF ALFRED HITCHCOCK: A MEMOIR FEATURING THE SCREENPLAY
  OF ALFRED HITCHCOCK'S "THE SHORT NIGHT," THE 1844
LAST METRO: FRANCOIS TRUFFAUT, DIRECTOR, THE 2143
LAST NEW WAVE: THE AUSTRALIAN FILM REVIVAL, THE 2158
LAST OF THE NOVELISTS, F. SCOTT FITZGERALD AND THE LAST TYCOON,
  THE 1111
LAST PICTURE SHOW, THE 996
LAST TYCOON, THE 1041, 1042, 1104, 1109, 1117, 1130, 1131, 1132, 1133,
  1134, 1135, 1148, 1158, 1161, 1162, 1247, 1492
LAST YEAR AT MARIENBAD: TEXT BY ALAIN ROBBE-GRILLET FOR THE FILM
  BY ALAIN RESNAIS 2137
LATIN AMERICA CINEMA: FILM AND HISTORY 2177
LAUGH AND LIVE 1400
LAUGHTER 1425
LAUGHTER THROUGH TEARS: THE YIDDISH CINEMA 845
LAUGHTON STORY: AN INTIMATE STORY OF CHARLES LAUGHTON, THE 1860
LAUREL AND HARDY 1690, 1691
LAUREL AND HARDY BOOK, THE 1691
LAUREL AND HARDY: THE MAGIC BEHIND THE MOVIES 1692
LAURENCE OLIVIER 1862, 2162
LE JOUR SE LEVE: A FILM BY MARCEL CARNE AND JACQUES PREVERT 1816
LEARNING FROM FILMS 51
LEARNING TO DREAM: THE NEW BRITISH CINEMA 540
LEFT SIDE OF PARADISE: THE SCREENWRITING OF JOHN HOWARD LAWSON,
  THE 1264
LEGEND OF CHARLIE CHAPLIN, THE 1421

LEGENDS ON THE SCREEN: THE AUSTRALIAN NARRATIVE CINEMA
1919-1929 2158
LEGEND: THE LIFE AND DEATH OF MARILYN MONROE 1138, 1965
LEGION OF DECENCY: A SOCIOLOGICAL ANALYSIS OF THE EMERGENCE AND
DEVELOPMENT OF A SOCIAL PRESSURE GROUP, THE 219, 964
LEISURE AND POPULAR CULTURE IN TRANSITION 457, 458, 733
LEMMON: A BIOGRAPHY 2058
LENA 879, 880, 950
LENI RIEFENSTAHL AND OLYMPIA 318
LENI RIEFENSTAHL: THE FALLEN FILM GODDESS 318
LENIN AND PHILOSOPHY AND OTHER ESSAYS 479
LENS AND ALL ITS JOBS, THE 81
LEONARD MALTIN'S TV MOVIES AND VIDEO GUIDE. 1987 Edition 66
LEOPARD'S SPOTS, THE 700, 1387
LES BROWN'S ENCYCLOPEDIA OF TELEVISION 650
LESSONS WITH EISENSTEIN 208, 1660
LET US NOW PRAISE FAMOUS MEN 145
LET'S GO TO THE MOVIES 1675
LETTER FROM AN UNKNOWN WOMAN: MAX OPHULS, DIRECTOR 1966, 1983,
2007
LETTERS OF F. SCOTT FITZGERALD, THE 1056, 1111, 1116, 1118, 1120, 1122,
1125, 1128, 1129
LETTERS OF NUNNALLY JOHNSON, THE 1036, 1130, 1249
LETTERS TO HIS DAUGHTER 1123, 1129
LIBERATED CINEMA: THE YUGOSLAV EXPERIENCE 2014
LIBRARY OF FILM CRITICISM: AMERICAN FILM DIRECTORS, A 1550
LIFE AND ADVENTURES OF CARL LAEMMLE, THE 1475
LIFE AND LILLIAN GISH 1365
LIFE GOES TO THE MOVIES 1757
LIFE OF DRAMA, THE 712
LIFE OF FORMS IN ART, THE 194
LIFE OF JOHN O'HARA, THE 1274
LIFE OF PYTHON 2159
LIFE OF RITA HAYWORTH, THE 1914
LIFE OF ROBERT TAYLOR, THE 1920
LIFE ON FILM, A 1679
LIFE WITH GROUCHO 1783
LIFE, A 1257, 1979
LIGHT AND SHADOWS: A HISTORY OF MOTION PICTURES 1519, 1559, 1586,
1671, 1749
LIGHT IN AUGUST 1213
LIGHT OF A STAR 1861
LIGHT ON HER FACE, THE 1676
LIGHT YEARS: CONFESSIONS OF A CINEMATOGRAPHER 81
LILIES OF THE FIELD 952
LILLIAN HELLMAN: HER LEGEND AND HER LEGACY 1230
LILLIAN HELLMAN: THE IMAGE, THE WOMAN 1096, 1230
LILLY: REMINISCENCES OF LILLIAN HELLMAN 1227
LIMEHOUSE NIGHTS 1388
LIMITS OF INFINITY: THE AMERICAN SCIENCE FICTION FILM 1950-1975,
THE 416
LINDSAY ANDERSON 2159
LION'S SHARE: THE STORY OF AN ENTERTAINMENT EMPIRE, THE 1482
LIPTON ON FILMMAKING 74
LITERARY IMAGE OF HOLLYWOOD, THE 1028, 1134
LITERATURE AND FILM 1026, 1298, 1315
LITERATURE AND FILM: AN ANNOTATED BIBLIOGRAPHY, 1909-1977 1163
LITERATURE OF THE FILM: A BIBLIOGRAPHIC GUIDE TO FILM AS ART AND
ENTERTAINMENT, THE 1525

LITERATURE STUDY IN THE HIGH SCHOOLS 980
LITTLE BIG MAN 1320
LITTLE CAESAR 1314
LITTLE FELLOW: THE LIFE AND WORK OF CHARLES SPENCER CHAPLIN,
  THE 1420
LITTLE FOXES, THE 1348
LITTLE GIRL LOST: THE LIFE AND HARD TIMES OF JUDY GARLAND 1138,
  1773
LITTLE SISTER, THE 1198
LIVELIEST ART: A PANORAMIC HISTORY OF THE MOVIES, THE 233, 263,
  1359, 1438, 1519, 1562
LIVING CINEMA: NEW DIRECTIONS IN CONTEMPORARY FILM-MAKING 51
LIVING IMAGES: FILM CRITICISM AND COMMENT 153
LIVING PICTURES: THEIR HISTORY, PHOTO-PRODUCTION AND PRACTICAL
  WORKING 1592
LIVING SCREEN: BACKGROUND TO THE FILM AND TELEVISION, THE 50
LIVING SCREEN: WHAT GOES ON IN FILMS AND TELEVISION, THE 106
LOBBY CARDS: THE CLASSIC COMEDIES--THE MICHAEL HAWKS COLLECTION,
  Volume II 1449
LOCKWOOD CONCERN, THE 1274
LOLITA 1272
LOLITA: A SCREENPLAY 1273
LONDON AFTER MIDNIGHT: A RECONSTRUCTION 1679
LONELY LIFE: AN AUTOBIOGRAPHY, THE 1766
LONG JOURNEY: A BIOGRAPHY OF SIDNEY POITIER, THE 886, 888, 951
LONG LIVE THE KING: A BIOGRAPHY OF CLARK GABLE 1773
LONG VIEW, THE 200, 216, 217, 1520, 1565, 1809, 1839, 1912, 1923, 1924, 1926,
  1934, 1936, 1937, 1938, 1946, 1949, 2012, 2018
LONG VOYAGE HOME, THE 1350
LOOK BACK IN ANGER 601
LOOK HOMEWARD ANGEL 2052
LOOKING AWAY: HOLLYWOOD AND VIETNAM 199, 231, 283, 359
LOOKING FOR MR. GOODBAR 1032
LORD OF THE FLIES 1001
LORENTZ ON FILM: MOVIES FROM 1927 TO 1941 153
LORETTA YOUNG: AN EXTRAORDINARY LIFE 1797
LOS ANGELES: A GUIDE TO THE CITY AND ITS ENVIRONS 1057
LOS ANGELES: BIOGRAPHY OF A CITY 1057, 1233
LOSER TAKE ALL: THE COMIC ART OF WOODY ALLEN 2046, 2072
LOSEY ON LOSEY 371, 1963
LOST FILMS 1524
LOST FILMS, 1895-1917 1595, 1600
LOST HORIZON 1328, 1799
LOST WEEKEND, THE 1029
LOST WORLDS OF 2001, THE 2083
LOTTERY, THE 1312
LOVE GODDESSES OF THE MOVIES 1447
LOVE IN THE FILM 498
LOVE LIFE 1260
LOVE SCENE: THE STORY OF LAURENCE OLIVIER AND VIVIEN LEIGH 1861
LOVED ONE, THE 1041, 1158
LOVE, LAUGHTER, AND TEARS: MY HOLLYWOOD STORY 1396
LOVING WITH A VENGEANCE: MASS-PRODUCED FANTASIES FOR WOMEN 463,
  468, 469, 517, 528, 537, 538, 592, 718
LOW COMPANY 1314
LUBITSCH TOUCH: A CRITICAL STUDY OF THE GREAT FILM DIRECTOR,
  THE 1639
LUCHINO VISCONTI 1884

LUCHINO VISCONTI: A BIOGRAPHY 1884, 1922
LUGOSI: THE MAN BEHIND THE CAPE 1782
LUIS BUNUEL 1721, 1728, 1729
LUIS BUNUEL: A CRITICAL BIOGRAPHY 1719, 1990
LURE OF THE TROPIX: A PICTORIAL HISTORY OF THE JUNGLE HEROINE,
  JUNGLE QUEENS, WHITE GODDESSES, HAREM GIRLS 498
LUST FOR LIFE 1015
LUTHERAN MILIEU OF THE FILMS OF INGMAR BERGMAN, THE 2185
LUV 2060
L136: DIARY WITH INGMAR BERGMAN 2188
L. J. M. DAGUERRE: THE HISTORY OF THE DIORAMA AND THE
  DAGUERREOTYPE 1591

M

M 1639
M-G-M STOCK COMPANY: THE GOLDEN ERA, THE 1484
M-G-M STORY: THE COMPLETE HISTORY OF FIFTY ROARING YEARS,
  THE 1482
MABEL 1411
MACBETH 1789
MACK SENNETT'S KEYSTONE: THE MAN, THE MYTH, AND THE
  COMEDIES 1412
MACK & MABEL 1410
MACMILLAN FILM BIBLIOGRAPHY, THE 66, 422, 513, 1541
MADAME BOVARY 1309, 1317
MAE WEST 1795
MAGIC AND MYTH OF THE MOVIES 170, 233
MAGIC IN THE MOVIES: THE STORY OF SPECIAL EFFECTS 81
MAGIC LANTERN, THE 1158
MAGIC LANTERN: AN AUTOBIOGRAPHY, THE 2182
MAGIC MOMMIES, TREMBLING SISTERS, PURITANS & PERVERTS: FEMINIST
  ESSAYS 519
MAGIC OF FILM EDITING, THE 82
MAGIC SHADOWS: THE STORY OF THE ORIGIN OF MOTION PICTURES 1580,
  1581, 1594, 1599
MAGIC WORLD OF ORSON WELLES, THE 1794
MAGICIAN AND THE CINEMA, THE 1588
MAGNIFICENT AMBERSONS, THE 1327
MAISON DE RENDEZ-VOUS, La 2140
MAJOR FILM THEORIES: AN INTRODUCTION 161
MAJOR FILM THEORIES: AN INTRODUCTION, THE 119, 124, 125, 132, 133,
  161, 169, 176
MAKE IT AGAIN, SAM: A SURVEY OF MOVIE REMAKES 1328, 1330
MAKE LIFE WORTH-WHILE 1400
MAKE YOUR OWN ANIMATED MOVIES: YELLOW BALL WORKSHOP FILM
  TECHNIQUES 87
MAKING FILMS YOUR BUSINESS 73
MAKING IT MOVE 91
MAKING MONEY MAKING MOVIES: THE INDEPENDENT MOVIE-MAKERS'
  HANDBOOK 76
MAKING MOVIES: FROM SCRIPT TO SCREEN 72
MAKING MOVIES: STUDENT FILMS TO FEATURES 88
MAKING OF A SCREEN CHARACTER, THE 1398, 1399
MAKING OF FEATURE FILMS: A GUIDE, THE 44, 63
MAKING OF KUBRICK'S "2001," THE 553, 2054
MAKING OF THE GREAT WESTERNS, THE 431
MAKING OF THE MOVIE "JAWS," THE 553

MAKING OF "CITIZEN KANE," THE 1790
MAKING OF "ONE DAY IN THE LIFE OF IVAN DENISOVICH," THE 554, 1319
MAKING OF "RAIDERS OF THE LOST ARK," THE 554
MAKING OF "STAR TREK: THE MOTION PICTURE," THE 554
MAKING OF "SUPERMAN," THE 554
MAKING OF "THE AFRICAN QUEEN" OR HOW I WENT TO AFRICA WITH
  BOGART, BACALL AND HUSTON AND ALMOST LOST MY MIND, THE 554,
  1915, 1979
MAKING OF "THE DARK CRYSTAL": CREATING A UNIQUE FILM, THE 411
MAKING OF "THE MISFITS," THE 554
MAKING OF "THE WIZARD OF OZ," THE 554
MAKING PICTURES MOVE 89
MAKING "TOOTSIE": A FILM STUDY WITH DUSTIN HOFFMAN AND SYDNEY
  POLLACK 554
MALCOLM LOWRY: A BIOGRAPHY 1265
MALTESE FALCON, THE 1222, 1914
MAN AND THE MOVIES 1028, 1316
MAN CALLED WHITE, A 879
MAN FOR ALL SEASONS: A PLAY IN TWO ACTS, A 970, 1020
MAN IN THE STRAW HAT: MY STORY, THE 1765
MAN RAY: AMERICAN ARTIST 1727
MAN RAY: THE RIGOUR OF IMAGINATION 1727, 1731
MAN WHO INVENTED HOLLYWOOD: THE AUTOBIOGRAPHY OF D. W. GRIFFITH,
  THE 1377
MAN WHO SHOT LIBERTY VALANCE, THE 1311
MAN WHO WOULD BE KING, THE 1312
MAN YOU LOVE TO HATE: ERICH VON STROHEIM AND HOLLYWOOD,
  THE 1699, 1708
MANIFESTES DU SURREALISME 1713
MANKIND IN BARBARY: THE INDIVIDUAL AND SOCIETY IN THE NOVELS OF
  NORMAN MAILER 1044, 1135
MANK: THE WIT, WORLD, AND LIFE OF HERMAN J. MANKIEWICZ 1266, 1271
MANUAL OF FILM-MAKING 87
MANUAL ON FILM EVALUATION. Rev. edition. 48
MARCH OF TIME, 1935-1951, THE 227, 280, 281, 296, 301, 319
MARILYN 1138
MARILYN IN ART 1138, 1966
MARILYN MONROE 1138, 1965
MARILYN MONROE CONFIDENTIAL: AN INTIMATE PERSONAL ACCOUNT 1138,
  1965
MARILYN MONROE: A COMPOSITE VIEW 1290
MARILYN MONROE: A LIFE OF THE ACTRESS 1138, 1965
MARILYN MONROE: A LIFE ON FILM 1138, 1965
MARILYN MONROE: HER OWN STORY 1138, 1964
MARILYN THE TRAGIC VENUS 1138
MARILYN: A BIOGRAPHY 1138, 1965
MARILYN: THE LAST MONTHS 1138, 1965
MARILYN: THE TRAGIC VENUS. New Edition 1965
MARK TWAIN IN THE MOVIES: A MEDITATION WITH PICTURES 1363
MARLENE 1767
MARLENE DIETRICH 1767
MARLON BRANDO 1958
MARLON BRANDO: THE ONLY CONTENDER 1958
MARLON: PORTRAIT OF THE REBEL AS AN ARTIST 1958
MARQUISE OF O: FILM BY ERIC ROHMER, STORY BY HEINRICH VON KLEIST,
  THE 2142
MARRIAGE OF MARIA BRAUN: RAINER WERNER FASSBINDER, DIRECTOR 2166
MARTIN DIES 832, 1077

MARTIN DIES' STORY, THE   832
MARTIN SCORSESE AND MICHAEL CIMINO   2209
MARTIN SCORSESE: A GUIDE TO REFERENCES AND RESOURCES   2209
MARTIN SCORSESE: THE FIRST DECADE   2209
MARVELLOUS MELIES   1604, 1616
MARX BROTHERS AND THE MOVIES, THE   1784
MARX BROTHERS SCRAPBOOK, THE   1784
MARX BROTHERS, THE   1783, 1784
MARX BROTHERS: THEIR WORLD OF COMEDY, THE   1783
MARXISM AND THE SCENOGRAPHIC BAROQUE IN THE FILMS OF LUCHINO
  VISCONTI   1874
MARY PICKFORD AND DOUGLAS FAIRBANKS: THE MOST POPULAR COUPLE
  THE WORLD HAS KNOWN   1398, 1403, 1406
MARY PICKFORD: COMEDIENNE   1379, 1395
MASCULINE FEMININE: A FILM BY JEAN-LUC GODARD   2129
MASS COMMUNICATIONS   543
MASS COMMUNICATION: AN INTRODUCTION   747
MASS CULTURE REVISITED   548, 552
MASS CULTURE: THE POPULAR ARTS IN AMERICA   67, 455, 547, 602, 814
MASS ENTERTAINMENT   455, 456, 461
MASS MEDIA AND MASS MAN   63
MASS MEDIA AND SOCIAL PROBLEMS, THE   438, 439, 445, 746
MASTER HANDBOOK OF STILL AND MOVIE TITLING FOR AMATEUR AND
  PROFESSIONAL, THE   75
MASTERING THE FILM AND OTHER ESSAYS   165
MASTERS OF MENACE: GREENSTREET AND LORRE   397
MASTERS OF STARLIGHT: PHOTOGRAPHERS IN HOLLYWOOD   1576
MASTERS OF THE AMERICAN CINEMA   1549
MASTERS OF THE SOVIET CINEMA: CRIPPLED CREATIVE BIOGRAPHIES   1651
MASTERWORKS OF THE BRITISH CINEMA   1940
MASTERWORKS OF THE GERMAN CINEMA: THE GOLEM, NOSFERATU, M, THE
  THREEPENNY OPERA   1635
MAT (MOTHER)   1667
MATINEE IDOLS, THE   1440
MATURE MIND, THE   1054
MAX OPHULS AND THE CINEMA OF DESIRE: STYLE AND SPECTACLE IN FOUR
  FILMS, 1948-1955   2006
MAX REINHARDT 1873-1973: A CENTENNIAL FESTSCHRIFT OF MEMORIAL
  ESSAYS AND INTERVIEWS   1635
MAY '68 AND FILM CULTURE   474
MAYER AND THALBERG: THE MAKE-BELIEVE SAINTS   226, 1117, 1118, 1483
MCQUEEN: THE UNTOLD STORY OF A BAD BOY IN HOLLYWOOD   2059
MCTEAGUE   1018, 1299
MEDIA AND THE AMERICAN MIND: FROM MORSE TO McLUHAN   458, 723, 772
MEDIA CONTENT AND CONTROL: TELEVISION AND SOCIAL BEHAVIOR, Volume
  1   459
MEDIA MADE IN CALIFORNIA: HOLLYWOOD, POLITICS, AND THE NEWS   573
MEDIA POWER AND SOCIAL CONTROL: THE MOTION PICTURE IN AMERICA,
  1896-1936   710, 718
MEDIA SEXPLOITATION   2037
MEDIA-MADE DIXIE: THE SOUTH IN THE AMERICAN IMAGINATION   913
MEIN KAMPF   205
MEL BROOKS: THE IRREVERENT FUNNYMAN   1294, 2047
MELODRAMA   712
MELODRAMA UNVEILED   712
MELODRAMATIC IMAGINATION: BALZAC, HENRY JAMES, MELODRAMA, AND
  THE MODE OF EXCESS, THE   712, 714, 716
MELODY LINGERS ON: THE GREAT SONGWRITERS AND THEIR MOVIE
  MUSICALS, THE   404

MELVILLE ON MELVILLE   2006
MEMBER OF THE WEDDING, THE   997
MEMO FROM DAVID O. SELZNICK   1124, 1486
MEMOIRS   1346
MEMOIRS OF A PROFESSIONAL CAD   1969
MEMOIRS OF A STAR   1695
MEMORABLE FILM CHARACTERS: AN INDEX TO ROLES AND PERFORMERS,
   1915-1983   1446
MEMORIES FOR TOMORROW: THE MEMOIRS OF JEAN-LOUIS BARRAULT   1909
MEMORIES OF UNDERDEVELOPMENT: THE REVOLUTIONARY FILMS OF
   CUBA   2164
MEN AND WOMEN   986
MEN IN BATTLE   1177
MEN WHO MADE THE MOVIES: INTERVIEWS, THE   1553
MERCHANT OF VENICE, THE   822
MERELY COLOSSAL: THE STORY OF THE MOVIES FROM THE LONG CHASE TO
   THE CHAISE LOUNGE   1676
MERRY WIVES OF WINDSOR, THE   1353
MERTON OF THE MOVIES   1041, 1059
MERVYN LEROY: TAKE ONE   1780, 1804
METAMORPHOSIS, THE   1153
METROPOLIS   1639
METROPOLIS: A FILM BY FRITZ LANG   1639
MEXICAN CINEMA: INTERVIEWS WITH THIRTEEN DIRECTORS, THE   2178
MEXICAN CINEMA: REFLECTIONS OF A SOCIETY 1896-1980   2178
MICHAEL BALCON PRESENTS A LIFETIME OF FILMS   1841
MICHAEL BALCON'S 25 YEARS IN FILM   1842
MICHAEL REDGRAVE, ACTOR   1863
MICHELANGELO ANTONIONI'S NEO-REALISM: A WORLD VIEW   1928
MICHELANGELO ANTONIONI: AN INTRODUCTION   1882
MIDDLE EAST AND NORTH AFRICA ON FILM: AN ANNOTATED FILMOGRAPHY,
   THE   2178
MIDNIGHT MATINEES: MOVIES & THEIR MAKERS 1975-1985   157
MIDNIGHT MOVIES   392
MIKE NICHOLS   2060
MIKHAIL CHEKHOV AS ACTOR, DIRECTOR, AND TEACHER   1648
MILDRED PIERCE   797, 800
MILESTONES IN MASS COMMUNICATION RESEARCH: MEDIA EFFECTS   747
MILLION AND ONE NIGHTS: A HISTORY OF THE MOTION PICTURE THROUGH
   1925, A   1382, 1467, 1519, 1555, 1615
MILOS FORMAN STORIES, THE   2164
MILTON   1013
MIND'S EYE   1842
MINDSCAPES OF ART: DIMENSIONS OF THE PSYCHE IN FICTION, DRAMA, AND
   FILM, THE   448, 453, 578, 586, 600, 601, 602
MINDSCREEN: BERGMAN, GODARD, AND FIRST-PERSON FILM   116
MINI-DOCUMENTARY--SERIALIZING TV NEWS, THE   82
MINUTES OF THE LAST MEETING   1770
MIRACLE IN MILAN   1929
MIRACLE OF THE MOVIES, THE   1596
MIRACLE WORKER, THE   2064
MIRROR AND THE LAMP: ROMANTIC THEORY AND THE CRITICAL TRADITION,
   THE   445
MIRROR FOR ENGLAND: BRITISH MOVIES FROM AUSTERITY, A   1939
MIRROR IMAGE; THE INFLUENCE OF THE DAGUERREOTYPE ON AMERICAN
   SOCIETY   1594
MISERY   601
MISLAID IN HOLLYWOOD   1057, 1243

MISS LONELY HEARTS 154, 1226
MISS TALLULAH BANKHEAD 1760
MISSING 1020
MISSION TO MOSCOW 259, 343
MISSION: A FILM JOURNAL, THE 553
MISTER ROBERTS 1264
MIZOGUCHI 1900
MOBILE MISE EN SCENE: A CRITICAL ANALYSIS OF THE THEORY AND
  PRACTICE OF LONG-TAKE CAMERA MOVEMENT, THE 112, 113
MOBILE MISE-EN-SCENE: A CRITICAL ANALYSIS OF THE THEORY AND
  PRACTICE OF LONG-TAKE CAMERA MOVEMENT, THE 1632
MOBY DICK 156, 1314
MODERN AMERICAN NOVEL AND THE MOVIES, THE 1315
MODERN CINEMA OF POLAND, THE 2179
MODERN CZECHOSLOVAK FILM 1945-1965 2013
MODERN EUROPEAN FILMMAKERS AND THE ART OF ADAPTATION 1139, 1310
MODERN FILM SCRIPTS 1511
MODERN FILM SCRIPTS: "THE THIRD MAN" 1219, 1329
MODERNISM IN THE NARRATIVE CINEMA: THE ART FILM AS GENRE 118
MODES, MOVIES, AND MAGNATES: EARLY FILMMAKING IN CHICAGO 621
MOGULS, THE 1468
MOGULS: INSIDE THE BUSINESS OF SHOW BUSINESS 662, 1951
MOMENTS WITH CHAPLIN 1426
MOMMIE DEAREST 1402, 1765
MONEY BEHIND THE SCREEN 630, 1103
MONOGRAPH NO. 2: GLOSSARY OF FILM TERMS, Rev. ed. 1528
MONOPOLY CAPITALISM 765
MONSTER MOVIE GAME 398
MONSTERS: TWENTY TERRIBLE AND WONDERFUL BEASTS FROM THE CLASSIC
  DRAGON AND COLOSSAL MINOTAUR 399
MONTAGE EISENSTEIN 1655
MONTGOMERY CLIFT: A BIOGRAPHY 1958
MONTY: A BIOGRAPHY OF MONTGOMERY CLIFT 1958
MOON OF THE CARIBBEES, THE 1350
MORE ABOUT "ALL ABOUT EVE" 1272
MORE FILMS KIDS LIKE: A CATALOG OF SHORT FILMS FOR CHILDREN 983
MORNING AFTER: SELECTED ESSAYS AND REVIEWS, THE 158
MORNING WATCH, THE 145
MOROCCO AND SHANGHAI EXPRESS: TWO FILMS BY JOSEF VON
  STERNBERG 1788
MOST IMPORTANT ART: SOVIET AND EASTERN EUROPEAN FILM AFTER 1945,
  THE 2011, 2013
MOTHER GODDAM: THE STORY OF THE CAREER OF BETTE DAVIS 801, 1766
MOTHER (MAT) 1667
MOTION PICTURE AND THE TEACHING OF ENGLISH, THE 54, 1021, 1807
MOTION PICTURE ANNUAL: 1988--COVERING FILMS OF 1987, THE 1538
MOTION PICTURE CAMERA TECHNIQUES 81
MOTION PICTURE DIRECTORS: A BIBLIOGRAPHY OF MAGAZINE AND
  PERIODICAL ARTICLES, 1900-1972 1554
MOTION PICTURE DISTRIBUTION HANDBOOK 75
MOTION PICTURE EMPIRE 607, 1075, 1467
MOTION PICTURE GOES TO WAR: THE U.S. GOVERNMENT FILM EFFORT
  DURING WORLD WAR I 308
MOTION PICTURE GUIDE 1927-1983, THE 1755
MOTION PICTURE IN THE SOVIET UNION, THE 1652
MOTION PICTURE INDUSTRY--A PATTERN OF CONTROL, THE 607, 619, 625,
  687
MOTION PICTURE INDUSTRY, THE 607, 617, 626, 733
MOTION PICTURE MOODS FOR PIANISTS AND ORGANISTS 407

MOTION PICTURE PATENTS COMPANY, THE 619
MOTION PICTURE PERFORMERS: A BIBLIOGRAPHY OF MAGAZINE AND
  PERIODICAL ARTICLES, SUPPLEMENT NO.1 1970-1974 1543
MOTION PICTURE PERFORMERS: A BIBLIOGRAPHY OF MAGAZINE AND
  PERIODICAL ARTICLES, 1900-1969 1543
MOTION PICTURES 43, 1303, 1306, 1307, 1333
MOTION PICTURES AND STANDARDS OF MORALITY 729
MOTION PICTURES AND THE SOCIAL ATTITUDES OF CHILDREN 729, 730, 732,
  865
MOTION PICTURES AND YOUTH: A SUMMARY 729
MOTION PICTURES AS A PHASE OF COMMERCIALIZED AMUSEMENT IN TOLEDO,
  OHIO 626, 724
MOTION PICTURES FROM THE LIBRARY OF CONGRESS PAPER PRINT
  COLLECTION 1894-1912 1593
MOTION PICTURES FROM THE LIBRARY OF CONGRESS PAPER PRINT
  COLLECTION 1912-1939 1533
MOTION PICTURES IN A TYPICAL CITY 710
MOTION PICTURES, TELEVISION AND RADIO: A UNION CATALOGUE OF
  MANUSCRIPT AND SPECIAL COLLECTIONS 1537
MOTION PICTURES: THE DEVELOPMENT OF AN ART FROM SILENT FILMS TO
  THE AGE OF TELEVISION 46, 1613, 1943
MOVEMENT IN TWO DIMENSIONS: A STUDY OF THE ANIMATED AND
  PROJECTED PICTURES 1584, 1589, 1590
MOVIE AND VIDEOTAPE: SPECIAL EFFECTS 72
MOVIE BOOK, THE 1235
MOVIE BRATS, THE 661
MOVIE BUSINESS BOOK, THE 608, 699, 754
MOVIE BUSINESS, THE 698
MOVIE BUSINESS: AMERICAN FILM INDUSTRY PRACTICE, THE 607, 676, 687
MOVIE COMEDY TEAMS 1754
MOVIE DIRECTORS STORY, THE 1549
MOVIE FACTS AND FEATS: A GUINNESS RECORD BOOK 1542, 1950
MOVIE FANTASTIC: BEYOND THE DREAM MACHINE 409
MOVIE INDUSTRY BOOK (HOW OTHERS MADE AND LOST MONEY IN THE MOVIE
  INDUSTRY), THE 66
MOVIE JOURNAL: THE RISE OF THE NEW AMERICAN CINEMA, 1959-1971 1955
MOVIE LOT TO BEACHHEAD: THE MOTION PICTURE GOES TO WAR AND
  PREPARES FOR THE FUTURE 263, 283, 346
MOVIE LOVER'S GUIDE TO HOLLYWOOD, THE 1232
MOVIE MAKERS: ARTISTS IN AN INDUSTRY, THE 1552, 2057
MOVIE MAKING FOR THE YOUNG CAMERAMAN 87
MOVIE MAKING--A GUIDE TO FILM PRODUCTION 72
MOVIE MAKING: A WORKBOOK FOR SUPER 8 FILM PRODUCTION 88
MOVIE MAN 144
MOVIE MOGULS: AN INFORMAL HISTORY OF THE HOLLYWOOD TYCOONS,
  THE 1466
MOVIE MONSTERS 390
MOVIE MUSICAL FROM VITAPHONE TO 42ND STREET: AS REPORTED IN A
  GREAT FAN MAGAZINE, THE 405
MOVIE MUSICAL, THE 407
MOVIE PALACES 1506
MOVIE PALACES: RENAISSANCE AND REFUSE 1507
MOVIE PEOPLE: AT WORK IN THE BUSINESS OF FILM 2041
MOVIE PRODUCER: A HANDBOOK FOR PRODUCING AND PICTURE-MAKING,
  THE 73
MOVIE PRODUCTION & BUDGET FORMS . . . INSTANTLY! 75
MOVIE QUOTE BOOK, THE 1529
MOVIE RATING GAME, THE 964

MOVIE STARS STORY, THE 1531
MOVIE STARS, REAL PEOPLE, AND ME 1264
MOVIE STARS, THE 1442
MOVIE WORLD OF ROGER CORMAN, THE 2049
MOVIE-MADE AMERICA: A SOCIAL HISTORY OF AMERICAN MOVIES 228, 560,
572, 607, 640, 729, 957, 1057, 1133
MOVIEMAKER'S HANDBOOK, THE 76
MOVIEMAKERS AT WORK 1548
MOVIEMAKERS, THE 1549
MOVIEMAKING ILLUSTRATED: THE COMICBOOK FILMBOOK 74
MOVIES 148
MOVIES AND CENSORSHIP 963
MOVIES AND CONDUCT 729, 730
MOVIES AND HOW THEY ARE MADE 66
MOVIES AND METHODS: AN ANTHOLOGY 170, 176, 799
MOVIES AND MONEY: FINANCING THE AMERICAN FILM INDUSTRY 608, 618,
627, 629, 630, 634, 637, 638, 645, 662, 663, 702, 1367
MOVIES AND MORALS 53
MOVIES AND SOCIETY 450, 471, 540, 679, 705, 775, 777, 1556
MOVIES ARE BETTER THAN EVER: WIDE-SCREEN MEMORIES OF THE
FIFTIES 647, 658, 1951, 1953
MOVIES AS ARTIFACTS: CULTURAL CRITICISM OF POPULAR FILM 564, 581,
733, 736, 753
MOVIES AS MASS COMMUNICATION 439, 463, 488, 577, 611, 613, 650, 674,
676, 677, 711, 752, 780
MOVIES AS MEDIUM, THE 65
MOVIES AS SOCIAL CRITICISM: ASPECTS OF THEIR SOCIAL
PSYCHOLOGY 550, 552, 777, 854, 978
MOVIES BEGIN: MAKING MOVIES IN NEW JERSEY, 1887-1920, THE 1595
MOVIES COME FROM AMERICA, THE 157, 173, 1055, 1757
MOVIES FOR A DESERT ISLE: FORTY-TWO WELL-KNOWN FILM LOVERS IN
SEARCH OF THEIR FAVORITE MOVIE 1539
MOVIES FOR KIDS: A GUIDE FOR PARENTS AND TEACHERS ON THE
ENTERTAINMENT FILM FOR CHILDREN. Rev. ed. 978, 983
MOVIES FROM THE MANSION: A HISTORY OF PINEWOOD STUDIOS 1940
MOVIES GO TO COLLEGE: HOLLYWOOD AND THE WORLD OF THE
COLLEGE-LIFE FILM, THE 989
MOVIES GROW UP 1940-1980, THE 661, 1519, 1913, 1944, 1951, 2038
MOVIES IN OUR MIDST: DOCUMENTS IN THE CULTURAL HISTORY OF FILM
IN AMERICA, THE 1536, 1600
MOVIES IN THE AGE OF INNOCENCE 1410
MOVIES INTO FILM 996, 1001, 1003, 1347, 1349, 1356, 2086
MOVIES INTO FILM: FILM CRITICISM 1967-1970 159
MOVIES MADE FOR TELEVISION: THE TELEFEATURE AND THE MINI-SERIES
1964-1986 1536
MOVIES ON TV 68
MOVIES ON YOUR MIND, THE 582, 598
MOVIES PLUS ONE: SEVEN YEARS OF FILM REVIEWING 154
MOVIES WITH A PURPOSE 88
MOVIES' GREATEST MUSICALS: PRODUCED IN HOLLYWOOD USA BY THE
FREED UNIT 403
MOVIES, CENSORSHIP AND THE LAW 225, 963, 2038
MOVIES, DELINQUENCY AND CRIME 729
MOVIES, MR. GRIFFITH, AND ME, THE 1369, 1375
MOVIES, THE 1562, 1571
MOVIES: A LANGUAGE IN LIGHT 69, 1298
MOVIES: A PSYCHOLOGICAL STUDY, THE 581, 602, 734, 740
MOVIES: AN AMERICAN IDIOM; READINGS IN THE SOCIAL HISTORY OF THE
AMERICAN MOTION PICTURE, THE 565, 664

MOVIES: THE HISTORY OF AN ART AND AN INSTITUTION 234, 1435, 1564
MOVIES: THE SIXTY-YEAR STORY OF THE WORLD OF HOLLYWOOD 1576
MOVIES: UNIVERSAL LANGUAGE--FILM STUDY IN HIGH SCHOOL 55
MOVIETONE PRESENTS THE 20TH CENTURY 298
MOVING IMAGE: A GUIDE TO CINEMATIC LITERACY, THE 88, 94
MOVING IMAGE: PRODUCTION PRINCIPLES AND PRACTICES 73
MOVING PICTURE BOOK, THE 65
MOVING PICTURES: MEMORIES OF A HOLLYWOOD PRINCE 1118, 1193, 1277
MOVIOLA 1041
MR. DOOLEY REMEMBERS 1204
MR. LAUREL AND MR. HARDY 1691
MR. RANK: A STUDY OF J. ARTHUR RANK 1862
MURIEL OSTRICHE: PRINCES OF SILENT FILMS AND EARLY AMERICAN FILM
  PRODUCTION 1440
MURNAU 1640
MUSIC FOR THE MOVIES 408
MUSIC SCHOOL, THE 1316
MUSIC SCORING FOR TV AND MOTION PICTURES 75
MUSICAL FILM, THE 406
MUSICAL: FROM BROADWAY TO HOLLYWOOD, THE 403
MUSIC, FILM, AND ART 141
MUSIQUE FANTASTIQUE: A SURVEY OF FILM MUSIC IN THE FANTASTIC
  CINEMA 412
MUTINY ON THE BOUNTY 1330
MUYBRIDGE: MAN IN MOTION 1596
MY AUTOBIOGRAPHY 1414, 1419, 1427
MY DARLING CLEMENTINE: JOHN FORD, DIRECTOR 1960
MY FATHER--MY SON 1091
MY FATHER, CHARLIE CHAPLIN 1420
MY FIRST HUNDRED YEARS IN HOLLYWOOD 226, 1498
MY FOUR YEARS IN GERMANY 1494
MY HOLLYWOOD--WHEN BOTH OF US WERE YOUNG: THE MEMORIES OF PATSY
  RUTH MILLER 1695
MY HUSBAND, MY FRIEND 2059
MY HUSBAND, ROCK HUDSON: THE REAL STORY OF ROCK HUDSON'S
  MARRIAGE TO PHYLLIS GATES 1962
MY JOURNEY ROUND THE WORLD 1817
MY LAST SIGHT 1720, 1990
MY LIFE AND MY FILMS 1822
MY LIFE EAST AND WEST 1687
MY LIFE IN PICTURES 1420
MY LIFE WITH CHAPLIN 1431
MY LIFE WITH CLEOPATRA 2043
MY PATHS AND DETOURS: AN AUTOBIOGRAPHY 1917
MY STORY 1138, 1965
MY STORY: AN AUTOBIOGRAPHY 1679
MY TEN YEARS IN THE STUDIOS 1759
MY WICKED, WICKED WAYS 989, 1771
MY WONDERFUL WORLD OF SLAPSTICK 1688
MYRA BRECKINRIDGE 1041
MYRNA LOY 1781
MYRNA LOY: BEING AND BECOMING 1781
MYSTIFYING MOVIES: FADS & FALLACIES IN CONTEMPORARY FILM
  THEORY 162
MYTH THAT WON'T GO AWAY, THE 1063
MYTHICAL WORLD OF NAZI WAR PROPAGANDA, 1939-1945, THE 206, 208, 228
MYTHMAKERS OF THE AMERICAN DREAM: THE NOSTALGIC VISION IN
  POPULAR CULTURE 1160

MYTHOLOGIES   177, 482, 487
M/FRITZ LANG   1830

N

NABOKOV'S DARK CINEMA   1272
NAKED CITY, THE   1975
NAME ABOVE THE TITLE: AN AUTOBIOGRAPHY, THE   281
NAMING NAMES   1067, 1075, 1085, 1086, 1092, 1093, 1096, 1097, 1098, 1099,
1100, 1155, 1189, 1205, 1282, 1284
NAPOLEON: ABEL GANCE'S CLASSIC FILM   1726
NARRATION IN LIGHT: STUDIES IN CINEMATIC POINT OF VIEW   119
NARRATION IN THE FICTION FILM   113
NARRATIVE STRATEGIES: ORIGINAL ESSAYS IN PROSE AND FICTION   1297
NARRATIVE, APPARATUS, IDEOLOGY   117
NARROW IS THE WAY   1766
NAT KING COLE   885
NATALIE & R. J. : HOLLYWOOD'S STAR-CROSSED LOVERS   1973
NATHANAEL WEST: A COMPREHENSIVE BIBLIOGRAPHY   1289
NATIONAL ASSOCIATION FOR THE ADVANCEMENT OF COLORED PEOPLE AND
THE AMERICAN THEATRE   879
NATIONAL BOARD OF CENSORSHIP (REVIEW) OF MOTION PICTURES,
1909-1922, THE   964
NATIONAL HEROES: BRITISH CINEMA IN THE SEVENTIES AND EIGHTIES   1940
NATIONAL SOCIETY OF FILM CRITICS ON THE MOVIE STAR, THE   1392, 1418,
1452
NATIVE SON   945
NATURE OF NARRATIVE, THE   175
NAZI CINEMA   207, 240
NAZI PROPAGANDA: THE POWER AND THE LIMITATIONS   202, 251
NEGATIVE SPACE   1013, 1015, 1296, 1325, 1352, 1912, 1981, 2085, 2086
NEGATIVE SPACE: MANNY FARBER ON THE MOVIES   148
NEGLECTED ART: A CRITICAL STUDY OF MUSIC IN FILMS, A   407
NEGRO COWBOYS, THE   893
NEGRO IMAGE AND THE MASS MEDIA, THE   860
NEGRO IN FILMS, THE   866, 877, 920, 938, 939, 1341
NEGRO IN HOLLYWOOD FILMS, THE   931
NEITHER RIGHT NOR LEFT: FASCIST IDEOLOGY IN FRANCE   1904
NEW AMERICAN CINEMA: A CRITICAL ANTHOLOGY, THE   489, 1955
NEW CINEMA IN BRITAIN   1939
NEW CINEMA IN EASTERN EUROPE   2013
NEW CINEMA IN THE USA: THE FEATURE FILM SINCE 1946   1954
NEW COURTS OF INDUSTRY: SELF-REGULATION UNDER THE MOTION PICTURE
CODE, INCLUDING AN ANALYSIS OF THE CODE   966
NEW DEAL IN ENTERTAINMENT: WARNER BROTHERS IN THE 1930s, A   1496
NEW DOCUMENTARY IN ACTION: A CASEBOOK IN FILMMAKING, THE   2042
NEW FILM INDEX: A BIBLIOGRAPHY OF MAGAZINE ARTICLES IN ENGLISH,
1930-1970, THE   1522, 1526, 1535, 1998
NEW GERMAN FILMMAKERS FROM OBERHAUSEN THROUGH THE 1970s   2166
NEW GERMAN FILM: THE DISPLACED IMAGE   2165
NEW HENRIETTA, THE   1406
NEW HOLLYWOOD: AMERICAN MOVIES IN THE 70's, THE   662, 675
NEW ITALIAN CINEMA: STUDIES IN DANCE AND DESPAIR, THE   2169
NEW LANGUAGES, THE   180
NEW LATIN AMERICAN CINEMA--AN ANNOTATED BIBLIOGRAPHY OF SOURCES
IN ENGLISH, SPANISH, AND PORTUGESE: 1960-1980, THE   2177
NEW PICTORIAL HISTORY OF THE TALKIES, A   1752
NEW THEATRE AND CINEMA OF SOVIET RUSSIA, THE   1649

NEW THEATRES FOR OLD 1339
NEW WAVE: CRITICAL LANDMARKS, THE 1102, 2123
NEW WAVE: TRUFFAUT, GODARD, CHABROL, ROHMER, RIVETTE, THE 2097, 2126
NEW YORK TIMES FILM REVIEWS, 1913-1968 1539
NEW YORK TIMES GUIDE TO MOVIES ON T.V., THE 70
NEW YORK'S FIRST THEATRICAL CENTER: THE RIALTO AT UNION SQUARE 1600
NEWSREELS ACROSS THE WORLD 1870
NEXT TIME DRIVE OFF THE CLIFF! 1456
NICHOLAS RAY 1968
NICHOLAS RAY: A GUIDE TO REFERENCES AND RESOURCES 1968
NICKELODEON THEATRES AND THEIR MUSIC 1588, 1600
NICOLAS ROEG 2209
NIGGER, THE 862
NIGHT AND FOG (NUIT ET BROUILLARD): A FILM STUDY 324
NIGHT BUS 1311
NIGHT OF THE IGUANA, THE 1345
NIGHTMARE MOVIES: WIDE SCREEN HORROR SINCE 1968 396
NINE AMERICAN FILM CRITICIS: A STUDY OF THEORY AND PRACTICE 143
NINE LIVES OF MIKE TODD, THE 1971
NINETEEN FORTY SEVEN HEARINGS OF THE HOUSE COMMITTEE ON UN-AMERICAN ACTIVITIES INTO COMMUNISM 1068
NIVEN'S HOLLYWOOD 1057
NO BED OF ROSES: AN AUTOBIOGRAPHY 1914
NON-BEING AND SOMETHING-NESS: SELECTIONS FROM THE COMIC STRIP "INSIDE WOODY ALLEN" 2045
NON-WESTERN FILMS OF JOHN FORD, THE 1685
NONFICTION FILM THEORY AND CRITICISM 217, 230, 255, 280, 295, 319
NONFICTION FILM: A CRITICAL HISTORY 215, 284, 294, 320
NONINDIFFERENT NATURE 1657
NOON WINE 2062
NORMA JEAN: THE LIFE OF MARILYN MONROE 1138, 1965
NORMA: THE STORY OF NORMA SHEARER 1786
NORTH BY NORTHWEST 1858, 2053
NOSTALGIA ISN'T WHAT IT USED TO BE 1910
NOT SO DUMB: THE LIFE AND TIMES OF THE ANIMAL ACTORS 1446
NOTES 367
NOTES OF A FILM DIRECTOR 1658
NOTES ON WOMEN'S CINEMA 471
NOVEL AND THE CINEMA, THE 1316
NOVELS INTO FILM: THE METAMORPHOSIS OF FICTION INTO CINEMA 1019, 1021, 1309, 1314, 1327
NOW, VOYAGER 797, 800
NUCLEAR WAR FILMS 355
NUREYEV VALENTINO: PORTRAIT OF A FILM, THE 1296

O

O'HARA CONCERN: A BIOGRAPHY OF JOHN O'HARA, THE 1110, 1273
O'NEILL ON FILM 1038, 1340
OBSCENITY AND FILM CENSORSHIP: AN ABRIDGEMENT OF THE WILLIAMS REPORT 968
OCTOROON, THE 862
ODD COUPLE, THE 2060
ODYSSEY OF A FILM-MAKER: ROBERT FLAHERTY'S STORY, THE 1681, 1704
OEDIPUS AT COLONUS 601

OEDIPUS REX 2171
OEDIPUS TYRANNUS 601
OF HUMAN BONDAGE 1312
OF MICE AND MAGIC: A HISTORY OF AMERICAN ANIMATED CARTOONS 1623
OF WALKING IN ICE: MUNICH-PARIS 11/23 TO 12/14, 1974 2166
OFF CAMERA: LEVELING ABOUT THEMSELVES 609
OFF WITH THEIR HEADS: A SERIO-COMIC TALE OF HOLLYWOOD 1394
OFF-HOLLYWOOD MOVIES: A FILM LOVER'S GUIDE 1543
OFFICIAL JAMES BOND MOVIE BOOK, THE 423
OKAY FOR SOUND 1758
OL' MAN ADAM AN' HIS CHILLUN: BEING THE TALES THEY TELL ABOUT THE
   TIME WHEN GOD WALKED THE EARTH LIKE A NATURAL MAN 930
OLD HOLLYWOOD/NEW HOLLYWOOD: RITUAL, ART, AND INDUSTRY 173, 176,
   179, 194, 1464, 1466
OLIVER MESSEL: A BIOGRAPHY 1676
OLIVER TWIST 822
OLIVIA DE HAVILLAND 1767
OLIVIER 1862
OLIVIER-SHAKESPEARE 1344, 1354
OLIVIERS, THE 1861
OLIVIER: THE COMPLETE CAREER 1862
OMNI'S SCREEN FLIGHTS/SCREEN FANTASIES: THE FUTURE ACCORDING TO
   SCIENCE FICTION CINEMA 415
ON BEING FUNNY: WOODY ALLEN AND COMEDY 2046
ON FILM 1326
ON FILM MAKING 1081
ON FILMMAKING 72
ON FILM: A HISTORY OF THE MOTION PICTURE 1519, 1558, 1584, 1625
ON LIES, SECRETS, AND SILENCE: SELECTED PROSE 1966-1978 468
ON MAKING A MOVIE: "BREWSTER MCCLOUD" 554
ON MOVIES 154
ON THE COMPOSITION OF THE SHORT FICTION SCENARIO 1658
ON THE OTHER HAND: A LIFE STORY 1795
ON THE SET OF FELLINI'S SATYRICON: A BEHIND-THE-SCENES DIARY 2170
ON THE SMALL SCREEN: NEW APPROACHES IN TELEVISION AND VIDEO
   CRITICISM 179, 180
ON THE VERGE OF REVOLT: WOMEN IN AMERICAN FILMS OF THE
   FIFTIES 368, 375, 498, 657
ON VISUAL RACISM: ASIANS IN THE AMERICAN MOTION PICTURES 453
ONCE UPON A TIME: THE FILMS OF SERGIO LEONE 2171
ONE FOR MY BABY 1177
ONE REEL A WEEK 1587
ONE TOUCH OF VENUS 1259
ONE WOMAN, THE 1378
ONE-DIMENSIONAL MARXISM: ALTHUSSER AND THE POLITICS OF
   CULTURE 479
ONLY GOOD INDIAN . . . THE HOLLYWOOD GOSPEL 427, 434
ONLY VICTIMS: A STUDY OF SHOW BUSINESS BLACKLISTING 1067, 1096, 1194
OPEN BOOK, AN 1087, 1915
OPERATIONAL THEORIES OF PERSONALITY 586
OPPONENTS OF WAR, 1917-1918 211
ORDINARY PEOPLE 1008
ORIGINAL SIN: A SELF-PORTRAIT, THE 1968
ORIGINS OF AMERICAN FILM CRITICISM 1909-1939, THE 120, 123, 124, 126,
   142
ORSON WELLES 1790, 1793, 1794
ORSON WELLES: A BIOGRAPHY 1793
ORSON WELLES: A CELEBRATION 1795
ORSON WELLES: A CRITICAL VIEW 1789

ORSON WELLES: THE RISE AND FALL OF AN AMERICAN GENIUS   1792
OSCAR AT THE ACADEMY AWARDS   1170
OSCAR DIRECTORS, THE   1164
OSCAR MOVIES FROM A TO Z, THE   1171
OSCAR: A PICTORIAL HISTORY OF THE ACADEMY AWARDS   1174
OTHELLO   862, 1034
OTHER HOLLYWOOD, THE   1057, 1240
OTHER SIDE OF THE RAINBOW: WITH JUDY GARLAND ON THE DAWN PATROL,
   THE   1138, 1774
OUR FILMS   1566
OUR MODERN ART, THE MOVIES   44, 1012, 1019, 1021
OUR MOVIE MADE CHILDREN   732, 778
OUT WITH THE STARS: HOLLYWOOD NIGHTLIFE IN THE GOLDEN ERA   1442
OUTLINE OF CZECHOSLOVAKIAN CINEMA   2013
OUTRAGEOUS CONDUCT: ART, EGO, AND THE "TWILIGHT ZONE" CASE   691
OVER MY SHOULDER: AN AUTOBIOGRAPHY   1862
OX-BOW INCIDENT, THE   1021, 1309
OXFORD COMPANION TO FILM, THE   1522
OZU   1892, 1893, 1900

P

PAINTING WITH LIGHT   79
PAL JOEY   1274
PAPERBOUND BOOKS IN PRINT   30
PAPPY: THE LIFE OF JOHN FORD   1683
PARADE'S GONE BY, THE   1392, 1519, 1609
PARADISE LOST (Clifford Odets)   1259
PARAMOUNT PICTURES AND THE PEOPLE WHO MADE THEM   1503
PARAMOUNT STORY, THE   1503
PARE LORENTZ AND THE DOCUMENTARY FILM   1871
PARKER ADDERSON, PHILOSOPHER   1316
PARODY OUTLINE OF HISTORY, A   1278
PASOLINI ON PASOLINI: INTERVIEWS   2171
PASOLINI: A BIOGRAPHY   2171
PASSAGE TO INDIA, A   548
PASSING JUDGMENTS   1034
PASSION AND DEFIANCE: FILM IN ITALY FROM 1942 TO THE PRESENT   1876,
   1926, 1928
PASSION FOR FILMS: HENRI LANGLOIS AND THE CINEMATEQUE FRANCAISE,
   A   2006
PASSION OF INGMAR BERGMAN, THE   2185
PAT AND ROALD   2059
PAT HOBBY STORIES BY F. SCOTT FITZGERALD, THE   1127, 1128, 1129, 1161
PATH OF FAME OF THE CZECHOSLOVAK FAME, THE   2013
PATHS OF GLORY   1314
PATRICIA NEAL AND MARGARET SULLAVAN   2059
PATTERNS OF REALISM: A STUDY OF ITALIAN NEO-REALISM   1928
PAUL MUNI: HIS LIFE AND HIS FILMS   1785
PAUL NEWMAN   2060
PAUL NEWMAN, SUPERSTAR: A CRITICAL BIOGRAPHY   2060
PAUL ROBESON   951
PAUL'S MISTRESS   2129
PAWNBROKER, THE   1314
PEARL WHITE, THE PEERLESS FEARLESS GIRL   1457
PECKINPAH: A PORTRAIT IN MONTAGE   2063
PECKINPAH: THE WESTERN FILMS   2063

PENTIMENTO: A BOOK OF PORTRAITS 1225, 1228
PEOPLE IN A DIARY: A MEMOIR 1176
PEOPLE WHO MAKE MOVIES 70
PEOPLE'S FILMS: A POLITICAL HISTORY OF U. S. GOVERNMENT MOTION
 PICTURES, THE 224, 230, 305
PERDIDO 1041
PERFECT BEHAVIOR 1278
PERIOD OF ADJUSTMENT 1345, 2052
PERSISTENCE OF VISION: A COLLECTION OF FILM CRITICISM 371, 1592
PERSISTENCE OF VISION: THE FILMS OF ROBERT ALTMAN 785
PERSONAL FILMMAKING 75
PERSONAL VISION OF INGMAR BERGMAN, THE 2185
PERSPECTIVES ON THE STUDY OF FILM 48
PETER FINCH: A BIOGRAPHY 1941
PETER LAWFORD STORY: LIFE WITH THE KENNEDYS, MONROE, AND THE RAT
 PACK, THE 1780
PETER O'TOOLE: A BIOGRAPHY 2160
PETER SELLERS 1941
PETER SELLERS: THE MASK BEHIND THE FACE 1941
PETIT SOLDAT: A FILM BY JEAN-LUC GODARD, LE 2134
PHANTOM OF THE OPERA 396
PHENOMENON OF THE SOVIET CINEMA, THE 1653
PHILOSOPHY IN A NEW KEY: A STUDY IN THE SYMBOLISM OF REASON, RITE
 AND ART 450, 583, 955
PHILOSOPHY OF ANDY WARHOL (FROM A TO B AND BACK AGAIN), THE 2069
PHILOSOPHY OF THE FILM: EPISTEMOLOGY, ONTOLOGY, AESTHETICS 163
PHILOSOPHY OF THE SOCIAL SCIENCES 608
PHOTOGRAPHIC THEORY FOR THE MOTION PICTURE CAMERAMAN 87
PHOTOGUIDE TO MOVIEMAKING, THE 75
PHOTOPLAY EDITION 1453
PHOTOPLAY TREASURY 1453
PHOTOPLAY: A PSYCHOLOGICAL STUDY, THE 124, 582
PICNIC 1002, 1264
PICTORIAL COMMUNICATION 67
PICTORIAL HISTORY OF SCIENCE FICTION FILMS, A 414, 416
PICTORIAL HISTORY OF THE MOVIES, A 1564
PICTORIAL HISTORY OF THE SILENT SCREEN, A 1613
PICTORIAL HISTORY OF THE WESTERN FILM, A 426
PICTURE 554, 1319, 1321
PICTURE DANCING ON THE SCREEN: POETRY OF THE CINEMA, THE 1557
PICTURE HISTORY OF THE CINEMA, A 1562
PICTURE PALACE AND OTHER BUILDINGS FOR THE MOVIES 1507
PICTURES WILL TALK: THE LIFE AND FILMS OF JOSEPH L. MANKIEWICZ 363,
 1123, 1269, 1354
PICTURES WITHOUT A CAMERA 90
PIECES OF TIME 146
PIER PAOLO PASOLINI 2171, 2176
PIER PAOLO PASOLINI AND THE THEATRE OF THE WORD 2172
PLACE IN THE SUN, A 1015
PLANNING AND PRODUCING AUDIO-VISUAL MATERIAL 89
PLAY IT AGAIN, SAM 2046
PLAY IT AS IT LAYS 1041
PLAY THEORY OF MASS COMMUNICATION, THE 463
PLAYBOY INTERVIEW, THE 609
PLAYED OUT: THE JEAN SEBERG STORY 1970
PLAYERS: A PROFILE OF AN ART, THE 1448
PLAYING DOCTOR: TELEVISION, STORYTELLING, AND MEDICAL POWER 812,
 816
PLAYWRIGHT AS THINKER, THE 1333

PLAZA SUITE 2060
PLEASE DON'T SHOOT MY DOG: THE AUTOBIOGRAPHY OF JACKIE
  COOPER 1679
PLEASURE DOME: GRAHAM GREENE, THE COLLECTED FILM CRITICISM
  1935-1940, THE 1220, 1320
PLEASURE OF THE TEXT, THE 482
POEMS 2171
POETICS OF HERESY 2171
POLANSKI A BIOGRAPHY: THE FILMMAKER AS VOYEUR 1355
POLANSKI BY POLANSKI 2179
POLANSKI: THE FILMMAKER AS A VOYEUR--A BIOGRAPHY 2179
POLANSKI: THREE FILM SCRIPTS--KNIFE IN THE WATER, REPULSION,
  CUL-DE-SAC 2179
POLISH FEATURE FILMS: A REFERENCE GUIDE 1945-1985 2012, 2014
POLITICAL BIOGRAPHY, A 1113
POLITICAL ILLUSION, THE 205
POLITICAL LANGUAGE OF FILM AND THE AVANT-GARDE, THE 1651
POLITICS AND CINEMA 156
POLITICS AND FILM 204, 208, 236
POLITICS AND THE MEDIA 252
POLITICS OF GLAMOUR: IDEOLOGY AND DEMOCRACY IN THE SCREEN ACTORS
  GUILD, THE 1156
POLITICS OF PROPAGANDA: THE OFFICE OF WAR INFORMATION, 1942-1945,
  THE 229
POLITICS OF RESCUE: THE ROOSEVELT ADMINISTRATION AND THE
  HOLOCAUST, 1938-1945, THE 831
POLITICS OF THE SOVIET CINEMA 1917-1929, THE 1644, 1652
POLITICS OF UPHEAVAL, THE 733, 736
POLITICS, ART AND COMMITMENT IN THE EAST EUROPEAN CINEMA 2013
POODLE SPRINGS STORY, THE 1197
POPCORN AND PARABLE: A NEW LOOK AT THE MOVIES 48
POPCORN VENUS: WOMEN, MOVIES AND THE AMERICAN DREAM 471, 497, 514,
  518
POPPY 1390
POPULAR CULTURE AND HIGH CULTURE 706
POPULAR FILM CULTURE IN FASCIST ITALY: THE PASSING OF THE REX 464,
  1873, 1874, 1877
POPULAR THEATRE, THE 1034
PORTABLE F. SCOTT FITZGERALD, THE 1111
PORTRAIT OF A DIRECTOR: SATYAJIT RAY 2167
PORTRAIT OF AN INVISIBLE MAN: THE WORKING LIFE OF STEWART
  MCALLISTER, FILM EDITOR 249
PORTRAIT OF JOHN GARNETT 1798
PORTRAIT-SOUVENIR 1817
POSITIVE IMAGES: A GUIDE TO NON-SEXIST FILMS FOR YOUNG PEOPLE 490
POSSIBLE CINEMA: THE FILMS OF ALAIN TANNER, A 2189
POSTMAN ALWAYS RINGS TWICE, THE 1161, 1162, 1314, 1924
POTEMKIN: A FILM BY SERGEI EISENSTEIN 1655
POWER 985
POWER OF THE IMAGE: ESSAYS ON REPRESENTATION AND SEXUALITY,
  THE 509
PRACTICAL MANUAL OF SCREEN PLAYWRITING FOR THEATER AND
  TELEVISION FILMS, A 85
PRACTICAL MOTION PICTURE PHOTOGRAPHY 87
PRATER VIOLET 1031, 1102
PREMINGER: AN AUTOBIOGRAPHY 643, 1967
PRESENTATION OF THE AMERICAN NEGRO IN HOLLYWOOD FILMS, 1946-1961,
  THE 860

PRESTON STURGES: A GUIDE TO REFERENCES AND RESOURCES 1918
PRETEND INDIANS: IMAGES OF NATIVE AMERICANS IN MOVIES, THE 425
PRETTY BABY: AN INSIDER'S LOOK AT THE WORLD OF THE HOLLYWOOD
 CHILD STAR 991
PRIDE AND PREJUDICE 1309, 1312, 1327
PRIMAL SCREEN: ESSAYS ON FILM AND RELATED SUBJECTS, THE 156, 1006,
 1015
PRIMARY CINEMA RESOURCES: AN INDEX TO SCREENPLAYS, INTERVIEWS,
 AND SPECIAL COLLECTIONS AT USC 1546
PRIME OF MISS JEAN BRODIE, THE 30, 1003
PRIMER FOR FILM MAKING: A COMPLETE GUIDE TO 16MM AND 35MM FILM
 PRODUCTION, A 91
PRIMER ON VISUAL LITERACY, A 45
PRINCESS GRACE 1350, 1962
PRISONER OF SECOND AVENUE, THE 2060
PRIVATE EYE, THE COWBOY AND THE VERY NAKED GIRL: MOVIES FROM CLEO
 TO CLYDE, THE 147, 1008, 1020
PRIVATE SCREENINGS: VIEWS OF THE CINEMA OF THE SIXTIES 159, 995,
 1006, 1020, 1022, 1024, 1328, 1350, 2086
PRIVATE VIEW, A 1488
PROCESS AND EFFECTS OF MASS COMMUNICATION, THE 201
PROFANE MYTHOLOGY: THE SAVAGE MIND OF THE CINEMA 162
PROFESSIONAL FILMMAKING 72
PROFESSIONAL SECRETS: AN AUTOBIOGRAPHY OF JEAN COCTEAU--DRAWN
 FROM HIS LIFETIME WRITINGS 1818
PROFESSOR UNRATH 1831
PROFESSOR UNRATH (THE BLUE ANGEL) 1830
PROJECTING BRITAIN: EALING STUDIOS FILM POSTERS 1841
PROMISE OF MELODRAMA: RECENT WOMEN'S FILMS AND SOAP OPERAS,
 THE 792
PROPAGANDA AND PERSUASION 239
PROPAGANDA AND THE GERMAN CINEMA 1933-1945 202, 249, 282
PROPAGANDA AND THE NAZI WAR FILM 206
PROPAGANDA COMES OF AGE 213
PROPAGANDA FOR WAR: THE CAMPAIGN AGAINST AMERICAN NEUTRALITY,
 1914-17 211
PROPAGANDA ON FILM: A NATION AT WAR 204, 241
PROPAGANDA, POLITICS AND FILM, 1918-45 210, 211, 212, 213, 214, 216, 217,
 225, 242, 255
PROPAGANDA: THE FORMATION OF MAN'S ATTITUDES 204, 241
PROPAGANDES 204
PSYCHOANALYTIC APPROACHES TO LITERATURE AND FILM 594
PSYCHOS: EIGHTY YEARS OF MAD MOVIES, MANIACS, AND MURDEROUS
 DEEDS 394
PSYCHOTONIC ENCYCLOPEDIA OF FILM, THE 419
PUBLIC AND THE MOTION PICTURE INDUSTRY, THE 627
PUBLIC ARTS, THE 158, 1055
PUBLIC IS NEVER WRONG, THE 1505
PUBLIC OPINION 541, 542, 546
PUBLIC RELATIONS OF THE MOTION PICTURE INDUSTRY, THE 954
PUBLISHED SCREENPLAYS: A CHECKLIST 1153
PUDOVKIN'S FILMS AND FILM THEORY 1662
PUPIL, THE 601
PUPPET ANIMATION IN THE CINEMA: HISTORY & TECHNIQUE 77
PURLIE VICTORIOUS 915
PURPLE ROSE OF CAIRO, THE 2208
PYLON 1209
P. S. I LOVE YOU: AN INTIMATE PORTRAIT OF PETER SELLERS 1941

Q

QU'EST-CE QUE LE CINEMA?   128
QUALITY OF MERCY: AN AUTOBIOGRAPHY, THE   1964
QUEER PEOPLE   1031, 1041, 1104, 1135, 1136
QUEST FOR PARADISE, THE   1326
QUEST FOR WEALTH: A STUDY OF ACQUISITIVE MAN, THE   1047, 1050
QUESTIONS OF CINEMA   167, 475, 592
QUIET AMERICAN, THE   363, 364
QUINLAN'S ILLUSTRATED DIRECTOR OF FILM STARS   1540
QUITE REMARKABLE FATHER, A   1778, 1858

R

RADIE'S WORLD   1057, 1243
RADIO AND POETRY   1025
RADIO AND TELEVISION   43
RAGE TO LIVE   1274
RAGGED DICK And MARK, THE MATCH BOY   1052
RAGMAN'S SON: AN AUTOBIOGRAPHY, THE   1959
RAGTIME   1032
RAINBOW: THE STORMY LIFE OF JUDY GARLAND   1138, 1773
RAISIN IN THE SUN, A   1009
RAISING HELL: THE REBEL IN MOVIES   812
RAJ QUARTET   548
RALPH RICHARDSON: AN ACTOR'S LIFE   1863
RALPH STEINER: FILMMAKER AND STILL PHOTOGRAPHER   252
RAPE OF THE LOCK, THE   1153
RASHOMON   2028
RASHOMON: A FILM   2028
RAYMOND CHANDLER AND FILM   798, 1198
RAYMOND CHANDLER IN HOLLYWOOD   1196
RAYMOND CHANDLER ON SCREEN: HIS NOVELS INTO FILM   798, 1198
RAYMOND CHANDLER SPEAKING   1197
RE-VISION: ESSAYS IN FEMINIST FILM CRITICISM   465, 466, 495
READ THIS AND THE WAR IS WON (KORE DAKE YOMEBA WARE WA
  KATERU)   1897
READER-RESPONSE CRITICISM: FROM FORMALISM TO
  POST-STRUCTURALISM   485
READER'S GUIDE TO CONTEMPORARY LITERARY THEORY, A   120
READING THE ROMANCE: WOMEN, PATRIARCHY, AND POPULAR FICTION   469
READINGS AND WRITINGS: SEMIOTIC COUNTER-STRATEGIES   134, 171
REAGAN: A POLITICAL BIOGRAPHY   1088
REAL AND THE UNREAL, THE   1057, 1242
REAL STARS: ARTICLES AND INTERVIEWS ON HOLLYWOOD'S GREAT
  CHARACTER ACTORS, THE   1446
REAL THING, THE   2060
REAL TINSEL, THE   609, 1468
REALISM AND THE CINEMA: A READER   166
REALISM AND TINSEL: CINEMA AND SOCIETY IN BRITAIN 1939-48   1841
REALITY FILMS: THE FILMS OF FREDERICK WISEMAN   2070
REALM OF PLEASURE: VON STERNBERG, DIETRICH, AND THE MASOCHISTIC
  AESTHETIC   1697
REAR WINDOW   1311
REBECCA   469, 1029
RECANTATION OF GALILEO GALILEI, THE   1178
RECKONING, THE   1387

RED BADGE OF COURAGE, THE   1319, 1321
RED FASCISM: BORING FROM WITHIN BY THE SUBVERSIVE FORCES OF
  COMMUNISM   1079
RED HARVEST   1222
REEL ART: GREAT POSTERS FROM THE GOLDEN AGE OF THE SIVER
  SCREEN   1238
REEL CHANGE: A GUIDE TO SOCIAL ISSUES FILMS   52
REEL CHARACTERS   1451
REEL FACTS: THE MOVIE BOOK OF RECORDS   608, 1544
REEL PLASTIC MAGIC: A HISTORY OF FILMS AND FILMMAKING IN
  AMERICA   1562
REEL POLITICS: AMERICAN POLITICAL MOVIES FROM "BIRTH OF A NATION"
  TO "PLATOON"   558
REEL POWER: THE STRUGGLE FOR INFLUENCE AND SUCCESS IN THE NEW
  HOLLYWOOD   698
REELING   150, 896, 993, 1011
REFERENCE GUIDE TO AMERICAN SCIENCE FICTION FILMS   417
REFERENCE GUIDE TO AUDIOVISUAL INFORMATION, A   1533
REFERENCE GUIDE TO FANTASTIC FILMS: SCIENCE FICTION, FANTASY AND
  HORROR   412
REFERENCE GUIDE TO THE AMERICAN FILM NOIR: 1940-1958, A   1947, 1956
REFLECTIONS ON THE CINEMA   1724
REFLECTIONS ON THE SCREEN   142
REFLEXIVITY IN FILM AND LITERATURE: FROM DON QUIXOTE TO JEAN-LUC
  GODARD   118
REGENERATION THROUGH VIOLENCE: THE MYTHOLOGY OF THE AMERICAN
  FRONTIER, 1600-1860   175
REGRESSIVE ANALYSIS OF PRIOR EXPERIENCE OF KEY PRODUCTION
  PERSONNEL AS PREDICTORS OF REVENUES   735
REIVERS, THE   1212
REMARKABLE ANDREW, THE   1282
REMEMBERING JAMES AGEE   146
REMEMBRANCE OF THINGS PAST   2137
RENAISSANCE OF THE FILM   137
RENE CLAIR   1725
RENE CLAIR: A GUIDE TO REFERENCES AND RESOURCES   1725
REPORT ON BLACKLISTING: I--MOVIES   1067, 1074, 1087, 1096, 1185
REPRODUCTIONS OF BANALITY: FASCISM, LITERATURE, AND FRENCH
  INTELLECTUAL LIFE   1558
RESEARCHER'S GUIDE TO BRITISH FILMS AND TELEVISION
  COLLECTIONS   310
RESEARCHER'S GUIDE TO BRITISH NEWSREELS   310
RESPONSE TO INNOVATION: A STUDY OF POPULAR ARGUMENT ABOUT NEW
  MASS MEDIA   456, 725
RESPONSES TO DRAMA: AN INTRODUCTION TO PLAYS AND MOVIES   1335
REST OF THE STORY, THE   1247
RETROSPECTIVE INDEX TO FILM PERIODICALS   1522
RETURN ENGAGEMENT: FACES TO REMEMBER--THEN & NOW   1452
REVERSE ANGLE: A DECADE OF AMERICAN FILMS   159, 993, 996, 1007, 1008,
  1011, 1016
REVOLUTIONARY SOVIET POSTERS   1650
REX INGRAM: MASTER OF THE SILENT CINEMA   1687
REX: AN AUTOBIOGRAPHY   1842
RE/SEARCH #10: INCREDIBLY STRANGE FILMS   418
RHETORIC OF FILM NARRATION, THE   114
RIBBON OF DREAMS, A   1791
RIBBONS IN TIME: MOVIES AND SOCIETY SINCE 1945   1923, 1924, 2122
RICHARD BURTON: A LIFE   1940
RICHARD BURTON: VERY CLOSE UP   1356, 1940

RICHARD II   1353
RICHARD LEITERMAN   2058, 2162
RISE AND FALL OF BRITISH DOCUMENTARY: THE STORY OF THE FILM
  MOVEMENT FOUNDED BY JOHN GRIERSON, THE   215, 248
RISE AND FALL OF FREE SPEECH IN AMERICA, THE   1367, 1376
RISE AND FALL OF THE MATINEE IDOL: PAST DEITIES OF STAGE AND
  SCREEN, THEIR ROLES, THEIR MAGIC, AND THEIR WORSHIPPERS   1440
RISE OF RONALD REAGAN, THE   1088
RISE OF SILAS LAPHAM, THE   1051
RISE OF THE AMERICAN FILM: A CRITICAL HISTORY WITH AN ESSAY,
  THE   262, 633, 710, 864, 872, 915, 1359, 1467, 1509, 1519, 1576
RISE OF THE NOVEL, THE   1297
RITA HAYWORTH   1914
RKO: THE BIGGEST LITTLE MAJOR OF THEM ALL   1477
ROAD MOVIES   409
ROAD TO GLORY: A SCREENPLAY, THE   1103, 1207
ROBERT ALDRICH: A GUIDE TO REFERENCES AND RESOURCES   2044
ROBERT BREER: A STUDY OF HIS WORK IN THE CONTEXT OF THE
  MODERNIST TRADITION   165
ROBERT BRESSON: A GUIDE TO REFERENCES AND RESOURCES   2005
ROBERT DONAT: A BIOGRAPHY   1842
ROBERT FLAHERTY: A GUIDE TO REFERENCES AND RESOURCES   1681
ROBERT FLOREY, THE FRENCH EXPRESSIONIST   1771
ROBERT J. FLAHERTY: A BIOGRAPHY   1682
ROBERT MITCHUM   1964
ROBERT MITCHUM ON THE SCREEN   1964
ROBERT MITCHUM STORY: "IT SURE BEATS WORKING," THE   989, 1964
ROBERT REDFORD   2066
ROBERT REDFORD: A PHOTOGRAPHIC PORTRAYAL OF THE MAN AND HIS
  FILMS   2066
ROBERTO ROSSELLINI   1882, 1883
ROBERTO ROSSELLINI: A GUIDE TO REFERENCES AND RESOURCES   1883
ROBINSON CRUSOE   1311
ROCK HUDSON, PUBLIC AND PRIVATE: AN UNAUTHORIZED BIOGRAPHY   1962
ROGER CORMAN: THE BEST OF THE CHEAP ACTS   2050
ROGER EBERT'S MOVIE HOME COMPANION 1987 EDITION   1526
ROLLING BREAKS AND OTHER MOVIE BUSINESS   643, 1235
ROMAN BY POLANSKI   1355
ROMAN POLANSKI STORY, THE   1355, 2179
ROMANCE IN THE HOLLYWOOD FILM AND IN POSTER PUBLICITY: STUDIO
  YEARS   792
ROMEO AND JULIET   1009
RONALD COLMAN: A VERY PRIVATE PERSON   1679
RONALD REAGAN, THE MOVIE AND OTHER EPISODES IN POLITICAL
  DEMONOLOGY   1785, 2077
ROOM AT THE TOP   1016
ROSE TATTOO, THE   1345
ROTHCHILD'S FIDDLE   601
ROUBEN MAMOULIAN   1782
ROUBEN MAMOULIAN: STYLE IS THE MAN   1782
ROVER, THE   1114
RULES OF THE GAME: A FILM BY JEAN RENOIR   1822
RUN-THROUGH: A MEMOIR   1340
RUNNING AWAY FROM MYSELF: A DREAM PORTRAIT OF AMERICA DRAWN
  FROM THE FILMS OF THE FORTIES   494

S

S-F 2: A PICTORIAL HISTORY OF SCIENCE FICTION FILMS FROM
  "ROLLERBALL" TO "RETURN OF THE JEDI"   414
SAINT CINEMA: SELECTED WRITING, 1929-1970   160, 1022, 1729
SAINT JOAN   1344
SALAD DAYS, THE   1404
SALT OF THE EARTH   1089
SAM PECKINPAH   2062
SAM PECKINPAH: MASTER OF VIOLENCE--BEING THE ACCOUNT OF THE
  MAKING OF A MOVIE AND OTHER SUNDRY THINGS.   2061
SAM SHEPHERD   1278
SAMBO: THE RISE AND DEMISE OF AN AMERICAN JESTER   861, 907
SAMUEL FULLER   1960, 1961, 1977
SAMUEL GOLDWYN PRESENTS   1473
SAMUEL GOLDWYN, THE PRODUCER AND HIS FILMS   1473
SAMURAI FILMS OF AKIRA KUROSAWA, THE   205, 807, 1732, 1734, 1735, 1888,
  2019, 2024, 2026, 2027, 2030
SAMURAI FILM, THE   1732, 1743
SANFORD MEISNER ON ACTING   76
SARAH BERNHARDT   1463
SARAH BERNHARDT: THE ART WITHIN THE LEGEND   1463
SATURDAY AFTERNOON AT THE BIJOU   421
SAVE ME THE WALTZ   1110, 1119
SCANDINAVIAN FILM   1624, 1628
SCARLET LETTER, THE   1314
SCARLETT, RHETT, AND A CAST OF THOUSANDS   1125
SCARLETT, RHETT, AND A CAST OF THOUSANDS: THE FILMING OF "GONE
  WITH THE WIND"   1318
SCENES FROM A MARRIAGE   2184
SCHOLAR'S GUIDE TO WASHINGTON, D. C. FILM AND VIDEO
  COLLECTION   1542
SCHOOL AND THE ART OF MOTION PICTURES, THE   191
SCHOOL FOR SCANDAL, THE   1267
SCIENCE FICTION   411
SCIENCE FICTION COLLECTOR'S CATALOG, THE   416
SCIENCE FICTION FILM IMAGE: THE ILLUSTRATED ENCYCLOPEDIA OF
  SCIENCE FICTION, THE   420
SCIENCE FICTION FILMS   410
SCIENCE FICTION IN THE CINEMA   410
SCIENCE FICTION IN THE MOVIES: AN A-Z   415
SCIENCE FICTION, HORROR & FANTASY FILM AND TELEVISION CREDITS   412
SCIENCE FICTION, HORROR & FANTASY FILM AND TELEVISION CREDITS
  SUPPLEMENT: THROUGH 1987   412
SCOTT FITZGERALD   1118
SCOUNDREL TIME   1096, 1225, 1229
SCREEN ACHIEVEMENT RECORDS BULLETIN, THE   1174
SCREEN ARTS: A GUIDE TO FILM AND TELEVISON APPRECIATION, THE   46
SCREEN DECO: A CELEBRATION OF HIGH STYLE IN HOLLYWOOD   1754
SCREEN EDUCATION YEARBOOK   95, 2189
SCREEN EDUCATION: TEACHING A CRITICAL APPROACH TO CINEMA AND
  TELEVISION   47
SCREEN EXPERIENCE: AN APPROACH TO FILM   46, 980
SCREEN FACTS REFERENCE GUIDE, A   1456
SCREEN GUIDE FOR AMERICANS   229
SCREEN IMAGE OF YOUTH: MOVIES ABOUT CHILDREN AND ADOLESCENTS,
  THE   978, 984
SCREEN OF TIME: A STUDY OF LUCHINO VISCONTI, A   1884
SCREEN WORLD   1523

SCREENING OUT THE PAST: THE BIRTH OF MASS CULTURE AND THE MOTION
  PICTURE INDUSTRY   711, 717, 718, 719, 720, 782, 784
SCREENING SPACE: THE AMERICAN SCIENCE FICTION FILM   417
SCREENING THE HOLOCAUST: CINEMA'S IMAGES OF THE UNIMAGINABLE   310
SCREENING THE NOVEL: REDISCOVERED AMERICAN FICTION IN FILM   1313
SCREENPLAY AS LITERATURE, THE   1163
SCREENPLAYS AND OTHER WRITINGS ON THE CINEMA: THE BLOOD OF A
  POET/ THE TESTAMENT OF ORPHEUS   1817
SCREENPLAYS OF LINA WERTMULLER: THE SEDUCTION OF MIMI, LOVE AND
  ANARCHY, SWEPT AWAY, SEVEN BEAUTIES, THE   2172
SCREENPLAYS OF MICHELANGELO ANTONIONI: IL GRIDO/L'AVVENTURA/LA
  NOTTE/L'ECLISSE   1012, 2169
SCREENPLAYS: AGUIRRE, THE WRATH OF GOD; EVERY MAN FOR HIMSELF
  AND GOD AGAINST ALL; LAND OF SILENCE AND DARKNESS   2166
SCREENPLAY: THE FOUNDATIONS OF SCREENWRITING. New expanded
  ed.   84
SCREENPLAY: "TO KILL A MOCKINGBIRD"   1325
SCREENWRITER LOOKS AT THE SCREENWRITER, THE   1104, 1150
SCREENWRITER: THE LIFE AND TIMES OF NUNNALLY JOHNSON   1063, 1254
SCREENWRITING   85, 1036
SCREWBALL: THE LIFE OF CAROLE LOMBARD   1781
SCRIPT CONTINUITY AND THE PRODUCTION SECRETARY IN FILM AND
  TV   85
SCRIPT SUPERVISING AND FILM CONTINUITY   85
SCRIPTWRITING FOR ANIMATION   84
SCRIPTWRITING FOR THE AUDIO-VISUAL MEDIA: RADIO, FILMS, TELEVISION,
  FILMSTRIPS, SLIDEFILMS   84
SCULPTING IN TIME   2181
SEARCH FOR SAM GOLDWYN: A BIOGRAPHY, THE   1129, 1471
SECOND MAN, THE   1176
SECOND SIGHT: NOTES ON SOME MOVIES, 1965-1970   156, 995, 1001, 1024
SECOND WAVE   2094, 2123
SECRET AGENT, THE   1153, 1312, 1838
SECRET LIFE OF TYRONE POWER, THE   1785
SECRETS OF CREWE HOUSE   212
SEE NO EVIL: LIFE INSIDE A HOLLYWOOD CENSOR   968
SEE YOU AT THE MOVIES: THE AUTOBIOGRAPHY OF MELVYN DOUGLAS   1769
SEEING IS BELIEVING: HOW HOLLYWOOD TAUGHT US TO STOP WORRYING
  AND LOVE THE FIFTIES   1952
SEEING THE LIGHT   80
SEEING WITH FEELING: FILM IN THE CLASSROOM   49
SEEN ANY GOOD DIRTY MOVIES LATELY? A CHRISTIAN CRITIC LOOKS AT
  CONTEMPORARY FILMS   42
SEESAW: A DUAL BIOGRAPHY OF ANN BANCROFT AND MEL BROOKS   2047
SELECTED ARTICLES ON CENSORSHIP OF THE THEATER AND MOVING
  PICTURE   963
SELECTED ATTEMPTS AT STEREOSCOPIC MOVING PICTURES   655, 1585, 1591
SELECTED FILM CRITICISM 1951-1960   143
SELECTED LETTERS BY JOHN O'HARA   1273
SELF AND CINEMA: A TRANSFORMALIST PERSPECTIVE   163
SELF PORTRAIT   1727
SELF-CONSUMING ARTIFACTS: THE EXPERIENCE OF SEVENTEENTH CENTURY
  LITERATURE   485
SELF-MADE MAN IN AMERICA: THE MYTH OF RAGS TO RICHES, THE   1047,
  1049, 1054
SELZNICK   1489
SELZNICK PLAYERS, THE   1487
SEMIOTICS AND LIGHTING: A STUDY OF SIX MODERN CAMERAMEN   165

SEMIOTICS OF CINEMA 164
SENTINEL, THE 1311, 2054
SEPARATE PEACE, A 601
SERGEI EISENSTEIN AND UPTON SINCLAIR: THE MAKING & UNMAKING OF
   "QUE VIVA MEXICO!" 1656, 1866
SERGEI EISENSTEIN'S "POTEMKIN": A SHOT-BY-SHOT PRESENTATION 1659,
   1666
SERGEI EISENSTEIN: AN INVESTIGATION INTO HIS FILMS AND
   PHILOSOPHY 1660, 1666
SERGEI M. EISENSTEIN: A BIOGRAPHY 830, 1646, 1647, 1656, 1660, 1661,
   1667, 1865
SERGEI PROKOFIEV, HIS MUSICAL LIFE 1868
SERIALS: SUSPENSE AND DRAMA BY INSTALLMENT, THE 1457
SERPENT'S EGG, THE 2184
SERPENT'S EYE: SHAW AND THE CINEMA, THE 1344
SEVEN LIVELY ARTS, THE 1055, 1358, 1676
SEVEN SAMURAI: A FILM, THE 2028
SEVENTEEN INTERVIEWS: FILM STARS AND SUPERSTARS 609
SEVENTEEN-SEVENTY-SIX 1095
SEVENTH ANNUAL GREATER HARTFORD FORUM 57
SEX GODDESSES OF THE SILENT SCREEN 1452
SEX ON CELLULOID 999, 2037
SEX PSYCHE ETCETERA IN THE FILM 1956
SEXUAL STRATAGEMS: THE WORLD OF WOMEN IN FILM 444, 451, 471, 496,
   498, 529
SEXUALITY IN THE FIELD OF VISION 519
SEX, VIOLENCE, AND THE MEDIA 2037
SHADOW MAN: THE LIFE OF DASHIELL HAMMETT 1223
SHADOW OF AN AIRPLANE CLIMBS THE EMPIRE STATE BUILDING: A WORLD
   THEORY ON FILM, THE 171
SHADOW OF SOUND, THE 1753
SHADOWLAND 1292
SHADOWS OF THE INDIAN: STEREOTYPES IN AMERICAN CULTURE 434
SHADOWS OF THE MAGIC LAMP: FANTASY AND SCIENCE FICTION IN
   FILM 416
SHAKESPEARE AND THE FILM 1343, 1408
SHAKESPEARE ON FILM 1343
SHAKESPEARE ON FILM: AN INDEX TO WILLIAM SHAKESPEARE'S PLAYS ON
   FILM 1343
SHAKESPEARE ON SILENT FILM: A STRANGE EVENTFUL HISTORY 1342
SHAKESPEARE ON TELEVISION: AN ANTHOLOGY OF ESSAYS AND
   REVIEWS 1342
SHAKESPEARE: TIME AND CONSCIENCE 1343
SHANE 1009
SHATTERED PEACE: THE ORIGINS OF THE COLD WAR AND THE NATIONAL
   SECURITY STATE 346
SHATTERED SILENTS: HOW THE TALKIES CAME TO STAY, THE 1759
SHELLEY: ALSO KNOWN AS SHIRLEY 1973
SHERLOCK HOLMES ON THE SCREEN 381
SHERLOCK HOLMES: A CENTENARY CELEBRATION 381
SHINMIN NO MICHI (THE WAY OF THE SUBJECT) 1897
SHIRLEY TEMPLE 1787
SHIRLEY TEMPLE: AMERICAN PRINCESS 1787
SHOOTING STARS: HEROES AND HEROINES OF WESTERN FILM 430
SHOOTING STAR: A BIOGRAPHY OF JOHN WAYNE 1081
SHORT FILM: AN EVALUATIVE SELECTION OF 500 RECOMMENDED FILMS,
   THE 1541
SHORT HISTORY OF THE MOVIES, A 1407, 1519, 1562
SHORT STORY/SHORT FILM 1312

SHORT TIME FOR INSANITY: AN AUTOBIOGRAPHY, A 1701
SHOWDOWN: CONFRONTING MODERN AMERICA IN THE WESTERN FILM 429
SIDNEY 886, 888, 951
SIDNEY LUMET: A GUIDE TO REFERENCES AND RESOURCES 2058
SIGHTS AND SOUND OF CINEMA AND TELEVISION: HOW THE AESTHETIC
  EXPERIENCE INFLUENCES OUR FEELINGS, THE 64
SIGHT, SOUND AND SOCIETY: MOTION PICTURES AND TELEVISION IN
  AMERICA 70, 801
SIGHT, SOUND, MOTION: APPLIED MEDIA AESTHETICS 107
SIGNAL, THE 2129
SIGNS AND MEANING IN THE CINEMA 133, 172
SILENCE OF GOD: CREATIVE RESPONSE TO THE FILMS OF INGMAR BERGMAN,
  THE 2186
SILENT CINEMA, THE 1610
SILENT CLOWNS, THE 1677
SILENT MAGIC: REDISCOVERING THE SILENT FILM ERA 1609
SILENT PARTNER: THE HISTORY OF THE AMERICAN FILM MANUFACTURING
  COMPANY 1910-1921, THE 1622
SILENT SCREAM: ALFRED HITCHCOCK'S SOUND TRACK, THE 1857
SILENT SCREEN AND MY TALKING HEART: AN AUTOBIOGRAPHY, THE 1450
SILENT STAR: COLLEEN MOORE TALKS ABOUT HER HOLLYWOOD 1695
SILENT VOICE--A TEXT, THE GOLDEN AGE OF THE CINEMA 1610
SINATRA 1918
SINATRA: AN AMERICAN CLASSIC 1918
SINATRA: AN UNAUTHORIZED BIOGRAPHY 1918
SINATRA: TWENTIETH-CENTURY ROMANTIC 1918
SINEMA: AMERICAN PORNOGRAPHIC FILMS AND THE PEOPLE WHO MAKE
  THEM 2037
SINGING COWBOYS, THE 433
SIRK ON SIRK 1970
SISTER CARRIE 1314
SIX-GUN MYSTIQUE, THE 182, 185, 188
SIXGUNS AND SOCIETY: A STRUCTURAL STUDY OF THE WESTERN 175, 184,
  293
SKIN OF OUR TEETH, THE 1259
SKOURAS; KING OF FOX STUDIOS 1492
SKYWALKING: THE LIFE AND FILMS OF GEORGE LUCAS 2209
SLAPSTICK QUEENS, THE 1756
SLOW FADE 1041
SLOW FADE TO BLACK: THE NEGRO IN AMERICAN FILM, 1900-1942 860, 863,
  867, 868, 876, 923, 924, 926, 927, 929, 1341
SMALL CHANGE: A FILM NOVEL 2149
SMART ALEC: THE WIT, WORLD AND LIFE OF ALEXANDER WOOLLCOTT 1064
SMUT PEDDLERS, THE 955
SOCIAL BASIS OF AMERICAN COMMUNISM, THE 830
SOCIAL CINEMA OF JEAN RENOIR, THE 1820
SOCIAL CONDUCT AND ATTITUDES OF MOVIE FANS, THE 729, 732
SOCIAL PROBLEMS: A MODERN APPROACH 459, 461
SOCIAL PSYCHOLOGICAL STUDY OF MOTION PICTURE BEHAVIOR: A CASE
  STUDY OF THE NEGRO IMAGE IN MASS COMMUNICATION, A 882
SOCIAL SIGNIFICANCE OF STARDOM, THE 1441
SOCIOLOGY OF FILM 580
SOCIOLOGY OF FILM ART, THE 1633, 1923, 1925
SOLDIER'S HOME 1316
SOME ARE BORN GREAT 1396
SOME SORT OF EPIC GRANDEUR: THE LIFE OF F. SCOTT FITZGERALD 1118,
  1121, 1122, 1125, 1127, 1129, 1132, 1133, 1280
SOME TIME IN THE SUN 1066, 1125, 1129, 1134, 1147

SOMETHING LIKE AN AUTOBIOGRAPHY 1735, 1738, 1739, 1886, 1891, 1895, 1899, 2016
SOMETHING TO DECLARE: TWELVE YEARS OF FILMS FROM ABROAD 160, 998
SONG OF ROLAND, THE 1153
SONGS OF DEATH: PERFORMANCE, INTERPRETATION AND THE TEXT OF RICHARD III 1342
SONS AND LOVERS 1010, 1312
SOON TO BE A MAJOR MOTION PICTURE: THE ANATOMY OF AN ALL-STAR, BIG-BUDGET, MULTIMILLION-DOLLAR DISASTER 554, 643
SOPHIE'S CHOICE 1032
SORROW AND THE PITY: A FILM BY MARCEL OPHULS, THE 317
SOUND AND THE CINEMA: THE COMING OF SOUND TO THE AMERICAN FILM 632
SOUND AND THE DOCUMENTARY FILM 86
SOUND AND THE FURY, THE 1212
SOUND RECORDING FOR MOTION PICTURES 86
SOUNDER 565
SOUNDS FOR SILENTS 405
SOUNDTRACK: THE MUSIC OF THE MOVIES 403
SOURCE MUSIC IN MOTION PICTURES 401
SOUTH AND FILM, THE 912
SOUTH PACIFIC 1264
SOVIET CINEMA 1650
SOVIET CINEMA IN THE SILENT ERA, 1918-1935 1653
SOVIET CINEMA: DIRECTORS AND FILMS 1649
SOVIET FILM INDUSTRY, THE 1648
SPAGHETTI WESTERNS: COWBOYS AND EUROPEANS FROM KARL MAY TO SERGIO LEONE 427
SPANISH CIVIL WAR IN AMERICAN AND EUROPEAN FILMS, THE 219, 277
SPANISH FILM DIRECTORS (1950-1985): 21 PROFILES 2182
SPARKS FLY UPWARD 1941
SPEAKING OF SOAP OPERAS 721, 722
SPECIAL EFFECTS: CREATING MOVIE MAGIC 80
SPECIAL EFFECTS: DISASTER AT "TWILIGHT ZONE"--THE TRAGEDY AND THE TRIAL 698
SPECIAL EFFECTS: WIRE, TAPE AND RUBBER BAND STYLE 79
SPECIAL ISSUE ON BERGMAN 2184
SPECIAL ISSUE ON SATYAJIT RAY 2168
SPECIAL ISSUE: ANTONIONI 1881
SPECIAL KIND OF MAGIC, A 1778
SPELLBOUND IN DARKNESS: READINGS IN THE HISTORY AND CRITICISM OF THE SILENT FILM 1594
SPENCER TRACY 1788
SPENCER TRACY: A BIOGRAPHY 1788
SPENCER TRACY: TRAGIC IDOL 1788
SPIDER BOY 1041
SPIEGEL: THE MAN BEHIND THE PICTURES 1490
SPLATTER MOVIES: BREAKING THE LAST TABOO 394
SPLIT FOCUS 1870
SPONSORED FILM, THE 73
SPORTS FILMS: A COMPLETE REFERENCE 422
SPORTS IN THE MOVIES 421
SPRINGTIME FOR HITLER 2047
SPRINGTIME IN ITALY: A READER ON NEO-REALISM 1928
SPURS 1311
STAGE TO LORDSBURG 1311, 1772
STAGE TO SCREEN: THEATRICAL METHOD FROM GARRICK TO GRIFFITH 1331, 1338
STAGECOACH: A FILM BY JOHN FORD AND DUDLEY NICHOLS 1772

STAGE/SCREEN DEBATE: A STUDY IN POPULAR AESTHETICS, THE   1030,
  1331, 1333, 1334, 1338
STAMBOUL TRAIN   1218
STAN BRAKHAGE: A GUIDE TO REFERENCES AND RESOURCES   1957
STANDARD EDITION   453
STANLEY KUBRICK DIRECTS   2057
STANLEY KUBRICK'S CLOCKWORK ORANGE: BASED ON THE NOVEL BY
  ANTHONY BURGESS   2055
STANLEY KUBRICK: A FILM ODYSSEY   2057
STANLEY KUBRICK: A GUIDE TO REFERENCES AND SOURCES   2056
STAN: THE LIFE OF STAN LAUREL   1690
STAR ACTING: GISH, GARBO, DAVIS   1388, 1438
STAR IS BORN: THE MAKING OF THE 1954 FILM AND ITS 1983 RESTORATION,
  A   1248
STAR MAKER: THE STORY OF D. W. GRIFFITH   1374
STAR-SPANGLED SCREEN: THE AMERICAN WORLD WAR II FILM, THE   203,
  329, 345
STARDOM: THE HOLLYWOOD PHENOMENON   1451
STARGAZER: ANDY WARHOL'S WORLD AND HIS FILMS, 2nd ed.   2068, 2091
STARMAKER: THE AUTOBIOGRAPHY OF HAL WALLIS   801, 1288
STARRING FRED ASTAIRE   1759
STARRING MISS BARBARA STANWYCK   799, 1786
STARRING ROBERT BENCHLEY: THOSE MAGNIFICENT MOVIE SHORTS   1177
STARS   487, 999, 1293, 1436, 1437, 1441, 1556
STARS AND STRIKES: UNIONIZATION OF HOLLYWOOD   1068, 1069, 1156, 1173
STARS AND STRIPES   1173
STARSPEAK: HOLLYWOOD ON EVERYTHING   1447
STARSTRUCK: THE WONDERFUL WORLD OF MOVIE MEMORABILIA   1529
STARS, THE   569, 1435, 1448, 1449
STATE OF THE ART, THE   151
STATISTICAL ABSTRACT OF THE UNITED STATES 1985, 105th edition   650
STAY OUT OF THE SHOWER: 25 YEARS OF SHOCKER FILMS BEGINNING WITH
  "PSYCHO"   397
STEINBECK AND FILM   1281, 1326
STELLA DALLAS   797
STEPS IN TIME: AN AUTOBIOGRAPHY   1759
STERNBERG   1697
STEVE MCQUEEN: STAR ON WHEELS   2059
STEVE MCQUEEN: THE UNAUTHORIZED BIOGRAPHY   2059
STEVEN SPIELBERG   2209
STEVEN SPIELBERG STORY: THE MAN BEHIND THE MOVIES, THE   2209
STOP THE PRESSES! THE NEWSPAPERMAN IN AMERICAN FILMS   408
STORIES INTO FILM   1311
STORIES OF F. SCOTT FITZGERALD: A SELECTION OF 28 STORIES,
  THE   1113, 1116, 1119
STORY AND DISCOURSE: NARRATIVE STRUCTURE IN FICTION FILM   114
STORY BEHIND "THE EXORCIST," THE   554, 1319
STORY OF ADELE H.: THE COMPLETE SCRIPT OF THE FILM, THE   2149
STORY OF THE FILMS, THE   619
STORY OF THE LOST REFLECTION: THE ALIENATION OF THE IMAGE IN
  WESTERN AND POLISH CINEMA   2013
STORY OF WALT DISNEY, THE   1768
STORYTELLING AND MYTHMAKING: IMAGES FROM FILM AND
  LITERATURE   798, 1153
STRANGE CASE OF ALFRED HITCHCOCK, OR, THE PLAIN MAN'S HITCHCOCK,
  THE   1843
STRANGE CASE OF DR. JEKYLL AND MR. HYDE, THE   1277

STRATEGIC PSYCHOLOGICAL OPERATIONS AND AMERICAN FOREIGN
  POLICY 201
STREAK OF LUCK: THE LIFE AND LEGEND OF THOMAS ALVA EDISON,
  A 1586, 1615
STREETCAR NAMED DESIRE, A 1260, 1345, 1489
STREETCAR NAMED DESIRE, A (Play) 1848
STROHEIM 1699
STROHEIM: A PICTORIAL RECORD OF HIS NINE FILMS 1700
STRUCTURAL STUDY OF MYTH AND TOTEMISM, THE 175
STRUCTURALISM 480
STRUCTURE OF SCIENTIFIC REVOLUTIONS, THE 1571
STRUGGLES OF THE ITALIAN FILM INDUSTRY DURING FASCISM,
  1930-1935 1872, 1875, 1878
STUDIES IN FICTION 109
STUDIES IN THE ARAB THEATER AND CINEMA 2178
STUDY OF FILM AS AN ART FORM IN AMERICAN SECONDARY SCHOOLS,
  THE 39, 54
STUDY OF THE ATTITUDES OF WRITERS OF THE NEGRO PRESS TOWARD THE
  DEPICTION OF THE NEGRO IN PLAYS AND FILMS, THE 860
STUDY OF THE TECHNOLOGY OF COLOR MOTION PICTURE PROCESSES
  DEVELOPED IN THE UNITED STATES, A 654
STUNTING IN THE CINEMA 76
STYLES OF RADICAL WILL 1356
SUBJECT OF SEMIOTICS, THE 165
SUCCESS AND OPPORTUNITY: A STUDY OF ANOMIE 1047
SUCCESS IN AMERICA: THE YEOMAN DREAM AND THE INDUSTRIAL
  REVOLUTION 1046, 1049, 1051
SUCCESS TRIP: HOW THEY MADE IT, HOW THEY FEEL ABOUT IT, THE 609
SUDDENLY LAST SUMMER 1345
SUMMER AND SMOKE 1345
SUN ALSO RISES, THE 1323
SUN AND SHADOW: AN AUTOBIOGRAPHY 1909
SUNDAY NIGHT AT THE MOVIES 48
SUNDOWN BEACH 1260
SUNRISE AT CAMPOBELLO 1485
SUNSHINE AND SHADOW 1395
SUPER SECS, THE 1237
SUPER 8 BOOK, THE 74
SUPER 8 FILMMAKING FROM SCRATCH 74
SUPER 8: THE MODEST MEDIUM 73
SUPERFILMS: AN INTERNATIONAL GUIDE TO AWARD-WINNING EDUCATIONAL
  FILMS 1539
SUPERTALK 609
SURPRISED BY SIN: THE READER IN PARADISE LOST 485
SURREALISM AND FILM 1718
SURREALISM AND THE CINEMA (OPEN-EYED SCREENING) 1716
SURREALISME AU CINEMA, LE 1722
SURVEY FOR THE MPAA, A 742
SURVIVOR: AN ANATOMY OF LIFE IN THE DEATH CAMPS, THE 223
SUSAN HAYWARD: PORTRAIT OF A SURVIVOR 1777
SUSAN HAYWARD: THE DIVINE BITCH 1777
SUSAN LENNOX: HER FALL AND RISE 1313
SUSPENSE IN THE CINEMA 391
SVENGALI 1798
SWANSON ON SWANSON 1454
SWASHBUCKLERS, THE 423
SWEDEN 1: AN ILLUSTRATED GUIDE 1624, 1627
SWEDEN 2: A COMPREHENSIVE ASSESSMENT OF THE THEMES, TRENDS, AND
  DIRECTORS IN SWEDISH CINEMA 1627

SWEDISH CINEMA 1624, 1627, 1628
SWEDISH FILM CLASSICS: A PICTORIAL SURVEY OF 25 FILMS FROM 1913 TO
  1957 1625, 1628
SWEDISH FILMS 1628, 1630
SWEET BIRD OF YOUTH 1261, 1345
SWEET SWEETBACK'S BAADASSSSS SONG 942, 953
SWEETHEART: THE STORY OF MARY PICKFORD 1396
SWORDSMEN OF THE SCREEN: FROM DOUGLAS FAIRBANKS TO MICHAEL
  YORK 423
SYDNEY POLLACK 2065
SYMBOL, THE 1177
SYNDICATION OF FIRST-RUN TELEVISION PROGRAMMING: ITS DEVELOPMENT
  AND CURRENT STATUS 678
S. J. PERELMAN: A CRITICAL STUDY 1275
S. J. PERELMAN: A LIFE 1275
S. J. PERELMAN: AN ANNOTATED BIBLIOGRAPHY 1275
S. M. EISENSTEIN: SELECTED WORKS. VOLUME I: WRITINGS, 1922-34 1662
S/Z 472, 482

T

TABLE, THE ASS, AND THE STICK, THE 601
TAIYO NO KISETSU/SEASON OF THE SUN. 2023
TAKE BACK THE NIGHT: WOMEN ON PORNOGRAPHY 565
TAKE TWO: A LIFE IN MOVIES AND POLITICS 272, 1059, 1067, 1087, 1203
TAKE 22: MOVIEMAKERS ON MOVIEMAKING 609
TALE OF TWO CITIES, A 1305, 1307, 1308
TALK-BACK TV: TWO WAY CABLE TELEVISION 93
TALKIES, THE 1757
TALKIES: ARTICLES AND ILLUSTRATIONS FROM A GREAT FAN MAGAZINE
  1928-1940, THE 1057
TALKING ABOUT THE CINEMA: FILM STUDIES FOR YOUNG PEOPLE 48
TALKING CLOWNS: FROM LAUREL AND HARDY TO THE MARX BROTHERS,
  THE 1755
TALKING PICTURES: HOW THEY ARE MADE, HOW TO APPRECIATE THEM 1754
TALKING PICTURES: SCREENWRITERS IN THE AMERICAN CINEMA
  1927-1973 1029, 1093, 1101, 1140, 1145, 1266, 1285, 1912
TALKING WITH INGMAR BERGMAN 2186
TALL AMERICAN: THE STORY OF GARY COOPER, THE 1081
TALLULAH 1760
TALLULAH, DARLING 1760
TALLULAH: DARLING OF THE GODS 1760
TALLULAH: MY AUTOBIOGRAPHY 1760
TALMADGE GIRLS: A MEMOIR, THE 1060
TARZAN OF THE APES 919
TEA AND SYMPATHY 1261
TEACHING A LITERATURE-CENTERED ENGLISH PROGRAM 36
TEACHING ABOUT FILM 1329
TEACHING ABOUT THE FILM 52
TEACHING FILM ANIMATION TO CHILDREN 87
TEACHING PROGRAM: EXPLORING THE FILM 49
TECHNICAL REPORTS OF THE US COMMISSION ON OBSCENITY AND
  PORNOGRAPHY I 546
TECHNIQUE OF DOCUMENTARY FILM PRODUCTION, THE 82
TECHNIQUE OF EDITING, THE 82
TECHNIQUE OF FILM AND TELEVISION MAKE-UP, THE 84
TECHNIQUE OF FILM ANIMATION, THE 77

TECHNIQUE OF FILM EDITING, THE 82
TECHNIQUE OF FILM MUSIC, THE 84
TECHNIQUE OF LIGHTING FOR TELEVISION AND MOTION PICTURES, THE 92
TECHNIQUE OF SCREENPLAY WRITING: AN ANLYSIS OF THE DRAMATIC
  STRUCTURE OF MOTION PICTURES, Revised 85
TECHNIQUE OF SPECIAL EFFECTS CINEMATOGRAPHY, THE 80, 98
TECHNIQUE OF TELEVISION PRODUCTION, THE 92
TECHNIQUE OF THE FILM CUTTING ROOM, THE 83
TECHNIQUE OF THE MOTION PICTURE CAMERA, THE 81
TECHNIQUE OF THE SOUND STUDIO: FOR RADIO, TELEVISION, AND FILM.
  3rd ed., THE 86
TECHNIQUE OF WILDLIFE CINEMATOGRAPHY, THE 76
TECHNOLOGICAL HISTORY OF MOTION PICTURES AND TELEVISION, A 654,
  1590
TECHNOLOGIES OF GENDER: ESSAYS ON THEORY, FILM, AND FICTION 494
TEENAGERS AND TEENPICS: THE JUVENILIZATION OF AMERICAN MOVIES IN
  THE 1950s 983
TELECOMMUNICATIONS MANAGEMENT: THE BROADCAST AND CABLE
  INDUSTRIES 75
TELEPRODUCTION SHORTCUTS: A MANUAL FOR LOW-BUDGET TELEVISION
  PRODUCTION IN A SMALL STUDIO 93
TELEVISION AND THE TEACHING OF ENGLISH 135
TELEVISION AS A CULTURAL FORCE 180
TELEVISION PRODUCTION HANDBOOK, 3rd ed. 93
TELEVISION: THE CRITICAL VIEW 780
TELL IT ON THE MOUNTAIN 1479
TELLING IT AGAIN AND AGAIN: REPETITION IN LITERATURE AND FILM 1310
TEN DAYS THAT SHOOK THE WORLD 1667
TEN NORTH FREDERICK 1274
TENDENCIES TO MONOPOLY IN THE CINEMATOGRAPH FILM INDUSTRY 1568
TENDER IS THE NIGHT 1110, 1115, 1116, 1117, 1119, 1120, 1136, 1158, 1217
TENNESSEE WILLIAMS AND FILM 1346
TENNESSEE WILLIAMS: AN INTIMATE BIOGRAPHY 1345
TENNESSEE: CRY OF THE HEART 1345
TENNY COMMITTEE: LEGISLATIVE INVESTIGATIONS OF SUBVERSIVE
  ACTIVITIES IN CALIFORNIA 1079
TEVYE AND HIS DAUGHTERS 850
TEX 998
THALBERG: LIFE AND LEGEND 226, 1490
THAT BOWLING ALLEY ON THE TIBER: TALES OF A DIRECTOR 1881
THE POLITICAL CONSCIOUSNESS: NARRATIVE AS A SOCIALLY SYMBOLIC
  ACT 417
THEATER AND FILM: A COMPARATIVE STUDY OF THE TWO FORMS OF
  DRAMATIC ART, AND THE PROBLEMS OF ADAPTATION 1337
THEATRE OF SCIENCE, THE 1519, 1555, 1614
THEIR HEARTS WERE YOUNG AND GAY 991
THEM OR US: ARCHETYPAL INTERPRETATIONS OF FIFTIES ALIEN INVASION
  FILMS 412
THEMES: SHORT FILMS FOR DISCUSSION 48
THEOLOGY THROUGH FILM 47
THEORIES OF AUTHORSHIP 162
THEORIES OF AUTHORSHIP: A READER 1999
THEORIES OF FILM 165
THEORIES OF MASS COMMUNICATION 721, 747
THEORY AND PRACTICE OF THE "CINE-ROMAN," THE 2112, 2113, 2114, 2127
THEORY AND TECHNIQUE OF PLAYWRITING AND SCREENWRITING 85, 1070
THEORY OF AMERICAN FILM: THE FILMS AND TECHNIQUES OF GEORGE
  STEVENS, A 1787
THEORY OF CAPITALIST DEVELOPMENT 634

THEORY OF COGNITIVE DISSONANCE, A 543
THEORY OF FILM PRACTICE 112, 167
THEORY OF FILM: THE REDEMPTION OF PHYSICAL REALITY 130, 168, 1027,
  1304, 1339
THEORY OF THE FILM: CHARACTER AND GROWTH OF A NEW ART 125, 166
THERE MUST BE A LONE RANGER: THE AMERICAN WEST IN FILM AND IN
  REALITY 425
THERE REALLY WAS A HOLLYWOOD: AN AUTOBIOGRAPHY 1962
THEY DIDN'T WIN THE OSCARS 1169
THEY SHOOT HORSES, DON'T THEY? 1161, 1162, 1314
THEY WENT THATAWAY; A FRONT ROW KID'S SEARCH FOR HIS BOYHOOD
  HEROES--THE OLD-TIME HOLLYWOOD COWBOYS 429
THIN MAN, THE 1222, 1806
THINGS TO COME: AN ILLUSTRATED HISTORY OF THE SCIENCE FICTION
  FILM 414
THINKING IN PICTURES: THE MAKING OF MATEWAN 554
THIRD CINEMA IN THE THIRD WORLD: THE AESTHETICS OF
  LIBERATION 917, 918
THIRD WORLD FILMMAKING AND THE WEST 2189
THIRTY YEARS OF TREASON: EXCERPTS FROM HEARINGS BEFORE THE HOUSE
  COMMITTEE ON UN-AMERICAN ACTIVITIES, 1938-1968 1067, 1179
THIRTY-NINE STEPS, THE 212, 1838
THIS 'N THAT 1766
THIS LIFE 886, 951
THIS LOVING DARKNESS: THE CINEMA AND SPANISH WRITERS 1920-1936 1723
THIS SIDE OF PARADISE 1110, 1113, 1125
THIS WAS HOLLYWOOD: AN AFFECTIONATE HISTORY OF FILMLAND'S GOLDEN
  YEARS 1057, 1233
THOMAS A. EDISON PAPERS--A GUIDE TO MOTION PICTURE CATALOGS BY
  AMERICAN PRODUCERS AND DISTRIBUTORS, 1894-1908 1586, 1600, 1615
THOSE CRAZY WONDERFUL YEARS WHEN WE RAN WARNER BROS. 1495
THOSE ENDEARING YOUNG CHARMS: CHILD PERFORMERS OF THE
  SCREEN 990
THOSE GREAT MOVIE ADS 1447
THOUSAND CLOWNS, A 1022
THREE 1225
THREE BRITISH SCREEN PLAYS: BRIEF ENCOUNTER, ODD MAN OUT, SCOTT
  OF THE ANTARCTIC 1939
THREE CLASSIC SILENT SCREEN COMEDIES STARRING HAROLD LLOYD 1693
THREE COMRADES 1148
THREE FACES OF THE FILM: THE ART, THE DREAM, THE CULT, THE 171
THREE FILMS BY WAJDA: ASHES AND DIAMONDS/ A GENERATION/
  KANAL 2014
THREE FILMS OF WOODY ALLEN: ZELIG, BROADWAY DANNY ROSE, THE
  PURPLE ROSE OF CAIRO 2208
THREE NOVELS OF F. SCOTT FITZGERALD 1115, 1119
THREE OF A KIND 798
THREE SCREENPLAYS: ALL THE KING'S MEN/THE HUSTLER/LILITH 1090
THREE SCREENPLAYS: BRIEF ENCOUNTER/ODD MAN OUT/SCOTT OF THE
  ANTARCTIC 1021
THREE SCREENPLAYS: I VITELLONI/IL BIDONE/THE TEMPTATIONS OF
  DOCTOR ANTONIO 2171
THREE SCREENPLAYS: ORPHEUS/ THE ETERNAL RETURN/ BEAUTY AND THE
  BEAST 2005
THREE SCREENPLAYS: VIRIDIANA/THE EXTERMINATING ANGEL/SIMON OF
  THE DESERT 1990
THREE SCREENPLAYS: WHITE NIGHTS/ROCCO AND HIS BROTHERS/THE
  JOB 2172

THREE-D MOVIES: A HISTORY AND FILMOGRAPHY OF STEREOSCOPIC
 CINEMA 694
THREE-QUARTER FACE: REPORTS & REFLECTIONS 148
THREE'S A FAMILY 1206
THRILLER: THE SUSPENSE FILM FROM 1946, THE 384
THROUGH PARISIAN EYES: REFLECTIONS ON CONTEMPORARY FRENCH ARTS
 AND CULTURE 2127
THROUGH THE LOOKING GLASS 1031
THUNDER IN THE DUST: CLASSIC IMAGES OF WESTERN MOVIES 428
TIME MACHINE, THE 1312
TIME OF THE TOAD: A STUDY OF INQUISITION IN AMERICA AND TWO
 RELATED PAMPHLETS, THE 1067, 1074, 1076, 1087, 1284, 1286
TIMEBENDS: A LIFE 1265
TIME/STEPS 1041
TIN STAR, THE 1019
TITLE GUIDE TO THE TALKIES, A 1752
TITLE GUIDE TO THE TALKIES, 1964 THROUGH 1974, A 2033
TO BE CONTINUED . . . 1457
TO FIND AN IMAGE: BLACK FILMS FROM UNCLE TOM TO SUPER FLY 852,
 895, 902, 936, 937, 938, 953, 2092
TO HAVE AND HAVE NOT 1214
TO KILL A MOCKINGBIRD 1325
TO SEE THE DREAM 1319
TO THE DISTANT OBSERVER: FORM AND MEANING IN THE JAPANESE
 CINEMA 733, 1601, 1732, 1733, 1734, 1735, 1738, 1739, 1740, 1741, 1742, 1743,
 1744, 1745, 1887, 1889, 1890, 1892, 1896, 1897, 1901, 1902, 2018
TOBACCO ROAD 914
TOM JONES 1029, 1312, 1316, 1328
TOM JONES: A FILM SCRIPT 1328
TOM SWIFT AND HIS WIZARD CAMERA; OR, THRILLING ADVENTURES WHILE
 TAKING MOVING PICTURES 1145
TOMORROW & TOMORROW & TOMORROW 1215
TOMS, COONS, MULATTOES, MAMMIES, AND BUCKS: AN INTERPRETIVE
 HISTORY OF BLACKS IN AMERICAN FILMS 852, 860, 885, 920, 921, 922, 923
TORN SPROCKETS: THE UNCERTAIN PROJECTION OF THE CANADIAN
 FILM 2162
TOTAL FILM-MAKER, THE 90
TOUCH OF EVIL: ORSON WELLES, DIRECTOR 2069
TOUGH GUYS AND GALS OF THE MOVIES 385
TOUGH GUYS, THE 386
TOUGH GUY: THE AMERICAN MOVIE MACHO. 812
TOWARD A CONCEPT OF CINEMATIC LITERATURE: AN ANALYSIS of
 "HIROSHIMA MON AMOUR" 2136
TOWARD A DEFINITION OF THE AMERICAN FILM NOIR (1941-1949) 1947, 1956
TOWARD A FILM HUMANISM 47
TOWARDS A SOCIOLOGY OF MASS COMMUNICATIONS 721
TOWER OF BABEL: SPECULATIONS ON THE CINEMA 1553, 1645
TRACY AND HEPBURN: AN INTIMATE MEMOIR 1777
TRAGEDY AND MELODRAMA: VERSIONS OF EXPERIENCE 712
TRANSCENDENTAL STYLE IN FILM: OZU, BRESSON, DREYER 1893, 2004
TRAVELS IN GREENELAND: THE CINEMA OF GRAHAM GREENE 1219
TREASURE OF THE SIERRA MADRE, THE 1022, 1314
TREE IS A TREE, A 1081, 1696
TREVOR HOWARD: A GENTLEMAN AND A PLAYER 1941
TRIAL, THE 1022, 2091
TRIAL: A FILM BY ORSON WELLES, THE 2070, 2092
TRILOGY: AN EXPERIMENT IN MULTIMEDIA. A CHRISTMAS MEMORY, MIRIAM,
 AMONG THE PATHS TO EDEN 1318

TRIUMPH OF PIERROT: THE COMMEDIA DELL'ARTE AND THE MODERN
  IMAGINATION, THE 1427
TROJAN HORSE IN AMERICA, THE 1077
TRUE WOMAN AND THE FAMILY-FILM, THE 794
TRUFFAUT BY TRUFFAUT 2147, 2155
TRUMAN CAPOTE: DEAR HEART, OLD BUDDDY 1196
TURN OF THE SCREW, THE 1324
TV AND SCREENWRITING 85
TV ARAB, THE 454
TWELVE ANGRY MEN 2058
TWENTY ALL-TIME GREAT SCIENCE FICTION FILMS 418
TWENTY BEST FILM PLAYS 378, 1007, 1015, 1018, 1320, 1326, 1327
TWENTY FIVE THOUSAND SUNSETS: THE AUTOBIOGRAPHY OF HERBERT
  WILCOX 1863
TWENTY YEARS OF BRITISH FILMS 1925-1945 216, 1871
TWENTY-FOUR TIMES A SECOND: FILMS AND FILM-MAKERS 154, 1327
TWINKLE, TWINKLE, LITTLE STAR: BUT DON'T HAVE SEX OR TAKE THE
  CAR 992
TWO FILMS: SAVAGES, SHAKESPEARE WALLAH 2167
TWO FOR THE SEESAW 2064
TWO HUNDRED DAYS OF 8 1/2, THE 2170
TWO LIVES OF ERROL FLYNN, THE 1771
TWO OR THREE THINGS I KNOW ABOUT HER: ANALYSIS OF A FILM BY
  GODARD 2110, 2111, 2131
TWO ORPHANS, THE 1389
TWO RUSSIAN FILM CLASSICS: "MOTHER," A FILM BY V. I. PUDOVKIN;
  "EARTH," A FILM BY ALEXANDER PUDOVKIN 1663
TWO SCREENPLAYS: LA TERRA TREMA/SENSO 1932
TWO SCREENPLAYS: THE BLOOD OF A POET/ THE TESTAMENT OF
  ORPHEUS 1817
TWO THOUSAND AND ONE: SPACE ODYSSEY, BASED ON A SCREENPLAY BY
  STANLEY KUBRICK AND ARTHUR C. CLARKE 2083
TWO WEEKS IN ANOTHER TOWN 1041
TWO WORLDS OF AMERICAN ARTS: THE PRIVATE AND THE POPULAR,
  THE 260
TWO-STEP FLOW HYPOTHESIS OF MASS COMMUNICATION: A REFORMULATION
  USING COGNITIVE DISSONANCE THEORY, THE 543
TYCOONS AND LOCUSTS: A REGIONAL LOOK AT HOLLYWOOD FICTION OF
  THE 1930s 1042, 1043, 1108, 1161
TYPES APPROACH TO LITERATURE, THE 181
TYRONE POWER: THE LAST IDOL 1785

U

UN-AMERICANS, THE 832, 1177
UNABRIDGED MARILYN: HER LIFE FROM A TO Z, THE 1965
UNCENSORED WAR: THE MEDIA AND VIETNAM 347
UNCLE TOM'S CABIN 156, 718, 940
UNDERGROUND FILM: A CRITICAL HISTORY 1956
UNDERSTANDING MOVIES, 4th ed. 104, 119, 122, 128, 131
UNDERSTANDING THE FILM 105
UNDERWORLD USA 174, 192, 386
UNFINISHED WOMAN: A MEMOIR, AN 1225, 1227
UNHEARD MELODIES: NARRATIVE FILM MUSIC 404
UNHOLY FOOLS--WITS, COMICS, DISTURBERS OF THE PEACE: FILM &
  THEATER 149

UNION LIST OF FILM PERIODICALS: HOLDINGS OF SELECTED AMERICAN
  COLLECTIONS 1523
UNITED ARTISTS STORY, THE 1371
UNITED ARTISTS: THE COMPANY BUILT BY THE STARS 1369, 1466
UNITED ARTISTS: THE COMPANY THAT CHANGED THE FILM INDUSTRY 686,
  1370
UNIVERSAL PICTURES: A PANORAMIC HISTORY IN WORDS, PICTURES, AND
  FILMOGRAPHIES 1476
UNIVERSAL STORY, THE 1476
UNIVERSITY FILM ASSOCIATION MONOGRAPH 2: GLOSSARY OF FILM TERMS.
  rev. ed., THE 2211
UNKINDEST CUTS: THE SCISSORS AND THE CINEMA, THE 965
UNTUTORED EYE: CHILDHOOD IN THE FILMS OF COCTEAU, CORNELL, AND
  BRAKHAGE, THE 1818
UP IN THE CLOUDS, GENTLEMEN PLEASE 1941
UPTON SINCLAIR PRESENTS WILLIAM FOX 624, 1471
USE OF THE FILM, THE 1871
USING VIDEOTAPE 93
USTINOV IN FOCUS. 1941

V

VAGABONDE, LA 508
VALENTINO 1060, 1695
VALENTINO: A BIOGRAPHY 1695
VALENTINO: THE LOVE GOD 1060
VALUABLE PROPERTY: THE LIFE STORY OF MIKE TODD, A 1971
VALUES IN CONFLICT 986
VAMPIRE FILM, THE 398
VAN DYKE AND THE MYTHICAL CITY OF HOLLYWOOD 1788
VANITY FAIR 1299, 1312
VANITY WILL GET YOU SOMEWHERE 1765
VARIETY FILM REVIEWS, 1913-1970 1545
VARIETY OBITS: AN INDEX TO OBITUARIES IN "VARIETY," 1905-1978 1540
VARIETY PRESENTS THE COMPLETE BOOK OF MAJOR U. S. SHOWBUSINESS
  AWARDS 1531
VARIETY'S COMPLETE SCIENCE FICTION REVIEWS 419
VARIETY: INTERNATIONAL MOTION PICTURE MARKETPLACE 1530
VARIETY: INTERNATIONAL SHOWBUSINESS REFERENCE 1531
VAUDEVILLE AND FILM 1895-1915: A STUDY IN MEDIA INTERACTION 440,
  710, 766, 767
VERNON YOUNG ON FILM: UNPOPULAR ESSAYS ON A POPULAR ART 161
VERSATILES: A STUDY OF SUPPORTING ACTORS AND ACTRESSES IN THE
  AMERICAN MOTION PICTURE, 1920-1955, THE 1451
VICHY FRANCE AND THE JEWS 1903
VICTOR DUNCAN PRODUCTION EQUIPMENT GUIDE 72
VICTOR SJOSTROM: HIS LIFE AND HIS WORK 1629
VIDEO AND UTOPIA: EXPLORATIONS IN A NEW MEDIUM 70
VIDEO CAMERA TECHNIQUES 92
VIDEO NASTIES: FREEDOM AND CENSORSHIP IN THE MEDIA, THE 962
VIDEO PRODUCTION HANDBOOK 92
VIE EXTRAORDINAIRE DE LOLA MONTES, LA 2009
VIETNAM IN PROSE AND FILM 218, 363
VIETNAM ON FILM: FROM THE GREEN BERETS TO APOCALYPSE NOW 218,
  341
VIEW FROM SUNSET BOULEVARD, THE 574
VINCENTE MINNELLI AND THE FILM MUSICAL 1784
VIOLENCE AND THE MASS MEDIA 749

VIOLENT AMERICA: THE MOVIES 1946-1964 383, 452
VIRGIN LAND: THE AMERICAN WEST AS SYMBOL AND MYTH 175, 176, 1048
VIRGIN SPRING, THE 2186
VIRGINIAN, THE 1314
VIRGINS, VAMPS, AND FLAPPERS: THE AMERICAN SILENT MOVIE
 HEROINE 503, 631, 632, 1365, 1374, 1391
VISIBLE AND THE INVISIBLE, THE 183, 185
VISIBLE FICTIONS: CINEMA, TELEVISION, VIDEO 549, 559
VISIBLE MAN, OR FILM CULTURE, THE 125
VISION OF ROBERT FLAHERTY: THE ARTIST AS MYTH AND FILMMAKER,
 THE 1681
VISIONARY FILM: THE AMERICAN AVANT-GARDE 1757
VISIONS OF WAR: HOLLYWOOD COMBAT FILMS OF WORLD WAR II 174, 175,
 178, 233, 328, 341, 349, 350
VISIONS OF YESTERDAY 1833, 1839
VISIONS, IMAGES, AND DREAMS: YIDDISH FILM PAST AND PRESENT 828,
 847, 848
VISUAL LITERACY 55
VISUAL SCRIPTING 84
VISUAL STUDY GUIDE, A 379
VIVA ZAPATA! THE ORIGINAL SCREENPLAY BY JOHN STEINBECK 1326
VIVIEN LEIGH: A BIOGRAPHY 1861
VIVIEN: THE LIFE OF VIVIEN LEIGH 1861
VOICES FROM THE JAPANESE CINEMA 1732, 1733, 1738, 1888, 2015, 2021,
 2024, 2025
VON STROHEIM 1698

W

WALL, THE 837
WALT DISNEY'S WORLD OF FANTASY 1767
WALT DISNEY'S "SNOW WHITE AND THE SEVEN DWARFS" 1769
WALT DISNEY: A GUIDE TO REFERENCES AND RESOURCES 1767
WALT DISNEY: AN AMERICAN ORIGINAL 1080, 1769
WALT DISNEY: MAGICIAN OF THE MOVIES 1769
WALT DISNEY: THE ART OF ANIMATION. THE STORY OF THE DISNEY STUDIO
 CONTRIBUTION TO A NEW ART 78
WALTER LANTZ STORY: WITH WOODY WOODPECKER AND FRIENDS, THE 1780
WALTHAM CONFERENCE: SCREEN EDUCATION IN THE UNITED STATES,
 THE 41
WANDERER: AN AUTOBIOGRAPHY 1092, 1097
WANDERING COMPANY: TWENTY-ONE YEARS OF MERCHANT IVORY FILMS,
 THE 2167
WAR FILM, THE 342, 348
WAR GAMES 363
WAR ON FILM: THE AMERICAN CINEMA AND WORLD WAR I, 1914-1941 203,
 223, 267
WAR WITHOUT MERCY: RACE AND POWER IN THE PACIFIC WAR 236, 1897
WAR YEAR 363
WARNER BROS. GOLDEN ANNIVERSARY BOOK: THE FIRST COMPLETE
 FEATURE FILMOGRAPHY, THE 1499
WARNER BROTHERS 1494
WARNER BROTHERS DIRECTORS: THE HARD-BOILED, THE COMIC, AND THE
 WEEPERS 800, 1495
WARNER BROTHERS PRESENTS: THE MOST EXCITING YEARS--FROM THE JAZZ
 SINGER TO WHITE HEAT 1497
WARNER BROTHERS, THE 1493

WARREN BEATTY 2046
WARREN BEATTY AND DESERT EYES: A LIFE AND A STORY 2047
WARREN BEATTY: HIS LIFE, HIS LOVES, HIS WORK 2047
WARRIORS, THE 973
WAR, THE WEST AND THE WILDERNESS, THE 204, 205, 209, 210, 212, 213,
  223, 259, 262, 263, 296
WASHINGTON JITTERS 1282
WASHINGTON SQUARE 1006
WASHINGTON TASK FORCE REPORT ON THE MOTION PICTURE INDUSTRY
  (1978), THE 659
WASTELAND, THE 1315
WAVES AT GENJI'S DOOR: JAPAN THROUGH ITS CINEMA, THE 2023, 2026,
  2029, 2031
WAY OF ALL FLESH TONES: A HISTORY OF COLOR MOTION PICTURE
  PROCESSES 1895-1929, THE 654
WAY OF SEEING: A CRITICAL STUDY OF JAMES AGEE, A 145
WAY OF THE SUBJECT, THE (SHINMIN NO MICHI) 1897
WAYS OF SEEING: BASED ON THE BBC TELEVISION SERIES 531, 538, 637
WE BARRYMORES 1760
WE MAKE THE MOVIES 1756
WE TALK, YOU LISTEN 916
WE THOUGHT WE COULD DO ANYTHING: THE LIFE OF SCREENWRITERS
  PHOEBE AND HENRY EPHRON 1206
WE'RE IN THE MONEY: DEPRESSION AMERICA AND ITS FILMS 441, 554, 555,
  556
WEEKEND AND WIND FROM THE EAST: TWO FILMS BY JEAN-LUC
  GODARD 2135
WEEP NO MORE MY LADY 1138, 1773
WELCOME TO HARD TIMES 1032
WERE WE OUR BROTHERS' KEEPERS? THE PUBLIC RESPONSE OF AMERICAN
  JEWS TO THE HOLOCAUST, 1938-1944 291
WEST GERMAN FILM IN THE COURSE OF TIME: REFLECTIONS ON THE TWENTY
  YEARS SINCE OBERHAUSEN 2166
WEST OF THE ROCKIES 1041
WESTERN ACTORS ENCYCLOPEDIA: FACTS, PHOTOS, AND FILMOGRAPHIES
  FOR MORE THAN 250 FAMILIAR FACES 429
WESTERN FILMS OF JOHN FORD, THE 1684, 2076
WESTERN FILMS: A COMPLETE GUIDE 428
WESTERN FILMS: AN ANNOTATED CRITICAL BIBLIOGRAPHY 431
WESTERN FILM, THE 434
WESTERN HERO IN FILM AND TELEVISION: MASS MEDIA MYTHOLOGY,
  THE 432
WESTERN MOVIES 433
WESTERN MOVIES: A TV AND VIDEO GUIDE TO 4200 GENRE FILMS 433
WESTERNS: A PICTURE BOOK QUIZ, THE 426
WESTERN: AN ILLUSTRATED GUIDE, THE 426
WESTERN: FROM SILENTS TO THE SEVENTIES. A NEW AND EXPANDED
  EDITION, THE 427
WHAT IS A FILM? 50, 142
WHAT IS CINEMA? VOLUME I 128, 167, 1297, 1334, 1414, 1509, 1814
WHAT IS CINEMA? VOLUME II 167, 1297, 1334, 1432, 1922
WHAT MAKES SAMMY RUN? 1041, 1091, 1104, 1117, 1135, 1158, 1161, 1162,
  1233, 1277
WHAT SHALL WE DO TOMORROW? 1941
WHAT'S WRONG WITH THE MOVIES? 725
WHATEVER BECAME OF . . . ? Volume 1 1444
WHATEVER BECAME OF . . .? Volume 2 1445
WHATEVER BECAME OF . . .? Volume 3 1445
WHATEVER BECAME OF . . .? Volume 4 1445

WHATEVER BECAME OF . . .? Volume 5 1446
WHATEVER HAPPENED TO HOLLYWOOD 1478
WHEN HOLLYWOOD RULES THE SKIES: THE AVIATION FILM CLASSICS OF
  WORLD WAR II 380
WHEN I WAS YOUNG 1325, 1861
WHEN MOVIES BEGAN TO SPEAK 1755
WHEN PICTURES BEGAN TO MOVE 1614, 1755
WHEN THE LIGHTS GO DOWN 151, 998, 1016, 1294
WHEN THE MOVIES WERE YOUNG 1376
WHEN THE SHOOTING STOPS . . . THE CUTTING BEGINS: A FILM EDITOR'S
  STORY 82
WHEN THE SMOKE HIT THE FAN 1761
WHERE WE CAME IN: SEVENTY YEARS OF THE BRITISH FILM INDUSTRY 1613
WHERE'S THE REST OF ME? THE RONALD REAGAN STORY 1088, 1785
WHISTLE AND HO--SING AS WE GO 1400
WHITE COLLAR: AMERICAN MIDDLE CLASSES 462
WHITE OVER BLACK 918
WHO IS THAT? THE LATE LATE VIEWERS GUIDE TO THE OLD OLD MOVIE
  PLAYERS 1447
WHO OWNS THE MEDIA?: CONCENTRATION OF OWNERSHIP IN THE MASS
  COMMUNICATIONS INDUSTRY 607, 613, 626, 647, 660, 678, 748
WHO WAS THAT MASKED MAN? THE STORY OF THE LONE RANGER 433
WHO WAS WHO ON THE SCREEN: ILLUSTRATED EDITION 1545
WHO WROTE THE MOVIE AND WHAT ELSE DID HE WRITE? AN INDEX OF SCREEN
  WRITERS AND THEIR FILM WORKS 1144, 1174
WHO'S WHO IN AMERICAN FILM NOW 1538
WHO'S WHO IN HOLLYWOOD 1900-1976 1541
WHO'S WHO IN THE SOVIET CINEMA: SEVENTY DIFFERENT PORTRAITS 2181
WHO'S WHO OF THE HORRORS AND OTHER FANTASY FILMS: THE
  INTERNATIONAL PERSONALITY ENCYCLOPEDIA OF THE FANTASTIC
  FILM 392
WHOLE FILM SOURCEBOOK, THE 1535
WHOLE TRUTH AND NOTHING BUT, THE 1057, 1243
WHY A DUCK? VISUAL AND VERBAL GEMS FROM THE MARX BROTHERS
  MOVIES 1783
WHY ME? THE SAMMY DAVIS STORY 950
WIDE-EYED IN BABYLON: AN AUTOBIOGRAPHY 1964
WIDE-SCREEN CINEMA AND STEREOPHONIC SOUND 86
WILD CHILD: A SCREENPLAY, THE 2150
WILD PALMS, THE 1209, 2114
WILL THERE REALLY BE A MORNING? AN AUTOBIOGRAPHY 1292
WILLIAM FAULKNER, THE MAN AND THE ARTIST: A BIOGRAPHY 1215
WILLIAM FAULKNER: AMERICAN WRITER 1211
WILLIAM GOLDMAN'S STORY OF "A BRIDGE TOO FAR" 554, 1318
WILLIAM HOLDEN 1350, 1778
WILLIAM PETER BLATTY ON "THE EXORCIST": FROM NOVEL TO FILM 554,
  1317
WILLIAM WYLER 322, 1086, 1795, 1988
WILLIAM WYLER: THE AUTHORIZED BIOGRAPHY 322, 1086, 1796
WILLOWBROOK CINEMA STUDY PROJECT 43
WINNERS OF THE WEST: THE SAGEBRUSH HEROES OF THE SILENT
  SCREEN 429
WISDOM OF EVE, THE 1981
WISECRACKS: THE FARCES OF GEORGE S. KAUFMAN 1064
WIT AND WISDOM OF HOLLYWOOD; FROM THE SQUAW MAN TO THE HATCHET
  MAN, THE 1241
WIT AND WISDOM OF MAE WEST, THE 1795
WITCHES OF EASTWICK, THE 1316

WITH EISENSTEIN IN HOLLYWOOD: A CHAPTER OF AUTOBIOGRAPHY 1867
WITH MALICE TOWARD ALL 609
WITNESS 1190
WIZARD OF OZ, THE 1801
WOMAN IN THE DUNES 2177
WOMAN'S FILM AT WARNER BROS., 1935-1950, THE 794
WOMANHOOD MEDIA: CURRENT RESOURCES ABOUT WOMEN 525
WOMEN AND FILM: A BIBLIOGRAPHY 509
WOMEN AND FILM: BOTH SIDES OF THE CAMERA 471, 504, 527, 532, 585, 591,
 792, 794
WOMEN AND THE CINEMA: A CRITICAL ANTHOLOGY 471, 507
WOMEN AND THEIR SEXUALITY IN THE NEW FILM 471, 515, 527, 669
WOMEN AS SEX OBJECT: STUDIES IN EROTIC ART 977
WOMEN IN COMEDY 513
WOMEN IN FILM 586
WOMEN IN FILM NOIR 469, 471, 507, 798, 1947
WOMEN IN FOCUS 491
WOMEN IN LOVE 1312
WOMEN OF COLOR: A FILMOGRAPHY OF MINORITY AND THIRD WORLD
 WOMEN 940
WOMEN ON FILM: THE CRITICAL EYE 513, 514, 531
WOMEN ON THE HOLLYWOOD SCREEN 471, 513, 791
WOMEN WHO KNEW TOO MUCH: HITCHCOCK AND FEMINIST THEORY,
 THE 1849
WOMEN WHO MAKE MOVIES 520
WOMEN'S FILM AND FEMALE EXPERIENCE 1940-1950 442, 443, 458, 461, 521,
 522, 523, 543, 614, 638, 800, 801
WOMEN'S FILMS IN PRINT: AN ANNOTATED GUIDE TO 800 16mm FILMS BY
 WOMEN 492
WOMEN'S PICTURES: FEMINISM AND CINEMA 471, 475, 509, 586, 588
WOMEN'S REFLECTIONS: THE FEMINIST FILM MOVEMENT 451, 519
WONDERFUL LIFE: THE FILMS AND CAREER OF JAMES STEWART, A 1787
WONDERFUL WORLD OF OZ, THE 1314
WOODY ALLEN'S "PLAY IT AGAIN, SAM" 2208
WOODY ALLEN: A BIOGRAPHY 2045
WOODY ALLEN: AN ILLUSTRATED BIOGRAPHY 2046
WOODY ALLEN: CLOWN PRINCE OF AMERICAN HUMOR 2044,
WOODY ALLEN: HIS FILMS AND CAREER 2045
WORD AND IMAGE: HISTORY OF THE HUNGARIAN CINEMA 2012, 2013
WORDS AND IMAGES: AUSTRALIAN NOVELS INTO FILM 2157
WORDS THAT WON THE WAR: THE STORY ON THE COMMITTEE OF PUBLIC
 INFORMATION, 1917-1919 223
WORK OF DOROTHY ARZNER: TOWARDS A FEMINIST CINEMA, THE 475
WORK OF THE FILM DIRECTOR, THE 75
WORK OF THE MOTION PICTURE CAMERAMAN, THE 81
WORK OF THE SCIENCE FILM MAKER, THE 76
WORLD CINEMA SINCE 1945 1519, 1914
WORLD ENCYCLOPEDIA OF CARTOONS, THE 77
WORLD ENCYCLOPEDIA OF THE FILM, THE 1543
WORLD FILM DIRECTORS, VOLUME ONE, 1890-1945 1554
WORLD FILM & TV STUDY RESOURCES: A REFERENCE GUIDE TO MAJOR
 TRAINING CENTERS AND ARCHIVES 52
WORLD IN A FRAME: WHAT WE SEE IN FILMS, THE 179, 180, 186
WORLD OF ENTERTAINMENT: HOLLYWOOD'S GREATEST MUSICALS, THE 404
WORLD OF FANTASTIC FILMS: AN ILLUSTRATED SURVEY, THE 414
WORLD OF FANTASY FILMS, THE 414
WORLD OF LAUGHTER: THE MOTION PICTURE COMEDY SHORT, 1910-1930,
 THE 1412
WORLD OF LUIS BUNUEL, THE 1720

WORLD OF LUIS BUNUEL: ESSAYS IN CRITICISM, THE 1722
WORLD OF MELODRAMA, THE 712
WORLD OF RAYMOND CHANDLER, THE 1197
WORLD OF ROBERT FLAHERTY 1681
WORLD ON FILM: CRITICISM AND COMMENT, A 33, 151, 221, 994, 997, 1004,
  1005, 1009, 1010, 1013, 1014, 1016, 1018, 1022, 1023, 1295, 1323, 1324, 1325,
  1328, 1348, 1349, 1350, 1352, 1353, 1356
WORLD VIEWED: REFLECTIONS ON THE ONTOLOGY OF FILM, THE 64, 528
WORLD WAR II COMBAT FILM: ANATOMY OF A GENRE, THE 280, 341
WRITERS IN AMERICA: THE FOUR SEASONS OF SUCCESS 1278
WRITERS ON THE AMERICAN SCREEN: A GUIDE TO FILM ADAPTATIONS OF
  AMERICAN AND FOREIGN LITERARY WORKS 1152
WRITERS ON THE LEFT: EPISODES IN AMERICAN LITERARY COMMUNISM 830
WRITING FOR FILM AND TELEVISION 84
WUTHERING HEIGHTS 1309, 1312, 1327
W. C . FIELDS IN "THE BANK DICK" 1770
W. C. FIELDS 1800
W. C. FIELDS AND ME 1770
W. C. FIELDS BY HIMSELF: HIS INTENDED AUTOBIOGRAPHY 1770
W. C. FIELDS IN "NEVER GIVE A SUCKER AND EVEN BREAK" AND "TILLIE
  AND GUS" 1770
W. C. FIELDS. 1771
W. C. FIELDS: A BIO-BIBLIOGRAPHY 1770
W. C. FIELDS: HIS FOLLIES AND FORTUNES 1771

Y

YEAR IN THE DARK: JOURNAL OF A FILM CRITIC 2085
YEAR IN THE DARK: JOURNAL OF A FILM CRITIC 1968-69 145
YEAR'S WORK IN THE FILM--1949 1021
YEARLING, THE 1010
YEKL: A TALE OF THE NEW YORK GHETTO 1313
YES I CAN: THE STORY OF SAMMY DAVIS, JR. 950
YESTERDAY'S CLOWNS: THE RISE OF FILM COMEDY 1678
YOU MIGHT AS WELL LIVE: THE LIFE AND TIMES OF DOROTHY PARKER 1274
YOUNG FILMMAKERS 89
YOUNG GOODMAN BROWN 1312
YOUNG JUDY 1773
YOUR CAREER IN FILM MAKING 89
YOUR FILM ACTING CAREER: HOW TO BREAK INTO MOVIES & TV & SURVIVE
  IN HOLLYWOOD 76
YOUR FILM & THE LAB 73

Z

Z 577
Z IS FOR ZAGREB 2014
ZANUCK: HOLLYWOOD'S LAST TYCOON 1499
ZANUCK: THE RISE AND FALL OF HOLLYWOOD'S LAST TYCOON 1501
ZAVATTINI: SEQUENCES FROM A CINEMATIC LIFE 1884, 1885, 1924
ZEFFIRELLI: THE AUTOBIOGRAPHY OF FRANCO ZEFFIRELLI 2172
ZELDA 1110, 1114, 1115, 1116, 1118
ZEMLYA: KNYIGA-FILM 1663
ZERO MOSTEL: A BIOGRAPHY 1179
ZOMBIES THAT ATE PITTSBURGH: THE FILMS OF GEORGE A. ROMERO,
  THE 390

Film Personalities Index

A

Abbott, Bud 1445, 1476, 1757
Abbott, George 371
Abe, Yutaka 1740
Abrahams, Harold 1013
Abrams, Hiram 1277, 1464
Acres, Birt 1567, 1570, 1586, 1610, 1613
Adams, Dawn 1432
Adams, Henry 179
Adams, Ken 79
Adam, Ken 786
Addison, John 408, 1328
Adelson, Marvin 536
Adjani, Isabelle 584
Adler, Alfred 587, 600, 601
Adler, Buddy 1256, 1466
Adler, Celia 829
Adler, Larry 1087
Adler, Luther 1151
Adler, Renata 145
Adler, Stella 1151, 1635
Adoree, Renee 1450
Adrian 1801
Adrian, Iris 1447
Agadzhanova, Nina 1659, 1666
Agar, John 396, 1445
Agee, James 127, 145, 146, 1147, 1148, 1150, 1154, 1311, 1426, 1979
Agel, Henri 161
Ager, Cecelia 139
Aikins, Zoe 1797
Aimee, Anouk 1023
Aitken, Harry E. 1384, 1386, 1399, 1412, 1463, 1467, 1622
Aitken, Spottiswoode 1387
Akerman, Chantal 497
Akins, Zoe 1154
Aladar, Laslo 1804
Alassane, Mustapha 2121
Albee, Edward 1034
Alberti, Rafael 1722
Albert, Eddie 1988
Albin, Fred 812, 1801
Alcoriza, Luis 1002
Alden, Mary 1387
Aldredge, Theoni V. 1322
Aldrich, Henry 971
Aldrich, Robert 348, 980, 1094, 1237, 1254, 1290, 1548, 1549, 1550, 1551, 2036, 2043, 2044, 2071
Aldrich, R. and detective films 2071
Aldrich, R. and FILM NOIR 2071
Aldrich, R. and RKO 2043
Aldrich, R. and television 2043
Aldrich, R. and United Artists 2043
Aldridge, Kay 498
Alejandro, Julio 1991
Alekan, Henry 1988, 2009

Alessandrini, Geoffredo   1874, 1878
Alexander I   298
Alexander the Great (Alexander Victor)   1588
Alexander, Jane   1007
Alexander, Lelia   1472
Alexander, William   947
Alexandrov, Grigori V.   1652, 1657, 1659, 1661, 1662, 1865, 1867
Alfalfa (See Switzer, Carl)   993
Alfred, John   1347
Alison, Joan   1288
Alland, William   992
Allegret, Marc   1869
Allende, President Salvador   1020
Allen, Dede   508
Allen, Jay Presson   30, 1219, 1293
Allen, Paul   1390
Allen, Rex   433
Allen, Woody   191, 196, 368, 530, 786, 833, 837, 841, 980, 1164, 1452, 1545,
  1548, 1551, 1626, 1954, 2036, 2044, 2045, 2046, 2072, 2073, 2194, 2195, 2208
Allen, W. and F. Scott Fitzgerald   2045
Allen, W. and gangster films   2072
Allen, W. and Ingmar Bergman's melodramas   2072
Allen, W. and Penelope Gilliatt   148
Allen, W. and Stanley Kauffmann   153
Allen, W. and THE NEW YORKER   2045
Allgood, Sara   1007, 1446
Allyson, June   575, 781, 1439, 1484, 1759
Almendros, Nestor   165
Almereyda, Miguel   1824
Alpert, Hollis   146
Alterman, Joseph   755
Althusser, Louis   134, 500, 587, 2003
Altman, Robert   379, 912, 914, 1175, 1552, 1758, 2195
Alton, John   1983
Alvarez, Santiago   299
Alwyn, William   323, 408
Alyn, Kirk   1446
Amada, Yukio   1000
Ameche, Don   1439, 1501
Ames, Preston   402, 1240, 1983
Amidei, Sergio   378
Amyes, Julian   1752
Anabella   1444
Anderson, Bibi   143
Anderson, Eddie "Rochester"   877, 921, 952, 1445
Anderson, Ernest   922
Anderson, Gilbert M. ("Bronco Billy")   429, 1415
Anderson, Lindsay   295, 1001, 1141, 1682, 1870, 1923, 1939, 2159
Anderson, Madeleine   901
Anderson, Marion   320, 920
Anderson, Maxwell   304, 371, 1176
Anderson, Robert   1257
Anderson, Roland   1350
Andersson, Bibi   606, 2183
Andersson, Harriet   2183
Andran, Stephane   2151
Andress, Ursula   419, 498
Andrews, Dana   375, 1021, 1294, 1472, 1499, 1979

Andrews, Del 371
Andrews, Julie 145, 790, 1237, 1295
Andrews, Laverne 1445
Andrews, Maxine 1445
Andrews, Patti 1445
Andreyev, Leonid 1651
Andrzejewski, Jerzy 2180
Angel, Heather 1446
Anger, Kenneth 1529, 2072
Anhalt, Edna 997
Anhalt, Edward 369, 997, 1150, 1154
Ankers, Evelyn 396
Ann-Margret 790
Annakin, Ken 1219
Annis, Francesca 1355
Anouilh, Jean 1908
Anstey, Edgar 215, 316, 1869
Antheil, George 408
Anthony, Joseph 1211
Anthony, Mark (Marcus Antonius) 383
Antonioni, Michelangelo 53, 56, 113, 117, 141, 466, 562, 918, 1012, 1163, 1310, 1316, 1547, 1553, 1566, 1874, 1881, 1882, 1927, 1928, 1932, 2034, 2169, 2170, 2172, 2173
Antonowsky, Marvin 2202
Anznavour, Charles 2155
Apollinaire, Guillaume 1709, 1717, 2106
Aragon, Louis 1710, 1717, 1718
Arbuckle, Roscoe "Fatty" 1223, 1241, 1374, 1380, 1395, 1410, 1493, 1504, 1505, 1677, 1678, 1687, 1695
Archer, Ernie 2084
Arciaga, Michael 611
Arden, Eve 798, 800
Ardrey, Robert 2087
Aristotle 601
Arkin, Alan 995, 2060, 2082
Arkoff, Samuel Z. 388, 744, 986, 1235, 2049
Arlen, Harold 83, 404, 405, 1801
Arlen, Richard 370, 990, 1445
Arletty (Leonie Bathiat) 1447, 1814, 1825, 1905, 1910, 1992
Arling, Arthur 1010
Arliss, George 219, 1499, 1759, 1833
Armat, Thomas 1586, 1590, 1593, 1615, 1731
Armes, Roy 1826
Armetta, Henry 1450
Armstrong, Louis 885
Armstrong, Robert 1865
Arnheim, Rudolf 54, 100, 124, 142, 144, 166, 1339, 1555
Arnold, General "Hap" 273
Arnold, Jack 565
Arnold, Malcolm 374
Arnold, Matthew 179
Arp, Hans 1716
Arrabal, Fernando 279
Artaud, Antonin 1342, 1729
Arthure, Robert Alan 2036
Arthur, Jean 64, 499, 502, 1009, 1449
Arvidson, Linda 1361, 1372, 1376, 1382, 1387
Arzner, Dorothy 466, 471, 475, 489, 497, 508, 519, 1277, 1549, 1747, 1797, 1798

Asakura, Setsu 2025
Ashby, Hal 376, 1758, 2082, 2195
Ashcroft, Peggy 1852
Ashley, Elizabeth 1346
Ashley, Sylvia 1401
Ashley, Ted 2035, 2197
Askew, Luke 429
Asner, Ed 2058
Asquith, Anthony 1357, 1549, 1565, 1566, 1567, 1833, 1841, 1863, 1934, 1942
Asquith, Herbert Henry 211, 1841
Astaire, Fred 219, 401, 402, 404, 407, 1164, 1235, 1242, 1443, 1449, 1484, 1487, 1759, 1798, 1952
Asther, Niles 1446
Astor, Mary 373, 600, 1444, 1445, 1452, 1484, 1679, 1683
Astruc, Alexandre 1790, 2094, 2095, 2116, 2122
Atherton, William 1291
Atkins, Zoe 1802
Atsuta, Yuharu 2032
Attasheva, Pera 1661
Attenborough, Richard 374, 548, 1318, 1934
Atwill, Lionel 396, 1215, 1447
Aubert, Pierre 2010
Aubrey, James 1002
Audran, Stephane 2098, 2100
Audry, Colette 1995
Auer, Mischa 1445, 1450
Auffay, Patrick 1006
August, Joseph H. 1806
Aumont, Jean-Pierre 1906, 1909, 2154
Aurel, Jean 318
Aurenche, Jean 377, 1908, 1993, 1995, 1998, 2008
Auric, Georges 2009
Auriol, Jean-Georges 1996, 1997, 2002
Austin, Albert 1416
Austin, Gene 1445
Austin, Michael 1037
Autant-Lara, Claude 1571, 1904, 1908, 1992, 1993, 1995, 2000, 2001
Autry, Gene 429, 430, 431, 432, 433, 1444, 1456
Avedon, Richard 1440
Axelrod, George 84, 1146, 2077, 2078
Axelrod, Jonathan 1150
Ayfre, Amedee 161
Ayres, Lew 346, 371, 1484, 1805

B

Baarova, Lida 238
Baby Dumpling (See Simms, Larry) 1446
Bacall, Lauren 554, 798, 1078, 1087, 1215, 1243, 1323, 1494, 1502, 1977
Bacharach, Burt 2078, 2161
Bach, Steven 535
Backus, Jim 997
Bacon, Kevin 1530
Bacon, Lloyd 1496, 1548
Bacon, Roger 1580, 1594
Baddeley, Hermione 1016
Baddeley, W. Hugh 82

Badel, Alan 269
Badham, John 415
Badham, Mary 1325
Baggot, King 1444
Baif 1313
Bailey, Pearl 885, 922
Baker, Bob 433
Baker, Carroll 383, 790, 1346, 1439, 1957
Baker, Chet 1439
Baker, Diane 849
Baker, Don 974
Baker, Josephine 870, 920
Baker, Kenny 1445
Baker, Stanley 2161
Bakshi, Ralph 2195
Bakshy, Alan 127
Balaban, Barney 613
Balazs, Bela 65, 100, 125, 144, 166
Balchin, Nigel 373
Balcon, Michael 216, 1566, 1569, 1571, 1833, 1834, 1837, 1838, 1839, 1840, 1841,
    1842, 1847, 1853, 1855, 1937
Balderston, John 1154
Baldwin, Evelyn 1368
Baldwin, James 540
Ballard, Lucien 80
Ballard, Lucinda 1352
Ballew, Smith 433
Ball, Derek 813
Ball, Lucille 1184, 1484, 1552, 1757
Balsam, Martin 1022, 2080
Balshofer, Fred J. 1587, 1595
Balzac, Honore de 1608
Bancroft, Anne 1016, 1350, 2047, 2085, 2086
Bancroft, George 1277, 1708
Banerji, Karuna 1004
Bankhead, Tallulah 390, 555, 1228, 1241, 1243, 1259, 1348, 1760, 1967
Banks, Lionel 1799
Banky, Velma 1448
Baraka, Imamu Amiri (LeRoi Jones) 159, 894, 1349
Bara, Theda 503, 631, 1112, 1374, 1434, 1443, 1444, 1447, 1449, 1453, 1470,
    1471, 1595
Barbaro, Umberto 1874, 1922
Barbie, Klaus 289
Barcroft, Roy 1447
Bardot, Brigitte 508, 1447, 2050, 2095
Barends, Edda 526
Bari, Lynn 1445
Barker, Jess 1439
Barker, Reginald 1623
Barker, William 1612
Barna, Yon 1661
Barnes, Binnie 1445
Barnes, George 606, 1846
Barnouw, Erik 201
Barrault, Jean-Louis 1814, 1905, 1909, 1910, 2127
Barrett, Laurinda 995
Barrie, Barbara 1004, 1005
Barrow, Clyde 2064
Barrymore, Ethel 1440, 1469, 1481, 1484, 1848

Barrymore, John 381, 1235, 1374, 1393, 1440, 1444, 1449, 1451, 1452, 1481,
    1484, 1494, 1498, 1578, 1579, 1798, 1803, 1967
Barrymore, John, Jr. 1439, 1446
Barrymore, Lionel 1207, 1387, 1397, 1440, 1481, 1484, 1488, 1595, 1803
Barry, Iris 127, 140, 1989
Barry, Joan 1421, 1424, 1426, 1433, 1864
Barry, John 402
Barry, Jon 813
Barry, Leon 1406
Barr, Charles 1752
Bartel, Paul 415
Barthelmess, Richard 1388, 1391, 1439, 1444, 1705
Barthes, Roland 134, 2124
Bartholomew, Freddie 990, 992, 993, 1444
Barthou, Jean Louis 298
Bartlett, Sy 261
Bartolini, Elio 1012, 2172
Baruch, Donald 230, 232, 361
Baryshnikov, Mikhail 1016
Basehart, Richard 1021, 1247, 1933
Basevi, James 1327
Basquette, Lina 1445
Bassman, Don 365
Bass, Saul 2053, 2054
Bat-Adam, Michal 601
Batalov, Alexei 1001
Batchelor, Joy 78
Bates, Alan 1006, 2076
Bathiat, Leonie (See Arletty) 1447
Baumann, Charles O. 1409, 1413, 1463, 1464, 1476
Baur, Harry 238, 1814, 1907
Bautzer, Greg 1136
Bava, Mario 382, 398
Baxter, Anne 575, 1167, 1471, 1957, 1981
Baxter, Keith 1353
Baxter, Leon 574
Baxter, Warner 431, 1207
Bayne, Beverly 1444, 1445
Bazin and screen education 40
Bazin, Andre 53, 474, 1339, 1790, 1996, 1997, 1999, 2002, 2097
Bazin, A. and adaptations 129
Bazin, A. and Alain Resnais 167
Bazin, A. and Bertolt Brecht 2125
Bazin, A. and CAHIERS DU CINEMA 1997, 2123
Bazin, A. and CITIZEN KANE 1792
Bazin, A. and Eric Rohmer 2141
Bazin, A. and feminist film theory 500
Bazin, A. and film theory 128, 163, 165, 167
Bazin, A. and Francois Truffaut 167
Bazin, A. and genres 129
Bazin, A. and Hollywood 128
Bazin, A. and humanist film criticism 129
Bazin, A. and Jean Cocteau 1818
Bazin, A. and Jean-Luc Godard 167
Bazin, A. and montage 129
Bazin, A. and Neo-Realism 129
Bazin, A. and Otis Ferguson 148
Bazin, A. and realist film theory 128

Beach, Rex 1061, 1472
Beard, Matthew "Stymie," Jr. 992, 1439, 1446
Beatles, The 376, 405, 2161
Beaton, Cecil 1440, 1761
Beatty, Warren 810, 1010, 1452, 2046, 2047, 2088
Beaudine, William 1398
Beaumont, Harry 1483
Beauregard, Georges de 2109, 2110, 2129
Beaverbrook, Lord 212, 213
Beavers, Louise 862, 872, 877, 880, 921, 939
Becker, Israel 848
Becker, Jacques 1821, 1992, 1993, 1994, 1995, 1999, 2001
Beckett, Samuel 485, 1155, 1178, 1311
Beckett, Scotty 992
Beddington, Jack 316
Bedoya, Alfonso 1022, 1979
Beerman, Jill S. 443
Beery, Noah 1407
Beery, Wallace 1164, 1407, 1410, 1481, 1803
Beethoven, Ludwig von 789
Beetson, Fred 1173
Begelman, David 537, 666, 2197
Beggs, Richard 367
Begley, Ed 1346
Behrman, Samuel Nathaniel 1176
Beighan, Thomas 1703
Beiles, Mendel 845, 2076
Belafonte, Harold George Harry, Jr. 879, 885, 889, 896, 901, 922, 935, 937,
    938, 950, 1251
Belasco, David 1331, 1392
Bellamy, Madge 193
Bellamy, Ralph 1237, 1761
Belleau, Remy 1313
Bellin, Olga 1211
Bellocchio, Mario 2173
Bellour, Raymond 471
Bell, Daniel 574
Bell, Hugo 1716
Belmondo, Jean-Paul 2129, 2151
Belushi, John 2202
Bemton, Robert 110
Ben-Ami, Jacob 829, 848
Benchley, Nathaniel 2082
Benchley, Robert 1063, 1177, 1265, 1269, 1278, 1797
Benet, Stephen Vincent 1386
Benjamin, Mary 325
Benjamin, Robert 1369, 1945
Benjamin, Walter 252, 474
Bennett, Arnold 1061
Bennett, Bruce 1022
Bennett, Charles 1855, 1857, 1864
Bennett, Enid 1407
Bennett, Heinz 2143
Bennett, Joan 1847
Bennet, Spencer Gordon 1758
Benny, Jack 1243
Benoit-Levy, Jean 1811, 1825, 1923
Benson, Erastus A. 702
Benson, Sally 1920

Benton, Robert 111, 143, 1007, 2088
Berard, Christian 2009
Berenger, Tom 368
Bergen, Edgar 1445
Berger, Mark 367
Bergman, Ingmar 45, 113, 141, 143, 466, 497, 516, 582, 583, 593, 606, 1141, 1163, 1297, 1311, 1547, 1549, 1552, 1625, 1626, 1627, 1628, 1882, 2033, 2034, 2048, 2072, 2170, 2182, 2183, 2184, 2186
Bergman, Ingrid 346, 372, 564, 606, 623, 1242, 1243, 1262, 1288, 1322, 1443, 1446, 1447, 1449, 1487, 1761, 1845, 1847, 1848, 1852, 1853, 1855, 1883
Bergner, Elisabeth 1444
Bergren, Eric 1292
Bergson, Henri 2118, 2136, 2139
Bergstrom, Janet 483
Berg, Gertrude 833
Berkeley, Busby 402, 1240, 1249, 1445, 1496, 1548, 1550, 1747, 1797
Berkeley, Martin 1096
Berle, Milton 833, 1294
Berlin, Irving 346, 405, 1241, 1478
Berman, Padro 1798
Berman, Pandro S. 1240, 1502
Berman, Shelley 2060
Bernds, Edward 1237
Bernhardt, Curtis 1496, 1550
Bernhardt, Sarah 1463, 1504, 1606, 1608, 1618, 1737
Bernstein, Elmer 83, 408, 1325
Bernstein, Leonard 1979
Bernstein, Maurice 1789
Bernstein, Sidney 1847, 1848, 1854
Bern, Paul 1152, 1396, 1481, 1484
Berri, Claude 2149
Berry, Chuck 405
Berry, John 1005
Bertolucci, Atilio 2170
Bertolucci, Bernardo 516, 583, 1927, 1932, 2006, 2174, 2200
Besserer, Eugenie 1350
Bessie, Alvah 1088, 1154, 1177, 1178, 1202
Best, Willie (Sleep n' Eat) 870, 877, 926
Betram, Charles 1603
Bettleheim, Bruno 289
Bevan, William 1412
Beymer, Richard 1445
Bezzerides, A. I. 2071
Biberman, Herbert 944, 1088, 1093, 1178, 1202
Bickford, Charles 370, 1259, 1680
Biden, Preston (Preston Sturges) 1918
Biggar, Helen 1840
Bikel, Theodore 2082
Billon, Pierre 1905
Billy the Kid (William S. Bonney) 434
Binger, R. O. 1351
Bioff, Willie 1186, 1493, 1500, 1504
Birdwell, Russell 1234
Birinski, Leo 1640
Biro, Lajos 1865
Bisset, Jacqueline 2154
Bitzer, Johann Gottlieb Wilhelm "Billy" 1362, 1371, 1372, 1373, 1377, 1378, 1379, 1380, 1387, 1389, 1390, 1391, 1397, 1588, 1618, 1680

Bjornstrand, Gunnar 2183
Blacher, Pierre 1814
Blache, Alice Guy 466, 497, 508, 519, 520, 620
Blackie, Boston 380
Blackton, J. Stuart 1113, 1588
Blackwell, Carlyle 381, 1444
Black, Karen 1291
Blair, Betsy 1008, 1982
Blair, Linda 971, 981, 991
Blaise, Pierre 377
Blake, Robert 605, 992, 993
Blalack, Robert 813
Blanc, Alberto 1573
Blane, Sally 1445
Blanke, Henry 1139
Blankfort, Michael 1181
Blasetti, Alessandro 1573, 1874, 1875, 1878, 1880, 1885
Blatty, William Peter 1319
Blees, Robert 1986
Bletcher, Billy 1468
Blixen, Karen (Isak Dinesen) 488
Bloch, Robert 388
Block, Ralph 1204
Blondell, Joan 1236, 1237, 1439
Bloom, Claire 1323, 1432
Blue, Ben 1445
Blue, Monte 1390, 1450
Bluhdorn, Charlie 2205
Blum, Leon 1903, 1992
Blythe, Betty 1445
Blyth, Ann 798, 800, 1484
Bodeen, DeWitt 1018
Boetticher, Budd (Oscar Boetticher, Jr.) 174, 429, 1548, 2042
Boetticher, Oscar, Jr. (Budd Boetticher) 174, 429, 1548, 2042
Bogarde, Dirk 371, 1567, 1934, 2161
Bogart and audience expectations 62
Bogart, Humphrey 346, 372, 373, 375, 385, 1137, 1164, 1215, 1232, 1235, 1243, 1250, 1262, 1265, 1288, 1290, 1558, 1952, 1977, 1979, 2078, 2129
Bogart, H. and DEAD END 1808
Bogart, H. and FILM NOIR heroes 809
Bogart, H. and Howard Hawks 1323
Bogart, H. and HUAC 1078, 1087
Bogart, H. and stereotypes of heroes 805
Bogart, H. and THE AFRICAN QUEEN 554, 1915
Bogart, H. and THE BIG SLEEP 798
Bogart, H. and THE MALTESE FALCON 1347, 1915
Bogart, H. and the star system 1443, 1449, 1452
Bogart, H. and the theme of loneliness 575
Bogart, H. and THE TREASURE OF THE SIERRA MADRE 1022
Bogart, H. and Warner Bros. 1494, 1497, 1498
Bogart, H. and World War II propaganda 375
Bogdanovich, Peter 146, 996, 1294, 1315, 1552, 1674, 1758, 2042, 2049, 2195
Bojangles (Luther Bill Robinson) 877
Bojm, Henryk 847
Boland, Bridget 1347
Boland, Mary 1450
Boles, John 1445
Bolger, Ray 1439
Bolt, Robert 1020

Bondi, Beulah 1445
Bond, Edward 1178
Bond, Ralph 1840
Bond, Ward 1080, 1188, 1192, 1254, 1976
Bone, Robert A. 35
Bonney, William S. (Billy the Kid) 434
Bonnot, Francoise 577
Boone, Ashley 902, 905
Boone, Pat 405, 2044
Boorman, John 416, 562, 2073
Booth, Charles G. 373
Booth, Margaret 1330
Booth, Walter R. 1588
Borau, Jose Luis 235
Borgnine, Ernest 1008, 1951, 1982
Borowczyk, Walerian 2192
Borzage, Frank 353, 1148, 1215, 1231, 1673, 1701, 1702, 1774, 2035
Bossak, Jerzy 2012
Bost, Pierre 377, 1908, 1993, 1995, 1998, 2008
Bottoms, Timothy 996
Boulle, Pierre 374, 1171
Boulting, John 1934
Boulting, Ray 323, 1934
Bourne, St. Claire 901, 937, 949
Bowers, William 1150
Bowman, Lee 1446
Bowser, Pearl 949
Bow, Clara 370, 502, 503, 631, 1060, 1443, 1444, 1447, 1449, 1453, 1477, 1504, 1679
Boxer, Nat 367
Box, Muriel 1752
Boyd, William 1445, 1579, 1750
Boyer, Charles 1264, 1443, 1675
Boyer, Francois 377
Boyle, Robert 850
Bracken, Eddie 1014, 1439
Brackett, Charles 84, 1140, 1151, 1803, 1971, 1972, 1987
Brackett, Leigh 508, 798
Bradbury, Ray 1315
Bradley, Omar 365
Brady, William A. 1399, 1505
Bragaglia, Anton Giulio 1879
Brakhage, Stanley 1818, 1951, 1957, 1974
Branda, Olympe 1439
Brando, Jocelyn 1186
Brando, Marlon 376, 805, 810, 1202, 1237, 1244, 1257, 1259, 1260, 1264, 1326, 1346, 1347, 1352, 1354, 1418, 1442, 1443, 1951, 1957, 1958, 1979, 2042, 2176
Brandt, Joseph 1469, 1502, 1670
Brand, Harry 1234
Brand, Neville 429
Braselle, Keefe 1439
Braseur, Pierre 1910
Brasillach, Robert 1903
Bravermann, Barnet 1382
Brazzi, Rossano 1439
Brecht, Bertolt 118, 130, 133, 358, 474, 489, 1088, 1151, 1155, 1180, 1187, 1196, 1229, 1287, 1335, 1633, 1651, 1675, 1829, 1922, 1963, 1968, 2109, 2125
Brecht, B. and CAHIERS DU CINEMA 2124, 2126

Brecht, B. and Denis Diderot 2125
Breen, Bobby 1444
Breen, Joseph I. 345, 572, 1497, 1749, 2037
Brejchova, Hana 2164
Brennan, Eileen 996
Brennan, Walter 430, 1323, 1976
Brennan, William J., Jr. 962, 2037
Brenner, Albert 1017
Brenon, Herbert 342
Brent, Evelyn 1445, 1708
Brent, George 1445
Bresson, Robert 53, 113, 141, 162, 1023, 1163, 1547, 1553, 1571, 1626, 1904, 1905, 1992, 1993, 1994, 1995, 1996, 1999, 2001, 2003, 2004, 2005, 2008, 2170
Breton, Andre 1710, 1713, 1716, 1717
Brewer, Roy Martin 1080, 1082, 1088, 1180, 1186, 1188, 1192, 1202
Brian, David 1209
Brian, Mary 1445
Brice, Fanny 836
Bridges, Jeff 996, 1351
Bridges, Lloyd 375, 1184, 1190, 1191, 1292
Bridge, Joan 1020
Bright, John 1070, 1192, 1193, 1494, 1807, 1808
Brimley, Wilfred 1017
Brinton, Ralph 1328
Briskin, Samuel 1169
Bristol, Howard 1349
Brittain, David 323
Britton, Sherry 1445
Broca, Phillipe de 2100
Broccoli, Albert R. 422, 423
Broderick, Matthew 1530
Brogger, Frederick 1318
Bromberg, Joseph Edward 1096, 1188
Bronco Billy (See Anderson, Gilbert M.) 429
Bronowski, Jacob 315
Bronson, Betty 1445
Bronson, Charles 385, 2071, 2198
Bronston, Samuel 354, 382
Brooke, Hillary 1446
Brooks, Clarence 934, 947, 948
Brooks, Geraldine 1087
Brooks, Louise 508, 1444, 1445
Brooks, Mel 191, 833, 837, 841, 1154, 1294, 1954, 2036, 2047, 2073, 2194, 2195
Brooks, Richard 274, 605, 1000, 1140, 1237, 1352, 1550
Brook, Clive 1445, 1708
Brook, Peter 1001, 1342, 1343, 2127
Broughton, James 1951, 1974
Broun, Heywood 123
Browder, Earl 1193
Browne, George 1186, 1493, 1504
Browne, Leslie 1016
Browne, Roscoe Lee 893, 901, 922
Browning, Ricou 415
Browning, Robert 1363
Browning, Tod 388, 1214, 1385, 1388, 1475, 1524, 1747, 1762, 1798
Brownlow, Kevin 1382, 1416, 1727
Brown, Clarence 1010, 1080, 1204, 1208, 1209, 1321, 1483, 1548, 1579, 1764
Brown, David 1552
Brown, Eleonora 2174

Brown, George 1500
Brown, Harry 1015, 1147, 1154
Brown, Jim 893, 894, 896, 901, 922, 935, 937
Brown, Joe E. 346, 990, 1445, 1449
Brown, Johnny Mack 1445
Brown, Karl 1372, 1385, 1387
Brown, Nacio Herb 1295, 1980
Brown, Tom 1446
Brown, Tony 905
Bruce, Lenny 836, 1146
Bruce, Virginia 1445
Bruckman, Clyde 1705
Bruckner, Robert 259, 343, 1219
Brunelin, Andre-G. 1821
Brunius, Jacques B. 1718
Brusati, Franco 1356
Bryan, Jane 1446
Bryan, John 1357
Bryher (Winifred Ellerman) 514
Brynner, Yul 2042
Buchanan, Edgar 1446
Buchan, Jack 211, 212
Buchman, Sidney 375, 1093, 1100, 1154, 1203, 1293
Buchsbaum, Jonathan 1947
Buckley, William F. 1187
Buck, Pearl S. 54
Buell, Jed 878
Bujold, Genevieve 1347
Bujones, Fernandos 1016
Bull, Edward 193
Bumstead, Harry 1325
Bunker, Archie 835
Bunny, John 1434
Bunuel, Leonardo 1721
Bunuel, Luis 53, 113, 141, 516, 598, 1002, 1094, 1310, 1311, 1547, 1553, 1561,
  1592, 1626, 1713, 1714, 1715, 1716, 1717, 1720, 1721, 1722, 1723, 1727, 1811,
  1923, 1989, 1990, 1991, 2118, 2170
Bunuel, L. and Alfred Hitchcock 1838
Bunuel, L. and Hollywood 1989
Bunuel, L. and Mexico 1989, 1990
Bunuel, L. and Paramount Pictures 1989
Bunuel, L. and the Spanish Civil War 1989
Bunuel, L. and Warner Bros. 1989
Bunuel, Maria Portoles 1721
Bunyan, John 485
Burch, Noel 167
Burch, Ruth 1240
Burham, James 1187
Burke, Kenneth 184
Burnette, Smiley 1447
Burnett, Charles 901
Burnett, Murray 1288
Burnett, W. R. 374, 1219
Burns, Bob 1450
Burns, George 1253
Burrell, Walter, Jr. 938
Burrows, Abe 1181, 1190
Burstyn, Ellen 1006, 1011, 2049

Burstyn, Joseph 1949
Burton, Richard 1243, 1347, 1356, 1940, 2086
Burtt, Benjamin, Jr. 813
Busch, Niven 1314
Bushman, Francis X. 1440, 1444, 1479
Bush, Anita 948
Butler, Bill 1324
Butler, Charles E. 942
Butler, Frank 1094
Butler, Hugo 1094, 1284
Butterworth, Charlie 1253
Byington, Spring 1445
Byrnes, Ed "Kookie" 1439
Byrnes, Marion 1252
Byrne, James F. 1992

C

Caan, James 2063
Cabanne, William Christy 1385, 1406
Cabral, Amilcar 917
Caesar, Sid 833, 2044, 2047
Cage, Nicolas 999
Cagney, James 62, 226, 385, 386, 409, 623, 643, 809, 1078, 1084, 1085, 1244,
  1288, 1369, 1436, 1442, 1443, 1445, 1452, 1494, 1496, 1497, 1499, 1558, 1750,
  1762
Caine, Michael 368, 2160
Cain, James M. 1105, 1107, 1108, 1196, 1273
Caldicott, Helen 325
Caldwell, Erskine 343
Calhern, Louis 1354
Calhoun, Rory 1439, 1487
Callahan, Gene 1014
Callenbach, Ernest 132
Calley, William 360
Calthrop, Donald 1864
Calvert, Corinne 1445
Calvert, Phyllis 1439
Calvino, Italo 492
Cambridge, Godfrey 893, 896, 901
Camerini, Mario 1573, 1874, 1878, 1879, 1880
Cameron, James 765
Cameron, Rod 1439
Cammell, Donald 2160
Campbell, Alan 1296, 1348
Campbell, Colin 1383
Campbell, Eric Stuart 1416, 1419
Campos, Raphael 1439
Camp, Colleen 998
Camus, Marcel 2097, 2118
Canale, Gianna Maria 1439
Canby, Vincent 1452
Cannon, David 1240
Cannon, Dyan 981
Canonero, Milena 1013
Cantor, Eddie 1188, 1474
Canudo, Riccioto 1709
Canutt, Yakima 429, 1758

Capolichio, Lino 2174
Capone, Al 188, 1468
Capote, Truman 1196, 1324
Capra, Frank 147, 162, 208, 209, 227, 241, 247, 281, 282, 294, 295, 304, 320, 321, 343, 346, 347, 556, 568, 572, 980, 1075, 1093, 1160, 1169, 1202, 1328, 1469, 1547, 1548, 1549, 1551, 1553, 1672, 1692, 1705, 1762, 1764, 1799, 1911
Capra, F. and sound films 1747, 1748, 1749, 1758
Caranovsky, Morris 1093, 1195, 1349
Cardiff, Jack 1010, 1943, 1979
Carey, Harry 193, 429, 1389, 1456, 1475, 1704, 1799
Carey, Harry, Jr. 1683
Carfango, Edward 1354
Carlino, Lewis John 1150
Carlin, Lynn 2074
Carlisle, Mary 1445
Carmichael, Hoagy 1323, 1445
Carney, Art 1006, 2044
Carney, William H. 906
Carne, Marcel 1571, 1714, 1812, 1813, 1816, 1825, 1881, 1904, 1905, 1908, 1910, 1922, 1992, 2001, 2127
Carol, Martine 2009, 2010
Carol, Sue 1446
Caronovsky, Morris 1259
Caron, Leslie 1265, 1484
Carpenter, Carleton 1439
Carpenter, Claude 1326
Carradine, John 396, 1683
Carreras, James 1569
Carrington, Cora 1397
Carroll, Diahann 888, 901, 937, 1005
Carroll, John 1445
Carroll, Madeleine 373, 1445, 1853, 1864
Carroll, Sidney 1014
Carruthers, Ben 2074
Carr, Alexander 828
Carson, Jack 1352
Carson, Johnny 1164, 1527
Carson, Robert 1101, 1295
Carson, Sunset 429
Carter, Maurice 1347
Cartier-Bresson, Henri 1993
Caruso, Enrico 1478
Cary, Diana Sierra (Baby Peggy) 426, 992, 1444
Casals, Melchor 299
Casanova, Judy 1444
Case, Theodore W. 272, 1745
Cash, Rosalind 862, 897
Casler, Herman 1371
Cassavetes and Ingmar Bergman 2048
Cassavetes, John 894, 922, 1548, 1549, 2033, 2039, 2047, 2048, 2071, 2074
Cassidy, Hopalong (See Boyd, William) 1750
Cassler, Herman 1586, 1592, 1593
Castellani, Renato 1009, 1573, 1874, 1878
Castle, Irene 1389, 1444
Castle, William 388, 415
Castro, Fidel 312
Cavalcanti, Alberto 141, 214, 215, 216, 244, 248, 249, 292, 294, 295, 304, 309, 315, 343, 1714, 1728, 1753, 1869, 1937

Cawelti, John G. 463
Cayrol, Jean 323, 2112, 2113, 2127, 2137
Cecchi, Emilio 1875, 1879, 1880
Cekalski, Eugene 2012
Cendrars, Blaise 1709, 1717
Cerf, Bennett 1130
Cezanne, Paul 1717
Chabrol, Claude 516, 1572, 1844, 1993, 2002, 2006, 2096, 2098, 2122, 2128, 2151
Chabrol, C. and Alain Resnais 2098
Chabrol, C. and Alfred Hitchcock 2128
Chabrol, C. and CAHIERS DU CINEMA 1997
Chabrol, C. and Eric Rohmer 2094, 2102, 2128
Chabrol, C. and Francois Truffaut 2098, 2099
Chabrol, C. and Friedrich W. Murnau 2099
Chabrol, C. and Fritz Lang 2099
Chabrol, C. and Georges Franju 2098
Chabrol, C. and Honore de Balzac 2099
Chabrol, C. and Jacques Rivette 2099, 2100
Chabrol, C. and Jean-Luc Godard 2098, 2099
Chabrol, C. and the AVANCE SUR RECETTES 2094
Chabrol, C. and the CINEMATEQUE FRANCAISE 1992
Chabrol, C. and 20th Century-Fox 2100
Chadwick, Cyril 193
Chaffey, Don 1752
Chagall, Marc 1709
Chaiken, Judy 1949
Chalais, Francois 1790
Chamberlain, Neville 257, 547
Chambers, Robert W. 1387
Champion (horse star) 1446
Champion, Marge 1439
Chandlee, Harry 365, 1293
Chandler, Raymond 381, 798, 1108, 1196, 1197, 1198, 1211, 1273, 1854, 1957, 1987
Chaney, Lon, Jr. 388, 1440
Chaney, Lon, Sr. 388, 1444, 1475, 1491, 1524, 1579, 1673, 1674, 1679, 1702
Chan, Charlie 380, 381
Chapin, Tom 1002
Chaplin, Charles Spencer 188, 192, 209, 250, 271, 297, 342, 726, 1396, 1418, 1426, 1542, 1547, 1549, 1551, 1552, 1564, 1567, 1570, 1622, 1687, 1750, 1756, 1956, 1974
Chaplin, Charles, Sr. 1427
Chaplin, C. and Alvah Bessie 1178
Chaplin, C. and AUTEUR criticism 2096
Chaplin, C. and blacklisting 1178, 1948
Chaplin, C. and Buster Keaton 1678, 1687, 1689, 2001
Chaplin, C. and comic traditions. 1427
Chaplin, C. and Communism 1418
Chaplin, C. and Darryl F. Zanuck 1501, 1502
Chaplin, C. and David O. Selznick 1847, 1848
Chaplin, C. and Douglas Fairbanks, Sr. 1398
Chaplin, C. and dream theory 583
Chaplin, C. and early film history 1410, 1594, 1595, 1621
Chaplin, C. and early silent films 1824
Chaplin, C. and Erich von Stroheim 1699, 1994
Chaplin, C. and film comedy 1421, 1578, 1579
Chaplin, C. and Francois Truffaut 2145
Chaplin, C. and Gilbert Seldes 157
Chaplin, C. and his emerging comic style 107

Chaplin, C. and Hollywood 1239, 1241, 1244, 1248
Chaplin, C. and independent filmmaking 639
Chaplin, C. and Jack L. Warner 1498
Chaplin, C. and Jacques Tati 2007
Chaplin, C. and Kon Ichikawa 2022
Chaplin, C. and Liberty Bonds 1417
Chaplin, C. and Louis B. Mayer 1479
Chaplin, C. and Mabel Normand 1411
Chaplin, C. and Mack Sennett 1411, 1412, 1413
Chaplin, C. and Mary Pickford 1393, 1397
Chaplin, C. and Max Linder 1619
Chaplin, C. and Mildred Harris 1421
Chaplin, C. and Miriam Cooper 1374
Chaplin, C. and Rene Clair 1724
Chaplin, C. and Robert Aldrich 2043
Chaplin, C. and Robert Parrish 1275
Chaplin, C. and Samuel Goldwyn 1473
Chaplin, C. and screenwriters 1254
Chaplin, C. and Sergei M. Eisenstein 1720
Chaplin, C. and silent film comedy 1672, 1673, 1674, 1676, 1677, 1678
Chaplin, C. and silent films 1360
Chaplin, C. and Stan Laurel 1691
Chaplin, C. and teenage films 984
Chaplin, C. and the American Dream 1046, 1054
Chaplin, C. and the art of the film 1553
Chaplin, C. and the AVANT-GARDE 1709, 1710
Chaplin, C. and the development of the film industry 1463, 1464, 1465, 1467
Chaplin, C. and the fifties 2035
Chaplin, C. and THE NUT 1407
Chaplin, C. and the Oscars 1164
Chaplin, C. and the star system 1434, 1443, 1449, 1452
Chaplin, C. and the Talkies 1417, 1757
Chaplin, C. and United Artists 1369, 1370, 1394, 1417, 1669
Chaplin, Geraldine 1432
Chaplin, Lita Grey 1446
Chaplin, Michael 1431
Chaplin, Saul 1983
Chaplin, Sydney 1414, 1422, 1424, 1426, 1429, 1432, 1502
Chapman, Robert H. 1018
Charleson, Ian 1013
Charles, Judge 193
Charters, W. W. 729
Chartoff, Robert 1294, 1296
Chase, Borden 424, 1101, 1145, 1146, 1147, 1154, 1982
Chase, Charlie 1578
Chase, Chevy 2202
Chasin, Asher 846
Chayefsky, Paddy 836, 1008, 1036, 1248, 1265, 1292, 1982, 2036
Chekhov, Anton 602, 1218
Chekhov, Mikhail 606, 1649
Chenal, Pierre 1880
Cherkasov, Nikolai 1866, 1868
Cherrill, Virginia 1424, 1429
Chevalier, Albert 1427
Chevalier, Maurice 1265, 1477, 1478, 1764
Chewing, Wallace 1433
Chew, Richard 813, 1324
Chiarini, Luigi 1874, 1878

Chomette, Rene (see Rene Clair) 1725
Chopin, Frederic 407, 789
Christensen, Benjamin 1624, 1626, 1630, 1726
Christians, Mandy 1096, 1188
Christian, Linda 1445
Christian, Roger 813
Christie, Julie 994
Christopher, Dennis 1004
Christopher, Sybil Burton 1439
Chukrai, Grigori 371
Churchill, Sara 1439
Churchill, Winston 547
Cilento, Diane 1328
Cimino, Michael 209, 218, 367, 604, 668, 2201, 2209
Ciotti, Charles 799
Claire, Ina 1445
Clair, Rene 582, 1571, 1606, 1711, 1713, 1714, 1716, 1717, 1724, 1725, 1810,
 1811, 1813, 1825, 1833, 1992, 1993, 2000, 2001, 2034
Clair, R. and film criticism 142, 144
Clanton family, the 1960
Clarke, Mae 1445
Clarke, Shirley 497, 508, 520, 894, 922, 937, 1348, 2039
Clarke, T. E. B. "Tibby" 1010, 1937, 1942
Clark, Al 1799
Clark, Benjamin Champ 203
Clark, Candy 605, 993
Clark, Dick 1242
Clark, James B. 996, 1007
Clark, Kenneth 91
Clark, Ron 1294
Clark, Walter Van Tilburg 1108
Clatworthy, Robert 2054
Clavell, James 374
Clayburgh, Jill 1452, 2194
Clayton, Jack 1016, 1321, 1324
Clayton, Jan 1439
Clement, Rene 57, 377, 1993, 1995, 2001, 2008
Cleopatra 383
Clever, Edith 2142
Clifford, Graeme 1292
Clifton, Elmer 1450
Clift, Montgomery 368, 369, 377, 810, 1007, 1015, 1202, 1272, 1347, 1951, 1989
Cline, Edward F. 1800
Clooney, Rosemary 1439
Cloquet, Ghislain 165
Close, Glenn 1174, 1530
Clouzot, Henri-Georges 1571, 1815, 1904, 1905, 1908, 1909, 1992, 2000, 2001,
 2008
Clurman, Harold 1257, 1258
Cobb, Humphrey 372
Cobb, Lee J. 1093, 1097, 1178, 1181, 1184, 1188, 1190, 1260
Cobo, Robert 1002
Coburn, James 2063, 2087
Cochise 199
Cochrane, Robert H. 1428, 1475
Cochran, Gifford 875
Cocteau, Jean 582, 1313, 1549, 1571, 1572, 1710, 1716, 1730, 1790, 1811, 1815,
 1816, 1817, 1818, 1819, 1821, 1826, 1905, 1908, 1910, 1993, 1995, 1997, 1999,
 2000, 2001, 2006, 2008, 2009

Cocteau, J. and AVANT-GARDE cinema 1818
Cocteau, J. and Childhood 1818
Cocteau, J. and film criticism 144
Cocteau, J. and Jean-Luc Godard 2129
Cody, Lew 1413
Coe, Fred 1022, 2064
Cogley, John 1195
Cohen-Seat, Gilbert 2002, 2003
Cohen, Albert J. 701
Cohen, Ernest Philip 1190
Cohen, Larry 604
Cohen, Manny 1031, 1277, 1478
Cohen, Meyer "Mickey" Harris 1242
Cohen, Octavus Roy 921
Cohen, Philip 1178
Cohen, Sammy 828
Cohl, Emile 1606, 1709
Cohn, Harry 244, 399, 534, 700, 754, 820, 1136, 1183, 1192, 1229, 1235, 1254,
   1263, 1290, 1435, 1466, 1468, 1469, 1475, 1490, 1496, 1502, 1670, 2043
Cohn, Jack 1469, 1475, 1502, 1670
Colbert, Claudette 1443, 1467, 1765, 1799
Colby, Anita 1446
Coleman, C. C., Jr. 1328, 1799
Coleman, Nancy 1439
Coleridge, Samuel Taylor 247
Colette (See Sidonie Gabrielle) 147, 508
Cole, Jack 402
Cole, Lester 1036, 1070, 1073, 1083, 1088, 1098, 1184, 1187, 1199, 1205
Cole, Nat "King" 885
Collinge, Patricia 1348
Collings, Esme 1606
Collings, Pierre 1800
Collins, Pat 961
Collins, Richard 1079, 1091, 1098, 1100, 1190, 1191
Colman, Ronald 423, 1305, 1443, 1444, 1448, 1451, 1472, 1488, 1679, 1799, 1975
Colonna, Jerry 1445
Comden, Betty 83, 404, 1145, 1295
Comer, Anjanette 1294
Comer, Sam 1350
Comingore, Dorothy 1269
Comolli, Jean-Louis 2124
Como, Perry 320
Compson, Betty 1445
Compton, Joyce 1445, 1446
Conklin, Chester 1410, 1413, 1432, 1444, 1545
Connelly, Marc 859, 874, 952, 994, 1063, 1253
Connery, Sean 422, 805, 810
Conrad, Joseph 366, 1432
Conreid, Hans 1446
Considine, John W. 1115
Considine, John, Jr. 1386
Considine, Tim 1439
Constantine, Eddie 2151
Conte, Richard 369, 826, 1087
Conway, Jack 1118, 1385, 1483
Coogan, Jackie 991, 992, 993, 1431
Cooke, Alistair 139, 140, 547, 1753
Cook, Elisha, Jr. 373, 1977

Cook, Fiedler 2067
Coolidge, Martha 977, 999
Cooper, Gary 348, 365, 369, 370, 431, 789, 803, 1019, 1080, 1088, 1146, 1160, 1178, 1180, 1232, 1243, 1244, 1262, 1274, 1319, 1322, 1443, 1449, 1452, 1453, 1472, 1504, 1806, 1952, 2194
Cooper, Gladys 800
Cooper, Jackie 970, 990, 992, 993
Cooper, James Fenimore 367, 1300, 1363
Cooper, Miriam C. 639, 1373, 1379, 1384, 1387, 1388, 1488, 1800, 1869
Cooper, Ralph 878, 929, 935, 942, 948
Coop, Denys 994
Copland, Aaron 408, 1007
Coppel, Alec 2080
Coppola, Francis Ford 57, 339, 341, 355, 362, 365, 367, 536, 558, 980, 1140, 1321, 1552, 2033, 2049, 2196, 2208
Corbett, James 861
Corbucci, Sergio 382
Corda, Maria 1859
Cordy, Raymond 1825
Corey, Jeff 952, 1093
Corio, Ann 498
Corliss, Richard 121, 1270
Cormack, Bartlett 1018
Corman, Roger 388, 389, 415, 744, 983, 986, 1549, 2049, 2050, 2075, 2197
Corman, R. and Allied Artists 2049
Corman, R. and Edgar Allan Poe 2049
Corman, R. and gangster movies 2049
Corman, R. and monster movies 2049
Cormon, Eugene 1389
Cornelius, Henry 1937
Cornell, Don 1439
Cornell, Joseph 1818
Cornell, Katharine 1176, 1445, 1789
Corrado, Gino 1406, 1447
Correll, Mady 1433
Cortese, Valentine 2154
Cortez, Ricardo 1445, 1478
Cortez, Stanley 1327, 2042
Corwin, Norman 1015
Cosby, Bill 938
Cosgrove, John R. 812, 1801
Costa-Gavras, Constantin 566, 577, 1020, 2126, 2127
Costa, Mario 1573
Costa, Mary 1439
Costello, Dolores 1445
Costello, Lou 1476, 1757
Costello, Maurice 1444
Cottafavi, Vittorio 382, 2032
Cotton, Joseph 1327, 1329, 1487, 1765, 1920
Couch, Lionel 1347
Coulouris, George 1807
Courant, Curt 1433
Courau, Pierre 2137
Courtenay, Tom 371, 374, 994, 997
Courtot, Marguerite 1459
Coutant, Andre 2120
Coutard, Raoul 2120, 2129
Cowan, Lester 642, 1125, 1129, 1329
Coward, Noel 371, 1243, 1860, 1943

Cowie, Peter 1792
Coxe, Louis O. 1018
Cox, Jack 1857
Crabbe, Larry "Buster" 415, 1444, 1456
Craig, Gordon 1342
Crain, Jeanne 1272, 1439, 1471
Crane, Stephen 53
Crawford, Broderick 1012
Crawford, Joan 409, 502, 631, 798, 800, 1137, 1240, 1271, 1402, 1437, 1440, 1443, 1447, 1452, 1481, 1484, 1487, 1529, 1556, 1766, 1803, 1985
Crawford, Wayne 998
Creature from the Black Lagoon 390
Creel, George 223, 224
Crichton, Charles 1937, 1942
Crichton, Kyle 1279
Crichton, Michael 415
Crisp, Donald 1007, 1015, 1387, 1388, 1405, 1497, 1705
Crist, Judith 147
Croce, Benedetto 1922
Crocker, Harry 1429
Crockett, Davy 474
Cromwell, John 1204, 1292, 1329, 1333, 1696
Cronenberg, David 394
Cronyn, Hume 1852, 1855
Crosby, Bing 803, 990, 1094, 1174, 1350, 1411, 1443, 1504, 1757
Crosby, Bob 1439
Crosland, Alan 1496
Cross, Ben 1013
Crowell, John 1248
Crowell, Josephine 1387, 1388
Crowther, Bosley 127, 147, 1250, 1372, 1792
Cruise, Tom 2206
Crum, Bartley 1192
Cruze, James 1248, 1702
Cukor, George 980, 1012, 1033, 1202, 1254, 1275, 1295, 1306, 1488, 1548, 1550, 1552, 1553, 1747, 1753, 1764, 1801, 1802, 1951, 1975
Cummings, Robert 1439
Cunard, Grace 1444, 1455
Cunningham, Cecil 1447
Cuny, Alain 1023
Curtis, Tony 383, 423, 1288
Curtiz, Michael 343, 372, 800, 1146, 1231, 1496, 1551, 1747, 1750, 1913
Cushing, Peter 381, 388, 390
Cutts, Graham 1833, 1837, 1855
Cybulski, Zbigniew 2012, 2180
Czesko, Bohdan 2014
Czinner, Paul 1356, 1833
Czugajewicz, Pierre 1591

D

D'Amico, Masolino 1356
D'Annunzio, Gabriele 1879
D'Orsay, Fifi 1445
Da Roma, Eraldo 1883
Da Silva, Howard 1093, 1136, 1181, 1195
Da Vinci, Leonardo 1580, 1582, 1594, 1660

Dafoe, Willem 368
Dagover, Lil 1439, 1632, 1641, 1643
Daguerre, Louis Jacques Mande 1584, 1591, 1598
Dahl, Arlene 1484
Daisuke, Ito 1742
Daley, Cass 1445, 1447
Dalio, Marcel 1232, 1814, 1822, 1826, 1827, 1906
Dali, Salvador 598, 1714, 1716, 1717, 1720, 1722, 1727
Dalrymple, Ian 216, 242, 309, 317, 352
Dana, Viola 1446
Dandridge, Dorothy 882, 885, 920, 922, 935, 945, 948, 950, 1474, 1967, 1968
Dane, Karl 367, 1450
Dangerfield, George 302
Daniell, Henry 1012, 1431
Daniels, Bebe 1444, 1450, 1703, 1705
Daniels, William 1352, 1708, 1976
Danischewsky, Monja 1937
Danska, Herbert 894
Dantine, Helmut 1439
Danto, Arthur 184
Darby, Ken 83
Darcell, Denise 1439
Darnell, Linda 502, 1271, 1707
Darrell, Donald 164
Darrow, Frankie 991, 1445
Darvi, Bella 1502
Darwell, Jane 1021, 1326
Dassin, Jules 386, 941, 944, 1946, 1948, 1951, 1976, 2043
Daste, Jean 1828
Davenport, Henry 1021
Davenport, Ken 1402
Daves, Delmer 369, 1140, 1142, 1147, 1178, 1284, 1496
Davidson, Max 828
David, Gail 1446
David, Hal 2078, 2161
Davies, Joseph E. 259, 343, 344, 1187, 1494
Davies, Marion 1395, 1396, 1417, 1444, 1450, 1484, 1489
Davies, Peter 325
Davis, Bette 385, 390, 409, 623, 686, 735, 797, 800, 801, 1164, 1169, 1202,
    1241, 1250, 1262, 1265, 1329, 1348, 1436, 1438, 1442, 1443, 1449, 1452, 1472,
    1494, 1496, 1497, 1499, 1502, 1748, 1756, 1766, 1915, 1952, 1981
Davis, Elmer 228, 351
Davis, George W. 849
Davis, James 1951, 1974
Davis, Marvin 663
Davis, Ossie 879, 896, 901, 915, 922, 923, 937, 938
Davis, Sammy, Jr. 901, 922, 937, 950
Dawley, Jay Searle 1383
Dawley, J. Searle 1361
Dawn, Hazel 1445
Day, Dennis 1439
Day, Doris 508, 523, 524, 643, 790, 1254, 1443, 1452, 1951, 1958, 1959
Day, Josette 2009
Day, Laraine 1445, 1484
Day, Richard 1007, 1352, 1708, 1808, 1980
Day, Robert 1752
De Benedetti, Aldo 1875
De Broca, Phillippe 1813
De Brulier, Nigel 1408

De Carlo, Yvonne 498
De Carmoy, Guy 1906
De Chirico, Giorgio 1716
De Forest, Lee 272, 1670, 1745
De Gaulle, Charles 260
De Gaulle, President Charles 1206
De Grasse, Sam 1407
De Groot, Roy 266
De Haven, Gloria 1439
De Havilland, Olivia 623, 913, 1007, 1448, 1449, 1767, 1801, 1915, 1945, 1952
De Hirsch, Storm 508
De Laurentiis, Dino 658, 1233
De Maupassant, Guy 1608
De MIlle, Cecil B. 209
De Niro, Robert 152, 367, 1233, 1293, 1452, 2049, 2194
De Palma, Brian 341, 399, 604, 1548, 1549, 2196
De Robertis, Francesca 1573
De Rochemont, Louis 78, 280, 283, 301, 302, 319, 1532
De Rochemont, Richard 301
De Santis, Giuseppe 1874
De Santis, Pasqualino 1356
De Saussure, Ferdinand 133
De Sica, Vittorio 127, 378, 1004, 1573, 1874, 1875, 1877, 1878, 1925, 1926, 1932, 1933, 2034, 2174
De Silva, Howard 1439
De Stafani, Alberto 1875
De Tocqueville, Alexis 179, 553
De Wilde, Brandon 975, 990, 992, 993, 997, 1001, 1009
Dead End Kids 987
Dean, Basil 1833, 1839, 1842
Dean, Eddie 433
Dean, James 805, 810, 975, 997, 1005, 1244, 1325, 1442, 1443, 1448, 1951, 1959, 1969
Dean, Priscilla 1444
Decae, Henri 165, 1006
DeCuir, John 1356
Dee, Frances 1329, 1446, 1452
Dee, Ruby 549, 901, 922, 1009
Dee, Sandra 790, 975
Degas, (Hilaire-Germain) Edgar 131
DeHaven, Carter 1424
Dekker, Albert 1188
Del Gallo di Roccagiovane, Alberto 1573
Del Giudice, Filippo 1567
Del Rio, Dolores 1444, 1445, 1709
Delamater, Jerome 191
Delannoy, Jean 162
Delaunay, Robert 1709
Delerue, Georges 1322, 1347
Dellannoy, Jean 1904
Delluc, Louis 40, 147, 1426, 1710, 1711, 1712, 1713, 1717, 1728
Dell, Gabriel 987
Delteil, Joseph 1729
Deluc, Germain 1717
DeLuise, Dom 1294
Demeny, Georges 1586
Demick, Irina 1502
DeMille, Beatrice 1239

DeMille, Cecil B. 269, 382, 426, 600, 980, 1172, 1239, 1241, 1254, 1260, 1272, 1395, 1396, 1449, 1463, 1477, 1478, 1491, 1504, 1549, 1550, 1553, 1579, 1594, 1607, 1673, 1680, 1681, 1703, 1709
DeMille, Cecilia (Mrs. Joseph Harper) 1680
DeMille, William 1239
Demme, Jonathan 2049
Dempster, Carol 1372, 1373, 1378, 1382, 1384, 1387, 1389, 1390, 1445
Dempsy, Mary Estelle 1918
Demutski, Daniel 1647
Demy, Jacques 562, 1572, 2119, 2122
Deneuve, Catherine 1721, 2050, 2143
Dennery, Adolphe 1389
Dennis, Sandy 2086
Depardieu, Gerard 2143
Dereck, John 1445
Derek, Bo 419
Deren, Maya 140, 497, 508, 1951, 1955, 1974
Dern, Bruce 376, 2049
Derrida, Jacques 134
DeSano, Marcel 1117, 1277
Desmond, William 1456
Desmouchceaux, Geory 2149
Desnos, Robert 1717, 1718
Desvignes, Pierre Hubert 1591
Detlef Sierck, Hans (Douglas Sirk) 1970
Devant, David 1588, 1603, 1616
Devine, Andy 430, 1445
DeVore, Christopher 1292
Dewey, John 260, 344, 1495
Diamond, I. A. L. 1150, 1291, 1552, 1971, 1972, 1987
Diaz, Jesus 299, 2163
Dickens, Charles 1163, 1363, 1837, 1944
Dickinson, Thorold 1566, 1833, 1934
Dickson, William Kennedy Laurie 293, 1371, 1586, 1590, 1592, 1593, 1598, 1599, 1615
Dickstein, Sam 1195
Diderot, Denis 2125
Didion, Joan 530
Dies, Martin 204, 832, 1192, 1195
Dieterle, William 376, 1015, 1496, 1635, 1750, 1758, 1800, 1948
Dietrich, Marlene 502, 508, 555, 1215, 1219, 1264, 1394, 1440, 1441, 1443, 1447, 1449, 1477, 1478, 1674, 1675, 1676, 1697, 1806, 1830, 1831, 1833
Dietrich, Otto 234
Dighton, John 1942, 1988
Diller, Barry 611, 666, 678, 2197
Dilley, Leslie 813
Dillman, Bradford 1351
Dillon, Carmen 1353, 1354
Dillon, Matt 970, 998
Dillon, Melinda 1017
DiMaggio, Joseph 1493
Dinemandi, Jean (Dorat) 1313
Dinesen, Isak (Karen Blixen) 488
Dingle, Charles 1348
Dintenfass, Mark 1463
Disney, Walt 78, 283, 306, 308, 487, 488, 572, 639, 1080, 1084, 1088, 1179, 1188, 1301, 1369, 1449, 1466, 1467, 1549, 1746, 1747, 1756, 1767, 1952, 1975, 2022
Disney, W. and television showcasing 653

Dixon, Ivan 901, 952, 1009
Dixon, Thomas 863, 933, 1366, 1377, 1382
Dix, Richard 1444, 1477, 1833
Dmytryk, Edward 72, 274, 369, 375, 849, 1079, 1088, 1092, 1098, 1178, 1179, 1180, 1181, 1190, 1192, 1202, 1204, 1287, 1354, 1485, 1758, 1946, 2043
Dobson, Tamara 896
Dockendorf, David 2078
Domarchi, Jean 1997
Donahue, Phil 544
Donald, James 374
Donati, Danilo 1356
Donat, Robert 373, 1328, 1753, 1833, 1834, 1841, 1864, 1865, 1934
Donen, Stanley 1295, 1954, 1980
Donfeld 2089
Doniol-Valcroze, Jacques 1996, 1997, 2002, 2119
Donnelly, Ruth 1445, 1497
Donner, Jorn 1628
Donner, Robert 429
Dooley, Paul 1004
Doran, Ann 997
Dorat, (Jean Dinemandi) 1313
Dore O. 1956
Dorn, Philip 1446
Dors, Diana 1439, 1567
Dos Passos, John 1153, 1156, 1157, 1924
Dos Santos, Nelson Pereira 2158
Dostoyevsky, Fyodor Mikhaylovich 1301, 1650, 1957
Dougherty, Lee 1387
Douglass, Robyn 1004
Douglas, Haldane 1322
Douglas, Helen Gahagan 1192, 1444
Douglas, James 297
Douglas, Kirk 372, 383, 386, 805, 1015, 1284, 1288, 1290, 1951, 1959, 2055
Douglas, Melvyn 1188, 1192, 1336, 1481, 1750, 1803
Dourif, Brad 1324
Dove, Billie 1405, 1445
Dovzhenko, Alexander P. 213, 304, 314, 1645, 1647, 1651, 1652, 1654, 1655, 1665, 1758, 1865
Dowd, Nancy 1037
Downey, Robert 1549
Downs, Johnny 1445
Dracula 391, 395, 398, 399
Drake, Tom 1445
Drake, William A. 1802
Draper, Paul 1188
Dratler, Jay 366
Dreier, Hans 1322, 1806
Dreifuss, Arthur 947
Dreiser, Theodore 1151, 1156, 1661
Dressler, Marie 1394, 1395, 1396, 1410, 1433, 1468
Drew, Ellen 1439
Drew, Robert 1557, 2040
Dreyer, Carl Theodor 65, 466, 1542, 1547, 1553, 1592, 1594, 1626, 1628, 1629, 1631, 1714, 1718, 1726, 1729, 1811, 2004, 2189
Dreyfuss, Richard 605, 836, 993
Driscoll, Bobby 990, 993
Drobashenko, Sergei 242
Drummond, Bulldog 380

Dru, Joanne 1439
Dr. Jekyll and Mr. Hyde 390, 399
Du Bellay, Joachim 1313
Du Hauron, Louis Ducos 1585, 1591
Du Maurier, Daphne 1439
Duboscq, Jules 1585
Duburau, Jean-Gaspard 1427
Ducados, Sarah (Sarah Maladoror) 508
Duca, Lo 1997, 2002
Duchamp, Marcel 1716, 1727
Duchesne, Roger 1905
Duck, Donald 283, 306
Duclos, Jacques 1193
Duell, Randall 402
Duff, Howard 1093
Dugger, Florrie 971
Duke, Patty 991, 992
Dulac, Germaine 147, 466, 497, 508, 1712, 1713, 1716, 1729
Dullea, Keir 995
DuLuca, Rudy 1294
Dumas, Alexandre 1408
DuMont, Henry 1591
Dumont, Margaret 1783, 1805
Dunaway, Faye 2088
Dunham, Katherine 944
Dunne, Finley Peter 1204
Dunne, Irene 1160, 1444, 1481, 1786, 1986
Dunne, John Gregory 530
Dunne, Philip 1001, 1007, 1066, 1071, 1079, 1087, 1147, 1154, 1182, 1192, 1203,
  1204, 1205, 1271, 1503
Dunning, George 1002
Dunning, William A. 864
Dunnock, Mildred 1346
Dupont, E. A. 1579, 1632, 1634, 1640, 1829
Durand, Jean 1606
Durante, Jimmy 1439, 1757
Duras, Marguerite 466, 505, 1313, 2112, 2113, 2127, 2136, 2137
Durbin, Deanna 991, 992, 993, 1750
Durgnat, Raymond 2130
Durham, Marcel 1322
Durham, Philip 430
Duryea, Dan 1348
Duse, Eleanora 1618
Dusty "Open the Door" Richard 882
Duvall, Robert 367, 1211
Duvivier, Julien 1811, 1812, 1813, 1922, 1992
Dvorak, Ann 1445
Dwan, Allan 1294, 1385, 1400, 1405, 1406, 1407, 1671, 1713
Dya, Richard 1472, 1473
Dykstra, John 813
Dylan, Bob 425
Dymling, Carl Anders 2184
Dynamov, Sergei 1657

E

Eady, Wilfrid 1936
Eagels, Jeanne 1242
Earp, Wyatt 1960
Easdale, Brian 1016
Eastman, Carole (Adrian Joyce) 516
Eastman, George 1585, 1589, 1614
Eastwood, Clint 378, 431, 437, 559, 576, 801, 805, 810, 1235, 1265, 1436, 1548,
    2036, 2206
Eaton, Walter P. 458
Eberson, John 1506
Ebert, Roger 976
Ecare, Desire 2121
Eco, Umberto 492
Eddy, Nelson 1443
Edeson, Arthur 1805
Edison, Thomas Alva 292, 293, 711, 766, 932, 1062, 1461, 1462, 1504, 1509,
    1586, 1593, 1594, 1595, 1598, 1599, 1601, 1610, 1615, 1675, 1715, 1731
Edlund, Richard 813
Edmundson, William 2078
Edson, Arthur 1408
Edwards, Blake 598, 980, 1237, 1295, 2195
Edwards, Hugh 1002
Edwards, James 375, 883, 922, 937, 952
Egan, Richard 1439
Eggeling, Viking 1711, 1717
Eilers, Sally 1445
Einstein, Albert 1400, 1709
Eisenhower, Dwight D. 365, 1318
Eisenhower, Milton S. 229
Eisenstein, Sergei M. 100, 141, 209, 213, 274, 281, 1030, 1509, 1547, 1553,
    1555, 1645, 1651, 1656, 1661, 1664, 1667, 1718, 1866, 1867, 1868, 1939, 1956
Eisenstein, S. and American films 304
Eisenstein, S. and BATTLESHIP POTEMKIN 1655
Eisenstein, S. and Charles Chaplin 1426
Eisenstein, S. and Charles Dickens 1301
Eisenstein, S. and David Wark Griffith 1656
Eisenstein, S. and Douglas Fairbanks, Sr. 1402
Eisenstein, S. and dream theory 583
Eisenstein, S. and Esther Shub 1658
Eisenstein, S. and European theater 1342
Eisenstein, S. and feminist film theory 500
Eisenstein, S. and film aesthetics 65, 68
Eisenstein, S. and film criticism 144, 172
Eisenstein, S. and film editing 1646, 1647, 1651, 1652
Eisenstein, S. and film theory 41, 163, 165, 1656, 1658, 1660, 1666, 1667
Eisenstein, S. and French censorship 1811
Eisenstein, S. and Hollywood 1227
Eisenstein, S. and ideology 474
Eisenstein, S. and Japanese films 1737
Eisenstein, S. and Jay Leyda 1651
Eisenstein, S. and Joseph V. Stalin 1657
Eisenstein, S. and Judaism 830
Eisenstein, S. and Leon Moussinac 1660
Eisenstein, S. and Luchino Visconti 1934
Eisenstein, S. and Marie Seton 1660, 1661
Eisenstein, S. and Maxim Straukh 1658

Eisenstein, S. and montage 99, 126
Eisenstein, S. and newsreels 1659
Eisenstein, S. and Nina Agadzhanova 1666
Eisenstein, S. and Pyotr Pavlenko 1868
Eisenstein, S. and Rene Clair 1724
Eisenstein, S. and screen adaptations 1311, 1316, 1331, 1339
Eisenstein, S. and state censorship 1655
Eisenstein, S. and the AVANT-GARDE 1710, 1712, 1715, 1758
Eisenstein, S. and the coming of sound 1865
Eisenstein, S. and the documentary movement 294
Eisenstein, S. and the origins of film 1579
Eisenstein, S. and Upton Sinclair 1866
Eisenstein, S. and Valery Pletniev 1666
Eisenstein, S. and Vladimir Nizhny 1660
Eisenstein, S. and William Faulkner 1212
Eisenstein, S. in Hollywood 1661, 1866
Eisenstin, S. and film theory 126
Eisler, Gerhart 1180
Eisler, Hanns 1180
Eisner, Lotte 1996
Eisner, Michael 537, 666
Ekberg, Anita 1023
Ekman, Hasse 1628
Elam, Jack 429
Elder, Lonne III 899
Eldridge, Florence 1192
Elfand, Martin 666
Eliot, George 1363
Elizabeth II, Queen 1854
Ellerman, Winifred (Bryher) 514
Elmes, Frederick 999
Elsie, Lily 1441
Elterman, Howard 443
Elton, Arthur 214, 215, 238, 248, 253, 309, 316, 1869
Eluard, Paul 1710
Emerson, Faye 1445
Emerson, John 1379, 1380, 1385, 1400, 1404, 1405, 1455
Emerson, Ralph Waldo 1324
Emert, Oliver 1325
Emmett, "Ted" 266
Empson, William 315
Engel, Samuel G. 1976
Engl, Erich 1828
Engl, Josef 1745
Enrico, Robert 379
Ephron, Henry 1206
Ephron, Phoebe 1206
Epstein, Jean 582, 1712, 1722, 1730, 1869, 1880, 1923
Epstein, Jerry 1427
Epstein, Julius J. 372, 1083, 1130, 1146, 1154, 1203, 1288, 1494
Epstein, Marie 1825
Epstein, Philip G. 372, 1130, 1146, 1154, 1203, 1288, 1494
Erens, Patricia 470
Erice, Victor 235
Erikson, Erik 600
Erlanger, A. L. 1379
Ermler, Friedrich 1647
Ernst, Max 1716
Espinosa, Julio Garcia 2163

Estabrook, Howard 1071
Etaix, Pierre 1572, 2119, 2122
Etkes, Raphael 535
Etzioni, Amitai 437
Evans, Dame Edith 1328
Evans, Joan 1439, 1472
Evans, Mark 403
Evans, Maurice 2090
Evans, Robert 1233, 2197
Everson, William K. 430
Ewell, Tom 1439, 1975
Eythe, William 1021

F

Fabrizi, Aldo 378
Fagin 822
Fairbanks, Beth Sully 1404
Fairbanks, Douglas, Jr. 346, 1396, 1402, 1404, 1451, 1806, 1833
Fairbanks, Douglas, Sr. 188, 423, 1395, 1396, 1397, 1398, 1402, 1404, 1405,
  1407, 1442, 1455, 1673, 1700, 1833
Fairbanks, D. and Adolph Zukor 1504
Fairbanks, D. and Anita Loos 1379
Fairbanks, D. and Charles Chaplin 1420
Fairbanks, D. and early film history 1385, 1610, 1622
Fairbanks, D. and Hollywood 1236
Fairbanks, D. and Liberty Bonds 1417
Fairbanks, D. and Mary Pickford 1393, 1398, 1402
Fairbanks, D. and Rene Clair 1724
Fairbanks, D. and Sergei M. Eisenstein 1656
Fairbanks, D. and silent films 1360
Fairbanks, D. and the American Dream 1054
Fairbanks, D. and THE AMERICANO 1578
Fairbanks, D. and THE BLACK PIRATE 1405, 1579
Fairbanks, D. and the development of the film industry 1464
Fairbanks, D. and THE IRON MASK 1406
Fairbanks, D. and THE LAMB 1406
Fairbanks, D. and THE MARK OF ZORRO 1407
Fairbanks, D. and THE MOLLYCODDLE 1407
Fairbanks, D. and the Motion Picture Academy of Arts and Sciences 1172
Fairbanks, D. and THE NUT 1407
Fairbanks, D. and the star system 1434, 1440, 1443, 1444, 1449, 1451, 1452
Fairbanks, D. and the talkies 1401
Fairbanks, D. and THE TAMING OF THE SHREW 1408
Fairbanks, D. and THE THIEF OF BAGDAD 1408, 1579
Fairbanks, D. and THE THREE MUSKETEERS 1408
Fairbanks, D. and the Triangle Film Corporation 1399, 1412, 1503
Fairbanks, D. and United Artists 1369, 1370, 1417, 1478, 1669
Falconetti, Renee (Maria) 1629, 1729
Falk, Peter 833, 2074
Faragoh, Francis Edwards 1071, 1804
Farber, Manny 127, 148
Farina (Allen Clayton Hoskins) 866, 920
Farkas, Antonia (Maria Corda) 1859
Farmer, Frances 1137, 1151, 1241, 1292
Farnum, William 1444, 1470
Farouk, King 1290

Farrar, Geraldine 1444, 1474
Farrell, Charles 1445, 1702
Farrell, Glenda 1497
Farrell, Suzanne 1016
Farrow, Mia 584, 786, 1321
Fassbinder, Rainer Werner 311, 1310, 1986, 2099, 2165
Fassini, Alberto 1573
Faulkner, William 152, 260, 370, 798, 913, 1065, 1101, 1103, 1106, 1108, 1146,
  1147, 1148, 1149, 1151, 1152, 1153, 1155, 1156, 1249, 1251, 1253, 1256, 1272,
  1273, 1274, 1323, 1977
Faulkner, W. and F. Scott Fitzgerald 1226
Faulkner, W. and Howard Hawks 1207, 1210, 1214
Faulkner, W. and Jean Renoir 1210, 1211
Faulkner, W. and John Frankenheimer 2051
Faulkner, W. and Samuel Marx 1213
Faulkner, W. and screen adaptations 1208, 1231, 1232
Faulkner, W. and television 1209
Faulk, John Henry 1100, 1188, 1189
Faure, Elie 1710
Faustman, Hampe 1628
Faye, Alice 1471
Faye, Safi 2121
Faylan, Frank 1987
Fazan, Adrienne 1295
Fearing, Franklin 778, 1192, 1193
Feinstein, Diane 974
Feldman, Marty 1294
Fellini, Federico 45, 53, 63, 117, 378, 583, 593, 1021, 1023, 1163, 1310, 1547,
  1553, 1929, 1930, 1931, 1932, 1933, 2034, 2170, 2171, 2174, 2175
Fellows, Anita 1446
Fengler, Fred 976, 977
Fenin, George 430
Ferber, Edna 1268
Ferguson, Otis 127, 139, 148, 1792
Ferguson, Perry 1807
Ferida, Luisa 1573
Fernandez, Emilio 2087
Ferno, John 314
Ferrer, Jose 1091, 1092, 1181, 1188, 1229, 1250, 1291
Ferrer, Mel 1484
Ferry, Jean 1998
Ferzetti, Gabriele 1012
Fetchit, Stepin (Lincoln Perry) 870, 872, 877, 915, 921, 926, 948, 1034, 1444
Feuillade, Louis 1571, 1605, 1606, 1617, 1709
Feyder, Jacques 1571, 1714, 1811, 1812, 1813, 1833, 1992
Fiedler, Leslie 1028
Fielding, Henry 1405
Fielding, Jerry 408
Fielding, Raymond 35, 633
Fields, Al 1807
Fields, Dorothy 1798
Fields, Gracie 1439, 1833, 1841
Fields, Verna 605, 1552
Fields, W. C. 555, 1385, 1390, 1410, 1443, 1449, 1487, 1749, 1755, 1770, 1800
Field, Betty 1002
Field, Connie 318
Field, Sally 1017
Field, Virginia 1446, 1447
Figueroa, Gabriel 1002

Finch, Jon 1355
Finch, Peter 1941
Fine, Morton 1314, 2084
Finkel, Abem 365
Fink, Harry Julian 576
Fink, Rita M. 576
Finney, Albert 1328, 2162
Fischbeck, Harry 1390
Fischer, Ruth 1180
Fischer, Terence 117
Fisher, Jim 1503
Fisher, Terence 388, 396
Fish, Hamilton 1195
Fiske, Minnie Maddern 1504, 1618
Fitzgerald, Barry 1174
Fitzgerald, F. and David O. Selznick 1489
Fitzgerald, F. and Donald Ogden Stewart 1278, 1280
Fitzgerald, F. and GONE WITH THE WIND 1036, 1801
Fitzgerald, F. and Hollywood 1244
Fitzgerald, F. and Irving Thalberg 1217, 1492
Fitzgerald, F. and screenwriters 1101, 1103, 1105, 1107, 1108, 1109, 1116,
  1127, 1133, 1134, 1139, 1147
Fitzgerald, F. Scott 631, 1109, 1146, 1147, 1148, 1151, 1155, 1156, 1157, 1216,
  1217, 1226, 1227, 1250, 1251, 1256, 1265, 1266, 1273, 1278, 1293, 1321, 1670
Fitzgerald, Geraldine 1006, 1327
Fitzgerald, Zelda 631
Fitzhamon, Lewin 1567
Fitzmaurice, George 1837
Flaherty, Frances Hubbard 100
Flaherty, Robert 141, 166
Flaherty, Robert J. 237, 243, 244, 246, 292, 294, 295, 296, 306, 309, 1490,
  1547, 1549, 1564, 1592, 1594, 1610, 1671, 1674, 1681, 1682, 1703, 1756, 1869,
  1871, 1939
Flaiano, Ennio 1021, 1023, 1933, 2174, 2175
Flanagan, Hallie 1180
Flannery, William 1002
Flebbe, Beulah Dix 1239
Fleischer, Richard 382
Fleming, Rhonda 1487
Fleming, Victor 117, 812, 854, 994, 1080, 1401, 1406, 1407, 1550, 1801
Fletcher, Louise 1164, 1324
Fletcher, Tex 433
Flint, Derek 422
Flint, Motley 1494
Flipper (dolphin star) 1446
Flitterman, Sandy 483
Florey, Robert 1771
Flowers, Bess 1446
Flynn, Errol 350, 423, 989, 1160, 1177, 1262, 1288, 1323, 1443, 1448, 1451,
  1494, 1498, 1771
Focillon, Henri 194
Foghorn (See Winslow, George) 993
Fonda, Henry 577, 803, 810, 1021, 1240, 1252, 1254, 1264, 1326, 1449, 1674,
  1683, 1771, 1920, 1976, 2089
Fonda, Jane 376, 508, 551, 552, 790, 799, 1202, 1235, 1265, 1318, 1322, 1436,
  1442, 1452, 1771, 2050, 2089, 2194, 2206
Fonda, Peter 1771, 2051, 2081
Fontaine, Joan 1251, 1288, 1452, 1486, 1487, 1846, 1847, 1852, 1853, 1914, 1983

Fontanne, Lynn 1176, 1782
Fonteyn, Margot 1356
Foote, Horton 1039, 1210, 1325, 2036
Foran, Dick 433
Forbert, Leo 847
Forbes, Bryan 374, 1552
Ford and heroes 809
Forde, Walter 1833
Ford, Aleksander 2012, 2013
Ford, Francis 381
Ford, Glenn 575, 810, 1000, 1284, 1707
Ford, Henry 1675
Ford, John 175, 191, 193, 194, 227, 283, 295, 477, 499, 1169, 1547, 1548, 1549,
  1551, 1673, 1674, 1682, 1683, 1684, 1685, 1686, 1704, 1747, 1750, 1756, 1802,
  1911, 1924, 1952, 1960, 1976, 2022, 2027, 2075, 2076
Ford, J. and Akira Kurosawa 1899
Ford, J. and Alfred Hitchcock 1847
Ford, J. and Carl Laemmle 1475
Ford, J. and Darryl F. Zanuck 1500, 1503
Ford, J. and David O. Selznick 1488
Ford, J. and Elia Kazan 1257, 1260
Ford, J. and Eugene O'Neill 1341
Ford, J. and Hollywood 1237
Ford, J. and HOW GREEN WAS MY VALLEY 1007
Ford, J. and ideology 479
Ford, J. and images of the South 912
Ford, J. and John Wayne 147
Ford, J. and Nunnally Johnson 1256
Ford, J. and political filmmaking 577
Ford, J. and Robert Parrish 1275
Ford, J. and Samuel Goldwyn 1472
Ford, J. and screenwriters 1204, 1208, 1220, 1254
Ford, J. and stereotypes of African-Americans 854
Ford, J. and teenage films 982
Ford, J. and the family in film 980, 981
Ford, J. and THE GRAPES OF WRATH 1326, 1351
Ford, J. and the Hollywood image 1160
Ford, J. and THE INFORMER 1019
Ford, J. and THE LONG VOYAGE HOME 1351
Ford, J. and UP TIGHT 916, 941
Ford, J. and war films 350, 369
Ford, J. and westerns 424, 425, 427, 434
Foreman, Carl 85, 220, 368, 375, 376, 944, 952, 987, 1019, 1028, 1035, 1036,
  1093, 1100, 1154, 1171, 1189, 1191, 1948
Foreman, Deborah 998
Forester, C. S. 1101
Forman, Lady Helen 242
Forman, Milos 562, 1175, 1324, 2164
Formby, George 1833, 1841
Forrest, Frederick 998
Forsdale, Louis 35
Forster, Margaret 1006
Forsyte, Robert 139
Fortas, Abe 1226
Fort, Garrett 1805
Fosse, Bob 407, 1165, 1551
Foster, Jodie 970, 971
Foster, Norman 1355
Foster, Susanna 1445

Foster, William 863, 920, 943, 947, 948
Foucault, Michel 492, 496
Fowler, Gene 226
Fowler, Hugh S. 365
Fox, Donald 1312
Fox, James 374, 2160, 2161
Fox, Richard 959
Fox, William 244, 272, 622, 624, 820, 1054, 1389, 1463, 1464, 1466, 1468, 1470, 1471, 1621, 1622, 1670, 1745
Fraga, Jorge 299
Frampton, Hollis 1754, 1956
Francisi, Pietro 382
Francis, Freddie 1010
Francis, Kay 1804
Francois, Camille 1827
Franco, Francisco 236, 267, 319, 1003
Franju, Georges 1870, 1993, 2006, 2098, 2119, 2122, 2128
Franju, Jacques 2006
Frankenheimer, John 1351, 1550, 2036, 2051, 2052, 2065, 2076, 2077, 2078
Frankenstein 391, 399, 1240
Franklin, Sidney 1320, 1385
Frank, Harriet 1212
Frank, Robert 2039
Frazee, Jane 1446
Freddi, Luigi 1875, 1879
Frederick the Great 228
Frederick, Pauline 1444
Freedman, John 1837, 1855
Freedman, Ronald 2037
Freed, Arthur 83, 404, 1173, 1184, 1295, 1801, 1945, 1980
Freeman, Al, Jr. 894, 922, 1349
Freeman, David 1844, 1854
Freeman, Mona 1439
Freeman, Morgan 903
Freericks, Bernard 1240
Fregoli, Leopoldo 1588, 1603
Freire, Dido 1820
Fremont, Marian 1390
Frend, Charles 371, 1934, 1937
Fresnay, Pierre 1826, 1992
Freud, Sigmund 133, 184, 188, 272, 448, 452, 453, 463, 483, 492, 531, 532, 580, 590, 599, 601, 603, 604, 714, 816, 1190, 1311, 1353, 1380, 1556, 1631, 1660, 1709, 1719
Freuler, John R. 1622
Freund, Karl 1320, 1632, 1633, 1640, 1642, 1802
Frey, Leonard 850
Friedhofer, Hugo 83, 375, 408
Friedkin, David 1314, 2084
Friedkin, William 1140, 1319, 2195, 2200
Friedman, Lester D. 1024
Friend, Arthur S. 1463, 1477
Friese-Greene, William 1567, 1585, 1586, 1591, 1606, 1610, 1612
Frijda, Nelly 526
Froeschel, George 370, 378, 522
Frohman, Daniel 1504
Froment, Raymont 2137
Frueler, John R. 1463
Frye, Dwight 396

Frye, Northrop   184, 188
Fuchs, Daniel   1154, 1314
Fuchs, Leo   829
Fuji, Yahiro   2031
Fuji, Yozo   1901
Fulchignoni, Enrico   1881
Fuller, Leland   1326
Fuller, Mary   1455
Fuller, Samuel   85, 261, 289, 386, 489, 1716, 1758, 1960, 1961, 1976, 1977, 2042, 2078
Funicello, Annette   1241, 1443
Furse, Margaret   1347
Furse, Roger K.   1353
Furthman, Hecht   1146
Furthman, Jules   798, 1147, 1151, 1214, 1323, 1330, 1706, 1806
Fusco, Giovanni   1881, 2152

G

Gabaldon, Guy   339
Gabin, Jean   1814, 1825, 1826, 2129
Gable, Clark   62, 121, 346, 370, 409, 623, 735, 805, 809, 812, 958, 1202, 1242, 1244, 1330, 1395, 1435, 1436, 1442, 1443, 1448, 1449, 1472, 1480, 1481, 1484, 1487, 1488, 1501, 1772, 1799, 1801, 1806, 2194
Gabrielle, Sidonie   147, 508
Galbraith, John Kenneth   198
Galeen, Henrik   1632
Galey, Louis-Emile   1906
Galiano, Carlos   299
Galileo   1981
Gallico, Paul   1101
Gallone, Carmine   1874, 1878
Gallup, George   733, 735
Gaman, Tom   1002
Gammon, Frank R.   702, 766
Gance, Abel   1571, 1592, 1709, 1712, 1713, 1714, 1717, 1722, 1725, 1726, 1730, 1999
Ganda, Oumarou   2121
Gang, Martin   1186, 1190
Gans, Herbert G.   778
Ganz, Bruno   2142
Gan, Aleksei   1664
Garbo, Greta   502, 503, 508, 515, 555, 631, 971, 1012, 1176, 1244, 1380, 1472, 1479, 1480, 1481, 1487, 1524, 1529, 1625, 1630, 1631, 1634, 1643, 1674, 1675, 1686, 1781, 1802, 1803
Garbo, G. and the star system   1438, 1440, 1441, 1443, 1444, 1447, 1448, 1449, 1450, 1452, 1453
Garcia, Allan   1429, 1432
Garci, Jose Luis   235
Garden, Mary   1472
Gardiner, Reginald   1431, 1445
Gardin, Vladimir   1662
Gardner, Ava   1244, 1248, 1290, 1323
Gardner, Herb   1022
Gardner, Robert   295
Garfield, John   346, 369, 882, 1087, 1093, 1096, 1136, 1151, 1188, 1191, 1259, 1442, 1497, 1949, 1985
Gargan, William   1446

Garland, Judy   377, 401, 600, 970, 991, 992, 993, 1138, 1241, 1242, 1243, 1244,
    1271, 1295, 1380, 1395, 1396, 1443, 1478, 1485, 1750, 1773, 1774, 1801, 1952
Garmes, Lee   1806, 2042
Garner, Don   1976
Garner, James   374, 2036
Garner, Peggy Ann   990, 991, 992, 1445
Garnett, Tay   1314
Garnier, Charles   396
Garrett, Betty   402
Garrett, Oliver H. P.   1064, 1071
Garrick, David   1338
Garson, Greer   346, 378, 522, 575, 1327, 1328, 1354
Gaudio, Tony   1494
Gaumont, Leon   520, 1590
Gavin, John   1970
Gaye, Howard   1388
Gaynor, Janet   502, 1295, 1445, 1452, 1471, 1702, 1706
Geer, Will   1093, 1181
Gegauff, Paul   2100, 2151
Gehr, Ernie   1956
Geissler, Harry   611
Gelber, Jack   1348
Gellhorn, Martha   1229
Genet, Jean   1311
Genina, Augusto   1874, 1878
George, Chief Dan   1006, 1320
George, Gladys   1446
George, Lloyd   211, 212, 213
Gerard, James W.   259, 297, 1494
Gerbner, George   545
Gere, Richard   62
Gerima, Haile   949
Germi, Pietro   1874
Gershwin, George   405, 831, 1176, 1983
Gershwin, Ira   1087
Gerson, Barry   1956
Gerstad, Harry   1019
Gersten, Berta   829
Gervasi, Luigi   1356
Gessner, Robert   88
Getchell, Robert   1011
Getino, Octavio   918
Getty, J. Paul   1426
Gheradi, Piero   2175
Giachetti, Fosco   1874
Giannini, Attilio Henry   618, 703, 704
Gibbons, Cedric   1001, 1010, 1080, 1165, 1354, 1801, 1983
Gibney, Sheridan   1800, 1804
Gibson, Althea   922
Gibson, Helen   1455
Gibson, Hoot   193, 429, 431
Gidding, Nelson   1323
Gielgud, John   1353, 1354, 1449, 1842
Gifford, Frances   498
Gilbert, Billy   1431, 1446
Gilbert, John   367, 1440, 1444, 1448, 1454, 1474, 1479, 1481, 1502, 1686, 1696,
    1700, 1803
Gilbert, Lewis   2160

Gilbert, Polly 1445
Gilbert, Roland 1449
Giler, David 1150
Gilford, Jack 1096, 1188
Gilks, Alfred 1983
Gillespie, A. Arnold 370, 378, 1240, 1801
Gilles, Genevieve 1502
Gillette, William 381
Gillett, John 1939
Gilliatt, Penelope 148, 149, 1147
Gill, David 1416
Gilpin, Charles 927, 948
Giono, Jean 1313
Giovannetti, Eugenio 1873
Giraudoux, Jean 1905, 1908, 2097
Gish, Dorothy 1375, 1384, 1385, 1388, 1389, 1390, 1578, 1700
Gish, Lillian 502, 503, 631, 970, 992, 1375, 1382, 1384, 1387, 1388, 1389, 1390, 1391, 1395, 1396, 1438, 1441, 1443, 1444, 1452, 1479, 1488, 1558, 1578, 1674, 1700, 1706
Glasmon, Kubeck 1494, 1807
Gleason, Jackie 1014
Glenn, Jack 302
Glenn, Pierre-William 998
Globus, Yoram 535
Glover, Danny 903, 904
Glyn, Elinor 631, 1061
Godard, Jean-Luc 53, 140, 466, 497, 562, 583, 1163, 1547, 1553, 1572, 1715, 1969, 2006, 2032, 2034, 2096, 2109, 2117, 2118, 2122, 2129, 2130, 2133, 2134, 2151, 2170
Godard, J. and Al-Fateh 2111
Godard, J. and Alfred Hitchcock 2129
Godard, J. and Andre Malraux 2129
Godard, J. and Bertolt Brecht 2124
Godard, J. and Brigitte Bardot 2131
Godard, J. and CAHIERS DU CINEMA 1997, 2002, 2124, 2126
Godard, J. and Carl Th. Dreyer 2131
Godard, J. and Charles-Pierre Baudelaire 2129
Godard, J. and CITIZEN KANE 2151
Godard, J. and Claude Chabrol 2098, 2099
Godard, J. and dialectics 2124
Godard, J. and Dziga Vertov 2111
Godard, J. and Edgar Allan Poe 2129
Godard, J. and Ernst Lubitsch 2131
Godard, J. and film criticism 141, 144
Godard, J. and film theory 129, 163
Godard, J. and Francois Truffaut 2129, 2149
Godard, J. and Francois Villon 2129
Godard, J. and Fritz Lang 2110, 2131
Godard, J. and George Wilhelm Friedrich Hegel 2134
Godard, J. and Henri Langlois 2111
Godard, J. and Hollywood genres 2095, 2129
Godard, J. and Howard Hawks 2131
Godard, J. and Jean Cocteau 2129
Godard, J. and Jean-Nicholas-Arthur Rimbaud 2129
Godard, J. and Jean-Paul Sartre 2129
Godard, J. and Jeanne Moreau 2131
Godard, J. and John Huston 2131
Godard, J. and LA NOUVELLE VAGUE 2108, 2126
Godard, J. and Luchino Visconti 2129

Godard, J. and Maoism 2111
Godard, J. and musicals 2129
Godard, J. and Raoul Coutard 2120
Godard, J. and Roberto Rossellini 2129, 2131
Godard, J. and Samuel Fuller 2131
Godard, J. and Sergei M. Eisenstein 2111
Godard, J. and the Algerian war 2134
Godard, J. and the Black Panther party 2111
Godard, J. and the CINEMATEQUE FRANCAISE 1992
Godard, J. and the Dziga Vertov Group 2111
Godard, J. and the events of May 1968 2111
Godard, J. and the narrative film 113
Godard, J. and the Vietnam War 2111
Godard, J. and the "new cinema" 2121
Godard, J. and westerns 2129
Godard, J. and William Shakespeare 2112
Goddard, Paulette 1418, 1423, 1424, 1431, 1432, 1433, 1444
Godfrey, Peter 1496
Godowsky, Dagmar 1444, 1468
Godsol, Frank Joseph 1473
Godzilla 390
Goebbels, Josef Paul 202, 206, 207, 219, 226, 227, 228, 234, 235, 236, 238,
    239, 240, 250, 251, 255, 256, 257, 258, 282, 292, 296, 352, 1636, 1829, 1904,
    1907, 1908
Goetz, Augustus 1006
Goetz, Edith 1489
Goetz, Ruth 1006
Goetz, William 1480, 1489, 1500, 1501, 1502
Golan, Menaham 535
Goldbergs, The 833
Goldberg, Bert 878, 881, 935, 937, 947, 948
Goldberg, Jack 878, 881, 935, 937, 947, 948
Goldberg, Jakub 2180
Goldberg, Ralph D. 639, 771
Goldberg, Whoopi 903, 904
Golden, Sydney M. (Goldin, Sidney M.) 845, 846, 847, 848
Goldin, Sidney M. (Golden, Sydney M.) 845, 846, 847, 848
Goldman, Bo 1324
Goldman, Marvin 753
Goldman, Philippe 2149
Goldman, William 1028, 2078
Goldsmith, Jerry 83, 408
Goldstein, Robert 223, 262, 343
Goldwyn, Samuel 776, 820, 1054, 1061, 1129, 1151, 1157, 1192, 1225, 1228,
    1229, 1236, 1255, 1273, 1369, 1393, 1395, 1396, 1411, 1435, 1466, 1468, 1471,
    1473, 1474, 1477, 1478, 1479, 1484, 1489, 1491, 1498, 1503, 1621, 1676, 1746,
    1973
Goldwyn, S. and Elia Kazan 1259
Goldwyn, S. and Eminent Authors 1062
Goldwyn, S. and independent filmaking 639
Goldwyn, S. and John Huston 1915
Goldwyn, S. and the development of the film industry 1463, 1464, 1466
Goldwyn, S. and William Wyler 1808
Gold, Ernest 850
Golitzen, Alexander 1325
Golovnya, Anatoli N. 1646
Gomez, Sara 466
Goodis, David 1101

Goodman, Hannibal 1585, 1595
Goodrich, Frances 849, 1151, 1191, 1192, 1806
Goosson, Stephen 1328, 1349, 1799
Gorcey, Leo 987, 1445, 1808
Gordon, Barry 1022
Gordon, Leon 1314
Gordon, Michael 1097
Gordon, Ruth 1145, 1975
Gordon, Vera 828
Gorelik, Mordecai 1339
Goring, Marius 1015
Gorin, Jean-Pierre 2111
Gorris, Marleen 501, 526
Gosha, Hideo 1743
Goshjal, Sumiron 1004
Gosho, Heinosuke 1740, 1743, 1887, 1888, 1896, 2017, 2018
Goskind, Shaul 848
Gossett, Lou, Jr. 903, 904, 905
Gottheim, Larry 1956
Gottschalk, Joachim 238
Goulding, Edmund 797, 800, 1496, 1802
Gould, Elliot 379, 2194
Goya, Chantal 2129
Grable, Betty 498, 692, 769, 990, 1254, 1443, 1447, 1471, 1529
Grahame, Gloria 1289, 1439
Graham, Sheila 1032, 1127, 1130, 1131, 1151, 1217
Granger, Bertram 1322
Granger, Dorothy 1446
Granger, Farley 1439, 1472
Granger, Stewart 423, 1439, 1941
Grant, Bud 726
Grant, Cary 369, 809, 1236, 1244, 1443, 1479, 1774, 1803, 1806, 1807, 1808, 2079, 2194
Grant, John Edward 1154
Grant, Lee 604
Granville, Bonita (Wrather) 991, 992, 1439
Grauman, Sid 1506
Graumont, Leon 1599
Grau, Albin 1632
Graves, Jesse 942
Graves, Ralph 1413, 1450
Grayson, Kathryn 1439
Gray, Billy 1445
Gray, Coleen 1440
Greaves, William 901, 902, 937
Greco, Juliette 1502
Greene, Abel 1497
Greene, Danford B. 379
Greene, Felix 2163
Greene, Graham 139, 358, 1033, 1156, 1218, 1219, 1300, 1301, 1329, 1753
Greene, Richard 1440
Greenfield, Josh 1006
Greenstreet, Sydney 372, 373, 397, 1447
Green, Adolph 83, 1145, 1295
Green, Alfred E. 1248, 1293
Green, Eddie 947
Green, F. L. 1021, 1943
Green, Howard J. 1804
Green, John 1240, 1983, 2089

Green, Joseph (Greenberg) 846, 848
Green, Sam 2069
Green, Walon 2087
Gregory XIII, Pope 210
Gregory XV, Pope 210
Gregory, Grace 1350
Gregor, Nora 1827
Gremillon, Jean 1904, 1908, 1992, 2001
Grenzbach, John 368
Greven, Alfred 1907
Grey, Lita 1421, 1423, 1424, 1428, 1429, 1431
Grey, Virginia 1440, 1446
Grierson, John 202, 206, 207, 214, 215, 236, 237, 241, 243, 244, 245, 246, 248,
    249, 255, 542, 1566, 1568, 1569, 1840, 1869, 1871, 1934
Grierson, J. and documentaries 294, 295, 303, 305, 306, 308, 309, 315, 318
Grierson, J. and film aesthetics 100
Grierson, J. and film theory 127, 165
Grierson, J. and propaganda 214
Grierson, J. and Robert J. Flaherty 1682, 1704
Grierson, J. and screen education 40
Grierson, J. and studio filmmaking 1753
Grierson, J. and war films 280, 292, 295, 302, 307, 308, 316
Grier, Pam 897
Griffith and Italian epics 1559
Griffith, Charles 2075
Griffith, Corrine 503, 1445
Griffith, David Wark 188, 209, 224, 297, 703, 912, 915, 1240, 1242, 1360, 1395,
    1396, 1397, 1403, 1406, 1413, 1488, 1509, 1547, 1549, 1550, 1671, 1674, 1701,
    1718, 1756
Griffith, D. and Adolph Zukor 1504
Griffith, D. and AMERICA 1578
Griffith, D. and Andy Warhol 2040
Griffith, D. and Billy Bitzer 1371, 1680
Griffith, D. and BROKEN BLOSSOMS 1509
Griffith, D. and Budd Schulberg 1277
Griffith, D. and Charlie Chaplin 1423
Griffith, D. and Douglas Fairbanks, Sr. 1399, 1404, 1405, 1409
Griffith, D. and dream theory 583
Griffith, D. and early film history 1338, 1360, 1383, 1385, 1386, 1410, 1593,
    1594, 1595, 1609, 1610, 1617, 1618, 1621, 1824
Griffith, D. and Elia Kazan 1257
Griffith, D. and film criticism 140, 162
Griffith, D. and filmmaking in New Jersey 1595
Griffith, D. and F. Scott Fitzgerald 1111
Griffith, D. and Gloria Swanson 1454
Griffith, D. and Henry N. Marvin 1378
Griffith, D. and his biographers 1381
Griffith, D. and Irving Thalberg 1491
Griffith, D. and Italian epics 1607
Griffith, D. and Karl Brown 1373
Griffith, D. and Lillian Gish 1375, 1377, 1378
Griffith, D. and Mabel Normand 1411
Griffith, D. and Mack Sennett 1411
Griffith, D. and Mary Pickford 1393, 1397
Griffith, D. and Miriam C. Cooper 1373
Griffith, D. and narrative films 122
Griffith, D. and President Woodrow Wilson 1382
Griffith, D. and racism 156, 863, 864, 933, 940, 1366

Griffith, D. and Rene Clair 1724, 1725
Griffith, D. and Scandanavian films 1626
Griffith, D. and screen adaptations 1311, 1331, 1374
Griffith, D. and screenwriters 1061
Griffith, D. and Sergei M. Eisenstein 1656, 1657
Griffith, D. and Shakespeare 1561
Griffith, D. and the American Dream 1054
Griffith, D. and the art of the film 572, 1172
Griffith, D. and the AVANT-GARDE 1709, 1712
Griffith, D. and the development of the film industry 1463, 1464
Griffith, D. and the family in film 980
Griffith, D. and the star system 1404, 1438
Griffith, D. and the suspense film 393
Griffith, D. and the Triangle Film Corporation 1412
Griffith, D. and United Artists 1369, 1370, 1417, 1669
Griffith, Hugh 1328
Griffith, Jacob Wark 1423
Griffith, Richard 140
Griggs, Loyal 1009
Grilling, John 396
Grimes, Stephen 851
Groesse, Paul 1010
Grot, Anton 1015, 1494
Groulx, Gilles 2123
Groves, George R. 2086
Gruault, Jean 2155
Gruber, Frank 85
Grumberg, Jean-Claude 2143
Guarini, Alfredo 1880
Guazzoni, Enrico 1573, 1607
Guerra, Ruy 2123
Guerra, Tonino 1012, 2172, 2173
Guffey, Burnett 193, 2088
Guffy, Burnett 368
Guichen, R. de 1828
Guinee, Jean (R. de Guichen) 1828
Guinness, Alec 107, 220, 374, 812, 1165, 1841, 1937, 1941, 1942
Guiol, Fred 1806
Guitry, Sacha 1313, 1907, 1908, 1992
Gunn, Moses 1351
Gupta, Pinaki Sen 1004
Guthrie, Arlo 2088
Guthrie, A. B., Jr. 1009, 1101
Guy-Blache, Alice 1551, 1606
Guzzetti, Alfred 982
Gwenn, Edmund 1327

H

Habermas, Jurgen 198
Hackett, Albert 849, 1151, 1191, 1192, 1203, 1806
Hackett, Buddy 2044
Hackett, Frances Goodrich 1203
Hackman, Gene 143, 2088, 2194
Haddock, William 1468
Hadley, Edwin J. 615, 1599
Haffenden, Elizabeth 1020
Hageman, Richard 1351

Hagen, Jean 1295, 1446, 1980
Hagen, Uta 1186
Haight, George 1228
Haik, Jacques 1906
Haim, Corey 997
Haines, William 1445
Hakim brothers 1906
Halas, John 78
Haley, Jack 1445, 1801
Hale, Alan 1497
Hale, Alan, Jr. 1440
Hale, Chester 1445
Hale, Creighton 1458
Hale, George C. 1600
Hale, Georgia 1430
Hale, John 1347
Hale, Monte 433
Haller, Ernest 812, 952, 1801
Hall, Conrad 80, 605, 2078
Hall, Huntz 987, 1808
Hall, John 1445
Hall, Peter 1343, 1355
Hall, Willis 994
Halop, Billy 987, 1445, 1808
Halsey, Forrest 1390
Hamilton, George 368
Hamilton, Guy 1934
Hamilton, Margaret 1801
Hamilton, Neil 1387, 1389, 1446
Hammerstein, Elaine 1124, 1444
Hammerstein, Oscar 1253
Hammer, Robert 1937
Hammer, Roger 1942
Hammett, Dashiell 373, 381, 1073, 1079, 1189, 1221, 1222, 1223, 1225, 1227, 1228, 1229, 1251, 1273, 1750, 1957
Hammett, Josephine 1221, 1223
Hammett, Lillian 1225
Hammett, Mary Jane 1221
Hanayaki, Yoshiaki 2031
Handel, Leo A. 742
Hanhardt, John G. 2040
Hani, Susumu 466, 1000, 2025
Hanke, Karl 239
Hanoun, Marcel 2119
Hansberry, Lorraine 1009, 1348
Hansen, E. H. 366, 1326
Hansen, Juanita 1444
Har 1004
Harburg, E. Y. 1801
Hardwicke, Cedric 1934
Hardy, Andy 971, 974, 975
Hardy, Forsyth 1753
Hardy, Oliver 621, 627, 1412, 1419, 1578, 1677, 1690, 1691, 1695, 1701, 1755
Harlan, Russell 1001, 1325
Harlan, Veit 218, 238, 240
Harlow, Jean 226, 502, 1117, 1235, 1244, 1247, 1290, 1395, 1430, 1440, 1443, 1447, 1448, 1449, 1452, 1468, 1480, 1481, 1484, 1701, 1772, 1774
Harnett, Vincent 1186, 1188

Harper, Jessica 786
Harriet, Frank, Jr. 1349
Harrison, Joan 1853, 1854
Harrison, Rex 1243, 1272, 1449, 1842, 1934
Harrison, Tom 242
Harris, Barbara 1022, 2060
Harris, Harry 1600
Harris, James B. 2055
Harris, John 1600
Harris, Julie 997, 1005, 1323, 1325
Harris, Mildred 1417, 1421
Harris, Richard 1265, 2160
Harris, Teresa 877
Harron, Robert 1372, 1376, 1385, 1387, 1388, 1389, 1390
Harryhausen, Ray 411, 415
Hartnoll, Gillian 1842
Hart, Moss 1018, 1296, 1485
Hart, William S. 429, 431, 434, 1240, 1396, 1397, 1405, 1412, 1434, 1440, 1449, 1504, 1579, 1687, 1704, 1709, 1737
Harvey, Anthony 1349
Harvey, Laurence 1009, 1016, 1329, 2077
Hashimoto, Shinobu 2030
Haskell, Molly 1452
Haskin, Byron 1548
Hasso, Signe 1440, 1975
Hass, Charles 998
Hathaway, Henry 366, 373, 383, 1204, 1500, 1502, 1952
Hatton, Rondo 396
Hauben, Lawrence 1324
Haver, June 1445
Havez, Jean 1705
Havlick, Gene 1328, 1799
Havoc, June 1087, 1188
Hawks, Howard 186, 187, 349, 350, 360, 382, 424, 425, 434, 508, 1207, 1210, 1211, 1215, 1231, 1253, 1496, 1542, 1547, 1551, 1552, 1553, 1702, 1708, 1747, 1749, 1752, 1756, 1758, 1774, 1777, 1803, 1952, 1977, 1985, 1999
Hawks, H. and Al Capone 1468
Hawks, H. and Alfred Hitchcock 1776, 1847
Hawks, H. and anti-Semitism 832
Hawks, H. and AUTEUR criticism 2096, 2124
Hawks, H. and Carl Gustav Jung 1775
Hawks, H. and Cary Grant 1776
Hawks, H. and Eric Rohmer 2102
Hawks, H. and Ernst Lubitsch 1776
Hawks, H. and film criticism 144
Hawks, H. and Frank Capra 1776
Hawks, H. and Humphrey Bogart 1776
Hawks, H. and John Ford 1776
Hawks, H. and John Wayne 147, 1776
Hawks, H. and MISE EN SCENE 1998
Hawks, H. and screenwriters 1147
Hawks, H. and THE BIG SLEEP 798
Hawks, H. and the family in film 980
Hawks, H. and William Faulkner 1149, 1152, 1207, 1210, 1214, 1250, 1323
Hawks, William 1207
Hawn, Goldie 1037, 2194
Hayakawa, Sessue 374, 1444, 1737
Hayasaka, Fumio 2030
Haycox, Ernest 1101

Hayden, Richard 1439
Hayden, Russell 1446
Hayden, Sterling 1087, 1091, 1092, 1097, 1179, 1180, 1181, 1190, 1191, 1439, 2083
Haydn, Franz Joseph 209
Hayer, Nicolas 2009
Hayes, Alfred 1247
Hayes, Gabby 430, 431, 1447
Hayes, John Michael 1154, 1854, 1855, 1978
Haymes, Dick 1445
Haynes, Daniel 939
Haynes, Stanley 1860
Hays, William Harrison 225, 956, 966, 1082, 1673, 1948, 2037
Hayward, Leland 1125, 1241
Hayward, Louis 346, 1446, 1451
Hayward, Susan 1777
Hayworth, Rita 515, 575, 1137, 1290, 1443, 1447, 1707, 1790, 1914
Hay, Ian 1857
Hay, Willie 1833, 1841
Haze, Jonathan 2075
Head, Edith 610, 1015, 1240, 1531, 1777, 1981, 1988
Hearst, William Randolph 1152, 1380, 1394, 1396, 1450, 1458, 1481, 1489, 1696, 1751, 1790
Heath, Stephen 167
Hecht, Ben 85, 606, 812, 1036, 1063, 1064, 1066, 1142, 1145, 1146, 1147, 1151, 1154, 1224, 1251, 1265, 1267, 1327, 1472, 1708, 1801, 1806, 1847, 1848, 1853
Heckerling, Amy 604
Heckroth, Hein 1016
Hedren, Tippi 1852, 1855
Heerman, Victor 1383
Heffner, Richard D. 959
Heflin, Van 1009, 1241, 1317, 1484
Hefner, Hugh 1355
Hegel, George Wilhelm Friedrich 2134
Heggen, Tom 1278
Heidegger, Martin 252
Heinreid, Paul 800
Heisenberg, Werner 1709
Heller, Lukas 2043, 2071
Hellinger, Mark 1466, 1976
Hellman, Lillian 523, 836, 990, 1067, 1073, 1083, 1095, 1101, 1151, 1179, 1181, 1192, 1206, 1217, 1221, 1223, 1225, 1226, 1227, 1228, 1229, 1230, 1259, 1260, 1289, 1322, 1348, 1472, 1474, 1750, 1796, 1808, 1949
Helmore, Tom 1852
Helm, Matt 422, 896
Helpern, David, Jr. 1293, 1985
Helpmann, Robert 1016, 1943
Heman, Roger 366
Hemingway, Ernest 179, 219, 279, 314, 319, 1039, 1101, 1103, 1151, 1153, 1156, 1214, 1217, 1227, 1231, 1232, 1250, 1272, 1300, 1311, 2051
Hemingway, Mariel 530, 971
Hemmings, David 2173
Henabery, Joseph 1387, 1388, 1406
Henderson, Randell 1240, 1413
Henderson, Robert M. 1382
Hendrix, Wanda 1439
Henie, Sonja 1444, 1449, 1471
Henreid, Paul 1087, 1440

Henrey, Bobby 1329
Henrikson, Anders 1628
Henry, Buck 1150, 2036, 2047, 2085, 2086
Henry, Justin 110, 1007
Henson, Jim 411
Hepburn, Audrey 508, 523, 524, 1243, 1855, 1937, 1951, 1952, 1988
Hepburn, Katharine 409, 502, 1164, 1192, 1243, 1341, 1346, 1350, 1352, 1443, 1448, 1449, 1452, 1484, 1487, 1777, 1778, 1803, 1952, 1967, 1975, 1979
Heppler, Fritz 227
Hepworth, Cecil 1549, 1567, 1588, 1607, 1611, 1612, 1617
Herald, Heinz 1015
Herbert, Joyce 1328
Herczeg, Geza 1015
Herlie, Eileen 1353
Herlihy, James Leo 1001
Herlth, Robert 1632, 1641, 1642
Hernandez, Juano 922, 1209, 1321
Herndon, Vanable 2088
Herold, Don 139
Heron, Julia 1472, 1473
Herrand, Marcel 1910
Herring, Robert 139
Herrmann the Great 1477
Herrmann, Bernard 83, 402, 403, 408, 1792, 1807, 1835, 1854, 2054
Herschel, John 1584
Hersholt, Jean 1803
Hertz, Carl 1588
Herzog, Werner 311, 2165, 2166
Hessling, Catherine 1820, 1822
Heston, Charlton 269, 383, 805, 1288, 1452, 1680, 2052, 2063, 2069, 2090
Heuschling, Andree (Catherine Hessling) 1820
Hewett, Christopher 2073
Heyle, Henry Renno 1585
Heyward, DuBose 875
Hickman, Darryl 990, 992, 993, 1446
Hickman, Howard 1623
Hickok, Wild Bill 193
Hidari, Sachiko 2025
Hilberg, Raul 291
Hildyard, David 850
Hildyard, Jack 374
Hilferding, Rudolph 702
Hiller, Wendy 1010, 1357, 1863
Hill, George Roy 1254, 1548, 1758, 2036, 2052, 2053, 2067, 2078
Hill, Walter 973, 2019
Hilton, James 378, 522, 1802
Himmler, Heinrich 234
Hines, Gregory 903, 904, 1530
Hines, Johnny 1444
Hinkel, Hans 250
Hirsch, Judd 1008
Hirsch, Paul 813
Hitchcock, Alfred 186, 187, 261, 1542, 1547, 1549, 1552, 1565, 1567, 1570, 1716, 1756, 1758, 1834, 1841, 1843, 1844, 1855, 1863, 1864, 1913, 1952, 2034, 2053, 2054, 2079, 2080, 2096, 2170
Hitchcock, A. and autobiographical filmmaking 1550, 1553
Hitchcock, A. and Ben Hecht 1853
Hitchcock, A. and Bernard Herrmann 402
Hitchcock, A. and British films 1833, 1834

Hitchcock, A. and CAHIERS DU CINEMA 1845, 1850
Hitchcock, A. and Charles Dickens 1837
Hitchcock, A. and Claude Chabrol 1845, 2128
Hitchcock, A. and Darryl F. Zanuck 1847
Hitchcock, A. and David O. Selznick 1486, 1488, 1844, 1845, 1846, 1847, 1848, 1849, 1851, 1853, 1978
Hitchcock, A. and detective fiction 1837
Hitchcock, A. and dramas 1857
Hitchcock, A. and Eric Rohmer 1845, 2102, 2141
Hitchcock, A. and Expressionism 1858
Hitchcock, A. and feminist film theory 492, 1849
Hitchcock, A. and film audiences 1978
Hitchcock, A. and film criticism 144
Hitchcock, A. and FILM NOIR 1844
Hitchcock, A. and Francois Truffaut 1845, 1856
Hitchcock, A. and Frank Capra 1847
Hitchcock, A. and Gainsborough Pictures 1834
Hitchcock, A. and Grace Kelly 1854
Hitchcock, A. and Hieronymus Bosch 1855
Hitchcock, A. and his collaborators 1852
Hitchcock, A. and his directorial debut 1837
Hitchcock, A. and his directorial style 107
Hitchcock, A. and Hollywood 1857
Hitchcock, A. and horror films 389
Hitchcock, A. and Howard Hawks 1847
Hitchcock, A. and Jean-Luc Godard 2129
Hitchcock, A. and John Ford 1847
Hitchcock, A. and Lew Wasserman 1854
Hitchcock, A. and Lewis Milestone 1847
Hitchcock, A. and Luis Bunuel 1721, 1838
Hitchcock, A. and Michael Balcon 1834, 1853
Hitchcock, A. and MISE EN SCENE 1998
Hitchcock, A. and montage 1836, 1838, 1845, 1851
Hitchcock, A. and MOVIE 1752
Hitchcock, A. and music 1857, 1858
Hitchcock, A. and Paramount Pictures 1848, 1854
Hitchcock, A. and Point of View 119
Hitchcock, A. and political activism in WWII 1851, 1852
Hitchcock, A. and psychoanalytic criticism 599
Hitchcock, A. and Raymond Bellour 511
Hitchcock, A. and Raymond Chandler 1854
Hitchcock, A. and RKO 1847
Hitchcock, A. and romantic comedies 1857
Hitchcock, A. and screenwriters 1254
Hitchcock, A. and Sergei M. Eisenstein 1845
Hitchcock, A. and slasher films 976
Hitchcock, A. and Soviet cinema 1858
Hitchcock, A. and studio filmmaking 1753
Hitchcock, A. and suspense 1836
Hitchcock, A. and television 1846
Hitchcock, A. and the American Film Institute 1854
Hitchcock, A. and the family in film 980
Hitchcock, A. and the FBI 1848, 1851
Hitchcock, A. and the Hollywood image 1160
Hitchcock, A. and the image of psychiatrists 606
Hitchcock, A. and the nature of evil 575
Hitchcock, A. and the Oscars 1846, 1848, 1854, 2054
Hitchcock, A. and the star system 1845

Hitchcock, A. and the Talkies   1753
Hitchcock, A. and THE THIRTY-NINE STEPS (1935)   373
Hitchcock, A. and the "double" motif   1920
Hitchcock, A. and Thomas Hobbes   1835
Hitchcock, A. and Three-D   1978
Hitchcock, A. and thrillers   1857
Hitchcock, A. and Universal-International   1849, 1854
Hitchcock, A. and voyeurism   592, 1978, 2081
Hitchcock, A. and Walter Wanger   1854
Hitchcock, A. and Warner Bros.   1844, 1848, 1854
Hitchcock, A. and World War II   353
Hitler, Adolf   203, 205, 206, 207, 219, 228, 234, 235, 238, 239, 240, 250, 258,
   264, 289, 291, 293, 302, 321, 358, 366, 1573, 1635, 1660, 1750, 1822, 1830,
   1880, 1948, 1971
Hively, George   1019
Hobbes, Thomas   2114
Hobson, Valarie   1439
Hodkinson, William Wadsworth   1464, 1466, 1467, 1503, 1504
Hoffe, Monckton   1921
Hoffman, Dustin   110, 554, 1007, 1151, 1320, 1538, 1544, 2054, 2063, 2085, 2086,
   2194, 2206
Holbrook, Hal   1322
Holden, William   374, 809, 1002, 1264, 1291, 1295, 1296, 1350, 1503, 1778, 1952,
   2087
Holder, Geoffrey   893
Hold, Jack   1444
Holliday, Billie   920, 938
Holliday, John "Doc"   1960
Holliday, Judy   1096, 1951, 1975
Holloway, Stanley   1934, 1937
Holloway, Sterling   1445
Holly, Buddy   1138
Holmes, Brown   1804
Holmes, Helen   1455, 1459
Holmes, Sherlock   380, 381, 608, 640
Holmes, William   365
Holm, Celeste   1018
Holm, Eleanor   1445
Holt, Seth   1752
Holt, Tim   600, 1022, 1327, 1445, 1976, 1979
Homer   565
Homolka, Oscar   1544
Honda, Ishiro   2019
Hood, Darla   1445
Hooks, Robert   923
Hoover, Herbert   1470, 1481
Hoover, J. Edgar   320, 384, 488
Hope-Jones, Robert   406
Hope, Bob   346, 739, 1094, 1160, 1174, 1452, 1757, 1954
Hopkinson, Peter   1870
Hopkins, Bo   429
Hopkins, George James   1352
Hopkins, Miriam   1804
Hopkins, Peggy Joyce   1417
Hopkins, Robert   1806
Hopper, Dennis   810, 2051, 2054, 2081
Hopper, Hedda   877, 1080, 1243
Hopper, Willian DeWolf   1243
Hopwood, Henry V.   1582

Horman, Charles 1020
Hornbeck, William 1015
Horner, Harry 1007, 1014, 2089
Horner, William George 1583
Horne, Lena 879, 880, 882, 920, 921, 929, 932, 944, 948, 950, 1093
Horning, William A. 1801
Horsley, David 1595
Horton, Edward Everett 1468
Hoskins, Allen Clayton (Farina) 866, 920
Houdini, Harry (Ehrich Weiss) 1235, 1444, 1588
Houseman, John 1237, 1263, 1354, 1751, 1789, 1983
Houston, George 433
Houston, Penelope 131, 516
Howard, Frances 1474
Howard, Leslie 809, 1329, 1357, 1778, 1833, 1834, 1841, 1858, 1863
Howard, Richard 2137
Howard, Ron 993
Howard, Sidney 812, 1036, 1065, 1176, 1474, 1801
Howard, Trevor 1010, 1502, 1934, 1941, 1943
Howe, James Wong 564, 995, 1240, 1439, 1552, 2042
Howlett, John 1001
Hrabal, Bohumil 994, 2165
Hubley, Faith 520
Hudson, Hugh 1174
Hudson, Rochelle 1445
Hudson, Rock 1970, 1986
Huelsenbeck, Richard 1716
Hugenberg, Alfred 1829
Huggins, Roy 1097
Hughes, Howard 958, 1099, 1137, 1244, 1290, 1697, 1912, 1919, 1949, 1967
Hughes, Mary Beth 1440
Hughes, Rupert 1061, 1073, 1080, 1088, 1192, 1248, 1472
Hulbert, Jack 1833
Hulburd, Merritt 1253, 1474
Hulce, Thomas 547
Hulette, Gladys 193
Hull, Henry 1215
Humberstone, H. Bruce 1758
Hunter, Ian McLellan 1988
Hunter, Kim 1188, 1346, 1352, 1487
Hunter, Ross 1986
Hunter, Tab 1440, 1498
Hunter, Tim 998
Hunt, Hugh 1354
Hunt, Hugh B. 1001
Hunt, Marsha 1087, 1445
Hurd, Gale Anne 681
Hurd, Hugh 2074
Hurley, Joseph 2054
Hurt, Mary Beth 1530
Hurt, William 1530
Hurwitz, Leo 1872
Hussey, Olivia 1356
Hussey, Ruth 1445, 1484
Huston, Anjelica 1916
Huston, Evelyn 1087

Huston, John 61, 203, 283, 322, 343, 365, 373, 386, 554, 965, 980, 1022, 1087, 1147, 1154, 1231, 1263, 1284, 1314, 1319, 1321, 1488, 1496, 1501, 1547, 1551, 1748, 1757, 1758, 1911, 1915, 1936, 1952, 1954, 1979
Huston, Reah Gore 1915
Huston, Walter 1022, 1386, 1915, 1916, 1979
Hutton, Betty 1440, 1921
Hutton, Brian 378
Hutton, Eleanor Post 1918
Hutton, Timothy 584, 1008
Huxley, Aldous 1065, 1103, 1106, 1147, 1148, 1150, 1151, 1157, 1327
Huyck, Willard 605, 993, 2195
Huygens, Christiaen 1580, 1581
Hyer, Martha 1439
Hyman, Bernie 1217

I

Ibbetson, Arthur 1347
Ichikawa, Kon 371, 1574, 1895, 1898, 2018, 2019, 2022, 2023, 2024, 2025, 2026, 2029
Ihnen, Willard 366
Ikeda, Tadao 1902
Imai, Tadashi 2016, 2017, 2018, 2025
Imamura, Shohei 1898
Imhoof, Markus 376
Inagaki, Hiroshi 1740, 1743, 2017, 2018
Ince, Thomas Harper 697, 700, 1350, 1381, 1384, 1405, 1412, 1463, 1464, 1491, 1577, 1578, 1622, 1623, 1687, 1709
Inda, Estela 1002
Inescort, Frieda 1445
Infontino, Joseph 756
Inge, William 1002, 1010, 1257, 1349
Ingram, Rex 375, 877, 881, 921, 931, 948, 952, 1119, 1446, 1480, 1545, 1687, 1707
Innis, Roy 855
Inslee, Charles 1387
Insull, Samuel 1267
Ionesco, Eugene 1034, 1155
Ireland, John 1012, 1976
Irving, Amy 1175
Irving, Henry 1331
Irwin, May 1480
Isherwood, Christopher 1032, 1065, 1102, 1151, 1294
Ishida, Tamizo 1743, 1887
Isola, Emile 1588
Isola, Vincent 1588
Itami, Mansaku 1887, 1888, 1896
Ito, Daisuke 1743, 1887, 2017, 2025
Ito, Takao 1896
Iturbi, Jose 1446
Ivan IV, Csar 1866
Ivan, Rosiland 1446
Ivens, Joris 177, 217, 292, 294, 295, 312, 313, 314, 319, 1714, 1869
Ives, Burl 1325, 1346, 1352
Ivey, Judith 1530
Ivory, James 548, 1323, 2167

J

Jackson, Peter 861, 925
Jacobi, Leo 849
Jacobs, Alexander 84, 2073
Jacobs, Lewis 127
Jacob, Max 1709
Jaenzon, Julius 1624, 1630
Jaffe, Sam 1799, 1806
Jagger, Dean 370
Jagger, Mick 2160
Jahraus, Donald 369, 370
Jakubowska, Wanda 2012
James, Henry 1324
Janco, Marcel 1716
Jandl, Ivan 1989
Janis, Elsie 991
Jannings, Emil 238, 584, 1579, 1632, 1633, 1634, 1640, 1642, 1675, 1697, 1830,
    1831
Janowitz, Hans 1632, 1643
Janssen, David 833, 1611
Janssen, Pierre Juels Cesar 292
Jansso, Miklos 2167
Jarman, Claude, Jr. 991, 1010, 1209, 1445
Jarrico, Paul 1099, 1181, 1192, 1195
Jarrott, Charles 1347
Jarvick, Laurence 291
Jarvis, Merrill 539, 763, 764
Jaubert, Maurice 998, 1828
Jeakins, Dorothy 851
Jean (dog star) 1446
Jeanson, Henri 1998
Jean, Gloria 992, 1445
Jefferson, Arthur Stanley (see Stan Laurel) 1675
Jefferson, Thomas 1204
Jeffers, Robinson 1108
Jefford, Barbara 1355
Jeffrey, R. E. 266
Jeffries, Herb (Herbert Jeffrey) 878, 948
Jenkins, Allen 1445
Jenkins, C. Francis 1582, 1586, 1590, 1593
Jenkins, Jackie "Butch" 992, 993, 1445
Jennings, Humphrey 216, 244, 249, 283, 295, 309, 315, 316, 317, 322, 323, 343,
    352, 1553, 1566, 1567, 1869
Jennings, Talbot 1320, 1330
Jergens, Adele 1446
Jerome, Victor Jeremy 1181, 1190, 1195, 1259
Jessel, George 828, 943, 1253
Jessner, Leopold 1714
Jewison, Norman 850, 905, 1550, 2036, 2082
Jhabvala, Ruth Prawer 1323, 1324
Jodelle 1313
Jodorowsky, Alexandro 392
Johann, Zita 1445
Johnson, Arthur 1387
Johnson, Ben 996, 998
Johnson, Celia 1934, 1943
Johnson, Clint 2092

Johnson, Dorothy M.   1101
Johnson, Dorris Bowdon   1252
Johnson, Dots   922
Johnson, George   627, 866, 947
Johnson, Jack   870, 920, 925
Johnson, Julian   1503
Johnson, J. Rosamond   875
Johnson, Kay   1329
Johnson, Lawrence   1188
Johnson, Lyndon B.   218
Johnson, Marjorie   1252
Johnson, Noble M.   627, 866, 870, 934, 947, 948
Johnson, Nora   1252, 1256
Johnson, Nunnally   366, 522, 1036, 1063, 1065, 1066, 1104, 1114, 1130, 1140, 1142, 1145, 1149, 1150, 1203, 1207, 1208, 1210, 1211, 1214, 1249, 1252, 1254, 1281, 1326, 1503, 1683, 2071
Johnson, Richard   1323
Johnson, Van   370, 1130, 1484
Johnston, Eric A.   1082, 1178, 1187, 1193, 1287, 1948, 2037
Johns, Arthur   812, 1801
Jolson, Al   346, 401, 805, 831, 872, 943, 1189, 1293, 1498, 1778
Jones, Allan   1446
Jones, Buck   429, 431, 1450
Jones, Everett L.   430
Jones, Fuzzy Q.   431
Jones, F. Richard   1413
Jones, James Earl   893, 897, 901, 903, 938, 953, 1005
Jones, Jennifer   502, 1254, 1317, 1440, 1486, 1487
Jones, LeRoi (Imamu Amiri Baraka)   159, 894, 1349
Jones, L. Q.   429
Jones, Marcia Mae   1445
Jones, Peter P.   863, 943
Jones, Quincey   605
Jones, Robert C.   376
Jones, Shirley   894
Joplin, Janis   1138
Jordan, Bobby   987, 1808
Jordan, Dorothy   1408
Jordan, Louis   882
Jory, Victor   1440
Josephson, Julien   1706
Joslyn, Allyn   1446
Jost, Jerry   1017
Jourdan, Louis   1487, 1983
Jouvet, Louis   1814
Jowett, Garth S.   35
Joyce, Adrian (Carole Eastman)   516
Joyce, Alice   1444
Joyce, Brenda   1439
Joyce, James   1156, 1211, 2138
Joy, Beatrice   1444
Julian, Rupert   1702
Jung, Carl   133
Jung, Carl Gustav   1775
Jurado, Katy   1440
Juran, Nathan   1007

K

Kadar, Jan 378, 2165
Kael, Pauline 132, 149, 150, 604, 1146, 1263, 1282, 1790
Kael, P. and film reviewing 121
Kaeriyama, Norimasa 1739, 1740
Kagawa, Kyoko 2031
Kahn, Felix E. 703
Kahn, Gordon 1091
Kahn, Gus 401
Kahn, Richard 947
Kahn, Sheldon 1324
Kalatozov, Mikail 1001
Kalmar, Bert 1805
Kamei, Fumio 2016
Kamenaka, Alexander 1714
Kaminska, Ida 378, 829, 2165
Kaminsky, Melvin (Mel Brooks) 2047
Kandinsky, Vassily 1711, 1717
Kane, Joseph 1758
Kanin, Fay 1150
Kanin, Garson 323, 1145, 1777, 1975
Kanzler, Rodolfo 1573
Kaoru, Osanai 1740
Kaper, Bronislau 408
Kaplan, Nelly 497
Karas, Anton 1329
Karina, Anna 2109, 2132, 2151
Karloff, Boris 388, 394, 395, 1237, 1456, 1467, 1502, 1592, 1779, 1808
Karmitz, Marin 2126
Karno, Fred (Fred Westcott) 1415
Kartozian, William F. 682, 959
Katzman, Sam 986
Katz, Charles 1192
Katz, Elihu 778
Katz, Gloria 605, 993
Katz, Joan 2195
Katz, Samuel 613, 1504
Kauffmann, Stanley 121, 132, 143, 151, 1790
Kaufman, Boris 1646, 1828, 1906, 1979
Kaufman, Denis Arkadievich (see Dziga Vertov) 1663
Kaufman, George S. 1063, 1096, 1267, 1268, 1269
Kaufman, Mikhail 1646, 1663, 1664, 1668, 1669
Kaufman, Millard 1986
Kaufman, Phillip 183
Kaufman, Victor A. 678
Kawakita, Kashiko 2025
Kawalerowicz, Jerzy 2012
Kaye, Danny 805, 1087, 1188, 1474
Kaye, Simon 368
Kayne, Celia 996
Kay, Beatrice 1446
Kazanjoglou, Elia (Elia Kazan) 1258
Kazan, Elia 53, 84, 386, 559, 1005, 1010, 1018, 1093, 1098, 1151, 1165, 1179,
  1181, 1184, 1189, 1190, 1191, 1204, 1229, 1257, 1288, 1293, 1325, 1326, 1352,
  1489, 1500, 1501, 1550, 1946, 1951, 1954, 1961, 1968, 1979, 2022
Kazan, Nicholas 1292
Keach, Stacy 419

Keaton, Buster 196, 914, 1241, 1247, 1248, 1393, 1412, 1423, 1426, 1432, 1443, 1449, 1450, 1454, 1479, 1548, 1551, 1564, 1579, 1592, 1672, 1674, 1677, 1678, 1687, 1688, 1689, 1690, 1691, 1704, 1705, 1756, 2001, 2067

Keaton, B. and Jacques Tati 2007

Keaton, Diane 1003, 1452

Keaton, Joseph Francis (see Buster Keaton) 1688

Keeler, Ruby 1444, 1452

Keene, Tom 431

Kehoe, Vincent J. R. 84

Kehr, Dave 1452

Keighley, William 952, 1496

Keith, B. F. 767

Kelland, Clarence Buddington 1101

Kellerman, Annette 1445

Kellerman, Sally 379

Keller, Marthe 1291

Kellner, Sandor-Laszlo (Alexander Korda) 1859

Kelly, Anthony Paul 1391

Kelly, Gene 401, 402, 407, 575, 1087, 1295, 1952, 1962, 1980, 1983

Kelly, Grace 62, 523, 524, 547, 1350, 1852, 1854, 1855, 1978

Kelly, Hetty 1421

Kelly, Patrick 2197

Kelly, Patsy 1444, 1446

Kennedy, Burt 424

Kennedy, Jacqueline 2192

Kennedy, John F. 359, 360, 425, 2193

Kennedy, Joseph P. 1369, 1454, 1493

Kennedy, J. J. 1379, 1505

Kennedy, Merna 1429

Kennedy, Robert J. 425, 2077, 2089

Kenney, Robert W. 1192

Kent, Sidney R. 1466, 1470, 1477, 1492

Kenyon, Charles 193

Kenyon, Doris 1445

Kerkorian, Kirk 662

Kernberg, Otto 600

Kern, Hal C. 812, 1801

Kern, Jerome 405, 831, 1798

Kerouac, Jack 53

Kerry, Margaret 992

Kerr, Deborah 1247, 1324, 1354, 1541

Kershner, Irvin 516, 2036, 2049

Kessel, Adam, Jr. 1409, 1413, 1463, 1464, 1476

Keyes, Evelyn 1087, 1445

Keynes, John Maynard 1176

Keystone Cops 1676, 1701

Khan, Aly 1380

Khill, Marcel 1817

Kiam, Omar 1472

Kibbee, Guy 1215

Kibre, Jeff 1186

Kienzle, Raymond Nicholas (Nicholas Ray) 1968

Kiernan, William 851

Kikuchi, Kan 2029

Kilburn, Terry 992

Killiam, Paul 1557

Killinger, Dorothy 1191

King Kong 390, 810

Kingsley, Ben 547, 1443

Kingsley, Sidney 1808, 2058
King, Alan 1293
King, Bradley 1350
King, Dusty 433
King, Henry 365, 370, 794, 1231, 1232, 1247, 1256, 1323, 1500, 1502, 1671, 1705, 1758, 1779, 1952
King, Martin Luther 425, 551
Kinoshita, Keisuke 1898, 2017, 2018, 2022
Kinugasa, Teinosuke 1740, 1742, 1743, 1744, 1887, 2017, 2018, 2029
Kircher, Athanasius 1580, 1582, 1589, 1594
Kirkpatrick, Theodore 1188
Kirkwood, James 1380
Kirk, Phyllis 1440
Kirk, Tommy 1439
Kirsanov, Dmitri 1714
Kitchen, Fred 1427
Kitt, Eartha 885, 920, 950
Kleine, George 1609
Klein, Charles 1379
Klemperer, Otto 1635
Kline, Herb 1279
Kline, Kevin 1530
Klingman, Lynzee 1324
Klos, Elmer 2165
Klove, Jane 996
Kluge, Alexander 2165
Knight, Arthur 1468
Knight, Eric 321
Knight, Shirley 1346, 1349
Knott, Frederick 1978
Knox, Alexander 365
Knudtson, Frederic 377
Kobayashi, Masaki 1743, 1898, 2025
Kobayashi, Takiji 2018
Kober, Arthur 1225, 1228, 1348
Koch, Howard W. 343, 365, 372, 1067, 1091, 1142, 1145, 1146, 1147, 1154, 1187, 1205, 1262, 1288, 1494, 1751, 1983
Koch, Karl 1814, 1827
Kohler, Fred 193
Kohut, Heinz 600
Kol'tsov, Mikhail 1663
Konigsberg, Allen Stewart (Woody Allen) 2044
Kookie (See Byrnes, Ed) 1439
Koopman, Elias B. 1371, 1586, 1592, 1593
Korda, Alexander 249, 418, 1229, 1329, 1369, 1401, 1431, 1565, 1567, 1569, 1571, 1619, 1697, 1725, 1746, 1753, 1809, 1833, 1834, 1840, 1842, 1859, 1865, 1935, 1936, 1937
Korda, Vincent 1833, 1840, 1859
Korda, Zoltan 375, 887, 1231, 1833, 1840, 1859
Korngold, Erich Wolfgang 83, 408, 1494
Korzybski, Alfred 913
Kosjus, Miliza 1446
Koster, Henry 1204, 1636
Kostner, Kevin 801
Kotani, Henry 1740
Kotto, Yaphet 896
Kovacks, Laszlo 152
Kozintsev, Grigori 1342, 1343, 1353, 1355, 1647

Kracauer, Siegfried 41, 100, 130, 144, 165, 168
Kramer, Robert 2126
Kramer, Stanley 375, 376, 377, 415, 945, 952, 987, 1189, 1191, 1237, 1550, 1777, 1778
Krams, Arthur 1240
Krasker, Robert 1009, 1021, 1329
Krasna, Norman 1018, 1140, 1146, 1147, 1151
Krauss, Werner 1632, 1643
Kress, Harold F. 378
Krimsky, John 875
Krim, Arthur 1369, 1945
Kristofferson, Kris 2063
Kroner, Josef 378, 2165
Krook, Margaretha 606
Krueger, Kurt 1446
Kruger, Otto 1445
Kubelka, Peter 1956
Kubrick, Stanley 53, 159, 356, 372, 553, 1140, 1154, 1254, 1272, 1273, 1314, 1549, 1552, 1566, 2054, 2055, 2056, 2057, 2058
Kubrick, S. and RKO 2055
Kubrick, S. and United Artists 2055
Kubrick, S. and Vsevolod I. Pudovkin 2055, 2057
Kuleshov, Lev V. 1644, 1645, 1646, 1652, 1653, 1656, 1661, 1662
Kurant, Willy 165
Kurihara, Thomas 1740
Kuri, Emile 1007
Kurnitz, Harry 1279, 1973
Kurosawa, Akira 140, 567, 1343, 1356, 1548, 1549, 1574, 1737, 1738, 1739, 1743, 1886, 1891, 1895, 1896, 1898, 1899, 2017, 2018, 2019, 2021, 2022, 2025, 2026, 2027, 2028, 2029, 2030, 2116
Kurosawa, Heigo 1899
Kyo, Machika 2030

L

L'Herbier, Marcel 1710, 1712, 1713, 1714, 1904
La Follette, Suzanne 1495
Lacan, Jacques 134, 480, 483, 492, 500, 531, 584, 605
Ladd, Alan 1917, 1952
Ladd, Alan, Jr. 536, 666, 902, 1009, 1241, 1321
Laemmle, Carl 224, 622, 820, 1054, 1157, 1428, 1463, 1466, 1467, 1468, 1469, 1475, 1491, 1505, 1560, 1621, 1622, 1708
Laemmle, Carl, Jr. 1475, 1502
Laemmle, Joseph 1475
Lagerlof, Selma 1630
Lahr, Bert 1801
Laidlaw, William R. 370
Lai, Francis 2119
Lake, Arthur 1445
Lake, Veronica 1444
LaMarr, Barbara 1242, 1408, 1444, 1453
Lamarr, Hedy 1440, 1443, 1445, 1467, 1780
Lambert, Gavin 1010
Lamb, Thomas W. 1506
Lamont, Peter 850
Lamour, Dorothy 498, 1439, 1449, 1452
Lampert, Zohra 2060
Lanagan, Glenn 1440

Lancaster, Burt   368, 377, 386, 431, 643, 810, 1443, 1451, 1951, 2162
Lanchester, Elsa   1833, 1860, 1865
Landau, Arthur   1774
Landau, Ely   837, 1034, 1351
Landru, Henri   1433
Land, Ben   901
Lane, Andrew   998
Lane, Charles   901
Lane, Lola   1445
Langdon, Harry   1410, 1412, 1449, 1551, 1579, 1672, 1674, 1677, 1678, 1692, 1701, 1705
Langdon, H. and Jacques Tati   2007
Langenheim, Frederick   1584, 1594
Langenheim, William   1584, 1594
Lange, Harry   2084
Lange, Hope   790
Lange, Jessica   1174, 1235, 1292
Langford, Frances   1445
Langley, Noel   1801
Langlois, Henri   128, 1996, 2006, 2111
Langston, Tony   947
Lang, Fritz   186, 187, 1018, 1160, 1256, 1468, 1548, 1550, 1553, 1631, 1632, 1633, 1634, 1636, 1637, 1638, 1640, 1641, 1642, 1643, 1714, 1722, 1750, 1753, 1756, 1829, 1948, 1951, 1952, 2035, 2088, 2096
Lang, F. and Claude Chabrol   2099
Lang, F. and communism   273
Lang, F. and Douglas Fairbanks, Sr.   1402
Lang, F. and dream theory   583
Lang, F. and film criticism   144
Lang, F. and gangster films   386
Lang, F. and Graham Greene   1033
Lang, F. and Jean Renoir   187
Lang, F. and Jean-Luc Godard   2110
Lang, F. and Luis Bunuel   1721
Lang, F. and Point of View   119
Lang, F. and racism   876
Lang, F. and screenwriters   1254
Lang, F. and the independent film movement   643
Lang, F. and World War II   353
Lang, June   1207, 1446
Lang, Walter   1758
Lansbury, Angela   383, 1951, 2077
Lantz, Adolf   1879
Lantz, Walter   1780
Lanzo, Mario   1478
LaPlante, Laura   1445
Lardner, Ring   2043
Lardner, Ring, Jr.   379, 1036, 1063, 1073, 1074, 1079, 1083, 1088, 1098, 1100, 1101, 1142, 1147, 1150, 1154, 1179, 1180, 1184, 1188, 1193, 1206, 1269
Larkin, Ailie Sharon   901
Larner, Jeremy   455
LaRocque, Rod   1444, 1468
Larsen, Roy Edward   296, 301
LaRue, Jack   1446
Lasky, Blanche   1477, 1479, 1780
Lasky, Jesse L., Jr.   85, 383, 1284, 1439, 1454, 1478
Lasky, Jesse L., Sr.   224, 1054, 1277, 1463, 1467, 1472, 1477, 1478, 1479, 1491, 1621, 1724, 1756, 1775, 1780

Lassie (dog star) 1446
Latham Family 1586, 1593
Latham, Woodville 1586
Latimore, Frank 1439
Lattuada, Alberto 1573, 1874
Laudi, Elissa 1450
Laufer, Bernard 323
Laughton, Charles 346, 1229, 1330, 1451, 1487, 1833, 1834, 1838, 1859, 1860, 1865
Launder, Frank 1934
Laurel and Hardy at MGM 1691
Laurel and Hardy at the Roach Studios 1691
Laurel and Hardy at 20th Century-Fox 1691
Laurel, Stan 1237, 1412, 1419, 1420, 1423, 1578, 1675, 1677, 1690, 1691, 1695, 1701, 1755
Laurel, Virginia Ruth 1691
Laurents, Arthur 851, 1016, 1147
Laurent, Arthur 274
Laute, Eugen Augustin 1590, 1745
Lavery, Emmett G. 1079, 1088, 1180
Lawford, Peter 1780
Lawrence, Carol 1349
Lawrence, Catalina 1240
Lawrence, D. H. 179
Lawrence, Florence 1377, 1428, 1434
Lawrence, Gertrude 145, 1243
Lawson, Arthur 1016
Lawson, John Howard 85, 100, 141, 164, 229, 232, 272, 273, 375, 376, 1070, 1073, 1083, 1087, 1088, 1098, 1152, 1156, 1178, 1179, 1180, 1182, 1184, 1190, 1195, 1196, 1205, 1259, 1263, 1264, 1284, 1750
Lawson, Ted 370
Lawson, Wilfred 1863
Law, John Phillip 2082
Laydu, Claude 2008
Layton, R. T. 1351
Lazersfeld, Paul 778
Le Maire, Charles 849
Le Mat, Paul 993
Le Picard, Marcel 1387
Le Prince, Louis Aime Augustine 1542, 1586, 1589
Leachman, Cloris 996
Leacock, Richard 1557, 1870
Leacock, Robert 2040
Lean, David 52, 220, 371, 374, 548, 1174, 1301, 1357, 1552, 1566, 1842, 1860, 1934, 1939, 1943, 2032
Lear, Norman 669, 672
Leaud, Jean-Pierre 1005, 2129, 2154, 2155
Leavitt, Sam 850
Lederer, Charles 1151, 1269, 1790
Lederer, Francis 219, 1078, 1445
Lee of Fareham, Lord 213
Leenhardt, Roger 2001, 2098
Lee, Canada 882, 922, 1096, 1188
Lee, Christopher 381, 388, 390, 399
Lee, Gypsy Rose 1967
Lee, Lila 1444
Lee, Robert N. 1708, 1804
Lee, Rowland V. 1204
Lee, Spike 903

Lefebvre, Jean Pierre 2123, 2162
Leger, Fernand 1709, 1713, 1717, 1730
Legge, Stuart 214, 215, 280, 309, 1869
Lehman, Ernest 1140, 1147, 1844, 1852, 1854, 1855, 2053, 2079, 2086
Lehman, Peter 598
Lehrman, Henry "Pathe" 1415, 1476
Leibman, Nina C. 1003
Leigh, Janet 62, 1951, 1962, 2053, 2080
Leigh, Vivien 121, 812, 913, 1243, 1346, 1352, 1357, 1447, 1487, 1801, 1833, 1834, 1859, 1861, 1934
Leiterman, Richard 2058
Lelouch, Claude 1571, 2135
LeMaire, Charles 1981
LeMay, Curtis 361
Lemberg, Aleksandr 1663
Lemmon, Jack 409, 1020, 1284, 1351, 2058
Lengyel, Melchior 1803
Lenin, V. I. 702
Leni, Paul 1714
Lennart, Isobel 1097, 1203
Leno, Dan 1427
Lenz, Kay 971
Leonard, Marion 1389
Leonard, Robert Z. 1313, 1327, 1483
Leonard, Sheldon 1323
Leone, Sergio 191, 382, 427, 2171
Lerner, Alan Jay 404, 1983
Leroy, Baby 990, 992, 993
LeRoy, Hal 1445
Leroy, Jean Aime 1586
LeRoy, Mervyn 50, 353, 370, 939, 1496, 1696, 1748, 1780, 1801, 1804
Leslie, Joan 1445
Lesser, Sol 1468
Lester, Jerry 1439
Lester, Mark 992, 993
Lester, Richard 1550, 2161
Levant, Oscar 301, 1529
Levels, Calvin 549
Levene, Sam 849
Levi-Strauss, Claude 184, 197, 492
Levielle, Gabriel 1605
Levine, Joseph E. 1236, 1318, 2047
Levine, Nat 1456
Levinson, Barry 1294
Levinson, Nathan 1015, 1352, 1804
Levinson, Sam 1096
Levin, Joni 61
Levin, Myer 139
Levy, Benn W. 1864
Levy, Robert 921
Lewin, Albert 1329, 1468
Lewin, Bertram 584
Lewis, Andy K. 799
Lewis, Cecil 1357, 1863
Lewis, Dave 799
Lewis, Edward 1284
Lewis, Herschell Gordon 393, 394
Lewis, Jerry 53, 90, 117, 1242, 1288, 1550, 1752, 1951, 1954

Lewis, Joseph H.   743
Lewis, Ralph   1387
Lewis, Sinclair   1151, 1176, 1278, 1472
Lewis, Ted   1445
Lewton, Val   388, 389
Leyda, Jay   140, 343, 1263
Libby, Fred   1976
Lichtman, Al   1481
Liddell, Eric   1013
Lieberson, Sandy   902
Liebmann, Robert   1831
Lighton, Louis D.   370
Lincoln, Abbey   952
Lincoln, Abraham   478, 804
Lincoln, Elmo   1444, 1456, 1459
Lindbergh, Charles   1400
Linder, Max   1239, 1419, 1423, 1426, 1571, 1605, 1619, 1677, 1709
Lindsay, Howard   1798
Lindsay, Vachel   123, 125, 147, 168
Link, John   1322
Lipman, Jerzy   2014
Lippmann, Walter   244, 294, 305
Lipscomb, W. P.   1357
Lipsett, Arthur   318
Lipton, Lenny   988
Liscomb, W. P.   1863
Lithgow, John   1530
Littin, Miguel   918
Littlefield, Lucien   1447
Little, Thomas   366, 1007, 1326
Litvak, Anatole   320, 321, 1259, 1496, 1502
Livadary, John P.   368, 1328, 1799
Lloyd, Frank   1330
Lloyd, Harold   922, 1412, 1423, 1426, 1445, 1449, 1473, 1551, 1564, 1578, 1672, 1674, 1677, 1678, 1692, 1693, 1695, 1705
Lloyd, H. and Jacques Tati   2007
Loach, Kenneth   1566
Loader, Jayne   324
Locke, Sandra   995
Lockhart, Calvin   923
Lockhart, Gene   1558
Lockwood, Margaret   1440, 1934
Loden, Barbara   520, 1261
Loder, John   1445
Loeb, Philip   1096, 1188, 1259
Loeff, Ted   658
Loew, David   642
Loew, Marcus   224, 622, 624, 767, 776, 820, 1480, 1481, 1482, 1504, 1506, 1621, 1670
Logan, Ella   1444
Logan, Jacqueline   1445, 1703
Logan, Joshua L.   1002, 1242, 1264, 2064
Lollobrigida, Gina   1447
Lombardo, Gustavo   1573
Lombard, Carole   346, 1160, 1235, 1395, 1410, 1449, 1701, 1772
Lombard, Thomas R.   702
London, Babe   1439
London, Jack   1363
Lone Ranger, the   433

Longanesi, Leo 1923
Longstreet, Stephen 1293
Long, Walter 263, 1387, 1388
Loos, Anita 85, 631, 1060, 1066, 1117, 1147, 1151, 1217, 1237, 1378, 1394, 1400,
  1403, 1404, 1405, 1468, 1595, 1805
Looten, C. L. 1799
Lorca, Garcia 1721, 1722
Lord, Daniel A., Father 1749
Lord, Marjorie 1439
Lorentz, Pare 127, 153, 203, 292, 305, 1870, 1871, 1872
Loren, Sophia 378, 1341, 1418, 1447, 2174
Loring, Eugene 402
Loring, Hope 370
Lorin, Joni 1915
Lorre, Peter 372, 373, 388, 396, 397, 1253, 1641, 1830
Losey, Harold 1963
Losey, Joseph 144, 371, 944, 1094, 1237, 1261, 1552, 1553, 1566, 1752, 1946,
  1949, 1951, 1962, 1963, 1981, 2043, 2161
Losey, J. and Bertolt Brecht 2124, 2125
Lotman, Jurij M. 492
Loughlin, Judge Martin 763
Louis, Joe 884
Lourie, Eugene 1827
Lovelace, Linda 2192
Love, Bessie 1385, 1388, 1439, 1444, 1541
Lowe, Edmund 1709
Lowe, James B. 870
Lowry, Malcolm 1265
Loy, Myrna 375, 382, 735, 1293, 1448, 1452, 1480, 1481, 1484, 1781, 1806
Lubitsch, Ernst 186, 187, 407, 555, 809, 1065, 1276, 1393, 1395, 1397, 1403,
  1480, 1498, 1500, 1502, 1504, 1671, 1674, 1675, 1694, 1706, 1748, 1756, 1803,
  1804, 1951, 2022, 2206
Lubitsch, E. and AUTEUR criticism 1542, 1548, 1549, 1639
Lubitsch, E. and feature films 1607
Lubitsch, E. and German silent films 1631, 1632, 1634, 1639, 1642
Lucas, George 56, 341, 604, 605, 673, 768, 902, 993, 1140, 1235, 2033, 2197,
  2199, 2200
Lucas, Marcia 605, 813
Lucas, Sam 920, 932
Luce, Henry 296, 301
Lucianni, Sebastiano Arturo 1873, 1879
Luedtke, Kurt 1017
Lugosi, Bela 385, 388, 394, 419, 1237, 1456, 1592, 1798, 1808
Luhr, William 598
Luick, Earl 1439
Luke, Keye 1447
Lumet, Baruch 2058
Lumet, Sidney 837, 1293, 1314, 1349, 1350, 2032, 2036, 2051, 2058, 2059, 2066,
  2084
Lumieres, The 122, 1558, 1586, 1602, 1619, 1643, 1924
Lumiere, Auguste 1586, 1593, 1594, 1598, 1599, 1601, 1731
Lumiere, Louis 292, 1571, 1586, 1588, 1590, 1593, 1594, 1598, 1599, 1601, 1606,
  1610, 1624, 1715, 1731, 2001
Lunacharsky, Anatoli V. 1649, 1661
Lundigan, William 1446
Lund, John 1440
Lunt, Alfred 1176, 1390, 1782
Lupino, Ida 489, 502, 508, 1236, 1548

Luther, Martin 2185
Lutter, Alfred 1011
Lydon, Jimmy 1445
Lyndon, Barre 373
Lynley, Carol 790, 1001
Lynn, Henry 846
Lynn, Jeffrey 1440, 1446
Lyons, Eugene 1188
Lyon, Ben 1445
Lyon, Elizabeth Hart 483
Lyon, Francis 1985
Lyon, William A. 368, 1002

M

Mabley, Jackie "Moms" 882
Mabry, Moss 851
MacArthur, Charles 1063, 1151, 1217, 1224, 1251, 1265, 1267, 1269, 1327, 1472, 1806
MacAvin, Josie 1328
Macdonald, Dwight 127, 132, 153, 179, 774, 1790
MacDonald, Jeanette 1443, 1806
MacDonald, Richard 79
MacDonald, R. A. 369
MacDougall, Don 813
MacDougall, Ranald 355, 798, 800
MacDougall, Roger 1937, 1942
Mace, Fred 1410
Macgowan, Kenneth 123
MacGraw, Ali 1233
Machaty, Gustav 1880
MacKaye, Steele 1331
Mackendrick, Alexander 1937, 1942
Mack, Marion 1687
MacLaine, Shirley 790, 1016, 1288
MacLeish, Archibald 228, 351
MacMillan, Kenneth 1356
MacMurray, Fred 798
MacPherson, C. B. 198
Macpherson, Jeanie 1703
Maddow, Ben 1147, 1208, 1321
Madge, Charles 315, 316
Madison, Cleo 520
Madison, Guy 1446, 1487
Maeterlinck, Maurice 1472
Maggiorani, Lamberto 1004
Magnani, Anna 378, 1346, 1933
Magnin, Rabbi Edgar 1504
Magnusson, Charles 1624
Mahin, John Lee 994, 1073, 1151, 1192, 1203
Mahler, Margaret 600, 601
Mahoney, Jack 1439
Mailer, Norman 1157, 1227, 1531, 1549
Main, Marjorie 1445, 1808
Majia, Alfonso 1002
Makavejev, Dusan 516, 2123
Makino, Masahiro 1742
Makino, Shozo 1736

Maladoror, Sarah (Sarah Ducados) 508
Malcolm X 425
Malden, Karl 1346, 1352, 1979
Malins, Geoffrey 297
Malkovich, John 1530
Mallarme, Stephane 131
Malle, Louis 293, 377, 1572, 2094, 2119, 2122, 2127, 2149
Malone, Dorothy 1439, 1978
Malraux, Andre 53, 278, 1313, 2129
Maltz, Albert 274, 369, 850, 1088, 1100, 1155, 1182, 1193, 1202, 1219, 1284, 1285
Mamet, David 1039, 1136
Mamoulian, Rouben 117, 874, 1254, 1550, 1551, 1707, 1748, 1782, 1803
Mancini, Henry 408
Mancuso, Frank 676
Mandell, Daniel 375, 1349, 1472, 1473
Mankiewicz, Donald Martin 1267
Mankiewicz, Herman J. 1063, 1073, 1142, 1148, 1151, 1154, 1192, 1253, 1263, 1266, 1268, 1269, 1270, 1271, 1277, 1279, 1485, 1751, 1793, 1807
Mankiewicz, Joseph L. 363, 372, 980, 1029, 1031, 1033, 1038, 1065, 1066, 1122, 1140, 1142, 1151, 1192, 1204, 1215, 1216, 1219, 1250, 1260, 1266, 1267, 1268, 1269, 1270, 1271, 1272, 1290, 1352, 1354, 1466, 1500, 1501, 1502, 1952, 1981
Manley, Nellie 1240
Manners, David 1444
Mannix, Edward 691, 1183, 1466
Mann, Abby 377, 1237
Mann, Anthony 144, 174, 382, 429, 434, 980, 1951, 1964, 1982, 2055, 2096
Mann, Daniel 1020
Mann, Delbert 84, 1008, 1349, 1951, 2036
Mann, Hank 1413
Mann, Thomas 1297
Mansfield, Jayne 1241, 1443
Manson, Charles 425
Marais, Jean 1818, 1905, 1910, 2009
March, Fredric 375, 809, 1078, 1164, 1192, 1207, 1232, 1295, 1351, 1449
March, Marvin 1017
Marey, Etienne-Jules 1594, 1598, 1599, 1601, 1611, 1615
Margo 1446
Margolin, Janet 995
Mariani, Giuseppe 1356
Marion, Frances 84, 519, 620, 1066, 1268, 1396, 1397, 1474, 1706, 1802
Marion, George F. 1350
Maris, Jean 2009
Marker, Chris 1818, 1993, 2112, 2115, 2116, 2117, 2122, 2152
Markey, Enid 1439
Markham, Dewey (Pigmeat) 882
Marklatt, Mark 1430
Markowski, Andrzej 2014
Marks, John 139
Marley, John 2074
Marlowe, Christopher 151, 1180
Marlowe, Philip 380, 1197, 1198
Marlow, Brian 1192
Marmstedt, Lorens 2184
Marple, Miss 380
Marquez, Evaristo 2176
Marriott, John 1348
Marshall, Edward 79

Marshall, Herbert 1329, 1804
Marshall, John 2092
Marshall, Ted 1328
Marshall, Tully 1388
Marshall, William 885, 904, 937
Marsh, Mae 1372, 1382, 1384, 1385, 1387, 1388, 1389, 1392, 1444, 1452, 1468, 1558, 1578
Marsh, Marian 1798
Mars, Kenneth 2073
Martelli, Otello 1021
Martino, Enrico di S. 1573
Martino, Sergio 419
Martins, Peter 1016
Martin, Dean 1288, 1951
Martin, Marcel 100
Martin, Steve 786, 1174
Martin, Strother 429, 2063
Marton, Andrew 361
Marvin, Arthur 1387
Marvin, Frank 61, 1915
Marvin, Henry N. 1371, 1378, 1379, 1586, 1592, 1593
Marvin, Lee 1265, 1351, 2071, 2075, 2084
Marx Brothers, The 192, 555, 957, 1383, 1449, 1477, 1749, 1755, 1783, 1784, 1805
Marx, Chico 1503, 1783
Marx, Groucho 1251, 1253, 1503, 1783, 1784, 1805
Marx, Gummo 1783
Marx, Harpo 1064, 1503, 1783, 1784, 2090, 2091
Marx, Karl 41, 188, 313, 483, 521, 702, 1556, 1651
Marx, Minnie 1783
Marx, Sam 1118, 1192, 1213, 1214, 1483, 1783
Marx, Zeppo 1445, 1783
Maschwitz, Eric 1328
Masina, Giulietta 1021, 1929, 1933
Maskelyne, John Nevil 1588, 1603, 1616
Mason, Alice 1252
Mason, James 366, 372, 1006, 1021, 1295, 1354, 1558, 1934, 1943, 2058, 2079
Mason, Marsha 1166
Mason, Perry 380
Mason, Sarah Y. 1383
Massey, Ilona 1444
Massey, Raymond 381, 418, 1005, 1325, 1439, 1833, 1861
Massine, Leonide 1016, 1943
Massolle, Josef 1745, 1828
Masterman, Charles F. G. 211
Masters, Tony 2084
Mastroianni, Marcello 1023, 2174, 2175
Matarazzo, Raffaello 1874, 1878
Mateos, Antonio 365
Mate, Rudolph 1729
Mathers, Jerry 1445
Matheson, Richard 388
Mathias, June 1396, 1480, 1707
Matsuyama, Zenzo 601
Matthau, Walter 1202, 1283, 1336, 1351, 2194
Matthews, Jessie 1833, 1841, 1862
Matthews, Joseph Brown 1186
Mattoli, Mario 1874, 1878
Mattson, Arne 1628

Mature, Victor 346, 423, 1445, 1976
Matuszewski, Boleslaw 304
Maugham, W. Somerset 1061, 1176, 1329
Maurice, Bernard 2010
Maurier, Claire 1006
Maxwell, Edwin 1408
Maxwell, Elsa 1290
Maxwell, John 1567, 1571, 1833
Mayakovsky, Vladimir 1644, 1664
Mayer, Arthur 50, 54, 1468
Mayer, Edith 1480, 1489
Mayer, Edwin Justus 1070, 1071
Mayer, Irene 1479, 1480
Mayer, Jacob 1489
Mayer, Karl 1632, 1633, 1636, 1642, 1643
Mayer, Louis B. 226, 244, 820, 886, 1156, 1157, 1158, 1159, 1173, 1183, 1192,
   1208, 1217, 1225, 1235, 1277, 1435, 1475, 1478, 1479, 1480, 1484, 1485, 1486,
   1488, 1489, 1491, 1496, 1500, 1502, 1750
Mayer, L. and Donald Ogden Stewart 1279
Mayer, L. and HUAC 1088
Mayer, L. and Irving Thalberg 844, 1239
Mayer, L. and Katharine Hepburn 1341
Mayer, L. and racism 876
Mayer, L. and the American Dream 1054
Mayer, L. and the creation of MGM 776
Mayer, L. and the Hollywood image 1136
Mayer, L. and the Motion Picture Academy of Arts and Sciences 1172
Mayer, L. and the rise of Hollywood 686, 1466, 1468
Mayer, L. and William Faulkner 1214
Mayer, L. and William Fox 1470
Mayer, Margaret 1489
Mayes, Wendell 1154
Maynard, Ken 431, 1445, 1456
Mayo, Archie 353
Mayo, Virginia 1440, 1472
Mayron, Melanie 526
Maysles, Albert 1870, 2041, 2042, 2084, 2121
Maysles, David 1870, 2041, 2084, 2121
May, Elaine 520, 680, 2060
May, Joe 1634
Mazursky, Paul 841, 1006, 1028
McAllister, Stewart 249
McAuliffe, Anthony 353
McAvoy, May 1445, 1706
McBride, James 355
McCallister, Lon 1445
McCallum, David 1440
McCallum, Gordon K. 850
McCambridge, Mercedes 1012, 1319, 1964, 1985
McCarey, Leo 273, 980, 1088, 1179, 1202, 1752, 1805, 2035
McCarthy, Frank 361
McCarthy, Joseph R. 229, 1188, 1190
McCarthy, Mary 1226, 1229, 1322
McCaughey, William 368
McCay, Winsor 1584
McClain, Florence 933
McCleary, Urie 365
McCleery, Albert 1240

McCord, Ted   1022
McCormack, Patty   992
McCoy, Horace   1108
McCoy, Tim   429, 431, 1439
McCrea, Joel   261, 429, 1445, 1808, 1921, 2086
McCulley, Johnston   1407
McCune, Grant   813
McCutcheon, George   1362
McDaniel, Hattie   812, 862, 872, 877, 880, 921, 929, 939, 1801
McDonald, J. Farrell   193
McDonnell, Fergus   1021
McDonough, Tom   81
McDowall, Malcolm   1001
McDowall, Roddy   990, 992, 993, 1007, 1862
McFarland, George "Spanky"   992, 993, 1445
McGraw, Ali   1293, 2063, 2191
McGuinness, James Kevin   1064, 1073, 1080, 1088, 1192
McGuire, Biff   995
McGuire, Dorothy   1018, 1319, 1349, 1440, 1446, 1487
McGuire, Kathryn   1705
McHugh, Frank   1497
McHugh, Jimmy   405
McIntyre, Bob   1472
McKay, Gardner   1439
McKay, Windsor   1583
McKee, Lotte   903
McKern, Leo   1020
McKim, Robert   1407
McKinney, Bill   429, 998
McKinney, Nina Mae   872, 873, 921
McKuen, Rod   1003
McLaglen, Victor   1019, 1709, 1806
McLaren, Norman   1975
McLean, Barbara   366, 1503
McLoughlin, Patrick   1347
McLuhan, Marshall   63, 457, 774, 776, 777
McMurtry, Larry   996
McNair, Barbara   937
McNeill, Claudia   862, 1009
McNichol, Kristy   991
McNutt, Patterson   1192
McQueen, Steve   374, 810, 889, 1233, 1443, 2036, 2059, 2063
McQueen, Thelma "Butterfly"   877, 921, 932, 939, 1445
Medavoy, Mike   666
Meehan, John   1007
Meeker, Ralph   2071
Meighan, Tommy   1444
Meiji, Emperor   1732, 1733
Meisel, Edmund   1661
Meisner, Sanford   76
Mekas, Adolfas   2039
Mekas, Jonas   65, 141, 1951, 2039, 2069
Melcher, Martin   524
Melchior, Lauritz   1445
Melies, Gaston   1604, 1616
Melies, Georges   410, 583, 1331, 1558, 1571, 1578, 1588, 1590, 1593, 1602, 1604,
   1606, 1610, 1616, 1619, 1620, 1709, 1715, 1718, 1728, 1812, 1824, 2001
Mellett, Lowell   229
Mellor, William C.   849, 1015, 1986

Melnick, Daniel 536, 666
Melville, Herman 373
Melville, Jean-Pierre 113, 386, 1995, 1999, 2093, 2094, 2101, 2122
Mencken, H. L. 1379
Mengers, Sue 1552
Menjou, Adolphe Jean 372, 1080, 1088, 1180, 1192, 1408, 1417, 1806
Menzel, Jiri 994, 2164, 2165
Menzies, William Cameron 1386, 1408, 1801, 1833
Mercanton, Louis 1618
Merchant, Ismail 548, 2167
Merchant, Vivien 2161
Meredith, Burgess 1237, 1291
Meredyth, Bess 1066, 1073, 1192
Merkel, Una 1445, 1446
Merriam, Charles Edward 244, 294
Merriam, Frank E. 225, 226
Merrick, David 1289
Merrill, Gary 1440
Merritt, Russell 297, 1382
Messel, Oliver 1676
Messter, Oskar 297, 1586, 1590, 1630
Meszaros, Marta 501
Metzger, Radley 2037
Metzler, Jim 998
Metzner, Erno 1632
Metz, Christian 108, 133, 168, 192
Meyerhold, Vsevolod E. 1342, 1644, 1649, 1656, 1661
Meyers, Carmel 631
Meyers, Russ 2037
Meyer, Carl 1876
Meyer, Johnny 1290
Meyer, Nicholas 415
Meyer, Russ 2037
Meyer, Sidney 1923
Micheaux, Oscar 860, 866, 869, 870, 909, 910, 911, 921, 927, 929, 934, 935,
     937, 940, 943, 947
Micheaux, Swan 948
Michelangelo 269
Mickey Mouse (cartoon character) 1240, 1797
Mielziner, Jo 1002, 1257
Mieville, Anne-Marie 2111, 2132
Mifune, Toshiro 1356, 2029, 2030
Miki, Shigeto 1901
Milestone, Lewis 261, 342, 354, 369, 371, 1091, 1236, 1275, 1281, 1469, 1500,
     1748, 1753, 1758, 1779, 1805, 1847, 2043
Miles, Sarah 2161
Miles, Vera 1854, 1855
Milford, Gene 1328, 1799, 1980
Milius, John 341, 367, 2197
Milland, Ray 272, 1978, 1987
Miller, Arthur 836, 1101, 1155, 1189, 1195, 1260, 1261, 1265, 1349, 1587
Miller, Arthur (cinematographer) 80, 1007
Miller, George 415
Miller, Glenn 320
Miller, Henry 901, 2098
Miller, Merle 2036
Miller, Patsy Ruth 1444, 1695
Miller, Robert Ellis 995

Miller, Seaton I. 1219
Miller, Walter 1456
Miller, Winston 1976
Millett, Kate 516
Mills, C. Wright 179
Mills, Earl 886
Mills, Hayley 790, 992, 993, 1439
Mills, John 1301, 1934, 1941
Mills, Reginald 1016, 1943
Mill, John Stuart 214
Milton, Paul 1186
Mimieux, Yvette 790
Minciotti, Esther 1008
Mineo, Sal 850, 997
Minkler, Bob 813
Minnelli, Liza 152, 1138
Minnelli, Vincente 402, 714, 874, 1015, 1290, 1317, 1553, 1707, 1753, 1784,
  1952, 1983, 2096, 2141
Minor, Worthington 2066, 2067
Minter, Mary Miles 966, 1444, 1505
Miranda, Aurora 1439
Miranda, Carmen 1471
Mirisch, Walter 361
Mishma, Yukio 2023
Mitchell, James 1410
Mitchell, Joseph 1705
Mitchum, Robert 386, 989, 1293, 1951, 1964
Mitra, Subrata 1004
Mitry, Jean 132, 133, 161, 169
Mix, Tom 193, 426, 429, 430, 431, 434, 810, 1440, 1456, 1470, 1674
Miyagawa, Kazuo 2030, 2031
Mizener, Arthur 1217
Mizner, Wilson 1379
Mizoguchi, Kenji 162, 466, 497, 567, 583, 1739, 1740, 1742, 1743, 1887, 1889,
  1890, 1895, 1896, 1898, 1901, 2017, 2018, 2022, 2026, 2027, 2031
Modot, Gaston 1821
Moffitt, John Charles 1088, 1179
Moguy, Leonide 1906
Moholy-Nagy 1717
Mohr, Hal 80, 1398, 1468
Molander, Gustaf 1628
Mollo, John 813
Mongiardino, Renzo 1356
Monks, John, Jr. 373
Monnier, Antoine 2004
Monroe, Marilyn 508, 515, 523, 524, 551, 575, 586, 587, 789, 1138, 1235, 1241,
  1243, 1244, 1248, 1251, 1252, 1254, 1256, 1260, 1264, 1282, 1292, 1471, 1493,
  1499, 1558, 1951, 1964, 1965, 1966, 1967, 2039
Monroe, M. and the star system 1442, 1443, 1447
Monroe, Vaughn 1445
Montagu, Ivor 65, 100, 142, 1833, 1840, 1857, 1867
Montaigne, Michel [Eyquem] de 457
Montand, Yves 379, 577, 2152
Montez, Maria 1443
Montgomery, Bernard Law 365, 1318
Montgomery, Frank 933
Montgomery, George 346
Montgomery, Robert 369, 1088, 1445, 1484
Montouri, Carlo 1004

Moonjean, Hank 1240
Moorcroft, Judy 1323
Moorehead, Agnes 1240, 1327
Moore, Brian 1855
Moore, Colleen 1385, 1445, 1479, 1695
Moore, Dickie 970, 992, 993, 1445
Moore, Mary Tyler 1008, 2036
Moore, Nancy Noret 763
Moore, Owen 1392
Moore, Roger 422
Moore, Ted 1020
Moore, Terry 1440
Moran, Lois 1116, 1119
Moreau, Jeanne 466, 1022, 1353, 1447, 1721, 2095, 2147, 2155
Moreland, Mantan 877, 878, 935, 948, 1445
Moreno, Tony 1444
More, Sir Thomas 461
Morgan, Dennis 1445
Morgan, Frank 1558, 1801
Morgan, Helen 1805
Morgan, Ira 1432
Morgan, James P. 1746
Morgan, Michele 1814, 1906
Morin, Edgar 2153
Morison, Patricia 498
Mori, Masayuki 2030, 2031
Mori, Paola 1790
Morley, Robert 1934
Morrison, Frederick Ernest (Pickaninny Sammy, Sunshine Sammy) 865, 866
Morrison, Kathleen (see Colleen Moore) 1695
Morrissey, Paul 2040, 2068, 2069
Morris, Gouverneur 1061
Morris, Oswald 850
Morrow, Vic 1000
Morse, Ella Mae 1445
Morse, Robert 1294
Moses 269
Moss, Carlton 901
Mostel, Zero 1179, 1188, 1260, 1293, 1975, 2073
Motte, Marguerite de la 1407
Moulton, Thomas T. 812, 1351, 1801
Mourlet, Michel 1998
Moussy, Marcel 1005, 2154, 2155
Mower, Jack 1456
Mudge, Estelle de Wolfe 1918
Muir, Jean 1188
Mulhall, Jack 1445
Muller, Renate 238
Mulligan, Richard 1295
Mulligan, Robert 1325, 2036
Mullin, Kevin 764
Mummy, the 390, 391
Muni, Paul 385, 386, 1015, 1020, 1320, 1485, 1494, 1497, 1756, 1800, 1804
Munk, Andrzej 2012
Munsterberg, Hugo 124, 161, 169, 1339, 1555
Murata, Minoru 1740, 1742
Murch, Walter 367, 1322
Murdoch, Rupert 663, 678

Murnau, Friedrich W. 162, 471, 1564, 1573, 1578, 1632, 1633, 1634, 1640, 1642, 1671, 1674, 1706, 1710, 1714, 1756, 1869
Murnau, F. and Claude Chabrol 2099
Murnau, F. and Eric Rohmer 2102
Murphy, Audie 360, 431, 564, 1319, 1321
Murphy, Bert 933
Murphy, Brianne 680
Murphy, Dudley 875, 878
Murphy, Eddie 62, 903, 904, 1443, 2202, 2206
Murphy, George 1088
Murphy, Richard 1979
Murray, Bill 62, 2202
Murray, James 1707
Murray, Mae 1380, 1444, 1453
Murrow, Edward R. 2051
Muse, Clarence 870, 877, 880, 921, 926, 928, 939, 948
Musschenbroek, Pieter van 1594
Mussolini, Benito 218, 1003, 1750, 1874, 1876, 1877, 1879, 1880
Mussolini, Vittorio 1922
Musto, David M. 973
Mutt and Jeff 1595
Muybridge, Eadweard 292, 1585, 1596, 1597, 1601, 1611, 1615
Myers, Carmel 1385, 1475

N

Nabokov, Vladimir 150, 1272, 1273
Nagel, Conrad 1156, 1173, 1468
Nagle, Anne 1919
Naldi, Nita 503, 631, 1444
Napoleon 228
Narizzano, Silvio 1006
Naruse, Mikio 1740, 1743, 1887, 1888, 1898, 2018, 2019, 2026
Narushima, Toichiro 2025
Naschy, Paul 396
Natan, Bernard 1815, 1903
Nathan, George Jean 1034, 1375, 1376, 1379
Navarre, Rene 1617
Neagle, Anna 1440, 1833, 1841, 1862
Neal, Patricia 1137, 1223, 2059
Neame, Ronald 30, 373, 1003, 1860
Neame, Roy 1934
Neckar, Vaclav 994
Nedell, Bernard 1447
Neff, Hildegard 1487
Negri, Pola 238, 631, 809, 1417, 1423, 1444, 1452, 1453, 1473, 1477, 1632, 1634, 1642, 1674, 1675, 1707
Negulesco, Jean 1496, 1550
Neilan, Marshall 1277, 1393, 1401, 1775
Neitzschmann, Erich 1641
Nelson, Charles 1002
Nelson, David 1446
Nelson, Lori 1440
Nelson, Ralph 952, 2036
Nelson, Willie 2065
Newcombe, Warren 370, 378
Newcom, James E. 812
Newell, James 433

Newhouse, David   2073
Newhouse, Rafe   2073
Newman, Alfred   83, 366, 403, 408, 1007, 1326, 1327, 1472, 1473, 1503
Newman, David   143, 2088
Newman, James E.   1801
Newman, Joseph   1806
Newman, Paul   564, 575, 584, 805, 810, 850, 889, 1014, 1017, 1346, 1352, 1436,
    1443, 2058, 2060, 2078, 2206
Newman, Walter Brown   1150
Newton, Robert   1934
Ngor, Haing S.   1174, 1175
Niblo, Fred   1172, 1173, 1407, 1408, 1707
Nicholson, Jack   983, 1235, 1324, 2049, 2051, 2061, 2194
Nicholson, James Harvey   744, 986
Nicholson, Jim   2049
Nicholson, Virginia   1790
Nichols, Barbara   1439
Nichols, Bill   170
Nichols, Dudley   85, 140, 142, 370, 1019, 1064, 1066, 1071, 1073, 1083, 1147,
    1151, 1192, 1203, 1231, 1322, 1341, 1350, 1683, 1747, 1750, 1772, 1802
Nichols, Mike   154, 516, 1165, 2060, 2061, 2086
Nichols, Peter   1006
Nico   2069
Nicolai, Otto   1355
Nicoll, Allardyce   1030, 1339
Nielsen, Asta   1625, 1626, 1631, 1632, 1643
Niepce, Isidore   1591
Niepce, Joseph Nicephore   1584, 1591, 1598
Nietzsche, Freidrich   1957
Nijinsky, Fomich   1973
Nikolayev, Vladimir   371
Nilsson, Torre   150, 1561
Nimoy, Leonard   415
Nitzsche, Jack   1324
Niven, David   272, 346, 1057, 1327, 1449, 1451
Nixon, Richard M.   218, 360, 425, 551, 1181, 1192, 1684, 2089
Nizer, Louis   1189
Nizhny, Vladimir   1660
Noble, William   1001
Noda, Kogo   2032
Nolley, Ken   1024
Normand, Mabel   1374, 1379, 1394, 1396, 1410, 1411, 1413, 1415, 1433, 1455,
    1474, 1505, 1622, 1696
Norris, Chuck   801, 2198
Northcliffe, Lord   212
North, Alex   1326, 1352
North, Edmund A.   1284, 1987
North, Edward H.   365
North, Jay   992
North, Sheree   1471
Nosseck, Max   846, 848
Novak, Jane   1444
Novak, Kim   523, 524, 1242, 1264, 1329, 1854, 1855, 2080
Novarro, Ramon   1440, 1444, 1450
Novotna, Jarmila   1989
Nugent, Elliott   1237, 1321
Nugent, Frank S.   1145, 1372, 1501, 1683, 2076
Nunez, Eslinda   527

Nunn, Bill 903
Nureyev, Rudolf 1296, 1356
Nye, Gerald P. 203
Nykvist, Sven 2183

O

O'Bannon, Dan 415
O'Brien, Edmund 1290, 1354, 1975
O'Brien, George 193, 431, 1445, 1706
O'Brien, Margaret 272, 990, 991, 992, 993, 1445
O'Brien, Paul 1369
O'Brien, Tom 367
O'Brien, Virginia 1445, 1447
O'Brien, Willis H. 411, 1800
O'Connell, Arthur 1002
O'Connor, Donald 991, 1295, 1980
O'Connor, Glynnis 971
O'Feeney, Sean Aloysius (see John Ford) 1682
O'Hara, John 1108, 1251, 1273, 1274
O'Hara, Maureen 1007, 1439
O'Neal, Ron 899, 901, 904, 923
O'Neal, Ryan 1294
O'Neal, Tatum 971, 992
O'Neill, Eugene Gladstone 1034, 1038, 1090, 1151, 1155, 1335, 1340, 1350, 1351
O'Neill, Oona 1432
O'Steen, Sam 2086
O'Sullivan, Maureen 1484
O'Toole, Peter 2160
Oakie, Jack 1271, 1431, 1445, 1800
Oakland, Simon 1852
Oates, Warren 2063
Oberon, Merle 1327, 1833, 1834, 1841, 1859, 1865
Oberson, Merle 1859
Oboler, Arch 1550
Odets, Clifford 836, 1093, 1151, 1154, 1181, 1188, 1189, 1195, 1229, 1257, 1258,
  1259, 1279, 1290, 1292, 1349
Oehler, Andrew 1602
Oes, Ingvald C. 1627
Oetel, Curt 238
Ogai, Mori 2031
Oglesby, Mary 1360
Oguni, Hideo 2030
Okada, Eiji 2152
Okochi, Denjiro 1888
Oland, Warner 219
Oleson, Ole 1625, 1626
Oliver, Edna May 1327, 1447
Olivier, Laurence 162, 272, 1013, 1164, 1176, 1327, 1343, 1344, 1353, 1354,
  1419, 1441, 1472, 1473, 1488, 1489, 1833, 1834, 1859, 1861, 1934, 2162
Olivier, L. and William Shakespeare 1343
Olivio, Robert (Ondine) 2069
Olmi, Ermanno 2034
Olson, Charles 1974
Olson, Nancy 1439
Ondine (Robert Olivio) 2069
Ondra, Anny 1864
Onoe, Matsunosuke 1736

Ono, Yoko 508
Opatoshu, David 829
Ophuls, Marcel 317, 324, 377, 2006, 2127, 2143
Ophuls, Max 119, 324, 497, 980, 1147, 1275, 1310, 1553, 1571, 1756, 1815, 1829,
  1880, 1906, 1946, 1966, 1983, 1999, 2000, 2001, 2006, 2009
Oppenheimer, George 1805
Orchard, Tom 302
Ornitz, Arthur J. 1022
Ornitz, Samuel 1071, 1084, 1085, 1088
Orpheus 1717, 1818
Osborne, John 1328, 2162
Osborne, Paul 1005, 1010, 1325
Oshima, Nagisa 567, 1651, 1898, 2025, 2123
Oswald, Gerd 1752
Oswald, Lee Harvey 586
Ouspenskaya, Maria 1447
Owen, Don 1008
Owen, Reginald 1330
Owen, Seena 1406
Oysher, Moisher 829
Ozawa, Sakae 2031
Ozu, Yasujiro 141, 567, 1742, 1743, 1887, 1888, 1891, 1892, 1893, 1894, 1896,
  1898, 1900, 1902, 2004, 2017, 2018, 2022, 2023, 2024, 2026, 2027, 2031, 2032

P

Paar, Jack 231, 2044
Pabst, Georg Wilhelm 342, 508, 1573, 1633, 1634, 1640, 1643, 1829
Pacelli, Ernesto 1573
Pacino, Al 2194, 2206
Paget, Debra 498, 1440
Page, Anita 1446
Page, Geraldine 790, 1346
Pagliero, Marcello 1884
Pagnol, Marcel 1313, 1809, 1826, 1905
Paige, Mabel 1446
Pakula, Alan J. 516, 799, 800, 1032, 2195
Palance, Jack 1009, 1136, 1290
Palermi, Amleto 1878
Pallette, Eugene 1388
Palmieri, Judge Edmund L. 646
Pal, George 411, 415
Pampanini, Silvana 1439
Pangborn, Franklin 1413
Pan, Hermes 1798
Paolieri, Germana 1874
Pappas, Irene 1347
Paramore, Edward E. 1122, 1216
Paris, John Ayrton 1582, 1594
Parker, Albert 1405
Parker, Bonnie 2064
Parker, Cecilia 1446
Parker, Dorothy 1063, 1073, 1079, 1101, 1151, 1184, 1188, 1192, 1227, 1253,
  1265, 1269, 1278, 1296, 1348
Parker, Eleanor 1440
Parker, Fess 1439
Parker, Jean 1446

Parker, Lottie Blair 1391
Parker, Suzy 1440
Parkman, Francis 1405
Parks, Gordon 894, 896, 900, 901, 922, 936, 937, 1551
Parks, Larry 1091, 1092, 1179, 1180, 1181, 1189, 1229, 1293, 1444, 1949
Parlo, Dita 1828
Parrish, Robert 1275, 1985
Parrondo, Gil 365
Parsons, Estelle 2088
Parsons, Louella 1243, 1249, 1396
Pascal, Ernest 1071
Pascal, Gabriel 598, 1344, 1357, 1567, 1863
Pasolini, Pier Paolo 493, 1932, 2022, 2171, 2175
Pasternak, Boris 1355
Pastrone, Giovanni 685, 1573, 1607
Pathe, Charles 1599, 1605
Patinkin, Mandy 1530
Patrick, Gail 1446
Patrick, Lee 1446
Patton, George S. 337, 365
Paul, Robert W. 1567, 1586, 1588, 1590, 1599, 1606, 1607, 1610, 1612, 1617
Pauzer, Paul 1458
Pavlenko, Pyotr 1659, 1868
Paxinou, Katina 1322
Paxton, John 375, 849
Payne, Freda 941
Payne, John 1445
Pearce, Larry 894
Pearson, George 342, 1567, 1833
Pechter, William S. 1452
Peckinpah, Sam 153, 174, 425, 429, 1758, 2019, 2036, 2061, 2062, 2063, 2086, 2087
Peckinpah, S. and Ernest Hemingway 2063
Peckinpah, S. and James Fenimore Cooper 2063
Peckinpah, S. and Norman Mailer 2063
Peckinpah, S. and Sergei M. Eisenstein 2063
Peck, Gregory 370, 606, 643, 1010, 1018, 1247, 1254, 1325, 1487, 1503, 1635, 1847, 1917, 1952, 1988
Peerce, Larry 601, 945
Peggy, Baby (Diana Sierra Cary) 426, 991, 992, 1444
Pegler, Westbrook 1188
Pendleton, Nat 1447
Peneria, Hal 1988
Pennebaker, Don 1557, 2042
Penn, Arthur 603, 1320, 1548, 1551, 2036, 2042, 2064, 2065, 2088
Peppard, George 368
Perary, Hal 1446
Percy, Eileen 1445
Pereira, Hal 1350
Perelman, S. J. 1275, 1783
Perilli, Ivo 1880
Perinal, Georges 1432, 1865
Perkins, Anthony 1022, 1265, 1319, 1336, 2053, 2080, 2091
Perkins, Gil 1468
Perkins, Millie 849
Perreau, Gigi 993
Perrin, Nat 1193
Perry, Eleanor 516, 601, 995, 1028, 1147, 1318
Perry, Frank 516, 601, 995, 1318

Perry, Lincoln ("Stepin Fetchit")   870, 872, 877, 878, 926, 937, 939, 948
Peschkowsky, Michael Igor (Mike Nichols)   2060
Peterson, Jerry   870
Peters, Bernadette   786, 1410
Peters, Brock   922, 2084
Peters, Jean   1439, 1977
Petrie, Daniel   1009, 1348
Petrova, Olga   1444, 1450
Pflueger, Timothy L.   1506
Phantom of the Opera, The   390
Phelps, William   1312
Piaget, Jean   600, 601
Picabia, Francis   1717, 1724, 1727, 1728
Picasso, Pablo   1717
Pichel, Irving   1091
Pickaninny Sammy (Frederick Ernest Morrison)   865
Pickens, Slim   2063
Pickford, Charlotte   1397
Pickford, Jack   1397
Pickford, Lottie   1397
Pickford, Mary   209, 502, 503, 523, 971, 1235, 1277, 1391, 1395, 1396, 1402, 1403, 1408, 1443
Pickford, M. and Adolph Zukor   1504
Pickford, M. and Billy Bitzer   1372
Pickford, M. and Charles Chaplin   1420
Pickford, M. and child stars   970, 992
Pickford, M. and Douglas Fairbanks, Sr.   1398, 1402, 1404
Pickford, M. and D. W. Griffith   1379, 1382
Pickford, M. and early film history   685, 1360, 1383, 1384, 1464, 1467, 1621
Pickford, M. and Ernst Lubitsch   1498
Pickford, M. and female stereotypes   631
Pickford, M. and filmmaking in New Jersey   1595
Pickford, M. and Gloria Swanson   1454
Pickford, M. and Hollywood   1236
Pickford, M. and Howard Hawks   1775
Pickford, M. and IMP   1476
Pickford, M. and Jesse Lasky   1478
Pickford, M. and Liberty Bonds   1417
Pickford, M. and Samuel Goldwyn   1473
Pickford, M. and SPARROWS   1398
Pickford, M. and Spyros Skouras   1493
Pickford, M. and the American Dream   1054
Pickford, M. and THE LONELY VILLA   1389
Pickford, M. and the Motion Picture Academy of Arts and Sciences   1172
Pickford, M. and THE NEW YORK HAT   1397
Pickford, M. and the star system   1434, 1444, 1447, 1449, 1452
Pickford, M. and United Artists   1369, 1370, 1417, 1669
Picon, Molly   829, 836, 846
Pidgeon, Walter   370, 378, 1007, 1484
Pierce, Jack   1798
Pierson, Frank   84
Pineapple   866
Pinelli, Tullio   1021, 1023, 1933, 2174, 2175
Pine, Lester   1005
Pine, Tina   1005
Pinter, Harold   1034, 1178, 1293, 1963, 1981, 2161
Pinza, Ezio   1265
Pirandello, Luigi   1335, 1873, 1879

Pirosh, Robert 354, 1805
Pittaluga, Stefano 1875, 1879
Pitts, Zasu 1018
Planer, Frank 1988
Plateau, Joseph 1583, 1589, 1594, 1598, 1599
Plato 324
Platt, Polly 1552
Pleshette, Suzanne 790
Pletniev, Valery 1666
Pliny the Younger 382
Plumpe, Friedrich Wilhelm (See Murnau, Friedrich W.) 1640
Plunkett, Walter 1983
Poe, Edgar Allan 381, 389, 393, 1300, 1363
Poe, James 85, 952, 1037, 1147, 1290, 1314, 1352, 2088, 2089
Poggioli, Ferinando Maria 1878
Poitier, Sidney 805, 890, 891, 892, 896, 901, 903, 916, 922, 935, 937, 938, 951, 952, 953, 1000, 1449, 1552, 1778, 1951, 2038, 2082
Poitier, S. and A RAISIN IN THE SUN 1009
Poitier, S. and African-American performers 851, 879, 893, 901, 905
Poitier, S. and First Artists Corporation 889
Poitier, S. and racism 885, 887, 888, 892, 906
Poitier, S. and THE BLACKBOARD JUNGLE 1000
Polanski, Roman 389, 1343, 1355, 1566, 1758, 2013, 2179, 2180
Polansky, Abraham 2043, 2044
Polan, Vicki 526
Polglase, Van Nest 1807
Polito, Sol 800, 1494, 1495
Polk, Oscar 929, 952
Pollack, Sydney 554, 851, 1017, 1314, 1758, 2065, 2066, 2088, 2089
Pollard, Michael J. 2088
Pollard, Snub 1412, 1705
Pollock, Gordon 1430
Polonsky, Abraham 882, 944, 1093, 1100, 1154, 1985, 2042
Polo, Eddie 304, 1456
Pommer, Erich 1631, 1632, 1633, 1640, 1643, 1706, 1714, 1829, 1833, 1838
Pontecorvo, Gillo 2172, 2176
Popkin, Harry 878
Popkin, Leo 878
Porta, Giovanni Battista Della 1580, 1594
Porter, Cole 405
Porter, Edwin S. 122, 618, 696, 1277, 1383, 1504, 1549, 1550, 1551, 1578, 1583, 1593, 1595, 1599, 1605, 1610, 1617, 1620, 1718
Porter, Katherine Anne 1383
Portman, Richard 368
Potamkin, Harry Alan 127, 140, 155
Potter, Dennis 786
Potter, H. C. 1237
Potter, Martin 2175
Pound, Ezra 1211
Powell, Dick 1249, 1289, 1960
Powell, Eleanor 1445, 1452
Powell, Michael 396, 801, 1015, 1566, 1833, 1842, 1934, 1943
Powell, Robert 383
Powell, William 382, 454, 809, 1160, 1445, 1448, 1504, 1772, 1806
Powers, Pat 1463
Power, Tyrone 219, 346, 423, 1232, 1323, 1401, 1451, 1499, 1501, 1707, 1782, 1833
Pratt, George 1382
Pratt, James 1240

Prejean, Albert 1728
Preminger, Otto 643, 841, 1033, 1206, 1253, 1474, 1500, 1501, 1635, 1752, 1948, 1949, 1952, 1966, 1967, 1984
Presley, Elvis 405, 1138, 1288, 2039
Pressburger, Emeric 1015, 1934, 1943
Presson, Jay Allen 1003
Preston, Robert 1295, 1349, 1410
Pretty, Arline 1444, 1445, 1455, 1459
Prevert, Jacques 1812, 1813, 1814, 1816, 1825, 1908, 1910
Previn, Andre 404
Prevost, Pierre 1591
Price, Frank 536, 666
Price, Vincent 388, 419
Priestley, J. B. 53
Priestly, Robert 1002
Pringle, Aileen 1444
Prinzler, Hans Helmut 2165
Private Snafu 320
Prokofiev, Sergei 1645, 1659, 1868
Pronay, Nicholas 242
Propp, Vladimir 184, 532
Proust, Marcel 1311, 2136, 2138, 2139
Pryor, Richard 903, 904
Pryor, Roger 1445
Psilander, Valdemar 1625, 1626
Pucholt, Vladimir 2164
Pudovkin, Vsevolod I. 99, 100, 126, 142, 144, 213, 304, 314, 1339, 1645, 1646, 1647, 1651, 1652, 1655, 1661, 1662, 1667, 1718, 1758, 1811, 1865
Pulman, Jack 1318
Punsley, Bernard 987
Purdom, Edmund 1439
Purkye, J. E. 1582
Purviance, Edna 1416, 1417, 1429, 1431
Puttnam, David 537, 671, 704, 1842

Q

Quasimodo 390
Quayle, Anthony 1347, 1353
Queen, Ellery 380
Quigley, Martin 1749
Quillan, Eddie 1445
Quine, Richard 937
Quinn, Anthony 1015, 1021, 1202, 1326, 1541, 1933, 1951, 1968

R

Rabier, Jean 165, 2100, 2151
Rabinovitch, Gregor 1906
Rabinowitz, Seymour 1403
Radiguet, Raymond 1993
Radnitz, Robert B. 996
Rafferty, Kevin 324
Rafferty, Pierce 324
Raff, Norman C. 702, 766
Raft, George 1445, 1785

Raimu 1814, 1826
Rainer, Luise 1078, 1320, 1444, 1452, 1484, 1802
Rainer, Peter 1452
Rainer, Yvonne 501
Rainey, Ma 920
Raine, Kathleen 315
Raine, Norman Reilly 1015, 1101
Rainger, Ralph 405
Rainier, Louis Henri Maxence Bertrand Rainier III 547
Rains, Claude 372, 800, 1288, 1357
Ralston, Esther 1445
Ralston, Vera Hruba 1445
Ramsaye, Terry 208
Randall, Jack 433
Randall, Tony 415
Randolph, Lillian 948
Randol, George 878, 942, 947
Rand, Ayn 1088, 1180, 1263
Rank, J. Arthur 1566, 1567, 1571, 1613, 1833, 1834, 1862, 1935, 1937
Rapf, Harry 1277, 1485
Rapf, Maurice 1073, 1192, 1193, 1277
Raphael (Raffaelo Sanzio) 57
Raphaelson, Samson 1070, 1142, 1145, 1192, 1276, 1804
Rapper, Irving 797, 800, 1496, 1550
Rapp, Cornelius Ward 1506
Rapp, George 1506
Raskin, David 408, 1097, 1424
Raskolnikov 1240
Rastus 938
Rathbone, Basil 381, 1451, 1863
Ratoff, Gregory 828
Rattigan, Terence 1942
Ravetch, Irving 1212, 1349
Rawlinson, Herbert 1444
Raye, Martha 1433
Raymond, Gene 1446
Ray, Allene 1444
Ray, Charles 1444
Ray, Man 1711, 1713, 1714, 1717, 1727, 1730, 1731
Ray, Nicholas 119, 386, 980, 997, 1237, 1259, 1548, 1721, 1752, 1951, 1963,
  1968, 1969, 1984, 1985, 2002, 2088, 2096
Ray, Satyajit 466, 548, 1004, 1553, 1566, 2167, 2168, 2169
Read, Herbert 1939
Reagan, Ronald 431, 437, 1088, 1180, 1192, 1289, 1293, 1527, 1529, 1531, 2181,
  2200
Rebush, Roman 848
Rector, Enoch 1593
Redford, Robert 671, 851, 1008, 1151, 1321, 1436, 1437, 2065, 2066, 2078, 2206
Redgrave, Lynn 1006
Redgrave, Michael 1863, 1934, 1942
Redgrave, Vanessa 547, 1265, 1322, 2173
Reed, Carol 323, 343, 1021, 1033, 1204, 1218, 1219, 1329, 1552, 1566, 1833,
  1842, 1934, 1939, 1941, 1943, 2034
Reed, Donna 368, 1167, 1446
Reed, Pamela 1530
Reed, Rex 155, 1175
Reed, Ted 1407
Reese, Mason 992
Reeves, Alf 1417

Reeves, Michael 396
Reeves, Steve 1440
Reggio, Godfrey 598
Reid, Carl Benton 1348
Reid, Mrs. Wallace 519
Reid, Wallace 966, 1242, 1375, 1396, 1440, 1444, 1504, 1505
Reimann, Walter 1632, 1643
Reiner, Carl 2047
Reiner, Rob 2036
Reinhardt, Gottfried 1319
Reinhardt, Max 1331, 1573, 1631, 1632, 1633, 1634, 1635, 1642, 1675, 1967
Reisch, Walter 1191, 1803
Reisman, Arnie 1293
Reiss, Stuart R. 849
Reisz, Karel 82, 1939, 2162
Rejane, Gabrielle 1618
Reles, Abe 833
Remick, Lee 790, 1323
Remy, Albert 1006
Renaldo, Duncan 1445
Renan, Sheldon 107
Renick, Ruth 1407
Rennahan, Ray 812, 1322, 1801
Rennie, Michael 1987
Renoir, Jean 186, 187, 242, 261, 274, 277, 466, 648, 912, 914, 1211, 1548, 1551,
    1571, 1714, 1756, 1815, 1826, 1827, 1906, 1922, 1924, 1946, 1951, 1992, 1993,
    1994, 1996, 1999, 2000, 2001, 2027, 2034, 2043, 2096, 2155
Renoir, J. and Akira Kurosawa 1899
Renoir, J. and Eric Rohmer 2102
Renoir, J. and Ernest Hemingway 1232
Renoir, J. and film criticism 144
Renoir, J. and Fritz Lang 187
Renoir, J. and ideology 474
Renoir, J. and Luchino Visconti 1884
Renoir, J. and MISE EN SCENE 1998
Renoir, J. and RKO 1820
Renoir, J. and screen adaptations 1316
Renoir, J. and screenwriters 1147
Renoir, J. and social cinema 1812, 1813, 1814
Renoir, J. and the Popular Front in France 1821
Renoir, J. and THE RULES OF THE GAME 1827
Renoir, J. and the 1940s 1821
Renoir, J. and the 1950s 1821
Renoir, J. and Universal Pictures 1820
Renoir, J. and William Faulkner 1149, 1210, 1256
Renoir, J. and World War II 352, 353
Renoir, J. and 20th Century-Fox 1820
Renoir, Marguerite 1994
Resnais, Alain 305, 323, 355, 379, 1311, 1553, 1572, 1715, 1882, 1993, 2006,
    2033, 2097, 2112, 2114, 2115, 2117, 2122, 2127, 2134, 2135, 2136, 2137, 2138,
    2139, 2149, 2152, 2153
Resnais, A. and Claude Chabrol 2098
Resnais, A. and the "new cinema" 2121
Rettig, Tommy 992, 993, 1445
Reverdy, Pierre 1710
Revere, Anne 1093, 1444
Reville, Alma 1838, 1847, 1852, 1853, 1855, 1857, 1864, 1920
Revuelta, Raquel 527

Rex (horse star) 1446
Reynauld, Emile 1583, 1585, 1589, 1598
Reynolds, Ben 1708
Reynolds, Burt 2036
Reynolds, Debbie 523, 524, 790, 1295, 1969, 1980
Reynolds, Marjorie 1439
Reynolds, Norman 813
Reynolds, William 1017
Rey, Fernado 1722
Rhodes, Erik 1439
Rhodes, Majorie 143
Rice, Elmer 836, 1061, 1176, 1189
Rice, John 1480
Richardson, Ian 1355
Richardson, Ralph 418, 1007, 1329, 1350, 1863, 1934, 1943
Richardson, Tony 997, 1013, 1294, 1328, 1939, 2118, 2162
Richards, Dick 1758
Richards, Robert L. 1982
Richard, Edmond 165
Richman, Harry 1444
Richter, Hans 292, 1711, 1717
Rich, Irene 1444, 1502, 1706
Rich, John 1427
Rich, Lee 536, 662
Rich, Marc 663
Rich, Robert 1171
Riddle, Nelson 1322
Riefenstahl, Leni 209, 218, 238, 240, 250, 292, 293, 295, 296, 317, 321, 466, 497, 508, 539, 1439, 2177
Riera, Albert 1828
Rigg, Diana 1355
Rin Tin Tin (dog star) 1288, 1446, 1495, 1500
Rinaldo, Ben 878, 942
Rinehart, Mary Roberts 1061, 1472
Ripley, Arthur 1708
Riskin, Robert 346, 1066, 1073, 1093, 1151, 1154, 1203, 1328, 1747, 1799
Ritchard, Cyril 1864
Rittau, Gunther 1642
Ritter, Karl 238, 240
Ritter, Tex 433
Ritter, Thelma 1977, 1978
Ritt, Martin 913, 945, 1212, 1293, 2036
Riva, Emmanuelle 2152
Rivette, Jacques 1553, 2006, 2094, 2096, 2098, 2100, 2122, 2125
Rivette, J. and CAHIERS DU CINEMA 1997
Rivette, J. and the CINEMATEQUE FRANCAISE 1992
Rivkin, Allen 1071
Roach, Hal, Sr. 866, 920, 1146, 1240, 1410, 1468, 1491, 1691, 1692, 1695, 1701
Robards, Jason, Jr. 549, 1022, 1322, 1350, 1351, 2062, 2063
Robbe-Grillet, Alain 416, 1156, 1311, 1313, 1572, 2112, 2113, 2114, 2127, 2137, 2139, 2153
Robbins, Harold 1236
Robbins, Jerome 1164, 1181, 1188
Robbins, Jim 763
Robert-Houdin, Jean-Eugene 1588, 1616
Robertson, Cliff 2078, 2089
Robertson, Etienne Gaspard (Robert) 1588, 1602
Robertson, John 117
Robertson, Stanley 905

Roberts, Eric 1530
Roberts, Rachel 2160
Roberts, Tony 1293
Robeson, Paul 870, 875, 876, 877, 921, 929, 937, 939, 942, 943, 948, 951, 953, 1179, 1181, 1195, 1445, 1567, 1833
Robeson, Paul, Jr. 905
Robey, George 1427
Robinson, Andrew 429
Robinson, Casey 797, 800
Robinson, Edward G. 385, 386, 798, 799, 1091, 1093, 1181, 1188, 1229, 1240, 1289, 1443, 1494, 1499, 1750, 1804
Robinson, Jackie 884
Robinson, Luther Bill "Bojangles" 877, 882, 921, 939
Robson, Flora 1009, 1357
Robson, Mark 375, 952, 1550
Rocha, Glauber 2123, 2158
Rochester (See Anderson, Eddie) 921
Rochin, Aaron 368
Rockefeller, John D. 630, 1746
Rockefeller, Nelson 307
Rockerfeller, Nelson 1789
Rock, Joseph 1468
Rodgers, Jimmie 1439
Rodgers, Richard 405
Rodney, Richard 402
Roeg, Nicolas 492, 493, 495, 2160, 2209
Roemer, Michael 894, 922, 952
Rogers, Charles "Buddy" 370, 1393, 1396, 1445
Rogers, Ginger 219, 402, 502, 990, 1164, 1202, 1449, 1452, 1759, 1786, 1798
Rogers, Howard Emmett 1073, 1080, 1088, 1192
Rogers, Lela 1088, 1179
Rogers, Roy 431, 433, 1449, 1750, 1757
Rogers, Will 1160, 1444, 1474, 1578, 1673, 1686, 1701
Roget, Peter Mark 1582
Rogosin, Lionel 2089
Rohmer, Eric 516, 598, 1844, 1996, 2096, 2100, 2102, 2123, 2124, 2125, 2127, 2142
Rohmer, E. and Alfred Hitchcock 2102, 2141
Rohmer, E. and Andre Bazin 2141
Rohmer, E. and CAHIERS DU CINEMA 1997, 2002, 2141
Rohmer, E. and Claude Chabrol 2094, 2102, 2128
Rohmer, E. and Francois Truffaut 2102
Rohmer, E. and Fredrich W. Murnau 2102
Rohmer, E. and Howard Hawks 2102
Rohmer, E. and Jean Renoir 2102
Rohmer, E. and LA NOUVELLE VAGUE 2108
Rohmer, E. and MISE EN SCENE 1998
Rohmer, E. and the CINEMATEQUE FRANCAISE 1992
Rohmer, E. and the "new cinema" 2121
Rohmer, E. and Vincente Minnelli 2141
Rohrig, Walther 1632, 1641, 1642, 1643
Roland, Gilbert 1439, 1455
Roland, Ruth 304, 1455
Rolfe, Ben 1477
Rolling Stones, the 376, 405
Romanoff, Mike 1498
Romero, George A. 389, 390, 392, 394, 397, 399, 604
Rommel, Erwin Johannes Eugen 323, 365, 366

Romm, May 1847
Romm, Mikhail Ilyitch 237, 1652
Rondi, Brunello 1023, 2174, 2175
Ronsard, Pierre 1313
Room, Abram 1647
Rooney, Mickey 735, 970, 991, 992, 993, 1242, 1341, 1750, 1786
Roosevelt, Franklin Delano 200, 258, 260, 273, 292, 343, 344, 365, 1191, 1494, 1496, 1789
Roosevelt, Theodore 296, 1400, 1405
Root, Well 1071
Rosay, Francois 1814, 1906
Rosemond, Clinton 859
Rosenberg, Alfred 234
Rosenberg, Meta 1190
Rosenblatt, Sol 1192
Rosenbloom, "Slapsie" Maxie 1445
Rosenfelt, Frank E. 642
Rosenman, Leonard 408, 1552
Rosen, Robert (Robert Rossen) 1969
Rose, Reginald 2036, 2058
Rose, William 1279, 1937, 2072, 2082
Rosher, Charles 1010, 1398, 1403
Rossellini, Renzo 1883
Rossellini, Roberto 127, 186, 187, 352, 378, 564, 648, 1316, 1440, 1548, 1573, 1874, 1875, 1878, 1881, 1883, 1922, 1923, 1924, 1925, 1926, 1932, 1933, 1995, 2002, 2094, 2096
Rossellini, R. and Jean-Luc Godard 2129
Rossen, Hal 80
Rossen, Harold 370, 994, 1801
Rossen, Robert 139, 354, 369, 882, 944, 1012, 1014, 1018, 1091, 1154, 1178, 1195, 1275, 1551, 1946, 1951, 1969, 1985, 2043
Rossif, Frederic 222, 319
Ross, Diana 905, 920
Ross, Herbert 786, 1016
Ross, Katharine 2078, 2085, 2086
Ross, Larry 1444
Ross, Lillian 1319
Ross, Steven J. 2205
Rosten, Norman 1349
Rostovtsev, I. 1662
Rothafel, Samuel L. "Roxy" 1506
Rothapfel, Samuel L. "Roxy" 1379
Rotha, Paul 144, 214, 215, 216, 243, 245, 248, 283, 292, 294, 295, 302, 323, 1840, 1869
Rothman, Stephanie 508
Rothstein, Arnold 833
Roth, Joe 2206
Roth, Lillian 1445
Roth, Philip 1315
Rouch, Jean 293, 2119, 2120, 2121, 2122, 2143, 2153
Roundtree, Richard 899, 901, 904, 923, 935
Rouquier, Georges 1993, 2001
Rouse, Russell 1752
Rove, La 1717
Rowlands, Gena 2074
Rowland, Richard 1393, 1464, 1481
Rozier, Jacques 2119
Rozov, V. 1001
Rozsa, Miklos 83, 403, 408, 606, 799, 1354

Ruban, Al   2049
Rubin, Benny   828
Rubin, Robert   1481, 1483, 1489
Ruby, Harry   1253, 1805
Ruggles, Wesley   1807
Rumkowski, Chiam   290
Runkle, Theodora Van   2088
Ruskin, Harry   1314
Russell, Harold   375, 1445
Russell, Jane   1917
Russell, John L.   2054
Russell, Ken   583, 1296, 1552, 1566
Russell, Louis J.   1180
Russell, Rosalind   502, 1002, 1240
Rutherford, Ann   992, 1445, 1456
Rutherford, Margaret   1934
Ruth, Babe   1400
Ruth, Roy Del   1548
Ruttenberg, Joseph   402, 1018, 1216, 1354
Ruttmann, Walther   292, 294, 1711, 1714, 1717, 1869, 1880
Ryan, Cornelius   1501
Ryan, Kathleen   1021
Ryan, Peggy   1439
Ryan, Robert   331, 375, 386, 849, 1018, 1351, 1635, 1986, 2071
Ryan, Sheila   1439
Ryan, Thomas C.   995
Rydell, Mark   516
Ryder, Loren   799
Ryerson, Florence   1801
Rye, Stellan   1631
Ryskind, Morrie   226, 1088, 1147, 1154
Ryu, Chishu   2032

S

Sabinson, Lee   1195
Sack, Alfred   935
Sadoul, Georges   1996
Sagan, Leontine   497, 1829, 1923
Sahl, Mort   2044, 2087
Saint, Eva Marie   850
Sais, Marin   1444
Saks, Gene   1351
Salfrank, Hermann   1641
Salter, Hans J.   408
Saltzman, Harry   422
Salt, Waldo   376, 1091, 1100, 1181, 1195, 1291
Salvani, Robert   947
Sambo   883, 938
Samoilova, Tatiana   1001
Samuelson, G. B. (Bertie)   1567
San Juan, Olga   1446
Sanchez, Jaime   2084
Sanda, Dominique   2174
Sandburg, Carl   1265
Sanders, Denis   379
Sanders, George   1329, 1451, 1981

Sanders, Helke   501
Sanders, Robert (See Stan Brakhage)   1957
Sandford, Stanley J.   1406
Sandrich, Mark   194
Sands, Diana   901, 922, 1009
Sands, Tommy   1440
Sanford, John   1038
Sanjines, Jorge   918
Sargent, Alvin   1008, 1228, 1322
Sargent, Epes Winthrop   123
Saroyan, William   1065, 1108, 1278
Sarrayte, Nathalie   2112, 2137
Sarris, Andrew   1141, 1270, 1426, 1452, 1592, 1792, 1926
Sarris, A. and Andre Bazin   156
Sarris, A. and film criticism   155
Sarris, A. and film reviewing   121
Sarris, A. and Jean-Luc Godard   156
Sarris, A. and the AUTEUR theory   132
Sartov, Hendrik   1372, 1378, 1387, 1388, 1390, 1391, 1397
Sasdy, Peter   396
Sassard, Jacqueline   2151
Satie, Erik   1728
Saul, Oscar   1352
Saunders, Russ   1015
Saura, Carlos   235, 278, 598
Savage, John   367
Savalas, Telly   378, 2071
Savaleva, Era   371
Saville, Victor   1567, 1833, 1834, 1837, 1841, 1855
Savini, Robert   935
Savini, Tom   394
Sawyer, Gordon   1472
Sayer, Jay   2075
Sayles, John   415
Sayre, Joel   1103, 1207, 1806
Schach, Max   1840
Schaefer, George J.   735, 1789
Schafer, Natalie   1439
Schaffner, Franklin J.   365, 382, 2036, 2066, 2067, 2089, 2090, 2175
Schary, Belle   1485
Schary, Dore   691, 849, 1088, 1205, 1208, 1209, 1236, 1319, 1466, 1468, 1485
Schary, Herman Hugo   1485
Schell, Maria   790
Schell, Maximilian   377, 1202, 1322, 1354
Schenck, Joseph M.   537, 622, 820, 1075, 1369, 1395, 1455, 1470, 1482, 1493, 1500, 1501, 1967
Schenck, Nicholas   244, 622, 820, 1235, 1479, 1481, 1482, 1485, 1488, 1500
Schickel, Richard   121, 156, 1379, 1385, 1452
Schiffmann, Suzanne   998, 2143
Schildkraut, Joseph   849, 1015, 1264, 1390
Schlesinger, John   516, 562, 994, 1291, 1552
Schlondorff, Volker   311, 2165
Schmidt, Godfrey   1186
Schneer, Charles H.   411, 1289
Schneiderman, George   193
Schneider, Alan   2067
Schneider, Alfred   973
Schneider, Romy   1022
Schoedsack, Ernest B.   1800, 1869

Schoenberg, Arnold 1711, 1717
Schott, Gaspar 1594
Schrader, Paul 341, 2195
Schub, Esther 466, 497
Schufftan, Eugen (Eugene Schuftan) 1014, 1642
Schulberg, Benjamin P. 1202, 1268, 1277, 1486, 1488
Schulberg, Budd 238, 836, 1065, 1073, 1092, 1098, 1106, 1109, 1116, 1125,
  1127, 1144, 1148, 1154, 1155, 1157, 1181, 1184, 1188, 1190, 1192, 1193, 1217,
  1257, 1260, 1261, 1277, 1670, 1750, 1979, 2048
Schultz, Benjamin 1188
Schwartz, Maurice 829, 846, 847, 848
Schwarzenegger, Arnold 2198
Schweizer, Richard 1989
Scofield, Paul 970, 1020, 1449
Scorsese, Martin 341, 604, 1011, 1758, 2033, 2049, 2196, 2209
Scott, Adrian 849
Scott, Allan 1798
Scott, Emmett J. 867, 926, 934, 949
Scott, Fred 433
Scott, George C. 365, 547, 1014, 1452, 2036, 2067, 2083
Scott, Hazel 879, 921, 944
Scott, Jay 157
Scott, Lizabeth 1445
Scott, Randolph 431, 1160, 1445, 2086
Scott, Ridley 415
Scott, Walter M. 849
Scott, (Robert) Adrian 1088, 1202, 1287, 1485
Scully, Frank 226
Sears, Heather 1016
Sears, Zelda 1313
Seaton, George 1140, 1203, 1350, 1805
Seberg, Jean 1967, 1970, 1985, 2151
Seeber, Guido 1717
Seeger, Pete 1188
Segal, George 374, 1541, 2086
Segal, Vivienne 1445
Seiden, Joseph 829, 845, 846, 848
Seitz, John 799
Selander, Lesley 1758
Seldes, Gilbert 127, 140, 157, 173
Seldte, Franz 297
Sellers, Coleman 1585, 1591
Sellers, Peter 1941, 2083
Selpin, Herbert 238
Seltzer, David 997
Selwyn, Archibald 1472, 1480, 1503
Selwyn, Edgar 1472, 1480, 1503
Selznick, David O. 244, 273, 572, 639, 812, 820, 929, 958, 1054, 1124, 1192,
  1219, 1254, 1264, 1277, 1288, 1289, 1369, 1435, 1466, 1479, 1480, 1485, 1486,
  1487, 1488, 1489, 1490, 1503, 1746, 1839
Selznick, D. and Alfred Hitchcock 1846, 1847, 1848, 1849, 1853, 1978
Selznick, D. and Charlie Chaplin 1847, 1848
Selznick, D. and GONE WITH THE WIND 1801
Selznick, D. and Peter Bogdanovich 146
Selznick, D. and RKO 1848
Selznick, D. and United Artists 1847, 1848
Selznick, Howard 1486
Selznick, Irene Mayer 1489

Selznick, Lewis J. 1467, 1468, 1486, 1488, 1621
Selznick, Myron 1124, 1486, 1488, 1489
Selzter, David 972
Sembene, Ousmane 909, 910, 911, 918, 919
Semon, Larry 1412, 1578
Semprun, Jorge 577, 2113, 2136, 2137
Sennett, Mack 142, 188, 1248, 1360, 1379, 1384, 1409, 1411, 1412, 1413, 1415, 1420, 1423, 1424, 1426, 1433, 1463, 1464, 1474, 1476, 1491, 1549, 1550, 1551, 1578, 1595, 1606, 1618, 1619, 1621, 1677, 1692, 1701, 1824
Serandrei, Mario 1922
Serling, Rod 2036, 2090
Serna, Jacques 1439
Serre, Henri 2155
Sersen, Fred 366
Sessions, Almira 1447
Sewall, Blanche 1801
Sewell, Vernon 396
Seymour, Clarine 1384
Shagan, Steve 836
Shakespeare, William 151, 156, 191, 594, 1009, 1311, 1342, 1343, 1353, 1354, 1355, 1356, 1398, 1408, 1561, 1608
Shamroy, Leon 366
Sharaff, Irene 1356, 1983, 2086
Sharitis, Paul 1956
Sharp, Don 396
Shawn, Dick 2073
Shaw, Artie 1096
Shaw, George Bernard 151, 1151, 1170, 1243, 1340, 1344, 1357, 1797, 1863
Shaw, Irwin 369, 1144, 1279
Shaw, Robert 1020
Shaw, Wini 1439, 1468
Shearer, Douglas 369, 370, 378, 1468, 1801
Shearer, Moira 1015, 1440, 1943
Shearer, Norma 1214, 1440, 1444, 1450, 1479, 1481, 1502, 1786
Shea, John 1020, 1530
Sheedy, Ally 972
Sheed, Wilfrid 158
Sheehan, Winfield 692, 1466
Sheen, Charlie 368
Sheen, Martin 367
Sheffield, Johnny 992, 993, 1445
Shenberg, Margaret 1480
Shentall, Susan 1009
Shepard, Richard 666
Shepherd, Cybill 913, 996
Shepherd, Sam 1278
Sherdeman, Ted 996
Sheridan, Ann 346
Sherman, Lowell 1374, 1808
Sherman, Vincent 1496
Sherriff, R. C. 1021, 1328, 1943
Sherrif, Paul 1354
Sherwin, David 1001
Sherwood, Robert E. 127, 228, 351, 375, 1063, 1176
Shields, Brooke 970, 981
Shils, Edward 179
Shimazu, Yasujiro 1887, 1888, 1894, 2017
Shimizu, Hiroshi 1743, 1887, 1891, 1892
Shimura, Takashi 2029, 2030

Shindo, Kaneto 2018, 2019, 2025
Shinoda, Masahiro 1743, 1898, 2025, 2026
Shipman, Nell 1450
Shirley, Anne 1446
Shore, Dinah 346
Short, William 729
Shostakovich, Dimitri 1343
Shtraukh, Maxim 1661
Shub, Esther 213, 304, 1645, 1647, 1656, 1658, 1661
Shulman, Irving 997
Shumyatsky, Boris 1661, 1865
Shurlock, Geoffrey 2037
Shylock 822
Sickner, Roy N. 2087
Sidney, George 828
Sidney, Sylvia 1018, 1277, 1445, 1808
Siegel, Benjamin "Bugsy" 1241, 1242
Siegel, Donald 183, 191, 343, 386, 576, 1146, 1231, 1237, 1762, 1916, 1946, 1951, 2061
Siegmann, George 263, 1387, 1388
Signoret, Simone 1016, 2152
Sigurd, Jacques 1998
Sillen, Sam 1286
Silliphant, Stirling 937, 1150, 2082
Sillitoe, Alan 997, 2162
Sills, Milton 1444
Silver (horse star) 1446
Silvera, Darrell 1807
Silverblatt, Howard 1095
Silverheels, Jay 1445
Silverstein, Elliot 1550
Silverstein, Mort 2042
Silver, Joan Micklin 604, 1313
Simmons, Jean 383, 1353
Simms, Ginny 1445
Simms, Larry "Baby Dumpling" 1446
Simoni, Dario 1356
Simon, John 121, 158
Simon, Michel 1814, 1828
Simon, Neil 1028, 1155, 1351
Simon, Simone 1445
Simpson, Claire 368
Simpson, Mickey 1976
Simpson, Robert E. 1326
Sim, Alistair 1934
Sinatra, Frank 62, 368, 426, 690, 1089, 1188, 1206, 1242, 1272, 1917, 1918, 2077
Sinclair, Upton 225, 226, 574, 624, 1233, 1656, 1661, 1750, 1866
Sindler, Irving 1472, 1473
Sindlinger, Albert 302
Singer, Isaac Bashevis 598, 836
Singleton, Penny 1445
Sintzenich, Hal S. 1387, 1390
Siodmak, Robert 386, 1813, 1829, 1906, 1948
Sirk, Douglas 489, 794, 980, 1548, 1757, 1758, 1829, 1951, 1970, 1971, 1986, 2035
Siskel, Gene 976
Sjoberg, Alf 2183

Sjoman, Vilgot 1628
Sjostrom, Victor 1524, 1624, 1626, 1627, 1629, 1630, 1671, 1674, 1706, 2189
Skelton, Red 1241
Skerritt, Tom 379
Skinner, Richard Dana 1429
Skladanowsky, Emile 1586, 1630
Skladanowsky, Max 1586, 1590, 1630
Skolimowski, Jerzy 2123, 2180
Skolsky, Sidney 1244
Skouras, Charles 1466, 1492
Skouras, George 1466, 1492
Skouras, Spyros 1206, 1235, 1251, 1254, 1256, 1466, 1470, 1492, 1501
Skulnick, Menasha 829
Sleep n' Eat (Willie Best) 870, 877, 926
Slesinger, Tess 1320
Sleznick, D. and GONE WITH THE WIND 1436
Slide, Anthony 1382
Sloane, Everett 992, 1188
Slocombe, Douglas 1322
Sloman, Edward 1383
Slos, Elmar 378
Small, Edward 1296
Smith, Albert E. 1588
Smith, Alexis 1452
Smith, Bessie 870
Smith, Charlie Martin 993
Smith, Frank Leon 1457
Smith, Fred Y. 1240
Smith, George Albert 1606, 1612
Smith, Henry Nash 430
Smith, Jack Martin 402
Smith, James 1387
Smith, Leonard 1010
Smith, Maggie 30, 1003
Smith, Mildred Joanne 922
Smith, Pete 1234, 1445
Snowball 877
Snow, Marguerite 1459
Snow, Michael 492, 493, 1956
Soderberg, Theodore 1017
Sokolove, Richard 1347
Sokolsky, George E. 1186, 1188
Solanas, Fernando 918, 2110, 2157
Solas, Humberto 526
Soldati, Mario 1573, 1878
Solinas, Franco 2172, 2176
Sologne, Madeleine 1910
Solow, Eugene 1281
Solt, Andrew 1293, 1469
Sommer, Edith 1001
Sommer, Elke 1244
Sondergaard, Gale 1093, 1181, 1195, 1444, 1446
Sontag, Susan 516
Sorlin, Pierre 444
Sorrell, Herbert 1082, 1180, 1186, 1191, 1192, 1202
Soupault, Philippe 1710, 1718
Southern, Ann 1484
Southern, Terry 1294, 2051
Souto, H. Mario Raimondo 81

Spaak, Charles   1812, 1813, 1814, 1826
Spacek, Sissy   1020, 2209
Spade, Sam   380
Spanky (See McFarland, George)   992
Spatz, Jonas   1144
Spellman, Francis Cardinal   1260
Spencer, Kenneth   879, 922, 939
Sperber, Dan   138
Sperling, Karen   516
Sperling, Milton   1192, 1502
Spiegelman, Gaye   1235
Spiegel, Sam   220, 1225, 1284, 1352, 1490
Spielberg, Steven   56, 341, 604, 668, 760, 905, 1140, 1154, 1550, 2196, 2199, 2209
Sponable, Earl I.   272, 1745
Spottiswoode, Raymond   54
Stahl, John   1986
Staiola, Enzo   1004
Stalin, Joseph V.   228, 259, 261, 344, 1656, 1657, 1661, 1750, 1866, 1868
Stallings, Laurence   304, 367
Stallone, Sylvester   801, 1164, 1538, 2198, 2206
Stander, Lionel   1179, 1181, 1188
Stanford, Governor Leland   1585, 1596, 1597
Stanford, Leland   1597
Stanislavsky, Constantin   1648, 1649
Stanley, Kim   1292
Stannard, Eliot   1857
Stanwyck, Barbara   502, 798, 799, 1443, 1452, 1786, 1920, 1970
Stapleton, Maureen   1346, 1349
Stark, Ray   1235
Starrett, Charles   431, 1440, 1446
Stears, John   813
Steele, Barbara   396
Steele, Bob   429, 431
Steelman, Barry   763
Stefano, Joseph   2054
Stefan, Jerzy   2180
Steiger, Rod   143, 816, 1136, 1290, 1294, 1979, 1982, 2082, 2084
Steinbeck, John   135, 1103, 1108, 1153, 1156, 1232, 1251, 1260, 1261, 1272, 1274, 1278, 1281, 1325, 1326
Steinbeck, J.   2051
Steinem, Gloria   1531
Steiner, Fred   408
Steiner, Max   83, 408, 800, 812, 1015, 1019, 1468, 1494, 1801
Steiner, Ralph   252, 1872
Steinhoff, Hans   238, 240
Steinkamp, Frederick   2089
Steinore, Michael   369
Stein, Gertrude   1311
Sten, Anna   1444, 1472
Stephanoff, Blagoe "Bob"   1472
Stephenson, Jill   251
Stephenson, William   778
Sterling, Ford   1410, 1415, 1622
Sterling, Jan   1529
Sternberg, Jonas (see Josef Von Sternberg)   1696
Stern, Julius   1708
Stern, Stewart   997, 1240

Steuermann, Salka 1102
Stevenson, Adlai E. 1485, 2089
Stevenson, Edward 1237
Stevens, Charlie 1403
Stevens, George 849, 1009, 1015, 1169, 1552, 1787, 1798, 1806, 1952, 1954
Stevens, George, Jr. 1787
Stevens, Rise 1445
Stewart, Donald Ogden 1020, 1063, 1066, 1073, 1083, 1104, 1124, 1142, 1182, 1192, 1203, 1278, 1750
Stewart, James 346, 383, 735, 789, 803, 990, 1160, 1264, 1443, 1449, 1674, 1787, 1799, 1850, 1951, 1952, 1978, 1982, 2075, 2080
Stiller, Mauritz 1395, 1479, 1624, 1626, 1627, 1630, 1631, 1671, 1674, 1706, 1710
Stirling, Linda 1446
Stockwell, Dean 990, 992, 1010
Stoler, Mark 344
Stompanato, Johnny 1242
Stonehouse, Ruth 520
Stoney, George C. 293
Stone, Flora Shallcross 1597
Stone, Lewis 1803
Stone, N. B., Jr. 2086
Stone, Oliver 368
Stone, Peter 1146
Storaro, Vittorio 367
Storm, Gale 1446
Stothart, Herbert 1330, 1801
Strand, Paul 1872
Strasberg, Lee 1258, 1261, 2060
Straub, Jean-Marie 2126
Straukh, Maxim 1658
Strauss, Robert 374
Streep, Meryl 62, 110, 1007, 1530
Street, James 1101
Streisand, Barbra 62, 842, 851, 889, 1233, 1235, 1243, 1295, 1436, 2206
Strickling, Howard 1234
Stringer, Michael 850
Stripling, Robert E. 1180, 1187
Strode, Woody 885, 901, 904, 922, 937
Stroheim, Erich Oswald (see Erich Von Stroheim) 1699
Stromberg, Hunt 642, 1149
Strongheart (dog star) 1446
Stroub, Jean-Marie 2123
Struss, Karl 1386, 1398, 1431, 1432
Stuart, Gloria 1446
Sturges, John 374, 1951, 1986
Sturges, Preston 1014, 1065, 1145, 1147, 1154, 1548, 1912, 1918, 1919, 1920, 1921, 1954
Sturges, Solomon 1918
Stymie (See Beard, Matthew) 992
Styron, William 1032
St. Jacques, Raymond 893, 896, 922, 935, 941
St. John, Adela Rogers 1453
Subotsky, Milton 388
Sullavan, Margaret 1123, 1151, 1215, 1264, 2059
Sullivan, Barry 1289
Sullivan, C. Gardner 1154, 1623
Sullivan, Ed 1188
Sullivan, Frank 1216
Sully, Anna Beth 1399

Summers, Hope 1446
Summer, Donna 920
Sunday, Billy 1400, 1405
Sunshine Sammy (Frederick Ernest Morrison) 865, 866, 922
Surtees, Robert L. 370, 996, 1016, 1208, 1290, 2086
Survage, Leopold 1711, 1717
Susskind, David 1188
Sutherland, Donald 378, 379, 1291, 2071
Sutton, Grady 1446
Svilova, Elizaveta Ignat'evna 1663, 1669
Swain, Mack 1410, 1429, 1430
Swanson, Gloria 502, 503, 631, 809, 1248, 1296, 1369, 1393, 1394, 1395, 1401,
   1410, 1440, 1443, 1444, 1447, 1449, 1454, 1477, 1503, 1504, 1560, 1578, 1674,
   1700, 1703, 1797
Swanson, William 1463
Sweet, Blanche 1350, 1384, 1389, 1444, 1452, 1468
Swerling, Jo 812, 1151
Swift, David 1237
Swink, Robert 1988
Switzer, Carl "Alfalfa" 992, 993
Syberberg, Hans-Jurgen 362, 2165
Sylbert, Anthea 1322, 1552
Symonds, Julian 373

T

Tacitus, Publius Cornelius 382
Taffel, Bess 1182
Takahashi, Michio 2152
Taka, Miiko 1440
Talbot, William Henry Fox 1584, 1598
Tallents, Stephen 214, 216, 244, 295
Tally, Thomas L. 1416, 1600
Talmadge, Constance 1060, 1115, 1116, 1379, 1385, 1388, 1400, 1444, 1454
Talmadge, Natalie 1454, 1688
Talmadge, Norma 1060, 1379, 1385, 1400, 1412, 1444, 1454
Talmadge, Richard 1403, 1405
Tamblyn, Russ 992
Tamiroff, Akim 1022, 1322
Tanaka, Eizo 1740
Tanaka, Kinuyo 2031
Tandy, Jessica 1346, 1852
Tanen, Ned 666
Taniguchi, Senkichi 2017
Tannura, Phil 297
Tapiovarra, Nyrki 1627
Taradash, Daniel 368, 1237
Tarkington, Booth 1327
Tartikoff, Brandon 678
Tashlin, Frank 1146
Tate, Sharon 1244, 1355
Tati, Jacques 1571, 1999, 2000, 2001, 2007, 2010, 2118, 2122
Tati, J. and Buster Keaton 2007
Tati, J. and Charlie Chaplin 2007
Tati, J. and Harold Lloyd 2007
Tati, J. and Harry Langdon 2007
Tati, J. and silent film comedy 2010

Tattloli, Elda 2173
Tatum, Art 320
Taurog, Norman 355
Tavel, Ronald 2069, 2091
Tavernier, Bernard 2127
Taviani, Paolo 377
Taviani, Vittorio 377
Taylor, Donald 1869
Taylor, Elizabeth 62, 159, 508, 523, 524, 913, 991, 992, 1015, 1130, 1219, 1235, 1242, 1243, 1250, 1346, 1352, 1356, 1440, 1443, 1447, 1484, 1502, 1951, 2042, 2086
Taylor, John 215, 1869
Taylor, Kent 1440
Taylor, Laurette 1346
Taylor, Libby 877
Taylor, Peter 374
Taylor, Robert 209, 350, 1012, 1080, 1088, 1180, 1187, 1192, 1215, 1229, 1443, 1920, 1986
Taylor, Rod 2036
Taylor, Samuel 1408, 1852, 1855, 2080
Taylor, William Desmond 1410, 1411, 1695
Tchaikovsky, Pyotr Ilich 209
Tcherina, Ludmilla 1943
Teisch, Steve 1004
Tellegen, Lou 1440
Temple, Shirley 970, 971, 990, 991, 992, 993, 1129, 1219, 1220, 1401, 1443, 1452, 1471, 1487, 1529, 1750, 1787
Tenney, John 1192, 1193
Tennyson, Alfred Lord 1363
Terayama, Shuji 2025
Terrhune, Max 1447
Terry, Alice 1444, 1450, 1707
Teshigahara, Hiroshi 2025, 2177
Tetzel, Joan 1487
Tevis, Louise Sargent 1919
Tewkesbury, Joan 2195
Thacher, Molly 1259
Thalberg, Irving 226, 1117, 1131, 1156, 1184, 1192, 1256, 1330, 1435, 1455, 1466, 1476, 1480, 1481, 1483, 1484, 1486, 1489, 1490, 1492, 1502, 1670, 1697, 1708, 1803
Thalberg, I. and Budd Schulberg 1277
Thalberg, I. and Carl Laemmle 1475
Thalberg, I. and Donald Ogden Stewart 1279
Thalberg, I. and Francis Marion 1395
Thalberg, I. and F. Scott Fitzgerald 1117, 1217, 1227
Thalberg, I. and Howard Hawks 1775
Thalberg, I. and Louis B. Mayer 844, 1239
Thalberg, I. and MUTINY ON THE BOUNTY 1330
Thalberg, I. and producers in the 1980s 669
Thalberg, I. and screenwriters 1066, 1254
Thalberg, I. and THE GOOD EARTH 1320
Thalberg, I. and the Motion Picture Academy of Arts and Sciences 1172
Thalberg, I. and the Screen Playwrights 1152, 1271
Thalberg, I. and William Faulkner 1210, 1211, 1214
Thaxter, Phyllis 1439
Thevent, Pierre-Louis 365
Thew, Harvey 1808
Thomashevsky, Boris 828, 829
Thomasi, George 2053

Thomas, Elton (See Fairbanks, Douglas, Sr.)   1407, 1408
Thomas, J. Parnell   1187, 1190, 1192
Thomas, Olive   503, 1242
Thompson, Donald   297
Thompson, Jim   372, 1314
Thompson, J. Lee   366, 383
Thompson, Robert E.   1314, 2088, 2089
Thomson, Virgil   1872
Thorndike, Andrew   304
Thorndike, Annelie   304
Thorpe, Jim   1485
Thorp, Margaret Farrand   742
Three Stooges, The   1445
Thulin, Ingrid   2183
Thurber, James   269, 1130
Tierney, Gene   1446, 1471
Tierney, Lawrence   1440
Tillery, Millard   1283
Tilly, Meg   998
Tinney, Frank   1432
Tiomkin, Dimitri   403, 408, 1019, 1328, 1799
Tisch, Laurence A.   678
Tisse, Eduard K.   1646, 1661, 1666, 1667, 1867, 1868
Tobin, Genevieve   1445
Toddy, Ted   882, 937, 947, 948
Todd, Ann   1859, 1860, 1863, 1934, 1943
Todd, Mike   1950, 1971
Todd, Richard   1439
Todd, Sherman   1322, 1351
Toeplitz, Jerzy   2012
Tokugawa, Ieyasu   1732
Tokunaga, Frank   1740
Toland, Gregg   375, 1207, 1225, 1226, 1228, 1326, 1327, 1348, 1351, 1472, 1473,
    1792, 1807, 1808
Tolstoy, Leo   1608
Tol, Henriette   526
Tone, Franchot   1078, 1151, 1215, 1484
Topol   850
Torme, Mel   1774
Torn, Rip   549
Tors, Ivan   85
Totheroh, Roland H. "Rollie"   1416, 1427, 1429, 1430, 1431, 1432, 1433
Tourjansky, Victor   1714
Tourneur, Jacques   1550, 1752
Tourneur, Maurice   1395
Toutain, Roland   1827
Tover, Leo   996, 1001, 1007
Towne, Robert   1028, 1037, 1174, 2049, 2195
Townsend, Colleen   1439
Townsend, Leo   1293
Townsend, Robert   903
Tracy, Arthur   1444
Tracy, Dick   2116
Tracy, Lee   1488, 2090
Tracy, Spencer   377, 735, 994, 1018, 1164, 1202, 1244, 1443, 1448, 1449, 1479,
    1481, 1484, 1485, 1777, 1778, 1788, 1806, 1975, 1986
Trauberg, Leonid   1647
Traven, B.   1022

Travers, Bill 1009, 1355
Travers, Henry 378
Tree, Herbert Beerbohn 1385
Tressler, George 1355
Trevor, Claire 1242, 1440, 1452, 1808
Trewey, Felicien 1588, 1610
Trigger (horse star) 1446
Trintignant, Jean-Louis 577, 2151, 2174
Trotsky 259
Trotti, Lamar 366, 577, 580, 1021, 1066, 1140, 1203, 1503
Troy, William 127
Truffaut, Francois 53, 313, 771, 998, 1005, 1310, 1542, 1548, 1566, 1572, 1856,
  1969, 1993, 2034, 2043, 2094, 2096, 2097, 2098, 2106, 2117, 2118, 2122, 2127,
  2143, 2146, 2148, 2150, 2151, 2154, 2155, 2170
Truffaut, F. and Alfred Hitchcock 2107, 2146, 2155
Truffaut, F. and Andre Bazin 1999, 2107, 2144, 2146
Truffaut, F. and CAHIERS DU CINEMA 1997, 2002, 2144
Truffaut, F. and Claude Chabrol 2098, 2099
Truffaut, F. and Eric Rohmer 2102
Truffaut, F. and film criticism 142
Truffaut, F. and film theory 128
Truffaut, F. and Francis Ford Coppola 2107
Truffaut, F. and George Lucas 2107
Truffaut, F. and Henri Langlois 2006, 2107
Truffaut, F. and Henry James 2106
Truffaut, F. and Hollywood genres 2095
Truffaut, F. and Jean Renoir 2107, 2146, 2148, 2154, 2155
Truffaut, F. and Jean Vigo 2155
Truffaut, F. and Jean-Luc Godard 2129
Truffaut, F. and Jean-Pierre Leaud 2148
Truffaut, F. and LA NOUVELLE VAGUE 2108, 2123, 2126
Truffaut, F. and Orson Welles 2155
Truffaut, F. and Roberto Rossellini 2155
Truffaut, F. and Steven Spielberg 2107
Truffaut, F. and the Antoine Doniel cycle 2143
Truffaut, F. and the Cannes Film Festival 2097
Truffaut, F. and the CINEMATEQUE FRANCAISE 1992
Truffaut, F. and the "new cinema" 2121
Truffaut, F. and United Artists 2107
Truman, Harry S. 344, 1500
Trumbo, Dalton 342, 370, 850, 1036, 1067, 1073, 1083, 1087, 1088, 1098, 1099,
  1100, 1146, 1147, 1154, 1155, 1171, 1182, 1184, 1185, 1186, 1188, 1196, 1202,
  1203, 1205, 1263, 1282, 1286, 1949, 2043, 2076
Trumbull, Douglas 674
Tryon, Tom 1291
Tuchock, Wanda 1806
Tucker, Lorenzo 871, 931
Tufts, Sonny 1445
Tuhock, Wanda 1313
Tully, Jim 226
Turin, Victor 1647
Turner, Lana 1241, 1242, 1289, 1443, 1484, 1970, 1971
Turner, Ted 59, 662, 663, 678
Turpin, Ben 1410, 1412, 1456, 1578, 1622, 1701, 1800
Twain, Mark 1300, 1363
Tyard, Pontus de 1313
Tyler, Parker 170
Tyler, Tom 431
Tyler, Walter 1988

Tynan, Kenneth 1355
Tyson, Cicely 893, 904, 913, 920, 923, 995
Tzara, Tristan 1716

U

Uchida, Tomu 1896
Uekusa, Keinosuke 2029
Ullmann, Liv 508, 606, 2183
Ullman, Ellwood 1237
Ulman, H. C. 1398
Ulmer, Edgar G. 829, 845, 846, 848, 1548, 1702, 1774
Umemura, Yoko 1901
Uncle Remus 922
Urban, Charles 203, 204, 1612, 1617
Ustinov, Peter 1018, 1934, 1941, 2010
Uyeda, Akinari 2031

V

Vache, Jacques 1717
Vadim, Roger 1571, 2094, 2095, 2119, 2122, 2149
Valentino, Rudolph 1060, 1236, 1247, 1296, 1393, 1394, 1395, 1434, 1440, 1441,
  1443, 1444, 1449, 1450, 1453, 1477, 1504, 1529, 1579, 1595, 1674, 1695, 1707
Valentino, R. and feminist criticism 471
Valenti, Jack 545, 647, 682, 752, 759, 760, 764, 959, 2038, 2198
Valery, Frederick Henry 1585, 1591
Valli, Alida 1487
Vallone, Raf 1349
Van Cleef, Lee 429
Van Dongen, Helen 314
Van Doren, Mamie 983
Van Doren, Mimi 1439
Van Druten, John 812
Van Dyke, Dick 2036
Van Dyke, Willard S. "Woody" 54, 295, 296, 1483, 1490, 1788, 1806, 1870, 1872
Van Enger, Charles 1494
Van Every, Dale 994
Van Fleet, Jo 1005, 1325
Van Hamel, Martine 1016
Van Peebles, Melvin 879, 889, 894, 899, 901, 909, 910, 911, 936, 937, 949, 953,
  1551
Van Sloan, Edward 396
Van Voorhis, Cornelius Westbrook 301, 302
Vance, Philo 380
Vanderbeek, Stan 2090, 2091
Vangelis 1013
Vardac, A. Nicholas 1339
Varda, Agnes 466, 516, 562, 2112, 2114, 2115, 2122, 2149, 2157
Varga, Marina 1417
Varnel, Marcel 1833
Vaughn, Robert 1194, 1295, 2068
Vazak, P. H. 1037
Veidt, Conrad 1632, 1634, 1640, 1643, 1833
Velde, James 896
Velez, Lupe 1450

Venable, Evelyn 1445
Ventigmilia, Baron 1857
Vera-Ellen 1439, 1472
Vergano, Aldo 1880
Vernon, Elmo 994
Vertov, Dziga 213, 295, 304, 1549, 1645, 1646, 1651, 1652, 1654, 1655, 1661, 1663, 1664, 1668, 1669, 1811, 1865, 1869
Vertov, D. and Jean-Luc Godard 2111
Vesey, Denmark 252
Vickers, Martha 1977
Victor, Alexander (Alexander the Great) 1588
Vidal, Gore 1352, 2089
Vidor, Florence 1444
Vidor, King 304, 342, 367, 532, 556, 794, 796, 854, 872, 941, 980, 981, 1080, 1164, 1237, 1248, 1445, 1472, 1488, 1550, 1551, 1553, 1671, 1674, 1696, 1707, 1713, 1748, 1753, 1801, 1806, 2035
Vierny, Sascha 2152
Viertel, Berthold 1102
Viertel, Peter 1102, 1323, 1979
Vigo, Eugene Bonaventure de (Miguel Almereyda) 1823
Vigo, Jean 162, 292, 1553, 1571, 1714, 1811, 1823, 1824, 1828, 1869
Vilandebo, Carlos 319
Villa, Pancho 1340
Violet, Ultra 2069
Viot, Jacques 1825
Visconti, Luchino 516, 1297, 1308, 1573, 1874, 1878, 1884, 1922, 1925, 1926, 1934, 2118, 2129, 2172
Vitti, Monica 1012, 2172, 2173
Viva 2069
Vogt, Gunther 1828
Vogt, Hans 1745
Voight, Jon 376
Vollmoeller, Karl 1831
Von Braun, Wernher 366
Von Harbou, Thea 1636, 1637, 1641, 1830
Von Seyffertiz, Gustav 1398
Von Stampfer, Simon Ritter 1583, 1589, 1599
Von Sternberg, Josef 53, 119, 161, 306, 980, 1277, 1484, 1504, 1548, 1553, 1674, 1697, 1708, 1716, 1748, 1756, 1788, 1806, 1829, 1830, 1831, 1833, 2035
Von Stroheim, Erich 263, 297, 965, 1018, 1277, 1296, 1388, 1395, 1456, 1475, 1479, 1480, 1484, 1492, 1503, 1511, 1594, 1610, 1671, 1674, 1697, 1698, 1699, 1700, 1708, 1709, 1724, 1814, 1822, 1826, 1955, 1994
Von Sydow, Max 2183
Von Trotta, Margarethe 466, 505
Von Uchatius, Baron Franz 1585, 1589, 1594
Vorkapich, Slavko 140, 1216

W

Wada, Natto 2029
Wagenknecht, Edward 1382
Wagner, Fritz Arno 1632, 1633, 1641, 1642
Wagner, Rob 1758
Wajda, Andrzej 1553, 2012, 2013, 2014, 2180
Wakely, Jimmy 433
Walbrook, Anton 1015, 1943
Walburn, Raymond 1447
Waldekranz, Rune 2184

Wald, Jerry 797, 800, 1206, 1212, 1247, 1466
Waleffe, Maurice de 1709
Walgensten, Thomas 1580, 1581
Walken, Christopher 367, 368, 786
Walker, Robert 1242
Wallace, Edgar 700, 1833
Wallach, Eli 1449, 1916
Walling, William 193
Wallis, Gladys 1267
Wallis, Hal B. 801, 1139, 1225, 1288, 1466, 1493, 1497, 1552
Walls, Tom 1833
Walsh, Raoul 348, 434, 1294, 1373, 1408, 1496, 1553, 1579, 1671, 1672, 1674, 1701, 1709, 1748, 1985, 2035
Walters, Charles 194, 1548
Walters, John 392
Walthall, Henry B. 1373, 1387, 1389, 1444, 1450
Walton, William 1353, 1354
Wanger, Walter 272, 639, 1125, 1127, 1250, 1264, 1369, 1468, 1485, 1750, 1846, 1847, 1854, 2043
Warden, Jack 2058
Ward, Fannie 1444
Warhola, Andrew, Jr. (Andy Warhol) 2068
Warhol, Andy 56, 1549, 1717, 1956, 2039, 2040, 2068, 2069, 2091
Warm, Hermann 1632, 1641, 1643, 1729
Warner, Abe 1493
Warner, Albert 1494
Warner, David 820, 1355
Warner, Harry 244, 622, 1466, 1493, 1494, 1670, 1703
Warner, H. B. 1328, 1799
Warner, Jack L. 226, 227, 302, 343, 345, 622, 820, 1066, 1178, 1179, 1184, 1187, 1192, 1215, 1235, 1241, 1288, 1295, 1435, 1468, 1493, 1494, 1498, 1501, 1635, 1670, 1945, 1950, 2086
Warner, Sam 1435, 1493, 1494
Warner, William 1468
Warren, Earl 1485
Warren, Harry 405
Warren, John F. 1350
Warshow, Robert 127, 160
Warwick, Dione 937
Warwick, Richard 1001
Washburn, Bryant 1444
Washburn, Derec 367
Washington, Booker T. 867, 926
Washington, Denzel 903
Washington, Fredi 875, 877, 921
Washington, Kenny 937
Washington, Ned 1019
Wasserman, Lew 1849, 1854, 1951, 2035, 2197
Waterbury, Ruth 1237
Waterhouse, Keith 994
Waters, Ethel 870, 879, 880, 920, 921, 922, 939, 944, 951, 997, 1260, 1445
Waters, John 2210
Watkins, David 1013
Watkins, Peter 1024, 1566, 2042
Watt, Harry 214, 215, 216, 244, 248, 249, 283, 294, 308, 309, 316, 322, 352, 1869, 1937
Waugh, Evelyn 1157, 1294
Waxman, Franz 83, 408, 1015, 1216

Wayne, David 1975
Wayne, John 147, 209, 339, 348, 350, 360, 361, 369, 426, 430, 431, 432, 434, 474, 781, 805, 809, 811, 897, 938, 990, 1032, 1080, 1160, 1192, 1236, 1254, 1264, 1289, 1351, 1401, 1442, 1443, 1449, 1452, 1456, 1674, 1802, 1952, 2075, 2076, 2194
Wead, Frank 369
Weavers, The 1096
Weaver, Doodles 1445
Weaver, Sigourney 415, 1530
Webber, Frank 1864
Webber, Robert 1295
Webb, Clifton 373, 1235
Webb, Elven 1356
Webb, Jack 376, 1752
Weber, Andrew Lloyd 396
Weber, Lois 508, 519, 620
Wegener, Paul 1632, 1635
Weicher, Karyl 835
Weidler, Virginia 992, 993
Weigle, Edwin F. 297
Weil-Curiel, Andre 1908
Weill, Claudia 526, 604, 680
Weill, Kurt 65, 1259, 1633
Weinberg, Herman G. 127, 160, 1480
Weinstein, Hannah 1263
Weir, Peter 583
Weissmuller, Johnny 219, 919, 1444, 1484
Weiss, Ehrich (Harry Houdini) 1588
Weiss, Emil 1977
Weiss, Peter 1628
Weitzenkorn, Louis 1070
Welch, Raquel 390, 1471
Welland, Collin 1013
Weller, Peter 1530
Welles, Beatrice Ives 1789
Welles, Orson 175, 981, 1020, 1022, 1160, 1327, 1343, 1353, 1355, 1548, 1551, 1560, 1592, 1750, 1751, 1756, 1790, 1791, 1792, 1793, 1794, 1807, 1954, 1961, 1963, 1996, 2035, 2049, 2091
Welles, O. and AUTEUR criticism 2096
Welles, O. and censorship 965
Welles, O. and Charlie Chaplin 1433
Welles, O. and CITIZEN KANE 127, 1269, 1792, 1807
Welles, O. and Dalton Trumbo 1283
Welles, O. and Darryl F. Zanuck 1502
Welles, O. and Donald Ogden Stewart 1279
Welles, O. and Elia Kazan 1257, 1259
Welles, O. and film criticism 162
Welles, O. and Francois Truffaut 2145, 2155
Welles, O. and Howard Koch 1262, 1263
Welles, O. and John Houseman 1263
Welles, O. and Rene Clair 1725
Welles, O. and screenwriters 1063
Welles, O. and THE EXORCIST 981
Welles, O. and the family in film 980
Welles, O. and the Oscars 1164
Welles, O. and THE THIRD MAN 1329
Welles, O. and THE TRIAL 159
Welles, O. and William Shakespeare 1790
Welles, Richard Head 1789

Wellman, William A. 261, 350, 361, 370, 1021, 1240, 1256, 1295, 1488, 1496, 1500, 1503, 1553, 1674, 1675, 1701, 1748, 1758, 1913, 2043
Wells, Paul 1017
Wenders, Wim 311, 2006, 2165
Werner, Oskar 2010, 2155
Wertmuller, Lina 117, 152, 466, 497, 508, 1927, 2172
Weschler, David 1989
Weschler, Lazar 1988
Westerbeck, Colin L. 1452
Westmore, Perc 1240
West, Billy 1578
West, Claudine 378, 522, 1320, 1328
West, Jessamyn 1319
West, Mae 219, 502, 516, 555, 921, 957, 1296, 1443, 1504, 1676, 1749, 1755, 1795, 1807, 1808
West, Nathanael 580, 1065, 1103, 1105, 1107, 1108, 1147, 1148, 1150, 1156, 1157, 1227, 1278, 1289, 1670
West, Raymond B. 813, 1623
Wexler, Haskell 1324, 2086, 2090
Wexley, John 1202
Whalen, Michael 1446
Whale, James 261, 388, 389, 1748, 1808, 1834
Wheatstone, Charles 1584, 1585, 1591
Wheeler, Burton K. 203
Wheeler, Hugh 1219
Wheeler, Lyle R. 812, 849, 1326, 1801
Whipper, Leigh 879, 922, 1021
Whitaker, Clem 574
White, Byron R. 962
White, Pearl 304, 1247, 1455, 1458, 1459, 1595, 1709, 1780
White, Walter 879, 930, 934
Whiting, Leonard 1356
Whiting, Richard 405
Whitman, Walt 1363
Whitney, John Hay (Jock) 1486
Wicker, Irene 1188
Widerberg, Bo 1628
Widmark, Richard 377, 1499, 1674, 1977
Wieland, Joyce 508
Wiene, Robert 1632, 1633, 1634, 1643, 1829
Wiesel, Elie 289, 311
Wilcoxon, Henry 1237, 1439
Wilcox, Daeida 1233
Wilcox, Harvey 1233
Wilcox, Henry 1680
Wilcox, Herbert 1567, 1571, 1833, 1863
Wilder Samuel (Billy Wilder) 1971
Wilder, Billy 374, 798, 799, 980, 1065, 1140, 1142, 1145, 1146, 1151, 1198, 1236, 1254, 1291, 1296, 1550, 1552, 1753, 1758, 1803, 1829, 1948, 1952, 1954, 1971, 1972, 1973, 1987
Wilder, Gene 2073, 2194
Wilder, Thornton 1789, 1920
Wilde, Cornel 415, 423, 1439, 1451, 2092
Wilde, Oscar 1706
Wilding, Michael 1243, 1440, 1446
Wiles, Gordon 1314
Williamson, James A. 1606, 1612
Williamson, Thames 798

Williams, Bert 921, 933
Williams, Billy Dee 920
Williams, Douglas O. 365, 1017
Williams, Elmo 1019
Williams, Esther 498, 1445, 1449
Williams, JoBeth 1530
Williams, John D. 813, 850, 1416
Williams, J. Terry 2082
Williams, Kathlyn 1444, 1455
Williams, Patrick 1005
Williams, Raymond 1877
Williams, Spencer 881
Williams, Tennessee 1155, 1257, 1260, 1261, 1340, 1346, 1352, 1489
Williams, Treat 1530
Williams, Whitney 1424
Willingham, Calder 372, 1314, 1320, 2085, 2086
Willis, Bruce 1437
Willis, Edwin B. 1001, 1010, 1354
Willis, Gordon 786
Willkie, Wendell Lewis 203, 879
Wills, Mary 849
Wilmer, Douglas 381
Wilson, Ben 1444
Wilson, Carey 1330
Wilson, Dooley 372, 881
Wilson, Edmund 1188, 1217, 1278
Wilson, Jack 1430
Wilson, John 371
Wilson, Lois 1446
Wilson, Margery 519, 1385, 1388
Wilson, Michael 372, 1015, 1036, 1094, 1147, 1171, 1949, 2090
Wilson, Scott 605
Wilson, Woodrow 211, 262, 337, 1400
Wimperis, Arthur 378, 522, 1865
Windsor, Claire 1445
Windsor, Duke of 1290
Winkler, Irwin 1143, 1294, 1296
Winkler, Max 1907
Winnicott, D. W. 600, 601
Winnington, Richard 1910
Winslow, Dick 991
Winslow, George "Foghorn" 992, 993, 1446
Winters, Grant 1976
Winters, Jonathan 1241, 1294
Winters, Shelley 849, 1015, 1975
Winter, Keith 1943
Wirth, Franz Peter 1354
Wiseman, Frederick 293, 295, 1870, 2040, 2042, 2070, 2092, 2121
Wise, Robert 145, 415, 1164, 1323, 1327, 1550, 1807, 1951, 1987
Withers, Jane 991, 992, 993
Witney, William 1758
Wohl, Stanislaus 2012
Wolcott, Jersey Joe 922
Wolf man, the 390, 399
Wolfe, Nero 380
Wolfe, Thomas 1156
Wolff, Lothar 302
Wolfman Jack 993
Wolheim, Louis 1390

Wollen, Peter 171
Wolper, David 549
Wong, Anna May 1450, 1477
Woodberry, Bill 901
Woodbury, Albert 2089
Woodlawn, Holly 2069
Woods, Frank E. 123, 124, 1387, 1389
Woods, Lotte 1408
Woodward, Joanne 790, 913
Woody Woodpecker 1780
Wood, David 1001
Wood, John S. 1180
Wood, Natalie 790, 990, 991, 992, 993, 997, 1010, 2076
Wood, Peggy 1445
Wood, Robin 1752, 2130
Wood, Sam G. 278, 370, 1080, 1179, 1231, 1269, 1289, 1322, 1328, 1483, 1549,
   1779, 1805
Wooley, Monty 1215
Woolf, Alan 1801
Woolf, C. M. 1837
Woolf, Virginia 1156
Woollcott, Alexander 1063
Woolsey, Ralph 1351
Worsley, Wallace 1702
Wrangell, Basil 1320
Wrather, Bonita (See Granville, Bonita) 992
Wray, Fay 396, 1445, 1452, 1795, 1800
Wray, John Griffith 1350
Wright, Basil 214, 215, 248, 309, 315, 316, 1753, 1869, 1870, 1871, 1939
Wright, Richard 922
Wright, Teresa 375, 376, 378, 1348, 1852, 1920
Wurlitzer, Fanny 1588
Wurtzel, Stuart 786
Wyatt, Jane 369, 1087, 1328, 1439
Wyler, William 283, 923, 1006, 1087, 1169, 1204, 1225, 1226, 1228, 1254, 1319,
   1327, 1348, 1438, 1472, 1473, 1474, 1475, 1503, 1548, 1550, 1551, 1721, 1748,
   1750, 1758, 1808, 1911, 1913, 1916, 1952, 1954, 1988
Wyler, W. and epic films 382
Wyler, W. and war films 322, 346, 375, 378
Wyman, Jane 1010, 1986
Wyman, Thomas H. 678
Wynette, Tammy 789
Wynn, Ed 849, 1241
Wynn, Keenan 1293, 2083
Wysbar, Frank 238

Y

Yamada, Isuzu 1356, 1901
Yamamoto, Kajiro 1886, 1896, 1899, 2021
Yamamura, So 2019
Yamanaka, Sadao 1887, 1889
Yasui, Shoji 371
Yates, Peter 1004, 1549
Yeats, William Butler 1311
Yoda, Yoshikata 1901, 2031
Yordan, Phillip 1984

York, Alvin 337, 348
York, Michael 423
York, Susannah 2089
Yoshimura, Kimisaburo 2017, 2018
Youngblood, Denis J. 1644
Youngstein, Max 362
Youngston, Robert 1557
Young, Clara Kimball 1444, 1450
Young, Gig 2089
Young, Hal 1857
Young, Loretta 502, 1471, 1781, 1786, 1797
Young, Nedrick 944, 1099
Young, Robert 894, 952, 1215, 1484, 1833
Young, Vernon 161
Young, Victor 403, 1322
Yule, Lady 1567
Yurka, Blanche 1445, 1446
Yutkevitch, Sergei Iosipovitch 1651, 1652

Z

Zampa, Luigi 1573, 1874
Zangwill, Israel 864
Zanuck, Darryl F. 219, 229, 231, 261, 572, 690, 1117, 1139, 1149, 1192, 1204,
  1207, 1208, 1210, 1211, 1244, 1249, 1250, 1253, 1254, 1255, 1256, 1281, 1435,
  1466, 1469, 1470, 1479, 1493, 1496, 1497, 1499, 1501, 1684, 1847, 1967, 2200
Zanuck, D. and Elia Kazan 1260
Zanuck, D. and war films 354, 361
Zanuck, Frank 1502
Zanuck, Louise 1502
Zanuck, Richard D. 690, 1470, 1500, 1501, 1502, 1552, 2200
Zanuck, Virginia 1502
Zapata, Emiliano 1326
Zavattini, Cesare 127, 1004, 1876, 1884, 1885, 1926, 1932, 1933, 2174
Zavitz, Lee 1801
Zecca, Ferdinand 1605, 1606, 1621, 1709
Zeffirelli, Franco 159, 602, 1009, 1356, 2172
Zemtsova, Anna Nicolaevna 1662
Zetterling, Mai 497, 1570, 1628
Zimmerman, Don 376
Zinnemann, Fred 361, 368, 376, 970, 980, 997, 1019, 1020, 1322, 1549, 1552,
  1829, 1946, 1950, 1951, 1988, 1989, 2032
Zinner, Peter 368
Zorina, Vera 1445
Zucco, George 396
Zuckerman, George 1147
Zuckmayer, Karl 1675
Zugsmith, Albert 2069
Zukor, Adolph 224, 244, 572, 621, 622, 624, 685, 820, 1054, 1061, 1157, 1277,
  1368, 1463, 1466, 1467, 1468, 1471, 1477, 1482, 1491, 1504, 1621, 1622, 1670,
  1837
Zwillman, Abner "Longy" 1242

Subject Index

A

AB Svensk Film Industri (AB Svenska Biografteatern Company) 769, 1624
AB Svenska Biografteatern Company (AB Svensk Film Industri) 769, 1624
abortion 491, 520
above-the-line costs 702
Abraham Lincoln Brigade 1177
Academy Awards 192, 193, 323, 325, 364, 366, 368, 370, 404, 405, 411, 698,
  1171, 1172, 1173, 1174, 1452, 1477, 1531
Academy Conciliation Committee, the 1069
Academy of Motion Picture Arts and Sciences (AMPAS) 680, 1156, 1171, 1172,
  1173, 1174, 1365, 1391, 1544, 1670
Acoustic Sound Recording 674
acting coaches 1232
acting in film 76
Actor's Studio, the 1260, 1261
Actors' Equity Association 1072, 1172, 1174
Actualities Reconstituees 1601
adaptations 158, 189, 190, 191, 274, 776, 1152, 1499, 1658, 1709
admission prices 687, 755
adolescence 565
adolescents in film 601, 779
adult education 47
adult westerns 1982
adventure films 191, 192, 371, 1526, 2044
advertising 204, 765, 1360, 1384, 1386, 1437, 1438, 1447, 1455, 1467, 1486
aesthetics 93, 179, 180, 182, 190, 197, 215, 218, 236, 245, 259, 267, 273, 275,
  333, 418
AFFS NEWSLETTER 1522
AFI EDUCATION NEWSLETTER, The 35
Africa 283, 328
Africa and film 910, 918, 919
African-American actor, the 937
African-American athletes-turned-performers 945
African-American audiences 884, 938, 947
African-American exhibitors 884, 938, 947
African-American film genres 923, 924
African-American films 427, 936, 937, 2038
African-American Hollywood extras 881
African-American independent filmmakers 938
African-American independent films 943
African-American literature 949
African-American press 926, 938
African-American stereotypes 569, 874, 899, 920, 930, 941, 944
African-American stereotypes and cartoons 874
African-American theaters 921, 935, 947
African-American two-reelers 928
African-American women in film and video 902, 941
African-Americans and Brazilian Cinema 2158
African-Americans and Jews 859, 926
African-Americans and television 854, 923
African-Americans and the Academy Awards 877
African-Americans and the coming of sound 939
African-Americans as movie heroes 900
African-Americans in film 559, 779, 1386, 1577, 1976, 2038

African-Americans in Hollywood during WWII   916
African-Americans in theater   938
agents   524, 1232, 1234, 1486
AGITKI films   1662
AIDS and the arts   2204
AJYM (Chabrol's production company)   2100
Alco   1481
ALCOA HOUR, THE (TV series)   2058
alcoholism in films   569
Aldgate Trustees   1840
Aldrich and Associates Company   2043
Aldrich Studios, the   2043
ALFRED HITCHCOCK HOUR, THE   1849, 1854
ALFRED HITCHCOCK PRESENTS   1849, 1854, 2036
Algonquin Round Table   1101, 1269
Alice Restaurant's Massacre, The   2088
ALL IN THE FAMILY   835
Alliance of Theatrical Stage Employees and Motion Picture Operators   1172
Allied Artists   651, 986
Allies and film propaganda   224, 234, 331, 334, 349, 352
AMAZING STORIES television series   760
America and the AVANT-GARDE   1542, 1716
America and Yiddish films   847
American Academy of Dramatic Arts   2048
American Broadcasting Corporation (ABC)   489, 549, 671
American culture   386
American documentary movement   1902
American Dream, The   190, 387, 484, 501, 550, 598, 801, 874, 982, 1398, 2048
American family life   987
American Federation of Labor, the   1172, 1173
American film bureaus   771
American film exhibition in the twenties   685
American film feminists   466
American film industry, the   775, 776
American Film Institute (AFI), The   33, 41, 47, 495, 1169, 1240, 1552, 1577,
   1684, 1854
American Film Manufacturing Company, the   1622
American Film Theatre   1351
American films and the Holocaust   311
American foreign film policy   694
American influence on European film production   664
American Institute of Public Opinion, the   735
American International Pictures (AIP)   699, 744, 2049
American Jews   291
American Multi-Cinema   682
American Museum of Natural History   489
American Mutoscope and Biograph Company   1361, 1371
American myths   1686
American Negro Theatre (ANT)   944
American newsfilm 1914-1919   269
American screenwriters   1152
American Telephone and Telegraph Company (AT&T)   695, 703
American underground films   1951
American values and the woman's film   521, 797
American Vitagraph Company   618, 1616
American war films   304
American-International   986
American-Japanese relations in Japanese films   1575
Americans United for World Government   2066

AMERIKA controversy between ABC and Russia   489, 549
Amsterdam and the Holocaust   849
androgyny in films   491, 598
animal actors   1444
animation   76, 299, 307, 321, 411, 414, 1468, 1583, 1588, 1623, 1716
animation stand, the   78
annual box-office champs   1544
ANSCHLUSS . 226
antebellum Southern mythology   943
antebellum South, the   864, 926, 943
anthropological concerns   253
anti-American films   1949
anti-fascism films   568
Anti-Feudal Drama, the   2027
anti-intellectualism   181
anti-isolationist films   568
anti-Nazi films   356
Anti-Peonage law, The   1945
anti-Semitism   203, 204, 219, 222, 223, 226, 235, 236, 237, 238, 239, 240, 248,
  251, 257, 274, 289, 301, 311, 316, 317, 369, 375, 378, 568, 849, 1156, 1215,
  1629, 1946
anti-Semitism in France   2143
anti-Semitism in Hollywood in the 1980s   836
anti-Semitism in Russia   847
anti-Semitism in the movies   941
anti-war films   194, 220, 221, 223, 262, 325, 342, 348, 568
anticipatory socialization   779
antitrust film legislation   639
apartheid   2089
Arab films   2178
archeology of film   1581
Archers, The   1935
archetypes   173, 183, 190, 233, 250, 262, 385, 789, 1175
ARCHITECTURAL FORUM, THE   630
archives, film   265, 275, 292, 304, 307
Argentine films   771
ARK ROYAL   235
Army Signal Corps   346
ARMY-NAVY SCREEN MAGAZINE, THE   281, 320
Art Deco and Hollywood   1754
art decoration   1002
art films   767
art houses   691
Artcraft   1400
ARTS   2002, 2100
Ashkenazic Jews   818
Asia   328, 340, 352, 359, 363
assimilation   311
Assistant Secretary of Defense for Public Affairs   361
associate producer   66
Associated Actors and Artists of America   1072, 1172
Associated British Cinemas (ABC)   1939
Associated British Picture Corporation (ABPC), The   1935
Associated Features   948
Associated Realist Film Producers   243, 244, 249
Associated Talking Pictures   1839
Astor Pictures   948
Asynchronism   100

atomic bomb, the 298, 324
Attorney General's Commission on Pornography 961
audience 239, 250, 253, 255, 257, 258, 259, 262, 265, 266, 267, 268, 275, 278,
  280, 284, 285, 293, 325, 342, 359, 1240, 1359, 1603
audience and genres 192
audience and social effects 573
audience and spectator 436
audience and subcultures 458
audience and the new feminism 492
audience attitudes 535
audience composition 728
audience gratification 745, 801
audience identification 781
audience profiles 700
audience research 735, 751, 754, 770, 775
Audience Research Institute (ARI) 733, 735
audience-centered models 438
audiences and early psychological theory 124
audiences and film criticism 146
audiences and film theory 129, 135
Audit of Marquee Values 735
Auschwitz 222, 305, 323
Australia and television movies 672
Australian novels into film 2157
Australian silent films 1590
Austria and Yiddish films 847
AUTEUR theory and Andrew Sarris, the 162
AUTEUR theory and Edward Buscombe, the 162
AUTEUR theory and film criticism, The 165, 170
AUTEUR theory and Jean Narboni, the 162
AUTEUR theory and Jean-Louis Comolli, the 162
AUTEUR theory and Lindsay Anderson, the 162
AUTEUR theory and Louis Marcorelles, the 162
AUTEUR theory and Nick Browne, the 162
AUTEUR theory and Pauline Kael, the 150
AUTEUR theory and Peter Wollen, the 162
AUTEUR theory and Robin Wood, the 162
AUTEUR theory and Roland Barthes, the 162
AUTEUR theory and Stephen Heath, the 162
AUTEUR theory, the 55, 129, 178, 189, 190, 191, 194, 328, 334, 350, 603, 1141,
  1204, 1993, 2032, 2097, 2123, 2124
Authors League of America, The 1172
AUTORENFILM 1631
AVANCE SUR RECETTES 1993
AVANT-GARDE filmmaking in Soviet silent films 1664
AVANT-GARDE films 188, 225
AVANT-GARDE movement 1663
Avco-Embassy 669
Aviation films 380
Axelbank Collection of the Hoover Archives, the 281
Axis film propaganda 217, 329, 346, 349
A. C. Nielsen Company 760

B

B films 147, 356, 498, 701, 702, 1548, 1945
B'nai B'rith Anti-Defamation League 825
backstage musicals 555
Balaban & Katz theaters 622
balance models 438
BALTIMORE AFRO-AMERICAN, THE 948
Bank of America, The 704
banking and film 700, 702, 703, 704
Basic Studio Agreement, the 1156
basic versus surplus repression 604
basketball films 421
Bathing Beauties 518
Battle of Britain 234
Battle of Stalingrad, The 235, 282
Battle of the Bulge, The 353
beach party films 530, 982
beer hall putsch 321
behavior modification 779
behavior theories 535
behaviorism 600
Belgium Cinematheque 1699
Belgium film market 693
Belle-Vista 1236
below-the-line costs 702
BEN CASEY (TV series) 2065
BENSHI 1736, 1740, 1741, 1742, 1885, 1886
Beograd Film Institute 200
Bergen-Belsen 323
Berlin Film Festival 1171
Berlin Wall 231
best boys 76
Beverly Hills 574
Biblical films 182, 832, 1517, 1526
bikers films 339, 418
bilateral oligopoly 660
BILLBOARD 123
binary sets 198
Biograph Company, the 381, 766, 1358, 1361, 1364, 1366, 1370, 1371, 1373,
    1374, 1375, 1376, 1377, 1378, 1379, 1380, 1381, 1383, 1384, 1385, 1386, 1389,
    1392, 1394, 1395, 1397, 1409, 1423, 1434, 1595, 1608
Biograph editing 1409
biographical films 191, 256, 1497, 1914
biographical war films 337, 365
Birth of a Race Photoplay Corporation, The 868, 934, 948
Black Artists Alliance (BAA) 942
BLACK CREATION 936
Black Film Center 1545
Black Hundred, The 845
BLACK JOURNAL 902
Black Maria, The 1617
Blackburn Velde Productions 870
blackface 933, 939
blacklisting 345, 372, 802, 832, 849, 882, 944, 987, 1036, 1171, 1202, 1204,
    1260, 1261, 1285, 1293, 1915, 1948, 1951, 1985
blacklisting and Nicholas Ray 1985
blacklisting and THE FIXER 2077

blaxploitation films   150, 385, 895, 896, 898, 900, 906, 923, 937, 941, 942, 946
blind buying   638
blind-bidding   676, 698, 781
blind-booking   677, 1465
blind-selling   687
BLITZKRIEG   298
block booking   421, 645, 677, 781, 1464, 1465, 1482, 1944
block-booking   638, 687
blockbusters   59, 564, 2191
blocked film revenues   693
blood and soil (BLUT UND BODEN)   250
Blum-Byrnes Agreement   1992
Board of Trade, the   1935
Bolshevism   1670
bond issues   702
Bond, James   421, 422, 486, 896, 1569
boomerang effect, the   543
Box Office Attractions Company   1470
box-office receipts   703, 755, 781
boxing films   421
Brazilian films   236, 771
Breen Office, The   572, 1497, 1792
Brewster Color   654
Bridgewater State Prison Hospital   2092
Brighton School, the   1606, 1612
Britain   244, 245, 246, 267, 273, 322, 339, 351, 352, 372, 373, 374
British Academy Awards   1171
British Air Ministry, the   218
British and French pantomimes   1604
British animation   1567
British audience studies   1568
British Board of Film Censors (BBFC)   224, 225, 1571
British Broadcasting Corporation   222, 319, 744, 1024
British Cinematograph Act of 1938, The   641
British documentaries in the post-WWII period   1568
British Documentary Movement   283, 294, 295, 302, 303, 306, 308, 309, 315, 323,
   352, 1902
British film attendance in the 1950s   699
British film audience research   744
British film censorship   1840
British film feminists   466
British film genres   1569
British film industry, the   699, 751, 775
British Film Institute Summer School   507
British Film Institute, The   192, 243, 244, 249, 1833, 2006
British film market, the   693
British film theaters   699
British film unions   1831
British films   236, 248, 273, 274, 294, 295, 309, 342, 352, 396, 1401
British films and sexuality   567
British films from 1895 to 1896   1610
British films in the post-World War II period   1569
British films in the 1930s   1840
British films in the 1940s   1569
British films in World War II   1938
British Foreign Office   212
British Independent films in the post-World War II period   1569
British International Pictures (BIP)   1344, 1838, 1843
British Labour movement, the   239, 242, 1569

British Lion Films 1568
BRITISH MOVIETONE NEWS 310
British news media during World War II 242
British newsreels 255, 310
British propaganda and World War II 1571
British publications 348
British quotas 1935
British war films 265, 304
British working class 214
broadcast copywriting 74
Broadway 370, 1489
Bronco Pictures 1409
Buchenwald 323
Buena Vista 659
bullfighting films 421
Bund, German-American 263
BUNRAKU plays 1734, 1735
Bureau of Intelligence, the 229
Bureau of Motion Picture Affairs, The (BMPA) 229
Bureau of Motion Pictures Affairs, The (BMPA) 881
Burma 371
BURSTYN v. WILSON 686
Burton Lane's Dramatic Workshop 2048
business people in film 568
By Request News Features 320
Byzantine spiritual art 2004
B. F. Keith vaudeville circuit 766

C

cable television 704, 762, 769
CAESAR'S HOUR (TV series) 2047
cafe-concerts 1604
Cagney Productions 643
CAHIERS DU CINEMA 41, 128, 131, 133, 167, 474, 475, 1237, 1997, 1999, 2002,
    2072, 2096, 2099, 2100, 2125, 2126
California and the media 573
California gubernatorial race of 1934 1069
California Production Company 1919
CALIFORNIA (operetta) 1477
camera angles 97
CAMERA OBSCURA 41, 483, 1589, 1591
CAMERA OBSCURA: A JOURNAL OF FEMINISM AND FILM THEORY 483
camera perspective 479
Canadian films 249, 280, 293, 307, 771, 1590
Cannes Film Festival 324, 437, 1171, 2097, 2137
Cannon Group, Inc. 535, 672, 682
caper movie 190
capitalism 270
career women comedies 521, 523
cars in American films 559
cartoons 266, 307, 320, 414, 874
casting process 1847
castration theory 590, 604
Catholic Church, the American 219
CBS, Inc. 671, 677, 726, 961, 2051
celebrities 566

censorship   209, 211, 216, 224, 225, 228, 242, 247, 260, 271, 272, 274, 284, 325, 339, 768, 778, 979, 981, 988, 1198, 1344, 1432, 1497, 1504, 1537
censorship and African-American films   941
censorship and D. W. Griffith   1376
censorship and horror films   394
censorship and human rights   560
censorship and MISSING   772
censorship and newsreels   298, 300
censorship and silent films   296, 572, 954
censorship and the Holocaust   317
censorship and the Office of War Information   229
censorship and the star system   1447
censorship and TITICUT FOLLIES   772
censorship and war films   361
censorship and World War II   203, 351, 352
censorship in documentaries   288
censorship in the 1930s   270
censorship in the 1940s   686
censorship in the 1960s   2036, 2037
Center for Advanced Film Studies   1552
Center for the Humanities (University of Southern California), the   495
Center Kamerny theater   1649
central artists' bureau   1071
Central Information Bureau, the   223
Central Office of Information   317
Central Powers, the   211, 296
CENTRE DU CINEMA   2094
CENTRO SPERIMENTALE DI CINEMATOGRAFIA   1876, 1879, 1881, 1883, 1922
CERCLE DU CINEMA, LE   2006
Chamba Productions   937
CHAMBARA   1742
character actors   189, 429, 1443, 1444, 1446, 1447, 1451
Charlie Chan movies   879
chase and robbery films   384
Chase National Bank   1492
chaser theory, the   767
CHICAGO DEFENDER, THE   948
Chicago film market   689
child custody   520
child stars   992, 993
childbirth   491
childhood innocence and psychoanalytic film theories   598
children's live-action musical films   404
children's rights   520
Chile   1021
China   226, 283, 331, 334, 340, 357
CHINA SMITH (TV series)   2043
Chinese Kung Fu films   565
Chinese Nationalists   298
Chinese Reds   298
Chronochrome   654
CHRYSLER THEATER (TV series)   2065
Cinderella image in movies, the   503
CINE-ROMAN   2127, 2137, 2140, 2141
Cine-Structuralism   477
CINEACTION: A MAGAZINE OF RADICAL FILM CRITICISM   483
CINEASTE   41
CINEASTES   609, 1522, 1711
Cineguild   1860

Cineliteracy   108
CINEMA '68   1818
Cinema Advertising   771
CINEMA D'ART movement, the   1710
Cinema Histories, Cinema Practices I Conference (May 1981)   495
CINEMA JOURNAL   41, 1522
CINEMA MAGAZINE   1711
CINEMA NOVO, the   2158
CINEMA QUARTERLY (1932-1935)   216
CINEMA VERITE   305, 309, 1557, 1715, 2040, 2048, 2072, 2120, 2121, 2123, 2153
Cinema 16   1716
CinemaScope   655, 1493, 1500, 1950, 1969, 2002
CINEMATEQUE FRANCAISE   128, 132, 1992, 1996, 2006, 2099, 2111
cinematic apparatus   591
cinematic modes of representation   277
CINEMATICS   165
Cinematograph Film Act (1927)   1569, 1831, 1840
Cinematograph Film Act (1938)   1832
Cinematographe   1586, 1602
Cinematographe-Lumiere, the   1610
cinematography   79
cinephilia   2126
Cineplex Odeon Theatres   682
Cinerama   1730, 1950
Cinerama Corporation   1481
CINETHIQUE   41, 2103
CINETRACTS   41
Circle Theater, The   1426
circuses   1604
Civil Censorship Division   2016
Civil Information and Education Section (CI&E)   2016
Civil Rights movement   2034
civil rights movement and feminist film criticism   502
Civil War films   379
Civil War, the   478, 864, 912, 932
civilian war film   376
classic Hollywood realist style   522
classical film theory   134, 163
classical Hollywood film   59, 60, 61, 62, 63, 70, 111, 113, 477, 603
classical plot, the   197, 198
Classification and Ratings Administration, the   2038
cleanliness   181
clearances   612, 687, 1944
cliffhangers   55
CLIMAX (TV series)   2051
CLOSE UP   126, 514, 1567
close-up shots   1409
closed film   186, 187
clozentropy   164
Coca-Cola Company   663, 669, 678
Cockatrice-Basilisk, the   399
Code of Fair Competition   687
codes   134, 472, 1071
cognitive dissonance   543
Cold War, the   241, 270, 288, 293, 324, 334, 342, 348, 356, 430
COLGATE COMEDY HOUR (TV series)   2064
collaborative-structural process, the   551
collective behavior   552

collective consciousness   780
collective experience   778
collective heroes   195
collective perceptions   181
college-related films   989, 990
Colonial Office propaganda films   1569
color films   59, 697, 1386, 2033
Colored and Indian Film Company, the   867, 948
Colored Players Film Corporation, the   928, 948
Columbia Broadcasting Corporation, Inc. (See CBS, Inc.)   671
Columbia Pictures   252, 301, 536, 635, 653, 660, 671, 672, 677, 704, 905, 1093,
   1467, 1469, 1485, 1509, 1944, 1945
Columbia Pictures Entertainment Inc.   2205
Columbia University   1240
combat photography   224, 314
comedians   1447
comediennes   1383, 1395, 1411
comedies   182, 190, 192, 271, 328, 342, 348, 400, 406, 426, 498, 508, 767, 1177,
   1416, 1532, 1709, 1784, 1914
comedies in the 1980s   762
comedy   188, 189, 191, 269, 273, 1379, 1409, 1410, 1411, 1412, 1413, 1418, 1420,
   1424, 1429, 1433, 1447, 1449, 1479, 1497, 1500
comedy and bigotry   835
comedy and Mary Pickford   1392
comic strips   1239, 1583, 1587
coming of sound in France   1809
coming of sound, the   697, 782, 1424, 1451, 1467, 1671, 1673, 1675, 1677, 1748,
   1751, 1759
COMITE D'ORGANIZATION DE L'INDUSTRIE CINEMATOGRAPHIQUE
   (COIC)   1906
COMITE D'ORGANIZATION (CO)   1906
COMMEDIA DELL'ARTE   1427, 1646
commercial film industry and censorship   67
commercial film industry and copyrights   67
commercial film industry and limited partnerships   67
commercial film industry and magazine reviews   67
commercial film industry and obscenity   67
commercial film industry and short contracts   67
commercial film industry and uniform commercial codes   67
commercial film industry and working forms   67
commercial film industry, the   56
commercial film production library   275
Commercial Kino   1649
Commissariat General A L'Information (Department of Information)   223, 247
Committee for the First Amendment   1203
Committee for the Liberation of the French Cinema, the   1991
Committee for the Negro in Arts (CNA)   944
Committee on Public Information (CPI), the   223, 224
Commonwealth Theaters   682
Commonwealth, The   213
communication research   745
Communism   204, 213, 215, 227, 229, 240, 273, 274, 306, 334, 1258, 1259, 1431,
   1433, 1977
Communist China   312
Communist Party Central Committee, the   223
company movie theaters   630
company union   1172, 1173
Compass Players, The   2060
COMPASS ROSE   371

compilation films 222, 304, 318
completion guarantees 700
composers 403, 405, 408
composition 1362
computer animation 77
concessions in movies theaters 667
Conference of Cinema Workers 1657
confessional films 176
conglomerates 612, 661, 662, 671, 673, 686, 691, 697, 699, 704
Congregatio de Propanda Fide 209
Congress 292, 305, 1944
Congress of Racial Equality, the (CORE) 893
Congress of the FEDERATION INTERNATIONAL DES ARCHIVES DU FILM 1510
Conscience-liberalism 274
conscious parallelism 689
consciousness 466
Conseil Superieur de Cinema 1811
consent decrees 687
constructivism 1664
consumerist culture 765
contemporary film theory 134
content analysis 265, 268, 356, 524, 708, 728
CONTES MORAUX 2142
contextual criticism 176
contextualism 38
CONTINENTAL FILM SOCIETE A RESPONSABILITE LIMITEE 1907
continuity scripts 58, 685
contract adjustments 645, 677
contract players 421
contractual obligations 1447
conventions 173, 179, 182, 183, 184, 187, 188, 194, 196, 200, 202, 204, 206,
  257, 258, 265, 278, 285, 339, 348, 349, 350, 357, 358, 359, 363, 364, 385, 386,
  397, 408, 427, 434, 463, 1784
convergent selectivity 463
conversion hysteria 714
convicts in films 568
Cooper-Randol Productions 948
Coordinator of Information's Foreign Information Service 229
Coordinator of Inter-American Affairs, the 307
coproductions 694
corporate capitalism 198
corporate loans 702
corporate stocks 702
COSBY SHOW, THE (TV sitcom) 833, 972
Counterpoint 100
courtroom dramas in American films 560
Creel Committee, the 213, 224, 236, 297
Crewe House 212
cricket films 421
crime films 176, 192, 197, 386, 559
crime in Hollywood 1234
CRISIS, THE 915
Criterion Collection: THE GRADUATE, The 2085
critical subjectivity 501
Crown Film Unit, the 217, 242, 317
Cuban Film Industry 299, 312
Cuban Institute of Cinematographic Art and Industry (ICAIC), the 299
Cubism 1713, 1715, 1717, 1727, 1730

Cubo-Futurism 1664
cult films 392, 419
cult of celebrity, the 550
cultural hegemony 521, 800
Cultural Ratification Model 451
cultural vs. ideological codes 917
culture and propaganda 566
culture and society 614
culture, high 179, 195, 260, 278
culture, mass 179, 278
Curse of Capistrano, The 1407
Czech New Wave 141
Czechoslovakian films 2013
C. B. C. Film Sales Company 1469

D

Dadaism 1710, 1713, 1716, 1727, 1728, 1730
daguerreotype 1591
Dai-Nihon Eiga (The Greater Japan Motion Picture Company) 1895
Daiei Motion Picture Company, the 2016, 2021, 2024
Daito Motion Picture Company, the 2018
DALLAS (TV series) 536
dance in film 402
DANGER (TV series) 2051
Danish Film Museum 1629
Danish films 693, 1626
David O. Selznick Productions 1486
daydreams 448, 531, 532, 581
De Havilland decision against Warner Bros. 1945
De Laurentiis Entertainment Group, the 672
debt financing 631, 702
Decla-Bioscop 1632, 1636
deconstruction 475, 1956
DECOUPAGE 112
Deep and Solid Laboratories 988
deep-focus cinematography 63, 1951
defamation and invasion of privacy 699
DEFENDERS, THE (TV series) 2065, 2067
Defense Department, the 358
Democracy Film Corporation, the 867, 948
Denham Studios 1840, 1859
Department of Agriculture 305
Department of Defense 231, 305
Department of Defense Public Affairs Office, the 230
Department of Enemy Propaganda 212
Department of Information 211, 212, 213, 247
Department of the Treasury 307
Depression, the 176, 190, 272, 309, 555, 564, 565, 568, 572, 640, 736, 782
depth psychology 600
Depth-of-field photography 479, 1814
designated play dates 687
DeStijl 1717
detective films 194, 373, 380, 386, 1175
detective novels 178
determinate space 195
development of cross-cutting 1605
devils in film 415

DFZ Productions   1500
diachronic mode of historical vision   486
dialectical montage   311
DICK POWELL REYNOLDS ALUMINUM SHOW, THE (TV series)   1960, 2061
DIE WALKURE   209
diegesis   472
Diet, the   1733
dime novel   1583
Dimension Pictures   643
Diney Studios and TV   672
dinner-movie theaters   770
diorama   1591
direct cinema   188, 295, 2040, 2041, 2121
direct lie   250, 251
director interlocks   702
directors   1234, 1238, 1239, 1240
Directors Guild, the   1260, 2044
DIREZIONE GENERALE PER LA CINEMATOGRAFIA   1879
disaster movies   189, 753, 2193
DISCORS theory   507
discourse theory   472, 495, 591
Disney films   668
Disney Studio, the   306, 308, 321, 660
distortions   246, 254, 255, 256, 260, 265, 274, 291, 292, 298, 302, 317, 344,
   347, 355
distribution   698, 1358, 1399, 1438, 1463, 1464, 1465, 1466, 1470, 1481, 1486,
   1494, 1499
distribution and exhibition of British feminist films   492
distribution of foreign films in America   771
distribution policies in the 1970s   666
diversification   704
divorced theater circuits   686
DNIPRO   1655
doctors in the movies   1239
DOCTOR, THE (TV series)   2043
docu-dramas   222, 605
documentaries and historical evidence   252, 261
documentaries and music   405, 407
documentaries and realism   779
documentaries in Cuba   299
documentaries in the silent era   296
documentaries in World War II   353
documentaries, armed forces   305
documentary   81, 188, 215, 230, 237, 238, 240, 243, 244, 248, 253, 266, 268,
   272, 280, 285, 288, 289, 291, 292, 294, 304, 306, 317, 322, 325, 339, 347, 364,
   1947, 2040
documentary film movement   213, 214, 215, 216, 243, 244, 245, 1281, 1569
documentary films   173, 216, 217, 245, 246, 255, 256, 280, 281, 284, 288, 289,
   291, 292, 293, 296, 303, 305, 318, 333, 342, 352, 355, 1542, 1646, 1661, 1664,
   1668, 1669, 1681, 1682
DOCUMENTARY NEWSLETTER OF BRITAIN (1940-1947), THE   216, 315, 316
documentary techniques in fiction films   303
dog movies   1500
Dolby   674
Domino Films   1409
domino theory, the   363
Don'ts and Be Carefuls List   224
double bills   421, 640, 700

double text 657
Douglas Fairbanks Picture Corporation   1400
Douglas Fairbanks, Jr. Presents   1403
Dracula/Frankenstein films   389
DRAGNET   1564
dramas in the 1980s   762
dramatic license   291
DRAMATIC MIRROR, THE   123
dramatic-personal process, the   551
dream   180, 181, 182, 188
dream screen   584
Dresden   218, 360
drive-in theaters   767, 769
drugs   224, 988, 1396, 1411
dual consciousness   500, 501
dubbing   1885
Dunbar Film Corporation, the   948
Dunkirk   234, 321, 378
duping   619
Duquesne Amusement Supply Company   1494
Dutch cinema   2178
Dynamation   411
Dziga Vertov Group, the   2111, 2126

E

E & R Productions   889
Eady Levy   1936
Eagle-Lion Films, Ltd.   1935
Ealing Studios   352, 1568, 1569, 1839, 1840, 1841, 1937, 1938
early American paintings   874
early British films   1617
early filmmaking in Chicago   621
early filmmaking in Colorado   626
early filmmaking in New Jersey   1595
early films and the fairgrounds   1599
Easman Kodak   41
East River National Bank   1465
Eastern Europe films and the Holocaust   311
Eastern European Jews and Hollywood   818
Eastern Front   234
Eastman Kodak   654, 1461, 1463, 1945
Ebony Film Company, the   867, 948
Eclair Cameflex 35mm camera, the   2120
Eclipse   1459
economic film history   195, 198, 684, 770, 781
economic patterns in the entertainment world   686
Edict of Isolation   1731
Edison films   1608
Edison laboratories   1542
Edison Manufacturing Company, the   684, 766, 1462
Edison National Historic Site   1545
Edison Studio   1358, 1361, 1423
EDISON v. AMERICAN MUTOSCOPE COMPANY (1902)   1537
editing   314, 1363, 1737
educational films   283, 307, 1538
Edwardian London   1427
Effects Model   451

effects of movies on attitude development   767
effects of the media   728
ego-psychology   600
EIGA GEIJUTSUKA KYOKAI (The Motion Picture Artists Association)   2021
Eight Lancashire Lads   1415
eight mm sound film   65
Ekstatics   1028
El Alamein   323
Electric Theatre   1600
Electrical Research Products Inc. (ERPI)   700
electronic cinematography   81
electronic media   779
elements of film   93
Eleven East 14th Street   1361, 1376
Em Gee Film Library   1705
Emergency Committee   1174
Eminent Authors   1062
Emmys   1531
Emotional Response Index System Company (ERIS), the   782
Empire Marketing Board, The   213, 214, 238, 243, 244, 248, 295, 306, 308
empirical research   773
Empress Theater, the (Kansas City)   1415
England   235, 236, 240, 243, 293, 331, 342, 371, 378
English music halls   1427
Enterprise Studios   1136, 2043
entertainment   455, 460
epic films   182, 188, 189, 192, 382, 383
epic war films   177, 342
equity financing   631, 702
escapism and experimental films   166
Espionage Act, the   223
Essanay Film Manufacturing Company, the   1358, 1401, 1416, 1426, 1427, 1454,
  1595, 1616
ethics in documentary filmmaking   537
ethics in the film industry   537, 771
ethnicity   864
ethnographic filmmaking   2120
Europe   328, 329, 352
European AVANT-GARDE, the   1716
European book illustrations   874
European cinema in the twenties   1709
European Competition Law   664
European directors in Hollywood, 1922-1931   1676
European film industries   693
European film market   572
European filmmaking and feminist film criticism   502
European paintings   874
euthanasia   240
evidence   259, 270
evolution of period dramas in Japanese films   1575
exhibition   1358, 1359, 1399, 1438, 1463, 1464, 1465, 1466, 1475
exhibition licenses   700
exhibitionism   592
EXODUS and Arab boycotts   849
EXODUS and Israel   849
EXPERIMENTAL CINEMA   126
experimental films   187, 188, 1715, 1716
experimentation with color films in Britain   1840

exploitation films   393, 651, 743, 770, 982
Expressionism   1637, 1707, 1742, 1858, 1948, 2040
expressive montage   100
expressive realism   213

F

Factors Etc. Inc.   611
Factory, the (Andy Warhol's studio)   2068
factual films   284, 305, 352
fairy tales   253, 415, 601
faking   254, 267, 275, 292
Falcon Lair   1236
fallen women films   555
family films (see maternal melodrama)   794
family in Japanese films   1575
family melodramas   194, 195, 712, 792, 793, 794
FAMILY TIES (TV sitcom)   972
Famous Players Film Company, the   1383, 1392, 1400, 1463, 1465, 1467, 1471,
    1477, 1479, 1504
Famous Players Theaters   682
Famous Players-Lasky Corporation   621, 622, 703, 1837
fan magazines   993, 1234, 1237, 1450
FANTASMAGORIE   1588
fantastic films   412
fantasy films   192, 409, 411, 414, 415, 416, 801, 1913
fascism in films   568, 569
Fascist Italy   247, 1877
fashions   298
feature film financing   700
feature film production   63
feature films   1358, 1461, 1463
feature films and vaudeville   766
Federal Bureau of Investigation (FBI), the   373, 1418, 1848
federal litigation   690
Federal Theatre   1789
Federated Motion Picture Crafts, The (FMPC)   1750
FEERIES   1604
FELIX THE CAT series   928
female communists in Hollywood films   1945
female Gothics   517
female sexuality in films   516
feminine narrative   522
feminism and FILM NOIR   1948
feminist documentary cinema   512
feminist film criticism   134, 270, 470, 474, 476, 492, 493, 494, 495, 497, 499,
    500, 501, 507, 513, 521, 585, 603, 795, 1441, 1849
feminist filmmaking in Australia   491
feminist readership   793
fetishism   461, 589, 590
fiction film   173
field-of-focus   1362
fight films   301
filler   1970
film acting   1234, 1240, 1366, 1374, 1434, 1453
film advertising   537, 754, 769, 782
film and cultural pluralism   661
film and entertainment   711

film and formalism   161
film and politics   444
film and psychology   492, 493, 494, 594, 775, 781, 782
film and realism   130, 161, 166
film and reality   124, 127
film and semiotics   493
film and sociology   176, 775, 1441, 1447
film and television   655, 691, 762, 782
Film and Television Study Center   1537
film and theater   594, 602, 655, 666
film and vaudeville   685, 766, 767
Film Art Institute of the State Film Archive of the USSR   242
film as language   68, 95, 96, 101, 104, 108, 163, 168, 172, 493
film as literature   135
film attendance   745, 756, 1172, 1944, 1950
film audience research   754, 767, 768, 769
film audiences   745, 768, 769, 776, 782
Film Booking Office of America, Inc.   1493
film bureaus in America   658
film canons   42, 446, 2081
film censorship and verbal taboos   438
film censorship in the 1930s   685
Film Centre   244, 249
film coloring   656
film comedy   502, 1532
film comedy in the thirties   555
FILM COMMENT   1522
film commissars   534
film company management   700
film concepts   769
film connotations   99
film content   776
film continuity   85
film contracts   699
film credits   698
film criticism   119, 120, 137, 745, 775, 777, 1507, 1754
film criticism and Andrew Sarris   137, 143
film criticism and CITIZEN KANE   141
film criticism and Dwight Macdonald   143, 159
film criticism and genres   127
film criticism and James Agee   141, 143, 159
film criticism and John Simon   137, 143
film criticism and Judith Crist   137
film criticism and Parker Tyler   143
film criticism and Pauline Kael   137, 143, 159
film criticism and Robert Warshow   143
film criticism and Stanley Kauffmann   137, 143, 159
film criticism and the AUTEUR theory   138
film criticism and Vernon Young   143
film criticism and Vincent Canby   137
film criticism and "B" films   127
film critics   145
FILM CULTURE   1522
film cycles   463
FILM D' ART   1608
FILM D'ART   1338, 1558, 1709, 1833
FILM DAILY, THE   781
film denotations   99

film distribution 690, 702, 781
film distribution and vaudeville 767
film distribution and videocassettes 762
film distribution handbook 75
film economics 697, 702, 768
film editing 82
film equipment 1371
film exchanges 684, 1463, 1470, 1494
film exhibition 684, 702, 781, 782
film exhibition and vaudeville 767
film exporting 693
FILM FAN MONTHLY 1237
film fashions and the fashion world 610
film financing 58
film funding 781
film genres 1561
film genres and vaudeville 767
film grammar 96, 97, 99
FILM HERITAGE 1522
Film Hour for the Young (JUGENDFILMSTUDEN) 250
film images of women in early films 1587
film language 1362, 1364
film lens 81
FILM LIBRARY QUARTERLY 1522
film lighting in the silent era 719
film loans (1933-1939) 687
film magazines 1383, 1447
film marketing 698, 767, 768, 770, 781
film melodrama in 1907 1361
film melodramas 792, 794
film movements 125
film music 83, 611
FILM MUSIC NOTES 406
film narratives 195, 472, 493, 494
FILM NOIR 188, 197, 373, 505, 507, 522, 798, 800, 1637, 1712, 1913, 1947, 1948,
1952, 1956, 2129
FILM NOIR and American paranoia 559
FILM NOIR and anti-Semitism 849
FILM NOIR and families 1003
FILM NOIR and heroes 809
FILM NOIR and LA NOUVELLE VAGUE 2096
FILM NOIR and Stanley Kubrick 2057
FILM NOIR and women's films 522, 523
film populism 1713
film preferences 535, 769, 782
film previews 738, 769
film production 68, 71, 702, 781
film psychology and westerns 745
film punctuation 98
FILM QUARTERLY 41, 1522
film ratings 700, 959, 961
film ratio 97
film realism 112, 113
film reception and foreign films 748
film reception in Chile 748
film remakes 772
film rental 1475
film reviewers 121
film scandals 1374, 1376, 1400, 1411, 1417, 1423, 1426, 1432, 1433, 1505

film scheduling   75
film scholarship   1523
film seating capacities   781
film securities   628
film sequels   772
film series   772
film settings   98
film size   97
FILM SOCIETY REVIEW   1522
Film Society, 1925-1939, The   1567
film sound systems   782
film styles   103, 114, 164
film subsidies   699, 700
film subtitles   1383
film systems   120
film technology   675, 697, 700, 782
film theaters   755, 1944
film theaters owned by the majors in the U. S. (1940)   687
film theorists   166
film theory   119, 120, 161
film theory and adaptations   130
film theory and Free Cinema   131
film theory and LA NOUVELLE VAGUE   131
film theory and Marxism   130
film theory and Neo-Realism   127, 131
film theory and the British documentary movement   127
film titles   769
film trailers   769
film violence   555, 745, 769
FILM & HISTORY   41
film "sleepers"   745
film-banking relationship   702
Film-Maker's Cooperative, the   2039
filmic motivation   100
filmic rhythm   101
filmic space   97, 98, 126
filmic time   98, 126, 1363
Filmliga   314
Filmology Movement, the   2002
films about Israel   841
films about the Jewish family   841
films and entertainment   776
FILMS AND FILMING   1522
films and rape   295
films as "chasers"   685
FILMS DU CARROSSE, LES   2107
FILMS IN REVIEW   1522
Filmways Pictures   535, 2049
FILMWELT (German film world)   250, 251
FILM: THE FRONT LINE series   235
financing   627, 645, 1464, 1465, 1486
financing film production in Europe   664
Fine Arts Company   1384
Finnish film market   684, 693
Finnish films   234, 1627
FIRESIDE THEATER   653
First Artists Corporation   889
first film shown at the White House   685

First National Exhibitors' Circuit, the   686, 1393, 1416, 1426, 1428, 1429, 1464, 1465, 1492
first-run audiences   745
first-run films   763
first-run movie theaters   687, 1465
Five o'clock look   677
fixed shots   97
Flaherty Papers   1682
flapper movies   523
Florida and early filmmaking   1599
Florida and the motion picture industry   621
folk art   403
folk culture   781
folktale   190, 253
football films   421
FORD THEATER (TV series)   2066
foreign distribution   700
foreign film markets   224, 226, 227, 686, 693, 703
foreign film subsidies   694
foreign filmmakers commenting on America   562
Foreign Information Service   229
Foreign Language Film Academy Awards' process   1165
foreign policy, American   273
foreign tax incentives   700
formalism   127, 1654, 1657, 1664
formula deals   623, 1944
formula film and popular culture   422
formula filmmaking   567, 691
formula films   173, 178, 182, 183, 187, 188, 189, 190, 192, 194, 197, 233, 273, 285, 403, 465, 690, 1360, 1399, 1438
Fort Lee, New Jersey   520, 621, 1675
FORTUNE   685
Forty-Five Hundred Sunset Boulevard   1372, 1384
Foster Photoplay Company, the   863, 934
four-walling   666, 754
Fox Film Corporation   624, 678, 703, 1464, 1470, 1471, 1478, 1479, 1492, 1500, 1502, 2205, 2206
Fox Metropolitan Theatres   1492
Fox Movietone News   298, 300, 346
Fox Theater in Atlanta, The   1506
Fox-Case Corporation   298
framing   97
framing devices   1362
France   234, 331, 351, 367, 379
France and the AVANT-GARDE   1716
France and the Holocaust   317
Frankfurt Institute of Social Research, the   537, 774
Frankfurt School   521
Fred Karno's Pantomine Company   1415
Frederick Douglas Company, the   867
Free Cinema   129, 2039, 2121
free market models   438
FREEDMAN V. MARYLAND, 380 U. S. 51 (1965)   2037
French cinema of the Occupation   1571, 1905
French existentialism   1927
French film audiences   733
French film industry   225, 273, 352, 567, 693, 693, 771, 1409
French films and the Holocaust   311
French films during World War I   1571

French films in the 1920s   441, 1571, 1631
French Foreign Legion   1813
French New Wave, the   567, 1924
French Resistance   317, 324
French Revolution, The   277, 474, 1591
French Union of Young Communists   2111
French/Indochinese War   363
Front Line Cinemas   297
Frontier Films   292
Fuenteduena   319
future of the film industry   782
Futurism   1583, 1664, 1713, 1879
futuristic films   415
F. Warde Company   1399

G

G-Man movies   556
Gabrielinos, the   1233
gaffers   76, 80
Gainsborough Pictures   1834, 1837, 1843
gallery shots   1451
game strategies   182, 188
gangster films   173, 175, 176, 188, 189, 190, 191, 194, 195, 255, 373, 382, 385,
   386, 522, 555, 568, 572, 776, 785, 1494, 1500, 2035, 2036, 2064
gangster films and African-Americans   878, 935
gangster films and Jews   819
gangster films and Robert Aldrich   2044
gangster films and Samuel Fuller   1977
GARRY MOORE SHOW, THE (TV series)   2051
Gate Theatre   1789
Gaumont Pictures   266, 1459, 1606, 1843
Gaumont Studio   1725
Gaumont-British studios   1834, 1838, 1860
Gay and lesbian cinema   573
gay liberation   1441
Gencorp Incorporated   663
GENDAI-GEKI   1733, 1741, 1742, 1886, 1893
General Cinema Theatres   682
General Film Company   1460, 1461, 1463, 1494
General Motors   252
General Post Office, The   214, 215, 217, 238, 244, 249, 295, 306, 308, 315, 316,
   317
generative mechanisms   1555
genocide   323
genres   188, 203, 204, 206, 246, 248, 251, 253, 255, 258, 265, 272, 273, 278,
   281, 284, 292, 304, 334, 339, 355, 771, 1175
genres and audiences   192, 193
genres and CAHIERS DU CINEMA   2002, 2099
genres and classic films   187
genres and conventions   603
genres and cultural significance   564
genres and documentary films   285
genres and double bills   640
genres and dream theories   598
genres and epic films   382
genres and feminist film criticism   521

genres and film criticism 165
genres and film economics 608
genres and film history 188
genres and film theory 170
genres and historical evidence 252, 291
genres and history on film 270
genres and Hollywood 178, 182
genres and iconography 197
genres and ideology 463
genres and musicals 408
genres and newsreels 300
genres and nuclear war films 355
genres and popular reviews 68
genres and propaganda 202
genres and psychoanalytic criticism 599
genres and screen education 181, 185, 186, 188, 191, 192
genres and the Hollywood musical 400
genres and the Old South 912
genres and the star system 1442
genres and the 1940s 1913
genres and Vietnam War films 359, 364
genres and war films 325, 335, 361, 367
genres and World War II 284, 334, 345, 349, 350
genres in the 1980s 669
genres vs. movements 507
German Expressionism 785, 1633, 1923
German feminist films 2165
German films 236, 240, 250, 273, 311, 352
German films and the Holocaust 311
German films in the 1920s 441, 1631
German newsreels (DEUTSCHE WOCHENSCHAUEN) 250
German Romanticism 362
German silent films 1573
Germany 226, 238, 250, 256, 262, 264, 293, 301, 340, 342, 351, 357, 365, 370,
  372, 373, 377
Germany and the AVANT-GARDE 1716
GET SMART (TV series) 2047
ghost films 415
Gilded Age, the 1238
GIROT 919
Globe Enterprises 1960, 2078
Gold Rush of 1849, the 1597
Golden Age of Yiddish films 848
Goldman Sachs 632
Goldwyn Pictures Corporation 1464, 1471, 1472, 1473, 1479, 1480
Golem, the 399
golf films 421
Gos-Kino 1649, 1653
gossip columnists 1234
Gothic literature and the women's film 522
Gothic romance films 794
Gothic spiritual art 2004
government agencies 769
government films 271, 296, 305, 307, 309, 324, 346
government public relations 305
Gower Gulch 426, 1456
gradients of depth in film 116
GRAF SPEE, the 235
Grammys 1531

Grand Opera 714
Grauman's Chinese (Hollywood) 1506
Great Stone Face 1688
Greater Japan Film Machinery Manufacturing Company, Limited. 1736
Greater Japan Motion Picture Company, The (Dai-Nihon Eiga) 1895
Greater New York Film Rental Company 1460, 1470
Greek tragedy 1336
Greenfilm 846
Griffin, the 399
Griffith versus Borzage 1701
Griffith's Biograph shorts 44
grips 76
group behavior 777
Group Theatre, the 1258, 1259, 1292
GROWING PAINS (TV sitcom) 972
Gryphon Group, the 1716
Gulf & Western Industries, Inc. 671
GUNSMOKE (TV series) 2061

H

Hal Roach Studio 1787
Hale's Tours 1504, 1505, 1600
HALES TOURS 1492
Halsey, Stuart, and Company 629, 685
Hammer Film Productions 390
Hammer Films 388, 390, 396, 398, 1569
hand tinting 654
hand-colored films 654
Hang-the-Kaiser films 213, 263
harem women 498
Harlem Productions 948
Harlem Renaissance, the 870, 887
Harlequin Romances 517
Harris-Kubrick Productions 2055
HARVARD LAMPOON 1544
Hate-the-Hun movies 211
Hawaii 359
Hayart 1456
Hays Office, the 225, 641, 797
heads of production 536
Hearst International Newsreel 300
Hearst Metrotone News 300
heliography 1591
Hemingway in film 373
Herald Pictures 881
Herodotus 382
heroes 195, 1400
heroes and Afro-Americans 860
heroes in silent films 804
heroes, American war 232
heroines 993, 1384, 1411, 1444, 1447, 1455, 1457
High Arts Pictures Corporation 848
hillbilly films 912
HINDENBERG, the 298
Hiroshima 298
Hispanic films 826

Hispanic horror productions 390
Hispanics and the media 574
historians, social 273
historic preservation 1507
historical accuracy 284, 291
historical documents 273
historical dramas 222, 255
historical epics 1945
historical evidence 253, 254, 256, 258, 260, 265, 267, 268, 272, 274, 275, 276,
    277, 278, 285, 288, 289, 296, 304, 311, 318, 334, 348, 382, 1387
historical evidence and documentary films 288
historical evidence and propaganda 252
historical reconstructions 313, 314
historical war films 379
historiography 276
history films and costume design 269
history in film 254, 272, 289, 296
history of mentalities 261
history on film 254, 271, 289, 296, 333
Hit Parade 1000
hoboes in film 568
HOGANS'S HEROES 374
Holland 314
Hollywood 242, 244, 245, 246, 258, 259, 262, 263, 264, 267, 272, 278, 281, 292,
    331, 339, 344, 348, 349, 352, 355, 1160, 1223, 1233, 1234, 1235, 1236, 1237,
    1238, 1239, 1240, 1241, 1243, 1275, 1295, 1496
Hollywood and Adolph Zukor 1477, 1504
Hollywood and African-Americans 870
Hollywood and Alexander Korda 1859
Hollywood and Alfred Hitchcock 1221, 1839
Hollywood and Anita Loos 1380
Hollywood and anti-Semitism 125, 223
Hollywood and assimilation 823
Hollywood and bisexuality 603
Hollywood and blacklisting 1963
Hollywood and British films 1607, 1840, 1935
Hollywood and Broadway actors 1399
Hollywood and Carl Laemmle 1475
Hollywood and Communism 836
Hollywood and Darryl F. Zanuck 1500
Hollywood and David O. Selznick 1486
Hollywood and Dore Schary 1485, 1486
Hollywood and Douglas Fairbanks, Sr. 1402
Hollywood and D. W. Griffith 1373, 1377, 1969
Hollywood and Eisenstein 1866
Hollywood and Elia Kazan 1259
Hollywood and epic films 382
Hollywood and Ethnicity 454
Hollywood and Eugene O'Neill 1341
Hollywood and feminism 604
Hollywood and film criticism 146
Hollywood and film scandals 1374, 1423
Hollywood and Foreign Affairs 454
Hollywood and foreign films 647, 691
Hollywood and F. Scott Fitzgerald 1031
Hollywood and gangster films 385, 386
Hollywood and genres 177, 178, 182, 193, 195, 198
Hollywood and HBO 653
Hollywood and history on film 270

Hollywood and Irving Thalberg   1491
Hollywood and isolationism in World War II   203, 345
Hollywood and Israel   832, 837
Hollywood and Jesse Lasky   1478
Hollywood and Jews   819, 827
Hollywood and MGM   1239
Hollywood and movie series   420, 421
Hollywood and musicals   402, 408
Hollywood and Native Americans   425
Hollywood and New Jersey   1595
Hollywood and PHOTOPLAY   1453
Hollywood and Pickfair   1400
Hollywood and political film criticism   573
Hollywood and post-WWII Germany   647
Hollywood and Poverty Row   1456
Hollywood and pro-Soviet propaganda   351
Hollywood and propaganda   204, 207, 213, 217, 218, 219, 220, 224, 225, 226,
   232, 233, 236, 340, 346
Hollywood and puppet films   411
Hollywood and racism in World War II   351
Hollywood and Samuel Goldwyn   1471
Hollywood and science fiction films   411
Hollywood and silent films   1360
Hollywood and stage mothers   1455
Hollywood and studio publicity posters   792
Hollywood and technology   681
Hollywood and teenage films   974, 986
Hollywood and television   648, 653, 656, 686
Hollywood and the American Dream   61, 125, 1046
Hollywood and the civil rights movement   856
Hollywood and the conversion to color   654
Hollywood and the Depression   521
Hollywood and the development of the film industry   1465, 1468
Hollywood and the Holocaust   311, 837
Hollywood and the image of Roman Catholicism   1754
Hollywood and the movie moguls   1466
Hollywood and the new feminism   492
Hollywood and the New Wave   2123
Hollywood and the newspaper genre   408
Hollywood and the NRA   640
Hollywood and the Office of War Information   229, 230, 351
Hollywood and the Spanish Civil War   345
Hollywood and the star system   64, 171, 1440, 1441, 1444, 1451
Hollywood and the studios   1467
Hollywood and the Trust   685
Hollywood and the Vietnam War   335, 360, 363, 364, 2035
Hollywood and the youth market   748
Hollywood and the 1950s   1953
Hollywood and war films   328, 331, 349, 356, 359, 361
Hollywood and westerns   430
Hollywood and World War I   370
Hollywood and World War II   340, 345, 349, 353, 358, 370, 372, 521, 559, 856,
   1911
Hollywood architects   1233, 1236, 1507
Hollywood choreographers, 1915-1937   1676
Hollywood designers   1236
Hollywood domestics   1234, 1236
Hollywood extras   671

Hollywood feuds 1235, 1236
Hollywood finances 1235
Hollywood gossip 1242
Hollywood guilds 1156
Hollywood in the post-World War I era 1962
Hollywood in the post-World War II era 523, 568
Hollywood in the teens 1463
Hollywood in the 1920s 502, 1561, 1675, 1715
Hollywood in the 1930s 502, 555, 567, 568, 685, 697, 778, 874, 944, 1561
Hollywood in the 1940s 494, 502, 567, 568, 797, 881, 944, 1561, 1911
Hollywood in the 1950s 502, 524, 559, 565, 653, 770, 883, 887, 983, 1561, 2035
Hollywood in the 1960s 393, 502, 603, 779, 1561, 2035, 2037, 2041, 2123, 2124
Hollywood in the 1970s 502, 558, 603, 660, 946, 2190, 2192
Hollywood in the 1980s 672, 2190
Hollywood musicals 83
Hollywood novels 1145
Hollywood parochialism 779
Hollywood politics 1234, 1235, 1236
Hollywood pranks 1234
Hollywood Productions 881, 948
HOLLYWOOD QUARTERLY 1522
Hollywood Reds, the 1084
Hollywood restauranteurs 1234
Hollywood Roosevelt Hotel 1165
Hollywood scandals 1242
Hollywood studio system 691
Hollywood Ten, the 572, 1187, 1293
Hollywood unions 1232
Hollywood war film (1916-1930) 223
Hollywood's impact on British filmmaking 1567
Holocaust 152, 222, 289, 293, 311, 312, 324, 833
Holocaust films 291, 323, 333, 841, 2084
Holographic films 655
Home Box Office (HBO) 548, 653, 677, 678
home entertainment 769
homosexuality 274, 491
Hopi Concept of "Life out of Balance," the 598
horizontal splitting 677
horror films 176, 182, 185, 188, 189, 190, 191, 197, 278, 388, 389, 392, 393,
   395, 396, 399, 409, 415, 419, 496, 497, 604, 785, 982, 1171, 1175, 1475, 1913,
   2035
horror movies and the women's film 794
horse racing films 421
Horst Wessel 321
House Un-American Activities Committee (HUAC) 204, 273, 340, 559, 569, 572,
   686, 836, 1089, 1155, 1177, 1187, 1235, 1257, 1258, 1260, 1261, 1485, 1945, 1969
human rights 560
humanist critics 124
Hungarian films 2012, 2013
Huntington Park Civic Center, the 2061
huntresses 498
hypodermic theory, the 778

I

I SPY (TV series)   443
icon 173, 174, 190
iconography 174, 189, 192, 196, 258, 349, 359, 385, 386, 389, 416, 425, 427,
  434, 451
idea films 294
identification films 307
ideology 135, 277, 468, 769
ideology and dream theory 584
ideology and the star system 1441
ideology and the Third World 559
ILLUSTRATED LONDON NEWS 1570
image of doctors on TV 812
image-objects 1710
Imax 674
imperial films 1569
Impressionism 1711, 1713, 1742
Improvisational theaters 1649
in-home entertainment 760
incandescent lighting 1814
independent African-American film companies 863
independent African-American films 942, 946, 947, 948
independent exhibitors 686, 700, 763
independent film and TV producers 73
independent film financing 704
Independent film producers 643, 686, 698, 700, 1377, 1463, 1483, 1491
independent filmmaking 573, 681, 704, 1622
Independent Motion Picture Company (IMP) 1392, 1475
independent women directors in the seventies 508
Independents 1459, 1461, 1462, 1463, 1505, 1885
indeterminate space 195
India Maria, La 453
Indians (see Native Americans) 427
indirect lie 250
individual psychology 600
industrial films 1746
influence of foreign films on Japanese cinema 1575
influence of psychoanalysis in American movies 797
informal vision 1716
Information and Education Division (I&E) 247
informational films 324
Initiative of Jewish Actors and Artists, the 848
insanity and film 569, 597, 598
INSIDE WOODY ALLEN (comic strip) 2045
INSIGHT 42
INSTITUTO LUCE 1873
intellectual historians 258, 260, 270, 275
intellectual montage 1647, 1667
Internal Revenue Service 643
International Film and Radio Guild, the (IFRG) 939
international film financing 769
international filmmaking 697
International Olympic Committee 250
international relations 242
International Roadshows 881, 948
internationalization 704
Interstate Television (Monogram) 653

Intertitles 1388, 1748
InterUniversity History Film Consortium, the 242
interventionism 227
inventions 182, 183, 184, 200, 202, 204, 206, 258, 265, 285, 463
investigation movies 197
IRON HORSE, THE (TV series) 1960
IRONSIDES (TV series) 1267
Irving G. Thalberg Memorial Award, The 1492, 1846
Islington studios 1834, 1837
isolationism 225, 227, 273, 320, 376
Israel 833
Israeli cinema 2169
Italian Fascist cinema 1574, 1874, 1875, 1876, 1877, 1878
Italian film market, the 693
Italian films 236, 246, 427, 1573, 1574, 1608, 1873, 2126
Italian films and the Holocaust 311
Italy 226, 283, 301, 351, 369, 378
itinerant movie shows 1599

J

Jack Paar Show, The 2060
JACKSON PARK case, the 689
Japan 298, 301, 328, 329, 351, 357, 358, 359, 374
Japan and talkies 1885
Japanese and American film genres 1734
Japanese audiences 748
Japanese cinematic techniques 1575
Japanese film heroes 801, 1743
Japanese film heroines 1575, 1743
Japanese film villains 802, 1575
Japanese films 209, 352, 1885
Japanese films in the 1930s 1898
Japanese films in the 1950s 1898
Japanese films in the 1960s 1575, 1898
Japanese newsreels 283
Japanese serials 2018
Japanese silent films 1731, 1736, 1739
Japanese war films 1575, 1894
Jeffersonian democracy 1686
JERUSALEM 1013
Jesse L. Lasky Feature Plays Company, The 1463, 1477, 1504
Jew in American films, the 836, 839
Jewish American Princess, the 842
Jewish and Irish relationships in film 840
Jewish film festivals 836
Jewish immigration 845
Jewish Media Services 835
Jewish-American authors 833
Jewish-American characters 840
Jewish-American Drama 836
Jewish-American film, the 840, 841
Jews and the silent film 825, 842
Jews in World War II movies 883
JIDAI-GEKI (historical films) 1733, 1741, 1742, 1886
John Frankenheimer Productions 2051
JOHN WESLEY HARDING (record album) 425

JOSEPH BURSTYN, INC. v. WILSON, COMMISSIONER OF NEW YORK, ET AL.
 (1952) 1537
JOURNAL OF FILM AND VIDEO 41
JOURNAL OF POPULAR FILM AND TELEVISION, THE 41, 564
JOURNAL OF POPULAR FILM, THE 564
journalists in film 555
Jubilee Pictures 948
Judea Pictures Corporation 846, 848
JUMP CUT 41, 573
JUNBUNGAKU, 1892
jungle heroines 498
Justice Department and "political propaganda" 962
juvenile delinquency films 418
juvenile delinquency in films 556, 568, 982, 986
J. O. film company 2022

K

KABUKI and American film genres 1734
KABUKI films 1736
KABUKI plays 1733, 1734, 1735
KAISER ALUMINUM HOUR, THE (TV series) 2067
Kalem Company 1373, 1379, 1595, 1616
Kaminsky troupe, the 847
KAMMERSPIELFILM 1632, 1640, 1728, 1742
Kanto earthquake 1741
Karlovy Vary Film Festival 1171
Karno Company, the 1416, 1421, 1423
katsuben 1736
Kay-Bee Productions 1384, 1409
KEIKO EIGA ("tendency films") 1886
Keith Theatre Circuit 616
Keith-Albee vaudeville circuit 632
Kent State 425
Keystone Film Company 1384, 1409, 1411, 1412, 1413, 1415, 1416, 1423, 1427,
 1593, 1595
Kinemacolor Studio 654, 1372
kinesics 600, 601
Kinetophone, the 1585
Kinetoscope 122, 293, 685, 1386, 1586
Kinetoscope Exhibition Company, the 860
Kinetoscope in Britain, the 1610
Kinney National Service 663
KINO-NEDELYA 1658
KINOR 848
KLEINBURGERTRUM 251
Kodachrome 654
KODAN 1733
Korean War combat films 342
Korean War films 334, 359, 1976
Korean War, the 200, 328, 334, 340, 354, 356, 366, 430
KRAFT TELEVISION THEATER (TV series) 2048, 2052, 2058
Ku Klux Klan 1386, 1387, 1423
Kuhn, Loeb and Company 618, 703, 1465
Kung Fu films 191

L

lab processing   73
labor disputes   1172, 1173, 1174
labor problems in post-World War II films   569
Lacanian psychology   2126
LAMP UNTO MY FEET (TV series)   2051
LANGUE   482
LaSalle Street investment houses   629
Lasky Feature Plays   1471
Latian American cinema   2177
Latin America film history   245
Latin American film history   252
Laurel Award   1064, 1285
Le Bon   251
leadership cult (FUHRERPRINZIP)   250
Leadership of the American Jewish Community   291
League of Nations, the   365
LEBENSBAUM (living-space)   234
left-wing documentary filmmakers   247
legal problems in the film industry   770, 1360
Legion of Decency   219, 220, 1232, 1749
Leigh Whipper Film Company, the   948
leisure time   564
Leni Riefenstahl documentaries   1829
lesbianism in films   516
Lewis J. Selznick Enterprises, Inc.   1486
Liberty Bond drives   224
Liberty Productions   1169
Library for the Performing Arts at Lincoln Center, the   1365, 1374, 1391
Library of Congress   1577
LIFE   203, 301
lighting   98, 1362
Lillian Gish clippings, the   1365
Lillian Gish papers, the   1365
Lillian Gish scrapbook, the   1365
Lincoln Motion Picture Company, the   866, 934, 947, 948
line producers   700
linguistics, structural   277
literary agents   700
literary life in Hollywood in the 1930s   1153
Literary New Wave, the   2112
Literary Projects Company, the   658
literature and horror films   397, 398, 399
location shooting   661, 1386
Loew's Consolidated Enterprises   1482
Loew's Incorporated   624, 630, 635, 646, 686, 692, 1284, 1481, 1482, 1500, 1944
Loew's Theatres   678, 682, 763
London blitz   323
London Film Productions   1859
long-takes   1950, 1951
LOOK magazine   2055
Lorimar Telepictures Corporation   536, 662, 663, 672, 905
Los Angeles   1233
LOS ANGELES TIMES, THE   1169
Louis B. Mayer Pictures Corporation   1481
love teams   1447
Lubin Company   1358
Lucas "THX" sound   674

Lumiere Company, the   684, 766
Lumiere films   1590
LUSITANIA, the   262, 297
Lux Radio Theatre   1681
lynching in film   568
lyricists   405

M

M-G-M PARADE   653
MacGuffin   1864
Mack Sennett's Bathing Beauties   1502
MacMahonian theater, the   1998
MacMahoniens, the   1998
made-for-Cable TV films   68
made-for-TV movies   68
madonna-whore syndrome   599
magazine films   280, 281, 352
magic in films   415, 416
magic lanterns   1588, 1590, 1594
Maginot Line, the   298
magnetic sound   1950
Majestic-Reliance   1373, 1378, 1392, 1463
major studios and theater ownership in the 1980s   2207
make-up   84
male gaze, the   504, 590, 592
male vs. female viewing behavior   745
Malibu Beach   1238
Manifesto of the 121, the   2147
Mann Theaters Corporation of California, Inc.   682
Manticore, the   399
MARCH OF TIME, The   226, 237, 246, 280, 281, 292, 296, 301, 303, 319, 352,
   1601, 2066
MARCH OF TIME, The (radio show)   301
MARCUS WELBY, M.D. (TV series)   1267
market capitalism   198
marketing research   773, 1447, 1847
marketing strategies in the 1940s   1847
Marlowe, Philip   1198
marriage in film   779
Martial Arts films   565
Martin Theaters   682
Martinique   1215
Marxist film criticism   474, 484, 587, 603, 1442
Maryland State Censorship Board   2037
Mascot Pictures   1456
masquerade   589, 590
mass art as popular art   537
mass communication models   438, 780
mass communications research   734
mass media and children   745
mass media and reception theory   745
mass media and society   67
mass media and the concept of escape   745
mass media and the public interest   648
mass media preferences   533
MASS OBSERVATION   315

MASSES AND MAINSTREAM   911, 1286
Massilia Episode, the   317
master agreements   623
Material aesthetics   130
maternal melodrama   521, 522, 523, 794, 795
Mayflower Productions   1838
MCA and anti-Semitism   836
MCA Inc.   671
McCarthy era and Robert Aldrich, the   2071
McCarthyism and westerns   430
meaning of "life" in Kurosawa's films   1575
Meiji Restoration   1732
MEISTERSINGER   209
Melies Manufacturing Company, the   1459, 1616
melodrama and early films   1587
melodrama and the Japanese cinema   1894
melodrama and the women's film   522
melodrama and the 1940s   1913
melodramas   180, 209, 331, 531, 714, 792, 794, 1784, 2044
melodramatic conventions   311
melodramatic traditions   564
mental concepts   363, 542
MENTSHLEKHKAYT   829
Mercury Theatre   1789
Mercury Theatre of the Air   1789
mergers   704
Mers-el-Kebir   234, 317
Meschrabpom Company, the   928
methodological problems   176
Metro Pictures Corporation   1393, 1440, 1464, 1472, 1479, 1481
Metro-Goldwyn-Mayer   226, 273, 367, 398, 404, 630, 635, 663, 672, 686, 776,
  934, 1000, 1204, 1237, 1239, 1394, 1396, 1440, 1464, 1467, 1469, 1472, 1478,
  1479, 1481, 1482, 1483, 1484, 1485, 1486, 1488, 1490, 1491
Mexican films   771, 2178
MGM film library   662
MGM-British and Alexander Korda   1859
MGM-Entertainment Company   662
MGM/UA Communications Company   662, 678
Micheaux Film Corporation, the   947, 948
Middle Ages in literature and film, the   416
Middle East cinema   2178
military films   307, 361
military, American   246, 360
MILLER v. CALIFORNIA (1973)   962
Million Dollar Productions   948
MILWAUKEE JOURNAL   42
minimal movies   1716
Ministry of Information, The   202, 212, 213, 216, 217, 223, 242, 247, 316, 317,
  323, 1569
Ministry of Popular Enlightenment and Propaganda, the   223
Ministry of Propaganda   202, 1907
minorities in film   568
minority audiences   565
Minotaur, the   399
minstrel tradition   943
mirror phase, the   480, 588, 590, 596
MISE EN SCENE   102, 104, 107, 112, 129, 170, 1709, 1950, 1952, 2032, 2123,
  2124
MISSION IMPOSSIBLE (TV series)   443

mobile MISE EN SCENE   113
Modac Indian War, the   1597
modeling in film and television   72
modeling in Hollywood   1232
modern British cinema   2159
modern Canadian cinema   2162
modern Chilian cinema   2163
modern Chinese cinema   2163
modern Cuban cinema   2163
modern Czechoslovak cinema   2164
modern German cinema   2165
modern Greek cinema   2166
modern Hungarian cinema   2166
modern Indian cinema   2167
modern Italian cinema   2169
modern Japanese cinema   2176
Modern Polish cinema   2179
modern Swedish cinema   2182
modernism   118, 1715, 1739
moguls and African-Americans   853
MONO NO AWARE   1738
Monogram Pictures   640, 651, 2151
Monogram (Interstate Television)   653
monopoly capitalism   702, 703, 765
monster films   189, 190, 565, 975
montage   99, 100, 129, 304, 1657
montage of attractations   1660
Monument Valley   1674
moral turpitude clauses   1234
Morales, Gerardo Machado y   1214
Mormons and silent films   826
Moscow   344
Moscow Art theater   1649
Moscow Cinema Committee   1663
Moscow Film Festival   1171
motifs   1175
Motion Picture Academy of Arts and Sciences, The   700, 1402, 1409, 1429, 1481,
   1492, 1504
Motion Picture and Television Relief Fund, the   1240
Motion Picture Artists Association, The (EIGA GEIJUTSUKA KYOKAI)   2021
Motion Picture Association of America (MPAA)   647, 694, 738, 1948, 1949, 2038,
   2086
Motion Picture Association of America, the (MPAA)   1948
Motion Picture Board of Trade (1915), the   701
Motion Picture Code   894
Motion Picture Committee Co-operating for National Defense   346
Motion Picture Export Association (MPEA)   694
MOTION PICTURE HERALD   198
MOTION PICTURE MAGAZINE   264
motion picture marketing   700
Motion Picture Patents Company (MPPC), The   572, 607, 633, 685, 954, 1358,
   1459, 1460, 1462, 1463, 1496, 1609, 1616, 1622, 1885
Motion Picture Players Union, the   1072
Motion Picture Producers and Distributors of America (MPPDA)   224, 687, 738,
   1504
Motion Picture Producers of America (MPPA)   1949
Motion Picture Producers of America, the (MPPA)   752, 961
Motion Picture Production Code, the   146, 357, 685, 744, 1537

Motion Picture Relief Fund, the 1240
Motion Picture Research Bureau 734
motion picture wage rates 647
motion shots 97
mountain films 1829
MOVIE 41, 1237, 1522, 1752, 2096
movie by-products 781
movie posters 1453
movie production and budget forms 75
movie theaters 1507
movies and entertainment 782
movies as mass communication 781
movies as social communication 711
movies on television 545
movies on video tapes 762
movies vs. television 780
Movietone News 266, 298
MOVING PICTURE NEWS 123
MOVING PICTURE WORLD, THE 123
MUJO 2025
multichannel recording 86
multinational film corporations 1950, 1952
multiplex theaters 752
MURNAU VEIDT FILMGESELLSCHAFT 1640
Musee Grevin 1558
Museum of Modern Art, The 1370, 1371, 1372, 1382, 1403, 1442, 1473, 1989,
  2006, 2055
Music Corporation of America (MCA) 653, 662
music halls 1604, 1824
music in fantastic films 412
music in film 402, 403, 406, 407, 408, 1424
music videos 584
musical scoring for TV and film 75
musicals 176, 182, 187, 188, 189, 190, 191, 192, 194, 195, 197, 251, 328, 331,
  361, 400, 401, 403, 404, 405, 406, 407, 408, 426, 555, 564, 1476, 1494, 1497,
  1500, 1784, 1914, 1945, 2036
musicals and African-Americans 878, 935
Mutoscope 1361, 1386
MUTUAL FILM CORPORATION v. INDUSTRIAL COMMISSION OF OHIO
  (1915) 955, 1537
Mutual Film Corporation, The 1366, 1369, 1416, 1426, 1427, 1463
mysteries 191, 328
myth 175, 177, 178, 180, 181, 182, 183, 184, 188, 190, 195, 197, 199, 206, 207,
  209, 233, 234, 235, 236, 239, 251, 268, 277, 299, 335, 1291
myth of success 1293
mythologizing history 205
mythology and psychoanalysis 602

N

Nagasaki 299
NAKED CITY (TV series) 2065
narcissism 601
narcissistic personalities 600
narrative film music 404
narrative films and modernism 118
narrative film, the 58, 104, 107, 129
narrative logic 60

narrative montage 100
narratives 174, 177, 180, 182, 184, 1360, 1362
national accreditation 35
National Aeronautics and Space Administration, the 305
National Association for the Advancement of Colored People (NAACP) 855, 866,
   877, 915, 929, 930, 934, 939, 1382
National Association of Theater Owners (NATO) 753, 755, 959
National Board of Censorship, the 723
NATIONAL BOARD OF REVIEW MAGAZINE, THE 140
National Board of Review of Motion Pictures 954, 1171
National Broadcasting Corporation (NBC) 678
National Center for Jewish Film 1545
national cinemas 1944, 1950
National Coalition of Television Violence, the (NCTV) 961
National Film Archives, the 1833
National Film Board of Canada, the 236, 249, 280, 294, 296, 306, 318, 323, 2162
National Film Finance Corporation, The 1935
National Film Preservation Act, The 1514
National Film Study Project 200
National Film Theatre, the 1521
National Industrial Recovery Act (NIRA), the 700
National Kinney Corporation 1495
National Labor Relations Board, the 1156
National Legion of Decency, the 1530
National Recovery Administration (NRA) 640, 687, 697
National Screen Service 700
National Socialism 234, 240, 250, 251, 256
National Society of Film Critics 143
National Theatres Corporation 1493
National Urban League, The 915
Native American Women 454
Native Americans 425, 427, 434
Nazi Architecture 251
Nazi espionage 320
Nazi films 206, 222, 239, 246, 255, 257, 292, 295, 296, 304, 323, 1573, 1635
Nazi Germany 196, 203, 206, 207, 216, 219, 226, 228, 235, 236, 238, 239, 240,
   259, 262, 264, 289, 293, 305, 311, 312, 321, 322, 323, 324, 344, 349, 352, 353,
   357, 358, 360, 366, 369, 373, 377, 568, 849, 1430
Nazi Germany and the Holocaust 311
Nazi newsreels (DEUTSCHE WOCHENSCHAUEN) 206, 247, 255, 282, 300
Nazi propaganda 206, 207, 208, 228, 234, 235, 236, 238, 240, 241, 250, 251,
   305, 321
Nazi war films 222, 282
Nazi-Soviet Pact of 1939 227, 248, 1661
Negro Theatre of Harlem 1789
neo-realism 128, 146, 378, 779, 1633, 1875, 1921, 1922, 1923, 1927, 1929, 1930,
   1946, 2002
neo-realism and the Japanese cinema 1894
Neutrality Laws (1935) 226
New American Cinema, the 2039, 2074
New Cinema 2124
New Criticism 108
New Deal, the 272, 400, 564, 568, 1497, 1750
New Economic Policy (NEP) 1649, 1664
New German Cinema 152, 618
New Hollywood, the 772
New Left, the 2112, 2113, 2115
NEW REPUBLIC, THE 124

New Right, the 574
New Russian Theater 1649
New World Entertainment Ltd. 673
New World Pictures 2049
New York bankers 776
New York Board of Motion Picture Censorship 954
NEW YORK DRAMATIC WRITER, THE 123
New York Film Critics Circle 852, 1171, 1174
New York Film Festival 1544
New York Motion Picture Company 1409
New York Times Company 671
NEW YORK TIMES, THE 2027
NEW YORKER, THE 1101, 1268, 1273
Newport 1238
News of the Day 300, 346
newspaper films 408
newsreel library 275
newsreels 203, 206, 217, 222, 224, 225, 237, 246, 253, 254, 255, 256, 257, 265,
   266, 267, 268, 274, 275, 276, 280, 281, 282, 285, 292, 293, 294, 296, 298, 299,
   300, 301, 303, 304, 306, 318, 319, 346, 352, 369, 1664
newsreels and historical evidence 252, 261
newsreels in World War II 208
nickelodeons 572, 617, 619, 685, 696, 719, 766, 767, 1386, 1462, 1492, 1537,
   1600
nickelodeons and narrative films 767
Nielsen Company, A. C. 760, 789
Nielsen Ratings, the 552, 1138
Nikkatsu Motion Picture Company, the 1736, 1737, 1741, 1742, 1885, 1886, 2018
NIMAIME 1734
nineteenth-century entertainment 771
nineteenth-century magic shows 1588
nineteenth-century melodrama 711, 1604
nineteenth-century naturalism 1583
NIPPON HOSO KYOKAI (NHK) 247
NIPPON KATSUDO SHASHIN, the (Japan Cinematograph Company) 1736
Nisei 1976, 1986
nitrogen prints 618
NOH plays 508, 1734, 1735
non-fiction films 214, 224, 230, 253, 254, 255, 292, 293, 294, 295
non-genre films 194
non-governmental censorship 769
Non-Intervention Committee of 1936, the 267
nonfeature film activities in the 1930s 1749
Nordisk Film Company 1625, 1626, 1627
Normandy Invasion, the 283, 323, 373
North Africa 323, 372
Norway 230
Norwegian Resistance Movement 230
Nostalgic Samurai Drama, the 2027
NOUVEAU NOUVEAU ROMAN 2139, 2140
NOUVEAU ROMAN 2113, 2114, 2137, 2139, 2140, 2152
NOUVELLE VAGUE 129, 133, 505, 1669, 1969, 1999, 2039, 2093, 2112, 2113,
   2123, 2153
NOUVELLE VAGUE and CINEMA D'ART 2096
NOUVELLE VAGUE and John Huston 1916
novels into films 188, 191, 192, 2113
novelty 200
November 20, 1940, Consent Decree 687
nuclear family 516

nuclear war comedy 355
nuclear war films 325, 355, 1024
Nuremberg 289, 321, 377

O

object "You," the 482
OBJECTIF '48 2002
objections to psychological interpretations 601
obscenity 962
occult, the 414
October Group, the 1820
Odessa 274
ODYSSEY and 2001: A SPACE ODYSSEY, THE 2054
Oedipus complex, the 493, 531, 532, 588, 590, 601
off-screen space 1362
Office of Strategic Services 229
Office of War Information, the (OWI) 201, 228, 229, 230, 273, 305, 323, 329,
   344, 346, 349, 642, 881, 1848, 1911
Official Code Objectives of 1968 1537
oligopoly 704
Olympia Film Gmbh 250
Olympic films 296
Olympic Games 296, 421
Olympics (1924) 1013
OMNIBUS (TV series) 2048, 2058
one and two reelers 1401
ONNAGATA 1735
open film 186
OPERA NAZIONALE DOPOLAVORO 1873
Opinion Research Corporation, the (ORC) 754
OPPORTUNITY 915
optical distortions 98
oral history 1240
Organization for Economic Co-Operation and Development (OECD), the 782
organizing a feminist film series 492
organizing a film society 55
original screenplays 660
Orion Pictures 974
Oscar Micheaux Film and Book Company 947
Oscars 545, 1165, 1175
Oscars and source material 666
outlaws 430
OVER THE RAINBOW (song) 1801
over-budget protection 700
overbuying 687
overseas audiences 748
overseas markets 647, 672
OYAMA 1735, 1739, 1741

P

Pacific War, the   331, 349, 369, 1899
pacifism   210, 340
pacifist films   210, 221, 223, 342, 568
package deals   611, 1945, 2035
Pale of Settlement   847
Palestine   841
panachromatic film   1947
panchromatic stock   1814
panoramas   1589
para-social interaction   544
Parafamet Agreement   1633
parallel editing   1363, 1409
Parallelism   100
Paralta   1383
Paramount and the Office of War Information   229
Paramount Communications Inc. vs. Time Warner   2204
Paramount Communications, Inc.   662
PARAMOUNT Decree reassessed   686
PARAMOUNT Decree, the   572, 639, 644, 883, 1944, 1945, 1948, 1952
Paramount News   266, 300
Paramount Pictures and Eisenstein   1866
Paramount Pictures and TV   672
Paramount Pictures Corporation   226, 278, 346, 621, 624, 635, 653, 660, 676,
   678, 974, 1271, 1392, 1397, 1464, 1467, 1469, 1477, 1478, 1479, 1486, 1488,
   1490, 1491, 1492, 1504, 1505, 1944, 1945
paranoia in films   521, 522, 714
PAROLE   482
pastoral romances and heroes   804
patent wars   272
Pathe Entertainment, Inc.   673
Pathe Freres Pictures   618, 1605, 1606
Pathe News   266, 300, 310, 346, 1456, 1459
Pathe-Cinema   1815
patriotic films   217, 218
Paul Rotha Productions   215
pay television   672, 769
Payne Fund Studies   40, 729, 775, 778, 957
Pearl Harbor   283, 298, 302, 346, 368
pedophilia   981
peep shows   1371, 1589
penny arcade   1470, 1481, 1504
Pensacola   346
Pentagon Motion Picture Bureau   361
Pentagon-Hollywood relationship   231, 232
Pentagon, the   230, 231, 348, 360, 361, 362
percentage reductions   677
perception theory   442
perceptual faith   183
performers   1239
Perry, Matthew Calbraith   1732
persistence of vision, the   1583, 1590
PERSON TO PERSON (TV series)   2051, 2066
personal genre, the   312
personality formation   552, 777, 778
PETITS GENS   1713
phallic symbols   532
PHANTASMAGORIA   1589

PHANTOM OF THE OPERA, THE   396
phenakistiscope   1598
phenomenology   132, 192
phi phenomenon   169
PHILCO PLAYHOUSE (TV series)   2064
Phony War, the   216
Photo Chemical Laboratories (P. C. L.)   1886, 1899
Photo League, the   225
Photo Play Editions   1453
photographic slide shows   1590
Photophone   633
PHOTOPLAY, ART (August 1916)   1623
physiological responses to motion pictures   754
Pickfair   1236, 1400
Pickford-Lasky Productions, Inc.   1478
picture palaces   629
pin-ups, the   167, 769
Pinewood Studios   1940
PITTSBURGH COURIER, THE   948
Platonic types   181
play date   612
PLAYBOY   565
PLAYHOUSE 90 (TV series)   2048, 2051, 2052, 2058, 2064, 2067
plays into films   192
Playwright's Company   1176
pleasure gratification   779
pleasure in film   493, 494
pleasure principle, the   478, 529, 533
Plitt Theatres   682
pluralism   446
poetic films   312
poetic realism   1825
pogroms   845, 847
Poland   216, 320
Poland and Yiddish films   847, 848
Polish church and the Holocaust   311
Polish film tastes   745
Polish films and the Holocaust   311
Political Satire theaters   1649
politicians in film   555, 568
politics in film   196, 242, 430
polysemy   1436
Polyvision   1727, 1730
pooling arrangements   1944
popular arts, the   179, 180, 181
popular culture   173, 188, 382, 457, 521, 564, 781
Popular Front in France, 1935-37, The   1813
Popular Front, the   225, 242, 274, 1075, 1156, 1750
populism in films   247, 567, 1713
pornographic films   981
pornography   512, 565, 778
pornography and videocassettes   960
pornography and violence   961
POSITIF   41, 1997, 2096
positive images of women   492
Post-Freudian object-relations theory   600
Post-Structualism   587
posters from the 1930s   1238

postmodern theory and the contemporary horror film 388
poverty row 399, 640, 1456, 1469, 1548
PRAVDA 212
praxinoscope 1598
Pre-Oedipal theory and film criticism 596
pregnancy 491
pregnant moments 475
prehistoric feature films 498
presence of women and men 531
Presidency, the 305
Presidential convention, 1968, Chicago 425
price fixing 1944, 1945
pricing policies 1460
Princeton University 1264
print advertising 769
private detectives 494
pro-Soviet films 259
pro-war films 226, 342
producer-audience process 173, 174, 177
producers 1238, 1239, 1240, 1360, 1400
producers in the 1980s 669
product splitting 677
production 1358, 1359, 1360, 1399, 1438, 1455, 1463, 1464, 1465, 1481, 1482,
  1507
Production Code Administration, The 345, 685, 1848, 2038
Production Code revisions, November, 1968 691
Production Code, the 358, 449, 523, 555, 686
production loans 702
production managers 1240
production of theatrical movies in U. S. (1930-1931 to 1938-1939) 687
Productive Art 1664
Professional Plot, the 198, 199
professional warriors 334, 357, 358
Progressive era 825
progressive film 568
Progressive movement 804
Prolet-Kino 1649
Proletkult Theater 1649, 1658, 1660, 1661, 1666
propaganda 201, 203, 239, 240, 241, 242, 243, 244, 245, 246, 247, 248, 251,
  255, 259, 260, 263, 265, 268, 272, 273, 274, 282, 284, 292, 303, 314, 320, 352,
  547
PROPAGANDA ABTEILUNG 1907
propaganda analysis 773
propaganda and Alexander Korda 1859
propaganda and anti-Semitism 203, 222, 236
propaganda and British films 212, 213, 214, 215, 216, 217
propaganda and censorship 209, 224
propaganda and documentary films 238, 288, 304, 305, 307
propaganda and educational films 166
propaganda and entertainment 826
propaganda and feminist film criticism 501
propaganda and historical evidence 252, 274, 291
propaganda and Hollywood 211, 224, 225, 230, 231
propaganda and myths about Africa 919
propaganda and Nazi Germany 318
propaganda and newsreels 217
propaganda and pro-Soviet films 259
propaganda and THE BIRTH OF A NATION 1387
propaganda and the Holocaust 291

propaganda and the Soviet Union 1653
propaganda and the Spanish Civil War 220
propaganda and the structure of the film industry 776
propaganda and the Vietnam War 325, 363
propaganda and the 1940s 1913
propaganda and TRIUMPH OF THE WILL 317, 318
propaganda and Vietnam 1674
propaganda and war films 202, 348, 351, 361
propaganda and World War I 308
propaganda and World War II 209, 229, 234, 235, 236, 321, 344, 346, 347, 349,
  351, 352, 358, 369, 378, 856
propaganda films 280, 281, 284, 292, 297, 304, 319
propaganda films and the silent era 296
propaganda for study in the classroom 239
propaganda, definition of 201, 233
prostitution 491
protection of film titles 699
proxemics 600, 601
Prudential Insurance Company, the 1840
psychedelic movies 418
psychoanalysis and feminist criticism 519
psychoanalysis and the 1950s' melodramas 792
psychoanalysis, film, and television 579
psychoanalytic film criticism 483, 538, 585, 586, 599, 600
psychoanalytic studies and women's films 797
psychoanalytical film theory 582, 603
psychographic correlates 770
psychographics 748
psycholinguistics 600
psychological considerations 182, 184, 188, 190, 191, 192, 196, 197, 203, 204,
  205, 207, 211, 216, 236, 253, 261, 265, 274, 284, 314, 355, 359, 370, 767, 1447
psychological rearmament 242
psychological studies and women's films 521
psychological studies on movie audiences 752
PSYCHOTRONIC 419
public nuisance laws 769
public opinion analysis 773
Public Opinion Research Centre of Polish Radio and Television 745
publicity campaigns 637, 1234, 1847
Publix Theatres 697
Pulitzer Prize plays 1531
pulp literature 177
puppet animation 77
puppet shows 1589
Puppetoons 411
Python, Monty 2159

Q

quadraphonic sound 674
QUARTERLY REVIEW OF FILM STUDIES 41
QUARTERLY REVIEW OF FILM, RADIO AND TELEVISION 1522
quickies 55
Quota Act of 1927, the 1567
quota system 1840, 1926

R

race relations 1946
race relations between African-Americans and Jews 858
racial films 271, 274, 863, 928, 934, 935, 937
racism 181, 205, 217, 218, 222, 235, 248, 270, 276, 277, 301, 328, 340, 346, 349, 355, 363, 364, 367, 375, 376, 427, 430, 462, 478, 551, 569, 779, 1378, 1381, 1383, 1386, 1387, 1468, 1471, 1479, 1494
radical French films 508
radical theater movement 1963
Radio City Music Hall 1506
Radio Corporation of America (RCA) 671, 703, 1670, 1809
Radio Luxembourg 247
radio personalities 1757
Radio-Keith-Orpheum Corporation, the (RKO) 635, 703, 934, 1344, 1467, 1477, 1478, 1486, 1488, 1490, 1500, 1751, 1944, 1945
radio-TV copy 92
Rambo war toys 437
Rank Organization, the 1569, 1939
rape 491
Ratings System, the 43, 753, 959, 2038, 2088, 2198
RCA 1490
reading a text 468
readjustment theme in movies, the 568
Realart Pictures 744
realism 59, 249, 268, 273, 275, 277, 280, 352, 776, 1555, 1654, 1715, 2124, 2125
realism and AVANT-GARDE cinema 492
realism vs. realistic 603
realist film theory 130
recall 533
reception theory 135, 485, 486, 507
recidivism 754
reconnaissance films 284
reconstructing lost films 1524
Reconstruction period, the 864
record reviews 405, 406
recuperation 591
recycled scripts 673
Red Scares 1670
Redstone Theaters 682
Reference Group theory 456, 779
referential cross-cutting 100
reflection hypothesis, the 459
reflexivity 118
refreshment sales 700
regional filmmaking 626
regression and film criticism 596
Reich Security Main Office 250
Reichstag, the 264
reincarnation 415
reinforcement of values 779
RELACHE 1728
Reliance-Majestic 1366
religion in film 382, 416
remakes 420, 426, 673
RENSA-GEKI 1735
Reol Production Company, the 867, 921, 948
Repertory Theatre of Lincoln Center 1261
repetition compulsion 188, 463

report films   280, 281
reportage documentary   283
repositories, film   275
representation   468, 492, 1231
repressed bisexuality in film   604
repression and film   603
repression and oppression   604
Republic Pictures   640
Research Branch of the War Department   734
Resettlement Administration, The   153, 292
RESIDENCIA DES ESTUDIANTES   1720
Resolution 152   204
retakes   1483
reviews vs. critiques   777
Revillon Freres Fur Company   1703
Revolutionary Theatre   1649
Revolutionary War films   270
Revolutionary-Kino   1649
REVUE DU CINEMA   2002
REVUE INTERNATIONALE DE FILMOLOGIE, LE   2002
rhythmic montage   1666
Rialto, the   1600
RIFLEMAN, THE   (TV series)   2061
rise of American feature films, the   685
rise of Hollywood   572
rise of the studio system   1622
RISORGIMENTO   277
ritual   182, 199
Riverside Studios   317
RKO Pantages Theatre   1174
road films   409
Roadshows   1950
robber barons   1238
ROCK AROUND THE CLOCK   1000
Rock films   982, 1000, 2199
rock music in film   405
Rockefeller Foundation, The   51
romance films   177, 182, 188, 192, 498, 769, 1532
Romantic Tradition, the   179, 1818
RONIN   1888
Roosevelt, President Franklin Delano   200
Roosevelt, Theodore   297
Roper poll   437
rota pools   300
ROTH v. UNITED STATES, 354 U.S. 476 (1957)   962
ROUTE 66 (TV series)   2061
rugby films   421
runaway productions   1936, 1950
rural problems in films   568
Russia   212, 235, 259, 273, 277, 314, 331, 334, 340, 344, 351, 357, 1653
Russia and the Yiddish film   847
Russian films   273, 305
Russian Formalist critics of the 1920s   113
Russian-Japanese Non-Aggression Pact of 1941   227

S

Sack Amusement Enterprises 948
Sack Cinemas 763
SACRA CONGREGATIO DE PROPAGANDA FIDE 210
salaries for film executives 536
SALLE DES AGRICULTEURS 2006
sample exhibition contracts 700
Samuel Goldwyn Productions, Incorporated 1472
Samuel Goldwyn Studio Sound department 2082
Samurai films 191, 1743, 2027
Samurai hero, the 1743
Samurai in fiction 1743
Santa Mira 183
satire 311
saturation advertising 770
SATURDAY EVENING POST 238, 1101
SATURDAY NIGHT LIVE (TV show) 2202
scenarios in the silent era 1455
SCHAUER films 1632
science fiction films 188, 190, 191, 195, 196, 395, 396, 398, 409, 411, 412, 415,
   417, 418, 419, 565, 756, 769, 1175, 1234, 1946, 2035
Science fiction films and Stanley Kubrick 2057
science fiction films and the 1950s 412, 1988
science filmmaking 76
scopophilia 512
SCREEN 41, 168, 192, 1567
screen acting 1364
Screen Actors Guild, the (SAG) 895, 1069, 1156, 1174, 1481, 1951
Screen Actors of America, the 1072
screen adaptations 1145, 1218, 1913
Screen Directors Guild 1272, 1951
screen education 32, 42, 46, 136
screen education and acting 44
screen education and adaptations 63, 69
screen education and African-Americans 52
screen education and aging 52
screen education and animation 45
screen education and art design 44
screen education and Asians 52
screen education and audience values 50
screen education and censorship 50, 52, 63
screen education and cinematography 44
screen education and composing 44
screen education and directing 44, 47
screen education and ethnic issues 52
screen education and film criticism 47, 52, 69
screen education and film genres 69
screen education and film history 47, 50, 103
screen education and film movements 103
screen education and filmmaking 43, 49
screen education and Gay issues 52
screen education and genres 45, 46, 103, 107
screen education and Hispanics 52
screen education and Hollywood 63
screen education and literature 51
screen education and McCarthyism 51
screen education and narrative films 43, 69
screen education and Native Americans 52

screen education and political movements 52
screen education and producing 44
screen education and religion 42
screen education and screenwriting 44
screen education and sequels 63
screen education and special effects 44
screen education and stereotyping 107
screen education and the documentary film 43
screen education and the experimental film 43
screen education and the image of crime 51
screen education and the image of marriage 51
screen education and the image of war 51
screen education and the influence of TV 50
screen education and theology 47, 48, 52, 53, 55
Screen Gems (Columbia Pictures) 653
Screen Playwrights, the 685, 1172
Screen Producers Guild 1505
screen sizes 674
screen tests 1234
Screen Writers Guild, the (SWG) 1156, 1172, 1481, 1485
SCREEN WRITER, THE 1186
screenplays 58, 192, 986
screenwriters 690, 691, 1237, 1239, 1240
Screenwriters Wars, The 1489
screenwriting 84, 1028, 1234, 1344
SCREEN, 41
screwball comedies 190, 194, 195, 556, 572, 1532, 1920
script supervising 85
scripts 1360
SD reports (SICHERHEITSDIENST DER SS) 250
Second City, The 2060
second director 1483
Second French AVANT-GARDE 1902
second-run movie theaters 1465
Section for the Wehrmacht Propaganda (ABTEILUNG FUR
  WEHRMACHTPROPAGANDA) 228
Select Pictures Corporation 1486
selective contracts 687, 781
selective exposure 543, 778
self-censorship in the movies 212, 697
Selig Company 1358, 1379
Selznick International 1486, 1490
Selznick Pictures Corporation 1486
Selznick Releasing Organization 1848
semiology 67, 96, 133, 134, 165, 168, 170, 173, 192, 195, 197, 198, 277, 474,
  482, 600, 1441, 1956
semiology and the AUTEUR theory 172
Sensurround 674
Sephardic Jews 818
sequels 421, 673, 761, 1171
serializing TV news 82
serials 272, 304, 420, 426, 498, 1455, 1456, 1457, 1458, 1709, 1717
series films 420, 421, 673
SESAME STREET (TV series) 983
set decoration 1002
sets 1234
Seven Arts 1495
SEVENTEEN 609

sex in the cinema 196, 567
sex role stereotypes 789
sexism 270, 462, 478, 551, 793
sexploitation films 1371, 2037
sexual repression 278
shadow plays 1579, 1582, 1589, 1590, 1594
shadow shows 1580, 1581, 1589
SHAKESPEARE ON FILM NEWSLETTER 1332
Shell Film Unit 244
Shell International Marketing Branch 316
Shepperton Studios 1859
SHERLOCK HOLMES 1423
Sherman Anti-Trust Act of 1890 1463
SHIMPA films 1735, 1742
SHIMPA plays 1734, 1735
SHISHOSETSU 1887
SHO WEST '85 545, 755
SHO WEST '86 759
SHO WEST '89 682
Shochiku Cinema Company, the 1737, 1742, 1885, 1886, 2016, 2018, 2021
SHOMIN-GEKI 1742, 1888, 1891, 1892, 1898
short films 355, 1716
short subjects 224, 266, 272, 346
showcase theaters 1465
Showscan 674
Showtime 653
SHTETLS 845
shyster films 555, 568
Sighisoara 395
SIGHT AND SOUND 131, 243, 249, 1522
signification 133, 468
signified 133, 134
signifier 133, 134
Sila 847
silent era, the 209, 296, 408, 414, 426, 1243
silent film comedy 804, 1294, 1678
silent film westerns 429
silent films 187, 298, 402, 615, 684, 1344, 1587
silent films and women directors 519
silent movies heroines 1365
silent newsreels 298
silent Yiddish films 847
siphoning 677
Six Day War 833
skimming 677
Slade Film History Register 310
slavery 478
SLON (SOCIETE POUR LE LANCEMENT DES OUVRES NOUVELLES) 2115, 2116
Snagov 395
sneak previews 574, 1234, 1847
snuff films 1145
soap operas 517, 522
Sobibor 222, 334
soccer films 421
social cinema 1812, 1813
social conformity 430
social content 1367
social control 463, 728
social criticism 1416

Social Engineering   320
social film history   1516
Social Gospel, the   1405
social history of women in the 1940s   522
social implications   182, 1367
social problem film, the   567, 568, 569, 944, 1204, 1475
social psychology   552, 773, 777
social types   551
socialism   216, 225
socialist ideology   500
socialist realism   1650, 1653, 1654, 1664
socialization   552, 777, 778
SOCIETE FILM D'ART   1608
Society of devotees of the Artistic Film (START)   2012
sociological films   1913
sociological issues   188
soft-focus   1372, 1387, 1397
Soldier's Show Company   2064
Sons of the Desert   1691
Sony Corporation   2205
Sony Corporation's purchase of Columbia Pictures   2205
sound   98
sound and African-American stereotypes   928
sound comes to Britain   1840
sound comes to the Soviet film industry   1654
sound film comedy   1678
sound films   187, 238
sound manipulations   99
Sound 360   674
South African film audiences   771
South America   307
South American audiences   748
South China Seas   359
Southeast Asia   288
Southern heroines   857
Southland fiction   1145
Sov-Am Productions   848
Soviet and Japanese filmmakers   1737
Soviet children's theaters   1649
Soviet documentaries   243
Soviet expressive realism   1633, 1923
Soviet Film Agency   1651
Soviet films   237, 241, 246, 304, 1367, 1648, 1650, 1902
Soviet films in the post-WWII period   1949
Soviet Information Bureau   247
Soviet Jewish theaters   1649
Soviet newsreels   243
Soviet propaganda   241
Soviet silent films   1653
Soviet State theaters   1649
Soviet studio theaters   1649
Soviet Union   212, 213, 227, 228, 234, 236, 312, 343
Soviet Union and the AVANT-GARDE   1716
Sovkino   1653, 1654
spaghetti westerns   1483
Spain   220, 226, 265, 301, 379
Spanish cinema   235
Spanish Civil War films   319

Spanish Civil War, the 216, 220, 221, 222, 265, 266, 267, 277, 278, 298, 314, 319, 376, 379, 1177, 1750, 1989
Spanish films 235, 693
Spanish writers and the cinema 1723
Special Assistant for Audio Visual (Department of Defense) 230
special effects 81, 411, 414, 416, 1319
spectacules 188, 406
spectator positioning 544
spectator sports and filmgoing 770
spectator theory 584
Sphinx Films 846
splatter movies 390, 394
split personalities 398
sponsored films 73, 303
sports movies 189, 190, 298, 299, 421, 884, 929, 945, 1239
spy films 373, 422, 423
spy novels 423
stage melodrama 1583
stage mothers 993, 1442, 1455, 1478
stage techniques and psychological theory 600
stage vs. screen 187, 191, 237, 1963
Standardized Achievment Tests (SATs) 439
Star Film Company 1604, 1616
star system and FILM NOIR 507
star system and women's films, the 797
star system in Yiddish films 848
star system, the 297, 426, 523, 564, 685, 743, 777, 993, 1234, 1360, 1383, 1404, 1434, 1435, 1437, 1441, 1442, 1447, 1449, 1450, 1451, 1453, 1456, 1468, 1472, 1484, 1486, 1491, 1497
stars 189, 1396
State Department, the 344
State Institute of Cinematography 1662
state-commissioned movies (STAATSAUFTRAGSFILME) 250
State's Rights 1464
state-supported propaganda films (TENDENZFILME) 250
statistics on shot lengths 2198
stereophonic sound 63
stereoscopes 1584
stereoscopic photography 655
stereotypes 179, 188, 210, 211, 217, 222, 224, 236, 250, 251, 258, 262, 263, 265, 268, 271, 293, 297, 325, 346, 349, 450, 551, 782, 1369, 1386
stereotypes and African-American women 872
stereotypes and African-Americans 780, 851, 887, 2038
stereotypes and Africans 918, 919
stereotypes and audience research 709
stereotypes and cultural hegemony 742
stereotypes and ethnic images 440
stereotypes and feminist film criticism 502
stereotypes and film theory 135
stereotypes and GONE WITH THE WIND 1801
stereotypes and Hispanic images 826
stereotypes and Italians 826
stereotypes and Mexican-Americans 826
stereotypes and Mormons 826
stereotypes and Orientals 826
stereotypes and pre-World War II films 348
stereotypes and public opinion 542
stereotypes and racism 868
stereotypes and THE BIRTH OF A NATION 1387

stereotypes and the Chinese 826
stereotypes and the PARAMOUNT case 660
stereotypes and the star system 1437, 1447
stereotypes and the Vietnam War 334
stereotypes and women's films 400, 495, 498, 516, 521
stereotypes and World War II 328, 356
stereotypes of actresses in the 1950s 523, 524
stereotypes of Arabs 454, 826
stereotypes of businessmen 486
stereotypes of Chinese women 789
stereotypes of Jews 916
stereotypes of Native Americans 425, 427, 434, 916
stereotypes of silent film heroines 503
stereotypes of women in FILM NOIR 507
stereotypes vs. conventions 776
still photography 1583
stimulus-response models 438
story conferences 691
story editors 700
Strand Films 244
Strategic Air Command 361
stratification 733
structural binary oppositions 197
structural cinema 1716
structural film studies 184, 197
structuralism 277, 600, 1442
structure 109, 111, 135
structuring absences 477
student filmmaking 87
Student Non-Violence Coordinating Committee, the (SNCC) 893
Studio Basic Agreement, the 1173
STUDIO ONE (TV series) 2048, 2058, 2066
studio system 193, 194, 449, 567, 697, 1238, 1360, 1561
study of film history 1568
stunt men 296, 424, 1403, 1405, 1468
stunting in films 76
style versus structure 111
subcultures 458, 779
subject "I," the 482
subjective play theory 463
subjectivity 493
subtitles 1885
summer movies 762
Super Panavision 655
Super Technirama 655
Super 8 filmmaking 74
suprematism 1664
Supreme Command of the Armed Forces (OBERKOMMANDO DER
 WEHRMACHT 228
Supreme Commander for Allied Powers (SCAP) 2015, 2016
Supreme Court and censorship 962
Supreme Court of California, the 1945
Supreme Court, the 686
Surrealism 1710, 1713, 1716, 1717, 1718, 1722, 1727, 1989
Surrealist Manifestos 1717
suspension of disbelief 781
suture 591
SVENSK FILMINDUSTRI 2183, 2184

swashbuckler films   192, 423
Swedish films   693, 769, 1625, 1627, 1628
Sweetheart Suits   763
Swiss cinema   2189
Switzerland   376
Sword Film, the   2027
symbolic annihilation   459
symbols   178
synchronic mode of historical vision   486
Synchronism   100
Synfy Theatres   682
syuzhet   114

T

TAIYOZOKU genre, the   2023
TAKE ONE   1522
talent agencies   1232
talent agents   700
talkies   1368, 1401, 1429, 1475, 1478
Tanhouser Company   1358, 1383
Tarzan film series   927
TATEYAKU   1734
tax shelters   698
teacher training   47
Technicolor   63, 654, 1405
Technicolor Corporation, the   1560, 1945
technological changes   633
teenage films   419, 743, 982, 983
telecommunications management   75
telefilm production   653
TELEFONO BIANCO ("white telephone" cinema)   1876
televised cartoons   789
television   179, 180, 218, 272, 273, 295, 300, 305, 317, 545, 691, 704, 1235,
  1436, 1452, 1485
television acting   1453
television and dream theory   584
television and film   572, 754, 779, 1949, 2036
television and realism   1715
television and westerns   425
television commercials   769, 1232
television documentaries   276
television news   299
television production   91, 93
television sitcoms   544
television studio system design and maintenance   92
television-technologies and their relationship to film   770
televison library   275
Temporary National Economic Committee   687
TEN OF US (TV sitcom)   972
tendency films (KEIKO EIGA)   1886
tennis films   421
territories   1465
terrorism   437
Texas in Hollywood films   428
textual criticism   132
Thalberg type, the   1158
theater acquisitions   700

theater holdings 629
theaters 700, 1172, 1234, 1359, 1386, 1465, 1470, 1492, 1506
Theatre Ambigu-Comique 1591
THEATRE ENTERPRISE case 689
Theatre Robert-Houdin 1588, 1616
theatrical techniques 187
Theda Bara clippings, the 1374
themes 1175
theories about motherhood 795
Third Reich 207, 238, 240, 250, 321
Third World cinema 559, 573, 917
Third World Film Company 938
Three-D movies 655, 699, 1950, 2033
thrillers 192, 342, 353, 386
tight oligopoly 671
Time Inc. 301, 653, 671
Time Inc. merger with Warner Communications Inc. 2204
Time Warner 2204
Time-Life, Inc. 280
Times-Mirror Company 671
tinted films 2033
Tobias-Klangfilm 632, 1809, 1828
Todd-AO 655, 1950
Toei Motion Picture Company, the (Tokoyo Film) 2018
Toho Motion Picture Company, the 1886, 2016, 2018, 2021
Tokyo 283, 369, 370
TOM AND JERRY film series 928
Tom Moyer Theaters 682
toning 654
TONY BROWN'S JOURNAL (TV series) 905
Tonys 1531
topical films 176, 767
Toyoko Film (the Toei Motion Picture Company) 2018
Tradition of Quality 129
tragic mulatto, the 862, 883
training films 280, 281, 283, 284, 307, 346
Transamerica Corporation, The 662, 671
Transatlantic Pictures 1848, 1854
transcendentalism in film 2004
Transformalism 163
Transitional Theme, the 198
transvestism 589, 590
Transylvania 395
treatments 58, 66
Treblinka 222, 323
Tri-Ergon patents 632, 1470
Tri-Star and United Artists Theaters 682
Tri-Star Pictures 678, 763
Tri-State Theatre Corporation 639, 771
Triangle Film Corporation 1368, 1379, 1384, 1399, 1403, 1412, 1464, 1560, 1680
Triangle-Fine Arts 1400
trick photography 1409, 1588
trope 115, 134
tropical musicals 498
tropical serials 498
tropical television shows 498
Trust, the 771, 1377, 1463, 1470, 1475, 1505
Turkey 372

Turner Broadcasting Company, The 812
Twentieth Century Pictures 1500
Twentieth Century Studies (University of Wisconsin-Milwaukee), the 495
Twentieth Century-Fox 298, 536, 635, 660, 671, 678, 886, 934, 939, 1204, 1467, 1486, 1493, 1499, 1502, 1944, 1950
TWENTIETH CENTURY-FOX HOUR, THE 653
Twentieth Century-Fox Sound department 1981
Two Cities 1935
two way cable TV 93
two-reelers 1358, 1409, 1416, 1463
two-step flow models 438
Typage 1646
typecasting 101, 187
T. A. T. Communications 669

U

umbrella organizations 704
unemployment in film 568
Unicorn, the 399
unionization in Hollywood 568, 1156
Unique Film Company, the 867, 948
Unit Four 2067
unit manager 66
United Artists 535, 635, 643, 660, 662, 672, 685, 686, 875, 1204, 1368, 1369, 1378, 1382, 1383, 1386, 1387, 1393, 1394, 1397, 1400, 1416, 1417, 1421, 1431, 1464, 1467, 1474, 1478, 1486, 1493, 1944, 1945, 1949
United Artists and Communism 1418
United Artists and MGM 669
United Artists Theatre Circuit Inc. 682
United Auto Workers (UAW) 252
United Nations 365
United States Catholic Conference (USCC), the 1530
United States Film Service, The 153
United States Information Agency (USIA) 230, 294, 305, 1674
United States Supreme Court 1470, 1945, 1949, 2037
UNITED STATES v. PARAMOUNT PICTURES, INC., (1947) 1537
United World Films (Universal) 653
United World Pictures 1935
Universal City 1475, 1560
Universal Film Manufacturing Company 1463, 1475
Universal News 266, 300
Universal Pictures 346, 535, 635, 660, 662, 672, 682, 701, 927, 974, 1397, 1456, 1467, 1476, 1491, 1502, 1935, 1944, 2035
Universal (United World Films) 653
Universal-International Pictures 662, 934
University of California at Los Angeles 1240
University of Southern California Performing Arts Council 1169
University of Southern California (USC) 495
University of Wisconsin-Milwaukee 495
Universum Film Aktiengesselschaft 1631
urban geography and American film history 623
Urban League 877
USA Cinemas 763
Uses and Gratification Model 451
USO 346
utopianism 460, 546
U. S. Department of Justice 686, 687

U. S. Film Service   305
U. S. Information Agency (USIA)   748
U. S. Supreme Court   955, 962
U. S. v. TECHNICOLOR, INC. TECHNICOLOR MOTION PICTURE CORP., AND EASTMAN KODAK CO., (S.D. Cal. 1947)   654

V

VALERIE'S FAMILY (TV sitcom)   972
values in films   535
vampire films   395, 398, 399, 415
vamp, the   631
VARIETY   123, 2027
VARIETY BOXOFFICE INDEX (VBI)   753
vaudeville   718, 767, 1824
VCR's and violence   961
vengeance hero, the   198
Vengeance Variation, the   198
Venice Film Festival   1171, 1737
VERFREMDUNG effect, the   2103, 2125
vertical splitting   677
Viacom   662
Vichy government, the   234, 247, 317, 372
Victorian London   1427
videocassettes   31, 92, 93, 174, 365, 545, 672, 704, 755, 756, 759, 760, 762, 764, 769, 782, 2202
Videoscope   183
Vietnam War and Hollywood   2089
Vietnam War films   217, 289, 334, 335, 342, 347
Vietnam War films vs. World War II films   337
Vietnam War, the   178, 200, 218, 232, 233, 259, 272, 288, 298, 324, 325, 328, 339, 340, 342, 346, 347, 354, 359, 360, 361, 363, 364, 366, 367, 376, 425, 430, 443, 484, 562, 604, 1517, 2071
VIEWS AND FILM INDEX   123
VILLAGE VOICE, THE   1522, 2027
Vim Comedy Company   621, 627, 771
violence   175, 176, 190, 191, 217, 334, 355, 359, 361, 386, 394, 422, 565, 722, 778, 793, 974, 2038, 2124
VIRGINIAN, THE (TV series)   1960
Viscentini   1427
VISION   1522
Vistar Films   535
VistaVision   655, 1950
visual literacy   47, 55, 66, 96
visual pleasure   2124
Vitagraph   210, 700, 1379, 1456, 1462, 1595, 1601
Vitaphone   624, 633
Vitascope Company, the   766, 1602
VLSE (merger of Vitagraph, Lubin, Selig, and Essanay companies)   1467
voice-over narration   116
Volk   206
VOLKISCH tradition, the   250
voyeurism   512, 589, 592, 605, 1838
VSESOYUZN GOSUDARSTVENYI INSTITUT KINEMATOGRAFIA (V.G.I.K.)   1645, 1658, 1662

W

Wagner Act, the 1156
Waldorf Declaration, the 1485
Wall Street 628, 629, 1238, 1465, 1670
Walt Disney Company, the 537, 672
WALT DISNEY'S WONDERFUL WORLD OF COLOR 653, 2036
WALTONS, THE (TV series) 536
War Activities Committee, the 229, 642, 1911
War Co-operating Committee 224
war comedies 361, 1532
war correspondants 297
war documentaries 312, 314
war film documentaries 294
war films 178, 186, 188, 191, 192, 194, 195, 196, 197, 199, 200, 218, 224, 230,
  233, 234, 255, 257, 258, 262, 263, 264, 265, 268, 273, 278, 280, 281, 284, 296,
  329, 331, 342, 348, 349, 352, 522, 1497
war films and historical evidence 252, 291
war films and post-WWII period 1945
war films and propaganda 202, 203, 205, 340, 348, 349, 353, 356, 357, 360,
  361, 362
war films and Robert Aldrich 2044
war films and Samuel Fuller 1976
war films and THE BIRTH OF A NATION 1387
war films and the Holocaust 289, 291
war films and the Vietnam War 325, 359, 360, 363
war films and the 1940s 1913
war films and the 1960s 2071
war films and World War II 284, 331, 340, 350, 351, 352, 358, 375
war films "faked" 210
war heroes 357, 494
WAR OF THE WORLDS, THE (radio show) 1262, 1263, 1789, 1794
Warde 1403
Wardour Street 1567
Warner Bros. 260, 273, 343, 397, 471, 535, 556, 624, 635, 660, 672, 686, 692,
  974, 1177, 1319, 1464, 1467, 1469, 1478, 1479, 1492, 1494, 1495, 1496, 1497,
  1498, 1499, 1500, 1502, 1944, 1945, 2035
Warner Bros. and HBO 653
Warner Bros. and the woman's film 794
Warner Bros. in the forties 797
Warner Bros. in the thirties 508
Warner Bros. Library of the Wisconsin Center for Film and Theater
  Research 798
Warner Bros. story department, the 691
Warner Bros. with a conglomerate structure 686
WARNER BROTHERS PRESENTS 653
Warner Communications 663, 671, 686
Warner-Pathe News 300
Warsaw Ghetto, the 222, 240
wartime film propaganda 568
Watergate 484, 604
Webb-Pomerene Export Trade Act of 1918, the 694
WEFT series (Wings, Engine, Fusilage, and Tail) 307
Weimar Republic 212
Wellington House 211, 212
WELTANSCHAUUNG 256
werewolves 398, 415
Wesco Corporation 1493
Wessex Films 317

Western Electric 1670, 1809
Western European audiences 748
Western European Jews 818
WESTERNER, THE (TV series) 2061
westerns 173, 175, 176, 177, 178, 182, 184, 187, 188, 189, 190, 191, 192, 193,
    194, 195, 197, 198, 199, 232, 237, 255, 270, 297, 325, 339, 424, 532, 726, 785,
    1517, 1709, 1946, 2027, 2035, 2036, 2087
westerns and African-American films 935
westerns and African-American stereotypes 878, 893, 945
westerns and Andre Bazin 167
westerns and cultural significance 564
westerns and gangster films 776
westerns and heroes 804
westerns and ideology 559
westerns and Italian filmmakers 427
westerns and John Ford 1674, 1772
westerns and male-oriented films 522
westerns and Native American women 454
westerns and Robert Aldrich 2044
westerns and Robert Altman 1175
Westerns and samurai films 1734
westerns and the Nickelodeon era 619
westerns and the pleasure principle 534
westerns and war films 328, 357
westerns in the 1930s 556
westerns in the 1950s 2035
White House, the 292
White Rats Strike 767, 1386
white telephone films 1875
Whitney Museum of American Art 902, 2040
WIDE ANGLE 41
widescreens 63, 86, 1950, 2033
wilderness films 297
wildlife cinematography 76
WILLOWBROOK CINEMA STUDY PROJECT, the 43
Wilson, Woodrow 213, 224, 365, 1378, 1382
Wisconsin Center for Film and Theatre Research, the 343, 1369
Wisconsin/Warner Bros. Screenplay Series 797
wish fulfillment 188
witchcraft 415
WOMEN AND FILM 41, 481, 482
women and World War II 521
women directors 516, 520
women editors 520
women filmmakers in the silent era 520
women in comedy films 513
women in film 269, 277, 318, 350, 425, 516, 680, 977, 993, 1363, 1384, 1392,
    1394, 1396, 1410, 1411, 1440, 1447, 1471, 1474, 1494
women in FILM NOIR 507
women in westerns 431
women screenwriters 516, 520
women-in-distress films 976
women-in-prison films 418
Women's counter-cinema 573
women's documentaries 495
women's film and horror movies 794
women's film festivals 495
women's films in Britain 1569

women's film, the 196, 495, 496, 502, 521, 522, 615, 638, 793, 795, 797, 1914
Wood, John 1190
work documentaries 312
Workers Film and Photo League 292
Workers' Film Movement 214
working girl movies 522
WORLD FILM NEWS (1936-1938) 216
World Films 1486
World Union of Documentary 245
World War I 196, 203, 205, 210, 212, 216, 223, 224, 242, 262, 263, 264, 265, 267, 268, 270, 284, 318, 334, 337, 1359
World War I and Biograph films 1371
World War I and Charles Chaplin 1429
World War I and Darryl F. Zanuck 1499, 1500
World War I and documentary filmmaking 238, 296
World War I and Douglas Fairbanks, Sr. 1400
World War I and early film history 1621
World War I and historical evidence 277
World War I and Hollywood 1622
World War I and Loew's Incorporated 1482
World War I and MY FOUR YEARS IN GERMANY 259
World War I and newsreels 298, 300
World War I and propaganda 205, 209, 210, 224, 340, 346, 361, 367
World War I and THE BIRTH OF A NATION 1387
World War I and the Skouras brothers 1492
World War I and war films 325, 326
World War I and Yiddish films 845, 846
World War II 178, 196, 200, 201, 206, 216, 221, 222, 233, 234, 238, 242, 243, 245, 247, 255, 257, 262, 263, 271, 272, 280, 282, 284, 293, 297, 1160, 1241, 1246
World War II and African-American films 947
World War II and aviation films 380
World War II and bankers 703
World War II and biographical films 337
World War II and British documentary films 1568
World War II and British theatrical films 1568
World War II and Charlie Chaplin 1431
World War II and Communism 334
World War II and documentary films 249, 280, 284, 285, 293, 295, 305, 306, 315, 316, 322
World War II and female stereotypes 318
World War II and fiction films 328
World War II and FILM NOIR 507
World War II and genres 373
World War II and historical evidence 274
World War II and Jewish films 825, 845
World War II and morale 769
World War II and newsreels 298, 300
World War II and propaganda 204, 206, 209, 213, 214, 216, 217, 218, 224, 227, 228, 230, 233, 236, 321, 340, 343, 346, 349, 351, 356, 358, 361
World War II and racism 328, 883
World War II and stereotypes 356, 781
World War II and the Holocaust 222, 291, 311, 317
World War II and the Spanish Civil War 319
World War II and the Vietnam War 359, 364
World War II and the women's film 522, 523, 800
World War II and war films 334, 349, 353, 354
World War II combat films 341, 342
Wortheim and Company 686

wrestling films   421
Wurlitzer pipe organ   406
WWI and German films   1634
Wyatt Earp-Doc Holliday friendship   1976
W. T. Henley Telegraph Company   1855

X

X-rated audiences   754
X-rated films   960

Y

YAKUZA   2023
YAKUZA ("gangster") genre   2027
YAKUZA-EIGA   1742
Yale Motion Picture Research Project, The   51
Yiddish film in America   846
Yiddish film in Poland   846
Yiddish films   627, 829, 845, 847, 848
Yiddish literature   845
Yiddish theater   828, 829, 836, 845, 846, 847, 848
YIDDISHKEIT   845
Yosemite Valley   1597
YOU ARE THERE (TV series)   2051, 2058
Young Men's Christian Association (YMCA)   630
YOUR SHOW OF SHOWS (TV series)   2047
youth market and "B" films   651
youth subcultural studies   770
Yugoslavian films   2014

Z

Zagreb cartoon studio   2014
ZAIBATSU   1741
Zen Fighters   2027
Zen spiritual art   2004
Zionism   311
Zoetrope Studios   536, 2196
zones   612, 1460
zoning   687
Zoopraxiscope   1596
Zukor-Lasky Feature Film Company   1392

Film Titles Index

A

A BOUT DE SOUFFLE (BREATHLESS) 1515, 2130, 2133, 2134, 2151
A NOUS LA LIBERTE (GIVE US FREEDOM) 1724, 1725, 1810, 1825
A PROPOS DE NICE 1811, 1824
ABBOTT AND COSTELLO MEET FRANKENSTEIN 394
ABBY 923
ABE LINCOLN IN ILLINOIS 1095, 1333, 1530
ABIE'S IMPORTED BRIDE 822
ABIE'S IRISH ROSE (1922) 825
ABILENE TOWN 428, 1089
ABOUT LAST NIGHT . . . (SEXUAL PERVERSITY IN CHICAGO) 738
ABOVE ALL IN THE WORLD (UBER ALLES IN DER WELT) 240
ABOVE AND BEYOND 339
ABOVE SUSPICION 331
ABRAHAM LINCOLN 1368, 1386
ABSENCE OF MALICE 1017, 1530, 2065
ABSOLUTION 1213
ACCIDENT 990, 1293, 1530, 1963, 2161
ACCUSED, THE 2206
ACROSS THE PACIFIC 331, 1911
ACROSS 110th STREET 896
ACTION IN THE NORTH ATLANTIC 331, 1070, 1178
ACTIVIST, THE 338
ADAM'S RIB 521, 523, 1449, 1951, 1975
ADVENTURES OF DOLLIE, THE 1361, 1362, 1387
ADVENTURES OF EMPEROR CHIEN LUNG, THE 1164
ADVENTURES OF MARK TWAIN, THE 1478
ADVENTURES OF ROBIN HOOD, THE (1938) 488, 1288
ADVENTURES OF ROBIN HOOD, THE (1952) 1951
ADVENTURES OF ROBINSON CRUSOE (LAS AVENTURAS DE ROBINSON
  CRUSOE) 1094, 1311, 1990
ADVENTURES OF TARZAN, THE 1456
ADVENTURE, THE (L'AVVENTURA) 1012, 1881, 2036, 2169, 2172
ADVISE AND CONSENT 1966, 1967
AEROGRAD (AIR CITY/FRONTIER) 1655
AFRICAN QUEEN, THE 62, 145, 150, 554, 657, 1086, 1169, 1250, 1530, 1757,
  1915, 1916, 1936, 1952, 1979
AFTER HOURS 1530
AFTER MEIN KAMPF 287
AFTER THE THIN MAN 1222
AFTERMATH OF WORLD WAR II: PROLOGUE TO THE COLD WAR 287
AGAINST ALL ODDS 1526
AGE D'OR, L' (THE GOLDEN AGE) 1721, 1722, 1723, 1811, 1989, 1990
AGE OF THE ATOM, WORLD WAR II: 1935-1965 287
AGENT ORANGE: A STORY OF DIGNITY AND DOUBT 290
AGNES OF GOD 680, 787, 2204
AGONY AND THE ECSTASY, THE 1203
AGUIRRE, DER ZORN GOTTES (AGUIRRE, THE WRATH OF GOD) 598, 2166
AGUIRRE, THE WRATH OF GOD (AGUIRRE, DER ZORN GOTTES) 598, 2166
AH, WILDERNESS! 1341
AINE DES FERCHAUX, L' 2000
AIR CITY (FRONTIER/AEROGRAD) 1655
AIR FORCE 331, 348, 349, 350, 351, 361, 370, 831
AIR RAID 1217, 1280
AIRPORT 803, 2191

AKAHIGE (RED BEARD)   2028
AKANISHI KAKITA (KAKITA AKANISHI)   1888
AKASEN CHITAI (RED-LIGHT DISTRICT)   2019
ALAMO BAY   338
ALAMO, THE   474, 857
ALEXANDER NEVSKY (ALEXANDR NEVSKII)   402, 1658, 1659, 1661, 1866, 1868
ALEXANDR NEVSKII (ALEXANDER NEVSKY)   402, 1658, 1659, 1661, 1866, 1868
ALFIE   2038, 2160
ALGIERS   1070
ALICE ADAMS   1305, 1787
ALICE DOESN'T LIVE HERE ANYMORE   508, 512, 588, 668, 1011, 2197
ALICE IN WONDERLAND   1031, 1270
ALICE'S RESTAURANT   88, 149, 163, 338, 558, 2064, 2088
ALIEN   589, 611, 676, 2200
ALIEN'S PLACE, THE   289
ALIENS   765, 2200, 2201
ALKAZAR   278
ALL ABOUT EVE   117, 791, 1269, 1272, 1500, 1952, 1954, 1981
ALL FALL DOWN   2051
ALL QUIET ON THE WESTERN FRONT (1930)   220, 221, 262, 297, 328, 342, 348,
  371, 568, 730, 1090, 1475, 1517, 1576, 1805
ALL THAT HEAVEN ALLOWS   499, 657, 794, 980, 1970
ALL THAT JAZZ   2199
ALL THE KING'S MEN   44, 568, 1012, 1091, 1315, 1469, 1969
ALL THE PRESIDENT'S MEN   438, 1151, 2198
ALL THE YOUNG MEN   334, 893
ALL-AROUND REDUCED PERSONALITY, THE   501
ALPHAVILLE   2151
ALTERED STATES   2200
ALVAREZ KELLY   1201
AMACHUA KURABU (AMATEUR CLUB)   1740
AMADEUS   539, 2204
AMANTS, THE (THE LOVERS)   2094
AMARCORD (I REMEMBER)   1874, 1929
AMATEUR CLUB (AMACHUA KURABU)   1740
AMAZING HOWARD HUGHES, THE   1137
AMBULANCE   334
AMBUSH BAY   332
AMERICA   1386, 1387, 1578
AMERICA AMERICA   1261
AMERICA MUST CONQUER (KING OF THE HUNS)   213
AMERICA UNPREPARED   285
AMERICA--FROM HITLER TO MX   288
AMERICA'S ANSWER   285
AMERICAN DREAM, THE (L'AMERIQUE REVE)   2115
AMERICAN GRAFFITI   558, 565, 605, 611, 987, 993, 2193, 2196, 2197, 2200
AMERICAN GUERRILLA IN THE PHILIPPINES   331
AMERICAN IN PARIS, AN   404, 595, 1173, 1784, 1952, 1983
AMERICAN ISM: JOE MCCARTHY, AN   288
AMERICAN MADNESS   1073
AMERICAN MATCHMAKER (AMERICAN SHADCHAN)   829
AMERICAN PEOPLE IN WORLD WAR II, THE   287
AMERICAN SHADCHAN (AMERICAN MATCHMAKER)   829
AMERICAN TRAGEDY, AN   1866, 1867
AMERICANIZATION OF EMILY, THE   330, 348
AMERICANO, THE   1578
AMERICA: A PERSONAL HISTORY OF THE UNITED STATES, NO. 11--THE
  ARSENAL, PARTS 1 & 2   287

AMERIQUE REVE, L' (AMERICAN DREAM, THE)   2115
AMI DE MON AMIE, L' (BOYFRIENDS AND GIRLFRIENDS)   2105
AMITYVILLE HORROR, THE   393, 976
AMORE, L' (WAYS OF LOVE)   1929
AMOUR A VINGT ANS, L' (LOVE AT TWENTY)   2148
AMOUR EN FUITE, L'(LOVE ON THE RUN)   2148
AMOUR L'APRES-MIDI, L' (CHLOE IN THE AFTERNOON)   2104
AMOURS DE LA REINE ELISABETH, LES (QUEEN ELIZABETH)   685, 1386, 1463,
  1504, 1505, 1618
AMY!   506
ANATOMY OF A MURDER   560, 1966, 1967
AND GOD CREATED WOMEN (ET . . . DIEU CREA LA FEMME)   2094
AND NOW MY LOVE (TOUTE UN VIE)   2119
AND NOW TOMORROW   1198
AND THE SHIP SAILS ON   1931
AND THEN THERE WERE NONE (1945)   939, 1725
AND WHEN THE WAR IS OVER: THE AMERICAN MILITARY IN THE 70'S   356
ANDALUSIAN DOG, AN (UN CHIEN ANDALOU)   595, 598, 1713, 1720, 1721,
  1722, 1723, 1727
ANDERSON PLATOON, THE   290
ANDERSON TAPES, THE   2192
ANDY HARDY film series   420, 421
ANGEL   1276
ANGEL EXTERMINADOR, EL (THE EXTERMINATING ANGEL)   1721, 1723, 1990
ANGEL WORE RED, THE   278, 1251
ANGELS FROM HELL   338, 339
ANGELS OF THE STREETS (LES ANGES DU PECHE)   1904, 1994, 2003
ANGELS WITH DIRTY FACES   195, 556, 975, 986, 987
ANGES DU PECHE, LES (ANGELS OF THE STREETS)   1904, 1994, 2003
ANGRY HILLS, THE   2043
ANI TO SONO IMOTO (A BROTHER AND HIS YOUNGER SISTER)   1894
ANIKOSEN (CRAB-CANNING BOAT)   2019
ANIMAL CRACKERS   1088, 1383
ANIMAL FARM   78
ANIMAL HOUSE   989
ANIMATED CARTOONS: THE TOY THAT GREW UP   1598
ANNA BOLEYN (DECEPTION)   1631
ANNA CHRISTIE (1923)   1340, 1350, 1394
ANNA CHRISTIE (1930)   638, 1341, 1394, 1492
ANNA KARENINA (1935)   1176, 1305
ANNA LUCASTA   885
ANNE OF THE THOUSAND DAYS   1288, 1347
ANNEE DERNIERE A MARIENBAD, L' (LAST YEAR AT MARIENBAD)   150, 539,
  579, 1317, 2118, 2124, 2137, 2139, 2140, 2152
ANNIE   488
ANNIE HALL   117, 530, 558, 668, 1017, 2045, 2208
ANOTHER COUNTRY   1331
ANOTHER PART OF THE FOREST   1225
ANOTHER WOMAN   2045
ANSIKTE MOT ANSIKTE (FACE TO FACE)   2184
ANSIKTET (THE MAGICIAN/THE FACE)   2183, 2184, 2186
ANTHONY ADVERSE   1497
ANTHONY AND CLEOPATRA (MARCANTONIO E CLEOPATRA)   383
ANTOINE AND ANTOINETTE   1994
ANZIO   330
AOI SAMMYUKA (GREEN MOUNTAINS)   2017
APACHE   2043
APACHE WOMAN   744
APARAJITO (THE UNVANQUISHED)   1004

APARTMENT, THE   1291, 1971, 1972, 2036
APOCALYPSE NOW   178, 269, 271, 335, 338, 339, 341, 361, 362, 364, 366, 550,
  558, 580, 1312, 1517, 2196, 2200
APOSTASY (HAKAI)   2017
APPLAUSE   1782, 1805
APPOINTMENT IN TOKYO   286
APPRENTICESHIP OF DUDDY KRAVITZ, THE   835, 838, 1032
APRIL FOOL   827
ARASHI NO NAKA NO SHOJO (MAIDEN IN THE STORM)   1894
ARCH OF TRIUMPH   1090
ARGENT DE POCHE, L' (SMALL CHANGE)   998, 2106, 2107, 2146, 2149
ARGENT, L'   1994
ARISE, MY LOVE   272, 329
ARMORED ATTACK (NORTH STAR)   262, 331, 1090, 1225, 1226, 1228, 1913
ARMORED COMMAND   330
ARMS AND SECURITY: HOW MUCH IS ENOUGH   356
ARMS AND THE MAN   1344, 1345
AROUND THE WORLD IN EIGHTY DAYS   1370
ARRIVAL OF EXPRESS AT LYONS (L'ARRIVEE D'UN TRAIN)   1619
ARRIVEE D'UN TRAIN, L' (ARRIVAL OF EXPRESS AT LYONS)   1619
ARROWSMITH   922, 1472, 1685
ARSENAL   1655, 1665
ART OF THE FILM, THE   107, 983
ARTS VIETNAM   290
ARUYO NO TONOSAMA (LORD FOR A NIGHT)   2017
AS IF IT WERE YESTERDAY (COMME SI C'ETAIT HIER)   289
AS THE WORLD ROLLED ON   986
ASCENSEUR POUR L'ECHAFAUD, L' (ELEVATOR TO THE
  SCAFFOLD/FRANTIC)   2094, 2119
ASHES AND DIAMONDS (POPIOL I DIAMENT)   311, 331, 334, 2014, 2180
ASHI NI SAWATTA ONNA (THE WOMAN WHO TOUCHED THE LEGS)   1740
ASK ANY GIRL   499
ASPHALT JUNGLE, THE   923, 1086, 1915, 1948, 1952, 1954
ASSASSINATION OF THE DUC OF GUISE, THE   1061
ASSASSINS, THE   1257
ASSAULT, THE   331
ASTRAY FROM STEERAGE   1413
ASU O TSUKURU HITOBITO (THOSE WHO MAKE TOMORROW)   2020
AT CLOSE RANGE   2207
AT LONG LAST LOVE   536
AT THE EARTH'S CORE   414
AT THE FRONT   286
ATALANTE, L'   1714, 1811, 1824, 1827
ATLANTIC PARTNERSHIP, 1939-1941   287
ATOMIC CAFE, THE   288, 324
ATTACK OF THE CRAB MONSTERS   419
ATTACK ON THE IRON COAST   330
ATTACK!   331, 348, 362, 2043
ATTACK! THE BATTLE OF NEW BRITAIN   286
AU HASARD BALTHAZAR (BALTHAZAR)   114, 2003
AU REVOIR LES ENFANTS (GOODBYE MY CHILDREN)   334
AUBERGE ROUGE, L' (THE RED INN)   1993
AUDREY ROSE   414, 976
AUNTIE MAME   657
AUS DEM LEBEN DER MARIONETTEN (FROM THE LIFE OF THE
  MARIONETTES)   2184
AUSCHWITZ STREET   289
AUTHOR! AUTHOR!   484

AUTUMN LEAVES 2043
AVANTI! 1971
AVENTURAS DE ROBINSON CRUSOE, LAS (ADVENTURES OF ROBINSON
  CRUSOE) 1094, 1311, 1990
AVIATOR'S WIFE, THE (LA FEMME DE L'AVIATEUR OU ON NE SAURAIT PENSER
  A RIEN) 2105
AVVENTURA, L' (THE ADVENTURE) 1012, 1881, 2036, 2169, 2172
AWAY ALL BOATS 332
A. K.: THE MAKING OF "RAN" 2116

B

BABES IN ARMS 404
BABY BOOM 2207
BABY DOLL 858, 959, 981, 1261, 1345, 2036
BABYLON REVISITED 1125
BABY, IT'S YOU 977
BACK AT THE FRONT 334
BACK ROADS 913
BACK TO BATAAN 331, 359
BACK TO SCHOOL 2202
BACK TO THE FUTURE 761, 2200, 2201
BACK TO THE FUTURE II 762, 2200
BACK TO THE FUTURE III 762
BACK-SEAT GENERALS, THE 290
BACKSTAIRS (HINTERTREPPE) 1714
BAD AND THE BEAUTIFUL, THE 1136, 1290, 1952
BAD BOYS 972
BAD BOYS (FURYO SHONEN) 802, 1000
BAD DAY AT BLACK ROCK 306, 331, 569, 1485
BAD TIMING--A SENSUAL OBSESSION 493, 495
BAISERS VOLES (STOLEN KISSES) 2145, 2148
BAKER'S WIFE, THE (LA FEMME DU BOULANGER) 1809, 1826
BALL OF FIRE 1971
BALLAD OF A SOLDIER, THE (BALLADA A SOLDATE) 371
BALLAD OF CABLE HOGUE, THE 2061, 2062, 2063, 2193
BALLADA A SOLDATE (THE BALLAD OF A SOLDIER) 371
BALLET MECANIQUE 1730
BALLET MECANIQUE (MECHANICAL BALLET) 1713, 1717
BALTHAZAR (AU HASARD BALTHAZAR) 114, 1994, 2003
BAMBA, LA 611, 2203
BAMBINI CI GUARDANO, I (THE CHILDREN ARE WATCHING US) 1875
BAMBOO PRISON, THE 334
BANANAS 2044, 2194
BAND OF ANGELS 884
BAND WAGON, THE 404, 1784, 1952
BANDERA, LA (ESCAPE FROM YESTERDAY) 1813
BANGIKU (THE LATE CHRYSANTHEMUM) 2019
BANGOKU NO ISSHO (THE LIFE OF BANGOKU) 1889
BANJO ON MY KNEE 1207, 1256
BANK DICK, THE 1770, 1800
BANSHUN (LATE SPRING) 2017, 2031
BAPTISM OF FIRE (FEUERTAUFE) 206, 282, 287
BARBARY COAST 1265
BARBED WIRE 297, 327
BARBERSHOP, THE 1411
BAREFOOT CONTESSA, THE 1136, 1137, 1245, 1269, 1290
BARON FANTOME, LE (THE PHANTOM BARON) 1995

BARON OF ARIZONA, THE 1960
BARRETTS OF WIMPOLE STREET, THE (1934) 1279, 1336, 1481, 1492
BARRY LYNDON 382, 1312, 2055, 2057
BARTLEBY: A STORY OF WALL STREET 1312
BAS-FONDS, LES (THE LOWER DEPTHS) 353, 1813, 1814
BASIC FILM TERMS 107
BASTILLE 334
BAT 21 338
BATAAN 209, 248, 331, 341, 342, 349, 361, 831, 879, 939
BATAILLE DU RAIL, LA (THE BATTLE OF THE RAILS) 1995
BATMAN 762, 2206
BATTAGLIA DI ALGERI, LA (THE BATTLE OF ALGIERS) 2172, 2176
BATTLE AT BLOODY BEACH, THE 336
BATTLE CIRCUS 334, 359
BATTLE CRY 332, 1700
BATTLE CRY OF PEACE, THE 211, 268, 297, 328, 342
BATTLE CRY OF WAR, THE 210
BATTLE FOR LEYTE GULF 287
BATTLE FOR THE MARIANAS, THE 286
BATTLE HELL 334
BATTLE HYMN 334
BATTLE OF ALGIERS, THE (LA BATTAGLIA DI ALGERI) 2172, 2176
BATTLE OF BRITAIN (CBS) 287
BATTLE OF BRITAIN (WOLPER) 287
BATTLE OF BRITAIN, THE (WHY WE FIGHT) 287
BATTLE OF BRITAIN, THE (1969) 331, 1319
BATTLE OF CHICAGO, THE 290
BATTLE OF CHINA, THE (WHY WE FIGHT) 287
BATTLE OF MIDWAY, THE 283, 287
BATTLE OF RUSSIA, THE (WHY WE FIGHT) 287
BATTLE OF SAN PIETRO 283, 284, 287, 322, 1915
BATTLE OF THE BULGE--THE BRAVE RIFLES, THE 287
BATTLE OF THE BULGE, THE 331, 345
BATTLE OF THE CORAL SEA 332
BATTLE OF THE RAILS, THE (LA BATAILLE DU RAIL) 1995
BATTLE OF THE SEXES, THE 1368
BATTLE OF THE SOMME, THE 285
BATTLE OF THE UNITED STATES--ISSUE 42 320
BATTLE STATIONS 332
BATTLE TAXI 334
BATTLE ZONE 336
BATTLEGROUND 257, 331, 354, 361, 1485
BATTLESHIP POTEMKIN (BRONENOSETS POTEMKIN) 144, 209, 241, 274, 282,
 345, 1576, 1654, 1655, 1656, 1658, 1659, 1665, 1666, 1667, 1840
BATTLING BUTLER 1688
BAY OF PIGS 917
BEACH HEAD AT ANZIO 287
BEACH RED 331
BEACHHEAD 332
BEACHHEAD FOR BERLIN 286
BEAST AT BAY, A 1380
BEAST FROM TWENTY THOUSAND FATHOMS, THE (1953) 1946
BEAST OF THE CITY 568
BEAST WITH A 1,000,000 EYES, THE 744
BEAST WITHIN, THE 976
BEASTS OF BERLIN (GOOSE STEP/HELL'S DEVILS) 329
BEAT THE DEVIL 1936
BEAU GESTE (1939) 1701

BEAU MARRIAGE, LE 2105
BEAU SERGE, LE (HANDSOME SERGE/BITTER REUNION) 2094, 2100, 2128
BEAUTE DU DIABLE, LA (THE BEAUTY OF THE DEVIL) 1725, 2000, 2005
BEAUTIES OF THE NIGHT, THE (LES BELLES-DE-NUIT) 1725, 2005
BEAUTIFUL BLONDE FROM BASHFUL BEND, THE 1919
BEAUTIFUL LAUNDRETTE, MY 2203
BEAUTY AND THE BEAST (LA BELLE ET LA BETE) 417, 1730, 1818, 1995, 2005, 2006, 2008
BEAUTY OF THE DEVIL, THE (LA BEAUTE DU DIABLE) 1725, 2000, 2005
BECAUSE OF YOU 701
BECKET 1288
BECKY SHARP 1312, 1749, 1782
BED AND BOARD (DOMICILE CONJUGAL) 2145, 2148
BEDFORD INCIDENT, THE 334, 356, 888, 891
BEER DRINKER'S GUIDE TO FITNESS AND FILMMAKING, THE 671
BEETHOVEN 1712
BEETLEJUICE 2203
BEFORE SPRING 312
BEGINNING OR THE END, THE 331, 355, 356
BEHOLD A PALE HORSE 278
BEILIS CASE, THE (DELO BEILISA) 845
BEING THERE 536
BELL FOR ADANO, A 331
BELLE DE JOUR 144, 516, 596, 598, 1721, 1723
BELLE EQUIPE, LA (THEY WERE FIVE) 1813
BELLE ET LA BETE, LA (BEAUTY AND THE BEAST) 417, 1730, 1818, 1995, 2005, 2006, 2008
BELLE FILLE COMME MOI, UNE (SUCH A GORGEOUS KID) 2144
BELLES-DE-NUIT, LES (THE BEAUTIES OF THE NIGHT) 1725, 2005
BELLS OF ST. MARY'S, THE 1064, 1911
BELOVED INFIDEL 1032, 1245, 1247
BEN HUR (1926) 1481, 1492
BEN HUR (1959) 547, 805, 832, 1484, 1517, 1748
BEND OF THE RIVER 1946, 1964
BERLIN 287
BERLIN: THE SYMPHONY OF A CITY 1714
BERORINGEN (THE TOUCH) 2184
BEST FRIENDS 1044
BEST MAN, THE 2067, 2089
BEST YEARS OF OUR LIVES, THE 160, 259, 270, 331, 375, 472, 568, 1472, 1946, 1952
BETE HUMAINE, LA (JUDAS WAS A WOMAN) 353
BETRAYAL, THE 866, 878, 921, 948, 1331
BETRAYED 2206
BETTER ACTIVE TODAY THAN RADIOACTIVE TOMORROW 288
BETWEEN HEAVEN AND HELL 332
BEVERLY HILLS COP 539, 761, 903, 904, 2201
BEVERLY HILLS COP II 904, 2205
BEWITCHED 414
BEYOND A REASONABLE DOUBT 1637
BEYOND THE LIMIT 1218, 1301
BEYOND THE POSEIDON ADVENTURE 753
BEZHIN LUG (BEZHIN MEADOW) 1645, 1657, 1661, 1866
BEZHIN MEADOW (BEZHIN LUG) 1645, 1657, 1661, 1866
BICHES, LES 2101, 2128, 2151
BICYCLE THIEVES (LADRI DI BICICLETTE) 44, 144, 1004, 1576, 1926, 1928, 1932
BIDONE, IL (THE SWINDLE) 2171
BIG BROADCAST OF 1936 1071

BIG CHILL, THE   2193
BIG HEAT, THE   657, 1952
BIG HOUSE, THE   1394
BIG JIM MCLAIN   348, 1949
BIG KNIFE, THE   1095, 1136, 1137, 1245, 1248, 1290, 1470, 2043
BIG LEAGUER, THE   2043
BIG LIFT, THE   331
BIG MAN, THE (L'HOMMAGE DU LARGE)   1713
BIG PARADE, THE   257, 297, 304, 328, 342, 348, 354, 361, 367, 1481, 1696
BIG RED ONE, THE   262, 331, 1542, 1960, 1977
BIG SKY, THE   1064
BIG SLEEP, THE   494, 798, 980, 1147, 1149, 1197, 1210, 1214, 1315, 1747, 1947,
  1948, 1952, 1977, 1978
BIG STORE, THE   984
BIG TROUBLE   2048
BIG WEDNESDAY   338
BIGGER THAN LIFE   1985
BILDDOKUMENTE   285
BILLIONAIRE, A (OKUMAN CHOJA)   2023
BILLY BUDD   1018
BILLY JACK   565, 666
BILLY LIAR   994
BILLY THE KID (1941)   1073
BILOXI BLUES   2060
BIOGRAPHY OF THE MOTION PICTURE CAMERA   1598
BIRDMAN OF ALCATRAZ, THE   2051
BIRDS, THE   389, 1835, 1843, 1844, 1849, 1852, 1854, 1855, 1858
BIRDY   288, 338
BIRTH OF A NATION and epic film conventions, THE   383
BIRTH OF A NATION and film styles, THE   64
BIRTH OF A NATION and ideology, THE   472
BIRTH OF A NATION and INTOLERANCE, THE   1374, 1381, 1388
BIRTH OF A NATION and Lillian Gish, THE   1375
BIRTH OF A NATION and political films, THE   558
BIRTH OF A NATION and racism, THE   700, 857, 863, 864, 865, 866, 867, 895,
  908, 912, 920, 925, 933, 939, 940, 941
BIRTH OF A NATION and screenwriters, THE   1141
BIRTH OF A NATION and silent film music, THE   405
BIRTH OF A NATION and stereotyping of African-Americans, THE   915
BIRTH OF A NATION and the American Dream, THE   1053
BIRTH OF A NATION and the image of the Old South, THE   912
BIRTH OF A NATION and the White House, The   685
BIRTH OF A NATION and war film conventions, THE   348
BIRTH OF A NATION and WAY DOWN EAST, THE   1391
BIRTH OF A NATION and William A. Dunning, THE   914
BIRTH OF A NATION, THE   123, 254, 271, 276, 277, 1366, 1367, 1369, 1371,
  1373, 1382, 1385, 1386, 1387, 1405, 1481, 1515, 1576, 1608, 1657, 1740, 1910
BIRTH OF A RACE, THE (LINCOLN'S DREAM)   867, 926, 949
BIRTHRIGHT   866, 947
BIRUMA NO TATEGOTO (THE HARP OF BURMA/THE BURMESE HARP)   331,
  371, 2018, 2021, 2023
BISHOP'S WIFE, THE   408
BITCH, THE (LA CHIENNE)   1814, 1820
BITTER REUNION (LE BEAU SERGE/HANDSOME SERGE)   2094, 2100, 2128
BITTER VICTORY   328
BLACK AND TAN   928
BLACK CAESAR   896
BLACK CAT, THE   417, 829

BLACK FURY 556, 1497
BLACK GIRL 899, 919
BLACK GOD AND WHITE DEVIL 2158
BLACK HUNDREDS, THE (TERRORS OF RUSSIA) 847
BLACK JOURNAL 902
BLACK LEGION 556, 568, 1497
BLACK ORPHEUS (ORFEU NEGRO) 923, 2097
BLACK PANTHERS 2114
BLACK PIRATE, THE 1400, 1405, 1578
BLACK SUNDAY 2051
BLACK THURSDAY (LES GUICHETS DU LOUVRE) 311, 334
BLACK 107, THE 846
BLACKBOARD JUNGLE, THE 743, 816, 887, 892, 944, 986, 1000, 1485, 2207
BLACKMAIL 131, 1565, 1835, 1838, 1843, 1849, 1850, 1863, 1864
BLACULA 896
BLADE AF SATANS BOG (LEAVES FROM SATAN'S BOOK) 1626
BLADE RUNNER 2200
BLAUE ENGEL, DER (THE BLUE ANGEL) (1929) 131, 598, 1317, 1576, 1697,
  1806, 1829, 1830, 1831
BLAZING SADDLES 2047, 2194
BLE EN HERBE, LE (THE GAME OF LOVE) 1993
BLECHTROMMEL, DIE (THE TIN DRUM) 152, 311, 334
BLEEDING GERMANY (BLUTENDES DEUTSCHLAND) 321
BLEEDING HEARTS 847
BLEIER ZEIT, DIE (THE GERMAN SISTERS) (MARIANNE AND JULIANE) 505
BLIND HUSBANDS 1700, 1708
BLINKETY BLANK 1975
BLITHE SPIRIT 1860, 1935
BLITZKRIEG 209
BLITZKRIEG IM WESTEN (BLITZKRIEG IN THE WEST) 206
BLITZKRIEG IN THE WEST (BLITZKRIEG IM WESTEN) 206
BLOCK-NOTES DI UN REGISTA (FELLINI: DIRECTOR'S NOTEBOOK) 117
BLOCKADE 219, 278, 376, 568, 1070, 1184, 1194
BLONDE VENUS 504, 505, 529, 555, 638
BLONDIE film series 420, 421, 1469
BLOOD AND SAND (1922) 1579, 1707
BLOOD AND SAND (1941) 1707, 1782
BLOOD BEACH 976
BLOOD FEAST 393, 418
BLOOD OF A POET, THE (LE SANG D'UN POETE) 1811, 1817, 1818, 1826
BLOOD OF JESUS, THE 924
BLOOD ON THE BALCONY 287
BLOOD ON THE SUN 331, 1199
BLOOD SIMPLE 1526
BLOODY MAMA 2049
BLOW-UP (1966) 44, 45, 53, 117, 138, 558, 1310, 1311, 1576, 1881, 1928, 2169,
  2170, 2173
BLUE ANGEL, THE (DER BLAUE ENGEL) (1929) 131, 598, 1317, 1576, 1697,
  1806, 1829, 1830, 1831
BLUE DAHLIA, THE 740, 1197, 1198
BLUE DENIM 1001
BLUE GARDENIA, THE 507
BLUE HOTEL, THE 145
BLUE LIGHT, THE 1829
BLUE MAX 328
BLUE THUNDER 454
BlUEBEARD (LANDRU) 2100, 2128
BLUME IN LOVE 834
BLUTENDES DEUTSCHLAND (BLEEDING GERMANY) 321

BOAT IS FULL, THE (DAS BOOT IST VOLL)   311, 334, 376
BOAT, THE (DAS BOOT)   331
BOB LE FLAMBEUR   2000
BOBBY DEERFIELD   2065
BODU SAUVE DES EAUX (BODU SAVED FROM DROWNING)   1814
BODU SAVED FROM DROWNING (BODU SAUVE DES EAUX)   1814
BODY AND SOUL (1925)   867, 927, 948
BODY AND SOUL (1947)   569, 838, 882, 1091, 1094, 1151, 1275, 1946, 1969, 1985
BODY DOUBLE   787, 788, 802
BODY HEAT   590
BOGIE   1137
BOLD AND THE BRAVE,   330
BOMBA film series   420
BONHEUR, LE (HAPPINESS)   2114
BONNES FEMMES, LES   2098, 2100, 2124, 2128
BONNIE AND CLYDE   45, 53, 138, 143, 270, 387, 748, 804, 810, 1495, 2036,
   2038, 2064, 2088, 2193
BOOK OF NUMBERS, THE   923, 941
BOOM   1345
BOOMERANG   301, 1260, 1500, 1979
BOOT IST VOLL, DAS (THE BOAT IS FULL)   311, 334, 376
BOOT, DAS (THE BOAT)   331
BORDER RIVER   702
BORINAGE (MISERE AU BORINAGE)   312, 314
BORN FREE   150, 1093
BORN LOSERS   338, 987
BORN TO KILL   1948
BORN TO WIN   516
BORN YESTERDAY   1470, 1951
BOROM SARRET   919
BOSKO AND THE CANNIBALS   874
BOSTON BLACKIE film series   420, 1469
BOSTONIANS, THE   1324
BOUCHER, LE   2128
BOULANGERE DE MONCEAU, LA   2104
BOULEVARD NIGHTS   974, 975
BOUT DE SOUFFLE, A (BREATHLESS)   2036, 2109, 2110, 2129, 2156
BOWERY BOYS film series   420
BOXER AND DEATH, THE   334
BOY WITH GREEN HAIR, THE   1963
BOYFRIENDS AND GIRLFRIENDS (L'AMI DE MON AMIE)   2105
BOYS FROM BRAZIL, THE   312, 334, 2067
BOYS IN COMPANY C, THE   338, 341, 2200
BOYS TOWN   1485
BRASHER DOUBLOON, THE (THE HIGH WINDOW)   1197
BRASS TARGET   330
BRAVE BULLS, THE   1954
BRAVE COWBOY, THE   1284
BRAVE ONE, THE   1099, 1171, 1282, 1284
BREAKER MORANT   448
BREAKFAST AT TIFFANY'S   664
BREAKFAST CLUB, THE   815, 971, 972
BREAKING AWAY   975, 1004
BREAKING POINT, THE   1231
BREAKING THE SOUND BARRIER   1861, 1937, 1943
BREAKTHROUGH   331
BREATHLESS (A BOUT DE SOUFFLE)   1515, 2036, 2109, 2110, 2129, 2130, 2133,
   2134, 2151, 2156

BREWSTER MCCLOUD 554, 912, 1176
BRIDE COMES TO YELLOW SKY, THE 145, 1147
BRIDE OF FRANKENSTEIN, THE (1935) 417, 599
BRIDE WORE RED, THE 1256
BRIDGE AT REMAGEN, THE 330
BRIDGE ON THE RIVER KWAI, THE 196, 220, 331, 354, 374, 664, 1036, 1093, 1094, 1165, 1171, 1469, 1861, 1954
BRIDGE TO THE SUN 331, 340
BRIDGE TOO FAR, A 330, 345, 554, 1151, 1318
BRIDGES AT TOKO-RI, THE 334, 359, 361
BRIDGE, THE 314, 330
BRIEF ENCOUNTER 1021, 1335, 1336, 1860, 1936, 1940, 1943
BRIGADOON 1784
BRIGHT LEAF 912
BRIGHT ROAD 885, 886
BRIGHT VICTORY 883, 921, 1946
BRINGING UP BABY 1064, 1515, 1803
BRITISH SOUNDS 2111
BRIVELE DER MAMEN, A (A LITTLE LETTER TO MAMA) 846, 848
BROADCAST NEWS 2201, 2207
BROADWAY BILL 1073
BROADWAY DANNY ROSE 2045, 2208
BROKEN ARROW 193, 198, 569, 1946
BROKEN BLOSSOMS 405, 1368, 1372, 1373, 1386, 1388, 1390, 1397, 1439, 1509
BROKEN HEARTS (TSEBROKHENE HERSTER) 847
BROKEN LANCE 1201
BROKEN LULLABY (THE MAN I KILLED) 328, 343, 568, 1276, 1804
BROKEN VIOLIN 866, 940
BRONENOSETS POTEMKIN (BATTLESHIP POTEMKIN) 144, 209, 241, 274, 282, 345, 1576, 1654, 1655, 1656, 1658, 1659, 1665, 1666, 1667
BROTHER AND HIS YOUNGER SISTER, A (ANI TO SONO IMOTO) 1894
BROTHER FROM ANOTHER PLANET, THE 902, 905
BROTHER JOHN 888
BROTHER SUN, SISTER MOON 602
BROUGHT TO BERLIN 286
BROWN OF HARVARD 989, 1279
BROWNING VERSION, THE 1841, 1937, 1942
BRUTE FORCE 1951, 1976
BRUTE, THE 927
BUCCANEER, THE 1071, 1681
BUCK AND THE PREACHER 855, 858, 889, 899, 2193
BUCK PRIVATES 272, 329
BUDDY HOLLY STORY, THE 1138, 2193
BUFFALO BILL AND THE INDIANS, OR SITTING BULL'S HISTORY LESSON 425, 584, 595, 786, 811
BUGLE SOUNDS, THE 327
BULL DOGGERS, THE 868
BULL DURHAM 2203
BULLDOG DRUMMOND STRIKES BACK 1252, 1253
BULLETS OR BALLOTS 556
BULLITT 410, 960
BUNNY LAKE IS MISSING 1966
BURGLAR 904
BURMA OUTPOST--ISSUE 22 320
BURMESE HARP, THE (THE HARP OF BURMA/BIRUMA NO TATEGOTO) 331, 371, 2018, 2021, 2023
BURN! 2176
BUS STOP 1281
BUSH MAMA 901

BUSTER KEATON STORY, THE   1247
BUSYBODIES   1690
BUTCH CASSIDY AND THE SUNDANCE KID   149, 193, 196, 197, 199, 804, 960,
  1151, 2035, 2052, 2053, 2078
BUTLEY   1034
BUTTERFIELD 8   664
BUTTON, BUTTON: A DREAM OF NUCLEAR WAR   288
BYE, BYE BRAVERMAN   834

C

C'ERA UNA VOLTA IL WEST (ONCE UPON A TIME IN THE WEST)   427
CABARET   312, 334, 348, 558, 841, 1165, 1317
CABIN IN THE COTTON   914
CABIN IN THE SKY   404, 880, 916, 921, 934, 939, 944, 1784
CABINET OF DR. CALIGARI, THE (DAS KABINETT DES DR. CALIGARI)   388,
  579, 1308, 1576, 1632, 1635, 1643
CABIRIA   382, 685, 1607
CAESAR AND CLEOPATRA   1345, 1357, 1935
CAINE MUTINY, THE   331, 598, 1201
CALAMITY JANE   589
CALIFORNIA SPLIT   604, 1176
CALL NORTHSIDE   1952
CALL OF THE WILD, THE   1701
CALLING BULLDOG DRUMMOND   1073
CAMILLE   504, 505, 529, 532, 638, 1012, 1151, 1154, 1394, 1439, 1481, 1576,
  1802
CAMPANADAS A MEDIANOCHE (CHIMES AT MIDNIGHT/FALSTAFF)   1353, 1791
CANADA CARRIES ON series   280
CANDIDATE, THE   454, 985, 2193
CANDIDE   1317
CANNERY ROW   1281
CANTOR'S SON, THE (DEM KHAZNS ZUNDL)   848
CANYON PASSAGE   198
CAPORAL EPINGLE, LA (THE ELUSIVE CORPORAL/THE VANISHING
  CORPORAL)   1821
CAPTAIN JANUARY   1219
CAPTAIN MILKSHAKE   338
CAPTAIN NEWMAN, M. D.   330, 1206
CAPTAINS COURAGEOUS   994
CAPTIVE HEART   331
CARABINIERS, LES (THE SOLDIERS)   2110, 2124
CARMEN JONES   885, 886, 915, 916, 921, 941, 1966
CARMEN (1938)   598
CARNAL KNOWLEDGE   516, 558, 989, 2060, 2192, 2209
CARNET DE VIAJE (CARNET DE VOYAGE)   312
CARNET DE VOYAGE (CARNET DE VIAJE)   312
CARNETS DU MAJOR THOMPSON, LES (THE FRENCH THEY ARE A FUNNY
  RACE)   1919
CARNEY   738
CARNIVAL IN FLANDERS (LA KERMESSE HEROIQUE)   1812
CAROUSEL   401, 1206
CARRIE   393, 414, 976, 985, 1952
CARRIERE DE SUZANNE, LA   2104
CARROSSE D'OR, LE (THE GOLDEN COACH)   187
CARRY ON film series   1569

CASABLANCA 274, 328, 331, 372, 494, 599, 623, 881, 1021, 1083, 1215, 1262, 1263, 1288, 1446, 1494, 1577, 1913
CASE OF LENA SMITH, THE 1071
CASE OF SERGEANT GRISCHA, THE 568
CASE OF THE LEGLESS VETERAN: JAMES KUTCHER 288
CASINO ROYALE 2044
CASS TIMBERLANE 1279, 1280
CAST A GIANT SHADOW 805, 832
CASTLE KEEP 331
CASUALTIES OF WAR 338
CAT BALLOU 893, 1168, 2084
CAT ON A HOT TIN ROOF (1958) 858, 1352
CAT PEOPLE 410, 1912, 2195
CATCH-22 154, 231, 331, 348, 361, 1312, 1317, 2060
CAUGHT 615, 714, 1946, 2007, 2010
CAUGHT FIRE 356
CAUGHT IN THE DRAFT 272, 329
CAVALCADE 328
CBS'S GREAT WAR (TV SERIES) 285
CEASE FIRE 338
CEASE FIRE! 334
CENERE 1618
CERCLE ROUGE, LE 2000
CET OBSCUR OBJECT DU DESIRE (THAT OBSCURE OBJECT OF DESIRE) 1722, 1723
CHACAL DE NAHUELTORO, EL 917
CHAGRIN ET LA PITIE, LE (THE SORROW AND THE PITY) 246, 289, 303, 311, 317, 324, 377, 2143
CHAIRMAN, THE 334
CHALLENGE, THE 2051
CHAMPAGNE MURDERS, THE (LE SCANDALE) 2128
CHAMPION 1093, 1946
CHAMP, THE (1931) 1164, 1394, 1395
CHANT DU STYRENE, LE 2136
CHAOS (RAN) 2019, 2116
CHAPEAU DE PAILLE D'ITALIE, UN (THE ITALIAN STRAW HAT) 1728
CHAPLIN REVIEW, THE 1428
CHAPTER TWO 1166
CHARADE 150
CHARGE OF THE LIGHT BRIGADE, THE 218
CHARIOTS OF FIRE 421, 1013, 1570
CHARLIE CHAN film series 420, 421
CHARLIE CHAN'S GREATEST CASE 1199
CHARLY 1151
CHARME DISCRET DE LA BOURGEOISIE, LE (THE DISCREET CHARM OF THE BOURGEOISIE) 516, 596, 1723
CHASE, THE 603, 1225, 2064
CHELOVEK'S KINOAPPARATOM (THE MAN WITH THE MOVIE CAMERA) 1664, 1668, 1669
CHELSEA GIRLS, THE 2068, 2091
CHESS KING, THE (OSHO) 2017
CHEYENNE AUTUMN 1500, 1501, 1683
CHICHI ARIKI (THERE IS A FATHER) 1902
CHIEN ANDALOU, UN (AN ANDALUSIAN DOG) 595, 598, 1713, 1720, 1721, 1722, 1723, 1727
CHIENNE, LA (THE BITCH) 1814, 1820
CHILD OF THE GHETTO, A 826
CHILDREN ARE WATCHING US, THE (I BAMBINI CI GUARDANO) 1875
CHILDREN FROM NUMBER 67, THE (DIE KINDER AUS NO. 67) 334

CHILDREN HAND IN HAND (TE O TSUNAGU KORA) 2017
CHILDREN IN THE WIND (KAZE NO NAKA NO KODOMO) 1892
CHILDREN OF A LESSER GOD 672
CHILDREN OF PARADISE (LES ENFANTS DU PARADIS) 1904, 1909, 1910
CHILDREN OF THE ATOMIC BOMB (GENBAKU NO KO) 2019
CHILDREN OF THE BEEHIVE (HACHI NO SU NO KODOMOTACHI) 2017
CHILDREN'S HOUR, THE 1225
CHILLY SCENES OF WINTER 604
CHIMES AT MIDNIGHT (FALSTAFF/CAMPANADAS A MEDIANOCHE) 1353, 1791
CHINA 331
CHINA DOLL 332
CHINA GATE 338, 359, 885, 1960
CHINA IS NEAR (LA CINA E VICINA) 2173
CHINA SYNDROME, THE 454, 551, 700
CHINA (CHUNG KUO) 918
CHINATOWN 190, 2193
CHINOISE, OU PLUTOT A LA CHINOISE, LA 2109, 2130, 2134
CHLOE IN THE AFTERNOON (L'AMOUR L'APRES-MIDI) 2104
CHOIRBOYS, THE 2043
CHORUS LINE, A 2199
CHRISTMAS CAROL, A 1094, 1312
CHRISTMAS IN JULY 1919
CHRISTOPHER STRONG 1797
CHRONICLE OF A SUMMER (CHRONIQUE D'UN ETE) 2120, 2153, 2154
CHRONIQUE D'UN ETE (CHRONICLE OF A SUMMER) 2120, 2153, 2154
CHUJI TABI NIKI (A DIARY OF CHUJI'S TRAVELS) 1887
CHUNG KUO (CHINA) 918
CHUTE DE LA MAISON USHER, LA (THE FALL OF THE HOUSE OF
  USHER) 1722, 1730
CID, EL 806
CIEL LA TERRE, LE (THE SKY AND THE EARTH) 312
CINA E VICINA, LA (CHINA IS NEAR) 2173
CINCINNATI KID, THE 810, 893, 1073, 1100, 2062
CINDERELLA 1392
CINDERELLA LIBERTY 231, 1166
CINERAMA HOLIDAY 1950
CIRCUS WORLD 984
CIRCUS, THE 1416, 1417, 1429
CISCO KID, THE film series 421
CITADEL, THE 1839
CITIZEN KANE 44, 104, 116, 144, 568, 598, 992, 1063, 1153, 1248, 1263, 1266,
  1267, 1269, 1317, 1321, 1322, 1327, 1515, 1577, 1750, 1751, 1789, 1790, 1791,
  1793, 1794, 1807, 1948
CITIZEN KANE and Pauline Kael 149, 150
CITY ACROSS THE RIVER 986
CITY FOR CONQUEST 1259
CITY LIGHTS 271, 1275, 1417, 1424, 1425, 1429, 1515, 1542
CITY OF WOMEN 593, 1931
CITY STREETS 555, 1222
CIVILIZATION 211, 328, 342, 1623
CLAIRE'S KNEE (LE GENOU DE CLAIRE) 2104
CLANSMAN, THE 1366, 1369, 1387, 1412
CLASS 977
CLASS THAT WENT TO WAR, THE 290
CLASSMATES 989
CLAUDIA 1088
CLAUDINE 899, 1005
CLEO DE CINQ A SEPT (CLEO FROM 5 TO 7) 2114, 2156

CLEO FROM 5 TO 7 (CLEO DE CINQ A SEPT)   2114, 2156
CLEOPATRA JONES   896, 898
CLEOPATRA (1899)   383
CLEOPATRA (1910)   383
CLEOPATRA (1917)   383
CLEOPATRA (1928)   383
CLEOPATRA (1934)   383, 1090
CLEOPATRA (1963)   383, 664, 748, 1093, 1270, 1493, 1499, 1500, 2043
CLEVER DUMMY, THE   1413
CLIVE OF INDIA   218
CLOAK AND DAGGER   1073, 1089
CLOCKWORK ORANGE, A   418, 1317, 2055, 2056, 2057, 2058, 2199
CLOSE ENCOUNTERS OF THE THIRD KIND   611, 668, 1154, 2199
CLOSELY WATCHED TRAINS (OSTRE SLEDOVANE VLAKY)   994, 2165
CLOWN PRINCES, THE   1578
CLOWN'S EVENING, THE (SAWDUST AND TINSEL/THE NAKED
 NIGHT/GYCKLARNAS AFTON)   2183, 2187
CLOWNS, THE (I CLOWNS)   117
CLUNY BROWN   1694
COAL FACE   245, 249, 315
COBWEB CASTLE (KUMONOSU-JO/THRONE OF BLOOD)   1356, 2019, 2021
COCAINE COWBOYS   988
COCKEYED WORLD, THE   327
COCOON   2200, 2206
CODUTA DELGI DEI, LA (THE DAMNED)   310, 334, 348, 1884
COEUR FIDELE (FAITHFUL HEART)   1712
COFFY   896
COHENS AND THE KELLYS, THE   825
COLLECTIONNEUSE, LE (THE COLLECTOR)   2103, 2104
COLLECTOR, THE (LE COLLECTIONNEUSE)   2103, 2104
COLLEGE   989, 1688
COLLEGE WIDOW, THE   989, 1213
COLLISION COURSE   334
COLOR OF MONEY, THE   1014
COLOR PURPLE, THE   904, 905, 906, 2202
COLORED TROOPS DISEMBARKING   861
COLOSSUS--THE FORBIN PROJECT   418
COMA   787
COMANCHE STATION   197
COME BACK, AFRICA   2089
COME BLOW YOUR HORN   834
COMEDIANS, THE   893, 1219
COMING HOME   259, 338, 341, 376, 550, 551, 558, 1090, 2200
COMING TO AMERICA   2204
COMMAND DECISION   331, 339, 370
COMMANDO   2201
COMME SI C'ETAIT HIER (AS IF IT WERE YESTERDAY)   289
COMMENT CA VA?   2112
COMMUNICANTS, THE (WINTER LIGHT/NATTVARDSGASTERNA)   2186, 2187,
 2188
COMPARTIMENTS TUEURS (THE SLEEPING CAR MURDERS)   566
COMPULSION   560, 598
COMRADES   1413
COMRADESHIP (KAMERADSCHAFT)   1829
CONAN THE DESTROYER   2200
CONDAMNE A MORT S'EST ECHAPPE, UN (A CONDEMNED MAN ESCAPES)   1994
CONDEMNED MAN ESCAPES, A (UN CONDAMNE A MORT S'ECHAPPE)   1994
CONDEMNED OF ALTONA, THE   334
CONFESSIONS OF A NAZI SPY   203, 226, 262, 329, 345, 357, 568, 1497

CONFESSIONS OF WINIFRED WAGNER, THE 334
CONFIDENTIAL AGENT 278, 1219
CONFIDENTIAL REPORT (MR. ARKADIN) 1790, 1791
CONFIDENTIALLY YOURS! (VIVEMENT DIMANCHE!) 2144, 2147
CONFIRM OR DENY 329
CONFLAGRATION (ENJO) 2021, 2023
CONFORMISTA, IL (THE CONFORMIST) 1310, 2174
CONFORMIST, THE (IL CONFORMISTA) 1310, 2174
CONNECTION, THE 1348
CONQUEST 1176
CONQUEST OF THE POLE, THE (LA CONQUETE DU POLE) 1620
CONQUETE DU POLE, LA (THE CONQUEST OF THE POLE) 1620
CONSPIRACY OF HEARTS 334
CONTEMPT 1317
CONTEMPT (LE MEPRIS) 1310, 2110
CONTRACT 244
CONVERSATION, THE 2197
CONVOY 2062
COOL BREEZE 923
COOL HAND LUKE 45, 669, 985
COOL WORLD, THE 894, 945, 987
COOLEY HIGH 899
COQUETTE 1394
COQUILLE ET LE CLERGYMAN, LA (THE SEA SHELL AND THE
  CLERGYMAN) 1713, 1729
CORBEAU, LE (THE RAVEN) 1904, 1909
CORBETT-JACKSON FIGHT, THE 861
CORNER OF WHEAT, A 1366
CORNERED 1089, 1201, 1948
CORSAIR 555
CORSICAN BROTHERS, THE 1403
COSMOPOLITAN 1217
COTTON CLUB, THE 802, 902
COTTON GOES TO HARLEM 896, 923, 935, 941, 946
COUNSELLOR-AT-LAW 828, 841
COUNT OF MONTE CRISTO, THE (1934) 1203
COUNTDOWN 1176
COUNTDOWN TO ZERO 356
COUNTERFEIT TRAITOR, THE 330
COUNTERPOINT 330
COUNTESS FROM HONG KONG, THE 1418
COUNTRY 485, 1174
COUNTRY GIRL, THE (1954) 62, 498, 499, 657, 1095, 1335, 1349, 1350
COUP DU BERGER, LA 2094
COUP POUR COUP 2126
COURT MARTIAL OF BILLY MITCHELL, THE 328, 339, 1079, 1966
COUSINS, LES (THE COUSINS) 2094, 2097, 2098, 2100, 2128
COUSINS, THE (LES COUSINS) 2094, 2097, 2098, 2100, 2128
COVERED WAGON, THE 1372, 1477, 1702
COWARDS 338
COWARD, THE 328
COWBOY 1284
COWBOYS, THE 434
CRAB-CANNING BOAT (KANIKOSEN) 2019
CRAIG'S WIFE 472
CRANES ARE FLYING, THE (LETYAT ZHURAVLI) 1001
CRASH DIVE 331

CRAZY PAGE, A (A PAGE OUT OF ORDER/PAGE OF MADNESS/KURUTTA
   IPPEIJI) 1742, 1744
CRAZY RAY, THE (PARIS QUI DORT) 1725
CRAZY WORLD OF LAUREL AND HARDY, THE 1690
CREATURE FROM THE BLACK LAGOON 410, 565
CREATURES THE WORLD FORGOT 390
CREDO 919
CRIES AND WHISPERS (VISKNINGAR OCH ROP) 2183, 2184
CRIME DE MONSIEUR LANGE, LE (THE CRIME OF MONSIEUR LANGE) 274,
   1714, 1814
CRIME DOCTOR film series 420
CRIME IN THE STREETS 2048
CRIME OF MONSIEUR LANGE, THE (LE CRIME DE MONSIEUR LANGE) 274,
   1714, 1814
CRIME WITHOUT PASSION 1265
CRIMSON KIMONO, THE 1960
CRIMSON PIRATE, THE 150
CRISIS 287
CRISIS (KRIS) 2183
CRITICAL CONDITION 904
CRITIC, THE 2047
CROCODILE DUNDEE 2202, 2203
CROCODILE DUNDEE II 762
CROIX DE BOIS, LES (WOODEN CROSSES) 1207
CROSS CREEK 1011
CROSS OF IRON 331
CROSSFIRE 274, 334, 375, 384, 568, 575, 831, 849, 1089, 1176, 1946, 1948
CROSSING DELANCEY 2204, 2206, 2207
CROSSWAYS (SHADOWS OF THE YOSHIWARA/JUJIRO) 1742
CROWD, THE 980, 1481, 1576, 1696, 1707, 1713
CRUEL SEA, THE 331, 371, 1841
CRUISING 604
CRY DANGER 1275
CRY FREEDOM 905
CRY HAVOC 331, 349
CRY OF THE WORLD, THE 285
CRY, THE BELOVED COUNTRY 887, 892, 1860
CUBA SI (CUBA, YES) 2115
CUBA, YES (CUBA SI) 2115
CUL-DE-SAC 2179
CUMBERLAND STORY, THE 249
CURE, THE 1416
CYRANO DE BERGERAC 1093
CYRANO ET D'ARTAGNAN 1712
CZECHOSLOVAKIA: FROM MUNICH TO MOSCOW 287

D

D-DAY 287
D-DAY, THE SIXTH OF JUNE 330
D'OU VIENT-IL? (WHENCE DOES HE COME?) 1621
DADDY LONG LEGS 1206, 1392, 1393
DAGUERRE: THE BIRTH OF PHOTOGRAPHY 1598
DAISY KENYON 1966
DAME AUX CAMELIAS, LA 1618
DAMES 497
DAMES DU BOIS DE BOULOGNE, LES (THE LADIES OF THE BOIS DE
   BOULOGNE) 1994, 1995, 1996

DAMNATION ALLEY 536
DAMNED, THE (LA CODUTA DELGI DEI) 310, 334, 348, 1884
DANCE, GIRL, DANCE 508
DANCING DARKIES 861
DANCING LADY 1177
DANGEROUS 1169
DANIEL 334, 1032, 2059
DANZIG-1939 289
DARBY'S RANGERS 330
DARK ANGEL, THE 328, 1225
DARK AT THE TOP OF THE STAIRS, THE 1349
DARK CIRCLE 288
DARK CRYSTAL, THE 411
DARK HORSE, THE 555, 568
DARK MANHATTAN 878, 935, 942
DARK MIRROR, THE 1948
DARK PASSAGE 740
DARKTOWN JUBILEE 921
DARLING LILI 331
DATE WITH JUDY, A 975
DAUGHTER OF DESTINY 213
DAUGHTER OF THE CONGO, A 947
DAUGHTER RITE 506, 512
DAVID 334
DAVID AND BATHSHEBA 832, 1499, 1503, 1517, 1950
DAVID AND LISA 601, 816, 995, 1095
DAVID COPPERFIELD (1913) 1612
DAVID COPPERFIELD (1935) 1305, 1306, 1307, 1308, 1312, 1749
DAVID COPPERFIELD (1970) 1318
DAWN AT THE SOGA BROTHERS' HUNTING GROUND (SOGA KYODAI NO
  AKEBONO) 1735
DAWN OF THE DEAD 390
DAWN PATROL, THE (1930) 268, 328, 1152, 1403, 1775
DAWN PATROL, THE (1938) 328, 354
DAY AFTER TRINITY 288
DAY AFTER, THE 287, 334, 1024
DAY AND THE HOUR, THE (L'JOUR ET L'HEURE) 330
DAY AT THE RACES, A 421, 1804
DAY FOR NIGHT (LA NUIT AMERICAINE) 2107, 2143, 2144, 2145, 2148
DAY IN THE COUNTRY, A (UNE PARTIE DE CAMPAGNE) 1884, 2155
DAY IN THE VITAGRAPH STUDIO, A 1044
DAY OF THE DEAD 390, 806
DAY OF THE DOLPHIN, THE 2060
DAY OF THE FIGHT 2055
DAY OF THE JACKAL, THE 2199
DAY OF THE LOCUST, THE 1041, 1090, 1245, 1246, 1291, 1315
DAY OF WRATH (VREDENS DAG) 1629, 1726
DAY OUR LIVES SHINE, THE (WAGA SHOGAI NO KAGAYAKERU) 2017
DAY THE EARTH STOOD STILL, THE 334, 418, 1946, 1987
DAY THE WORLD ENDED, THE 2049
DAYBREAK (LE JOUR SE LEVE/THE LONG NIGHT) 353, 1714, 1813, 1816, 1825
DAYS OF GLORY (GIORNI DI GLORIA) 1884
DAYS OF WINE AND ROSES 2036
DE GAULLE STORY, THE 1206
DEAD END 195, 556, 975, 986, 987, 1151, 1225, 1439, 1472, 1808
DEAD RECKONING 331, 1064
DEADLY COMPANIONS, THE 2061, 2063
DEAD, THE 1916

DEAR AMERICA: LETTERS HOME FROM VIETNAM 290
DEAR BRIGITTE 1250
DEAR RUTH 1336
DEATH BY HANGING (KOSHIKEI) 2025
DEATH FACTORIES (TOYTMILN) 848
DEATH IN VENICE (MORTE A VENEZIA) 1308, 1317, 1884
DEATH RAY, THE (LUCH SMERTI) 1653
DEATH WISH 558, 811
DEBAJO DEL MUNDO (UNDER THE WORLD) 334
DEBT, THE 863
DEBUTS D'UN PATINEUR, LES (MAX LEARNS TO SKATE) 1619
DECADE PRODIGIEUSE, LA (TEN DAYS WONDER) 2101
DECEIVED SLUMMING PARTY 988
DECEMBER 7TH--DAY OF INFAMY 287
DECEPTION (ANNA BOLEYN) 1631
DECISION BEFORE DAWN 331
DECISION TO DROP THE BOMB 287, 288
DEEP SIX, THE 332
DEEP THROAT 686, 960, 2037, 2192
DEEP, THE 554, 668, 781
DEER HUNTER, THE 152, 178, 209, 335, 337, 338, 341, 367, 550, 558, 580,
  604, 668, 801, 2200
DEER PARK, THE 1041
DEFEAT OF THE GERMAN ARMIES NEAR MOSCOW, THE (MOSCOW STRIKES
  BACK/RAZGROM NEMETZKICH VOISK POD MOSKOVI) 287, 1089
DEFEATED PEOPLE, A 249
DEFIANT ONES, THE 887, 890, 892, 945, 1099
DEKIGOKORO (PASSING FANCY) 1902
DELICATE BALANCE, A 1034
DELIVERANCE 421, 596, 801, 2073
DELO BEILISA (THE BEILIS CASE) 845
DEMONSTRATION, THE 290
DENTIST, THE 1411
DERNIER METRO, LE (THE LAST METRO) 334, 2107, 2143
DERSU UZALA 2019
DESCRIPTION D'UN COMBAT 2115
DESERT ATTACK (ICE COLD IN ALEX) 328
DESERT FOX, THE 264, 328, 339, 349, 366, 1250, 1253, 1256, 1952
DESERT PATROL 332
DESERT RATS, THE 328
DESERT VICTORY 249, 287
DESERTO ROSSO, IL (RED DESERT) 144, 1881, 2173
DESIGN FOR LIVING 555
DESIGN FOR PEACE: SURRENDER OF JAPAN AND AFTERMATH OF WAR 287
DESIRE 1071
DESIRE UNDER THE ELMS 1335, 1341
DESK SET, THE 1206
DESPERATE DECISION (REVENGE AT DAYBREAK) 2037
DESPERATE HOURS, THE 816
DESPERATE JOURNEY 331
DESPERATELY SEEKING SUSAN 469
DESRSU UZALA 2020
DESTINATION GOBI 328
DESTINATION MOON 411, 412, 418, 1090, 1946
DESTINATION TOKYO 331, 369, 1088
DESTINY (DER MUDE TOD) 1402, 1631, 1641, 1722
DESTINY (1987) 331
DESTROYER 329
DET SJUNDE INSEGLET (THE SEVENTH SEAL) 2036

DEUTSCHLAND, ERWACHE! (WAKE UP, GERMANY!) 240
DEUX ANGLAISES ET LE CONTINENT, LES (TWO ENGLISH GIRLS) 2145, 2148, 2155
DEUX HOMMES DANS MANHATTAN 2000
DEUX OU TROIS CHOSES QUE JE SAIS D'ELLE (2 OR 3 THINGS I KNOW ABOUT HER) 497, 2110, 2131
DEUXIEME SOUFFLE, LE (SECOND WIND) 2000
DEVIL DOGS OF THE AIR 1497
DEVIL IN THE FLESH, THE (LE DIABLE AU CORPS) 1993
DEVIL IS A WOMAN, THE 119, 272, 592
DEVIL'S BRIGADE, THE 330
DEVIL'S DISCIPLE, THE 1344, 1345
DEVIL'S OWN ENVOYS, THE (LES VISITEURS DU SOIR) 1904
DEVIL'S PASSKEY, THE 1700
DEVILS, THE 410
DIABLE AU CORPS, LE (THE DEVIL IN THE FLESH) 1993
DIABLE PROBLEMENT, LE (PROBABLY THE DEVIL) 2004, 2005
DIABOLIQUE (LES DIABOLIQUES) 1954, 2000, 2008
DIABOLIQUES, LES (DIABOLIQUE) 1954, 2000, 2008
DIAL M FOR MURDER (1954) 1848, 1978
DIAMOND JIM 1919
DIAMOND LIL 1795
DIAMONDS ARE FOREVER 422
DIARY FOR TIMOTHY, A 249
DIARY OF A COUNTRY PRIEST, THE (LE JOURNAL D'UN CURE DE CAMPAGNE) 751, 1310, 1994, 2008
DIARY OF A MAD HOUSEWIFE 516
DIARY OF ANNE FRANK, THE (1959) 310, 311, 334, 833, 849, 1787
DIARY OF CHUJI'S TRAVELS, A (CHUJI TABI NIKI) 1887
DICK TRACY RETURNS 1456
DILLINGER 2197
DINER 995
DINNER AT EIGHT 1268, 1279, 1394, 1468, 1481
DIPLOMATIC COURIER 334
DIRECTED BY JOHN FORD 1674
DIRTY DANCING 971, 2199
DIRTY DINGUS MAGEE 62, 2191
DIRTY DOZEN, THE 233, 331, 348, 357, 669, 893, 1250, 1251, 2043, 2048, 2071
DIRTY EDDIE 1104
DIRTY HARRY 384, 558, 576, 669, 802, 810, 2192, 2199
DISCREET CHARM OF THE BOURGEOISIE, THE (LE CHARME DISCRET DE LA BOURGEOISIE) 402, 516, 596, 1723
DISENCHANTED, THE 1041
DISHONORED 328
DISRAELI 828
DISTANT THUNDER 338
DIVE BOMBER 272, 329
DIVIDE AND CONQUER 321
DIVIDED HEART 331
DIVINE WOMAN, THE 1524
DIX-SEPTIEME PARALLELE, LE (THE SEVENTEENTH PARALLEL) 289, 312
DO THE RIGHT THING 903
DOBBIN, THE (DI KLYATSHE/THE LIGHT AHEAD/FISHKE DER KRUMER) 829
DOCTOR FAUSTUS 1335
DOCTOR IN THE HOUSE, THE film series 421
DOCTOR ZHIVAGO 328, 1027, 1861
DOCTOR'S DILEMMA, THE 151, 1841
DOCTOR'S SECRET, THE (HYDROTHERAPIE FANTASTIQUE) 1620

DODESKADEN (DODESUKADEN)   2019, 2020
DODESUKADEN (DODESKADEN)   2019, 2020
DODGE CITY   198
DODSWORTH   1151, 1472
DOG DAY AFTERNOON   551, 604, 811, 2059, 2199
DOG'S LIFE, A   1416, 1428
DOG-STAR MAN   595
DOLCE VITA, LA (THE SWEET LIFE)   1023, 1315, 1929, 1930, 2036, 2169, 2170,
  2174
DOMICILE CONJUGAL (BED AND BOARD)   2145, 2148
DON JUAN   1746
DON QUIXOTE   1790
DON'T KNOCK THE ROCK   743
DON'T LOOK NOW   389
DONOVAN'S BRAIN   418
DONZOKO (THE LOWER DEPTHS)   2019
DOORWAY TO HELL   1497
DOROTHY VERNON OF HADDEN HALL   1392, 1393
DOUBLE INDEMNITY (1944)   494, 798, 799, 1197, 1198, 1948, 1971, 1987
DOUBLE LIFE, A   1951, 1975
DOUBLE SUICIDE (SHINJU TEN NO AMIJIMA)   2025
DOUBLE TOUR (WEB OF PASSION/LEDA)   2100, 2128
DOUBLE TROUBLE   1399
DOUCE (LOVE STORY)   1904
DOULOS, LE   2000
DOWN TO EARTH   1089
DRACULA (1931)   389, 398, 599, 984, 1475, 1578, 1798
DRAGNET   2205
DRAGONWYCK   1269
DREAM OF ALLAN GRAY, THE (VAMPYR)   397, 1629, 1726
DREAMS OF A RAREBIT FIEND   595, 1583
DREIGROSCHENOPER, DIE (THE THREEPENNY OPERA)   1633, 1635, 1829
DRESSED TO KILL   512, 816, 961
DRESSER, THE   1331
DRIFTERS   214, 243, 244, 245, 294, 303
DRUMS   1833
DRUMS ALONG THE MOHAWK   270, 1207, 1686
DRUM, THE   858, 1569
DRUNKEN ANGEL (YOIDORE TENSHI)   1899, 2017, 2020, 2029
DR. CHRISTIAN film series   420, 421
DR. CYCLOPS   412
DR. DOLITTLE   748, 893, 1500, 1501, 2041
DR. JEKYLL AND MR. HYDE (1920)   117
DR. JEKYLL AND MR. HYDE (1932)   117, 397, 1164, 1277, 1312, 1578, 1782
DR. JEKYLL AND MR. HYDE (1941)   117, 1305
DR. JOHN HANEY SESSIONS, THE   290, 291
DR. KILDARE film series   420, 421
DR. NO   422
DR. STRANGELOVE OR: HOW I LEARNED TO STOP WORRYING AND LOVE THE
  BOMB   44, 231, 270, 271, 334, 356, 418, 1046, 2036, 2055, 2056, 2057, 2058,
  2082, 2083
DR. ZHIVAGO   2199
DU UND MANCHER KAMERAD (YOU AND OTHER COMRADES)   304
DUCK SOUP   555, 1153, 1748, 1805
DUCK, YOU SUCKER   917
DUEL AT DIABLO   888, 891
DUEL IN THE SUN   531, 532, 1064, 1486, 1488, 1847, 1848, 1946
DUET FOR CANNIBALS   516
DUKE IS TOPS, THE   935

DUNGEON, THE   947
DUNKIRK   331
DUTCHMAN   159, 894, 923, 945, 1349, 2038
DWIGHT D. EISENHOWER: FROM SOLDIER TO PRESIDENT   287
D. I, THE   334
D.O.A. (1949)   1948

E

EACH OTHER   601
EAGLE AND THE HAWK, THE   328
EAGLE SQUADRON   329, 331
EAGLES OVER LONDON   330
EAGLE, THE   1579
EARTH TREMBLES, THE (LA TERRA TREMA)   1925, 1926, 1932, 1934
EARTH (TSUCHI)   1896
EARTH (ZEMLYA)   1645, 1647, 1655, 1663, 1665
EARTHQUAKE   803, 2193
EAST AND WEST (OST UND WEST)   846, 847
EAST IS RED, THE   287
EAST LYNN   1612
EAST OF EDEN   1005, 1261, 1281, 1325, 1494
EAST OF SUMATRA   701
EASY LIVING   150, 1919
EASY RIDER   341, 558, 669, 748, 804, 810, 912, 987, 2037, 2038, 2051, 2081
EASY STREET   1416
ECLIPSE, THE (L'ECLISSE)   150, 1012, 1881, 2169
ECLISSE, L' (THE ECLIPSE)   150, 1012, 1881, 2169
EDDIE CANTOR STORY, THE   1247
EDEN AND AFTER (L'EDEN ET APRES)   2141
EDEN ET APRES, L' (EDEN AND AFTER)   2141
EDGE OF DARKNESS   331
EDGE OF THE CITY   815, 890, 913, 945, 2048
EDIPO RE (OEDIPUS REX)   2171
EDISON MINSTRELS, THE   861
EDISON THE MAN   1094
EDOUARD ET CAROLINE   1994
EDWARD MY SON   1279
EDWARD TELLER--AN EARLY TIME   287
EEN SCHISM VAN TWIJFEL (SHADOW OF A DOUBT)   289, 1913
EGYPTIAN, THE   882
EHE DER MARIA BRAUN, DIE (THE MARRIAGE OF MARIA BRAUN)   2166
EICHMANN AND THE THIRD REICH (EICHMANN UND DAS DRITTE REICH)   287
EICHMANN UND DAS DRITTE REICH (EICHMANN AND THE THIRD REICH)   287
EIGHT IRON MEN   330
EIGHT MINUTES TO MIDNIGHT: A PORTRAIT OF DR. HELEN CALDICOTT   288,
325
EIGHT-AND-ONE/HALF (OTTO E MEZZO)   44, 138, 599, 600, 1927, 1929, 1930,
2170, 2175, 2180
EIGHTEEN SIXTY   277, 1885
EIGHTY-FIRST BLOW, THE   289
EIGHTY-FOUR CHARING CROSS ROAD   2203
EIGHTY-FOUR CHARLIE MOPIC   338
EINER VON VIELEN (ONE OF MANY)   321
EL CID   1964
EL DORADO   1747, 1777
EL DORADO (1921)   1712

ELEANOR AND FRANKLIN: THE WHITE HOUSE YEARS 339
ELECTRA 1337
ELECTRIC HORSEMAN, THE 2065, 2066
ELEGANT SWORDSMAN, THE (FURYU KATSUJINKEN) 1889
ELENA ET LES HOMMES 2000
ELEPHANT BOY 1833, 1859
ELEPHANT MAN, THE 595
ELEVATOR TO THE SCAFFOLD (FRANTIC/L'ASCENSEUR POUR
  L'ECHAFAUD) 2094, 2119
ELLERY QUEEN film series 420
ELMER GANTRY 664, 2036, 2162
ELUSIVE CORPORAL, THE (THE VANISHING CORPORAL/LA CAPORAL
  EPINGLE) 1821
ELVIS--THAT'S THE WAY IT IS 1138
EMAK BAKIA (LEAVE ME ALONE) 1713, 1730
EMERALD FOREST, THE 2200
EMITAI 919
EMPEROR JONES, THE 875, 876, 921, 928, 939, 944, 1341, 1577
EMPEROR OF THE NORTH POLE 2043
EMPIRE 2040, 2068
EMPIRE STRIKES BACK, THE 2200
EN RADE 215
END OF INNOCENCE 288
END OF ST. PETERSBURG, THE (KONYETS SANKT-PETERBURGA) 1668
END OF SUMMER, THE (KOHAYAGAWA-KE NO AKI) 2024
ENEMY AGENT 329
ENEMY BELOW, THE 264, 331
ENFANT SAUVAGE, L' (THE WILD CHILD) 155, 2107, 2146, 2150
ENFANTS DU PARADIS, LES (CHILDREN OF PARADISE) 1904, 1909, 1910
ENFANTS TERRIBLES, LES (THE STRANGE ONES) 1995, 2000
ENFORCER, THE 810
ENGLISHMAN'S HOME, AN 342
ENJO (CONFLAGRATION) 2021, 2023
ENOCH ARDEN 1363
ENSIGN PULVER 332
ENTER LAUGHING 834
ENTERTAINER, THE 1013, 1335, 2162
ENTHUSIASM: SYMPHONY OF THE DON BASIN (ENTUZIAZM: SIMFONIIA
  DONBASSA) 1645
ENTR'ACTE 1711, 1713, 1724, 1725, 1728
ENTUZIAZM: SIMFONIIA DONBASSA (ENTHUSIASM: SYMPHONY OF THE DON
  BASIN) 1645
EQUUS 975, 2059
ERASERHEAD 392
EROS PLUS MASSACRE (EROSU PURASU GYAKUSATSU) 2025
EROSU PURASU GYAKUSATSU (EROS PLUS MASSACRE) 2025
EROTIKON 1624
ESCAPE 263, 348, 353, 357, 1271
ESCAPE FROM ALCATRAZ 676
ESCAPE FROM SOBIBOR 334
ESCAPE FROM YESTERDAY (LA BANDERA) 1813
ESCAPED FROM SIBERIA 846, 847
ESTHER AND THE KING 832
ET DIEU CREA LA FEMME (AND GOD CREATED WOMEN) 2094
ETERNAL CITY, THE 1473
ETERNAL JEW, THE (DER EWIGE JUDE) 236, 1829
ETERNAL RETOUR, L' (THE ETERNAL RETURN) 1904, 1910, 1995, 2005
ETERNAL RETURN, THE (L'ETERNAL RETOUR) 1904, 1910, 1995, 2005
ETERNAL SEA, THE 339

ETOILE DE MER, L' (THE STARFISH)   1713
EUROPEANS, THE   1323
EVA   1094
EVACUEES, THE   334
EVERY MAN FOR HIMSELF AND GOD AGAINST ALL (JEDER FUR SICH UND
   GOTT GEGEN ALLE)   2166
EVERY MAN FOR HIMSELF (SAUVE QUI PEUT/LA VIE)   2112
EVERYTHING YOU ALWAYS WANTED TO KNOW ABOUT SEX   2045
EWIGE JUDE, DER (THE ETERNAL JEW)   236, 1829
EXCALIBUR   416
EXECUTION OF EDDIE SLOVIK, THE   1089
EXECUTIVE SUITE   814, 2053
EXILE, THE   866, 947
EXODUS   334, 805, 832, 837, 841, 1282, 1285, 1966, 1967
EXORCIST, THE   279, 388, 389, 399, 546, 554, 558, 597, 923, 976, 981, 985,
   1171, 1317, 1319, 2200
EXPLOITS OF ELAINE, THE   1456
EXTERMINATING ANGEL, THE (EL ANGEL EXTERMINADOR)   1721, 1723, 1990
EXTRA GIRL, THE   1245, 1413
EXTRACT OF GREAT EXPECTATIONS   1304
EXTRAORDINARY SEAMAN, THE   332, 2051
EYES OF LAURA MARS, THE   976
EYES WITHOUT A FACE (THE HORROR CHAMBER OF DR. FAUSTUS/LES YEUX
   SANS VISAGE)   2128
E. T.: THE EXTRA-TERRESTRIAL   410, 413, 484, 488, 554, 604, 979, 2196,
   2200, 2201

F

F FOR FAKE   1794
FACE IN THE CROWD, A   985, 1261, 1277
FACE OF BRITAIN, THE   244
FACE OF WAR, A   290
FACE TO FACE   1317
FACE TO FACE (ANSIKTE MOT ANSIKTE)   2184
FACES   2048, 2074, 2125
FACES OF IMPERIALISM   290
FACE, THE (THE MAGICIAN/ANSIKTET)   2183, 2184, 2186
FAHRENHEIT 451   412, 2107, 2150
FAIL-SAFE   231, 334, 356, 357, 558, 2036, 2058
FAITHFUL HEART (COEUR FIDELE)   1712
FAITHLESS   555
FALBALAS (PARIS FRILLS)   1994
FALCON AND THE SNOWMAN, THE   802
FALCON film series, THE   420
FALCON TAKES OVER, THE   1198
FALKENEAU, THE IMPOSSIBLE: SAMUEL FULLER BEARS WITNESS   289
FALL OF BABYLON   1578
FALL OF THE HOUSE OF USHER, THE (LA CHUTE DE LA MAISON
   USHER)   1722, 1730
FALL OF THE ROMAN EMPIRE, THE   382
FALL OF THE ROMANOV DYNASTY   304
FALLEN IDOL, THE   52, 1033, 1219, 1329, 1860, 1936
FALLEN SPARROW   278, 1948
FALSTAFF (CHIMES AT MIDNIGHT/CAMPANADAS A MEDIANOCHE)   1353, 1791
FAME   2199
FAMILY PLOT   1849, 1852, 1853, 1854, 1855, 2053

FAMILY WAY, THE 143
FANNY AND ALEXANDER (FANNY OCH ALEXANDER) 2183, 2184
FANNY OCH ALEXANDER (FANNY AND ALEXANDER) 2183, 2184
FANNY (1961) 1176
FANTASTIC NIGHT, THE (LA NUIT FANTASTIQUE) 1904
FANTASTIC VOYAGE 410, 690
FANTOMAS 1605, 1617
FANTOME DE LA LIBERTE, LE (THE PHANTOM OF LIBERTY) 1720, 1723
FANTOMES DU CHAPELIER, LES 2101
FAR COUNTRY, THE 1964, 2035
FAR FROM THE MADDING CROWD 1312
FAR FROM VIETNAM (LOIN DU VIETNAM) 290, 2116, 2118
FAR PAVILIONS, THE 548
FAREWELL MY LOVELY 1197
FAREWELL TO ARMS, A (1932) 328
FAREWELL TO ARMS, A (1957) 328, 1486, 1488
FAREWELL TO MANZANAR 331
FARMER'S DAUGHTER, THE 1485
FARREBIQUE 1993
FAST AND THE FURIOUS, THE 744
FAST FORWARD 890
FAST TIMES AT RIDGEMONT HIGH 604, 2207
FAT CITY 1916, 2199
FATAL ATTRACTION 788, 2204, 2205, 2206, 2207
FATAL GLASS OF BEER, THE 555, 1411
FATE OF EUROPE, THE - BLACK SEA, SOUTH OF FRANCE, SURRENDER 287
FATHER GOOSE 332
FATHER OF THE BRIDE 1952
FATHER'S HONOR, A (L'HONNEUR D'UN PERE) 1621
FDR: THIRD TERM TO PEARL HARBOR 287
FEAR AND DESIRE 2056, 2057
FEAR ON TRIAL 288
FEAR STRIKES OUT 421
FEDORA 1136, 1137, 1291, 1971, 1972
FEEL IT COMING 338
FEELING (SENSO) 1884, 1932
FELLINI SATYRICON 144, 1310, 1927, 1929, 2175
FELLINI'S CASANOVA 1931
FELLINI: DIRECTOR'S NOTEBOOK (BLOCK-NOTES DI UN REGISTA) 117
FELLOWS WHO ATE THE ELEPHANT, THE (ZO O KUTTA RENCHU) 2017
FEMALE ON THE BEACH 1529
FEMME DE L'AVIATEUR OU ON NE SAURAIT PENSER A RIEN, LA (THE
  AVIATOR'S WIFE) 2105
FEMME DE NULLE PART, LA (THE WOMAN FROM NOWHERE) 1712
FEMME DOUCE, UNE (A GENTLE WOMAN) 2003
FEMME DU BOULANGER, LA (THE BAKER'S WIFE) 1809, 1826
FEMME EST UNE FEMME, UNE (A WOMAN IS A WOMAN) 2110, 2131
FEMME INFIDELE, LA (THE UNFAITHFUL WIFE) 2101, 2128
FEMME MARIEE, UNE (A MARRIED WOMAN) 2131
FERRIS BUELLER'S DAY OFF 815, 2202
FEUERTAUFE (BAPTISM OF FIRE) 206, 282, 287
FEVER (FIEVRE) 1712, 1728
FIANCEE, THE (DIE VERLOBTE) 334
FIDDLER ON THE ROOF 834, 841, 850
FIEVRE (FEVER) 1712, 1728
FIFTH HORSEMAN IS FEAR, THE 334
FIFTY-TWO PICK-UP 2051
FIGHT FOR LIFE, THE 153, 1872
FIGHT FOR THE SKY 287

FIGHTER SQUADRON 330
FIGHTERS FOR DEMOCRACY 287
FIGHTING COAST GUARD 332
FIGHTING FOR THE FATHERLAND/WORLD WAR AS SEEN THROUGH GERMAN
 SPECTACLES/DER WELTKREIG 285
FIGHTING LADY, THE 283, 284, 286, 287
FIGHTING MAN: THE STORY OF GENERAL GEORGE S. PATTON 287
FIGHTING SEABEES 332
FIGHTING 69TH, THE 328, 1911
FILLE DE L'EAU, LA (THE WATER GIRL/THE WHIRLPOOL OF FATE) 1821
FILM 2067
FILM ABOUT A WOMAN WHO . . . 501, 505
FILM D'AMORE E D'ANARCHINA (LOVE AND ANARCHY) 2172
FILMGUIDE TO "THE BATTLE OF ALGIERS" 2176
FILMING OTHELLO 1353
FILMS OF GEORGES MELIES, THE 1619
FINAL COUNTDOWN, THE 332
FINEST HOURS, THE 287
FINIAN'S RAINBOW 2197
FINNEGAN'S WAKE 1311
FIRE 290
FIREMAN, THE 1449
FIRES ON THE PLAIN (NOBI) 331, 2021, 2023, 2029
FIRES WERE STARTED 249, 283, 287, 316, 322, 1934, 1938
FIRST BLOOD 337, 801, 2200, 2201
FIRST MEN ON THE MOON 410
FIRST OF THE FEW, THE 343
FIRST STRIKE 288
FIRST TO FIGHT 332
FIRST WORLD WAR, THE 285, 304
FISH CALLED WANDA, A 2203
FISHKE DER KRUMER (DI KLYATSHE/THE DOBBIN/THE LIGHT AHEAD) 829
FISTFUL OF DOLLARS, A (PER UN PUGNO DI DOLLARI) 427, 2019
FIUME, IL (THE RIVER/LE FLEUVE) 1820
FIVE 355, 1946
FIVE EASY PIECES 516, 558, 789
FIVE FINGER EXERCISE 330
FIVE FINGERS 372, 1270, 1500, 1952
FIVE GRAVES TO CAIRO 328, 1971
FIVE GUNS WEST 744
FIVE ON THE BLACK SIDE 896
FIXED BAYONETS 262, 334, 359, 1960
FIXER, THE 834, 1282, 2051, 2076
FLAMES IN THE ASHES 334
FLAMING CRISIS, THE 868
FLAMING YOUTH 1695
FLAMINGO KID, THE 971
FLASH GORDON 417
FLASH GORDON CONQUERS THE UNIVERSE 1456
FLASHDANCE 151, 598, 2199
FLAT TOP 332
FLEET THAT CAME TO STAY, THE 286
FLESH 2040, 2068
FLESH AND THE DEVIL 592
FLEUVE, LE (THE RIVER/IL FIUME) 1820
FLIGHT 1281
FLIGHT COMMAND 329
FLIGHT NURSE 336

FLIGHT OF THE PHOENIX, THE   2043
FLOATING CLOUDS (UKIGUMO)   2019
FLOWING (NAGARERU)   2019
FLYING ACE, THE   868
FLYING DOWN TO RIO   1797
FLYING FORTRESS   331
FLYING LEATHERNECKS   331
FLYING THE MAIL   1213
FLYING TIGERS   331
FLY, THE (1986)   2200
FM   611
FOCUS ON 1939: EUROPE GOES TO WAR   287
FOCUS ON 1941: AMERICA GOES TO WAR   287
FOCUS ON 1945   287
FOG   283
FOOLISH WIVES   472, 1511, 1698, 1699, 1700, 1708
FOOTLIGHT PARADE   555
FOOTLOOSE   2199
FOOTNOTES ON THE ATOMIC AGE   356
FOR A FEW DOLLARS MORE (PER QUALCHE DOLLARO IN PIU)   427
FOR ATT INTE TALA OM ALLA DESSA KVINNOR (NOT TO SPEAK ABOUT ALL
  THESE WOMEN)   2185
FOR HIS MOTHER'S SAKE   870
FOR LIFE, AGAINST THE WAR   290
FOR MASSA'S SAKE   862
FOR ME AND MY GAL   404, 1073
FOR THE LOVE OF MIKE   1253
FOR US (FUR UNS)   321
FOR WHOM THE BELL TOLLS   278, 331, 623, 1064, 1217, 1231, 1232, 1305, 1322
FORBIDDEN   334
FORBIDDEN GAMES (LES JEUX INTERDITS)   331, 377, 1923, 1995, 2008
FORBIDDEN PLANET   417, 418, 419
FORCE OF ARMS   330
FORCE OF EVIL   1094
FORCE TEN FROM NAVARONE   330, 331
FOREIGN AFFAIR   331
FOREIGN CORRESPONDENT   262, 331, 353, 357, 1177, 1847, 1852, 1911
FOREVER AMBER   1073, 1203, 1966, 1967
FOREVER AND A DAY   331
FORGOTTEN CHILDREN (WASURERARETA KORA)   2017
FORGOTTEN IMPERIAL ARMY (WASURERARETA KOGUN)   288
FORGOTTEN MEN (1933)   285
FORGOTTEN VILLAGE, THE   1280
FORSYTH SAGA, THE   1457
FORT APACHE   427, 433, 1208, 1500, 1501, 1673, 1684, 1686, 1946, 1952
FORT TI   428
FORTUNE COOKIE, THE   1971
FORTUNE, THE   2060
FORTY GUNS   1960
FORTY-NINTH PARALLEL   343, 1938
FORTY-SECOND STREET (1933)   405, 555, 1249, 1496, 1748, 1797
FORTY-SEVENTH RONIN: Part II/A TALE OF ROYAL RETAINERS IN THE
  GENROKU ERA (GENROKU CHUSHINGURA)   1901
FOUNTAINHEAD, THE   980
FOUR FEATHERS, THE   1488, 1569, 1833, 1860
FOUR FRIENDS   2064
FOUR HORSEMEN OF THE APOCALYPSE, THE (1921)   328, 343, 1707, 1708
FOUR HORSEMEN OF THE APOCALYPSE, THE (1962)   328, 1707

FOUR HUNDRED BLOWS, THE (LES QUATRE CENT COUPS) 1005, 2097, 2106,
  2107, 2143, 2144, 2145, 2148, 2150, 2154
FOUR HUNDRED MILLION, THE 287, 312, 314, 315
FOUR IN THE AFTERNOON 1974
FOUR NIGHTS OF A DREAMER (QUATRE NUITS D'UN REVEUR) 2003
FOUR SONS 263, 327, 329, 348, 353
FOUR STEPS IN THE CLOUDS (QUATTRO PASSI FRA LE NUVOLE) 1875
FOURTEENTH OF JULY, THE (LE QUATORZE JUILLET) 1714, 1810
FOURTH ESTATE, THE 244
FOX MOVIETONE NEWS 304
FOX, THE 1262
FRAGMENT OF AN EMPIRE 1592
FRANCES 1044, 1136, 1137, 1140, 1245, 1291
FRANCOIS THE POSTMAN (JOUR DE FETE) 2000, 2001
FRANKENSTEIN (1910) 391, 395
FRANKENSTEIN (1931) 388, 389, 391, 394, 599, 984, 1312, 1475, 1502, 1808
FRANKENSTEIN'S MONSTER film series 421
FRANKLIN D. ROOSEVELT, PART 2: THE WAR YEARS (WOLPER) 287
FRANKLIN D. ROOSEVELT: DECLARATION OF WAR 287
FRANKLIN ROOSEVELT: THE WAR YEARS (HISTORY MAKERS) 287
FRANKLIN ROOSEVELT: WAR COMES TO AMERICA 287
FRANTIC (L'ASCENSEUR POUR L'ECHAFAUD/ELEVATOR TO THE
  SCAFFOLD) 2094, 2119
FRAU IM MOND, DIE (WOMAN IN THE MOON) 412
FREAKS 417, 1311, 1798
FREDERICK DOUGLAS: AN AMERICAN LIFE 902
FRENCH CAN CAN (ONLY THE FRENCH CAN) 1814, 2000
FRENCH CONNECTION II, THE 2051
FRENCH CONNECTION, THE 359, 384, 472, 669, 804, 2192
FRENCH THEY ARE A FUNNY RACE, THE (LES CARNETS DU MAJOR
  THOMPSON) 1919
FRENCH WITHOUT TEARS 1841
FRENZY 669, 1567, 1836, 1838, 1849, 1850, 1854, 1855, 2199
FRENZY (TORMENT/HETS) 2183, 2185
FRESHMAN, THE 421, 989, 1160, 1693, 1705
FREUD 816, 1089
FREUDLOSE GASSE, DIE (THE JOYLESS STREET) 342, 1632, 1643
FRIDAY THE 13TH 802, 976
FRIDAY THE 13th series 2200
FRIENDLY FIRE 338, 341, 2200
FRIENDLY PERSUASION, THE 1319
FRISCO KID, THE 836, 841
FRITZ THE CAT 835
FROGMEN, THE 331
FROM HERE TO ETERNITY (1953) 231, 331, 361, 368, 499, 657, 1167, 1469
FROM KAISER TO FUEHRER 287
FROM OUT OF THE ASHES 334
FROM RUSSIA WITH LOVE 422
FROM THE LIFE OF THE MARIONETTES (AUS DEM LEBEN DER
  MARIONETTEN) 2184
FROM THESE ROOTS 902
FRONT PAGE WOMAN 638
FRONT PAGE, THE 408, 555, 828, 1081, 1090, 1224, 1265
FRONTIER (AIR CITY/AEROGRAD) 1655
FRONTLINE 290
FRONT, THE 334, 802, 1975, 2045, 2199
FU MANCHU film series 421
FUGITIVE KIND, THE 790, 1345, 2058

FUGITIVE, THE 1457
FULL CIRCLE 399
FULL METAL JACKET 338, 2055, 2201
FULL MOON IN PARIS (LES NUITS DE LA PLEINE LUNE) 2105
FUN FACTORY 1578
FUNNY FACE 461
FUNNY FARM 2052
FUNNY GIRL 748, 834, 960, 2036
FUNNY LADY 841
FUR UNS (FOR US) 321
FURY 556, 568, 876, 1018, 1270, 1636, 1637
FURY IN THE PACIFIC 286
FURYO SHONEN (BAD BOYS) 802, 1000
FURYU KATSUJINKEN (THE ELEGANT SWORDSMAN) 1889

G

G-MEN 387, 476, 556, 1497
GABLE AND LOMBARD 1245
GABRIEL OVER THE WHITE HOUSE 556, 568
GAI SAVOIR, LE (JOYFUL KNOWLEDGE) 2111
GALILEO 1963
GALLANT HOURS, THE 331, 339
GAME OF LOVE, THE (LE BLE EN HERBE) 1993
GANDHI 548, 1570
GANGSTER, THE 1314
GANJA AND HESS 899
GARDEN OF ALLAH, THE 1264
GARDEN OF DELIGHTS, THE 278
GARDEN OF EDEN 1579
GARDEN OF THE FINZI-CONTINIS, THE (IL GIARDINO DEI
 FINZI-CONTINI) 310, 311, 334, 1874, 1877, 2174
GARDENS OF STONE 338, 903
GARMENT INDUSTRY, THE 2043
GASLIGHT 521, 523, 976, 1155, 1336, 1948
GATE OF HELL (JIGOKUMON) 2019, 2029
GATE OF PARIS, THE (PORTE DES LILAS) 2000
GATHERING OF EAGLES, A 231, 357, 362
GATTOPARDO, IL (THE LEOPARD) 277, 1884
GAY DIVORCEE, THE 1177
GENBAKU NO KO (CHILDREN OF THE ATOMIC BOMB) 2019
GENERAL DELLA ROVERE (IL GENERALE DELLA ROVERE) 311, 334, 1883, 1954
GENERAL DIED AT DAWN, THE 1090, 1095, 1274
GENERAL GEORGE C. MARSHALL 287
GENERAL GEORGE PATTON 287
GENERAL LINE, THE (OLD AND NEW/STAROIE I NOVOIE) 1645, 1661, 1866
GENERALE DELLA ROVERE, IL (GENERAL DELLA ROVERE) 311, 334, 1883,
 1954
GENERAL, THE 914, 1576, 1579, 1688, 1704
GENERATION APART, A 334
GENERATION, A (POKOLENIE) 2014
GENOCIDE (1981) 289
GENOU DE CLAIRE, LE (CLAIRE'S KNEE) 2104
GENROKU CHUSHINGURA (FORTY-SEVENTH RONIN: Part II/A TALE OF ROYAL
 RETAINERS IN THE GENROKU ERA) 1901
GENTE DEL PO 1881
GENTLE WOMAN, A (UNE FEMME DOUCE) 2003
GENTLEMAN JIM 1700

GENTLEMAN'S AGREEMENT   375, 569, 831, 842, 849, 859, 1018, 1256, 1260,
  1261, 1499, 1500, 1503, 1946
GENTLEMEN ARE BORN   568
GENTLEMEN PREFER BLONDES   533, 1281, 1454, 1952
GEORGE RAFT STORY, THE   1247
GEORGE STEVENS: A FILMMAKER'S JOURNEY   1787
GEORGY GIRL   1006, 2038
GERMAN SIDE OF THE WAR, THE   285
GERMAN SISTERS, THE (MARIANNE AND JULIANE) (DIE BLEIER ZEIT)   505
GERMANIA, ANNO ZERO (GERMANY, YEAR ZERO)   1883, 1923
GERMANY IN WARTIME   285
GERMANY ON THE FIRING LINE   285
GERMANY PALE MOTHER   331
GERMANY TODAY   287
GERMANY--THE ROAD OF RETURN   287
GERMANY, YEAR ZERO (GERMANIA, ANNO ZERO)   1883, 1923
GERTIE THE DINOSAUR   414
GERTRUD   1629, 2189
GETAWAY, THE   153, 409, 2061
GETTING STRAIGHT   338
GHETTO SEAMSTRESS   822
GHOST AND MRS. MUIR, THE   1271
GHOST GOES WEST, THE   1833
GHOST STORY (WAR BIRDS)   1213
GHOST THAT NEVER RETURNS, THE   1592
GHOSTBUSTERS   484, 902, 2200
GHOSTBUSTERS II   762, 2200
GIANT   1787
GIARDINO DEI FINZI-CONTINI, IL (THE GARDEN OF THE
  FINZI-CONTINIS)   310, 311, 334, 1874, 1877, 2174
GIGI   404, 1784
GILDA   507, 575, 1948
GINGER AND FRED   1929
GINREI NO HATE (TO THE END OF THE SILVER-CAPPED MOUNTAINS)   2017
GION NO SHIMAI (SISTERS OF THE GION)   1890, 1901
GIORNI DI GLORIA (DAYS OF GLORY)   1884
GIRL AT THE DOJO TEMPLE, A (MUSUME DOJOJI)   2022
GIRL FROM CHICAGO, THE   911
GIRL I LOVED, THE (WAGA KOI SESHI OTOME)   2017
GIRLFRIENDS   491, 510, 512, 526, 604, 2199
GIRLS IN DANGER   1578
GIRLS IN THE NIGHT   701
GIRLS IN UNIFORM (MAEDCHEN IN UNIFORM)   495, 1829, 1923
GIULIETTA DELGI SPIRITI (JULIET OF THE SPIRITS)   593, 1929, 1930, 2171
GIVE US FREEDOM (A NOUS LA LIBERTE)   1724, 1725, 1810, 1825
GLASS KEY, THE   1948
GLASS MENAGERIE, THE   1347
GLASS WEB, THE   701
GLEN AND RANDA   355
GLENN MILLER STORY, THE   885
GLORIA   501, 2048
GLORY   905
GLORY ALLEY   882
GLORY BRIGADE, THE   334
GLOW OF LIFE, THE (SEI NO KAGAYAKI)   1739
GO TELL THE SPARTANS   338, 341, 2200
GO WEST   1688
GO-BETWEEN, THE   984, 1293, 2161

GOD DOESN'T BELIEVE IN US ANYMORE   289
GOD IS MY CO-PILOT   331, 332
GOD'S LITTLE ACRE   858, 1964
GOD'S STEPCHILDREN   948
GODDESS, THE   815, 1136, 1137, 1248, 1292
GODELUREAUX, LES   2100, 2128
GODFATHER PART II, THE   387, 565, 666, 1171, 2192, 2193, 2197
GODFATHER, THE   190, 194, 384, 385, 387, 558, 565, 666, 668, 980, 1153, 1165,
  2192, 2193, 2197
GODS OF METAL   288
GODZILLA (GOJIRA)   2019
GOERING   287
GOIN' ALL THE WAY   976
GOING BACK: A RETURN TO VIETNAM   290
GOING BYE-BYE   1690
GOING HOLLYWOOD   1245
GOING MY WAY   1094, 1174, 1911
GOJIRA (GODZILLA)   2019
GOLD DIGGERS OF 1933   401, 461, 555, 1288, 1797
GOLD DIGGERS OF 1935   1797
GOLD OF ROME, THE (L'ORO DI ROMA)   334
GOLD RUSH, THE   103, 144, 595, 1417, 1430
GOLDEN AGE OF COMEDY, THE   1701
GOLDEN AGE, THE (L'AGE D'OR)   1721, 1722, 1811, 1989, 1990
GOLDEN BOY   828, 1095
GOLDEN CHILD, THE   904
GOLDEN COACH, THE (LE CARROSSE D'OR)   187
GOLDEN EARRINGS   328, 1094
GOLDEN VOYAGE OF SINBAD, THE   411
GOLDFINGER   422
GOLEM UND DIE TANZERKIN, DER (THE GOLEM)   1635
GOLEM, THE (DER GOLEM UND DIE TANZERKIN)   1635
GOLEM, THE (DER GOLEM: WIE ER IN DIE WELT KAM)   1632, 1635
GOLEM: WIE ER IN DIE WELT KAM, DER (THE GOLEM)   1632, 1635
GOLUB   289
GONE ARE THE DAYS   915, 922
GONE WITH THE WIND   59, 121, 277, 400, 461, 526, 539, 565, 575, 595, 623,
  812, 912, 915, 929, 932, 939, 944, 958, 1036, 1124, 1151, 1169, 1217, 1224,
  1310, 1418, 1435, 1436, 1483, 1486, 1489, 1577, 1800, 1801
GONE WITH THE WIND and racism   852, 857, 876, 877, 904
GOOD EARTH, THE   1305, 1320, 1802
GOOD EXAMPLE, A   288
GOOD GUYS WEAR BLACK   338
GOOD LITTLE DEVIL, A   1392
GOOD MORNING, VIETNAM   338, 2201
GOOD MOTHER, THE   2207
GOOD NEWS   404
GOODBYE BILLY--AMERICA GOES TO WAR 1917-18   285
GOODBYE GIRL, THE   1166
GOODBYE MY CHILDREN (AU REVOIR LES ENFANTS)   334
GOODBYE, COLUMBUS   834, 916
GOODBYE, MR. CHIPS (1939)   1169, 1328, 1839
GOOSE STEP (HELL'S DEVILS/BEASTS OF BERLIN)   329
GORDON'S WAR   896, 898
GOSPEL ACCORDING TO ST. MATTHEW, THE (IL VANGELO SECONDO
  MATTEO)   2175
GOSTA BERLING'S SAGA (THE STORY OF GOSTA BERLING)   1625, 1630
GOTTERDAMMERUNG: FALL OF THE THIRD REICH   287
GRADUATE, THE   53, 138, 472, 558, 748, 975, 990, 1146, 1165, 2036, 2060, 2085

GRAND GAME, THE (LE GRAND JEU) 1812
GRAND HOTEL 1481, 1492, 1516, 1803, 2193
GRAND ILLUSION (LA GRANDE ILLUSION) 209, 220, 221, 254, 261, 277, 328,
  1232, 1576, 1813, 1814, 1822, 1826, 1827, 1924
GRAND JEU, LE (THE GRAND GAME) 1812
GRAND MANEUVER, THE (LES GRANDES MANOEUVRES) 1725, 2000, 2005
GRAND PRIX 409, 2051
GRANDE ILLUSION, LA (GRAND ILLUSION) 209, 220, 221, 254, 261, 277, 328,
  1232, 1576, 1813, 1814, 1822, 1826, 1827, 1924
GRANDES MANOEUVRES, LES (THE GRAND MANEUVER) 1725, 2000, 2005
GRANDMA'S BOY 1693
GRANTON TRAWLER 243, 1871
GRAPES OF WRATH, THE 194, 227, 271, 428, 472, 565, 978, 980, 1151, 1169,
  1250, 1252, 1253, 1256, 1280, 1305, 1309, 1312, 1326, 1351, 1499, 1500, 1673,
  1684, 1686, 1924
GREASE 2199
GREAT ACTRESSES OF THE PAST PROGRAM, THE 1618
GREAT BARRIER, THE 1569
GREAT DICTATOR, THE 209, 250, 271, 310, 334, 357, 568, 831, 1417, 1430,
  1433, 1911
GREAT DIRECTOR, THE 1369
GREAT ESCAPE, THE 196, 331, 354, 374
GREAT EXPECTATIONS (1947) 1301, 1305, 1306, 1307, 1308, 1312, 1860, 1936,
  1939
GREAT GATSBY, THE (1949) 1095, 1321
GREAT GATSBY, THE (1974) 553, 1095, 1321, 1322, 1436, 2193
GREAT KING, THE (GROSSE DER KONIG) 240
GREAT MCGINTY, THE 1912, 1919, 1920
GREAT NORTHFIELD MINNESOTA RAID, THE 433
GREAT ROAD, THE 304
GREAT SANTINI, THE 484, 738, 971, 2193
GREAT SIOUX UPRISING, THE 701
GREAT TRAIN ROBBERY, THE 428, 434, 696, 708, 1423, 1605, 1617, 1620
GREAT WALDO PEPPER, THE 1151, 2052
GREAT WAR, THE 304, 327
GREAT WHITE HOPE, THE 899, 945
GREATEST MOTHER OF THEM ALL, THE 2043
GREATEST SHOW ON EARTH, THE 1950
GREATEST STORY EVER TOLD, THE 382, 383
GREATEST THING IN LIFE, THE 1372
GREED 1018, 1299, 1317, 1480, 1576, 1698, 1699, 1700
GREEN BERETS, THE 209, 218, 231, 338, 339, 341, 348, 357, 359, 364
GREEN FIELDS (GRINE FELDER) 829, 846
GREEN HORNET, THE 1456
GREEN MOUNTAINS (AOI SAMMYUKA) 2017
GREEN PASTURES, THE 859, 874, 877, 878, 928, 930, 931, 934, 939, 944, 952
GREETINGS 338
GREMLINS 488, 1526
GREY GARDENS 2085
GREYSTOKE: THE LEGEND OF TARZAN, LORD OF THE APES 1037, 1174
GRIDO, IL (THE OUTCRY) 1012, 1881
GRIDO, IL (THE PASSENGER) 1881, 2169
GRINE FELDER (GREEN FIELDS) 829, 846
GRISSOM GANG, THE 2043
GROSSE DER KONIG (THE GREAT KING) 240
GROUP, THE 990, 1093
GROWING UP FEMALE 505
GUADALCANAL DIARY 248, 331, 349, 831

GUADALCANAL--ISLAND OF DEATH, PART I & II   287
GUADALCANAL, MIDWAY IS EAST. . . . JAPANESE VICTORIES AND THE
 BATTLE OF MIDWAY   287
GUERNICA--THE TREE OF LIBERTY   278
GUERRE EST FINIE, LA (THE WAR IS OVER)   278, 379, 2118, 2136, 2139
GUESS WHO'S COMING TO DINNER?   488, 855, 888, 892, 894, 896, 945, 2038
GUICHETS DU LOUVRE, LES (BLACK THURSDAY)   311, 334
GUILTY BY REASON OF RACE   287
GUILTY OF TREASON   1949
GUNFIGHTER, THE   199, 1252, 1500, 1779, 1946, 1952
GUNG HO!   332
GUNGA DIN   150, 272, 1214, 1224, 1265, 1403, 1787, 1806, 1833
GUNNAR HEDE'S SAGA   1625
GUNS OF NAVARONE, THE   331, 1093
GUNS OF THE TREES   894
GUNSAULUS MYSTERY, THE   947
GUY NAMED JOE, A   331, 1282
GUYS AND DOLLS   403, 1270
GYCKLARNAS AFTON (THE CLOWN'S EVENING/THE NAKED NIGHT/SAWDUST
 AND TINSEL)   2183, 2187
GYPSY MOTHS, THE   2051

H

H-BOMB OVER U. S.   356
HACHI NO SU NO KODOMOTACHI (CHILDREN OF THE BEEHIVE)   2017
HAIL THE CONQUERING HERO   331, 1014, 1912, 1919, 1921
HAIL, HERO!   338
HAIR   338, 401, 2199
HAIRCUT   2040
HAIRY APE, THE   1341
HAKAI (APOSTASY)   2017
HALLELUJAH!   730, 872, 873, 915, 921, 928, 934, 939, 941, 943, 980, 1696, 1806
HALLELUJAH, I'M A BUM   1090
HALLOWEEN   484, 961
HALLOWEEN series   2200
HALLS OF MONTEZUMA   331
HALSEY VS. YAMAMOTO: TURNING POINT   287
HAMBURGER HILL   337, 338, 2201
HAMLET (1948)   1342, 1353, 1936
HAMLET (1964)   1343, 1353, 1354
HANDSOME SERGE (LE BEAU SERGE/BITTER REUNION)   2094, 2100, 2128
HANGMEN ALSO DIE   331, 1637, 1911
HANKY PANKY   890
HANNAH AND HER SISTERS   368, 2045, 2207, 2208
HANOI   290
HANOI HILTON, THE   338
HANOVER SQUARE   404
HANOVER STREET   331, 345
HANS WESTMAR   321
HANUSSEN   334
HAPPINESS OF US ALONE, THE   601
HAPPINESS (LE BONHEUR)   2114
HARD TIMES   2087
HARDER THEY COME, THE   392
HARDER THEY FALL, THE   421
HARD, FAST AND BEAUTIFUL   421
HARLEM GLOBETROTTERS, THE   421

HARLEM IS TOPS 935
HARLEM ON THE PRAIRIE 935
HARLEM RIDES THE RANGE 935
HARLOW 1137, 1245
HARP OF BURMA, THE (BIRUMA NO TATEGOTO/THE BURMESE HARP) 331,
  371, 2018, 2021, 2023
HARPER 1151
HARRY AND SON 1436
HARRY AND TONTO 1006
HARRY S. TRUMAN: SUDDENLY, MR. PRESIDENT 287
HASARD BALTHAZAR, AU (BALTHAZAR) 1994
HATFUL OF RAIN, A 815
HAUNTING, THE 1323
HAWAII 2052
HAWK'S TRAIL, THE 1456
HAXAN (WITCHCRAFT THROUGH THE AGES) 1626, 1630
HAZARDS OF HELEN, THE 1456, 1458
HE WHO GETS SLAPPED 1483
HEART IS A LONELY HUNTER, THE 858, 995
HEART OF A JEWESS, THE 826, 846
HEART OF NEW YORK, THE 828
HEARTBREAK KID, THE 834, 838
HEARTBURN 2060
HEARTS AND MINDS 290, 303, 325, 364, 558
HEARTS IN DIXIE 872, 873, 915, 916, 921, 928, 934, 939, 941, 943
HEARTS OF THE WEST 841
HEARTS OF THE WORLD 297, 328, 1368, 1375, 1376, 1378, 1385, 1388
HEAT 2040, 2068
HEAT AND DUST 548
HEAVEN CAN WAIT (1943) 1276, 1694
HEAVEN KNOWS, MR. ALLISON 332, 499, 657
HEAVEN'S GATE 535, 553, 558, 604, 668, 2201
HEIDI 1401
HEIR TO GENGHIS-KAHN, THE (STORM OVER ASIA/POTOMOK
  CHINGIS-KAHN) 1668
HEIRESS, THE 1006, 1317
HELDENLIED, KOMSOMOL (SONG OF HEROES) 312, 314
HELL AND HIGH WATER 1960
HELL DIVERS 327
HELL IN THE PACIFIC 331
HELL IS FOR HEROES 331, 354
HELL TO ETERNITY 339
HELL'S ANGELS 328, 592
HELL'S DEVILS (BEASTS OF BERLIN/GOOSE STEP) 329
HELL'S HIGHWAY 568
HELL'S HOLIDAY 285
HELL'S HORIZONS 334
HELLCATS OF THE NAVY 332
HELLO, DOLLY 834, 1500, 1501, 2041
HELPING HAND, THE 1368
HELP! 2161
HENRY V 1337, 1342, 1354, 1935
HER FIRST BISCUITS 1392, 1394, 1395
HER SECOND MOTHER (IR TSYVEYTE MAME) 829
HERCULES AND THE CAPTIVE WOMEN 2032
HERE AND ELSEWHERE (ICI ET AILEURS) 2112
HERE COMES MR. JORDAN 1093, 1336
HERE COMES THE NAVY 327

HEROES 259, 338
HEROES ALL 285
HEROES FOR SALE 556
HEROES OF TELEMARK, THE 330
HERR ARNES PENGAR (SIR ARNE'S TREASURE) 1625, 1628
HESTER STREET 836, 838, 841, 850, 1313
HETS (TORMENT/FRENZY) 2183, 2185
HIDDEN FORTRESS, THE (KAKUSHI-TORIDE NO SANAKUNIN) 2019, 2027
HIGH AND THE MIGHTY, THE 1701
HIGH ANXIETY 2047
HIGH NOON 193, 198, 433, 472, 987, 1019, 1093, 1169, 1946, 2027
HIGH SCHOOL 290, 770
HIGH SCHOOL HERO 421
HIGH SIERRA 387, 1288, 1577, 1700, 1915, 1948
HIGH STREET (RUE HAUTE) 311, 334
HIGH WALL 740, 1187
HIGHWAY DRAGNET 2049
HILL, THE 328, 893
HINTERTREPPE (BACKSTAIRS) 1714
HIROSHIMA MON AMOUR 150, 355, 790, 2097, 2117, 2118, 2136, 2137, 2139,
 2152
HIROSHIMA-NAGASAKI, AUGUST 1945 287, 356
HIS BREAD AND BUTTER 1413
HIS GIRL FRIDAY 150, 521, 523, 1160, 1265, 1747
HIS MAJESTY, THE AMERICAN 1388, 1405
HIS PEOPLE 827
HIS PICTURE IN THE PAPERS 1380, 1399
HIS TRUST 1380
HIS TRUST FULFILLED 1380
HISTOIRE D'ADELE H., L' (THE STORY OF ADELE H.) 584, 2107, 2144, 2145,
 2149
HISTORY 331
HISTORY BOOK, VOLUME 7 - THE COMING OF DARKNESS 287
HISTORY IS MADE AT NIGHT 1264
HISTORY OF THE WORLD, PART I, THE 2047
HISTORY OF U. S. FOREIGN RELATIONS, PART 3 - THE RELUCTANT WORLD
 POWER 287
HIT PARADE, THE 1071
HITLER INVADES POLAND 287
HITLER YOUTH (HITLERJUNGE QUEX) 206, 236, 240
HITLER--A CAREER 339
HITLER'S CHILDREN 331, 1201, 1202
HITLERJUNGE QUEX (HITLER YOUTH) 206, 236, 240
HITLER, EIN FILM AUS DEUTSCHLAND (OUR HITLER, A FILM FROM
 GERMANY) 289
HITLER: ANATOMY OF A DICTATORSHIP 287
HITLER: NAZI-SOVIET WAR: PARTISAN 287
HITLER: THE LAST TEN DAYS 330
HITORI MUSUKO (THE ONLY SON) 1893, 1901
HI, MOM! 338
HOAXERS, THE 1949
HOBSON'S CHOICE 1861
HOLCROFT COVENANT, THE 2051
HOLD BACK THE DAWN, 1971
HOLE, THE 356
HOLIDAY 1093, 1279
HOLIDAY ON SYLT 304
HOLLYWOOD 1248
HOLLYWOOD HOTEL 1245, 1249

HOLLYWOOD ON TRIAL 288, 1293
HOLLYWOOD SHUFFLE 903, 2203
HOLLYWOOD: THE GOLDEN YEARS 663
HOLOCAUST (1978) 311, 312, 334, 837
HOME AND THE WORLD, THE 548
HOME BEFORE DARK 833
HOME OF THE BRAVE 274, 375, 569, 859, 882, 884, 887, 931, 935, 944, 952,
  987, 1093, 1946
HOMECOMING 330
HOMECOMING, THE 1034
HOMER 338
HOMESTEADER, THE 866
HOMEWORK 977
HOMMAGE DU LARGE, L' (THE BIG MAN) 1713
HOMME ET UNE FEMME, UN (A MAN AND A WOMAN) 2135
HOMME QUI AIMAIT LES FEMMES, L' (THE MAN WHO LOVED WOMEN) 2145
HONDOO ANNIE 1384
HONEYSUCKLE ROSE 2065
HONKYTONK MAN 1436
HONNEUR D'UN PERE, L' (A FATHER'S HONOR) 1621
HONOR GUARD 338
HOODLUM PRIEST, THE 987
HOOK, THE 334
HOOSIERS 2203
HOPALONG CASSIDY film series 420, 811
HOPE AND GLORY 331
HORA DE LOS HORNOS, LA 2157
HORIZONS WEST 701
HORNET'S NEST 330
HORROR CHAMBER OF DR. FAUSTUS, THE (LES YEUX SANS VISAGE/EYES
  WITHOUT A FACE) 2128
HORRORS OF WAR, THE 342
HORSE FEATHERS 421, 989, 1268
HORSE (UMA) 1896
HORSEMAN, THE 2051
HOSTAGES 331
HOT RODS TO HELL 419
HOTEL BERLIN 331
HOTEL DES INVALIDES 287, 2128
HOTEL DU NORD 1714, 1813
HOTEL IMPERIAL (1927) 328, 1625, 1706
HOTEL TERMINUS: THE LIFE AND TIMES OF KLAUS BARBIE 289
HOUDINI 984
HOUR OF THE WOLF, THE (VARGTIMMEN) 2184
HOUSE I LIVE IN, THE 1089
HOUSE OF BAMBOO 1960
HOUSE OF FRIGHT, THE (THE TWO FACES OF DR. JEKYLL) 117
HOUSE OF ROTHSCHILD, THE 828
HOUSE OF THE SEVEN GABLES, THE 1305
HOUSE OF USHER, THE 1317, 2049
HOUSE ON CARROLL STREET, THE 334
HOUSE ON 92ND STREET, THE 301, 373, 384, 1952
HOUSEBOAT 984
HOUSING PROBLEMS 245
HOW GIRLS GET UNDRESSED 1371
HOW GIRLS GO TO BED 1371
HOW GREEN WAS MY VALLEY 117, 980, 1007, 1203, 1204, 1499, 1500, 1503,
  1587

HOW I WON THE WAR 330
HOW THE JEWS TAKE CARE OF THEIR POOR 847
HOW THE WEST WAS WON 374, 383, 1684
HOW TO MARRY A MILLIONAIRE 1250, 1252, 1281
HUCKLEBERRY FINN (1939) 1305
HUD 150, 433, 564, 2036
HUMAN CONDITION 331
HUMANITY AND PAPER BALLOONS (NINJO KAMIFUSEN) 1889
HUMORESQUE (1920) 825, 827
HUMORESQUE (1946) 328, 589, 1529
HUNCHBACK OF NOTRE DAME, THE (1923) 1491, 1579, 1702
HUNGER 1317
HUNTERS, THE 334
HURDES, LES (LAND WITHOUT BREAD) 303, 1721, 1989
HURRICANE, THE 1064
HUSBANDS 2048
HUSH . . . HUSH, SWEET CHARLOTTE 2043
HUSTLE 2043
HUSTLER, THE 150, 575, 664, 810, 1014, 1091, 1311, 1969
HYDROTHERAPIE FANTASTIQUE (THE DOCTOR'S SECRET) 1620

I

I ACCUSE (J'ACCUSE) 833, 1712
I AIM AT THE STARS 339, 366
I AM A CAMERA 334
I AM A FUGITIVE FROM A CHAIN GANG 556, 568, 876, 915, 939, 944, 1288,
  1493, 1494, 1748, 1804
I AM CURIOUS: YELLOW 278, 1956
I AM IRELAND (MISE EIRE) 305
I CLOWNS (THE CLOWNS) 117
I CONFESS 1848
I LOVE YOU, ALICE B. TOKLAS 834
I MARRIED A COMMUNIST 1949
I MARRIED A DOCTOR 1305
I MARRIED A WITCH 1725, 1919
I REMEMBER MAMA 521, 1336
I REMEMBER (AMARCORD) 1874, 1929
I SHOT JESSE JAMES 1960, 1961
I VITELLONI (THE YOUNG AND THE PASSIONATE) 1927, 2171
I WALK THE LINE 2051
I WALKED WITH A ZOMBIE 1912
I WANT TO BE A MOTHER (IKH VIL ZAYN A MAME) 829
I WANT TO LIVE! 560
I WANT YOU 334
I WANTED WINGS 327, 329
I WAS A COMMUNIST FOR THE FBI 241, 334, 1949
I WAS A MALE WAR BRIDE 589, 1952
I WAS A SPY 328
I WAS BORN BUT . . . (UMARETE WA MITA KEREDO) 1893, 1901
I'LL CRY TOMORROW 1247
I'M A STRANGER HERE MYSELF 1985
I'M NO ANGEL 555, 1807
ICE COLD IN ALEX (DESERT ATTACK) 328
ICE STATION ZEBRA 334
ICEMAN COMETH, THE 1034, 1340, 1351, 2051
ICI ET AILEURS (HERE AND ELSEWHERE) 2112
IDOL DANCER, THE 865

IF . . .   990, 1001, 1562, 1923
IF I WERE A KING 1919
IF YOU LOVE THIS PLANET 288
IKERU SHIKABNE (THE LIVING CORPSE) 1740
IKH VIL ZAYN A MAME (I WANT TO BE A MOTHER) 829
IKIRU (LIVING) 2018, 2019, 2021, 2028, 2030
ILLEGALS, THE 290
ILLUSION TRAVELS BY STREETCAR (LA ILLUSION VIAJA EN TRANVIA) 1723
ILLUSION VIAJA EN TRANVIA, LA (ILLUSION TRAVELS BY STREETCAR) 1723
IMA HITOTABI NO (ONCE MORE) 2017
IMAGE BEFORE MY EYES 290
IMAGES 1176
IMITATION OF LIFE (1934) 551, 793, 863, 876, 915, 916, 939, 944, 1970
IMITATION OF LIFE (1959) 793, 863, 884, 980, 1970
IMMIGRANT, THE 1416
IMMORTAL ONE, THE (L'IMMORTELLE) 2140
IMMORTAL SERGEANT 328
IMMORTELLE, L' (IMMORTAL ONE, THE) 2140
IMPORTANCE OF BEING EARNEST, THE 1841, 1937
IMPOSSIBLE OBJECT (L'IMPOSSIBLE OJECT) 2051
IMPOSSIBLE OJECT, L' (IMPOSSIBLE OBJECT) 2051
IN A LONELY PLACE 1136, 1968
IN CALIENTE 1797
IN COLD BLOOD 580, 605, 2038
IN COUNTRY 338
IN DARK PLACES: REMEMBERING THE HOLOCAUST 289, 334
IN HARM'S WAY 331
IN OLD CHICAGO 1090
IN OLD KENTUCKY 1380
IN POLISH WOODS (IN POYLISHE VELDER) 847
IN POYLISHE VELDER (IN POLISH WOODS) 847
IN THE BEGINNING 1598
IN THE CZAR'S NAME 827
IN THE HEAT OF THE NIGHT 143, 805, 888, 894, 895, 896, 905, 916, 945, 1165,
  2036, 2038, 2082
IN THE NAVY 329
IN THE YEAR OF THE PIG 290
IN THIS OUR LIFE 1305
IN WHICH WE SERVE 331, 353, 371, 1860, 1861, 1938
INCHON 334
INCREDIBLE SHRINKING MAN, THE 410, 419
INCREDIBLY STRANGE CREATURES WHO STOPPED LIVING AND BECAME
  MIXED-UP ZOMBIES, THE 418
INDIA 1883
INDIANA JONES AND THE LAST CRUSADE 762, 2200
INDIANA JONES AND THE TEMPLE OF DOOM 2200, 2201
INDUSTRIAL BRITAIN 214, 244, 306
INDUSTRIAL SYMPHONY/PHILIPS-RADIO 314
INEZ FROM HOLLYWOOD 1248
INFIDELITY 1122, 1123, 1217
INFORMER, THE 44, 400, 461, 916, 941, 1019, 1064, 1169, 1309
INGEBORG HOLM 1625, 1628
INHERIT THE WIND (1960) 560
INHUMAINE, L' (THE INHUMAN) 1713
INHUMAN, THE (L'INHUMAINE) 1713
INN IN OSAKA, AN (OSAKA NO YADO) 2018
INNOCENTE, L' (INNOCENT) 1884
INNOCENTS, THE 1324

INNOCENT, THE (L'INNOCENTE) 1884
INSECTS AS CARRIERS OF DISEASE 418
INSIDE DAISY CLOVER 1137
INSIDE NAZI GERMANY-1938 227, 302
INSIDE NORTH VIETNAM 290
INSIDE THE THIRD REICH 287, 331
INSIDE VIETNAM 290
INTERIORS 530, 2045, 2072, 2208
INTERNATIONAL LADY 329
INTERNATIONAL SQUADRON 329, 357
INTERVIEW WITH MY LAI VETERANS 290
INTOLERANCE 825, 1367, 1373, 1374, 1375, 1378, 1379, 1382, 1385, 1386, 1388,
  1409, 1514, 1527, 1576, 1578, 1608, 1646, 1657, 1662, 1666, 1740
INTRUDER IN THE DUST 569, 882, 883, 884, 887, 916, 931, 935, 944, 1037,
  1208, 1315, 1321, 1946
INTRUDER, THE 935, 945
INVADER FROM MARS 418, 1946
INVASION OF THE BODY SNATCHERS (1956) 183, 270, 334, 397, 410, 412, 417,
  418, 2035, 2061
INVASION OF THE BODY SNATCHERS, THE (1978) 183
INVASION QUARTET 330
INVISIBLE MAN, THE 1919
INVISIBLE MAN, THE film series 421
IR TSYVEYTE MAME (HER SECOND MOTHER) 829
IRMA LA DOUCE 1971
IRON CURTAIN, THE 334, 348, 357
IRON EAGLES 904
IRON HORSE, THE 192, 193, 1704
IRON MASK, THE 1401, 1406
IS MONEY EVERYTHING? 1373
IS PARIS BURNING? 57, 254, 330
ISADORA 2036
ISHTAR 535, 2201
ISLAND IN THE SUN 884, 885, 886, 945, 1091, 1251, 1500
ISLAND OF LOST SOULS 874
ISLAND OF THE BLUE DOLPHINS 996
ISLAND WOMAN (SHIMA NO ONNA) 1740
ISLANDS IN THE STREAM 1231, 2067
ISLE OF THE DEAD 1912
ISN'T LIFE WONDERFUL 328, 1389
ISPANIYA (SPAIN) 287
IT 503
IT CAME FROM BENEATH THE SEA 411
IT CAME FROM OUTER SPACE (1953) 1946
IT HAPPENED HERE 330
IT HAPPENED ONE NIGHT 556, 623, 809, 1073, 1311, 1469, 1799
IT LIVES AGAIN 414
IT STARTED IN NAPLES 984
IT'S A WONDERFUL LIFE 569, 1160
IT'S ALIVE! THE CLASSIC CINEMA SAGA OF FRANKENSTEIN 389, 976
IT'S ALWAYS FAIR WEATHER 401, 2036
IT'S GRITS 913
ITALIAN STRAW HAT, THE (UN CHAPEAU DE PAILLE D'ITALIE) 1728
IVAN 1655
IVAN GROZNY II (IVAN THE TERRIBLE PART II) 1658
IVAN GROZNY (IVAN THE TERRIBLE) 477, 1153, 1658, 1661, 1866, 1867, 1868
IVAN THE TERRIBLE PART II (IVAN GROZNY II) 1658
IVAN THE TERRIBLE (IVAN GROZNY) 477, 1153, 1658, 1661, 1866, 1867, 1868
I. F. STONE'S WEEKLY 288

J

J'ACCUSE (I ACCUSE) 833, 1712
JACK ARMSTRONG, THE ALL AMERICAN BOY 1457
JACKIE ROBINSON STORY, THE 884
JACKNIFE 338
JACOB, DER LUGNER (JACOB, THE LIAR) 334
JACOB, THE LIAR (JACOB, DER LUGNER) 334
JAGGED EDGE 680, 2201, 2207
JAMAICA INN 1838
JAMES BOND film series 420, 421
JAMES DEAN STORY, THE 1246
JANE EYRE 1147, 1305, 1312, 1317, 1790
JANE SHORE 1612
JANIE 975
JANIE'S JANIE 505, 512
JANIS--THE WAY SHE WAS 1138
JANSENOVAC 289
JAPANESE TRAGEDY, A (NIHON NO HIGEKI) 2018
JAPANESE WAR BRIDE 334
JAPAN: A NEW DAWN OVER ASIA 287
JAWS 399, 414, 553, 554, 558, 611, 668, 781, 820, 985, 1514, 2197, 2200
JAWS OF JUSTICE 399
JAWS series 2200
JAZZ SINGER, THE (1927) 59, 407, 632, 805, 825, 827, 842, 872, 908, 943,
  987, 1276, 1498, 1499, 1500, 1746, 1797
JAZZ SINGER, THE (1981) 841
JE T'AIME, JE T'AIME (1968) 2139
JEAN DE FLORETTE 2 1538
JEANNE DIELMAN, 23 QUAI DU COMMERCE, 1080 BRUXELLES 501, 512
JEDER FUR SICH UND GOTT GEGEN ALLE (EVERY MAN FOR HIMSELF AND
  GOD AGAINST ALL) 2166
JENNY LAMOUR (QUAI DES ORFEVRES) 2000
JEREMIAH JOHNSON 1155, 2065, 2199
JEREMY 996
JERICHO MILE, THE 421
JESSE JAMES 1252, 1253, 1256, 1500, 1779
JESTER, THE (DER PURIMSPILER) 846, 848
JESUS CHRIST SUPERSTAR 160, 1530
JESUS OF NAZARETH 383
JET ATTACK 334
JETEE, LA 2115
JETZT . . . NACH SO VIELEN JAHREN (NOW . . . AFTER ALL THESE
  YEARS) 289
JEUNNE FILLE, LA (THE YOUNG ONE) 1094
JEUX INTERDITS, LES (FORBIDDEN GAMES) 331, 377, 1923, 1995, 2008
JEW SUSS (JUD SUSS) 218, 240, 257, 1906
JEWEL IN THE CROWN, THE 548
JEWEL OF THE NILE, THE 761, 2202
JEZEBEL 638, 857, 912, 944, 1439, 1915
JIGOKUMON (GATE OF HELL) 2019, 2029
JIM THORPE, ALL AMERICAN 421
JOAN OF ARC 589
JOB, THE 2172
JOE 558, 2038
JOE BUTTERFLY 340
JOE LOUIS STORY, THE 884
JOE SMITH, AMERICAN 331

JOHN HUSTON: THE MAN, THE MOVIES, THE MAVERICK 61, 1915
JOHNNY ANGEL 1948
JOHNNY GOT HIS GUN 328, 342, 343, 1530
JOHNNY GUITAR 197, 198, 589, 1968, 1984
JOHNNY O'CLOCK 1969
JOLI MAI, LE 2116, 2152
JOLSON SINGS AGAIN 401, 831, 1089
JOLSON STORY, THE 401, 831, 1089, 1189, 1244, 1245, 1247, 1293
JOSEPH ANDREWS 1312
JOSEPH MCCARTHY 288
JOUR DE FETE (FRANCOIS THE POSTMAN) 2000, 2001
JOUR DES PARQUES, LE (RUPTURE) 2101
JOUR ET L'HEURE, L' (THE DAY AND THE HOUR) 330
JOUR SE LEVE, LE (DAYBREAK/THE LONG NIGHT) 353, 1714, 1813, 1816, 1825
JOURNAL D'UN CURE DE CAMPAGNE, LE (THE DIARY OF A COUNTRY
  PRIEST) 751, 1310, 1994, 2008
JOURNAL D'UN SCELERAT 2103
JOURNEY FOR MARGARET 272
JOURNEY INTO FEAR 1751, 1789
JOURNEY THROUGH ROSEBUD, A 338
JOURNEY TO THE SUN 917
JOURNEY'S END 261, 328, 343, 568, 1834
JOYCE AT 34 505
JOYFUL KNOWLEDGE (LE GAI SAVOIR) 2111
JOYLESS STREET, THE (DIE FREUDLOSE GASSE) 342, 1632, 1643
JUAREZ 1288, 1800, 1915
JUD SUSS (JEW SUSS) 218, 240, 257, 1906
JUDAS WAS A WOMAN (LA BETE HUMAINE) 353
JUDEX 1605
JUDGMENT AT NUREMBERG 311, 331, 334, 377, 560, 837, 841
JUDGMENT OF THE NATIONS (SUD NARADOV) 289
JUDITH OF BETHULIA 1370, 1389, 1608
JUGGLER, THE 832
JUJIRO (SHADOWS OF THE YOSHIWARA/JUJIRO) 1742
JULES AND JIM (JULES ET JIM) 138, 1310, 2036, 2107, 2120, 2145, 2146, 2155,
  2156
JULES ET JIM (JULES AND JIM) 138, 1310, 2036, 2107, 2120, 2145, 2146, 2155,
  2156
JULIA 331, 485, 512, 551, 803, 841, 1225, 1227, 1228, 1322, 2199
JULIET OF THE SPIRITS (GIULIETTA DELGI SPIRITI) 593, 1929, 1930, 2171
JULIUS CAESAR (1953) 1269, 1354
JUMPING JACK FLASH 904
JUNGFRUKALLAN (THE VIRGIN SPRING) 2183, 2186, 2187
JUNGLE BOOK, THE 1833, 1860
JUNGLE FIGHTERS 331
JUNGLE JIM film series 420, 986
JUNGLEFIGHTERS 332
JUNIOR BONNER 2061
JUNIOR MISS 975
JUPITER'S THUNDERBOLTS 1619
JUST BETWEEN FRIENDS 2207
JUST GREAT (TOUT VA BIEN) 2111, 2126
JUST TELL ME WHAT YOU WANT 1136, 1293
JUSTE AVANT LA NUIT 2101
JUVE CONTRE FANTOMAS (JUVE VS. FANTOMAS) 1617
JUVE VS. FANTOMAS (JUVE CONTRE FANTOMAS) 1617
J. R. OPPENHEIMER AND THE ATOMIC BOMB 288

K

KABINETT DES DR. CALIGARI, DAS (THE CABINET OF DR. CALIGARI) 388,
  579, 1308, 1576, 1632, 1635, 1643
KAGEMUSHA (SHADOW WARRIOR) 2019, 2020, 2027
KAISER--BEAST OF BERLIN, THE 327
KAISER'S FINISH, THE 213
KAKITA AKANISHI (AKANISHI KAKITA) 1888
KAKUSHI-TORIDE NO SANAKUNIN (THE HIDDEN FORTRESS) 2019, 2027
KAMERADSCHAFT (COMRADESHIP) 1829
KAMIKAZE 287
KANAL 311, 334
KANAL (SEWER) 2014, 2180
KANNIBAL KAPERS 874
KAPO 289
KARAKURI MUSUME (TRICKY GIRL) 1740
KARATE KID III, THE 762
KARATE KID II, THE 2202
KARATE KID series, THE 2200
KARLEK OCH JOURNALISTIK (LOVE AND JOURNALISM) 1624, 1628
KARMA 338
KAROL LIR (KING LEAR) 1343, 1355
KAZE NO NAKA NO KODOMO (CHILDREN IN THE WIND) 1892
KEEP 'EM FLYING 329
KEEP AN EYE ON AMELIA! (OCCUPE-TOI D'AMELIE!) 1993
KEEP PUNCHING 929
KEEPER OF THE FLAME 331, 568, 1279, 1280
KEEPING COMPANY 1089
KELLY'S HEROES 330, 378
KENNEDY 334
KERMESSE HEROIQUE, LA (CARNIVAL IN FLANDERS) 1812
KEY LARGO 331, 1915
KEYS OF THE KINGDOM, THE 419, 1269
KHAZNS ZUNDL, DEM (THE CANTOR'S SON) 848
KID GALAHAD 1497
KID, THE 984, 1416, 1465, 1527
KILLER ELITE, THE 2061
KILLER OF SHEEP 901
KILLER'S KISS 2057
KILLERS, THE (1946) 191, 384, 387, 1231
KILLERS, THE (1964) 384, 1231
KILLER! (THIS MAN MUST DIE/QUE LA BETE MEURE) 2098, 2101
KILLING FIELDS, THE 151, 338, 472, 539, 802, 1174, 1530
KILLING OF A CHINESE BOOKIE, THE 2048
KILLING OF SISTER GEORGE, THE 2043
KILLING, THE 2035, 2055, 2056, 2057
KIND HEARTS AND CORONETS 1937, 1940, 1942
KINDER AUS NO. 67, DIE (THE CHILDREN FROM NUMBER 67) 334
KING AND COUNTRY 327, 343, 371
KING AND I, THE 886, 2053
KING DAVID 62
KING IN NEW YORK, A 1418, 1424, 1431
KING KONG (1933) 411, 417, 556, 599, 700, 874, 1169, 1576, 1577, 1748, 1800
KING KONG (1977) 414
KING LEAR (KAROL LIR) 1343, 1355
KING OF HEARTS (LE ROI DE COEUR) 328, 392, 1530
KING OF KINGS (1927) 382, 1449, 1702
KING OF THE HUNS (AMERICA MUST CONQUER) 213

KING OF THE NEWSBOYS 1071
KING OF THE ROARING TWENTIES 833
KING RAT 196, 331, 374
KING SOLOMON'S MINES (1937) 919, 1569
KING SOLOMON'S MINES (1950) 919
KING SOLOMON'S MINES (1985) 919
KINGS GO FORTH 330
KINOGLAZ 1664
KINONEDELIA newsreels 1664
KINOPRAVDA 1663, 1664, 1668
KISMET 1784
KISS 2040, 2068
KISS ME DEADLY 384, 2043, 2071, 2072
KISS OF DEATH 1952
KISS, THE 2037
KISS, THE (1896) 1617
KITTY FOYLE 1202, 1282, 1284, 1305
KITTY: RETURN TO AUSCHWITZ 289, 311
KLUTE 507, 508, 516, 558, 799, 2192
KLYATSHE, DI (THE DOBBIN/THE LIGHT AHEAD/FISHKE DER KRUMER) 829
KNIFE IN THE WATER (NOZ W WODZIE) 2179
KNIGHTRIDERS 390
KNOCK ON ANY DOOR 1968
KNOW YOUR ENEMY--JAPAN 281, 1897
KNUTE ROCKNE, ALL AMERICAN 421, 989, 1497
KOHAYAGAWA-KE NO AKI (THE END OF SUMMER) 2024
KOLBERG 240, 251
KOLCHAK: THE NIGHT STALKER 414
KONGI'S HARVEST 899, 937
KONYETS SANKT-PETERBURGA (THE END OF ST. PETERSBURG) 1668
KORKARLEN (THE PHANTOM CHARIOT) 1625, 1630
KOSHIKEI (DEATH BY HANGING) 2025
KOYAANISQATSI 598
KRAJOBRAZ PO BITWIE (LANDSCAPE AFTER BATTLE) 334
KRAMER VS. KRAMER 110, 111, 484, 501, 666, 680, 787, 971, 1007, 1046, 1530
KRIEMHILD'S REVENGE 1631
KRIS (CRISIS) 2183
KUDZU 913
KUMONOSU-JO (THRONE OF BLOOD/COBWEB CASTLE) 1356, 2019, 2021
KURUTTA IPPEIJI (PAGE OF MADNESS/A CRAZY PAGE/A PAGE OUT OF
  ORDER) 1742, 1744
KWAIDAN 410

L

L'CHAIM--TO LIFE 289
LACOMBE, LUCIEN 311, 334, 377, 2119
LADIES OF THE BOIS DE BOULOGNE, THE (LES DAMES DU BOIS DE
  BOULOGNE) 1994, 1995, 1996
LADRI DI BICICLETTE (BICYCLE THIEVES) 44, 144, 1004, 1576, 1926, 1928,
  1932
LADY AND THE TRAMP 1530
LADY EVE, THE 150, 1912, 1919, 1920, 1921
LADY FROM SHANGHAI, THE 384, 504, 505, 1790, 1791, 1948
LADY GAMBLES, THE 791
LADY IN ERMINE, THE 1276
LADY IN THE DARK 521, 523, 1336
LADY IN THE LAKE, THE 1197

LADY OF THE PAVEMENTS 1371
LADY SINGS THE BLUES 899, 938
LADY VANISHES, THE (1938) 1838, 1843, 1853
LADY WINDERMERE'S FAN 1694, 1706
LADYBUG, LADYBUG 355
LADYHAWKE 2200
LADYKILLERS, THE 1937
LAFAYETTE ESCADRILLE 261, 327
LAMB, THE 1399, 1404, 1406
LANCELOT DU LAC (LANCELOT OF THE LAKE) 2003
LANCELOT OF THE LAKE (LANCELOT DU LAC) 2003
LAND DES SCHWEIGENS UND DER DUNKELHEIT (LAND OF SILENCE AND
  DARKNESS) 2166
LAND OF LIBERTY, PART 5 287
LAND OF SILENCE AND DARKNESS (LAND DES SCHWEIGENS UND DER
  DUNKELHEIT) 2166
LAND OF THE PHARAOHS 1207
LAND WITHOUT BREAD (LES HURDES) 303, 1721, 1989
LANDRU (BLUEBEARD) 2100, 2128
LANDSCAPE AFTER BATTLE (KRAJOBRAZ PO BITWIE) 334
LAND, THE 1681
LAOS, THE FORGOTTEN WAR 290
LAS VEGAS STORY, THE 791, 1099
LASKEY JEDNE PLAVOVLASKY (THE LOVES OF A BLONDE) 2164
LASSIE COME HOME 1094
LAST AMERICAN HERO, THE 409, 421
LAST AMERICAN VIRGIN, THE 976
LAST ANGRY MAN, THE 833, 1020
LAST BLITZKREIG, THE 330
LAST CHAPTER, THE 290
LAST DETAIL, THE 362, 1469
LAST EMPEROR, THE 331
LAST EPIDEMIC 288
LAST ESCAPE, THE 330
LAST FLIGHT, THE 328
LAST GRAVE AT DIMBAZA 917
LAST HURRAH, THE 1500, 1501
LAST LAUGH, THE (DER LETZE MANN) 584, 595, 726, 1632, 1642, 1706, 1714
LAST METRO, THE (LE DERNIER METRO) 334, 2107, 2143
LAST OF THE MOBILE HOT-SHOTS 1347
LAST OF THE MOHICANS, THE (1936) 1203
LAST PICTURE SHOW, THE 913, 996, 1530, 2193
LAST SEA, THE 289, 290
LAST STOP, THE (OSTANTI ETAP) 334
LAST SUNSET, THE 2043
LAST TANGO IN PARIS 150, 2192, 2200
LAST TRAIN FROM GUN HILL, THE 806
LAST TRAIN FROM MADRID, THE 272, 568
LAST TYCOON, THE 1041, 1261, 1293
LAST WAVE, THE 596
LAST WILL OF DR. MABUSE, THE (DAS TESTAMENT DES DR. MABUSE) 1829
LAST WOMAN ON EARTH, THE 2049
LAST YEAR AT MARIENBAD (L'ANNEE DERNIERE A MARIENBAD) 150, 539,
  579, 1317, 2118, 2124, 2137, 2139, 2140, 2152
LATE CHRYSANTHEMUM, THE (BANGIKU) 2019
LATE GEORGE APLEY, THE 1203, 1271
LATE SHOW, THE 381
LATE SPRING (BANSHUN) 2017, 2031

LAUGHTER 1279
LAURA 400, 461, 1073, 1500, 1966, 1967
LAVENDER HILL MOB, THE 1937, 1942
LAW OF NATURE, THE 947
LAWLESS, THE 569
LAWRENCE OF ARABIA 267, 327, 1036, 1861, 2032
LAWYER MAN 555
LAZY RIVER 1213
LEADBELLY 899
LEARNING TREE, THE 894, 896, 900, 936, 2038
LEAVE HER TO HEAVEN 590, 791
LEAVE ME ALONE (EMAK BAKIA) 1713, 1730
LEAVE ON WORD OF HONOUR (URLAUB AUF EHRENWORT) 240
LEAVES FROM SATAN'S BOOK (BLADE AF SATANS BOG) 1626
LEBEN ADOLF HITLER, DAS (THE LIFE OF ADOLF HITLER) 287, 339
LEDA (DOUBLE TOUR/WEB OF PASSION) 2100, 2128
LEFT-HANDED GUN, THE 810, 2064, 2065
LEGACY OF THE BLACKLIST 1949
LEGEND OF LYLAH CLARE, THE 1094, 1137, 2043
LEGION OF TERROR 568
LEGIONS OF THE NILE 383
LENINGRAD AT WAR (LENINGRAD V. BORBE) 287
LENINGRAD V. BORBE (LENINGRAD AT WAR) 287
LEON MORIN, PETRE (LEON MORIN, PRIEST) 2000
LEON MORIN, PRIEST (LEON MORIN, PETRE) 2000
LEOPARD, THE (IL GATTOPARDO) 277, 1884
LET GEORGE DO IT 1938
LET KATY DO IT 1384
LET THERE BE LIGHT 140, 284, 287, 598, 1911, 1915
LET'S DO IT AGAIN 889
LET'S SCARE JESSICA TO DEATH 976
LETHAL WEAPON 904, 2205
LETHAL WEAPON II 762
LETTER FROM AN UNKNOWN WOMAN 119, 1262, 1946, 1983, 2007
LETTER FROM SIBERIA (LETTRE DE SIBERIE) 2115
LETTER TO JANE (LETTRE A JANE) 2111
LETTER TO THREE WIVES, A 521, 1269, 1500, 1952
LETTER, THE 1262, 1439
LETTRE A JANE (LETTER TO JANE) 2111
LETTRE DE SIBERIE (LETTER FROM SIBERIA) 2115
LETYAT ZHURAVLI (THE CRANES ARE FLYING) 1001
LETZE MANN, DER (THE LAST LAUGH) 584, 595, 726, 1632, 1642, 1714
LEVI AND COHEN--THE IRISH COMEDIANS 840
LIAISONS DANGEREUSES, LES 1310, 1317
LIBE UN LAYDNSHAFT (LOVE AND PASSION/LOVE AND SACRIFICE) 829
LIBERATION OF AUSCHWITZ, THE 289
LIBERATION OF L. B. JONES, THE 894, 923, 945, 2038
LIED DER STROME, DAS (SONG OF THE RIVERS) 312
LIES MY FATHER TOLD ME 841
LIFE AND DEATH OF COLONEL BLIMP, THE 202, 1569
LIFE AND TIMES OF JOHN HUSTON, ESQUIRE, THE 1915
LIFE AND TIMES OF JUDGE ROY BEAN, THE 1916, 2199
LIFE AND TIMES OF ROSIE THE RIVETER 287, 318
LIFE OF A WOMAN, THE (SAIKAKU ICHIDAI/THE LIFE OF OHARU) 2019
LIFE OF ADOLF HITLER, THE (DAS LEBEN ADOLF HITLER) 287, 339
LIFE OF AN AMERICAN FIREMAN, THE 1605, 1620
LIFE OF BANGOKU, THE (BANGOKU NO ISSHO) 1889
LIFE OF BRIAN 1530
LIFE OF DON JUAN, THE 1401

LIFE OF EMILE ZOLA, THE 840, 1015, 1221, 1288, 1800
LIFE OF JIMMY DOLAN, THE 556
LIFE OF LOUIS PASTEUR, THE 1221, 1288
LIFE OF OHARU, THE (THE LIFE OF A WOMAN/SAIKAKU ICHIDAI) 2019
LIFE WITH FATHER 1160, 1279
LIFEBOAT 331, 881, 939, 1281, 1847, 1852, 1911, 1913
LIGHT AHEAD, THE (DI KLYATSHE/THE DOBBIN/FISHKE DER KRUMER) 829
LIGHT IN THE PIAZZA 404
LIGHT THAT FAILED, THE 1305
LIGHTNING OVER WATER 1968
LIGHTS OF NEW YORK 1797
LIGHTS OUT IN EUROPE 287
LIGNE DE DEMARCATION, LA (THE LINE OF DEMARCATION) 2098, 2128
LILAC TIME 328, 1695
LILI MARLEEN 331, 334
LILIES OF THE FIELD 887, 891, 894, 946, 952
LILITH 1091, 1969, 1985
LILOM 1637
LIMBO 338
LIMELIGHT 1418, 1426, 1432, 1689
LINCOLN'S DREAM (THE BIRTH OF A RACE) 867, 926, 949
LINE OF DEMARCATION, THE (LA LIGNE DE DEMARCATION) 2098, 2128
LION AND THE EAGLE, THE, PARTS 1 & 2 287
LION IN WINTER, THE 2036
LION'S LOVE 516, 562, 2114
LIPSTICK 787, 788, 1115
LISA 334, 841
LISTEN TO BRITAIN 287, 316
LITTLE AMERICAN, THE 209, 328, 342
LITTLE ANNIE ROONEY 1392, 1393
LITTLE BIG MAN 425, 428, 433, 558, 811, 1320, 2064, 2065, 2193, 2194
LITTLE CAESAR 191, 384, 385, 387, 555, 1071, 1240, 1288, 1403, 1516, 1748,
  1804
LITTLE DRUMMER GIRL, THE 2052
LITTLE FOXES, THE 858, 1225, 1275, 1348, 1439, 1472, 1913
LITTLE GIANT 1476
LITTLE LETTER TO MAMA, A (A BRIVELE DER MAMEN) 846, 848
LITTLE LORD FAUNTLEROY 1392, 1393
LITTLE MATCH GIRL, THE (LA PETITE MARCHANDE D'ALLUMETTES) 1814
LITTLE MOTHER (MAMELE) 846, 848
LITTLE NIGHT MUSIC, A 403
LITTLE NIKITA 890
LITTLE ORPHAN ANNIE 1071
LITTLE PRINCESS, THE 1392, 1775
LITTLE PRINCE, THE 416
LITTLE REBEL, THE 857
LITTLE ROMANCE, A 2052, 2053
LITTLE SHOP OF HORRORS (1986) 1530, 2075, 2199
LITTLE SHOP OF HORRORS, THE (1960) 419, 2049, 2075
LITTLE SOLDIER, THE (LE PETIT SOLDAT) 2134
LITTLE THIEF, THE (LA PETITE VOLEUSE) 2106
LITTLE WOMEN 521
LITTLEST REBEL, THE 916, 944
LIVE AND LET DIE 422
LIVES OF A BENGAL LANCER 218, 1833
LIVES OF PERFORMERS 505, 512
LIVING CORPSE, THE (IKERU SHIKABNE) 1740
LIVING DESERT, THE 1951

LIVING (IKIRU) 2018, 2019, 2021, 2028, 2030
LLOYDS OF LONDON 218
LOCAL HERO 802
LODGER, THE 1838, 1843, 1851, 1858
LODZ GHETTO 290
LOG OF THE U-35, THE 285
LOIN DU VIETNAM (FAR FROM VIETNAM) 290, 2116, 2118
LOLA MONTES 2000, 2007, 2009
LOLITA 150, 558, 981, 1272, 1273, 2036, 2055, 2057
LONDON AFTER MIDNIGHT 1679
LONDON CAN TAKE IT 287, 309, 316
LONE RANGER, THE 811
LONELINESS OF THE LONG DISTANCE RUNNER, THE 985, 997
LONELY ARE THE BRAVE 1282, 1283, 1285
LONELY VILLA, THE 1366, 1379, 1389, 1618
LONELYHEARTS 154
LONESDALE OPERATOR, THE 405, 1366
LONESOME COWBOYS 2068
LONG DAY'S DYING, THE 330
LONG DAY'S JOURNEY INTO NIGHT (1962) 1337, 1341, 1350, 2058
LONG GOODBYE, THE 1176, 1197, 2194
LONG HOT SUMMER, THE 1212
LONG RIDERS, THE 428
LONG SHIPS, THE 888
LONG VOYAGE HOME, THE 1341, 1685
LONGEST DAY, THE 231, 254, 262, 331, 345, 354, 361, 806, 1499, 1500
LONGEST YARD, THE 2043
LOOK BACK IN ANGER 790, 1569, 1939
LOOKING FOR MR. GOODBAR 604, 668, 1032
LOONY TOM 1974
LORD FOR A NIGHT (ARUYO NO TONOSAMA) 2017
LORD JIM 1317
LORD OF THE FLIES 1001
LORDS OF FLATBUSH, THE 984, 2193
LOSER TAKES ALL 1219
LOSERS, THE 338
LOSIN' IT 977
LOST BOUNDARIES 301, 569, 859, 882, 883, 887, 931, 935, 944, 1946
LOST COMMAND, THE 338, 359
LOST HONOR OF KATHARINA BLUM, THE (DIE VERLORENE EHRE DER
 KATHARINA BLUM) 1310
LOST HORIZON (1937) 59, 460, 1073, 1169, 1328, 1799
LOST IN THE STARS 1034
LOST MAN, THE 888, 945
LOST PATROL, THE 328, 1064
LOST WEEKEND, THE 194, 569, 597, 1095, 1911, 1946, 1952, 1971, 1972, 1987
LOTTE INTALIA (LUTTES EN ITALIE/STRUGGLE IN ITALY) 2111
LOTTERY, THE 1312
LOUISIANA STORY 1681
LOVE AND ANARCHY (FILM D'AMORE E D'ANARCHINA) 2172
LOVE AND DEATH 2045
LOVE AND JOURNALISM (KARLEK OCH JOURNALISTIK) 1624, 1628
LOVE AND PASSION (LIBE UN LAYDNSHAFT/LOVE AND SACRIFICE) 829
LOVE AND SACRIFICE (LIBE UN LAYDNSHAFT/LOVE AND PASSION) 829
LOVE AT TWENTY (L'AMOUR A VINGT ANS) 2148
LOVE BUG, THE 960
LOVE IS A MANY-SPLENDORED THING 334, 1952
LOVE LETTERS 793
LOVE ME OR LEAVE ME 1247

LOVE ON THE RUN (L'AMOUR EN FUITE) 2148
LOVE PARADE, THE 1694
LOVE STORY 558, 2191, 2193
LOVE STORY (DOUCE) 1904
LOVE STREAMS 2048
LOVE UNDER FIRE 278
LOVED ONE, THE 1041, 1294
LOVEJOY'S NUCLEAR WAR 288
LOVER COME BACK 1176
LOVERS, THE 790, 2119
LOVERS, THE (LES AMANTS) 2094
LOVES OF A BLONDE (LASKEY JEDNE PLAVOVLASKY) 2164
LOVES OF MADAME DE, THE (MADAME DE . . .) 497, 2000, 2007
LOVING 516
LOWELL THOMAS REMEMBERS; (6 FILMS, 1939-1944) 287
LOWER DEPTHS, THE (DONZOKO) 2019
LOWER DEPTHS, THE (LES BAS-FONDS) 353, 1813, 1814
LUCAS 972, 997
LUCH SMERTI (THE DEATH RAY) 1653
LUCI DEL VARIETA (VARIETY LIGHTS) 1929
LUCIA 497, 526
LUCIANO SERRA, PILOTA 1883
LUCKY LADY 536, 2200
LUMIERE D'ETE (SUMMER LIGHT) 1904
LUST FOR LIFE 1015
LUSTIGEN WEIBER VON WINDSOR, DIE (THE MERRY WIVES OF WINDSOR) 1355
LUTHER 1034
LUTTES EN ITALIE (STRUGGLE IN ITALY/LOTTE INTALIA) 2111
LYDIA BAILEY 791, 885

M

M 144, 1635, 1639, 1641, 1829, 1830
MA NUIT CHEZ MAUD (MY NIGHT AT MAUD'S) 598, 2104, 2105
MABEL'S DRAMATIC CAREER 1413
MACARTHUR 254, 331, 339
MACBETH (1916) 1385
MACBETH (1948) 1342, 1355, 1790, 1791
MACBETH (1971) 1337, 1355
MACHI NO IREZUMI MONO (THE VILLAGE TATTOOED MAN) 1889
MACHI NO TEJINASHI (THE STREET JUGGLER) 1742
MACHINE GUN KELLY 2049
MACK SENNETT PROGRAM 1413
MACOMBER AFFAIR, THE 421, 1231
MAD LOVE 417
MAD WOMAN OF CHAILLOT, THE 2148
MADAME BOVARY 1309, 1317
MADAME CURIE 1122, 1124, 1217
MADAME DE . . . (THE LOVES OF MADAME DE) 497, 2000, 2007
MADAME DUBARRY (PASSION) 1631, 1642
MADAME SANS-GENE 1618
MADAMU TO NYOBO (THE NEIGHBOUR'S WIFE AND MINE) 1888
MADE FOR EACH OTHER 834, 835
MADE IN U. S. A. 562
MADELEINE 1860
MADIGAN 1094, 1100, 2035
MAE WEST 1136

MAEDCHEN IN UNIFORM (GIRLS IN UNIFORM) 495, 1829, 1923
MAGIC 598
MAGIC LANTERN, THE 1619
MAGIC OF MELIES 1619
MAGICIAN, THE (THE FACE/ANSIKTET) 2183, 2184, 2186
MAGNETIC MONSTER, THE 418
MAGNIFICENT AMBERSONS, THE 1169, 1305, 1327, 1751, 1789, 1791, 1794
MAGNIFICENT OBSESSION (1935) 1970, 1986
MAGNIFICENT OBSESSION (1954) 1970, 1986
MAGNIFICENT SEVEN, THE 193, 199, 2019
MAGNIFICENT YANKEE, THE 1079
MAGNUM FORCE 810
MAID OF THE DEEP MOUNTAINS (MIYAMA NO OTOME) 1739
MAIDEN IN THE STORM (ARASHI NO NAKA NO SHOJO) 1894
MAIN EVENT, THE 421, 676
MAJDANEK 289
MAJOR AND THE MINOR, THE 1971, 1972
MAJOR BARBARA 1344, 1860
MAJOR DUNDEE 893, 894, 945, 2061, 2063, 2087
MAJORITY OF ONE, A 340
MAKES A FACE 516
MAKING LOVE 551, 604
MAKING OF A LEGEND: "GONE WITH THE WIND," THE 812, 1801
MAKING OF BUTCH CASSIDY AND THE SUNDANCE KID, THE 2079
MAKING OF "STAR WARS," THE 813
MALAYA 331
MALE AND FEMALE 1703
MALE ANIMAL, THE 989
MALTESE FALCON, THE (1941) 373, 397, 494, 590, 599, 1086, 1169, 1288, 1347,
 1547, 1914, 1915, 1947, 1948
MAME 407
MAMELE (LITTLE MOTHER) 846, 848
MAN ABOUT TOWN (LE SILENCE EST D'OR/SILENCE IS GOLDEN) 1725, 2000,
 2005
MAN AND A WOMAN, A (UN HOMME ET UNE FEMME) 2135
MAN CALLED HORSE, A 425, 433
MAN FOR ALL SEASONS, A 970, 1020
MAN FROM LARAMIE, THE 198, 1964
MAN HUNT 203, 331, 353, 1637, 1911
MAN I KILLED, THE (BROKEN LULLABY) 328, 343, 568, 1276, 1804
MAN I MARRIED, THE 333
MAN IN THE GLASS BOOTH, THE 312, 334
MAN IN THE GREY FLANNEL SUIT 1252
MAN IN THE MIDDLE 332
MAN IN THE WHITE SUIT, THE 418, 1569, 1937, 1942
MAN OF A THOUSAND FACES 1247
MAN OF ARAN 309, 1153, 1681, 1834, 1841, 1871
MAN OF THE WEST 1964
MAN ON A TIGHTROPE 357, 1081, 1261
MAN WHO CAME TO DINNER, THE 1288
MAN WHO KNEW TOO MUCH, THE (1934) 1834, 1837, 1838, 1843
MAN WHO KNEW TOO MUCH, THE (1956) 1155, 1849, 1851, 1854
MAN WHO LOVED WOMEN, THE (L'HOMME QUI AIMAIT LES FEMMES) 2145
MAN WHO NEVER WAS, THE 373
MAN WHO SHOT LIBERTY VALANCE, THE 62, 117, 194, 199, 894, 1311, 1684,
 1686, 2075
MAN WHO WOULD BE KING, THE 1312, 1916, 2199
MAN WITH A GOLDEN ARM, THE 1949, 1966, 2036
MAN WITH THE GOLDEN GUN 422

MAN WITH THE MOVIE CAMERA, THE (CHELOVEK'S KINOAPPARATOM)   1664,
  1668, 1669
MAN WITH X-RAY EYES, THE   2049
MANCHURIAN CANDIDATE, THE   150, 334, 359, 384, 2036, 2051, 2077, 2078
MANDABI   919
MANDINGO   855, 857, 909
MANDY   1567
MANHANDLED   1401, 1713
MANHATTAN   530, 2045, 2046, 2208
MANHATTAN MELODRAMA   1064, 1269
MANILA CALLING   332
MANON   2000
MANON DES SOURCES (MANON OF THE SPRING)   1538
MANON OF THE SPRING (MANON DES SOURCES)   1538
MANSERVANT   1213
MANSON MASSACRE   418
MAN, THE   938
MARATHON MAN   312, 334, 802, 841, 1151
MARCANTONIO E CLEOPATRA (ANTHONY AND CLEOPATRA)   383
MARCH OF THE YEARS, THE   301
MARCH OF TIME   281, 306, 352, 693
MARGIN FOR ERROR   331
MARIANNE AND JULIANE (DIE BLEIER ZEIT) (THE GERMAN SISTERS)   505
MARIE   680
MARIE ANTOINETTE   1122, 1279
MARIE-CHANTAL CONTRE LE DOCTEUR KHA   2128
MARIJUANA   986
MARINE RAIDERS   331
MARINES, LET'S GO!   334
MARIUS   1809
MARJORIE MORNINGSTAR   833, 834, 842
MARK OF THE HAWK, THE   885
MARK OF ZORRO, THE (1920)   1400, 1407
MARK OF ZORRO, THE (1940)   1073, 1782
MARKED WOMAN   638
MARK, THE   816, 1093
MARLOWE   1197
MARNIE   793, 1835, 1843, 1849, 1854, 1858
MARQUISE D'O . . . , LA (THE MARQUISE OF O)   2105, 2142
MARQUISE OF O, THE (LA MARQUISE D'O . . .)   2105, 2142
MARRIAGE CIRCLE, THE   1694
MARRIAGE OF MARIA BRAUN, THE (DIE EHE DER MARIA BRAUN)   2166
MARRIED WOMAN, A (UNE FEMME MARIEE)   2131
MARRYING KIND, THE   499, 657
MARSEILLAISE, LA   274, 277, 474
MARTIN   390, 399
MARTY   499, 657, 810, 1008, 1370, 1982
MARTYRS OF THE ALAMO   1384
MARY BACKSTAGE, NOBLE WIFE   1457
MARY OF SCOTLAND   1685
MASCULIN FEMININ (MASCULINE FEMININE)   163, 2129
MASCULINE FEMININE (MASCULIN FEMININ)   163, 2129
MASHER, THE   862, 938
MASK   551, 2202
MASK OF THE RED DEATH, THE   2049
MASQUERADE   1151
MASSACRE   556, 1497
MASTER RACE, THE   1089

MAT (MOTHER) 314, 1647, 1663, 1667
MATA HARI 328
MATERNELLE, LA 1811, 1825, 1923
MATEWAN 554
MATT HELM film series 420
MAUPRAT 1722
MAUVAISES RECONTRES, LES 2094
MAX AND HIS DOG (MAX ET SON CHIEN DICK) 1619
MAX AND THE STATUE 1619
MAX ET SON CHIEN DICK (MAX AND HIS DOG) 1619
MAX LEARNS TO SKATE (LES DEBUTS D'UN PATINEUR) 1619
MCCABE AND MRS. MILLER 431, 1176, 2193
MCCONNELL STORY, THE 334
MCKENZIE BREAK, THE 330
ME AND THE COLONEL 805, 833, 1176
MEAN STREETS 2197
MECHANICAL BALLET (BALLET MECANIQUE) 1713, 1717
MEDAL FOR BENNY, A 1281
MEDITATION ON VIOLENCE 1974
MEDIUM COOL 338, 558
MEET JOHN DOE 227, 556, 568, 1073, 1160
MEET ME IN ST. LOUIS 404, 1515, 1784, 1911
MEET NERO WOLFE 1089
MEIN KAMPF 287
MELIES COLOR FILMS 1619
MELINDA 896
MELO 2137
MEMBER OF THE WEDDING, THE 858, 885, 922, 992, 997
MEMORANDUM 323
MEMORIES OF PRISON 2158
MEMORY OF JUSTICE, THE 289, 312, 324
MEMPHIS BELLE 283, 284, 287, 322
MEN IN WAR 334, 883, 1964
MEN OF BRONZE 285, 328
MEN OF THE FIGHTING LADY 334
MEN OF THE LIGHTSHIP 287
MEN WHO TREAD ON THE TIGER'S TAIL, THE (TORO NO O FUMU
   OTOKOTACHI) 2020
MENSCHEN AM SONNTAG (PEOPLE ON SUNDAY) 1971
MEN, THE 331, 376, 1093, 1347, 1946
MEPHISTO 311, 331, 334
MEPHISTO WALTZ, THE 976
MEPRIS, LE (CONTEMPT) 1310, 2110
MERMAID, THE 1619
MERRILL'S MARAUDERS 262, 339, 1960
MERRY GO ROUND 1700
MERRY WIDOW, THE (1925) 1481, 1492, 1698, 1699, 1700
MERRY WIDOW, THE (1934) 401, 1276, 1694
MERRY WIVES OF WINDSOR, THE (DIE LUSTIGEN WEIBER VON WINDSOR) 1355
MERTON OF THE MOVIES (1924) 1059, 1060, 1104, 1111, 1118, 1136, 1139, 1245,
   1246, 1248, 1670
MERTON OF THE MOVIES (1932) 1245, 1670
MERTON OF THE MOVIES (1947) 1245, 1670
MER, LE (THE SEA) 278
MESHES OF THE AFTERNOON 1974
METROPOLIS 187, 410, 417, 1515, 1632, 1638, 1641, 1642
METRO, LE 2128
MEXICAN BUS RIDE (SUBIDA AL CIELO) 1723
MEXICO: THE FROZEN REVOLUTION 917

MICHURIN 1655
MICKEY 1413
MICKEY ONE 2064
MIDDLE OF THE NIGHT, THE 833
MIDNIGHT 1071
MIDNIGHT COWBOY 562, 668, 960, 1090, 1100, 2037
MIDSUMMER NIGHT'S DREAM, A (1935) 1342, 1343
MIDSUMMER NIGHT'S DREAM, A (1969) 1337, 1355
MIDSUMMER NIGHT'S SEX COMEDY, A 2045
MIDWAY 331, 361
MIGHTY JOE YOUNG 411
MILDRED PIERCE 471, 507, 511, 521, 523, 532, 575, 793, 797, 800, 975, 1913, 1948
MILESTONE OF THE CENTURY 287
MILLION DOLLAR LEGS 555, 1268, 1269, 1271, 1800
MILLION, LE (THE MILLION) 1725, 1810, 1825
MILLION, THE (LE MILLION) 1725, 1810, 1825
MIMI METALLURGICO FERITO NELL'ONORE (THE SEDUCTION OF MIMI) 2172
MIN AND BILL 1394, 1395
MIND OF MR. SOAMES, THE 418
MINE OWN EXECUTIONER 1935
MINE YIDDISHE MAME (MY YIDDISH MAMA) 846
MINISTER OF HATE 287
MINISTRY OF FEAR, THE 1219
MINNIE AND MOSKOWITZ 834, 2048
MIRACLE OF MORGAN'S CREEK, THE 1912, 1919, 1921
MIRACLE OF THE BELLS, THE 1090
MIRACLE ON MAIN STREET 1071
MIRACLE WOMAN, THE 1073
MIRACLE WORKER, THE (1962) 1350, 2064
MIRACLE, THE 686, 1949
MIRACLE, THE (IL MIRACOLO) 1929
MIRACOLO, IL (THE MIRACLE) 1929
MISCHIEF MAKERS, THE (LES MISTONS) 2143, 2146
MISE EIRE (I AM IRELAND) 305
MISERABLES, LES 1305
MISERE AU BORINAGE (BORINAGE) 312, 314
MISFITS, THE 421, 428, 554, 657, 1916
MISS JULIE 1337
MISS LULU BETT 1577
MISS NYMPHET'S ZAP-IN 393
MISSILES OF OCTOBER 288, 334
MISSING 454, 566, 772, 1020
MISSING IN ACTION 338, 2200
MISSING IN ACTION II 338, 801
MISSION OVER KOREA 336
MISSION TO MOSCOW 230, 259, 260, 270, 331, 343, 344, 353, 569, 693, 1180, 1187, 1191, 1262, 1263, 1494, 1495, 1577, 1913
MISSION, THE 553
MISSISSIPI MERMAID (LA SIRENE DU MISSISSIPPI) 2145, 2146, 2147
MISSISSIPPI BURNING 255, 905
MISSOURI BREAKS, THE 433, 2064
MISTONS, LES (THE MISCHIEF MAKERS) 2143, 2146
MIYAMA NO OTOME (MAID OF THE DEEP MOUNTAINS) 1739
MIYAMOTO MUSASHI (MUSASHI MIYAMOTO) 2018
MOANA 303, 1564, 1681
MOBY DICK (1956) 1936
MODEL SHOP, THE 562

MODERN MUSKETEER, A 1401
MODERN TIMES 271, 1417, 1432
MODE, A LA 2090
MOGAMBO 1685
MOLE, THE (EL TOPO) 392
MOLLYCODDLE, THE 1407
MOMMIE DEAREST 1136, 1137, 1245
MON ONCLE D'AMERIQUE 2118
MON ONCLE (MY UNCLE) 2000
MONDO BIZARRO 290
MONKEY BUSINESS (1931) 1268
MONOLITH MONSTERS, THE 419
MONSIEUR VERDOUX 160, 194, 494, 1417, 1433
MONSTER FROM THE OCEAN FLOOR 2049
MONTAGNA DI DIO CANNIBALE, IL (SLAVE OF THE CANNIBAL) 419
MONTY PYTHON'S LIFE OF BRIAN 705, 769
MONTY PYTHON'S THE MEANING OF LIFE 152
MOON AND SIXPENCE, THE (1942) 1329
MOON IS BLUE, THE 959, 1370, 1949, 1966, 1984
MOON IS DOWN, THE 331, 1090, 1251, 1252, 1253, 1281
MOON PILOT 488
MOONRAKER 422, 676
MOONSTRUCK 472, 2201, 2207
MORE AMERICAN GRAFFITI 338
MORE THAN A SECRETARY 638
MORITURI (THE SABATOUR: CODE NAME--MORITURI) 330
MORLEY 290
MOROCCO 1788, 1806, 1885
MORTAL STORM, THE 263, 348, 353, 357, 568
MORTE A VENEZIA (DEATH IN VENICE) 1308, 1317, 1884
MOSCOW ON THE HUDSON 2204
MOSCOW STRIKES BACK (THE DEFEAT OF THE GERMAN ARMIES NEAR
 MOSCOW/RAZGROM NEMETZKICH VOISK POD MOSKOVI) 287, 1089
MOSQUITO SQUADRON 330
MOST DANGEROUS MAN ALIVE, THE 1402
MOTHER (MAT) 314, 1647, 1663, 1667
MOTHER (OKAASAN) 2019
MOUCHETTE 2003
MOULIN ROUGE 791, 1916, 1936
MOUNTAIN EAGLE, THE 1837, 1838
MOUNTAIN, THE 421
MOURIR A MADRID (TO DIE IN MADRID) 319
MOURNING BECOMES ELECTRA 1341
MOUTHPIECE, THE 555
MRS. MINIVER 331, 378, 521, 522, 1911
MRS. SOFFEL 802
MR. AND MRS. SMITH 1847
MR. ARKADIN (CONFIDENTIAL REPORT) 1790, 1791
MR. DEEDS GOES TO TOWN 556, 568, 1073, 1469
MR. HULOT'S HOLIDAY (LES VACANCES DE MONSIEUR HULOT) 2000, 2007,
 2010
MR. KLEIN 310, 334
MR. MOTO film series 420, 421
MR. POO (PU-SAN) 2022, 2023
MR. SMITH GOES TO WASHINGTON 64, 556, 568, 985, 1093, 1168, 1169, 1799
MUDDY WATERS (NIGORIE) 2018
MUDE TOD, DER (DESTINY) 1402, 1631, 1641, 1722
MUMMY'S CURSE, THE 1311
MUMMY'S GHOST, THE 1311

MUMMY'S HAND, THE 1311
MUMMY'S REVENGE, THE (LA VENGANZA DE LA MOMIA) 391
MUMMY'S TOMB, THE 1311
MUMMY, THE 1311
MURDER INC. 833
MURDER ON THE ORIENT EXPRESS 2059
MURDERER AMONG US (M) 1830
MURDERERS AMONG US, THE 331
MURDER! 1843, 1851
MURDER, MY SWEET (1944) 494, 738, 1089, 1197, 1201, 1948
MURIEL, OR THE TIME OF A RETURN (MURIEL, OU LE TEMPS D'UN
  RETOUR) 2116, 2118, 2139
MURIEL, OU LE TEMPS D'UN RETOUR (MURIEL, OR THE TIME OF A
  RETURN) 2116, 2118, 2139
MURMUR OF THE HEART (LE SOUFFLE AU COEUR) 2119
MURPHY'S WAR 330
MUSASHI MIYAMOTO (MIYAMOTO MUSASHI) 2018
MUSIC BOX, THE 1690
MUSIC IN AMERICA 320
MUSIC IN THE AIR 1797
MUSIC MAN, THE 403
MUSKETEERS OF PIG ALLEY, THE 387, 1366
MUSSOLINI 287
MUSUME DOJOJI (A GIRL AT THE DOJO TEMPLE) 2022
MUTINY ON THE BOUNTY (1935) 1330, 1481, 1492, 1577
MUTINY ON THE BOUNTY (1962) 1090
MY BEST GIRL 1392, 1393
MY BRILLIANT CAREER 501
MY DARLING CLEMENTINE 194, 199, 1153, 1500, 1684, 1686, 1946, 1952, 1976
MY DINNER WITH ANDRE 2119
MY FAIR LADY 1495
MY FAVORITE BLONDE 1094
MY FAVORITE WIFE 1251
MY FOUR YEARS IN GERMANY 259, 297, 328, 569, 1263, 1494
MY FRIEND FLICKA 1071
MY LIFE TO LIVE (VIVRE SA VIE) 2032
MY MAN GODFREY 568, 1088, 1160
MY NIGHT AT MAUD'S (MA NUIT CHEZ MAUD) 598, 2104, 2105
MY SON JOHN 241, 1949
MY TUTOR 977
MY UNCLE (MON ONCLE) 2000
MY YIDDISH MAMA (MINE YIDDISHE MAME) 846
MYRA BRECKINRIDGE 1041
MYSTERY SEA RAIDER (SUBMARINE ZONE) 329
MYSTIC HOUR, THE 399
MYSTIC PIZZA 2204
MYTHICAL LATIN-AMERICAN KINGDOM STORY 1213
M*A*S*H 334, 359, 379, 558, 1073, 1176, 2191, 2194

N

NADA 2101
NAGARERU (FLOWING) 2019
NAGAYA SHINSHI ROKU (THE RECORD OF A TENEMENT GENTLEMAN) 2017
NAKED AND THE DEAD, THE 233, 331, 841
NAKED CITY, THE 384, 1089, 1948, 1952, 1975
NAKED KISS, THE 1961

NAKED NIGHT, THE (THE CLOWN'S EVENING/SAWDUST AND
 TINSEL/GYCKLARNAS AFTON) 2183, 2187
NAKED PREY, THE 2092
NAKED SPUR, THE 1964
NANA (1927) 1814
NANIWA EREJI (OSAKA ELEGY) 1890
NANNY, THE 984
NANOOK OF THE NORTH 237, 245, 306, 1576, 1681, 1703, 1869
NAPALM 290
NAPOLEON VU PAR ABEL GANCE 1515, 1712, 1726, 1727, 1730
NASHVILLE 138, 912, 914, 1176
NATHALIE GRANGER 505
NATIONAL LAMPOON'S ANIMAL HOUSE 2193
NATIONAL VELVET 1208
NATIVE SON (1951) 923, 944, 945
NATIVE SON (1986) 903, 945
NATTVARDSGASTERNA (WINTER LIGHT/THE COMMUNICANTS) 2186, 2187,
 2188
NATURAL, THE 1174
NATURE'S PLAYMATES 393
NAVE BIANCA, LA (THE WHITE SHIP) 1875, 1883
NAVIGATOR, THE 44, 1688, 1705
NAZARIN 1990
NAZI CONCENTRATION CAMPS 287
NAZI GERMANY: YEARS OF TRIUMPH 287
NAZI HUNTER: THE BEATE KLARSFELD STORY 331
NAZIS STRIKE, THE (WHY WE FIGHT) 287, 320
NEGRO SOLDIER, THE 246, 271, 287, 303, 881, 924
NEIGHBORS 1975
NEIGHBOUR'S WIFE AND MINE, THE (MADAMU TO NYOBO) 1888
NETWORK 2059, 2198
NEVADA SMITH 198
NEVER GIVE A SUCKER AN EVEN BREAK 1770
NEVER SAY NEVER 2204
NEVER SO FEW 332
NEW EARTH (NIEUWE GRONDEN) 312
NEW GENTLEMEN, THE (LES NOUVEAUX MESSIEURS) 1812
NEW SPIRIT, THE 307
NEW YORK HAT, THE 1366, 1397
NEW YORK STORIES 2045
NEW YORK, NEW YORK 152
NEXT OF KIN 343, 1938
NGUYEN HUN THO SPEAKS TO THE AMERICAN PEOPLE 290
NIAGARA 1281
NIBELUNGEN, DIE 1631
NICHOLAS AND ALEXANDRA 2067
NICK MAZZUCO: BIOGRAPHY OF AN ATOMIC VET 288
NICKELODEON 1143, 1294
NIEUWE GRONDEN (NEW EARTH) 312
NIGGER, THE 863
NIGHT AND FOG (NUIT ET BROUILLARD) 140, 289, 293, 305, 310, 323, 2117
NIGHT AT THE OPERA, A 708, 1088, 1481, 1492, 1805
NIGHT HAS A THOUSAND EYES, THE 1948
NIGHT MAIL 249, 309, 1871
NIGHT MOVES 2064
NIGHT MUST FALL (1937) 1336
NIGHT OF THE GENERALS, THE 331
NIGHT OF THE HUNTER, THE 145, 751
NIGHT OF THE LIVING DEAD 389, 390, 392, 397, 2036

NIGHT OF THE QUARTER MOON, THE 935
NIGHT OF THE SHOOTING STARS, THE (LA NOTTE DI SAN LORENZO) 331,
  377
NIGHT PEOPLE 241, 334, 357, 1250, 1252, 1253, 1256
NIGHT PORTER, THE (IL PORTIERE DI NOTTE) 312, 334
NIGHTMARE IN RED 287
NIGHTS OF THE CABIRIA (LE NOTTI DI CABIRIA) 1929
NIGHT, THE (LA NOTTE) 150, 1012, 1881, 2169
NIGORIE (MUDDY WATERS) 2018
NIHILIST VENGEANCE 846
NIHON NO HIGEKI (A JAPANESE TRAGEDY) 2018
NIJUSHI NO HITOMI (TWENTY-FOUR EYES) 2018
NINE TO FIVE 501
NINETEEN EIGHTY-FOUR 334, 1317
NINETEEN FORTY-ONE 668
NINETEEN HUNDRED 1874, 2200
NINETEEN THIRTY-NINE: EUROPE GOES TO WAR 287
NINETY-NINE 44/100% 2051
NINJO KAMIFUSEN (HUMANITY AND PAPER BALLOONS) 1889
NINOTCHKA 419, 1169, 1639, 1694, 1781, 1803, 1971, 1973
NINTH CONFIGURATION, THE (TWINKLE, TWINKLE KILLER KANE) 338
NISEI: THE PRIDE AND THE SHAME, THE 287
NO LIES 295
NO MAN IS AN ISLAND 332
NO PLACE TO HIDE 288
NO REGRETS FOR OUR YOUTH (WAGA SEISHUN NI KUINASHI) 2017
NO SAD SONGS FOR ME 1263
NO VIETNAMESE EVER CALLED ME NIGGER 290
NO WAY OUT (1950) 887, 890, 922, 935, 944, 1269, 1946
NO WAY TO TREAT A LADY 834
NOA NOA 145, 146
NOBI (FIRES ON THE PLAIN) 331, 2021, 2023, 2029
NOBODY WAVED GOODBYE 1008
NOCES ROUGES, LES WEDDING IN BLOOD) 2101
NONE BUT THE BRAVE 331
NONE BUT THE LONELY HEART 1095
NONE SHALL ESCAPE 331
NORAINU (STRAY DOG) 2017, 2021
NORMA RAE 485, 512, 801, 909
NORMANDY D-DAY 287
NORMANDY TO BERLIN: A WAR REMEMBERED 287
NORTH BY NORTHWEST 44, 119, 1153, 1843, 1846, 1849, 1852, 1854, 1858,
  2053, 2079
NORTH SEA 243, 309
NORTH STAR (ARMORED ATTACK) 262, 331, 1090, 1225, 1226, 1228, 1913
NORTHERN PURSUIT 1177
NORTHWEST MOUNTED POLICE 1478
NOSFERATU THE VAMPIRE 1312
NOSFERATU (1922) 388, 399, 410, 1632, 1635, 1640, 1642
NOT TO SPEAK ABOUT ALL THESE WOMEN (FOR ATT INTE TALA OM ALLA
  DESSA KVINNOR) 2185
NOTHING BUT A MAN 894, 922, 924, 935, 936, 937, 945, 952, 2038
NOTHING SACRED 1160, 1224
NOTORIOUS 331, 1224, 1526, 1835, 1843, 1845, 1847, 1848, 1849, 1852, 1853
NOTTE DI SAN LORENZO, LA (THE NIGHT OF THE SHOOTING STARS) 331,
  377
NOTTE, LA (THE NIGHT) 150, 1012, 1881, 2169
NOTTI BIANCHE, LE (WHITE NIGHTS) 1884, 2172

NOTTI DI CABIRIA, LE (NIGHTS OF THE CABIRIA) 1929
NOUVEAUX MESSIEURS, LES (THE NEW GENTLEMEN) 1812
NOW THAT THE BUFFALO'S GONE 74
NOW . . . AFTER ALL THESE YEARS (JETZT . . . NACH SO VIELEN
 JAHREN) 289
NOW, VOYAGER 521, 523, 589, 590, 598, 797, 800
NOZ W WODZIE (KNIFE IN THE WATER) 2179
NUIT AMERICAINE, LA (DAY FOR NIGHT) 2107, 2143, 2144, 2145, 2148
NUIT ET BROUILLARD (NIGHT AND FOG) 140, 289, 293, 305, 310, 323, 2117
NUIT FANTASTIQUE, LA (THE FANTASTIC NIGHT) 1904
NUITS DE LA PLEINE LUNE, LES (FULL MOON IN PARIS) 2105
NUMBER TWO (NUMERO DEUX) 2111
NUMERO DEUX (NUMBER TWO) 2111
NUN'S STORY, THE 499, 657, 919
NUREMBERG TRIALS, THE 287
NUREMBERG (NURNBERG) 289
NURNBERG (NUREMBERG) 289
NUTTY PROFESSOR, THE 117
NUT, THE 1402, 1407

O

OBCHOD NA KORZE (THE SHOP ON MAIN STREET) 310, 311, 334, 378, 2165
OBJECTIVE BURMA! 331, 332, 349, 700, 705, 769, 1160, 1177, 1199, 1913
OBSCUR OBJECT DU DESIRE, CET (THAT OBSCURE OBJECT OF DESIRE) 1310
OBSESSION (OSSESSIONE) 1884, 1922, 1924, 1926
OBYKONOVENN FASCHISM (ORDINARY FASCISM) 237, 287
OCCUPATION OF SUMATRA 209
OCCUPE-TOI D'AMELIE! (KEEP AN EYE ON AMELIA!) 1993
OCCURRENCE AT OWL CREEK BRIDGE, AN 379
OCTOBER (TEN DAYS THAT SHOOK THE WORLD/OKTIABR) 277, 1658, 1659,
 1667, 1668
OCTOPUSSY 269
ODD COUPLE, THE 1351
ODD MAN OUT (1947) 1021, 1935, 1936, 1943
ODDS AGAINST TOMORROW 885, 945
ODE TO BILLY JOE 975
OEDIPUS REX (EDIPO RE) 2171
OEDIPUS WRECKS 2045
OF HUMAN BONDAGE (1934) 623, 1169, 1305, 1312, 1329, 1749
OF HUMAN BONDAGE (1964) 1312, 1329
OF MICE AND MEN (1940) 1090, 1280, 1281, 1315, 1695
OFF TO BLOOMINGDALE ASYLUM 938
OFFICER AND A GENTLEMAN, AN 484, 905
OHM KRUGER (UNCLE KRUGER) 209, 240
OH! WHAT A LOVELY WAR 328, 343
OIL DU MALIN, OPHELIA, L' (THE THIRD LOVER) 2100
OKAASAN (MOTHER) 2019
OKLAHOMA 1950, 2032
OKTIABR (TEN DAYS THAT SHOOK THE WORLD/OCTOBER) 277, 1658, 1659,
 1667, 1668
OKUMAN CHOJA (A BILLIONAIRE) 2023
OLD AND NEW (THE GENERAL LINE/STAROIE I NOVOIE) 1645, 1661, 1866
OLD ISAACS, THE PAWNBROKER 822, 836
OLD MAID, THE 638
OLD SOLDIER: DOUGLAS MACARTHUR 287
OLD SOLDIER: DUTY, HONOR, COUNTRY, THE 287
OLIVER TWIST (1933) 992, 1090

OLIVER TWIST (1948)   1860, 1936
OLIVER!   403
OLVIDADOS, LOS (THE YOUNG AND THE DAMNED)   917, 978, 1002, 1923, 1990
OLYMPIA (OLYMPIADE)   240, 250, 303, 318, 321, 2177
OLYMPIADE (OLYMPIA)   240, 250, 303, 318, 321, 2177
OMEN, THE   279, 389, 397, 976, 985, 2192
ON A CLEAR DAY YOU CAN SEE FOREVER   401, 1784, 2191
ON AND UNDER COMMUNICATION (SUR ET SOUS LA COMMUNICATION)   2112
ON HER MAJESTY'S SECRET SERVICE   422
ON THE BEACH   231, 334, 355, 1953
ON THE TOWN   403, 404
ON THE WATERFRONT   271, 559, 569, 815, 1190, 1261, 1277, 1469, 1979
ON THE 8TH DAY   288
ONCE IN A BLUE MOON   1095
ONCE MORE (IMA HITOTABI NO)   2017
ONCE UPON A TIME IN AMERICA   191, 836
ONCE UPON A TIME IN THE WEST (C'ERA UNA VOLTA IL WEST)   427
ONE AND ONLY, THE   421
ONE A.M.   1416
ONE DAY IN THE LIFE OF IVAN DENISOVICH   554
ONE FLEW OVER THE CUCKOO'S NEST   597, 666, 802, 1315, 1324
ONE FRIGHTENED NIGHT   399
ONE FROM THE HEART   558, 2199
ONE HOUR WITH YOU   555, 1276, 1694
ONE HUNDRED AND ONE DALMATIANS   2202
ONE HUNDRED RIFLES   894, 945, 2038
ONE MILLION B. C.   269
ONE MINUTE TO ZERO   334, 359
ONE NIGHT IN LISBON   329
ONE OF MANY (EINER VON VIELEN)   321
ONE OF OUR AIRCRAFT IS MISSING   353, 1860, 1934
ONE PLUS ONE (SYMPATHY FOR THE DEVIL)   2130
ONE POTATO, TWO POTATO   894, 922, 935, 945, 2038
ONE SINGS, THE OTHER DOESN'T   2114
ONE THAT GOT AWAY   331
ONE WAY OR ANOTHER   506, 512
ONE WOMAN'S STORY (THE PASSIONATE FRIEND)   1860
ONE WONDERFUL SUNDAY (SUBARASHIKI NICHIYOBI)   1899, 2017, 2020
ONE-EYED JACKS   198
ONE, TWO, THREE   1971
ONLY ANGELS HAVE WINGS   1577, 1777
ONLY GAME IN TOWN, THE   1787
ONLY SON, THE (HITORI MUSUKO)   1893, 1901
ONLY THE FRENCH CAN (FRENCH CAN CAN)   1814, 2000
ONLY THE STRONG   356
ONLY WHEN I LAUGH   1166
OPEN SECRETS   290, 291
OPENING NIGHT   2048
OPERA MOUFFE   2114
OPERATION BOTTLENECK   336
OPERATION CIA   338
OPERATION CROSSBOW   331
OPERATION MICHAEL (UNTERNEHMEN MICHAEL)   240
OPERATION PACIFIC   332
OPERATION SNAFU   330
OPERATION TEUTONIC SWORD   304
OPIUM SMOKERS   988
ORCHESTRA REHEARSAL   1931

ORDERS TO KILL 331
ORDET (THE WORD) 1629, 1726
ORDINARY FASCISM (OBYKONOVENN FASCHISM) 237, 287
ORDINARY PEOPLE 484, 584, 680, 971, 1008, 1167
ORFEU NEGRO (BLACK ORPHEUS) 923, 2097
ORGANIZATION, THE 888
ORIENT EXPRESS 1218
ORIGINS OF THE MOTION PICTURE 1599
ORMENS AGG (THE SERPENT'S EGG) 311, 333, 2184
ORO DI ROMA, L'(THE GOLD OF ROME) 334
ORPHANS OF THE STORM 1368, 1375, 1382, 1385, 1389, 1578
ORPHEE (ORPHEUS) 579, 1572, 1995, 2005, 2009
ORPHEUS (ORPHEE) 579, 1572, 1995, 2005, 2009
OSAKA ELEGY (NANIWA EREJI) 1890
OSAKA NO YADO (AN INN IN OSAKA) 2018
OSHO (THE CHESS KING) 2017
OSSESSIONE (OBSESSION) 1884, 1922, 1924, 1926
OST UND WEST (EAST AND WEST) 846, 847
OSTANTI ETAP (THE LAST STOP) 334
OSTERMAN WEEKEND, THE 2062
OSTRE SLEDOVANE VLAKY (CLOSELY WATCHED TRAINS) 994, 2165
OTHELLO (1952) 1790, 1791
OTHELLO (1965) 1342
OTHER, THE 976
OTTO E MEZZO (8 1/2) 44, 138, 599, 600, 1927, 1929, 1930, 2170, 2175, 2180
OUR DAILY BREAD 556, 1269
OUR GANG film series 866, 920, 992, 1237, 1275, 1412, 1695
OUR HITLER, A FILM FROM GERMANY (HITLER, EIN FILM AUS
  DEUTSCHLAND) 289
OUR HOSPITALITY 1688
OUR MAN FLINT 690
OUR MAN IN HAVANA 334, 1219
OUR NEIGHBOR MISS YAE (TONARI NO YAE-CHAN) 1894
OUR RUSSIAN FRONT 286, 1090
OUR TIME IN THE GARDEN 289
OUR VINES HAVE TENDER GRAPES 1282
OUT OF AFRICA 2065, 2066, 2201, 2202
OUT OF THE INKWELL series 928
OUTCRY, THE (IL GRIDO) 1012, 1881
OUTLAW JOSEY WALES, THE 810
OUTLAW, THE 167, 958, 1370
OUTRAGE, THE 2028
OUTSIDE THE LAW 702
OUTSIDER, THE 262
OVER THE EDGE 974
OVER THERE, 1914-1918 285, 318
OVER TWENTY-ONE 1336
OVERLANDERS, THE 1841
OVERLORD 331
OX-BOW INCIDENT, THE 44, 568, 575, 580, 879, 939, 944, 1021, 1309, 1587,
  1701, 1913

P

PACIFIC BOILS OVER--PEARL HARBOR, DECEMBER 7, 1941, THE   287
PACIFIC PATTERN   287
PACT WITH THE DEVIL (PACTO DIABOLICO)   391
PACTO DIABOLICO (PACT WITH THE DEVIL)   391
PAGE OF MADNESS (A PAGE OUT OF ORDER/A CRAZY PAGE/KURUTTA
   IPPEIJI)   1742, 1744
PAGE OUT OF ORDER, A (A CRAZY PAGE/PAGE OF MADNESS/KURUTTA
   IPPEIJI)   1742, 1744
PAINT YOUR WAGON   2041, 2191
PAISA (PAISAN)   44, 331, 1883, 1925, 1926, 1929, 1932
PAISAN (PAISA)   44, 331, 1883, 1925, 1926, 1929, 1932
PALACE OF THE ARABIAN NIGHTS, THE (LE PALAIS DES MILLE ET UNE
   NUITS)   1619, 1620
PALAIS DES MILLE ET UNE NUITS, LE (THE PALACE OF THE ARABIAN
   NIGHTS)   1619
PALM BEACH STORY, THE   1912, 1919
PANDORA'S BOX   508
PANIC IN NEEDLE PARK, THE   516, 810, 975
PANIC IN THE STREETS   1260
PANIC IN YEAR ZERO   355, 419
PAPER CHASE, THE   989
PAPER MOON   2193
PAPILLON   1282, 2067, 2198
PARACHUTE BATTALION   329
PARADE   2007
PARADINE CASE, THE   1848
PARALLEX VIEW, THE   2192
PARAPLUIES DU CHERBOURG, LES (THE UMBRELLAS OF CHERBOURG)   408
PARATROOPER   328
PARENT TRAP, THE   1176
PARENTS TERRIBLES, LES (THE STORM WITHIN)   1995, 1997
PARIS BLUES   888, 894, 945
PARIS CALLING   329
PARIS FRILLS (FALBALAS)   1994
PARIS NOUS APPARTIENT   2098
PARIS QUI DORT (THE CRAZY RAY)   1725
PARK ROW   1961, 2078
PARNELL   62, 1176, 1221
PARTIE DE CAMPAGNE, UNE (A DAY IN THE COUNTRY)   1884, 2155
PARTIE DE PLAISIR, UNE (A PIECE OF PLEASURE)   2101
PARTISANS OF VILNA, THE   289
PASO DOBLE   2048
PASQUALINO SETTEBELEZZE (SEVEN BEAUTIES)   117, 152, 311, 312, 334, 2172
PASSAGE TO INDIA, A   539, 548, 1174, 1861
PASSAGE TO MARSEILLES   331, 494
PASSENGER, THE (IL GRIDO)   334, 1881, 2169
PASSING FANCY (DEKIGOKORO)   1902
PASSING THROUGH   901
PASSION DE JEANNE D'ARC, LA (THE PASSION OF JOAN OF ARC)   144, 1629,
   1725, 1726, 1729
PASSION OF ANNA, THE (EN PASSION)   2184
PASSION OF JOAN OF ARC, THE (LA PASSION DE JEANNE D'ARC)   144, 1629,
   1725, 1726, 1729
PASSION (MADAME DUBARRY)   1631, 1642
PASSIONATE FRIEND, THE (ONE WOMAN'S STORY)   1860
PASSION, EN (THE PASSION OF ANNA)   2184

PASSPORT TO PIMLICO 1569, 1937
PASSWORD IS COURAGE, THE 330
PAST OF MARY HOLMES, THE 638
PAT AND MIKE 421, 1951
PAT GARRETT AND BILLY THE KID 2061, 2063
PATCH OF BLUE, A 888, 891, 2036
PATENT LEATHER KID, THE 1061
PATHER PANCHALI 2168
PATHS OF GLORY 267, 328, 372, 558, 1081, 1314, 2055, 2056, 2057, 2058
PATRICIA NEAL STORY, THE 1137
PATRIOTEN (PATRIOTS) 240
PATRIOTS (PATRIOTEN) 240
PATTERNS 1176
PATTON 231, 254, 331, 339, 354, 361, 365, 2067, 2090, 2175, 2191, 2193
PAUL JACOBS AND THE NUCLEAR GANG 288
PAUL ROBESON: TRIBUTE TO AN ARTIST 288, 952
PAULINE A LA PLAGE (PAULINE AT THE BEACH) 2105
PAULINE AT THE BEACH (PAULINE A LA PLAGE) 2105
PAWNBROKER, THE 334, 837, 841, 893, 946, 1314, 2036, 2058, 2084
PAWNSHOP, THE 1416
PAY OR DIE 1090
PEARL, THE 1280
PEGGY SUE GOT MARRIED 2200
PENNIES FROM HEAVEN 786, 2199
PENNY SERENADE 1088
PENSION MIMOSAS 1812
PEOPLE AND THEIR GUNS, THE (LE PEUPLE ET SES FUSILS) 289, 312
PEOPLE IN ARMS (PUEBLO ARMADO) 312
PEOPLE OF THE CUMBERLAND 1259
PEOPLE ON SUNDAY (MENSCHEN AM SONNTAG) 1971
PER QUALCHE DOLLARO IN PIU (FOR A FEW DOLLARS MORE) 427
PER UN PUGNO DI DOLLARI (A FISTFUL OF DOLLARS) 427, 2019
PERCEVAL LE GALLOIS 2101, 2105
PERFORMANCE 2160
PERILS OF NYOKA, THE 1456
PERILS OF PAULINE, THE (1914) 1456, 1457, 1458
PERILS OF THE JUNGLE 1456
PERIOD OF ADJUSTMENT 334, 2052
PERSHING'S CRUSADERS 224
PERSONA 143, 595, 598, 605, 2183, 2186, 2187
PERSONAL BEST 492, 590
PETER PAN (1924) 405
PETIT SOLDAT, LE (THE LITTLE SOLDIER) 2134
PETITE MARCHANDE D'ALLUMETTES, LA (THE LITTLE MATCH GIRL) 1814
PETITE VOLEUSE, LA (THE LITTLE THIEF) 2106
PETRIFIED FOREST, THE 385, 876, 944
PETT AND POTT 315
PEUPLE ET SES FUSILS, LE (THE PEOPLE AND THEIR GUNS) 289, 312
PEYTON PLACE 1457, 1954
PHANTOM BARON, THE (LE BARON FANTOME) 1995
PHANTOM CHARIOT, THE (KORKARLEN) 1625, 1630
PHANTOM OF LIBERTY, THE (LE FANTOME DE LA LIBERTE) 1720, 1723
PHANTOM OF THE OPERA, THE (1925) 396, 1702
PHANTOM OF THE PARADISE 2194, 2197
PHARMACIST, THE 1411
PHILADELPHIA STORY, THE (1940) 980, 1168, 1270, 1279, 1336
PHILO VANCE film series 420
PHONE CALL FROM A STRANGER 1250, 1252
PICKININNIES, THE 861

PICKPOCKET 1994
PICKUP ON SOUTH STREET 1960, 1977
PICNIC (1956) 499, 657, 1002, 1954
PIECE OF PLEASURE, A (UNE PARTIE DE PLAISIR) 2101
PIECE OF THE ACTION, A 889
PIED PIPER, THE 1090
PILGRIMAGE FOR PEACE: POPE PAUL VI VISITS AMERICA, A 290
PILGRIM, THE 1429
PILOT NUMBER FIVE 568
PILOTS IN PYJAMAS 290
PIMPERNEL SMITH 331, 1911, 1938
PINK FLAMINGOS 392
PINKY 526, 569, 859, 882, 883, 884, 931, 935, 944, 1064, 1204, 1256, 1260,
 1499, 1500, 1503, 1946
PIPPA PASSES 1380
PIRATE GOLD 1457
PIRATE, THE 1784, 1945, 1952
PIT AND THE PENDULUM, THE 2049
PLACE IN THE SUN, A 1015, 1094, 1155, 1787, 1952, 1954
PLACES IN THE HEART 485
PLAGUE OF THE ZOMBIES 390
PLAINSMAN, THE 556
PLAISIR, LE 2007
PLANET OF THE APES 2035, 2067, 2090
PLANET OF THE APES, THE (series) 389, 421
PLATOON 117, 270, 337, 338, 368, 558, 2201, 2205
PLAY DIRTY 328
PLAY IT AGAIN, SAM 2045, 2194, 2208
PLAYA GIRON 917
PLAYGIRL 702
PLAYING FOR TIME 312, 334
PLEASURE GARDEN, THE 1837, 1838, 1843, 1845, 1850
PLENTY 680, 2207
PLOW THAT BROKE THE PLAINS, THE 153, 1870, 1872
PLUNDER 1457, 1458
POIL DE CAROTTE 1811
POINT BLANK 387, 562, 2036, 2073
POINT OF ORDER 288
POINTE-COURTE, LA 2114
POKOLENIE (A GENERATION) 2014
POLICE ACADEMY 539
POLLYANNA 1081, 1392, 1393
POLTERGEIST 1526, 2196, 2200
POLTERGEIST series 2200
PONTCARRAL, COLONEL D'EMPIRE 1910
POOR LITTLE RICH GIRL, A 1392
POPIOL I DIAMENT (ASHES AND DIAMONDS) 311, 331, 334, 2014, 2180
PORGY AND BESS 885, 886, 888, 890, 1473, 1966
PORK CHOP HILL 262, 334, 359, 1090
PORKY'S 484, 539, 976
PORKY'S DUCK HUNT 414
PORT OF SHADOWS (QUAI DES BRUMES) 1813
PORTE DES LILAS (THE GATE OF PARIS) 2000
PORTIERE DI NOTTE, IL (THE NIGHT PORTER) 312, 334
PORTNOY'S COMPLAINT 834, 835
PORTRAIT OF JENNIE, A 1486
POSEIDON ADVENTURE, THE 753, 2193
POSSESSED 521

POSTMAN ALWAYS RINGS TWICE, THE (1946) 494, 505, 1314, 1948
POSTMAN ALWAYS RINGS TWICE, THE (1981) 505, 536
POTASH AND PERLMUTTER 825
POTOMOK CHINGIS-KAHN (STORM OVER ASIA/THE HEIR TO GENGHIS
 KAHN) 1668
POWER AND THE GLORY, THE 1479, 1919
POWER AND THE LAND 314, 315
POWER GOD, THE 1456
PRAESIDENTEN (THE PRESIDENT) 1626
PRAVADA 2111
PRESENTS 493
PRESIDENT VANISHES, THE 556, 568
PRESIDENT'S ANALYST, THE 894
PRESIDENT'S MYSTERY, THE 1098
PRESIDENT, THE (PRAESIDENTEN) 1626
PRESSURE POINT 816, 894
PRESTIGE 944
PRETTY BABY 975, 981, 2119
PRIDE AND PREJUDICE 1147, 1305, 1309, 1312, 1327
PRIDE OF THE MARINES 331, 568, 1088
PRIDE OF THE YANKEES, THE 421, 1269, 1472
PRIME OF MISS JEAN BRODIE, THE 30, 1003
PRIME TIME, THE 393
PRINCE OF THE CITY 2059
PRISE DU POUVOIR PAR LOUIS XIV, LA (THE RISE OF LOUIS XIV) 1883
PRISONER OF SHARK ISLAND, THE 944, 1252, 1253, 1502
PRISONER OF WAR 231, 334
PRISONER OF ZENDA, THE (1937) 1279, 1403
PRISONER, THE 414
PRIVATE BENJAMIN 787, 788, 840
PRIVATE LIFE OF HENRY VIII, THE 1833, 1834, 1859, 1865
PRIVATE PROPERTY 790
PRIVATE SCHOOL 977
PRIZZI'S HONOR 1086, 1916, 2202
PROBABLY THE DEVIL (LE DIABLE PROBLEMENT) 2004, 2005
PROCES DE JEANNE D'ARC, LE (THE TRIAL OF JOAN OF ARC) 1023, 1994
PROCES, LE (THE TRIAL) 159, 1022, 1791, 2070, 2091
PRODUCERS, THE 833, 2037, 2047, 2073
PROFESSIONALS, THE 198, 426, 668, 2036
PROFESSOR MAMLOCK 334, 830
PROJECT X 670
PROLOGUE U. S. A. 287
PROM NIGHT 976
PROPHECY 288, 676, 2051
PROUD AND THE PROFANE, THE 331
PROVIDENCE 593, 2137, 2138
PSYCHO 62, 166, 389, 397, 592, 599, 816, 976, 1843, 1845, 1849, 1851, 1852,
 1854, 1855, 1858, 1978, 2035, 2036, 2053, 2054, 2080
PU-SAN (MR. POO) 2022, 2023
PUBLIC ENEMY'S WIFE 556
PUBLIC ENEMY, THE 270, 385, 387, 472, 555, 1070, 1494, 1497, 1576, 1701
PUDOVKIN 1668
PUEBLO AFFAIR, THE 288
PUEBLO ARMADO (PEOPLE IN ARMS) 312
PUMPKIN EATER, THE 1293
PUNISHMENT ROOM (SHOKEI NO HEYA) 2023
PURIMSPILER, DER (THE JESTER) 846, 848
PURPLE HEART, THE 217, 248, 262, 331, 338, 343, 345, 349, 831, 1090
PURPLE PLAIN, THE 331

PURPLE ROSE OF CAIRO, THE (1985)   786, 2045
PUTNEY SWOPE   558, 894
PUTTING ON PANTS   1690
PYGMALION (1935)   1344, 1863
PYGMALION (1938)   1170, 1336, 1337, 1344, 1357, 1841, 1860, 1863
P. O. W.   338
P. T. 109   331, 339

Q

QB VII   334
QUAI DES BRUMES (PORT OF SHADOWS)   1813
QUAI DES ORFEVRES (JENNY LAMOUR)   2000
QUATORZE JUILLET, LE (THE FOURTEENTH OF JULY)   1714, 1810
QUATRE CENT COUPS, LES (THE FOUR HUNDRED BLOWS)   1005, 2097, 2106,
   2107, 2143, 2144, 2145, 2148, 2150, 2154
QUATRE NUITS D'UN REVEUR (FOUR NIGHTS OF A DREAMER)   2003
QUATTRO PASSI FRA LE NUVOLE (FOUR STEPS IN THE CLOUDS)   1875
QUE LA BETE MEURE (THIS MAN MUST DIE/KILLER!)   2098, 2101
QUE VIVA MEXICO!   1661, 1866
QUEEN CHRISTINA   638, 1176, 1782, 1803
QUEEN ELIZABETH (LES AMOURS DE LA REINE ELISABETH)   685, 1386, 1463,
   1504, 1505, 1618
QUEEN KELLY   1699, 1700
QUEEN OF SPADES, THE (1949)   1937
QUESTION OF SILENCE, A (DE STILTE ROND CHRISTINE M)   492, 501, 526
QUIET AMERICAN, THE   338, 359, 364, 442, 1219, 1270
QUIET MAN, THE   499, 657, 1500, 1501, 1674, 1684, 1952
QUIET ONE, THE   1923
QUILLER MEMORANDUM, THE   1293
QUIXOTE   290
QUO VADIS?   382, 1176, 1386, 1607

R

RACHEL AND THE STRANGER   1090
RACK, THE   334
RADIO DAYS   2045, 2203
RAGE   2193
RAGING BULL   604
RAGS   1392
RAGTIME   802, 840, 1032
RAID ON ROMMEL   328
RAIDERS OF THE LOST ARK   484, 554, 2196, 2200
RAIDER, THE (WESTERN APPROACHES)   287, 331, 1938
RAILWAY BATTLE   331
RAIN   592, 1090, 1714
RAIN MAN   816
RAIN PEOPLE, THE   2197
RAINTREE COUNTY   1201
RAISIN IN THE SUN, A   862, 893, 945, 1009, 1348, 2038
RAISING ARIZONA   2203
RAMBO III   671
RAMBO IV   2204
RAMBO: FIRST BLOOD PART II   337, 338, 437, 472, 549, 761, 2200
RAMONA   1380

RAMPARTS WE WATCH, THE 285, 303, 304, 319
RAN (CHAOS) 2019, 2116
RANCHO NOTORIOUS 1952
RANDOM HARVEST 328
RASHOMON 410, 1576, 1737, 1899, 1954, 2018, 2021, 2024, 2025, 2027, 2028, 2029, 2030
RASPUTIN AND THE EMPRESS 1265
RASTUS IN ZULULAND 862
RAVAGER, THE 338
RAVEN, THE 2049
RAVEN, THE (LE CORBEAU) 1904, 1909
RAYON VERT, LE (SUMMER) 2105
RAZGROM NEMETZKICH VOISK POD MOSKOVI (MOSCOW STRIKES BACK/THE DEFEAT OF THE GERMAN ARMIES NEAR MOSCOW) 287, 1089
RAZOR'S EDGE, THE (1946) 1167, 1587
RAZOR'S EDGE, THE (1984) 62
REALIZATION OF A NEGRO'S AMBITION, THE 866, 947
REAR GUNNER 272
REAR WINDOW 1311, 1843, 1844, 1848, 1858, 1952, 1978
REBECCA 469, 615, 714, 1486, 1835, 1846, 1847, 1853
REBECCA OF SUNNYBROOK FARM 1392, 1394
REBEL WITHOUT A CAUSE 119, 558, 743, 810, 816, 986, 997, 998, 1442, 1968, 1969, 1984
RECKLESS 2207
RECKLESS MOMENT, THE 793, 2010
RECLAIMING THE SOLDIERS' DUDS 224
RECORD OF A TENEMENT GENTLEMAN, THE (NAGAYA SHINSHI ROKU) 2017
RED BADGE OF COURAGE, THE (1951) 1319, 1321, 1916, 1952
RED BALL EXPRESS 331
RED BEARD (AKAHIGE) 2028
RED DANUBE, THE 1949
RED DAWN 335, 2204
RED DESERT (IL DESERTO ROSSO) 144, 1881, 2173
RED DUST 1394, 1395
RED HEAT 2204
RED INN, THE (L'AUBERGE ROUGE) 1993
RED LINE SEVEN THOUSAND 1152
RED MENACE, THE 1949
RED PONY, THE 1281
RED RIVER 193, 270, 1146, 1347, 1747, 1777, 1946, 1952
RED SHOES, THE 1015, 1016, 1935, 1936, 1943
RED SNOW 1949
RED-HEADED WOMAN 1117, 1217, 1380
RED-LIGHT DISTRICT (AKASEN CHITAI) 2019
REDS 328, 558
REED: INSURGENT MEXICO 917
REEFER MADNESS 986
REGLE DU JEU, LA (THE RULES OF THE GAME) 144, 472, 1153, 1232, 1814, 1821, 1822, 1827, 1996, 2145, 2154
REIVERS, THE 858, 1212
REMBRANDT 1833, 1834, 1859
REMEMBRANCE (YISKER) 828, 846, 847
RENDEZ-VOUS DE JULLIET 1994
REPORT FROM THE ALEUTIANS 284, 286, 287, 1915
REPULSION 389, 392, 2179
RESCUED BY ROVER 1607, 1617
RESCUED FROM AN EAGLE'S NEST 1277, 1361, 1617
RESCUERS, THE 414
RESURRECTION 738

RETOUR A RAISON (RETURN TO REASON)   1713
RETOUR, LE (REUNION)   284, 287, 1993
RETREAT, HELL!   334, 359
RETURN FROM THE ASHES   334
RETURN OF FRANK JAMES, THE   1637
RETURN OF THE JEDI   414, 484, 2200
RETURN OF THE SOLDIER, THE   328, 551
RETURN TO POLAND   289, 311
RETURN TO REASON (RETOUR A RAISON)   1713
REUNION (LE RETOUR)   284, 287, 1993
REVEILLE   342
REVENGE AT DAYBREAK (DESPERATE DECISION)   2037
REVOLT IN THE EARTH   1212
REVOLT OF JOB, THE   334
REVOLT OF MAMIE STOVER, THE   532
REVOLUTION EN RUSSIE (REVOLUTION IN ODESSA)   1621
REVOLUTION IN ODESSA (REVOLUTION EN RUSSIE)   1621
RHAPSODY   1649
RHAPSODY IN BLUE   831, 1478
RHINOCEROUS   1034
RHODES OF AFRICA   1221, 1569
RICH AND FAMOUS   2199
RICHARD III (1911)   1612
RICHARD III (1955)   1860
RIDDLES OF THE SPHINX   506
RIDE THE HIGH COUNTRY   558, 2035, 2061, 2063, 2086
RIEN QUE LES HEURES   215, 1714, 1728
RIGHT STUFF, THE   151, 443
RING OF TREASON   288
RIO BRAVO   198, 433, 980, 1747, 1777
RIO CONCHOS   893
RIO GRANDE   427, 1686, 1946
RIO LOBO   1747, 1775
RIO RITA   1797
RIOT   894
RIOT IN CELL BLOCK 11   1090, 2061
RIPTIDE   1265
RISE AND FALL OF LEGS DIAMOND, THE   188
RISE OF LOUIS XIV, THE (LA PRISE DU POUVOIR PAR LOUIS XIV)   1883
RISING OF THE MOON, THE   1684
RISKY BUSINESS   2207
RITA HAYWORTH: THE LOVE GODDESS   1137
RIVER OF NO RETURN   1281, 1966
RIVER'S EDGE, THE   2207
RIVER, THE   44
RIVER, THE (LE FLEUVE/IL FIUME)   1820
RIVER, THE (1937)   153, 246, 1870, 1872
RIVER, THE (1984)   485, 1174
RKO: THE HOLLYWOOD YEARS   1670
ROAD TO CORINTH, THE (LA ROUTE DE CORINTHE)   2100
ROAD TO GLORY, THE   327, 328, 1207, 1212, 1213, 1249, 1250, 1253, 1775
ROAD TO MANDALAY, THE (1926)   1268
ROAD TO MANDALAY: CHINA, BURMA, INDIA AND INDIAN OCEAN   287
ROAD TO MOROCCO   1094
ROAD TO SINGAPORE   1094
ROAD TO YESTERDAY   1579
ROAD, THE (LA STRADA)   1021, 1815, 1929, 1930, 1933, 1954
ROARING TWENTIES, THE   476, 1091, 1700

ROBE, THE 1203, 1950
ROBIN HOOD (1922) 1400, 1401, 1407, 1408
ROBINSON CRUSOE ON MARS 418
ROCCO AND HIS BROTHERS (ROCCO E I SUOI FRATELLI) 1884, 2172
ROCCO E I SUOI FRATELLI (ROCCO AND HIS BROTHERS) 1884, 2172
ROCK AROUND THE CLOCK 743
ROCKY 270, 421, 802, 803, 2198
ROCKY HORROR PICTURE SHOW, THE 392
ROCKY II 676
ROCKY IV 761, 2201
ROCK, PRETTY BABY 743
ROGUE'S REGIMENT 359
ROI DE COEUR, LE (KING OF HEARTS) 328, 392, 1530
ROJO NO REIKON (SOULS ON THE ROAD) 1740, 1741
ROLIN COMEDIES 865
ROLLERBALL 414
ROLLING THUNDER 259, 338
ROLLOVER 1436
ROMAN HOLIDAY 547, 1748, 1952, 1988
ROMAN RENAISSANCE: SICILY AND THE ITALIAN CAMPAIGN 287
ROMANCE 1071
ROMANCE OF A MILLION DOLLARS, THE 986
ROMANCE OF ROSEY RIDGE, THE 1199
ROMANCE OF THE RAILS, A 1617
ROMANCING THE STONE 2200
ROMA, CITTA APERTA (ROME, OPEN CITY) 138, 331, 378, 1883, 1924, 1925,
1926, 1929, 1932, 1933, 1995
ROMEO AND JULIET (1954) 1009, 1335, 1342
ROMEO AND JULIET (1966) 1356
ROMEO AND JULIET (1968) 960, 1356
ROME, OPEN CITY (ROMA, CITTA APERTA) 138, 331, 378, 1883, 1924, 1925,
1926, 1929, 1932, 1933, 1995
ROMOLA 1385
RONDE, LA 1310, 2000, 2007, 2010
ROOM AT THE TOP 790, 1016, 1569, 1939, 2036
ROOM SERVICE 1088
ROOM WITH A VIEW, A 2203
ROOSEVELT AND U. S. HISTORY (1930-1945) 287
ROOSEVELT VS. ISOLATION 287
ROOSTER COGBURN 160
ROOTS 780, 855, 857
ROPE 1336, 1835, 1848, 1851
ROSEMARY'S BABY 388, 389, 392, 393, 584, 595, 976, 2035, 2036, 2048
ROSE, THE 1138
ROSITA 1392, 1393
ROUE, LA (THE WHEEL) 1712
ROUGH HOUSE ROSIE 1253
ROUTE DE CORINTHE, LA (THE ROAD TO CORINTH) 2100
ROYAL SCANDAL, A 1071
RUE HAUTE (HIGH STREET) 311, 334
RULES OF THE GAME, THE (LA REGLE DU JEU) 144, 472, 1153, 1232, 1814,
1821, 1822, 1827, 1996, 2145, 2154
RUMOR OF WAR, A 338
RUMOURS OF WAR 356
RUN OF THE ARROW 1960
RUN SILENT, RUN DEEP 331
RUNNING ON EMPTY 2059, 2207
RUNNING SCARED 904
RUPTURE (LE JOUR DES PARQUES) 2101

RUSSIA AT WAR 287
RUSSIA OF NIKOLAI II AND LEV TOLSTOY, THE 304
RUSSIANS ARE COMING, THE RUSSIANS ARE COMING, THE 334, 2082
RUSSIA, THE LAND OF OPPRESSION 845
RYAN'S DAUGHTER 1861

S

SABATOUR: CODE NAME--MORITURI, THE (MORITURI) 330
SABOTAGE (1936) 1312, 1834, 1838
SABOTEUR (1942) 331, 1275, 1847, 1852
SABRE JET 334
SABRINA 2053
SACRIFICE, THE 1380
SAD CLOWNS 1579
SAD SONG OF YELLOW SKIN 290
SADAT 488
SADDLE THE WIND 2048
SADIE MCKEE 638
SAFAR'S VIETNAM 290
SAFE IN HELL 555
SAFETY LAST 1693
SAGA OF ANATAHAN, THE 1697, 1698
SAHARA 328, 361, 375, 881, 1070, 1913
SAIGON 338, 359
SAIKAKU ICHIDAI (THE LIFE OF A WOMAN/THE LIFE OF OHARU) 2019
SAINT JOAN 1335, 1966
SAINT, THE film series 420, 421
SALEM'S LOT 393
SALESMAN 2041, 2084
SALLY OF THE SAWDUST 1368, 1385, 1390
SALOME 1790
SALT OF THE EARTH 512, 569, 1089, 1094
SALUT LES CUBAINS 2114
SALVATION HUNTERS, THE 1697
SAMBIZANGA 508
SAMOURAI, LE 2000
SAMSON 334
SAMSON AND DELILAH 832, 1478, 1950
SAN FRANCISCO 1380, 1481, 1805
SAN QUENTIN 1070
SANCTUARY 858
SAND PEBBLES, THE 359
SANDERS OF THE RIVER 1569, 1833
SANDRA (VAGHE SETLLE DELL'OREA) 334
SANDS OF DEE, THE 1392
SANDS OF IWO JIMA 331, 359, 1155, 1401
SANG D'UN POETE, LE (THE BLOOD OF A POET) 1811, 1817, 1818, 1826
SANG DES BETES, LES 2128
SANJURO 2027
SANS TOIT NI LOI (VAGABOND) 2114
SANSHIRO SUGATA (SUGATA SANSHIRO) 2028
SANSHO DAYU (SANSHO THE BAILIFF) 2019, 2031
SANSHO THE BAILIFF (SANSHO DAYU) 2019, 2031
SANTA 961
SANTA FE 289
SANTA FE TRAIL 1160

SARATOGA TRUNK 882
SASOM I EN SPEGEL (THROUGH A GLASS DARKLY) 2183, 2186
SATAN'S SADISTS 339
SATURDAY NIGHT AND SUNDAY MORNING 815, 1569, 1940, 2162
SATURDAY NIGHT FEVER 611, 802, 975, 987, 2199
SATYRICON 389, 2170
SAUVE QUI PEUT (LA VIE/EVERY MAN FOR HIMSELF) 2112
SAVAGE EYE, THE 790
SAVAGES 2167
SAVE THE TIGER 834, 838, 2193
SAWDUST AND TINSEL (GYCKLARNAS AFTON/THE NAKED NIGHT/THE
  CLOWN'S EVENING) 2183, 2187
SAYONARA 331, 340
SCALPHUNTERS, THE 894, 2038, 2065
SCANDALE, LE (THE CHAMPAGNE MURDERS) 2128
SCAR OF SHAME, THE 270, 868, 921, 924, 928
SCARECROW 604
SCARFACE (1932) 385, 387, 730, 1224, 1468, 1708, 1747, 1777
SCARLET EMPRESS, THE 638, 1403
SCARLET LETTER, THE (1926) 1394, 1625, 1706
SCARLET PIMPERNEL, THE 1833, 1834, 1859
SCARLET STREET 1637
SCEICCO BIANCO, LO (THE WHITE SHEIK) 1929, 1931
SCENER UR ETT AKTENSKAP (SCENES FROM A MARRIAGE) 2184
SCENES FROM A MARRIAGE (SCENER UR ETT AKTENSKAP) 2184
SCHATTEN (WARNING SHADOWS) 1592
SCHOOL DAZE 903
SCIUSCIA (SHOESHINE) 331, 1925, 1926
SCORCHED EARTH 286
SCORPIO RISING 1241, 2072
SCOTT OF THE ANTARCTIC 1021
SCOUNDREL, THE 1265
SCROOGE 2191
SCUTTLING OF THE GRAF SPEE 287
SEA AND SAND: INVASION OF NORTH AFRICA 1942-1943 287
SEA CHASE, THE 264, 345
SEA DEVILS 327
SEA GULL, THE 2058
SEA HAWK, THE 1262, 1263
SEA OF GRASS 1260
SEA SHELL AND THE CLERGYMAN, THE (LA COQUILLE ET LE
  CLERGYMAN) 1713, 1729
SEA WOLF, THE 1095, 1305
SEA WOLVES, THE 330
SEARCH FOR GREEN EYES 290
SEARCHERS, THE 117, 194, 197, 427, 449, 478, 529, 810, 980, 1686, 2076
SEARCHING WIND, THE 568, 1225
SEARCH, THE 331, 1988
SEA, THE (LE MER) 278
SECOND WIND (LE DEUXIEME SOUFFLE) 2000
SECONDS 2051
SECRET AGENT, THE 1834, 1838
SECRET INVASION, THE 327
SECRET OF MY SUCCESS, THE 2205, 2206
SECRET OF SANTA VITTORIA, THE 330
SECRET SIX, THE 176, 568, 1394, 1395
SECRET WAYS 288
SECRETS OF A SOUL 579, 584, 593
SEDUCTION OF MIMI, THE (MIMI METALLURGICO FERITO NELL'ONORE) 2172

SEE HERE, PRIVATE HARGROVE   331
SEI NO KAGAYAKI (THE GLOW OF LIFE)   1739
SEINE A RECONTRE PARIS, LA (THE SEINE HAS MET PARIS)   312
SEINE HAS MET PARIS, THE (LA SEINE A RECONTRE PARIS)   312
SEISAKU NO TSUMA (SEISAKU'S WIFE)   1742
SEISAKU'S WIFE (SEISAKU NO TSUMA)   1742
SELLING OF THE PENTAGON, THE   290, 303
SEMINOLE   428
SENATOR WAS INDISCREET, THE   1250, 1251
SENSO (FEELING)   1884, 1932
SENTINEL, THE   414
SEPARATE PEACE, A   601
SEPTEMBER   2045
SERGEANT RUTLEDGE   427, 894, 945, 1673, 1684, 2038
SERGEANT RYKER   334
SERGEANT YORK   203, 328, 339, 348, 365, 568, 913, 992, 1262, 1288, 1478,
   1911, 1915
SERGEI EISENSTEIN   1667
SERPENT OF THE NILE   383
SERPENT'S EGG, THE (ORMENS AGG)   311, 333, 2184
SERPENTINE DANCERS   1371
SERPICO   1090, 2058, 2199
SERVANT, THE   103, 1293, 1963, 2161
SET-UP, THE   1946
SEVEN BEAUTIES (PASQUALINO SETTEBELEZZE)   117, 152, 311, 312, 334, 2172
SEVEN CHANCES   1688
SEVEN DAYS IN MAY   231, 334, 2036, 2051, 2077
SEVEN DAYS TO NOON   1936
SEVEN SAMURAI (SHICHI-NIN NO SAMURAI)   2019, 2020, 2021, 2027, 2028, 2030
SEVEN WOMEN   1673, 1683, 1685
SEVEN YEAR ITCH, THE   657, 1282
SEVEN YEARS BAD LUCK   1619
SEVENTEENTH PARALLEL, THE (LE DIX-SEPTIEME PARALLELE)   289, 312
SEVENTH CROSS, THE   331
SEVENTH HEAVEN   328, 1701
SEVENTH SEAL, THE (DET SJUNDE INSEGLET)   44, 138, 144, 1628, 2036, 2183,
   2184, 2186, 2188
SEVENTH VEIL, THE   1935
SEVENTH VICTIM, THE   1912
SEVENTH VOYAGE OF SINBAD, THE   411
SEVENTY NINE SPRINGTIMES   290
SEWER (KANAL)   2014, 2180
SEX KITTENS GO TO COLLEGE   419
SEX LIFE OF THE POLYP, THE   1797
SEXUAL PERVERSITY IN CHICAGO (ABOUT LAST NIGHT . . .)   738
SGT. PEPPER'S LONELY HEARTS CLUB BAND   2199
SHADOW OF A DOUBT   1835, 1843, 1847, 1851, 1853, 1920
SHADOW OF A DOUBT (EEN SCHISM VAN TWIJFEL)   289, 1913
SHADOW WARRIOR (KAGEMUSHA)   2019, 2020, 2027
SHADOWS   894, 2039, 2048, 2074, 2075
SHADOWS OF THE YOSHIWARA (CROSSWAYS/JUJIRO)   1742
SHAFT   896, 898, 899, 900, 923, 937, 946, 949
SHAKESPEARE WALLAH   2167
SHAME   2033
SHAME (SKAMMEN)   2183
SHAMPOO   438, 2192
SHANE   103, 193, 197, 198, 433, 499, 657, 806, 1009, 1169, 1787, 1946, 1952
SHANGHAI EXPRESS   730, 1698, 1788

SHARK 1960
SHAW TALKS FOR MOVIETONE 1797
SHE 874
SHE DONE HIM WRONG 555, 1070, 1807
SHE GOES TO WAR 327
SHE WORE A YELLOW RIBBON 193, 427, 1500, 1501, 1686, 1946, 1952
SHE'S GOTTA HAVE IT 903
SHENANDOAH 857
SHERLOCK HOLMES 1424
SHERLOCK HOLMES BAFFLED 381
SHERLOCK HOLMES film series 420, 421
SHERLOCK, JR. 595, 1248, 1688
SHICHI-NIN NO SAMURAI (SEVEN SAMURAI) 2019, 2020, 2021, 2027, 2028, 2030
SHICHIMENCHO NO YUKUE (TURKEYS IN A ROW) 1740
SHIMA NO ONNA (ISLAND WOMAN) 1740
SHINING, THE 393, 976, 2055, 2056, 2057, 2200
SHINJU TEN NO AMIJIMA (DOUBLE SUICIDE) 2025
SHIP OF FOOLS 1168
SHIP THAT DIED OF SHAME, THE 1567
SHIPMATES FOREVER 327
SHIPYARD 244
SHOAH 289
SHOCK CORRIDOR 1960
SHOCKING NIGHT, A 728
SHOES OF THE FISHERMAN, THE 2041
SHOESHINE (SCIUSCIA) 331, 1925, 1926
SHOKEI NO HEYA (PUNISHMENT ROOM) 2023
SHOOT THE MOON 971
SHOOT THE PIANO PLAYER (TIREZ SUR LE PIANISTE) 2107, 2144, 2155
SHOOTING STRAIGHT 1685
SHOOTIST, THE 2199
SHOP AROUND THE CORNER, THE 1276, 1694
SHOP ON MAIN STREET, THE (OBCHOD NA KORZE) 310, 311, 334, 378, 2165
SHORS 1655
SHORT CIRCUIT 972
SHORT NIGHT, THE 1844, 1854
SHORT VISION, A 356
SHOULDER ARMS 328, 348, 1416, 1417, 1429
SHOW BOAT (1929) 863
SHOW BOAT (1936) 863, 876
SHOW BOAT (1951) 863, 884, 921
SHOW GIRL IN HOLLYWOOD 1245
SHOW PEOPLE 1060, 1245, 1248, 1670
SHRIKE, THE 657
SIEG IM WESTEN (VICTORY IN THE WEST) 206, 282
SIEGE 287
SIEGFRIED 1631
SIERRA DE TERUEL 278
SIGHET, SIGHET 289
SIGMUND FREUD'S DORA: A CASE OF MISTAKEN IDENTITY 501, 506
SIGN OF THE CROSS, THE 1093, 1468
SIGN OF THE LION (LE SIGNE DU LION) 2103
SIGNE DU LION, LE (SIGN OF THE LION) 2103
SILENCE DE LA MER, LE 2000, 2093, 2094
SILENCE EST D'OR, LE (SILENCE IS GOLDEN/MAN ABOUT TOWN) 1725, 2000, 2005
SILENCE IS GOLDEN (LE SILENCE EST D'OR/MAN ABOUT TOWN) 1725, 2005
SILENCE, THE 290
SILENCE, THE (TYSTNADEN) 2183, 2186

SILENT MOVIE 1294, 2047
SILENT SIX, THE 555
SILENT THREAD, THE 2066
SILENT VILLAGE, THE 287, 316, 323
SILK STOCKINGS 589
SILKWOOD 454, 801, 2060
SIMON OF THE DESERT 1990
SIN OF MADELON CLAUDET, THE 1265
SINBAD THE SAILOR 1403
SINCE YOU WENT AWAY 273, 331, 353, 521
SINGIN' IN THE RAIN 150, 404, 575, 1136, 1169, 1244, 1245, 1248, 1295, 1515,
  1670, 1980
SINGING BLACKSMITH, THE (DER ZINGENDIKER SHMID) 829, 846
SINGING FOOL, THE 943
SINK THE BISMARCK 331
SIR ARNE'S TREASURE (HERR ARNES PENGAR) 1625, 1628
SIRENE DU MISSISSIPPI, LA (MISSISSIPI MERMAID) 2145, 2146, 2147
SISTERS 399, 2197
SISTERS OF THE GION (GION NO SHIMAI) 1890, 1901
SIX CHARACTERS IN SEARCH OF AN AUTHOR 1879
SIX HUNDRED THIRTY-THREE SQUADRON 328
SIXTEEN CANDLES 959
SJUNDE INSEGLET, DET (THE SEVENTH SEAL) 44, 138, 144, 1628, 2183, 2184,
  2186, 2188
SKAMMEN (SHAME) 2183
SKEZAG 290
SKI PATROL 329
SKIDOO 356
SKIN GAME, THE 899
SKOKIE 334
SKY AND THE EARTH, THE (LE CIEL LA TERRE) 312
SKYLARK 1336
SLAPSHOT 2052
SLAPSTICK 1578
SLAUGHTER 338, 896
SLAUGHTER'S BIG RIP-OFF 896
SLAUGHTERHOUSE FIVE 217, 331, 360, 558, 2052, 2193, 2199
SLAVE OF THE CANNIBAL (IL MONTAGNA DI DIO CANNIBALE) 419
SLAVE SHIP 1207
SLAVES 858, 894, 909, 945, 1089, 2038
SLEEP 2040, 2068
SLEEP MY LOVE 521, 523
SLEEPER 2045
SLEEPING BEAUTY 78
SLEEPING CAR MURDERS, THE (COMPARTIMENTS TUEURS) 566
SLENDER THREAD, THE 946, 2065
SLEUTH 1270, 2194
SL1 288
SMALL CHANGE (L'ARGENT DE POCHE) 998, 2106, 2107, 2146, 2149
SMART MONEY 176
SMASH-UP 1946
SMASHING OF THE REICH 287
SMILES OF A SUMMER NIGHT (SOMMARNATTENS LEENDE) 1628, 2183, 2184,
  2187
SMILING LIEUTENANT, THE 1276
SMILING MADAM BEUDET, THE (LA SOURIANTE MADAME BEUDET) 1712
SMULTRONSTALLET (WILD STRAWBERRIES) 595, 599, 600, 751, 1625, 1628,
  2183, 2184, 2186, 2189

SNAKE PIT, THE 271, 569, 793, 1256, 1500, 1946
SNIPER'S RIDGE 334
SNIPER, THE 987
SNOW WHITE AND THE SEVEN DWARFS 487, 1769
SNOWS OF KILIMANJARO, THE 1231, 1232, 1500, 1952
SO DEAR TO MY HEART 1073
SO ENDS OUR NIGHT 333
SO PROUDLY WE HAIL 331
SO RED THE ROSE 877, 939, 941, 944
SO THIS IS LOVE 1247
SO THIS IS PARIS 1694
SOAK THE RICH 1265
SOCRATE 1883
SODOM AND GOMORRAH 2043
SOGA KYODAI NO AKEBONO (DAWN AT THE SOGA BROTHERS' HUNTING
  GROUND) 1735
SOLARIS 410
SOLDIER BLUE 339, 425, 811, 2193
SOLDIER'S STORY, A 551, 902, 905, 2204
SOLDIERS, THE (LES CARABINIERS) 2110, 2124
SOLOMON AND SHEBA 832, 1517, 1696
SOME EVIDENCE 290
SOME KIND OF HERO 338
SOME LIKE IT HOT 499, 589, 657, 1971, 1972
SOMEBODY UP THERE LIKES ME 2053
SOMEONE TO WATCH OVER ME 2203, 2204, 2207
SOMETHING OF VALUE 887, 945
SOMETHING'S GOT TO GIVE 1251, 1252
SOMEWHERE IN FRANCE 331, 1911
SOMMARNATTENS LEENDE (SMILES OF A SUMMER NIGHT) 1628, 2183, 2184,
  2187
SON OF THE SHEIK 1578
SONG OF BERNADETTE, THE 1587, 1911
SONG OF CEYLON 249, 303, 1871
SONG OF HEROES (HELDENLIED, KOMSOMOL) 312, 314
SONG OF RUSSIA 331, 1090, 1649, 1913
SONG OF THE RIVERS (DAS LIED DER STROME) 312
SONG OF THE SOUTH 855, 857, 882, 904, 921, 1073
SONG TO REMEMBER, A 589, 738
SONGWRITER 2065
SONO YORU NO ONNA (THE WOMAN THAT NIGHT) 1894
SONS AND DAUGHTERS 290
SONS AND LOVERS 1010, 1312
SOPHIE'S CHOICE 334, 1032
SORCERER 2200
SORROW AND THE PITY, THE (LE CHAGRIN ET LA PITIE) 246, 289, 303, 311,
  317, 324, 377, 2143
SORROW OF ISRAEL, THE 846, 847
SORROWS OF SATAN, THE 1368
SORRY, WRONG NUMBER 976, 1288, 1948
SORTIE DES USINES, LA (WORKERS LEAVING THE LUMIERE FACTORY) 1619
SOUFFLE AU COEUR, LE (MURMUR OF THE HEART) 2119
SOULS FOR SALE 1248
SOULS ON THE ROAD (ROJO NO REIKON) 1740, 1741
SOUND AND THE FURY, THE 152
SOUND FILM ANTHOLOGY 1797
SOUND OF MUSIC, THE 150, 748, 1500
SOUNDER 551, 565, 899, 909, 936, 941, 945, 1530, 2199
SOURIANTE MADAME BEUDET, LA (THE SMILING MADAM BEUDET) 1712

SOUS LES TOITS DE PARIS (UNDER THE ROOFS OF PARIS) 404, 1714, 1725, 1810, 1825
SOUTH PACIFIC 331
SOUTHERNER, THE 912, 914, 1147, 1149, 1160, 1210, 1256, 1814, 1820, 1946
SPAIN (ISPANIYA) 287
SPANISH EARTH, THE 303, 312, 313, 314, 319, 352, 1870
SPANISH TURMOIL, THE 319
SPARE TIME 316
SPARROW 89
SPARROWS 1392, 1393, 1398
SPARTACUS 547, 1282, 1285, 2055
SPECTER OF THE ROSE 1649
SPELLBOUND 595, 606, 1224, 1649, 1843, 1852, 1853, 1911, 1913
SPHINX 2067
SPIES LIKE US 2202
SPIES WHO NEVER WERE, THE 289
SPIRIT OF '76, THE 328
SPIRIT OF ST. LOUIS, THE 1155
SPIRIT OF YOUTH, THE 929
SPLENDOR IN THE GRASS 664, 975, 1010, 1261
SPLIT, THE 894
SPOOK WHO SAT BY THE DOOR, THE 896
SPORTING BLOOD 421
SPORTING LIFE, THE 421
SPRING BREAK 977
SPY IN BLACK 328
SPY WHO CAME IN FROM THE COLD, THE 334, 2036
SPY WHO LOVED ME, THE 414, 422, 1569
SPY, THE 328
SQUAW MAN, THE 1472, 1477, 1681
STACHKA (STRIKE) 1658, 1666, 1667
STAGE DOOR CANTEEN 331
STAGE FRIGHT 1848, 1920
STAGECOACH (1939) 44, 114, 193, 194, 197, 433, 1064, 1169, 1311, 1370, 1684, 1686, 1772, 1802
STAIRWAY TO HEAVEN 331
STAKEOUT 2205, 2206
STALAG 17 196, 331, 348, 374, 1952, 1966, 1971
STALINGRAD 287
STAND BY FOR ACTION 331
STAND BY ME 2202, 2203
STAR IS BORN, A (1937) 112, 1060, 1073, 1081, 1136, 1151, 1176, 1245, 1246, 1275, 1295, 1675, 1701
STAR IS BORN, A (1954) 112, 1136, 1176, 1244, 1245, 1246, 1248, 1275, 1295, 1296, 1494, 1495, 1952
STAR IS BORN, A (1976) 112, 1138, 1176, 1295
STAR TREK films 2200
STAR TREK III: THE SEARCH FOR SPOCK 151, 2200
STAR TREK II: THE WRATH OF KAHN 2200
STAR TREK IV: THE VOYAGE HOME 2200
STAR TREK V 762
STAR TREK: THE MOTION PICTURE 554, 676, 2200
STAR WARS 410, 411, 414, 415, 536, 539, 554, 668, 768, 802, 803, 902, 1017, 2199, 2200
STAR 80 1044, 1137
STARDUST 2199
STARDUST MEMORIES 153, 2045, 2208
STARFISH, THE (L'ETOILE DE MER) 1713

STARK LOVE 1372
STARMAN 151, 2200
STAROIE I NOVOIE (THE GENERAL LINE/OLD AND NEW) 1645, 1661, 1866
STARSHIP INVASIONS 414
STARTING OVER 512
STAR! 145, 748, 1500, 1501, 2041
STATE FAIR 1779
STATE OF THE UNION 1081
STATE'S ATTORNEY 555, 568
STAVINSKY 2118
STAYING ALIVE 802
STEAGLE, THE 834
STEAMBOAT 'ROUND THE BEND 270
STEAMBOAT BILL, JR. 1672, 1688
STEAMBOAT WILLIE 1797
STEEL FIST, THE 1949
STEEL HELMET, THE 231, 262, 334, 359, 1960, 1976
STELLA DALLAS (1925) 793, 794, 1394, 1779
STELLA DALLAS (1937) 793, 794, 795, 796
STELLA MARIS 1392
STEPFATHER, THE 2203
STEPFORD WIVES, THE 1151
STERILE CUCKOO, THE 975, 1039
STILTE ROND CHRISTINE M, DE (A QUESTION OF SILENCE) 492, 501, 526
STING, THE 105, 2052, 2199
STIR CRAZY 890
STOLEN KISSES (BAISERS VOLES) 2145, 2148
STOP THE WORLD--I WANT TO GET OFF 403
STORM OVER ASIA (THE HEIR TO GENGHIS-KAHN/POTOMOK
 CHINGIS-KAHN) 1668
STORM WITHIN, THE (LES PARENTS TERRIBLES) 1995, 1997
STORMY WEATHER 880, 921, 939
STORY OF A THREE DAY PASS 894
STORY OF ADELE H., THE (L'HISTOIRE D'ADELE H.) 584, 2107, 2144, 2145,
 2149
STORY OF CHIAM RUMKOWSKI AND THE JEWS OF LODZ, THE 290
STORY OF GOSTA BERLING, THE (GOSTA BERLING'S SAGA) 1625, 1630
STORY OF G. I. JOE, THE 331, 349, 361, 1675, 1701, 1913
STORY OF LOUIS PASTEUR, THE 1497, 1800
STORY OF RUTH, THE 832
STORY OF THE LAST CHRYSANTHEMUM, THE/TALE OF LATE
 CHRYSANTHEMUMS (ZANGIKU MONOGATARI) 1901
STORY OF WILL ROGERS, THE 1247
STRADA, LA (THE ROAD) 1021, 1564, 1815, 1929, 1930, 1933, 1954
STRAIGHT FROM HEAVEN 935
STRAIGHT SHOOTING 1684
STRAIT-JACKET 389
STRANGE INTERLUDE 1154, 1341
STRANGE LOVE OF MARTHA IVERS, THE 1160
STRANGE ONES, THE (LES ENFANTS TERRIBLES) 1995, 2000
STRANGER ON THE THIRD FLOOR 1948
STRANGERS ON A TRAIN 150, 1197, 1198, 1843, 1844, 1846, 1848, 1854, 1858,
 1952
STRANGER, THE 334, 1317, 1790, 1791
STRATEGIC AIR COMMAND 262
STRAW DOGS 359, 558, 669, 804, 811, 2061, 2087
STRAWBERRY STATEMENT, THE 338
STRAY DOG (NORAINU) 2017, 2021
STREAMERS 338

STREET JUGGLER, THE (MACHI NO TEJINASHI) 1742
STREET SCENE 840, 841, 1472
STREETCAR NAMED DESIRE, A 791, 1260, 1337, 1347, 1352
STRIKE (STACHKA) 1658, 1666, 1667
STRIPPER, THE 2067
STRONG MAN, THE 328, 1705
STRONGHEARTS 989
STRUGGLE IN ITALY (LOTTE INTALIA/LUTTES EN ITALIE) 2111
STRUGGLE, THE 1368
STUDENT OF PRAGUE, THE (DER STUDENT VON PRAG) 1631
STUDENT PRINCE, THE (1927) 1694
STUDENT VON PRAG, DER (THE STUDENT OF PRAGUE) 1631
ST. ELMO'S FIRE 815, 972
ST. LOUIS BLUES, THE 924, 928
ST. VALENTINE'S DAY MASSACRE, THE 2049
SUBARASHIKI NICHIYOBI (ONE WONDERFUL SUNDAY) 1899, 2017, 2020
SUBIDA AL CIELO (MEXICAN BUS RIDE) 1723
SUBMARINE COMMAND 334, 336
SUBMARINE PATROL 327, 1207
SUBMARINE PIRATE, A 327
SUBMARINE RAIDERS 328
SUBMARINE X-1 330
SUBMARINE ZONE (MYSTERY SEA RAIDER) 329
SUCH A GORGEOUS KID (UNE BELLE FILLE COMME MOI 2144
SUCH GOOD FRIENDS 834, 835
SUD NARADOV (JUDGMENT OF THE NATIONS) 289
SUDDEN IMPACT 437, 801
SUDDENLY LAST SUMMER 858, 1270, 1352
SUDS 1392, 1393
SUEZ 1401
SUGARLAND EXPRESS, THE 409
SUGATA SANSHIRO (SANSHIRO SUGATA) 2028
SUICIDE ATTACK 286
SULLIVAN'S TRAVELS 1244, 1912, 1919, 1921
SULLIVANS, THE 331
SUMMER HOLIDAY 401, 1341
SUMMER LIGHT (LUMIERE D'ETE) 1904
SUMMER WORLD, A 2067
SUMMER (LE RAYON VERT) 2105
SUMMERTIME 1489
SUMMERTIME (SUMMER MADNESS) 1861
SUMMERTREE 338
SUN ALSO RISES, THE (1926) 1315
SUN ALSO RISES, THE (1957) 328, 408, 1231, 1232, 1323, 1500
SUNA NO ONNA (WOMAN IN THE DUNES) 2177
SUNDAY DINNER FOR A SOLDIER 331
SUNDAY, BLOODY SUNDAY 148, 516
SUNDOWN 328
SUNRISE 472, 1394, 1398, 1555, 1706
SUNSET BOULEVARD 376, 499, 657, 1136, 1137, 1169, 1244, 1245, 1246, 1248,
  1291, 1503, 1952, 1953, 1971, 1972
SUPER FLY 898, 899, 923, 946, 978, 988
SUPERMAN 414, 554, 2200
SUPERMAN III 409
SUPERMAN series 2200
SUR ET SOUS LA COMMUNICATION (ON AND UNDER COMMUNICATION) 2112
SURF GIRL, THE 1413
SURVIVAL . . . OR SUICIDE 288

SURVIVORS 288
SUSAN LENNOX: HER FALL AND RISE 555, 638, 1313, 1748
SUSAN SLADE 975, 987
SUSPICION 521, 523, 1486, 1847, 1913
SUTTER'S GOLD 1212, 1867
SUZY 328
SVENGALI 1798
SWANEE RIVER 944
SWARM, THE 414, 753
SWEET BIRD OF YOUTH 1248
SWEET CHARITY 2041, 2191
SWEET DREAMS 680
SWEET LIFE, THE (LA DOLCE VITA) 1023, 1315, 1929, 1930, 2036, 2169, 2170,
2174
SWEET LOVE, BITTER 894
SWEET SMELL OF SUCCESS 150, 838, 2053
SWEET SWEETBACK'S BAADASSSSS SONG 894, 896, 898, 911, 923, 924, 937,
942, 949, 953
SWEETHEARTS 1275
SWEPT AWAY (TRAVOLTI DA UN INSOLITO DESTINO NELL'AZZURRO MARE
D'AGOSTO) 2172
SWINDLE, THE (IL BIDONE) 2171
SWING SHIFT 1037
SWING TIME 401, 1787, 1798
SWINGTIME 150
SWISS MISS 1690
SWORD IN THE DESERT 832
SYMPATHY FOR THE DEVIL (ONE PLUS ONE) 2130
SYMPHONIE PASTORALE, LA 1310
SYMPHONY OF 6,000,000, THE 828
S. O. B. 536, 598, 1136, 1137, 1140, 1294

T

TABU 1640, 1671
TAILOR-MADE MAN, A 822
TAKE A GIANT STEP 893, 945
TAKE THE HIGH GROUND 334
TAKE THE MONEY AND RUN 833, 834, 2044
TAKING OFF 562
TALE OF LATE CHRYSANTHEMUMS/THE STORY OF THE LAST
CHRYSANTHEMUM (ZANGIKU MONOGATARI) 1901
TALE OF ROYAL RETAINERS IN THE GENROKU ERA, A/FORTY-SEVENTH
RONIN: Part II(GENROKU CHUSHINGURA) 1901
TALE OF TWO CITIES, A (1935) 1305, 1306, 1307, 1481, 1749
TALES OF HOFFMAN, THE 1860, 1935, 1937
TALES OF MANHATTAN 939, 944
TALK OF THE TOWN, THE 568, 1093
TAMANGO 858, 886
TAMING OF THE SHREW, THE (1929) 1343, 1344, 1401, 1403, 1408
TAMING OF THE SHREW, THE (1967) 159, 1356
TANKS ARE COMING, THE 330
TARGET FOR TONIGHT 249, 283, 287, 293, 309, 322
TARGET SURIBACHI: IWO JIMA 287
TARGET ZERO 334
TARGETS 2064
TARIS 1824
TARNISHED ANGELS, THE 794, 1039

TARZAN AND JANE REGAINED . . . SORT OF 2068
TARZAN film series 420, 421, 874, 879, 918, 1174
TARZAN movies 929
TARZAN, THE APE MAN (1932) 919
TARZAN, THE APE MAN (1981) 419
TASK FORCE 332, 369
TASTE OF BLOOD, A 393
TAUSEND AUGEN DES DR MABUSE, DIE (THE THOUSAND EYES OF DR.
 MABUSE) 1636, 1637
TAXI DRIVER 338, 339, 341, 558, 570, 811, 981, 1153, 1526, 2198
TAXI FOR TOBRUK 328
TAZA, SON OF COCHISE 1757
TCHAPAEV 261, 275
TE O TSUNAGU KORA (CHILDREN HAND IN HAND) 2017
TEAHOUSE OF THE AUGUST MOON, THE 331, 340
TELL IT TO THE MARINES 327
TELL ME A RIDDLE 604
TELL ME THAT YOU LOVE ME, JUNIE MOON 1966, 1967
TELL THEM WILLIE BOY IS HERE 1094
TEMPEST 1579
TEMPEST, THE 2048
TEMPS DETRUIT, LE (TIME DESTROYED) 287
TEMPS DU ONETTO, LA (THE WITNESSES) 289
TEMPTATION 867, 947
TEMPTATIONS OF DOCTOR ANTONIO, THE 595, 2171
TEN COMMANDMENTS, THE (1923) 382, 1703
TEN COMMANDMENTS, THE (1956) 269, 382, 383, 832, 885, 1478, 1517
TEN DAYS THAT SHOOK THE WORLD/OCTOBER (OKTIABR) 1658, 1659, 1667,
 1668
TEN DAYS WONDER (LA DECADE PRODIGIEUSE) 2101
TEN LITTLE INDIANS (AND THEN THERE WERE NONE) 939
TEN LITTLE NIGGERS (AND THEN THERE WERE NONE) 939
TEN NIGHTS IN A BARROOM 921
TEN NORTH FREDERICK 1203
TEN SECONDS TO HELL 2043
TENDER COMRADE 331, 1201, 1202, 1284
TENDER IS THE NIGHT 1217
TENDER TRAP, THE 499, 657
TENNESSEE JOHNSON 274, 856
TERESA 331
TERJE VIGEN 1625
TERMINATOR, THE 802, 2200
TERMS OF ENDEARMENT 501, 787, 792, 971, 1167, 2199
TERRA TREMA, LA (THE EARTH TREMBLES) 1925, 1926, 1932, 1934
TERRORS OF RUSSIA (THE BLACK HUNDREDS) 847
TERRY WHITMORE, FOR EXAMPLE 290
TESS OF THE STORM COUNTRY (1914) 1392
TESS OF THE STORM COUNTRY (1922) 1393
TESTAMENT 334
TESTAMENT D'ORPHEE, LE (THE TESTAMENT OF ORPHEUS) 1817, 1995, 2009
TESTAMENT DES DR. MABUSE, DAS (THE LAST WILL OF DR. MABUSE) 1829
TESTAMENT OF ORPHEUS, THE (LE TESTAMENT D'ORPHEE) 1817, 1995, 2009
TETE CONTRE LES MURS, LA (THE KEEPERS) 2128
TEVYE DER MILKHIKER (TEVYE THE MILKMAN) 828, 829
TEVYE THE MILKMAN (TEVYE DER MILKHIKER) 828, 829
TEX 977, 998
TEXAS CHAINSAW MASSACRE, THE 392, 976
TEXAS RANGERS, THE 556

THAT CERTAIN FEELING 885
THAT COLD DAY IN THE PARK 1176
THAT DARN CAT 488
THAT NIGHT IN RIO 1073
THAT OBSCURE OBJECT OF DESIRE (CET OBSCUR OBJECT DU DESIRE) 1310,
  1722, 1723
THAT ROYALE WIFE 988
THAT'S ENTERTAINMENT 1483
THAT'S ME 985
THAT'S MY BOY 1954
THE ATTACK ON ZEEBRUGGE 285
THEIR MUTUAL CHILD 728
THEM (1954) 418, 1946
THEODORA GOES WILD 1093
THERE IS A FATHER (CHICHI ARIKI) 1902
THERE WAS A CROOKED MAN 1270
THERE'S NO BUSINESS LIKE SHOW BUSINESS 1206, 1281
THESE THREE 1225
THEY ALSO SERVE 287
THEY CALL ME MR. TIBBS 888, 896
THEY DARE NOT LOVE 329
THEY DIED WITH THEIR BOOTS ON 1700
THEY DRIVE BY NIGHT 1497, 1968, 2088
THEY LIVE BY NIGHT 1948
THEY SHOOT HORSES, DON'T THEY? 1314, 2065, 2088
THEY WERE EXPENDABLE 331, 349, 369, 1684
THEY WERE FIVE (LA BELLE EQUIPE) 1813
THEY WON'T BELIEVE ME 1948
THEY WON'T FORGET 556, 568, 836, 859, 939, 944, 1091
THIEF 769
THIEF OF BAGDAD, THE (1924) 1400, 1402, 1408, 1478, 1578, 1700
THIEF OF BAGDAD, THE (1940) 417, 1619, 1833, 1860
THIEVES LIKE US 912, 1176
THIN MAN, THE film series 420, 421, 1222, 1226, 1806
THIN RED LINE, THE 332
THING FROM ANOTHER WORLD, THE 1777
THINGS TO COME 410, 412, 417, 418, 460, 1859
THING, THE (1951) 417, 418, 1152, 1224, 1946, 1952
THIRD LOVER, THE (L'OIL DU MALIN, OPHELIA) 2100
THIRD MAN, THE 331, 343, 1033, 1218, 1219, 1329, 1790, 1860, 1936, 1937,
  1940
THIRTEEN RUE MADELEINE 331
THIRTY SECONDS OVER TOKYO 217, 331, 370, 595, 1282, 1911
THIRTY YEARS AFTER 866
THIRTY-FOUR YEARS AFTER HITLER 289
THIRTY-NINE STEPS, THE (1935) 114, 373, 1834, 1838, 1843, 1851, 1853, 1864
THIRTY-SIX HOURS 331
THIS ABOVE ALL 331
THIS DAY AND AGE 556
THIS GUN FOR HIRE 1088, 1219, 1948
THIS HAPPY BREED 1860
THIS IS AMERICA 280, 285
THIS IS EDWARD R. MURROW 287
THIS IS THE ARMY 331
THIS ISLAND EARTH 418
THIS MAN MUST DIE (KILLER!/QUE LA BETE MEURE) 2098, 2101
THIS PROPERTY IS CONDEMNED 2065
THIS SIDE OF PARADISE 1113
THIS SPORTING LIFE (1963) 74, 1569, 2160

THIS STRANGE PASSION 1990
THOMAS GRAAL'S BEST FILM 1624
THOMAS L'IMPOSTEUR (THOMAS THE IMPOSTER)   2128
THOMAS THE IMPOSTER (THOMAS L'IMPOSTEUR)   2128
THOROUGHLY MODERN MILLIE 2052
THOSE DARING YOUNG MEN IN THEIR JAUNTY JALOPIES 2041
THOSE WERE THE HAPPY TIMES 1501
THOSE WHO MAKE TOMORROW (ASU O TSUKURU HITOBITO) 2020
THOUSAND CLOWNS, A 1022
THOUSAND CRANES: CHILDREN OF HIROSHIMA, A 356
THOUSAND EYES OF DR. MABUSE, THE (DIE TAUSEND AUGEN DES DR
  MABUSE) 1636, 1637
THREADS 287
THREE BRAVE MEN 334
THREE CABALLEROS, THE 307, 984
THREE CAME HOME 331
THREE COINS IN THE FOUNTAIN 499
THREE COMRADES 328, 568, 1039, 1114, 1122, 1148, 1151, 1215, 1216, 1217,
  1250, 1270, 1271
THREE DAYS OF THE CONDOR 811, 2065, 2192
THREE FACES OF EVE, THE 793, 1252, 1253
THREE FACES WEST 329
THREE IN THE ATTIC 894
THREE LITTLE WORDS 1176
THREE LIVES 516
THREE MEN AND A BABY 762, 2205, 2206
THREE MUSKETEERS, THE (1921) 1081, 1400, 1408
THREE MUSKETEERS, THE (1974) 269, 382, 2194
THREE SISTERS (1964) 1034, 1337
THREE STRIPES IN THE SUN 340
THREE WOMEN 593
THREEPENNY OPERA, THE (DIE DREIGROSCHENOPER) 1633, 1635, 1829
THRILLER 506, 512
THRONE OF BLOOD (KUMONOSU-JO/COBWEB CASTLE) 1356, 2019, 2021
THROUGH A GLASS DARKLY (SASOM I EN SPEGEL) 2183, 2186
THROUGH THE LOOKING GLASS 1974
THUNDER ROCK 1938
THUNDERBALL 422
THUNDERBIRDS 332
THUNDERBOLT AND LIGHTFOOT 604
THX 1138 2196
TIGER LIKES FRESH BLOOD, THE (LE TIGRE AIME LA CHAIR FRAICHE) 2100
TIGHT LITTLE ISLAND (WHISKEY GALORE) 1937
TIGRE AIME LA CHAIR FRAICHE, LE (THE TIGER LIKES FRESH BLOOD) 2100
TILL THE CLOUDS ROLL BY 831
TILL THE END OF TIME 331, 1946
TILL WE MEET AGAIN 1071
TILLIE AND GUS 1770
TILLIE'S PUNCTURED ROMANCE 1416, 1433
TIME DESTROYED (LE TEMPS DETRUIT) 287
TIME HAS COME, THE 288
TIME LIMIT 334
TIME MACHINE, THE 411, 412, 1312
TIME OF THE LOCUST 290
TIME OF THEIR LIVES, THE 1476
TIME OUT OF WAR, A 379
TIME TO KILL 1198
TIME TO LOVE AND A TIME TO DIE, A 331, 2134

TIN DRUM, THE (DIE BLECHTROMMEL) 152, 311, 334
TIREZ SUR LE PIANISTE (SHOOT THE PIANO PLAYER) 2107, 2144, 2155
TITFIELD THUNDERBOLT, THE 1937
TITICUT FOLLIES 815, 2040, 2092
TKIES KAF (THE VOW) 847
TO BE OR NOT TO BE (1942) 311, 334, 1071, 1694
TO BE OR NOT TO BE (1983) 331, 334, 2047
TO CATCH A THIEF 499, 1848, 1952, 1978
TO DIE IN MADRID (MOURIR A MADRID) 319
TO DIE, TO LIVE: THE SURVIVORS OF HIROSHIMA 288, 356
TO EACH HIS OWN 521, 523
TO HAVE AND HAVE NOT 150, 331, 1147, 1214, 1215, 1231, 1315, 1323, 1747, 1777
TO HELL AND BACK 331, 334, 339
TO KILL A MOCKINGBIRD 858, 894, 945, 1325, 2038
TO LIFE--L'CHAIM 289
TO LIVE AND DIE IN L. A. 806
TO REMEMBER THE FALLEN: CONFLICT IN JAPAN 287
TO SIR WITH LOVE 891
TO THE END OF THE SILVER-CAPPED MOUNTAINS (GINREI NO HATE) 2017
TO THE SHORES OF HELL 338
TO THE SHORES OF IWO JIMA 286
TOBACCO ROAD 858, 980, 1499, 1686
TOBRUK 254, 328
TODAY WE LIVE 328, 1207, 1213
TOKYO MONOGATARI (TOKYO STORY) 2019, 2025, 2032
TOKYO OLYMPIAD (TOKYO ORIMPIKKU) 2177
TOKYO ORIMPIKKU (TOKYO OLYMPIAD) 2177
TOKYO STORY (TOKYO MONOGATARI) 2019, 2025, 2032
TOKYO TRIAL, THE 287
TOL'ABLE DAVID 1705, 1779
TOLL GATE, THE 1704
TOM AND JERRY film series 1237
TOM JONES 1312, 1316, 1328
TOM SAWYER 1305
TOMB OF LIGEIA, THE 2049
TOMORROW 913
TOMORROW IS FOREVER 1790
TOMORROW THE WORLD 1073
TONARI NO YAE-CHAN (OUR NEIGHBOR MISS YAE) 1894
TONI 1714, 1814
TONIGHT WE RAID CALAIS 1090
TOO HOT TO HANDLE 1672
TOO LATE THE BLUES 2048
TOO LATE THE HERO 331, 2043
TOO MUCH, TOO SOON 1247
TOO YOUNG THE HERO 331
TOOTSIE 554, 588, 802, 2065
TOP GUN 2202
TOP HAT 150
TOP SECRET--THE HISTORY OF THE GERMANS 289
TOPAZ 334, 1849, 1854
TOPO, EL (THE MOLE) 392
TOPPER film series 1695
TORA! TORA! TORA! 231, 279, 331, 2191
TORMENT (FRENZY/HETS) 2183, 2185
TORN CURTAIN 1849, 1854, 1858
TORO NO O FUMU OTOKOTACHI (THE MEN WHO TREAD ON THE TIGER'S TAIL) 2020

TORPEDO ALLEY   336
TORPEDO RUN   331
TORTILLA FLAT   1281
TOUCH OF EVIL   1790, 1791, 2069, 2091
TOUCH, THE   516
TOUCH, THE (BERORINGEN)   2184
TOUR OF DUTY   232
TOUT VA BIEN (JUST GREAT)   2111, 2126
TOUTE UN VIE (AND NOW MY LOVE)   2119
TOWED IN A HOLE   1690
TOWERING INFERNO, THE   803, 2193
TOWN WITHOUT PITY   331, 1282
TOWN, THE   306
TOYS IN THE ATTIC   1225, 2052
TOYTMILN (DEATH FACTORIES)   848
TRACKS   338
TRADE WINDS   1275
TRADER HORN (1931)   874, 919
TRADER MICKEY   874
TRAFFIC   2007
TRAIN, THE   331, 2051
TRAMP, THE   1416
TRANSPORTS OF DEATH   289
TRASH   2040, 2068
TRAVELS WITH MY AUNT   1219
TRAVOLTI DA UN INSOLITO DESTINO NELL'AZZURRO MARE D'AGOSTO (SWEPT
    AWAY)   2172
TREASURE ISLAND (1950)   1951
TREASURE OF THE SIERRA MADRE, THE   62, 191, 599, 1022, 1086, 1091, 1169,
    1314, 1315, 1915, 1916, 1952, 1979
TREE GROWS IN BROOKLYN, A   521, 1259, 1260, 1968
TRIAL   816
TRIAL AT NUREMBERG (CBS)   287
TRIAL OF BILLY JACK, THE   338, 666
TRIAL OF JOAN OF ARC, THE (LE PROCES DE JEANNE D'ARC)   1023, 1994
TRIAL OF THE CATONSVILLE NINE, THE   2193
TRIAL, THE (LE PROCES)   159, 1022, 1317, 1791, 2070, 2091
TRIBUTE   484
TRICKY GIRL (KARAKURI MUSUME)   1740
TRIP DOWN MEMORY LANE, A   318
TRIP TO THE MOON, A (LE VOYAGE DANS LA LUNE)   410, 411, 413, 417, 1620
TRIPLE CROSS   330
TRIP, THE   558
TRISTANA   1310, 1720, 1721
TRIUMPH DES WILLENS (TRIUMPH OF THE WILL)   218, 236, 238, 239, 240, 241,
    246, 251, 254, 287, 295, 303, 317, 321, 539, 540, 1515, 1910
TRIUMPH OF THE AXIS   287
TRIUMPH OF THE SPIRIT   334
TRIUMPH OF THE WILL (TRIUMPH DES WILLENS)   218, 236, 238, 239, 240, 241,
    246, 251, 254, 287, 295, 303, 317, 321, 539, 540, 1515, 1910
TRIUMPH OVER VIOLENCE   287
TRON   409, 2200
TROOPER OF COMPANY K, THE   947
TROUBLE IN PARADISE   555, 1276, 1639, 1694, 1804
TROUBLE MAN   896
TROUBLE WITH HARRY, THE   1849
TROUBLES OF A GRASS WIDOWER   1619
TRUE GLORY, THE   249, 287, 323

TRUE GRIT 160, 960, 1288
TRUE HEART SUSIE 1368, 1390
TSEBROKHENE HERSTER (BROKEN HEARTS) 847
TSUCHI (EARTH) 1896
TSUMA YO BARA NO YO NI (WIFE! BE LIKE A ROSE!) 1891
TUESDAY THE 13TH 290
TUMBLEWEEDS 431
TUNISIAN VICTORY 286
TURKEYS IN A ROW (SHICHIMENCHO NO YUKUE) 1740
TURN ABOUT 1213, 1214
TURN IN THE ROAD, THE 1696
TURN OF THE SCREW 976
TURNING POINT, THE 472, 558, 803, 1016, 2199
TWELVE ANGRY MEN 560, 2033, 2058, 2059
TWELVE CHAIRS, THE 2047
TWELVE O'CLOCK HIGH 262, 331, 354, 370, 1500, 1952
TWENTIETH CENTURY 305, 828, 1224, 1265, 1335, 1747
TWENTY MILLION MILES FROM EARTH 411
TWENTY THOUSAND LEAGUES UNDER THE SEA 410, 417, 1951
TWENTY-FIFTH HOUR, THE 330
TWENTY-FOUR EYES (NIJUSHI NO HITOMI) 2018
TWENTY-THIRD PSALM BRANCH 290
TWILIGHT ZONE 691
TWILIGHT'S LAST GLEAMING 338, 2043
TWINKLE, TWINKLE KILLER KANE (THE NINTH CONFIGURATION) 338
TWISTED CROSS 287
TWO ARABIAN NIGHTS 1090
TWO DECADES OF HISTORY 287
TWO ENGLISH GIRLS (LES DEUX ANGLAISES ET LE CONTINENT) 2145, 2148,
   2155
TWO FACES OF DR. JEKYLL, THE (THE HOUSE OF FRIGHT) 117
TWO MULES FOR SISTER SARA 1100
TWO NIGHTS WITH CLEOPATRA 383
TWO OF US, THE (LE VIEIL HOMME ET L'ENFANT) 311, 334
TWO OR THREE THINGS I KNOW ABOUT HER (2 OU 3 CHOSES QUE JE SAIS
   D'ELLE) 497, 2110, 2131
TWO RODE TOGETHER 1673
TWO THOUSAND AND ONE: A SPACE ODYSSEY 159, 410, 412, 415, 418, 553,
   1169, 1311, 2054, 2055, 2056, 2057, 2058, 2083
TWO THOUSAND AND TEN 2083, 2200
TWO WEEKS IN ANOTHER TOWN 1041
TWO WOMEN 330, 331, 378, 1310, 2174
TWO YEARS BEFORE THE MAST 1095
TYSTNADEN (THE SILENCE) 2183, 2186

U

UBER ALLES IN DER WELT (ABOVE ALL IN THE WORLD) 240
UGETSU MONOGATARI (UGETSU) 2019, 2025, 2029, 2031
UGETSU (UGETSU MONOGATARI) 2019, 2025, 2029, 2031
UGLY AMERICAN, THE 334, 359
UKIGUMO (FLOATING CLOUDS) 2019
ULZANA'S RAID 339, 425, 433, 2043
UMA (HORSE) 1896
UMARETE WA MITA KEREDO (I WAS BORN BUT . . .) 1893, 1901
UMBERTO D 1926, 1932, 1933
UMBRELLAS OF CHERBOURG, THE (LES PARAPLUIES DU CHERBOURG) 408
UNCLE KRUGER (OHM KRUGER) 209, 240

UNCLE MOSES 829
UNCLE TOM'S CABIN (1903) 718, 857, 862, 906, 908, 920, 938
UNCLE TOM'S CABIN (1914) 920, 932
UNCLE TOM'S CABIN (1927) 927
UNCLE YANCO 2114
UNCOMMON VALOR 338, 442, 2200
UNDER CAPRICORN 1848
UNDER FIRE 454
UNDER THE ROOFS OF PARIS (SOUS LES TOITS DE PARIS) 404, 1714, 1725,
  1810, 1825
UNDER THE WORLD (DEBAJO DEL MUNDO) 334
UNDER TWO FLAGS 1073
UNDERCOVER HERO 330
UNDERGROUND 329
UNDERWORLD U. S. A. 1960, 2078
UNDERWORLD (1927) 387, 1224, 1708
UNDERWORLD (1936) 948
UNFAITHFUL WIFE, THE (LA FEMME INFIDELE) 2101, 2128
UNFAITHFULLY YOURS 1912, 1919
UNFINISHED BUSINESS 287
UNION MAIDS 505, 512
UNION PACIFIC 1478
UNITED WE STAND 286
UNKNOWN CHAPLIN 1416
UNMARRIED WOMAN, AN 472, 512
UNNATURAL CAUSES 338
UNQUIET DEATH OF JULIUS AND ETHEL ROSENBERG 288
UNSEEN, THE 1198
UNSUSPECTED, THE 1073
UNTERNEHMEN MICHAEL (OPERATION MICHAEL) 240
UNTOUCHABLES, THE 2205
UNVANQUISHED, THE (APARAJITO) 1004
UP FROM THE BEACH 331
UP PERSICOPE 332
UP THE DOWN STAIRCASE 985
UP THE SANDBOX 1436
UP TIGHT 916, 937, 941, 1951, 2038
UPTOWN SATURDAY NIGHT 889
URLAUB AUF EHRENWORT (LEAVE ON WORD OF HONOUR) 240

V

VACANCES DE MONSIEUR HULOT, LES (MR. HULOT'S HOLIDAY) 2000, 2007,
  2010
VAGABOND (SANS TOIT NI LOI) 2114
VAGABONDE, LA (THE VAGABOND) 508
VAGABOND, THE 1416
VAGABOND, THE (LA VAGABONDE) 508
VAGHE SETLLE DELL'OREA (SANDRA) 334
VALENTINO (1951) 1245, 1246, 1247, 1296
VALENTINO (1977) 1143, 1245, 1296
VALLEY GIRL 977, 998
VALLEY OF THE DOLLS 1137
VALPARAISO, A 312
VAMPIRES, LES 1605
VAMPYR (THE DREAM OF ALLAN GRAY) 397, 1629, 1726, 1811
VAN GOGH 2117, 2136, 2137

VANGELO SECONDO MATTEO, IL (THE GOSPEL ACCORDING TO ST.
  MATTHEW) 2175
VANISHING AMERICAN, THE 1577
VANISHING CORPORAL, THE (THE ELUSIVE CORPORAL/LA CAPORAL
  EPINGLE) 1821
VANISHING POINT 409
VANITY FAIR 1618
VARGTIMMEN (THE HOUR OF THE WOLF) 2184
VARIETE (VARIETY) 1579, 1632, 1640
VARIETY LIGHTS (LUCI DEL VARIETA) 1929
VARIETY (VARIETE) 1579, 1632, 1640
VEILS OF BAGDAD, THE 701
VENGANZA DE LA MOMIA, LA (THE MUMMY'S REVENGE) 391
VENT D'EST (VENTTO DELL'EST/WIND FROM THE EAST) 2111, 2135
VENTTO DELL'EST (VENT D'EST/WIND FROM THE EAST) 2111, 2135
VENUS IM PELZ (VENUS IN FURS) 2037
VENUS IN FURS (VENUS IM PELZ) 2037
VERDICT, THE 560, 2059
VERLOBTE, DIE (THE FIANCEE) 334
VERLORENE EHRE DER KATHARINA BLUM, DIE (THE LOST HONOR OF
  KATHARINA BLUM) 1310
VERTIGO 144, 976, 1515, 1843, 1849, 1850, 1852, 1854, 1855, 1858, 2080, 2081
VICAR OF WAKEFIELD, THE 1612
VICTORS, THE 233, 331, 368, 1093
VICTORY 312, 334, 1305
VICTORY AT SEA 287
VICTORY IN EUROPE 287
VICTORY IN THE SOUTH PACIFIC 287
VICTORY IN THE WEST (SIEG IM WESTEN) 206, 282
VICTORY THROUGH AIR POWER 286, 307
VICTOR, VICTORIA 589, 604
VIEIL HOMME ET L'ENFANT, LE (THE TWO OF US) 311, 334
VIETNAM 290
VIETNAM DOCUMENTARY 290
VIETNAM EPILOGUE 290
VIETNAM IN TURMOIL 290
VIETNAM REQUIEM 290
VIETNAM! VIETNAM! 1674
VIETNAM: A TELEVISION HISTORY 290
VIETNAM: AN AMERICAN JOURNEY 290
VIETNAM: PICKING UP THE PIECES 290
VIEW FROM THE BRIDGE, A 1349, 2058
VIE, LA (EVERY MAN FOR HIMSELF/SAUVE QUI PEUT) 2112
VIKING WOMEN AND THE SEA SERPENT, THE 2075
VILLAGE OF THE DAMNED 418
VILLAGE TATTOOED MAN, THE (MACHI NO IREZUMI MONO) 1889
VIOLETS ARE BLUE 2207
VIOLIN MAKER OF CREMONA, THE 1380, 1392
VIOLONS DU BAL, LES 334
VIRGIN SPRING, THE (JUNGFRUKALLAN) 2183, 2186, 2187
VIRGINIAN, THE (1929) 433, 1305, 1503
VIRGINIAN, THE (1946) 433
VIRIDIANA 138, 1721, 1990, 1991, 1992
VIRTUOUS VAMP, A 1455
VISITEURS DU SOIR, LES (THE DEVIL'S OWN ENVOYS) 1904
VISITE, UNE (A VISIT) 2147
VISITORS, THE 1261
VISIT, A (UNE VISTE) 2147
VISIT, THE 1250

VISKNINGAR OCH ROP (CRIES AND WHISPERS)   2183, 2184
VITAGRAPH ROMANCE, A   1246
VITELLONI, I (THE YOUNG AND THE PASSIONATE)   1929
VIVA LA MUERTE   278
VIVA VILLA!   1152, 1488
VIVA ZAPATA!   270, 1260, 1280, 1281, 1288, 1326, 1500
VIVACIOUS LADY   990
VIVEMENT DIMANCHE! (CONFIDENTIALLY YOURS!)   2144, 2147
VIVRE   319
VIVRE SA VIE (MY LIFE TO LIVE)   2032
VIXENS   2037
VLADIMIR AND ROSA (VLADIMIR ET ROSA)   2111, 2130
VLADIMIR ET ROSA (VLADIMIR AND ROSA)   2111, 2130
VOICE FROM THE ATTIC   290
VON RYAN'S EXPRESS   196, 331, 690
VOW, THE (TKIES KAF)   847
VOYAGE DANS LA LUNE, LE (A TRIP TO THE MOON)   410, 411, 413, 417, 1620
VOYAGE OF THE DAMNED   334, 841
VREDENS DAG (DAY OF WRATH)   1629, 1726

W

WAGA KOI SESHI OTOME (THE GIRL I LOVED)   2017
WAGA SEISHUN NI KUINASHI (NO REGRETS FOR OUR YOUTH)   2017
WAGA SHOGAI NO KAGAYAKERU (THE DAY OUR LIVES SHINE)   2017
WAGES OF SIN, THE   867, 940
WAGON MASTER   427, 1684
WAKE ISLAND   331, 341, 343, 361, 1911
WAKE UP, GERMANY! (DEUTSCHLAND, ERWACHE!)   240
WALK EAST ON BEACON   1949
WALK IN THE SUN, A   233, 262, 331, 350, 354, 369, 831, 1090, 1911
WALK PROUD   974
WALKING DOWN BROADWAY   1700
WALKING TALL   811
WALL STREET   802
WALLENBERG: A HERO'S STORY   334
WALLS OF HELL, THE   332
WALL, THE   311, 334
WANDA   1261
WANDERERS, THE   974
WANNSEE CONFERENCE, THE   334
WAR AND PEACE (1958)   980
WAR AND REMEMBRANCE   334, 2205
WAR AT HOME, THE   290
WAR BIRDS (GHOST STORY)   1213
WAR BRIDES   211, 328, 342
WAR COMES TO AMERICA   287
WAR GAMES   409
WAR GAME, THE   356, 389, 1024
WAR HUNT   231, 334
WAR II: TOTAL WAR   287
WAR IS HELL   334
WAR IS OVER, THE   328
WAR IS OVER, THE (LA GUERRE EST FINIE)   278, 379, 2118, 2136, 2139
WAR LOVER, THE   330, 1262
WAR OF THE SATELLITES   2049
WAR OF THE WORLDS, THE   411, 418, 1946

WAR STORY, A 287
WAR WITHOUT WINNERS 288
WAR--ISSUE--10, THE 320
WARGAMES 972
WARM DECEMBER, A 889
WARNING SHADOWS (SCHATTEN) 1592
WARRENDALE 815
WARRIORS' WOMEN 290
WARRIORS, THE 973, 974, 975, 987
WARSAW GHETTO, THE 222, 287
WASHINGTON MERRY-GO-ROUND 568
WASHINGTON SQUARE 1952
WASURERARETA KOGUN (FORGOTTEN IMPERIAL ARMY) 288
WASURERARETA KORA (FORGOTTEN CHILDREN) 2017
WATCH ON THE RHINE 331, 521, 522, 1222, 1225, 1226, 1227, 1288, 1336
WATER GIRL, THE (THE WHIRLPOOL OF FATE/LA FILLE DE L'EAU) 1821
WATERLOO BRIDGE 1176
WATERMELON MAN 894, 923
WATTSTAX 405
WAY AHEAD, THE 1934
WAY DOWN EAST 138, 270, 1368, 1372, 1375, 1391, 1527, 1657, 1708
WAY TO SHADOW GARDEN, THE 1974
WAY TO THE FRONT, THE 290
WAY TO THE STARS, THE 331, 1841, 1934, 1938
WAY WE WERE, THE 834, 836, 841, 842, 851, 989, 1136, 1140, 2065, 2193, 2199
WAY WOMEN LOVE, THE 728
WAYS OF LOVE (L'AMORE) 1929
WAYWARD BUS, THE 1281
WE ARE MARINES 286
WE DIVE AT DAWN 1841
WE'LL BURY YOU 287
WEAPONS OF THE SPIRIT 290
WEAVERS: WASN'T THAT A TIME, THE 288
WEB OF PASSION (LEDA/DOUBLE TOUR) 2100, 2128
WEDDING IN BLOOD (LES NOCES ROUGES) 2101
WEDDING MARCH, THE 1698, 1699, 1700
WEE WILLIE WINKIE 1219, 1220, 1833
WEEK THAT SHOOK THE WORLD, THE 287
WEEK-END, LE (WEEKEND) 2109, 2111, 2120, 2130, 2131, 2133, 2135
WEEKEND (LE WEEK-END) 2109, 2111, 2120, 2130, 2131, 2133, 2135
WEEKENDS AT DUNKIRK 330
WELCOME HOME 338, 2067
WELCOME HOME JOHNNY BRISTOL 290
WELCOME HOME, SOLDIER BOYS 338
WELCOME TO HARD TIMES 1032
WELL, THE 334
WELTKREIG, DER (FIGHTING FOR THE FATHERLAND/WORLD WAR AS SEEN
  THROUGH GERMAN SPECTACLES) 285
WENT THE DAY WELL? 1938
WEST SIDE STORY 377, 987, 1164
WESTERN APPROACHES (THE RAIDER) 287, 331, 1938
WESTFRONT 1829
WESTWARD THE WOMEN 791
WHAT A WIDOW! 1401
WHAT DID YOU DO IN THE WAR, DADDY? 330
WHAT EVER HAPPENED TO BABY JANE? 389
WHAT MAKES SAMMY RUN? 1041
WHAT NEXT, CORPORAL HARGROVE? 330
WHAT PRICE GLORY? (1926) 268, 297, 304, 328, 342, 348, 361, 1700, 1709

WHAT PRICE GLORY? (1952)   328, 1206
WHAT PRICE HOLLYWOOD?   1176, 1246
WHAT'S NEW, PUSSYCAT?   2044
WHAT'S UP, TIGER LILY?   2044, 2046
WHATEVER HAPPENED TO BABY JANE   2043
WHEEL, THE (LA RUOE)   1712
WHEN A STRANGER CALLS   976
WHENCE DOES HE COME? (D'OU VIENT-IL?)   1621
WHERE EAGLES DARE   331
WHERE'S POPPA?   834
WHICH WAY TO THE FRONT?   330
WHILE THE SUN SHINES   1935
WHIP HAND   348
WHIRLPOOL OF FATE, THE (THE WATER GIRL/LA FILLE DE L'EAU)   1821
WHISKEY GALORE (TIGHT LITTLE ISLAND)   1937
WHISTLE AT EATON FALLS, THE   569
WHITE BUFFALO, THE   414
WHITE CHRISTMAS   1950
WHITE CLIFFS OF DOVER   331
WHITE HEAT   387, 580, 1700, 1948
WHITE LIGHTNING   914
WHITE LINE FEVER   559
WHITE NIGHTS   2202
WHITE NIGHTS (LE NOTTI BIANCHE)   1884, 2172
WHITE SHADOWS OF THE SOUTH SEAS   1490
WHITE SHEIK, THE (LO SCEICCO BIANCO)   1929, 1931
WHITE SHIP, THE (LA NAVE BIANCA)   1875, 1883
WHITE ZOMBIE   874
WHO KILLED ROGER RABBIT?   2203
WHO SHALL LIVE AND WHO SHALL DIE?   289, 290
WHO'LL STOP THE RAIN   338, 364
WHO'S AFRAID OF VIRGINIA WOOLF?   45, 62, 271, 989, 1169, 1337, 1495, 1942,
   2036, 2038, 2060, 2086
WHOSE CHOICE?   512
WHOSE LIFE IS IT ANYWAY?   2048
WHY AMERICA WILL WIN   213
WHY VIETNAM?   290
WHY WE FIGHT series   208, 247, 281, 284, 287, 320
WIDE BLUE YONDER, THE   332
WIFE! BE LIKE A ROSE! (TSUMA YO BARA NO YO NI)   1891
WILBY CONSPIRACY, THE   889
WILD AND WOOLLY   1400
WILD ANGELS, THE   558, 986, 987, 2049
WILD BOYS OF THE ROAD   556, 568, 1675, 1701, 1748
WILD BUNCH, THE   193, 196, 197, 199, 433, 558, 2037, 2038, 2061, 2063, 2087
WILD CHILD, THE (l'ENFANT SAUVAGE)   155, 2107, 2146, 2150
WILD GEESE, Yhe   328
WILD ONE, THE   405, 986, 1311, 2207
WILD RIVER   894, 1261
WILD STRAWBERRIES (SMULTRONSTALLET)   595, 599, 600, 751, 1625, 1628,
   2183, 2184, 2186, 2189
WILL ROGERS   1578
WILLOW   673
WILSON   254, 271, 328, 339, 365, 568, 1517
WINCHESTER '73   197, 1946, 1951, 1964, 1982
WIND AND THE LION, THE   2197
WIND FROM THE EAST (VENTTO DELL'EST/VENT D'EST)   2111, 2135
WINDFLOWER: THE STORY OF A DRAFT DODGER   338

WINDS OF WAR, THE 331
WIND, THE 1625
WING AND A PRAYER, A 331, 343
WINGS 261, 297, 328, 343, 361, 370, 1477, 1701
WINGS OF EAGLES, THE 334, 339, 1673
WINGS OF THE NAVY 327
WINNING 153, 409, 421
WINNING OF BARBARA WORTH, THE 1394
WINNING TEAM, THE 421
WINSLOW BOY, THE 1841, 1860, 1936
WINTER CARNIVAL 990, 1073, 1125, 1129, 1199, 1277
WINTER LIGHT (THE COMMUNICANTS/NATTVARDSGASTERNA) 2186, 2187, 2188
WINTER SOLDIER 290
WINTERSET 828
WISH YOU WERE HERE 2203
WITCHCRAFT THROUGH THE AGES (HAXAN) 1626, 1630
WITCHES OF EASTWICK, THE 2205
WITCHFINDER GENERAL, THE 410
WITH A SONG IN MY HEART 1246
WITH A SOUTH VIETNAMESE MARINE BATTALION 290
WITH THE MARINES AT TARAWA 286
WITHIN OUR GATES 870, 947
WITHOUT HONOR 1090
WITNESS 151, 761, 2201
WITNESS FOR THE PROSECUTION (1958) 560, 1971, 1972, 1973
WITNESSES, THE (LA TEMPS DU ONETTO) 289
WIZARD OF OZ, THE (1925) 1801
WIZARD OF OZ, THE (1939) 59, 404, 554, 599, 1169, 1208, 1801
WIZ, THE 2199
WOLF MAN, THE film series 389, 421
WOMAN FROM NOWHERE, THE (LA FEMME DE NULLE PART) 1712
WOMAN IN THE DUNES (SUNA NO ONNA) 2177
WOMAN IN THE MOON (DIE FRAU IM MOND) 412
WOMAN IN THE WINDOW, THE 1637
WOMAN IS A WOMAN, A (UNE FEMME EST UNE FEMME) 2110, 2131
WOMAN OF PARIS, A 1081, 1417
WOMAN OF THE YEAR 521, 523, 1073, 1270, 1787
WOMAN ON TRIAL 1625
WOMAN THAT NIGHT, THE (SONO YORU NO ONNA) 1894
WOMAN TO WOMAN 1837
WOMAN UNDER THE INFLUENCE, A 508, 598, 668, 2048
WOMAN WHO TOUCHED THE LEGS, THE (ASHI NI SAWATTA ONNA) 1740
WOMAN'S FILM, THE 505
WOMEN 501
WOMEN IN LOVE 1312
WOMEN IN WAR 329
WOMEN OF THE NIGHT (YORU NO ONNATACHI) 2017
WOMEN OF THE RHONDDA 512
WOMEN OF VALOR 331
WOMEN, THE 1122, 1124, 1217, 1280, 1336, 1380
WONDER OF WOMEN 1073
WOODEN CROSSES (LES CROIX DE BOIS) 1207
WOODEN HORSE, THE 1936
WOODSTOCK 558, 1171, 2199
WOOING AND WEDDING OF A COON, THE 862
WORD INTO IMAGE: WRITERS ON SCREENWRITING 1028
WORD, THE (ORDET) 1629, 1726
WORKERS LEAVING THE LUMIERE FACTORY (LA SORTIE DES USINES) 1619

WORKING GIRL 470, 2060, 2204
WORLD ACCORDING TO GARP, THE 2052
WORLD AT WAR, THE 286
WORLD AT WAR, THE (26 FILMS) 287
WORLD AT WAR: THE FINAL SOLUTION, THE 289
WORLD HISTORY FROM 1917 TO PRESENT, 5 FILMS: THE RISE OF HITLER,
  HITLER'S WAR 287
WORLD IN ACTION, THE (series) 280, 293, 305
WORLD OF APU, THE 2169
WORLD OF HENRY ORIENT, THE 1252, 1256, 2052
WORLD OF PLENTY 249, 283, 287, 323
WORLD OF SUZIE WONG, THE 664
WORLD WAR AS SEEN THROUGH GERMAN SPECTACLES (DER
  WELTKREIG/FIGHTING FOR THE FATHERLAND) 285
WORLD WAR II 287
WORLD WAR II: BACKGROUND AND CAUSES 287
WORLD WAR II: GI DIARY 287
WORLD WAR II: 1939-1941 287
WORLD WAR II: 1942-1945 287
WORLD, THE FLESH AND THE DEVIL, THE 355, 884, 885, 945
WRITTEN ON THE WIND 794, 980, 1970
WRONG MAN, THE 1843, 1849, 1854
WUSA 2192
WUTHERING HEIGHTS (1939) 1169, 1224, 1265, 1305, 1309, 1312, 1317, 1327,
  1472, 1473
WUTHERING HEIGHTS (1971) 1327
W. C. FIELDS AND ME 1245, 1246

X

XALA 919

Y

YANK AT OXFORD, A 1122, 1839
YANK IN INDOCHINA, A 338, 359, 442
YANK IN KOREA, A 334
YANK IN THE RAF, A 218, 272, 331, 357, 1911
YANK IN VIETNAM, A 338, 359
YANK ON THE BURMA ROAD, A 332
YANKEE CLIPPER 1578
YANKEE DOODLE DANDY 62, 209, 328, 1288, 1911, 1913
YANKS 331
YANKS ARE COMING, THE 328
YANKS BOMB TOKYO 287
YEAR OF LIVING DANGEROUSLY, THE 802
YEARLING, THE 1010, 1208
YELLOW ROLLS ROYCE, THE 1841
YENTL 62, 801, 834, 836, 1032
YES, GIORGIO 2067
YEUX SANS VISAGE, LES (EYES WITHOUT A FACE/THE HORROR CHAMBER
  OF DR. FAUSTUS) 2128
YIDDLE WITH A FIDDLE (YIDL MITN FIDL) 846, 848
YIDL MITN FIDL (YIDDLE WITH A FIDDLE) 846, 848
YISKER (REMEMBRANCE) 828, 846, 847
YOIDORE TENSHI (DRUNKEN ANGEL) 1899, 2017, 2020, 2029

YOJIMBO 2027
YORU NO ONNATACHI (WOMEN OF THE NIGHT) 2017
YOU AND OTHER COMRADES (DU UND MANCHER KAMERAD) 304
YOU ARE FREE 289
YOU CAN'T TAKE IT WITH YOU 556, 568, 1073, 1827
YOU ONLY LIVE ONCE 119, 2088
YOU ONLY LIVE TWICE 422
YOU'RE A BIG BOY NOW! 2197
YOUNG AND INNOCENT 1838
YOUNG AND THE BRAVE, THE 334
YOUNG AND THE DAMNED, THE (LOS OLVIDADOS) 978, 1002, 1923, 1990
YOUNG AND THE PASSIONATE, THE (I VITELLONI) 1927, 1929, 2171
YOUNG BLOOD 1164
YOUNG EAGLES 328
YOUNG FRANKENSTEIN 2047, 2194
YOUNG GOODMAN BROWN 1312
YOUNG LIONS, THE 331, 369, 841, 1201
YOUNG MAN WITH A HORN 1093
YOUNG MR. LINCOLN 477, 478, 479, 576, 1686
YOUNG MR. PITT, THE 1938
YOUNG ONE, THE (LA JEUNNE FILLE) 1094
YOUNG RACERS, THE 2049
YOUNG SAVAGES, THE 2051, 2065
YOUNG STRANGERS, THE 2051
YOUNG TOM EDISON 1094, 1485
YOUNG WARRIORS, THE 330
YOUNG WINSTON 339
YOUNGER GENERATION, THE 827
YPRES 285

Z

Z 384, 566, 577
ZABRISKIE POINT 562, 565, 1874, 1881, 1928
ZANDY'S BRIDE 428
ZANGIKU MONOGATARI (TALE OF LATE CHRYSANTHEMUMS/THE STORY OF
  THE LAST CHRYSANTHEMUM) 1901
ZAZA 1401
ZAZIE DANS LE METRO 2119
ZEEBRUGGE 285
ZELIG 786, 836, 2045, 2208
ZEMLYA (EARTH) 1645, 1647, 1655, 1663, 1665
ZERO DE CONDUITE (ZERO FOR CONDUCT) 404, 1811, 1824, 1828
ZERO FOR CONDUCT (ZERO DE CONDUITE) 404, 1811, 1824, 1828
ZIEGFELD FOLLIES, THE 1784
ZINGENDIKER SHMID, DER (THE SINGING BLACKSMITH) 829, 846
ZO O KUTTA RENCHU (THE FELLOWS WHO ATE THE ELEPHANT) 2017
ZOOT SUIT 2199
ZVENIGORA (ZVENYHORA) 1645
ZVENYHORA (ZVENIGORA) 1645